LOVE TRIANGLE

RONALD REAGAN, JANE WYMAN, & NANCY DAVIS

ALL THE GOSSIP UNFIT TO PRINT

A Word About Phraseologies

Since we at Blood Moon weren't privy to long-ago conversations as they were unfolding, we have relied on the memories of our sources for the conversational tone and phraseologies of what we've recorded within the pages of this book.

This writing technique, as it applies to modern biography, has been defined as "conversational storytelling" by *The New York Times,* which labeled it as an acceptable literary device for "engaging reading."

Blood Moon is not alone in replicating, "as remembered" dialogues from dead sources. Truman Capote and Norman Mailer were pioneers of direct quotes, and today, they appear in countless other memoirs, ranging from those of Patti Davis to those of the long-time mistress (Verita Thompson) of Humphrey Bogart.

Some people have expressed displeasure in the fact that direct quotes and "as remembered" dialogue have become a standard—some would say "mandatory"—fixture in pop culture biographies today.

If that is the case with anyone who's reading this now, they should perhaps turn to other, more traditional and self-consciously "scholastic" works instead.

Best wishes to all of you, with thanks for your interest in our work.

Danforth Prince
President and Founder
Blood Moon Productions

LOVE
TRIANGLE

RONALD REAGAN,
JANE WYMAN, &
NANCY DAVIS

DARWIN PORTER &
DANFORTH PRINCE

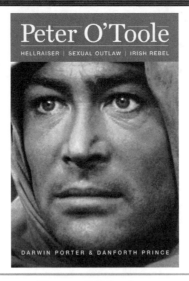
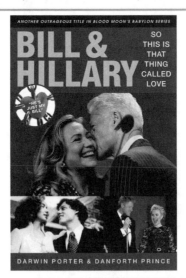

Other Books by Darwin Porter

Biographies

Jacqueline Kennedy Onassis
A Life Beyond Her Wildest Dreams

Pink Triangle
*The Feuds and Private Lives of
Tennessee Williams, Gore Vidal, Truman Capote,
and Famous Members of their Entourages.*

Those Glamorous Gabors
Bombshells from Budapest

Inside Linda Lovelace's Deep Throat
Degradation, Porno Chic, and the Rise of Feminism

Elizabeth Taylor
There is Nothing Like a Dame

Marilyn at Rainbow's End
Sex, Lies, Murder, and the Great Cover-up

J. Edgar Hoover & Clyde Tolson
Investigating the Sexual Secrets of America's Most Famous Men and Women

Frank Sinatra
The Boudoir Singer. All the Gossip Unfit to Print

The Kennedys
All the Gossip Unfit to Print

***Humphrey Bogart, The Making of a Legend** (2010) , and*
***The Secret Life of Humphrey Bogart** (2003)*

Howard Hughes
Hell's Angel

Steve McQueen
King of Cool, Tales of a Lurid Life

Paul Newman
The Man Behind the Baby Blues

Merv Griffin
A Life in the Closet

Brando Unzipped

Katharine the Great
Hepburn, Secrets of a Lifetime Revealed

Jacko, His Rise and Fall
The Social and Sexual History of Michael Jackson

and, co-authored with Roy Moseley
Damn You, Scarlett O'Hara*,*
The Private Lives of Vivien Leigh & and Laurence Olivier

FILM CRITICISM

Blood Moon's 2005 Guide to the Glitter Awards
Blood Moon's 2006 Guide to Film,
Blood Moon's 2007 Guide to Film, *and*
50 Years of Queer Cinema
500 of the Best GLBTQ Films Ever Made

NON-FICTION

Hollywood Babylon—It's Back! *and*
Hollywood Babylon Strikes Again!

NOVELS

Butterflies in Heat,
Marika, Venus (a roman à clef based on the life of Anaïs Nin)
Razzle-Dazzle,
Midnight in Savannah,
Rhinestone Country,
Blood Moon,
and **Hollywood's Silent Closet**

TRAVEL GUIDES

Many Editions and Many Variations of
The Frommer Guides, The American Express Guides, and/or TWA Guides, et alia to:

Andalusia, Andorra, Anguilla, Aruba, Atlanta, Austria, the Azores, The Bahamas, Barbados, the Bavarian Alps, Berlin, Bermuda, Bonaire and Curaçao, Boston, the British Virgin Islands, Budapest, Bulgaria, California, the Canary Islands, the Caribbean and its "Ports of Call, " the Cayman Islands, Ceuta, the Channel Islands (UK), Charleston (SC), Corsica, Costa del Sol (Spain), Denmark, Dominica, the Dominican Republic, Edinburgh, England, Estonia, "Europe by Rail, " the Faroe Islands, Finland, Florence, France, Frankfurt, the French Riviera, Geneva, Georgia (USA), Germany, Gibraltar, Glasgow, Granada (Spain), Great Britain, Greenland, Grenada (West Indies), Haiti, Hungary, Iceland, Ireland, Isle of Man, Italy, Jamaica, Key West & the Florida Keys, Las Vegas, Liechtenstein, Lisbon, London, Los Angeles, Madrid, Maine, Malta, Martinique & Guadeloupe, Massachusetts, Morocco, Munich, New England, New Orleans, North Carolina, Norway, Paris, Poland, Portugal, Provence, Puerto Rico, Romania, Rome, Salzburg, San Diego, San Francisco, San Marino, Sardinia, Savannah, Scandinavia, Scotland, Seville, the Shetland Islands, Sicily, Sint Maarten & St. Martin, South Carolina, Spain, St. Kitts & Nevis, Sweden, Switzerland, the Turks & Caicos, the U.S. Virgin Islands, Venice, Vienna and the Danube, Wales, and Zurich.

BLOOD
MOON
Productions, Ltd.

LOVE TRIANGLE
Ronald Reagan, Jane Wyman, & Nancy Davis

Darwin Porter and Danforth Prince

www.BloodMoonProductions.com

Manufactured in the United States of America

ISBN 978-1-936003-41-9

Special thanks to the Stanley Mills Haggart Collection,
the Woodrow Parrish-Martin Collection, the H. Lee Phillips Collection, the Fredric
and Grace Smithey Collection, and Elsa Maxwell Café Society.

Cover designs by Richard Leeds (Bigwigdesign.com)
Videography and Publicity Trailers by Piotr Kajstura

Distributed worldwide through National Book Network
(www.NBNbooks.com)

1 2 3 4 5 6 7 8 9 10

Thanks for the Memories
THIS BOOK IS DEDICATED TO

JOAN BLONDELL AND VAN JOHNSON

AND TO STANLEY MILLS HAGGART AND WILLIAM HOPPER

Ω

PLUS A CAST OF HUNDREDS OF OTHER PLAYERS FROM THE
ENTERTAINMENT INDUSTRY, SOME OF WHOM DID NOT WANT TO BE NAMED.

RONALD REAGAN WAS THE FIRST U.S. PRESIDENT TO TRIUMPH OVER WHAT HAD BEEN CONSIDERED, PRIOR TO HIS ELECTION, AN INSURMOUNTABLE STIGMA: HE WAS A *DIVORCÉ* WHO HAD BEEN MARRIED TWICE.

THIS IS THE STORY OF THE LOVE TRIANGLE WHOSE COMBATANTS ARE FEATURED BELOW.

HOLLYWOOD STARS

Ronald Reagan with Jane Wyman. Love is in bloom. Their marriage lasted from 1940 to 1948.

Ronald Reagan with Nancy Davis. Their "until-death-do-us-part" union lasted from 1952 until 2004.

Contents

Scenes from the Life of an American President

"Back in Dixon, Illinois, a rich older woman wanted me to be her kept boy. But I had other plans. I headed for Hollywood."

"Talk about getting your ass beat. When I returned to my *alma mater*, Eureka College, in 1947, my TKE frat brothers left me with red buns."

(Left) "If there's one thing I liked to do, it was playing Cowboys and Indians."

"Here, I'm ready to scalp a few, although Barbara Stanwyck (*right*, his co-star in *Cattle Queen of Montana; 1954*) preferred to shoot them down off their horses."

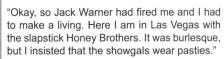

"Okay, so Jack Warner had fired me and I had to make a living. Here I am in Las Vegas with the slapstick Honey Brothers. It was burlesque, but I insisted that the showgals wear pasties."

"In 1955, John Payne and I made *Tennessee's Partner*. People in Hollywood always claimed that Jane had this thing for Payne."

"Here, he and I take a break and absorb some sun. You decide which of us is the hottie."

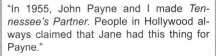

Michigan governor George Romney (yes, Mitt's father) watches as Reagan fails to flip a jelly bean into his mouth. The setting was the Governors' Conference in Washington, D.C., on March 17, 1967.

Running for Governor of California in 1966, Reagan on horseback waves his cowboy hat in San Jose during Mexican Independence Day. He told friends, "Sacramento is the first act before I gallop off to the White House."

"When Nancy and I arrived in Sacramento, we realized that that Victorian monstrosity of a governor's mansion was a damn fire trap. We moved out. Here I am, carrying our dishes."

During his Governorship, the Reagans' housing dilemma was solved by rich friends, who bought them an elegant home in an exclusive suburb of Sacramento.

"At Eureka College, they wouldn't let me on the baseball team. I showed them."

"Here, as Governor of California, I threw out the first ball of the 1972 World Series at Oakland."

"Here, I am at my ranch in California on a foggy day, August 13, 1981."

"Whereas Hitler danced a jig at the fall of France, I'm tossing my leg into the air after signing the largest tax reduction and spending control bill in American history."

"At my ranch in California, I drove my Jeep to clear some dead limbs from my property."

"In Washington, I set out to clear deadwood from the government."

"Forget Milton Berle! That Liz from across the pond could wow them with her jokes about the heavy rains of California."

On March 10, 1983, Queen Elizabeth II visited the flooded Reagan spread, Rancho del Cielo.

Nancy told the press, "Thank god she didn't spend the night! Our guest bedroom could house a Munchkin or two from *The Wizard of Oz*. And Ronnie used to say, 'If you sat down on the can, your legs stuck out the door.'"

Reagan shook the hand of John F. Kennedy, Jr., as Caroline Kennedy looks on. It was their first visit to the White House since the Presidential regime of Richard Nixon in 1973.

Reagan told the handsome young man, "I believe I'm shaking the hand of a future President of the United States."

After JFK Jr. departed, Reagan told Nancy, "I hope my prediction never comes true."

A former First Lady, Jacqueline Kennedy Onassis *(on the right),* greets a presiding First Lady, Nancy, as a smiling and indulgent President Reagan looks on. The June 25, 1985 rendezvous occurred in Boston at a fund-raiser for the John F. Kennedy Presidential Library.

Later, Reagan told his aide, Donald Regan, "I first met Jackie in Hollywood in the late 1950s, when she was screwing my best friend, Bill Holden."

(Left) In the Oval Office, President Reagan shows off his golfing stance, hitting a ball within the sightlines of a real golf pro (Ray Floyd), who's standing outside the frame of this photo.

When this photo was published on June 24, 1986, golf pros thought Reagan's pose was "effeminate."

When he heard that, Reagan, always fast with a quip, told aides, "They don't know the half of it. In private, I give the best pansy imitation in the history of the Presidency."

(Above) Reagan and Nancy appear to be admiring a sculpted replica of a Komodo Dragon presented to them in Bali in May of 1986.

His shirt was a gift from the Indonesian people. As he later quipped, "The only thing louder was the mouth of Jimmy Carter."

(Left) President Reagan welcomes the Iron Lady of Britain, Margaret Thatcher, to Camp David on November 6, 1986. There was press speculation that he had always been drawn to strong-willed women. "Take his two wives or his mother, Nelle, as an example," wrote one reporter.

Another had a different view. "I think Mrs. Thatcher had the hots for him."

Reagan and Nancy dig into the earth at a ground-breaking ceremony for the Ronald Reagan Presidential Library and Museum in Simi Valley, California, on November 21, 1988.

Again, Reagan was fast with a quip, telling reporters, "Nancy learned the use of a shovel by scooping up horse shit on my ranch in Malibu."

President Reagan certainly earned his place in the sun in American history. But was it good for his nose? Apparently not.

In August of 1987, he appeared at a press briefing in the Old Executive Office Building in Washington. He'd just had surgery on his nose for cancer.

(Left) In January of 1989, after eight years residency in the White House, President Reagan and Nancy bid farewell to their assembled well-wishers at Washington's Andrews Air Force base, before a plane hauled them away to their retirement in California. The occasion caused them to shed tears.

When Reagan was later asked about it, he said, "Richard Nixon in his farewell address also shed tears—and so did his wife, Pat. But Dick and I were tearing up for very different reasons during our exit from the White House."

Ronald Reagan

(1911-2004)

The Heartland's Heartthrob Becomes the Horny, Hard Working, "Gay Blade and Most Desirable Bachelor" in Des Moines

Young Reagan in the arms of his first love, "Mugs," who cautioned him to get a grip on his raging hormones.	The Reagan family *(left to right)*: Jack, Moon, Baby Dutch, and Nelle. Young Reagan is "all dressed up."

The son of an alcoholic Irish father and a Bible-thumping religious zealot mother, Ronald Wilson Reagan entered the world on February 6, 1911. As viewed through the windows of the family's apartment, in the hamlet of Tampico, in northwestern Illinois, the scene could have been from the 1880s, with horse-drawn carriages traversing Main Street.

1

The infant son, who would grow up to be called "The Great Communicator," started early by crying his head off day and night. "For such a little bit of a fat Dutchman, he sure makes a hell of a lot of noise," said Jack Reagan.

The boy was nicknamed "Dutch."

The devout Nelle Clyde Wilson had previously given birth to another son, John Neil Reagan, who was nicknamed "Moon" after the cartoon character of Moon Mullins.

When he was sober enough, Jack sold shoes and his friends admitted he had "the gift of Blarney and the charm of a Leprechaun."

Auburn-haired Nelle, of Scottish-English descent, had an ample bosom, narrow hips, and a strong jaw. She'd taken out one of her large breasts in church for Dutch to suckle. Later, she complained to Jack, "He sucked voraciously for his mother's milk, practically biting my nipple off. He can't get enough."

"That means in twenty or so years from now, he's gonna be a tit man, chasing all the big bosom dames, if I know my son," Jack said.

The family was poor. As a boy, Dutch went to the butcher, where liver was given away free, as it was viewed not fit for human consumption. The boy said the liver was for their cats, except it usually was the main course at Nelle's Sunday dinner.

In later years, Dutch recalled growing up with Moon, "Ours was a Tom Sawyer-Huck Finn idyll."

In the years to come, the Reagans moved five times, including a dismal existence in a cold-water flat in Chicago, where they were called "trashy Micks." Jack enjoyed Chicago, as it was labeled "the most drunken town in the Middle West."

Reagan inherited his love of acting from "Jack & Nell," who appeared in amateur theatricals, his father scoring his greatest hit as a female impersonator,

Trim and fit, Dutch became a lifeguard in Dixon, saving 77 lives.

In his high school football uniform, Dutch was getting an early rehearsal for his first famous movie, *Knute Rockne— All American*.

Nelle and Jack in a 19th Century pose

with lots of powder, rouge, and bright red lipstick.

In school, Dutch was known as a bookworm. "I got my ass beat a lot," he recalled. "Those rough-and-tumble farmboys called me a sissy. I got used to black eyes and bloody noses, but I wanted to learn."

The highlight of his young life came in 1926, when he was made Dixon's lifeguard along Rock River, a position he'd hold down for seven summers, during which time he heroically saved 77 lives—men, women, and children. Muscled, bronzed, and handsome, he became the most pursued young man in Dixon.

Wanting to play football, but too skinny, Dutch became a baton twirler for the school band. Moon called him "a majorette." By his junior year, he also became an actor in school plays.

Along came love into his life, Margaret Cleaver, nicknamed "Mugs," a sparkling brunette with brown eyes. As he later revealed, "She told me to control my raging hormones. She always wore that chastity belt."

Washing dishes helped pay his tuition at Eureka College. He'd later joke, "The road to the presidency was paved with masses of dirty dishes."

Dutch's first love, Margaret Cleaver (Mugs), in 1928. She looked like a flapper, but was a "Bible Thumper."

As he physically filled out, he got to play football, his passions being football, drama, politics, and Mugs.

Although he qualified for the football team, the basketball team rejected him because of his poor eyesight. He became a cheerleader instead. The players called him "Sister Boy." But he was elected the captain of the swimming team.

Taunted by Moon for being a virgin, Dutch finally lost it to Peggy Hannah, 28, who charged young men from the nearby college $1.50 a throw.

After a vagabond life, the Reagans settled in Dixon, Illinois, a hundred miles west of Chicago, on the banks of the Rock River. Dixon became the role model for President Reagan's "a Shining City on the Hill."

Dutch's favorite spot for having a cold lemonade was President's Park with its statue of Abraham Lincoln. In 1823, the future president with his volunteers had roared through town to rout some hostile Black Hawk Indians, driving them north into Canada. Later, when Peggy got pregnant, she admitted, "It could have been any one of forty guys." Both Moon and Dutch drove her to Chicago for an illegal abortion.

After college, he drifted to Des Moines where, in time,

Eureka College Man, Reagan, with his hair parted in the middle, starred in school plays.

he was hailed as "The Radio Sports Voice of the Middle West." In his own words, "I became the Gay Blade of Des Moines." He dated an array of beautiful young girls. Even a rich older widow fell for him.

While there, Durch's first major league seduction occurred when Aimee Semple McPherson, the most famous evangelist in America, seduced him after he interviewed her at his radio station. Big name Hollywood stars would follow.

One winter day, his life changed when he was invited by the managers of the Chicago Cubs to watch their training on Catalina Island off the coast of Southern California. He shouted, "California, here I come!" and he was off.

He was twenty-six years old, and the year was 1936, when he hit Tinseltown.

In Des Moines, he'd interviewed a singer, Joy Hodges. He found out that she was the star nightlife attraction at Los Angeles' Biltmore Hotel, where he was staying. She stood him up on a date, but, in remorse, arranged for him to meet a blonde starlet, Betty Grable, with whom she'd recently worked on an RKO picture, *Follow the Fleet* (1936). This close friend of another starlet, Jane Wyman, turned out to be the most glamorous woman Reagan had ever met.

On their first date, Grable seduced him. "She taught me more tricks than a whore learns in a whorehouse," he later bragged to Moon.

That spring of 1937, he returned to Catalina Island, ostensibly as part of an assignment from his work as a sportscaster to watch the Chicago Cubs in training. But after his re-arrival in California, he shifted his focus, heading for Hollywood instead. He stayed at the Biltmore once again. This time, Hodges kept her date with him.

He told her, "I want to be a movie star." In Des Moines, he would have been laughed at, but in Hollywood, that statement was typical. Issuing a warning, she told him, "Men who wear glasses don't get

Reagan achieved early fame in Des Moines, broadcasting sports and chasing corn-fed beauties.

Aimee Semple McPherson, America's most famous evangelical faith healer, had Reagan singing "Ave Maria."

passes." She translated that phrase for him, explaining that men who wear glasses don't get screen tested.

Hodges arranged an interview with her own talent agents, who handled big stars like Robert Taylor, as well as minor starlets like Grable and Wyman.

In Reagan, these agents thought they had discovered "the next Robert Taylor," and a screen test was arranged for him at Warner Brothers.

Reagan later recalled, "Some homos in wardrobe and makeup treated me like

4

a slab of beef, but remade me to face the camera. On his report, the head of wardrobe wrote—"Greek god physique but not Johnny Weissmuller. Broad shoulders, slim waist, slight over six feet, face that would get a second look from Joan Crawford."

His test went smoothly, but he had to get approval from Jack Warner.

He could not wait around and returned to his broadcasting job in Des Moines.

Five days later, back in Iowa, he received an urgent telegram from his agent. It read: WARNERS OFFER CONTRACT SEVEN YEARS. ONE YEAR OPTIONS. STARTING AT $200 A WEEK.

It was late at night when he received the telegram. "I think I yelled so loud I woke up every coyote in Iowa."

In his newly purchased Nash convertible, he headed for the "Dream Factory" that was Hollywood in those days, in the full flower of what is known as "its Golden Age."

Starlet Betty Grable, on the dawn of World War II fame, was Reagan's first conquest in Hollywood.

***

To his new friends in Hollywood, especially Dick Powell, Reagan recalled that screen test. "It was my introduction to Hollywood, which I found crawling with homos. I met a lot of them in makeup and wardrobe. They sure took liberties with my body, feeling and fussing, a little to much for my tastes. But they did turn a hayseed from the Middle West into a passable leading man."

Warner Brothers promoted Reagan as a body beautiful.

Ronald Reagan, a former hayseed, now one of Hollywood's leading men.

Years later, Ron Reagan, Jr. would write about his father's "physical beauty" at the time, citing his "charisma as a man who harbored an unquenchable flame of ambitions and believed in his dreams."

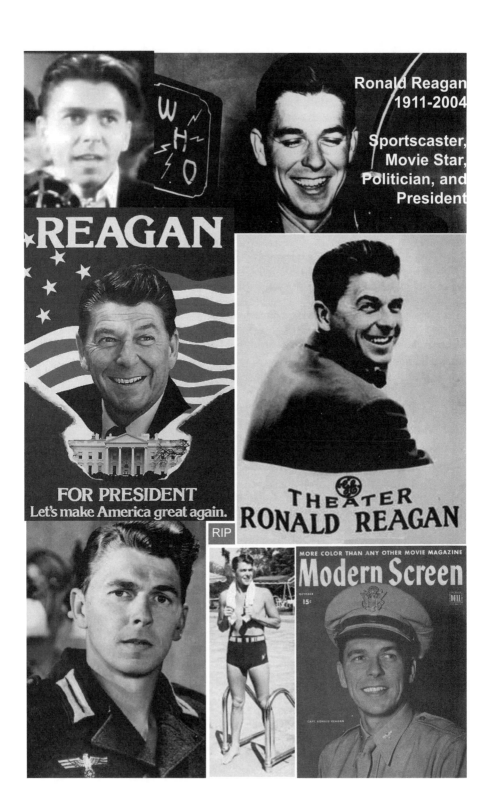

Ronald Reagan
1911-2004

Sportscaster,
Movie Star,
Politician, and
President

REAGAN

FOR PRESIDENT
Let's make America great again.

RIP

GE THEATER
RONALD REAGAN

MORE COLOR THAN ANY OTHER MOVIE MAGAZINE
Modern Screen

Jane Wyman
(1917-2007)

A Lonely Teenage Girl
Meets "A Walking Streak of Sex"

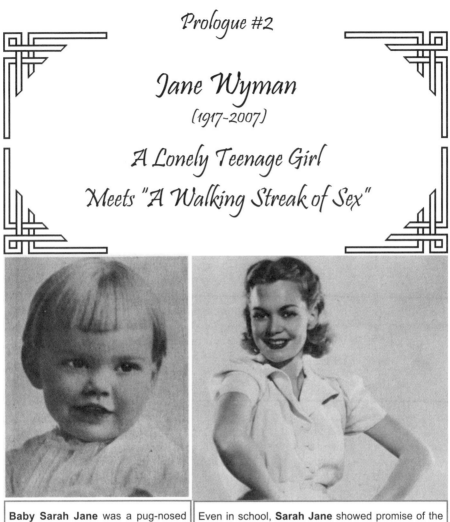

Baby Sarah Jane was a pug-nosed cutie abandoned by her parents.	Even in school, **Sarah Jane** showed promise of the Hollywood chorus girl she'd become.

Nicknamed "Saint Joe," St. Joseph, Missouri, lies on the Missouri River on the Kansas/Missouri border in the northwestern part of the "Show Me" state. It was the starting point of the Pony Express and the death place of the outlaw, Jesse James. It is also the home of Missouri Western State University. Once, it was the last supply point before a pioneer ventured into the "Wild West." Deep in this heartland of America, a movie star was born.

Even though she was married to a man who became one of the most famous of the 20th Century, and even though she became an A-list, Oscar-winning movie star, much about the life of the screen star Jane Wyman remains a mystery.

Her birthday, her actual parents, and the basic facts of her background and upbringing are consistently misreported.

Much of the false information about her emanated not only from the Warner Brothers' publicity department, but from Jane herself.

In defiance of her status as a minor, and as a vehicle to combat the possibility that she'd be rejected for employment because she was under-aged, Jane herself "invented" her birth date as January 4, 1914. In St. Joseph, authorities representing the state of Missouri registered her actual birth as January 5, 1917. Her biological parents were Gladys Hope Christian and Manning J. Mayfield, who had married in Kansas City, Missouri, on May 17, 1916, only eight months before her actual birth.

Jane Wyman's humble birthplace in St. Joseph, Missouri. From this, a multi-millionaire actress emerged into world fame.

The infant's original name was Sarah Jane Mayfield, although most of the official records associated with her early life report her last name as Fulks. That was the surname of her foster parents, who never legally adopted her. Officially, her maiden name was never officially changed. Her surname of Wyman came from a mysterious young husband, a brief interloper who has since disappeared into the dustbin of history.

Jane's mother, Gladys (1891-1960), worked in St. Joseph as a stenographer and office assistant for Dr. Jackson Elam. Jane's father, Manning (1885-1922), was a worker at a local factory that turned out food products made from grain.

When Jane was five years old, her father unexpectedly opted to leave St. Joseph without his family, heading alone for San Francisco, where he found employment as an office worker at a local shipping company. He divorced Gladys in October of 1921, having taken a mistress in San Francisco. He died on January 21, 1922 at the age of twenty-seven, having contracted a severe case of pneumonia.

Back in Missouri, when Dr. Elam's wife discovered that her husband was having an affair with his stenographer, Gladys was fired. Instead of remaining to face disgrace in St. Joseph, she decided to take the train to the bright lights of then-burgeoning Cleveland, Ohio, to try her luck there.

Gladys told her associates that she wanted to find another husband, and she believed that bringing a young child to her uncertain future in Cleveland would be "too much baggage" for her. She also couldn't afford to hire a part-time babysitter for her young pre-school daughter.

During her employment with Dr. Elam, she had met the Fulks couple. Richard Fulks, 65, the husband, was rather stern and didn't have much to say, but his German wife, Emma, 60, seemed interested, perhaps, in arranging a future adoption.

In an impulsive moment, Gladys proposed that she leave Sarah Jane with the Fulks family, who would take care of her and supervise her schooling. She promised that as soon as she found work in Cleveland, she would send child support.

> "Little Miss Wyman is a mystery no one ever bothered to solve."
>
> — Marlene Dietrich

Although somewhat reluctant at first, the Fulks agreed to take responsibility for the child.

Jane's foster parents were a hardworking, battered-by-life couple. Emma Reiss (1866-1951) had emigrated many years before from her native Saarbrucken, Germany, to Missouri. Jane's foster father, Richard D. Fulks (1862-1928), had been progressively promoted from beginnings as a low-level municipal bureaucrat to the community's chief detective.

Young Jane's new home was a gloomy house she'd later call "a Victorian gingerbread monstrosity, something out of an Addams Family cartoon."

Her foster parents were stern disciplinarians. Her new stepfather was an aging, balding man with a walrus mustache. The sound of laughter was never heard in this decaying pile. It was a sad, lonely place for Jane.

Once settled in Cleveland, Gladys did not send child support. Except for a brief visit with Jane in Los Angeles in 1933, Gladys never saw her daughter again, dying in New York City at the age of sixty-five in 1960.

Later in life, Jane could not recall one pleasurable memory from her girlhood. "I was raised in such a bitter household that it took me years to recover from the memories that remained."

In a rare interview given to *Guidepost* Magazine in 1964, Jane said, "I was extremely shy as a child. Shyness is no small problem. It can cripple a whole personality. It crippled me for many years. As a child, my only solution to the problem of shyness was to hide myself and make myself as small and insignificant as possible. Through grade school, I was a well-mannered little shadow who never spoke above a whisper."

On September 10, 1923, "Sarah Jane Fulks" was enrolled in the Noyes School in St. Joseph. She had little interest in schoolwork and was not a good pupil. If called upon to answer a question, her vocal chords would become almost paralyzed with fear. Eventually, she dropped out of school.

Every afternoon on her way home from school, Jane would walk by Edward A. Prinz's Dancing School, where young girls could enroll for lessons for fifty cents. His students called him Dad.

From the street below, Jane could hear the echo of staccato, syncopated taps. She dreamed that one day, she might become a dancer.

Since coming to live with the Fulks, Jane had never asked for anything, but she began to beseech Emma to enroll her in the dancing school. For the first few weeks, Emma resisted, but when Jane's teacher summoned her for a discussion about her foster daughter, she warned her that Jane's extreme shyness was growing more severe. "It's almost a sickness that can lead to social retardation. The only thing she expressed an interest in involves dancing lessons. It might bring her out of her shell. Right now, if a grown up speaks to the poor child, she bursts into tears. Something has to be done to help her, and I think dancing lessons will help a lot."

Even though her husband, Richard, remained adamantly opposed, Emma bundled Jane up one afternoon and enrolled her in Ed Prinz's School. For the first time, Jane met a man she could idolize.

As the weeks progressed, Prinz singled Jane out for special attention, devoting two hours a day to training her after the classes had "officially" ended. Even though his resources were limited, he purchased three beautiful white dresses for her and bought her red ribbons. He took special care in dressing and undressing

9

her in her dance costumes, which he paid for himself.

In later years, she would remember his excessive fondling of her during costume changes. In those days, most of the residents of St. Joseph didn't even know what a pedophile was.

Later, Jane said, "At no point did I feel I was being used. I was just delighted that a grown-up was doling out love and affection to me, something I never got at home."

Working extensively with her, Prinz took an ugly little duckling and transformed her into a beautiful swan.

***

By 1922, Emma had saved up enough money for Jane and herself to head west, by train, to Los Angeles. Ostensibly, as she explained to her husband, she wanted to visit her children, Morie and Elsie, who were now married and had families of their own. She'd never seen her grandchildren. Richard's son, Raymond, had moved to Texas years earlier, and had never been heard from again.

Richard agreed to come down to St. Joseph's railway station to see Emma and Jane off to California. Jane noticed that he was walking with a limp. Lately, he'd gone to a doctor to see what was wrong with him. The doctor had found nothing, suggesting that he was far too ambitious and was working too hard, keeping long hours. His physical condition had deteriorated during the previous years.

Frugally, Emma had packed provisions in a basket for them to eat along the way en route to Los Angeles. By the time the train had crossed the Missouri State Line, heading west, Emma made a confession to Jane.

"Actually, I may never come back to your Papa," she said. "If my plans go well, you're going to be discovered in Hollywood and made a child star."

***

As Hollywood ségued into the Roaring Twenties, the studios were no longer the precarious enterprises they had been during the previous decade. Studios had become film factories, and talent was being devoured as a means of meeting weekly production quotas. Movie theaters were springing up across the country,

At first anonymous, stars had now emerged as distinctive icons in their own right. Household names included Rudolph Valentino, Gloria Swanson, Mary Pickford, Charlie Chaplin, William S. Hart, and Douglas Fairbanks, Sr., among many others.

If at this early stage, Jane had a role model, it was Diana Serra Cary, billed as "Baby Peggy." At the time, the "Million Dollar Baby" was receiving 1.2 million fan letters annually. Emma had taken Jane to see the star's first film, Playmates, in 1921, in which the actress had appeared with the canine star of Century

Wyman's role model, and the wealthiest pre-teen in Hollywood: BABY PEGGY.

Studios, Brownie the Wonder Dog. Emma bought Jane a Baby Peggy doll, and the young girl drank milk from a container that featured a portrait of Baby Peggy on the label.

Child star **Jackie Coogan** is seen here in a tender embrace with **Charlie Chaplin** in *The Kid* (1919).

Young Sarah Jane wanted to be in their next picture. She discovered that The Little Tramp was even fonder of little girls.

***

One of the first magazines Emma ever purchased at a Hollywood newsstand featured a headlined, ambition-fueling story—"YOUR CHILD SHOULD BE IN PICTURES."

"Just think of it," Emma told Jane. "You could be earning a million dollars a year, like Jackie Coogan with Charlie Chaplin in *The Kid* (1919). I heard those were real tears the boy cried."

Every weekday morning, Emma, with a carefully dressed Jane, set out to make the rounds of the studios, beginning at Century Studios. Jane said, "I soon learned that the world was filled with blonde, curly haired little girls being pushed before a bored director."

Emma eagerly read the trade papers, and she came across an item announcing that Charlie Chaplin was considering making a film in which he plays the errant father of a little orphan boy and girl he adopts, which leads to a series of wild antics. It had already been announced that Jackie Coogan, who had played Chaplin's irascible sidekick in *The Kid*, had been contracted to play the boy. But the search was on to find a girl to appear opposite Coogan and The Little Tramp. Emma was convinced that Jane would be ideal as Coogan's little sister.

Arriving at Chaplin's office, Jane and Emma were disappointed to find at least twenty blonde little girls waiting to see the superstar. They had to wait four hours before they were ushered into Chaplin's office. Emma wanted to accompany Jane, but the secretary insisted that Jane go in alone.

What happened that late afternoon between Chaplin and Jane became part of Hollywood's whispered lore. Years later, Jane spread the scandalous story about what took place, claiming that during the course of her interview with the star, he unbuttoned his trousers and exposed himself to her.

Unfamiliar with male anatomy, she was said to have giggled nervously at his exposed penis. For her, it must have been a daunting introduction to the male body, as Chaplin claimed he possessed a twelve-inch appendage, which he defined as "the eighth wonder of the world." Because Chaplin's fondness for little girls was well documented, the story of the alleged encounter between Jane and Chaplin gained traction. Previously, he had gone on record as saying, "The most beautiful form of life is a very young girl just starting to bloom."

Regardless of what happened that day, Jane was rudely kicked out of Chaplin's office.

After making all the rounds with no ensuing job offer, Emma and Jane received more bad news. Morie Fulks (one of Emma's biological children and their host during their time in L.A) told them one night over their meager dinner that he could no longer support them and that he had already purchased two one-way tickets for their transit back to St. Joseph.

***

After her return to St. Joseph, Jane sank into a deep depression. The town had never looked so bleak.

On March 25, 1928, Richard Fulks died, leaving Emma a widow at the age of sixty-two. She managed to sell the house, but because it was heavily mortgaged, there was very little left over. Nonetheless, with her meager savings, she decided to pack her things and return to Hollywood with Jane. Arriving in Los Angeles, Jane and Emma found a cheap room in a shabby boarding house that mostly catered to out-of-work actors.

Still a lackluster student, Jane enrolled in Los Angeles High School, which she found "was overrun with predatory boys."

She wanted both singing and dancing lessons. She lied about her age and found a job as a waitress at Mannings, a coffee shop, burger joint, and ice cream parlor, where she worked for tips, sometimes coming home with two dollars a night.

During the day, she took singing and dancing lessons. Frustrated that her calendar was overloaded, she dropped out of school without telling Emma.

***

One spring night in 1933, when Jane was only sixteen, a tall, well-built young man came into the coffee shop and ordered a chocolate malt. She'd never seen such a handsome male. He looked older than her. Actually, he was twenty-seven.

Sipping his malt, he stared at her, not taking his eyes off her. "I felt he was undressing me," she recalled.

"Listen, gal," he said to her. "I don't care how many boyfriends you have. From now on, you're going to be my girl, belonging just to me. Is that understood?"

She was flattered but pretended otherwise. "I understand nothing of the sort. You just walk in here and think you can take over my life. I don't even know who you are."

"Let me introduce myself," he said in a husky, masculine voice. "I'm Eugene Wyman. I dropped out of school, and I've got this job as a mechanic at a nearby garage. So now that you know who I am, just who in hell are you, other than being a soda jerk?"

"Sarah Jane Fulks," she said, already mesmerized by him.

"The name of Sarah has got to go," he said. "Sounds like some old maiden aunt. I like the name of Jane, however. I'll let you keep it. But the Fulks will have to go, too. Sounds like a dirty word. But don't worry about it. Before the end of the month, I will have changed that name from Fulks to Jane Wyman."

"You're pretty sure of yourself," she said.

"Baby Doll, I've got a lot to be sure about. The girls call me a walking steak of sex. I'm gonna hang out here till you get off from work. Then I'm gonna take you dancing. If you're a good girl, I might even tell you I'm in love with you."

12

Prologue #3

Nancy Davis
(1921-)

Born in a Trunk, "Cuddles" Davis Becomes a Debutante in a World of Theatrical Celebrities

Handsome, red-haired **Sangston Hettler, Jr.**, always claimed he was the first man to "deflower" **Nancy Davis**. Did she discover why he was nicknamed "Sock?"	Nancy's mother, actress **Edith Luckett**, nicknamed "Lucky," was a beauty, a bigot, and "slept on both sides of her bed," as it was called then.

Born Anne Francis Robbins on July 6, 1921 (not in 1923, as she'd later claim), the future First Lady, Nancy Davis, grew up a theatrical world of make-believe. She was the daughter of the actress, Edith ("Lucky") Luckett.

For some reason, her mother chose to call her "Nancy," instead of Anne. After a difficult delivery, the infant entered the world at Sloane Hospital in Flushing, Queens, a borough of New York City.

As a weapon in her campaign of remaining "eternally young" on stage, Edith claimed she'd been born in 1896, although the actual year of her birth was 1888,

13

when Grover Cleveland was president. She invented a glamorous background for herself, a Tara-like setting inspired by something from the life of Scarlett O'Hara, falsely claiming that she was a Southern belle from one of the first families of Virginia.

Actually, she was born the youngest into an expansive and boisterous brood of nine children, the daughter of Charles Edward Luckett, a clerk for Railway Express. To make ends meet, her mother, Sarah Frances Whitlock, ran a boarding house near the railroad tracks in Washington, D.C.

The family lived in rooms over buggy stables near the theater where Abraham Lincoln had been assassinated. It was called "Swampoodle," (a swamp filled with puddles), and was inhabited mostly by working class Irish Catholics. As Edith remembered it, "all the men got drunk on Saturday night."

Six years younger than Edith, Nancy's father was Kenneth Seymour Robbins, who grew up in Pittsfield, Massachusetts. His family had deep colonial roots.

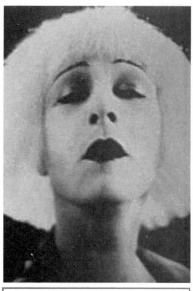

The infamous movie star lesbian, **Nazimova,** was designated as Nancy's godmother.

From all reports, Kenneth was a mama's boy, the type of kid his mother attired in white and dressed until he was nine years old. He wore his hair in long blonde curls, evocative of Mary Pickford.

He always claimed that he was a graduate of Princeton, although no record has ever surfaced to prove that. He attended a theatrical performance at the Colonial Theater in Pittsfield, Massachusetts, where he spotted Edith in a small part. He went backstage and introduced himself. Soon, they were dating, which eventually led to their marriage on June 27, 1916.

When America went to war in 1917, Kenneth volunteered and served until January of 1919, when he was honorably discharged.

Shortly after his return from the Army, he and Edith separated. He was not living with her when Nancy was born. After she recovered from childbirth, Edith took the infant girl on the road with her, as she traveled from town to town as part of a touring theatrical troupe. She hired babysitters along the way.

"When Judy Garland later sang about being born in a trunk, I knew what she meant," Nancy later recalled. "Before I was three, I had greasepaint in my veins. My ambition from the age of five was to become an actress like my mother."

In the meanwhile, Edith had grown into a beautiful young girl with blonde hair and larkspur blue eyes. She matured early, dressing like the fashion-conscious soubrettes of the day, with cloche hats, silk stockings, peacock feathers, and hobble skirts.

She preferred to hang out with the male actors and learned "to curse like a Turkish sailor." No joke was too bawdy for her potty mouth. Many of the women who worked with her found her vulgar, but the men seemed to adore her.

In the selection of Nancy's godmother, Edith made an odd choice, designating Alla Nazimova, the Russian-Jewish actress, born in Yalta in 1879, and the reigning queen of MGM in Hollywood and its highest paid star in 1920.

Edith had met Nazimova on Irving Place in Manhattan at the townhouse of the city's most celebrated literary agent, Bessie Marbury. Her lists of clients had included Oscar Wilde, W. Somerset Maugham, H.G. Wells, and George Bernard Shaw. Marbury lived with her love, the society decorator Elsie de Wolfe, who later became famous as Lady Mendl.

Nazimova was said to have been enthralled with Edith's youthful beauty and had taken her as a lesbian lover the night they met.

Edith and Loyal at their wedding. She lied about her age.

Later, Nazimova cast Edith in a small role in 'Ception Shoals, which opened on Broadway on January 10, 1917.

***

After years on the road, Edith decided that her vagabond lifestyle was hardly ideal for bringing up a daughter. She took her to the home of her older sister and brother-in-law, Virginia and C. Audley Galbraith, who lived in a small house in Bethesda, Maryland, outside Washington, D.C. For herself, Edith rented an apartment in Manhattan in the theater district.

Married since 1904, the Galbraiths were a tightly knit, conservative family who offered Nancy a stable environment. A small little corner of an upstairs porch was converted into a sleeping quarters for the newly arrived Nancy.

As Nancy entered grade school, Edith began to face the fact that she'd always be a second tier actress appearing in "third rate productions," for which she usually earned $60 a week. She was approaching middle age, recognizing that if stardom were to come to her, it would have visited her during her twenties.

However, based to some degree on her bubbling personality, she had developed a friendship with big name stars.

One by one, Nancy got to meet such greats as Lillian Gish, Colleen Moore, Walter Huston, and ZaSu Pitts. Edith became extremely intimate with Spencer Tracy, who in time practically became a member of the household. As a young girl, Nancy suspected that Tracy and her mother were having an affair, although he had a wife, Louise, and a deaf son, John.

***

Before the 1920s came to an end, life changed drastically for Edith and ultimately for Nancy, too. Sailing for Europe from the port of New York aboard the *SS New York*, Edith met Dr. Loyal Davis, who hated his first name. Edith was at the "dangerous" age of thirty-nine, back when a woman that old found it almost impossible to find a second husband.

Davis was only thirty-one and an associate professor of surgery at Northwestern University. He had earned his M.D. in 1918, and five years later, had studied with Dr. Harvey Cushing, later hailed as the pioneer of modern neurosurgery in America.

Davis himself had become the first neuro-surgery specialist in Chicago. "I operate on man's most delicate parts, his brain and his spinal cord," Loyal said.

A shipboard romance was launched, though Edith was disappointed after learning that he already had a wife, Pearl, in Chicago, and a two-year-old son, Richard. He assured Edith that his marriage was all but over.

After he delivered a speech at a medical conference in London, he headed with Edith for an

Nancy Robbins Davis at graduation from Girls' Latin.

adulterous holiday on the French Riviera, settling into chic Cannes.

Although they went their separate ways after their return to America, they vowed to meet again after he solved his domestic problems in Chicago.

In a fit of delayed good intentions during a stopover in New York, the recently divorced Dr. Loyal married Edith in a union that would survive till the end of their respective lives. Huston functioned as their best man at their wedding in October of 1928. Young Nancy, back in Chicago, did not attend.

The newly married couple soon provided a home in Chicago for Nancy.

Loyal could afford to send Nancy to the exclusive Girls' Latin School of Chicago. He was charging $500 for a major brain operation; $150 for a prefrontal lobotomy.

His marriage to Edith would last fifty-three years and became, in time, a sort of role model for Nancy's long-enduring marriage to Ronald Reagan.

Politically, at the time, Edith was perceived as "a short, gay Democrat," and Loyal labeled as a "tall, serious Republican."

Although Loyal did not officially adopt Nancy until 1938, she always referred to him as "my father." Later in her life, when challenged about that claim, she said, "I don't care. Loyal was my father in my mind." In her memoirs, she wrote: "Since Kenneth Robbins was such a small part of my life, it is impossible for me to think of him as my father."

At the time of her adoption by Loyal, she legally changed her name to Nancy Davis.

At school in Chicago, Nancy became an avid movie fan and was allowed to go to the cinema with girlfriends whenever she wanted. She developed a very serious crush on Tyrone Power. A girlfriend remembered that she eventually collected enough pictures and articles for the compilation of a thick scrapbook on the handsome movie star, whom she defined as "a living doll." She also maintained a crush on fast-rising Jimmy Stewart, whom she would later meet.

Ironically, one of her acquaintances, Mary Beth Langford, had a crush on a different handsome new star at Warner Brothers. Nancy, however, was rather dismissive of the girl's infatuation. "I just don't understand what you see in Ronald Reagan."

Nazimova came through Chicago, appearing in her hit play, Ibsen's *Ghosts*. Nancy's godmother introduced her to her new lover, Glesca Marshall.

Edith had such an attractive personality that she became friends with two of the biggest names in the theater or in cinema, both Lillian Gish and Helen Hayes, each of whom visited her in Chicago. There, the two great stars were introduced to young Nancy.

***

It had to happen. When Nancy proclaimed herself "sweet sixteen," her interest in boys overpowered her fascination with the movies and its male stars.

Her friends maintained that she had many beaux, and, in the words of one jealous rival, "Nancy was determined to lose her virginity before the rest of us. She was a very pushy person and always had to be the first in everything."

Into her life came a tall, red-haired young man, Sangston Hettler, Jr., a student in Chicago at Boys' Latin. Nicknamed "Sock," he was popular with the girls and admired for his good looks and athletic body. According to reports, he fell madly in love with Nancy.

Young men, out to prove their emerging manhood, liked to boast of their affairs. Whether it was true or not, Sangston bragged, "I taught Nancy about the birds and bees."

For a while, Nancy continued to date Sock, who invited her once a week to Chicago's chic Fortnightly Club, a members' only dinner and dancing club in a stately Georgian mansion. One night, Nancy took the microphone and sang "Pennies from Heaven" to the other patrons. Sock later said, "Nancy wasn't exactly Dinah Shore, but she wasn't as bad as I feared."

When she heard that Sock was telling his friends that he'd taken her virginity, she dropped him.

After Nancy broke up with Sock, she tried to get dates with Robert Crane, scion of a wealthy plumbing contractor, and with Buddy Baird, whose family had made a million or two in real estate.

"Although she pursued Bobby and me, we weren't that interested in taking her out," Baird said. "We had far prettier girls chasing after us. I noticed that Nancy pursued only guys from rich families. I called her 'La Belle,' as did most of her classmates behind her back."

Baird also claimed that Nancy "shopped" around Chicago for the scions of dynastic fortunes—Armours and Swifts, the meatpackers; McCormicks of farm machinery; Palmers and Fields in retail; or the Wrigleys in chewing gum.

At the age of sixteen, Nancy's birthday present was her first car, a black Mercury convertible with red leather

Nancy Robbins Davis as a debutante at the "official beginning" of her adult life.

17

upholstery.

Ironically, in her senior year, she was cast in her school's production of the George S. Kaufman play, *The First Lady*, which had premiered on Broadway at the Music Box Theatre in 1935.

The plot spun around two determined women intent on putting their men into the Oval Office. One of the politicians was identified as "Good looking, a Westerner, and he doesn't know a thing." In the 1980s, the same charge would be leveled against Ronald Reagan.

According to the plot, through various means of treachery, Nancy's character succeeded in getting her man into the White House after delivering a slogan that she remembered years later as one of her favorites: "The American people ought to elect the First Lady and then let her husband be President."

As Europe went to war in 1939, Nancy graduated from Chicago's Girls' Latin School.

***

With a major in English and drama, coed Nancy Davis enrolled at Smith College in September of 1939. For the world at large, it was a dreadful time. In Berlin, Hitler ordered a Nazi attack on Poland, launching World War II. Wartime deprivations at Smith lay in the immediate future, but Nancy didn't seem overly concerned. "I have no interest whatsoever in politics," she proclaimed.

She was attending the largest women's resident liberal arts college in America. Within the Ivy League's circle of elite schools, Smith was included among the prestigious "Seven Sisters" colleges.

As Nancy herself confessed in her memoirs, *My Turn*, "At Smith College, I majored in English and drama—and boys."

Returning to Chicago for the Christmas holidays of 1939, Nancy was to face one of the milestones of her life. On December 28, at a tea dance, she would launch herself as a debutante at the Casino Club and acquire a new beau while doing it.

Fifty Princeton men, in Chicago as escorts for the various debutante launches, were invited. In walked Frank Birney, Jr. The son of a Chicago banker, he was a member of the Triangle Theater Club at Princeton.

When they were introduced, Nancy found Birney "charming, gracious, witty, and very good looking."

"Nancy was not everyone's *cuppa*," said one of the guests, William Barton, unchivalrously. "But Frank seemed to go for her, although the guys at Princeton didn't think he liked girls all that much. Nancy appeared open and friendly and looked like she was an easy lay if you wanted it."

Back at Smith, Nancy began to date Birney on weekends and was intrigued that he, too, wanted

Although lovely, cosmetic surgery after college changed Nancy's look and especially her nose, into something more in synch with prevailing standards of "pert and sassy."

to become a stage actor.

In Manhattan, they often met "under the clock at the Biltmore Hotel." He claimed to his classmates that he was having an affair, hoping to squelch rumors that he was a "sissy boy." Ever since enrolling at Princeton, he had endured taunts from his more "traditionally masculine" classmates.

His roommate, Geoffrey Talbot-Jones, said, "Frank was a manic-depressive and frequently talked about suicide. He was despondent, worrying about flunking out of Princeton because of his poor grades. Toward the end of his life, he was also deeply troubled by some recent involvement he'd had. I presumed he'd had a disastrous sexual encounter with some stranger, and the experience had wounded him in some way. I can't speculate on what that was, but he was demoralized."

Another of Birney's friends, James Easton, said, "I knew Frank was dating Nancy. They seemed to live in a world that, after the war began, no longer existed. They resided in a theatrical world, absolutely oblivious to the Battle of Britain or Hitler's killing of the Jews. He dated her, but I don't think he was in love with her."

Suddenly, in New York City, Birney committed suicide by deliberately darting toward an oncoming train. The *Daily Princetonian* ran a story about his suicide, quoting the train's engineer: "I saw the young man dart out from behind a pole right in front of my oncoming train. I gave a long blast on my whistle, but he kept coming. I applied the brake, but was not able to bring the train to a stop before we struck him. His body was mutilated beyond recognition."

Birney's roommate at Princeton discovered a suicide note, which he turned over to the dead man's family. Nancy flew to their side and offered what comfort she could.

***

Back at Smith, Nancy was a poor student, especially in science and math. She was accused of majoring in extracurricular activities.

After America entered the war during the immediate aftermath of the December, 1941, Japanese attack on Pearl Harbor, eligible men became fewer and fewer. Many of the Smith undergraduates had already kissed their boyfriends goodbye before sending them off to die on the battlefields of Europe or North Africa.

Nancy was not caught up in the war effort, preferring to spend her free time within any of the three movie houses of Northampton, watching films starring such actors as Mickey Rooney or Judy Garland.

She still collected photo albums of movie stars. Tyrone Power remained her favorite, followed by Jimmy Stewart. At some point, Errol Flynn became one of the movie idols she worshipped. After seeing *Kings Row,* she added another young actor, Ronald Reagan, to her growing list of heartthrobs. She'd never cared for Reagan before.

She remained steadfast in her goal of becoming a Broadway star, if not a movie actress.

Much to Nancy's disappointment, neither Loyal nor Edith could attend her graduation ceremonies. Edith faced wartime travel restrictions, and Loyal was on duty as a surgeon for the U.S. Army in England.

But at long last, diploma in hand, Nancy was free to return to Chicago.

Funds were still low, so Nancy went to work as a nurse's aide at the Cook County Hospital. The job, which often consisted of carrying out bedpans, was, to her at least, demeaning. She quit and became a sales clerk at the mammoth Marshall Field Department Store. Her most frightening moment there involved stopping a woman carting off stolen jewelry. When Nancy confronted the thief, she retaliated by ripping off Nancy's dress.

It was during the summer of 1944 that Nancy launched her second "most serious" love affair.

James Platt White, Jr. was a handsome student from Amherst College, in Massachusetts, and the scion of a wealthy family, During World War II, he had joined the Navy.

Later, his college classmates claimed that he spent a great deal of time grooming himself and dressing immaculately. He did not like sports, and preferred theater to football. He shared this common interest in the theatrical world with Nancy. "He didn't really fit in too well with the other frat brothers," a classmate said. "Some guys thought he was a bit of a sissy."

When White's ship docked at San Diego, Nancy visited him. When they went to Hollywood, Nancy, with White accompanying her, paid to visit to Nazimova, a year before her death in 1945.

On June 24, 1944, Loyal and Edith announced Nancy's engagement to White. She was presented with a diamond engagement ring his parents had purchased at Tiffany's. Their engagement lasted until right after the Navy transferred White to the South Pacific.

In her memoirs, Nancy wrote: "I broke off the engagement later that summer. It was a heady, exhilarating time, and I was swept up in the glamour of war, wartime engagements, and waiting for the boys who were away. I realized I had made a mistake. It would have been unfair to him and to me. It wasn't easy to break off an engagement, but it was the best thing for both of us. We weren't meant to be married, but we remain friends to this day."

After years of delay and endless frustration, Nancy decided to launch herself as a stage actress. Edith told her, "I have your back. We'll contact every big name we have, from Lillian Gish to Spencer Tracy, to get you roles. We'll be shameless about it, letting nothing stand in our way."

In the middle of the night, Edith awakened Nancy, telling her about a vivid dream she'd just had. "I dreamed that you're going to become a big star, one of the biggest, right up there with Joan Crawford and Bette Davis. Not only that, but you're going to marry a movie star and have two children with him—a boy and a girl. A future Oscar is already having your name engraved on it."

Chapter One

Jane Wyman Marries a Sex Maniac and Later, a Trannie Who Sold Dresses

Her First Marriage is Suppressed, the Other Forgotten

Mating Games: Jane's Romantic "Detours" with George Raft, Errol Flynn, & Bing Crosby

In these early publicity stills, Jane Wyman could be pouty or fun-crazed. "I didn't exactly take Hollywood by storm, cast as a chorus girl cutie or some star's sidekick for more than a decade," she said. "The directors were retarded in taking notice of me, but the male stars of the 30s found I had a certain allure. If only they'd stop calling me 'Pug Nose.'"

Eugene Wyman carried through on his promise to change the name of Sarah Jane Fulks to Jane Wyman, although she would continue to bill herself with her former name for months to come.

To the horror of her foster mother, Emma Fulks, Jane ran away to marry Eugene, falsifying her real age, since she was still a minor.

When she first went to work in Hollywood, appearing in the chorus line of *The Kid from Spain,* (1932), she told her fellow chorines, Paulette Goddard and Lucille Ball, about her early marriage. But after those revelations, she would remain silent, allowing any link to, or memory of, her first husband to disappear into the vast landscapes of America.

No record has ever been discovered that she divorced Eugene, the implication of which was that she became a bigamist when she remarried.

As relayed to her new friends, Eugene turned out to be some sort of a sex fiend. As Jane confided, "He didn't just want to make love to a girl, he wanted to devour her." On her honeymoon night in a cheap roadside motel, he had sex with her six times, followed by three more bouts before noon the following day.

Since she had no basis for comparison, she initially thought all men were like Eugene. During her first week of marriage, she also learned that his heavy drinking sometimes made him violent.

She had to endure several beatings, and she plotted to run away from him. But she really had no place to go. Emma had virtually disowned her.

When Jane threatened to leave him, he vowed that he'd carve up her face with a broken beer bottle.

Early Cheesecake: Jane *(right figure)* in *King of Burlesque* (1935)

He earned enough at his garage that he did provide her with food and lodging in a cheap apartment in West Hollywood. The marriage limped along for a month, going from bad to horrific.

One night, when he came home drunk, he was with his best friend, a studly farmboy he'd known when he lived in Bakersfield. She was asleep when the two men entered her bedroom and Eugene ripped the covers off her. He also tore off her flimsy garment, as she tried to cover her nudity in front of this stranger.

As she'd later relate to Goddard and Ball, Eugene not only held her down while his burly friend raped her, he then mounted her himself, deliberately trying to hurt her. She spent the rest of the night as the prisoner of both of these strong young men, as she was mauled and repeatedly attacked.

She stayed awake all night, and Eugene's friend left shortly before six. Since Eugene didn't work on Sundays, he was still sound asleep. Quietly, she gathered up her clothing and found his wallet on the dresser. It contained eighty dollars, which she removed. Then she silently made her way out the door with her battered suitcase and into the early morning air. Her body ached.

Later that day, she took a bus to southern Los Angeles, where she found a room for rent at eight dollars a week in a shabby boarding house filled mostly with Mexican laborers.

For the next few weeks, she found what jobs she could—waitress, switchboard operator, manicurist, but nothing worked out. One day, she heard that LeRoy Prinz was becoming one of the lead choreographers of Hollywood. He was the son of Edward ("Dad") Prinz, who had been her dance instructor in St. Joseph.

On her day off, she showed up at his studio, which was very informal. She walked in and introduced herself to the choreographer, who had been working on musicals since 1929 with the advent of the Talkies.

She found him charismatic, and he liked her in spite of her shyness. Apparently, "Dad" had told him about her, and he was eager to meet her.

During the next few days, as he practiced dance routines with her, she came to know him quite well. As she remembered LeRoy, he "was a little giant standing five feet, five inches, with a potty mouth. He was a feisty little man, who always had a cigarette dangling from his lips and looked more like a bartender than a choreographer."

In a profile in *The New York Times,* LeRoy's life story was compared to that of a script for an Errol Flynn adventure picture.

The Times had not exaggerated. He'd been sent to reform school after chasing his stepmother with a carving knife. Later, upon his release, he formed a song-and-dance act on the vaudeville circuit. Called "Prinz and Buck," he danced onstage with a young black man.

As he grew older, he became a cabin boy aboard a ship heading for France. When he got there, he hitchhiked to Marseille, where he joined the French Foreign Legion, serving as a bugler in Algiers. When World War I erupted, he became a pilot for Captain Eddie Rickenbacker's 94th Aero Squadron, where he crashed eighteen planes and was nicknamed "America's German Ace."

At war's end, he drifted to Paris, where he was hired as a choreographer for the *Folies Bergère.*

Returning to the Americas, he ferried ammunition for Nicaraguan rebel leader, Augusto César Sandino. When that came to an end, he flew to Mexico City, teaching young wannabee pilots how to fly.

Finally, he returned to the States, first settling in Omaha, Nebraska, where he danced in a bordello, Heading east to Chicago, he became for a time the producer of special shows for Al Capone and his gangsters. Eventually, he made it to New York, where he was hired as a dancer by the famous nightclub entrepreneur, Texas Guinan.

With the advent of sound, after Hollywood began to produce musicals, LeRoy headed West, where he found jobs directing dance sequences for Paramount and then Warner Brothers.

Using his influence, LeRoy obtained a job for Jane dancing as one of the Goldwyn girls in the chorus line of *The Kid from Spain* (1932).

LeRoy told her that Samuel Goldwyn was "always on the look-out for pretty young fillies to add to his stable of stunning chorines."

It was on the set of this slapstick comedy (Jane's first-ever film role) that she was befriended by Goddard and Lucille Ball, and also by the young star, Betty Grable.

Grable later recalled meeting Jane. "She and I were regarded as 'ponies' in the Goldwyn stable be-

After leading a wild life of high adventure, LeRoy Prinz, Jane's dance teacher, rehearses Mary Martin for a 1939 appearance in *The Great Victor Herbert.*

cause we were the smallest of the dancing girls."

"I had signed a contract claiming I was sixteen years old," Grable said. "Jane, too, lied about her age, making herself older. I would have to stand still for two years until my real age caught up with me. Jane, too."

"Lucy, Paulette, Betty, and I were on the long road to stardom," Jane said. "For Lucy and Betty, and for me, it was a long, tortuous road. But, frankly, Paulette took a few shortcuts to stardom, but I never wanted to play the casting couch game."

After Jane's violent rape by Eugene and his

The Kid from Spain: Jane Wyman is lower right; Lucille Ball is second from top; Paulette Goddard fourth from the bottom.

friend, she confided to Goddard, "I feel I don't have any morality left to hold onto, not now, not after what happened to me. I was used like a cheap whore."

"You can turn that to your advantage," Goddard said. "Now that you're already a fallen woman, fuck your way to the top, baby."

Goddard certainly took her own advice, sleeping with Joseph M. Schenck, who became chairman of 20th Century Fox. She also bedded such big box office draws as Gary Cooper and Clark Gable before landing in the marriage bed of the very successful, very rich Charlie Chaplin, who had once exposed himself to Jane.

The comedian—frenetic, goggle-eyed Eddie Cantor—was the star of the picture. Other than waiting around between scenes, Jane didn't have that much to do, so she watched Cantor emote in front of the camera, doing the eye-rolling song-and-dance routines whose oft-repeated gags made him famous. They had earned him the nickname, "Banjo Eyes."

Even though her part was miniscule, and limited just to the chorus, Jane exchanged pleasantries with the film's well-established director, Leo McCarey, who had been working in silent films since 1921.

Jane also met Busby Berkeley, who choreographed some of *The Kid From Spain's* dance numbers. He gave Jane her first screen close-up, as part of the technique he had developed, the "parade of faces"–individualizing each chorus girl with a loving close-up.

Jane's first Hollywood seduction was with a young Robert Young, who was ridiculously cast in *Kid from Spain* as Ricardo, a Latin Lover type with a pencil-thin mustache. Before breaking into pictures, he'd been a bank teller, a reporter, and a shoe salesman.

After three dates, he seduced her on a Saturday night. The following Monday, Goddard asked her, "How was it?"

"I was screwed by a real gentleman," Jane said. "After my disastrous marriage, I thought all men were brutes in bed. Robert did it with courtesy and such politeness. He even thanked me profusely at the end."

That same Monday, the film's director, McCarey, confronted Young and told him, "You don't have any screen eroticism. I don't think you'll make it in pictures."

Weeks after the picture was wrapped, Jane had a chance encounter with Young on Hollywood Boulevard. "The reviews of *The Kid from Spain* have come out," he said. "One paper wrote, 'Robert Young is less noticeable than the rest of the cast.'"

"I'm sorry Robert. Better luck next time," she said, giving him a kiss on the cheek before moving on.

***

Meanwhile, Paulette Goddard was sleeping with director Mervyn LeRoy, who, in time, would become known for helping launch such stars as Edward G. Robinson, Clark Gable, Loretta Young, and Robert Mitchum. LeRoy was also known for seducing some of the great beauties of Hollywood, including blondes such as Ginger Rogers and Lana Turner.

Goddard used her influence with LeRoy to get him to cast Jane in a small part in a film he was directing, *Elmer the Great* (1932), an ode to the Great American Sport, wherein a country hick bats his way to stardom.

Elmer the Great was conceived as a vehicle for the endless corny vaudevillian character actor, Joe E. Brown, whose wide mouth was frequently compared to the Grand Canyon. The female lead was awarded to Patricia Ellis, the self-proclaimed "Queen of the Bs" at Warner.

At Goddard's urging, Jane hinted to LeRoy that she'd be available for dates, but he didn't seem that interested. He later boasted that he had "discovered" Jane Wyman. "Jack Warner had signed her. I first spotted her walking around the lot in a yellow polo coat. I decided she'd be right for this part in *Elmer*. I cast her and she did a swell job. Her career was launched."

In contrast to LeRoy, Brown made many seductive hits on Jane, as she confessed to Goddard. "I think he's goofy looking," Jane said. "He's not my type at all. Unlike you, I'll sleep with a director or a star, but only if he's good looking, I insist on that."

During the filming, Jane and Goddard became close friends. Goddard, by now a star in her own right, confessed to Jane that she had gotten her start on Broadway "by letting Florence Ziegfeld fuck

Chorine, Betty Grable

Chorine, Paulette Goddard

Chorine, Lucille Ball

25

me."

Goddard's advice to Wyman was to continue to pursue her screen career, providing that she had married "some rich businessman who pays for your upkeep and isn't stingy with mink coats and diamond rings."

Why was Joe E. Brown called "Mr. Big Mouth?"

 ***

Robert Young in the 1930s... "No erotic fire."

Chicago-born director, Norman Taurog, who in time would helm eighty films, offered Jane a small role in the latest Jack Oakie film, *College Rhythm. [Its plot involves the college rivalry of a piccolo player and an All-American halfback who both love the same coed.]* Oakie had appeared in so many of these collegiate films that he was known as "The World's Oldest Freshman."

Although he liked Jane, Taurog failed to see her potential. "I'm not surprised," she recalled. "My God, in the past few months, he'd directed Gary Cooper, George Raft, Charles Laughton, W.C. Fields, and Carole Lombard. How could I measure up to those guys?"

In *College Rhythm*, Oakie played the role of "Love 'n' Kisses Finnegan," a once-celebrated college quarterback who, after graduation, falls on hard times. He finds work at a department store, where his status as a former football star is broadcast as an advertising ploy.

Jane told Taurog that "Oakie made a pass at me, but didn't score a touchdown off screen." Even though she turned him down, she respected his comedic talent.

Jane asked Taurog if he thought she'd ever graduate from a bit-part player in the chorus line into a major actress. "Your speaking voice is poorly pitched and unsteady in tone," he responded. "It doesn't match your face. And that heart-shaped face of yours! I don't know how it would go over in a dramatic role. The cast members call you 'Dog Puss.'"

Jane spent much of her time on the movie set, laughing and talking with Franklin Pangborn, one of Hollywood's most visible stately homos of the 1930s. His fussy and effeminate mannerisms were matched only by those of Edward Everett Horton.

Pangborn showed her an article written by the militant film censor Joseph Breen in 1932. Breen had claimed that

Busby Berkeley, a neurotic perfectionist, directing *Babes on Broadway* in 1941.

sexual perversions were rampant among the Hollywood colony, alleging that many directors and male stars were queer.

[Between 1934 and 1955, Breen, a strict (some say rabid, with a sense of mis-

sionary zeal) Roman Catholic, was a film censor with the Motion Picture Producers and Distributors of America.He zealously applied the stuffy and punitive Hays Code to film production, much to the rage and frustration of avant-garde directors, actors, writers, and civil libertarians.]

Pangborn also showed her an article from *Variety.* "Effeminate boys have crept into motion pictures," it stated. "Winked at, they are now a comedy staple."

"If a director needs a swishy interpretation, I'm his boy," Pangborn told Jane.

Movie director, Mervyn LeRoy (*right*), boasted of launching the career of Jane Wyman. Matinee heartthrob Robert Taylor would discover Jane in a more intimate way.

On the set of *College Rhythm,* Jane met a fellow bit player billed as Clara Lou Sheridan. She would later become famous as the movie star, Ann Sheridan. She appeared in two scenes, first as a glove saleswoman and later as a spectator at the department store football game.

Jane spoke to her only casually, never realizing that she would, in the years to come, become a frequent visitor at her home during her marriage to Ronald Reagan, with whom Sheridan would later star.

When Jane went to see the final cut of *College Rhythm,* she said, ruefully, "Goo-Goo," the mascot duck for the football team, walked off with the picture."

***

Jane went on to play a very small role in the frothy 1935 film, *All the King's Horses*, a mediocre musical about a movie star who exchanges places with lookalike king from the mythical kingdom of Ruritania, causing political and romantic complications for both of them.

Non-Collegians: Jack Oakie with Mary Brian.

Its director, Frank Tuttle, had helmed movies since 1922, including *The Untamed Lady* (1926), with Gloria Swanson, and *Kid Boots* (also in 1926), starring Eddie Cantor and Clara Bow.

A former prizefighter, the Danish film actor and singer, Carl Brisson, was the film's dashing star, cast into the double roles of both the King (Rudolf XIV) and the hapless actor (Carlo Rocco) who temporarily "replaces" him.

A star from the British stage, Mary Ellis, was cast as the film's dignified female lead, Elaine, Queen of Langenstein. Known for her roles in musical theater, Ellis had sung at New York's Metropolitan Opera House with operatic superstar Enrico Caruso.

Two character actors, Eugene Pallette and Edward Everett Horton, became two of the most unusual characters Jane would ever meet. Early in his career, Pallette was a slender leading man, but he morphed into a very obese actor with a large stomach and a deep, gravelly voice.

[Pallette liked Jane as a friend and would remain friendly with her throughout the war years. In 1946, he became convinced that a "world blow-up" was imminent, fearing—with some justification—that the planet was threatened by atomic bombs.

He purchased a 3,500-acre mountain fortress in Imnaha, Oregon, to await the nuclear holocaust.

Jane was among the people to whom he extended an invitation there for survival. On his ranch, he had a large herd of prize cattle, a vast amount of food, and his own canning plant and lumber mill.

Jane meets the two most visible and reliable homos of Hollywood—Franklin Pangborn *(left)* and Edward Everett Horton.

Jane thanked him, but turned down his invitation. When the world blowup did not happen within two years, as he had predicted, he sold the ranch and returned to Hollywood, but never made another movie.]

After working with Pangborn, Edward Everett Horton became the second "stately homo" of Hollywood with whom Jane would work. She found him vastly amusing. He told her, "Even though homosexuality can't be depicted on the screen, it is hiding in plain sight. I entered films at the height of the so-called Pansy Craze. It pays for me to be a sap or a mouse on screen. Those are euphemisms for queers. If a director wants a bumbling, stuttering, fluttering, actor, here I am. If the macho leading man needs a fairy friend, here I am, twinkle toes and all."

***

Jane's next picture was *Rumba* (1935). *[A bored debutante pursues, romantically, a Latino dancer in a Broadway show.]* Its 71-minute screenplay featured two big stars, George Raft and Carole Lombard. As its director, Paramount selected Russian-born Marion Gering. Before arriving in Hollywood to direct some Sylvia Sidney movies, he had helmed many plays on Broadway.

Raft and Lombard had had a hit when they'd filmed *Bolero* together the previous year. Paramount was hoping—in vain—that lightning would strike twice. In *Bolero*, Raft and Lombard had created fireworks both privately and onscreen, but their torrid romance seemed to have fizzled before filming began on *Rumba.*

The film is perhaps best remembered for a scene in which Raft, in tails, dances sublimely with Lombard, in shimmering silver lamé against a backdrop of stylized tropical vegetation. But in spite of its impressive cast, *Rumba* didn't project the sparks that *Bolero* did.

Also appearing in *Rumba* as an uncredited chorus girl, like Jane, was Texas born Ann Sheridan, an actress

Carl Brisson

28

known for her acerbic wit, her come-hither looks, and her deep, suggestive voice. She would soon be christened the "Oomph Girl" by Hollywood Publicists. She became friends with Jane on the set of *Rumba*. Despite its commercial appeal, however, Sheridan despised the "Oomph" label, telling Jane, "*Oomph* is a noise a fat man makes when he bends over to tie his shoelace in a phone booth."

Like Paulette Goddard and Lucille Ball, Sheridan planned to "sample the wares" of some of the leading stars of Hollywood—and she did.

Apocalytic visionary: Eugene Pallette

Jack Benny said, "Annie was just a plain, simple girl. She liked her sex simple and her liquor plain, and she liked a lot of men and a lot of liquor." Ultimately, Sheridan agreed with the comedian's assessment of her.

While making *Rumba,* Sheridan took Jane on a "troll" of the Hollywood bars. "After a few drinks, I passed out," Jane said, "but Annie was just starting her binge."

During the making of *Rumba,* Sheridan agreed to pose for some publicity stills, trying to make herself look super sexy. Privately, she told Jane, "I have the body of a skinny young man."

Since her figure was less than shapely, wardrobe made a chest harness for her, with rubber, size-38 breasts.

As Jane looked on, and as the day grew hotter, it became time for lunch. Annoyed at the discomfort of the harness, Sheridan took it off and slung it at Jane. "Honey, hold my tits for me while I change into something more comfortable."

During her early days at Warners, Jane, like Sheridan, would also be asked to seductively pose for cheesecake. Jane herself was soonafter reminded of how Hollywood bestowed breasts upon its flat-chested stars and wannabees. As she was walking by Lombard's dressing room, the blonde-haired star opened the door and called out to one of the wardrobe men. "Okay, faggot, bring me my tits."

When Jane completed her work on *Rumba*, she bid farewell to the cast and crew, hoping they might work together on some future project. When she approached Raft, he said, "I like your looks, Pug Nose. How about a date with me tonight? I think there's a role for you in my next picture."

"I'd be honored to go out with you, Mr. Raft," she answered.

***

To Jane, and to thousands of his fans, Raft was exciting, intriguing, and charismatic. A Broadway dancer, a Hollywood tough guy, a gambler, and a Don Juan with a life-long involvement in the Underworld, he had emerged from Hell's Kitchen in New York. Having been born there in 1895, he was a juvenile delinquent and a member of a rough-and-tumble street gang before becoming a boxer.

Deciding that boxing wasn't for him, he became a dancehall gigolo, rooming with and loving his counterpart, Rudolph Valentino. Together, they worked the "tea rooms"

George Raft romances Carole Lombard, with Jane on the side, in *Rumba*

29

of Manhattan and later made professional love to aging, rich women before returning to their shared apartment and their mutual bed.

One client fell in love with Raft and nearly fatally stabbed him when she learned that he was dating her so-called best friend.

Eventually, Raft fell into the bed of the queen of New York City nightlife, Texas Guinan. She typecast him as a gigolo, an association that would remain with him throughout the rest of his career, in her movie, *Queen of the Night Clubs* (1929).

From that lowly beginning, he drifted into movie work.

After his hit film, *Scarface* (1932), he joined the pantheon of Warner Brothers' screen gangsters, the most visible of which included Edward G. Robinson, James Cagney, and the emerging Humphrey Bogart.

Ann Sheridan admitted, "I have no tits," but Hollywood billed her as *"über-glamorous, über-sexy."*

Raft also starred in Mae West's first film, *Night After Night* (1932), and had an affair with her. Later, after he saw the final cut, he turned on her. "The bitch committed armed robbery in stealing the picture from me."

After 1932, he perfected his evil sneer and rude, stoic manner that would carry him through the 1930s. But with the passage of youth, his wooden presence on the screen would grow more dreary with each lackluster picture.

Jane would go out on two separate dates with Raft, both of which led to violence. Early on the evening of the first date, he'd taken her to the Café Trocadero on Sunset Strip. Almost overnight, it had become the place for Hollywood stars to be seen. A black tie, French-inspired supper club in the posh Sunset Plaza section of the Strip, it had quickly become one of the most famous nightclubs in the world.

But when a waiter served Raft a gin and tonic that was not to his liking, the movie star tossed the drink into the young man's face. Jane was horrified at such behavior, but said nothing.

Many sources claim that Raft did not drink, but many of his dates, including Jane, differed, suggesting that he was a binge drinker who could go for weeks without a drink before having a heavy bout with liquor.

Raft had been drinking heavily that night and invited Jane back to his apartment. With reluctance, she accepted the invitation, her decision based to some degree on her hopes of snagging a role in his next picture.

Inside his apartment, furnished in what she called "gangster modern," she was introduced to Mack Grey. Raft referred to him as "My Man Friday."

Raft put on some recorded music. To her astonishment, he ordered Grey to dance for him. When his servant wasn't dancing fast enough to please his boss, Raft removed a revolver and shot two .38 caliber bullets at the floor, narrowly missing Grey's feet. After that, he danced faster.

One of the two bullets had penetrated through to the floor below, embedding itself into the sofa of Mrs. Jack Warner, the former Irma Solomons, an heiress. It caused a small scandal that was quickly hushed up.ᶠ

As Jane later reflected, "That bullet could have ended both my future career at Warners and Raft's, too."

In spite of her disastrous first date, she agreed to return to the Trocadero with Raft on a second date. She still wanted that part in his next movie.

When Raft escorted Jane to the dance floor at "The Troc," the two professional dancers created such a sensation that the other couples quit dancing and formed a circle around them to watch the exhibition.

Later, at table, Raft told her, "I could have become mainstream Hollywood's first X-rated dancer. I was very erotic in my dances in New York. I caressed my body, especially Black Snake. To make it bigger, I fondled it as I danced, and it grew bigger and bigger, much to the delight of the squealing women in the audience."

Raft always referred to his large penis as "Black Snake," and, according to women who had gone to bed with him, it was an apt description.

As Jane would later tell Lucille Ball, "Grey wasn't there at his apartment that night. Raft didn't attempt to seduce me with any subtlety. He was drunk and attacked me, ripping my dress. He raped me, although, frankly, I didn't put up much resistance."

To Jane's surprise, she learned later that both of her friends, Ball and Betty Grable, had each had flings with Raft, too.

Once, Ball confessed that she'd become involved with Grey before her involvement with Raft. "He doesn't have a pretty face, but he can have any woman he wants when he takes off his clothes." Grey had risen from the back streets of Brooklyn and had been known by the mob as "The Killer."

Ball admitted that Raft finally seduced her himself, although Tallulah Bankhead had warned her that she'd gotten gonorrhea from Raft. Before his involvement with Ball, Raft had assured her that he'd been cured.

"We had several fights," Ball claimed. "One time he got so mad at me, he broke into my apartment and cut up all my clothing with a pair of tailor scissors."

Ball also confided, "Did that guy like to screw. On his day off, he devoted at least twelve hours a day to prolonged screwing. He told me he averaged at least two women a day."

Years later, Grable also told Jane about her own disastrous involvement with Raft, who beat her on occasion. "He said he wanted to marry me. No way! Personally, I think he's a latent homosexual, in spite of his womanizing."

Raft carried through on his promise to Jane and got her a small part in *Stolen Harmony* (1935), directed by Alfred L. Werker, who had been involved in filmmaking beginning with the Silents in 1917. He had earned the undying animosity of the temperamental director, Erich von Stroheim, when Fox called him in to reshoot and re-edit the director's film, *Hello Sister!* (1933).

After working with Jane and others, Werker, in the early 1940s, had directed a number of comedies for Laurel and Hardy.

In *Stolen Harmony,* Raft was cast as a dancer/actor/gangster who, after his release from prison, joins Ben Bernie's Swing Band, playing a mean saxophone. Various misadventures take place before Raft finally saves the day and rescues the band.

Band leader Ben *["The Old Maestro,"]* Bernie and his band starred in the movie. Bernie was a jazz violinist and radio personality known for his showmanship and memorable bits of snappy dialogue. Jane had often danced to his hit record, "Sweet Georgia Brown."

To beef up her income, Jane asked if she could appear as a vocalist with his band, since she was also a singer. He turned her down, later picking Dinah Shore for the spot instead.

Lloyd Nolan, born in San Francisco, made his film debut in *Stolen Harmony*. He would go on to become one of the leading character actors in Hollywood.

Jane was on the set of *Stolen Harmony* as a witness to one of the most violent cops-and-robber shootouts in the history of the movies. After the film's release, it was determined that some of its scenes were so violent that a few states refused to allow the movie to be screened until parts of it were cut.

Variety infuriated Raft when it suggested that a double was used in many of his dance numbers. "I don't need a fucking double. I'm a dancer. There are two dancing gangster actors in Hollywood, George Raft, number one, and James Cagney, a distant second."

***

Jane was beginning to despair at the direction of her career, since she seemed stuck as an uncredited cutie in the film industry's chorus line. Yet when she was offered another uncredited part, this time in *King of Burlesque* (1936), she accepted. During those Depression years, any paycheck, even a meager one, was welcomed.

But 1936 would turn out to be one of her best years so far, as she appeared in six movies.

At Paramount, Jane was not under contract, but was simply an extra, hired whenever a "perky" blonde was called for. She stood 5'5", tall for the day, and her hair and trim figure were in style. She had large brown eyes and high cheekbones. She photographed well, but she was still self-conscious about her appearance, working hard to gain confidence.

She had also picked up an agent, actually an actor/agent. Minnesota-born William Demarest had worked in vaudeville before coming to Hollywood in 1926 to begin a career in silent films. He'd have his greatest film success with Preston Sturges, appearing in such hits as *Sullivan's Travels* and *The Miracle of Morgan's Creek*. Like Jane, he'd go on to big success in television, notably in the sitcom *My Three Sons [it ran from 1965 to 1972]*, in which he appeared opposite Fred MacMurray.

In the mid-1930s, when acting jobs were scarce, he hustled roles for other actors, including Jane.

She later commented on that period of her life. "A lot of men had tried to exploit me, and it had toughened me up. I heard a lot of sweet talk and heaps of promises that amounted to nothing. But a few along the way genuinely had my welfare at heart, notably William Demarest."

Years later, she spoke of this time to *Guidepost* magazine. "For a girl who grew up in terror at being looked at, it was agony for me to appear on camera. Then I made a discovery: A good shield for shyness is a bold exterior. Did my heart turn over when the man with a megaphone bellowed my name? Were all the other dancers prettier? Never mind. I covered up my shyness by becoming the cockiest of all, by talking the loudest, laughing the longest, and wearing the curliest, most blatantly false eyelashes in Hollywood."

Even thought her role was small in *King of Burlesque,* Jane was thrilled to be working with some top professionals in the business. The one-time jazz musician and vaudevillian star, Sidney Lanfield, had signed to direct. He had been working at Fox since 1930. In 1955, he and Jane would work together again on television's *Fireside Theater.*

She wasn't thrilled to see Jack Oakie again, this time cast in third billing, but she was impressed with the film's other star, Warner Baxter, who at the time was the highest paid male movie actor in Hollywood, and the blonde singer, Alice Faye, goddess of the 20th Century Fox lot until she was replaced in the 1940s by Jane's friend, Betty Grable.

At the wrap party, Demarest, her agent, told Jane, "You've got to do a quickie with Big Mouth."

"Oh, no, not Joe E. Brown again," she protested. "Oh, yes," he said.

***

On the set of *Polo Joe* (1936), Jane once again faced Joe E. Brown, whose contract with Warners was nearing its end. As his farewell gesture to the studio, Brown and his gaping mouth appeared in this lackluster slapstick directed by William McCann.

Years later, Jane claimed she could not remember what she had to do in the movie. All that she recalled was Brown telling her what pleasure he could provide her with his canyon of a mouth.

William Demarest, Jane's first Hollywood agent: "God, she was jumpy. Thought I was going to rape her."

On the set of *Polo Joe,* Jane escaped from the hot pursuit of Brown and fell into the strong, muscular arms of Wayne Morris, a tall, good-looking blonde with a slow drawl who had just signed a contract with Warners.

To Jane, Wayne represented the ideal American male. She told her friends, "Every high school has a Wayne Morris type. He's usually the captain of the football team. I could easily fall in love with him, but I held my heart in check when I learned that he went out with a different girl at least four nights a week. With him, the line of beauties pursuing him formed on both the left and the right."

"Until I learned more about him, I was in love with him," Jane said. "Yes, it led to a sleepover in his apartment. He's completely skilled in the art of lovemaking. Wayne was like a kid in the Hollywood candy store, wanting to sample all the sugary goodies, of which I was a nugget."

*[*Polo Joe *marked Jane's long association, both professional and private, with Morris.*

A native of Los Angeles, Morris played football at Los Angeles Junior College. Later, he worked as a forest ranger. He returned to Los Angeles and studied acting at the Pasadena Playhouse, where a Warner Brothers talent agent spotted him in 1936. Blonde and open-faced, he was the perfect type for "the boy-next-door" parts.]

***

Co-starring Carole Lombard and William Powell, *My Man Godfrey* (1936) was a comedy-drama directed by Gregory La Cava, a freelancer throughout most of his career. The story was about a Depression-era socialite (Lombard) who hires a dignified, handsome derelict (Powell) to be her family's butler, only to fall in love with him.

Both Constance Bennett and Miriam Hopkins had been considered for the role, but Powell had insisted on Lombard. *[The couple had been married from 1931 until their divorce in 1933. Their cinematic pairing was interpreted at the time as a rare example of friendship triumphing over heartbreak in the aftermath of a stormy marriage.]*

As he had during the course of their real-life marriage, Powell continued to object to Lombard's obscene vocabulary, every other word being "fuck" or "shit." During her divorce proceedings, she had accused him of being a very emotional man "cruel and coarse in manners of language who displayed his temper repeatedly." Ironically, at least for the purposes of their reappearance on screen, their former courtside acrimonies were set aside.

Jane agreed with Graham Greene's 1936 assessment: "Mr. Powell is a little too immaculate, his wit is too well-turned, just as his clothes are too well-made; he drinks hard but only in the best of bars. He is rather like an advertisement of a man about town in *Esquire."*

Although an aging actor, born in 1892, Powell was still an attractive, sophisticated man. Jane was reluctant to flirt with him, because all of Hollywood knew that he was in love at the time with the platinum blonde bombshell Jean Harlow.

[In June of 1937, Harlow's early death would shock the world. Clark Gable forced his way into her home after she had been absent from the studio, and incommunicado for a week. He discovered that the star was dying because her mother, a Christian Science devotee, refused to send her to the hospital for an operation.]

Wayne Morris was a Warner Brothers' heartthrob of the 1930s. Jane had nothing but praise for "his football player physique and his virility."

On the set, Jane spotted the director, La Cava, sitting by himself after lunch. She approached him and asked for advice about her career. He looked her over very carefully. "My suggestion is that you learn to play sickeningly sweet, pure honey type of roles," he told her. "That way, you can replace Loretta Young on the screen."

Jane was at first delighted to have been cast in *My Man Godfrey,* calling it "my first big break." I've got two lines of dialogue with Lombard. In the 20s, I heard that Howard Hughes had taught her about the birds and the bees. I flubbed my lines three times, but Carole was very helpful."

Jane recalled, "I faced real competition to get noticed from the other players in this film. In the supporting cast was Alice Brady, who stole the picture, along with Gail Patrick, Jean Dixon, my old buddy, Eugene Pallette, Alan Mowbray, and Mischa Auer. How do you follow acts like theirs?"

Jane was cast in a scavenger hunt scene, but most of the footage ended up on the cutting room floor. "I'm still in the picture," she said. "You can catch me next to the organ grinder and this damn vicious little monkey. The bastard bit me so hard, I screamed."

***

Running only one hour, *Here Comes Carter* was the fifth Warners' short film to be directed by William Clemens, a Hollywood veteran best known for having previously helmed the three of the studio's most durable series: Philo Vance, Nancy Drew, and The Falcon.

The charming and boyish-looking Ross Alexander was cast as the film's lead—a radio commentator in a convoluted plot that involves vengeance of an old wrong through whistle-blowing on some shady Hollywood scandals.

On the set, Jane launched a friendship with Ross. Born in Brooklyn, his life would end, shortly after their first meeting, in suicide. Ironically,

Carole Lombard and William Powell in *My Man Godfrey.* At their divorce, she complained of his temper, and he attacked her obscenity.

Warners would almost immediately replace him with a young radio announcer from Des Moines named Ronald Reagan. Jane would later refer to his tragic life story as "a bad Hollywood movie."

He had a bubbly personality and spoke in a voice that Jack Warner later defined as "very similar to young Reagan's."

With Jane, at least, Ross did not conceal his homosexuality.

During his dialogues with her, he enlightened her about Hollywood actors. "Many of the biggest stars are actually homos or at least bisexual." As an example, he cited his best friend, Henry Fonda, who had become his lover in 1933 when they first started rooming together during their joint appearances in summer stock. "Hank's true love is Jimmy Stewart, but Jimmy is not always available, so he settles for me."

For years, Ross had been under pressure to camouflage his homosexuality. As a means of doing that, he had married, in February of 1934, as part of a lavender arrangement of convenience, the Broadway actress, Aleta Friels. Faced with a failed marriage and a stalled career, she committed suicide less than a year later, in December of 1935, shooting herself with a rifle in the barn of their home in the Hollywood Hills.

[To her astonishment, Alexander revealed that he had pursued Bette Davis for three years. "If I had been able to get her to marry me, it would have been the publicity coup of my life, and I'd be a big star today. But she uncovered my secret. Bette, you know, detests homosexuals."

Ross's big break came when he was chosen to play Demetrius in the all-star cast of A Midsummer Night's Dream *(1935).*

The same year, he starred in Captain Blood *in the role of Jeremy Pitt, cast as the friend and navigator to the character played by swashbuckler Errol Flynn. Alexander told Jane that he had fallen in love with the bisexual Australian actor, and that the two men were currently involved in a torrid affair.*

"So far in my screen career, I've been nothing but a second rate Dick Powell, signing on to any role he rejects," Ross told Jane.

Before meeting Jane, Ross had entered yet another marriage, this time to Anne Nagle, an actress from Massachusetts, who was to work for 25 years in film adventures, mysteries, and comedies.

Anne Nagel is not to be confused with Anna Neagle, Britain's biggest female draw for seven years, and the wife of producer Henry Wilcox.]

Also appearing in *Here Comes Carter* was the brassy-*personaed* Glenda Farrell, who had arrived in Hollywood toward the end of the Silent Era. Finding no work immediately, she worked temporarily in a whorehouse, seducing, among others, clients who included a young Humphrey Bogart.

Like Joan Blondell, Farrell specialized in wise-cracking, hard-boiled, and somewhat dizzy blonde roles. She and Blondell were often paired together in films. During a period of her career, Jane's screen *persona* would be compared to that of both Blondell and Farrell.

Jane and Wayne Morris didn't have much to do in the film. Her relationship with him almost collapsed when she saw him leaving Farrell's dressing room late one afternoon as she was heading home. She confronted him and accused him of having an affair

The doomed Ross Alexander.

with her rival.

He freely admitted it. "The broad wanted to find out if all those stories about 'Jumbo' were true," he said. "I plowed her. Listen, you don't own me. I know you sleep around quite a bit yourself."

"He'd nailed me," Jane later confessed. "He and I didn't have any special arrangement. I decided to hold onto him. I'd have to be very understanding. When I wasn't with him, I was free to date other men, so I thought it was a fair deal between us."

He asked to go home with her. "After two or three beers and a steak, I'll have recovered from Farrell, and I'll be all yours for the night."

"It's a deal, Jumbo," she said. "Forgive me for being so silly. It's just that Farrell and I are rivals, and I resent her taking roles I want. That's why I got so pissed when I saw her going after my man, too."

Demarest sent over the latest script with a brief role for Jane. She read it one night and called the next morning, with her assessment of the script. "This sounds like another turkey masquerading as a tiger."

She was referring to the 1936 *Bengal Tiger.*

***

Ross invited Jane to attend an intimate dinner at the home of Errol Flynn, the swashbuckling, relatively new star at Warners. Ever since appearing together in *Captain Blood,* Ross and Flynn had been lovers, even though Flynn was married at the time to the French actress, Lili Damita.

The Flynns lived on Appian Way, a narrow, hairpin-curved mountain path positioned off Laurel Canyon Boulevard in the Hollywood Hills. Ross notified Jane that Damita would not be present at the dinner, as she and Flynn had had a violent argument the night before.

Before meeting him, Jane had heard many lurid stories about Flynn—that he was a lecherous, lovable rebel, a sexual pervert, and a drunkard. In the flesh, he evoked none of those qualities. Critics at the time suggested that he was the true heir to the handsome, swashbuckling traditions of Douglas Fairbanks, Sr. At the time, Flynn was at the peak of his male beauty, on the verge of interpreting the title role in the aptly name *The Perfect Specimen.*

As he kissed her hand, Flynn was the epitome of graciousness, and initially, at least, Jane had a very favorable view of him. Later, she referred to him as the "Tasmanian Devil," a reference to his birthplace.

Her future husband, Ronald Reagan, who would make two movies with Flynn, had a very negative view of the Australian.

As Flynn introduced Jane to his six other guests, none of whom she had ever heard of, he was most solicitous of her. His softly accented voice was especially alluring and seductive. As she would later say, "A gal would have a hard time saying no to this guy."

Glenda Farrell, often Jane's rival for roles, once made a confession: "My first job was in a bordello, where I learned how to act by telling johns how great they were as lovers."

By the time she met him, Flynn had already seduced hundreds of women and dozens of men, claiming that he lost his virginity at the age of twelve to the family maid in Australia.

[Before Flynn's early death at the age of 50 in 1959, he claimed that he had made some 12,000 to 14,000 sexual conquests with persons from all walks of life, including— during the course of one especially prolific afternoon in his dressing room—four starlets.]

Jane remembered his eyes, a seductive tool unto themselves. "They twinkle when he talks to you," she said, "and they are flecked with gold."

His sometimes roommate, David Niven, described Flynn "as a great athlete of immense charm and evident physical beauty, crowing lustily atop the Hollywood dung-heap."

Flynn seated Jane with him at the head of the table, talking mostly about himself. He claimed that he got his start in life as a slave trader and prospector in New Guinea.

He also spoke about the time when Jack Warner hired him. "He said I reminded him of John Barrymore, a hard-drinking, wenching, lovable, handsome man. I think Warner wanted to be like John and me, but he wasn't."

"I'm supposed to be a great swordsman," he said. "Well, I guess I am in one department. But on the screen as a dueling swordsman, I stink. I'm horrible at fencing. In the beginning, Michael Curtiz had to reshoot many of my scenes because of my inadequacies. Or else he'd call in one of the stunt doubles."

The dinner party broke up before midnight, because of early shooting schedules the next morning. Flynn already was rather drunk when he told Jane, "I feel as horny as a three-peckered billy goat."

"What a flattering invitation," she said.

However, she accepted his offer to stay over. When Flynn relayed that information to Ross, he got angry and stormed out of the house.

In spite of the liquor, Flynn lived up to his reputation as a great lover. After the sex act, she cuddled in his arms until he made a confession. "I lied to you. I pretended I used precautions, but I didn't. What's the point of eating dinner with your gloves on?"

Horrified, she jumped up from the bed and headed for his kitchen. There, she removed a bottle of white cider vinegar from his cabinet and then raced to the bathroom for a serious douche.

[During the weeks ahead, Jane feared that Flynn might have impregnated her. If so, she planned to have an abortion. Maybe it was that vinegar. Whatever, she never became pregnant.]

The next morning, on the set of *Here Comes Carter*, Jane told Glenda Farrell, "Every girl should enjoy the manly charms of Errol Flynn. And, at the rate he's going, every girl will have her chance at him."

***

Jane's next film was *Bengal Tiger* (1936), directed by Louis King and starring Barton MacLane and June Travis. MacLane was cast as the blustering lion-tamer who marries his assistant's poverty-

Errol Flynn shows off why he was selected as the star of *The Perfect Specimen* (1937). Overnight, he became a pinup boy.

37

stricken daughter, as played by Travis. To advance the plot, she then falls in love with the man on the flying trapeze (Warren Hull).

To Jane, the real star of the film was "Satan," a tiger who did the best acting job, mauling a double, chewing up a chair, and snarling at a whip.

King was a Southern gentleman from Virginia, who had become known in the 1920s for directing westerns and adventure stories. He was the brother of the famous director, Henry King.

In her future, Jane would often be attracted to her leading man. But MacLane was a big turn-off to her. He was cast as the furrow-browed tough guy giving someone a hard time. He seemed menacing, with his squinty eyes and his mouth clamped tightly shut.

Jane told Travis, "I think the script writer got it perfect. Barton ends up as cat food in the final reel. I'll never understand why he ever became a star. He has little talent and is both ugly and obnoxious."

Travis seemed rather contemptuous of Jane and soon wasn't speaking to her. She was from Chicago, the daughter of Harry Grabiner, vice president of the Chicago White Sox. With her dark brown hair and green eyes, she stood 5'4". It was understandable why Ronald Reagan, in his first picture, was attracted to her, but ever so briefly.

Travis not only snatched Reagan from Jane before she got a chance at him, but she fell into the slot at Warners that Jane wanted for herself. Travis became another actress known as the "queen of the B's," something Jane had been striving for, since she feared that super stardom was but a dream.

***

When William Demarest called to tell Jane that Paramount had offered her a small role in the film version of the hit Broadway musical, *Anything Goes* (1936), she was elated. Later, she was disappointed to learn "just how small a small part can be."

With music, at least some of it by Cole Porter, the film would star Bing Crosby, Ethel Merman, character actor Charles Ruggles, and a newcomer, Ida Lupino, taking the role Jane really wanted, that of "Hope Harcourt."

An odd choice of director for a musical was Lewis Milestone, a Russian-born Jew who had achieved fame for winning two Oscars as the director of *Two Arabian Knights* (1927) and *All Quiet on the Western Front* (1930).

On the set, Merman befriended Jane, and the bigger star often complained to her about her newly written role in the film. On Broadway, she had appeared in 420 performances, but she detested the new film script. "Everything in this movie is geared to promote that stuck-up asshole, Crosby," she told Jane. "Those jerks, Howard Lindsay and Russel Crouse, have written one dumb line after another for me. 'What are you doing here?' What's the idea?' Crap like that. The censors even nixed my big number, 'Blow, Gabriel, Blow.' Too suggestive, they say."

Porter was furious when he heard that many of his songs with their suggestive lyrics had been removed from the film, and that new composers had been called in to fill the gap. However, they allowed "You're the Top," to stay in, perhaps not realizing that for a gay audience, that was a very suggestive line.

Merman knew Porter and spoke to Jane about him. "We are two very different ducks," Merman said. "He likes cute young men, and I prefer something else. He's Yale educated, and I never opened a book. He prefers elegant food and wine, and I'm a hamburger gal with lots of onions and catsup. He wears Savile Row suits, and I prefer loud hats and flashy costume jewelry."

The film was about a shipboard romance in which Crosby chased after Lupino. Merman called the British-born actress "a limey bitch."

Lucille Ball dropped by the set one day to have lunch with Jane. In the commissary, Jane whispered a secret. "Ethel is one butch broad. Would you believe it, she invited me to her dressing room and put the make on me. I got out of there—and damn fast."

"I should have warned you," Ball said. "Ethel is a lesbian."

[Escaping from the embrace of Merman, Jane became friends with Lupino. In a few short years, Lupino would also become a close friend of Jane and her new husband, Ronald Reagan. She visited the Reagans frequently at their apartment at 1326 Londonderry Road in Beverly Hills. To Jane's dismay, Lupino and Reagan would talk politics all night. Both of them were liberal Democrats and supporters of FDR.

At Warners, Lupino became known as "the poor man's Bette Davis," accepting whatever "leftover parts" the grand diva turned down.]

As filming progressed on *Anything Goes (1936)*, and Jane heard Crosby sing and emote on camera, she developed a crush on him. Somehow word of her interest reached him. He approached her one day. "I hear you like me," he said. "Let's do something about that. A date tonight, perhaps?"

June Travis and Barton MacClane were the stars of *Bengal Tiger*. Jane could never figure out how MacLane became a leading man.

The beautiful starlet, Travis, would soon be in the arms of Ronald Reagan, both on and off the screen.

***

In the days ahead, Jane and Bing Crosby launched what evolved into a long-enduring affair for each of them. It would be put into storage in the 1940s during her marriage to Reagan, but it would resume in the 50s when they made two more pictures together.

The crooner, with his trademark bass-baritone, sometimes preferred pretty but demure young women with delicate features, and Jane fitted that bill. There was a fourteen-year difference in their ages, but that didn't matter to her.

As the 1930s had moved on, Jane had ceased to care if a man were married or not. Paulette Goddard had told her, "All movie stars, married or single, sleep around. It's how we play the game out here."

Jane was aware that Crosby in 1930 had married the Tennessee-born singer and showgirl, Dixie Lee (aka Dixie Carroll). Jane had heard reports that both were alcoholics, but that whereas Crosby had brought his liquor consumption under control, his wife had become more and more depressed.

[The 1947 film, Smash-Up—The Story of a Woman,

Bing Crosby with Ethel Merman performing "You're the Top," with its suggestive Cole Porter lyrics.

According to Merman, "I thought Crosby was somewhat of a girlie man, and he claimed I was far too macho. Nothing ever happened between us, but if it ever did, I bet I'd be the one on top."

39

starring Susan Hayward, was loosely based on the tragic life of Dixie Lee. She had had a brief film career at Crosby's Paramount Studio, her most notable movie being Love in Bloom *(1935).]*

Crosby had a history of seducing some of his leading ladies. Of course, on the set of *Anything Goes,* he certainly did not plan to go after Merman. He could have made a play for Lupino, but he chose to pursue bit player Jane instead.

Crosby had bedded Miriam Hopkins (his co-star in *She Loves Me, '34);* Joan Bennett (his co-star in *Mississippi, '35);* Joan Blondell (his co-star in *Two for Tonight, '35);* and most recently the mentally disturbed Frances Farmer (his costar in *Rhythm on the Range, '36).*

Since Crosby was well known and a married man, he had to be very secretive about sexual trysts with Jane. Their love affair could not be carried out at Chasen's, the Troc, or at the Cocoanut Grove.

Fortunately, director Frank Tuttle was only too willing to give them the use of his guest cottage. He hardly remembered Jane from her brief stint in his *All the King's Horses.* Crosby was Tuttle's friend, referring to him as "my favorite director."

Tuttle had helmed Crosby's *Here Is My Heart* (1934) and would go on to direct him in such pictures as *Waikiki Wedding* (1937); *Doctor Rhythm* (1938); and *Paris Honeymoon* (1939).

Many stars, directors, and other entertainers detested Crosby. His rival, Rudy Vallee, claimed, "Bing has ice water in his veins instead of warm blood." The public, however, adored him, and he remained a beloved singer throughout the dizzy Prohibition era, during the bleak years of the Depression, and through the darkest days of World War II. She had heard stories about his troubled marriage to the beautiful but tragic Dixie Lee and his difficulties with his own sons. He was said to beat them severely.

With Jane, on occasion, he displayed a streak of cruelty, "but he never hit me," she claimed. "However, I did on that rare occasion piss him off, but I never went too far. I learned that if you make one major wrong move with Bing, he'll never speak to you again. For the most part, we had a very good relationship."

One night, when Crosby and Jane were sitting out on a breeze-swept terrace in the Hollywood Hills, taking in the panoramic view of Los Angeles at night, she broached a delicate subject. She asked him if he had ever considered divorcing Lee.

"Never!" he shouted at her. "Don't ever ask me that again. "I'll never divorce Dixie. It's truly an 'until death do us part' kind of thing."

For all his dark side, Crosby was wonderful with minorities, according to Jane. He not only related to African Americans, including the great Louis Armstrong, but he brought the same respect to the shoeshine boy at the front gates of Paramount. He'd stop and talk to the boy and joke with him. "He was never patronizing, like most stars of the 30s to minorities," Jane claimed.

As Jane later told Glenda Farrell, "Bing is not the stud that Wayne Morris and Errol Flynn are, but he's adequate for the job—and I like him a lot. But he's very distant emotionally, not physically. Nobody seems to get close to him, certainly not his family."

***

At one point, Jane drifted into a deep depression once again, as she had so many times before, feeling that her career had stalled. The 1930s were passing, and she still hadn't made it big. Every day, chorus girls, some no more than sixteen, were arriving from the hinterlands.

She finally decided to take Paulette Goddard's advice and find some wealthy man to marry. "If he's nice and charming, or even handsome, that's all to the good, but don't ask for everything," the star advised. "If he's got enough money, you can't insist on all those other redeeming qualities."

Along came Myron Futterman. He was a clothing manufacturer from New Orleans, who specialized in ladies' gowns. He always lied about his age, but she suspected that he was at least twenty years older than she was. He had been born in 1903, making him fourteen years older than Jane.

Like her friend, Lucille Ball, Jane was a party girl. A studio such as Paramount or Warners could call upon her to entertain an important out-of-town client. Futterman had important connections in the business world, and someone at Warners called Jane and asked her if she'd entertain him during his visit to Los Angeles. Hoping to get cast in another Warners film, Jane agreed.

Although not as attractive as she would have preferred, Futterman was a gracious Southern gentleman, who treated her kindly, although she realized he wanted to have sex with her. She managed to hold him off until the third date. He was far from the greatest lover she'd known, but, on the other hand, he was not a disaster. As she later told Goddard, "Myron is competent in bed."

"Count yourself lucky," Goddard said. "Most men are incompetent between the sheets, and I should know. But if the bank account is big enough, competent is just rosy pink."

It was Jane who pressed marriage onto him. He'd been married before and still spoke favorably of his first wife, and seemed to be mourning her loss.

He flew with Jane to New Orleans for Mardi Gras. That wasn't all. A diamond engagement ring was followed in two days by a wedding band placed on her finger at City Hall before a justice of the peace. The date was June 29, 1937.

To her, it seemed that almost overnight, she'd become Mrs. Myron Futterman, although she had never divorced Eugene Wyman. "Who's to know?" was her cavalier attitude.

During her honeymoon, she realized that she'd married the wrong man, as she'd later relate to Goddard. She hadn't realized how conservative her new husband was. Although he marketed gowns with plunging *décolletage,* he didn't want Jane to wear such a dress or gown. For days at a time, he sank into a sullen mood and didn't want to see or talk to her. He was so withdrawn at times, he reminded her of her foster father.

For her, the worst was yet to come. He did not want her to pursue a career in Hollywood. "That's something whores do," he told her. He had plenty of ammunition to back up that outrageous statement. "I've dated plenty of starlets. All of them put out. In fact, let's face it: That's how I met you. I want to rescue you from the life of a tramp."

She wasn't as shy as she used to be, standing up to him and telling him she was going to pursue her career—"or else!"

"Faced with such a strong statement from me, he caved in," she told Goddard.

William Demarest didn't give the marriage much of a chance for success. "When Jane married that Futterman guy, I was really put off by him when I met him. Wherever they went, he was taken for her father. I think she married him for a sense of security, but his demands made her insecure. It was a money thing. Before she got married, she had told me that one day, she'd be thirty years old, with only $100 in her bank account."

Fortunately for Jane, Futterman was on the road most of the time, leaving her to her own devices. That meant she could show up at the Troc or the Cocoanut Grove with a series of come-and-go beaux, becoming the dutiful wife the moment he hit town again.

"Myron is tight with the purse strings," Jane told Demarest, "but generous with the wardrobe."

For the first time in her life, she had all the dresses and gowns she wanted, showing up at various night clubs with a different outfit every time.

"It was just assumed that she had some sugar daddy," Demarest said, "and at least in the clothing department, she did. Otherwise, he gave her an allowance of $50 a week."

She and Futterman had nothing in common. She liked nightclubs and movies. He wanted to go to bed at ten o'clock. For relaxation, he attended a ball game or else went to the fights. Not only that, he wanted to live in New Orleans, not Hollywood.

Whenever he came back to Hollywood, he accused her of flirting with everybody from Errol Flynn to Bing Crosby. Actually, he was right about that.

What he didn't know was that in the final weeks of their marriage, she had met a handsome young man that she felt "I could really go for."

The inevitable confrontation between Futterman and Jane occurred one rainy afternoon. Jane came home early from Warners, feeling sick. When she turned the key in the door, she sensed something unusual going on in the apartment. Loud music was coming from the bedroom.

When she opened the door, she discovered Futterman in drag, wearing a white satin gown with large red polka dots. To his astonished face, she said the first thing that flashed in her mind. "Myron, you're far too big to wear polka dots."

She left soon after, packing an overnight bag. Divorce was inevitable.

For $200, Demarest got Jane a divorce lawyer and arranged for her court date. Before a judge, she told him that Futterman had refused to conceive a child with her. She also claimed that he abandoned her for weeks at a time, returning to her and charging her with adulturous affairs. "I was constantly harassed and compared unfavorably to his first wife. He made me insecure and neurotic."

The judge granted the divorce on December 6, 1938. As part of the settlement, Jane was awarded $1,000 in cash, plus her attorney's fees. The title to her car was still in his name, but he transferred it to her.

At 1326 Londonderry Terrace, overlooking Sunset Strip, he'd lived in an apartment with her during his trips to Hollywood. During their marriage, he had allowed her to furnish the apartment with the modern pieces she preferred, although he wanted more traditional choices. After their divorce, he told her, "Take all of this crap. I'm just removing my clothes—and that's it. Enjoy!"

Many years later, Futterman gave a brief interview to a reporter. He said, "I knew that Jane would blossom into a great screen actress one day. Stardom was everything to her, and it was backed up by a steely determination. She really wanted to be a big Hollywood star, and she didn't want a husband to block that pursuit."

As Jane's star rose on the horizon, Futterman became a footnote in the history of a great actress. However, an inveterate grave finder tracked down his tombstone, discovering that he had moved to California and had died in Los Angeles on March 6, 1965. He was buried in the Garden of Everlasting Peace on lot 5298 in the Forest Lawn Memorial Park at Glendale.

When this evidence was presented to her, she snapped, "Gone and forgotten."

Chapter Two

Ronald Reagan in Hollywood —
Warners' "Errol Flynn of the B's"

"Leading Lady-itis"
(Falling In Love Again...and Again...and Again)

In Ronald Reagan's first movie, *Love Is on the Air,* June Travis took him to her breast both on and off the screen, although she later denied it. The former sports reporter, age 26, made his Hollywood debut as a crusading radio announcer.

As a young Lothario, Regan found "love" again, at least for three weeks when he was teamed with pretty, perky Mary Maguire in *Sergeant Murphy* (1938). Here, she salutes him for a job well done. Exactly what performance was she praising?

'It's a tough racket, but when you consider the rewards you're shooting at—fame such as couldn't be won in any other profession and wealth that amounts to dizzying heights—it's worth the chances you take."
—Ronald Reagan

"When I was young and had just arrived on the Warners lot, I shacked up with any female who caught my eye—and I got an eyeful."
—Ronald Reagan

For twenty hours, without sleep, Reagan had driven his Nash convertible across the desert, heading west for Los Angeles. He had stopped only for food and gas. "By the roadside, I watered a lot of cactus along the way, since I had dry throat all the way. At the wheel, I must have drunk enough bottled water to flood the banks of the Colorado River."

Eventually, his battered, dust-covered car pulled up at the entrance to the Biltmore Hotel in downtown Los Angeles. "After I got there, I think I slept for the first twenty-four hours," he recalled.

He had checked into the Biltmore because his friend, the singer, Joy Hodges, had returned for another singing engagement in the nightclub there. He called her to thank her for arranging a screen test for him.

Reluctantly, she admitted why she had stood him up on what was supposed to have been their first date several months before. "You wanted to go riding,

Warners Four: *left to right*, Albert, Harry, Sam, and Jack. As young Polish immigrants, the sons of a cobbler, they did everything—butchering hogs, making leather shoes, selling homemade soap (later, bicycles).

In time, they would become movie moguls, the bosses of Humphrey Bogart, Bette Davis, and a young Ronald Reagan.

and I didn't have any riding clothes, but I was too ashamed to admit it. Since then I've bought an outfit that makes me look like the Queen of the Sagebrush."

That Sunday, the two of them went riding together. She later admitted, "There was no sexual chemistry between us, in spite of what people said. He was new to Hollywood and lonely, and he needed someone to talk to."

"I knew he needed some action, so once again, I called my friend, Betty Grable, to the rescue," Hodges said. "I knew she'd soon be knocking on his door at the Biltmore. Later, when I saw Ronnie in the movies, I realized that I'd missed out on something, and regretted turning him over to Betty."

[Hodges, had previously appeared with Grable in Old Man Rhythm.*]*

"When I went on a promotional tour with Ronnie, months later, I was about to move in on him, until I learned that both Jane Wyman and Susan Hayward were already fighting over him."

In spite of Grable's upcoming marriage in November of 1937 to the former child star, Jackie Coogan, she seemed more than willing to slip around town on Reagan's arm.

When he asked her about Coogan, she told him, "He's probably visiting some whorehouse tonight. He likes very experienced gals who will do everything." She went on to tell him that when she'd first started to date him, she thought Coogan was rich. As a child star, he earned $4 million *[the equivalent of some $50 to $65 million in the U.S. currency of 2014]*.

"But now, I usually have to pick up the restaurant or nightclub tab," she said. "He has no money. As a grief-stricken 20-year-old, after his father died in an accident, he turned all his assets over to Lillian, his mother. She's got a greedy lover, Arthur Bernstein."

[In an interview, Lillian had shamelessly informed the press, "Every dollar a kid

44

earns before he is 21 belongs to his parents. His money is now mine to spend on fur coats, diamonds, expensive cars—whatever I want. The little devil won't get a cent of it. He's been a bad, bad boy."]

"Jackie went to Chaplin, since he'd made millions for him," Grable said, "but all he got from Chaplin was a thousand dollars."

[Coogan would later sue his mother and Bernstein, but all he rescued from his previous earnings was $126,000. His legal battle with his mother led to the enactment of the California Child Actor's Bill, often called "The Coogan Law," which requires a child actor's employer to set aside 15% of his earnings in a trust.]

One morning, Betty, in her car, drove Reagan around Hollywood, his new home. He had never really seen much of it, and was shocked at buildings painted Halloween orange, chartreuse, or pink. "Out here, we call it pussy pink," Grable said. Her potty mouth sometimes startled him.

As their friendship intensified, Grable got him a pass to enter the grounds of Paramount, where he had lunch with her in the commissary. She told him she was making a movie called *This Way, Please,* starring Charles ("Buddy") Rogers, who was struggling to rescue his sagging film career.

"LeRoy Prinz is my dance instructor," Grable said. "The talented little midget is often screwing around with my fellow starlet, Jane Wyman. He's teaching her dance steps 'movie star style'—among other lessons."

Unlike the women Reagan had previously known, Grable had no hesitation about discussing "Who's screwing who," as she put it. She suggested that she had been shacking up with Rogers ever since they had appeared together in the 1935 *Old Man Rhythm.* "He's not getting much from Mary"

[She was referring to "America's sweetheart," Mary Pickford, who, prior to her decline, had been the most lucrative female star of the silent era. She had married Buddy Rogers in 1937, in the wake of her divorce from Douglas Fairbanks, Sr.]

Later, when Hodges joined Grable and Reagan for a rendezvous, she complimented Reagan on his new eyewear. She turned to Grable, "I got him to get rid of those damn horn rim glasses. Now he's leading man material."

After a few days at the Biltmore, shacked up during some of them with Grable, Reagan moved into less expensive lodgings, in this case, the Hollywood Plaza. His agent, George Ward, had instructed him that he should live closer to Warner Brothers.

On Wednesday, Ward retrieved Reagan at his new hotel for an appointment at Warners. It would be his introduction to the co-producers and director who were thinking about casting him in his first movie role.

"Our agency has high hopes for you," Ward said. "We've already warned one of our highest-paid clients, Robert Taylor, that Warners is aggressively interviewing and grooming his competition. Bob may be prettier, but you're a good looker yourself. At least your shoulders are broader than Bob's, and I'm sure your dick is bigger. Bob is rather deficient in that department."

Such talk embarrassed Reagan. Later that day, he complained to Grable, "Men shouldn't talk about each other's personal equipment that way. I don't like it."

"Get used to it, sweet cheeks," Grable warned him. "Out here in Hollywood, when we're not talking about upcoming pictures, and whether there'll be a role for us, movie stars talk about dick sizes and the measurements of a woman's breasts. Bette Davis said that Hollywood lives in a tit culture. She might have said in a 'tit and dick' culture."

When he was alone, Reagan wrote to Nelle and Jack, informing them that he was having a difficult time adjusting to "this semi-desert environment in a city without a past."

He had heard that immigrant moguls from Eastern Europe, often one-time peddlers and junk dealers, ran the film studios of Hollywood, ruling with iron fists and autocratically hiring and firing dancers, singers, comedians, cowboys, real-life gangsters, beauty queens, and handsome leading men. Many, he learned, had escaped Hitler's "final solution" in the gas chambers of Central Europe, and now lived in harmony with Okies fleeing the Dust Bowl, hundreds of whom worked as laborers in the film studios.

***

In his new status as a contract player at Warners, Reagan was paid $200 a week to join a roster of big name stars including James Cagney, Edward G. Robinson, Errol Flynn, and the queen of the lot, Bette Davis. Humphrey Bogart was also on hand in case a director needed an actor who could play a convincing villain.

Before signing with Warners, Reagan had read whatever he could about the studio.

Jack Warner was its vice president in charge of production. He was one of four Polish-Jewish brothers—Harry, Albert, Sam, and the youngest, Jack himself. Around the turn of the century, each of them had settled in the United States, where they were among the first to envision the future of the movie industry. By 1903, they had opened their first theater—in Newcastle, Pennsylvania—featuring early films such as *The Great Train Robbery*, a historic short (12 minutes long) silent film.

Based on their objections to the payment of licensing fees to Thomas A. Edison, within seven years, they were producing their own films. Edison seemed to dislike Jews intensely, wanting to bar them from an involvement in the movie industry. When the Warner brothers started to produce their own films, Edison accused them of exploiting sex on the screen.

Near the end of World War I, the Warner brothers moved to Los Angeles, opening a studio on Sunset Boulevard in Hollywood, then a boom town in the making. They scored a big success with "The Wonder Dog," Rin Tin Tin. The dog, an exceptionally intelligent German shepherd, had been brought to America by a soldier who had found it wandering about after his master, a French soldier, was slain by the Germans.

During their early debut in Hollywood, Warners hired wisely, employing Darryl F. Zanuck and the brilliant director, Ernst Lubitsch. In addition, they wisely signed stage actor John Barrymore to a contract, scoring a big hit with *Beau Brummel* (1924).

Before the end of the 1920s, Warners was the first studio to become a pioneer of talkies, although Harry had initially (and loudly) objected. "Who in hell wants to hear an actor talk?"

Jack shot back, "Ever hear of Shakespeare, brother dear?"

Jack ventured into sound, casting Al Jolson in *The Jazz Singer,* which featured a limited number of sound segments. It became a sensation, signaling the twilight of the Silents

Depicted here at the peak of his power and glory, Jack Warner, the tycoon who ran Warner Brothers, established his studio, along with his brothers, in Hollywood in 1923. They wanted to escape the licensing fees of the anti-Semitic Thomas A. Edison.

Jack never believed Reagan would be a star—"perhaps a leading man, or the pal of the leading man."

and the end of the careers of many big stars who did not have a voice suitable for Talkies.

In the 1930s, Warners produced musicals along with socially realistic films "drawn from the headlines. After turning out such hit films as *The Public Enemy,* which made James Cagney a star in 1931, and *Little Caesar,* which did the same thing the same year for Edward G. Robinson, Warners became known as the gangster studio.

Their pre-Code Talkies were daring and provocative.

By 1934, censors from the Production Code Administration (PCA), as spearheaded by Joseph Breen, tightened their control over Warners movies, ordering that it restrict itself to more moralistic, less gritty, and more idealized storylines. As a response to their increasingly strident demands, Jack turned to historical dramas, along with swashbucklers, women's pictures, and adaptations of best-selling novels. Some of their pre-Code stars, "tainted" as they were with reputations for sexual profligacy and indiscretion, ended up working for low budget studios along "Poverty Row."

To help buttress the revenues of their A-list pictures, the Warner brothers needed quickies, usually shot in three weeks to a month and sometimes running no more than 60 minutes. Bryan Foy ("The Keeper of the Bs") was hired to supervise and organize their production.

"Brynie," as he was nicknamed, had been the youngest member of the famous vaudeville act, "Eddie Foy and the Seven Little Foys."

Ironically, Ronald Reagan, at Warners—usually under Foy's supervision during the late 1930s, would become famous as "The King of the Bs," and as "The Errol Flynn of the Bs."

Foy himself came out to greet Reagan and welcome him to the studio. Foy told him that he'd been named co-producer of Reagan's first film, *Love Is On the Air,* a 59-minute B-movie released in 1937. "You'll play a radio announcer."

According to the plot, Reagan is an aggressive radio announcer who investigates a local crime wave. When sponsors complain, Reagan is demoted to the humiliating job of hosting a kiddie show on the air. He usurps the job from Jo Hopkins, a character played by June Travis. Eventually, she falls for him and joins his anti-crime crusade. In the end, good guy Reagan triumphs heroically over the mob.

"Type casting," said Reagan. "I was a radio announcer."

"But now, you've got to become one on the screen, which takes another kind of talent," Foy cautioned.

The producer handed him a copy of the script. "I'm taking you to meet Jack Warner. He's a very busy man, and we can't take more than four or five minutes of his time. He'll do all the talking. Listen to him as if God himself were speaking. You don't have to curtsy, but suck up!"

***

The flamboyant showman, Jack Warner, lived up to his billing and a magazine's description of him. "He was always smiling through a tan under his thin, oiled hair." He was also the self-proclaimed "court jester" at the Roosevelt White House, where, in his capacity as head of Warners, he was a frequent visitor. Like Reagan, Jack was a liberal supporter of the social policies of FDR—a "New Dealer."

In his $35 suit, Reagan was introduced to Jack in his $1,000 Savile Row tailored clothing, which included a silk handkerchief and a necktie. To Reagan, he was an intimidating figure. Jack did almost all the talking.

"Here at Warners, we're a peddler of dreams, the creator of illusions," Jack said.

"During the depression, Warners has been the American drug of choice."

Later, when he was alone, making use of his fantastic memory, Reagan wrote down Jack's pronouncements.

"With the coming of a World War, which I know is inevitable, we're hiring patriotic, all-American white Protestant guys like yourself—guys with good looks. Catholics we can cast as priests, Jews as intellectuals. Leggy blondes will play bad gal roles, and aging brunettes will be mothers baking apple pies. Actors with foreign accents will be Nazi spies."

"We've replaced Al Jolson with a very wholesome Dick Powell—no more blackface shit. Negroes will be cast as servants, usually lazy and retarded, just shuffling along. We'll cast anti-heroes like Bogart with heroic types like yourself."

"Your agent [George Ward] told me you're a shirt-chasing, red-blooded American boy with a perpetual hard-on—there's not a homo streak in you. That'll be a change from our popular hero, Errol Flynn, who will stick it in any hole. That one's heading for trouble. You're free to chase after our beautiful starlets, but don't knock them up. In case you do, we've employed a resident abortionist to take care of unwanted babies."

"Of course, you don't really have to chase after the skirts. These horny pussies will be calling you. If you're a stud, our gals will keep you busy. Most of them can't get enough. I sample a different one every day myself."

Reagan was finally allowed to say something. In the brief moment allotted, he thanked Jack for letting him become a member of the Warners family.

"You're welcome, and you seem personable enough," Jack said. "But don't get difficult like that god damn mutt, Rin Tin Tin, the Wonder Dog. He was our 'mortgage lifter' in the 20s, but I fired him in '29. The first time I met the beast, he bit off a hunk of my flesh. He often attacked his director, too."

"I'm eager to cooperate," Reagan said.

Jack glanced at his watch, "I've got Miss Bette Davis waiting, and she's threatening to scratch my eyes out, wanting better roles. What a bitch!"

In the anteroom to Warner's office, Reagan was introduced to Hal B. Wallis, who told him he would be the co-producer of *Love Is On the Air*. Reagan shook his hand and said how eager he was to begin shooting his first film. Wallis would later refer to Reagan as "that hick radio announcer from the Middle West."

Foy then introduced him to Bette Davis, who wore a funny hat. "I'm honored to meet you, Miss Davis," he said. "I consider you the greatest *tragedienne* on the screen."

"Of course you do, dear boy," Davis snapped.

"You were thrilling in *Of Human Bondage,*" he said

"Of course I was," she replied. "So why didn't I get the fucking Oscar?"

After she abruptly departed, heading in to Jack's office, she continued talking. Apparently, Jack had slipped into his adjoining toilet, leaving Bette and Wallis together and alone.

From his position in Warner's anteroom, Reagan heard Davis say, "What a silly boy."

"The kid's name is Ronald Reagan, some hayseed Jack has put under contract," Wallis said. "He was hired to replace Ross Alexander."

"Poor pathetic homo Ross," Davis said. "Even though he was always pestering me to marry him, I was sorry to hear he committed suicide. He thought that by marrying me, his perversion would be camouflaged. It figures that Jack would hire another homo like this Reagan boy to replace Ross."

Wallis suddenly shut the door to Warner's office, and Reagan could hear no more. He was infuriated, but maintained a polite façade. Davis had insulted him, but he didn't dare strike back.

Foy sensed his anxiety. "Lesson number one in the film business: Take it on the chin until you have the power to get even."

Foy introduced Reagan to his first-ever film director, Nick Grinde. Grinde was married at the time to actress Marie Wilson, with whom Reagan would work on the 1938 film, *Boy Meets Girl.* Like Reagan, Grinde was from the Middle West, hailing from Wisconsin. He'd written the script for the film *Toyland* (1934), which had co-starred Laurel and Hardy and some of the music (including "March of the Toys") by the noted composer, Victor Herbert.

"I heard you were a radio announcer in Des Moines," Grinde said. "You may end up playing the role of Andy McLeod as yourself."

Co-starring in the film as its second lead was Eddie Acuff, a minor actor and another Middle Westerner who would become better known playing the recurring role of the postman, Mr. Beasley, in the *Blondie* movie series. He and Reagan quickly became friends and started having lunch together in the commissary.

Director Nick Grinde recalled, "I had to teach Reagan how to kiss on camera. He was wet-lipping Travis and ruining her makeup. I made the ultimate sacrifice and used my own lips to show the fucker how it's done. He learned fast after that."

For the remainder of his first day at Warners, George Ward drove him to the Santa Monica Pier. Reagan wanted to go swimming.

As he was emerging from the water, Ward came up to him. "My God, you're an Adonis from the deep. We're going to have to pose you in a bathing suit for publicity photos.

That weekend he arranged for a Warner photographer to take "beefcake" pictures of Reagan in swimwear. *[Of course, they weren't called beefcake back then.]*

Reagan said, "I used to be a four-letter man in college, but I didn't think that gave me an excuse to stick out my chest and expand my biceps publicly, every time someone mentioned the word 'health.'"

Even before the release of *Love Is On the Air,* these beefcake photos, when published, generated fan mail. Most of it originated with teenage girls, but a number of homosexuals wrote to him too, relaying in graphic detail what the letter-writer would do to him if and when he removed his trunks. He found fan mail from either gender embarrassing. "For the first time in my life, I was being treated like a slab of beef."

The next day, he reported to casting director Max Arnow. "Good to see you again, Reagan," he said. He looked him up and down. "Where in hell did you get that bargain basement white jacket? You look like a Filipino refugee." He was then informed that he'd have to supply his own wardrobe. Throughout the course of his involvement in *Love Is On the Air,* there would be a dozen changes of suits, and he owned only four.

He solved that dilemma by "doubling," which involved wearing the same suits at the beginning of the film and again at the end, hoping that the audience would have a brief attention span.

He also met Percival ("Perc") Westmore, who was widely acknowledged as the best makeup artist in Hollywood. Reagan would later become friends with both Westmore and his wife, actress Gloria Dickson. Perc regularly applied the makeup of such Warner stars as Kay Francis and Bette Davis, and was credited with the creation of thirty-five shades of blonde.

With his razor-sharp instincts, he appraised and evaluated Reagan's physicality: "Your neck's too short, Kid," he said. "Jimmy Cagney has the same problem. I'll send you to his shirt maker, who can design a trick collar that will conceal your deficiency."

Westmore continued, oblivious to the alarm his appraisals were causing: "And your head is too small. It doesn't leave room for your brain. We'll have to disguise that fact as well, Ronald."

Having been called Dutch for most of his life, Reagan was not yet accustomed to the name "Ronald." Throughout his life, he had always regretted having been named that.

Then Westmore introduced him to the writers in Warner's publicity department, instructing them to "hide the fact that he's a no-necker with a pinhead."

Reagan later said, "It's amazing that Perc and I became friends after all his insults to my physicality."

Almost immediately, the Publicity Department ground out a press release, citing Reagan's broad shoulders and slender waistline. According to the release, the Hollywood newcomer "was almost proficient in every sport, an expert marksman and horseman."

With his newly coiffed pompadour, his hair no longer parted in the middle, Reagan showed up on the set for his kissing scene. Director Grinde was there waiting to introduce him to his leading lady, June Travis.

Young Reagan, after his transformation by Warners' Wardrobe and Makeup Departments.

He later complained, "Too many homos took liberties with my physique in both makeup and wardrobe, but they did a god damn good job. You've got to hand it to these guys. They're outrageous, but they know their business."

***

Love Is On the Air was a minor crime drama whose plot and premises had already appeared, in another variation, on the screen. Its plot was a rehash of the 1934 movie, the badly titled *Hi, Nellie,* one of Paul Muni's less impressive films. In it, Ronald Reagan, age 26, was making his screen debut.

Reagan was shown a memo that Grinde had received from the Breen office, the official censor of Hollywood films. New to both movie making and to censorship, he read it with embarrassment and astonishment:

"Mr. Reagan, in the role of the radio announcer, must not be unduly exposed in the scene where he strips off his pajamas and starts to dress. If he is photographed in his underwear, make sure he wears white boxer shorts with an athletic supporter underneath. At no point should there be a mound of his genitalia on display, even if it's covered by fabric."

At that point, his leading lady, June Travis, emerged from makeup. With her dark brown hair, her green eyes, and her round, rosy cheeks, she was beautiful, standing 5'4", and relatively new to films. Born in Chicago, she was the daughter of Harry Brabiner, who in the 1930s was vice president of the Chicago White Sox.

Two years earlier, she'd appeared in *Stranded* with Kay Francis and George Brent. Howard Hawks had directed her in *Ceiling Zero* (1936), starring James Cagney and Pat O'Brien. For her role in that film, Amelia Earhart, a friend of her family, had instructed Travis in flying, aeronautical navigation, and parachute jumping.

50

She was very flirtatious with him. "Those green eyes were practically begging me to take her out...or whatever," he said to Grinde.

During his first hour with Travis, shooting a kissing scene, Reagan got to know her rather well, at least insofar as her succulent lips were concerned. "I was so eager to get at her that I pressed my face against hers so hard I think I turned her features into pudding. Grinde stepped in to teach me how to screen kiss, using his own stinking mouth on mine."

"You don't come at a gal with your tongue hanging out like *Tyrannosaurus rex* about to swallow whole some primeval beast." Then he showed Reagan how to kiss on camera.

"I learned my lesson, which helped me kiss dozens of beautiful stars in my future. It's true. I had moved toward June's mouth like there was no tomorrow. I practically sucked the tongue out of her mouth. Grinde told me I had to kiss the girl without shoving her face out of shape. He told me that our lips should barely meet. I had to leave her as beautiful as she was, even though giving the impression of a fervent kiss."

Working with Travis, Reagan developed his first case of "a disease called *Leadinglady-itis.*" That's when an actor falls in love with his leading lady and has an affair with her, but only during the shoot. When the picture is wrapped, both parties move on. In some cases, the affair is resumed when the two appear in another picture together. Occasionally, it leads to marriage." *[Such was the case with Jane Wyman and Reagan when they made* Brother Rat *in 1938.]* It's also common for an actress to develop "*Leadingman-itis.*"

At the end of their kissing scene, when Travis whispered into his ear, "I want some more of where that came from," their affair was launched.

That was all the encouragement he needed. For the next three weekends, she was in his arms, mostly when he was alone with her in his bachelor apartment. When they wanted diversion, he took her to shoot clay pigeons in an amusement arcade at the Santa Monica pier.

"June was a great shot," he said, "knocking off every clay pigeon in the shooting gallery. She even licked me throwing baseballs at milk bottles. She was also great at water sports and at hockey, a real girl jock in spite of her delicate beauty. She was also a fine horsewoman, as she demonstrated when I took her riding in Griffin Park."

The ultimate late 30s chic: June Travis, the woman who set the pattern for Reagan's chronic and oft-repeated syndrome, "LeadingLady-itis."

Travis later told the press that she went out with Reagan on only one date, the focal point of which involved a shooting match at a carnival. When he heard that, Grinde said, "Of course, June said that. but that doesn't mean we have to believe her. After all, a gal has to protect her reputation in this town."

One night during dinner together in Hollywood, Reagan and Travis encountered James Cagney, with whom she had previously appeared on the screen. He kissed Travis and chatted with her. Reagan reminded him that he'd conducted an interview with him at his radio station in Des Moines. "I remember that, "Cagney said, "but I have no memory of you. You know, stars meet so many people. It's all in a day's work."

During the short time he knew her, Reagan was

getting serious enough with Travis that he contemplated proposing marriage. There was much speculation about why his affair with her ended so abruptly.

As he was to learn painfully, she had another suitor who was also ardently pursuing her. He was Walter Annenberg. A playboy born to a wealthy Jewish family in Milwaukee, he eventually evolved into a major media mogul, philanthropist, and patron of the arts. He showed her a far more glamorous life than Reagan could. Annenberg and Travis were seen cruising together along Hollywood Boulevard in his custom-made Lincoln, at his luxurious bungalow on the grounds of the Beverly Hills Hotel, and in Palm Springs. He also escorted her to San Simeon, the exclusive mountaintop castle of the press baron, William Randolph Hearst and his actress/mistress, blonde-haired and vivacious Marion Davies.

[Reagan eventually retreated from his affair with Travis, surrendering her to Annenberg. There were no hard feelings. In fact, Annenberg and the woman he eventually married, Leonore Cohn, became best friends with Reagan and Nancy.

After Annenberg convinced Reagan to switch his allegiance from the Democratic Party to the Republicans, he arranged for his friend's first big break: a job as the host of TV's General Electric Theater *from 1954 to 1961. He later encouraged Reagan to enter politics and subsequently became one of his biggest campaign contributors.*

Reagan, with his wife Nancy, often spent New Year's Eve with the Annenbergs at Sunnylands, their palatial winter estate in Rancho Mirage, near Palm Springs. "Although born Jewish, Walter and Leonore, whom we called Lee, did not practice Judaism. Nancy and I often celebrated Easter and Christmas with them," Reagan said.

By this time, Annenberg was a publisher, owning The Philadelphia Inquirer, Seventeen *magazine, and the popular* TV Guide. *As a philanthropist, he donated $2 billion during the course of his lifetime to educational institutions and art galleries.*

Richard Nixon appointed Annenberg ambassador to the United Kingdom from 1969 to 1974. It was Annenberg who introduced Reagan to Britain's "Iron Lady," Margaret Thatcher.

After Reagan's election as U.S. president, he appointed Leonore as the U.S. State Department's Chief of Protocol.]

***

William Hopper, cast in a small role in *Love Is on the Air,* was an engaging and extremely handsome actor, the only child of singer and comic stage actor, DeWolf Hopper, Jr., and actress Hedda Hopper. His mother would become a famous Hollywood gossip columnist, the rival of Louella Parsons.

William is best remembered today for playing detective Paul Drake in more than 250 episodes of TV's long-running Perry Mason series. He is also known for his role as the father of the Natalie Wood character in James Dean's *Rebel Without a Cause* (1955).

William had made his film debut when he was one year old. His father had cast him in his 1916 silent movie, *Sunshine Dad.* Hedda divorced DeWolf in

At a reception, President Reagan welcomes his chief backers, the Annenbergs. Reagan later said, "I was never happier than when I rode around Palm Springs on Walter's golf cart."

1922, and subsequently moved from New York to Hollywood with her son.

For William, his role in *Love Is On the Air* was a bit of a comedown, since in the same year (1937), he'd been Jane Wyman's leading man in *Public Wedding,* a picture also directed by Nick Grinde. During the shooting of that film, he'd escorted Jane on two dates. William also had a major role that same year, co-starring with Ann Sheridan in *The Footloose Heiress.* He had also dated Sheridan, mainly for publicity purposes, hoping that their photos would appear in the newspapers.

Ironically, therefore, William Hopper bears the double-barreled honor of having dated Ronald Reagan's future wife, and his longest and most enduring mistress (Ann Sheridan) too.

Voyeuristically, Grinde watched the burgeoning friendship between Reagan and William. "The boy had stars in his eyes every time Ronnie walked onto the set," Grinde recalled. "All of us knew that William was a homosexual—all of us except Ronnie. William dated women as camouflage to conceal his sexual proclivities. He'd later marry twice and serve heroically as a Navy frogman during World War II, but he was always known in Hollywood for having a boyfriend on the side. As William got older, the boyfriends got younger."

At one point, William introduced Reagan to his mother, Hedda, who would become his future political ally. In 1937, Reagan was still a New Deal Democrat, and he interpreted Hedda's opinions as "politically to the right of Attila the Hun."

She liked Reagan and told him, "I'm glad to see my boy Billy running around with a real red-blooded American boy and not one of those queers who are always chasing after him."

At the time Reagan met Hedda, her lackluster movie career had nose-dived into cine-matic oblivion. "I need a new gig," she told him. To find another source of income, she was developing a new career as a gossip columnist, something she was adept at. On Valentine's Day of 1938, her first column, "Hedda Hopper's Hollywood," would make its debut in the *Los Angeles Times.*

William invited Reagan for a weekend of boating offshore from Catalina Island, where his mother had arranged, through a friend, for their occupancy of a small vacation cottage.

Much of that weekend remains a mystery, although Grinde later shed some light on what happened: "Ronnie

Hedda Hopper, the vindic-tive "Hellion of Hollywood," photographed in a rare in-stance without a hat.

Hedda's son, William Hop-per, who worked with Rea-gan on his first picture, is seen here as Paul Drake on *Perry Mason,* the TV series.

In Reagan's first picture, *Love Is on the Air,* he appeared with young William Hopper *(left).* To his chagrin, Reagan learned that he was "becoming the dreamboat of Hopper's sexual fantasies."

was incredibly naïve at the time about the ways of Hollywood," Grinde said. "He didn't know it, but William was actually 'dating' him, even though they were taking out two girls at the time. William's real goal involved seducing Ronnie and making him his lover. Hedda's son really had the hots for Ronnie."

"When he returned from Catalina and reported for work on Monday morning, Ronnie was reluctant to talk about his weekend," Grinde said. "I finally got it out of him: The two men had shared a double bed. In the middle of the night, Ronnie was awakened by William going down on him. He pulled away from that encounter in horror and spent the rest of the night on the sofa."

"Most straight actors I've known will let a homo go down on them if no women are available," Grinde said. "Not so Ronnie. I don't think he had a queer streak in him."

"He was very upset, and I tried to wise him up to the ways of Hollywood," Grinde said. "I told him that the industry was populated by homos. 'Every day, a dozen or more are getting off the train at Union Station, fresh from the hinterlands.' I warned him that as a good-looking guy, he'd be solicited, frequently."

"You've got to turn them down firmly but politely," Grinde told Reagan. "They'll be co-starring with you, applying your makeup, styling your hair, dressing you, shooting your publicity stills while you're in a bathing suit, and even directing your pictures. I think you should make up with William, shake his hand and assure him you still want to be friends. Don't treat him like a pariah. He probably feels like a shit because of your rejection. And lest you forget, you certainly don't want to piss off Hedda."

Reagan obviously took Grinde's advice. In a few weeks, he was once again seen on double dates with William, who was escorting actress Isabel Jewell, his arm candy for the evening. At the time, Reagan seemed to be dating a different woman six nights a week. Sundays were reserved for family dinners with Jack and Nelle.

Grinde's advice to Reagan was astute. Hedda's son would play a New York reporter in one of Reagan's most famous films, *Knute Rockne—All American* (1940). In fact, he would appear in an amazing total of nine films with Reagan between 1937 and 1942.

During its filming, Reagan frequently viewed the advance rushes of *Love Is On the Air.* "When I first saw myself on the screen, as others see me, I sank into my seat. I've been doing that in every movie since."

The film opened on November 12, 1937, at the Palace Theater in Manhattan, where it played second fiddle in a double feature that included the prestigious *Stage Door,* starring Katharine Hepburn and Ginger Rogers.

Love Is On the Air, Reagan's quickie, had been cobbled together in just three weeks for a budget of $119,000.

The film's makeup chief, Perc Westmore, had issued a warning to the cameraman: "When Reagan gets tired, his left eye starts to travel."

Although *Love Is On the Air* was akin to a frivolous and minor potboiler, it received generally favorable reviews. The *Hollywood Reporter* defined Reagan as "a natural," and *Variety* labeled him as "a find."

Jack Warner was impressed enough to pick up Reagan's option and raise his salary to $250 a week.

Confidant that he'd succeed as a movie star, Reagan purchased a house in West Hollywood for his parents, Jack and Nelle. He sent them the train fare to Hollywood, and eventually moved them into 9031 Phyllis Avenue, the only home they'd ever owned in their lives.

In failing health, Jack had given up drinking after his heart attack, although he remained a chain smoker. "So Dad won't feel he was on relief," Reagan gave him a job, paying $25 a week, answering his fan mail, which had begun arriving at Warners. He told his father that he didn't have to respond to letters from homosexual men.

With his increase in salary, Reagan moved into a cottage at 1128 Cory Avenue, a block north of Sunset Boulevard. He boasted to his male friends, "It's become known as the love cottage of Hollywood."

Soon, his brother Moon followed his family to Hollywood, and Reagan succeeded in getting him a job as an announcer at WFWB, a radio station owned by Warner Brothers.

***

It was Priscilla Lane, the singer and actress, who sought him out when she learned that he had lived in her native state of Iowa. She was from the small college town of Indianola, south of Des Moines, and had sung, live, at the radio station in Des Moines where Reagan had been a sports announcer.

Priscilla was the youngest of the singing Lane Sisters, a trio which included Lola and Rosemary. The sisters had made their professional debut at Des Moines' Paramount Theater. During his residency in the city, Reagan had been one of the theater's best customers.

Orchestra leader and radio personality Fred Waring heard the Lane sisters and subsequently lured them to Hollywood for appearances with his band, the Pennsylvanians, in the bemusedly frothy *Varsity Show* (1937), starring Dick Powell.

Priscilla turned out to be the most promiscuous of the three sisters, engaging in an affair with Powell before moving on to Wayne Morris, with whom she was later cast in *Love, Honor, and Behave* in 1938. Morris was also dating Jane Wyman, even though she was married at the time to Myron Futterman, who, as a salesman, was often out of town and on the road.

"Priscilla liked to date different men," Waring said. "At Warners, she told me, 'I've died and gone to heaven. So little time, so many men. She got really busy when Busby Berkeley cast her in *Men Are Such Fools* (1938)—one night with Morris, another night with Humphrey Bogart, another co-star in that movie. She also spent an occasional weekend with this handsome newcomer, Ronald Reagan. Warners was a very incestuous place in the late 1930s, with everybody sleeping around with everybody else."

Over their first lunch together in the commissary, Reagan and Priscilla shared different memories of how they broke into show business.

She told him she'd had her first screen test in New York, with two other aspiring actresses, Margaret Sullavan and Katharine Hepburn, whom she described as "a strange-looking girl with her hair slicked back in a sort of bun and with a weird voice. Not very pretty. All three of us were turned down when MGM saw our screen tests. Fortunately, other studios had better taste."

Reagan later recalled, "Priscilla and I came roughly from the same part of America, and both of us were just feeling our way around Hollywood and learning its special kind of morality. My friend Mugs would definitely not approve. The girls I dated didn't go to church on Sunday."

"Nelle met some of my dates. My mother told me, 'I wish you'd find some nice girl and settle down instead of running around with those painted hussies from Warner Brothers.'"

Priscilla became a frequent visitor to Reagan's love cottage. They would sometimes be spotted leaving for the studio together during the early morning hours when it was still dark.

After watching a movie, Priscilla and Reagan often dined together at Barney's Beanery on Santa Monica Boulevard in West Hollywood. Both of them loved Barney's chili and his cold beer. They always began their meal with his famous onion soup, enjoying it under a crude sign that read FAGOTS *(sic)* STAY OUT.

Barney, explaining his stance to them, and later to *Life* magazine, which had to censor his provocative comments, said: "I just don't like queers. There's no excuse for them. They'll approach any good looking guy and put the make on him. Anybody who does any recruiting in my place is shown the door. I've seen them take a guy home and turn him into a queer for life.

Priscilla Lane, one of the singing Lane Sisters, liked to make love to her leading men both on and off the screen. Lane courts the young Hollywood newcomer, Ronald Reagan.

Some guys completely give up with women once a queer has bedded them. That's because a queer will do things no decent woman will do. I say, shoot 'em. Who gives a fuck if one more faggot bites the dust? What I can't understand is why any man in his right mind would prefer plugging a smelly asshole to a juicy pussy."

Reagan said nothing and appeared embarrassed at these comments. Priscilla chimed in, "Barney, you've got a lot to learn about sex, my friend. I understand homos to my toenails. Who wouldn't like dick?"

***

Shortly thereafter, Reagan was assigned the lead in another film, *Sergeant Murphy* (1938). He was a last minute choice, based on the fact that the highly temperamental James Cagney had originally intended to star in the film. But Cagney had objected to the final script by Warren Jacobs, based on a true story by Sy Bartlett. With a running time of only 57 minutes, the picture would be directed by B. Reeves Eason, and produced by Bryan Foy ("The Keeper of the Warner Bs") who had been in charge of Reagan's first film.

Sergeant Murphy, set against a backdrop of the pre World-War I U.S. cavalry, was inspired by a racehorse with that name. Eason was a logical choice to direct a picture about horses. He had staged the most famous racing scene in pictures, the frenzied chariot race in the original (1926) version of *Ben Hur,* starring Ramon Novarro and Francis X. Bushman.

In *Sergeant Murphy*, Reagan's starring vehicle, the horse is an expert jumper, but freaks out at the sound of gunfire, which, of course, makes him useless as a military animal. He's destined for a meat factory until Reagan, cast as Private Dennis Murphy, saves his life and acquires him. The horse is smuggled into England, where it enters the prestigious Grand National Steeplechase. The film was a low-budget quickie, so location shooting at the fabled British course was not possible. As a substitute, Eason used the Santa Ana Racetrack in California instead.

He wrote a dispatch to the *Des Moines Register*, claiming, "I'm no hero, but if you're yellow and refuse to risk a few bruises, and occasionally something more serious, you might as well leave Hollywood."

The film would later generate protests from the Screen Actors Guild because real military men were used, denying jobs for Hollywood actors. But Jack Warner, based to some extent on his contacts with the Roosevelt White House, had obtained the permission of Harry Woodring, U.S. Secretary of War. The secretary claimed, "It is essential for the public to see a true picture of the Army rather than one based on a director's imagination."

In *Sergeant Murphy,* on a much more limited scale than what he'd later bring to fruition in 1939, the director made use of Reagan's equestrian skills and his love of horses. After receiving approval from Warners not to use a stunt man, Reagan did his own riding himself. Jack Warner had sent a threatening memo, warning about any cruelty to the horses. "If a horse is forced into a scene where it breaks a leg and has to be put down, I'll break a few legs myself," the studio mogul had threatened.

Eason sent a memo to Foy. "Reagan is very professional, shows up on time, and knows his lines. Unlike many actors I've worked with, he arrives on the set sober."

Cast in the film as the Army's post commander was veteran actor and director, Donald Crisp, a Londoner. Previously, he had played General Ulysses S. Grant in D.W. Griffith's controversial masterpiece, the racist silent drama, *The Birth of a Nation* (1915). Crisp was an experienced horseman himself, having served as a trooper in the 10th Hussar during the Boer War, where he had befriended a young Winston Churchill.

On the set of *Sergeant Murphy,* Reagan contracted another case of "*Leadinglady-itis*" when he was introduced to an eighteen-year-old Australian beauty, Mary Maguire. Her father was Mickey Maguire, a racehorse owner. "She knew her way around a stable," Reagan said.

Almost immediately, she asked him to call her Peggy and told him, "I think you're one handsome man. You should have been an Aussie. We need more men like you Down Under."

Reagan was delighted when Eason sent the actors and crew on location to the Monterey Peninsula, the home of the 11th U.S. Cavalry. After work, Reagan and Maguire went together on long, romantic walks along the sea shore, which she claimed reminded her of her native Australia. The red-tiled roofs and adobe buildings, however, evoked the era when Mexico ruled over the land.

They stayed in separate rooms at the local lodge, which was rather elegant, requiring formal wear at dinner.

When the picture was released and the reviews came out, several critics claimed that Reagan appeared to be more in love with Sergeant Murphy (the horse) than with his leading lady. Off the screen, that was not the case.

On several occasions, Eason spotted Maguire leaving Reagan's bedroom before dawn. When interviewed years later, Eason said, "Reagan's affair with the sophisticated, smart-talking Priscilla Lane prepared him for his marriage to Jane Wyman, and his romantic fling with Mary

At first, Reagan, in uniform, was attracted to "my delicate, petite Aussie," Mary Maguire.

After the war, he'd have nothing to do with her, having heard that she'd been closely associated "with a coven of British Nazis."

Maguire, more demure in demeanor, was a rehearsal for his wedded bliss with Nancy Davis."

Although only eight years younger than Reagan, Maguire came to view him as a kind of father/lover, according to both Crisp and Eason. A fellow Australian expat, John Farrow (later, the father of actress Mia Farrow), had arranged an interview for Maguire with the casting director at Warners, who ordered a screen test for her.

"So far, I don't like these *ingénue* roles," she told Reagan. "I'm a serious actress. The script on this clunker says I'm to say my lines in four different ways, 'sweetly, frigidly, impulsively, or excitedly.' How insulting to me as an actress!"

After the location shooting was completed in Monterrey, and after their return to Hollywood, Maguire and Reagan had a strong disagreement. Contrary to Reagan's strongly expressed advice, she threatened to instigate "a mutiny" against Jack Warner. Ignoring her lover's caution, she stormed into Warner's office, demanding better and more dramatic parts, "the kind you assign to Olivia de Havilland or Bette Davis."

Predictably, the mogul refused. Her militancy led to the abrupt end of Maguire's career at Warners.

Before her eventual return to England, she paid a farewell visit to Reagan, who seemed to have lost his romantic interest in her, having moved on to other starlets. They shared, however a mutual disappointment in the fact that Warners had delayed the release of *Sergeant Murphy* for eighteen months.

When it was eventually released, its critical reception did virtually nothing for either of their careers.

In reference to *Sergeant Murphy,* film critic Dorothy Masters, writing in *The New York Daily News,* issued a prophetic pronouncement, alluding to the virtually unknown medium of television: "In the movies, only because television isn't yet equipped to do him justice, Ronald Reagan's erstwhile radio announcer's looks and personality scoop out toeholds for a plot that can barely make the grade. These are the thrills attendant to daring horsemanship, comedy is in abundance, but the scenario has no villain (and therefore, no suspense)."

Bert Harland in the *Hollywood Spectator* issued faint praise: "Reagan has gained noticeably in ease, in sureness of gesture, and in ability to get his thoughts and emotions into the camera."

After her humiliating failure in Hollywood, shunned by the studios because of her outburst in Jack Warner's office, McGuire moved to England. There, in 1939, she married the controversial British fascist Robert Gordon-Canning, thirty years her senior. The widely detested leader of the British Union of Fascists, he was a rabid anti-Semite.

In the summer of 1940, during the Battle of Britain, he was jailed under the Defence Regulation Act and not released until 1943.

McGuire wrote to Reagan and others in Hollywood, claiming, "I do not share my husband's Fascist sympathies. I will not be a party to his political agenda, and I oppose Hitler's policy regarding the Jews. As you know, I worked with many Jews in Hollywood with no prejudice against these people."

Maguire divorced her husband in 1945 when he purchased a large marble bust of Hitler from a sale of German Embassy property. Gordon-Canning had announced to the press, "Jesus, 2,000 years ago, was mocked, scorned, and crucified. Today, he is a living force in the hearts and minds of millions of people. The same fate awaits Hitler, a charming and fine man."

Maguire returned to Hollywood in an attempt to revive her career, but her reputation remained tainted. She later blamed "Hollywood Jews for blocking my return to the screen."

***

Having been cast as the lead in his first two pictures, Reagan proclaimed, "I'm on top of the world." Then reality set in. During the context of his next three pictures, he either ended up on the cutting room floor or in bit parts.

He had hardly stripped off his U.S. Cavalry uniform before he had to don the uniform of a Navy flier, and rush south to Coronado, California, where his first A-list movie, *Submarine D-1* (1937), was nearing completion.

Pictured above: Wayne Morris, Doris Weston, and Pat O'Brien. Reagan ended up on the cutting room floor.

Directed by Lloyd Bacon, the film offered many insights into the U.S. Navy submarine force on the eve of World War II.

[One of its plot devices focused on then high-tech new devices, including the Momsen lung, an experimental underwater breathing device which some experts say may have killed more submariners than it rescued.]

Warners had cast three of its A-list male stars as the movie's male leads: Pat O'Brien, George Brent, and Wayne Morris.

Reagan was disappointed to find that his role was hardly more than a walk-on. As he later wrote, "Some place in the studio higher echelons, it had been decided to provide a surprise ending to the picture so that neither *(sic)* of the three stars would end up with the girl. I would come in as her fiancé in the last reel."

Uncharacteristically, Reagan didn't succumb to *Leadinglady-itis* after his introduction to Doris Weston, the female star of the picture. They had lunch at a café one day, finding that both of them hailed from Illinois.

The Chicago-born singer, actress, nightclub singer, and radio performer had been chosen to replace Ruby Keeler opposite Dick Powell in *The Singing Marine* (1937).

During lunch, she revealed that while filming *The Singing Marine,* she'd befriended "a cute little thing with a button nose. Her name is Jane Wyman. She saw you in a movie and thought you were good looking. She wants to meet you. I invited her to join us here, but she's needed for a scene."

"Some other time," he said.

On the set, Reagan met Pat O'Brien, a fellow Irishman, who was a close friend of James Cagney. They had become lifelong friends after their first encounter in 1926. During the course of his career, O'Brien became known for playing Irish cops or priests. The Milwaukee-born actor would loom large in Reagan's future. He invited Reagan to join him for lunch and to meet James Cagney. Reagan told him he'd already interviewed Cagney in Des Moines, but the actor hadn't remembered him. Later, during that encounter, Cagney finally remembered being introduced to Reagan.

Another of the film's male leads, Wayne Morris, would also loom in Reagan's future when they had a conflict over who had "squatters' rights" to Jane Wyman. At the time Reagan met Morris, he was also seducing Wyman, as well as Priscilla Lane, Reagan's other girlfriend.

On his second day on the set, Reagan met veteran actor Frank McHugh. This Pennsylvania-born actor had been performing ever since he was a child. He had been a workhorse contract player at Warner's since 1930, playing an occasional lead, but most often a sidekick to the leading man, consistently providing a film's comedy relief.

McHugh introduced Reagan to the actress, Veda Ann Borg, who had a minor role in *Submarine D-1.*

Born of Swedish parents, Borg was a beautiful, shapely blonde, who had broken into films the same year as Reagan. In her career, she had been in 100 films, including a small role in the 1945 *Mildred Pierce,* starring Joan Crawford. *[Ironically, the daughter in that movie was also named Veda.]*

Veda Ann Borg: A visionary about the future role of television, and a newcomer to Hollywood from Sweden, she preferred her romantic encounters "down and dirty."

"Veda had seen Reagan on the set and wanted to meet him," McHugh said. "I sorta played Cupid and brought them together. She accepted his invitation to spend a weekend at his cottage. When I saw her the following Monday, I asked her, 'How did it go?' She was very frank with me, almost too frank."

She told him, "It was good, clean fun in the missionary style. But as Wayne Morris and George Brent can tell you—yes, I've had both of them, too—I like it more lowdown and dirty."

Reagan's fling with Borg lasted for a few months, but in 1939, he visited her in the hospital after a car crash. She had been so badly injured that plastic surgeons had to drastically reconstruct her face.

She was one of the first actresses in Hollywood to recognize the importance of television. When she met with Reagan in the 1950s, she recommended that he, too, enter the medium. In time, he agreed, becoming the host and occasional star of the *General Electric Theater.* Perhaps based to some extent on his influence there, she eventually appeared in one of G.E.'s televised dramas.

McHugh also introduced Reagan to George Brent, who had the second male lead. He was one of Warner's major leading men and a famous womanizer in Hollywood. "Morris dates B-movie starlets," McHugh told Reagan. "Brent, on the other hand, goes for the big names—Bette, Olivia, Garbo, and Young."

[He was referring to Brent's affairs with Bette Davis (his costar in Housewife*; '34); Olivia de Havilland when she wasn't otherwise occupied with Errol Flynn; Greta Garbo (his costar in* The Painted Veil*; '34); and Loretta Young (his co-star in* They Call It Sin*; '32). When Brent bothered to come home, he was married to Ruth Chatterton (his co-star in* The Rich Are Always With Us*; '32).*

In the early 1940s, Reagan and Brent would conflict over yet another movie star, Ann Sheridan.]

At the last minute, the script of *Submarine D-1* was drastically revised. Reagan's scenes ended up on the cutting room floor, and Morris got the girl (Doris Weston). Ironically, however, before the film's release, based on subsequent cuts and edits, none of these four men, including Reagan, got the girl. In the final reel, their love and patriotic dedication to their submarine won the hearts of all four of the Navy men.

Reagan had originally been publicized as one of the stars of the film. Amazingly, he got fan mail praising his performance, even though he was not in the final cut. "After that, I learned to take fan mail with a grain of salt."

That Saturday night, Reagan was on a date with Priscilla. "Guess what?" he said.

"I've been assigned another picture, although I don't know in which role. It's called *Hollywood Hotel,* and your two sisters, Rosemary and Lola, have already been cast in it."

"I know, I know," she said, showing irritation. "I've warned my bitch sisters that I saw you first."

***

Priscilla Lane need not have worried that Reagan would become intimately involved with either of her sisters, Rosemary or Lola, during the filming of *Hollywood Hotel* (1937). All he managed was a brief handshake and a hello to each singer.

His role as a radio announcer was small. It involved an appearance with Louella Parsons, publicized at the time as "the Queen of Hollywood," because of her gossip column, which was religiously read by everybody in the film industry as well as by the public at large.

Whether he was scheduled for a scene that day or not, he showed up every day for lunch and for talks with the film's other actors and top-rated musicians. He had never been included within such an A-list cast of star players before.

Dick Powell, the star of the movie, formed a bond with Reagan, becoming his favorite golfing partner. Likewise, Jane Wyman, cast in other pictures, was also forming a bond with Joan Blondell, who would soon marry Powell.

Joining the singing Lane sisters (Rosemary and Lola) was another popular singer of that era, Frances Langford.

As Mona Marshall, Lola delivered a strong comedic performance, showing she could act as well as sing.

The director, Busby Berkeley, had assigned Reagan only a small role. Jerry Wald wrote the weak script. The movie was helped by the wonderful songs of Johnny Mercer and Richard Whiting, as interpreted by Benny Goodman and his orchestra.

"Busby's personal tribulations seem to weigh heavily on him, and about the last thing he wanted to do was direct *Hollywood Hotel,"* Reagan said. "Privately, the stars complained that he wasn't telling them what to do, and I didn't like my role, especially as I had been the star in my last efforts."

Reagan had lunch with Wald, who at the time was a writer at Warners, although he'd later become more celebrated as a producer. He was the same age as Reagan, and would play a future role in the careers of both Reagan and Jane Wyman. Wald was the inspiration for the horrid character of Sammy Glick in the Budd Schulberg novel, *What Makes Sammy Run?*

Reagan, who derived from the same town (Dixon, Illinois) as the dreaded columnist, Louella Parsons, appeared in her star-studded revue, *Hollywood Hotel.*

From left to right, Lola Lane, Dick Powell, Ted Healy, Reagan himself, and Allyn Joslyn.

Reagan found him intimidating, or, as film critic David Thomson described him, "Certainly, he was a vulgarian in the David O. Selznick mold, combining a brutal instinct for the lowest common denominator with earnest literary pretensions."

Reagan formed many relationships during the filming of *Hollywood Hotel*, notably with Parsons herself. When she learned that he, too, was from Dixon, Illinois, she was immediately taken with him, admiring his good looks and athletic build. She began to promote him in her column, defining him frequently, in print, as one of the most exciting newcomers to Hollywood.

The idea for the film grew out of Parsons' radio show, which was also called "Hollywood Hotel." Launched in 1934 and sponsored by Campbell's Soup, the program became one of the most listened to in America. The audience thought it was coming from a glamorous hotel, but in reality it was broadcast from a dreary booth at a radio station.

William Paley, head of CBS, had come up with the idea for Parson's radio program, and for four years running, it was one of the most popular on the airwaves. On a typical show, its Master of Ceremonies, Dick Powell, sang at least one song, and Frances Langford came out and did a blues number.

Stars who included Jean Harlow and Clark Gable showed up for chats with Parsons, who interviewed them about their latest happenings, which usually meant they had a new movie to promote. In those days, most stars got $1,000 for an appearance on radio, but in this case, Parsons gave each of them a crate of canned soup, usually tomato, as a gift from the sponsor.

The plot of *Hollywood Hotel* (the movie) was relatively simple. Powell, the lead, played a singer and saxophone player, Ronnie Bowers, in the immediate aftermath of signing a ten-week movie contract. His (now redundant) employer, Benny Goodman, with his band, gives him an enthusiastic send-off, performing "Hooray for Hollywood," as composed by Johnny Mercer, as part of the farewell. The number is belted into a microphone, onstage, by Langford and Johnnie Davis, an actor, singer, and trumpeter from Indiana who was making his film debut.

"Hooray for Hollywood" (the song) became a standard and is still performed at movie award ceremonies, including some of the annual Academy Award presentations.

As part of the film's zany plot, Lola Lane, cast as the temperamental star Mona Marshall, doesn't show up for a premiere. Instead, her lookalike, played by Lola's real-life sister, Rosemary Lane, appears as an emergency substitute, fooling both Parsons and Reagan. Thus follows a series of convoluted misadventures, with the character played by Powell eventually falling for Virginia (Rosemary), who works as a waitress.

Two future movie stars, blonde-haired Carole Landis, and a redhead, Susan Hayward, appear in the film in uncredited roles. *[Reagan would become intimately involved with both of them.]* Landis was cast in the film as "the most glamorous hatcheck girl in Hollywood," helping Mona's daffy father, Hugh Herbert, on with his overcoat. At the age of nineteen, Hayward played the role of "a starlet at table."

On the set, Reagan arranged a reunion with actor Eddie Acuff, who had been his co-star in *Love Is On the Air*. Acuff later recalled, "Reagan and I often had a drink together after

Eddie Acuff *(left)* was Reagan's confidant, but did a poor job of keeping his secrets.

work. His reputation as a Hollywood horndog began on the set of *Hollywood Hotel.* I think he was trying to topple Errol Flynn's seduction record. Apparently, Reagan didn't make it with Rosemary and Lola Lane; he had already had Priscilla. He seemed to be lusting after Glenda Farrell, Frances Langford, Carole Landis, and especially a new-comer, Susan Hayward, who made the mistake of falling in love with him. He dated all of them, even though Frances was married to Jon Hall and our director, Busby Berke-ley, was banging Landis. Undoubtedly, never again in his screen career would he meet so many beautiful young starlets willing to do his bidding. You might say that *Hollywood Hotel* represents the peak of his off-screen career as a Don Juan with a roving eye. Of course, never again would he be so young, so virile, and look that great, either."

"That Reagan was a sneaky little devil when he came to getting some nookie," Acuff continued. "That year I also made a picture called *The Singing Marine,* in which this cute little dish, Jane Wyman, had a small part. I took her out on two occasions, but I don't think she dug me at all. I was no Casanova like Reagan."

The film had an array of big name musicians, and Reagan often took his dates to hear one of the stars perform in the local nightclubs. He met Johnny Mercer, "The Ge-nial Southern Gent from Savannah."

After talking with Reagan, Mercer said, "You'd be perfect for the role of Ashley Wilkes."

"Who in hell is Ashley Wilkes?" Reagan asked.

"That means you haven't read Margaret Mitchell's novel, *Gone With the Wind,"* Mer-cer said. "I hear Jack Warner might buy it. You could be Ashley, with Errol Flynn in the male lead as Rhett Butler, and with Bette Davis playing Scarlett O'Hara."

"I'll try to get a copy of it," Reagan said.

Later, Parsons shared some indiscreet gossip about Mercer: "He's a perfect gen-tleman during the day. But at night, he can become vicious when he hangs out with Bing Crosby's hard-drinking cronies. Bing is dating this starlet, Jane Wyman, who is right cute."

"My God," Reagan said. "Everybody I meet keeps talking about this Jane Wyman."

"The other night at this out-of-the-way club, Mercer got really loaded and wrecked the joint," Parsons said. "Bing paid for all the damages."

Reagan also met Georgia-born Harry James, who had appeared with Benny Good-man's Orchestra before assembling his own swing band. In 1939, James became the first director of a "big-name band" to hire the young vocalist, Frank Sinatra. Reagan was conducting an on-again, off-again affair at the time, as mentioned previously, with Betty Grable, who would later marry James after her divorce from Jackie Coogan.

Reagan also met Gene Krupa, a jazz and big band drummer, known for his high en-ergy and flamboyant style. The Chicago-born musician invited Reagan to hear him play in a local dive. After watching his performance, Reagan defined him as "a Ball of Fire."

[In an ironic touch, Ball of Fire *became the name of a 1941 film in which Krupa made a cameo appearance with Barbara Stanwyck and Gary Cooper.]*

Reagan was also drawn to Lionel Hampton. An African-American from Louisville, Kentucky, and the first jazz Vibraphone player, he was destined to become one of the great names in jazz history.

Unlike some of his contemporaries, Reagan was not a bigot and was delighted to hear Hampton performing with the first racially integrated jazz group. As a drummer, Hampton performed stunts with several pairs of sticks, twirling and juggling without miss-ing a beat.

Hampton later said, "Those were hard days in 1937. Appearing with white musi-cians made it possible for Negroes to have their chance in baseball and other fields."

While hanging out with the stars of *Hollywood Hotel,* Reagan for the first time became interested in "the politics of the screen actor," a commitment that would lead to his election, in 1941, to the Board of Directors of the Screen Actors Guild.

He quickly learned that most actors were narcissistic, and didn't want to talk about anything except themselves. In contrast, he was genuinely interested in their welfare, as he would demonstrate as president of the Screen Actors Guild.

"I also learned the ropes of the movie business by listening to veteran actors share their experiences with me," he said. "Those actors were Allyn Joslyn, Alan Mowbray, and Ted Healy. My experiences with each of them was different, but very enlightening in the ways of Hollywood."

Ted Healy, murdered by Wallace Beery

After meeting Ted Healy one day on the set, the Texan invited him to bring a date and join him and his wife, Betty Hickman, to hear Gene Krupa on the drums. Healy had been instrumental in launching the slapstick comedy style of The Three Stooges. He appeared on stage with them until they broke with him in 1931 after a dispute over a movie contract. He had seen better days, having made a staggering (for the time) $9,000 a week when he was the highest-paid performer in vaudeville.

Reagan, with Priscilla Lane on his arm, found the Healys delightful and amusing company, and a friendship was formed. "Let's do this again," Healy said at the end of the evening. He would later call and invite Reagan and Priscilla to a New Year's Eve party scheduled at his house.

They never attended that party. On December 21, 1937, Reagan was listening to the radio when he heard that Healy had died suddenly at the age of 41. Initial reports listed the cause of death as a heart attack. However, it was later reported that immediately prior to his death, he had suffered recent wounds, including a "discolored" left eye, a deep cut over his right eye, and bruises on his head, neck, and chest. Witnesses claimed that he had been involved in some altercation the night of his death at the Trocadero nightclub on Sunset Strip. His assailants were identified as a trio of "college boys."

Months later, the real culprits were revealed, but no charges were ever filed against them for either murder or manslaughter. The leader of the attack was said to have been actor Wallace Beery, the gravel-voiced, jowly, superstar and a "lovable lug" onscreen in many an MGM film. His cohorts were Albert ("Cubby") Broccoli, later a producer of the James Bond films. Pat DiCicco, Cubby's cousin, was also said to have been involved. He was no stranger to scandal, having been implicated in the murder of his first wife, actress Thelma Todd. He later entered into an unsuccessful marriage to heiress Gloria Vanderbilt, during which he brutalized her.

Reagan later said, "Hollywood is good at covering up a scandal and letting the real culprits take a walk."

***

During the filming of *Hollywood Hotel,* its producer, Hal B. Wallis, had shown up on the day where a shot involved Louella Parsons. He lavishly greeted her. When she left "to check my makeup," he turned to Reagan. "I cast her because I decided that no one can play Louella better than Louella."

Perc Westmore had applied both Reagan's and Parson's makeup that day, and Orry-Kelly had created a simple black dress for her as a means of making her appear thinner. He then borrowed $165,000 worth of jewelry, a virtual fortune back them, to add to her glamour.

As Parson's biographer, George Eels, wrote: "During the filming, when Louella saw Lola Lane's splashy movie queen gown, she found her simple black too drab. When Orry-Kelly refused to give her another, Louella screamed, swore, threatened, and threw a full-fledged tantrum. Finally, the temperamental designer, who was accustomed to having his way—even with stars—pretended to give in. The result: He designed a gown for Louella that made her look like a large floating island."

Weeks later, Reagan, a fellow by-product of Dixon, Illinois, escorted a very nervous Parsons to a screening of their newest film. "In the dark theater that awful night, I thought I heard a local critic laugh loudly when I appeared on the screen," she later wrote.

Grabbing Reagan's hand, she rushed, sobbing, out of the theater and into the street. "I have never been so unhappy in my life."

So was Reagan. He protested, "But, Louella, my scene has not come up yet. You left too soon!"

***

When Reagan met Glenda Farrell on the set of *Hollywood Hotel,* he didn't really want to date her. She had made several flirtatious advances toward him, each of which he had ignored. "She's practically begging me to take her to bed," he confided to Acuff, "but she's not my type. She's a bit trashy, if you ask me."

"She got her start in Hollywood working in a whorehouse," Acuff told him.

"The Blonde from Oklahoma," as she was sometimes billed, was seven years older than Reagan, having migrated to Hollywood at the end of the Silent era. Her big break came in July of 1930 when she was given the female lead in *Little Caesar,* starring Edward G. Robinson. Along with another brassy blonde, Joan Blondell, Farrell personified a wise-cracking, hard-boiled, and somewhat dizzy blonde—an on screen archetype during the early talkies.

Farrell carved out a niche for herself playing the articulate and street-smart Torchy Blane, girl reporter. Billed as "The Lady Bloodhound With a Nose for News," she was shoehorned into one of the limited roles in American cinema that positively portrayed women as competent, career-oriented, and self-reliant. As Torchy, Farrell solved crimes that baffled the police.

When Reagan met Farrell, she was between husbands, and occasionally dating, among others, fellow contract player Humphrey Bogart.

Late one night, when Reagan was alone in his cottage reading a script, there was a knock on his door. When he opened it, he discovered Farrell standing there in a mink coat she'd borrowed from wardrobe.

He invited her in, perhaps beginning to reappraise her. She was more beautiful at night, or so it seemed, standing 5'4", with devilish blue-green eyes.

It was a cool night in Los Angeles, and she kept on her coat as he went to mix her a drink.

As he shared a cocktail with her in front of his fireplace, she talked about herself, as did most of the actresses he met.

Her father was a horse trader of Irish and Cherokee descent, and she'd made her first appearance on the stage playing Little Eva in *Uncle Tom's Cabin* at a theater in Wichita, Kansas. "At every performance, I went to heaven on a pulley," she said.

Long before Shirley Temple acquired squatter's rights to *Rebecca of Sunnybrook Farm* (1938), Farrell had appeared in the role as a child actor on a stage in San Diego.

After her drink was downed, Farrell stood up before him.

"You're leaving?" he asked.

"No, but we both have an early call," she said, "so I figured time is wasting." In front of the flickering light of the fireplace, she opened the mink coat, letting it glide to the floor. She was completely nude underneath it. "Hop to it, big boy," she ordered.

***

As a frequent listener to Parson's "Hollywood Hotel" radio show, Reagan had often heard Florida-born Frances Langford sing, especially her cheerfully upbeat signature songs, "I'm In the Mood For Love," and "You Are My Lucky Star," both of which were among his favorites.

Short (5'1" tall), vivacious, and pretty, she had made her film debut two years earlier in *Every Night at Eight* (1935). He was aware that she'd married the B-actor Jon Hall in 1934. Tall, athletic, and handsome, he was the scantily clad star currently appearing with another relative newcomer, Dorothy Lamour, in *The Hurricane* (1937), which eventually became a box office success and later, a camp classic.

Over lunch, as the talk drifted to relationships, Langford suggested that Reagan not get married: "Better that you remain the most sought-after bachelor in Hollywood."

"I fear you flatter me," he said, modestly.

"I'm finding marriage a roller-coaster ride," she said. "It's very difficult maintaining both a marriage and career, too. "

"I plan to get married in the future, as I keep telling people," he said. "But right now, I'm having too good a time. A wifey and kiddie will have to wait."

"Jon and I seem to operate on different time schedules," she said. "When I'm home, he's off somewhere. First, he's got to settle on a name. He appeared in pictures first as Charles Locher and later as Lloyd Crane before becoming Jon Hall. He's not much of an actor, but if he sticks to swashbucklers, fairy tales, Westerns, and South Sea adventure films, he'll do all right. He's got a great body, especially when he appears in a male sarong. Speaking of great bodies, you seem to have one yourself."

Before she married Elliott Roosevelt, singer Frances Langford *(above)* was wed to Jon Hall *(lower photo)*, famous on screen for wearing a sarong.

Known as "the swinging duo" of Hollywood, Frances and Jon invited Reagan for a *ménage à trois.*

"I don't think it wise for me to strip down here in the commissary," he said.

"I agree, but why not come over Saturday afternoon and go swimming with Jon and me in our pool, followed by a barbecue?"

"That sounds wonderful," he said. "I need to make new friends. Right now, my social life consists of a series of dates, no real friends."

"As actors just sinking their teeth into Hollywood, I'm sure you and Jon will have much to talk about," she said. "I might even sing 'You Are My Lucky Star' for you."

"That would be swell," he said. "Should I bring a date?"

"No, just yourself. We can entertain you."

The following Monday over lunch, Acuff pressed Reagan for details of his Saturday night fiesta with Jon Hall and Frances Langford.

Reagan seemed reluctant to talk about it. "A bomb. I've heard about decadent lives in the movie colony. On Saturday night, I experienced it. Frances and Jon are the weirdest couple I've met out here."

"I should have warned you," Acuff said. "They throw some wild parties and occasionally have orgies. At some parties, Jon strips down and masturbates while a circle forms around him, urging him on."

"You've got to be kidding," he said.

"I think I know what happened," Acuff said. "They tried to lure into a three-way?"

"Right you are."

"Did you enjoy it?" Acuff asked.

"Like hell, I did," Reagan said. "After thanking Frances for her barbecue, I got up and walked out the door. I won't go there again. Even if the setup had been with two gals and me, I still wouldn't have gone for it. I may be a bit square, but I believe in one man, one woman at a time. Of course, for variety's sake, there can be two or three ladies within the same week, but only one at a time."

"At some parties, I've seen a guy screwing a gal while another guy bangs him at the same time," Acuff said. "I might try that myself one night."

"That's disgusting," Reagan said. "Let's change the subject."

At that point, Acuff signaled to a young, blonde actress carrying her lunch on a tray to come and share their table. She walked over. He said, "Ronald Reagan, meet Carole Landis, who's got this bit part in *Hollywood Hotel*. She's god's gift to all cheesecake shutterbugs."

After smiling and shaking Reagan's hand, she signaled she'd be right back after rushing off to get a Coke.

When she was out of earshot, Acuff whispered to Reagan. "Carole might be a new experience for you if you decide to take on two gals at the same time. She sleeps with both men and women, so it might be interesting. At least you'd get to see two gals in action at the same time."

"Eddie, I think you're one great guy, but did anyone tell you you're a real sickie?"

***

After meeting Carole Landis, Reagan wasted no time in asking her out on a date. Unknown to him at the time, the blonde goddess (whose measurements were widely publicized at the time as 37-24-35), had launched a torrid affair with Busby Berkeley, whom she called "Buz." He had been instrumental in getting her a minor part in *Hollywood Hotel*.

After seducing Betty Grable, Reagan took on her chief rival at Fox, Carole Landis *(above)*, the "Queen of Cheesecake."

She concealed that fact from Reagan, but suggested that she did not want to accompany him, publicly, to a nightclub. Presumably, that might have made Berkeley suspicious and jealous.

"In that case, why not drop by my place for a supper?" he asked. "That is, if you like grilled hamburgers and spinach salad, my specialties."

That night, she arrived promptly at seven for drinks, followed by a simple yet tasty dinner he cooked himself.

He liked to exchange stories and experiences with all newcomers to Hollywood. He told her how easy it had been for him to get a screen test and a contract at Warners.

"Your life seems so conventional," she said. "My becoming a Hollywood starlet took a more circuitous route. If a film were ever made of my life, it would have to star Jean Harlow."

Landis' father had been a "drifting railroad mechanic" from Wisconsin, who had left home before she was born with the name of Frances Lillian Mary Ridste. She had been the youngest of five children. Tragically, two of her brothers had died young and violently. They included Jerome who, as a 17-month-old baby, was fatally scalded to death when a pot of boiling water spilled on him. Later, her 11-year-old brother, Lewis, was accidentally shot by a "gun nut" next door. He had been recklessly firing at some crows perched on his fence.

She told Reagan that just before she had dropped out of high school at the age of fifteen, she had tried to join the football team.

"A girl on the team?" he asked. "That would have caused a riot in the locker room, especially when the guys went to take a shower."

"That's what the coach thought, too," she said, "so I formed an all-female football team."

Reagan was reluctant to get involved with a married woman, and he pointedly asked her if she had a husband.

"Yes, unfortunately, and I'm still married to the jerk. He stole his father's car and we eloped to Yuma, Arizona, in January of 1934. He told me his name was Irving Wheeler and that he was a writer. Age nineteen. Actually, his name was Jack Roberts, and he was a part-time usher in a movie theater—and a full-time sleazeball."

She said that the marriage had lasted for only twenty-five days, and that her mother had arranged for it to be annulled before the end of February.

"Stupidly, we slipped away again and remarried on August 25. That time, the marriage lasted just three weeks. He was into it for the sex. When we weren't having sex, we fought all the time."

"Why haven't you gotten a divorce?" he asked.

"I've been meaning to, but I haven't gotten around to it yet."

"You should, you know. What if you meet some guy you'd like to marry?"

"You mean, like yourself?"

"I didn't exactly mean *that*."

After running away from her teenage husband, Landis arrived in San Francisco "with exactly $16.82 in my flimsy little purse."

"I went to all the clubs, trying to find a job as a showgirl," she said. "Nothing. I got a lot of propositions. Older guys just love to screw teenagers. I'm not proud of it, but for a time, I worked as a call girl. A gal has to do what a gal has to do."

She revealed why she had changed her name to Carole Landis, the Carole coming from her favorite star, Carole Lombard. "I dyed my hair blonde, and that seemed to work. Two days later, I was hired as a hula dancer at a night club, although I didn't know my left foot from my right."

When she'd saved up enough money, she took the train from San Francisco to Los Angeles. "Unlike you, I auditioned for bit parts on the casting couch."

Then, she revealed to him that she was currently involved in a torrid affair with Berkeley.

"Studio heads like Jack Warner routinely demand sex from their wannabe starlets. Unless you're a super star, you've got to trade sex for a bit part in almost any picture. Right now, I'm, appearing in more films, albeit shitty little parts, than any other actress in Hollywood, all coming from my lying on that damn casting couch."

[She was not exaggerating. In 1937 alone, the year Reagan started out in films, Landis was cast in at least ten films, maybe more, since some of her scenes in movies ended up on the cutting room floor.]

"Unlike you ladies, being a man, I'll never be called upon to lie on any casting couch," Reagan said. "It doesn't work that way for guys."

"Like hell it doesn't!" she answered. "You haven't been asked to drop your pants because you haven't worked with a queer director yet. I predict your day will come. With all the homos directing pictures these days, you'll get propositioned!"

"If any director ever comes on to me like that, he'll end up with a bloody nose," Reagan answered.

"You should be more cooperative. John Wayne didn't have a problem dropping his pants for John Ford. Hell, Gary Cooper got hired as a stuntman by bedding Rudolph Valentino. And later, during the making of *Wings,* he even had to make whoopee with Howard Hughes."

"I never knew that," Reagan said. "It's hard to believe. They're such he-men."

"Those are the ones the queers go after," she said. "You're very good looking and—although I'm not entirely sure—you seem to have a great body hidden under all those clothes."

"Thanks," he said. "Maybe you'll see more of it before the night ends. But tell me about some other films you worked on."

"I slept with Mervyn LeRoy, the director, as a means of getting a part in *The King and the Chorus Girl* (1937)*,"* she said. "LeRoy kept me busy when he wasn't balling Lana Turner."

She revealed that her unwanted husband, then billing himself as Irving Wheeler, once showed up on the set. "I got LeRoy to give him a tiny little part in *The King and the Chorus Girl,* but Jack has no talent at all. The last I heard from him, he was selling his big dick to queers cruising Hollywood Boulevard. He charges five dollars for a blow-job, more if a homo wants rough sex."

"During the filming of that chorus girl turkey, I made friends with another chorine named Jane Wyman," she said.

"There's that name again," he said. "It seems everybody I meet has just seen Jane Wyman."

"Jane and I started out as rivals," Landis said. "She and I both wanted to be moved to the front of the chorus line. But partly because LeRoy was screwing me at the time, I got the spot. Jane plays around a bit, but there's no one else like 'legs apart' Landis here."

Over cognac at the end of their meal, she shared some of her ambitions and fears. "I want to prove myself as a real actress and not be known as some curvaceous cutie. I desperately want to be a star, and I don't want to end up like most film actresses, living in some sleazy rooming house and sleeping on a piss-stained mattress, with an empty liquor bottle beside me, a woman with full scrapbooks of past successes, but with an empty stomach."

"It's getting late," she said, starting to unbutton her blouse. "In case Busby won't propose to me, you might be interested. I fully believe a man should try out a woman before proposing to her."

"My mother, Nelle, wouldn't agree," he said. "And if I had a daughter, I wouldn't advocate that. But for myself, I believe it."

"Then you don't mind if I sleep over tonight?" she asked.

"It would be a dream come true," he said.

[In the weeks, months, and even years to follow, Reagan must have found sex with Landis most agreeable. Their affair would continue through the early years of his marriage to Jane Wyman.]

Reagan's friend, Eddie Acuff, was kept abreast of the Landis/Reagan affair. After all, he was the man who introduced them. He later commented on their special relationship.

"I think they had different reasons for being attracted to each other, aside from the sex, which I heard was good. Carole told me that herself."

"Although Carole had a brother, Lawrence Ridste, still left, they never saw each other," Acuff said. "Reagan became not only her lover, but a big brother to her. She told me that she could depend on Reagan for good, solid advice, even though she lived on the sharp edge of the sword."

"His attraction to her, however, was harder to figure. Of course, she was a blonde cutie, and that's enough for most men. But it was more than that. There was a side of Reagan that he never wanted people to know about, a darker side. In spite of his philandering during his early days at Warners, he was still known as Mr. Goodie Two-Shoes. He maintained that reputation regardless of his private life."

"Carole was that bad girl type Reagan's mother had warned him about," Acuff continued. "It was like a Jewish mama warning her little Bernie, or whomever, about the forbidden fruit, a blonde, gentile, Christian *Shiksa*."

***

Acuff also became aware of an even more tempestuous affair Reagan launched during the shooting of *Hollywood Hotel*. It was with another "dress extra" (i.e., "bit player"), Susan Hayward, a fiery, short-tempered redhead from Brooklyn. While he was having lunch with Acuff in the commissary, Hayward came right up to Reagan and sat down beside him.

Her opening line was a new one for him: "This is your lucky day."

"Hi, I'm Ronald Reagan."

"And I'm Susan Hayward," she said provocatively and seductively.

"Is this the beginning of a beautiful friendship?" he asked.

Acuff later recalled, "Susan and Reagan just ignored me, caught up in their own private flirtation. I was witnessing the beginning of his most tumultuous, even violent, affair of the 30s. The question was, was he man enough to handle a firecracker like Hayward? Correction: I mean 'a stick of dynamite' like Hayward."

Chapter Three

Jane Wyman

The Chorus Girl Cutie Successfully Pursues

Clark Gable, Henry Fonda, & Robert Taylor

Overdressed, Ambitious, & Adorned with Fake Jewelry,
"The Hey-Hey Girl" Dances the Night Away

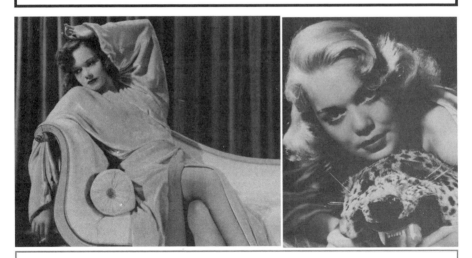

She was just a plucky young woman with a baby face spotlighted by a pug nose. Her talent was wasted in uninspired musicals, *clichéd* Westerns, insipid comedies, and amateur detective stories. But then the girl discovered she could make you cry in *Johnny Belinda* ('48).

As Jane herself claimed, "It was a hell of a long trip getting there, even if it took a movie of uncut corn to do it for me."

At Warner Brothers, and for the first time, Sarah Jane Fulks was billed as Jane Wyman when she was assigned a small speaking part in *Stage Struck (1936)*, starring Dick Powell, Warren William, and Joan Blondell, who stole the picture.

Jack Warner had decided to give Jane what the studio called "the build-up" to see if fans gravitated to her. "We don't really have a star here," he said. "Maybe a gal pal to a star."

The studio's casting director, Max Arnow, told Warner, "This Wyman gal has something, but I can't figure out what it is."

The build-up seemed designed to turn her into a major rival of the studio's other wisecracking chorus girl types, as exemplified by Blondell and Glenda Farrell.

As Jane posed endlessly for countless cheesecake photos and "girlie shots," the studio coaches went to work on her image, giving her dancing, singing, and acting lessons. Perc Westmore, the studio's resident makeup genius, worked on her face. In addition, a voice coach was brought in, as her speech was considered at the time as "unsteady."

Hey-Hey-Hey, from Jane Wyman, the Hey-Hey Girl.

As part of the campaign to improve her public image, men from the studio's wardrobe department told her she should tone down her clothing. She had become known for overdressing, having frequently appeared in "overly flamboyant" garb during nighttime excursions to the Cocoanut Grove or the Trocadero. Since she couldn't afford real jewelry, she had adorned herself with fake emeralds and diamonds.

Yet even when the wardrobe department critiqued her for "dressing like a Saturday night floozie seeking a sailor pickup who's been at sea for six months," she refused to listen.

During her filming of *Stage Struck,* she told Blondell, "I'm a dancing, good-time girl, and I'm not ashamed of it."

"I've been through hard times with rotten husbands and fickle boyfriends," she claimed. "I've known hunger, joblessness, and abuse. I've stood in the chorus line watching women of lesser talent get ahead."

"I'm still in the fucking chorus line, so I've decided to have some fun, now that I've dumped Myron Futterman. I've had 23 years of high energy—that's why I'm the 'Hey-Hey Gal,' but I've packed in 60 to 75 years of life experience—and that includes all the disillusion that goes with them."

"Everybody says I'm taking over the 'Resident Tough Gal Blonde' roles at Warners from you and Glenda Farrell. Hell, I've been living that Tough Gal role for the past

"Paradise depends on what a man is between the sheets."

—Jane Wyman

decade. I'm no longer the little virgin who lives next door."

"It's not true that all the leading men like James Cagney and others at Warners have fucked me," she told Blondell. "Some of them didn't even give me a second look."

When Jane saw her latest part, she complained to her agent, William Demarest, "I think I'll be typecast as a gum-chewing chorine until I'm thirty-eight, when I'll be too young to play grandmother roles and too old for the chorus line."

Her complaints to Demarest continued. "I don't like being billed as 'The Hey-Hey Girl.'"

That's because you're so lively," he said. "Jumping around all over the joint. You can't keep still for a minute. After a day's work on your feet, you continue dancing in night clubs until dawn breaks."

In her one scene with Dick Powell, he was impressed with her, telling Berkeley, "Jane can sing, she can dance, and she can act. You should give her more to do. We have a budding Ginger Rogers here."

When he saw the rushes of their scene, Powell was amused.

POWELL: *"What's your name?*
WYMAN: *"My name is Bessie Fufnick. I swim, I dive, I imitate wild birds, and play the trombone."*

Jane had wanted to make a play for Powell, although she didn't find him very sexy. She told her friend, Frank McHugh, who had fourth billing, "Blondell's already got him. They're going to get married."

Even though she had little to do, Jane was allowed to remain on the set to watch Blondell emote. She was interpreting the role in an outrageous "camp" style, years before the word was coined.

Her character seemed to be based on that scandal-soaked tabloid outrage of the time, Peggy Hopkins Joyce, whom one critic decades later would define as "the Paris Hilton of the 1930s."

With a pencil-thin mustache, Powell was not cast in the movie as a singer.

Jane had wanted the role of the *ingénue*, but Berkeley had cast newcomer Jeanne Madden in that part instead. "Her role should have gone to me," she complained to Busby Berkeley.

"Jeanne can't act, but I needed a singer, A Ruby Keelerish type, and I thought she'd do," Berkeley said. "But after directing her in her first two scenes with Powell, I think I've made a horrible mistake."

When he saw the rushes, he said, "Warner has put me in a financial strait-jacket on this movie. Powell is tepid in his role, and Madden delivers her lines with such flatness, she makes Ruby Keeler sound like Bette Davis. As for Blondell, she flashes her pearly whites, bats her eyelashes, and flaps about like an over-the-top Carole Lombard. In all, the movie tastes like yesterday's piss."

Jane need not have worried that Madden would be much competition for her. "I ceased to be jealous of her when her star flickered out so fast, she won't even merit a footnote in the history of Tinseltown. As for me, I was going places, except it would take a few more years to climb up that ladder."

At one point, Blondell invited Jane into her dressing room. Years later, Blondell told one of the authors of this book, "The press had begun to define Wyman as 'the future Joan Blondell,' and since I was still around, I figured I should get to know my competition better. I took the same approach with Jane that Betty Grable would eventually take with Marilyn Monroe when Fox was grooming her as Betty's replacement."

Jack Warner had decided to give the busty blonde the ultimate star treatment, and as such, Jane was awed by Blondell's dressing room. It incorporated a large living room, a fireplace, two bedrooms, a fully stocked kitchen, and a separate room for wardrobe and makeup.

Powell emerged from her bathroom wearing nothing but a pair of boxer shorts. Giving Jane a quick hello, he dressed hurriedly and left to shoot a scene, still complaining of his sore throat.

Perhaps to make clear to Jane who was the star, Blondell asked her to take two wire-haired dachshunds, collectively known as "The Thundering Herd," for a walk on the grass.

When Jane returned with the dogs, Blondell was being interviewed by a handsome young feature writer for *The Hollywood Reporter.*

Addressing Blondell, the reporter asked: "The fashion designer, Orry-Kelly, recently asserted that you have 'the most beautiful lips in Hollywood.' What do you think of that honor?"

"Blondell appraised him. "Why don't you try them out for yourself."

"Oh, no," he said. "I couldn't do that."

On Jane's final day on the set, she and Blondell lunched together in the commissary. "It's no secret that Dick and I are going to get married, so my romantic future was settled during the making of this film," she said. "But how did it go for you?"

"Usually, I at least find someone to date on a film," Jane claimed. "But not this time around. The only proposition I got was from Spring Byington. I turned her down."

"I did too," Blondell said. "That sweet charming woman certainly likes pussy—that's Hollywood for you!"

In spite of any potential rivalry, Blondell and Jane liked each other, and would spend many future evenings together. Dick Powell would in time become one of Ronald Reagan's best friends, and the two married couples—Powell and Blondell, Reagan and Wyman—became a social fixture on the Hollywood scene until 1944, when the Powells divorced.

The studio knew at the time that Jane was married, but that fact was deliberately not publicized, and no one had ever seen her mysterious husband. Therefore, Jack Warner felt it important for Jane to attend premieres on the arm of one of his handsome contract players. Ronald Reagan was suggested as an ideal escort, but he rejected the idea, based on his knowledge that she was married. "It would hurt my image to be seen dating a married woman," he protested.

"A lot of guys I was assigned to date put the make on me when we attended a premiere or whatever," Jane told Blondell. "I fought off most of them, but not always, if you get my drift. Of course, if my date was a star, he found me most accommodating. Privately, even though I was married, I dated a few big stars who had wives at the time. The pot can't call the kettle black."

Hope bloomed anew for Jane when Demarest called with news that he'd gotten her a role in an upcoming film, *Cain and Mable (1936)* that would star Clark Gable and Marion Davies.

***

On her first day on the set of *Cain and Mabel,* Jane was greeted by the film's director, Lloyd Bacon, who seemed deeply experienced in almost any genre of filmmaking—comedies, westerns, musicals, and gritty crime dramas "torn from the headlines."

By the end of her first day, Jane was disappointed that once again, "I'll get lost in the chorus line."

Even though her contract called for only a week's work on the film, Jane also showed up on days when the stars were shooting their big scenes. She had learned to ingratiate herself with the big names, hoping they would use their influence to either expand her roles, or get her future parts. Over a period of a few days, she managed to meet both Gable and Davies.

More gifted as a *comedienne* than as a dramatic actress, with past credits that included a stint as a Ziegfeld chorus girl, Davies was the publicly acknowledged mistress of press baron William Randolph Hearst. Born in Brooklyn, Davies had been educated in a Manhattan convent.

"Come on, honey," Davies said. "Let's have a snort together in my dressing room." She was referring to a twelve-room house that had been specifically moved for her use onto the Warner's lot. Jane was impressed at how lavish it was.

With the help of her maid, while she removed one outfit and got into another, Davies told Jane that she'd worked with Gable on *Polly of the Circus* (1932). It was obvious from her tone and from her wording that he'd seduced her.

"Clark was determined to seduce every female star at MGM, and by now, he virtually has. And now, while he's here at Warner's, he'll probably work his way through the gals on this lot, too. You're cute. I bet you'll be next on his list."

"I'd be honored," Jane gushed. "I'd love to go out with Clark Gable."

"Stick around, sweetie," Davies said. "Perhaps I can arrange something."

Davies asked Jane to fetch her more ice. "I'm about to collapse from heat stroke. It's a god damn 122° F. on that set. I've got to dance in a fur costume that could get me through a winter in Alaska."

"By the way, I used my star power and ordered Bacon to make Clark shave off that mustache of his. It tickles me when he kisses me. While I do my next big scene, keep bringing me ice," Davies said. "I'll put it on my wrists to keep cool."

Jane's favorite moment in the film came when Gable insults Davies as follows: "If the galloping you do is dancing, I've seen better ballet in a horse show." Davies slaps him before emptying a bucket of ice cubes over his head.

Jane appears as one of the dancers who suddenly explode, manically, onto the sound stage near the end of the movie. At the finale, a 100-foot-high pipe organ bursts apart, releasing 150 bridesmaid chorus girls, grinning like Cheshire cats and wailing, "I'll Sing You a Thousand Love Songs." The elaborate dance sequence lasted onscreen for only nine minutes, but it took a week to shoot.

Near her final day on the set, Davies approached Jane. "I told Clark about you. He wants to see you in his dressing room."

With trepidation, Jane headed for his dressing room and knocked on the door. "I was nervous as hell," she later recalled, "but I decided to cover it up with a brassy bravado."

When he invited her in for a drink, she delivered the opening line she'd rehearsed: "Are you really, as your press agents claim, a lumberjack in evening clothes?"

"One and the same, babe," Gable said.

"I've seen all your films with Jean Harlow," she said. "And I loved every one of them. But as you can

Marion Davies with Clark Gable in *Polly of the Circus*

see, unlike Harlow, I wear a bra."

"Bras can be removed," he said, "and I'm good at that."

Gable was suddenly called to the set. He turned to her. "Marion's invited us to San Simeon this weekend," he said. "I'd like you to ride up with me."

"That is so thrilling," she said. "I've always wanted to see that castle. I read something about it every day."

"I assure you that once you're there, I'll be more interesting than that damn castle," he said. "Now give me a kiss and we'll meet later and set up a time and place for me to pick you up."

"I can't wait," she said.

"Keep it on ice for me, you sweet little thing."

***

On Saturday morning, Jane had hoped to leave early for San Simeon, but Gable had something to do, and they didn't depart until late in the afternoon. She'd read about the many lavish parties Hearst and Davies had hosted at the castle for such guests as Charlie Chaplin (her secret lover), Douglas Fairbanks, Sr., and such unlikely guests as a very young John F. Kennedy. When George Bernard Shaw visited the castle, he famously remarked, "This is what God would have built if he had had the money."

Since they arrived late, most of the other guests had already retired for the evening. Gable told Jane he'd see her later, as he left to join the male guests who were having cigars and brandy in the library before retiring.

Appearing drunk, Davies was there to greet Jane and show her to her room. But first, she invited her into the powder room, where she removed a bottle of gin kept cool in her toilet tank. "Let's have a belter," she said. "I have to hide my liquor because Willie doesn't like for me to drink."

An hour later, Jane, in her sole *négligée*, had gone to bed and was about to drift off to sleep when Gable entered her room. "Clark," she said, sitting up in surprise.

"Didn't Marion tell you?" he asked. "I'm sharing the room with you."

The next morning over breakfast, Jane was introduced to one of the world's most powerful media barons, the portly William Randolph Hearst himself, along with other guests. Hearst told her, "You're a real cutie with that button nose of yours. It looks really kissable."

What happened between Gable and Jane that weekend didn't emerge until a few days later, when Blondell invited Jane for lunch at the Brown Derby. There, Blondell more or less guessed what had taken place. After all, Gable had seduced her way back in 1931 when they worked together on *Night Nurse* for Warner Brothers.

When Jane appeared somewhat reluctant to discuss her seduction by Gable, Blondell as-

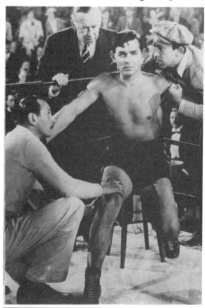

Gable, as a pro boxer, in *Cain & Mabel*. Earlier in his career, his manly physique had been rejected as "unfit to play Tarzan."

sured her, "I know the routine, and I'm sure that the same thing happened to you. He comes into your bedroom and pours you a drink and then begins some harmless chit-chat. He asks you about your ambitions as a movie actress. Then he gets into bed with you, kisses you, and fondles your breasts before he gets up and removes his clothes. Then, there's no more petting, no more foreplay, no more kissing: It's down to the dirty deed. It's all over in about a minute or so. He's a fast shooter. Then he's up and heading for the shower. By the way, he shaves his armpits and his chest."

"Joan, you've nailed it," she said. "That's exactly the way it happened!"

Years later, Blondell said. "Clark adored women—not in a lechy way. He loved beauty. His eyes would sparkle when he saw a beautiful woman. And if he liked you, he let you know it. He was boyish, mannish, a brute—all kinds of goodies. When he grinned, you'd have to melt. If you didn't want him as a lover, you'd want to give him a bear hug. He affected all females, unless they were dead."

Her involvement in *Cain and Mabel* did nothing for Jane's career. She wasn't even noticed. It didn't help Davies or Gable either, as it was a flop at the box office. *Newsweek* summed it up: "The studio's cycle of musical spectacles, begun with the successful *42nd Street,* reaches a new low. Clark Gable and Marion Davies fit into this picture like a fat hand squeezed into a small glove. Too much talent for such a skimpy, thinly woven plot that unravels in a trite series of moments."

***

During negotiations for her next movie, *Smart Blonde* (1937), Jane, as a Warner Brothers contract player, accepted whatever role she was given, no matter how meager. She didn't want to go on suspension.

Once again, she was disappointed that she'd been cast as a hatcheck girl. Having previously been uncredited in so many movies, she was relieved to hear that she'd get a screen credit, albeit in very small type.

The star of the picture was Glenda Farrell, playing a wisecracking female reporter, Torchy Blane. Jane decided she'd approach Farrell, if at all, with some caution. "By then, I was not only being billed as 'the next Joan Blondell,' but as 'the next Glenda Farrell,' too," Jane said. "I didn't think Miss Farrell would be particularly happy that her rival was in the same movie with her."

On the third day of shooting, when Jane accidentally crossed paths with Farrell, she greeted her and reminded her that she'd worked on her film, *Here Comes Carter,* in which her friend Ross Alexander had the male lead. "Oh, were you in that?" Farrell asked. "I hadn't noticed." Then she walked on.

The director of *Smart Blonde was* Frank MacDonald, a railroad employee who had quit his job and begun working for Warners in 1933 as a dialogue director. He told Jane that her voice was weak, but that because she had only a line or two of dialogue in the film, "It doesn't really matter, because your scene will probably end up on the cutting room floor."

She was not impressed with MacDon-

In *Smart Blonde,* Jane as a hatcheck girl is trapped in a bit part between the picture's two stars, Barton MacLane and Glenda Farrell.

77

ald, and neither was Jack Warner. MacDonald eventually drifted over to Poverty Row.

***

Jane's first impression about the possibility of finding a lover, or even a suitable date, on the set of *Smart Blonde* seemed virtually non-existent

How wrong she was. At the last minute, Wayne Morris was assigned a bit part and showed up on the set. He invited her for a weekend at a friend's vacation retreat in Palm Springs. She'd heard a lot about the place, but had never been there and was anxious to go.

She almost canceled her commitment to the plan when she saw him once again emerging from Farrell's dressing room.

Wayne Morris: Aviator, movie star, and patriot.

He realized that she had spotted him and he walked over to her immediately. "Listen, babe, remember our agreement."

"I remember," she said. "But I'm still jealous of that bitch."

"Honey, she means nothing to me. But she's the star of the picture. Like many of you chorus gal types, a man with a body like mine sometimes has to lie on the casting couch, the same as you babes. You won't believe some of the big names at Warners who have wanted to play with Jumbo. "

"I'd believe it," she said, sarcastically.

She couldn't stay mad at him for long, and she left the next morning for the hot, sticky drive to Palm Springs.

The town evoked a desert landscape and movie stars sipping cocktails around pools attached to lavish homes. Back in the days of Rudolph Valentino and Theda Bara, the resort had become a mecca for discreet, off-the-record weekends.

Jane fell in love with the place. *[It would become her hideout in years to come. Eventually, she leased a house there after her divorce from her third husband, Ronald Reagan.]*

Once they arrived inside the two-bedroom house, Morris pulled off all his clothes and jumped into the pool. He urged her to strip down, but she refused. She finally agreed to swim topless with him, but she retained her bottom. "I may be a chorus girl, but I'm still a lady," she said.

That Saturday night, he told her that he'd invited four other couples over for drinks and a swim in the cool of the evening. She put on a cocktail dress and returned to the pool area, finding him still lying, nude, on a chaise longue.

"Aren't you going to get dressed?" she asked. Then, she heard the doorbell. "For God's sake, throw a towel around you."

Jane answered the door and greeted Morris' friends. He hung out with people on the fringe of the movie industry—grips, technicians, a wardrobe woman, no big stars. She ushered them onto the patio.

Morris' bath towel fell down as he was mixing drinks for his guests. He didn't bother to recoup it. "He was stark raving naked in front of the women and their dates," she later told Blondell.

"Soon, all the couples were stripping down and jumping into the pool," Jane said. "Wayne urged me to get naked and join them. Instead, I retreated into the house until they left. I feared the whole thing would turn into my first Hollywood orgy, but it didn't. I learned something about Wayne—it was my first encounter with an exhibitionist."

Later that evening, he told her, "In Hollywood, it pays to advertise your best assets. The news will spread. A lot of the producers and directors in this town are homos, and this kind of word of mouth will lead to steady work in films, maybe even a major role."

"Dear one, don't you see that that makes you a whore?" she asked.

"It's Hollywood, baby, where a pretty boy doesn't have to go hungry."

Morris had completed his brief appearance in *Smart Blonde,* and he agreed to call her in a few days. "Something big is cooking for me."

She felt lonesome and abandoned on the set that Monday morning. She read a book until it was time for lunch, as she had nothing to do.

Later, as he was strolling into the commissary, she encountered a tall, very good looking man who held open the door for her. "Hi," he said. "I'm Craig Reynolds. Where have you been hiding all my life?"

"I'm Jane Wyman," she said.

"Since we both appear to be alone, why don't you share a bite with me?"

"I thought you'd never ask," she said.

"He was drop dead gorgeous," as she'd later tell her friend, Lucille Ball. "When he trained his left eye on me, I melted."

She didn't mention anything about his right eye. "It was one of those 'if you blow in my ear, I'll follow you to the ends of the earth,'" Jane said.

"Craig was creamy, dreamy, my kind of man, the ideal beau I've been seeking in Hollywood, but never found," Jane claimed. "By the time the blueberry pie was served, I was ready to roll if he wanted me, although I feared my passion for him was not matched."

She had never met him before, even though she'd played bit parts in two of his movies, including *Here Comes Carter,* which had starred her friend, Ross Alexander, as well as Farrell. Reynolds had also played minor roles in her just-completed *Stage Struck* and, before that, in *Rumba,* with Carole Lombard and George Raft.

"Well," he said, "on the occasion of this, our fourth picture together, it's time I remedied that with a hot date tonight."

"I'm game," she said.

"Craig and I began dating that very night," Jane told Blondell, who had become her confidant. "When Craig took off his clothes, I nearly fainted. He's an Adonis, the type high school girls dream about. Unlike Clark Gable, he's got an impressive piece of equipment and can go all night."

Jane began to learn more about Reynolds, a native of Anaheim, California, over breakfast the next morning. Fortunately for her, he was unmarried, and would remain so until 1943. In his early films, he'd been billed by his real name, Hugh Enfield.

In many ways, his career at Warners evoked her own. Both had used their original names in the beginning, and now they were being evaluated by Jack Warner as potential stars. Previously, Reynolds had been cast as the second lead in *Paris in Spring* (1935). Although he was nine years older than Jane, he looked much younger.

[In 2014, an online fan, identifying herself as "Caftan

Craig Reynolds, an early love of Jane Wyman's. When he "turned it on," his left eye was said to be the most seductive in Hollywood.

Woman," was still raving about Reynold's sex appeal. She, too, cited his seductive left eye, evoking Jane's comment in the late 1930s. *Caftan Woman* defined Reynolds as "Versatile, energetic, tough, and as dashing and charming as Errol Flynn."

Caftan Woman went on to write: "In 1936, Reynolds was at home on the range as the villain opposite Dick Foran in Treachery Rides the Range. He seemed born to the tuxedo in the Warren William comedy, Times Square Playboy. Stage Struck *(1936) was a fine showcase for Reynolds as Gilmore Frost, a ham actor with a way with the ladies. He had the opportunity to display his comedic talents along with his good looks.")*

When *Stage Struck* opened in Pasadena as a sneak preview, Reynolds escorted Jane to see it, later taking her back to his apartment until dawn broke over Los Angeles.

"I wanted to marry him, but he never asked me," Jane recalled to Blondell. "I was at least willing to move in with him, but he had time for me only two nights a week. He was busy on those other nights, but never told me how. It was obvious that he was leading a double or even a triple life."

All the people who had worked with Jane and Reynolds were predicting stardom for them. It was even suggested that Reynolds and Jane might co-star together in their own series of films, based on the detective character created by Erle Stanley Gardner.

Eventually, however, Reynolds ended up getting cast in *The Case of the Black Cat* (1936), playing in a minor role. Ricardo Cortez was cast as Perry Mason, with June Travis as his secretary, Della Street, the role Jane coveted.

Jane would later learn from Carole Lombard, during the filming of an upcoming movie, *Fools for Scandal,* that Reynolds and she often joined "my homo pals, Ricardo Cortez and Cesar Romero, for wild nights on the town at the queer bars." The outspoken Lombard told Jane that "Reynolds and Cortez had been taken with each other during the filming of the Perry Mason movie."

"At least I know how Craig occupies some of his nights," Jane later said. "But there are still nights unaccounted for. In gossipy Hollywood, I was sure to find out sooner than later."

***

Based on her familiarity with the other actors in its cast, Jane referred to her brief appearance in the 1936 release, *Gold Diggers of 1937,* as "old home week." It brought her together again with previous stars on whose films she had worked, notably Dick Powell and her friend Joan Blondell, now a happily married couple. Once again, she encountered a very icy Glenda Farrell, cast in the third lead. The director, Lloyd Bacon, had helmed Jane's brief appearance in Clark Gable's *Cain and Mabel.*

Another familiar face, Busby Berkeley, arrived on the set to direct what evolved into some of the decade's most lavish musical num-

Blondell with then-husband Dick Powell, in the swing of things.

bers. Among other composers, Harold Arlen contributed to the music.

[*Blondell's stirring rendition of "Remember My Forgotten Man," the keynote song within that movie, became an anthem for the frustrations of the unemployed and the government's failed economic policies, especially those of Herbert Hoover. "I Can't Sing Worth a Damn," Blondell said, "but in that Forgotten Man number, I mostly talked and acted my way through what evolved, in terms of socialist propaganda, at least, into a very important and controversial song."*]

Blondell seemed concerned for her future. "Right now, I'm one of the

Joan Blondell singing one of the great but thinly disguised odes to socialism after WWI, "Remember My Forgotten Man."

most sought-after actresses in America. But how long can it last? Wrinkles and gray hair are on the way. But I'm excited by my upcoming movie. I'm going to appear opposite Errol Flynn in a film aptly entitled *The Perfect Specimen."*

"Remember me to that perfect specimen," Jane responded. "He's probably forgotten me by now. After all, Errol is king of the one-night stand."

"You don't have it so bad, kid," Blondell said. "At least you can call Craig Reynolds honey one or two nights a week."

Jane finally received a copy of the script of *Gold Diggers of 1937*, wondering what was in it for her. Character actor Victor Moore was cast in it as a meek, aging hypochondriac who thinks he's dying. He plans to back a Broadway show, but finds that his partners have lost his capital in bad stock market investments.

Cast as one of the chorus girls, Jane soon discovered that the script granted her only one line of dialogue. It consists of the words: "Girls, we're saved!" shouted to her fellow chorines when the money for the show is finally raised.

The movie's theme song was, "With Plenty of Money and You." Identified by its secondary title, *"The Gold Diggers Lullaby,"* it became a big hit.

The film's finale, an elaborate chorus-line-dance-number, quickly evolved into a major-league Busby Berkeley spectacular. Jane appeared in it as one of 104 women wearing white military uniforms, tapping in military formations and geometric patterns, singing "All's Fair in Love and War."

During the Academy Awards that followed the release of this film, and based on this lavish production number, Berkeley was nominated for an Oscar for Best Dance Direction of the year.

At the end of filming, Jane was anxious for news and details about her next assignment.

"I got you a part in *The King and the Chorus Girl,"* her agent, William Demarest told her.

"I hope I get to play the chorus girl," Jane said.

"No such luck," he said. "That role goes to the co-star, Joan Blondell. I think you know her."

***

81

Actor Craig Reynolds continued to date Jane, taking her out at least two nights for dinner every week, followed by a sleepover at her apartment. For some reason, he never invited her to his own apartment. She kept hearing reports of his various involvements with both men and women, but she never confronted him about it. Neither had pledged fidelity to the other.

Reynolds at that point in his life claimed, "I'm shooting skyward in Hollywood." It certainly seemed so at the time. In 1937 alone, he appeared in a total of eleven films, either in bit parts or in starring roles, including *Smart Blonde* with Jane.

"I must be setting a record with the number of film appearances. If this keeps up, by 1939, I'll be a household word throughout America."

Double Trouble: Billy (*left*) and Bobby Mauch. Before actor James Craig came along, these twins were Gore Vidal's "ultimate sexual fantasy."

He invited her to a sneak preview in Pasadena of his latest film, *Penrod and Sam,* in which he had been cast as "Dude" Hanson, a gangster with a mean streak. She noticed that he sat nervously on the edge of his seat, waiting for his image to appear on the screen.

Although she found his brief appearance riveting, she felt the film actually belonged to Billy Mauch, one of the famous Mauch twins. The other twin was Bobby, and both of them had starred with Errol Flynn in Mark Twain's *The Prince and the Pauper* (1937).

The plot of *Penrod and Sam,* was based on the short stories of Booth Tarkington. It concerned a gang of junior G-Men, a secret club where all the members were sworn to uphold the law and turn in crooks.

During their exit from the theater, Reynolds spotted Billy Mauch, who had slipped into the theater, unnoticed, to catch the final cut of his performance. He introduced the twin to Jane, before inviting both of them to join him for late night hamburgers.

Over a beer, Jane found the young Billy to be winsome and blue-eyed. She had seen the Errol Flynn movie. "Were you the prince or the pauper? I couldn't tell the difference."

"Neither can our mother, although she claims she can," Billy said. "Sometimes Bobby and I secretly trade roles. We tricked Flynn that way, even the director and crew."

[*Bobby and Billy Mauch would reunite to film two more movies based on Tarkington's tales,* Penrod and His Twin Brother *and* Penrod's Double Trouble. *They'd flip a coin to see which brother would play which role.*

During World War II, they'd serve in the military together. After the war, the sun set on their film careers. Billy, however, would appear on the screen for a final cameo with Ronald Reagan and a chimpanzee in Bedtime for Bonzo *(1951).]*

***

With so little work, Jane continued to visit actor friends on the sets of their respective movies. Other than as a means for passing the time, she had a motive for these visits. She was hoping that one of her friends would introduce her to the right director, who'd say, "You fit perfectly into this choice role I haven't cast yet."

When an invitation to visit Bing Crosby filming the Depression-era musical, *Pennies from Heaven* (1936) arrived, she eagerly accepted.

The Crooner warmly welcomed her, inviting her to his dressing room, where he indulged in heavy petting with her. Called to the set, he said, "I promise there's more to come later tonight."

She got to hear him sing, "Ev-ry time it rains, it rains pen-nies from heav'en." Later, *Down Beat* magazine reported that the recording was among the best-selling in America for three solid months.

When he broke for lunch, Crosby asked Jane to join him in the commissary, where he introduced her to Louis Armstrong. The jazz trumpeter and singer was also appearing in the film. Noted for his flashy cornet and trumpet playing, along with his raspy singing voice, the African American musician was a favorite of Jane's. Crosby admitted that Armstrong's velvety lower register and bubbling cadences in such songs as "Lazy River" had exerted a powerful influence on him.

After the closing of Harlem's Cotton Club in 1936, Armstrong had moved to Los Angeles, where he was appearing at the local Cotton Club, along with Lionel Hampton on drums. Jane and Crosby were invited to watch them perform.

Paramount executives didn't want to hire Armstrong to perform within the movie, but Crosby had insisted. The trumpeter was consequently featured within a musical number and as part of two comic exchanges. He was among the first black stars to get billing in an otherwise white picture. Crosby had wanted to perform a duet with him, but the bosses at Paramount rejected that idea, a bow to the segregated color line of that era.

Armstrong told Jane, "I could run my mouth all day about My Man Bing. He's got a heart as big as the world. Carry on Papa, I say."

After work, Crosby drove Jane to his new house at 10500 Camarilly Street, telling her that "Dixie and the boys are away."

As his car pulled into his driveway, she asked him, "Is this a mansion or a palace?" It was the first of dozens of invitations to come, where she'd be invited to the home of a movie star. At the time, in 1930s dollars, Crosby was making $150,000 per picture, plus $3,500 for a radio broadcast.

To her, that was a vast fortune. "I don't think I've ever been known to carry more than fifty bucks at a time," she said.

After offering her a drink, he took her on a tour of the grounds, which included a bathhouse next to a luxurious swimming pool, along with a tennis court. Back in the house, he escorted her downstairs to his den and bar, which was adjacent to a playroom and a living room, complete with fireplace and a large Murano chandelier. The house was a mixture of styles, ranging from Regency to Victorian. In all, a very informal style.

For her girlfriends, Jane later summed up her night with Crosby: "After being mauled by Wayne Morris, a brute in bed, my time with Bing was a cake-walk. I've decided that if I don't make it in the movies, I'm going to marry a movie star, and lie around all day on a sofa, calling out, "Beulah, peel me a grape.'"

***

Two days after her visit to Bing Crosby's home, Jane was invited to visit Wayne Morris on the set of his latest film, *Kid Galahad* (1937). He showed her into his dressing room and gave her passionate kiss before telling her, "This is my big break. I play a boxer, the title role. Jack Warner is grooming me for stardom as the next Errol Flynn."

"Who else is in this picture?" she asked.

"The big names: Edward G. Robinson, Bette Davis, and Humphrey Bogart."

The film concerned an aggressive promoter (as played by Robinson) who transforms a naïve bellhop into a boxing star. During the course of the movie, he tangles with mobster Bogart at every turn.

Veda Ann Borg and Jane Bryan were cast in minor roles. Ironically, during the making of *Kid Galahad,* Ronald Reagan was having an affair with Borg, and he would soon develop a crush on Jane Bryan when they made a picture together.

In a role she hated, Davis was cast in *Kid Galahad* as a torch singer, the on-screen mistress of the character played by Robinson. She hated her character's name, "Fluff" Phillips. "Whether I like it or not, I'm forced to play, once again, this annoying cardboard character," she had said.

In addition to the affair she was conducting with one of its stars, Wayne Morris, Jane had other reasons that motivated her visits to the set of *Kid Galahad.* Not knowing if Davis would be available, Jack Warner had recommended Jane for the role of Fluff. It was to be Jane's first big break at Warners.

As a champion prizefighter in *Kid Galahad,* Wayne Morris, the tall, blonde, and well-built actor, saw this publicity still from Warners. "My best asset, 'Jumbo,' is hidden by those droopy shorts."

"I lived in a dream for at least for two weeks, thinking I'd achieved my first starring role, and with Bogart and Robinson, no less! But then I got a call that Davis had suddenly become available, and consequently, I would no longer be needed."

Although Morris was delighted to have been given such a big part, he was furious at the size of his paycheck. "It's criminal—that's what it is." He was receiving $66 a week, whereas Robinson was earning $50,000 for his role in the film, with Davis getting $18,000.

During the early days of the shoot, Bette Davis had repeatedly—and seductively—invited Morris to her dressing room, and he kept refusing. He'd even asked Bogart, "How do I get this hot-to-trot mama off my back? I'm not into mothers this year."

Morris was 23 at the time, Davis only 29.

"Why don't you throw her a mercy fuck?" Bogart asked.

"I get it up only for teenage gals," he said. "Perhaps if they're hot enough, a gal in her early twenties might do."

Jane learned that in an effort to get to Morris, Davis had even approached Curtiz and asked him to write in a passionate love scene between Morris and her. The director had refused.

Jane didn't realize that she was being used when Morris invited Jane to join him, with Davis for lunch. At first, Davis ignored Jane, completely, directing all of her comments to Morris.

"I just had another argument with Curtiz," Davis said. "He hates me, you know. He didn't want me in the picture. In the early 1930s, he seduced me. 'You're no bigger than a little piece of okra,' I told him later. He's despised me ever since."

"No wonder," Jane said.

"That's certainly not my problem, is it Jane?" Morris asked.

Jane didn't immediately answer, but she noticed that Davis' face seemed immediately consumed in a jealous rage.

Davis stood up and, for the first time, addressed Jane directly, this time as a means of insulting Morris: "When you see *Kid Galahad,* Miss Wyman, expect to give one big yawn. There's no excitement except what I generate."

The next day, when Jane once again showed up on the set of *Kid Galahad,* she encountered Davis. She reached for Jane's arm. "Listen, Kid, if you think Morris is faithful to you, forget it. He's making it with this bimbo, Veda Ann Borg, when she's not screwing this Ronald Reagan. Borg's role in the picture is so small, she's identified in the cast as only 'the Redhead.'"

Jane politely thanked Davis for her warning, and headed for Morris' dressing room. She had long ago accepted the fact that he slept with other women, much in the same way that she slept with other men.

At lunch, Morris introduced Jane to Humphrey Bogart, who would soon be making a picture with Ronald Reagan. Like Bette Davis, he too, was disenchanted with his role in *Kid Galahad.*

"Can you believe that I play this creepy character whose name is Turkey? I complained to that bastard Curtiz, telling him my role was one-dimensional. He told me, 'I make this film go so fast nobody notice character.'"

"I don't want to bitch too much, however, because I've heard that Jack Warner is considering dropping me when my contract is up," Bogart said.

Later, he said, "I ran into Robinson. I told him I had to learn to shoot better. I explained to him that in the film, I get shot and a blanket is put over me. But when I shoot him, the bullet doesn't kill him right away, and he survives for a curtain speech he gets to deliver in the arms of Bette Davis. So while he gets to deliver this big *Pietà*-like death scene, I'm covered up in a flea-infested blanket."

Later, when Morris introduced Jane to Robinson, he spoke kindly of Bogart. "For all his outward toughness, insolence, *braggadocio,* and contempt, there comes through a kind of sadness, loneliness, and heartbreak, all of which are very much part of Bogie the man. I always feel sorry for him—sorry that he imposes upon himself the façade of the character with which he has become identified."

As Jane was leaving the studio with Morris, she thanked him for letting her visit the set of *Kid Galahad.* "At least I got a preview of the stars I would have worked with if I'd been allowed to play the role of Fluff."

"Honey," he said from behind the wheel of his car. "You can Fluff me any time of the day or night."

***

As Demarest, her agent, had predicted, Jane was awarded with a role in *The King and the Chorus Girl* (1937). This time, instead of a role as hatcheck girl, or inclusion as an unbilled chorine, her character would have a name: Babette Latour. "How phony can a name be?" she asked Joan Blondell, the female star of the film. "But I'm glad that at least I have an identity."

The film was notable for a screenplay officially credited to Groucho Marx. The plot focused on Alfred VII, a young and rich deposed king in exile in Paris, who is monumentally bored. That leads to his involvement with a chorus line cutie. The plot seemed inspired by the abdication of Edward VIII in England, followed by his exile to France.

Jane was anxious to meet the handsome, dashing, star of the movie, Fernand Gravey, *[an actor billed in the U.S. as Fernand Gravet.]* He had been cast in the role of King Alfred Bruger VII.

When Blondell introduced him to Jane, the Belgium-born actor bowed and kissed her hand. She found him enchanting, and it was obvious that he was attracted to her. He suggested that they might get together later in his dressing room for a drink.

"I'll count the hours," she said, before he bid her *adieu.*

Later, in Blondell's dressing room, she said, "Not that it would matter to you, but Fernand got married last year to this French actress, Jane Renouardt, who is fifteen years older than he is. Perhaps he likes older women."

"Perhaps he'd like a little variety in his life," Jane shot back.

"This is his first film in America," Blondell said. "Jack Warner is giving him a big build-up, thinking he can be the studio's leading Gallic lover, ready and available whenever a picture calls for a good-looking Continental with impeccable manners."

Later that afternoon, the drink with Gravey led to a sleepover at Jane's apartment. During the evening, she learned more about this charming new import from the Continent.

He had started performing at the age of five under his father's direction. His parents, Geôrges Mertens and Fernande Depernay, had each been film actors during the silent era. Born

Fernand Gravey (aka Gravet): "I may be married, but the heart wants what the heart wants."

in 1905, Gravey had made four movies himself in 1913 and 1914. His first good movie role was in *L'Amour Chante,* released in 1933.

His first English-language movie, *Bitter Sweet* (1933), an adaptation of an operetta by Noël Coward, was followed by a more famous reincarnation when Nelson Eddy and Jeanette MacDonald re-configured and re-filmed it in 1940.

Gravey told Jane that he could make both English and French-language movies because he'd been educated in Britain.

"I wondered why you spoke such perfect English," Jane said.

The King and the Chorus Girl was Gravey's first film for Warner Brothers, and he was anxious to succeed.

Over dinner at the Brown Derby, she found Gravey to be a gentleman of impeccable manners and Gallic charm. "Too bad you're already married," she said.

"Marriage is a legal contract, but it does not place a limitation on my desires. I'm free to follow the rhythms of my heart."

"I agree with you," she said. "Marriage is such a limitation."

The next day, Blondell was eager to hear a report on her date with Gravey.

"He's the kind of man any woman could really fall for," Jane said. "I'm sure he has a dark side—perhaps smothering babies to death, or something like that—but he showed none of that to me. Unlike Wayne Morris, he told me his ultimate aim in bed is to please a woman—and that he did. I wonder, though, if all Frenchmen are that oral in bed."

"I haven't sampled enough Frenchmen to make a learned judgment," Blondell said. "When are you seeing him again?"

"Would you believe tonight?" Jane asked.

"I'd believe it," Blondell said. "How long do you think this is going to last?"

"At least until the end of the picture," Jane said, "and then, I'm certain he'll return to his other Jane, his wife from the 19th Century."

"Can you add him to your growing list of *beaux*?" Blondell asked.

"Women down through the ages have managed to have more than one lover, and I'm sure I can, too. In fact, tomorrow, when I have the day off, I'll be visiting Craig

Reynolds on the set of his new movie."

On the second day of shooting, Jane encountered Mervyn LeRoy, who was directing the picture. He kissed her on the cheek, recalling that he'd directed her in her second film, *Elmer the Great,* starring Joe E. Brown.

He told her that the Hays Office was objecting to the plot line of the Gravey/Blondell movie. It had issued a mandate that no film in Hollywood could be made, even under the disguise of fiction, that exploited the abdication of King Edward VIII and his subsequent marriage to the twice-divorced Wallis Warfield Simpson, a (scandal-soaked) American socialite.

As part of a spirited defense, LeRoy argued that the movie had gone into production before the abdication scandal had erupted, and that therefore, the objection of the Hays Office was without merit.

LeRoy revealed that Warners was investing a whopping $2 million in the production and filming of *The King and the Chorus Girl.* "I'm having the last laugh on the Hays Office. I'm directing Gravey as an effete, brandy-swilling ex-monarch, evocative of Edward VIII himself. Did you know that the jerk who gave up the throne of England 'to marry the woman I love,' is actually a homo?"

"I didn't," she said. "But now that I do, I'll know not to proposition him if I'm ever introduced."

Later, LeRoy invited her to the set to witness Blondell emote her way through one of her big scenes.

Even though Blondell was the star's friend, Jane wished that the role of the chorus girl had gone to her. From what she'd seen of Blondell's performance, this was her best yet. Later, the *Los Angeles Evening Herald Express* would agree, asserting that her portrayal was "the finest she has ever put on the screen. She has the subdued finesse of a Lubitsch heroine."

Blondell would later assert that the film, with its undercurrent of star-crossed love, was her favorite.

"Dorothy was a sympathetic role for me," Blondell said. "A woman with some intelligence and character, though ignorant of royal protocol. The kind of person chorus gals often are. It was one of those lucky breaks that sometimes comes along when you're under contract, have made a dozen poor pictures, and are wondering if the public will ever forgive and forget them."

On the set, Jane was happy to be reunited with Edward Everett Horton, playing Count Humbert Evel Bruger. He had previously worked with her during the filming of *All the King's Horses.* "You and I seem stuck in pictures with 'King' in the title. For me, maybe I should be making movies with 'Queen' in the title."

"If that happens, I'm sure you'll get the title role," Jane said, laughing with him.

On the set, Jane bonded with a blonde-haired actress, Carole Landis, who had been cast as an unbilled dancer in the chorus line at the Folies Bergère. Carole confided to Jane that she was dating a handsome newcomer to the Warners family, Ronald Reagan.

"Who isn't?" Jane asked, sarcastically, tired of hearing the name.

Two days later, she got to witness Landis perform as a chorus girl. "I admire that gal's guts," she recalled. "She had a real independent streak back then, long before she became a star. She demanded—yes, demanded—that LeRoy place her at the head of the chorus line. Amazingly, she got her way. I learned something from that. Being mousy Sarah Jane Fulks would get me nowhere. I had to become more assertive."

An uncredited actor appearing in the film was identified as "Jack Roberts." He seemed to be annoying Landis, hanging around her uninvited. When he left, Landis told

Jane, "I married the jerk back home when I was sixteen years old, and the marriage lasted one night, if that. Now the creep is trying to break into the movies. His real name is Irving Wheeler. I've got to get rid of him. Maybe I'll have my new boyfriend, Ronnie Reagan, beat the shit out of him. Ronnie's very athletic and in good shape."

Jane and Landis gravitated to each other. Their careers seemed to share, more or less, the same position, although Landis was far more aggressive in sleeping with producers and directors as a means of procuring roles.

One night, Landis suggested that she (with Reagan) and Jane (with Gravey) go out together on a double date. At the last minute, Gravey had to cancel because Jack Warner had invited him to his home to discuss, over dinner, his upcoming build-up at Warners.

Jane later claimed that at that point in her life, she had come to accept Warners as an extended big family. "Of course, there are all sorts of families, and sometimes members don't get along. There are petty jealousies, whatever."

***

A Warners luminary, Kay Francis, met Jane through LeRoy. To Jane's surprise, Francis seemed to take an interest in her.

Jane had seen a number of her movies and was enthralled that such a big star would take time out to talk with her. She invited her on several occasions to her dressing room, and one afternoon had lunch with her in the commissary.

She was impressed with this Oklahoma-born star, particularly her style of dress.

She learned that Francis had made her debut as an actress by understudying for Katharine Cornell on Broadway in *The Green Hat,* She told Jane that her big break had come when she'd appeared opposite Walter Huston on Broadway in *Elmer the Great.* Jane told her that when the play was adapted into a movie, she'd been a member of the cast.

"I saw the movie, but don't remember you in it," Francis said.

"You're forgiven," Jane said. "If you blinked, you would have missed me."

Jane had to cancel two dates, one with Reynolds another with Morris, to accept an invitation to spend the weekend at Francis' home. The star had promised "to give you some pointers on wardrobe and makeup. I know what it takes to become a star, and I think I can groom you to become one yourself."

Jane later conceded to Blondell that Francis taught her many secrets, especially "how to be an illumination when the camera is turned on you." The Saturday afternoon had gone beautifully, and Jane felt she'd found a new friend.

But, according to Jane's confession to Blondell, their relationship collapsed later that night. "She put the make on me and grabbed me and kissed me. I felt a foot-long tongue down my throat. I left her place at once. She screamed after me and called me a lot of names. I don't object to the casting couch. I've been there. Lain there. Or is it 'laid' there? But there's one thing I always insist upon. The person seducing me on that casting couch has to have a dick."

Kay "Fwancis," as she called herself.

88

Months later, a British film distributor refused to release *The King and the Chorus Girl* in the U.K., because of the use of the word "King" within its title. Like the character in the film, Britain's recently abdicated king was living in exile in France. The film's reference to the fallen monarch (Edward VIII, aka the Duke of Windsor) was too obvious.

However, when Warners agreed to change the name of their movie to *Romance Sacred*, it was released throughout the U.K. Despite the change in its title, U.K. audiences immediately recognized its references to their former monarch.

***

On a Sunday night, Craig Reynolds called Jane after midnight. She was asleep when the phone rang. From the background noise, she realized that he was at a wild party. His slurred voice indicated that he'd been drinking.

"It's finally happened, Janie," he shouted into the phone. "I'm a star." He told her that for the first time, he was playing the leading male role in a movie, *The Footloose Heiress* (1937), opposite Ann Sheridan.

"I'm so happy for the both of you," said a sleepy Jane, who tried to sound as enthusiastic as possible. She couldn't help but be jealous of her fellow actors. Top billing seemed to be happening to everybody but her.

Concealing her true feelings, she agreed to have lunch with Sheridan and Reynolds on Monday at noon. It took a long time for her to go back to sleep, as she was disillusioned with both her career and the men in her life.

The day before, she'd called her former chorus line girl friend, Paulette Goddard, who had married Charlie Chaplin in 1936. "How much longer do I have to wait to become a star?" Jane asked.

"Well, honey, I did it by marrying Charlie," Goddard said. "Perhaps you, too, can hook your wagon to a bigtime star, or perhaps to a director or producer. It's working for me. Charlie has become my Svengali, he wants to create an image of me as a spirited girl of the gutter, not easily given to surrender, or so he says."

"Good luck with that, whatever it means," Jane said. "Perhaps only Charlie knows." She must have recalled the time Chaplin had exposed himself to her when she was a teenager.

On the set of *The Footloose Heiress,* Jane discovered that Reynolds, despite his status as the star of the picture, had not been given a private dressing room, but shared one with both William Hopper, Hedda Hopper's son, and the character actor, Frank Orth.

In the commissary, Jane and Reynolds waited until Sheridan's arrival to begin eating.

Sheridan told them that she had lingered too long at Paramount in uncredited parts. When she signed with Warners in 1936, she was hoping for star roles.

Born in Texas and the winner of a beauty contest, Sheridan claimed she came from a straight-laced southern Baptist family. "My mother told me that 'Vanity is bad'—just tell that to a screen actress—and she also claimed that 'marriage is the only role for a woman.' Like hell it is! She's still urging me to return to Texas and become a school teacher."

"Even though I've got no tits, Jack Warner told me he's going to launch a big publicity campaign featuring me as a sex symbol," Sheridan confided to Jane.

She studied the star closely, hoping to learn the secret of how she had sprung from the chorus line into starring roles. There was a no-nonsense quality to her, and she appeared down-to-earth. Hedda Hopper, the mother of her co-star, William, would later write, "Ann Sheridan is the kind of girl that wouldn't seem an intruder at a stag party."

89

Partly because Jane wasn't otherwise employed at the time, she showed up on the set of *The Footloose Heiress* every day, since she had nothing else to do.

She told Sheridan, "My romance with Craig has gone from white hot passion to maintenance."

Reynolds emerged from his dressing room jauntily attired in a leather jacket and fedora, a kind of prototype of "Indiana Jones," a movie character that loomed in Hollywood's future.

He introduced her to William, whom she found "extraordinarily handsome." While he was filming a scene, Reynolds noted Jane's interest in Hedda's son. "Don't get your hopes up. He's a homo. I found that out when I undressed in front of him."

Later that day, Reynolds and Jane had drinks with William, who promised her he'd get his mother to plug her in her column. He spoke of his friend, Ronald Reagan, suggesting to Jane and Reynolds that they go out together on double dates.

During her third day on the set, Jane was introduced to Anne Nagel, who had married her friend, Ross Alexander, in September of 1936. The marriage had transpired shortly after the suicide of Alexander's first wife, Aleta Freel.

Nagel had met Alexander on the set of *Here Comes Carter.* Jane was astonished. "I was in that picture, but I haven't seen it yet. We obviously worked on it on different days."

"Ross is a very secretive man," Nagel said. "Perhaps he didn't want us to meet. Of course, Ross has a lot to be secretive about."

Both women described the torturous trail they'd followed since their arrival in Hollywood.

Born in Boston, Nagel had originally planned to be a nun before becoming a photographer's model.

Two days later, during Jane's final visit to the set, Nagel approached her. "Good news. Ross just called. He's just learned that he's going to star in the next Ruby Keeler film, and you're in it, too."

"He has the male lead, and you have a credited role! Its title is *Ready, Willing, and Able.*"

"Thank God I can go back to work and quit hanging out," Jane said.

***

On her first day on the set of *Ready, Willing, and Able* (1937), Jane was handed a copy of the script by director Ray Enright. It was a musical, conceived mainly as a vehicle for tap-dancing Ruby Keeler. Instead of Dick Powell, Ruby's usual co-car, it starred Jane's friend, Ross Alexander, in the male lead.

Before noon, Jane had skimmed the script, finding to her disappointment that her role was that of an unnamed receptionist. Becoming more assertive, she confronted Enright later that afternoon, asking if her role could be expanded.

He told her to be patient, claiming that he would give her a better part in the next two films he was directing.

Jane later said, "Unlike most of Hollywood, where telling a lie is an art form, Enright kept his promise to

Ruby Keeler in 1933. The dancer told Jane, "My husband, Al Jolson, is a sex pervert."

90

me, even though my upcoming roles weren't the star parts I wanted. At least I was working."

Ready, Willing, and Able is memorable for two reasons: It introduced the (later) immensely popular song "Too Marvelous for Words;" and it featured a campy, easy-to-satirize scene in which Keeler tap dances on the keys of a gigantic, tap-tap-tapping typewriter.

Jane was not included in the film's publicity campaign, but her name appeared in advertisements in tiny, eight-point type as opposed to the larger 20-point type reserved for Keeler.

She spoke briefly with Jerry Wald, one of the film's scriptwriters. She complained to him about her difficulties in finding a good part. He warned her to be patient. "Your day will come," he said. "Some stars are born overnight, but they are the rare and lucky ones. Most stars become stars by painfully climbing that ladder in Hollywood one rung at a time."

"I thought he was just bullshitting me," Jane said. But years later, she recalled, "Jerry was absolutely right. Look what he did for my career."

During the shoot, Jane saw more of her new friend, Ross Alexander, than she ever had before. One day at noon, he invited her to join Keeler and himself for lunch in the commissary. Jane had already seen most of the film repertoire of this Canadian-born actress and dancer, including her breakthrough role in *42nd Street* (1933), opposite Dick Powell.

From 1928 to 1940, Keeler had been famously married to Al Jolson. Over lunch, Jane was rather surprised at how she referred to her husband with contempt. "Every day I'm married to Jolson, I have to go to confession," Keeler said.

After lunch, Keeler was called to the set, but Jane and Alexander remained behind to chat. She was intrigued by Hollywood gossip, and her actor friend was a font of information.

"Jolson is not a faithful husband," Alexander said. "He occasionally fucks from A-list—Barbara Stanwyck, for example—but mostly, he hires prostitutes, showgirls, and what he really prefers, 'colored gals,' as he calls them. Some of his conquests tell me his favorite thing is having oral sex performed on him. I also hear he demands 'unusual positions'—especially those not approved of by missionaries."

Despite Jane's envy of Keeler's stardom, she wanted to see her perform on camera whenever possible.

[Budd Schulberg, in The Harder They Fall, *wrote: "Even in the scantiest attire, Ruby Keeler carried herself with an air of aloof respectability, which has the actual effect of an intense aphrodisiac. Seeing her with her black lace stockings, forming a sleek and silken path to her crotch was like opening a wrong door by mistake and catching your best friend's sister in the act."]*

One afternoon, when Jane was watching Keeler dance in front of the cameras, Jolson himself arrived at the studio and was suddenly standing beside her. She introduced herself.

Jane is *Ready, Willing, and Able.*

91

"I can't remember names," he said. "So I'll remember you as 'Pug Nose.'"

At one point, he asked her to step outside with him. "I expected him to offer me a role in his next picture. How naïve I was." She relayed the details of her encounter with Jolson to Alexander. "He rudely propositioned me, wanting me to sneak off with him somewhere and perform oral sex on him. He told me it would a smart career move on my part."

"Did you accept?" Alexander asked.

"I turned him down," she said, "but I configured it into a most flattering rejection. I told him that I had heard that his penis was so mammoth I feared it would choke me to death."

During the shoot, Jane visited Alexander at his home—a ranch in Encino— with his second wife, Anne Nagel. They seemed to be having difficulty in their marriage. Privately, he had told Jane, "I can't be a real husband to Anne. It's not in my nature."

Jane had been escorted to the Alexander/Nagel home by her former co-star, Fernand Gravey, to spend one of the pre-Christmas holidays with the unhappily married couple. Nagel told them that, "Ross and I are planning a long-delayed honeymoon in New York when Enright tells him it's a wrap."

Gravey volunteered to go into the kitchen with Nagel to help her prepare a French sauce for a dish she was serving. Alexander invited Jane to go for a walk.

He had a confession to make, telling her that he'd picked up a hobo hitchhiker and had performed an act of oral sex on him. The stranger recognized Alexander's face from his screen images, and threatened to blackmail him.

"He could ruin my career," Alexander lamented. "He demanded $10,000 in cash from me, which I don't have. I had to go to Jack Warner, who agreed to lend me the money to avoid a scandal."

"I fear that because of this, Warners isn't going to renew my contract. Publicity told me he considers me 'too hot to handle.'"

She offered him her deepest sympathy, promising "to stand by you until this blows over."

The day after Christmas, Jane received a call from Cornelius Stevenson, the butler at the Alexander household. "I wanted to talk privately with you. But I didn't have a chance."

He revealed that three weeks before, he found an intoxicated Alexander loading cartridges into his pistol. He was in a very dark mood, and I feared he was going to harm himself, maybe commit suicide like his first wife did out in the barn. But he claimed he was going to shoot some birds. Perhaps you could come over later this afternoon and be with him. He really trusts you."

She promised she could, but Craig Reynolds distracted her, asking her to host a private party he was giving for friends.

She heard no more from Ross's household until January 3. A distraught Nagel was sobbing into the phone. "Ross is gone," she said. "He shot himself."

Dressing immediately, Jane drove over to the house where the police admitted her after checking with Nagel. In tears and emotionally distraught, Nagel told her that Ross had taken a .22 pistol from his cabinet, claiming he was going to shoot a duck for tomorrow's dinner.

He went out to the barn, aimed the pistol at his temple, and shot himself. The butler found him slumped over a bag of grain in the hayloft.

Along with Glenda Farrell, Henry Fonda, and others in the Warner community, Jane attended Ross's funeral at Forest Lawn's Little Church of the Flowers.

Bette Davis had been pursued by Ross during the months he was begging for her to marry him, and she had bitterly rejected him. She told associates, "He's dead. One must not speak ill of the dead. Good!"

When she and Jane returned to the studio, Enright told her that future roles intended for Ross would be assigned to the newcomer, Ronald Reagan. "They're both handsome and they both have the same baritone voice."

When *Ready, Willing, and Able* was released, Warner ordered that Ross's name be demoted to fifth position in the credits, even though he was the film's lead male star.

Henry Fonda, according to Jane, had been distraught at Ross's funeral. Enright told her that he had been contracted to direct Fonda in his next picture, *Slim,* set for a 1937 release. "You're in it, too," he told her.

***

Jane's next picture for Warners, *Slim,* starred Pat O'Brien and Henry Fonda as two telephone linemen, with Margaret Lindsay playing their love interest. Jane was cast as the girlfriend of character actor Stuart Erwin, who played "Stumpy." Craig Reynolds had a small role as "the Gambler."

Emerging from Squaw Valley, California, Erwin was fourteen years older than Jane, a wide-eyed, fair-haired actor who was usually cast as an amiable, none-too-bright hayseed. "With Henry Fonda up for grabs, I'm assigned Erwin as a boyfriend," she lamented.

When he met Jane, Erwin told her, "I usually get to play slow-witted rubes. At the rate I'm going, I'll probably end up playing the same type of role on Poverty Row. Oh, and just because I'm your boyfriend in the movie, don't get the wrong idea. I'm happily married to an actress, June Collyer."

Of all my on-screen lovers, ranging from John Payne to Rock Hudson, I ended up in *Slim* as the girlfriend of Stuart Erwin (*left*)," Jane recalled. "Hollywood can be cruel to a working gal."

"Don't worry," she snapped back. "You're safe with me. My real life boyfriend, Craig Reynolds, is in the film, too, so all my needs are satisfied."

Jane bonded with the star of the picture, Pat O'Brien. She later recalled, "He took me under his wing and was like a big brother to me. There was no funny stuff. He was a happily married man, but he taught me many tricks of the trade. I'll always be grateful to him. He said he'd made a new male friend, Ronald Reagan, and that he'd introduce us sometime. He thought we'd make the perfect fit 'as a romantic couple.'"

Once again, Jane was disappointed that she didn't get to play the female lead. That role went to Margaret Lindsay, who plays Nurse Cally in a plot that calls for her to switch her romantic affections from the character played by O'Brien to Fonda.

The movie explores the hazards—including electrocu-

Young Henry Fonda, at around the time he was involved with starlet Jane Wyman.

93

tions—faced by telephone linemen under dangerous conditions such as storms, high winds, and lightning. Slim remains one of Fonda's lesser-known roles. He thought so little of it, he didn't even mention it in his autobiography, *My Life.*

Ray Enright, the director who had previously helmed her in *Ready, Willing, and Able,* appeared on the set to greet her. "I told you I'd cast you in my next picture, and so I did."

"Thanks, Ray, but you could have made my role a bit bigger and written in a love scene between Fonda and me. Would *you* like to kiss Stu Erwin?"

"That's not one of my fantasies," he answered.

When Lindsay met Jane, the Iowa-born actress told her, "We have a mutual friend in William Hopper. I'm dating Ronnie Reagan, and we often go out on double dates with William and his girlfriend, Isabel Jewell. She's an actress, too."

Jane had seen Fonda at a distance during the funeral of Ross Alexander. On the set of *Slim,* he came up and introduced himself. "You can call me Hank."

He commented on his role in *Slim.* "I know it's a B picture, but I like to play earthy guys like the lineman Slim. He's a real down-to-earth guy, the kind of blue collar man who makes America great."

She told him that she'd seen him at Ross's funeral. "Ross told me how close you guys were."

Since he wanted to discuss his departed friend, he invited Jane to lunch. "I assumed Ross clued you in on our very secret relationship," he said.

"He did indeed," she answered.

"That means, then, that I can speak frankly to you. You know, therefore, that he was passionately in love with me, a love that I could not reciprocate with equal emotion," Fonda said. "It was also a love I did not reject. During my first marriage to Margaret Sullavan, she had devastated me. I didn't feel like I was a man anymore. She can make any man feel like two cents—and two inches. She cheated on me constantly, and I felt castrated by her. How can you make love to a woman as she critiques your performance, loudly telling you that you're both a 'fast starter' and a 'lousy finisher.'"

"A lot of men wouldn't have put up with crap like that and would have bashed her face in," Jane said.

"Perhaps I should have, but I'm not a violent man. Ross built me up and constantly praised my manhood. I was attracted to him because of what he was doing to beef up my ego."

The death of his best friend had occurred so recently that Fonda seemed to want to unburden himself to Jane, finding her an attentive, sympathetic listener.

"I was the best man at Ross's wedding to Aleta Freel, whose suicide probably put the idea of his own suicide into Ross's head." Fonda said. "I knew the marriage wasn't going to work, though. Ross was really in love with me, but desperately trying to conceal his homosexuality by marrying Aleta."

"Ross and I went to Hollywood together and lived at this place on Woodrow Wilson Drive. Dogs and goats ran freely all over the place. I found Hollywood had an unreal quality. For a while, I lived with Aleta and Ross. But I have another close friend, Jimmy Stewart."

"Jimmy and I rented this Mexican style farmhouse in

Jimmy Stewart told Jane, "Hank and I share our women together sometimes."

94

Brentwood next door to Greta Garbo. Ross was furious at me for moving out and was very jealous of Jimmy. Jimmy and I were double dating, Lucille Ball for me and Ginger Rogers for him. I cooked dinner. Sometimes, Ross would drop in, but he obviously felt left out. He began to live dangerously, rarely returning home to Aleta. He told me he was spending his nights with studio grips, electricians, extras, messenger boys, whomever. I feared for his safety."

***

Craig Reynolds was planning to take Jane down to Laguna Beach for the weekend, but canceled at the last minute. She just assumed that he'd gotten a better offer from one of his girlfriends, perhaps a boyfriend.

She mentioned that to Fonda when he stopped to talk to her. He seemed upset. "I was going to drive Frances, my wife, to Lake Arrowhead this weekend, but we had a big fight, and she stormed out of the house last night, and hasn't come back."

He flashed on an idea. "Since we've both been stood up, why not drive there with me? I've got this real nice cottage that belongs to a friend."

On their way to Lake Arrowhead, Jane and Fonda felt free to talk to each other about their previous romantic failures. She admitted to having had two disastrous marriages, and he spoke about his failed marriage to Margaret Sullavan.

"I got started with women in a very bad way," he admitted. "When I was a teenager, I lost my virginity in a whorehouse in Omaha. It was one of the most humiliating experiences of my life. It turned me off women for a very long time."

"I guess I don't make a good husband. When I'm working on a film, I immerse myself in the role and even take it home with me. I come into the house, wanting a light supper. Then I toddle off to my study to learn tomorrow's lines. It's early to bed for me."

"Not only that, but all my friends, including Jimmy Stewart, have a burning interest in the movie industry. Frances just isn't interested. What does she care about rushes, close-ups, and billings?"

"When I first met Frances, I was banging Annabella, my co-star in *Wings of the Morning,* but Frances lured me away," he said. "But I don't think Frances is happy with what she got. She listens to all the shit spread about me. She ran into that horrid George Sanders at a party. He told her that I was a Don Juan homosexual who has to prove himself with one woman after another. She was always suspicious about my relationship with Ross. She's also terribly jealous of my friendship with Jimmy. She calls it 'too intimate.' Incidentally, Jimmy might drop in to share the cottage with us this weekend."

"I'd love to meet him," she said. "I think he's divine."

"So does Jean Harlow, and Ginger Rogers raves about him, too. Jimmy has a goal: He wants to get intimate with 263 glamour girls before it rises for a final time."

"Why such an odd number?" she asked.

"A fortune teller told him that was his destiny. He'll probably end up making a movie with my former wife, Margaret. I'm sure he'll seduce her during the course of the filming. Jimmy and I believe in sharing women."

"Include me in that, too," she said. "I'd love to date him."

"I'll try to set it up," he said. "I'm sure he'd be interested."

The screen goes black at this point. When she returned from Lake Arrowhead, Jane gave a "very limited" description to her confidant, Joan Blondell, of what happened. Blondell was eager for further details, but Jane would not provide them. All that Blondell got from her was that Stewart had arrived at the cottage late at night and had walked in on Fonda and Jane having sex.

"Oh, my God," Blondell said. "Did it turn into a three-way? I hear that Jimmy and Hank adore three-ways."

"All I can tell you is that I didn't behave like a lady that weekend—and I'll say no more."

***

In her next picture, *The Singing Marine* (1937), Jane was cast once again in a movie starring Dick Powell, Ronald Reagan's good friend and the husband of Joan Blondell. The film marked the third movie in a row in which she'd been directed by Ray Enright.

Marines, when they're not singing: Jane Wyman *(left)*, Dick Powell, and "Reagan's Swede," Veda Ann Borg.

Powell played a marine from Arkansas who becomes a popular radio singer.

Jane had a small role playing a "cutie" called Joan. *The Singing Marine* was the last of a trio of Warner films celebrating the military, beginning with *Flirtation Walk* (1934), a tribute to the Army, followed by *Shipmates Forever* (1935), honoring the men of the Navy.

She had worked with many members of the cast before, including Busby Berkeley, who was brought in to stage two musical sequences.

At first, Jane had been told that the movie would be another showcase for Dick Powell and Ruby Keeler, with Warners hoping to repeat the success of *42nd Street*. But Keeler had another commitment and consequently, was not available.

Jane had hoped that she might have been summoned to take the role intended for Keeler. She reminded Enright, "I sing and dance, too, and rather well, if I must say so myself."

He rejected her in favor of Doris Weston, a Chicago-born actress, radio performer, and nightclub singer. Jane, at one point, chatted briefly with Weston, who told her, "I was chosen because of my physical resemblance to Keeler. Frankly, I'm a much better singer than Miss Ruby."

Cast in a minor role was Guinn ("Big Boy") Williams. He stood 6'2", with a muscular frame from his years of working on ranches in his native Texas and playing semi-pro and pro baseball.

Eighteen years older than Jane, he'd made his screen debut in 1919 in the silent comedy, *Almost a Husband* with Will Rogers, Sr. He worked mainly in supporting roles in sports dramas, westerns, or outdoor adventure pictures. He was teamed frequently with Alan Hale, Sr. as a sidekick in Errol Flynn movies.

Williams relentlessly pursued her, and she finally relented, agreeing to go out with him on a Saturday night. The date evolved into a disaster.

Big, stupid, and abusive: Guinn Williams

Except to confide some of its details to Joan Blondell, she never spoke of it again. Apparently, Williams had assaulted her in his car when she refused to have sex with him. Based on his extreme strength and physicality, he overwhelmed her.

According to Blondell, he drove her home, and she left his car "humiliated and depressed." She had been bleeding. "He just ripped me apart."

Both Blondell and Jane agreed that she would not report the incident to the police, which would have catalyzed a frontpage scandal.

To help her recover, Blondell invited her to join Powell and herself for a weekend at her "love nest," on North Maple Drive in Beverly Hills. Powell was away at the studio when Jane arrived.

Blondell told her that she'd been considered to star in *The Singing Marine* when Keeler became unavailable.

"I protested, because I didn't want to work with Ray Enright again. I wrote a letter to Hal Wallis, telling him that Ray and I had already worked enough together. We knew each other's tricks, so—as a director—he had nothing else to teach me. I concluded the letter with: 'There's nothing more to be gained for the good of a picture by our continued association.'"

Blondell said that Powell had become a wonderful father to her son, Norman, who had been fathered by her former husband, the noted cinematographer (and abusive alcoholic), George Barnes. Powell had adopted her boy, changing his name to Norman Powell. In time, he would grow up to become an accomplished producer, director, and TV executive.

Over drinks, Blondell and Jane indulged in "girl talk." She admitted that Powell was a better father than lover. "It's a ritual every Friday night. We're sitting listening to one of his recordings when he gets this look on his face. It's a signal. He raises his eyebrows. As I lie in bed waiting for him, he spends a half hour in the bathroom. What a thorough cleansing job! A hot shower, hair wash followed by elaborate combing of his coiffure. He checks to see that his nails are clipped. Endless gargling with mouthwash. Finally, he enters the room for some pajama-clad action for exactly four minutes. He's got it perfectly timed. When it's over, he rushes back to the bathroom for another thorough cleansing."

Over Sunday dinner, Powell complained that at the age of thirty-two, "I'm still playing a juvenile. I can't keep this up much longer. I hear Jack Warner is grooming my replacement, Kenny Baker. You've worked with him before. I've just heard that you are going to star with him in *Mr. Dodd Takes the Air*. At long last, you've got co-star billing. You've made it, Pug Nose!"

"Well, it's about god damn time," she said. "Pardon my French."

Kenny Baker with Jane Wyman in *Mr. Dodd Takes the Air.* He was being groomed as Dick Powell's replacement. But where was the sex appeal?

***

Director Alfred E. Green welcomed Jane to the set of *Mr. Dodd Takes the Air* (1937). She had been told that her latest movie was a remake of the 1932 release of *The Crooner,* a cautionary tale about the dangers of stardom, a vehicle for the message that fame can be a terrible curse.

The star of the picture, Kenny Baker invited Jane to lunch in the commissary, where he seemed filled with career anxiety. "I can't seem to make it big like Bing Crosby or Rudy Vallée. I'm not even the equal of Dick Powell, whom I'm supposed to be replacing at Warners. As a singer, I'm referred to as milque-toasty, with no sex appeal. Vallée, in contrast, was attacked by Cardinal O'Connell. He was defined as a threat to the nation's moral safety. The cardinal claimed that Vallée's appeal was obviously rooted in raw lust. No one ever says that about me."

She assured him that he was a good-looking man, although privately, she agreed that he was no sexual menace to anyone.

In an uncredited role, William Hopper befriended Jane and had lunch with her. He spoke of his growing friendship with Ronald Reagan, and told Jane that they often double-dated at the Cocoanut Grove. Jane responded that she'd like to meet "this Reagan boy that everybody seems to be talking about."

He told her that he'd try to arrange it sometime, but first, he wanted her to meet his mother. Hedda Hopper was just launching her gossip column about the movie industry.

In her office, Hedda ruled like an imperial monarch, stridently ordering her two employees about. Jane had hoped that Hedda would interview her and devote some space to her in her column. But Hedda, worldly wise and sophisticated, seemed more intrigued with her own pronouncements.

She told Jane, "Hollywood is the ultimate Bitch Goddess, with the power to destroy. She has a taste for fresh blood, especially that of young starlets, who are a dime a dozen in this town. Very few will surface to the top as stars."

"When the lucky few get there, they'll find out that it isn't what it was cracked up to be. The Bitch Goddess can also destroy big stars—take Jean Harlow, for example. Sometimes, even when stardom is achieved, the Bitch Goddess turns actors into alcoholics, liars, cheats. You'll be lucky if you grab the prize, but if you do, know that it carries a wicked price."

After Hedda had finished her rant, she focused on her son, William, who was making coffee for them. "Bill is a nice boy, and I don't want him to get mixed up with bad company. Are you a bad girl? Tell me, how many men, married or otherwise, have you slept with since leaving Union Station?"

"I can't do that, Miss Hopper, I'm a respectable married woman...or was. My marriage is over now."

"You seem like a sweet gal, and I approve of your going out with Bill," Hedda said. "He's the victim of dreadful rumors. Some gossips claim he's a homosexual, which is definitely not true. He's the most red-blooded actor working in Hollywood, which I dub 'Pansyville.' Rumors are flying that Ronald Reagan and my Bill are lovers, which is definitely not true. That's pure bullshit! Just ask their girlfriends. If you want to be a star, you've got to put up with crap like that."

Later, over dinner that night, William talked frankly about his mother, whom he called Hedda. "All the stars call her for lovelorn advice. She'd be a success writing a Lonely Hearts column. Of course, I've got some dark secrets. I never share my private life with Hedda. She hates communists, Jews, and homosexuals."

"We were never close as mother and son. But she made sacrifices for me. In the middle of the Depression, she sent me to Catalina Island School. The tuition was $2,000 a year, and to cough up that kind of money, she had to live in a dreary basement apartment with rats."

"Hedda had a hard life," he said. "My father, DeWolf Hopper, was a singer and comic stage actor. Off stage, he was an abusive alcoholic. She divorced him and took me to Hollywood. Here I am, dreaming of stardom. Aren't you dreaming of stardom too?"

She admitted that she was. "I look up in the sky at Polaris, which seems to stand motionless in space. Other stars in the northern sky rotate around it. I picture myself as Polaris. One day, I want minor stars and supporting players, male or female, to gravitate around me."

"I've been told that Polaris is much brighter today than it was when Ptolemy first observed it thousands of years ago. That's what I want to be in my upcoming *[1940s]* films. Brighter and more visible than I ever was in these stupid B-films I've been making in the 30s."

"Go, girl, go," he said.

When *Mr. Dodd Takes the Air* was wrapped, Jane collapsed. As she later told Joan Blondell, "My candle was burning at both ends. I'd been rushing from one movie set to another, then going out dancing every night until 4:30 in the morning. Getting an hour's sleep before rushing to the studio. I've been filled with such anxiety about my career that I've been breaking out in red blotches."

On June, 22, 1937, she entered the hospital. Although not yet a star, she generated a headline in *Variety—JANE WYMAN HOSPITALIZED FOR NERVOUS BREAKDOWN.* The story appeared on page 67.

Blondell visited her a few times during her three days in the hospital before driving her home.

While resting in bed, a call came in from William Demarest. "You won't believe this, but you've got the star role in your next picture. Your leading man is William Hopper, Hedda's son. I think you know him. The film is called *Public Wedding.*"

***

A former vaudevillian, the B-movie specialist, Nick Grinde, is known today (if at all) as the director who helmed Ronald Reagan's first Hollywood movie. But he also directed Jane Wyman in the first film, *Public Wedding,* in which she was billed above the leading man. Even before reading the script, Jane knew that it would be a second-rate picture.

To her surprise, she learned that the well-known actress, Marie Wilson, had been cast in the film's third lead. Although details of Grinde's marriage to her are disputed, Jane had heard that Wilson and Grinde were married in the early 1930s, and subsequently divorced. Apparently, their relationship had survived the ordeal.

During the course of their chats, Wilson informed her that she'd soon be appearing in *Boy Meets Girl* (1938), with James Cagney, Pat O'Brien, and Ronald Reagan. "Nick said he would introduce me to Reagan. He's eligible marriage material, I heard, and I'm between husbands."

As an actress, she became so identified with the character of Irma that she ended up playing dumb blondes throughout the remainder of her career. She would later claim that, "Marilyn Monroe stole my dumb blonde *persona* when she saw me in *Satan Met a Lady." [Released in 1936, that film was the second screen adaptation of Dashiell Hammett's detective*

In *Public Wedding,* Jane appears with William Hopper in what might have become a rehearsal for the real thing.

novel, The Maltese Falcon.*]*

In *Public Wedding,* Jane was cast as "Flip Lane," part of a group of five street-smart employees of a carnival side-show. Broke and without jobs, they concoct a publicity scheme, a phony, "mock wedding" staged within the gaping open mouth of a (previously unprofitable) stuffed whale. Jane, as the star, plays the bride, with handsome William Hopper interpreting the role of her groom, Tony Burke. To make their plot livelier, the protagonists sincerely dislike each other. However, after the wedding, they discover that they are legally married.

During the filming, Jane encountered, once again, Veda Ann Borg, who played Bernice, a receptionist. Borg liked to have "a nip or two," as she put it. By three o'clock in the afternoon, she was usually intoxicated. One day, fearing for her safety, Jane agreed to drive her back to her apartment.

She was curious about why Borg had dumped Reagan, when half the young women she met, including Wilson, seemed to have set their sights on him for future seductions.

"I can answer that, but do you mind if I get down, dirty, and graphic?" Borg asked.

"Go ahead," Jane said.

"I'm European in my tastes," Borg said, "meaning I like the smell of a man. Reagan is always showering and always smelling like soap. To make our sex work, I asked him to wait for three days before taking a shower. I said that would make the sex all the better. I have a perversion. I like to go down on a man when he's got head cheese."

"What in hell is that?"

"Oh Jane, darling, you've got a lot to learn about sex. But I'm no teacher. Eventually, you'll find out for yourself what headcheese is, not during any sexual encounter with Mr. Clean, Ronald Reagan."

"I'm beginning to get the picture," Jane said. "Let's drop the subject."

During the shoot, William Hopper took Jane out on a few occasions, ending the evening "dancing at the Troc" on Sunset Strip. At the end of the night, he'd always kiss her on the cheek and hastily bid her goodnight.

She learned that after seeing her, he'd spend the night with Stanley Mills Haggart, who had a small house on Laurel Canyon Boulevard. She assumed that he and Haggart were lovers.

[At the time, Haggart, who had been intimately linked with both Cary Grant and Randolph Scott, worked at RKO Studios as an extra. He was a "night bird," regularly hitting the hot clubs of Los Angeles. Hedda liked to go to bed early, so Stanley and her son William often prowled through the night time landscapes of underground Los Angeles, ostensibly picking up items for Hedda's column. However, in those days, most of the "dirt" they unearthed could not, for legal reasons, be printed.]

One night, Hedda called Jane at Warners and asked her to visit her home after she got off from work. She thought that Hedda, as a nationally syndicated columnist, was finally going to interview her. Jane drove over with high expectations and a touch of fear.

When she got there, Hedda offered her a drink and said, "I'll get right to the point. I can give you a major star build-up in my column, but I want something in return."

"Within reason, I'll oblige," Jane promised.

"I want you to marry my son."

Jane was so startled that it took her a moment to recover.

It seemed that William had been caught in a sexual and romantic scandal with Jon Hall, who was enjoying great success as the hero of John Ford's epic, *The Hurricane* (1937). He co-starred in it, often wearing a sarong, opposite Dorothy Lamour, who also wore a sarong and hibiscus flowers, throughout most of the tropical-island action/adventure/romance.

At first, Jane was very reluctant to get involved, but Hedda could be very persuasive. After her third drink, Jane agreed to meet with William to discuss the arrangement's details and implications.

"Don't worry," Hedda said. "If you're discreet, you can see other men on the side. It's what we call in Hollywood a 'lavender marriage.'"

Jane immediately realized that Hedda had previously lied to her. Hedda had known that her son was a homosexual for years.

Shortly before her departure from Hedda's apartment at around midnight, after listening to the reams of publicity such a marriage would generate, Jane agreed to go through with it.

There was, however, one important problem: Hedda had not bothered to check with William. Although he adamantly refused to participate in the arrangement, Hedda assured Jane that she could talk him into it.

As it turned out, she could not. After less than a week, their so-called "engagement" was canceled.

Jon Hall survived that potential scandal with William Hopper, and many other scandals after that, and eventually, in the 1940s, became a star, often appearing with campy Maria Montez.

Later, during one of William's conversations with Jane, he asked her, "You're not mad at me for rejecting that offer of marriage, are you?"

"Not at all," she said, smiling and giving him a hug and a kiss on the cheek. "Let's be brother and sister instead. Besides, the marriage would never have worked. We just wouldn't have been right for one another." `

***

For Jane's next film, since Warner's had no immediate use for her, she was lent out to Universal Studios for a role in *The Spy Ring* (1938). Its director, Joseph H. Lewis, cast her as the female lead. Even though her role was secondary, Jack Warner decided to give her star billing, and for some reason, ordered that she be hailed as "The Year's Best Actress!" which she clearly was not.

With the same sinking feeling she'd associated with *Public Wedding,* she didn't have high hopes for this film, either.

Lewis was known for his stream of hastily produced B-movies, most of them low-budget westerns, action pictures, and thrillers. Around Universal, he was known as "Wagon Wheel Joe," for his cowboy movies, usually shown to the kiddies at Saturday matinees across the country.

Jane had never heard of the star of the picture, William Hall. Universal had recently signed this Brook-

Jane co-starred with William Hall before he began interpreting Hollywood as "the boulevard of broken dreams."

101

lyn-born actor, planning to groom him for major stardom. *The Spy Ring* was designed as a trial balloon to see if he appealed to audiences. Jane learned he was already thirty-five years old, which struck her as "a bit long in the tooth" to be launched as a possible matinee idol.

He played an army officer and the star player on the camp's polo team. Lewis, the film's director, shot so many miles of polo footage that to Jane, it appeared to be "another horsey oats opera" instead of a spy thriller.

The executives at Universal had so much faith in Hall that after shooting was completed, he was cast and contracted as the male lead in yet another film, *Escape by Night* (1938), even before *The Spy Ring* was released. Jane lunched with her friend, Anne Nagel, who was on the set that day for a meeting with Hall. She had been cast as his leading lady in his yet-to-be-shot spinoff film *[i.e.,* Escape by Night.*]*

She did not want Jane to speak about her late husband, Ross Alexander, who had recently killed himself. She still seemed in shock and would go into seclusion for three years after she finished her final film commitment. When she resurfaced, she joined Universal as one of its "scream queens" in B-picture horror flicks.

[Both the reviews and box office receipts for The Spy Ring *were disappointing. By the time William Hall's second film was released for public consumption, Universal had dropped him. Even though he played the lead, Hall's name was not used within the film's promotions and publicity.*

Consequently, Hall disappeared from the Hollywood scene. In 1986, Jane noticed a small obituary in Variety, *reporting that he had died in obscurity in Kerr County, Texas. She had only one comment. "Hall was tall in the saddle. The loftiest actor I ever worked with, towering at 6'4".")*

***

After her temporary loan-out to Universal Pictures, Jane's return to Warners, her home studio, was filled with disappointment. Her star roles had gone largely unnoticed, contained as they were within programmers designed to precede, in theaters, more noteworthy, A-list competitors.

The director, Mervyn LeRoy, who had helmed her in *The King and the Chorus Girl,* had cast her this time in a small role in *Fools for Scandal* (1938), starring Carole Lombard, with Fernand Gravey and Ralph Bellamy as her leading men.

The role was so small that Jane's name didn't even appear in some of the listings. "LeRoy was going around still claiming that he'd discovered me," Jane lamented. "But what had he discovered? Not a star, that's for god damn sure. He's doing better with Lana Turner in more ways than one."

The first day on the set, Jane resumed her affair with Gravey, with whom she had become involved during the shooting of *The King and the Chorus Girl.* She had been told that the film had greatly offended the Duke of

Recognizing that Fernand's last name, "Gravey," didn't sound romantic in English, the studio changed its spelling to "Gravet" on posters with Carole Lombard.

102

Windsor, who had threatened to sue.

Gravey hadn't called her since that movie, and he tried to explain why. "At the time I was temporarily separated from my wife *[the French actress Jane Renouardt]*. We had had a big fight around the time I met you. I got angry at her and told her that she was old enough to be my mother."

"I can see why a wife wouldn't like that," Jane said.

"My wife and I are now back together again and limping along in our marriage," he said. "But she's learned a big lesson. I'll stay married to her, but will also see other women. It's my nature."

On their first night out again, dancing at the Troc, he told her he didn't hold out much hope for the commercial success of *Fools for Scandal.* "Lombard and I have no chemistry. I don't see why Clark Gable finds her so hot. She's appealed to Gary Cooper and to John Barrymore, but not to me. Perhaps we Frenchmen have more exacting standards for women."

Even though he was predicting failure for their present movie, Gravey told her he was about to be loaned out, short-term, to MGM. "I've signed to play Johann Strauss in *The Great Waltz,* opposite Luise Rainer. I'm hoping this big production will put me over the top."

"I'll be cheering you on," she said. "I adore your Continental charm, unlike some of the jerks I've been cast with. Take Joe E. Brown, for instance."

During his nights with Jane, Gravey seemed morbidly depressed over what was about to happen to his beloved France. He feared an attack from Germany. "Hitler's Nazi war machine will overrun Paris," he predicted.

[Gravey's fears came true in 1940. MGM was set to star him in the film version of Rafael Sabatini's novel, Scaramouche. *But Gravey turned it down and returned to France just before the Nazi invasion. Throughout the war, he was a member of the French Secret Army, and later joined the French Foreign Legion to fight the Nazis. By war's end, the French people hailed him as a war hero.*

Renouardt forgave him his many indiscretions, and they stayed married until his death of a heart attack in 1970, her death following two years later.]

Fools for Scandal, the screwball comedy, had a convoluted, rather silly plot, with Lombard cast as Kay Winters, a film star living in Paris. She is pursued by both Gravey and Ralph Bellamy. Lombard remembered Jane from her brief stint in *My Man Godfrey.* She told her that she was sorry that her role didn't make the final cut of that previous movie, and she invited Jane to her dressing room for a few drinks.

At one point, Lombard pulled off her robe and stood nude in front of a full-length mirror. "Guess what?" she said, surveying her curves. "Only today, the *Hollywood Reporter* wrote that 'I'm a platinum blonde with a heart-shaped face, delicate, impish features, and a figure to be swathed in silver *lamé.'* That's what somebody on that paper thinks. Let me ask you. If you were a lesbian, would you be muff diving on me right now?"

"I'd be eating you up," Jane said, jokingly.

She was fascinated by Lombard's dialogue. *Life* magazine had asserted that off-screen, "Her conversation, often brilliant, is punctuated by screeches, laughs, growls, gesticulations, and the expletives of a sailor's parrot."

At the time of filming, all of Hollywood knew that Gable, despite his status as a married man, was involved in a torrid affair with Lombard. One day, she announced that Gable was going to show up on the set for lunch with her. She told Jane that she wanted her to serve as a "beard," along with Bellamy, Isabel Jeans, and Jenkins.

In spite of the fling Jane had had with Gable during the filming of *Cain and Mable,* he did not seem to remember her. Or perhaps he was pretending ignorance to throw

Lombard off the scent. Bellamy later told Jane, "Gable has had all the major female stars at MGM, and half the starlets. How can he remember every conquest?"

With nothing to conceal in front of her fellow actors, Lombard talked openly about her affair with Gable, although that didn't seem to set too well with him. She claimed that she'd been included in his otherwise all-male hunting and fishing trips. "In the future, I'm going to seriously limit the number of films I make every year. It was those conflicting schedules that ruined my marriage to William Powell."

"That and the fact that you two guys were not compatible," Gable interjected.

The talk inevitably turned to the upcoming filming of Margaret Mitchell's novel, *Gone With the Wind.* Most of America wanted Gable to play Rhett Butler. But Jane was shocked when Lombard claimed that its producer, David O. Selznick, had more or less promised her the lead female role of Scarlett O'Hara.

"Myron Selznick, David's brother, is my agent, and I can't stand him," Lombard said. "But I'm keeping him because I think he'll push David into signing a contract with me."

"You should be grateful to Myron," Gable cautioned. Then, addressing the other listeners present, he said, "He got her a contract with Paramount for $450,000 big ones a year."

"Well, you've got something there," she said. "That makes me the highest paid pussy in Hollywood."

Gable admitted that he was a bit leary about appearing in another period costume drama after the failure of his film *Parnell* (1937). "Carole here feels that the role of Rhett Butler will be the high point of my career."

"I know I have stiff competition for Scarlett," Lombard said. "Everybody from Lucille Ball, that low-rent RKO hooker, to Katharine Hepburn, a lesbian and Miss Box Office Poison herself, wants it. Joan Crawford and Bette Davis would each kill for it, and Paulette Goddard is telling everyone the role already belongs to her."

"Would you believe that my dear, departed Jean Harlow, whom I loved dearly, read that thick novel when it came out and began to imagine herself as Scarlett?" Gable said.

He warned Carole not to get her hopes up, because he'd heard rumors that Selznick feared that casting a pair of "illicit lovers," like Lombard and himself, in the same movie might cause a moral backlash if and when their affair were discovered, and lead to boycotts of the movie, nationwide.

Before the meal ended, Lombard lamented the script of *Fools for Scandal.* "I think I'm making my worst film, although how can it be more horrid than *The Gay Bride* (1934)?"

[Lombard's dire forecast turned out to be accurate. Even her most dedicated fans stayed away "in droves" from Fools for Scandal. *She was so disappointed with the film that for a while, at least, she opted to appear only in dramatic roles instead of comedies.]*

Since Jane had never read *Gone With the Wind,* and since everyone else was talking about it, she bought a copy one Friday afternoon and canceled all engagements. By late Sunday night, she had waded through it, savoring every scene that featured Melanie—the character who marries Scarlett's love, Ashley Wilkes.

When Jane encountered Carole the following Monday morning, she aggressively lobbied for the role. "I think I'd be perfect as Melanie."

Carole looked Jane over skeptically for a moment and then smiled. "Honey, I think you're mousy enough to pull off that sob sister role."

After a moment's hesitation, Carole continued: "Despite all the press about those other Scarlett wannabees—including that old hag, Tallulah Bankhead, for god's sake— I've got the role of Scarlett sewn up. I practically have Selznick eating breakfast out of my honeypot. I can promise you this: The role of Melanie is yours. I'll see to that."

"Do you really mean it? Jane asked. "You really think so?"
"My word is like a certified check that you can take to the bank."

***

By now, Jane viewed herself as a hard-working staple on the Hollywood wannabee scene, attending auditions, showing up on time for appointments, and generally emoting on and off the screen in efforts to advance her screen image and career.

Her next gig involved another star billing in *He Couldn't Say No*, a film released in 1938. Except for Frank McHugh, her leading man, Jane didn't know any of the actors appearing with her in this film directed by Lewis Seiler. Even though the movie had clearly, since its inception, been configured as a B picture, she was delighted that once again, she'd been awarded with a highly visible role.

She was less excited when she read the script. McHugh starred as a timid man who works for a linoleum company for $30 a month. Cast as Violet Coney, Jane plays his domineering girlfriend. When his boss gives him a ten-dollar-a-month raise, she and her mother decide that it's time for him to get married.

At an auction, he purchases a nude statue modeled after the girl of his dreams, whom he adores from afar. Regrettably, her father, a senator, is campaigning against public nudity and wants to confiscate the statue. After a series of complications, McHugh gets the girl of his dreams, and dumps the complaining, kvetching character played by Jane.

"It's just as well," she said. "I wouldn't want to end up in the arms of Frank anyway."

Released with low expectations as a B-list programmer, *She Couldn't Say No* was quickly tossed into the Hollywood's dustbin.

***

Jane was a bit heartsick, or so she claimed, when she was cast in *Wide Open Faces* (1938), once again appearing in a movie with "Big Mouth," character actor Joe E. Brown. This time, she was Brown's co-star, unlike the smaller role she had played years before in *Polo Joe,* their previous film.

When she met with the film's director Kurt Neumann, she told him, "I'll have to wear a chastity belt and throw away the key if that horndog Brown chases after me like he did on the set of *Polo Joe.*"

Neumann assured her that Brown, in spite of his lovable screen image, still "has a taste for the ladies, especially if they're young and pretty like you. I do, too."

"Are you going to take director's privilege with me?" she asked.

"We'll see," he said. "For the moment, I've got my eye on this hot little blonde number, Barbara Pepper. I've cast her in a bit part."

As she chatted with Neumann, she came to realize he'd been given the wrong picture to direct. Born in

Wide Open Faces: Ingenue Wyman with Joe E. Brown. She called him "a horny old toad."

105

Nürnberg, Germany, he'd come to Hollywood in the early talkie era to direct German-language versions of Hollywood films, as was the custom back then. Once he'd mastered English, he was also assigned low-budget programmers such as *The Big Cage* (1933).

Wide Open Faces, a short film of only 67 minutes, is a story of criminals gathering at a lakeside inn where a bank robber has stashed $100,000. Brown plays Wilbur Keeks, a soda jerk, and Jane a character called Betty Martin. She gets ensnared in the subterfuge when she and an aunt move into an abandoned mansion where the crooks believe that the

Starlet Barbara Pepper *(left)* was Lucille Ball's best friend. Ball introduced her to Craig Reynolds, Jane's beau, who immediately dropped her for Pepper.

Later, as a fat lady (right) she appeared in several episodes of *I Love Lucy.*

stash is hidden. Before long, the mobsters are chasing after both Jane and Brown. The script was poor, and the film—released during Brown's waning film career—bombed at the box office.

Lucille Ball, Jane's former friend from the chorus line, appeared on the set one day. At first, Jane thought her appearance was for a reunion with her, but it turned out that Ball's real reason for showing up was to greet her other friend, Barbara Pepper, who had a supporting role in *Wide Open Faces.*

Until Ball showed up, Jane hadn't noticed the blonde New York actress. During her stint as one of the Goldwyn Girls, Pepper had met her lifelong friend, Ball.

Ball invited Pepper and Jane to lunch in the commissary, where Jane's sometimes beau, Craig Reynolds, showed up to join them.

Ruefully, Jane would later inform Ball, "Your friend, Miss Pepper, stole Craig from me. I think they exchanged phone numbers when I went to the ladies' room. All I know is that three nights later, he was seen around town with Pepper when not dating one of his menfolk."

***

One Friday morning, Carole Lombard called Jane early at her apartment, extending an invitation to drive with her to Palm Springs for the weekend. "Of course, I want you with me, but there's a motive to this invitation: I want you to be my beard. We'll look like two playgirls at the resort, having fun on the golf course, dining out, whatever. But secretly, I'll be shacked up with Clark *[Gable]*. While the casting for *Gone With the Wind* is ongoing, we've been advised to *lay low.* Did you get the *double entendre,* darling?"

Thrilled at the prospect, Jane eagerly accepted. "Should I bring a date?" she asked.

"Skip it," Carole said. "We'll have a full house as it is. Robert Taylor and Barbara Stanwyck, another pair of so-called illicit lovers, will be joining us. As for you, I'll pick up some handsome tennis pro, or whomever, for you. In Palm Springs, you never have to import a stud. The place is overrun with them."

In Palm Springs, Gable arrived in time for lunch with Carole and Jane. He remembered her from their lunch in the commissary, but still seemed unaware that he had seduced her before that. Two hours after he disappeared into the master bedroom with

106

Carole, they emerged in bathing suits. Jane joined them in the pool.

An hour later, when she went to answer the phone, Gable looked quizzically at Jane. "I think I met you before that day in the commissary," he said.

"I had a small part in *Cain and Mabel*," she said.

"My God," he said, his memory jogged. "We did it, didn't we?"

"That we did," she answered. "But Carole doesn't have to know."

"Good thinking, kid," he said.

When Carole returned to the pool, she told them that Robert Taylor would be showing up alone at ten o'clock that evening. He and Barbara Stanwyck had had a big row, and she wouldn't be coming.

Taylor arrived at around ten, as promised, after a big Mexican dinner had been served and cleared away by a staff member. He seemed better looking in person than he was on the screen. Jane was entranced by his looks, although he paid little attention to her, directing all his remarks and most of his attention to Carole and Gable.

"Louis B. Mayer doesn't want Barbara and me to get married. He claims that it will greatly reduce my appeal as a matinee idol. He wants me to remain a bachelor. Barbara disagrees. She says, 'Fuck Mayer and marry me.' We had a fight."

Carole, Gable, and Taylor stayed up way past midnight, comparing notes and gossiping. As Jane recalled, "I was outclassed. I felt left out."

She retired slightly before midnight, as they continued talking late into the night.

At around 3AM, she woke up, sensing a presence in her bedroom. She switched on a lamp. Completely nude, Taylor stood at the foot of her bed.

"*What...?*" She was startled.

"Turn off the light and keep quiet," he ordered. "I don't want to disturb Clark and Carole. Can I crawl in with you?"

"If that's what you've got in mind," she said. "I thought you'd come to borrow a pair of pajamas."

Other than confiding in Carole, and giving only the briefest of details to Joan Blondell back in Hollywood, Jane didn't fully reveal what happened that night.

Her sexual interlude with Taylor would eventually, however, be discovered. Taylor apparently enjoyed his time with Jane so much that he promised to get her a small role in his next picture, MGM's *The Crowd Roars* (1938). She was excited at the prospect of working on an A-list movie after her string of Bs.

On the set of that movie, when it finally got underway, one of the co-stars, Edward Arnold, walked in on Jane and Taylor in his dressing room. "Don't you know how to knock?" an angry Taylor called out to the pudgy actor.

"Sorry," Arnold said. "Carry on, dear hearts. I was young once myself."

[Apparently, Barbara Stanwyck never found out that Taylor had cheated on her with Jane. Stanwyck married Taylor in 1939, and after Jane wed Ronald Reagan in 1940, the two couples became close friends and often visited each other's homes for dinner.]

***

On the set of Jane's next film, *The Crowd Roars* (1938), Richard Thorpe had been assigned to direct a very talented cast of supporting players. Jane's role was minor, the female lead going to Maureen O'Sullivan, who had previously appeared with Taylor in *A Yank at Oxford* (1938). The supporting players included Edward Arnold, Frank Morgan, William Gargan, Nat Pendleton, Lionel Stander, and Isabel Jewell.

Taylor told Jane he hoped that this macho prizefight drama would end his press lampooning as an effeminate pretty boy. "I've got hair on my chest," He showed her a shirtless picture of himself with a patch of black hair on his chest. The photo was being released by the MGM publicity department.

"No one will think I'm a faggot when they see me playing *sock-'em dead* Killer McCoy, the menace in the ring." Jane noticed that with his smudged face, mussed hair, and truculent stance, he did indeed look credible as a boxer. She complimented him on his hairy legs. "Bob, with legs like that, you're the male version of Betty Grable."

Born in Kansas, Thorpe, the film's director, had begun his career in vaudeville before coming to Hollywood, where he directed his first silent film in 1923. During the course of his long career, he had helmed 180 movies.

In *The Crowd Roars, a* macho boxing film, Jane's role was minor, eclipsed by the talents of the female lead, Maureen O'Sullivan.

Thorpe told her, "The only reason you're in the picture is because Bob requested you, and he's got a lot of clout. Actually, I had a much better actress in mind."

"Thanks for your confidence," she said. "I'll try to make you proud of me."

Jane envied O'Sullivan's status as the lead opposite Taylor. Despite her jealousy, and with the understanding that they'd be filming a scene together, Jane was most gracious when they met.

Originally from Ireland, O'Sullivan had gone to school with Vivien Leigh. When she had emigrated to Hollywood, she was first signed by 20th Century Fox, but had later gravitated to MGM.

Once there, "Boy Wonder," Irving Thalberg signed her to appear as "Jane" in a series of Tarzan movies, beginning with *Tarzan the Ape Man* (1932), opposite that hunk of beefcake, Johnny Weissmuller.

The Crowd Roars for Robert Taylor, here successfully portraying a professional, hard-hitting boxer.

When *The Crowd Roars* was released, Taylor told Jane, "The picture was therapeutic for me. When the public sees my smudged face, my mussed hair, my boxing stance, and my right crosses, they'll realize how macho I really am."

The movie did a respectable box office, and for the most part, Taylor got good reviews. One critic wrote: "He plays the pug with a good deal more command than he has mustered in the past. He takes his place with Clark Gable among the screen heroes."

Reacting to critics, who virtually ignored her, Jane asked, "Was *I* in the picture?"

Taylor came to her defense. "She was a sparkling little star on the way up. The director and the cameraman more or less neglected her. I did not!"

Chapter Four

Horndog Reagan: Conquering Warners, Starlet by Starlet

"He's a Greater Swordsman than Errol Flynn"

It was publicity pictures such as these that caused Warner's to promote its new rising star, former lifeguard Ronald Reagan, as a "male pin-up," here depicted teaching Susan Hayward how to swim. When they were shown to Jack Warner, he said, "My God, Ronnie's got better legs than this redhead from Brooklyn. Her legs are too fat, and she doesn't know how to pose for leg art."

Years later, in Fort Lauderdale, Hayward said, "My greatest film role would have been as Scarlett O'Hara in love with Ashley Wilkes, as played by Ronnie Reagan—perhaps with Errol Flynn as that cad, Rhett Butler."

109

"I've been out with her on only two dates, and already, she's acting like she owns my balls."

So said Ronald Reagan on the set of his latest movie, *Swing Your Lady* (1938). He was talking to the star of the picture, a depressed Humphrey Bogart, who hated his role. The lady Reagan was referring to was Susan Hayward.

"The trouble with you, "Bogart said, "is that you don't know how to handle women. You

Bogart and Reagan in *Swing Your Lady,* a career atrocity.

should take some lessons from the master himself, namely, me. Every now and then, you need to sock a bitch in the kisser to remind her who's boss."

At the time he made the movie with Reagan, Bogart was locked into his third marriage to the minor but tempestuous actress, Mayo Methot. Their arguments became so public, they became known around Hollywood as "The Battling Bogarts."

After having starred in pictures, Reagan found himself in this one in a forgettably minor role which he'd shoot in just five days. Once again, he'd been cast as a glib, fast-talking radio announcer, which, of course, had been part of his pre-Hollywood career.

"All I get to do in this stinker is to make unwise wisecracks," Reagan lamented.

Bogart had been forced to star in the picture that he would later assert was "the worst movie in my entire career."

In time, film critics Harry Medved and Randy Lowell agreed with him, selecting *Swing Your Lady* as among *The Fifty Worst Films of all Time (and How They Got That Way),* a round-up of the most awful atrocities ever cranked out by Hollywood studios.

Although Reagan and Bogart would conflict, politically, in their future, Reagan chose to remember him pleasantly in his first memoir, *Where's the Rest of Me?* He claimed that Bogie was a real pro, a very affable man in spite of his tough guy façade. He liked to rib Reagan, always referring to him as a skirt chaser whenever he encountered him in the years ahead, even during the course of his marriage to Jane Wyman.

Joan Blondell was the first to read the script of *Swing Your Lady.* Ray Enright, who had recently completed directing three separate films with Jane Wyman in bit parts, offered Blondell the role of "Cookie Shannon," which ultimately went to Penny Singleton. "I detested it," Blondell recalled. Her refusal to participate in its production forced Jack Warner to suspend her for four weeks.

She had told Bogart, "The picture is crap. A stupid hillbilly romp. You're supposed to be some barnstorming wrestling promoter in the Ozarks. I didn't think it was a good idea to jeopardize my health to make this cornpone hee-haw."

"Just because I was cast as a homo doesn't mean I am one."

—*Reagan on the set of Dark Victory*

Suffering from neuritis, Blondell had recently admitted herself into a hospital. Jane was her daily visitor.

Unwilling to risk suspension, and needing the money, Bogart accepted the role of the sleazy promoter. From the first day, he feuded with Enright. "My God," Bogart said, during a phone call to Blondell. "This creepy little guy was a gag writer for Mack Sennett comedies. He once directed the wonder dog, Rin Tin Tin, and now, he's trying to tell me how to act."

When Bogart had complained to Jack Warner about the lousy parts he'd been assigned, the studio chief said, "Bogie, I can hardly

Swinging Ladies: The cast is all here *(left to right)*, the Amazonian female blacksmith (Louise Fazenda), the charming Penny Singleton, Bogie, and a smiling Ronald Reagan, wondering why he was trapped in this clunker.

give you romantic leads. What beautiful gal would want to end up with your ugly kisser in the final reel?"

In his role of Ed Hatch, Bogart, as a wrestling promoter, finds himself broke in a small town in Kentucky. There, he is impressed with a female blacksmith, a muscled Amazon named Sadie Horn, a role played by Louise Fazenda, the wife of producer Hal B. Wallis. Behind her back, Bogart referred to Wallis as "The Prisoner of Fazenda. Imagine his marrying that ugly puss when he could have his pick of any of the beautiful gals of Hollywood."

Reagan agreed with Bogart's unflattering assessment of the talented *comedienne*, who played a country bumpkin with multiple pigtails and spit curls. Clad in calico dresses, she seemed inspired by Minnie Pearl and Judy Canova. She spoke only once to Reagan, telling him, "Hal is not impressed with you at all. He feels you can only play sports announcers—nothing else."

"Thank your husband for the compliment," Reagan shot back.

In the script, Bogart decides to stage a fight between Fazenda and a boxer he had promoted, Joe Skopapoulos (Nat Pendelton). Pendleton had recently worked on a picture where he'd tried unsuccessfully to seduce Wyman.

Reagan talked with the always reliable character actor, Frank McHugh, cast as "Popeye Bronson." Reagan had just seen McHugh's movie, *He Couldn't Say No*, in which he and Wyman were given star billing.

Perky Penny Singleton caught Reagan's eye. Bogart had told Reagan that "Penny is the only one in this clunker who looks good enough to fuck."

Reagan agreed, but he acted cautiously because he'd learned that she had recently married a dentist, Dr. Laurence Scogga Singleton.

During Reagan's second day on the film set, Singleton openly flirted with him. "Unlike Bogart, you are one good-looking man," she said to him. "How about lunch?"

In the commissary, she told him how unhappy she was in her marriage to the dentist. "After the first month, I realized I'd made a mistake. I'm going to divorce him after I let a respectable amount of time go by."

"At least you're getting free dental care," Reagan quipped.

At the end of the meal, she asked him, "Can I come over to your place tonight and cook dinner for you? I'll bring the steaks."

"I know I shouldn't, but it sounds like an offer I can't refuse." Reagan had begun to recant his personal rule of never dating a married woman.

Somehow, Bogart heard about Singleton's visit to Reagan's home. Later, Bogart, the voyeur, wanted details. He asked Enright, "What's your opinion? Did Reagan fuck Penny?"

Enright asserted that in all likelihood, the answer was yes.

At the time of Reagan's interlude with Singleton, she was a brunette. In time, she'd dye her locks blonde for her appearance as "Blondie" opposite "Dagwood," the comic strip characters. Partly in honor of that series, she remained a blonde for the rest of her life.

Reagan later said, "Penny was no dumb blonde, as I believed at first. She became the first woman president of an AFL-CIO Union and led a strike by the Radio City Rockettes."

The dire predictions of Blondell and Bogart about the upcoming doom of *Swing Your Lady* came true. It took in less than $25,000 at the box office, and Jack Warner pulled the plug on it after its release, nationwide, after only two days, playing to mostly empty houses.

After that, dreading his next film assignment, Reagan actually feared that his contract would not be renewed.

***

Through her husband, the well-connected Dick Powell, Blondell was alerted early to what films Warners planned to produce and who would star in them.

In a call to Reagan, she announced, "Bryan Foy is giving you the lead role in your next picture, *Accidents Will Happen* (1938)"

"I hope that film won't be just another accident," he said.

"I'm sure it will be a big hit," she said. "I have a personal interest in it. The female role will be played by none other than my sister, Gloria."

"Is she blonde and beautiful, like you?"

I'm warning you, Reagan. As it pertains to my sister, keep that much used dick of yours buttoned up. Or have you switched to zippers now for faster action?"

Don't worry about that," he told her. "That part of my anatomy is worn out now that I'm dating Susan Hayward."

***

When Susan Hayward first spotted Reagan on the set of *Hollywood Hotel,* she told fellow starlet, Carole Landis, "When Christmas comes this year, I want that hunk tied with a red ribbon, nothing else, and put under my tree. He's the most gorgeous thing I've seen here since taking the stagecoach from Brooklyn."

Unknown to Hayward at the time, Landis had more or less the same thoughts about young Reagan, too.

Hayward, the blunt, fiery, and very talented redhead, was born Edythe Marrener on June 30, 1917, at 3507 Church Avenue in the Flatbush section of Brooklyn. She was the daughter of Walter Marrener, a Coney island carnival barker, and his Swedish wife, Ellen. Young Edythe had to rise above poverty and a childhood automobile accident that came very close to crippling her for life.

As a teenager, she hawked copies of *The Brooklyn Eagle* on the streets of Flatbush.

For a time, she was in the stenographer's pool, deserting that to become a model for fashion photographers. After four months of that, she landed on the cover of *The Saturday Evening Post*.

There, she was evaluated by director George Cukor, who brought her to the attention of producer David O. Selznick, who was searching for a young actress to star as Scarlett O'Hara in *Gone With the Wind*.

Hayward accepted the free train ticket to Hollywood, and—abandoning Brooklyn forever—headed west for a screen test.

As the train rolled toward California, Hayward was determined to make it big, overcoming the disappointments and rejections she'd faced during the course of her frustrated young life. "When you grow up in Flatbush, and you're poor, you learn to roll with the punches," she later said.

Hayward, despite her best efforts, still spoke a husky Brooklynese. Cukor immediately ordered her to take elocution lessons.

During the late 1960s, while living in Fort Lauderdale, Hayward spoke wistfully to author Darwin Porter about those long-ago days in California when another rising young star, Ronald Reagan, was included among her first beaux.

"It was a golden time," she said. "There was no smog. The weather was always sunny, and there wasn't too much traffic. I remember the night-blooming jasmine that scented the air. It was a romantic place and a time to fall in love."

From the streets of Brooklyn, a young Susan Hayward developed a philosophy of life, which she later shared with Reagan.

"The only thing a woman should ever be afraid of in her life is not having lived it."

"For my screen test as Scarlett, I had to practice a Southern accent with a vocal coach," Hayward said. "After all, we girls in Brooklyn didn't speak like we had cotton in our mouths. They coiffed me and dressed me up like an antebellum Georgia peach."

"I made the test with Alan Marshall. It involved a scene between Scarlett and Ashley Wilkes, in the library of Twelve Oaks. I still remember my lines: "*Oh, my dear. I love you. I tell you, I love you. And I know you must care about me, because…Ashley, you do care.*"

Reagan surprised her by saying that he was being considered for the role of Ashley, "although Selznick isn't exactly beating my door down."

"Maybe if you'd put out a bit for George Cukor on his casting couch, the role might be yours," Hayward suggested, provocatively.

"I'm not that kind of guy," Reagan said.

"Susan was bubbling over with anticipation about that screen test," Reagan later recalled. "I feared she was heading for heartbreak."

Ben Medford, Hayward's first Hollywood agent, privately told Reagan, "The test was terrible, but I can't tell her that. She's a bitch to work with, but I see in her a deep emerging talent."

Her beauty and spirit attracted the attention of Howard Hughes, the aviator and movie producer, who ordered his pimp, Johnny Meyer, to set up a date with her.

Hughes later told Meyer, "Susan cooked the dinner herself. In Brooklyn, do they prefer bloody chicken? Even so, I see a possibility in her for future dates. As you know, I prefer 'wet decks.'" *[That was Hughes' reference to recently divorced women, or those who were "well-seasoned."]*

Hayward later told Cukor, "Hughes' favorite kind of sex is oral, both on the giving and receiving end."

During the next few weeks, Hayward shifted her interest in Hughes onto Reagan. She later confided to Medford. "Believe it or not, on my first date with Reagan, he didn't even kiss me on the cheek when he said good night. I decided to take matters into my own hands. I figured that this bashful boy needed some encouragement. When he went to kiss me on our second date, I invited him inside for a night cap. He stayed over for breakfast."

"Neither Reagan nor I were as sexually experienced as we pretended," Hayward, years later, told author Darwin Porter. "I mean, he knew where all the plumbing was, but he'd be no competition for more experienced men. But what the hell! One afternoon on Santa Monica Beach, I fell for him."

"Although we both knew that we had to conquer Hollywood, I actually began to think about settling down, getting married, stuff like that. He was one beautiful man."

"But there was a serious drawback," she said. "He talked too much, babbling on about baseball scores and the fear of a war in Europe—subjects that held no interest for me whatsoever. But I was willing to overlook that. In those days, most other actors talked about what they had read in *Variety* or in *The Hollywood Reporter,* perhaps the latest gossip from Louella Parsons."

"He bored me, but I dug him. I wondered how he managed to crowd all those facts into his small head. But I came alive when he made love to me."

Louella Parsons had taken a maternal interest in Hayward, who confided in the gossip maven.

"I want to mother him and make love to him," Hayward confessed. "Sometimes, I enjoy lying awake at night, listening to the sound of his breathing. I feel comfortable with him, fulfilled as a woman."

"It's about time you youngsters got married and settled down," Parsons advised. "I think the two of you would make an ideal couple."

Hayward and Reagan found themselves jointly enrolled in the Warners' Drama School under the tutelage of acting coach Frank Beckwith, a nervous little man who wore horn-rimmed glasses and was known to "pass wind" frequently.

Penny Singleton and Carole Landis were also in the class. Both of them, along with Hayward, were having affairs with Reagan.

Nervous at being exposed, he paid no undue attention to any of them. "Susan hawkeyes my every move," he told Beckwith, who was aware of his pupil's romantic liaisons with his fellow classmates. "I think Susan suspects there's something going on between Carole and me. She's always calling Carole a tramp."

Over lunch with Reagan one afternoon, the drama coach told him that of all the women in his class, Hayward had the best chance of making it as a star. "She's aggressively self-assured. She could play bitches, but not a woman with a heart. She would not be convincing as a vulnerable character. On the other hand, Jane Wyman, whom you haven't met, has heart—It would be hard for Wyman to convincingly play an icy bitch."

"Jack Warner told me I need to teach Hayward to cry on cue," Beckworth continued. "Perhaps if you drop her, you'll break her heart, and then she'll know how to act as if she's vulnerable."

"That's not a good idea," Reagan said. "Susan has threatened to castrate me if I dump her."

In Fort Lauderdale, more than twenty years later, Hayward recalled to Darwin Porter that in the beginning, during her brief stint at Warner's, her career was going nowhere. "I was a nothing in nothing roles. If nothing else happened, I realized I might at least end up with a steady boyfriend, namely Ronald Reagan. Actually, I wanted to move from Warners to Paramount, hoping to get a contract over there."

Reagan's seduction of Hayward and other starlets stirred up a debate at Warners. The head officer of his local U.S. cavalry branch told the press, "Ronnie is a greater swordsman at Warners than Errol Flynn." That comment, when he read it, infuriated Jack Warner, who preferred to promote an image of Reagan as a chaste, clean-cut, All-American boy, saving himself until the right woman came along.

The publicity department at Warners, reacting to pressure from above, developed an idea to promote the careers of both Hayward and Reagan by having them pose in swimwear—"a little cheesecake for the boys, a hunk of beef for the ladies." Those candid photographs appeared in newspapers across the country.

One of the photos was captioned *RONALD REAGAN SHOWS SUSAN HAYWARD THE RIGHT POSITION*. The publicist meant to suggest the right position in the water, but sexually sophisticated Hollywoodites interpreted it as a reference to the right position during sexual intercourse.

Warner studied the photographs carefully: "I'm not a faggot, but Reagan's legs are better than Hayward's. She has chubby calves and knobby knees. With these pictures, Reagan is going to become the pin-up boy for every fairy in the country. THAT IS NOT THE IMAGE I WANT FOR HIM."

Nearly everybody on the lot interpreted Reagan as a love 'em and leave 'em kind of Lothario. In contrast, a noted studio writer, Owen Crump, disagreed, defining Reagan as the studio's "porch warmer—that is, more gab than grab, with no threat to any virgin."

When Blondell heard that, she said, "Reagan might not have been a threat to any virgin at Warners, because no such animal existed there. All of our gals have already been laid end to end."

Reagan spent the night with Hayward when she learned that the coveted role of Scarlett O'Hara had been awarded to a relatively unknown British actress, Vivien Leigh.

"The only comfort I could give her," Reagan confessed to Medford, "was to make love to her all night."

Astonishingly, perhaps for reasons of political discretion, Reagan chose to completely exclude any mention of Hayward from his Hollywood memoirs, *Where's the Rest of Me?*, published in 1965.

***

Off the screen, a major turning point in Reagan's career came when super agent Jules Stein, founder of the Music Corporation of America (MCA), entered his life when he purchased William Meiklejohn's talent agency, the organization which had arranged for Reagan's first screen test and his original contacts with Warners.

Rising from South Bend, Indiana, Stein was more than forty years old when he first met Reagan. He had first opened shop in Hollywood in 1937, representing such stars at Warners as Bette Davis. He also branched out to other studios, luring Joan Crawford, Betty Grable, Ingrid Bergman, Greta Garbo, and Frank Sinatra to supposedly greener pastures.

By the mid-1940s, it was estimated that half of the movie industry's stars—including Jane Wyman and her first agent, William Demarest, now working mainly as an actor— were being represented by MCA, by then pejoratively nicknamed "The Octopus."

Through a lucrative bribe, Stein persuaded Louella Parsons to give Reagan the "star build-up" in her column.

Reagan didn't spend all his time dating. He became obsessed with his career. Whereas in one picture, he'd be the star, his follow-up assignment would involve only a minor role. He desperately wanted to be a major star, right up there with Pat O'Brien, Errol Flynn, James Cagney, and Edward G. Robinson.

He had high hopes, however, for his next B picture. Entitled *Accidents Will Happen,* it ran for only an hour, a drama/romance about phony insurance claims. Cast in the star role, he played an ambitious insurance claims adjuster, Eric Gregg.

Gloria Blondell, Joan's younger sister, was appearing in this, her second film, having made her screen debut in *Daredevil Drivers* (1938), co-starring Beverly Roberts and Dick Purcell. Unlike Joan, she would have only a minor career as an actress.

In 1938, just as it was emerging from the Depression, America was plagued with insurance frauds. The plot of *Accidents Will Happen* was, in the words of its director, William Clemens, "torn from today's headlines." A specialist in low-budget crime dramas, Clemens had previously directed Jane Wyman in *Here Comes Carter (1936).*

In the film, the character played by Reagan is married to the wrong woman, Nona (Sheila Bromley), who is collaborating, without her husband's knowledge, with the insurance fraud crooks.

Reagan's character, however, soon falls in love with a cigar stand sales clerk, Patricia Carmody (Gloria Blondell). In this jam-packed thriller, all ends happily, as Reagan, aided by Gloria, captures the crooks, including his own wife, and opts to spend the rest of his life with the blonde beauty hawking those cigars.

On the set, Reagan, according to Clemens, "went crazy" over Bromley.

The exact age as Reagan, Bromley, of San Francisco, had never quite agreed on her name, billing herself at various eras of her career as Sheila LeGay, Sheila Manners, Sheila Mannors, or Sheila Manors. She had launched her career in westerns at "Poverty Row's" Monogram Pictures during the early 1930s, appearing with such cowboy stars as Hoot Gibson, Johnny Mack Brown, and Bill Cody.

She had also made three films with John Wayne: *Westward Ho* (1935); *Lawless Range* (1935); and

Jules Stein, MCA's powerful boss, with connections to the mob, told Reagan: "I'm not only going to make you our million dollar baby during the next few years, but one day, when you're older, I'll make you a multi-millionaire, too."

"Of course, when we put you in a position of power, I'll want favors in return."

In the photo above, Jane, in a backless gown, goes into a huddle with Jules Stein in a restaurant on Hollywood Boulevard.

He allegedly told her, "Janie, I know you like to sleep around, but we're going to promote you and Reagan as 'the greatest romance of the 20th Century.'"

Idol of the Crowds (1937). After her affair with Wayne, she uttered a remark that was widely circulated throughout Hollywood, "There's not enough there to mess up your mouth with."

Although not known for beating up on ladies, Wayne once threatened her he'd mash her face if she didn't stop mocking his lack of endowment.

When Reagan became president of the United States in the 1980s, Bromley, then retired, was set upon by reporters eager to learn details of her affair with him.

In *Accidents Will Happen,* Reagan was cast as a naïve insurance adjustor married to a crooked wife (Sheila Bromley), but rescued by the love of a decent woman (Gloria Blondell, sister of Joan, depicted above playing a cigar stand salesgirl.)

She consistently denied that she'd ever had any involvement with the president during the 1930s.

However, those who worked on the picture with her claimed that she was lying. Clemens, who died as Reagan was running for election as president, said on one occasion, "Bromley spent four hours in his dressing room when I didn't need either of them for the scenes I was filming. During the shoot, he was also pumping it to Gloria Blondell. He was quite a stud in those days before Nancy put a chastity belt on him."

Cast as a crook in the movie, a New York trained actor, Elliott Sullivan, specialized in gangster roles, his characters usually named "Lefty" or "Mugsy." Before he became blacklisted in the 1950s, he made dozens of films, including *King of the Underworld* (1938).

"In the movie, on the screen, *[the character played by]* Reagan threatened to beat me up. I liked the guy. More to the point, I envied him. It was Bromley in the afternoon, Gloria Blondell at night, with Susan Hayward showing up on occasion, too. Hayward had stamped 'personal property' on the guy, but that didn't slow him down in his role as Don Juan. If only I had his looks. Clemens told me I looked like the average Joe in America who carries his lunchbox to a factory job."

Disregarding the pointed warning from Joan Blondell, Reagan went after her younger sister, Gloria. Joan seemed jealous of her sister, who not only resembled her, but had the same pretty, bubbly, vivacious, and curvaceous appeal.

Reagan learned that Gloria was a girl within the "stables" of Howard Hughes, that she was part of a bevy of relatively unknown actresses he kept available in case he had a sudden need for them in the middle of the night. Systematically, he told all of them, "I made Jean Harlow a star. I can do the same for you."

Reagan was afflicted with *"Leadinglady-itis"* specifically as it applied to Gloria, but only for the duration of the picture. "It was no more than a brief fling," Gloria later admitted to both Joan and her husband, Dick Powell, who rendezvoused with Reagan at least once a week for a game of golf.

According to Gloria, "Reagan was not serious about me, and I viewed him as a passing fancy. It might have gone on longer than it did, but Hughes learned of our affair and sent a warning to Reagan through one of his henchmen. Reagan didn't care enough for me to antagonize Hughes. Very soon after Reagan and I broke up, I fell really hard for someone else. Reagan didn't want to settle down in those days. He was like a hungry, greedy little bastard who wanted to sample every dessert on the buffet table. He provided the banana for the banana split, and I provided the cherry, so to speak."

[In the aftermath of her fling with Reagan, Gloria launched an affair with Albert R. ("Cubby") Broccoli, one of the aviator and movie mogul's employees and henchmen. When Hughes learned of this, he fired Broccoli and threw Gloria out of his "stable." In 1940, Broccoli defiantly chartered a plane to fly Gloria and himself to Las Vegas, where they were married.]

Cast in *Accidents Will Happen* in a minor role was Anderson Lawler. When Reagan met him, he was a part-time actor, but mainly a talent scout for Warners. "I'm already discovered," Reagan told the talent scout.

During one of Reagan's discussions with Lawler, the actor announced that he was expecting a guest, scheduled for arrival soon, for lunch with him in the commissary. "Stick around and meet him."

Within fifteen minutes, Reagan was shaking the hand of Gary Cooper, who would soon be seducing Susan Hayward when they co-starred together in *Beau Geste* (1939).

"If all goes well," Reagan told him, "I'll soon be playing your rival in *Gone With the Wind*, Ashley Wilkes to your Rhett Butler."

Before the production of *Accidents Will Happen*, Joan Blondell wanted to ensure, in her mind at least, that the virginity of her sister, Gloria *(depicted above)*, would still be intact at the end of filming.

After his first night with Gloria, Reagan learned that "she'd lost her cherry long ago, and was being kept by Howard Hughes."

Reagan, as President, was an avowed anti-communist. In this scene from *Accidents Will Happen*, he's seen beating up an insurance scammer and mobster, as played by Elliott Sullivan. Later, in real life, Sullivan was blacklisted as "a communist pinko."

"I doubt that," Cooper said. "I don't want to play Rhett. Let Gable have it! Anderson here keeps urging me to do it, though."

"I think it would be the role of a lifetime for Coop," Lawler said. "He can play Southern. His first talkie was *The Virginian* (1929). I'm from Alabama, so I taught him some good 'ol Southern dialect while he was rehearsing the role."

Later, Reagan talked to director Clemens, regretting that he'd not been given real he-man roles like Cooper. "He seems like a real man's man."

"He's a man's man all right," Clemens said. "He got sexually involved not only with Anderson, but with Cary Grant, William Haines, Rod La Rocque, Howard Hughes, David Lewis, Randolph Scott, and Cecil Beaton. When Edmund Goulding directed him in *Paramount on Parade,* I heard he 'worshipped' Cooper twice a day."

"I can't believe that," Reagan said. "He's so masculine."

"Wise up!" Clemens said. "Some of the most masculine men in Hollywood are queer. Don't tell me you think only effeminate men suck cock. Of course, Coop seduces women, too. Let's name them: Claudette Colbert, Marlene Dietrich, Tallulah Bankhead, Lupe Velez, Clara Bow."

When Cooper was later asked about how he differed from his image on the screen, he responded. "Hollywood personalities are really applesauce. We deceive the public and get paid for it. I get paid pretty well, so I deceive the public really, really good."

By now, Jack Warner no longer opposed his publicity department's policy of posing Reagan with the most beautiful women on the Warners lot for cheesecake photographs. Instead of spoiling his clean cut image, Warner felt it enhanced his sex appeal. He ordered more of the same.

It was at this same time that the studio mogul picked up on the refrain, calling Reagan "A better swordsman on the Warners' lot than Errol Flynn."

Here, Reagan gets cozy with Sheila Bromley's ankle. When he became President, she told reporters, "Ronnie and I, contrary to reports, did not have an affair."

"During the making of *Accidents Will Happen,*" director William Clemens claimed, "when he wasn't due on the set, our boy Ronnie was making the rounds from Gloria's dressing room to Sheila's."

He also wanted Reagan to systematically escort Warners starlets to premieres, events where they'd be widely photographed. When Hayward heard that he'd be escorting other women on studio-arranged "dates," she warned him: "Make sure you escort them and nothing else."

Ironically, she, too, was ordered to encourage photo ops with rising young male stars, so she came to realize it was strictly business.

Stubbornly, Reagan had not listened to Joan Blondell's mandate about keeping his hands off her younger sister, Gloria. He didn't listen to Hayward's mandate, either.

Soon, the publicity department notified him that he'd be Lana Turner's date at the next Warners' premiere.

***

Wearing a dinner jacket borrowed from Warners' wardrobe department, Reagan, with his hair slicked back, took a taxi to retrieve the starlet Lana Turner, at her home, as part of the process of escorting her to the world premiere of *Jezebel (1938),* starring Bette Davis and Henry Fonda.

The date was March 7, 1938. Months before, Jack Warner had bowed out of the competition for the film rights to Margaret Mitchell's *Gone With the Wind*. Subsequently, they'd been sold to David O. Selznick for just $50,000.

[At Jezebel's premiere, Davis was still fuming over her loss of the role of Scarlett O'Hara. Reagan, however, was more philosophical: "I had long ago accepted the fact that I was not going to play Ashley Wilkes, the Southern gentleman," Reagan said. "The part was better cast with this British actor, Leslie Howard, with Gable as Rhett Butler."

In releasing its own Civil War epic, Jack Warner was hoping to capitalize off the growing fame of Gone With the Wind *by "striking first." Selznick had already accused Warner of plagiarizing* Gone With the Wind. *When* Jezebel *was released,* Time *magazine claimed that it resembled the Mitchell novel like "chicory to coffee."*

Long before Vivien Leigh came onto the screen as Scarlett O'Hara, Davis in Jezebel *was hailed by Warner's publicity machine as "The Most Exciting Heroine Who Ever Lived and Loved in Dixie!"]*

Might it have happened? At least in the talking stage, there arose the possibility of casting Gary Cooper as Rhett Butler and Ronald Reagan as Ashey Wilkes in *Gone With the Wind* (1939).

Reagan arrived at a modest little apartment on Highland Avenue, above Hollywood Boulevard. It was a neighborhood filled with low-rent apartments, catering mostly to transients who had flocked to Hollywood to break into the movie business.

When he knocked on Turner's door, it was opened by director Mervyn LeRoy, who had discovered Turner and cast her in the now notorious opening scene of *They Won't Forget* (1937), where she played a young girl in a sweater who becomes a murder victim. LeRoy offered Reagan a drink.

He congratulated LeRoy on his casting of Turner in *They Won't Forget,* for a Warners release. Her appearance in the film had created a sensation, especially her bouncing bosom, which earned her an appellation as "the Sweater Girl."

"Lana signed a contract just four days after she turned sixteen," LeRoy claimed. "When I first met her, she was so nervous, her hands were shaking. She didn't have on any makeup, and she was so shy, she could not look me in the face. But there was something endearing about her. I thought she was the right gal to play a murder victim. I wanted to call her Lenore Turner or Lurlene Turner, but she came up with 'Lana' on her own."

For some reason, perhaps because he was overstocked with beautiful young women, Reagan had been somewhat reluctant to date Turner. He asked the publicists at Warners, "Do I have to go to the premiere of *Jezebel?*"

"No, but you'll be hanging out a lot longer at Warners if you do," the publicist had responded.

From the bedroom of her apartment, Turner emerged looking dazzling in a white gown borrowed from the wardrobe department at Warners. Reagan looked stunned when introduced. He finally said, "You're the most beautiful gal I've ever seen."

"You're not bad yourself, buster," she replied.

Like Reagan, she had emerged from origins in a small town, having been born in the mining hamlet of Wallace, Idaho. She was almost eighteen when she first met Reagan. After she kissed LeRoy goodbye, she headed out the door with Reagan.

Years later, in the Polo Lounge of the Beverly Hills Hotel, Turner recalled her first date with Reagan to author Darwin Porter. "He said I was the most beautiful girl he'd ever seen, but he was not the best looking man I'd ever seen. I mean, he was handsome but not a beauty contest winner. I found him very appealing, with the most wonderful manners, and he knew how to treat a lady. He made me feel grown up even though I was only a teenager, around eighteen at the time."

He complimented her on *They Won't Forget.*

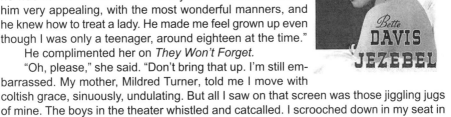

"Oh, please," she said. "Don't bring that up. I'm still embarrassed. My mother, Mildred Turner, told me I move with coltish grace, sinuously, undulating. But all I saw on that screen was those jiggling jugs of mine. The boys in the theater whistled and catcalled. I scrooched down in my seat in embarrassment. Later, I fled from the theater in horror. As I walked along, I tried to keep anything from bouncing."

He had rented a taxi to take her to the theater, because he felt that his own car was too battered to show up at a premiere with such a glamorous star.

"I hear that *Jezebel* is an unashamed rip-off of *Gone With the Wind,* even though Selznick's movie hasn't yet been released," he said.

"Like everyone else, I read *Gone With the Wind,* but I knew I could never play Scarlett," she said to him. "It wasn't right for me. But Warners sent me over to MGM to do a screen test. I was embarrassed to learn that a great director like George Cukor had been assigned to the test. I rushed through it as quickly as I could, both Cukor and I knowing that nothing would come of it."

[Years later, Turner was deeply embarrassed when screen tests, including hers, of actresses wanting to be cast as Scarlett were shown on TV. "I was held up to ridicule," she lamented at the time.]

Before arriving at the premiere, Turner turned to Reagan and gripped his hand. "I'm afraid! All eyes will be on us. Deep down, I'm still a frightened little girl. But when that car door opens, I'll try to camouflage my insecurities by throwing my head up high in the air and walking along the red carpet like I own Tinseltown."

At the theater, a pedestrian walkway had been built above the traffic of the boulevard in front. A reporter for *The New York Times* later wrote that "Lana Turner on the arm of Ronald Reagan made a dazzling appearance crossing the bridge of stars, even though they aren't stars yet. Klieg lights brightened the night sky over Hollywood, as hundreds of fans showed up."

After the premiere, where the night and most of its credits belonged to Bette Davis, Reagan invited Turner to dinner. He was happily surprised that she enjoyed the same type of food that he did: Hot dogs, macaroni and cheese, barbecued ribs, and spaghetti with meatballs.

When their food was served, she removed a bottle of chili peppers from her purse. She sprinkled it over the ribs, telling him that she was convinced that it removed toxins from one's body.

What happened after dinner has grown hazy in Hollywood lore, with various versions repeated, most of them inaccurate.

On the golf course the following Sunday, Reagan confided to Dick Powell that, "Lana is just as oversexed as I am. I spent the night with her after seeing *Jezebel,* and

I hope it'll be the beginning of many more nights to come. I've got to slip around, though, because I don't want Susan Hayward to find out."

Edmund Morris, Reagan's official biographer, noted, "Dutch was not yet a one-girl guy. He was soon seen squiring dishy Lana Turner around town, joking that he 'wasn't acting' in her company."

His pursuit of Turner was made easier when Warners' publicity department asked them to pose for pictures together for distribution nationwide.

In riding costumes, Lana Turner poses with Ronald Reagan for publicity shots. His friend, Dick Powell, later revealed, "Lana was one of Ronnie's grandest conquests, a flamoyant feather in his cap."

Later, Lana denied the affair, probably because of her friendship with Nancy Davis.

"Lana and I did whatever the studio wanted us to do," Reagan later said. "Put on our clothes, take off our clothes. Susan would kill me if she ever heard me say this, but Lana looks hotter in a bathing suit than she does."

Late one morning, Reagan, in his battered car, drove Turner to the Warners ranch outside Los Angeles, where they would be photographed together in riding costumes. An expert horseman, he taught her how to ride.

That night, back at her apartment, she cooked a meal for him, filet mignon coated with cracked peppercorns, lots of salt, and mustard. He was no longer surprised when she sprinkled hot sauce over it. "Too much sauce gives me the runs," he said. "You must have a cast-iron stomach." He also noted that she was "the world's slowest eater, chomping down on a piece of steak for at least fifteen minutes before swallowing it."

News of the Reagan/Turner affair eventually reached Wayne Morris at Warners. One afternoon, he confronted Reagan in the commissary. "What is this shit about you moving in on Lana? Before you, I was taking advantage of the big crush she had on me."

"Isn't Priscilla Lane enough for you?" Reagan said.

"Isn't Susan Hayward enough for you?" Morris asked.

"*Touché,*" Reagan answered.

In her memoirs, *Lana—The Lady, The Legend, The Truth,* she was discreet. She

When Lana Turner walked down the street in *They Won't Forget* (1937), she was dubbed "the Sweater Girl" and became an overnight sensation. She always claimed she wore a bra; viewers of the movie doubted that.

At the movie's preview, a young man in the audience yelled out, to almost universal applause: "Get a load of that kid! Whatta pair of tits!"

did recall posing for pictures with Reagan, defining him as "a nice young man," but provided no other insights.

In his memoirs, Reagan didn't even mention her.

***

A friendly young reporter from Des Moines visited Reagan at Warners. He had seen pictures of him posing with Turner, and he asked what it was like for a local boy to find himself dating glamour queens.

"Miss Turner is an actress of natural beauty that gets worked over by the studio makeup department that creates a make-believe character for her. She is very down to earth, kind and considerate. Young girls across America, so I'm told, are trying to imitate her. Of course, Hollywood publicists like to rewrite her story. If a girl gets a high school diploma, it suddenly appears in print that she's got a doctorate. If she spends all Saturday afternoon in the beauty parlor, that isn't talked about. Magazines and newspapers print that she spends all her spare time helping homeless refugees from Europe."

Reagan would have more or less agreed with Patrick Agan's conclusion in *The Decline and Fall of the Love Goddesses.* "To millions, the Love Goddesses were surrogate mistresses, ladies of incredible beauty who afford at least a visual satisfaction that men were able to indulge in even in the company of their wives. The Love Goddesses were an inspiration, Everests of glamour for both men and women."

After Reagan had been elected to the Oval Office, author Darwin Porter met with Turner in the Polo Lounge of the Beverly Hills Hotel. "Now that Ronnie is President, the press is always asking me about my former relationship with him," she said. "Somebody wrote that I didn't even remember dating him—that is pure crap! Of course, I remembered him. I've even been asked to describe what kind of lover he is. I'll never tell, but I'll give you a hint. He's a man who likes to take his time, unlike another future President of the United States I used to know."

"I liked Ronnie right from the beginning, and we became friends. Later, I got to know Nancy Davis when she was a starlet at MGM. After she married Ronnie, I visited their home on many occasions."

"I recall one very formal party I attended with Ronnie in the mid-50s," she said. "I was still trying to hold onto my beauty, but for the first time, I realized that he'd lost his looks. His face had aged a lot. That Midwestern farm boy appeal of his had faded with my romance with Artie Shaw. He still had that beautiful head of hair, perhaps dyed, but he had begun to look the way he did when he was governor of California."

"I liked Nancy, but detested Jane Wyman," Turner continued. "I first met her when we were both starlets at Warners. Later, for the 1982-83 season, I appeared with her on TV in *Falcon Crest.* After an initial introduction and a chat, she didn't even speak to me. She always resented my beauty. Not only that, but she learned that I

Now there's a movie star! A view of Lana Turner in 1947, during her filming of *Green Dolphin Street.*

had dated Reagan before she got her claws into him. She was one icy cold bitch."

Turner's daughter, Cheryl Crane, wrote: "After Reagan became President, mother couldn't help but think of him as that young guy from Warners. When she met him after the election, she said, 'Well, if it isn't *El Presidente.*'"

Along with a handful of other movie stars, Lana Turner joined that very exclusive club of women who had been seduced by both Reagan and John F. Kennedy.

***

When director Lloyd Bacon called Reagan with his next film assignment, *Cowboy from Brooklyn* (1938), the actor was disappointed when he learned of his role. After starring parts, he'd been demoted to seventh billing. "You wouldn't exactly call this climbing the ladder to success, now would you?" Reagan asked Bacon, who answered with a vague overview about how stardom isn't always achieved overnight.

The stars of the picture were Dick Powell, Pat O'Brien, Priscilla Lane, and Dick Foran, with Ann Sheridan and Johnnie Davis in supporting roles.

The plot for *Cowboys from Brooklyn* spoofed cowboy singing stars such as Roy Rogers and Gene Autry. Although he's afraid of animals, Brooklyn-born Elly Jordan (as played by Powell) becomes a singing cowboy at a dude ranch in Wyoming owned by Ma and Pop Hardy. Their daughter (as played by Lane) teaches him the ways of the West and also falls in love with him.

O'Brien and Reagan were cast as two Broadway hustlers looking for their next meal ticket. At the dude ranch, they discover the so-called singing cowboy and sign him to a radio contract. Typical of a 1930s comedy, complications inevitably follow as part of the light and fluffy plot.

O'Brien had become a sort of father figure to Reagan, who was all too aware that this tough-talking Irishman was a scene stealer. On screen, he was a fast talker. To counter that, in his scenes with him, Reagan spoke slowly and softly. "Bacon failed to tell me that I was screwing up every scene," he complained. "Without my knowledge, he was cutting my scenes and rewriting them, putting them into the mouths of other members of the cast."

One day, Elisabeth Risdon, a veteran English character actress, invited Reagan to lunch in the commissary. Before approaching the subject of his failure as an actor, she told him about herself.

Born in London in 1887, she had originally played beautiful society ladies. She spoke of her affair with George Bernard Shaw, who had cast her in some of his best plays. "I was once the leading lady to George Arliss," she said. "That long, bony face of his was such a turn-off for me, but I thought of God and country when he kissed me. I decided that a love scene with him was something to endure, like a kidney stone."

She finally got around to telling him what was going wrong with all his scenes with O'Brien. "Pat's got this high-pitched, rather nasal speedball patter. He comes on like he's

During the filming, Pat O'Brien *(right)* invited Reagan to become a member of the "Irish Mafia," an informal clique which pointedly excluded Jews like Edward G. Robinson

announcing that the building is on fire. Then you speak and you send the plot to the cellar with your slow drawl. Then he comes in again, with just a hint of Irish brogue, and he has to pick up the pace after you've put the audience to sleep. You seem to have trouble keeping up with the movie's race-to-the-finish comic pacing."

Heeding her advice, Reagan met privately in O'Brien's dressing room. Without the director's knowledge, O'Brien walked him through their next scene, telling him exactly how to play it opposite him.

In the next scene, after his coaching from O'Brien, Reagan was called upon to enter Grand Central Station in New York City to face the press. With a straw hat and cane, he did a carnival shill to introduce singing cowboy Powell. When Bacon called for action, "I came through like gangbusters," Reagan later wrote. "I bounced the cane off the floor, caught it in mid-air, and launched into my pitch. Bacon didn't have to give my lines away anymore."

Elisabeth Risdon in 1941...
Teaching Reagan how to act.

These two Irishmen, O'Brien and Reagan, bonded so well that Reagan was invited to become a member of the "Irish Mafia" clique in the commissary. "If you got invited to their table, you'd arrived," Reagan said. "On any given day, you could dine with Dick (Powell), Humphrey Bogart, James Cagney, and Frank McHugh. Edward G. Robinson wanted to join us, but Pat rejected him for being 'too Jewish.'"

One afternoon, when they weren't needed on the set, Reagan and Powell remained behind for extra cups of coffee. Powell appeared to be going through a career crisis. "I feel trapped by my Warners contract. How long can I go on playing a crooning man-boy? God damn it to hell and back, I was born in 1904. It'll soon be 1940. I'm not exactly a spring chicken anymore."

He confided to Reagan that he'd refused any involvement in the latest Busby Berkeley musical, and that Jack Warner had reacted by placing him on a twelve-week suspension with no pay.

"I've got to invent a new screen life for myself. If I don't, I'll be washed up in pictures."

"You've got more courage than I have to defy Warner," Reagan said. "I take whatever crap they throw at me."

"I'm desperate to expand my range, but Warner won't let me do it," Powell said. "He made me play Lysander in *A Midsummer's Night Dream* (1935), although I was wrong for the role. A Shakespearean actor I'm not. All this anxiety is fucking up my marriage to Joan (Blondell). She's pregnant, by the way."

"Congratulations," Reagan said.

"I don't know about that," Powell said. "I'm not a happy camper at home. After supper, I retreat."

Powell was instrumental in securing Reagan a seat on the board of the Screen Actors Guild (SAG).

The board included not only established stars like Walter Pidgeon and Robert Montgomery, but a broad representation of those who worked in the industry, including freelancers and extras. Reagan filled his seat on the board in his capacity as "a new, young contract player." SAG would play a large role in his future, and he referred to it as a "damned noble organization," although initially, he had opposed a union for actors.

During the course of filming *Cowboy from Brooklyn*, Reagan resumed his liaison with Priscilla Lane. He remained discreet, not letting Susan Hayward find out. She sometimes showed up unexpectedly on the set, perhaps hoping to catch him in something.

Lane certainly didn't limit her charms just to Reagan. On two different occasions, Reagan noticed Lane emerging from Powell's dressing room after long visits. Additionally, sometimes, Wayne Morris showed up to take Lane to lunch. In a private moment, alone with Reagan, Lane urged, "Don't tell Wayne about us," she warned Reagan. "He'd turn you into pulp."

"My lips are sealed," Reagan said.

One weekend, when Morris was out of town, Lane asked Reagan if she could spend the weekend with him. He told her that he had already committed himself to escort Hayward for an Italian dinner with his family on Sunday night.

"Don't worry about that," Lane said. "I'll come by your place late on Sunday morning. We'll go for a swim, have lunch, and later take care of business."

"It's a deal," he said. "But you've got to promise to leave something left over for Susan."

On the set that Monday, an exhausted Reagan, fresh from separate sexual performances with both Lane and Hayward, rendezvoused with Lane for coffee. She discussed a rising star, Ann Sheridan, who'd been given a small role in *Cowboy from Brooklyn*.

"Ann and I get together to talk about the men in our lives," she said. "Bogie's okay in bed, she told me, but when a gal lies under him, and he's kissing her, she has to swallow a pint of saliva."

"Thanks for warning me," Reagan said jokingly. "He'll not get into my bed, that's for damn sure."

Reagan later confessed to Powell, "When I met Ann, it was love at first sight."

He'd gotten off to a bad start with Sheridan, suggesting that she resembled June Travis, his girlfriend from the time they made *Love Is on the Air (1937)*. Her resemblance to Travis was an ongoing sore point with Sheridan, because in 1936, her first screen test had originally been turned down at Warners because—according to their wisdom at the time—she looked too much like Travis.

But she forgave him and invited him to her home out in San Fernando Valley. He lied to Hayward, telling her he was going mountain hiking that weekend "with some of the boys."

Having emerged from a childhood in Denton, Texas, Carla Lou Sheridan was four years younger than Reagan. After winning a beauty contest, she quit college and headed to Hollywood to pursue a career as an actress, making her film debut in 1934 at age 19.

Going nowhere at Paramount, she migrated to Warner Brothers in 1936, signing a long-term contract with them and changing her name to Ann Sheridan.

Tagged as "The Oomph Girl," a sobriquet she loathed, she became a popular pin-up girl, once receiving 250 marriage proposals from fans in the course of a single week.

When Reagan met her, she was unhappily married to the actor, Edward Norris. "We'll be divorced no later than next year," she confided to Reagan and others of her friends. "The marriage was a mistake."

That Saturday, Reagan drove out to Sheridan's home. They had a late morning swim in a nearby pool and enjoyed barbecued ribs, Texas style, for their lunch. His afternoon, as Reagan would later relate to Powell, was spent in bed with this former beauty queen from the Lone Star State.

Over sunset cocktails, she talked about having worked on the film, *Black Legion*

(1936), with Bogart. "I came right up to him and introduced myself. I said, "'How in the fuck are you, Mr. Humphrey Bogart?' He shot right back at me, 'You wanna feel it and find out?'"

"Bogie told me that what really attracted him to me was that I smoke three packages of cigarettes a day," Sheridan said.

That Monday at lunch, Reagan confided in Powell. "There's something so frank and down to earth about Ann that I'm very attracted to her. She has this come-hither look. What red-blooded American male can resist her? She's luscious," Reagan claimed. "After my weekend with her, I've nicknamed her the Texas Tornado. I've arranged to see her again two nights from now. "That is, unless Susan Hayward hears about it and gets militant. Perhaps you'll take Susan off my hands."

"Imagine having such delicious meat on your plate as Susan," Powell said. "And you want to scrape her off. Enjoy your run of luck while it lasts—and don't hand out any marriage proposals. A man's salad days last only a short while."

When *Cowboy from Brooklyn* was released, it didn't lose money, but didn't attract hordes at the box office either.

On July 14, 1938, *The New York Times* wrote: "To have built a standard length comedy out of an almost piteously frail satirical idea embodied in *Cowboy from Brooklyn* was an engineering achievement equivalent to the reconstruction of a giant diplodocus from a fossilized great toe. The best of the film's comic passages are slapstick, and the best, incidentally, are none too good."

A month after he'd finished work on the film, the director, Lloyd Bacon, called Reagan with news of his upcoming next picture. Entitled *Boy Meets Girl* (1938), it would star James Cagney and Reagan's friend, Pat O'Brien, once again.

When he heard the list of supporting players, he told Bacon, "That might be a problem for me. Not only is Susan Hayward likely to show up on the set, but you've cast two of my girlfriends, Carole Landis and Penny Singleton. How am I supposed to service so many starlets?"

"Listen, pal, at the rate you're going, it's gonna fall off by the time you're forty," Bacon said.

***

The respective fans of Susan Hayward and Ronald Reagan barely noted, or perhaps never realized, that both of them were associated with one of Humphrey Bogart's most unusual *films noir*, *The Amazing Dr. Clitterhouse* (1938). In it, Bogart co-starred with Edward G. Robinson and Claire Trevor. The screenplay was written by John Huston and John Wexley, and the picture was directed by Anatole Litvak, who was (unhappily) married at the time to Miriam Hopkins.

As the respected and "well-connected to society" Dr. Clitterhouse, Robinson is writing a book on the physiological reactions and psycholog-

Scary *Dr. Clitterhouse:* Edward G. Robinson, Claire Trevor, Humphrey Bogart. Bogie hated the film so much, he (unofficially) renamed it "Dr. Clitoris."

ical motivations of criminals, but decides he needs first-hand knowledge. Consequently, he becomes a criminal himself, robbing jewelry from the safes of the rich and famous. He later meets Rocks (as played by Bogart), a gangster and *bona fide* jewel thief who's working with a gang of safecrackers. Before the end of the film, the doctor realizes that he needs a final chapter—one on homicide. He gives Rocks a poisonous drink and studies his reaction as he dies.

On the set, Bogie encountered Reagan, who was complaining about his meager role in the film as a radio announcer. "They're not even letting me show my face in this film—just my voice."

"Would you say that's better than having to show your ass?" Bogie asked. "Listen to me, Reagan, you're a good looking guy—not my type, but good looking enough, I guess, although I prefer men with more kissable tits. I saw a picture of you without your shirt."

"You're kidding me," Reagan said. "I was told you like to put people on."

"You're gonna go to the top," Bogie said. "I've told you this before. You're going to become a bigger star than I could ever hope to be. It'll take a few more Bs for you, then it's Grade A prime rib beef movie roles for you. As for me, with my kisser, I'm stuck in the Bs. Jack Warner has told every director on the lot that I'm not good looking enough for a romantic role. He also considers me a midget. He complains that I'm losing my hair. Then there's the question of my lisp."

"Yes, I was wondering about that," Reagan said. "I was told to stay away from guys who lisp in Hollywood."

"Good advice, kid."

"I also got my report card from Jack Warner," Reagan said. "A little bird told me."

"You mean a certain secretary in Warner's office, the one with the shapely legs."

"Something like that," Reagan said. "Warner thinks I'm nice looking—of course, that's damning with faint praise. He says my best quality is my voice, very friendly. As for my acting, he thinks I'm a bit stiff but okay for B pictures. He thinks I have no comic timing, so I can only do drama. But, and here's the rub, he thinks I have 'no heat' on the screen."

"If you and I did a love scene together, we'd burn up the screen," Bogie said.

"You're such a kidder," Reagan said. "I was warned about you. Fortunately, man-on-man kissing scenes will never be shown on the screen—we can thank God for that."

"As I said, hang in there," Bogie said. "You can play romantic leads throughout the 40s and into the 50s. If you're still around in the 60s—and that's highly unlikely—you'll have to switch to villain roles."

"What about you?" Reagan asked. "Do you still plan to be a villain in the 1960s?"

"No, not me," Bogie said. "When the 60s roll around, I'll be resting comfortably in Forest Lawn."

"I'm going to hang around for two or three more years," Reagan said. "If I don't make it, I'm going home, back to radio."

In the final cut of *The Amazing Dr. Clitterhouse*, moviegoers didn't see Reagan, but they heard his voice as a radio announcer.

It was even worse for Hayward, who lamented to Reagan, "My walk-on part in the film ended up on the cutting room floor."

The Amazing Dr. Clitterhouse earned a profit of only $10,000. *The New York Times* defined it as "sad and aimless."

***

Reagan's eighth film, *Boy Meets Girl (1938),* was directed by Lloyd Bacon, who had just helmed him in *Cowboy from Brooklyn.* Although it had been successful as a play on Broadway, *Boy Meets Girl* had a rough launch as a film.

Two famous comedians, Olsen and Johnson, were slated to play the leads, but other commitments made each of them unavailable. Ultimately, the roles went instead to James Cagney, who had been absent from Warners for two years as part of a self-imposed exile, and Pat O'Brien, the star of Reagan's previous film.

The notoriously independent Cagney refused to accept George Abbott as director, but agreed to Bacon. Marion Davies, mistress of William Randolph Hearst, was cast in the female lead. She made so many demands on Bacon—ranging from her dressing room to what she defined as a poorly written script,

Reagan appears in *Boy Meets Girl* with Marie Windsor, who played a pregnant waitress, and with Dick Foran (*right*) who was cast as a celluloid cowboy.

that Bacon finally, in exasperation, replaced her with Marie Wilson.

In supporting roles was a talented cast, including Ralph Bellamy, Frank McHugh, and Dick Foran. Once again, Reagan was cast in a very minor role as a radio announcer. "If this keeps up, I'll be playing a radio announcer broadcasting the Second Coming," he said.

The film was actually a spoof of movie studio manias and politics, and Reagan was surprised that Jack Warner had personally approved the script. Bellamy plays a studio honcho with some subtle similarities to Warner himself.

The plot revolves around the studio's most visible cowboy star (Foran), who needs a hit movie to revive his fast-descending career. The two writers, as portrayed by Cagney and O'Brien, invent a plot that involves the infant son of a waitress in the studio's executive dining room, as played by Wilson. Subsequently, the baby, "Happy," becomes a star. Foran, partnered with the toddler, goes on to make a series of hit pictures.

Other than the cute baby, the picture clearly belonged to Cagney, who frequently jumps around like a crazed man, with O'Brien rather gloomily playing his more restrained counterpart. Reagan's role as a radio announcer, which appears only at the end of the picture, was so minor, he wasn't even given a screen credit.

Reagan arrived on the set several days before he was needed, mainly as a means of bonding with O'Brien and Cagney, his Irish Mafia friends. Though back on the lot, Cagney was still feuding with Jack Warner, frequently denouncing him in obscene Yiddish. Cagney was now the "bad boy" on the lot, known for his leftist politics and his court battle with Warners. The studio had violated his contract by billing another star over his name. Cagney also wanted to limit his films to four a year and to have a say in his choice of scripts. Reagan and O'Brien offered their support as friends, but each of them was terrified by the thought of antagonizing Warners the way Cagney had done.

Cast in a bit part, Penny Singleton sought Reagan out, chastising him for not calling her after the brief fling they'd had together. He used a standardized excuse, "I've been too busy." He also reminded her that she was a married woman.

"But my marriage is on the rocks," she told him. "I'm on the verge of divorcing that lout. We've each agreed to date other people."

"So," he said. "It's a typical Hollywood marriage."

She was very excited at a recent turn in her career. She had just signed for roles in a series of Blondie pictures with Arthur Lake, based on Chic Young's popular comic strip of Dagwood and Blondie.

Reagan resumed his affair with Singleton, visiting her dressing room on several occasions. She shared the space with Wilson, with whom she had an agreement. A red ribbon tied to the doorknob meant that Singleton was occupied. Wilson waited out the liaison by sipping cups of coffee in the commissary.

After one of their trysts, Singleton "introduced" Reagan to Carole Landis, who had been cast in an uncredited role as a commissary cashier. At the time of their "re-introduction," Landis and Reagan didn't give the slightest clue that they even knew each other as David knew Bathsheba.

Penny Singleton as Blondie Bumstead was cast opposite Arthur Lake in a series of Blondie movies based on the comic strip characters.

She'd later tell the future President, "Every picture is Blondie does this, Blondie does that. Why not you and me starring in *Blondie Fucks Reagan*?"

On a night off from Susan Hayward, Reagan visited Landis at her apartment. He later told O'Brien, "My lovemaking usually cheers her up, but she's very depressed these days."

Landis had already appeared in bit parts in an amazing twenty-one films. "Nobody ever talks about my talent," she had lamented to Reagan. "Rumors keep circulating that I'm sleeping my way to the top, and not just with Busby Berkeley. The rumors are so persistent, and so vicious, that a powerful group of studio wives are protesting to their husbands about using me in future pictures. Even worse, a blind item appeared recently in a gossip column about how 'a little blonde starlet is trading sex for fame.'"

"Don't let these women get to you," Reagan had urged. "I bet most of these studio wives began as starlets screwing their way to the top, or at least into a marriage license."

The following night, he met with Hayward, who also seemed far more concerned with her career than in lovemaking. "If Jack Warner would give me a decent role, I would succeed. I'm pulling in $150 a week mainly by posing for publicity shots and doing some one-line walk-ons. I've heard rumors that Warners is not planning to renew my contract. My option comes up in a few weeks."

Years later, Hayward's close friend, Martin Rackin, said, "Jack Warner used to boast that one actor on his ass was worth two on his feet, and he kept them that way. Susan was very shy and very insecure back then. She really got kicked around, and I think it got to her. After the Warner treatment, she never let down her guard. It made her a loner, and she never changed."

Hayward had told Reagan that she'd recently made a movie, *Men Are Such Fools* (1938), starring Wayne Morris, Priscilla Lane, and Humphrey Bogart. Then, with a veiled ferocity, she told him, "On the set, I met one of the bit players, this trampy blonde, Carole Landis. I told her that if she met up with you, she's to look on with admiration, but that she's not to touch."

On hearing that, Reagan opted not to tell her that he'd spent the previous evening in Landis' apartment.

In the final moments of *Boy Meets Girl,* Reagan appears as a radio announcer on a red carpet welcoming stars to a premiere. Known only to insiders, his scene was conceived as a subtly mocking satire of Errol Flynn.

For months, Flynn had been urging Warners to film a script he had (partially) written, *The White Rajah.* In the final moments of *Boy Meets Girl,* Reagan announces the arrival of stars at the premiere of a (non-existent) *The White Rajah,* with the subtle implication that it starred Errol Flynn.

Boy Meets Girl opened across the country on August 27, 1938, and—mainly because of Cagney's involvement—it attracted a respectable box office. Many fans went to see it, thinking—in spite of its title—that it was a gangster movie, perhaps a saga about Bonnie and Clyde.

***

Reagan was a last minute choice to play the young attorney in *Girls on Probation* (1938). Originally, it had been intended to star John Garfield, a newcomer to Warners.

A potboiling and pedestrian programmer, *Girls on Probation,* by anyone's estimation, was a Grade B flick with limp direction and a weak script by Crane Wilbur. Running only an hour, it didn't get much publicity or even a lot of notice at the time of its release in 1938. It made a "retro comeback," however, in the early 1980s when Reagan was president.

In spite of the picture's weakness, Reagan was glad to be cast as its male lead. Jane Bryan got first billing.

[In the film, Bryan plays the innocent young Connie Heath, who is falsely accused of theft by the witchy Gloria Adams (Susan Hayward). At a party, Gloria publicly accuses Connie of stealing her evening gown and Connie is arrested. As it turns out, the gown was illegally "borrowed" by Connie's bad-girl friend, Hilda (Sheila Bromley) from a local dry-cleaning shop.

Connie is subsequently tried for grand larceny, but a handsome, bright prosecuting attorney (Reagan) gets her off on probation. Later, based on a series of spectacularly foolish choices, Connie again hooks up with Hilda, once again gets into trouble, once again is publicly shamed, and once again is arrested.

She is ultimately rescued by Mr. Do-Right (i.e., Reagan), who gets her off again, this time because he's fallen in love with her.]

Reagan did more than fall in love with Bryan on screen. He fell for her off-screen, too, developing another case of *Leadinglady-itis.* But his luck in seducing his leading ladies had run out. She told him she liked him a lot, and although she wanted to be his

In the luridly titled *Girls on Probation,* Reagan, as a crusading district attorney, came down with another case of "Leadinglady-itis" when he met Jane Bryan, whom the script reveals is really a "nice girl," despite her embarrassing problems with the law.

Onscreen, her character revealed how much she appreciated his help in explaining things to the judge.

Offscreen, based partly on the hysterical jealousy she faced from Susan Hayward, she told him, "Let's confine our friendship to a handshake."

friend, "Let's keep it sealed with a friendly handshake and not a kiss."

A child of Hollywood, Bryan was a beautiful young woman being groomed for stardom at Warners during the late 1930s. She had already appeared in some memorable films, including *Marked Woman* (1937), with Bette Davis and Humphrey Bogart; *Kid Galahad* (1937), with Edward G. Robinson, Humphrey Bogart, and Davis, and *Each Dawn I Die* (1939), with James Cagney and George Raft.

Watching each of these movies, Reagan had been drawn to Bryan's winsome, fresh face, an innocent contrast to the cynicism of gangster-playing stars like Robinson, Raft, and Bogart. Bryan, even though she was only ten years younger than Davis, would play her daughter in four separate films. In two additional films, she would be cast as her sister.

Jane Bryan, a good girl on probation, dependent (in the film, at least) on the loving ministrations of a prosecuting district attorney (i.e., Ronald Reagan).

Girls on Probation would be the first of three films Bryan would appear in with Reagan, the others being *Brother Rat* and *Brother Rat and Baby.*

Bryan had become an almost inseparable *protégée* of Davis, the star. Based on their extremely close friendship, and based on Davis' penchant for demanding that she be cast in films with her, rumors spread of a lesbian love affair. Bryan appeared with her mentor in *The Sisters* (1938), and played her daughter in *The Old Maid* (1939).

Unusually generous for Davis, she predicted stardom for Bryan, suggesting that she was on the dawn of becoming one of the great stars of Hollywood. "Of all the younger actresses around, Jane, to me, is the most likely to develop amazingly." *[Oddly, in retrospect, Bryan's lackluster and unspectacular performances seem unworthy of such lavish praise from Warners' reigning diva.]*

Reagan's ego was soothed when he learned the reason for Bryan's rejection of his sexual overtures. At the time, she was secretly dating Justin Dart, "the Boy Wonder" of the pharmaceuticals industry. They would marry in 1939, the union lasting until his death in 1984.

In 1945, he'd take over the floundering Rexall drugstore chain, building it into a food and consumer products conglomerate which later merged with Kraft Foods.

Cast as the bad girl of *Girls on Probation,* Sheila Bromley wasn't as cozy with Reagan as she'd been when they'd made *Accidents Will Happen.* She resented the excessive attention he was paying to Bryan.

As a future budding politician, Reagan was always gracious to the supporting players in each of his films, and especially to their directors. He enjoyed his time with the Pennsylvania-born director of *Girls on Probation*, William C. McGann. In just one decade, beginning in 1930, he would helm fifty-two movies.

One evening, as previously arranged, Reagan picked up Hayward at her cheap bungalow court, where she was living with her brother, sister, and mother in a sleazy apartment with broken bed springs, a tattered sofa, and splintered chairs.

He took her to dinner at Chasen's. "At last, I've got a part in *Girls on Probation,* where I at least appear on the screen for ninety seconds, even though I play a bitch. My only problem is that I'm supposed to be a socialite, but with my Brooklynese, I sound more like one of the Dead End Kids than a debutante."

She claimed that whenever she could, she had attended various screenings of

Ronald Colman's *The Prisoner of Zenda* (1937). "He has perfect diction. I listen to it. I've seen the picture so many times I know all his lines. When I get home, in front of the mirror, I stand there and mimick his lines. I'll learn proper English yet."

At Chasen's, he noticed that she had brought a doggie bag. She bagged the entire bread basket and asked for another one. She even scooped up the leftovers on Reagan's plate. Previously, he'd taken her one day to lunch at Schwab's, where she had emptied the contents of their table's sugar bowl into a container she'd carried with her.

"Are things that bad at home?" he asked. "I'm far from rich, but I could lend you some money."

"I'm too proud to accept charity," she answered. "We'll get by."

She was carrying on bravely, always believing that she'd eventually achieve success by working harder. "I have to dream hard, too," she'd told him.

One night when he arrived on her doorstep, she was almost giddy with excitement. She'd just met with director William Keighley, who had cast her as the female lead of an upcoming movie, *Brother Rat*. Wayne Morris and Eddie Albert had been selected as two of the three male leads.

"It takes place in a military school," she told him. "Keighley said you're being considered for the third male lead."

Regrettably, Hayward's enthusiasm lasted for only a few days. Jack Warner had sat through a screening of *Four Daughters,* and had been so excited by the performance of Priscilla Lane that he'd decided to drop Hayward and cast Lane in *Brother Rat* instead. He told executives at Warners, "Priscilla, unlike her sisters, Rosemary and Lola, is headed for bigtime stardom."

Hayward's disappointment increased when Warner screened her brief scene in *Girls on Probation*. He immediately realized that she had not yet overcome her Brooklynese, a dialect that he considered inappropriate for her role in *Brother Rat*. Consequently, he ordered his staff not to renew her contract with Warners. "The bitch speaks pure Flatbush," he claimed.

Reagan spent almost an entire weekend trying to rescue Hayward from the depths of her despair. She was almost inconsolable. At one point, he feared she might commit suicide.

But by Monday morning, her steely determination had returned. She told him that she was going to hire an agent for herself and storm the gates of Paramount.

***

Carole Landis was among the young wannabees cast as inmates of a women's prison in *Girls on Probation*. A viewer would have to look closely to spot her.

Her affair with Busby Berkeley was winding down. She was last seen in public with him in the spring of 1938, when he took her to a costume party at the Hawaiian Paradise Club.

Her first husband, Irving Wheeler, had arrived on the scene and was trying to extort money from Jack Warner. He was not willing to give him one dollar.

Wheeler had hired a crooked lawyer and filed a lawsuit. A headline in *The Hollywood Reporter* read—BUSBY BERKELEY NAMED IN $250,000 LOVE THEFT SUIT. Although they'd only lived together for less than a month, way back in 1934, Wheeler's lawsuit charged that Berkeley had stolen his wife from him.

Berkeley's lawyer counter-filed with a demurrer that the case be thrown out of court, which it eventually was. But ultimately, the scandal hurt everyone's career, including Berkeley's. In the aftermath of the public shame the lawsuit caused, Berkeley's original choreography for the Scarecrow in MGM's *The Wizard of Oz* was scrapped.

During the course of the lawsuit, Landis made a powerful ally. Attracted to her beauty, Gregson (Greg) Bautzer, a handsome Hollywood attorney, had represented her.

Bautzer was known for seducing some of the stellar lights of Hollywood, which, over the years, would include Joan Crawford, Dorothy Lamour, Ginger Rogers, Paulette Goddard, Zsa Zsa Gabor, Jayne Mansfield, Ann Miller, and Lana Turner. In time, he would become the lover of Jane Wyman, too.

During Landis' turmoil and public humiliation, Reagan offered her whatever emotional support he could, but he rejected her proposal of marriage, fearing that she was far too controversial. On the other hand, she hoped that a stable marriage to Reagan would bring a stop to the barrage of bad publicity that had virtually earmarked her as a Hollywood whore.

Reagan allegedly informed his Irish Mafia friends, including Pat O'Brien and James Cagney, that "Carole is a girl you sleep with, but don't bring home to your mother."

Late one night, Landis called him in tears. "Jack Warner is not renewing my contract. I'm adrift."

***

The upcoming director of *Brother Rat,* William Keighley, called Reagan and invited him to lunch at the Warners' commissary. "The role of the third cadet is yours," he promised. "At lunch, I'll introduce you to Jane Wyman. I've cast her as your girlfriend in the movie."

Brother Rat had opened on Broadway on December 16, 1936, and had run for 577 performances. Eddie Albert as Bing Edwards would repeat his stage role on the screen, but the parts of the other

Two views of Carole Landis: *(left)* Coochey-coo? and *(right) Haute* fashion, circa 1942.

Looking as regal as an empress, the former prostitute, Carole Landis, one of the blonde bombshells of World War II, is seen on a date with ladies' man, Greg Bautzer, future lover of Jane Wyman.

Landis pleaded with Reagan to marry her, but he was turned off by her lifestyle, her emotional instablity, and her notorious past.

134

two male stars would be recast. Frank Albertson had starred as Bill Randolph in the play, but the movie role went to Wayne Morris. And although one of America's most outstanding actors, José Ferrer, had played Dan Crawford on Broadway, Reagan was assigned the role for the movie version.

When Reagan came together for the first time with Jane, he found her reasonably attractive, but no more so than any number of starlets he'd previously dated. In the beginning, she seemed more attracted to him than he was to her.

Her divorce from the dress peddler, Myron Futterman, would not be finalized until December of that year (1938). Consequently, Reagan still regarded her as a married woman and at first kept his distance. She signaled her willingness to date him, but "he took his god damn time getting around to it," she later complained to director Keighley, who had originally introduced them at lunch.

Privately, Reagan confided to the director, "I'm still hot for another Jane, Jane Bryan, who you've also cast in this movie. But her heart belongs to another."

The plot of *Brother Rat* ordained that Wayne Morris would romance Priscilla Lane, that Eddie Albert would be happily though somewhat dysfunctionally married to Jane Bryan; and that Reagan and Jane would fall passionately in love.

Brother Rat [the nickname used for each other by military cadets] had been on Broadway, staged by George Abbott. It had starred Albert in a breakthrough role, although his part had been considerably reduced in the film script written by Jerry Wald and Richard Macaulay. The setting for the film and its rowdy cadets was the Virginia Military Institute, defined as the West Point of the South.

Whereas Reagan was the more conservative cadet, the one who always seemed to be going "along for the ride," Morris' role was that of "someone who can get into more shakes than you can shake a shako at." Albert played the slow-thinking married cadet "who plugs along to accomplish things the hard way."

After sitting through the first rushes, watching the high-energy characters developed by Morris and Albert explode onto the screen, Reagan told Keighley, "I think I've gotten lost in the sandwich."

Reagan later recalled, "I was just a foil for Wayne and Eddie. I was this conservative roomie going along with Wayne's hare-brained shenanigans, but rather grudgingly."

To add some spark to his character, Reagan risks trouble by romancing the academy's stern Commandant's daughter, played by Jane as the bespectacled Claire. She's intent on becoming a bacteriologist. In one scene, as a means of making herself more alluring to Reagan, she removes her horn-rims and tosses them onto a cot. Her direction was to appear as "cutely alluring," and she does. The director noted the on-screen sexual chemistry between Jane and Reagan, which had not been fulfilled off screen.

Whereas George Abbott on Broadway was an impresario known for his fast-paced action on stage, Keighley, was known through his film work for cadenced melodramas, such as *Each Dawn I Die*. As a film, in comparison with the Broadway play, the action moved more slowly.

Fraternal Rats: *(left to right)* Ronald Reagan, Wayne Morris, and Eddie Albert.

For the first time, Reagan revealed on screen that he had a talent for comedy. Partly as a result of his work in *Brother Rat*, many other comedic roles lay in his future in the 1940s and 50s.

During the course of the comedy, Albert learns that his wife is pregnant, which threatens his ability to graduate. *[According to the plot premises, cadets are forbidden to marry while attending the academy.]*

Lane told Reagan that her part had been intended for Olivia de Havilland, who rejected it, and that his role had originally been cast with Jeffrey Lynn. For Lynn, an even bigger disappointment had involved losing the role of Ashley Wilkes to Leslie Howard in David O. Selznick's *Gone With the Wind*. "I lost out on Ashley, too," Reagan told Lane.

Priscilla Lane, the female star of the movie, was doing more than just sipping a shared soda with Wayne Morris *(left)* and Reagan.

[Handsome and tall, a schoolteacher from Massachusetts prior to his migration to Hollywood, Jeffrey Lynn was interpreted as the front runner for the role of Ashley Wilkes, partly because of his physical resemblance to the character, as defined by Margaret Mitchell in her novel. Lynn was used extensively during David O. Selznick's "Search for Scarlett," playing Ashley in the screen tests for many of the actresses who tried out, sometimes disastrously, for the part. Selznick eventually cast the more experienced British actor Leslie Howard, much to Lynn's disappointment.]

Although Reagan's sexual liaison with Lane had ended, he noticed that Morris was still visiting her dressing room. "Wayne and I are just rehearsing our roles," she jokingly told Reagan.

Unaware of Reagan's previous links to Lane, Jane complained to her, "Ronnie seems to prefer hanging out with his frat brothers who visit him on the set. I don't see him dating any girls."

"Honey," Lane said. "You just go on believing that fantasy."

Years would pass before Reagan learned that Jane was also carrying on an affair with Morris, one that would stretch on and off way into her future.

As was his custom, Reagan bonded with the rest of the cast. "Everybody liked him," Jane said.

He discovered that Albert hailed from Illinois like he did. "I was born with the name Heimberger, but I had to change it because of the anti-German prejudice." He told Reagan that he never planned to be an actor, and that instead, his original mission involved "conquering Wall Street." The crash of 1929 put an end to that.

Albert followed his stockbroking gig by accepting whatever job he could. "For a time, I was a man on the high-flying trapeze," he said. "Before becoming an actor, I even sang in a night club."

Eddie Albert, decades before his fame as the male lead in the TV sitcom *Green Acres*, in a broadcast studio for one of the networks during the 1940s.

Long before Reagan and Jane conquered the medium of television, Albert got there first. As early as 1936, in the "prehistoric" days of early TV, Albert became one of the first television actors, performing live in RCA's first television broadcast.

He also became a friend of Jane's, although he was decades away from interpreting the starring role of Carlton Travis on TV's *Falcon Crest* with her.

[Albert's life came to an end in 2005. Like Reagan, he suffered from Alzheimer's disease during his final days. He became one of four Illinois-born "nonagenarians" of Hollywood's Golden Age who lived until the 21st century. The other three included Buddy Ebsen, Karl Malden, and Reagan himself.]

***

Before meeting Reagan, Jane had dyed her hair platinum. "When I changed my hair, I actually changed my entire personality," she told him. Before I became a blonde, I had tried everything to get a start as an actress, but no one gave me a tumble." She paused. "So to speak."

When they met, she was only twenty-one, Reagan six years her senior. But in spite of his frequent seductions of starlets, the twice-married Jane was a decade or so ahead of him in life experience. At the time of her meeting with Reagan, she was emerging from the ruins of her disastrous marriage to Myron Futterman.

Reagan viewed her as markedly different from the archetypal image of an "over-painted, oversexed Hollywood glamour girl." As he relayed to Keighley. "She is not a brassy blonde like Joan Blondell, or a gal with a scandalous reputation like Carole Landis, so far as I know. She doesn't seem to have the fire and fury of a Susan Hayward, who is determined to get ahead at any cost."

As he confessed to Keighley, "When Jane trains those wide-set brown eyes on me, with that easygoing smile, I'm intrigued. It's not exactly love at first sight. But unlike some of the girls I'm dating, she's respectable enough to bring home to mother."

In addition to being attracted to Reagan's good looks and athletic body, she had other reasons to like him, as she once expressed in an interview with a reporter. "Until I met Ronnie, I viewed all men with suspicion. I felt men were just out to use women. But I was drawn to Ronnie because of his sunny personality. He seemed genuinely and spontaneously nice. He is also very kind, and I wasn't used to that."

"Neither of us was a star at the time," she recalled. "He was not a matinée idol like Errol Flynn, and I was no overdressed glamour girl."

In *Brother Rat,* Reagan breaks the rule, "Men don't make passes at girls who wear glasses," by wooing the commandant's daughter (Wyman), seated next to him.

She developed a crush on Reagan before he got around to her. Perhaps it was because she played "a brainy dame" in *Brother Rat.*

But when the cast and crew went to San Diego for location shooting, they took long walks along the moonlit beach at Coronado, and love, or something like it, blossomed.

like Kay Francis. We were just two kids climbing the ladder to what we hoped would be stardom for the both of us. Before I met him, I was the dancing fool, known as 'the Hey Hey Girl.' My nights were spent at the Cocoanut Grove or the Troc, wearing a big hat with a long cigarette holder coming out of my face."

"Ronnie asked me why I didn't do more daytime activities like horseback riding or playing golf," she said. "He also told me he was an expert swimmer, and invited me to go swimming with him. I needn't be afraid of the water, he told me, bragging that he had rescued 77 people when he'd been a young lifeguard in Illinois."

She told how Warners' publicity had arranged for Reagan to take her, along with Ann Sheridan, ice skating to pose for shots for the newspapers. "Both Ronnie and I already knew Ann, and she was a fine girl. I couldn't skate worth a damn, and I fell on my ass. He rescued me and stood me up for the photos. After that, we met often at the rink, and he actually taught me figure skating."

It was years before Jane became aware that Reagan's friendship with Sheridan extended way beyond a kiss on the cheek.

On his first formal date with Jane, he took her to the premiere of *Second Fiddle* (1939), starring the Norwegian ice-skating queen, Sonja Henie, and Tyrone Power.

Reagan wanted Jane Wyman to give up smoke-filled nightclubs and devote more time to outdoor sports and to him.

Shown above, in this carefully pre-arranged publicity photo, he teaches her to skate.

"He was a refreshing change of pace for me,' Jane told Lane. "I'm accustomed to men putting the make on me the first time out. He seemed like he's from a more innocent time, a Midwestern boy on a date with his college sweetheart. He never made a pass at me. At the end of the evening, he gave me a kiss on the cheek, and told me he respected me as a nice girl."

"He lectured me on a whole range of subjects," she said. "He's very smart and seems devoted to his parents. He supports them, you know."

"Because of all the abuse I've suffered in my life, I'm filled with resentments toward people. But I found him the very opposite. Mentally, he seems very healthy to me, although I'm sure he's got a darker side. Perhaps his pleasant façade is merely that. After midnight, he probably becomes a serial killer."

"I seriously doubt that," Lane said.

Lane told Keighley, "I think Ronnie is falling for Jane, but he plans to take his time. He's having too much fun being a much sought-after Hollywood bachelor. There are a lot of starlets at Warners who want him to fuck them. He's got a few steadies. Susan Hayward is a regular, Ann Sheridan a sometimes thing. I think at this point in his life, he wants to keep his options open. Unless he gets a gal pregnant, I don't think he'll want to settle down."

Once or twice a week, he took Jane dancing at his favorite night spot, the Grace Hayes Lodge. They frequented the place enough to adopt a favorite song, "Deep Purple," as a symbol of their shared affections. Sometimes, they double dated with Perc Westmore, Warner's expert makeup artist, and his actress wife, Gloria Dickson.

Morris took notice of the burgeoning relationship between Jane and Reagan. "I got the feeling those two couldn't wait to make love on camera. They were annoyed that the scriptwriters didn't have more love scenes for them. I saw an affair developing. I decided to give Reagan a break and cool down my affair with Jane. I didn't plan to give her up, not by a long shot, but I'd slip around behind his back and see her less frequently. She was just too turned on by me to give me up completely. I have this affect on women."

In his first memoir, *Where's the Rest of Me?*, Reagan mentioned *Brother Rat* in passing, although he made no mention of Jane. At the time he wrote it, he was married to Nancy Davis, who may have been the book's censor.

He barely concealed his disappointment that Eddie Albert stole the picture he'd made with Jane from both of them. "There is only one discovery in a picture, and it wasn't Jane or me," he claimed.

In its review, *The New York Times* wrote: "The cast of *Brother Rat* doesn't include strong marquee talent, but performances by the various members of the company are adequate."

After *Brother Rat* was wrapped, Reagan and Jane continued dating, although not exclusively. Priscilla Lane said, "It appeared to me that she was chasing after him, but that he was running faster than she was. The two of them eventually got married, but before that happened, two big affairs lay in each of their futures, along with some side action with other parties too. I don't think either of them wanted to retire to a rose-covered cottage to start dumping kids. Both of them hoped to make it big as movie stars. With them, love and marriage had to take second billing to seeing their names on the marquee."

***

Jane Wyman was surprised when she learned that Ray Enright, not her favorite director, had cast Reagan in *Going Places* (1938). At the time, he was unaware that it was a recycling of *Polo Joe,* a film she had made in 1936 opposite comedian Joe E. Brown.

"Jack Warner is certainly getting mileage out of that tired old horse," she told Reagan.

Originally a play by Victor Mapes and William Collier, Sr., the story was first filmed as a silent in 1923 starring Douglas MacLean. In 1929, it was made into a talkie with the very fluttery Edward Everett Horton in the lead.

In its reincarnated, 1938 version, Reagan once again was playing second fiddle to his friend, Dick Powell. The first day the two actors had lunch together, the veteran crooner lamented, "This is the kind of picture I've been trying to avoid."

Scriptwriters Jerry Wald, along with Sig Herzig and Maurice Leo, had been called in to pump new blood into the tired old script, which was enlivened with songs by Johnny Mercer and Harry Warren. *Going Places* produced only one memorable song, "Jeepers Creepers." It was not sung by Powell, but by Louis Armstrong, cast as the groom to the racing horse, Jeepers Creepers. He could race only if he heard that song playing.

In this B-rated flick, the plot was thin, involving a fake identity. Peter Mason (as played by Powell) poses as a famous gentleman jockey as a subterfuge for gaining access to the lavish estate of horse-breeding Colonel Tithering (Thurston Hall), a rich Maryland landowner. Powell is really after the colonel's niece, Ellen, as played by Anita Louise, a stunning blonde beauty in spite of her overbite.

Because he's presumed to be a prize-winning jockey, the colonel demands that

Powell ride Jeepers Creepers in a major race. Friends of the colonel plan to shadow the horse in a truck as it races alongside the track, loudly broadcasting the horse's theme song.

Reagan later said that the only thing he liked about the movie involved working with horses and being attired in natty riding garb. He played the colonel's none-too-bright son.

Part of the movie was shot at Los Angeles' Will Rogers State Park, a popular venue for the horsey set in Hollywood during the 1930s. With his *belle du jour*, Reagan often went to the park on weekends for horseback riding. One weekend, he encountered Walt Disney there. "Stick around, boy," Disney told him. "I might cast you in one of my movies. No, not as Prince Charming. Some other role."

It would be the female stars of *Going Places* that Reagan would remember best.

A pert blonde, the exquisite Anita Louise, born in New York, was one of filmdom's most beautiful, fashionable, and stylish stars. She was also known in Hollywood as a society hostess. Her parties, whose invitations were coveted, were attended by the Tinseltown elite.

Going Places was a comedown for her, as she'd previously appeared in minor roles in such prestigious productions as *A Midsummer Night's Dream* (1935); *The Story of Louis Pasteur* (1935); *Marie Antoinette* (1938) with Norma Shearer; and *The Sisters* (1938) with Bette Davis.

When Reagan met her, her once promising career was winding down. By the 1940s, she'd be reduced to appearing in minor B pictures, acting infrequently until the advent of television. She'd marry film producer Buddy Adler in 1940.

Before that, in the late 1930s, she dated Reagan, considering him as potential husband material except for one major flaw. She told Enright, "Ronnie doesn't have money, and I'm a girl with expensive tastes."

On one occasion, Reagan met Louise's mother. "Never again," he told Enright. "She is the ultimate stage mother from hell. She frankly told me I wasn't good enough for her daughter."

Years later, after he was discharged from the Army, Reagan encountered Louise dining at Chasen's. By then, she'd gone over to Columbia, appearing in such B movies as *Dangerous Blondes* (1943).

She told Reagan, "Those dreams of stardom I shared with you were merely to be dreamed. At best, I'll be a footnote in Hollywood history as one of those pretty ladies from the films of the 1930s."

She later shared her views on Reagan with her childhood friend, Stanley Mills Haggart, a sometimes actor and "leg man" for Hedda Hopper.

"Had I not married Buddy," Louise said. "I might have made something of Reagan. He looked great in the tailor-made tux I purchased for him. I asked him to be the host of several of

Here's Reagan, *Going Places*, torn between two blondes, man-hungry Minna Gombell *(left)* and social-climbing Anita Louise. Both women chased Reagan offscreen.

"If he weren't so poor, I might have made something of him," Louise said at the time.

my parties, introducing him to Hollywood bigwigs—Darryl F. Zanuck, Samuel Goldwyn, even Louis B. Mayer. After all, Jack Warner didn't seem to be doing all that much for him. But Ronnie seemed to prefer low-rent women—Jane Wyman, Susan Hayward, even Ann Sheridan. Had movies not come along, each of those gals would probably be working the truck stops."

During the making of *Going Places,* Reagan was also pursued by "the blonde terror," Minna Gombell, who was nearly two decades his senior.

"I like to chase after women," he told Enright. "I don't like it when they aggressively go after me. Gombell's first movie, *Bad Girl* (1931), must have been autobiographical. Thank god you don't have me doing any love scenes with her. I don't want to turn her on any more than I do. She told me she'd like to taste me, beginning at my earlobes and working her way down to my big toes."

At one point in his later life, Reagan was asked if he'd ever dated Rosella Towne, an Ohio-born actress who also appeared in *Going Places.* He had no memory of who she was and did not recall having ever worked with her. That did not signal that he had signs of his oncoming Alzheimer's disease at the time. He may not have remembered Towne, because her appearances in his films, with one exception, were so minor.

At the time she worked on *Going Places,* she was hoping for a breakthrough role, which came later during the course of that same year. She had been cast as the lead playing the comic strip character Jane Arden in *The Adventures of Jane Arden* (1939). Warners was hoping that the picture would lead to a series of adventure films, the way the cartoon character of Blondie did for Penny Singleton.

After *Going Places,* Towne would appear with Reagan in three more films, all of them in 1939—*Dark Victory, Secret Service of the Air,* and *Code of the Secret Service.* Critics touted her as a future star, but in 1943, following her marriage to Harry Kidman, she disappeared from the screen.

Towne was not featured in any future series based on Jane Arden or anyone else. A future series, however, did get awarded to Reagan, beginning with his next picture, in which he was cast as Secret Service agent Bass Bancroft, a character he'd eventually portray in a total of four films.

Jack Warner had predicted that Reagan—as a Secret Service hero—could have flourished through the production of at least a dozen more films if his movie career hadn't moved in a different direction and had he not entered the Army.

***

Ila Rhodes, a beautiful blonde beauty contest winner from Pasadena, emerges onto the scene to become a mysterious chapter in Reagan's love life. All of his previous biographers, if they knew about Rhodes at all, have misstated her links to him.

The actress aided in obscuring the details of her own biography. At one time, she claimed she was the daughter of a Cherokee Indian chief; at other times that she was the daughter of English aristocrats.

She also misrepresented her age, claiming that she was only twenty-one when she met Reagan, defining his age at the time as thirty. Actually, he was born in 1911 and she had been born in 1914, so her math

Years later, when Rosella Towne was told that Reagan didn't remember her, she lamented, "How quickly they forget!"

141

was off. Adding to the confusion was the fact that at various times during the course of her career, Rhodes billed herself as Rae Corncutt, and once as Rae Cornutt.

Rhodes was cast as Reagan's leading lady in the first of his four serial roles as Brass Bancroft. She would also appear in two more films with him, but in very minor roles.

In 1980, during the course of her marriage to a Brazilian industrialist, she discussed her affair with the press when Reagan was running for president.

She made the claim that she was engaged to him for eight or nine months in 1939. At any rate, it must have given Reagan a busy calendar for romancing, as he was also involved at the time with Ann Sheridan, Jane Wyman, Susan Hayward, and an occasional starlet on the side. As his friend, Pat O'Brien, said. "At Warners, Ronnie was known to have a more fully booked date book than Errol Flynn, if such a thing were possible."

Many of Reagan's friends, including Dick Powell, Joan Blondell, O'Brien, and co-stars John Litel and Eddie Foy, Jr., confirm that Rhodes showed them an engagement ring allegedly given to her by Reagan.

He did not meet Rhodes, as was his custom, when she was first announced as his leading lady. Instead, Blondell introduced Rhodes to Reagan when he came to visit O'Brien and herself when they were starring in a movie, *Off the Record* (1939). Rhodes appeared uncredited as a telephone operator in this film.

"Those two lovebirds really took to each other, and Ronnie was seen leaving the studio with her at five o'clock that afternoon," Blondell said. "What happened next, they'll have to tell you."

From the day of their first meeting, Reagan began an affair with the young beauty. But he was never seen in public with her, particularly at places where his romance would be reported to Jane or Hayward. Rhodes admitted that he never took her to Chasen's, or to any such posh dining venue.

"We ate at hot dog stands or at hamburger joints, and drank at taverns up the coast—you know, the kind with sawdust on the floor," Rhodes said. "We slipped away for a weekend in Palm Springs. We also went to this little beach house Pat O'Brien rented near Laguna Beach."

Blondell and others said that Rhodes had a "wild, wild reputation." One author claimed that she introduced Reagan to "sexual decadence." Other starlets reported that as a lover, Reagan was strictly "a missionary position type seducer."

Rhodes was known as a woman "who went all the way." In an interview, Rhodes said, "Ronnie was tall and attractive, very cute. I didn't have an antidote to ward off my attraction for him. Of course, he had a hectic schedule."

She might have been referring to all the B movies he was making, but she could also have been aware of his ongoing affair with Hayward or his "heavy dating" of Jane. How he managed to be engaged to Rhodes while seeing these other

The Pride of Pasadena: Ila Rhodes was a pretty blonde actress, but a very minor one.

As she later admitted—and her claim appears to be true—"Ronnie fell in love with me, and we were engaged for eight or nine months until I learned that he'd been seeing other women."

women has never been adequately explained.

Noel Smith, who later directed Rhodes and Reagan in *Secret Service of the Air,* said, "Ila practically lived in Ronnie's dressing room when they weren't due on the set. They even took their lunch there instead of going to the commissary."

It seemed that Reagan fell under her spell. "I don't know exactly what she was doing to him, but Ronnie just couldn't get enough of it," Smith said. "In those days, most men had to go to a whorehouse to get the services she was rumored to be performing on him."

He knew that a marriage to Rhodes, a woman with a dubious reputation, might jeopardize his standing at the studio. At one point, he went to Jack Warner to see if he would have any objection to his marrying her.

During the course of their private conversation, as Reagan later revealed to O'Brien, Warner admitted that he, too, had enjoyed the charms of Reagan's bride-to-be. But then he denounced her, claiming that Reagan's marriage to her would destroy a promising film career. Allegedly, he told Reagan, "You're a clean cut American boy. At least that's how we're promoting you. Marriage to the whore of Warners will ruin your name. You don't want to get messed up with a woman like that. Call off that god damn engagement—or else!!

It appeared that after his meeting with Warner, Reagan broke off his engagement to Rhodes, although he might have held out a promise of marriage at some future date. But he did not abandon her sexually, as he continued to see her on and off when she appeared in other films with him.

Blondell befriended her and tried to smooth over her rejection from Reagan. "Jack Warner has him by the balls," Blondell told her. "He controls all contract players."

One day after work, Blondell drove her to the Brown Derby for drinks. Over her second cocktail, Rhodes confessed, "I liberated Ronnie sexually. Apparently, he's never let himself go with a woman before. Even though he's been screwing Warners starlets, he still is incredibly naïve about sex. Or at least he was. A lot of guys I sleep with like to have me strap on a dildo. When I tried that with Ronnie, he almost went into a panic. He'd never heard of such a thing, although it is a common feature in all the whorehouses of Los Angeles."

Five months later, when Blondell ran into Rhodes on the Warners lot, the young beauty seemed depressed. "From leading lady, I've dropped down to appearing on the screen uncredited…you know, receptionist, telephone operator. I'll soon be leaving Hollywood, as I've planned another future for myself."

"And what might that be?" Blondell asked.

"While I'm young and beautiful, I'm going to marry some very rich man, preferably one with a private plane, three homes, a bank vault filled with stock certificates and bonds, and a man who has a tendency not to be stingy with diamonds."

"Good luck, kid," Blondell said.

***

In 1939—a year that has been cited as the most glorious, in terms of film production, in the history of entertainment—Reagan pioneered the first in a series of forgettable B films focusing on the adventures of a worker in the Secret Service.

That same year, other much more notable films were also being produced, and greeted with huge acclaim: Judy Garland was filming *The Wizard of Oz;* Vivien Leigh and Clark Gable were playing Scarlett and Rhett in *Gone With the Wind;* James Stewart was in *Mr. Smith Goes to Washington;* Laurence Olivier as Heathcliff was suffering through *Wuthering Heights;* Bette Davis was going blind in *Dark Victory;* and John Wayne became a big star in *Stagecoach.*

Conceived as Warners' programmers, the Bancroft series of adventure films were snappy, fast-paced, and action packed, complete with car chases, aerial stunts (often from the studio's stock footage library), train wrecks, and fistfights, some quite violent. The young, virile, clean cut Reagan, in the third year of his Warners contract, played an ex-Navy pilot turned commercial transport aviator, who is recruited by the Secret Service.

Released in 1939, *Secret Service of the Air* was the first time Reagan was cast as Brass Bancroft. The scriptwriter, Raymond Schrock, was asked, "Why the name of Brass?"

He responded. "Men in the audience will get it. Haven't you heard of brass balls?"

"I'll be competing with Flash Gordon and the Lone Ranger for the boys who attend Saturday matinees," Reagan said. "They don't want to see romantic mush. They want action, and I'll give it to them. I'll do my own stunts."

The 61-minute film was based very loosely on the memoirs of W.H. Moran, the former chief of the U.S. Secret Service. Moran had been hired at $250 a week as a consultant, but most of his job involved generating publicity for the film. The scriptwriter had to be inventive, because much of Moran's work for the government was classified as top secret.

The original villains in the film were supposed to be Nazis, who, under Hitler in real life, were soon to invade Poland, an act that ignited World War II in September of 1939.

[Ironically, during the course of the next two years, Joseph Breen of the censorship office ordered American film studios not to identify Nazis as evil or as wrongdoers in their films because of the neutrality policy of the United States in effect at the time. That ruling, however, did not pertain to Asians (read that as "Japanese") who could, without restriction, be depicted as the bad guys.

Any attempt on the part of the U.S. censorship office to treat the Nazis deferentially ended abruptly in December of 1941 with the entry of the Americans into World War II, as sparked by the bombing of Pearl Harbor. Nazis could, and have been, identified as bad guys in the huge majority of American films ever since.]

In the film, Reagan goes undercover to infiltrate a gang of spies. He poses as a counterfeiter to gain entrance to the illegal cabal. The villains are operating an airborne smuggling ring conceived as a means of bringing hostile aliens into the United States.

Despite his emotional involvement with the notorious starlet, Ila Rhodes, Warners publicity set out to promote a squeaky clean image of Reagan as a new hero in the movies. A statement claimed, "Ronald Reagan, both in appearance and personality, is the representative of all that is admirable in young American manhood. There is nothing pretty boy about him. Virility is his outstanding characteristic."

The mention of "pretty boy" was a veiled dig at Robert Taylor, the resident pretty boy at MGM. Ironically, Taylor was

Reagan, the Fighting Irish, as Secret Service Agent Brass Bancroft, balls his fists to confront the enemy

one of Reagan's closest friends, a relationship so close that his girlfriend, Barbara Stanwyck, once accused her bisexual beau of having a crush on Reagan.

"I don't want to be a candidate for glamour roles," Reagan told the press. "I don't care to have my hair curled." To promote his macho image, he was photographed working out with Mushy Callahan, the former junior welterweight boxing champion.

Warners assigned a Californian, Noel M. Smith, to direct the picture. He had helmed *Tooties and Tamales,* his first film, back in 1919, and would go on to direct 125 movies between then and 1952.

On being introduced to Smith, Reagan asked, "When do I fight? And whom?"

Smith later recalled, "Within an hour, my star had five skinned knuckles, a bruised knee, and a lump half the size of an egg on his head."

On the second week of the shoot, an actor in a minor role fired a blank .38 caliber cartridge too close to Reagan's ear, puncturing his ear drum. The damage couldn't be repaired, and he suffered a loss of hearing in that ear for the rest of his life.

Deep into the shoot, Reagan had another accident when, clad in his flying outfit, he stepped in front of a studio wind tunnel. As his parachute became unraveled, he was dragged by the hurricane-force winds across the railroad tracks of the props department and hurled against a wire fence. After the wind machines were shut down, he was rescued by two studio grips. An ambulance arrived and he was rushed to a hospital where he was examined. Doctors found no injuries, but he spent the night there and was released to recover at home that weekend before reporting back to work the following Monday morning.

Producer Bryan Foy had lined up an impressive supporting cast, including John Litel, James Stephenson, Rosella Towne, and Foy, Jr. "I've cast Ila Rhodes as your leading lady, although she's inexperienced," Bryan said. "She's the only one in the cast I'm taking a chance on. If she doesn't go over in this film, she's going to be reduced to uncredited role in programmers."

The role of Saxby, Reagan's boss at the Secret Service, was interpreted by veteran actor John Litel. The Wisconsin-born actor had enlisted in the French Army during World War II and had been decorated for his bravery. Reagan thought he was ideal for the role.

A Warner's contract player, Litel would appear in 200 films, most often as a hard-nosed cop or as a district attorney. He not only would make another Brass Bancroft films with Reagan, but would also appear in his classic, *Knute Rockne—All American.*

Dapper James Stephenson played the villain, Jim Cameron. Born in Yorkshire, England, the son of a chemist, Stephenson had been a stage actor in his native country until coming to the United States in 1937 at the age of 48. Jack Warner thought he'd be ideal cast as either an urbane villain or a disgraced gentleman.

Eddie Foy, Jr. played Bancroft's genial sidekick, Gabby. He and Reagan bonded and became close friends for years.

Eddie was introduced to show business in vaudeville as part of a family act, "The Seven Little

Robert Taylor *(depicted above)* was Reagan's best friend, but his occasional effeminacies were something that Reagan, in the promotion of his own career, wanted desperately to avoid.

Foys." He later branched out on his own, making his debut on Broadway in 1929 in *Show Girl*. In the 1940s, he would appear with Judy Canova in four films. She always played a hillbilly yokel, or a country bumpkin. One film had them battling Nazis.

Reagan interpreted Eddie as a genuine trouper, and he served as Reagan's "lookout" during filming, so he wouldn't be caught with Rhodes if Jane or Hayward arrived unexpectedly on the set.

Bancroft's dialogue, which Reagan was forced to deliver, sounded at times like something that tough-guy Edward G. Robinson might have said on screen.

John Litel *(right)* played the role of Saxby, Reagan's tough-as-nails boss at the Secret Service.

"He's a number one stool pigeon. Framing me so I'll get sent to Alcatraz. He called me a squealer. I'm not taking that from anybody."

In the film's most gruesome scene, the pilot, in his cockpit, pushes a stick on his control panel. The floor of the aircraft's passenger compartment suddenly opens for a view of earth thousands of feet below. The aliens are thus hurled to a squashy death.

This scene and others brought protests from the censors at the Joseph Breen office. It was suggested that the script be altered so that the captured criminals would be punished but not executed. Breen also wanted all references to opium smuggling eliminated. Additionally, a scene revolving around a café brawl was defined as "too violent a rough and tumble," and clipped from the final cut.

At the end of the movie, Reagan battles the villain in the cockpit of the airplane, as it plunges to the ground. This, although extremely violent, was deemed acceptable by the censorship board.

In response to protests from Jack Warner, Breen exclaimed, "I am the Code! I stand like a man on the seashore, trying to hold back the tides of the ocean with a pitchfork." He also said that he detested what he called "the whorehouse crap of Hollywood. A tide of immorality is engulfing the world." Privately, he blamed Hollywood's sexual indulgences on the Jews who operated most of the Hollywood studios.

The Breen office had even objected to the plot of Reagan's relatively harmless comedy, *Boy Meets Girl*. The censors cited veiled undercurrents of illegitimacy, bigamy, and abortion.

"The movies of one Ronald Reagan often contain nudity and promote promiscuity," Breen charged. "I also object to the treatment of marriage in Reagan films, along with rampant sexual innuendo."

Privately, he maintained a dim opinion of Reagan. "From what I hear, he's a horndog screwing every legs-apart star-

Producer Bryan Foy cast his brother, Eddie Jr., *(depicted above)* as Gabby, Bancroft's genial sidekick. "I liked Eddie a lot," Reagan said. "But he was one of those touchy-feely kind of friends. Couldn't keep his hands off me."

let at Warners."

Warners publicity played up the claim that Reagan as a reserve officer "made many training jumps from planes." A picture of Reagan outfitted as an ace pilot was placed in theater lobbies across the country, along with blowups of Charles Lindbergh, Amelia Earhart, the Wright Brothers, and Eddie Rickenbacker. In truth, Reagan had an absolute terror of flying.

The Secret Service of the Air was part of a political campaign to present the U.S. government in a good light long before the December, 1941, attack on Pearl Harbor. Jack Warner enjoyed a fine working relationship with the War Department, and sent many copies of Reagan's film to officials in Washington.

The pompous, dreaded, very judgmental, and much-despised Joseph Breen, the ferocious overseer of censorship issues associated with the movies.

In a letter to the War Department, Warner maintained that "with this film, we are trying to alert the American people about the dangers of subversive activities from foreign agents. We are also trying to rekindle some old-fashioned American patriotism."

At Warners, Reagan had become used to wearing military duds—a Navy uniform in *Submarine D-1,* even though his scene was cut from the final version; that of a U.S. Cavalry officer in *Sergeant Murphy;* and a military cadet's uniform in *Brother Rat.*

Throughout his varied interpretations of Brass Bancroft, Reagan continued his interest in politics. A left winger, Eddie Albert told him that Hollywood's Communist Party wanted to come the aid of the unemployed, the dispossessed, and the homeless, many of whom had lost their homesteads in the Middle West during the Depression and the Dust Bowl, and had drifted to California.

To the then-liberal Reagan, these goals sounded admirable, and he asked Albert if he could join the Communist Party. The chairman of the party, however, rejected Reagan's admission form, defining him as a flake and asserting that his political opinions changed every twenty minutes.

***

At long last, Reagan was cast in an A-list film, a soap opera tearjerker, *Dark Victory* (1939), a vehicle for Bette Davis. He hated his role of Alec Hamm, a repressed homosexual. He was fifth in billing, earning $1,258 for his work on the film, as opposed to the $35,000 paid to the film's female star.

There is evidence from Hal B. Wallis, the film's producer, that Reagan asked him to play the lead role of the brain surgeon, Dr. Frederick Steele. That role, however, went to George Brent, marking his eighth film with Davis.

Spencer Tracy was the first choice for the role if MGM would temporarily release him from his contract with them for a short-term stint with Warners. But after reading the script, Tracy turned it down. "This is Bette's picture," he wrote, as part of his rejection.

Basil Rathbone was then tested for the role of the doctor. After watching his own test, Rathbone wrote Jack Warner, "Would you either let me have the test or destroy it yourself?"

[Once again, Reagan would compete with George Brent for a role in yet another Bette Davis film, In This Our Life *(1942), co-starring Olivia de Havilland. Reagan lost the*

role of Craig Fleming to Brent. Perhaps Reagan enjoyed some revenge by continuing to seduce Brent's wife at the time, Ann Sheridan.]

***

As associate producer of *Dark Victory*, Wallis selected David Lewis, the lover of director James Whale, of *Frankenstein* fame.

Born in Colorado in 1903 to Russian Jewish immigrants, Lewis later trained under the "Boy Wonder," of MGM, Irving Thalberg. Originally, Lewis had wanted to be an actor himself, studying in New York under the *grande dame,* Maria Ouspenskaya.

He became known for taking any film script and making it better. Unlike others of Hollywood's closeted homosexuals, Lewis was rather frank about who he was, and did not attempt to camouflage his same-sex cohabitation with Whale. Because of that, Reagan was leary of Lewis' reputation when they met. Lewis shook his hand, but Reagan later complained to Brent that, "David held it far too long."

Although he had never been nominated for an Oscar, the bisexual director, Edmund Goulding, was one of the best directors of so-called women's pictures, competing with gay director George Cukor. Among many other films, Goulding had directed Greta Garbo and John Barrymore in *Grand Hotel* (1932). As regards Goulding's previous exchanges with Bette Davis, he had directed her in a 1937 film, *That Certain Woman,* and in the same year as *Dark Victory*, 1939, he'd helm another critical success for her, *The Old Maid.*

Born in London during the twilight of the Victorian era, Goulding was the son of a butcher. From a lowly beginning, he rose to become not only a great director, but a virtual Renaissance man too—playwright, novelist, screenwriter, singer, and composer.

Goulding was very friendly with Reagan during the first week of filming, almost paying him too much attention. It was obvious to Lewis that Goulding was maneuvering to seduce Reagan. Lewis called that fact to Goulding's attention. "You just want him for yourself, bitch," Goulding said.

"How true!" Lewis admitted.

Jack Warner had allotted only thirty shooting days and a budget of $500,000 for *Dark Victory*. Principal photography began on October 8, 1938.

Dark Victory had flopped on Broadway as a star vehicle for the formidable Tallulah Bankhead. As such, Jack Warner was able to purchase it for Kay Francis for $27,500. In a surprise move, Francis not only turned it down, but sued Warners, like Davis had done previously, to break her contract.

After that, even Bankhead herself was considered for the role. Then, for a brief time, the part belonged to newcomer Gale Page.

During the time David Selznick controlled the rights to the property, Barbara Stanwyck lobbied him to give her the lead. Selznick turned her down, offering the part to Merle Oberon instead.

At one point, Selznick even sent the script to Greta Garbo, but she returned it without reading it. Immersed in plans for *Gone With the Wind,* which was consuming all of his time, Selznick eventually allowed the rights go to Warners.

Films of the 1930s, for the most part, were supposed to

Dark Victory's Associate Producer David Lewis *(depicted above),* lover of James (*Frankenstein*) Whale , was willing to advance Reagan's career, providing he lay on his casting couch.

148

have happy endings. Not *Dark Victory.* The doomed heroine, Judith Traherne, has an incurable brain tumor and dies in the final scene as the world grows black. Davis was cast as a spoiled rich socialite on Long Island, interested in fast cars, beaux, race horses, drinking, and parties. In her early scenes, Davis almost hysterically overacts, but settles more comfortably into the portrayal later on.

Geraldine Fitzgerald, a little known Irish actress, was cast in the sympathetic role of Judith's best friend, Ann. Warners, through Wallis, had signed her to a seven-year contract.

Fitzgerald had been warned to expect "actress warfare" with Davis on the set. But they established a friendship and had mutual respect for each other's very different talents. That same year, Fitzgerald received an Oscar nomination for Best Supporting Actress in her role opposite Laurence Olivier in *Wuthering Heights.*

On the set, Reagan's girlfriend, Ila Rhodes, was heartbroken. Her brief position as his leading lady had come and gone after the release of *Secret Service of the Air.* In *Dark Victory,* she had an uncredited bit part playing a secretary.

Reagan offered her what comfort he could, and that involved making love to her in his dressing room. He was also balancing his ongoing affairs with Susan Hayward and Jane Wyman.

On the set, Reagan sometimes bonded with Humphrey Bogart, who for some strange reason played a horse trainer caring for Davis' stables. Like Reagan, he, too, was supposed to be in love with Judith Treherne. In those days, Reagan and Bogie often discussed their troubles with women.

"Both Susan and Jane seem to have marriage on their minds," Reagan said. "So does Ila Rhodes, that cutie I introduced you to the other day. Only problem is, marriage is about the last thing on my mind."

"Well, if you decide to get married, I'm prepared to divorce Mayo Methot and let you take her off my hands."

"Thanks, but no thanks," Reagan said.

Later, Bogie became less than friendly with Reagan when he heard that he had lobbied for his role as the horse trainer, urging Goulding to give his part of the repressed homosexual to Bogie. "The guy already has the lisp," Reagan had said to the director.

[Two weeks into the shoot, Bogie decided to play one of his practical jokes on his costar.

One hot afternoon, he waited until he saw Reagan heading for the men's room. Reagan was already there, urinating, when Bogie entered. There were eight urinals, but Bogie opted to stand at the one on Reagan's immediate left.

"To get even with the fucker and to frighten the hell out of him, I stared down at his dick," Bogie later said to Goulding. "I leaned over

In this scene from *Dark Victory,* Bette Davis as Judith Traherne was slowly going blind. Her close friend, Alex Hamm (an effete society gadabout portrayed not very convincingly by Reagan) provided sympathy, but not much else.

The script was subtle but clear—to Reagan's horror—that the character he was portraying was that of a frustrated, deeply closeted homosexual.

149

close to him and whispered in his ear. 'I can take care of that thing for you.' Reagan did-n't even finish pissing before he was zipping up and out of the toilet."

Throughout the remainder of his life, and despite overwhelming evidence to the contrary, Reagan always insisted in private that Bogie was a bona fide homosexual.]

Goulding extended an invitation to Reagan and Rhodes for a party at his spacious home. At the time, Reagan was unaware of the exact nature of Goulding's notorious parties, which most often degenerated into orgies. At Goulding's home, a butler showed them into the foyer where Gouldng came out to greet them.

Geraldine Fitzgerald *(left)*, the formidable Bette Davis, and Ronald Reagan as he appeared in his first A-list role, "although I didn't want to play it homo."

To Reagan's surprise, the director was dressed as a stern British nanny holding a wooden paddle. "I'm available tonight to deliver corporal punishment to those who have been naughty."

Almost speechless, Reagan later regained his voice. "I didn't know this was a costume party."

"Don't worry about it, darling," Goulding said. "Clothing is strictly optional. On the screen, I specialize in tasteful, cultured dramas. Off screen, my specialties include promiscuity and voyeurism."

Ushered into a large room, Reagan and Rhodes saw about fifty other guests, male and female, most of them in various stages of dress, mostly undress. Many of the women and men, too, were in their underwear. "You can strip down if you want to," Goulding told Reagan. "I've seen your publicity stills. Everything is casual here."

"No thank you," Reagan said. "We're fine."

He learned from fellow guest David Lewis that he and Rhodes had arrived in time for the orgy. Both Lewis and Goulding had rounded up "handsome hunks" from the various studios, along with beautiful young starlets.

Goulding left the room to check on the evening's "entertainment." Reagan whispered to Rhodes, "Let's have a polite drink and then get the hell out of here."

"C'mon, Ronnie," she said to him in front of Lewis. "Loosen up. The fun is about to begin."

Reagan told her he was leaving, but she said, "I'm staying."

He never really forgave Rhodes for staying behind. It certainly marked the end of their engagement and perhaps their relationship, too. She later reported to him what happened. "Goulding was the master of ceremonies, presiding over a very debauched scene—all combinations, with lots of role playing. At the orgy, Goulding obviously preferred the hunks."

Two days later, Goulding walked into Reagan's dressing room without knocking. The actor was changing for a scene, wearing nothing but a pair of white boxer shorts. He looked uncomfortable in Goulding's presence.

"Sorry you left the party," Goulding told him. "But you can make it up to me." He reached inside Reagan's shorts and fondled his genitals. Reagan immediately yanked his hand away and reached for his pants.

Goulding later told Lewis, "The kid rejected my advances. He's got a pretty good hang, though, but seems to be saving it just for the ladies."

"How unusual for a Hollywood actor," Lewis responded.

After that, Reagan and Goulding began to argue about how he should play the role of Hamm.

In the movie, Reagan had been cast as an alcoholic who, although in love with Judith, might have fitted more comfortably into the bed of Brent. Some latter-day reviewers suggested the role might better have been cast with Lew Ayres; others that either Van Heflin or Robert Walker might have developed the role into an Oscar-winning nomination for Best Supporting Actor of the year.

As Hamm, Reagan was supposed to play an inebriated idle dilettante, a character "full of chatter, as much so as a parrot or a woman."

Moody and tormented, director Edmund Goulding solicited sex from Reagan, but didn't get it.

He also invited him to one of his infamous Hollywood orgies.

When Reagan refused to play the role as a gossipy and—by inference—gay male, Goulding—rather than firing him outright—pared down his part to just a few scenes. In those scenes, Reagan appears as a rather dull and unimaginative man of few words, delivering a performance that's wooden, at best.

The character of Hamm had originally been conceived as "a drunkard, sexually ambiguous waste of a man." Goulding interpreted that to mean "a repressed homosexual."

"Goulding saw my part as a copy of his own earlier life," Reagan later wrote, an obvious reference to Golding's own homosexuality.

"I was playing, he told me, the kind of young man who could dearly love Bette but at the same time, the kind of fellow who could sit in the girls' dressing room dishing the dirt while they continued dressing in front of me."

"I had no trouble seeing him in that role, but for myself, I want to think that if I strolled where the girls are short of clothes, there will be a great scurrying about and taking to cover," he wrote.

"Goulding didn't get what he wanted, whatever the hell that was, and I ended up delivering my lines the way my instinct told me they should be delivered. It was bad."

Most reviewers agreed with Reagan's own assessment of his performance: It was bad.

Goulding later expressed his disappointment in Reagan's acting to Hal Wallis. "He refused to understand the nature of Hamm. He drank because he felt impotent, and he loved Judith because she was unattainable. The character was not necessarily a practicing homosexual, but a man battling his own sexual instinct and tragically losing, escaping to the bottle. Reagan saw only black and white in a character, never gray. He wanted to play good guys, supermachos like Brass Bancroft, the Secret Service agent. I went on and shot the film with him, but I should have fired him."

"Because Reagan refused to cooperate, I cut several possibly good scenes with him," Goulding later said. "It could have been a juicy part."

On the set of *Dark Victory,* Reagan had never been the object of so many sexual advances, some of which came from Bette Davis herself. She was at a turning point in her life, coming to an end of her affairs with Director William Wyler and aviator-film mogul Howard Hughes. She was also divorcing her first husband, Harmon Nelson, Jr.

One afternoon, she invited Reagan to her dressing room and was outrageously flirtatious with him. Finally, when he stubbornly refused to pick up on any of her come-hither signals, she openly invited him to go to bed with her. He politely refused and ex-cused himself. From that point on, she contemptuously referred to him as "little Ronnie Reagan."

If Davis struck out with Reagan, she at least got Brent to seduce her. She had been pursuing him for years. He had just divorced his actress wife, Ruth Chatterton, and was on the market again. Davis' most famous line in *Dark Victory* was "Darling, poor fool, don't you know I'm in love with you?" She delivered that same line in private to him. Their affair would continue even after *Dark Victory* was wrapped. But by the time he married Ann Sheridan, it was all over between them.

Orry-Kelly was selected to design Davis' costumes. For years, the flamboyant gay designer was her foremost costumer, beginning with *The Rich Are Always With Us* (1932), and ending with *A Stolen Life* (1946).

During the shoot, Davis had several feuds with Orry-Kelly over wardrobe. She wanted to show skin, even asking him to design what she called, "my naked dress."

When Reagan saw her in the revealing couture, he whispered to the designer. "Bette could be nude and she wouldn't turn me on."

Orry-Kelly misinterpreted the remark, assuming that Reagan was actually a ho-mosexual. Later, when the designer propositioned him, he learned differently.

After his rejection of Orry-Kelly *[the former lover of Cary Grant]*, Reagan asked Brent, "Are we the only heterosexuals making this movie?"

"I'm a heterosexual," Brent assured him. "I don't know about you. After all, you've been cast as the homo—not me!"

That snappy remark made Reagan dislike Brent even more than he had before. Ever since joining Warner Brothers, he'd felt that those gentlemanly roles assigned to Brent could have been better performed by him.

When *Dark Victory* was released in 1939, it had to compete with some of the great-est films Hollywood ever made. Even so, it drew mobs of fans at the box office. The re-views, however, were mixed. *Time Out London,* years after its release, defined it as "a Rolls Royce of the weepie world."

Reviews of Reagan were sometimes harsh. A critic wrote, "He doesn't do much of anything except guzzle vast quantities of alcohol and generally embarrass himself."

Bogart also didn't fare well as Traherne's horse trainer. A reviewer claimed that he played his role "with a creepy kind of sexuality."

At Oscar time, Davis received a nomination for Best Actress, losing to Vivien Leigh for her role in *Gone With the Wind,* a role Davis had coveted.

After shooting wrapped, Reagan entered a confused period of his life. The women he was involved with seemed to be wanting more of a commitment from him than he was willing to deliver.

After a sleepless night, he rose early one morning to greet the dawn.

He later wrote about his impressions: "I saw my first real California sunrise. It comes up over the rise of the mountains that hedge Hollywood on the East, with the misty clouds radiating all the colors of the rainbow."

Chapter Five

Fiery Susan Hayward

Battles Jane Wyman for Ronald Reagan
During His War with the Dead End Kids

Reagan Complains:
"Too Many Starlets Are Demanding My Services."

Until she met Reagan, Jane was not sports oriented, a nightclub with a drink being her favorite outing. At first, she liked to watch him at play, just to "check out his sexy body."

She later referred to this candid snapshot as "the happiest picture ever taken of Ronnie."

A picnic for two for the budding Warners starlets. They were being defined by the press as "a serious romantic item." Within a few months of this Sunday afternoon outing, they would be hailed as "America's Most Perfect Couple."

Actually, they weren't, but they were in love.

Movie historians cite 1939 as the greatest year in the history of motion pictures. That year, based on the release of *Gone With the Wind,* Scarlett O'Hara stood in the barren gardens of Tara, proclaiming, "As God is my witness, I will never go hungry again."

Starved for participation in A-list pictures, and yearning for good scripts, both Ronald Reagan and Jane Wyman were suffering from a different type of hunger as they rushed from one B-movie to another.

Reagan continued his role as a B-list matinee hero within a programmer series playing Brass Bancroft, Secret Agent. That's when he wasn't hitting the streets with the Dead End Kids or making love onscreen to his leading lady, a lesbian in private life.

Jane had graduated from the chorus line to at least eighth billing, but occasionally, she was awarded a starring role in a very minor film. For her, the highlight of 1939 involved meeting and starring "with the love of my life." The co-participant in that grand passion, however, wasn't Ronald Reagan.

Jack Warner was not pleased with Reagan's lackluster performance with Bette Davis in *Dark Victory.* "If you've got a weak script that none of our big male stars want, give it to Reagan," Warner told producer Bryan Foy. "Also, have him make some more of those Bass Bancroft adventure stories."

"I was proud of some of the B-pictures we made, but a lot of them were pretty poor," Reagan said. "They were movies the studio didn't want good, they wanted 'em Thursday."

Director Noel Smith was tapped once again to direct Reagan as Bass Bancroft in *Code of the Secret Service* (1938). Eddie Foy, Jr., repeating his earlier role, was signed on as his sidekick, Gabby. The female lead, such as it was, went to Rosella Towne.

A future U.S. president as Brass Bancroft, under arrest *(top photo)* and on a secret mission *(bottom).*

Running for only 58 minutes, the plot sends Reagan to a remote section of Mexico on the trail of a coven of counterfeiters using plates stolen from the U.S. Mint. At their headquarters, with the understanding that the paper used in the printing of U.S. currency is unique, the villains are bleaching real dollar bills and printing larger denominations on the same paper. The chief of the bad guys is a colorful, peg-legged character disguising himself as a Catholic priest.

Reagan didn't like any of his dialogue, especially the line, "*Oh, you wanna get tough, huh?*"

An expert horseman, Reagan is filmed jumping onto the back of a stallion and riding at a fast clip into the setting sun. At one point, he hides out in the river, escaping a Mexican posse. He breathes through the tube of a broken reed.

Bobbysoxers in Philadelphia Strip "Sexy Ronnie" Naked.

154

John Litel was not available to repeat his role of Saxby, Bancroft's boss, the part going instead to Joseph King. Reagan found him a bit wooden. A figure in silent films, King acted in 211 movies from 1912 to 1946.

When Reagan saw a screening of *Code of the Secret Service,* he was horrified. The producer, Bryan Foy, agreed with him. Both of them went to Jack Warner and pleaded with him not to release it. After viewing the film, the studio chief agreed.

But later, he retracted his word, releasing it across the coun-

One can only imagine the consequences if the circumstances in this picture had occurred in real life, with Reagan, during his presidency, as a terrorist's hostage. Reagan is tied up on the left, Rosella Towne on the right.

try as a minor programmer. To appease Foy, he agreed not to show it in the Los Angeles area, so as not to embarrass the producer and the actors in their home town.

On a trip back to Dixon, however, Reagan saw that his former favorite movie house was, indeed, showing the film. The ticket taker immediately recognized the hometown boy. "Mr. Reagan," he said. "Welcome home, but you should be ashamed of yourself for making this turkey."

In New York, a reviewer said, "I used to go see Pearl White in *The Perils of Pauline* at the Saturday matinee. Now the screen has a new Pauline facing even greater danger. Pauline is now Ronald Reagan."

After Warner betrayed Foy and Reagan and released the movie, Reagan said, "It was the worst film I ever made. Never has an egg of such dimensions been laid."

[One of Reagan's future security chiefs, Jerry Parr, when he was a child, had a different opinion. He went to see the movie eight times. Afterward, he told his parents, "When I grow up, I'm going to become a member of the Secret Service like Brass Bancroft."

Ironically, he eventually became not only a member of the Secret Service, but was designated as Reagan's Chief of Security. He accompanied Reagan on all his personal appearances, including a 1981 visit to the Hilton Hotel in Washington, where the President gave a speech to the Construction Trades Council.

After he left the hotel, the sound of gunfire cracked the air. As Reagan later wrote, "Jerry Paar grabbed me by the waist and literally hurled me into the back of the limou-

sine. When I landed, I felt a pain in my upper back that was unbelievable. 'Jerry, get off,' I said. 'I think I've broken one of my ribs.'"

Later, in the hospital, the President learned what really happened, as he suffered excruciating pain. He had taken a bullet from the demented John Hinckley, Jr. After ricocheting through his body, the bullet came to a stop about an inch from his heart.

"I began to realize that when Parr

Agent Jerry Parr, *right*, a childhood devotee of the Brass Bancroft series, pushes Ronald Reagan into his limousine during a 1981 assassination attempt in which the president was wounded.

had thrown his body on me, he was gallantly putting his own life on the line to save mine. I felt guilty that I'd chewed him out right after it happened."

Only the week before, Reagan had gone to Ford's Theater and looked up at the flag-draped box where Abraham Lincoln was assassinated.

Hinckley had gone to see Taxi Driver *starring Jodie Foster, and had become mesmerized by her. In his memoirs, Reagan wrote, "Although I have never seen the movie, I'm told there was a scene in it in which there was a shooting; For some reason, Hinckley decided to get a gun and kill someone to demonstrate his love of the actress."]*

***

When director Roy Del Ruth called Jane Wyman to tell her that he'd cast her in his upcoming aviation picture, *Tailspin,* she was mildly surprised to be playing an aviatrix. But when he revealed the formidable lineup of stars, she was not only awed, but a bit intimidated. Never had she faced such an array of stars, headlined by Alice Faye, Constance Bennett, Nancy Kelly, and Joan Davis, along with the former silent screen heartthrob Charles Farrell in the male lead.

Getting sixth billing in the 84-minute film, Jane learned that she would play a woman pilot named "Alabama." The movie was an oddity in that most films of the 1930s featured celluloid versions of only male pilots such as Clark Gable or Spencer Tracy.

According to the plot, Trixie (as played by Faye) takes off from her job as a Hollywood hatcheck girl and joins with another female aviator, Babe Dugan (Joan Davis), to enter a women's air race from Los Angeles to Cleveland. An oil leak causes their plane to crash, but the two women survive to continue with additional airborne adventures.

Trixie's rival, both in the air and for the romantic affections of the male lead, is socialite Gerry Lester (Constance Bennett), the daughter of a steel mogul. After lots of romantic scheming and scraping together the agreements and finances she needs to fly her plane, the optimistic and very perky Trixie eventually wins, although she was aided

by the kindly rich girl, Gerry, who at first fakes engine trouble as a means of letting Trixie win, but who then gets into serious danger when her plane crashes and she is injured.

Warners had lent Jane to 20th Century Fox since it had no immediate role for her. That didn't mean that Jack Warner was pushing her aside. He had taken out an ad in *The Hollywood Reporter,* naming her among his top ten contract players. On that list, only Jane and a New York actor, John Garfield, would ultimately achieve stardom.

While filming, Jane's final divorce papers came through from Myron Futterman. She had only kind words to say about him to the press, ignoring the harsh reality of their actual marriage. "I thought I was doing the right thing at the time," she said. "Myron was a lovely, charming man, but it just didn't work out. I guess I married too young." She defined her marriage to him as her first, ignoring completely her marriage to Eugene Wyman.

Jane Wyman, showcasing the *haute mode* of 1941.

For reasons of her own, she misled Warners' publicity department, asserting that her father, "Ernest Wyman," had died. There had never been such a person. *[Her screen name, Wyman, had derived from her first husband, Eugene Wyman.]*

During the shoot, the producer, Darryl F. Zanuck, with his cliché cigar, showed up on the set. He had come to see both Del Ruth and Faye. He met Jane briefly and said, "Welcome to Fox. Hope it won't be your last visit."

After a brief chat, he wandered over to Del Ruth before spending an hour with Faye. After all, Faye was his most bankable star. Jane had wanted to make a good impression on him, but she was sure he would have forgotten her by tomorrow.

Faye's husband, singer Tony Martin, came onto the set one afternoon. Faye was emoting before the camera. Unlike Zanuck, Martin paid a lot of attention to Jane.

As she'd later tell Joan Davis, "I find him very handsome and oh, so masculine. But I didn't want to interfere in Alice's marriage, although Tony flirted with me outrageously. I don't give that marriage a long life."

Jane was right, as Faye and Martin would divorce in 1940. She'd follow that with a 1941 marriage to Phil Silvers.

On the set, Jane turned down Martin's invitation to slip away for a drink. "He was some sharpie," she told Davis. "Too much hair oil, and I find his singing style a bit bland. He's no Bing Crosby. But I can see why Alice fell for the lug. He's very, very sexy. When

Tail Spin's female cast members, *left to right*: Jane Wyman, Joan Davis, Alice Faye, Constance Bennett, Nancy Kelly, Joan Valerie.

"I found myself lost in this lineup of hot-to-trot dames," Jane said.

he talks to a gal, he stands so close to her he rubs his ample package up against her."

The next day, Faye talked to Jane. "It seems that both of us started out as wise-cracking showgirls in films, but I, at least, have been told by Zanuck to soften my image. One reviewer said I was 'a singing version of Jean Harlow.' As you can see, my hairdresser has given my peroxide blonde hair a more natural look."

"Miss Faye, you look beautiful, and I loved you in *In Old Chicago.*" Jane said.

"Would you believe it, Zanuck initially turned me down for that role? He offered the part to MGM's Harlow, but she died, of course."

"I'm anxious to see you in *Alexander's Ragtime Band,*" Jane said. "With that divine Tyrone Power. I think he is the world's handsomest man."

"I do, too, but he's never given me a tumble. Most days, after work on that picture, Power rushed off with Errol Flynn, who always showed up at five o'clock. The world's second handsomest man made off with the world's first handsomest man. For we ladies, there is no justice."

Three days later, Faye encountered Jane on the set. "Did you hear the latest news? My newest claim to fame. I'm the favorite movie star of Adolf Hitler!"

That same day, Jane chatted with Charles Farrell, the matinee idol of the 1920s. Appearing in more than a dozen films with Janet Gaynor, they were once hailed as "the movies' favorite couple." With nostalgia, he discussed Hollywood in the 20s.

"Did you catch my latest?" he asked her. "I play Shirley Temple's dad in *Just Around the Corner* (1938). Alice has also played Temple's mother. Maybe Alice and I should get married and make the little lollipop brat legitimate."

Jane interpreted Del Ruth as a smooth, competent, director who managed to keep all those screen stars in line, along with a complicated plot that involved aerial competition and frequent wisecracks from both Davis and Jane. Del Ruth was a genuine professional, who, since 1932, had been the second highest-paid director in Hollywood.

Jane was awed by the blonde beauty of Constance Bennett, a New Yorker who was the daughter of famed actor Richard Bennett and the older sister and fellow actress, Joan Bennett. Constance seemed very independent, cultured, and rather candid.

For years, Jane had read about the star in fan magazines, learning that she liked to collect both money and men. One reporter asked her father, "Doesn't Constance know she can't take her money with her?"

Richard had responded, "If she can't take it with her, she won't go."

Everyone in the film industry had an opinion about Constance. Columnist Adela Rogers St. John said, "She has a reputation for attracting other girls' men." Bette Davis cattily remarked, "Her face is her talent. When that drops, there will go her career."

"I'm not quite the female Casanova that rumors have it," Constance told Jane. "In fact, I'm married at the moment. My husband will be arriving soon to take me to lunch, and I'll introduce you."

An hour later, Jane met James Henri Le Bailly de La Falaise, Marquis de La Coudraye, who had *[from 1925 to 1931]* been the third husband of Gloria Swanson. He had won Constance from the arms of her then-lover, Joseph P. Kennedy. Both Constance and Swanson had competed for the love of both Kennedy and the French nobleman.

In her capacity as *Tail Spin's* third lead, Nancy Kelly was just "walking through the picture." That same year, she was also making *Jesse James* (1939), interpreting the role of Tyrone Power's love interest. Emerging from New England, she had been a child actress and model, becoming "the most photographed girl in America" at the age of nine.

Rising from the plains of Minnesota, Joan Davis was a comedic actress who had gotten her start in vaudeville. Jane had lunch with her one afternoon in the commissary. By now, she was used to actresses talking about themselves. Davis revealed that she'd appeared in a picture, *Way Up Thar* (1935) with the then-unknown Roy Rogers. "He told me he would have made a pass at me, but didn't, because I was just too ugly," Davis said.

In her private life, Jane continued to date Reagan, but, as she told Joan Blondell, "He is hardly overcome with passion at the sight of me. He's also dating other starlets, casually playing the field. So am I. When 'God's gift to women' comes along, I'll know who he is at once. Perhaps he's waiting just around the corner."

She told Del Ruth, "When Ronnie goes for a while without calling me, I ring him up and ask him out. He's too polite to refuse such a request from a lady. I do wish he'd show more aggression in pursuing me."

Actually, as Jane would later concede to Louella Parsons, "I am much more concerned with my career than I am chasing after some man,."

For five days, she sat around idly until a call came in from Lewis Seiler. He told her that she would be returning to her home studio at Warners, as he'd cast her in *The Kid from Kokomo* (1939). She learned that her co-star would be Wayne Morris.

"Talk about a man who aggressively pursues women," she said. "He is the master of the forward pass."

***

Left to right: Gale Page, Dick Powell, and Ann Sheridan in *Naughty but Nice*

"This is my swan song to Warner Brothers," Dick Powell said, shaking Reagan's hand and welcoming him to the sound stage of their latest movie, *Naughty But Nice.* "I should be twenty years younger, playing my role."

Director Ray Enright had assembled a cast that, for a B-picture, was considered stellar. It included Reagan's sometimes lover, Ann Sheridan; Maxie ("Slapsie") Rosenbloom; newcomer Gale Page; plus such veteran performers as Helen Broderick, ZaSu Pitts, the ever-reliable Allen Jenkins, and band leader Peter Lind Hayes.

Naughty But Nice was filmed in October of 1938, but Jack Warner was so disappointed with it, he delayed its release until June of 1939.

The plot whirls around Donald Hardwick (as interpreted by Powell), a young and somewhat prim music teacher who comes to New York to try to get his symphony published and to visit

Although his role In *Naughty but Nice* was one of the smallest and least inspired in the film, Reagan managed to look "Presidential."

his colorful Aunt Martha, a role interpreted by Helen Broderick. His other two aunts are played by ZaSu Pitts and Vera Lewis.

When these idiosyncratic aunts appear on camera, they steal the show. Donald is introduced to Linda McKay (Gale Page), a lyric writer, who sees jazz and Big Band potential in Powell's symphonic music and also falls in love with him.

Torch Singer Zelda Manion (Sheridan) vamps the young composer, luring him away, at least temporarily from "nice girl" Linda. Playing the role of Ed Clark, Reagan was cast as an honest music publisher. Linda converts Donald's composition to swing, and the music ends up on *The Hit Parade*.

On the set, Page and Sheridan became friends. Sheridan told Reagan, "Gale and I are just two Cherokee squaws. I was told that Indian blood flows through our veins. Both of us are looking for a brave warrior—and you're it, Big Boy. Gale and I decided you're more Comanche than Cherokee."

Warners' Publicity Department gave Sheridan a major press buildup. No expert herself, *[she was in the process of divorcing Edward Norris at the time]*, she was encouraged to provide women with marriage tips, suggesting that in her pursuit of a happy marriage, a woman should be a good companion—and not just a wife. Posters advertised what was pre-defined as Sheridan's style of attracting men: "Not too much fire, not too much ice, it's best to be just a bit *Naughty But Nice.*"

Sheridan met Reagan in her dressing room for what she called "a very personal reunion." As she later told Page, "I wanted to make sure that all his equipment was still in working order and that Susan Hayward, perhaps in a fit of rage, hadn't snipped it off."

As he left her dressing room, Sheridan told him, "Don't tell Powell, but Jack Warner is giving me top billing. Warner's thinking is that it's better to promote one of his rising contract players than yesterday's news. Powell is on his way out the door."

After Reagan read the script for *Naughty But Nice*, co-written by Jerry Wald and Richard Macaulay, he told Powell, "You're getting a rather tepid send-off from Warner's with this turkey."

"Don't I know it," Powell said. "But let's struggle upward and onward."

Originally entitled *The Professor Steps Out, Naughty But Nice* was a minor musical with songs by Johnny Mercer and Harry Warren.

Reagan was pleased to be working with Powell. He later recalled, "I was one of the thousands who were drawn to this very kind man, and who would think of him as a best friend. Sometimes, our paths took us in different directions, and months would pass without your seeing each other. When we did meet again, it would be as if no interruption had occurred. I cannot recall Dick ever saying an unkind word about anyone."

Years later, in a memoir, Reagan credited one of his fellow cast members, veteran stage actress Helen Broderick, the mother of Oscar-winning actor, Broderick Crawford, of changing his mind about unions. "At first, I was not a union man, until one afternoon when Helen cornered me in the Warners Commissary. She lectured me for an entire hour about the facts of life. After that, I became the most devoted member of the Screen Actors Guild."

Gale Page and Ann Sheridan asked Reagan if he would escort them to hear the act of Peter Lind Hayes,the vaudeville entertainer, songwriter, and occasional actor. He had a small part in their movie.

Up to then, Reagan had not paid much attention to Page, whom he found demure and rather attractive. After the show, Page invited Sheridan and Reagan to her home, where she'd already baked a tray of lasagna.

He was only vaguely familiar with Page's short career. Both of them shared memories of their small contribution to *The Amazing Dr. Clitterhouse* (1938), the picture on which they'd worked with Edward G. Robinson and Humphrey Bogart.

Page's big break had come when she became a member of the "four daughters," three of which were played by the Lane sisters—Priscilla, Rosemary, and Lola—in the highly successful film, *Four Daughters* (1938). The picture had induced Jack Warner to sign Page to three more sequels with the Lane siblings.

Rumors of what happened that night at Page's apartment, where Reagan and Sheridan were guests of the young actress, eventually leaked out. The following Monday morning, Reagan confided in Powell the events of that Saturday night. "After eating, we engaged in a game of strip poker. The gals must have been con artists. They beat hell out of me, and I ended up stripped down to my underwear. After another game, even that came off, my last vestige of modesty."

"This was my first three-way," Reagan confessed, "and it'll be my last!"

The story was too tantalizing for Powell to keep to himself. That night, he told what had happened to his wife, Joan Blondell. She couldn't resist sharing it with her co-stars on the set of *The Kid from Kokomo.* Reagan's friend, Pat O'Brien, found it amusing, but Jane Wyman said she thought it was "disgusting."

On the last day of shooting for *Naughty But Nice,* Page visited Reagan in his dressing room to kiss him goodbye. "You have such a great figure," she told him. "You really should share it with others."

"I do enough of that already," he told her.

Months later, he would find out exactly what she meant by that strange suggestion.

Reviews of *Naughty But Nice* were tepid at best, or scathing at their worst. *Variety* called Sheridan "a slight menace, a mike siren who would break up the songwriting team just to be cut in on Powell's future songs." *Harrison's Reports* criticized "the silly plot and trite dialogue."

Bosley Crowther of *The New York Times* dismissed the film, claiming that it was "staffed by a competent cast of pranksters. This item might be steady fun if it were anything more than a bath of old gags strung together."

Even if Reagan's films were poor, it didn't seem to affect his ever-growing fan mail. Hundreds of women seemed to write letters that were almost love letters in tone. One woman found his voice "…irresistible. I like the way you breathe around words. What a pillow talker you must be."

Every week at least a dozen marriage proposals arrived. Most of them enclosed photographs of their senders in various states of dress, or undress, as the case might be.

Although Reagan's body was widely admired, he also had an eye for the female figure—that is, when he could see it.

Edmund Morris, in his officially sanctioned biography, *Dutch,* related a typical moment when Reagan went to the beach with Jane Wyman and a "friend."

"He must have been under orders not to wear his glasses in public," the friend claimed. "He squinted painfully as he watched her retreating figure go into the water. Then he jabbed at the sides of his eyes, pulling the flesh tight, and stared long and hard through sloed slits. The effect was of almost oriental lechery."

"All this adulation from fans is going to my head," Reagan told Powell. "I find myself walking around with my head in the clouds. But a call from the producer, Mark Hellinger, brought me down to earth with a thud."

The last day at the studio, Reagan went to Hellinger's office to pick up a script of his next movie, *Hell's Kitchen,* a feature he was ordered to make with the Dead End Kids.

"How could Jack Warner throw me into a hellhole with those juvenile delinquents?"

161

Reagan asked. "Unlike Bogie and Cagney, I've been a good boy. I don't cause trouble like Bette Davis. Why was I being singled out for punishment?"

***

Joan Blondell, the female star of *The Kid from Kokomo,* had been working a week on the movie before Jane Wyman reported to work as one of the supporting players. Blondell was there to greet her on the sound stage and invite her to share her dressing room, sparing her from the cramped communal salon reserved for the supporting female players.

Lewis Seiler, who had directed Jane in *He Couldn't Say No,* was also there to welcome her. She had read that he would next be directing Reagan and the Dead End Kids in *Hell's Kitchen.*

Pat O'Brien, the male lead, also greeted Jane. Reagan's close friend was like a father figure to her. In the starring role, O'Brien played Billy Murphy, a fast-talking boxing manager. Blondell was cast as his wily sweetheart, Doris Harvey.

Pat O'Brien and Joan Blondell, the stars of *The Kid from Kokomo.* He was a fast-talking boxing manager sharpie, and she was his wily secretary.

Jane's sometimes lover, Wayne Morris, arrived late on the set that day, since he had not been needed in early scenes. He passionately kissed Jane and invited her to have lunch with him in the Warners' commissary.

At first, he discussed his career woes, complaining about the script by Jerry Wald and Richard Macaulay. "I play this hayseed boxer who won't fight in the ring until he finds his mother who abandoned him on a doorstep as a baby. Incidentally, I think mama posed for that painting of *Whistler's Mother's.* I'm made to look like some sissy mama's boy. I'll be ridiculed like I was when I was a male cheerleader at Los Angeles High School."

"You were a cheerleader?" Jane asked in astonishment. "With your build, I thought you'd have gone out for football."

Usually Morris had a rather carefree personality. But on this day, he appeared worried and a little bit afraid. "I just learned that Warners is not going to renew my contract. Working with Bogie on *The Return of Doctor X* has done me in, along with this present turkey we're making. Bogie himself claimed that our Doctor X is a piece of shit. He's cast as the living dead in search of fresh blood."

"What are you going to do?" she asked.

"I hear Republic, which has combined with Monogram, is searching for a replacement for John Wayne," he said.

"You'd be perfect for John Wayne roles," she said.

I'm going over there to try to convince the brass that I can be their guy as soon as I finish making this cheesy farce."

At the end of the lunch, he saved other important news for last, revealing that he'd just married Leonora Hornblow.

She looked mildly shocked. "I hope the two of you will be very happy," she said, without trying to show any jealousy.

"It's not working out," he said. "We're only two months into the marriage and we're already talking divorce. That brings up the subject of you and me."

She reached for his hand. "Let's put you and me on hold for a while, at least until your divorce comes through. Are you okay with that?"

"Hell no!" he said, flashing anger. "But it's lady's choice. I'll predict something. You and me are going to get back together. You'll miss my kind of loving."

"That may be true," she said. "Do you realize this is our fifth picture together?"

"I'll predict something else," he said. "I bet we'll do five more. Fan magazines claim we make a cute couple, and that you should have gone for me in *Brother Rat* instead of Reagan."

"I must go," she said, rising from the table. "I'm sorry you've run into trouble so early in your marriage."

"You've had at least one or two husbands, so you know how things often don't work out."

"What seems to be the trouble?" she asked. "I know that whatever your problem may be, it's not in the bedroom. You're an artist in the boudoir."

"Of course it's not that," he said. "The bitch objects to my sleeping with other women."

Like Morris, Jane also wasn't pleased with her role in *The Kid from Kokomo.* At one point, she talked to Wald, the screenwriter. "I just wrote a film for your boyfriend, Reagan," he said. "*Naughty But Nice.* If he invites you out on a movie date to see it, turn him down."

She expressed her dissatisfaction with her role in *The Kid from Kokomo* as a girl reporter, the love interest of Morris.

"Eventually, when I'm a big-time producer, I'll bring stories by D.H. Lawrence and Ernest Hemingway to the screen," Wald said. "But for the moment, at least, I'm putting bread on the table."

Blondell's biographer, Matthew Kennedy, wrote: "If Jack Warner wanted to make Blondell happy again, he had a peculiar way of showing it. *The Kid from Kokomo* was so bad, in fact, that Warner more likely wished to bully Joan off the lot by giving her a Skid Row assignment. Predictably, *Kokomo* stunk up theaters for a few days, barely made its cost, then crept away to rightful obscurity."

Blondell, at age thirty-two, saw attention shifting to such younger actresses as Jane and Ann Sheridan. Jane stood with Blondell as she looked out over the empty sound stage at the end of the filming of *The Kid from Kokomo.* "The same fate awaits me one day," she said to Blondell.

"Where's the brass band playing for my send-off?" Blondell asked. She lamented not having campaigned for better roles. "They gave me the roles Carole Lombard turned down. I'll go down in film history as one of the Depression Blondes in movies of the 30s."

A messenger boy interrupted her and handed her an envelope. In front of Jane, she opened it. "It's dated January 7, 1939, my last paycheck from Warners. It totals $2,916.67—and that includes bonuses."

Then she turned to Jane. "Let's get the fuck out of here!"

Kokomo, Indiana, was never as glam as the implications of this photo by *haute* photographer George Hurrell, snapped as a publicity photo of Jane Wyman for her role in *The Kid from Kokomo.*

***

The producers of *Hell's Kitchen,* Bryan Foy (still "King of the Bs") and Mark Hellinger, sent Reagan its script, in which he discovered that once again, he had a disappointing role. It was obvious from the beginning that the picture would be stolen by the Dead End Kids.

"They'll make mince meat out of me," he complained to co-director Lewis Seiler, who had just completed helming *The Kid from Kokomo.*

"I don't think I'll be able to handle the rowdy scenes by myself," Seiler said. "I've called in E. A. Dupont as my co-director. "He's a German who's directed crime stories on film since 1918. He'll keep these unruly boys in line."

The underlying concept for the Dead End Kids had originated on Broadway in 1935 as a play, *Dead End,* which ran for 684 performances based on Sidney Kingsley's grim look at slum life on the Lower East Side of New York City. Producer Samuel Goldwyn had seen the play and decided to film it, paying $165,000 for the rights. In his film version, in starring roles, he cast six of the original Kids from the Broadway play.

During the filming of *Dead End,* the young actors ran wild around the studio, vandalizing and destroying property. At one point, they crashed a delivery truck into a sound stage while a film was actually being shot.

"I'm too old to put up with shit like this," Goldwyn had informed director William Wyler. "I'm selling these jerks' contract to Jack Warner. Let him deal with these aging brats."

The original film, *Dead End* (1937), had starred Sylvia Sidney, Joel McCrea, and Humphrey Bogart.

Before reporting to the set, Reagan placed a call to Bogie to learn about his experiences working with this motley crew. That actor told Reagan, "I did something that rubbed those jerks the wrong way. All of a sudden, all of them descended on me and stripped off all of my clothes, including my underwear. There I stood, jaybird naked, before cast and crew. With one hand covering my privates, I rushed to my dressing room listening to the catcalls and the jeers."

Bogie, in 1938, had also been cast in *Crime School,* with the Dead End Kids playing young hoodlums sentenced to reform school.

"I was miscast in *Crime School* as a do-gooder," Bogie said. "Not a role with my name written on it. Actually, *Crime School* was a rehash of Cagney's 1933 *The Mayor of Hell.* And now, Jack Warner is reworking virtually the same script with you in it. That bastard is sure getting his money's worth out of this old turkey."

Reagan also contacted Cagney, who had only recently filmed *Angels with Dirty Faces*

The Dead End Kids: Hollywood's romanticization of America's urbanized juvenile delinquents. Although movie audiences found them compelling, none of the actors who worked with them did—especially Reagan.

Upper row, left to right: Huntz Hall, Gabriel Dell and Billy Halop. *Bottom row:* Leo Gorcey, Bobby Jordan and Bernard Punsley.

(1938), with the Dead End Kids. It had also starred Bogie and his friends, Pat O'Brien and Ann Sheridan.

"You've got to watch the gang's leader, Leo Gorcey," Cagney warned Reagan. "He tries to throw you off by his constant ad-libbing. One day I snapped. I gave him a stiff arm above his nose and snapped his head back like I was going to break his neck. 'Now listen, punk,' I told him. 'There won't be any more of this god damn nonsense. You're going to do it like Michael Curtiz told you to. Or else...' The next day, the fucking ad-libbing stopped."

Reagan told Seiler, "If Cagney and Bogie each survived working with the Dead End Kids, I guess I can, too."

In *Hell's Kitchen,* Reagan was cast as a do-gooder, playing the role of lawyer Jim Donohue. He gets his uncle, Buck Caesar (Stanley Fields), a paroled convict with money, to make a contribution to the reform school which houses the Dead End Kids.

Regrettably, the school's superintendent, Krispan (Grant Mitchell), is a crook, keeping a double set of financial records. Eventually, as could be expected, the Kids expose Krispan's nefarious deeds, the most horrendous of which involves locking one of the Kids in a deep freeze, where he dies.

In the United Kingdom, because of its violence, the film was given an "H" rating (the equivalent of an "X" rating today).

For the female lead, Margaret Lindsay had been cast as a social worker. Reagan had already escorted her on two studio-sanctioned dates, each involving their attendance at Warners' premieres.

When he heard that Lindsay would play a role in the film, he told Seiler, "I think I'm losing my sex appeal with her. I didn't even rate a good night kiss on her doorstep."

"You're the wrong gender," Seiler told him.

"You mean, she's a lesbian?" Up until that point, Reagan seemed to feel that all lesbians were macho-strutting and butch. His mind had not yet wrapped around the concept of a lipstick lesbian, an archetype exemplified by Lindsay.

During the second week of shooting, it came as a complete shock to Reagan to learn that Seiler had cast Ila Rhodes in a small role in *Hell's Kitchen.* He had broken off his engagement to the actress four months before, and she was bitter toward him.

On the day of his scene with her, both of them were to appear with actors Grant Mitchell and Stanley Fields. For the first time in his life, he faced an actress who denounced him personally. Rhodes came up to him. "You turned out to be a second-rate asshole!"

He said nothing, but waited impatiently for direction from Seiler as a means of getting through the scene. He later told the director, "You didn't do me any favors. Here I am in this picture, facing an irate former girlfriend, pretending to make love to a lesbian on camera, and putting up with the Dead End Kids to boot."

Of all the gang members, Reagan held Huntz Hall, another New Yorker, in the deepest contempt. The son of an Irish immigrant, an air-conditioner repairman, Huntz got his nickname because of his "Teutonic-looking nose." At the

Hell's Kitchen: Reagan with Margaret Lindsay. "She batted for the other team," he said.

age of five, he'd become a performer on radio. In previous films, Hall and Bogie had practically declared war on each other. Bogie had warned Reagan, "Watch out for him."

Huntz maintained a total disdain for Reagan, referring to him as a square. Along with some of the gang members, Hunt plotted to give Reagan a "hot hat." On three separate occasions, he rolled newsprint around a hat, setting it on fire, and then slipping forward and shoving the burning headgear down onto Reagan's head. He would always yell in panic, but remove the burning hat before his hair caught on fire. "The Square was never seriously burned until one day," Hunt recalled years later.

Eventually growing bored with this prank, Hunt devised a devilish deviation on his arsonist theme: One day, as Reagan sat dozing in a director's chair, Hunt slipped up behind him and placed a powerful firecracker under the flimsy canvas of the chair's seat.

Huntz Hall: Bogie defined him as a "god damn psycho."

The firecracker blasted off, setting Reagan's trousers on fire. He screamed in panic as the flames engulfed his clothing.

"That fucking firecracker acted like a stick of dynamite," Huntz said. "Reagan must have jumped ten feet in the air."

As Hall stood laughing, looking like the dopey-looking kid he played on camera, another Dead End Kid, Bernard Punsley, rushed to Reagan's aid.

He smothered out the fire on his trousers and got two grips to carry him to Reagan's dressing room. An ambulance was summoned.

With a pocket knife, Punsley cut away at Reagan's burnt clothing. With a first aid kit, he applied a soothing salve to Reagan's burnt buttocks. When the ambulance and its crew arrived, Punsley told them he was a doctor in training, and rode beside his patient.

Even at the hospital, Punsley insisted on staying in Reagan's room. The actor agreed, because he'd come to his rescue. He visited Reagan every day and seemed to administer to him as if he were Reagan's doctor. He learned that Punsley, who was always reading medical books on the set of *Hell's Kitchen,* planned to become a physician.

Later, when he went into the Army, he received medical training. After the war, he entered the Medical College of the University of Georgia and obtained a degree. In time, he became the Chief of Staff at South Bay Hospital in Redondo Beach, California. When Reagan was Governor of California, he sent a note of thanks for his rescue, years before, along with his congratulations at his successful transition from acting to the medical fields.

In his letter, Reagan jokingly wrote, "You know better than anyone I've met how to deal with a hot-assed actor. Like you, I've changed professions, me going into politics, and you into medicine. You'll probably do better in helping people than I will in my new job."

Years later, Reagan recalled his horrid time working on set with the Dead End Kids. "It was an experience similar to going over Niagara Falls the hard way—upstream. Count-

A future doctor, Bernard Punsley later claimed, and rightly so, "I saved Reagan's ass...and I mean that literally."

166

ing noses and getting them all in one scene was a major chore, but sometimes it was a relief when they did take off and disappear for a few hours. You never knew when a canvas chair would go up in smoke or be blown apart by giant firecrackers they were never without. Having heard lurid tales from other actors, like Bogie and Cagney, I approached my first picture with them as something of a sweat. I barely survived that to find that Jack Warner had cast me in another picture with these hoodlums. They had graduated beyond juvenile delinquents at that point."

***

For her third film role of 1939, Jane Wyman was not thrilled to be cast as Torchy Blane, the girl reporter turned amateur detective. Beginning in 1937, Glenda Farrell, Jane's rival at Warners, had made the role her own in a series of seven movies, including *Smart Blonde* (1936), in which Jane had had a small part.

The first Torchy Blane movie was a box office hit, and Jack Warner ordered that it be developed into a series. It eventually included such installments as *Torchy Gets Her Man* and *Torchy Runs for Mayor*.

After Farrell bowed out of the series, the next Torchy role was awarded to Lola Lane, one of the famous Lane sisters. Lola's picture bombed at the box office, but Warner decided to give the series a final chance by casting Jane as the star of *Torchy Plays With Dynamite*.

The second female lead, that of bad girl Jackie Maguire, went to Shelia Bromley, who had made a film with Reagan. From time to time, Jane chatted briefly with her between takes, appearing pleasantly polite, although she didn't like her co-star. At one point, Bromley told Jane, "I think I'm the only one of Reagan's leading ladies that he didn't seduce. Not that he didn't try."

"How nice that you so bravely held out," Jane snapped, sarcastically.

Bromley's claim about being "a Reagan Virgin" was later disputed by her co-workers.

In the film, Bromley played the girlfriend of the notorious hoodlum, "Denver Eddie," who escapes a police raid, but Bromley is arrested and sent to jail. Torchy gets herself thrown into jail, too, by turning in eleven false alarms. In prison for eleven months, she befriends Maguire. Torchy's plan involves trailing Maguire after both of them are released from prison. The amateur detective rightly thinks Maguire will lead her to Denver Eddie—and so she does.

"By the time I took over the role of Torchy, the series had run out of steam," Jane later recalled. "Noel Smith, the director, wasn't much help to me."

"I watched all of Farrell's previous Torchy films in the Warners' screening room," Jane said. "She played her as a fast-talking, wisecracking, tough-acting broad, but I

In this, the final sequel of the Torchy Blane series, Jane *(right)* replaced Glenda Farrell *(left)*. Farrell had defined the role of a tough, fast-talking blonde, through four previous sequels.

Already out of steam by the time Jane arrived, the series was terminated after her first and final try.

wanted a different interpretation that was more who I was. Farrell's characterization of Torchy was rather annoying. I wanted to play her with more sympathy."

In the Torchy Blane movies that had featured Farrell, her none-too-bright boyfriend had been a detective played by Barton MacLane. Jane ended up with character actor Allen Jenkins, with whom she'd worked before. "I liked Allen," she said, "but I don't think any movie-goer will take us seriously as a romantic couple."

Smith not only helmed Jane in her debut as Torchy, but had also been assigned to her upcoming film, wherein she would also play a detective. At the end of the shoot, he had only praise for Jane. "She always showed up on time, perfectly made up, and with all her lines remembered. She was most cooperative."

"My, she was one good-looking dame, and my crew used to stare at her. Behind her back, they talked to each other about how they wanted to plug her. She'd joke and banter with them, but never give them any action. Frankly, the word back then was that Jane slept only with big-name stars like Henry Fonda or Clark Gable, perhaps an occasional director. But no cameramen, grips, lighting technicians, or messenger boys. Anytime Reagan called, she came running, even though he wasn't a big star."

One hot afternoon, Farrell showed up on the set to see how Jane's interpretation of Torchy was coming along. She and Jane chatted between takes.

"I'm leaving Warners," Farrell said. "Or, more accurately, it's leaving me. I hope I'll find work at Columbia and extend my career. But if I don't, I'll be like Blondell, one of those Depression-era film blondes of the 30s who tried to make Americans forget their troubles."

Jane wished her luck in her future career.

Years later, Jane tried to put a spin on her own B-pictures of the 1930s. "The writing, direction, and overall production values *[of those films]* may not have been much, but they did move fast and got all the action packed into less than an hour. I found that the shortcuts sharpened my timing and gave a razor-edge to my acting style. It was like being trained in an acting school. *[Thanks to them]* I learned how to be a stronger presence on the screen."

Jenkins more or less echoed Jane's sentiments. "The result was a hell of a lot of good pacing, compressed action with not a second wasted, and an overall *root-a-root-toot* effect that, I'm afraid, action films tended to lose when they got too long and careful."

"Of the three women who played Torchy, including Farrell and Lola Lane, Jane was the most attractive in purely physical terms," Jenkins said.

When the *Torchy Plays With Dynamite* came out, movie reviewers compared the three actresses who, over time, had interpreted the character of Torchy Blane. They defined Farrell as "the toughest broad of them all. For pure brass, she wins the prize," or so claimed the *New York Journal-American*. "Lane was more feminine and genial, less sure of herself. Wyman was less brassy, but more in control as Torchy, more her own woman."

For the most part, Jane's reviews were better than those for Lane. Most critics defined Lane as "a ghastly substitute for Glenda Farrell."

One reviewer asked, "Has any movie-goer ever seen Allen Jenkins get the girl until now?"

One of the worst reviews asserted, "If you've seen one Torchy film, you've seen them all. Jane Wyman does all the cutesy tricks she's learned from working in all those Warners' potboilers."

She liked *Variety's* appraisal of her performance best of all. She clipped it out to read it to Reagan on their next date.

"Jane Wyman is new to the title role of the newspaper scribbler and her casting as Torchy Blane is a happy choice. She clicks nicely with Allen Jenkins as her detective sweetheart, and goes through another exciting experience with mobsters. Wyman circumvents any temptation to overact and makes her romance with the detective lieutenant realistic."

"I'm grateful to *Variety* for saying that," Jane told Reagan. "But I didn't think my so-called romance with Allen looked realistic at all. Far from it!"

Torchy Plays With Dynamite had opened across the country as a B-list programmer on a bill that featured an A-list 1939 movie, *Dodge City,* starring the dashing Errol Flynn. Jane was disappointed when her picture flopped. Subsequently, the Torchy Blane series did not survive the 1930s.

Jane did not appear in *Dodge City*, but Warners publicity wanted to send her on a junket with Flynn to Dodge City, Kansas, for its premiere. She was told that the publicity she'd generate would help her career. Other Warners stars included Ann Sheridan and newcomer John Garfield.

Jane, of course, remembered, unfavorably, her one-night stand with the Australian star, Flynn, a major Hollywood seducer. She wondered if she'd be competing with Sheridan for his legendary romantic attentions.

***

One night, Reagan had dinner with his friend and Father Confessor, Pat O'Brien. He told the older actor that although he felt a strong need to become married with children, he did not want to abandon forever his life as a free-wheeling bachelor. He wondered if it were in him to dabble in the best of both worlds, although that would involve betrayal.

Susan Hayward, Jane Wyman, and Ann Sheridan were virtual fixtures in his life. He'd dropped Ila Rhodes, and now, he wanted to find time for two beautiful blondes, Carole Landis and Betty Grable, who had each been phoning him.

As he told Dick Powell over lunch at the Brown Derby, "I may be spreading myself a bit thin, but I think there's enough of me to go around."

When he discussed his dilemma with O'Brien, telling him, "If I accommodated all the starlets calling me, I wouldn't have time to make any movies," Reagan found him less than sympathetic.

"Poor Baby," O'Brien responded. "If only I had that problem. Even my wife turns me down more often than not."

***

On April 1, 1939, at Union Station in Los Angeles, Jane, with three big suitcases stuffed with wardrobe items from Warners, boarded a specially chartered train headed to Dodge City, Kansas, for the premiere of a Technicolor western starring Errol Flynn.

Jane was not in the cast of *Dodge City*. Warner's had commissioned Olivia de Havilland as the female lead. Jane was sent out as a Warners starlet, along with others, to publicize the film, but also to garner publicity for her own burgeoning career.

At the station, she joined some of the other passengers, including Humphrey Bogart, Ann Sheridan, Wayne Morris, John Garfield, De Havilland, Bruce Cabot, and another starlet, Jean Parker.

Sheridan and Jane were shown to their individual compartments by a porter. Jane whispered to her friend, "I wonder what the sleeping arrangements are going to be on this train ride."

"Errol already slept with me during the making of *Dodge City*," Sheridan confessed. "And Garfield and I have just made a thing called *They Made Me a Criminal* (1939). We've been spending some very hot nights together, but there's been absolutely no talk of marriage, which I'm glad about, 'cause I'm just recovering from a divorce. John feels he's got to share his dick with half the females of Hollywood, but he said it took a whole week before he got laid after arriving in Hollywood."

Although Jane wasn't in *Dodge City*, she was invited along on its promo tour.

Above, Olivia de Havilland and Errol Flynn, the featured stars of the picture, get dodgy.

"How tragic for him," Jane said.

"I'm sure Morris will be knocking on the door of your compartment soon," Sheridan said. "And perhaps Errol will throw you one, too."

"Been there, done that," Jane said. "But I could easily handle a second helping from that Tasmanian Devil."

Sheridan was riding the crest of her *Oomph Girl!* publicity buildup. Even though her role as a dance hall hostess was minor, she was nonetheless assigned third billing in *Dodge City*, one of Warners' "big budget" releases for 1939.

"I'm surprised Bogie is along for this trip," Sheridan said. "Maybe he's escaping from that harridan of his, Mayo Methot."

"I saw him slipping some little wren onto the train back at the station," Jane said. "She looked sixteen if she's a day. So I think we won't be seeing much of him."

The train stopped first in Pasadena, where De Havilland got off to report to the MGM sound stages to begin her role as Melanie in *Gone With the Wind*. Jane envied her, having coveted that part for herself.

After that, the train made sixteen stops en route to Dodge City. At each of them, all the actors, including the stars—with the visible exception of Bogie, who didn't seem to care—got off to pose for photos and to sign autographs.

Since Kansas was dry and because many of the stars were heavy drinkers, the prop department at Warners had converted one of the railroad cars into a replica of the hard-drinking bar *["The Gay Lady Saloon"]* that had been featured within the movie.

During the first night of their transit from L.A. to Kansas, Jane awoke after midnight and discovered that the light in her compartment didn't work. She exited from her compartment in search of a night porter. During her search, she spotted a young actor, William Lundigan, emerging from Flynn's compartment. She had already met him, finding him clean cut and good looking.

William Lundigan...Erotically involved with Errol Flynn

Sheridan had told her that Flynn had gotten him a small role in *Dodge City.* That would lead to future roles in Flynn's films, including *Santa Fe Trail,* in which Reagan would co-star.

The following evening, in the Gay Lady Saloon, Jane was surprised at how open Flynn was in flaunting his bisexuality.

Rising from his table at around midnight, he looked at Lundigan. In front of everyone, he said, "Fancy a poke, sport?"

The young actor dutifully rose from his chair and followed Flynn to his compartment.

Jane had expected Wayne Morris to come knocking on her door, but he hadn't. She soon found out why. He was spending his nights with Jean Parker, the Montana beauty, who had been working as a Warners starlet since 1932. Like Jane, she had unsuccessfully auditioned for the role of Melanie in *Gone With the Wind.* Parker had previously appeared with the Barrymores (John, Ethel, and Lionel) and with such performers as George Raft, Katharine Hepburn, and Robert Donat.

She was married to George E. McDonald, the prominent New York socialite and newspaperman, but her marriage was coming to an end, as indicated by her ongoing affair with Morris. Parker would divorce her husband in 1940. Jane viewed Parker as her rival, and managed to avoid her throughout the course of the train ride.

Jane found Garfield, a New York trained actor and "bad boy," immensely attractive and sexually appealing, but dangerous. She was reluctant to get involved with him because of her friendship with Sheridan. But any time Sheridan was not around, Garfield sent Jane "signals."

He told her that Warners had recently completed a survey of movie fans. "Jack said I have a powerful image on the screen, a certain *persona* that's very sexy. He claims I'm unique among actors because I appeal to both genders—I mean, regular guys, and not just the fags, seem to like me."

She assessed his cocky attitude and feared that it would soon catalyze some ongoing feuds with the Warners' brass.

"You know, I'm the obvious replacement for Bogie, and as you probably noticed, he's been avoiding me. I can also play those Edward G. Robinson roles. I find both Bogie and Robinson a bit creepy. You may not know this, but Robinson's a fag. And Bogie has no sex appeal at all. When are you going to let me provide you with one of my samples?"

"Give me a raincheck," Jane said.

***

Late one night, before the Warners train rolled into Kansas, Flynn knocked on the door of Jane's compartment. "How about it, sport?" he asked.

"I thought you'd never ask," she said, ushering him inside.

She offered him a drink, during which time he complained that he had been woefully miscast in *Dodge City.* "No one appreciates my acting. Everybody seems more interested in my thighs."

"That's because you encase them so well in those green tights," she said.

"I'm just a god damn sex symbol to the whole fuck-

Young John Garfield (from: *They Made Me a Criminal*).

171

ing world," he said.

"You should be flattered," she said. "I'm honored that you could include me in your busy schedule."

"Of course, sport," he said. "I adore you. Sheridan and Lundigan are just passing fancies. I really like quality gals like you."

Then he stood up. "Don't you think I should get out of my clothes and show you I'm still *The Perfect Specimen?* I'm sure you saw that movie I made with your buddy, Joan Blondell."

"I did indeed," she said. "But I prefer to see the real thing, not the screen image."

Flynn spent the rest of the night seducing Jane, promising to continue the adventure after they got to Dodge City.

During their final drunken night within the Gay Lady Saloon, "The Boys" gathered on the far side of the car. Jane still hadn't spoken to Big Boy Williams, having never forgiven him for his attack on her. His was the loudest voice, audible during conversations he conducted, respectively, with Alan Hale, Patric Knowles, Lundigan, Flynn, and Bruce Cabot.

Jane and Sheridan sat together at the far end of the railway saloon, in a position that allowed them to clearly overhear every word the men were loudly saying. Their topic was Venus's flytraps, which Jane quickly figured out was a reference to a vagina.

"When I married Lili Damita, her honeypot was so big it could stretch a country mile without tearing an inch," Flynn said.

"Since Bogie isn't here, I confess that I've had his wife, Mayo Methot," Cabot said. "So has Flynn here. So has Knowles. It was the biggest hole I've ever seen. A guy could fall in."

"My dear friend, John Barrymore, described the Venus's Flytrap better than anyone," Flynn said. "He once told me what it was like to fuck Tallulah Bankhead. You shove it in, a journey through the depth of a West Virginia coalmine, until you come to the main saloon and gallery. There, a cabin boy descends with a ladder, ringing a bell, inviting you to go on to the lower depths, if only human skin could stretch that far."

Jane later told Sheridan, "I was afraid to get up and leave. I didn't know what Big Boy would say about me."

When the train finally arrived at Dodge City, the passengers were met with a brass band and a parade. As they were driven through town in open cars, Jane waved to the adoring crowds.

Dodge City was previewed that night in three different movie houses. The film was shown around the clock until dawn, so that the town's entire population could see it if they wanted to.

The first night in Dodge City, Flynn kept his promise and visited Jane's suite. He left at two o'clock that morning, returning to his own suite which he shared with Lundigan.

As Jane told Sheridan over breakfast the next morning, "How could you and I go through the 30s as starlets at Warners without bedding Errol Flynn? If either of us hadn't, we'd be disgraced."

***

One night, when the sands from the desert winds were blowing into Los Angeles, an elated Susan Hayward arrived on Reagan's doorstep. "I'm a star!" she shouted, as she kissed and embraced him. "Perhaps not the biggest star in Hollywood, but I'm on my way."

Her first big break had come when she was cast in Paramount's 1939 remake of

Beau Geste, the original story based on a silent film, released in 1926, that had starred Ronald Colman. In the newer version, three brothers—Gary Cooper, Ray Milland, and Robert Preston—were the stars, with Hayward cast as their love interest and the female lead.

Even though she was broadcasting the news of her big break, Hayward was also aware of its limitations. "I'm the gal who says goodbye to the boys as they set off to war at the beginning of the picture, and I'm the one who's there to welcome them back."

"Congratulations and come on in," he said, taking her wrap. "I've got two steaks on the fire."

"At last my Flatbush accent is gone," she said gleefully. "The director, William Wellman, told me I now sound like a combination of Ronald Colman and Barbara Stanwyck."

Reagan tactfully avoided asking Hayward about her romantic life when she wasn't with him. Rumors were spreading that she and Cooper were engaged in an affair.

As a means of publicizing *Beau Geste,* Paramount had sent her on a splashy publicity tour to her native New York, where she received a lot of personal publicity, including her appearance on the front cover of *The Saturday Evening Post.*

The dream of every Hollywood starlet, Susan Hayward was the belle of the ball in *Beau Geste,* attracting the leering interest of Robert Preston, kneeling at her feet; Gary Cooper, standing guard over her; and Ray Milland, moving in on the right.

"Coop" won the prize in all departments, but later dumped her.

The next day, Reagan lunched with his new friend, Eddie Foy, Jr. During its course, they discussed their upcoming film, *Smashing the Money Ring,* another "Brass Bancroft, Secret Agent" thriller.

"He confided in me," Foy later said. "He told me that he'd never known Susan to be this wild and passionate. But he also expressed an unease about her, as if she were too vital and way too intense. His exact words to me were, 'Susan's a fiery tigress. I have this awful feeling that when she's in bed with me, she's going to sting me like a Black Widow spider after our dirty deed is finished.'"

Three nights later, Reagan entertained a very different, more angry, and more sullen Hayward. Her earlier sense of giddy elation had evaporated. At the end of the filming of *Beau Geste,* Gary Cooper, who seemed to have been afflicted with the same state of *Leadinglady-itis* that usually enveloped Reagan during filmings, had dropped Hayward and moved on to his next conquest.

Not only had Hayward lost Cooper, but those big roles she'd dreamed about had not been forthcoming from Paramount. Once again, she had been cast in two B-pictures. One was the lackluster *Our Leading Citizen (1939),* with Bob Burns, a former radio comic. The other, also from 1939, was *$1,000 a Touchdown,* co-starring Joe E. Brown and Martha Raye, two loud-mouthed troupers facing faltering screen careers.

Hayward did have some news that concerned him. That afternoon, she had had lunch with columnist Louella Parsons, who had asked her to join her in a vaudeville-inspired publicity tour scheduled for November. "She'll have a bevy of beautiful starlets, and she plans to ask you to be the sole male performer going with her on the jaunt."

"Who are the other gals?" he asked.

"She hasn't made up her mind yet, but I know she's going to ask Jane Wyman, that ugly little twat who performed so badly with you in *Brother Rat.* That role should have gone to me. I could have pulled it off."

***

With trepidation, Reagan reported to the Warners studio for his latest film, *The Battle of City Hall [Before its release in 1939, the title was changed to* Angels Wash Their Faces, *the sixth of seven films featuring the Dead End Kids.]* Its director was Ray Enright, who had previously helmed Reagan in the disastrous picture he made with Bogart, *Swing Your Lady,* and also in *Naughty But Nice,* where Reagan played a distant second fiddle to his friend, Dick Powell.

When Reagan shook Enright's hand, he was frank, admitting he wasn't looking forward to appearing once again with the Dead End Kids. He told Enright about the serious burns he had suffered on his buttocks after Huntz Hall had exploded a firecracker under his chair.

Reagan did not condemn all of the Dead End Kids, relaying to Enright the bravery of Bernard Punsley. "This doctor in the making put out the fire and ministered to my burns until the ambulance arrived. I'll always be grateful to him for that."

Jack Warner had ordered the film's title change as a means of cashing in on some of the success of a movie that Warners had released the previous year, *Angels with Dirty Faces,* a picture that had co-starred James Cagney, Ann Sheridan, Bogart, and the Dead End Kids. *Angels Wash Their Faces* was not really a sequel, but Warner hoped to trade off the wide visibility of the original title.

As the son of the District Attorney, (Henry O'Neill), Reagan was not pleased with his role, even though he shared top billing with Sheridan.

Enright told Reagan that he had conferred with his colleague, Michael Curtiz, the jaded survivor of many previous encounters with The Dead End Kids. *[Curtiz had directed* Angels With Dirty Faces *the year before.]* In this heavy Hungarian accent, Curtiz witnessed how the Dead End Kids had thrown a lit firecracker into Bogie's dressing room, and had painted obscene murals on the office walls of various high-placed Warner executives. They had also set off the fire sprinklers in the wardrobe department, ruining thousands of dollars worth of cos-

Reagan with Ann Sheridan in *Angels Wash their Faces.*

tumes.

Finally, as a means of policing the unruly delinquents, Curtiz called in a big ex-football player, Russ Saunders, to enforce security.

As Leo Gorcey later recalled about one of Saunder's disciplinary actions, "Anyone who has ever been hit, point blank—with water from a full-size, high-pressure fire hose can understand why we caused no more trouble."

As reported by Enright, "The first day Reagan encountered Hall on the set, he did something out of character for him. He punched Hall in the nose, giving him a bloody one. After what he did to Reagan on *Hell's Kitchen,* Hall certainly deserved that punch. He picked himself up off the floor and looked like he was going to fight Reagan. But he thought better of it and insulted him instead.

"Forgive me," Hall said to Reagan. "I know you have to keep those lily-white melons smooth and ready to receive the pricks of Errol Flynn and all the other studs at Warners who want to poke you."

Enright claimed that when he heard that, a genuinely furious Reagan looked like he wanted to continue beating up Hall, but turned and walked away instead. From then on, Hall and Reagan made it a point to stay out of each other's way.

Hall procured marijuana for the Dead End Kids. "They're going up in smoke with this Mexican weed," Reagan told Enright.

***

"It's good to work with Ann Sheridan," Reagan told Enright. "She's a great gal." In *Angels Wash Their Faces,* he falls in love with her.

According to Enright, Sheridan seemed to have a soothing influence on Reagan. "When they weren't needed on the set, they spent a lot of time together in his dressing room. Ann was very frank with me about their relationship."

"We're not in love," she told Enright. "But we have great sexual chemistry. If you can find a guy in Hollywood who knows how to fuck, you hold onto him."

For his part, Reagan never discussed his affair with Sheridan. "In spite of his busting Hall in the face, Reagan was a real gentleman," Enright said. "I knew he was dating Wyman at night. I had directed her pictures as well."

Once again, Reagan found himself working not only with Hall and Gorcey, but with Gabriel Dell and Bobby Jordan. He had lunch several times with Punsley. In the film, the character he played ended up badly. Trapped in a tenement fire, he is burned to death.

Punsley introduced Reagan to Frankie Thomas, who played Sheridan's brother. Reagan found him likable and talented, having worked on Broadway since he was eleven. He'd recently appeared in a hit film, *Boys' Town* (1938), starring Spencer Tracy and Mickey Rooney.

Sheridan was cast as the loyal sister of Gabe Ryan (Thomas), who is framed on a charge of arson and sent to prison. His gangland members work to clear his name, and the real arsonist is revealed at the end, as could be predicted.

"Other than being cast with Ann as my leading lady, what made the highlight of the picture for me involved meeting two delightful old broads, Margaret Hamilton and

Margaret Hamilton: Have you ever tasted an unripe persimmon?

175

Marjorie Main," Reagan said.

The same year Reagan met Hamilton, she was also starring as "The Wicked Witch of the West" in *The Wizard of Oz* with Judy Garland. "Thank God the movies had roles for an actress with a sour-apple expression and a beak-like nose. She was a natural to play the greatest female villain in celluloid history. To my surprise, I learned that before she became the terror of all little kids, she'd been a kindergarten teacher and had, for a while, run a nursery school. In the movies, she virtually cornered the market on playing schoolmarms, backfence gossips, spinsters, and acerbic old buzzards. In private, she was one of the nicest ladies I have ever met."

He had seen Hamilton in her role in *These Three,* based on Lillian Hellman's *The Children's Hour,* which had originated as a hit play on Broadway. In the film, Miriam Hopkins and Merle Oberon run a girl's school. A malicious little brat, played by Bonita Granville, spreads lies about them and endangers their livelihood.

"I loved it in the movie when you hauled off and smacked hell out of the little bitch," Reagan told her.

"Speaking of Bonita, here she comes," Hamilton said. "I'll introduce her. She's got a crush on you."

At that point, Reagan had not been informed that Granville was also in their movie. Hamilton later said, "Bonita met Reagan, but he seemed immune to the charms of this sharp-nosed, brazen young woman. Later, Bonita got Mickey Rooney to seduce her in those Andy Hardy films, but Reagan was a holdout. Of course, he had Ann Sheridan. What did he need with Bonita?"

Bonita Granville...a crush on Reagan

Main, who later became famous for her Ma Kettle roles, had appeared in the original Broadway production of *Dead End.* She was asked to repeat her role. In this movie version, she was cast as the mother of gangster Humphrey Bogart. She delivered a classic line, "*Ya yellow dog*!" before slapping hell out of Bogie.

She had heard about the trouble the Dead End Kids had caused Reagan. "If any of these hooligans cause you any more grief, send for me and I'll turn them into sopranos!"

During the final week of the shoot, John Garfield came onto the set to retrieve Sheridan. He was introduced to Reagan, who had been told that he'd accompanied Sheridan and Jane Wyman to Dodge City for that film's premiere.

He informed Reagan that he, along with Sheridan, had been cast as the stars of a new movie, *Castle on the Hudson,* with Reagan's good friend, Pat O'Brien.

When Garfield excused himself to go to the toilet, Reagan said to Sheridan, "My dear lady, I hear you and Garfield are becoming quite an item."

"That's because with Jane and Susan Hayward lusting after you, you're not always

Mom, roasted piglets, and Marjorie Main. She threatened to castrate the Dead End Kids.

available. With you, the line forms on the right."

"You flatter me," Reagan responded.

When she asked about his next picture, he said, "I'm back to playing Secret Agent Brass Bancroft chasing after counterfeiters. I'll end the 30s struggling through another B, heading for oblivion unless something breaks for me soon."

"Maybe Hollywood will get wise and cast us two heartbreakers together in an A-list picture," she said. "I feel it in my bones."

She had spoken like a prophet.

***

Dick Foran called Jane Wyman a "go-to-gal."

After sitting, bored, and watching Jane Wyman emote as Torchy Blane, Jack Warner pulled the plug on the series. To replace it, he immediately ordered the script department to launch a new series about a private woman sleuth that would be fresher and more tantalizing than the stale Glenda Farrell series.

The result involved Jane receiving star billing in *Private Detective,* where she was cast as Myrna ("Jinx") Winslow.

The 57-minute film would be screened as the bottom half of double bills throughout the country, opening at the end of 1939 and playing for a few weeks into 1940 when Europe had gone to war.

Screen writers Raymond Schrock and Earle Snell were hired to concoct a crime drama pitting Jane against her boyfriend detective, a role interpreted by Dick Foran in the part previously played by either Barton MacLane or Allen Jenkins.

Jane had never considered Foran a charismatic leading man. She told Noel Smith, the director of *Private Detective,* "Dick is hardly the type to set a gal's heart fluttering." Later, she re-evaluated him when he arrived on the set looking tall and handsome, a clean-cut all-American type like Ronald Reagan, standing six feet two with thick red hair.

She had always associated Foran with singing cowboy roles, where he had been directed by Smith. Occasionally, he had appeared in such A-list pictures as *The Petrified Forest* (1936), with Bette Davis and Humphrey Bogart, or *The Sisters* (1938), again with Davis. Jane had seen him in *Cowboy from Brooklyn* (1938), in which he had appeared with Reagan.

Although he was married at the time to Ruth Piper Hollingsworth, Foran signaled to Jane that he'd be interested in dating her. He explained, "My marriage is on the rocks, and I'll soon be filing for divorce."

"Welcome to the club," she said.

"If you're lucky, I'll sing my hit recording, 'My Little Buckaroo,' to you, something they featured in my film, *Cherokee Strip* (1937)."

"Thanks, but I'll skip it for the time being," she said.

Foran had nothing but praise for Jane, calling her "a real trouper, a good sport, no temperament, always a pleasure to play with."

In the same year, he'd directed Jane, Smith also helmed Reagan in *Secret Service of the Air.* "I always felt that Smith was the kind of director who wanted to rush through a movie, bringing it in on time and under budget," Jane said. "He didn't believe in giving an actor much guidance. His motto was, 'Show up on time, know your lines, and don't bump into the furniture.'"

The plot of *Private Detective* revolved around Jane, a detective who's involved in an investigation of a divorcée accused of murdering her ex-husband. A child is involved, as is a sleazy lawyer (Morgan Conway).

Jane and her boyfriend, a police officer, cross and criss-cross paths so often they decide to work together as a means of making more progress on the case. Her most dangerous moment occurs when she barely manages to escape carbon monoxide poisoning.

Jane was already a friend of her co-star, Gloria Dickson, who had made her film debut with Lana Turner in the 1937 *They Won't Forget*. She was the wife of Perc Westmore, the leading makeup artist at Warners. The Westmores often double dated with Jane and Reagan.

Gloria Dickson: NOT the luckiest girl in the world.

["There had been such hope for Gloria when she started out at Warners," Jane later recalled. "In 1937, she landed on the covers of several magazines, and featured in such articles as 'The Luckiest Girl in the World.' She wasn't lucky at all. I didn't see much of her after she and Perc divorced in 1941. There were two more husbands before she was burned to death in a fire in her Los Angeles home in 1945."]

As Jane feared, *Private Detective* met with lackluster or bad reviews. *Variety* summed it up like this: "Warners has put the Torchy Blane series into the garage for an overhauling and a repaint job. *Private Detective* has a new finish, but underneath, it's plainly the Torchy formula, with wider cruising range than was the case in the girl reporter series with Glenda Farrell."

When Jack Warner viewed *Private Detective*, he canceled the proposed follow-up installment that would have featured Jane. "Once again, I was back, along with the other starlets, in the Warners cow corral."

***

In the third of the Brass Bancroft Secret Service series, *Smashing the Money Ring* (1939), Reagan once again chased after counterfeiters, except that this time the crooks were already in prison.

The character he was playing had been defined as "an ace treasury operative," on a mission to bust up the ring, which was printing counterfeit money on the prison printing press and shipping it out into circulation by concealing it within bundles of their newspaper, *The Big House Bugle*.

Backed up with footage shot at San Quentin, Bancroft poses as a prison inmate so that he can live among the prisoners and learn how their operation works.

After Reagan read the script, mainly by Raymond Schrock, he knew at once that it was filled with all those prison movie *clichés* from the 1930s. The main villain, "Dice" Matthews, (played by the ratlike actor, Joe Downing), spouts dialogue such as "Don't forget what happens if you sing to the coppers!"

"A line like that might have worked coming from the mouth of George Raft," Reagan said.

"Dice" is feuding with the owner of a gambling ship, the *SS Kismet,* who he claims "double crossed me." When the investor is sent to prison, Dice goes after him with a shiv. But Reagan intervenes and saves his life, although (amazingly) that doesn't alienate him from Dice.

As the plot thickens, Reagan falls for the film's only female character, Peggy, the daughter of the owner of the *SS Kismet.*

Margot Stevenson was cast in the role. This sultry, blonde-haired, and glamorous New Yorker was also a stage and radio actress who was known mainly for her role of Margot Lane opposite Orson Welles in the radio adaptation of *The Shadow.*

The lovely Margot Stevenson.

Stevenson is incidental to the story, and appears mainly because Jack Warner wanted some romance in an otherwise all-male prison movie. On screen there was no chemistry between Reagan and the star. Apparently, there was no off-screen combustion, either. While making the movie, Reagan did not come down with his usual "disease" of "*Leadinglady-itis.*"

Once again, Reagan's friend and confidant, Eddie Foy, Jr., was cast as his goofy sidekick, Gabby.

Foy gave a good reason about why "Ronnie didn't pursue Margot, who was a very sexy broad. When she wasn't working, Jane Wyman was known to pop unexpectedly onto the set."

Reagan in jail!! with Eddie Foy, Jr. in *Smashing the Money Ring.*

Some of Foy's scenes were bizarre and perhaps suggestive. In one segment, he says, "I'll never forget the night I played Little Red Riding Hood aboard the *USS Arizona.* Did they salute me with 26 guns?"

No explanation is given as to why he was referencing this folkloric tale before the rugged seamen sailing the battleship.

Joe King played Reagan's boss, Saxby, although Reagan had wanted the more seasoned John Litel in the part instead.

The director, Terry O. Morse, a Missouri-born film editor since 1927, was new to Reagan. That same year, he was also helming *The Adventures of Jane Arden.* He complained to Reagan that he did not like to direct, "particularly the shitty material I'm assigned." In 1956,

Trigger-happy, and very *Film Noir.* Good Guy Reagan aims a pistol at actor Dick Rich in *Smashing the Money Ring.*

he did have a moment of glory when he directed the Raymond Burr scenes in *Godzilla, King of the Monsters!.*

Smashing the Money Ring was the second worst of the Brass Bancroft films, and

Reagan felt his character would go the way of the already-canceled Torchy Blane detective serials. He also spent many restless nights fearing that Jack Warner would not pick up his option.

He later recalled, "A lot of script changes went on every day. You never knew what the action was or what your lines were until you arrived on the set. Morse was working with a very small budget and a time clock that was ticking. The movie was released, warts and all."

Since the title, *Smashing the Money Ring,* revealed the ending, movie-goers felt no suspense during the 57 minutes the film was unwinding on the screen. "Everything was predictable," Reagan said. "The dialogue was boring, the action lame."

"I made many films in Hollywood I was not proud of," he said. "*Smashing the Money Ring* was one of them."

In a bizarre attempt to promote the movie, Jack Warner ordered that theater lobbies showing the serial be filled with fingerprint booths, WANTED posters, and "crime clue boxes." Patrons were encouraged to drop the names of suspicious neighbors into the boxes. Reagan objected to the promotion, defining it as "a Big Brother Is Watching You" kind of spying.

Reagan also objected to the way that he was being promoted both on and off the screen. Bancroft was defined in promotional materials as "a man with smashing fists when guns aren't handy."

"Reagan off-screen is much different," the publicity department trumpeted. "Don't get out of line around him, or you might get a taste in private of what the villains get on the screen."

Reagan pointedly informed the publicity people, "I'm not a violent person."

In response, one member of the staff said, "Get real! You should thank us for publicizing your testosterone quotient. It worked for Errol Flynn, didn't it?"

***

Jane visits Reagan, who's in prison garb, on the set of his Brass Bancroft movie, *Smashing the Money Ring.*

Jane Wyman embracing Kid Nightingale (John Payne), the "Singing Swinger."

Jane closed out her lackluster film career of the 1930s with yet another programmer, *Kid Nightingale,* co-starring John Payne. Thinking it would be "just another picture to grind out," she ultimately interpreted the experience of making that movie as "life-changing."

180

When she arrived on the set, her plans to marry Ronald Reagan had moved from the back of her brain to its frontal lobes. But, as she told her friend Paulette Goddard, "Life has this funny way of throwing you a curve ball. While dreaming of walking down the aisle with Ronald, along comes John Payne. God has this talent for creating exceptional men."

Since Goddard had never met Payne, Jane expressed her opinion: "He's a Southern gentleman from Virginia raised in an antebellum mansion. He is devastatingly handsome, with a devilish smile and an eye-catching cleft in his chin. He stands six feet four, and he can also sing a love song. Not only that, he exudes sex appeal with his super-wide shoulders and rocklike muscles, enough to make a weak-kneed girl swoon."

"There's just one major drawback," Jane said. "This Greek god is married to that little nobody actress, Anne Shirley. The lucky cow gets to paw those manly inches every night. Imagine waking up in the morning with a nude John Payne in bed with you? God, I detest that creature for snaring John when I want him. He could have his pick of Hollywood goddesses, and he chose Stella Dallas' bitch of an ungrateful daughter."

The devastatingly handsome John Payne and the pert, beautiful blonde, Jane Wyman, fell in love in both real and reel life.

She was referring to the 1937 movie *Stella Dallas,* the tearjerker soap opera that Shirley made with the long-suffering character who played her mother, Barbara Stanwyck.

The thin, silly plot of *Kid Nightingale* focuses on a singing waiter who gets into a fight with some obnoxious diners and knocks them out, for which he is fired. A shady boxing promoter, played by Walter Catlett, witnesses Payne's pugilistic skills and signs him up to become a boxer. "The quick buck artist" bills the character played by Payne (Steve Nelson) as "Kid Nightingale."

As the woman who falls for Payne, Jane, cast as Judy Craig, is a rehearsal pianist and singer.

The notorious "crotch shot" of John Payne from *Kid Nightingale* became an underground favorite of American homosexuals.

As Roddy McDowall recalled, "It did for John what that Betty Grable pinup pose did for her in World War II.

She and Payne get to perform a musical duet. He also sings operatic arias and Tin Pan Alley songs. Because of his studly physique, he attracts hordes of screaming females to his boxing matches, which are rather brief. His manager even hires an orchestra to accompany him, musically, after each of his knockouts.

"I got the role only because your friend, Dick Powell, turned it down as he was making his exit from Warners," Payne told Jane.

The director, George Amy, had a front-row position as he watched Jane fall hard for the seductive charms of Payne. "It was obvious to the whole cast that by the second day, Jane was madly in love," Amy said. "When they weren't due on the set, Jane spent all her time in Payne's dressing room. I didn't think Payne was going to divorce Shirley and marry Jane, although stranger things have happened. Jane was a sweet girl, but I feared she was heading for heartbreak. Like so many of Hollywood's leading men, Payne would probably drop her at the completion of the picture and return home to Shirley and their baby girl."

"Reagan showed up on two occasions," Amy said. "That guy liked to talk. I was known as a film editor more than as a director, and he asked me tons of technical questions, showing me he had a keen mind."

Amy was one of the best film editors in Hollywood, a favorite of other directors such as Howard Hawks and Michael Curtiz. His editing was one of the reasons Warners became known for turning out a steady stream of pictures with fluid style and at a breakneck pace.

Years later, Payne told the press, "When I made *Kid Nightingale* with Jane Wyman, she was so much in love with Reagan that she couldn't wait for our love scenes to end so she could rush to his arms."

Actually, however, in his capacity as a married man who was cheating on his wife, Payne was putting a good spin on his relationship with Jane, hoping to distract reporters from suspicions about his not-very-secret affair with his co-star.

Johnnie Davis *(center figure)* is cheerfully positioned between Reagan *(left)* and John Payne *(right)*. But it was actually Jane coming between the two men.

When Reagan heard about Jane's interest in Payne, he came over to work out with him in the studio gym. "Perhaps he wanted to check out the competition," Davis said.

When Payne was shown this candid shot, he said, "My chest is better developed than Ronnie's, and my legs are more muscular."

Jane wanted to know every scrap of information about Payne she could learn from him. "I was flattered," he told Amy. "No woman had ever shown that much interest in me."

She learned that he had attended a prestigious military school, the Mercersburg Academy, in Pennsylvania. Later, in 1930, he'd studied journalism at Columbia University, earning a living writing pulp fiction—"The bodice ripper type."

He had also studied drama and took voice lessons at Julliard in New York City. "I drifted from odd job to odd job," he said. "At one point, I was a wrestler billed as Alexei Petroff, 'the Savage of the Steppes.' I operated an elevator in a hotel, worked at the switchboard, and served beer to pool hall sharpies when not mopping up their vomit in the men's toilet. I was a male nurse and also a nanny to two unruly brats."

He later sang on the vaudeville stage. There, a talent scout for Samuel Goldwyn spotted him at Broadway's Shubert Theater in 1934. "Once I made it to Hollywood, I was bounced from studio to studio," he said. "I'll soon be leaving Warners and signing with Fox. I don't like the image, but they plan to turn me into a pretty boy to compete on screen with MGM's Robert Taylor."

It was pure speculation, but Amy suspected that one of the reasons Payne so easily strayed with Jane was because he'd heard that his wife was having a torrid affair with John Garfield on the set of the movie they were making, *Saturday's Child,* released in 1940.

His affair with Jane marked the beginning of Payne's roving-eyed conquests of many other screen goddesses, including Alice Faye, Betty Grable, Sonja Henie, Linda Darnell, Gene Tierney, and Susan Hayward.

As their affair quickly deepened, Jane confessed to Goddard, "John and I are in love, but he's not going to leave that dreadful little Shirley thing. He's made that painfully clear to me. But he had a counter-proposal: I couldn't turn that down. I'm crazy for him, and he's agreed to be my back alley lover, even if I marry Ronnie. That way, I can hold onto him. I mean, the sexual chemistry between us is explosive. I decided not to be greedy. If I can't devour the whole pie, I'll settle for a slice of it."

"Go, girl, go," Goddard advised.

"*Kid Nightingale* opened to rather bad reviews. *The New York Times* "yawned" through the picture, but praised Catlett as a "flibbertigibbet pug scout," Harry Burns as a fake singing teacher, and "Porky" Ed Brophy as "a dyspeptic manager."

Kid Nightingale also got a snicker from *Variety*. "The producer must have had his tongue-in-cheek. It's a combination of one film of every kind of pap, hokum, and comedy business that Hollywood has used since Mack Sennett and the Keystone Cops. It's so absolutely silly, it's almost good."

***

In the beginning, Susan Hayward did not view "pretty, pert" Jane Wyman as a romantic threat to her relationship with Reagan. She knew that he'd dated her during the filming of *Brother Rat,* a pattern he had followed with many of his other leading ladies. When his films were completed, so were his affairs, respectively, with these other starlets. At least that's what she had been led to believe.

She had also heard that Jane had divorced some dress manufacturer from New Orleans.

On several occasions, Reagan had told Susan that he always rejected invitations to date married women. "I don't care whether they are in the midst of a divorce or not. Until they get their papers, it's no dice with me."

She had taken him at his word, as he had seemed sincere in his dishonesty. It's true that he rarely dated married women. Jane had been an exception to his usual rule, but there had been others.

If anything, Hayward felt that her greatest competition for Reagan's affections derived from Priscilla Lane, who had been cast as the female lead in *Brother Rat.* Hayward, more or less, had been promised that role, fueling her resentment of Priscilla.

Years later, in her apartment in Fort Lauderdale, Hayward spoke with bitterness about that time in her life. "They called that whore, Priscilla, 'Warners' blonde sweetheart.' She pretended to be a Goodie Two-Shoes, but everyone knew what a slut she really was. She was not only fucking Reagan, but also Bogie, Wayne Morris, Bruce Cabot, Flynn, and for all I know, Edward G. Robinson, except I heard that he was a closeted gay who really preferred boys. Can you imagine that? Little Caesar himself chasing after pretty young boys? That was Hollywood back in those days."

"I remember Reagan as if it were only yesterday," Hayward ranted. "It was Friday night. I had spent the better part of the day working on my makeup and finding the sexiest dress I could wear. He had called me for a date, and I was very excited. I put clean sheets on my bed and stocked my medicine cabinet with his favorite gargle. He told me he had some important news to tell me. I knew what it was: He was going to propose!"

"When the doorbell rang that night, I took one look in my full-length mirror for reassurance. Then I went to the door. There he stood, in a white jacket, his hair slicked back. He smelled like he'd just stepped out of the shower. That was one clean man. I wanted to grab him, pull him inside, and rape him on the spot. But like Bette Davis said in some awful movie, 'I'd love to kiss you, but I just washed my hair.'"

Hayward recalled that he'd kissed her, but gently. She had thought that was because he didn't want to mess up her makeup. "I was in full warpaint, and we were heading for Cocoanut Grove."

"On the drive down, we made only small talk. I knew he was avoiding the subject of marriage. That would come later in the evening. I was almost certain he was carrying an engagement ring in his white jacket."

She remembered that "everything had gone swimmingly that night. He ordered champagne, but I asked for a Scotch to begin the evening. I found myself shaking. I thought a hard drink would steady my nerves."

She claimed that before dinner was over, she was wondering if she should keep her name of Susan Hayward, or else change it in future billings, to Susan Reagan.

"Since very few fans had even heard of Susan Hayward back then, it would have been no big deal. A lot of actors in the 1930s changed their names after appearing in only a couple of pictures."

Over an after dinner drink, Reagan told her that he had "an important secret to share with her."

"I won't get Louella on the phone right away," she said with a smirk. "I mean, she's got to know, sooner than later, but I promise to keep it a secret at least for forty-eight hours."

As she remembered, "He looked quizzically at me."

"You mean, you don't know?" he said. "God, I thought you'd heard the gossip by now. Word travels fast in this town."

"It suddenly occurred to me that Reagan and I were on two different pages. 'You're going to ask me to marry you tonight, and my answer is yes! There! That's out in the open even before you ask me. Us Brooklyn gals like to make it easy for our beaux.'"

Reagan looked startled before blurting out, "You don't understand. I've fallen in love with Jane Wyman. I'm going to ask her to marry me."

Blind with rage, Hayward rose from the table. She took a glass of champagne and tossed it in his face before storming out of the club, causing a scene.

"My tears were falling like a faucet," she said. "I called to the doorman to summon a taxi. When Reagan caught up with me, I hauled off and gave him the slap of his life. Growing up in Flatbush, I knew how to slap a man. He must have felt like he'd been stung by a nest of mad hornets."

Hayward claimed she spent the next ten nights alone, barricaded within her apartment. "Thank God I didn't have to report to the studio. I cried my eyes out. They got all puffy, and I looked like shit. The phone rang several times. I didn't know if it was Reagan or not. Finally, on the eleventh day, I picked up the receiver, expecting it to be either the studio or Reagan. It was neither."

Louella Parsons was on the other end of the line. "Susan, darling, I've been desperate trying to get in touch with you. I want to book you on a nationwide publicity tour. Jane Wyman and Ronald Reagan have already signed up for it."

***

Louella Parsons had rounded up a troupe of starlets, plus Reagan, to accompany her on a coast-to-coast personal appearance tour, a kind of vaudeville act billed as "Parson's Flying Stars." The tour was to last eleven weeks, for which Parsons would be paid $7,500 a week. The columnist allotted $4,200 of that to be divided among her six young subcontractees.

Before leaving Hollywood, she told Hayward that "the stars of the show will be those two lovebirds, Ronnie and Janie." That caused Hayward's face to turn as red as her hair. She confessed to Parsons that she was still carrying a torch for Reagan. "I can't believe any sane man would dump me for that little mouse, Wyman."

Ever the two-faced one, Parsons confidentially claimed that she agreed with Hayward. In contrast, she told Jane how happy she was for her to have snared Reagan.

"There's no way Jane's gonna become a star," the self-styled "Gay Illiterate" told Hayward. "She's not beautiful. She's not talented. Her career will be confined to bit parts, and I think her days before the camera will be very short. She'll probably become a housewife for Ronnie, raising his children."

"That won't be true for

Ronald Reagan with Louella Parsons, getting ready to make headlines on their return visit to Dixon, Illinois.

He knew how to handle "The Most Feared Woman in Tinseltown" better than any other actor.

me," Hayward predicted for herself. "I'm gonna have to build extra shelf space to store my Oscars."

Parsons assured her that she liked an actress with confidence.

When Hayward learned the names of the other starlets in the traveling troupe—Joy Hodges, Arleen Whelan, and June Preisser—she exclaimed, "I am not over-whelmed."

Hodges had scored a success on Broadway in a Rodgers and Hart musical, and had completed a co-starring role in *Little Accident* (1939) for Universal.

Reagan had always been grateful to her for helping him get launched in pictures in the aftermath of his early migration to Hollywood. Their dating had been "harmless," in his words. "No big deal, but we did have a love for each other."

Before she contracted for the tour, Parsons had visited the studios, including MGM, Warners, and 20th Century Fox, asking for suggestions about how to choreograph and promote her vaudeville preview of "The Stars of Tomorrow." As she admitted, "I've always had this soft spot in my heart for Ronnie. He and I share something in common. We both came from Dixon, Illinois."

Reagan was very nervous about having to be in such close intimacy with Hayward so soon after he'd dumped her. But he was delighted that his friend, singer Joy Hodges, was going along.

David Niven had described Parsons as "Short, dumpy, and dowdy, with large brown eyes and a carefully cultivated vagueness." But Reagan liked her, mainly because she was constantly plugging him and his career in her column.

He had, on occasion, been entertained at her home for intimate dinners with her third husband, Dr. Harry Martin, whom Parsons called "Docky." He specialized in treating movie stars who had contracted venereal diseases.

The first time Reagan had dined with the drunken doctor, he had loudly whispered to him, "I've just treated Clark Gable for the clap."

Because Parsons worked for the Hearst newspapers, she had booked her tour of just those cities where her boss, press baron William Randolph Hearst, owned a newspaper. That way, she would be assured of getting favorable reviews for her show. The hard-working starlets, along with Reagan, would be called upon to perform four or five shows a day, usually scheduled as part of the screening, in theaters, of a double feature._

For the big send-off from Los Angeles, and to cash in on free publicity, Parsons lined up major stars to see the troupe off at Union Station. The stars included Deanna Durbin, Sonja Henie, Eleanor Powell, and Hayward's nemesis, Priscilla Lane. Hayward remembered that Jane was furious when Priscilla gave Reagan a passionate kiss on the lips. "Wyman was even more enraged when that nymphomaniacal Norwegian skating star, Sonja Henie, practically lip-locked Reagan," Hayward said.

Jane later complained to Parsons, "I thought

Nymphomaniacal Norwegian Darling of the Nazi hierarchy, and former fuck-buddy of JFK—Sonja Henie the ice queen was going to suck out Ronnie's tongue."

Meanwhile, also as part of their very public departure, Hayward was kissed passionately by a trio of bisexual stars, Errol Flynn, Tyrone Power, and, somewhat less passionately, Fred Astaire. Slipping off afterward to conceal herself from photographers, she wiped her lips, later telling Parsons, "I don't know where those three cocksucking mouths had been the previous night."

Although he wasn't her type, she also accepted a big smack from the reigning box office champ, Mickey Rooney. She heard Parsons chide him for being two years older than his official MGM biography.

"I'll be Andy Hardy forever," Rooney said, "especially if Metro keeps finding these knockout sweethearts like Lana Turner for me."

June Preisser with Mickey Rooney. "Andy Hardy" appears to be resisting her advances on screen. That wasn't the case in private.

Pert, blonde-haired June Preisser showed up at the railroad station to greet Rooney. She had made *Babes in Arms* with him, and he gave her a warm embrace and a "very French kiss," as he called it.

Preisser, with her song-and-dance routines, had more vaudeville talent than any of the other starlets. Most of her acts opened with her "rolling" herself, like a tire, across the stage, using her hands and feet to imitate the rolling motion of a wheel.

Capitalizing on her skills as an acrobat, this Southern Belle from New Orleans would soon appear with Rooney and Judy Garland in *Strike Up the Band* (1940).

Another member of Louella's touring brigade was Arleen Whelan, born in Salt Lake City. During her twenty-year career, which began in 1937, she would make two dozen films, starting with Robert Louis Stevenson's *Kidnapped.* She broke into movies after one of 20th Century Fox's directors, H. Bruce Humberstone, received a manicure from her.

When Hayward met Whelan, she later confided to Parsons, "I thought redheads like me are supposed to flame. I'm on fire. Whelan can't light a candle to me. That red hair of hers is probably dyed."

To pacify her, Parsons privately agreed, although publicly, she tried to portray herself as a neutral and benificent monarch throughout all the backstage knife-stabbing to come.

After a tryout in Santa Barbara, the troupe opened at RKO's Golden Gate Theater in San Francisco after the audience had snoozed through a Jean Hersholt movie, *Meet Dr. Christian.* The date of that premiere was November 15, 1939.

Parson's 70-minute stage performance featured dance, music, comedy, and references to recent Hollywood gossip. On stage, her role involved sitting behind a desk, watching the hopefuls perform in front of her, while imperiously trying to figure out which of the "youngsters," as she called them, deserved a mention in her column. As corny as this was, audiences in the late 1930s "ate it up," Parsons gleefully reported.

Whelan recalled that Hayward usually stalked out onto the stage "like a red-haired panther. She planted her feet firmly, as if she owned the god damn theater and then she'd shout, 'Anyone here from Brooklyn?' Wherever we played, there was always a rowdy bunch from Brooklyn, or so it seemed."

187

The highlight of the show was a comedy sketch between Reagan and Hayward.

Hodges recalled seeing them perform. "Hayward put fantastic zeal into her performance. She was the least-known member of the troupe, but stood out the most. She came out on stage looking stunning in a blue velvet dress with all that flame-red hair."

"For her sketch with Reagan, she at one point 'stage stabs' him, but his head keeps bobbing up. Then she slugs him repeatedly. I don't mean a stage slug, but a down-and-out, fist-smashing attack. I don't know how Ronnie stood it."

From the beginning, Jane stood in the wings watching as Hayward pummeled her groom-to-be. She later complained to Parsons. "She is slapping him so hard just to make me mad. If she keeps this up, she's going to injure him. She's getting even with him for dropping her in favor of me."

Parsons later said, "Ronnie rolled with the punches and at no point did he complain of Susan's attacks. After the tour, he must have walked down the aisle with Jane black and blue."

Hayward, annoyed at Jane standing in the wings glaring at her, bitterly complained to Parsons, urging her to have her removed. "She's destroying my act. Instead of concentrating on what I'm doing, I'm staring at her."

When Parsons suggested that Jane remove herself from the sight lines of actors performing on stage, she refused. "To hell with this would-be Scarlett O'Hara. If I don't stand there watching over Ronnie, she'd kill him before our wedding day. She's just slapping him around like that to spite me."

"Or maybe to spite Ronnie," Parsons chimed in. Perversely, she seemed to enjoy the rivalry between the two actresses, each of whom would go on to become a superstar of Hollywood's Golden Age.

Louella had traveled with her own personal hairdresser and came out every night clad in mink and pearls. As she settled behind a desk, onstage, she read phony items ["William Powell and Ginger Rogers have been seen holding hands"] from a fake teletype machine. Then, after delivering her "update from Hollywood," she'd surrender the stage to Whelan, who sang a *Bossa Nova* tune. A San Francisco paper wrote, "She moves with mild undulations of her torso."

Variety found Reagan "very personable, deft, and obviously at home on the stage," suggesting that he might consider Broadway as an option one day.

The Hearst-owned *San Francisco Chronicle* defined the show as "sparkling—great dramatic flair from Louella."

Non-Hearst papers were critical, however, one of them suggesting that Parsons spoke her lines in a "muffing, spluttering, stumbling voice."

After San Francisco, Parsons and her "Flying Stars" were off to tour America, landing in such cities as Pittsburgh, where they played to "standing room only" audiences.

In Philadelphia, Reagan came to realize for the first time that he'd become a sex symbol to hundreds of young American women, along with a few grandmothers who had joined his fan club.

That was demonstrated one night when he left his hotel room, passed through the lobby, and walked out onto the street. He was immediately confronted with dozens of bobbysoxers, most of them with autograph books.

He later recalled, "Somehow, the crowd got out of control. I'd never seen women this aggressive before. They tore at my clothing, wanting a piece of me. I felt several hands grabbing my crotch. Before the hotel security guards rushed out to save me, I was practically stripped naked. Thank God I wore a clean pair of underwear. I thought things like that happened only to Frank Sinatra. Now I was experiencing it. That's what I get for being so god damn handsome and having such a masculine physique."

"On the tour, Louella was a bit mischievous," Hodges said. "She reported to Arleen that Susan had been making unflattering remarks about her."

Whelan set out to get her revenge, and went to Jane. "I hate to tell you this, but last night at around two o'clock in the morning, I saw Reagan leaving Susan's bedroom. I was coming home late from a date."

Jane believed Whelan's lies, later denouncing her future bridegroom, calling him "a whoremonger."

At one point during the tour, Jane got so angry, she wouldn't speak to Ronnie except on stage," Hodges claimed. "Finally, they had to appeal to their fairy godmother, Louella herself, to impose an uneasy truce upon these ill-matched lovers."

During the tour, while Jane was alienated from Reagan, Whelan decided to move in on him, hoping to take advantage. In Chicago, where Parsons was fêted, there was a swimming pool in the basement of their hotel.

"Arleen pursued Ronnie there," Hodges said. "When he put on his trunks, and went for a swim—he was quite the athlete—Arleen put on her most seductive bathing suit and followed him downstairs."

"Arleen told me, 'Ronnie's package looks promising, and I intend to sample it before this damn tour is over,'" Hodges claimed. "She was also mad at Louella for inviting only one male star along on the tour."

The players moved on to Washington, D.C. There, Parsons invited Eleanor Roosevelt to attend one of the performances, but the First Lady politely declined the invitation. Parsons fumed, "That bitch. I'm more famous than she is, and she snubs me."

Hodges later recalled, "There was something so alone about Hayward. She was the most unpopular of all the gals on the tour. I was a brand new bride. And Dutch (Reagan) and Jane had each other. Arleen was very gay, with plenty of beaux. She was to marry Alexander D'Arcy in 1940. June already had a career on the stage with her sister, Cherry. But Susan—she seemed to have nothing except her natural talent."

"Hayward had absolutely no sense of humor," Hodges continued. "She was grumpy all the time. We later learned that Jane had stolen Ronnie from her. I avoided Hayward whenever I could. She could be so blunt. You never knew when she was going to say something biting, hateful, or just plain sarcastic. Hayward sucked up to Louella, but gave everybody else a rough time, especially Ronnie and Jane."

At one point during the tour, a drunken Parsons took Jane outside and lectured her, "You're wearing far too much costume jewelry. It detracts from your natural beauty and makes you look cheap. You don't want to look like a Saturday night hooker when you go out."

For Jane, the highlight of the cross-country tour came when Reagan presented her with a fifty-two carat amethyst engagement ring. She proudly showed it to the girls.

A promotional tour makes whoopee about the Ronnie-Jane wedding nuptials to come.

Joy Hodges *(left)* and Arleen Whelen *(hovering over the happy couple)* look on with a certain envy.

When Hayward found out about it, she jealously snapped, "The man I'm going to marry will give me a fifty-two carat diamond."

En route back to Hollywood, their TWA plane stopped in Albuquerque, where the Pueblo Indians made Parsons an honorary member of their tribe. They gave her the name of "Ba Ku La," which translates as "Princess Starmaker."

Later, in her hotel room, the newly christened "Indian Princess" telephoned her editors, demanding that her previous submission be rewritten, as follows:

"Ronnie Reagan and Janie Wyman are to be married as soon as our personal appearance tours end in Hollywood. These two lovebirds are made for each other. It will be the third marriage for Jane, the first for Ronald."

When he read the column, Reagan said to Jane, "Louella says that your marriage to me will be number three. Where did she get that wrong information?"

"Not from me, darling," Jane said. "I was only married once. I've told you that."

During her years-long marriage to Reagan, she never revealed to him her first marriage to Eugene Wyman.

Years later, when Reagan was the emcee for *The General Electric Theater,* a reporter asked him about his involvement with Susan Hayward. All he said was, "Fire and Ice," before walking away.

During the months she spent in Fort Lauderdale early 70s, Hayward said, "It was men like Oleg Cassini, Jeff Chandler, John F. Kennedy, Porfirio Rubirosa, and oh, yes, Ronald Reagan, that led me to say, 'Men! I'd like to fry 'em all in deep fat!'"

Chapter Six

"Louella Parsons' Favorite "Lovebirds,"

Ronnie and Jane,

Begin Married Life.
But Will They Be Faithful?

Reagan's Movie Line "Win One for the Gipper" Morphs Into a Vote-Getting Slogan for His Future Campaigns.

Jane Wyman began her "married life" with Ronald Reagan months before the actual wedding, although he didn't come home every night.

"He's a great dancer," she told Joan Blondell, "and you know how much I like to dance. I prefer to go nightclubbing six nights a week, but he can settle happily for two. It's a possible conflict."

Here, Jane is pictured with her baby daughter, whose name became Maureen.

"He talks of having more children," Jane said to Blondell. "I told him to have the orphanage send over as many kids as he wanted, but he'd have to hire some god damn nannies to take care of them. I've worked too hard to become a movie star to let it all slip away from me now. It's a possible conflict."

Before he entered into marriage with Jane Wyman, Ronald Reagan called on Pat O'Brien, his fellow actor and "father confessor."

"I've slept with a lot of Hollywood starlets," he admitted, "and I've come to the conclusion that none of them is ideal marriage material. I'm looking for a gal I could proudly take home to dear old Dad...and Mom, too. Nelle believes I won't find such a gal in show business."

"What about Jane?" O'Brien asked.

"She's the best candidate so far," Reagan admitted, "but she didn't make a very good wife to this guy, Myron Futterman. My fear is that once again, Jane will not honor her marriage vows and that she'll go out with other men when I'm away, perhaps on location. She cheated on Futterman with a lot of other men, including yours truly. Since Futterman was out of town a lot, she had plenty of chances."

"Let me ask you this," O'Brien said. "Would you be faithful to her? You're a real ladies' man, bouncing from the bed of one starlet after another. From what I've seen, you don't have to ask them. They throw themselves at you. Could you resist such temptation and go home to a wife and maybe kids night after night? As we Irishmen know, the flesh is weak."

"I've got to be truthful with you, as I always am—no bullshitting with you," Reagan said. "In all honesty, I think I'd become a husband with a cheating heart."

"I believe that, too, my boy," O'Brien said.

Reagan later told Dick Powell, "Just before I stepped up to marry Jane, I had been in the toilet throwing up. No, not because the idea of marriage either terrifed me or disgusted me. I had history's worst case of the flu, and felt dizzy-headed and faint."

"On our honeymoon night, Jane didn't get a rise out of me."

"My answer might be different twenty or so years from now," Reagan said. "Maybe then I'll be ready to settle down: But right now, I'm living my salad years. Only a fool or a homosexual would turn down some of the offers I'm getting. For instance, Betty Grable and Carole Landis are still calling me. On the other hand, I'd like to start a family...You know, have three or four kids."

"I have some advice for you that goes against the *clichéd* rule," O'Brien said. "Why not have your cake and eat it, too?"

Reagan looked startled at first, then seemed to mull it over. "I think that might be

---

"All Married Male Stars in Hollywood Have Something on the Side."

—*Gale Page*

some of the best advice a young married man can ever receive."

***

After talking to O'Brien, Reagan proposed marriage to Jane, but how he went about that remains a source of widely different speculation. Some of Reagan's closest friends, including Dick Powell, Eddie Foy, Jr., and Eddie Albert claimed that Jane forced him into marriage with a suicide threat.

In a surprise move, First Lady Nancy Reagan confirmed those assertions in an interview in 1989 with Reagan's biographer, Edmund Morris. She claimed that Jane swallowed a lot of pills, but summoned an ambulance herself to rush her to the hospital to have her stomach pumped.

Stepping out, Jane Wyman and Ronald Reagan made a dashing, handsome, and romantic couple.

As this picture indicates, they had liberated themselves from their early Middle West dress codes and had "gone Hollywood."

According to Nancy, when a messenger delivered the suicide note to Reagan, he rushed to the hospital. When he was allowed to see her after her stomach was pumped, he was alleged to have said, "Of course, I'll marry you.":

"You know how softhearted Ronnie is," Nancy said to Morris. "Jane Wyman knew which buttons to push."

The story of Jane's suicide attempt was widely publicized at the time. Nancy's source obviously must have been Reagan himself.

Over the years, Jane consistently denied the story to her friends, labeling it "a gross exaggeration. It was Nancy who tricked Ronnie into marriage by getting pregnant—not me. She should not be spreading lies about me concerning an event that happened so very long ago."

As would be expected, Jane had a very different version. "Ronnie's proposal was about as unromantic as anything that happened. We were about to be called for a take on the set of *Brother Rat and a Baby*. Ronnie simply turned to me as if the idea were brand new and had just hit him and said, 'Jane, why don't we get married?' I couldn't think of any reason we shouldn't. I'd been wondering for a whole year—ever since I first saw him—why he hadn't asked me. I was just about to give him a definite yes when we were called before the cameras. In trying to step down off my personal cloud, I managed to muff a few lines and toss in a whispered 'yes,' after the director yelled, 'Cut!'"

Louella Parsons supplied her own version, claiming that "One lovebird proposed to the other lovebird during our cross-country tour."

When Reagan became president—the first divorced man to ever do so—there was a renewed interest within the press about his first marriage. Many reporters sought copies of his first memoir, *Where's the Rest of Me?*, for a rundown of his version of his first marriage. The book had been published in 1965 at the culmination of his film career.

In an almost shocking omission, which his editors at Duell, Sloan, and Pearce let him get away with, Reagan didn't even mention that he married Jane.

[In March, 1961, Duell, Sloan and Pearce became an affiliate of Meredith Publishing Company, which later sold parts of it to the Academic Learning Company, LLC and to

Prentice-Hall.]

Parsons had plenty to say about the upcoming marriage. "Jane was always so nervous and tense before she found Ronnie. She was a girl on the make—for life, for love. I think she wanted, well, *everything.* Steady, solid, decent young Ronnie has slowed down her pace, and it is all for the best. It is an opposites-attract thing, but I'm predicting here and now that these opposites will celebrate their 25th and 50th wedding anniversaries—together."

where's the rest of me?

The Ronald Reagan Story
Ronald Reagan with Richard G. Hubler

Joy Hodges, who had accompanied Parsons on her cross-country vaudeville tour, saw potential trouble in the upcoming marriage. "Even back in 1940, Ronnie was almost fanatically interested in politics, always talking about the war, Hitler, FDR, Lend-Lease, whatever. Jane was clearly bored with such talk. She made that rather obvious. She told everybody, 'Don't ask Ronnie what time it is, or he'll tell you how a watch is made.' She liked talking about movies and gossiping about the latest indiscretions within the Hollywood colony."

"I knew both of them pretty well, especially Jane, if you get my drift," said Wayne Morris. "I thought their attraction was almost entirely sexual. For that reason, when the novelty wore off, I predicted the marriage was due for a crash landing. I don't believe that a zebra can change its stripes. Jane was a playgirl who loved night clubs and handsome men, especially guys like me. Reagan was a magnet for the babes, attracting most of the little hotties running around the Warners' lot. He was also smarter, better educated. She didn't know what he was talking about half the time. Their temperaments were entirely different. Except for sex, the marriage had little going for it."

Eddie Albert, who once again had co-starred with them in *Brother Rat and a Baby,* talked to Reagan two days before the marriage. "Ronnie described Jane as 'lots of fun to be with' and 'a good sport.' That didn't sound like a man too deeply in love. I think she pressured him into marriage with that suicide attempt. I was convinced that my good buddy couldn't give up his pastime of screwing beautiful babes."

By the time Reagan entered into marriage, he was making $1,650 a week, whereas Jane was drawing only $500 a week as a contract player at Warners.

Although a so-called movie star, Jane had not yet been able to cash in on her growing fame. He knew he was not marrying a woman of

Although Reagan was dating other women, even doing more than dating, he and his blonde starlet, Jane Wyman, more or less let the world know that they were "an item."

All dolled up, they descended the steps of the Biltmore Hotel on February 23, 1939, after the Oscar ceremony. Jane's coat was a gift from Myron Futterman, her second husband.

194

means, but he soon learned his bride-to-be was not only flat broke, but heavily in debt, too.

For the November, 1941 issue of *Screenland*, Jane had given an interview to writer Virginia Wood. "When I married Ronnie, I was drowning in debt. I was marrying a man who could not let a bill lie on his desk for more than ten days. I tried to pay all my debts before I walked down the aisle, but I was not making enough money to pay them off. On one account, I was paying it off at two dollars a week."

"Ronnie told me that when we were married, he would see to it that both of us saved half of everything we made," she said.

Before their marriage, Joan Blondell and her husband, Dick Powell, took the Reagans to the Cocoanut Grove where Powell was invited to sing a song for the guests.

"Later, Jane and I went to the powder room," Blondell said. "She made a confession to me."

"I can't help wondering if Ronnie's easy nature is some sort of an act," Jane said. "He's just too god damn good natured. It doesn't seem possible that a man could have so even a disposition consistently. I'll let you know in two weeks if I'm marrying a Dr. Jekyll who turns out to be Mr. Hyde."

Jane didn't wait long between marriages. Her divorce from Futterman was finalized right before Christmas of 1939. She married Reagan on January 26, 1940. The rite of marriage was celebrated at the Scottish-themed Wee Kirk o' the Heather Chapel in the Forest Lawn Memorial Park in Glendale, California.

Jane later joked to Blondell, "It was

Warners' Publicity wanted to use their budding romance to promote their careers. So they posed for a series of pictures demonstrating what a happy couple they were.

Louella Parsons *(left)*, the gossipy columnist and "Tinseltown Tarantula," came down hard on many relationships, including Clark Gable, a married man, living with Carole Lombard.

Although she was known for exposing indiscretions, she always gave Reagan and Jane a pass when she heard of one of their adulterous scandals.

Nelle Reagan's idea to have the marriage performed in a cemetery. I practically had to stumble over the graves of Lon Chaney (Senior) and Marie Dressler to get to the chapel on time." The chapel had been the setting for the 1937 funeral of Jean Harlow.

The Rev. Cleveland Kleihaur performed the ceremony, which was traditional in every sense except for the bridal kiss. Jane didn't even get a peck on the cheek. That showed sensitivity on Reagan's part, not the reverse. "To get to the chapel, I had to rise from my deathbed, where I was suffering from the flu. I felt so weak during the ceremony, I thought I was going to pass out."

In a gown with accessories borrowed from the wardrobe department of Warners, Jane made a dazzling bride in her floor-length, high-necked, long-sleeved blue satin gown with a mink fur hat and a matching muff.

For his best man, Reagan selected Bill Cook, a friend from his Des Moines days as a radio announcer. Cook had been a member of Reagan's barbershop quartet.

Jane introduced her maid of honor, Elsie Watt, as her sister. Technically, Elsie was not her sister, but the

Two generations of Reagans at the "Ronnie and Janie" wedding. Nelle, in the frumpy finery of her era, and Reagan's father, Jack, flank the groom and bride.

daughter of Emma Fulks, who had reared Jane as a young girl when her real parents had abandoned her. To give the bride away, Louella Parsons had arranged for her husband, Dr. "Docky" Martin, to walk Jane down the aisle.

Blondell was rather cynical about the wedding. "I met Moon Reagan, Ronnie's brother. He held down jobs in media, but I found him rather dumb and boorish. But he was a doll compared to Ronnie's mother, Nelle. She looked like some severe religious fanatic, a real Midwest Puritan. His father, Jack, was already drunk before the ceremony began. I heard Jack approach Jane and beg her 'not to take Dutch away from us.'"

"Louella hovered over the newlyweds like some devouring mother hen," said Dick Powell. "She even hosted the reception at her home on North Maple Drive in Beverly Hills. Louella was so excited, she wet her pants. I mean that literally. But she did that at most of the parties she attended. Weak kidneys, I suppose."

The couple left for their honeymoon in Palm Springs, a resort that would more or less become her home in time to come.

Unusual for the desert resort, it rained almost every day, ruining Reagan's plans about playing golf, a game that Jane also enjoyed. He was going to teach her to swim, but that plan also fell through.

Fifty years after that honeymoon, and at the same resort, correspondent Bob Colacello asked Jane to recall her rainy honeymoon.

"Is there anything about it that stands out in your mind?" he asked.

"No, not particularly," she said.

He later claimed, "She flashed me such a cold and angry look that I thought she might murder me right there in her pink-and-lavender retirement condominium."

When Reagan and Jane drove back to Los Angeles, he moved his meager belongings into her modest three-bedroom apartment at 1326 Londonderry View, off the Sunset Strip.

That Monday, Blondell called and invited Jane to lunch at her favorite spot, the Brown Derby. "Ducky, how's married life?"

"We've had our first argument," she answered. "He wants to start a family right away, and I want to stay lean and mean and continue my movie roles, waiting for the big one."

"And now for the most important question," Blondell said, even though she knew the answer. "How is Ronnie in bed?"

"He's about as good in bed as he is on the screen," Jane answered.

***

Back in Hollywood, Reagan became suspicious that the mobs of crazed bobbysoxers in Philadelphia, who had previously disrobed him, had actually been paid to do so. The prime suspect was his aggressive new agent, Lew Wasserman, representing the Music Corporation of America (MCA).

Born in Cleveland to Jewish-Russian immigrants, Wasserman had begun a meteoric rise, beginning in 1933 as a theater usher at a movie house in Cleveland and eventually evolving, under the MCA baton, into the most powerful actors' and entertainment industry agent in the world.

His clients included not only Reagan and Jane Wyman, but Warners' *über*-diva, Bette Davis. In fact, most of the big stars at Warners were represented by him.

"If Hollywood was Mount Olympus Lew Wasserman *(depicted above)* was Zeus," said the late Jack Valenti, former president of the Motion Picture Association of America.

If Wasserman were indeed the culprit who had staged the mob scene in Philadelphia, he had a reason. It was his attempt to convince Jack Warner that his new client was a sex symbol, with the intention of getting him a breakthrough role in an A-list picture.

Warner believed that Errol Flynn and George Raft were sex symbols, but not "a clean-cut boy like Ronnie, whom I like personally, inviting him to my dinner parties."

"My male stars—Bogie, Ronnie, and Edward G. Robinson—are not sex symbols. Bogie and Edward G. are too ugly, almost repulsive, and Ronnie is every gal's big brother, but not one she wants to commit incest with."

Wasserman had met with Warner to try to get him to cast Reagan in an A-picture, the role of George Gipp in *Knute Rockne—All American,* which was to star Pat O'Brien as the coach.

For a while, William Holden and John Wayne had been leading contenders for the role of Gipp, although Robert Young and Robert Cummings provided heavyweight competition.

At one point, a handsome Canadian actor from Manitoba five years older than Reagan, Donald Woods, was in the lead. He had appeared in several B pictures, making his film debut in 1928, at the dawn of the Talkies. Occasionally he got to appear in an A-list picture, too, including *A Tale of Two Cities* (1935) and *Anthony Adverse* (1936). Warner finally concluded that Woods "is even more clean cut than Reagan. I hear he's faithful to his wife. My god, from what I heard, those two lovebirds fell in love with each other in the first grade."

[Woods had married Josephine Van der Horck in 1933, and he was still married to her when he died in Palm Springs in 1998.]

"The role of George Gipp is not particularly romantic," Wasserman protested.

"Okay, I'll consider Ronnie and get back to you," Warner promised.

It was believed that after this meeting, Wasserman then hired young women in Philadelphia to forcibly disrobe Reagan when he emerged onto the street through his hotel's front door.

But, then again, maybe not. No smoking gun was ever discovered, and Wasserman, of course, denied the charge.

"Ronnie's come a long way since he got rid of those god damn horn-rimmed glasses," Warner had told Wasserman.

[After 1940, Reagan was never again seen in any film with glasses. He had been among the first Hollywood star to wear contact lenses, something new on the market then in America. But there were problems. "Each lens has a little bubble over the cornea that you have to keep filed with a saline solution," Reagan told his friends. "Every couple of hours, the solution turns gray and you go blind. You've got to take them out, remove the liquid, and put in a clear solution. They're difficult to wear, but vanity prevails."]

Knowing that Wasserman also represented Jane Wyman, Warners issued an order concerning her appearance, too. "I don't want her to wear glasses like she did in those *Brother Rats.* It makes her look too scholarly. Also, I want her to be blonder. Tell her hair stylist to make her hair lighter. I'll invent a name for the kind of hair color I want. Call it 'Vroom Blonde.'"

Wasserman succeeded in negotiating more money for each of these soon-to-be-married clients of his. He arranged a seven-year contract for Reagan at $3,500 a week, referring to him as "my first million-dollar client."

He also convinced Warner to raise Jane's salary from $500 a week. He secured a three-year contract for her, beginning at $1,500 a week, with the stipulation that it would eventually climb to $2,500 a week.

Since she was still heavily in debt, she was delighted with the money. But as each new role came in for her, and she read yet another lackluster script associated with a B-picture, she continued to harass Wasserman to get her better parts. "I've got money in the bank, but I'm still a B-picture baby."

That long-anticipated A-picture role, her breakout movie, would not come until war's end in 1945.

In contrast to Jane, who was always complaining, Reagan became "the darling of MCA."

"Reagan was unlike all of our other clients, who bombarded us with complaints day and night," said Taft Schreiber, an MCA executive. "Bette Davis constantly storms our

Newlyweds for hire: An artfully staged, skilfully choreographed (by the studio) marriage. Three views of "America's most ideal couple."

citadel with one complaint after another. The diva even came to us one time to complain that Jack Warner had never felt her up."

"I understand that Mr. Warner likes to put his filthy paws up a girl's dress," Davis said. "But he's never done that to me. Does that mean he thinks I'm not a sex symbol like Kay Francis?"

"If a star gets trapped in a rotten flick, we're to blame," Schreiber said. "But Ronnie never blames us. He suffers through the B with good spirits, knowing that his big break will come, feeling secure that we're working to build him up."

Wasserman predicted that Reagan would become one of the biggest wartime stars in Hollywood. "Let's face it," Wasserman said to Reagan. "Sooner or later the United States will be attacked. All the glamour boys, unless some of them are too old, will be in the service. You're blind. They won't draft you. You can take over those matinee idol roles. Just be patient a little longer."

***

Whereas *Brother Rat* (1938) had been a hit, its sequel, *Brother Rat and a Baby* (1940), was lackluster. However, Warners hoped that the publicity generated by the marriage of Reagan with Jane would beef up the box office receipts.

In the sequel, the original cast was reunited—Wayne Morris, Priscilla Lane, Jane Bryan, and Eddie Albert, plus Reagan and Jane. Instead of William Keighley, a new director, Ray Enright, a familiar face to both Jane and Reagan, was brought in to helm the script, written by Jerry Wald and Richard Macaulay. A strong supporting cast included such stalwarts as Arthur Treacher, Paul Harvey, Berton Churchill, and Humphrey Bogart's quarrelsome wife, Mayo Methot.

The baby in the movie, the one supposedly belonging to Eddie Albert and Priscilla Lane, was the usually congenial toddler, Peter Good. At one point during the filming, Elsa Maxwell, the famous hostess, threw a party for him at the Hollywood Roosevelt Hotel. The kid was brought screaming into the party, and he continued screaming for another fifteen minutes until he was finally removed.

The film's most memorable and prophetic line was delivered when Jane says to Reagan: "You might as well back down, because I'm gonna get you."

Reagan noted that Enright was frequently impatient and seemed to deliberately rush through the script. At one point, he told Reagan, "Speed it up. I want out of this shit pile."

On the set, Reagan met a struggling, young, and rather handsome actor, Alan Ladd, who was appearing in a small role.

"My great dream is to become a big star like you," Ladd said to Reagan.

"You flatter me," Reagan answered. "I'm hardly a big star."

Ironically, the stardom during World War II that might have gone to Reagan, had he not been drafted, went to Ladd, after he appeared as the laconic gunman in the 1942 *This Gun for Hire*.

"Hollywood's two midgets, Ladd and his frequent co-star, Veronica Lake, became the screen team that Jane and I dreamed of becoming," Reagan said. "Jane and I never made it, but they sure did. No hard feelings, kids."

Critic George Browne wrote, "What was mildly amusing when Morris, Albert, and Reagan were enrolled at the Virginia Military Institute as cadets seems silly and rather childish now that they have graduated to being so-called 'adults.' Their antics don't seem to work anymore, and we've heard that Jack Warner has ruled, 'No more glasses for Wyman.'"

Another critic noted, "Reagan looks distinctly uncomfortable kissing Wyman on the screen. Maybe they should practice more at home. Dare I point out that all the principal stars were far too old to play the roles assigned?"

Another reviewer suggested that "If Reagan is trying to succeed in screwball comedy, as this film suggests, somebody should tell him Cary Grant he ain't."

Enright told Reagan that their film, *Brother Rat,* had angered some graduates of V.M.I., and that consequently, all references to that military institution were eliminated from the sequel.

Jane Bryan in 1939, off-camera, and her husband, drugstore czar Justin Dart, Sr. They evolved into major financial backers of political Reagan.

By the time Reagan worked again with Jane Bryan on the sequel, his original crush on her had gone the way of the summer wind. She was engaged to wealthy Justin Dart. Dart was unaware of Reagan's former passion for his wife-to-be, and he and Reagan bonded in spite of their differences. A staunch Republican, Dart was large, gruff, with a brilliant grasp of economics. Mostly, they debated FDR, Reagan in his capacity as a liberal Democrat, wanting FDR to seek re-election, and Dart fearing that he would.

Dart was in the process of divorcing heiress Ruth Walgreen, the daughter of the drugstore magnate, Charles Walgreen. Even with the divorce, Dart still controlled a large share of the fortune. He would turn his share into millions of dollars. He later recalled, "I played music whose siren sounds eventually lured Reagan into the Republican orchestra."

Bryan retired from the screen after *Brother Rat and a Baby,* and Dart became president of the Rexall Drugstore chain.

They remained Reagan's personal friends, surviving the collapse of his marriage to Jane and encouraging a relationship with his new wife, Nancy Davis. "We didn't have

The gang's all here: Fellow "Rats" *(left to right)* Wayne Morris, Eddie Albert, and Ronald Reagan carry their women *(left to right)* Priscilla Lane, Jane Bryan (and baby), and Jane Wyman

to convert Nancy to the Republican side," Dart later said.

The Darts first urged Reagan to run for governor of California and later for President of the United States. In the decades to come, the drugstore czar would become the bluntest and most outspoken of Reagan's so-called "Kitchen Cabinet" of longtime friends invited to the White House.

***

Her career on the skids, Mayo Methot was the third wife (all of them actresses) of Humphrey Bogart, Helen Menken and Mary Philips having preceded her. Methot had been cast in a small role—that of a larcenous passenger on a bus—in *Brother Rat and a Baby.* Once designated as "The Portland Rosebud," during her youth in her native Oregon, she had lost her looks, thanks to her very heavy drinking over the years.

By the time she married Bogie in 1938, her alcoholism had taken its toll. In the 1920s, she had been a popular actress on Broadway. Signing with Warners in the '30s, she had specialized in the portrayal of tough-talking dames in such pictures as *Marked Woman* (1937), co-starring Bogie and Bette Davis.

On the set, Methot chatted with Reagan and Jane, who were each well aware of her reputation as the more combative of "The Battling Bogarts." Both were heavy drinkers known for their violent excesses under the influence. She was such a warrior that Bogie had nicknamed her "Sluggy." During one fight in their kitchen, she'd taken a butcher knife and stabbed his left shoulder. After that, the press dubbed their home "Sluggy Hollow."

Bogie arrived one day on the set, congratulating Jane and Reagan on their marriage and inviting them to lunch with Methot and him in the commissary. "I hope your marriage will be as successful as mine," he said, presenting a straight face to Jane and Reagan.

Against Reagan's better judgment, he accepted an invitation to dress in formal wear and attend a gala at the Cocoanut Grove with them.

As they were dressing for the event, Reagan warned Jane, "We'd better confine our drinking to one glass, because we'll have to carry Bogie and Methot home in our car."

At the Ambassador Hotel, Reagan and Jane nursed their respective drinks, while the Bogarts belted down quite a few. Jane couldn't help but notice Methot's "conspicuous cleavage." When she dropped her purse and bent over, her left breast popped out of her gown.

"Stuff in your tit, bitch!" Bogie snarled at her. Angered, she straightened up, lifted her glass of vodka, and tossed it into his face. Although Reagan expected an immediately violent response from him, Bogie, for the moment at least, gave the appearance of remaining calm. Meanwhile, Jane looked pointedly in another direction.

But as he sat there, with liquor dripping from his face, it was obvious that Bogie was fuming. Slowly, he picked up a napkin and wiped away the vodka.

At the end of the evening, Bogie and Methot headed for the lounges to freshen up. Jane and Reagan remained behind to pay the bill. "We survived the night, but barely," he said. "Now, let's get these two home and call it a night."

"Never again," she vowed.

With Reagan behind the wheel, driving them home, Methot suddenly demanded to be taken to the Cock n' Bull Restaurant & Bar on Sunset Boulevard for a nightcap. Reagan demurred, saying that he and Jane had to get up early, but Bogie joined his wife in insisting.

"Take us to the fucking Cock n' Bull!" Bogie ordered Reagan.

Finally, to keep the peace, Reagan drove them there in spite of Jane's signals that she wanted to go home.

The restaurant and bar was one of the favorite watering holes of the stars. In 1931, Methot had married its co-owner, Percy T. Morgan, and she still liked to patronize the bar because the staff never presented her with a bill.

Seated at table, both Bogie and Methot each ordered vodka and tonic, the Reagans preferring coffee. When Methot's drink was served, she spit it out. "This is gin and tonic, you fucker," she called out, loudly, to the waiter. "I SAID VODKA, AND I MEAN VODKA."

The waiter moved forward to replace her drink. With condescension, showing his utter disdain for his wife, Bogie thanked her for not having tossed the drink into the waiter's face. "That's what she usually does," he said to Reagan, "like she did with me tonight at The Grove."

Reagan glanced at Jane, noticing that she was growing decidedly uncomfortable as the night progressed.

When the waiter returned with a different drink, Methot slugged down a fourth of it before turning to Bogart with a certain ferocity.

He shot a glance at Reagan, saying to him in an undertone, "Take a good god damn look at that face on her. She's getting ready for the kill. I can always see it coming." Then he turned his full attention in her direction.

"What is it now, my fair lady? What is going on in that vodka-soaked brain of yours?"

She ignored him, focusing instead first on Reagan and then on Jane.

"I found out today that my husband has been fucking Ann Sheridan."

Reagan squirmed in his seat, knowing that he was guilty of the same pleasure.

Almost as if for the first time, Jane spoke up. "Mayo, that's not true, Ann is a dear friend of mine, and she confides in me. She never once has mentioned Bogie, except as a vague reference as a friend."

Cocktail Parties That End Badly: The photo above shows the early stages of a stylish and formal gathering that devolved into a gunslinging disaster. *Left to right*: Mayo Methot, Humphrey Bogart, Ronald Reagan, and a very blonde starlet, Jane Wyman.

"Listen, sweet cheeks, I know better," Methot said. "Nothing gets by me."

"C'mon, bitch," Bogie snarled. "We're heading out of this joint."

Bogie stood up, along with Jane and Reagan, Methot rose on her unsteady feet, looking angry and distraught and also as if she were about to topple over.

When Bogie reached to support her, she slugged him in the face, bloodying his nose. He struck her back, knocking her down onto the floor. When Reagan offered to help her up, she pushed his arm away. "I can rise on my own fucking feet," she said, using the table to brace herself as she rose.

Then, facing Bogart in all her fury, she reached into her purse and pulled out a revolver. "Okay, Mr. Gangster, Mr. Tough Guy, it's twilight time." Then she pointed the gun at Bogie.

"I dare you," he said, defying her.

At first not knowing what to do, Reagan lunged toward her, impulsively wrestling the gun from her hand.

"You bastard," she shouted at Reagan. "I should shoot you, too."

Jane nervously intervened, taking the gun from Reagan's hand and passing it to the restaurant manager, who had rushed to their table as the noise had escalated.

"Come on," Jane said to Reagan. "We're going home. I'm sure that these two will get to their own home on their own steam if they don't kill each other first. If not, it's hardly our problem."

Reagan dutifully followed his new wife. As he exited from the restaurant, the entire place could hear the Bogarts screaming at each other.

[As far as it is known, that incident at the Cock n' Bull was the third time during her marriage to Bogart that Methot had threatened her husband with a gun.]

Louise Brooks in her memoir, *Lulu in Hollywood,* summed it up: "Bogie found Methot at a time of lethargy and loneliness, when he might have gone on playing secondary gangster parts at Warner Brothers for years and then been out. But he met Mayo and she set fire to him. Those passions—envy, hatred, and violence, which were essential to the Bogie character—which had been simmering beneath his failure for so many years—she brought to a boil, blowing the lid off all his inhibitions forever."

***

The marriage of Jane Wyman and Ronald Reagan attracted such nationwide attention that the couple became known as "America's Sweethearts." Jack Warner ordered that another script be found for them, insisting that in this latest picture that they be jointly configured as man and wife.

Top billing for their next project, *An Angel from Texas* (released in 1940), actually went to Eddie Albert and Wayne Morris, their *Brother Rat* cohorts.

A face familiar to both Reagan and Jane, Ray Enright, was called in to helm the pair once again in this 69-minute B-picture released by Warner Brothers.

The female lead went to Rosemary Lane, sister of the famous trio which also included Lola and Priscilla, Reagan's former girlfriend.

Enright assembled a strong supporting cast that included Ruth Terry, John Litel, Hobart Cavanaugh, Ann Shoemaker, Tom Kennedy, Milburn Stone, and Elliott Sullivan.

An Angel from Texas represented an oft-repeated, unimpressive film concept with an overused, somewhat experimental history, a re-configuration of a tired old workhorse that should have been sent out to pasture years before. Its script, written by George S. Kaufman (not one of his better works), had originated in 1925 as a play on Broadway entitled *The Butter and Egg Man*. Its plot involved a folksy out-of-towner who is persuaded to invest in an iffy but eventually successful Broadway play, finding love in the intrigue associated with the production.

The "Angel" in the film's title represented a show-biz term for a financial backer. In the 1940 film, a good-looking, rather innocent Texan (Albert) sends his girlfriend (Lane) to Broadway, hoping she can break in as a working actress. Instead, she becomes a secretary to a fast-talking sharpie, a Broadway producer as portrayed by Morris, and his more restrained partner.

Albert arrives with $20,000 of his mother's life savings to invest in a hotel. But he's lured into investing the money into a Broadway show, instead.

Warners was hoping that by teaming Ronald Reagan and Jane Wyman as a husband-and-wife in *An Angel From Texas,* the studio could cash in on the massive publicity generated by their recent marriage.

Jane was cast in the film as Reagan's wife. She easily outwits both her husband and his con artist partner and helps back their Broadway show with money from a winning sweepstakes ticket registered in her own name.

***

During the first year of her marriage to Reagan and her subsequent pregnancy, Jane did not see John Payne, refusing to return his persistent phone calls.

Reagan also temporarily abandoned his sometimes girlfriend, Ann Sheridan, at least until they started making more movies together.

Sheridan, however, was a frequent visitor at the Reagan household, praising Jane's cooking. Toward the end of the year, she began showing up at the Reagan apartment with George Brent, whom she would eventually marry.

Joan Blondell later delivered a rather revealing insight into Jane's relationship with her new husband. Blondell was aware of Jane's romantic interest in Payne.

"If you were making a movie with Payne and Ronnie, how would you cast it?" Blondell asked.

"I'd cast John as the romantic lover," Jane responded, "and I'd ask Ronnie to play the role of an older brother, who is a sort of a father figure to the heroine."

During their days off from the studio, both Reagan and Jane liked to play golf, so they applied for membership in the Lakeside Country Club. Their boss, Jack Warner, applied at the same time. Whereas his application was rejected, Jane and Reagan were granted membership.

Later, Reagan asked the club's president why Warner had been turned away. "We don't want Jews in our club," he told Reagan, who resigned from the club the following day, along with Jane.

Subsequently, both Jane and Reagan joined the Hillcrest Country Club in Beverly Hills, where they were befriended by other golf-loving couples, including George Burns and Gracie Allen and Jack Benny and Mary Livingston.

When *An Angel from Texas* opened across America, audiences were not particularly mesmerized. *Variety* referred to Albert's "befogged cranial machinery," and to Lane as "his school Bernhardt girlfriend."

The paper went on to say, "*[Angel from Texas]* wasn't made with the hope of knocking critics for a loop or lining up standees at the box office, but it serves its purpose of a good little audience picture with a fair share of laughs, once the patrons are in."

The New York Times characterized the film as "a bright little farce about a couple of yokels from Texas who outwit a pair of Broadway theatrical sharpies. Ray Enright has directed it in a breezy, farcical manner."

Another critic said the script should never have been reactivated after its 1928 release as a silent.

An Angel from Texas did absolutely nothing to advance the film careers of either Jane or Reagan. They were still hampered with reputations as actors limited to roles in B-pictures, hoping their big break would come soon. The sun would shine on Reagan far sooner than it would cast its powerful rays on Jane. Whereas he'd have to wait for only a few months, she would spend years languishing in the shadows.

***

Lewis Seiler had already directed Jane Wyman in *He Couldn't Say No* and in *The Kid from Kokomo.* For the third time around, he gave her fifth billing in his latest picture, *Flight Angels,* scheduled for release in 1940. The other stars included Virginia Bruce, Wayne Morris, Dennis Morgan, and Ralph Bellamy. She had worked with Bellamy before in *Fools for Scandal,* starring Carole Lombard and Fernand Gravet *[aka Fernand Gravey]*, whom Jane had dated.

The excitement within the cast was generated by Dennis Morgan, Warners' handsome new leading man. Jane had heard the gossip: Now that Reagan had married her, he was no longer the favorite handsome hunk of Warners starlets. Almost overnight, Morgan became the most sought-after heartthrob, even though he had married his childhood sweetheart way back in 1933.

Jane was most anxious to meet him, but in the meantime, she had to deal with her sometimes errant beau, Morris. In her dressing room, he told her that his divorce from Leonora Hornblow would be finalized as soon as he received some court documents.

"Even though you're now an old married woman, I still have the hots for you," he

Flight Angels: Wayne Morris, Jane Wyman, Virginia Bruce, and Dennis Morgan.

ungracefully informed her.

She thanked him for his continuing interest, but claimed, "I'm not ready yet to start cheating on my husband."

"I bet you won't say that when you meet Dennis Morgan," he said. "All my girlfriends are dumping me and going for him. Are you going to join the stampede?"

"I haven't met God's gift to women yet, and I'm still very much in love with Ronnie," she said.

"You will be until he starts to bore you," Morris responded. "When that day comes, think of old Wayne here. I can always rise to the occasion."

"I'm well aware of your manly charms," she said. "Right now, I've got to put on my air wings to take flight with this B picture we're making."

A 74-minute programmer, *Flight Angels* was an inside look at the pilots and stewardesses who work for a fictional airline. Morgan played an ace supervised by Bellamy, who grounds him when he learns his eyesight is failing. Bruce and Jane were cast as stewardesses, Bruce is in love with Morgan, who—in the film—eventually marries her. Morris was cast as an engineer working on a secret research aircraft called "the Stratosphere Ship." If all goes well, the aircraft will fly higher and faster than any other plane.

During the compilation of the film, Morris became so fascinated with flying that he told Jane that planned to study to become a naval aviator. "War is coming to America," he said, "and I want to be ready to shoot the bastards down when it comes."

Seiler introduced Jane to Margot Stevenson, who had been cast in a minor role of a woman named "Rita." Jane was rather cold and distant to this actress, because she suspected that the New York beauty had had an affair with Reagan when she had co-starred with him in the picture, *Smashing the Money Ring.*

On the set of *Flight Angels,* Stevenson was spotted leaving Morris' dressing room on two separate occasions. As Jane told Seiler, "Since Wayne isn't getting anything from me, he's wasting no time finding it elsewhere."

At one point, John Garfield arrived late one afternoon for a date with Stevenson. Their affair would continue when she was cast in his next two films, *Castle on the Hudson* (1940) and *Saturday's Children* (also 1940).

***

At long last, the eagerly anticipated Dennis Morgan walked into Jane's life. His romantic image had not been overly sold, as he was extremely handsome, radiating charm with his curly hair, broad shoulders, tall physique, and "Oscar-winning smile."

Jane agreed with the recent assessment of Ginger Rogers, who defined him as "the personification of the Arrow Collar Man." *Variety* had announced that Morgan was set to co-star with Rogers in *Kitty Foyle* (1940), each in meaty and highly dramatic roles.

Morgan had a natural spontaneity and winning charm. As he kissed Jane's hand, he said, "What a bonny lass. I know that sounds corny, but Jack Warner has ordered me to act more Irish."

In *Flight Angels,* Dennis Morgan seemed to have been typecast. On screen, he played a pilot with a roving eye for the ladies, much to the distress of his on-screen wife, Virginia Bruce.

Off screen, Morgan's roving eye focused on Jane.

"Actually, I was born in Wisconsin to a Swedish father and a Scottish mother. But Warner plans to cast me Irish."

"Your secret is safe with me," she said.

"For keeping it secret, I'll sing 'When Irish Eyes Are Smiling' one night to you."

"I can hardly wait for that moment," she said, flirtatiously.

"I'm supposed to be the new boy on the block at Warners," Morgan told Jane. "I'm hot, at least according to the publicity, but you may not agree with my build-up."

"But I do," she said. "You look like a dream walking. I hope I'm not being too forward. I just blurted that out without thinking."

"I love hearing that from you, Button Nose," he said. "I might even belt out a song for you right now."

"I know what a great voice you have," she said. "Ronnie took me to see *The Great Ziegfeld* (1936). You were dazzling when you emerged dressed to the nines and looking gorgeous, surrounded by a birthday cake of the most beautiful women in the world. I practically swooned when you sang 'A Pretty Girl Is Like a Melody.'"

"I hate to disappoint you," Morgan said, "but those idiots over at MGM dubbed my own singing voice and substituted that of Allan Jones instead. I can sing so much better than he can."

"I'm sure that's true," she said. "That won't happen at Warners."

"Already, the attacks on me have begun," he said. "Today I read that I'm being referred to as a 'muscle-bound canary.'"

"We have to expect that in this business."

"I'd like to get to know you better," he said.

"For you, I'll be an open book," she said. "But for now, you've got to go. If you stick around for another minute, I'll fall madly in love with you. After all, I'm only flesh and blood."

He kissed her on the cheek, but hadn't gone far until he glanced back at her, promising, "I'll be back!"

Flight Angels opened to predictably bad reviews, *Variety* claiming, "It's as obvious as the nose on your face and a typical Grade B second feature."

Another critic, Clive Hirschhorn, wrote, "The corn is high as an elephant's eye (8,000 feet, to be precise) in this soap opera of the air, which zeroes in on the private lives and public duties of air stewardesses and the men who pilot planes in which they serve. Romance, drama, and excitement cohabit shamelessly in Maurice Leo's familiar screenplay."

Years later, Morris recalled fondly his working on that picture and on other films with Jane, Reagan, Eddie Albert, Priscilla Lane, and Jane Bryan. "We were the 'One-for-All and All-for-One' Society of Busy Bees. 'B,' of course, for B pictures. But those days were fun."

***

After Lewis Seiler directed Jane Wyman in *Flight Angels,* he helmed her husband, Reagan, that same year in *Murder in the Air* (1940). This would be the fourth (and last) film in which Reagan would star as secret agent Brass Bancroft.

He was reunited with his friend and confidant, Eddie Foy, Jr., who had starred with him in *Smashing the Money Ring.* John Litel, who had interpreted the role of his boss in the first Bancroft film, returned to the series in the same role of Saxby. The British actor, James Stephenson, was a familiar face, having co-starred with Reagan in *Cowboy from Brooklyn, Boy Meets Girl,* and *Secret Service of the Air,* each of the three released in 1938.

In their latest endeavor, Stevenson would interpret the role of the spy, Joe Garvey, who speaks with an intentionally indeterminate foreign accent. He directs an allegedly patriotic society with hints of Fascist bad-guy overtones, "Loyal Naturalized Americans."

With a length of 55 minutes, *Murder in the Air* was the shortest of the Bancroft films, but also the best for fight scenes and aerial combat on the screen. Reagan's increasing number of female fans, as well as his gay ones, thought he looked "really cute" in his sailor uniform and swooned when he appeared shirtless.

As the war deepened in Europe, the United States was still not officially involved, although the FBI and other agencies were arresting alleged saboteurs and ferreting out spies on the home front. Even though he fully recognized the commercial value of releasing a film about the spy industry into espionage-crazed America in 1940, Jack Warner accused the producer, Bryan Foy, of "stretching a five-paragraph story on page eighteen into five or six reels."

"Hello Sailor." Brass (Reagan) Bancroft with Foy, embarking on his secret mission.

To beef up the plot, Bryan Foy had obtained footage of a dirigible crashing into the ocean. Scriptwriter Raymond Schrock was ordered to configure that footage into the film's dramatic climax.

After a well-known spy is killed in a train wreck, Reagan, as Brass Bancroft, is ordered to assume his identity and penetrate the inner circle of the spy ring. That part in the film turned out to be a bit of a stretch for his acting ability. One reviewer found his impersonation of an America-hating tough guy unconvincing. "Reagan is just too clean-cut and patriotic to be a Nazi spy."

Brass Bancroft's goal in the film involved preventing the spies from obtaining a new super weapon, a death ray projector that could destroy any airplane within a distance of four miles. *[It was widely speculated in some quarters that Hitler already possessed such a weapon.]* In the film, the death ray was called "The Inertia Projector," the ownership of which will determine the outcome of the war.

Of course, as anticipated, our hero, Reagan, will save the day and bring down the plane in which the chief bad guy—assisted by his use of the death ray—is making his escape.

Future historians have noted that in the 1980s, President Reagan's "Strategic Defense Initiative"— more commonly known as his Star Wars plan—was inspired by memories of the death ray, whose concept he had been so closely involved with during his crafting of *Murder in the Air.*

Prior to Reagan's involvement, the film's title had been renamed twice. Previous names had included both *The Enemy Within* and *Uncle Sam Awakens* before they were declared as not commercial enough. The title that eventually stuck was *Murder in the Air.* According to Jack Warner, "'Murder,' the audience understands, and 'In the Air' makes it all the more intriguing."

Long before it became notorious to liberals, HUAC (the House Un-American Activities Committee) was presented favorably in the film, a life-supporting voice that warned about the dangers of saboteurs and spies who operated destructively within the fabric of the American infrastructure.

The film's attack on "Reds" and "Wobblies" (a pejorative name for labor unions) provided a preview of Reagan's future as a conservative politician.

Reagan, as Brass Bancroft, on the verge of both a scary discovery, and an attack from James Stephenson.

Among the many studios in Hollywood, Warners had become anti-Nazi before MGM, Fox, or Paramount. In 1939, Warners' had released *Confessions of a Nazi Spy,* starring Edward G. Robinson. Because America was supposedly neutral at the time, that film had set off a wave of protests.

"Jack had a lot of balls to make this anti-Fascist film," Reagan said after seeing the movie.

Some congressmen had accused the Warners, especially Jack and Harry, of "warmongering." Immediately after its release, *Murder in the Air* was banned in Germany, Japan, and in some Latin American countries, including Argentina.

Months before its script went before the cameras, Jack's brother, Harry Warner, had delivered a blistering speech before the American Legion. He called upon Legionnaires to "fight unwelcome un-American forces. Drive them from their secret hiding places, destroy their insidious propaganda machines, and drive out the 'Bunds' and their leagues, their clans and Black Legions, the Silver Shirts, the Black Shirts, and the Dirty Shirts!"

After the release of *Confessions of a Nazi Spy,* the censors at the Breen Office wanted to avoid another controversy about America's neutrality. In an early draft of *Murder in the Air,* a coven of saboteurs, obviously German, were ripping apart railroad tracks as a means of derailing an oncoming train. Censors demanded that the scene be reshot and the saboteurs reconfigured as members of "mixed nationalities."

The months before America went to war represented a troubled time, with opinions sharply and rancorously divided. German Americans were raising loud objections against an unfavorable depiction of their homeland. Irish Americans opposed Lend Lease, America's initiative that sent supplies and equipment to a battered Britain, Ireland's long-standing oppressor. Many U.S. senators remained firmly isolationist, urging Americans to stay out of "Europe's War." Reagan learned that the Breen office was often, at its core, anti-Semitic, blaming Jews, not Hitler, for the troubles in Europe.

Even at that early stage, Reagan was aware of the dangers of Fascism. He was firmly committed to the belief that America was in imminent danger of an attack. He endorsed the first draft of *Murder in the Air,* with the full realization that it was obvious pro-American propaganda. Within a relatively short time, he would be making propaganda films for the War Department.

Originally *Murder in the Air* had opened with stock footage of goose-stepping Nazis on (malevolent) parade. The chief of the Secret Service proclaimed in a voice-over, "Once again, the world is rushing headlong into a maelstrom of death and destruction which would wipe civilization from the face of the earth."

After depicting the horrors of Europe, the screen turns peaceful, showing America going about its daily pursuits, feeling secure in its policy of isolation. But warnings are sounded that espionage agents are seeking to paralyze American industry, bomb its defense plants, and destroy its natural resources.

The Breen office demanded that these anti-German scenes be removed. However, some of the footage of the original version remained, wherein against a backdrop of fires and explosions, a headline reveals the gravity of the situation—PRESIDENT PLANS NATIONWIDE DRIVE ON SPIES AND SABOTEURS.

Reagan was already familiar with Lya Lys, the actress cast as *Murder in the Air's* leading lady. He had already seen her performance in *Confessions of a Nazi Spy.* In this newest film, she'd been cast as the scheming and crafty Hilda Ryker, who exposes Brass Bancroft's cover when he is on the trail of the spies.

Although he played a villain in *Murder in the Air,* Stephenson, in *Confessions of a Nazi Spy,* had been cast as a British Military Intelligence Agent. In *Confessions,* Lys had been cast as Erika Wolff, the mistress of Dr. Karl Klassel (Paul Lukas) who arrives in America to rally support for the Nazi cause among German Americans.

When Reagan met Lys, she had just married John Gunnerson, a Chicago vending machine manufacturer who had once been married to the famous silent screen star Anna Q. Nilsson. During the shooting of *Murder,* Lys used Reagan as a kind of Big Brother confidant, pouring out her woes. "After being married to John for only three days, I realized it was a mistake."

He found Lys an intriguing woman, originally thinking she was German, having been born in Berlin. But she told him she was actually French and Russian.

Three years older than Reagan, she was among a group of French actors who had arrived in Hollywood in the late 1920s to make French language versions of American films. Their members included the future matinee idol Charles Boyer.

Lys told Reagan that in the 1930s, she had returned to Paris to star in the surrealistic film by Salvador Dalí and Luís Buñuel, *L'Age d'Or,* delivering her finest performance.

She returned to Paris during the late 1930s, and was appearing there in a play entitled *The King's Dough* when war broke out. "I was among thousands of refugees fleeing Europe," she told Reagan. "But I couldn't get passage on a ship sailing from France. I was told to use a Scandinavian port. On the way to Denmark, I was detained for three days by the Nazis, even though I had become an American citizen. It seems that Josef Goebbels wanted me to stay in Berlin and make propaganda films for the Nazis at UFA Studios. Like Marlene Dietrich, I re-

Lya Lys, a European actress, fled the Nazis, refusing to make propaganda films for Josef Goebbels.

210

fused. They finally let me go, warning me never to return to Germany, telling me that if I did, I would be imprisoned."

Rightly thinking that *Murder in the Air* was a timely film, Warners geared up a massive publicity campaign, unusual for a programmer. In real life, Reagan had a morbid terror of flying, but in Warners' publicity releases, he was depicted as an ace pilot with a reputation for daring parachute jumps.

His friend, Foy Jr., asked him if he were embarrassed, in spite of his aversion to flying, at being promoted as a modern day Charles Lindbergh.

"It's all fantasy, my dear friend," Reagan said. "You forget we slave every day in a dream factory. Since when did Hollywood ever concern itself with telling the truth?"

Warners' Publicity Department devised a marketing plan wherein young boys across the country, for a fee, could join the Junior Secret Service. Membership included an 8" x 10" autographed photo of Brass Bancroft, signed by Reagan himself.

Ads across America asked countrymen to join Reagan in battling what was defined as "A Fifth Column of up to 20,000 secret and concealed enemies" seeking to sabotage America's infrastructure and to steal America's secrets. Schools were urged to set up essay contests, addressing the question of, "What steps do you think government must take to combat espionage and spying?"

Variety wrote that *Murder in the Air* "is strong on novelty in the Buck Rogers vein," and *The New York Tribune* pronounced Reagan "a dashing hero and a two-fisted man." But despite their patriotic preachings, Brass Bancroft movies did not routinely receive good reviews. One critic interpreted Reagan as "a heroic youngster playing Bancroft with vigorous conviction as he faces danger."

As Reagan moved into the 1940s, his increasing popularity was reflected in an avalanche of fan mail. Warners' mail department claimed that he was receiving almost as much fan mail as Errol Flynn.

[Writing in 2010, the Memphis-based film critic John Beifuss said, "The Warner archive collection of Brass Bancroft films raises a question. Why aren't these movies better remembered today? Is it because Reagan was a bit too immature and (even then) square to appeal to kid audiences, while also a bit boyish (and the films too juvenile) to interest adults? Whatever the reason, they're worth rediscovering for old movie buffs in general and for Reagan fans in particular."]

***

Carole Landis no longer called, especially after Reagan got serious about his relationship with Jane Wyman. He figured that the sexy blonde starlet had moved on with her life, although he'd always been attracted to her.

Variety had reported that she'd landed the female lead in an A-list picture, *One Million B.C.* (1940), opposite a muscle-bound newcomer, Victor Mature. It appeared that he was being groomed for stardom. Reagan had seen pictures in the newspapers of this actor, with his muscular frame, thick lips that opened to a toothy smile, and slick waves of dark hair. *Variety* also noted that in *One Million B.C.*, Mature as a skin-wearing caveman would battle giant lizards while projecting grunts at Landis.

One night, when Jane was involved in an evening shoot, Reagan called Landis, who agreed to meet him at an out-of-the-way club. He signaled that now that he was married, it would not be a romantic date, but a "chance for old friends to catch up."

She agreed to meet with him with the understanding that she'd have to leave before nine o'clock, for an important engagement.

Over drinks at the Blue Parrot, she told him how thrilled she was to be starring as the lead in a new movie. "I think it's going to make me a star. Of course, I have to wear skimpy animal skins and show off my body, but what the hell. Today, Victor Mature and I had to shoot a scene in this tree where a fifteen-foot python slithers down to join us. I nicknamed it Pete. The film is being directed by Hal Roach, Senior and Junior. They had to film a dozen takes because Vic is deathly afraid of snakes. I'm sort of a tomboy and wasn't scared. However, I wasn't quite prepared for my closeup with Pete when the god damn reptile darted his tongue out to give me a kiss."

Rather abruptly, he asked, "How's your love life?"

"Now that you no longer come around, I've found a beau or two. Of course, as anticipated, Vic comes on strong with me. He's the son of an Italian-speaking immigrant knife sharpener from Kentucky. Roach has signed him to a contract at $250 a week. When one of his talent agents discovered him, Vic was living in a tent on the bank of a small river in San Fernando Valley, where he bathed every morning. Getting fucked by him is like having a log shoved up you."

"That doesn't sound like much fun," Reagan said. "Are you and Zanuck finished?"

"Not at all," she said. "He keeps promising to make me a star. I still come running whenever he calls me and summons me to his office for love in the afternoon. All business at Fox slows down between noon and 2pm, when he takes his conquest of the day."

"I gathered you've moved," Reagan said.

"I rented this little bungalow at 1130 South Clark in Los Angeles. It's a neighborhood filled with underpaid studio employees and young actors hoping for the big break."

At the end of their meeting, Landis wrote down her new address and phone number. "One night when there's a full moon, why don't you drop in?"

"I love seeing you, but it doesn't seem that you have any night free."

"You've got a point there, gorgeous," she said. "What the hell! For old time's sake, you can at least give me a lip-lock before we depart."

***

After making eight B pictures in 1939, Reagan had grown impatient with producers or directors who never cast him in quality movies. He knew his days as the King of the Bs were numbered. Since no one would offer him a good script, he decided to write one himself, although he was not a writer. Jane volunteered to help him, but since she was far less well educated, her writing skills were even worse than his.

He obviously needed a subject, and he thought he'd like to write the script for a football picture. He decided to focus on the careers of George Gipp and Knute Rockne. Ever since he'd been a young boy, Reagan had admired the football exploits of George Gipp.

Michigan-born Gipp (1895-1920) had been a football player for Notre Dame, designated as that university's first All-American. During his senior season, he died at the age of 25 of a streptococcal throat infection days after leading Notre Dame to a win against Northwestern.

Of course, as Reagan soon learned, the story of Gipp could not be accurately transmitted without examining the life of his coach, Knute Rockne.

Born in Norway in 1888, and educated as a chemist, Knute Rockne is regarded as one of the greatest coaches in the history of college football. He popularized the forward pass. During his thirteen years as head coach at Notre Dame, his "Fighting Irish" won 105 victories, including three national championships.

Rockne's death in Kansas on March 31, 1931, shocked the nation. His TWA flight

599 crashed while he was en route to participate in the production of the film *The Spirit of Notre Dame*. President Herbert Hoover referred to Rockne's death as "a national loss."

To his surprise, Reagan one morning read that Warners', his home studio, was coincidentally moving ahead to film the life story of Knute Rockne, which would, of course, include an episode that featured the short, brilliant, and tragic life of Gipp.

He had never done this before, but Reagan set out to lobby for a role, scheduling an appointment with Hal B. Wallis, the producer of the upcoming film, which would eventually be entitled *Knute Rockne—All American,* after trying out two other titles, including *The Life Of Knute Rockne* and *Touchdown.*

Left: George Gipp, movie star and college football hero, who died of a streptococcal throat infection in 1920. *Right:* Ronald Reagan personifying George Gipp in 1940.

Before attending the meeting, Reagan talked to the film's first director, William Howard, who was hoping for a comeback. This talented, once-promising director had fallen on bad days.

During the first weeks of the shoot, Howard was drinking heavily, and Wallis fired him, replacing him with Lloyd Bacon. That director had helmed both Reagan and Pat O'Brien in the two films they had made together, *Cowboy from Brooklyn* and *Boy Meets Girl.*

To Reagan's astonishment, he had learned from Howard that William Holden and John Wayne had each been tested for his role of Gipp, and that each had been rejected by Wallis.

Left: Knute Rockne, revered by sports fans as one of the most inspirational football coaches who ever lived. *Right:* Pat O'Brien personifying Knute Rockne in the film.

"Wayne looks better on a horse," Howard had said, "and Holden is better as a violin player than a boxer, much less a football player." He was referring to Holden's role in the recent release of *Golden Boy* (1939), in which he'd starred with Barbara Stanwyck.

After a screen test, Robert Young was also rejected. "Put him in a dinner jacket in some parlor," Wallis said in a memo. "Certainly not on the football field."

Robert Cummings was another actor considered. "This Missouri kid might play a dapper playboy, but he can't play football," said Wal-

lis in yet another rejection memo.

Howard had suggested Dennis Morgan, who was making a picture with Jane Wyman, but Wallis wouldn't even sanction a screen test. "Morgan looks like he just stepped out of a beauty parlor to get his hair waved. He doesn't belong on a football field. Sports fans would mock him."

The Canadian actor, Donald Woods, was given the most serious consideration. Before Reagan claimed the title, Woods was another actor known on the Warners lot as "the King of the Bs." Woods had a better physique than Reagan, and was taller, standing 6'4".

Although Wallis thought Woods would be most convincing as a football player, he had another assignment for him. He and Lupe Velez had stirred up some box office in *The Girl from Mexico*. Wallis ordered a sort of sequel, *Mexican Spitfire,* in which he wanted the stars to appear together once again. "By the time Velez gets through fucking Woods, he won't have the energy to run across a football field," Wallis claimed.

In his office, the producer was not impressed with Reagan's physical presence. "You're not big enough to play a football player. Those guys are fucking bruisers."

Reagan protested. "Gipp weighed five pounds less than I do. He walked with a sort of slouch and a limp. He looked like a football player only when he was on the field."

To convince Wallis that he knew his way around a football field, Reagan went home and returned with pictures of himself in a uniform from the years when he played for Eureka College. That seemed to do it for Wallis, but he still wanted Reagan to be tested on camera.

By the time he got home that day, before Jane returned from the studio, the phone was ringing. It was Wallis' secretary. "The boss man wants you to show up for an eight o'clock shooting in the morning. You're to be tested for the role of George Gipp."

Reagan was elated. His big chance had come at last.

For his screen test, Reagan thought he would appear opposite some contract player, as was the custom. To his surprise, when he showed up, Pat O'Brien, in his coach's uniform and in full makeup, was there to shake his hand. He'd agreed to participate as Knute Rockne, conferring on camera with Reagan playing George Gipp.

The test went smoothly, and was completed before noon, when O'Brien invited Reagan to the commissary for a hamburger. Over coffee, he told Reagan that Jack Warner had wanted James Cagney to play Knute Rockne, because he was number four in terms of star power at the box office.

"In terms of star power, I'm not even in the top fifty," O'Brien said. "But both Bonnie Rockne, Knute's widow, and the Catholic Church objected to Cagney because he'd appeared in all those gangster films. After that, Warner went after Spencer Tracy, but MGM wouldn't release him. I was the last resort. I got the role only because Bonnie approved."

Two days later, Wallis called Reagan, granting him the role. "You're going to be on the screen for only ten minutes, but your role is vital to the script."

Screenwriter Robert Buckner, an amateur historian who had known Rockne slightly, got advice from Bonnie, as well as from the brass at Notre Dame. He told Reagan, "Bonnie claims there are too many football scenes and not enough scenes relating to her husband's academic achievements."

He also revealed that he was writing a new screenplay, a Western called *Santa Fe Trail.* There's a great role in it—that of George Armstrong Custer. You should lobby for it.'

Despite that advice, Reagan was not intrigued enough to follow it.

On the set, he had an embarrassing encounter with Gale Page, with whom he had had a notorious three-way with Ann Sheridan. She had been cast as Bonnie Skiles, the sweetheart that Rockne eventually marries. Reagan told O'Brien, "Thank God I have no love scenes with her. One night, things got out of hand between us."

O'Brien responded, "All of us adventurous Irishmen take a detour here and there, and no man should be held responsible for mistakes along the way."

On the set of *Knute Rockne*, Reagan was reunited with veteran actor Donald Crisp, with whom he had co-starred in *Sergeant Murphy*. Crisp had been cast as Father Callahan, who ran the university. Later, some reviewers cattily commented, "Crisp forgot he was playing Father Callahan. He thought he was playing God himself."

Reagan also had a reunion on the set with William Hopper, Hedda's son. In *Knute Rockne*, Hopper had been cast in an uncredited role as a New York reporter.

William had continued to call Reagan frequently, but he had always put him off. He wanted to maintain his friendship with William, mainly because he was the son of such a powerful columnist, but knowing about William's sexual interest in him, he didn't want to get too close. Reagan complained to O'Brien, "William's always after me."

Over lunch, William told Reagan that married life to Jane Gilbert "is something to endure. I prefer another kind of action. How is married life with you?"

"Jane and I are very happy, but unless we're making a picture together, we don't see a lot of each other. Two movie stars who get married rarely lead a life of domestic bliss—that is, if both of them are employed."

William said that he wished Reagan well, hoping that his portrayal of George Gipp "will put you over the top. As for me, I'm working steadily, but I'm just part of the scenery—a bank cashier who gets murdered, a cowboy in the background, often a reporter, once a Yale tennis player and a society gent in a top hat."

Hedda joined them for lunch and sympathized with her son's career frustration. She had experienced the same problems when she had tried to be a movie star. "When bad days come, all your hard work seems to be waiting to fall on you like a ton of bricks. I remember when I lost my seven-year contract at MGM. I was never a star, always a featured player, letting the spotlight shine on the stars. I was the mean woman who slapped children, made myself a gossipy and annoying guest, or else a matron on the make for someone else's husband. On the screen, I looked ridiculous. I once asked Mayer why I was always cast as a bitch. He told me, 'It takes one to play one.'"

Most of the film's football scenes were shot at Loyola University. The most difficult scene called for Reagan to run eighty yards for a touchdown. On that hot summer morning, he'd arrived in time for a heavy, high-cholesterol breakfast, consisting of a greasy bacon-and-egg sandwich, a can of pineapple juice, and coffee.

After his first run, a difficult dolly shot, Bacon ordered Reagan to do the run again. On the second time around, the cameraman still wasn't pleased with his shot. Bacon yelled out, "Once more, Reagan!"

On the third try, Reagan, with a lump in his stomach, made the dash. He raced past the goal line and headed for a wooden fence that enclosed the field. There, he vomited up all that bacon fat. "My director's name would also be Bacon—you figure," he said, after having soiled his football uniform.

Gipp's final words, supposedly uttered to Rockne before his death in 1920, were repeated by Reagan in the film: "Some day when things are tough, maybe you could ask the boys to go in there and win just one for the Gipper."

[The American Film Institute ranked the quote "Win one for the Gipper," as number 89 on its poll of the top 100 most famous quotes ever uttered in a movie. When Reagan ran for president in 1980, he used "Let's win one for the Gipper" as a political slogan. At that point, he was often referred to as "The Gipper."]

Years later, looking back on his role as the Gipper, Reagan recalled, "It was a springboard that bounced me into a wider variety of parts in pictures. It's true, I got some unmerited criticism from sports writers. One of them wondered why the producers never shoehorned real football players into key roles. But since I practically earned my way through college playing football—that disturbed me. However this criticism was balanced by some unmerited praise from the same general source, because another sports writer said I was so accurate in my portrayal of the Gipper that I even imitated his slight limp. Actually, I wasn't trying to limp. I just wasn't used to my new football shoes and my feet hurt."

For the gala premiere of *Knute Rockne—All American,* Warners rented two trains to chug their way from Los Angeles to South Bend, Indiana. Stars were commissioned, not only Jane and Reagan, but Rudy Vallée, Donald Crisp, Gail Patrick, Ricardo Cortez, Gale Page, and even Kate Smith, with the understanding that she'd be belting out frequent renditions of "God Bless America." Bob Hope also traveled to Indiana to serve as toastmaster. Taking time off from his father's 1940 presidential campaign, Franklin D. Roosevelt, Jr. also showed up to read a letter of congratulations from the president.

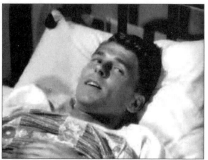

Still suffering from a heart condition, Jack Reagan was invited to go along with the troupe. "He revered fellow Irishman Pat O'Brien, putting him in the special category of Al Smith," Reagan said. "Dad and Pat became instant friends. Unfortunately, they went out every night boozing, returning in the early morning. I was worried about Dad's heart."

When Jack returned home to Nelle, he told her, "I've had everything now. I've seen Dutch get to be a star. Oh, I know the studio hasn't made him one yet, but the folks back there know he's arrived. I wish you could have heard the welcome they gave him. As far as I'm concerned, nothing will ever top it. I'm ready to go any time now."

For the first time, Reagan was acclaimed as an actor. He noticed it when he walked onto the Warners' lot every day. "Suddenly, people who had never spoken to me before were calling out, 'Good morning, Mr. Reagan!'"

[Reagan did not live to see the ghoulish exhumation of the body of his beloved role model, George Gipp, on October 4, 2007. Gipp's body was dug up for DNA testing to determine if he'd fathered a child out of wedlock with an 18-year-old high school student. His right thighbone was removed from his grave, and the rest of his decaying corpse was reburied the same day, much to the horror of Gipp's relatives. The tests showed that Gipp was not the father of the child that was born

Top photo: George Gipp, dying, is interpreted by Ronald Reagan in a screen interpretation that lasted for no more than ten minutes of the film's total running time.

Lower photo: During his second bid for the office of President of the U.S. Reagan invoked the role he'd played and the line ("Win one for the Gipper") he'd delivered in 1940.

within days of Gipp's death way back in 1920.]

***

As contract players at Warners, it seemed inevitable that Jane Wyman would end up in a picture (*My Love Came Back; 1940*) with her nemesis, Olivia de Havilland. She didn't have anything against Olivia personally, "Other than her being born," she confided to Reagan and others.

Perhaps inaccurately, Jane claimed that she would

Left to right: Eddie Albert; Olivia de Havilland (who had no musical talent); and Jane (who could sing and dance, but who only mimed at playing the violin) in *My Love Came Back.*

have become a big star on the Warner lot had it not been for Olivia, "who got all those roles with my name on them, beginning with Melanie in *Gone With the Wind* (1939)"

"I also should have starred opposite David Niven in *The Private Lives of Elizabeth and Essex* (1939), with Errol again in *Dodge City* (also 1939), and most definitely with that gorgeous hunk, John Payne, in *Wings of the Navy* (1939)."

Jane recalled her first meeting with Olivia. "The bitch had a chip on her shoulder. After *Gone With the Wind*, and after her suspension, she thought she was entitled to the roles reserved for Bette Davis. We were both cast in this little romantic comedy, *My Love Came Back*, but Miss Olivia didn't think the film was worthy of her talents. She actually told me that her part was the kind of role that might normally have been assigned to 'a little starlet like me.'"

"My role is such crap that even Priscilla Lane turned it down," Olivia told Jane.

Warners' assigned the German film director, Curtis Bernhardt, to "this little slice of strudel," as he characterized the film. Bernhardt had been arrested by the Nazis because he was a Jew, but he managed to escape in 1933 and had fled first to France and England, and then to Hollywood. The year Jane met him, he had just come to work for Warners.

He told Jane that in an upcoming film, based on a script then being written, he was considering casting her husband. "It's called *Million Dollar Baby.*"

In addition to Jane and Olivia, Bernhardt had assembled an all-star cast of supporting players, including Jeffrey Lynn, Eddie Albert, Charles Winninger, Spring Byington, Grant Mitchell, William T. Orr, and S.Z. Sakall.

In the film, Olivia was cast as a talented, high-strung violin student at a New York academy. She walks out on her music teacher, the cuddlesome S.Z. Sakall.

Later, she is accused of being the mistress of a wealthy and distinguished patron of the arts, as portrayed by Winninger. When he cannot attend a concert with Olivia, he sends his young business manager, the dashingly handsome Tony Baldwin (Jeffrey Lynn). The two fall in love.

Jane was cast as a musical friend of Olivia's. Her boyfriend is played by Eddie Albert, who had made those two *Brother Rat* movies with her.

To prepare for their roles, both Jane and Olivia each took violin lessons. *[In the final version of the film, the music supposedly emanating from their instruments would be dubbed.]* But whereas Jane learned how to handle the fingering and bowing on a dummy instrument, Olivia did not, losing patience and frequently shouting at the director.

In his cold German accent, Bernhardt told her, "I do not like incompetence. You should have learned how to finger the instrument like Miss Wyman here."

That did not endear Jane to Olivia.

Bernhardt told Jack Warner that Olivia complained about every single thing. "She is imperial and haughty. She dislikes everybody. The only person who can control her is Jimmy Stewart when he comes onto the set to make love to her in her dressing room."

On the first day Stewart arrived, he kissed Jane. "I enjoyed our previous time together with Hank (Henry Fonda). But I'd better steer clear of you now that you're married to my buddy, Ronnie."

In the middle of the shoot, Olivia, feigning illness, disappeared for a week. "Curtis was cursing her in German, and life was miserable on the set," Jane said.

One day, Bernhardt invited Jane to lunch in the commissary, where he complained at length about Olivia. Jane recalled their meal. "Beer in a large tankard, pretzels, and several slices of Bavarian chocolate cake. Chocolate cake and beer have never been my favorite taste treats."

By now, Eddie Albert and Jane were friends. He had worked on pictures with her before, and, amazingly, would also be appearing on TV with her in the 1980s. They always maintained an innocent but flirtatious relationship.

Jane became very fond of Lynn, and would co-star with him in a future movie. She found the New Englander handsome and exceedingly charming.

"On the screen, and in person, too, you look like the kind of clean-cut fellow you could take home to meet dear ol' mom," Jane said.

"I suffer from always appearing on screen with stronger personalities," he claimed. "In *Four Daughters,* John Garfield attracted most of the attention. In *The Roaring Twenties,* I was up against James Cagney and Humphrey Bogart. Now, I've been assigned to film a movie called *All This and Heaven Too.* What chance do I have when Bette Davis lights up and starts puffing on that god damn cigarette?"

For the most part, critics dismissed *My Love Came Back,* one calling it "a fluffy little romantic comedy. It's like Chinese food. An hour later, you're hungry. The same holds for this film. An hour later, you'll have forgotten all about it in your search to sink your teeth into something more substantial. The stellar talents of Olivia De Havilland and Eddie Albert are completely wasted. This movie is more suited to the limited talents of Jeffrey Lynn and Jane Wyman. Actually, the supporting stars such as Cuddles Sakall steal any scene they're in."

***

In May of 1940, Reagan was invited to pose in the nude for a sculpture class at the University of Southern California. Gale Page, who had played Knute Rockne's wife in their recent film, was enrolled in an art class there. She informed Reagan that her fellow classmates had voted him "The Most Nearly Perfect Male Body" among Hollywood's male stars.

Page later recalled, "Ronnie appeared extremely flattered, but also embarrassed, especially about posing in the nude."

After she cajoled him, he finally agreed to model for the class, but only if they allowed him to wear bathing trunks. "They'll have to settle for me in the same swimwear I'd appear in on the beach."

"I think we can make that work," she said. "I have a vivid memory of your genitals, and I'm a very good artist. The assignment is to draw a nude male body. The artists can sculpt your body, but they'll mold a replica of your genitals from my sketch. Of course, regarding those genitals, I would like a refresher course."

"We'll see about that," he said. "As you know, I'm a married man."

"Surely, you wouldn't be the only married man in Hollywood to have something on the side. That's virtually mandatory for a male movie star."

Dressed in a business suit, Reagan drove with Page to the USC campus the following evening. Outside the classroom, he faced her in the hall. She directed him to the men's room, telling him he could change into his trunks there.

A few moments later, he appeared in the classroom, where he was warmly greeted by a group of young women. About five or six young men also crowded around him, asking for his autograph. Some of them wanted him to autograph the publicity picture in which he'd posed in swimwear with Susan Hayward.

The class instructor called him aside. "I hope you'll change your mind about posing in the nude. It's all for art. It has nothing to do with sex. Our students are very sophisticated."

"I'm wearing trunks, or else it's no deal," Reagan responded. He opened his robe to display his body in a white bathing suit.

"Many of your greatest fans are here to sculpt your body," the instructor responded. "Several of them are young men who view you as a dreamboat. They collect pictures of you."

"Why aren't these guys collecting cheesecake pictures of Betty Grable or Carole Landis?"

Reagan, chaste and modest, modeling in Grannie's panties.

219

"Art students have varying sexual tastes," the teacher said. "Just imagine that you're David posing for Michelangelo."

"I will feel red-faced just posing for these gals," Reagan said. "But having all these guys ogling me, too…I don't know about this."

"After five minutes, you'll be relaxed. I'm sure you'll take off that bathing suit. I've seen you shirtless in movies. In one film, you stripped down to your underwear. Here, you can take the final step."

"I think not!"

"All right," the teacher responded. "We'll take you any way we can get you. Perhaps you'll change your mind and do what comes naturally, so we won't have to imagine your genitals. Several in my class have told me that they suspect you have beautiful genitals, nothing to be ashamed of."

During the session, Reagan had to pose uncomfortably, balancing a football in his right hand. Tiring easily, he had to take several breaks. Never in his life had his body been admired by so many at such close range. "Many young women, and even the men, were lusting for my body," as he'd later confide to Jane.

She became angry at him for having agreed to pose in the first place.

En route back to Page's apartment, she asked him to drop in for a nightcap. "I really want to see you again completely nude. If I'm going to draw your genitals, I don't want to rely on a distant encounter, but on a recent memory."

"I don't know how I feel about this," he said.

"Please don't be so square," she said. "You're going to be immortalized with thirty nude sculptures. I bet someday they'll be collectors' items."

"One thing," he said. "You didn't warn me that a photographer would arrive to snap my picture as a nude model. I don't know if I like that kind of body beautiful publicity. My male friends will make fun of me."

"Listen, Ronnie, as I'm sure you've been told by others, especially directors: You've got to start selling yourself as a sex symbol so that you can compete with Clark Gable, Robert Taylor, Tyrone Power, and, most definitely, with Errol Flynn. Flynn would have posed nude for the class, but they voted for you instead."

"I hope you're not giving me bad advice, you cute little vixen," he said, climbing up the stairs to her apartment.

***

Jane Wyman was reunited with Wayne Morris, her former boyfriend, on the set of their next movie, *Gambling on the High Seas* (1940). His divorce from Leonora Hornblow had just been finalized, and he was on the prowl again. According to Jane, "Wayne never let a marriage license cramp his romantic pursuits."

She also revealed, "He wasn't interested in the B picture we were making. All he could think and talk about, other than romance, was his fascination with flying. It began when we made *Flight Angels* together."

"War is in the wind," he told her, "and I've joined the Naval Reserve. Any day, I expect the United States will join the Allies in World War II. When I'm not in front of the camera, I'm studying to be a Navy flier."

Both of them agreed that their first three movies, *Here Comes Carter, Polo Joe,* and *Smart Blonde,* had done absolutely nothing for their careers. Their first *Brother Rat* movie had done well at the box office, but the sequel didn't go over. Nor did their two most recent movies, *Flight Angels* and *An Angel from Texas.*

"Whether you like to face it or not, we're a screen team," Morris told her. "Think

Hepburn and Tracy, William Powell and Myrna Loy, Clark Gable and Joan Crawford, even Garbo and Gilbert."

"I don't think we play ball in those leagues," she cautioned him.

He bent down and gave her a kiss on her pug nose. "I know you don't like to admit it, but we're also a winning team between the sheets."

"Is that any way to talk to a married lady?" she asked.

"I'll give you a pass for now," he said. "But on our next picture, I bet you'll come home to daddy."

"You're assuming we'll be teamed again."

"It's in the cards," he accurately predicted.

Jane Wyman with Wayne Morris in *Gambling on the High Seas*.

Very *noir*, her performance evoked something akin to a female version of Brass Bancroft.

The script for *Gambling on the High Seas* might have been better titled "*Mobsters, Mayhem, and Murder.*" Its complicated plot revolves around a casino boat operating in international waters off the coast of the United States. Gambling aboard the boat is strictly for suckers who get fleeced. Morris stars as Jim Carver, an investigative reporter accessorized with a big camera and flashbulbs.

Jane was cast as Laurie Ogden, a rather demure young woman who is Morris' love interest. She is also the bookkeeper to crime boss Greg Morella (Gilbert Roland), who owns the crooked gambling ship. With Morris' urging, she agrees to testify against her boss in court, but he learns of her scheme and orders her kidnapped and imprisoned aboard his ship. Morris, eventually and inevitably, comes to her rescue.

The gimmick aboard the casino ship is a rigged roulette wheel with a concealed camera, one reviewer noting that the director, George Amy, gave the roulette wheel more close-ups than he gave either Morris or Jane.

Cast as a mobster, Mexican-born Gilbert Roland, dashingly handsome and masculine, was planning to marry screen goddess Constance Bennett, with whom Jane had starred in *Tailspin.*

She remembered Roland "as an aggressive Latin Lover type, always feeling that he had to flirt with every pretty *gringa* he met."

"Originally, before I got hooked on acting—and actresses, I might add—I wanted to be a bullfighter," he told Jane. "I would have been a *big* attraction in my suit of lights, if you get my drift."

"I get your drift," she shot back. "But let it keep on drifting."

Even though she turned down a forward pass, she found him an intriguing character. "Gilbert could make me swoon," Jane said to director George Amy.

To put Roland off, she said, in jest, "I'd go to bed with you, but I suspect you'd tell half of Hollywood, including Ronald Reagan. You're obviously the kiss-and-tell Mexican bandit."

After Jane became a major star, Roland recalled working with her, "There was talent written all over her, but she was a late bloomer in movies, struggling for fifteen long years in programmers. She had a surface bravado. She appeared to be very confident, but I think she was plagued with self-doubt. Over the years, she always had this driving determination to be a big star—and she made it. She knew she had this certain flame burning inside her, and she fanned it, increasing its fire."

When *Gambling on the High Seas* was released, *Variety* wrote: "Could the newspapers of the country but hire the see-all, know-all, tell-all reporters trained in the B-picture corner of the Warner lot, there'd doubtlessly be not even space on page one for news from the war in Europe. They would be too full of underworld inside and cracking wide open crooked gambling joints through the smart work of newspapermen who look like the Boy Scouts of America personified."

In spite of the awkward wording of that review, Jane was pleased to read this appraisal of her own involvement in the film: "Miss Wyman makes a very aesthetic *vis-à-vis* to American Boy Morris."

That night, she showed the review to Reagan. He told her, "Don't worry, hon, you'll do better in your next picture."

She stormed out of the room, heading for the bedroom, where she locked the door from the inside. When he came knocking later, she didn't open it until it was time for her to report to work early the next morning.

***

Although the previous onscreen pairing of Jane with Reagan, *An Angel from Texas,* had not generated a lot of excitement at the box office, director Lewis Seiler and producer Bryan Foy decided to take one more chance and re-team them together in *Tugboat Annie Sails Again* (1940). The picture was conceived as a sequel to Marie Dressler's highly successful *Tugboat Annie* in 1933.

Based on its success, Dressler had been immediately scheduled to make a sequel, but she died in 1934, a year after the original film's release. Louis B. Mayer searched for a character actress to follow in her shoes, but found no suitable candidate.

Finally, Jack Warner acquired the rights, and cast the character actress Marjorie Rambeau as the grizzled old salt.

In the film's original version, crusty old Wallace Beery played the role of Annie's husband. But in the sequel, Annie is a widow, skippering a vessel called the *Narcissus* from the fictional port of "Secoma," a combined depiction of both Tacoma, Washington, and the larger port of Seattle. Most of the outdoor shots, however, were filmed on location in the Port of Los Angeles.

Jane and Reagan worked smoothly with Seiler, who had helmed Jane in *He Couldn't Say No* and in *Flight Angels,* and had directed Reagan in *Hell's Kitchen* with the Dead End Kids.

Appearing with her husband for the fourth and final time, Jane was cast as Peggy Armstrong, a rich young socialite who falls for Reagan, who plays the role of a poor sailor, Eddie King.

Seiler selected a strong cast of character actors to support his three stars, notably Alan Hale, Sr., who played Annie's major rival, the scheming Captain Bullwinkle. Others included Clarence Kolb as Joe Armstrong, Paul Hurst as Pete, and Chill Wills as "Shiftless."

Reagan also arranged a small role for his brother, Moon, in the film.

Maureen Reagan, the first child of Reagan and Jane, claimed that she made her film debut in *Tugboat Annie Sails Again.* Her face doesn't appear on the screen, as she was still in her mother's womb. In her memoir, *First Father, First Daughter,* she wrote: "There's a scene in the movie in which Mother gets knocked into the water, and I cringe every time I see it, knowing that I took the fall with her." She later referred to it as her "in utero" performance.

Perhaps Maureen didn't know this, but Jane's dive from the pier required four takes. "I ruined four dresses and got a thorough drenching. When Ronnie found out, he was furious with Seiler, fearing taking such falls would make me have a miscarriage."

In yet another scene, Jane pushes Reagan off the pier as a means of punishing him for giving her a public spanking when she backed her automobile into his, sending his vehicle into the water. In her role as the daughter of a shipping tycoon, before the film's happy ending, she arranges for it to be dredged up and repainted, returning it to him in good condition.

Reagan setting sail with Rambeau & Wyman.

The script of *Tugboat Annie Sails Again* involves a "tug" of war Rambeau fights with her arch-rival, Captain Bullwinkle (as played by Hale). Annie faces financial troubles, canceled contracts, fights over salvage laws, and a violent storm at sea.

Both Reagan and Jane later asserted that they enjoyed working with Rambeau. "Like *Tugboat Annie,* Marjorie was a tough old broad," Reagan said. "Born in San Francisco, she was deserted by her father and taken to remote Nome, Alaska, for some reason."

Because Nome was a rough town, filled with far more men than women, Rambeau's mother dressed her as a boy. She sang in and played the banjo in music halls and rowdy saloons. What her mother didn't realize was that an effeminate, rather pretty young boy might also invite lust in the horny frontiersmen. Reportedly, as an early teenager, Rambeau was raped three times, the men perhaps delighted to find that the boy was actually a girl.

Eventually landing in New York, Rambeau made her Broadway debut in the spring of 1911. After that, she drifted to Hollywood, where she starred in silent films.

Jane Wyman and Ronald Reagan were feuding and fighting—and eventually loving—in *Tugboat Annie Sails Again* aboard the *Narcissus.*

Ironically, as an early talkie, one of the films she played a role in was *Min and Bill* (1930), starring Wallace Beery and Marie Dressler, the original stars of *Tugboat Annie.* Rambeau was cast as a waterfront floozie. Later, one of her best showcases was as the trampy mother of Ginger Rogers in *Primrose Path* (1940), for which she received an Oscar nomination as Best Supporting Actress.

Although Jane's role in *Tugboat Annie Sails Again* did not particularly challenge her, Seiler praised her nevertheless. "In spite of the nothing assignments she was given, she seemed to me to be always trying to give the banal lines and situations something extra. We had a lot of great character actors in the film, and she studied them like she was taking acting lessons."

In a release from Warners' publicity department, Jane was quoted as saying, "Rambeau's seasoned talent and enormous thespic self-assurance awed me at first, and then I discovered the big heart and the wonderfully supportive nature of this fine woman."

Those words reflected Jane's sentiment but not her exact language. Most of the time, she spoke in vernacular slang, never using words like "thespic"

Rambeau also appraised Jane: "I think she was the greater talent, far more so than Ronnie. He had more book learning, but she was street smart and had her own kind of intelligence. She could size up people quicker than Ronnie."

As shooting progressed, Jane's pregnancy began to show. Seiler ordered his cameraman to conceal her expanding belly behind items of furniture or other actors. A dressmaker was hired to design costumes to make her look thin.

When the picture was released, most critics cited Jane and Reagan only in passing. Rambeau attracted most of the attention, and the critics were harsh, stating the obvious: Marjorie Rambeau was no Marie Dressler.

In the film, Reagan got to show off his athletic physique not once, but twice. As one reviewer said, "His torso looks better than this movie."

During the filming of *Tugboat Annie Sails Again*, Reagan had been so sure that Jane was going to have a son that he printed birth announcements to that effect. "Sperm like mine can only produce a boy," he bragged to Pat O'Brien.

"Don't count on the kid being born with a dick," the veteran actor warned him. "Mother Nature plays some wicked games."

On January 4, 1941, the day before Jane's 24th birthday, she gave birth to a baby girl weighing five and a half pounds. She was named Maureen Elizabeth Reagan. Following in the footsteps of her father, she would become a screen actress before venturing into politics.

When Reagan was shown his baby girl, he told the nurse, "She's a homely little thing, isn't she?"

With his usual frugality, he crossed out the word "boy" on his pre-printed birth announcements and wrote in "girl."

Reagan was fretting not only about the health and welfare of Jane and little Maureen, but about his new role in an upcoming movie. So far, Warners' hadn't notified him of his next assignment as a contract player.

He learned about it in a most unusual way when he was called back to the Warners lot to reshoot a scene with Rambeau.

As he waited for the scene to be set up, he sat in a director's chair reading the latest news about the war in Europe. Suddenly, a man approached him from behind. As he turned around to see who it was, he experienced a close encounter. He was shocked as a tongue darted into his mouth as part of a sudden and passionate kiss.

"You're gonna star with me in my next picture," the man said. "I've been yearning to give you a few pokes, sport, and here is my chance."

It was Errol Flynn.

Chapter Seven

When Quoted by His Enemies, Reagan's Most Famous Line

"Where's the Rest of Me?"

Becomes a Mockery of His Shortcomings

The Press Hails "Jane & Ronnie" as America's Perfect Couple—But Were They?

Above, in a scene he rehearsed endlessly, Reagan discovers he has no legs. Ann Sheridan *(right figure in photo, above)* is there to comfort him.

In 1940, the Reagans were captured on camera, at home, cracking nuts, as a depiction of America's most perfect, most adorable, and most wholesome couple.

In 1940, Jane appeared in *Honeymoon for Three*, a film released in January of 1941, the month Maureen was born.

She heard that she'd been cast when Joan Blondell called her one morning at eight o'clock. "Have you read *Variety* this morning?" her friend asked. "It's been announced you've been cast in *Honeymoon for Three* with George Brent and Ann Sheridan. "Those two are having such a hot affair that I hope they have something left for the camera."

Reagan had left early for the studio that morning, and Jane and Blondell had a long woman-to-woman talk about husbands, careers, and motherhood.

Blondell surprised Jane by telling her that her upcoming role was part of a remake of a movie that she had appeared in back in 1933. "I have no idea why Jack Warner is recycling this old script again," Blondell said. "When I filmed it, it had already been a hit on Broadway called *Goodbye Again*. I appeared with Warren William and Genevieve Tobin. It was a passable little piece of fluff, but it was quickly buried in the graveyard of forgotten films."

"We made it pre-Code, before the Breen office began tampering with it, so your writers will have to clean it up to get it past the censors," Blondell said. "There was a scene in our version where it was implied that Warren is taking a piss. It turned out to be running water. And in my version, I slept in the same hotel room with my boss—and it was understood that we weren't married. That's pretty *risqué* stuff, wouldn't you say?"

"I'd like to see it—sounds like fun," Jane said. "I met Warren William when we appeared together in *Stage Struck* with you. I saw Tobin in *The Petrified Forest* with Bogie and Bette Davis. Then Tobin's husband, William Keighley, directed Ronnie and me in *Brother Rat.*"

"I know all that," Blondell said.

"Just trying to let you know what a Hollywood insider I've become."

"I made *Goodbye Again* when I was recovering from yet another abortion," Blondell confessed. "George Barnes didn't like the idea of having children. He believed that kids take the romance out of a relationship. Unfortunately, he didn't believe in using rubbers."

[She was referring to the famous cinematographer, George Barnes, whom she married in Arizona in 1933, the union surviving until 1936. During the short run of that marriage, Blondell insisted on carrying a child to term. A son was born to the couple in 1934. She named him Norman. The boy was later adopted by her second husband, Dick Powell, and his name was changed to Norman S. Powell."]

"Ronnie wants to have children, but I don't want to settle into the role of a bored housewife looking out for a lot of little Reagans running around the place. I'm going to continue to pursue my film career, as hopeless as it looks at the moment."

"That's not what the fan magazines are claiming," Blondell said. "They say that Ronnie has domesticated you."

Ruth Waterbury of *Photoplay* was among the hacks promoting Jane's image as a woman wanting to settle down in the kitchen and bedroom as a dutiful wife playing second fiddle to her husband.

Waterbury overlooked the fact that in 1941 alone, Jane would release four different movies. "Jane is madly in love with Ronnie and is devoted to him," Waterbury wrote. "His every wish is her command. He comes first in her life, even if it means sacrificing her own career. She works constantly to build up his ego and confidence."

Blondell later said, "The Jane that Waterbury described was not the Janie I knew. She lacked confidence in her own talent, and didn't spend much time building up Ronnie's confidence as a screen actor from what I saw. She had a steely determination to succeed at all costs. Instead of being a wife and mother, she talked constantly about chasing that elusive dream of stardom."

Two "Dreamboats," John Payne & Dennis Morgan, Pursue Jane, as Reagan is Ensnared by Rival Blondes, Betty Grable & Carole Landis.

"I think Ronnie is cute," Jane told Blondell. "If only he would stop talking about politics, he'd be a hell of a lot cuter. I've failed twice at marriage, and, frankly, I don't know if I can make a go of it this time around, either. We put on our smiling faces for our fans, who read those pulp magazines, but in private, we can be a lot less charming."

Even at that point in her life, Jane showed a fierce independence. When her friend, Lucille Ball, had called to congratulate her on her marriage, Jane made a frank admission. "Even though I'm married, I still have my eye trained on every good-looking guy I meet, especially if they're named John Payne or Dennis Morgan. A really gorgeous guy can make me forget about home and hearth, at least put aside enough time for love in the afternoon. Which would your rather do, change some kid's shitty diaper or let John Payne make love to you?"

"You know me well enough to answer that question for yourself," Ball said.

The *Motion Picture Herald and Fame Poll* had designated Jane as a "Star of Tomorrow," but after their forecast was released, she lamented to Ball, "But will tomorrow ever come if I keep appearing in one highly forgettable film after another? I'm on the rocky road to thirty, and still turning out these god damn programmers. Who do you have to sleep with to get ahead in this town!"

"Try Jack Warner, Louis B. Mayer, and Darryl F. Zanuck, and most definitely Harry Cohn," Ball said.

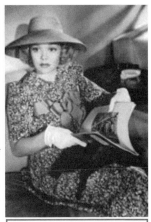

Young Jane evolved into the odd girl out, appearing in a wardrobe disaster she hated. Warners' wardrobe department promoted it as "a *foulard* dress with a wide-brimmed hat." Jane denounced it as "frumpy."

***

The script for *Honeymoon for Three* arrived that afternoon. When Jane read it, she was shocked at how small her part was. More than her role as Elizabeth Clochessy, she'd have preferred the part that went to Osa Massen, a Danish actress who had come to America in 1937, after having begun her career as a newspaper photographer. The same year Jane met her, she'd been cast as Melvyn Douglas' unfaithful wife dealing with blackmailer Joan Crawford in *A Woman's Face* (1941).

That night, when Reagan came home, Jane complained to him about her career frustration. "I was called the *Hey Hey* Girl. Now I should be renamed the Queen of the Sub-Plots. I'm living through the paper doll years of my career."

"I don't expect much from Lloyd Bacon," she said. "He's the director. He races through a film like he did my appearance in *Gold Diggers of 1937.*"

"I did all right when he directed me in *Knute Rockne,*" Reagan said.

Grannie Nelle, childminding Baby Maureen.

227

"I applaud your good luck," she said, sarcastically. "Lady Luck hates me."

"She doesn't at all," he said. "After all, she brought me to you. How lucky can a gal get?"

Sheridan was clearly the star of the picture, playing the secretary to George Brent, cast as the novelist, Kenneth Bixby, who is a literary Don Juan, eagerly sought after by hordes of women fans. One woman, Julie Wilson (Osa Massen, who, it's revealed, is married to the character played by Charles Ruggles), sneaks into his hotel room in the hopes of getting her book published. Thus the action begins. Elizabeth (as played by Jane) is Julie's cousin, who has followed her to Bixby's hotel. Elizabeth is engaged to the character played by William T. Orr, with whom Jane had worked before in *My Love Came Back.* She remembered him talking obsessively about America's possible entry into World War II.

Jane's competition: Danish beauty, Osa Massen.

"I plan to become an Army Air Force officer," he had told Jane.

At the war's end, Orr would marry Joy Page, Jack Warner's stepdaughter. A rosy future in media, especially the fast-emerging field of television, awaited him.

In *Honeymoon for Three,* Anne (Sheridan) gets her man Bixby (Brent) in the end.

Key roles were also played by Walter Catlett, who has some funny bits as a waiter, and by Lee Patrick, who seemed adept at playing eccentric characters who included nurses, floozies, and dithery socialites. In the movie, as Mrs. Pettijohn, she names her children after her favorite authors, including Booth Tarkington.

Jane enjoyed seeing Charles Ruggles again, an actor whose career would span six decades, a hundred pictures, and a reputation for playing absent-minded authority figures.

On the set, Jane met the screenwriting twins, Julius and Philip Epstein. They were filled with bitterness toward Jack Warner. In spite of their commercial success, Warner despised them, resenting their pranks, their work habits, and the odd hours they kept.

In 1952, the producer would turn their names over to the house Un-American Activities Committee. When asked if they were ever members of any subversive organization, the twins wrote, "Yes, Warner Brothers."

After their farce in which Jane appeared, the brothers went on to better things, winning an Oscar for the screenplay of Bogie's *Casablanca* (1942). They worked on that script with Howard Koch.

Like some other cast members, Catlett, defined by Jane as "the ugliest actor I ever met," was going on to greater things. Playing a testy and pompous waiter in *Honeymoon for Three*, he would soon be cast in *Yankee Doodle Dandy* (1942) with James Cagney.

Jane had never appeared this unglamorous on the screen before. Ironically at the same time she was posing for some of the most glamorous publicity shots for Warners. Some critics ridiculed her film outfits, calling them "in preparation for playing an old maid."

George Brent and Ann Sheridan, the stars of *Honeymoon for Three*, outshone Jane in this frothy romp, but Jane claimed, "My Day Will Come."

Another critic noted, "If Jane Wyman dressed like that in private life, she would never have nailed heartthrob Ronald Reagan."

During the filming of the movie, Hollywood writers made frequent visits to the set, looking for hot copy about the romance between Brent and Sheridan. Jane was with Sheridan when she was asked if she planned to marry Brent before Christmas. "Honey, I wouldn't spoil Christmas that way," she answered.

Even when Brent gave her a square-cut diamond, placing it on the third finger of her left hand, she still denied any engagement. "It's just a gift from a friend," she told reporters. "I place it on the finger where it fits best—and that's all there is to it. We're not engaged. Every time George gives me something, the press declares we're on the verge of eloping."

Walter Catlett..."The ugliest actor ever."

Honeymoon for Three was an obvious attempt to capitalize off the current flood of Brent-Sheridan publicity. But when the film was released, one critic wrote, "Brent and Sheridan may go up in flames off screen, but on screen, they make one burned-out couple."

To Jane, Sheridan confessed that they were having an affair, and that she was considering marrying him. Up to then, after her divorce, she'd been playing the field, dating David Niven, Allan Jones, and Frederick Brisson, along with directors Jean Negulesco and Anatole Litvak after he escaped from the clutches of Miriam Hopkins. Her dates with César Romero, "The Latin from Manhattan" were strictly platonic, as he was really lusting after Desi Arnaz, much to the annoyance of Lucille Ball.

"Frankly, George doesn't have a good marriage record," Sheridan said. "His first marriage to Helen Campbell lasted less than thirty days. Although he was married to Ruth Chatterton for two years, they didn't live together for most of that time. His third marriage to Constance Worth didn't survive the honeymoon."

Charles Ruggles... Specializing in mousy, stuttering, henpecked husbands.

"What's the matter with him?" Jane asked.

"I don't know for sure," she said. "As for me, I have a sexual problem with him."

"What kind of problem?" Jane asked.

"Brent *bent!*" Sheridan said before being called to the set.

[Sheridan's comment about Brent's sexual equipment, unprintable at the time, was made to Hedda Hopper, in explaining why their marriage broke up so quickly.]

Honeymoon for Three opened to bad reviews. The reasons most often cited for its failure included its direction, its acting, and its script. One critic in New York wrote, "George Brent is cast as a Lothario novelist, but it's not apparent why the ladies throw themselves at this dull character. Clark Gable he isn't."

Julius *(left)* and Philip Epstein: Irreverent and identical screenwriting twins working feverishly on the script for *Casablanca*

The film opened in January of 1941, the month Reagan and Jane added Baby Maureen to their household.

Many of Jane's friends, such as Paulette Goddard, called to congratulate her. Jane was rather frank. "Thanks, but no thanks. I am terribly disappointed. I was carrying around a girl all these months, and I wanted a boy, *really* wanted a boy. I had even selected a name for the kid: Ronald Reagan, Jr."

As a new father, Reagan was also being interviewed by the press. "The experience *[of having a baby]* made all this cartoon stuff about prospective fathers seem cheap. After work at the studio, I would go directly to Jane's hospital room. I was glad to be working because it took my mind off worrying about Jane. When she went into labor, she threw aside the hands of both the nurse and doctor. She grabbed mine and hung on for dear life. That gave me such a thrill, as I can't believe."

After the birth of their daughter, the Reagans found their living space too cramped. Although he held back, she urged him to go into debt and build a house. He had taken her to see the Rosalind Russell film, *This Thing Called Love* (1940), and she had fallen in love with the house depicted in the movie. She sought out the designer, asking him for a copy of his architectural plans, which he turned over to her.

After searching every weekend, Jane and Ronald bought a plot of land on a steep hill overlooking Hollywood Boulevard. A contractor was hired, and a new eight-room home was built. Jane decorated and furnished the house without any help from Reagan. "All he did was remind me that I was spending too much money," she lamented to her friends.

She was glad when he was cast in *Santa Fe Trail* (1940) with Errol Flynn. That gave her a chance to put some finishing touches on the house. She, too, was excited to have been cast, almost simultaneously, in another picture, *Bad Men of Missouri* (1941). As she told Blondell, "It stars my former lover, Wayne Morris, and my future lover, Dennis Morgan."

"Are you worried about Ronnie appearing in a movie with Flynn?" Blondell asked. "Do you think he'll tell Ronnie about the fling you two guys had?"

"No," Jane said. "Errol will be too busy chasing after Ronnie. I think I'll write a message for Flynn on Ronnie's dick—'This dick is mine.'"

***

For the most part, Reagan continued to ignore calls from Carole Landis, the celluloid blonde goddess, perhaps wanting to forget their romantic liaisons of the late 1930s. Nonetheless, he continued to tell friends such as Pat O'Brien, Robert Taylor, and Dick Powell, that, "Carole is one of the most luscious dames in Hollywood, but she's also among the most promiscuous where the competition is stiff for that honor."

His friends agreed, perhaps having sampled Landis' charms themselves. He knew that Powell had.

Unexpectedly, an urgent call came in from Landis that he felt he had to take. She informed him she was in the hospital, having been severely beaten. "I trust you as my friend. I need you to come to the hospital and help me figure out what to do."

When he got there, he found part of her face bandaged, and her nose was causing her a great deal of pain.

After a few minutes, she revealed what had happened. She'd become romantically involved with Pat DiCicco, a so-called Hollywood agent with no clients. He was in reality the front man for gangster Lucky Luciano's illegal activities in the Los Angeles area. Luciano was the city's major drug dealer, and those foolish enough to move in on his territory usually ended up with bullets in their bodies.

Reagan talked very earnestly to her, telling her that although he didn't want to dictate to her, "If you continue to hang out with DiCicco, you might end up dead. He's already been involved in at least two famous murders, and god knows how many gangland slayings. I know the guy's handsome and charming when he wants to be, but he's lethal."

DiCicco was an already well-documented beater of women. During his marriage to actress Thelma Todd (1932-34), he sent her to the hospital several times after assaulting her. Later, he was implicated in her murder.

In time, he'd marry heiress Gloria Vanderbilt, who, as published in her memoirs, stated that he beat her, too.

DiCicco had earned his negative reputation with Reagan because he had been partially responsible for the beating death of Reagan's friend, comedian Ted Healy. Wallace Beery and Albert ("Cubby") Broccoli were also involved in that fatal beating.

Landis promised to dump DiCicco. "If I do, I hope that means you'll start calling on me again," she told Reagan.

"Maybe sometime in the future, but right now, I'm trying to stay true blue to Jane. Maybe you should get married, too. Settle down."

Pat DiCicco...a documented henchman of Lucky Luciano, a brutalizer of women, and an omnisexual gigolo.

"If you'd divorce Jane and agree to marry me, I'll straighten out. You're the kind of guy who can help me."

"I can't." he said. "I'm taken. But if you try hard enough, you can find the right man. Just make sure he's not already married."

After Landis was released from the hospital three days later, she kept her promise to Reagan and dropped DiCicco. She even followed his advice and in 1940, she got married, a state of affairs that remained intact for only two months.

Her groom was an infamous playboy of the time, Willis Hunt, Jr., scion of a wealthy California society family in the yacht business. He lived in the Art Deco-style Sunset Towers Apartments on Sunset Boulevard, former home of John Wayne, Errol Flynn, director Howard Hawks, and gangster Bugsy Siegel.

Hunt thrived on speeding, and officers in the L.A.P.D. let him dress up in a police officer's uniform and arrest speeders along Santa Monica Boulevard and in the Hollywood Hills. At night, he was a party boy, often throwing orgies described as featuring "sex without gender" inside his deluxe apartment.

"I'm not really a homo cocksucker, because I'm always the top," he assured Landis.

During his two-month marriage to Landis, they were often seen cruising around Beverly Hills in his custom-made Lincoln convertible. On weekends, he took her flying, piloting his own plane. Later, in the evening, they were seen dancing and drinking at the Mocambo or at the Trocadero.

Bon vivant Willis Hunt, Jr., with Carole Landis at their wedding. He preferred "sex without gender" and desired Reagan.

When Landis could take him no more, she walked out, filing for divorce. The very next night, he was seen dating Betty Grable, who had divorced Jackie Coogan. Landis later told Reagan, "I'm seriously pissed off. He's going out with Grable because he knows she's my rival at Fox, and he's dating her to spite me."

Hunt was also seen dating New York actress Eleanor Frances, a dead ringer for Landis. He was also involved with starlet Carol Gallagher.

Hunt's most serious involvement was with Florida-born Martha O'Driscoll, who had appeared in 1939 with Mickey Rooney in *Judy Hardy and Son*. She was also set to have a minor role in Preston Sturges' classic comedy *The Lady Eve* (1941), starring Barbara Stanwyck, and also in Cecil B. DeMille's *Reap the Wild Wind (1942)*.

Dysfunctional playboy Willis Hunt chased blondes. In addition to Carole Landis, he heavy-dated Martha O'Driscoll.

Hunt called Reagan and invited him—"without Jane"—to one of his infamous parties. Reagan politely turned him down. Not put off, he phoned Reagan two days later and invited him to Bakers Field. He explained that at the airfield, he had become friends with some Royal Air Force pilots, who had a fleet of six two-seater fighter planes. They were training Americans who wanted to volunteer to shoot down Nazi planes flying over England during the Battle of Britain. With his fear of flying, Reagan turned down that offer. Hunt, however, was persistent, consistently calling Reagan and annoying him with his invitations.

Finally, he called Landis to protest Hunt's calls. "Why does he keep calling me? Are you behind this? Have you told him about us?"

"I hope you don't mind, but I did," she said. "He's not jealous—in fact, he finds you really cute. Actually, he wants to make it with you, perhaps join us in a three-way. He keeps calling because he never accepts the word 'no.'"

"Tell him to butt out, god damn it!"

"I'll not only do that, but I'm divorcing the fucker. I've had it. Since he can't get you, he's settled for Douglas Fairbanks, Jr., who swings both ways. If you don't believe me, ask Joan Crawford. Of course, she swings both ways, too."

After her divorce, in reference to her brief marriage, Landis told the press that, "It took exceptional forbearance just to make it through those sixty days."

She called Reagan to ask him to come by her home one night after work, but he refused. A short time later, she phoned him again, telling him she was going on a location shooting in Florida and asking him to slip away with her for a short vacation.

"The star of the picture is that bitch, Betty Grable, whom I detest. She claims she knows you, Like I'd believe you'd hang out with trash like that bleached blonde whore."

He wanted to say, "It takes one to know one," but he held his tongue. "I can't go away now. I'm making a movie with Errol Flynn."

"Better take along your chastity belt, darling," she said before hanging up.

***

A call from Warner Brothers came in to the Reagan home at six o'clock that morning. Jane was already awake, but Reagan was still sleeping. She called him to the phone. "It's Warners."

On the line, he learned that he was to report at eight o'clock for a costume fitting for Errol Flynn's new picture, *Santa Fe Trail.*

"Wayne Morris is off the picture," the voice said. "You're taking over the role of General Custer."

In the wardrobe department, a bright new cavalry uniform, blue with gold braid, had been crafted specifically for him. On the floor, he noticed a crumpled, discarded uniform with Morris' name pinned to it.

In his memoirs, Reagan recalled that that uniform had made a lasting impression on him. "It occurred to me that it would be just as easy someday to throw my clothes in the corner and hang some other actor's in their place. It's a highly competitive business."

Ronald Reagan impersonated George Armstrong Custer *(right)* in *Santa Fe Trail,* a loosely historical tale of an anti-slavery rebellion in Kansas.

Santa Fe Trail was the only film set in the Old West that Reagan would make for Warners. On the set, he was greeted by screenwriter Robert Buckner, who had also written the script for *Knute Rockne—All American.* "I've just been polishing your lines,"

"Michael Curtiz will be on the set soon," Buckner said, "But I've got to warn you: The bastard didn't want you in the role. He didn't want Morris either. Those two guys had a big fight and the Mad Hungarian ordered Morris off the set. Curtiz wanted John Wayne, who turned it down. He sent Curtiz a note: 'I REFUSE TO PLAY FLYNN'S PUSSY."

Before leaving Reagan to read the script, Buckner told him, "Actually, it was Jack Warner who wanted you to play Custer. He said war is coming, and he was about to lose his leading male actors. He told us the Army won't take you because you're blind as a bat."

Reagan sat down to read the script through his contact lenses. "Do I make my last stand against the Indians?"

"It's not that kind of role," Buckner said. "The plot revolves more around John Brown, the abolitionist crusader. It's not history. I've taken poetic license."

As he read Buckner's script, Reagan realized that little of it made sense from a standpoint of historical fact. The script called for Flynn to interpret the early military career (i.e., during the 1850s) of J.E.B. ("Jeb") Stuart, later the Confederacy's most renowned cavalry commander. Reagan had been hired for a sanitized (and chronologically incorrect) interpretation of George Armstrong Custer's career before the Civil War, covering events which might have happened years before the 1876 massacre by Native Americans of his military contingent at the Battle of the Little Bighorn.

When the film opens, Custer and Stuart are graduating from West Point in 1854, although in reality, Custer was a fifteen-year-old schoolboy at the time. Jefferson Davis also factors into the narrative, as do future Civil War generals such as Philip Sheridan, James Longstreet, James Hood, and George Pickett. Raymond Massey was cast as John Brown, a fanatical American abolitionist who advocated the use of armed insurrection as the only means of overthrowing slavery in the United States.

From behind him, Reagan heard the thick Hungarian accent of the film's flamboyant director, Michael Curtiz. "I want you to do good job. Earl Flint will be asshole as usual." *[The director always botched the names of people.]*

To many viewers, Buckner's script seemed to haphazardly combine the dramas associated with the westward expansion of the U.S. with a retelling of the abolitionist crusade of John Brown, a love story between the characters played by Errol Flynn and Olivia de Havilland; and a story about the growth of the Atchison, Topeka, and Santa Fe Railroads.

[The railroad was the subject of a popular song composed by Johnny Mercer and Harry Warren, "On the Atchison, Topeka, and The Santa Fe," written for the film, The Harvey Girls *(1946), and sung by, among others, Judy Garland.]*

Left: John Brown (1800-1859), from a 19th century photo of the idealistic abolitionist, and *(right)* Raymond Massey, interpreting John Brown as an unhinged fanatic.

"It's eight parts entertainment, two parts fact," Bruckner told Reagan. "Or, as Curtiz with his accent says, '*It's not the exact facts and we haff the facts to prove that.*'"

Before the day was over, Reagan met most of the cast—some new faces, but a lot of familiar ones with whom he'd worked before. Guinn ("Big Boy") Williams shook his hand, and Reagan smiled at him, though he detested the braggart. Ward Bond came up to greet Reagan. "I play Windy Brody," he said. "I think they mean for me to fart a lot."

Olivia de Havilland was most gracious, extending her hand to Reagan. She discussed working with Jane Wyman on *My Love Came Back.* In *Santa Fe Trail*, she played Kit Carson

Warners' re-enactment of salad days at West Point in the years immediately preceding the Civil War:

Left to right, Reagan in a loose interpretation of the student with among the lowest test scores (Custer); Flynn as J.E.B. Stuart; David Bruce; and in the right foreground, William Lundigan, Flynn's off-screen lover.

Halliday. "In the movie, both you and Errol are in love with me. In the end, he wins. But in real life, I'd much prefer you."

"Thank you," he said. "I'm flattered."

"Alas, Jane saw you first," De Havilland said. "But fortunately, right now, I have James Stewart to keep my company. He keeps talking about marriage, but his voice doesn't have a sincere ring."

De Havilland later told her biographer and film archivist, Tony Thomas, "My problems with Errol on the set of *Santa Fe Trail* are purely personal. He deliberately and provocatively upstaged me in two scenes, something he had never done before. Since then, I have wondered if his behavior might have something to do with the fact that I was seeing a lot of James

A shifty villain in an era of shifting alliances: Van Heflin

234

Stewart and that our affable co-star, Ronald Reagan, spent a lot of time talking to me on the set. Errol was still married to Lili Damita, albeit unhappily, and he was hardly in a position to court me, but I knew he was fond of me, as I was of him. Someone else paying attention to me seemed to bother him a bit."

Flynn was not scheduled to appear on the set for a few more days, so Reagan went around greeting the cast.

Alan Hale had just made *Tugboat Annie Sails Again* with Jane and him. Before that, he had been a regular sidekick of Flynn in such movies as *The Adventures of Robin Hood*. Hale and Reagan, in their near future, would be making more films together. Hale later said, "I like guys you can hang out with—Errol Flynn, Ward Bond, John Wayne. Reagan was too stiff and formal for my tastes."

Reagan also greeted such familiar faces as Henry O'Neill, who had been cast as De Havilland's father. He had a warm reunion with John Litel, who had played his boss in two of the Brass Bancroft movies. Hobart Cavanaugh also greeted him.

Reagan met an up-and-coming star, Van Heflin, who had been cast as Rader, a disciple of John Brown. In the movie, he too attends West Point, though he is discharged for distributing anti-slavery pamphlets.

Emerging from the bowels of Oklahoma, stage actor Heflin seemed to hold Reagan in contempt, though it was not obvious. He'd later refer to both Reagan and Flynn as "Hollywood pretty boys. They're not actors at all."

Reagan losing De Havilland.

Flynn winning De Havilland.

Heflin had appeared on the Broadway stage with Katharine Hepburn in *The Philadelphia Story*. He was still angry that he had not been cast in the play's screen version, the role eventually going to James Stewart.

In one of the coincidences of that day, Stewart himself showed up on the set to take his girlfriend, De Havilland, for lunch in the commissary. An angry Heflin confronted him, eventually cursing him. Before they came to blows, Reagan came between them. "C'mon, guys, if I fought every actor in Hollywood who got a part I wanted, I'd be beating up someone every day...or getting my ass licked."

When Heflin wasn't needed on the set, he hopelessly pursued De Havilland.

Unlike Reagan, Heflin would achieve early success in Hollywood, winning an Oscar as Best Supporting Actor for his role in *Johnny Eager* (1942), wherein he played the boozy, philosophical pal of gangster Robert Taylor.

Reagan chatted with William Lundigan, learning that most of the cast shunned him, dismissing him as "Flynn's plaything." Flynn consistently placed him in minor roles within his films. Reagan and Lundigan shared joint memories of their days as radio announcers.

He told Reagan, "If the United States goes to war, I'm joining the Marine Corps."

"Will your buddy, Flynn, join too?" Reagan asked.

"He doesn't want this known, but he can't pass the physical. From the outside, he looks gorgeous, but inside, he's a mess."

The craggy-faced Canadian actor, Raymond Massey, seemed so self-absorbed in his portrayal of the spooky fanatic, John Brown, that he had little time for Reagan. Jack Warner had personally supervised his makeup to ensure that he came off looking like a lunatic. A critic later defined Massey's interpretation of John Brown in *Santa Fe Trail* as "frighteningly demented, vaguely echoing Hitler's evil."

[Massey would make a far more lasting cinematic impression the same year when he appeared as Hollywood's definitive Abraham Lincoln in Abe Lincoln in Illinois *(1940). Two years later, he would appear with Flynn and Reagan again in the wartime action and aviation story,* Desperate Journey *(1942). And in 1955, Massey would star in the low-budget film,* Seven Angry Men, *in which he presented the character of John Brown as a far more sympathetic figure than his portrayal of him in* Santa Fe Trail.*]*

Finally, four days later, Flynn arrived on the set. He attempted to kiss Reagan on the mouth as he'd done before. Since Reagan was now aware that the swashbuckler was a kissing bandit, he turned away. Flynn's lips only managed to brush against Reagan's ear. "Just a friendly gesture, sport, since we'll be making our first picture together, I thought we might as well get cozy."

"I don't go in for man kissing," Reagan said, "although I know it's a show biz tradition. Everybody kisses everybody in Hollywood."

"And ain't it fun, sweet cheeks?" Flynn said. "I'd better read the god damn script. That asshole Curtiz has been shooting scenes with Massey for four days without one call for me, the fucking star of this flick. If that doesn't change soon, Curtiz is going to face big trouble and a one-way ticket back to the goulash factories of Budapest."

Although he tried to conceal his jealousy, Reagan envied Flynn as America's fourth-ranking box office star in America. Reagan didn't even place in the first one hundred.

"I once swore I'd never speak to you again," Flynn said. "Perhaps bloody your nose if we ever met up. But time has passed, and I'm in a more forgiving mood."

Reagan was dumbfounded and wanted an explanation, but none was forthcoming from Flynn.

Years later, a Flynn biographer, David Bret, provided a possible clue. "It was rumored that Ross Alexander had taken his life because he believed that Ronald Reagan had been signed by Warner Brothers to replace him. Although he would work with Reagan in the future, Errol would always detest him and hold him personally responsible for his friend's death."

If Flynn had felt such an emotion, it wasn't obvious when they co-starred together. Actually, during the making of *Santa Fe Trail*, Flynn spent a lot of time talking to Reagan, enough to incite a jealous rage in Lundigan.

Flynn discussed his troubled marriage to Lili Damita. "We are in a connubial war," he said. "I play the field from my base in a bachelor apartment. Damita doesn't accept this. She watches and pursues me as Javert pursued Jean Valjean."

"Her possessiveness upset our marriage from the start. As you'll find in your marriage to Jane, it's not man's nature to be monogamous. Neither is it woman's. The proof of this is in the well-known rejection of the whole standard of monogamy by so many people. You'll find what I'm saying to be true in your own marriage once you and Jane settle in. You'll stray and so will she. Movie stars are faced with challenges to their morality that are far greater than what's faced by 99% of the population."

"I plan to remain faithful," he protested.

"Time will tell," he answered. "Actually, you're lucky to have Jane. She's one hot little piece of ass with a twitching pussy."

"How would you know that?" Reagan asked, his anger growing. "You don't talk like that to a man about his wife."

"I was just speculating," Flynn said. "Call it a wild guess. Of course, I don't have any personal experience...with your maiden fair."

"If only I could believe that," Reagan said. "Let's drop the subject."

Seething with anger, he turned and walked away.

He soon forgave Flynn, mostly because of De Havilland's urging: "Errol can't help being Errol."

"I guess you're right," Reagan said.

The very next afternoon, between takes, Flynn was talking with Reagan again, yesterday's embarrassment seemingly forgotten.

"I want to be taken seriously," Flynn said. "I feel I'm inwardly serious, thoughtful, even tormented, but in practice I yield to the fatuous, the nonsensical. I allow myself to be understood abroad as a colorful fragment in a drab world."

Later, Reagan would write in his first memoir, "Errol was a strange person, terribly unsure of himself, and needlessly so. He was a beautiful piece of machinery, likable, with great charm, and yet convinced he lacked ability as an actor. As a result, he was conscious of every minute of scenes favoring other actors and their positions on the screen in relation to himself. He was apparently unaware of his own striking personality."

As a means of proving his point, Reagan recalled an all-night shoot at the Warner ranch. "My fellow actors and I were sitting around the campfire with Errol. I was right next to him, and he asked Curtiz to move me. I was placed behind two actors taller than me. My face would barely show in the shot—in effect, there would be only a glimpse of me. But I set out to protect myself. During rehearsal, I secretly piled up a mound of loose earth with my feet. When the cameras rolled, I quietly moved to the top of my newly created gopher mound so that my head showed above the two actors in front of me. I then dropped my one line like the gentle rain from heaven on the heads of the tall ones in front."

But when Reagan saw the final version, he was horrified. Flynn had demanded that Reagan's only line, uttered from the top of a low mound next to the campfire, be cut.

Late one afternoon, a luscious Tarheel beauty from North Carolina arrived on the set. Ava Gardner introduced herself to Reagan. She had arrived to meet Flynn, who had promised to take her to Palm Springs for the weekend.

She told him, "If I were a man in a picture with Errol Flynn, I'd be terrified—the competition would be too great. He's probably the most beautiful man I've ever dated. He has a perfect body—one that's at home in a swimsuit or on a horse. Actually, *The Perfect Specimen* (did you catch his movie?) looks better with no clothes on at all. He's fun, gallant, well mannered, and with a sense of humor. When he walks into a dark room, it's like a light being turned on. He drinks too much, and he fucks too much, but he's got style, *honeychile*. Real style."

Before heading off to Flynn's dressing room, she kissed

Ava Gardner: At a party, Mickey Rooney described this sultry star to Reagan. "She has big brown nipples which, when aroused, stand out like some double-long, golden California raisins."

Reagan on the cheek. "Give Ava a call some night. I might help liberate you. I've been known to turn many a square into a bouncing ball."

During the shoot, Reagan couldn't believe how vicious Curtiz was. The Hungarian threw a fit when he learned that he had to use a dummy instead of Massey's real body during his hanging scnee. "Wardrobe knows how to put choke to protect Massey's neck. Maybe he won't really hang, maybe. I don't want god damn dummy. But Warner moron insists."

When the filming began, an elderly actor playing the minister stood on the scaffold with Massey, who would then disappear as a *ségué* shot showed the dummy dangling. Curtiz kept yelling, again and again, for the elderly actor to step back. After he screamed to step back a final time, the older actor fell off the scaffold, a vertical distance of twelve feet.

"That ruthless tyrant, Curtiz, walked over and looked down at the actor, who was in agonizing pain, and crying out for help," Reagan said. "He'd broken his leg. Curtiz took one look at him and then yelled at his production assistant, 'Get me another god damn minister!'"

A handsome young actor, Gene Reynolds, played Jason Brown, John Brown's son. In a scene, as he lay dying, Errol Flynn bends over him, offering him loving comfort. When Warners' released a publicity still of Reynolds together with Flynn, Lundigan was furious. "Hell, Errol, you look like you're playing a love scene with Reynolds. I bet you want him more than you want me."

Flynn rushed to Lundigan's side to assure him that "You're my one and only."

During the second week of the shoot, Reagan was introduced to a young beauty, Susan Peters (formerly known as Suzanne Carnahan) from Spokane. Spotted by a talent scout, she had recently been given a contract at Warners.

Although the script of *Santa Fe Trail* ordained that Reagan would lose De Havilland before the end of the movie, it called for him to be introduced to "the right girl" and for him to subsequently fall for the character played by Peters. He found her a lovely girl, and befriended her, and she seemed to view him as a kind of father figure, although he was only a decade or so older than her.

During the months ahead, after the picture was finished, Peters continued to call Reagan for advice. She felt lost and lonely in Hollywood, and he offered her reassurance.

In 1942, in a panic, she came to him after Warners' failed to renew her contract. Consequently, he advised her to go to MGM. Within weeks, she had a contract with Metro, which had offered her a role in Greer Garson's *Random Harvest* (1942). *[This film eventually brought Peters an Academy Award nomination as Best Supporting Actress.]*

[For Peters, at least, triumph was followed by tragedy. She had married Richard Quine, the film actor and director. On January 1, 1945, he had invited her to go duck hunting with him. During the hunt, his rifle accidentally discharged and a bullet lodged in Peters' spinal cord.

When Reagan visited her in the hospital, he learned from her doctor that she would be permanently paralyzed, and that she'd have to live in a wheelchair.

Because of her physical limitations, she appeared in only a few productions after that. (One of them was a role in a regional production of Tennessee Williams' The Glass

The doomed and very depressed Susan Peters turned to Reagan as a father figure, not as a lover.

238

Menagerie.) *In 1952, she died at the age of 31. Doctors noted that her death was hastened by starvation and dehydration because Peters' had "lost interest" in eating and drinking, and had lost the will to live.]*

The shooting schedule of *Santa Fe Trail* took place in the oppressive heat of midsummer, the temperature often soaring to 110°F. The men were dressed in heavy military uniforms, the women in long 19th-century dresses. One location was Sun Valley in the arid Santa Susanna Mountains, a short distance north of Los Angeles. Stars and first-tier cast members were housed in small cabins. There weren't enough cabins for singles, so even the stars doubled up, Flynn sharing his cabin with Lundigan. The extras and crew slept dormitory style.

William Hopper, Hedda's son, had been assigned an uncredited role in the film as a military officer. When he arrived on the set, he informed the production assistant making housing assignments that he was Reagan's closest friend, and that he wanted to share his cabin.

Reagan had continued his friendship with William and occasionally went out with him, but he felt uncomfortable sharing such small quarters with him. William made it even worse when he told Reagan, "My passion for you has continued unabated."

"Get over it!" Reagan cautioned him.

"I won't get over it until my curiosity is satisfied," William said.

"If you think having sex with me one time will satisfy you, you're wrong. It would only whet your appetite. You'd be begging me every night for more."

"Perhaps you're right." William said.

The two men slept peacefully in a double bed, and William respected Reagan's privacy and did not move in on him during the night.

The next morning, Reagan woke up hot and sweaty and headed for the shower. He turned on the cold water. When he emerged, William, in his underwear, was sitting on the toilet, holding up a bath towel for him.

"What the hell?" Reagan said. "Get out of here."

"You mean I can't even look? What harm is that causing?"

"None, I guess," Reagan said, taking the towel. "Look, but don't touch."

"You really know how to break a guy's heart," William said.

He faced more disappointment when he went to a screening of the final cut of *Santa Fe Trail*. His only scene had been removed from the narrative.

During location shooting, some of the staff suffered injuries. Flynn got a saber cut on his thigh, and Massey's right leg was seared with a blank cartridge. Some of the horses also suffered leg injuries and had to be put down, which prompted an investigation by the ASPCA.

At the end of the shoot, Flynn, against Reagan's wishes, gave him a kiss on the mouth. Reagan wanted to pull away, but didn't want to antagonize Flynn, since he'd learned that they might be co-starring soon in another picture together.

He would later tell Jane, "Now I know how a woman feels when she suffers unwanted attention from the male animal."

"You live in Hollywood," Jane said. "Get used to it. Every third guy here is a homo."

Reagan did not attend the film's premiere in Santa Fe, but De Havilland accompanied Flynn. Warners sent three men from their publicity department to ensure that their star stayed sober for the premiere. They did not succeed. On the night of the big event, Flynn showed up drunk.

When the film opened across the country, it was a big success, earning some one and a half million dollars, a lot of money in the early 40s.

Reviews were mixed. The highly critical Bosley Crowther of *The New York Times* had faint praise: "It's got everything that a high-priced soap opera should have—hard riding, hard shooting, hard fighting, and a bit of hard drinking by Errol Flynn."

Variety weighed in with slight praise for Reagan, claiming, "He also scores."

He was annoyed by a review written by Charles Whittaker. "Ronald Reagan recedes into the scenery when confronted with Errol Flynn's charismatic and magnetic on-screen personality."

Many critics noted that politically, the movie seemed to reflect a Southern point of view, with Brown cast as a villain. Another noted that "blacks are depicted as wide-eyed simpleton Sambos. However, Reagan's Custer seems more sympathetic to Brown wanting to rid America of slavery."

[In later years, Santa Fe Trail *is often confused with another loosely historic Flynn movie,* They Died With Their Boots On *(1941). Directed by Raoul Walsh, it represented the eighth and final film collaboration of Flynn with Olivia de Havilland. In this release— in vivid contrast to* Santa Fe Trail—*Flynn portrayed General George Armstrong Custer in a not historically accurate rundown of his life and career, including a heroic spin on his last stand, and death, in the Battle of Little Bighorn.*

In 1968, United Artists Television, the owner of the copyright for Santa Fe Trail, *did not renew it, and the Flynn/Reagan movie entered the public domain.]*

Reagan learned that after the premiere of *Santa Fe Trail*, Flynn invited Lundigan and some other friends to go on what he defined as a "Good Will Tour" of Central and South America. The exact venue of that tour would be hotly disputed for decades to come.

Among Flynn supporters, it was said that he was on a spying mission for British intelligence. His detractors, however, including author Charles Higham, claimed that he was meeting with foreign agents, especially in Buenos Aires, turning over secret information to the Nazis.

As a film star, Flynn was invited by various U.S. ambassadors to visit American Army and Navy installations.

As part of his South American tour, Flynn took along his pimp, Johnny Meyer, also known for working for Howard Hughes. On what became defined as Flynn's "chicken hawk" tour, Meyer rounded up beautiful boys and girls in the twelve-to-fourteen year old bracket. They were invited aboard Flynn's yacht for sex orgies.

Lundigan later told his gay friends, "Usually Errol has to go to Mexico for such pleasures. Hell, in the States, he could be charged with statutory rape."

Reagan later discussed these rumors about Flynn with key administrators of the Screen Actors Guild. "I don't trust Flynn," Reagan told the board. "Never did, never will. I think he's capable of almost anything, at least in sexual terms. But thinking of this Aussie as a Nazi spy is a bit much for me, although he does have a number of suspicious friends."

***

In a phone call to Paulette Goddard, Jane Wyman was ecstatic. "I can't believe my good luck," Jane said. "Although I don't like Ray Enright as a director, the bastard called to tell me I'm going to co-star with my dream man, Dennis Morgan, in this thing called *Bad Men of Missouri* (1941). Of course, Wayne Morris is in the picture, too, but I can keep him at bay. Tell me, am I going to break my marriage vows?"

"Such vows are made to be broken," Goddard claimed. "Imagine pledging to be faithful to just one man. It's inhuman. I'm sure Ronnie is slipping around on the side since he's always surrounded by all these beauties at Warners'."

"Do you really think so?" Jane asked.

"The only faithful husband in Hollywood is my dear Charlie *[Chaplin]*," Goddard claimed.

"Now you're being sarcastic, my dear," Jane said.

"Keep me posted on this Morgan thing," Goddard said. "And pray that he doesn't have a small dick. I've been so disappointed by these so-called Hollywood studs—Clark Gable and John Wayne come to mind. Of course, Charlie makes up for it. Right now, he's sleeping with this blonde bitch, Carole Landis. I think your Ronnie knows her. Watch out for her! On a movie set, she's known as 'Legs Apart' Landis."

Not all men from Missouri (the "Show-Me-State") are bad: In the photo above, Wyman appears with Wayne Morris *(left)* and Dennis Morgan, each of whom were or would become her lover.

Jane's script was sent over to her that afternoon. As usual, *Bad Men of Missouri* was a disappointment to her. It told the story of the Younger brothers who, enraged by carpetbaggers infringing on the war-ravaged American South, move to the lawless frontier in this fictional western. They include Cole (Dennis Morgan); Bob (Wayne Morris); and the very talented Arthur Kennedy, cast as Jim. Jim is in love with Mary Hathaway, the character played by Jane. Ohio-born Alan Baxter had been hired to play a ruthless Jesse James.

After reading the script, Jane felt that its writer "should be horsewhipped. I have to repeat lines to the Younger brothers like, 'They say you did a lot of bad things—but a lot of good things, too.' I get to kick Walter Catlett in the shins and call Victor Jory a 'no good, low-down carpetbagger.'"

When Jane reported to wardrobe, she learned that she was to wear a snood and shapeless gingham dresses in many of her scenes. "I'd dyed my hair a whorish blonde, but it was to be hidden in some scenes with a bonnet. Actually, a snood was coming back into fashion since women were using them to secure their hair when working with machinery in defense plants."

When she met the film's scriptwriter, Charles Grayson, she protested, "I wish you'd given me something more to do. I'm playing second fiddle to a bunch of men who outnumber me by a thousand to one. Now and then, amidst all that gunfire, I'm permitted a *meow* or two. I get to look through a window as the rain comes down. I get to shake the hand of Dennis Morgan. Imagine with Dennis in the movie, you cast Kennedy as my lover. Who in hell is going to believe that? Wayne Morris would be better as a lover than Kennedy. Kennedy's very average looking—not the kind of guy a girl would go for when hunks like Dennis and Wayne are in the picture."

When she met her on-screen boyfriend, he introduced himself as "John Kennedy" of Massachusetts. "I thought Grayson said your name was Arthur Kennedy."

"It is," he said. "But I haven't gotten used to it yet. Arthur, which is my middle name, is my new billing. Up to now, I've billed myself as John Kennedy."

He had just appeared with James Cagney, playing his brother in *City for Conquest* (1940). "Jimmy discovered me. He likes to discover young men." He sighed. "To each his own."

[This was not the only picture Jane would make with Arthur Kennedy. In their future lay Tennessee Williams' The Glass Menagerie.*]*

Enright appeared with Victor Jory, introducing the actor to Jane. He'd been cast in

241

their upcoming movie as the villain, William Merrick, a crooked banker who buys warrants on back taxes and then dispossesses farmers and their families. As the plot unfolds, the Younger brothers set out to avenge his misdeeds. Their father, Henry Younger (Russell Simpson), had been killed by Merrick's henchman. The brothers then begin a series of bank and train robberies, often stealing from Merrick, before turning their loot over to the impoverished farmers.

Jane congratulated Jory on his success playing Jonas Wilkerson, the brutal and opportunistic overseer in *Gone With the Wind.* "I don't think I can ever forgive you for being so mean to Scarlett," Jane said. "You were such a bastard. I think you're terrible."

"You won't believe that when I started out, I was cast in romantic leads," Jory said. "Then directors got a glimpse of my coal-black and threatening eyes. I've been the bad guy ever since."

Jane also met actor Howard da Silva, thinking he was Portuguese. He corrected that impression. "I was born to Bertha and Benjamin Silverblatt, two Yiddish-speaking Jews in Cleveland. I have no relatives in Brazil or Portugal. I just liked the sound of Da Silva."

[She would later work with Da Silva and Ray Milland during her breakthrough role in The Lost Weekend *at the end of the war.]*

Jane was intrigued with Faye Emerson, a Southern belle who would later marry into the First Family at the White House. By the end of the 1940s, she would become "The First Lady of Television." Reagan was soon to work with her in one of his future movies, and he'd get to know her far better than Jane did.

Although Emerson had married a naval aviator, William Crawford, she was known to be sleeping around. She aroused Jane's jealousy by making a play for Morgan, who spurned her advances. When she didn't get him, she pursued Morris, finding him an easy conquest. Jane saw her leaving Morris' dressing room on several occasions.

During the making of the film, Jane had several intense talks with Virginia Brissac, born in San Jose, California, in 1883. Upon meeting her, Brissac asked Jane for her autograph. "I want to add it to my collection, along with those of Sarah Bernhardt, Eleonora Duse, Henry Irving, and Rudyard Kipling."

"I'll be in distinguished company," Jane said, signing her book.

Brissac had had a long stage career when she was young, later appearing in such movies as *Dark Victory* with Bette Davis and Ronald Reagan and in *Destry Rides Again* (1932), with Marlene Dietrich and James Stewart. Brissac would retire from the screen in 1955 after playing James Dean's grandmother in *Rebel Without a Cause.*

Jane always found comic actor Walter Catlett amusing, having appeared with him in *Kid Nightingale* with John Payne and more recently, in *Honeymoon for Three.*

During a rainy afternoon, when she was told she wouldn't be needed for the rest of the day, Catlett approached her. "One of your dear friends is waiting for you in a car outside."

At first, Jane refused to approach the car in the pouring rain unless he told her who was waiting for her inside. "He wants it be a surprise. He's a dear friend."

Under a heavy black umbrella, she approached the car on its passenger side as the door was thrown open for her. Sitting behind the wheel was Payne himself.

Once inside, he took her in his arms and passionately kissed her. "I've missed you so, darling. My heart is breaking for being separated from you for so long." Then he started

Jane on Howard da Silva: "He is the kind of man so easy to detest."

the motor. "I'm taking you away to my hideaway."

As she'd reveal to Catlett the next day, "I once made a movie called *He Couldn't Say No*. Well, you're looking at *The Girl Who Couldn't Say No*. Let's keep my little rendezvous with John our secret."

"My lips are sealed," Catlett promised.

From that day forth, Payne became a fixture in Jane's life, coming and going at frequent intervals. His marriage to Anne Shirley was falling apart. He told Jane that she was still involved in an affair with her co-star, John Garfield.

"Shirley is out of her mind," Jane said. "What gal in the world would want Garfield when John Payne, the sexiest man in pictures, is available?"

Linking up romantically with Payne again didn't diminish Jane's passion for the dashing Dennis Morgan. She eagerly awaited their reunion on the set.

During her absence from him, he was often the subject of Hollywood gossip. He'd made *Kitty*

When Jane saw this publicity still of John Payne, she exclaimed, "the fantasy come true of every fair maiden."

Foyle, The Natural History of a Woman (1940) with Ginger Rogers, the former dancing partner of Fred Astaire, in a drama about a working girl, which had brought her a Best Actress Oscar.

In the picture, Rogers found herself caught between two of the handsomest actors in Hollywood, not only Morgan, but James Craig, hired as a "replacement" for Clark Gable, to whom he bore some resemblance.

Rogers later wrote about Morgan in her memoirs, finding him "extremely handsome and intensely romantic, without manufactured overtones." However, in the celluloid world of *Kitty Foyle,* the character she played found only unhappiness after she married him.

Morgan had also completed *Affectionately Yours* (1941), a charming comedy *[which somehow flopped at the box office]* starring Merle Oberon and Rita Hayworth. Rumors abounded that both Oberon and Rogers had taken "leading lady's privilege," and seduced Morgan.

As regards her involvement in *Bad Men of Missouri,* Jane later told Goddard, "I'm the leading lady in this Missouri western, and I, too, am going to take leading lady's privilege with this super cute guy."

During the shoot, Jane got to know Morgan, and she took delight in their romance. She began to arrive later and later at home every night, telling Reagan that she was held up at the studio. He couldn't understand why such a small role in the picture would be such a burden to her, requiring so many late hours. She didn't bother to explain.

Nine years older than Jane, Morgan, whose birth name had been Earl Stanley Morner, had briefly worked under the acting pseudonym of Richard Stanley. At the debut of his association with Warners, the studio assigned him the new name of Dennis Morgan.

He told Jane that if not for a whim of fate, she might have been playing opposite Humphrey Bogart instead of with him. At the last minute, Bogie had turned down the script and had been placed on suspension.

Jane interpreted Morgan as the antithesis of the gritty Bogart, and wondered why Jack Warner had assigned him as Bogie's replacement. That would happen again when

243

Bogie rejected the script for *God Is My Co-Pilot* in 1945, and Morgan had great success with the role.

He had married his childhood sweetheart, Lillian Vedder, way back in 1933. "It was love at first sight," he said, "when I saw her selling poppies to passersby at a war veterans' benefit."

Originally, he was signed by MGM as a "threat" to Nelson Eddy, the singer-actor who often co-starred with Jeanette MacDonald.

As Morgan would later confide to his best friend, Jack Carson, "MGM didn't quite know what to do with me. Off the screen, even though I love my wife, I had the time of my life. Let me see: Jean Harlow in *Suzy* (1936)."

"Instead of fucking these MGM beauties, who did nothing for my career, maybe I should have let some of MGM's homo directors blow me, but that's not my style."

As one reporter claimed, "Warner's put Dennis Morgan on the assembly line with Wayne Morris, Arthur Kennedy, Jeffrey Lynn, Eddie Albert, and Ronald Reagan—likable young lugs squiring the heroine until Bogart, Cagney, or Flynn came crashing down to sweep her up."

Later, Jane told Goddard, "Dennis stands six feet two inches, and weighs 175—and he's all man. And yes, even in that department you worried about."

Jane later talked with Goddard about her affair with Morgan and the understanding they'd reached. He'd told her, "We're very attracted to each other, but we won't let our romance interfere with our marriages. In fact, by letting off some pent-up love steam with each other, I'll be a better husband to my wife and you'll be a better wife to Ronnie."

"You're very special to me, and I'd marry you in a minute if both of us were free," she'd told him. "But I think you're right. Instead of getting married, we'll have a back street affair."

"It's more fun to get out of that stinking alley and slip off to a perfumed boudoir," he said.

As she'd later relate to Goddard, "*Bad Men of Missouri* was, for me at least, the worst of my movies. But I'd rate Dennis a ten on a scale of ten. John Payne is more sex driven, but Dennis combines romantic love with kindness. He worships a woman and makes her feel like a goddess."

One night, he'd told her, "You fit into my body so smoothly, it's like you were meant to stay by my side forever. I think we're going to know each other for many a year."

"If not decades," she accurately predicted.

As he once told Jane, "I'm always faithful to my wife in my heart. Where I put my prick is my own god damn business."

Before its release, cast members were shown the final cut of *Bad Men of Missouri*. In the darkened screening room, Jane sat next to Morgan, and he held her hand.

After he'd seen it, Kennedy later recalled how unhappy Jane was with her role. "There's talent in that girl, and Enright should have taken advantage of it. The film would have been better if there were less horse chases and more of Jane. She gave it her best. But bigger and better things awaited her in her future roles."

Critic Jennifer Logan wrote, "The love scenes with Jane Wyman and Arthur Kennedy go by in a blur of speed. Wyman, a very pretty girl, has what must be one of the shortest romantic roles in the history of horse opera."

Variety weighed in: "*Bad Men of Missouri* is a cinematic glorification of that daring band of desperadoes, the Younger Brothers, operating in Missouri after the Civil War. It's strictly a shoot-em action melodrama, with plenty of excitement for a programmer. Expect lots of tough riding, robberies, and dusty chases."

***

In between films, Reagan took time off to catch up with Betty Grable, who was finally getting star billing after years of slaving in minor roles. Her divorce from child star Jackie Coogan had been finalized a few months before, and she told Reagan that she was enjoying "my role as a bachelor gal with a roving eye."

She had just completed *Moon Over Miami* (1941), a Fox Technicolor musical co-starring Don Ameche and Robert Cummings. "Unfortunately, that bitch Carole Landis was in it, too. She hates me. She wanted to be me, and resents Zanuck for building me up. Zanuck is fucking her, not me. When he called me to his office and took his dick out for me, I said, 'Darryl, that's very beautiful, but you can put it back now."

"I'm having a turbulent private life, but at least stardom has come to me," she said. "After I rejected Zanuck's sexual advances, he's gotten even by casting me with Landis. He has this thing about pitting one star against another. He used me to remind Alice Faye to stay in line. Now he's using Landis to remind me that I can be replaced. She and I hated each other on sight."

"That's understandable, because of the position Zanuck put you in," Reagan responded.

"Landis makes it worse than it is with her big mouth," Grable said. "She's telling everybody that she stole *Moon Over Miami* from me. She also claims she's far more beautiful than I am. She told Zanuck, Don Ameche, and others that 'Grable is so full of herself, it's a wonder she doesn't explode.'"

"It sounds as if a big catfight is shaping up," he said. "Count me out."

In the passenger seat of his car, she hiked up her dress. "I don't want you to have an accident, but my gams have been voted the most beautiful in the world. Fox has insured them for $1,250,000."

"How do you feel about all this publicity about your legs?" he asked.

"It would have been fine when I was a struggling chorus girl," she answered. "But right now, I'd rather the guys wrote about me as an actress. Frankly, I always felt the face of an actress was more important than her figure."

"I'm not so sure about that, except for someone like Garbo or Katharine Hepburn," he said.

At that point, Grable asked about the welfare of Jane Wyman. "I haven't seen her for some time. You may not know this, but Jane and I, along with Paulette Goddard and Lucille Ball, got our starts together in this clunker called *The Kid From Spain,* a vehicle for Eddie Cantor way back in '32. Jane was billed as Sarah Jane Fulks. Give the kid my love, won't you? Congratulate her on snaring a prize like you. I know what a treat it is to get pounded by you."

"I'll give her your regards, but leave out that bit about what a prize I am," he said. "Sometimes, I don't think she appreciates me like some of my gal pals."

After they'd talked and had a few drinks, Grable asked Reagan to drive her home, since it was starting to rain heavily. She'd been driven to Warners that morning by a dancer friend.

En route back to her place, she suggested that

Hot, Competitive Blondes: Landis with Grable in *Moon Over Miami.*

she would be willing to become his "mistress in waiting," as she defined it.

"You're the most gorgeous gal in Hollywood, and I may be a god damn fool, but I'd better take a raincheck, although that is the most tempting offer I think I'll ever receive in my life."

"Too bad," she said. "I'm even more experienced than I was since our last round. It looks like I've got to take the bull by the horn." Then she reached over and swiftly unzipped his pants. Before he fully realized what was happening, she was voraciously fellating him.

[Long before the world heard of Linda Lovelace and her movie, Deep Throat, Betty Grable's oral skills became an underground legend during World War II.

Biographer Mart Martin, among others, wrote, "Grable had a lifelong affection for chorus boys and dancers, many of whom were homosexual. When she couldn't find other sexual partners, she'd press her demands on them to service her. But she really preferred rough men of the truck driver and bartender type and especially liked to fellate them."]

As she later bragged, "I brought Ronnie to a climax that rivaled the eruption of Vesuvius." As she got out of the car, she blew him a kiss. "That will have to do until next time, Big Guy."

He looked a bit stunned at first, trying to recover from the assault. He seemed to have changed his mind about her offer. "When can I call you again?"

"Come over Saturday afternoon at around two o'clock," she said. "Tell Jane you're playing golf with Dick Powell, or some such shit."

She later relayed details of her sexual encounters of the 1930s and the World War II era to her homosexual dancer friend, Bob Foster, who wrote *Betty Grable's Men,* whose publication was ultimately rejected by a number of publishers. In it, he described her affairs with Jackie Coogan (she married him), Desi Arnaz, Victor Mature, George Raft, Tyrone Power, Mickey Rooney, Robert Stack, Don Ameche, John Payne, Dick Haymes, Buster Crabbe, George Montgomery, and Ronald Reagan.

The final two chapters were devoted to her second husband, band leader Harry James.

***

After appearing in some twenty-three films for Warners', Reagan was cast in the 1941 version of MGM's *The Bad Man.*

[Note that Reagan's The Bad Man *is an entirely different film from* Bad Men of Missouri, *a Jane Wyman film, which, confusingly, was also released in 1941. The Bad Man represented Reagan's first loan-out by Warner to another studio, in this case, MGM.]*

MGM had requested Reagan for the role of Gil Jones, an impoverished but well-intentioned American running a ranch in Mexico. MGM's decision to hire him was based on executives there who saw his performances as George Gipp in *Knute Rockne* and as General Custer in *Santa Fe Trail.*

Conceived as a remake of a remake of what had originated as a Broadway play more than twenty years before, *The Bad Man*, in addition to Reagan, featured Laraine Day, cast as his leading lady, and the veteran warhorses Wallace Beery, playing a noble-hearted Mexican bandit, and Lionel Barrymore.

[Earlier versions of its script had been released in 1923 as a silent film, starring Holbrook Blinn, and again in 1930 as a pre-Code talkie starring Walter Huston.

Beery had been selected as a leading player in the 1941 version because of his authenticity as a Mexican bandit in Viva Villa! (1934). *But in this 1941 reincarnation, he*

*played the character like a buf-
foon, blustering and mugging,
booming out his lines in an annoying rendering of pidgin English.]*

The film's director, Richard
Thorpe, was in a bad mood when
Reagan greeted him. *Variety* had
just revealed in painful detail the
circumstances of his firing as director of Judy Garland's *The Wizard of Oz* after only two weeks of
shooting. He was pondering a
libel suit.

Among his previous achieve-
ments, Thorpe had directed Jane
Wyman in a bit role in *The Crowd
Roars* (1938), starring Robert
Taylor.

Thorpe warned Reagan that
Beery and Barrymore were noto-

Who's The Bad Man? *Left to right*: Laraine Day; golden
oldies' Lionel Barrymore; Wallace ("wifebeater") Beery;
and the future President of the United States.

rious scene stealers, "using every trick in the book and adding a few never invented.
That asshole Beery even stole a picture from Rin-Tin-Tin, The Wonder Dog."

For that and for other reasons, Reagan approached Beery with a certain disdain.
He'd never liked him on the screen. He held a personal grudge against him as well:

In the 1941 version of *The Bad Man*, Beery plays a kind of *Mexicano* Robin Hood,
helping Gil Jones (Reagan) and his wheelchair-bound Uncle Henry (Barrymore) avoid
the loss of their ranch to greedy bankers. Complications materialize when Gil's childhood
sweetheart (Laraine Day) arrives at the ranch with her difficult and quarrelsome husband
(Tom Conway). Predictably, the ranch will be saved, Conway will be chased away, and
Reagan will be free to get involved once again with his love from yesteryear.

Beery, a veteran actor who during the course of his lifetime would be a player in 205
films, originated in Missouri, He ran away from home in 1901 at the age of 16 to work
for the Ringling Brothers Circus as an elephant trainer until he was attacked and mauled
by a leopard.

From there, he migrated to Hollywood, appearing with his future wife, Gloria Swanson, in *Sweedie Goes to College* (1915). He married the vamp a year later, and she
wrote about her horrendous time with this brute, beginning with his drunken, bloody
rape of her on her wedding night. His violence and alcoholism led to her divorce from
him in 1919.

One of his most successful pictures had been *Min and Bill* (1931), starring the formidable Marie Dressler. For *The Champ* in 1931, he'd won an Oscar as Best Actor.
He'd also appeared with Dressler in *Tugboat Annie* (1933).

When he met Reagan, he told the young actor that he'd seen the sequel, *Tugboat
Annie Sails Again,* and that he was not impressed. "You and your blonde floozie wife
sure fucked up that picture. Poor Dressler must be turning over in her grave."

"How can anyone, even Marjorie Rambeau, follow in Dressler's footsteps?" Reagan
asked. "And Jane is not a floozie. She's a lady."

"You might also wonder how any actor can follow in the footsteps of yours truly
here," Beery loutishly answered.

During his heyday in the 1930s with MGM, this unlikely star became the highest paid actor in the world, starring with such luminaries as Clark Gable, Jean Harlow, George Raft, Fatty Arbuckle, Douglas Fairbanks, Sr., and Joan Crawford.

Although during the shoot, Reagan never directly confronted Beery, he held him responsible for the December, 1937 death of his friend, Ted Healy. Following a dispute in a tavern, Beery, along with Albert ("Cubby") Broccoli and Pat DiCicco, had attacked Healy and severely beaten him, kicking him in the head, abdomen, and ribs, knocking his left eye from its socket, delivering major bruises and lacerations to his head, neck and trunk.

An autopsy and subsequent investigation deemed these men not guilty of (directly) causing his death, but Reagan knew better. He blamed Eddie Mannix *[VP and General Manager of MGM]* and Howard Strickling *[MGM's Head of Publicity]* for covering up the scandal.

Because the editors feared libel, this frontpage of New York's *Daily News* was yanked at the last minute, before the newspapers hit the streets.

In the version that replaced it, the Wallace Beery photo *(on the right)* was removed, along with a caption which identified him as a murder suspect.

In its place, the editors ran a photo of a woman from an unrelated story.

Reagan had always been fascinated by Lionel Barrymore's screen work, ever since he'd seen *A Free Soul* (1931), in which he played an alcoholic lawyer alongside Norma Shearer and Clark Gable. For his performance in that film, Lionel, the older brother of the famous siblings, Ethel and John, won an Oscar as Best Actor.

Lionel had begun his stage career in the 1890s. By 1911, he was making films with D.W. Griffith at Biograph Studios. In 1915, he starred with the legendary Lillian Russell in the movie *Wildfire*. Like Beery, he had worked with all the big names, including John Gilbert, Gable, Greta Garbo, Spencer Tracy, Jean Harlow, Marie Dressler, Lon Chaney, Sr., and even his sister, Ethel. He'd faced off on the screen with Beery before, appearing with him in *Grand Hotel* (1932), and with John, his younger brother.

Thorpe seemed to take delight in telling Reagan about all the rumors swirling around Lionel's head. Because of the pain from his crippling arthritis, Lionel was said to be a morphine addict. It was also rumored that Louis B. Mayer was purchasing $400 worth of cocaine every day as a means of keeping him out of pain and allowing him to get some sleep.

In addition to having broken his hip twice, Lionel, again according to rumor, suffered from having contracted syphilis in 1925 during an affair with a young stage actor. Lionel was known for developing crushes on actors, notably Clark Gable when they co-starred together in *A Free Soul*. It was said that the fellating of young men was his favorite form of sex.

Reagan later said, "Lionel was theater through and through. An actor such as myself was made better by his great ability—provided you keep from being run over. He was confined to his wheelchair at the time, and he could whip that contrivance around on a dime. It's hard to smile in a scene when your foot has been run over and your shin is bleeding from a hubcap blow."

Originating in Utah, Laraine Day was Reagan's leading lady. This time, he didn't fall in love—far from it. She was dating Ray Hendricks at the time, a singer turned airline executive. She'd marry him a year later, but divorce him in 1947. The following year, she married Leo Durocher, manager of the baseball team then known as the New York Giants. Subsequently, she became known as "The First Lady of Baseball."

[In 1957, after being sold and moving to California, the team was renamed the San Francisco Giants.]

Lionel Barrymore in December of 1939, performing *A Christmas Carol* for radio broadcast.

Reagan told Thorpe that Laraine, a devout member of the Church of Jesus Christ of Latter-day Saints (i.e., the Mormons), was the most rigidly puritanical of his many leading ladies. She was so intensely dedicated to the teachings of her faith that she did not smoke, drink, or swear, and refused to even drink tea or coffee. "Nothing tastes better than a glass of cold milk, or ice water, on a hot day," she told Reagan.

An MGM contract player, she was known as "Nurse Mary Lamont," the title character she played in a string of seven Dr. Kildare movies, beginning with *Calling Dr. Kildare* in 1939, where she co-starred with Lew Ayres.

On occasion, Laraine and Reagan discussed politics. Whereas he was still a liberal Democrat, she was a staunch Republican. She told him, "If your friend, Dick Powell, doesn't make you see the light politically, I'll enlist César Romero, Ginger Rogers, Adolphe Menjou, Irene Dunne, even Mary Pickford, to convert you."

Onscreen with Laraine Day, Reagan cozied up to his co-star, but didn't develop any particular case of "Leadinglady-itis."

Like Reagan, she detested Beery, refusing to speak to him except on camera. When she'd played his daughter in *Sergeant Madden* (1939), she claimed he'd pinched her bottom until the cheeks of her buttocks were black and blue. "He's nothing but a filthy, dirty old man," she complained to Reagan.

One day, when Jane arrived on the set for lunch with her husband, he introduced her to Laraine. Later, Jane told him, "She's pleasant enough, but she lacks star quality. She'll never be a front-rank actress. Hollywood is filled with these fluffy bits. I think she'd be passable playing the secretary to some boss."

"*Meow!*" was Reagan's response.

He got along better with the film's supporting actors than he did with the stars. He met Russia-born Tom Conway, the brother of the more famous actor George Sanders. Conway would be remembered in the '40s for taking over the role from his brother of the sleuthing "Falcon" in a detective serial.

When Reagan met Conway, he was already showing signs of alcoholism, which in time would lead to his sad death in a flophouse in Venice, California.

Over lunch one day, Reagan found him very resentful of his brother, George Sanders. "I love George, but I also hate him, too. I live in his shadow...He takes roles from me that I could have performed better. He is so imperious, so suave, so sure of himself. He looks down on the whole world, including me. His shit stinks just as much as mine. So do his farts. I used to sleep with him."

Cast as Red Giddings in *The Bad Man,* Texas-born Chill Wills was folksy and shaggy-haired, always bringing a dollop of color to any western. "He was the type you'd expect to find sitting around the campfire under a full moon some night in Texas," Reagan said.

Actually, Wills had started out as an amateur singer in minstrel and medicine shows, later forming a group called "Chill Wills and His Avalon Boys."

After the release of *The Bad Man,* critics suggested that the picture should have been far better. Beery and Barrymore got most of the attention. Reagan was barely mentioned in most critiques.

He told Jane, "I don't think Mayer will be using me again anytime soon."

Later he described his experience making that film.

"I survived the Dead End Kids. And I survived Hollywood's two curmudgeons, Wallace Beery and Lionel Barrymore. Even so, I probably couldn't survive playing a leading man to Joan Crawford, even though I'm one tough *hombre."*

"I learned one thing working for Mayer," Reagan said. "MGM is the Tiffany's of Hollywood, whereas Warners is a hash house specializing only in meat and potatoes."

***

Late in April of 1941, Reagan and Jane stopped by the house of Jack and Nelle Reagan. He wanted to say goodbye to his parents before heading to the East Coast on a publicity jaunt, with Jane, to promote *The Bad Man.* He hugged Jack and kissed his mother goodbye. Then, on an impulse, he exited from his car to wave a final goodbye to them. Standing near their doorstep, his parents waved back. It was the last time he'd ever see his father alive.

The night of May 17, Jack had been out on an all-night drinking binge with his newly minted friend, Pat O'Brien. "When two Irishmen get together to gab, there is some serious drinking of good ol' Irish whiskey, the nectar of the gods," he said.

Nelle had begged him not to go, citing his ill health. "I'm as robust as an ox," Jack had boasted.

During a stopover of his tour in Atlantic City, New Jersey, Reagan received the call from Nelle that he had long anticipated. She informed him that his father, age 57, had died of a heart attack on May 18.

He had collapsed on the floor of their living room, and she had immediately summoned an ambulance. She had phoned the wrong company, an inadvertent error whose timing might have contributed to Jack's death.

It seemed that there was a jurisdictional dispute between emergency medical teams serving Beverly Hills and West Hollywood. Whereas she should have contacted a service based in West Hollywood, she had phoned one in Beverly Hills instead. When the company researched the Reagans' street address, they discovered that their home lay outside the city boundaries of Beverly Hills. Therefore, they opted not to answer the call, and failed to ring Nelle back to inform her of that. During all the confusion and delay, Jack had died unattended.

Nelle fully understood that her son had a fear of flying, despite all his daring aerial exploits in those Brass Bancroft Secret Service movies. "If you and Jane got in a plane to fly back, and something went wrong, I could never forgive myself. The thought of burying my younger son and my husband on the same day would kill me. Take the train. I'll delay the funeral until you and Jane return."

When Jack Warner called Reagan, offering him the use of his personal plane—a TWA DC-21, which happened to have been at Idlewild Airport in New York City at the time—Reagan graciously rejected the offer.

It would take five days before Reagan, with Jane, could arrive in Los Angeles. Years later, he would recall the moment of their arrival to his daughter Maureen. "It was a grand California day when your mother and I arrived at Union Station. We hadn't been in the state long enough not to grasp the beauty of a California day. But despite the lovely weather, I was desolate."

The funeral was held at St. Victor's Catholic Church in West Hollywood, which attracted a small group of mourners, the most notable of which was Pat O'Brien. As Reagan recalled, "I'm sure Jack knew that Pat and his new friends were there in that little church off Sunset Boulevard to say goodbye."

Before the funeral, Reagan learned that Jack had started attending church—a Catholic one—again. As James Cagney later described it to Reagan, "Your father heard the flutter of wings in heaven."

Moon Reagan was at the funeral, and he appeared grief stricken. "Dutch's older brother had always been closer to Jack than Dutch was to him," Nelle claimed.

With a stoic face, Reagan listened to the funeral service for his father, the former shoe salesman, wanderer, binge drinker, and lapsed Catholic. Nelle, in a dress of lavender prints, sat between her son and Jane. The light from the stained-glass windows illuminated her Gothic American face, and in her lap rested a tattered Bible with dogeared pages.

At the end of the service, she looked over at her son with her gray-blue eyes. "Dutch," she said, taking his hand and holding it tightly. "You're all that I have left in the world now. I know you'll be there for me until the end."

Weeks later, Reagan talked to his friends about his feelings during the burial of his father. "I was beyond crying. My soul was desolate, desolate and empty. All of a sudden, I heard somebody talking to me, and I knew it was my father. He was saying, 'I'm all right. I'm in a place that's very nice. Please don't be unhappy and take care of Nelle for me. Give my love to Jane and my new grandchild.' After I heard that soothing voice, my desolations just went away. The emptiness was all gone."

[As a contract player with a steady income, Reagan had been giving Jack and Nelle $175 a month to live on. Since they had almost no house or car expenses, that represented a most adequate income early in 1941.

During World War II, after Reagan was drafted, he made a deal with Warners' to provide Nelle with $75 a week to answer his fan mail. Because of the number of movies he'd made in the early 1940s, his fan mail had continued, though not in the volumes before. Jack Warner agreed to deduct all the paychecks sent to Nelle from Reagan's future services to the studio upon his return from the Army.

Baby Maureen was only five months old when Jack died, and, of course, she had no memory of him. But she had great and lasting affection for Nelle, whom she called "Gramsie."

She later claimed that her grandmother "was something of a clairvoyant. She was absolutely convinced that one of her sons, 'My beloved Moon or Ronnie,'' would one day become President of the United States. One afternoon, she told me, 'My greatest goal in life is to travel with you and Dutch to Washington for the swearing in of Moon to lead our nation.'"]

One night in her living room, Jane turned to Reagan, dropping the latest script she'd received (*The Body Disappears;* 1941) onto her coffee table. "It's just a silly little comedy," she said, "by Erna Lazarus and Scott Darling, whoever the fuck they are."

Although Reagan didn't seem to care too much about the script, he urgently wanted to know who her leading man would be. "Am I in danger of losing my gal to some hot stuff?"

"I'm going to play opposite that darling Jeffrey Lynn," she said. "He's such a gentleman, unlike the other ruffians at Warners."

"What a coincidence," he said. "He's also the leading man in my next picture, *Million Dollar Baby* (1941). I resent him. He's getting star billing over yours truly."

In addition to Lynn, Jane's co-stars included her gay friend, the very prissy Edward Everett Horton; a former New York model, the sultry Marguerite Chapman; David Bruce; Ivan Simpson; and Willie Best. The director, Ross Lederman, was unknown to Jane.

Two days later, at Warners, she met Lederman. He annoyed her, telling her, "I'm the only prima donna on this lot. Get it right the first time. I don't go in for retakes."

At home that night, she accused Lederman of being "brusque, crude, rude, and a son of a bitch."

It was obvious to Jane that the storyline of *The Body Disappears* had been stolen from James Whale's *The Invisible Man* (1933). As she'd later recall, "It was the worst movie I ever appeared in in the 40s."

In this daffy comedy, a young millionaire, Peter de Haven (Lynn), is behaving outrageously. His fellow partygoers, each of them studying to be doctors, decide to teach him a lesson. When Lynn passes out drunk, some of the young men kidnap him and place him on a slab of marble in the college dissecting room reserved for cadavers.

As an outrageous and mad scientist, Horton is working on a serum which will make a person invisible. He injects Lynn with an experimental serum, making him appear headless when he awakens. Jane is cast as Horton's daughter and as Lynn's love interest. She, too, receives the serum and loses her head.

As predictable, both Lynn and Jane get their heads restored before the end of the final reel. Science fiction is combined with romance and what passes as mystery in this cinematic flop.

Jane enjoyed renewing her friendship with Horton, whom she had met while filming her bit part in *All the King's Horses* (1935). He would later invite her to visit his 22-acre tract of land in Encino. Dubbing it "Belly Acres," (actually Belleigh Acres), he told her. "All it lacks is its own post office."

"I brought my Scottish mother to live there," he said, "although she objects to my acting as a sissy on film. She demands that I attend church more often. When reporters come snooping around, I tell them I'm a confirmed bachelor. I hide my lover *[Gavin Gordon]* in the closet

In *The Body Disappears,* Jane maneuvers a face-off with Edward Everett Horton, that champion scene stealer and comic mugger champ.

until the press departs."

"All the actors, including myself, learned a lot from Edward," Jane said. "The director offered us no guidance. We more or less had to direct ourselves."

"I hold Jane in the highest esteem," Horton later said. "It took a long time for her big break to come."

[In the late 1950s, during one of Jane's visits to "Belly Acres," Horton was complaining that the State of California was forcing him to sell a portion of his land to make way for the Ventura Freeway, a major traffic artery that opened in 1960.]

Jane found her leading man, Jeffrey Lynn, "dreamy. If I didn't have Ronnie, I would have dated him. The trouble with Jeff was that he was too polite to

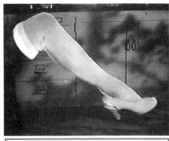

No, It's not a prosthesis...It's Jane's leg, the only part of her body still visible after ingesting "The Serum."

fight the gang of carpetbaggers who ran the studios. He didn't know how to become a star. He did just what they told him to do. He made all those movies with the Lane sisters, including *Four Daughters* (1938). The year I worked with him, *Four Daughters* had inspired yet another family melodrama starring Lynn, *Four Mothers* (1941)."

"I didn't see Jeffrey for years after the movie was made," she said. "I heard from Ronnie that he was in Army Intelligence. He and this blonde starlet, Marilyn Monroe, had small roles in *Home Town Story* (1951). And he did a little bit better in *BUtterfield 8* (1960), with Elizabeth Taylor. But the Hollywood sun never shone bright enough on this leading man. He ended up leaving show-biz to sell real estate. Actually, he never recovered from the loss of the role of Ashley Wilkes in *Gone With the Wind* (1939). He once confessed to me that he would have been a bigger star were it not for Ronnie, who got the roles most suited for him."

Craig Stevens had only a bit role in Jane's newest film, but he would figure into her future after the war. She found him handsome and charming, noting that he exuded masculinity. Horton admitted to her that although he had a crush on Stevens, "It won't do me any good. I'm not in his league."

Stevens would later marry actress Alexis Smith, who would become Reagan's leading lady in his first movie role after the war. Reagan would then follow that role by co-starring with Stevens in his next film after that, too.

By now, Jane was critically inspecting every young beauty appearing in her movies, attempts to evaluate any player who might one day challenge her tenuous position as a Warners' contract player. It was commonplace for a starlet's options not to be renewed, and Jane had been lucky to hold onto her contract, such as it was.

She turned an envious eye on one of the movie's supporting stars, Marguerite Chapman, a former switchboard operator who evolved into a New York model. She had parlayed her victories into a Hollywood contract, making her film debut in 1940.

Jane was right about sensing future stardom for the lovely young woman. In time, Chapman would appear opposite such stars as Edward G. Robinson and George Sanders. Big stardom never came, however, and Chapman ended up in supporting roles. One of them was a 1955 appearance with Marilyn Monroe in *The Seven Year Itch.*

Chapman later recalled an unpleasant experience she had with Reagan when dining with three other cast members, including Jane, in the Warner commissary. Reagan had joined his young wife for lunch.

"He was a real big shot back then," Chapman said. "Headed for stardom, as everybody thought. I was sitting at table between Jane and Horton. When Reagan joined us, he immediately embarrassed me."

"I heard from Jane that you're Catholic," Reagan said. "Why are you Catholic?"

"Because I was born one," she answered.

"That doesn't mean you have to stay one," Reagan said.

"I never liked the man after that," she said, "and I certainly never voted for him in future elections."

Other than its silly plot, *The Body Disappears* sometimes causes additional embarrassments when screened today on such networks as Turner Movie Classics. They revolve around the on-screen behavior of Willie Best, known back then as "Sleep n' Eat." An African American actor from Sunflower, Mississippi, he was a rival of the now notorious Stepin Fetchit, an actor who's reviled today because of his screen portrayals of dark-skinned, stereotypically lazy simpletons. That was exactly the role that Best was called upon to play in *The Body Disappears,* in which he was filmed as an eyeball-popping illiterate fool.

Best, who would soon appear in *High Sierra* (1941) with Humphrey Bogart and Ida Lupino, had been playing a variation of this role in other films since 1930. As he told Jane, "I don't mind acting witless. That is, if the paycheck is fat enough. I call it 'bringing home the bacon.' It's better than pickin' cotton in Mississippi on a dog day in August."

Marguerite Chapman—a serious threat to Jane's sovereignty at Warners, or so she thought at the time.

Jane talked mostly about the frustration of her new career," Lynn said. "She seemed 'put upon' by her new duties as a wife and mother."

"I'm tired of playing a sidekick to a bigger star," she told him. "I'm always cast in that secondary position, or else as a reporter turned detective or a glasses-wearing bookworm. I should have some of the roles going to Ida Lupino. There's got to be something better for me—and for Ronnie, too. All the roles I want to play go to either Lupino or to Ann Sheridan, who is my friend, or else to Olivia de Havilland. If you think I'm turning green with envy, you've got that right."

The release of *The Body Disappears* ended up as a second-tier programmer, and didn't even play in some of North America's major cities. Instead, it was dumped into small town movie houses from Peoria, Illinois, to Pocatelo, Idaho.

Critic Clive Hirschhorn claimed that, "The only thing not injected with an invisible serum was the film itself—which, in the circumstances, was an oversight and not easily forgiven."

***

Back at his home studio, after his brief stint for MGM, Reagan was once again cast opposite Priscilla Lane, this time in *Million Dollar Baby* (1941). Although the ardor which had once blazed between them had dimmed, they remained very friendly and supportive of each other.

After Reagan read the script of *Million Dollar Baby,* he told Priscilla that he was delighted to get the girl in the end. "I was afraid that Jeffrey Lynn would walk off with you. After all, he's billed before me in the credits."

It's somewhat ridiculous plot was based on a Leonard Spigelgass story called "Miss Wheelwright Discovers America." For some reason, it took three of Warners' most talented writers—Casey Robinson, Richard Macaulay, and Jerry Wald, to come up with an only mildly entertaining film script.

As the plot unfolds, a young attorney, James Amory (Lynn), travels to England to meet with an American multi-millionaire, Cornelia Wheelwright (May Robson), who has been living abroad for thirty years. He tells her that her father earned his fortune by defrauding his former business partner. She is also told that the granddaughter, Pam McAlister (Lane), of the defrauded partner is alive and living in a very modest boarding house in New York.

Feeling guilty, Robson journeys to America and checks into the boarding house herself, where she discovers Pam living across the hall from her pianist boyfriend (Reagan). She anonymously makes a gift of a million dollars to the shocked young woman, who works as a sales clerk in a department store. Elated, Pam immediately buys gifts for her friends in the boarding house—including Reagan, her true love.

Their reaction is not what she expects—in fact, she finds them resentful. Her newfound wealth threatens her relationship with Reagan, who does not "want to marry money. I prefer to make my own way in the world."

In a totally unbelievable development in the plot, Lane ultimately donates her fortune to charity, winning back the heart of her hard-working musician boyfriend. Presumably at the end of the movie, they start out on their life together as poor as they were when they were dating.

Unusual for him, Reagan had gone to work two weeks in advance of the shooting date, hoping to master some of the visual aspects, at least, of his role as a pianist. He went to Warners' Music Department, where he engaged a pianist to teach him how to play a piano keyboard, if not musically, at least for how it would appear on camera. Up to then, he had no musical background except for singing with a barbershop quartet in the Middle West. He was taught how to manipulate his fingers on a dummy keyboard, making no sound.

"A lot of acting is imitation anyway," he later said, "and I became pretty good, as long as the piano remained silent. For a while, I almost convinced myself I could play."

Although his hands seem to be playing the piano in the film, the actual sound came from dubbing by a concert pianist.

For several days, as Reagan studied the keyboard, David Lewis, the associate producer of *Million Dollar Baby,* showed up to take him to lunch.

Reagan had tangled with Lewis before, in his earlier capacity as associate producer of *Dark Victory* with Bette Davis. He resented Lewis for his continued sexual pursuit of him. "God, you're aggressive," he told Lewis. "Why not accept a no as a no?"

"Because I firmly believe that if you spent one night with me, I'd win you over and you'd switch to my side."

"That would be the day," Reagan said, sarcastically.

"I'm not a studio hack, and if you play along with me, I can really help make you an A-list star by get-

"Don't hate me because I'm rich!" *The Million Dollar Baby*, as interpreted by Priscilla Lane, begs her strange-valued fiancé, Reagan.

ting the right roles for you. I believe that the producer and the writer account for 80 percent of a film's success, the director and actor (or actors) only twenty percent. I like emotional dramas like the work I did on *Camille* with Garbo and Robert Taylor. I did a lot for Taylor, and he was most cooperative with me."

"I learned everything from Irving Thalberg at MGM, and he was the best in the business. I found out that the script based on a controversial novel, *Kings Row,* is in pre-production. It includes themes relating to both incest and homosexuality, but that can be toned down for a movie. I could use my influence to get you one of the screen's top roles. I could be a breakthrough for you. I see an Oscar in it for you."

"Why can't you help me win the role without turning me into a male whore?" Reagan asked. "C'mon, give me a break."

"And you want me to do this for you without anything in return?" Lewis asked. "That's not how we play the game in Tinseltown."

"Are we negotiating?" Reagan asked.

"Think over my offer," Lewis said. "I can get the role for you if you'll cooperate. Jeffrey Lynn on this very picture is practically signing a contract that he'll do my bidding if I get the role for him. You're so goddamn stubborn."

"Listen, I want to cooperate, and I need your help. But I can't...I just can't."

"Will you meet me halfway?" Lewis asked.

"Exactly what would that entail?" Reagan asked.

"Nude massages. You've been massaged before in the nude at your golf club. I know that for a fact. The masseurs there working you over are homos. So you've already been that route before—and you ended up paying the guys to paw your beautiful body."

"But nothing happened with those guys," he protested. "It was just a massage."

"If you'll let me massage you, nothing will happen either," Lewis said. "I promise I won't go all the way."

"Well, since you put it that way, and since such a thing has already happened to me at the golf club, I'll have to consider it. I really want a breakthrough role. I guess we might make some sort of deal."

"You're one hard bargainer," Lewis said. "Years from now, after you become a big star—with my help—you can omit this sordid detail from your memoirs."

"You can count on me doing that," Reagan vowed.

[Lewis penned the first draft of a tell-all memoir, devoted in large part to his long relationship with director James Whale (1930-1952), filling it with tantalizing tidbits about his troublesome relationships with Ronald Reagan, Robert Taylor, Bette Davis, Greta Garbo, Norma Shearer (with whom he claimed he had an affair), Elizabeth Taylor, Montgomery Clift, Irving Thalberg, Spencer Tracy (with whom he also claimed an affair), Jean Harlow, Ingrid Bergman, and Charles Boyer, who he claimed was a closeted homosexual.

Several of his friends read the manuscript and urged him to destroy it. Later, instead of a tell-all, he wrote a rather vanilla and harmless book, The Creative Producer: A Memoir of the Studio System.*]*

On his first day on the set, Reagan met with the film's German director, Curtis Bernhardt. He discussed not about Reagan's role in the movie, but about events in Germany, out of which he had escaped from the Nazis. He was morbidly worried about his Jewish family and friends he'd left behind.

"Bernhardt really filled me in on what was actually going on," Reagan later said. "The massacre of the Jews and other atrocities. He convinced me that America was asleep at the wheel, claiming that the country should mobilize. He predicted that the Nazis would one day invade the U.S. from the East Coast, the Japs from the West."

"He was actually a very talented director," Reagan said. "He shouldn't be handling the fluff he'd been given. He'd directed both Jane and Olivia in *My Love Came Back* and now he was tackling our project, with its stupid plot. In my role, I was virtually insisting my girlfriend give away a million bucks. If Jane brought home a million bucks, I'd be worshipping at her altar."

During the shoot, Reagan lunched with Priscilla Lane, his leading lady. Instead of romancing her, as he'd done during his past, he listened to her pour out her career woes. "Even when I was big box office at Warners, I made only $750 a week. I was constantly demanding more money from Jack Warner. I also turned down roles and went on suspension."

She showed him a copy of the London publication, *Picturegoer*. "Even the magazine is asking, 'Why is Priscilla Lane still knocking on the door of major stardom?' The magazine got it right. I've just been a stooge to John Garfield or Cagney. I deserve much larger and bigger parts."

Then she congratulated him on his marriage to Jane.

"Men are going to be scarce during the war," Reagan said. "Maybe it'll last until war's end."

After six decades on the stage and screen, the Australian actress, May Robson, was coming to the end of a distinguished career. As the eccentric lady of wealth and good conscience, she virtually stole the picture, *Million Dollar Baby,* from its other actors. She would die the following year at the age of eighty-four. During the shoot, she invited Reagan to see a screening of her recent film, *Granny Get Your Gun* (1940). "An amusing little trifle," she told him, and he agreed.

She claimed that there was a certain irony in her appearance in *Million Dollar Baby*. "I feel I've made this movie in reverse. In 1932, I starred in a film called *If I Had a Million.* I played the resident of an old folks' home who suddenly gets a new lease on life when I'm given a check for one million big ones from a dying business tycoon. Now, in your movie, I'm playing a dying lady dispensing a million—you figure."

Reagan had not gotten to know Johnny Sheffield when he'd played the childhood version of the title character in *Knute Rockne—All American* the year before. But he made it a point to meet and talk to the ten-year-old on the set of *Million Dollar Baby,* where he'd been assigned the minor role of Alvie Grayson.

His father had once read in the *Hollywood Reporter* an article entitled "Have You a Tarzan Jr. in Your Backyard?" Reginald Sheffield felt that his son, Johnny, fitted the bill, physique and all, and arranged for an interview for him to appear as the adopted son of Tarzan in the next jungle movie, starring Johnny Weissmuller and Maureen O'Sullivan.

During the audition, Weissmuller selected Johnny from among 300 juvenile actors interviewed. He soon appeared as "Boy" in *Tarzan Finds a Son* (1939). That same year, Sheffield also starred with Judy Garland and Mickey Rooney in *Babes in Arms.*

It was bound to happen that a fellow actor would eventually transmit gossip about Jane Wyman to her husband, Ronald Reagan. The comic actor, Walter Catlett, had recently appeared in *Bad Men of Missouri* with Jane. A heavy drinker, he always carried around a secret flask, although his large consumption of alcohol never seemed to interfere with his work. He was living proof that the art of gossip wasn't confined to women.

One day, he cornered Reagan during a break in filming, claiming, "I want to speak to you man to man. I promised Jane I wouldn't squeal on her, but I was never good at keeping a secret. I think a husband should know what a wife is up to so he can put a stop to it."

"And what is this hideous secret?" Reagan asked. "She's a Nazi spy? A lesbian in the closet?"

"I hate to be the bearer of bad news, but Jane is slipping around seeing John Payne on the side. I know. I arranged a rendezvous between them during our last picture together."

Reagan looked stunned. "Spare me—I don't really want to know the details."

"I'm sorry I had to tell you that, but I got fed up reading in all those fan magazines about what a perfect couple you guys were," Catlett said. "If you confront her, don't let her know that I was the one who let the cat out of the bag."

"I won't," Reagan said. "Actually, I don't plan to confront her at all. Jane's business is her own."

"You're a very understanding husband—far more than I would be," Catlett said. "If I found out that my wife was cheating on me, I'd beat the shit out of her."

"I'm sure you would," Reagan said before walking away.

Two days later, when Betty Grable called to confirm a Saturday afternoon date, he went to it, as he'd later confide to Dick Powell, "with less guilt than before."

Swinging on a vine, Johnny Weissmuller teaches Johnny Sheffield how it's done.

***

Over drinks on Betty Grable's terrace, Reagan laughed at the title of her latest movie, *Hot Spot,* co-starring Victor Mature and her nemesis, Carole Landis. It was based on a novel, *I Wake Up Screaming,* by pulp fiction writer Steve Fisher.

"I can't believe the Breen Office is letting Fox get away with a title like that. Guys all over the country will be making jokes. Do you play the title role of Hot Spot?"

In private, they became "Big John" and "Little John," and developed a strong affection for each other during the decade in which they made eight Tarzan movies together, including *Tarzan Finds a Son* (1939).

[Reagan was right. Producer Darryl F. Zanuck ordered the title of Fisher's novel restored. Although the posters had already been printed defining the film's name as Hot Spot, *it was retitled* I Wake Up Screaming *after violent objections from the Legion of Decency.]*

At one point, publicly and on the set, Grable and Landis had become embroiled in a hair pulling catfight until they were separated by Mature. "Not only is the blonde whore my worst enemy," Grable told Reagan. "She and I are sharing the sexual favors of Victor."

"I'm surprised you're making such a stark drama," he said. "No song-and-dance numbers?"

"My mother wants me to take my place up there with the marquee drama queens—Barbara Stanwyck, Joan Crawford, and Bette Davis. But Zanuck figures I'd better stick to musicals. In fact, many fans came to see *Hot Spot* thinking it was a musical."

"Landis won't shut up bad mouthing me," Grable continued. "She's played third lead in two of my recent pictures, not only *Hot Spot* but *Moon Over Miami.* The hooker is telling everyone that she's stolen both pictures right out from under me."

Grable tossed Reagan a copy of a newspaper with a column by Jimmy Fiddler. It read: "20th Century biggies are boasting that if any of their singing stars go temperamental, they have an ace in the hole—Carole Landis, who has been improving her fine natural voice by industrious study."

Grable also showed him a copy of *American Magazine*. "Though Carole has appeared in big roles in only four pictures, she has been dubbed by columnists from coast to coast as Hollywood's top glamour girl with the most gorgeous figure in moviedom."

"What does that make me?" Grable demanded to know. "Chopped liver?"

"You have a unique talent," Reagan told her, "and you need to concentrate on it and develop it. You can never escape competition. The same is true at Paramount and especially at MGM. At Warners I've got plenty of competition. Right now, Jeffrey Lynn is breathing down my neck, wanting parts assigned to me. And I want the roles given to George Brent. That's how studio politics work."

"After divorcing Jackie Coogan, I was looking forward to my new life as a swinging bachelor gal, but it has its dark side. I'm doing a lot better than Jackie. I don't think he's worked since we did *Million Dollar Legs* (1939). We're still friends. But both of us agreed that ours was just a childhood affair—we were too young to settle down. Unlike me, this former child star isn't finding any demand for his services. He claims that his fickle public couldn't stand for him to ever grow up."

"I think the same thing will happen to ShirleyTemple," he answered. "She lacks the talent to endure as an adult star."

After Reagan had helped cool Grable's rage about Landis, he suggested they go inside. Over a second drink, he confessed that he'd learned that Jane was having an affair with John Payne, with whom Grable had worked before.

She did not look surprised. "John and I had an affair when we made *Tin Pan Alley* (1940), and, years before that, we were a singing duet on a 15-minute daily show for CBS. Like you and Jane, John and that wife of his, Anne Shirley, are written up as 'The Perfect Couple,' but we both know that that isn't true. Both of them cheated on each other all the time."

"John plans to do what Gable did at MGM—that is, seduce all the beautiful leading ladies like you did at Warners. Not just me, but Linda Darnell, too. Now, he's making *Sun Valley Serenade*. When she's not on her skates, Sonja Henie summons him to do the dirty deed. I suspect he's already had Alice Faye, and he's got Gene Tierney in his sights right now, too. His thing with your Jane will be over before it really begins."

"I certainly hope so," he said. "I'm worried. Payne is a tough act to follow. I have doubts I can't satisfy Jane the way he does."

"Have no doubts," she assured him. "You do just fine. That reminds me." She got up and excused herself, appearing fifteen minutes later in a see-through black *négligée*. "Let's quit talking about all these other hunks and hussies, and get down to the main attraction of this

Sexual innuendo, censorship, film noir, Betty Grable, A corrupt NYPD, and Victor Mature

259

fast-fading afternoon—you and me, baby!"

***

Jane would later remember her 1941 film, *You're In the Army Now,* because of one scene with the Pittsburgh-born actor, Regis Toomey, who played her love interest, Captain Radcliffe. They indulged in what had been until then the longest kiss in cinematic history, lasting three minutes and five seconds, or four percent of the film's duration.

She later told Reagan, "Thank god our director, Lewis Seiler, didn't call for retakes. Regis had bad breath. He must have eaten skunk meat for supper. The sacrifices I make for my career!"

Alerted the day before the kissing scene was to be filmed, Reagan appeared on the set as an observer. Jane complained that his presence there made her uncomfortable, but her husband handled it very well, according to Toomey. At the end of the liplock, Reagan approached Toomey. "I didn't know if he was going to punch me in the nose—or what. Actually, he was quite friendly and shook my hand. He said, 'How did you get Jane to sit still that long'?"

Betty Grable, the #1 pinup girl in the world.

The film dealt with a timely topic. President Franklin D. Roosevelt knew that the United States would eventually enter World War II, and he had re-instated the draft. It became the topic of the day, as young men throughout the nation speculated on getting drafted and how it would disrupt their lives, or even end their lives.

Warners had cast Jimmy Durante and Phil Silvers as Jeeper Smith and Breezy Jones, two vacuum cleaner salesmen who accidentally get inducted into the Army.

Jane played "Bliss Dobson," the daughter of Colonel Dobson (Donald MacBride), who is opposed to Jane dating Toomey. Her leading man had started out in romantic roles in 1929. His scenes with Jane would virtually be the last of those kind of parts, as he'd soon switch to character roles minus his toupée.

Emerging from the streets of the Lower East Side of New York, Jimmy Durante was known as "Schnozzola," because of his big nose. When Jane worked with him, he was one of the most popular comedians in America, known for his throaty way with a song, his jovial good spirits, his one-liners, and his clipped gravelly speech, along with his comic butchery of language, all of it delivered with a New York accent.

On the surface, Durante had a bubbling, upbeat personality, yet Jane sensed a deep sadness in him. Fi-

After the longest kiss *(upper photo)* in cinematic history until then, Jane told her leading man, Regis Toomey *(lower photo)*, "Don't even think about ever trying that again."

260

nally, he told her the bad news. A doctor had informed him that his wife, the former Jean Olson, whom he'd married in 1921, had a serious heart ailment and had only months to live.

[His wife died on Valentine's Day of 1943 at the age of 46.]

Emerging from Brooklyn, the son of Russian Jews, Phil Silvers was hailed as "The King of Chutzpah." A veteran of vaudeville and burlesque, he'd been appearing on stage since the age of eleven. Jane found him "all frantic *schtick*, acting with buffoonish, idiotic behavior, even stealing scenes from Durante."

Although the film clearly belonged to Durante and Silvers, within its context, Jane had at least one moment in the spotlight, including the long kiss.

In a sexy dress that revealed her legs—and as Silvers claimed, "she has beautiful gams"—Jane sang "I'm Glad My Number Was Called" for a USO show. She was followed by Silvers, who, as Jeepers, performs an Apache Dance.

His comic behavior was just a front he put up. She discovered that most of the time, he suffered from a deep depression. Sometimes he had to be physically dragged out of his dressing room to perform on camera. He always managed to pull himself together to go through his routine.

Jane had no trouble working with Seiler again. He'd directed her in *He Couldn't Say No* (1938), and he'd also helmed Reagan in *Hell's Kitchen* (1939). He told her how sorry he was that the public didn't line up to see the other film he'd directed, *Tugboat Annie Sails Again* (1940), in which he'd cast Reagan and Jane as a screen team. "This new picture is a cinch," he told her. "Silvers and Durante will direct themselves."

Jane reported to work every day, but often was not needed, since Silvers and Durante were monopolizing most of the scenes—two comedians and an Army tank.

Seiler noted that during the movie's shooting, John Payne paid many visits to Jane's dressing room. She was getting to know the handsome actor, and liked what she learned.

"Before hitting pay dirt at Fox, where they are building me up as a big star, I drifted around Paramount and also Warners," he said. "They didn't know what to do with me."

In 1940 alone, Payne had been cast in six films at Fox, including *Star Dust,* in which Linda Darnell had made her screen debut, and *The Great Profile,* in which John Barrymore spoofed himself during his dying days.

"Like most Hollywood hunks, John is worried that he'll be sucked up into the war," Jane told Paulette Goddard.

"If we go to war, I'm going to enlist in Army pilot training, and I hope I'll be stationed in Long Beach, so I can continue seeing you," he'd told Jane.

She said to Goddard, "John does not take acting very seriously. He views it merely as a fun job with good pay."

"A lot of people seem to think he's just a pretty boy with a lot of gals fluttering around him, but he's a real gentleman with a serious side," Jane said. "He's much deeper than people think or the roles he plays. I mean, he reads philosophy, stuff like that."

"I've fallen into the Robert Taylor category at MGM," he told Jane. "Fox is build-

"Instead of Errol Flynn, I get Phil Silvers (*left*), 'the King of *Chutzpah*,' and Jimmy Durante (*right*), '*Schnozzola*,' as my leading men," Jane (*center*) said. "How lucky can a gal get?"

ing me up as the studio's pretty boy, their rival to Taylor."

When Jane poured out her feelings to Lucille Ball, the actress said, "You sound like you're in love."

"I am," Jane said, "but in John's case, love and marriage don't necessarily go together. He told me that when he divorces that Anne Shirley thing, he may never marry again. But then again, he might. He seems very confused. Do you think I should continue sleeping with John and betraying Ronnie?"

"Get it while you can, honey," Ball responded. "That's what I do, since Desi *[Arnaz]* is always on the road. I'm sure he knocks off a piece or two in every town in which he appears."

When *You're In the Army Now* was released, Jane didn't expect good reviews, knowing that all the attention would be devoted to the manic comedy of its male leads. One reviewer did single her out, however, citing her for "playing a piquant, saucer-eyed good sport, looking like she was having some fun." For the most part, the movie was attacked for its heavy slapstick and corny situations.

A week later, Lloyd Bacon, the director, called her. "In our last picture, Olivia (De Havilland) had the female lead, but in my new picture, *Larceny, Inc.* (1942). I'm giving the female lead to you. You're going to be the leading lady to Edward G. Robinson."

"In my last picture, I had a record-breaking kiss of three or so minutes. If you're telling me I've got to kiss Ol' Liver Lips for that long, I'm walking."

"It's not that kind of picture," Bacon said. "Show up on the set at 7AM tomorrow morning."

***

Before the final casting of *Casablanca (1942)*, many actors were suggested. The drama had originated as an unpublished play, *Everybody Comes to Rick's.* Stephen Karnot, the first reader at Warners, had suggested for the male lead (Rick Blaine), either Humphrey Bogart, James Cagney, or George Raft, with Mary Astor cast in the female lead.

The story was set in that Moroccan city of mystery, Casablanca, the action occurring after the fall of France, as refugees from that Nazi-occupied country gathered there, many of them waiting for exit visas.

Karnot called it "sophisticated hokum," but predicted, "It will play." Based on his favorable report, Jack Warner agreed to pay $20,000 for the adaptation, the highest amount ever paid for an unproduced play.

When the director, Michael Curtiz, read the first draft of the script, he thought that the role of Rick would be a good vehicle for Raft. The actor read the script and immediately rejected the role. He said he was tired of playing gangsters and that in his past, Rick had been a hoodlum.

As for Hal B. Wallis, after he reviewed the script, and as he was mulling over which actors might populate it, he sent out a "trial balloon," a list of candidates. It was published in newspapers nationwide on January 5, 1942. His tentative cast nominated Ronald Reagan as Rick, Ann Sheridan as Ilsa, and Dennis Morgan as Victor Laszlo, the Czech freedom fighter.

[When he was in the White House, Reagan was asked if he had ever been offered the role of Rick. "It appeared as an item in The Hollywood Reporter,*" he answered, "but I don't recall ever seriously being offered the part."*

When Ann Sheridan was asked about it, she said, "The female lead was originally to have been that of an American heiress, but the writers turned her into a European

262

woman. I was never formally offered the role."

Morgan corroborated his colleagues' statements, saying, *"I was never asked to play Victor Laszlo."*

As for Raft, although some movie writers claim that he was never offered the role of Rick, Raft's biographer, James Robert Parrish, wrote, *"Warners decided to test Raft in a more or less 'straight' role, that of Rick Blaine, ex-smuggler and present café owner. World War II had dampened the gangster film cycle (or, more correctly, Adolf Hitler and crew becoming the new gang-*

We remember it well—*Casablanca:* "We'll always have Paris." Depicted above, Ingrid Bergman and Humphrey Bogart.

sters). Raft rejected the role, reportedly because he did not like the taint of ex-gangster."

Years later, at a casino in London, Raft—who was fully aware of Hollywood commentators who claimed that he was never offered the role of Laszlo—was asked about his inclusion in the list of possible contenders for the role of Rick in Casablanca. In response, he asserted, "Warners wanted me to play Rick, and I turned them down. Anybody who says that isn't true is a god damn cunt!"]

Before shooting began, Wallis changed his mind, recasting the roles with Bogie, Ingrid Bergman, and Paul Henreid as the three main protagonists.

Hedy Lamarr had lobbied for the role of Ilsa, but MGM would not release her. Actually, Bergman had not wanted the role, viewing it as a B picture, little realizing that she was the star of a movie that would be hailed as the greatest ever made, even better, in the eyes of many critics, than Orson Welles' *Citizen Kane.*

When *Casablanca* was released in November of 1942, Reagan expressed his regrets to Dick Powell that he never got to play Rick. He stood idly by, looking on in envy as the role of Rick became a personal triumph for Bogie, establishing him as a romantic star and not just a screen villain. *Casablanca* brought him his first Oscar nomination, and also made him the reigning male star at the studio, "The King of Warner Brothers."

***

To his regret, Reagan ended up assigned instead to a routine sixty-three minute programmer, *Nine Lives Are Not Enough* (1941), to be directed by the London-born A. Edward Sutherland.

At first, he was delighted to learn that Jane Wyman would be his leading lady, but he was later informed that she'd been assigned to another picture.

Reagan's first question was, "Who is going to be my new leading lady?" He was told it would be the very beautiful Joan Perry, the Florida-born New York City model, a career which had led to a Hollywood contract with Columbia 1935. She had previously appeared with such actors as Melvyn Douglas, Lew Ayres, and Ralph Bellamy. But her biggest coup involved receiving a proposal of marriage from the studio boss, the much-feared Harry Cohn.

During the hour that the film's director, A. Edward Sutherland, spent with Reagan on the first day, he talked more about himself than he did Reagan's upcoming role. Arriving in Hollywood from England, he'd appeared as a bungling police officer in *Tillie's Punctured Romance* (1914), starring Charlie Chaplin, Mabel Normand, and the formidable Marie Dressler. Sutherland had become known for directing comedians, claiming, "I'd rather dine on tarantula than make another movie with Stan Laurel." However, he got along with the acerbic W.C. Fields.

Among Sutherland's five wives was the legendary Louise Brooks (1926-1928). During their tumultuous marriage, both of them were known for numerous affairs on the side.

Finally, Sutherland, who had been a *protégé* of Chaplin, got around to giving Reagan his overall direction as the newspaper reporter, Matt Sawyer, in *Nine Lives Are Not Enough*. "Play the role with a flip brashness. You know, the aggressive reporter with his hat resting on the back of his head. You can be resourceful and come up with some moves on your own. Play it frantic, like you're always in a jam. But, remember, you always land on your feet."

"With those directions, I should surely win an Academy Award nomination," Reagan said, sarcastically.

He studied his script. As a reporter for "The Daily News," he is known around the office as the "Boy Crusader." He is constantly getting into trouble with his tough boss, Howard da Silva. Reagan writes an *exposé* of a local mob boss (Ben Welden), but the gangster clears his name and files a libel suit against the paper.

Enraged, Da Silva demotes Reagan to the police beat, and threatens to assign him to writing the lonely hearts column if he slips up again.

Reagan makes the nightly rounds with two policemen (James Gleason and Edward Brophy) in their patrol car. Reagan particularly liked working with Gleason, who was also a playwright and screenwriter. He always played tough but warmhearted characters. Known as the master of the double-take, he was bald, with a loud, craggy voice.

According to the plot, during their patrol one night, Reagan and the cops discover the body of a missing millionaire. Reagan, as journalist, writes it up for his paper as a murder, although the coroner rules it as a suicide. Once again, Reagan is in trouble with Da Silva, who fires him.

He is determined to prove it was murder, and he enlists the help of the slain millionaire's daughter (played by Joan Perry in her role of Jane Abbott.)

Complications ensue, but in the end, Reagan discovers that it was murder after all. In the meantime, Perry falls in love with Reagan and marries him. She also buys the *Daily News* for him. His first move as its new owner involves assigning Da Silva the lonely hearts column.

During filming, actress Faye Emerson, cast as Rose Chadwick, paid special attention to Reagan, although he more or less ignored her. He would later regret that.

As he told Dick Powell, "I wish I had sucked up more to Faye. She was divorcing her first husband, William Crawford. How did I know that within months, she'd be married to Elliott Roosevelt and would move into the White House. If I had become a close friend of hers, I, too, would have been a frequent visitor to the White House, advising Franklin Roosevelt on how to conduct the war."

The character played by Reagan didn't like Da Silva in his screen role, and Reagan, as a private individual, detested him in private. The actor had just completed *Bad Men of Missouri* (1941) with Jane,

Reagan with Joan Perry in *Nine Lives*. Before filming began, Reagan received a memo from Harry Cohn, the mogul who ran Columbia: "Hands off Joan. Got that, Reagan?"

Like Walter Catlett, who had blabbed to him about Jane and John Payne, Da Silva was also a nasty gossip. He and Reagan got into several bitter political arguments. Although still a liberal Democrat, Reagan viewed Da Silva as a card-carrying communist.

[Da Silva was later blacklisted by the House Committee on Un-American Activities. After that, he was unable to find work in the movies or on television.]

One day, after Reagan had angered Da Silva, he struck back. "When I made *Bad Men of Missouri* with your wife, she spent more time with Dennis Morgan than she did before the camera. You'd better check to see what's going on. Sometimes, a husband is the last to know."

Coming so soon after the equivalent allegation about Jane and John Payne, Reagan became deeply depressed, trying to convince himself that Da Silva was a liar.

In the middle of the shoot, Jane invited Joan Blondell and Dick Powell for dinner. They were obviously having their own marital difficulties.

Concealed behind the draperies in *Nine Lives:* Reagan, playing a nosy reporter (*"Give me the City Desk"*) looks unpresidential.

Blondell recalled, "I sensed that Ronnie was greatly depressed. He was polite and he even told a few jokes, but he kept looking at Jane when she wasn't looking back. It was like he was studying her with a questioning look on his face. I suspected that some nasty little shit had been spreading gossip about Jane. But he had his own guilt. I'd heard through the grapevine that he was slipping around knocking off a piece here and there. Dick was doing the same with me. I just brushed off his infidelities. I referred to arrangements such as ours as a typical Hollywood marriage."

Cast in a small role as a mechanic, John Ridgely had appeared with Reagan in *Secret Service of the Air* (1939) and with Jane in *He Couldn't Say No* (1938). Now, he observed Reagan closely, sensing something was wrong. "He had changed," Ridgely said. "He

James Gleason: Played tough guys or cops, always with a suspicious whine in his voice.

seemed depressed, and his heart wasn't in his work. I felt he was going through marital troubles, like most couples do after they get hitched. He also talked about the draft, wondering if he'd be called up. Because of his bad eyesight, he couldn't fight on the front lines, but he might end up in some desk job. With his contact lenses, he could always push papers."

During the shoot, Reagan spent most of his time with Joan Perry. The two bonded and often had lunch together, but it wasn't a case of *"Leadinglady-itis."*

He knew that Perry was marrying one of the most powerful figures in Hollywood. He feared that Jack Warner might not renew his contract, and that he might find himself pounding on the door of Columbia, looking for work. The way he figured it, if he were a close friend of Harry Cohn's new wife, he'd have a better chance of getting a contract with that studio.

To his surprise, he found that Perry had also been announced as the leading lady in his next picture, *[The title of that film, originating as* Eagle Squadron *and later changed to* Flight Patrol, *would eventually be released in 1941 as* International Squadron.*]*

As regards his acting technique in *Nine Lives Are Not Enough*, Reagan had taken Sutherland's advice. One critic defined his performance as "helter-skelter."

The film had taken just twenty-two days to shoot, and Jack Warner had ordered the rough cut sent to his office for a screening. In a somewhat confusing memo, he claimed that *Nine Lives Are Not Enough* was "a peachy picture." But then he wrote, "I have about a half dozen more revamping shots, inserts, and effects to put in, and I cannot understand why they were not done in the first place, especially in the off-scene fight where Reagan slugs the newspaper reporter and throws him off-scene. Undoubtedly, they had mufflers on their black jacks."

John Ridgely: He found the future president "a troubled soul."

Sutherland was left to figure out what all that meant.

Warner also said that he detested the title *Nine Lives Are Not Enough,* since it had little connection to the plot. He promised he'd send over a new title, but he never did.

Reviews were tepid, as were attendance and box office receipts. One critic called the film, "a mystery-comedy—and not much of either."

***

In a Manhattan night club, in 1935, a beautiful model, Betty Miller, 21, danced by the table of Harry Cohn, aged 44, the chief honcho at Columbia pictures. Miller was in the arms of another man, but Cohn was intrigued by her striking figure.

As a fast worker, he offered her a Hollywood contract before the night was over, telling her "to dump that faggot you're with."

When she reached Hollywood, she found that he was in the process of trying to divorce his first wife, the former Rose Barker, whom he had married in 1923. Cohn personally drove Miller to Columbia, where he ordered both makeup and wardrobe to transform her natural beauty into something very glamorous for her screen test. He approved the test himself, and the newly re-christened "Joan Perry" found herself co-starring in *The Case of the Missing Man* (1935) opposite Roger Pryor. Cohn had told her that "Betty Miller" was too commonplace. "Sounds like a cobbler's daughter."

Perry moved in with Cohn long before his divorce was finalized. They lived together on Lexington Drive in Beverly Hills. After marrying her on July 30, 1941, at the St. Regis Hotel in Manhattan, he returned with her to their home in Hollywood. Now that she was his bride, they began to entertain the Hollywood elite, including Louis B. Mayer, Irene Dunne, Katharine Hepburn, Mae West, Cary Grant, even Sabu and Humphrey Bogart.

On the set of *Nine Lives Are Not Enough,* Perry invited Reagan and Jane to one of her fabulous dinner parties. As a stunning hostess, she appeared in a gown designed by Jean Louis of the Columbia Wardrobe department. She presided at one end of the table, with Cohn at the other end. Placed on either side of him were phones which were constantly ringing.

After dinner, Reagan joined Cohn in his library, where the male guests gathered for cigars and brandy. Perry was entertaining the women guests, including an emerging star, Rita Hayworth, in the adjoining saloon.

"Did Joan tell you?" Reagan asked Cohn. "She's starring in my next picture, *Flight Patrol.*"

"I prefer for you to refer to her as Mrs. Cohn," he said.

In spite of that slight embarrassment, Reagan was amused by Cohn, who seemed more well-versed in Hollywood legend and lore than anybody he'd ever met.

Before meeting Cohn, Reagan had heard many stories about him. He'd been born in 1893 into a working class Jewish family in New York City. Eventually, he landed in Hollywood and helped open Columbia Pictures on Poverty Row. His fortunes changed after the release of *It Happened One Night* (1934), a Frank Capra comedy starring Clark Gable and Claudette Colbert. The picture swept up five major Oscars at the Academy Awards ceremony that year.

Behind his back, Cohn was derisively called "White Fang," ruling like a tyrant, and presiding over Columbia like it was his own private police state.

Perry had admitted to Reagan that her new husband had a personality like Dr. Jekyll and Mr. Hyde. He was loud, brash, and had an intimidating personality. On his desk rested an autographed portrait of Mussolini, which he'd obtained in Rome during a visit there in 1933.

He was also known for demanding sex from his starlets as part of their employment. Over the years, he would seduce an array of established actresses, starlets, and extras, often deflowering A-list stars who included Marlene Dietrich, Marilyn Monroe, and Lucille Ball.

He maintained a secret passageway that led directly from his office into a dressing room filled with starlets, in a style something akin to a harem.

Everyone in Hollywood had an opinion about Cohn, usually negative. Hedda Hopper told Reagan, "He's a man you stand in line to hate."

Director Elia Kazan asserted, "Cohn is the biggest bug in a pile of horse shit."

In the library of his home, Cohn put his arm around Reagan and whispered in his ear, "Let me tell you about Hollywood: It's all about horses and cunt."

Reagan later recalled him: "Cohn was a great vulgarian, but at moments he had a certain charm. To him, all women were broads who could be had. At one point during our dinner party, when he cornered my Jane, he told her, 'If that Reagan boy can't satisfy you, you're looking at a man who can.' On that very night, he told me, 'I kiss the feet of talent. I won't be kissing your feet, Reagan.'"

Joan Perry (*aka* Betty Miller, *aka* Mrs. Harry Cohn).

That night, he also told Reagan that he'd seen him only once on the screen—and that was with Bette Davis in *Dark Victory* (1939). "You were supposed to be playing a homo, but you didn't do it right. In that bar scene with Bette, when you held up your drink to your mouth, you should have raised your little pinkie. That way, you'd signal the audience that you were a homo."

"I didn't see the role that way," Reagan protested.

"Bullshit!" Cohn said. "Edward Everett Hor-

Above is the logo/avatar inspired by the physicality of Mrs. Harry Cohn. It became recognizable throughout the world. Hail Columbia!

ton could have given you lessons in how to play a fag."

He told Reagan that long after she'd been a silent screen goddess, Gloria Swanson arrived at Columbia with two screen treatments she wanted him to produce. "I scanned both of them and turned each of them down. Three weeks later, the little over-dressed dwarf arrived with another screen treatment, which she insisted on reading to me, all twenty-five pages of it. I found it far too depressing, about a heroine who goes blind at the end of the picture. You guessed it. I turned down *Dark Victory.*"

Before Reagan left Cohn's home at around midnight, the drunken mogul approached him. "I know you'll be working with Mrs. Cohn again, and that you'll be in close proximity to her, perhaps even playing love scenes. I also know what can happen when a hot-to-trot stud like you meets a horny broad like my young wife."

Despite the pedestal on which he placed his wife, Joan Perry, Harry Cohn continued to fuck around with, among others, Rita Hayworth, who's depicted above.

"I assure you, Mr. Cohn, I'll be a perfect gentleman," Reagan said. "You can count on that. Any love scene between us will be strictly in the script."

"Thanks for that," he answered. "It's not just having my wife cheat on me. It's a health issue."

"I don't understand," Reagan said. "I'm not contagious."

"It's like this," Cohn said. "You guys with uncut dicks can cause a vaginal infection in women. Joan is used to clipped men like me. We Jews are a hell of a lot safer than you Protestant germ carriers."

***

Cast as "Denny Costello," Jane Wyman had the female lead in her latest movie, *Larceny, Inc.* (1942), wherein she played the adopted daughter of "Pressure" Maxwell (Edward G. Robinson).

They worked with three strong supporting players: Broderick Crawford as "Jug" Martin, a dim-witted gangster; Jack Carson as Jeff Randolf, a fast-talking salesman; and Anthony Quinn as the villainous gangster, Leo Dexter. Its plot was based on a Broadway play, *The Night Before Christmas,* by the distinguished humorist, S.J. Perelman, although this comedy-drama was not one of his greatest achievements.

Its director, Lloyd Bacon, welcomed Jane to the set and gave her a copy of the script, where she learned that Carson was the unlikely choice for her love interest. Bacon had most recently helmed Jane in *Honeymoon for Three* (1941).

The plot of *Larceny, Inc.* evokes Woody Allen's much later film, *Small Time Crooks* (2000). It spins around a supposed bank robbery that never quite comes off. A fellow inmate at Sing Sing, Dexter (Quinn) tries to intrigue Pressure (Robinson) and Jug (Crawford) into joining him in a bank robbery after their release from prison.

Pressure actually wants to purchase a dog-racing track in Miami with Jane, but the bank turns down his request for a loan. Along with Jug, he purchases a luggage shop next door to the bank. From the basement of the luggage store, they plan to dig a tunnel into the bank's vault.

In the meantime, a slick salesman (Carson) arrives to entice them into buying an

268

inventory of fine luggage, wholesale, for their otherwise virtually empty store. Advertising gimmicks are devised by Carson to line up customers. Eventually, based on the spectacular success of his luggage business, Pressure decides to become legitimate and stops digging the tunnel.

Tension rises after Dexter (who's still in jail) hears that Pressure has "stolen" his idea about digging a tunnel, and that he'll pocket the money from its success. Vengefully, Dexter breaks out of jail, with the intent of extorting money from Pressure. Burglar alarms are set off, there's gunfire, a police raid, and the luggage store erupts into flames. Dexter is captured and returned to Sing Sing, Pressure rebuilds his store and becomes a mogul in the merchandising of luggage and a civic-minded patriarch. Jane and Carson end up in each other's arms.

Robinson told Jane that he had accepted the comic role of Pressure Maxwell to offset the tough guy image he'd established in his star-making role of "Rico" in *Little Caesar* (1931).

Perhaps awed by his reputation, she was prepared not to like Robinson until she actually met him. In private, he was soft-spoken, cultured, and spoke seven languages. Born to Romanian Jews in Bucharest, he had emigrated to Manhattan, where he launched his acting career in Yiddish theater on the Lower East Side. His success in *Little Caesar* typecast him into gangster roles at Warners. His chief rivals for parts became George Raft, James Cagney, and Humphrey Bogart.

With the world at war, Warners was making fewer films. In 1942, Jane's only release was *Larceny, Inc.* In it, she was teamed with "tough guy" Edward G. Robinson. He turned out to be a man of culture, unlike his portrayals on screen.

"Eddie wasn't the prettiest mug ever to appear on the screen, but I learned a lot from this sensitive, talented man," Jane recalled. "He was a real pro."

He later said, "I found Jane a delight, totally professional and very pretty. I'm amazed that Jack Warner kept her dangling on the vine for so long before giving her a meaty roles like Ginger Rogers had in *Kitty Foyle*. Jane was one hell of a dame, who could do both serious drama and light comedy, each equally well."

Although Robinson praised Jane's talents to reporters, she was disappointed when he published his memoirs, *All My Yesterdays* in 1973. He didn't even mention her. All he wrote about their film was this line: "Then back to Warners' for *Larceny,*

Larceny, Inc. Jane appears here with Jack Carson, marking the beginning of a long friendship.

269

Inc."

"Eddie had this pug face with a snarling, snapping delivery that I had a hard time keeping up with," Jane later said. "He could play a milquetoast on occasion, although he excelled as a tough guy. No, he did not begin every sentence by saying, 'See.' I was a bit nervous working with him. When I met him, he'd just made *Manpower* (1941) with Marlene Dietrich. I could hardly imagine at the time that one day *little ol' me* would be cast opposite the formidable 'Kraut' in a movie shot in London."

Jack Carson, from the windswept plains of Manitoba, had made it to Hollywood, "kicking around" in movies since 1937. Usually, he was cast as an overbearing boor or some beefy lug, a hapless target of derision. But by the 1940s, he had been recognized by Warners as a first-rate comic actor who deserved better roles. At the time Jane met him, both of them were getting bigger parts. Between 1937 and '38, Carson had appeared as a minor player in some two dozen films. *Larceny, Inc.* marked the first of several movies in which he would be cast with Jane.

Today, Carson is best remembered for his dramatic roles, including that of the rejected suitor to Joan Crawford in *Mildred Pierce* (1945), and the oafish brother of Paul Newman and the father of those "no-neck monsters" in *Cat on a Hot Tin Roof* (1958) by Tennessee Williams, co-starring Elizabeth Taylor.

"Jane and I truly bonded," Carson later said. "We'd both survived a lot of crappy movies, and she, like myself, was a real trouper. I was also the best friend of Dennis Morgan, and he truly adored her. The three of us often hung out together. I was used as the 'beard' to cover up their romance. I didn't mind at all. I knew when I'd served my purpose. I'd frequently disappear into the night back in those days."

"On the set, I had to watch Jane," he said. "If not, she'd steal every scene we were in. I thought she had real potential. For all I know, one day she'd be the Queen of Warners after she dethroned Bette Davis. I knew she'd have to compete with Olivia de Havilland for the crown."

According to Jane, the screen didn't reveal just how big Carson was, standing 6'2" and weighing some 225 pounds. "Over the course of a life, he was married four times. At the time I met him, he was wed to Kay St. Germain Wells. *[For many years, Kay was the radio voice of Elsie the Cow.]* When they divorced in 1950, Jack indulged in some heavy dating with Doris Day and wanted to marry her.

Day was also indulging in heavy dating with another divorced man I knew so very well—Ronnie himself. Doris dumped both Ronnie and Jack to marry Martin Melcher, and brother, did she live to regret that choice."

Actress Helen Broderick's son, Broderick Crawford, was burly and brutish on the screen, but, in Jane's view, "a lovable lug off the screen." In 1937, he'd become famous for brilliantly playing Lennie in the Broadway production of *Of Mice and Men*. Ironically, and to his deep chagrin, he was not awarded that role in that drama's Hollywood remake in 1939. The role Broderick had developed (and coveted) went to Lon Chaney, Jr. instead.

"When Broderick and I used to go for a drink," Jane later reflected, we never thought for a moment that B picture stars like us would each end up one day winning an Oscar for Best Actor or Best Actress of the Year." *[Cast as Willy Stark, a charismatic, rough-edged character based on the crooked Louisiana politician, Huey Long,* All the

Broderick Crawford: He had an unlikely look for a movie star.

King's Men *(1949) would bring Crawford a Best Actor Oscar.]*

During the filming of *Larceny, Inc.,* Jane and Reagan invited Crawford to join them at a steak house, a style of restaurant he'd specifically requested. "That night, I saw the beginning of his downfall: Lots of liquor and heaps of food. I couldn't believe it. He ordered three big steaks cooked blood rare and told the waiter to keep his glass of liquor full at all times."

When Jane met Anthony Quinn, he'd just finished playing Chief Crazy Horse in *They Died With Their Boots On* (1941), starring Errol Flynn. Throughout his career, Quinn would not only play Indian chiefs, but Hawiian chiefs, Filipino Freedom fighters, Chinese guerilas, and, in *Lawrence of Arabia* (1962), a clever and dynamic desert sheik.

Malevolently handsome Anthony Quinn under arrest at the conclusion of *Larceny, Inc.*

"A seductive bundle of impish charm," is how Jane described him. Born in 1915 during Mexico's revolution, Quinn had always claimed that whereas his mother was of almost pure Aztec descent, his father, Francisco (Frank) Quinn, had been the offspring of a Mexican mother and an Irish immigrant father from County Cork. Francisco Quinn had ridden with Pancho Villa, the Mexican revolutionary.

Quinn became the first Mexican-American actor to win an Oscar—in his case, in 1952 for his supporting role in *Viva Zapata!.* Marlon Brando, its star, lost the Oscar that year to Gary Cooper for his role in *High Noon.* Actually, Quinn had originally wanted to play Zapata, but director Elia Kazan preferred Brando.

On the set of *Larceny, Inc.,* Quinn told Jane he was a master painter, and surprised her with his request to paint her in the nude. She politely refused, but he persisted. He told her that his painting would immortalize her the way Goya's *The Naked Maja* had done for the Duchess of Alba. Jane still refused.

"If you won't let me paint you in the nude, can I fuck you in the nude?" he asked.

"I must also turn down your gracious offer, your request put so delicately," she said.

In 1937, Quinn had married Katherine DeMille, the adopted daughter of Cecil B. DeMille. He was never faithful to his wife. When he tangled with Jane, he was also having an affair with Rita Hayworth, his co-star in *Blood and Sand* (1941). Other recent conquests had included Mae West and Carole Lombard.

He'd told actress Ruth Warrick, "I want to impregnate every woman in the world." Years later, to author Darwin Porter, Warrick mused, "I didn't realize at the time how literally he meant that."

Evelyn Keyes, "Scarlett O'Hara's younger sister," said "There was simply too much of Tony. Yes, down there, too."

At the conclusion of filming of *Larceny, Inc.,* Robinson threw a wrap party, and most of the stars and supporting actors showed up. Broderick Crawford arrived already drunk.

Quinn appeared to be suffering that evening from a deep depression. Speaking to her privately, he told Jane he'd be leaving the party soon. His two-year-old had drowned in the lily pond of his next door neighbor, W.C. Fields. After having a drink, and greeting the other guests, he quietly departed. She noticed tears running down his cheeks, and she ran out into the yard and embraced him warmly.

Robinson, the party's host, pointed out some of his choice paintings. She was very

271

impressed with his knowledge of art, of which she knew virtually nothing.

At the party, Jane made the rounds, talking with a Brooklyn-born actor, Jackie C. Gleason, who played a soda shop clerk in their film. "He told me he'd been born a pool hustler and a night club comic before trying to break into the movies," Jane said. "I found his brief role in our film uninspired, and I told him so. He said he was off to play Bogie's pal in a picture, *All Through the Night* (1941). I stupidly predicted he should try some field other than acting. How wrong I was! He did much better when he billed himself as Jackie Gleason."

Young Jackie Gleason..."How sweet it is!"

***

As Reagan moved into production of the fourteen films he made that were released between 1940 and 1943, a Gallup poll conducted during the summer of 1941 placed him at number 82 in the roster of American box office attractions. The number one spot went to Clark Gable, largely because of the success of his portrayal of Rhett Butler in *Gone With the Wind* (1939), which, in 1940, was still playing in movie houses across America.

Much to her disappointment, Jane Wyman did not rank among the top one hundred box office draws.

As far as paychecks went, "The King" (Gable) made $210,000 per picture; Errol Flynn $157,000; and Reagan $52,000 per film.

A more in-depth survey of movie audiences found that Jack Warner's attempt to turn Reagan into a romantic lead had largely failed. Reagan's greatest fans were young men and boys eighteen and under, no doubt stemming from his roles as Secret Service agent, Brass Bancroft.

Surveys showed that one out of ten movie fans would go see a film if Reagan's name was on the marquee. In contrast, 30 to 40 percent of Americans asserted that they would go see any film starring Flynn.

Reagan was slightly more popular with women than with men. Most of them seemed to feel, "He's a Mr. Average Nice Guy, but he's no Adonis." One woman wrote, "I find his crinkly eyes and wide grin a good substitute for glamour."

One fan wrote, "My Mom would approve of him if I brought him home."

Another commented, "Ronald Reagan suggests home for Christmas, football games, summer jobs at gas stations, junior proms with white carnations, and a fraternity pin worn on a girl's sweater."

Responding to the polls, Reagan admitted, "I know I'm no Errol Flynn or Charles Boyer. A man doesn't have to stand out from his fellow man to make his mark in the world. Average will do."

Flight Patrol (whose name would later be changed to *International Squadron;* 1941) was Reagan's 27th film. When he asked its director, Lothar Mendes, the names of his leading ladies, it was confirmed that he'd be working with Joan Perry (Mrs. Harry Cohn) again. This time, she'd been reduced to fifth position in the star lineup. His other two leading ladies included Olympe Bradna and Julie Bishop, actresses unfamiliar to him.

Reagan was a bit leery of Berlin-born Mendes because he had a negative stereotype of German and Austrian directors, gained in part from the stormy legend of Erich von Stroheim during the Silent era.

Mendes' most famous film was the 1934 *Jew Süss. [In the U.S., it was released as Power—Jew Süss. That film, which condemned Nazi atrocities, is not to be confused with the notorious anti-Jewish film, Jud Süss (1940), which was commissioned by Josef Goebbels through the UFA Studios in Berlin.*

Jew Süss was a British historical drama based on Lion Feuchtwanger's 1925 novel of the same name. It starred the German actor, Conrad Veidt, who later achieved screen immortality in Casablanca *(1942).]*

Screenwriters Kenneth Gamet and Barry Truivers met with Reagan to talk over how they had conceived his role of Pilot Jimmy Grant in *International Squadron.* "Grant is a cocky man, a real son of a bitch," Trivers said. "His devil-may-care attitude leads to the death of two of his comrades. This experience turns him from a trouble maker and a braggart into an aviator hero."

In the early part of the film, Grant appears as a playboy, a loner, full of bravado. Behind the wheel of a plane, he says, "I'm going to get this baby to six hundred (MPH) If I have to get out and push. I can fly any crate they give me."

As a Yank in war-torn Britain, he joins fellow pilots from such countries as Nazi-controlled Poland, Belgium, and Czechoslovakia. "Sounds had a Notre Dame backfield," Grant quips.

The dreaded Breen office raised objections to the first draft of the script, which depicted Grant (i.e., Reagan) as a fun-loving womanizer. No sweetheart of any pilot was safe from his amorous advances. Facing the objections, one of the producers, Edmund Grainger, ordered the writers to tone down the seductively manipulative aspect of Grant's character. As Grainger so graphically phrased it in a memo, "Don't have Reagan's tongue hanging out to lap pussy every time he sees a broad."

In its promotion of Reagan, Warners went to great lengths to portray Reagan as a great aviator, labeled in private and on the screen as an "unconquerable and intrepid pilot." For the release of *International Squadron,* the men in Warners' publicity department pulled out the stops, writing that "Reagan plays an avenging angel hurtling out of the heavens to shoot down Herman Göring's *Luftwaffe* pilots before they could bomb London." Another line associated with the role Reagan had been assigned shouted, "He is a man who lives only for today, because he might be placed in a hole in the ground tomorrow."

At the time America entered the war in December of 1941, Reagan was one of only a handful of men associated with valor in the air, even though his only experience in aviation had been faked in a movie studio. After one dreadful experience during a flight, he swore he'd never take another. Of course, by the time he became President of the United States in the 1980s, he had overcome that fear of flying he'd had as a young man.

In *International Squadron*, Reagan (as Jimmy Grant) plays a crack stunt pilot who accepts the job of delivering, transatlantic, a U.S. bomber to the embattled R.A.F. in war-torn Britain. After his successful arrival in England, he meets friends from the States, including squadron commander Charles Watt (James Stephenson) and Reg Wilkins (William Lundigan), another fighter pilot.

Reagan isn't interested in joining the R.A.F. until he witnesses a *Luftwaffe* air raid over London during the Battle of Britain. After he sees a child killed, he changes his mind and joins the Eagle Squadron, a British-sponsored air unit composed entirely of foreign fighters, including Americans, flying for Britain against the Nazis.

As described in a 1941 critique by *The New York Times*, "No ace among war films, it is none the less a brisk, brash flier in pulse-quickening entertainment…it is the familiar yarn of the cocky American *[as played by Reagan]* who joins the squadron, creates romantic havoc among his buddies' *fiancées*, and grows up after his breaches of discipline have cost the lives of two companions…Ronald Reagan is excellent as the slaphappy hell-diver who finally pays for his moral failures with his own death in combat."

A week into the shoot, Reagan learned that *International Squadron* was "the bastard copycat of an equivalent movie, *Ceiling Zero* (1935), that had starred two of his friends, James Cagney and Pat O'Brien. That picture had two starring male leads, each cast as a pilot. Originally, Jack Warner had wanted the script of *International Squadron* to have two male leads, Errol Flynn and John Wayne, each cast as a pilot. But when they weren't available, the script was refashioned to make Reagan, as a pilot, the sole male star.

An oddly distorted portrait of Reagan, supposedly windblown during one of his (nonexistent) flights.

Within ten days from the debut of shooting, Mendes visited Warner and complained to him about Reagan. "He's supposed to be so sexy that he creates havoc among the girlfriends of his fellow pilots. Flynn could have pulled off a role like that. But try as I might, I can't find any overpowering sex appeal in this Reagan boy. He's too clean cut, too American, the kind of guy you'd find coaching a Little League team."

The fabled aviator, Frank Wead, a stunt pilot turned screenwriter, had written the script for *Ceiling Zero*. During one of his visits to California, he visited Reagan on the set of *International Squadron* to see how this recycled version of his story was coming along. Based on Warners' flood of advance publicity, he just assumed that Reagan was a daring aviator

A smiling Ronald Reagan represents the Face of America in *International Squadron.*

like himself. With that preconceived notion in mind, he shared several long talks with him, discussing his own former exploits in the air.

Like Reagan, Wead was originally from Illinois. But, unlike Reagan, he was a *bona-fide* American aviation hero. During World War II, he had been promoted to the rank of commander.

As a screenwriter, Wead, in 1938, had received two Academy Award nominations, one for Best Original Story for *Test Pilot,* starring Clark Gable and Spencer Tracy, and a second for Best Screenplay for *The Citadel* with Robert Donat, Rosalind Russell, and Rex Harrison.

At one point, Wead invited Reagan to drive from Los Angeles south to San Diego with him so he could make a test flight, accompanied by Reagan, of an experimental Naval aircraft.

Frank Wead, aviator, screenwriter, and critic of Reagan's reputation as an aviator.

Reagan politely refused, claiming that Warners wouldn't permit him to take such a risk during the shooting of a movie.

Wead became very friendly with Reagan, proposing that the young actor should refer to him by his nickname of "Spig." Reagan later told Pat O'Brien, "Spig's life story should become the subject of a film, entitled *Spig,* about his life's involvement with aviation."

In *International Squadron,* Reagan was surrounded with an array of talented supporting players, including Julie Bishop, a California-born actress who'd begun making films in 1923. As a child, she'd appeared in Laurel and Hardy movies. During her work with Reagan, she would sign for roles in *Princess O'Rourke* (1943) with Olivia de Havilland, Robert Cummings, and Jane Wyman; and also with Humphrey Bogart in *Action in the North Atlantic* (also 1943).

Lovely and patriotic Julie Bishop, as portrayed by YANK magazine as one of their choices for Armed Forces "pinup girl" of 1944

Bishop would appear in a few more movies, including a role in *The Sands of Iwo Jima* (1949) as a down-on-her-luck waitress, with John Wayne, but that dream of a big career faded. In 1944, she married General Clarence A. Shoop, a test pilot for Howard Hughes who later became a vice president of Hughes Aircraft.

Perry was upset that the film's lead female role had gone to Olympe Bradna and not to her. The French dancer and actress was born in Paris, and Reagan found her an intriguing personality, the daughter of two world famous bareback riders. At the age of eight, she'd become a professional acrobatic dancer, later joining the *Folies Bergère* in Paris. After moving to Hollywood, she launched her film career in 1933, appearing over the years with such notables as Gary Cooper and George Raft.

Ironically, Bradna would pose no further career threat to Perry or to any other actress either. After she completed *International Squadron,* she retired from acting and settled into a marriage with Douglas Woods Wilhoit, CEO of the Stockton, California, Chamber of Commerce and a political appointee to the Juvenile Parole Board and the local Board of Corrections. After seventy years together, both of them died in 2012.

Before Bradna settled down with Wood, she had a final fling with Anthony Quinn, who had just made a movie with Jane. Although married to Katherine DeMille at

French-born Olympe Bradna, a former dancer at the *Folies Bergére*, being courted by "The Face of America" (Reagan) in *International Squadron.*

the time, Quinn visited the set of *International Squadron* five times for rendezvous with Bradna. They had become romantically involved when they'd starred together in the 1941 Warners' movie, *Knockout,* which had cast Arthur Kennedy as a boxer.

Reagan had met Quinn at the home of Edward G. Robinson. Although he had only recently recovered from the drowning of his young son, he was back on his familiar circuit of seducing starlets.

One day, as he was leaving, Quinn spoke to Reagan. "I love my wife, as I know you love Jane—she's a dear—but speaking man to man, a guy like me has to have something on the side. It's my hot Latin blood."

"I understand," Reagan assured him.

***

By now, thanks to her wedding to studio autocrat Harry Cohn, Reagan's friend and third female co-star, Joan Perry, had become one of Hollywood's most gracious hostesses. Jane and Reagan were often invited to her formal dinners or cocktail parties. Sometimes, Jane would opt out, claiming, "I have to look after Maureen."

Reagan actually liked to arrive stag at Joan and Harry's parties, enjoying the flirtatious attention bestowed on him by such beautiful starlets as Rita Hayworth or the sultry Evelyn Keyes.

It was at the home of the Cohns that Reagan was introduced to some of the power brokers who would later lend him political and financial support during his bids for governorship of California and President of the United States.

On the set, Reagan sometimes lunched with Perry. One afternoon, she discussed her honeymoon with Harry Cohn. "I headed for the pool, and he told me he'd join me there. But when I got there, I realized I had forgotten my suntan lotion. I returned to the room to discover Harry fucking our very young Mexican maid."

"What did you do?" Reagan asked.

"I told them to carry on, as I went to the bathroom and retrieved my lotion, then headed back to the pool."

"That's what I call an understanding wife," he said.

"I knew about Harry's reputation before I married him, and I didn't think he would change after we exchanged our vows. You can't expect Harry to be faithful. I talked it over with Virginia Fox, who married Darryl Zanuck back in 1923. She told me she never expected Zanuck to be faithful, and I couldn't demand fidelity from Harry, either. We had to enjoy the money, the luxury, the power, and prestige of being married to a studio mogul, and we had to forgive their womanizing. Every day at the studio, Harry, at around noon, has what he calls a 'fuck break,' and he summons the starlet of his choice for an afternoon lay."

Reagan had worked previously with his co-star, James Stephenson, most recently in the final installment of the Brass Bancroft films, *Murder in the Air.*

He learned from Stephenson that he had signed to play the psychotic Dr. Gordon in *Kings Row* (1942), an upcoming picture in which Reagan also wanted to be cast. But on July 29, 1941, Reagan heard over the radio that Stephenson had died. He later recalled, "He was to have been the doctor who cut off my legs in *Kings Row.* But instead of him, Charles Coburn had to perform that sadistic act."

The handsome, blonde-haired actor, Helmut Dantine, born in Vienna, had a brief role in *International Squadron.* He'd already been assigned another part in the upcoming film, *Casablanca* (1942). In it, he'd appear as a desperate Norwegian newlywed gambling as a means of raising money for an exit visa out of Morocco.

Dantine told Reagan that since 1938, he'd been involved in the anti-Nazi movement in his native Vienna. When the Nazis took over Austria during their *Anschlüss*, he was arrested and imprisoned in a concentration camp outside Vienna. His father had used his influence to get him released, after which he'd fled to California.

In addition to his performance in *Casablanca,* he would also make a startling appearance as a Nazi soldier in *Mrs. Miniver* (1942) with Greer Garson.

Reagan renewed his friendship with William Lundigan, Errol Flynn's boyfriend, with whom he had worked on *Santa Fe Trail.*

When Reagan had lunch with him, the handsome young actor was very candid. "Errol treats me like a Saturday night pussy. He ignores me for days, then calls and expects me to come running, which I always do. He never treats me like an equal, but like some boy in his harem. Right now, he's seeing a lot more of Bruce Cabot than he is of me. He calls him 'Big Bruce,' for obvious reasons, I guess."

Helmut Dantine, as a Nazi aviator in *Mrs. Miniver.*

"I find Errol a bit hard to take," Reagan said.

"I find him hard to take, too," Lundigan said.

"I didn't mean it that way," Reagan said. "You boys always twist a man's words."

"Sorry…And by the way, I've got some news for you," Lundigan said. "It's been announced that Errol is going to make *Desperate Journey* (1942), an anti-Nazi movie. He asked Jack Warner to designate you as his co-star. He liked you a lot when we made *Santa Fe Trail.* In fact, he told me that he's going to get you yet. How do you think that makes me feel?"

"Rest assured," Reagan said. "I can fend off any advances from Mr. Flynn. He should know by now I don't go that route."

"Perhaps you will," Lundigan said. "Others, both men and women, have said that, but they finally collapse under Errol's charms. He's very persuasive. If his charm fails, he can revert to rape."

"I'll call for your help if he tries that," Reagan said.

One afternoon, Flynn arrived on the set and greeted Reagan. "How's about a kiss, sport?"

"Instead of that, how about a punch in the nose?" Reagan asked.

While waiting for Lundigan to complete a scene, Flynn was introduced to Dantine. As Reagan stood witnessing it, Flynn was instantly attracted to the Austrian actor, and made his intentions obvious. The young actor seemed mesmerized by Flynn, in a way that implied, according to Reagan, that Lundigan would suddenly face competition for Flynn's affections.

It came as no surprise, months later, when Dantine was announced as one of the supporting actors in Flynn's upcoming picture, *Desperate Journey.*

Tod Andrews was cast in *International Squadron* as a French pilot, the boyfriend of the character played by Bradna. In their movie, Andrews played a character named Michele Edmé. He liked the name so much, he changed his professional name to an English-language derivation of it, being henceforth known as "Michael Ames." Reagan would soon find himself competing with Ames for the role he wanted in *Kings Row.*

The brass at Warners' became upset at the slow pace of *International Squadron,* and Mendes was replaced by Lewis Seiler as director. He had previously helmed Reagan in *Hell's Kitchen* with the Dead End Kids. "I thought Mendes was a rough taskmaster, but Seiler, anxious to conclude filming on schedule, was reckless," Reagan said. "He almost caused me to go up in flames."

Reagan had requested a double for one or two of his character's dangerous stunts, but Seiler rejected his requests. In one scene unfolding inside the cockpit of a plane, Reagan was to set a mop on fire, open the cockpit's hood, and toss the blazing mop outside. That stunt was intended to incite Luftwaffe pilots into thinking that his plane was on fire and to move on to other targets.

Reagan ignited the mop. But then, when he tried to open the hood of the cockpit, it jammed, and the cockpit began filling up with flames and smoke. Two grips eventually forced the hood open and rescued him. Reagan was rushed to the hospital for treatment of smoke inhalation.

When he was released two days later, Seiler demanded that the scene be reshot immediately. Against his better judgment, Reagan performed the same scene with a new mop. This time, the scene went off without incident.

International Squadron bore remarkable similarities to 20th Century Fox's *A Yank in the R.A.F.* (1941), a "hero aviator" film co-starring Tyrone Power and Betty Grable.

Consequently, Darryl F. Zanuck at Fox wrote threatening letters to Jack Warner, accusing him of stealing the plot of *A Yank in the R.A.F.* "You're planning a low-budget picture to capitalize off the fame of our movie," Zanuck charged.

Warners' position was that *International Squadron* was a remake of its 1935 movie, *Ceiling Zero.* Consequently, they went ahead and released the Reagan film without going to court to defend it.

Upon the release of *International Squadron,* many reviewers hailed the movie as Reagan's best work to date, although he had little competition for that honor, considering the lackluster reviews generated by his previous string of B movies.

However, when the film was screened in England, some technically savvy members of the audience laughed. The "Spitfire" Reagan's character had piloted was nothing more than a doctored-up Ryan monoplane that didn't even have a retractable landing gear. In his memoirs, Reagan wrote that "people accepted our makeshift props with the same kindly understanding they gave the local high school play." In writing that, perhaps he didn't hear the mocking laughter that howled out of England at the time.

Although America had not yet entered World War II, Jack Warner ordered major promotion of the film, knowing that audiences, except for "America Firsters" and German-Americans, were siding with the British. *International Squadron* was blatantly anti-Nazi, a slant which censors interpreted as a flagrant violation of America's neutrality.

Warner wanted to promote Reagan as a star, with the understanding that if he was rejected by the Army because of his eyesight, he'd become the biggest star at Warners, especially in wartime movies about airplane pilots.

Patriotic Fervor: Tyrone Power with Betty Grable in Darryl Zanuck's sword-rattling answer *(A Yank in the RAF)* to Jack Warner's *International Squadron.*

Ads for *International Squadron* proclaimed: "This is the role that zooms Ronald Reagan to the heights of stardom." History would demonstrate, of course, that that advertising slogan was a gross exaggeration.

Isolationists in Washington were outraged by the anti-German slant of *International Squadron*. Warners was accused of "war-mongering," and the Warner Brothers were specifically blamed as "Jews selfishly maneuvering American troops into World War II."

A politically motivated investigation was called. A Subcommittee of the House Committee on Interstate Commerce summoned Harry Warner to Washington for questioning. Since the release of *Confessions of a Nazi Spy,* Warners was considered the most anti-Nazi film studio in Hollywood.

Before the committee, Warner delivered an eloquent defense of his studio, claiming a responsibility to let the American public know about what was happening in Europe and the world. He said that of all the books published the previous year in America, seventy percent of non-fiction books were anti-Nazi, and ten percent of all fiction reflected the same point of view. He also claimed that ten percent of all film scripts submitted to Warners were virulently anti-Nazi.

But in early December of 1941, within days of the surprise Japanese attack on Pearl Harbor, the committee's war-mongering charges against Warners were dropped. At that point, all Hollywood studios began churning out pro-America wartime propaganda films that were not only anti-Nazi, but anti-Japanese as well.

***

A sprinkling of snow early one morning hinted at a cold upcoming autumn in Dixon, Illinois. Louella Parsons set out with Ronald Reagan to celebrate "Louella Parsons Day" in their native town of Dixon, where both of them had grown up.

Seizing the moment, Jack Warner rushed an early cut of *International Squadron* to a movie theater in Dixon for a world premiere.

Using her power as a ruthless Hollywood columnist, Parsons rounded up a bevy of Hollywood stars, spearheaded by Bob Hope, to accompany Reagan and her on their tour of her native Midwest.

Others in her all-star troupe included the comedian Jerry Colonna, along with Ann Rutherford, who had played Scarlett O'Hara's sister, Coreen, in *Gone With the Wind.* The handsome leading man, George Montgomery, went along too, as did silent screen star, Bebe Daniels. She was accompanied by Ben Lyon, who had scored such a hit in the Howard Hughes production of *Hell's Angels* in 1930, the year in which he'd married Daniels.

Jane Wyman, recovering from minor surgery, was not able to make the trip, so Reagan's mother, Nelle, accompanied her son instead, lamenting, "I'm so sorry that Jack didn't live to see this day." Her husband (Reagan's father) had died that May.

To take over when Hope's humor failed him, comedian Joe E. Brown, Jane Wyman's least favorite film partner, also joined the troupe aboard the train heading east.

A few moments after the train's arrival at Dixon's railway station, Parsons stepped in front of a waiting microphone to deliver a "thank you, thank you, thank you," to the assembled crowd.

Then Hope claimed the microphone from her. "Ladies and gentlemen," he said. "Over there is the birthplace of your townswoman, Louella Parsons. Do you wonder that this glamour girl—ablaze with orchids, dressed to the teeth, bedecked and bejeweled—wants to forget it? Do you wonder that the little lady is overcome with emotion?"

Parsons was irritated at such an enigmatic and downbeat introduction, but flashed an insincere smile nonetheless.

A crowd of 50,000, many from neighboring homesteads and hamlets, had journeyed to Dixon to see the stars. A ten-block parade, with five bands and fifteen floats, was staged along the elm-lined Galena Street, the shop-flanked main artery of the little city. Parsons would recall the parade that seemed "to spin in my memory like a happy but dizzy dream."

She rode in an open convertible, waving her white-gloved hand to the bystanders in a style she'd lifted from watching newsreels of British royalty moving through the streets of London.

In all his Brylcreemed glory, Reagan rode in a separate car with a frail Nelle, as both waved to the crowds. The parade ended near Geisenheimers Department Store, where Parsons had once worked as a sales clerk in the corset department, merchandizing contoured undergarments to restrain the flesh of her corn-fed customers. This was near the old store where Jack Reagan had once fitted shoes onto local farmers who came from outlying fields into Dixon to shop.

Later, Parsons dedicated the Louella Parsons Children's Ward, a new facility within the town's Katherine Shaw Bethea Hospital.

The hospital visit was followed by speeches in the park. At the podium, Reagan delivered a rather long-winded speech, much to Parsons' obvious annoyance.

Louella Parsons, accompanied by Ronald Reagan, returns to the little town of Dixon, where she once sold undergarments and corsets to farmers' wives.

"I want all of you to know that I did not sleep last night, thinking of my trip back here, where I could meet old friends. I counted the seventy-seven persons whom I have been credited with pulling out of the Rock River at Lowell Park many times during the night."

Then, Parsons managed to grapple the microphone from Reagan. Before that, Colonna had whispered in her ear, "Reagan thinks he's running for Congress."

Two hundred special guests were invited to a "rubber chicken" luncheon paid for by Warners. These box lunches were served on the lawn of Hazelwood, the Myrtle Walgreen estate.

In the afternoon, Reagan visited Lowell Park, where he discovered that the log on which he'd notched a record of the seventy-seven men and women he'd saved from the Rock River had washed away. At a ceremony, he was presented with a clock with the engraving, "From 77 Grateful People." Before the crowd, he said, "I came to know the victims better in five minutes than their mothers did in a lifetime."

Following a banquet at Dixon's Masonic Temple, a local movie house held the premiere of *International Squadron,* which, at its conclusion, received a standing ovation.

Parsons announced that director Frank Capra wanted Reagan to star in his upcoming film, *Arsenic and*

Snapped in Dixon, and portraying a finger-pointing Ronald Reagan, the face of the mystery woman in the photo above is obscured in shadow.

Some newspapers labeled her as Louella Parsons; others as Nelle Reagan. You be the judge.

Old Lace (1944). That role, however, was later awarded to Cary Grant. Parsons also announced that Jack Warner wanted Reagan to star in *The Will Rogers Story*. That didn't happen either.

[Ironically, a decade later, in 1952, The Will Rogers Story *would be made, but its star was Will Rogers, Jr., playing opposite Jane Wyman, by then divorced from Reagan.]*

Reporters from Hollywood interviewed the locals for firsthand memories of either Parsons or Reagan. Several women remembered Louella as "a silly romantic girl, a big sentimentalist with dreams of being a writer." Several recalled " her gooey personality." She had attended Dixon College followed by a year of teaching in a country school. Later, she worked part time as a reporter on the *Dixon Star*.

Biographer Edmund Morris rounded up some opinions of Reagan at the time: "Loves to talk, hates to listen. Exaggerates his college football prowess. Dislikes tennis and tomatoes. Combs his hair the wrong way. Keeps on his shoes as he undresses. Also keeps a scrapbook of flattering news clips of himself. Nurses a beer longer than Carrie Nation. Likes Bing Crosby and macaroni and cheese. Steals jokes from George Burns and Jack Benny. Dick Powell and some Republicans want him to run for Congress on their ticket, but Reagan remains a passionate New Dealer."

A reporter for the *Dixon Star* wrote: "If beauty-starved Dixonians were looking forward to ogling Ronald Reagan's curvaceous wife, they were doomed to disappointment. Instead of an eyeful of Jane Wyman, they got an earful of Louella Parsons." Newspapers proclaimed that Louella Parson's Day generated more excitement than did the parade dedicated to Charles Lindbergh when the fabled aviator visited Dixon. All media hailed the rags-to-riches story of both Parsons and Reagan, citing them "as typically American Sunday supplement heroes."

On a broadcast over CBS's Chicago affiliate, Reagan proclaimed that the event in Dixon "fulfilled a dream which probably every boy has at some time—that of coming home and being acclaimed by the local folks."

***

After recovering from minor surgery (a curettage), Jane Wyman reported to work as a loan-out to RKO. Her next picture, a vehicle for bandleader and singer Kay Kyser, was entitled *My Favorite Spy* (1942), a comedy caper revolving around Nazi spies working undercover in America. After reading the script, she was displeased with her role, regarding the film as a vehicle for the musician. "I'm just the blonde fluff," she claimed in a call to Reagan.

"So what else is new?" he asked her.

During her brief stint in the hospital, she'd been discreetly visited, on separate occasions, by both John Payne and Dennis Morgan. They brought flowers and well wishes, and Payne even talked about the possibility of marriage if they ever divorced their respective spouses.

In response, she told him she had no intention of divorcing Reagan. "But check with me later," she said. "I might change my mind."

Morgan, as he'd told her before, never planned to divorce his wife, but preferred their present sexual arrangement. Jane seemed in agreement.

During his final visit, Payne brought casting news: "I heard from Gregory Ratoff, who's directing, that you're going to be loaned out again, this time to Fox. We're going to appear in this thing called *Footlight Serenade* (1942) with Betty Grable and Victor Mature. Those two are involved in a torrid affair."

In the aftermath of her surgery, she'd returned home. There, the producer of *My Fa-*

vorite Spy, Harold Lloyd, the famous silent screen comic, dropped in for a visit.

As a little girl, she'd seen him on the screen playing bespectacled nebbishes in peril. In the pantheon of silent screen comics and their popularity with movie-goers of that era, he had placed third after Charlie Chaplin and Buster Keaton.

In a moment of levity, she told him, "The last time I met Chaplin when I was a little girl, he tried to molest me. How safe am I with you?"

Kay Kyser, bandleader and entertainment mogul, gets amorous with Jane in *My Favorite Spy.*

"Very safe," Lloyd said. "I molest no one. I'm the one who's usually molested."

She told him that as regards their upcoming *My Favorite Spy,* she'd been disappointed to find herself taking third billing after Kyser and Ellen Drew, a former beauty contest winner who, in the film, would play Kyser's bride.

"I think it'll be a big hit," Lloyd predicted, not addressing her concern.

Kyser, at the time, was a popular bandleader and singer, a well-known radio personality of the 1930s and the war years. His big hit on radio was as the quizmaster of an ongoing variety show, "Kay Kyser's Kollege of Musical Knowledge."

[A native of North Carolina, Kyser was also a vocalist, a Big Band director, and a master of swing and jazz. To capitalize off his fame, Hollywood had cast him in a number of movies, including That's Right You're Wrong *in 1939 and* You'll Find Out *in 1940. His last film had also been John Barrymore's last,* Play-

Ellen Drew

mates, made in 1941. Barrymore died in the spring of the following year.]

Before shooting of *My Favorite Spy* began, Jane lunched with its director, Tay Garnett. He was very blunt. "I asked RKO to hire you because I wanted your fine acting and style to camouflage the fact that Kyser is a swinging musician, but a lousy actor."

A native of Los Angeles, Garnett won Jane's approval. She'd seen two of the films he'd directed, including *Eternally Yours* (1939), which had co-starred Loretta Young and David Niven. *[In future years, Jane would appear with Niven in film, and Young would become her best friend.]* Before the end of their lunch, Garnett invited Jane to a screening of his latest movie, *Seven Sinners,* starring John Wayne and Marlene Dietrich as a torch singer.

On the set, Jane had a reunion with William Demarest, who'd been cast in a minor role. In the 1930s, he'd been her friend, mentor, and agent. She chided him: "After you discovered her in an ice cream parlor, you seemed to do better with Ellen Drew's career than with mine."

"Those are the breaks, sweetheart," Demarest said. "I did my best for you, gal. At least I kept you working."

[Like Jane, Drew, an early beauty contest winner, had emerged from Missouri. Her status as a beauty queen had brought her to the attention of Demarest, who managed to find a position for her at Paramount. Soon after, she appeared in several pictures, including Sing You Sinners *(1939) with Bing Crosby and* The Lady's From Kentucky

(1939) with George Raft.

In 1944, she'd switch from Paramount to RKO, where she appeared on screen with leading men who included William Holden, Basil Rathbone, Robert Preston, and Ronald Colman.

In the 1950s, as Drew's career faded, Jane's spiraled upward.]

When *My Favorite Spy* opened across America, this whirlwind of dizzy intrigue received lackluster reviews. As the sultry blonde, Jane personified most of its sexual energy. Movie posters provocatively presented her as bosomy in a filmy black *négligée.*

Screenland magazine defined the zany film like this: "A spy comedy with Kay Kyser playing a not-too-bright bandleader who is called to Army Service on his wedding day. He is later released and made a counter-espionage agent. Of course, Kyser bags the spies in the end, returns to his bride (Drew), while Jane plays his blonde secret operator-partner. It's not our favorite Kyser film."

Another movie magazine asked, "How can we win WWII with bandleader Kyser as our spy? Nonsensical music-comedy tried to explain."

In 1973, Kyser, in an interview, remembered Jane, reflecting on her sense of humor and her keen sense of loyalty. "She had a heart as big as the outdoors. She's also big on soul, too, and can sing a pretty darn good song herself."

"She also gave me many good tips on acting, though claiming she couldn't act herself," Kyser said. "After she won an Oscar for *Johnny Belinda,* I accused her of being a liar for telling me she couldn't act."

Garnett, the film's director, later commented, "Because of Jane, our troupe had great chemistry on the set while making *My Favorite Spy.* Too bad that chemistry wasn't reflected on the screen. The picture should have been much better than it was."

***

The surprise is that *Kings Row,* a controversial novel by Henry Bellamann, ever made it to the movie screens of America in 1942. Its release coincided with the debut of America's entry into World War II.

It seemed that every theme in this novel about a small town in the Middle West in the 1890s was flagrantly contrary to the Hayes Production Code: Homosexuality, incest, suicide, insanity, premarital sex, nymphomania, sadism, and mercy killing.

Jack Warner first asked Wolfgang Reinhardt to produce the film. But after reading the novel, he wrote back: "As far as the plot is concerned, the material in *Kings Row* is for the most part either censurable or too gruesome and depressing to be used. The hero finding out that his girl has been carrying on incestuous relations with her father; a host of moronic or otherwise mentally diseased characters; people dying from cancer, suicides—these are the principal elements of the story."

Warner turned to Hal B. Wallis and asked him if he'd produce the film, and he agreed, signing David Lewis as his associate producer. As he'd promised Reagan months before, Lewis began to lobby for the role of the second male lead, the character of Drake McHugh, to go to Reagan.

However, Wallis had other stars in mind. But first, he sent galley proofs of the novel to screenwriter Casey Robinson, who had scripted the film *Dark Victory* with Bette Davis in which Reagan had played a homosexual. Robinson had also worked on the script of *Million Dollar Baby,* starring Reagan.

Wallis hired producer Sam Wood as director. He'd already directed many films that evolved into hits, beginning his career in 1915 as an assistant to Cecil B. DeMille. Over the years, he'd helmed some of Hollywood's biggest stars, including Gloria Swanson, the doomed Wallace Reid, Marion Davies, Clark Gable, and Jimmy Durante.

A liberal, Jack Warner admired Wood's talents, but found him such a right winger as to be objectionable. Groucho Marx had worked with him on *A Night at the Opera* (1935) and *A Day at the Races* (1937), calling him a "fascist," denouncing him as anti-Semitic, and abhorring his racist comments about black people.

Wood had previously directed Robert Donat in *Goodbye, Mr. Chips* (1939), which had brought that actor an Oscar. That same year, Wood had been nominated for an Oscar as Best Director, but lost to Victor Fleming for his direction of *Gone With the Wind* (1939). *[Ironically, Wood had been an uncredited director of many of that film's scenes.]* The following year, he'd been nominated as the year's Best Director for *Kitty Foyle* (1940), but lost to John Ford for his *The Grapes of Wrath*.

Setting out on a cruise in Asia, Robinson leisurely read *Kings Row* and was horrified, although he admitted he found it a page-turner. "I also found it personally revolting," he later said. "It seemed to be an attack on the very moral fiber of an American small town at the turn of the century. After finishing it, I took the galley proofs and tossed them into the Sulu Sea near Bali. But no sooner had the galleys hit the water than I realized how the story might be saved. Step by step, I'd have to eliminate the controversial scenes without losing the power of the book. For example, instead of the doctor committing incest with his daughter, I would have him covering up her insanity. I wired Wallis to purchase it, but warned him that we'd have trouble with those censors at the Breen Office.

On Robinson's recommendation, Wallis purchased the film rights to the novel for $35,000, just $5,000 less than he'd unsuccessfully offered for the film rights to *Gone With the Wind*, *[David O. Selznick eventually paid $50,000 for them.]*

Originally, Fox had wanted *Kings Row* with Henry Fonda, but later rejected it because of its censorship problems. Jack Warner liked the idea of Fonda playing the sensitive role of Drake that eventually went to Reagan. Warner even suggested to Darryl F. Zanuck at Fox that he'd consider hiring Tyrone Power to play the lead role of Parris Mitchell, but Fox refused to release its major star.

After it had become clear that neither Fonda nor Power was available, Wallis and Warner penciled in several actors who might be ideal for the role of Parris, including Laurence Olivier (an odd choice for a dyed-in-the-wool resident of a small Midwestern town), Cary Grant, Robert Taylor, Douglas Fairbanks, Jr., Glenn Ford, Alexander Knox, Arthur Kennedy, John Garfield, Errol Flynn, and even Ronald Reagan. Warner rejected both Flynn and Garfield as "too sexy for the part."

For the role of Drake—the trust fund playboy who loses his money and later, his legs—the

Bellamann's view of small-town America as a sexually decadent, sadistic Hell was not compatible with the patriotic fervor then sweeping over the entertainment industry.

The miracle, partly because of the howls of protest from censors, was that Reagan's acclaimed film ever got made at all.

284

list of contenders being considered included Robert Cummings (who eventually was cast as Parris), Lew Ayres, Dennis Morgan, Franchot Tone, Fred MacMurray, Ray Milland, Lew Ayres, Robert Preston, Eddie Albert, John Garfield, Arthur Kennedy, and, finally, at the bottom to the list, Ronald Reagan.

Wallis was more intrigued with an unknown newcomer, a young and handsome actor, Michael Ames, who had previously appeared in a brief role with Reagan in *International Squadron* (1941) when he was identifying himself, professionally, as Tod Andrews.

Wallis had more or less assigned the role to Ames, but then news came in that the actor had been drafted into the Army. There went his one big chance, an acting opportunity which would never come again. Ames remained resentful throughout the rest of his life for losing the role.

The role of Cassandra Tower, the neurotic daughter of the incestuous Dr. Alexander Tower (as played by Claude Rains), attracted far more interest from actresses than the more wholesome female lead of Randy Monoghan, the tomboy from the wrong side of the tracks.

Bette Davis actively campaigned for the role of Cassandra, but Wallis thought she'd be overpowering and would distort the focus of the movie. Ida Lupino was sent the script, but returned it, finding it "degenerate." Ginger Rogers was mailed the script, but didn't respond. Warners' own Olivia de Havilland was a distinct possibility, but she wasn't interested. Vivien Leigh was under consideration until she left Hollywood, returning to war-torn Britain with Laurence Olivier.

Linda Darnell and Anita Louise were two other candidates, along with a virtually unknown actress, Adela Longmire. Warner sent a memo to Wallis, asserting that "Adela is a great actress," but Wallis didn't agree. Warner came up with some other actresses, none of whom met with Wallis' approval either. They included Susan Peters, Joan Leslie, and Priscilla Lane, who had appeared with Reagan in those *Brother Rat* movies. Wallis strongly approved of Gene Tierney, finding her ideal, but Zanuck at 20th Century Fox had already signed her to another film, *Tobacco Road* (1941).

Then, unexpectedly, the publicist for Marlene Dietrich announced that she had won the role of Cassandra, but nobody in Hollywood believed that.

The part finally went to Betty Field, a Bostonian with sad, sultry eyes. She had scored a success in Hal Roach's production of *Of Mice and Men* (1939), playing Curley's sad, slatternly wife.

Humphrey Bogart had read *Kings Row,* and he called his friend, Ann Sheridan, to suggest that she pursue the role of Randy, the well-adjusted girl who ultimately wins Drake's heart. She read the novel, thinking at first it would never reach the screen because of its taboo subjects.

When she became convinced that it could, she settled her contract dispute with Warners and aggressively sought the role—and won it. In fact, in the ads, she would take star billing, followed by Robert Cummings, Ronald Reagan, and Betty Field.

Wallis lined up one of the best supporting casts of any drama ever filmed at Warners—Charles Coburn, Claude Rains, Judith Anderson, Nancy Coleman, Maria Ouspenskaya, Harry Davenport, and many lesser but very talented lights. He also had to cast child actors, Ann Todd; Scotty Beckett; Douglas Croft; and Mary Thomas to play childhood versions of the lead roles.

"As I read the novel, with all its hypocrisy and narrow-minded people, it evoked for me my memories of growing up in Denton, Texas, where I fought against those traits and those people," Sheridan recalled in 1966. "Like Ronnie, I would give my best performance in any picture."

By the time Robinson sent his fourth screenplay to the Breen office, he had eliminated any hint of homosexuality between Parris and Drake; cut out Parris' mercy killing of his grandmother; and axed the death scene where Drake dies of cancer. Everything connected with Dr. Tower's incest with his daughter, Cassandra, was replaced with a theme of insanity. Tower kills her instead, thus keeping her from marrying Parris and ruining his life.

Kings Row was a precursor of Grace Metalious' *Peyton Place* that dominated the bestselling novel lists of the 1950s.

The Breen office even objected to the dialogue between Cummings and Reagan when Parris had to sleep over at his friend's home. Originally, Reagan was to say: "You have to bunk with me. I hope you don't mind the change."

In a decision that left its actors trying to figure out their motivation and meaning, the Breen censors ordered that the dialogue be changed to: "You have to bunk with me. I hope you don't mind, Mr. Mitchell."

Wood didn't want Reagan to wear a lot of makeup in *Kings Row*. But Cummings, a drag queen in private life, insisted on heavy makeup, so much that a critic later said, "In *Kings Row*, Robert Cummings looks like he's made up to be third girl in a chorus line."

Reagan knew from the beginning that he was facing his most challenging role. He recalled, "I drew upon some of the traits of Moon *[his brother, Neil Reagan.]* My brother was rakish, charming, and of good humor, a spicier version of myself. I felt the town of Kings Row in the movie could easily have been Dixon."

During the course of the filming, Reagan spent a lot of time with Sheridan. Always attracted to each other, they resumed their romance, as Wood closely observed. "I made sure that Reagan got advance notice when Jane visited him on the set. I knew she and Ann were good friends, a friendship that would have come to an abrupt end if she'd caught her husband banging Ann in her dressing room. Fortunately, that never happened."

"The role of Drake was an acting chore that got down and deep inside me and kind of wrung me out," Reagan recalled, years later. "The early scenes were easier. In those, I played a gay blade who cut a swathe among the ladies."

"Ann was a great help, practically giving me acting lessons. We spent a lot of time rehearsing the scenes, not just of the two of us. Sometimes, she played Parris when Cummings wasn't around to rehearse with me."

During the making of *Kings Row*, Sheridan told him that she'd heard "a rumor that Bette Davis wants your strong brown arms around her in her upcoming film, *Now, Voyager.*"

"I thought Bette detested me," Reagan said.

"Don't kid yourself," Sheridan said. "She wants you to fuck her in spite of your rejection of her offscreen in *Dark Victory.*"

Two views of Betty Field, seen in the lower photo with Reagan in *Kings Row*. She took on the difficult role of the emotionally maladjusted Cassie, stealing the part from Bette Davis.

286

Both Sheridan and Reagan knew that Cummings was better suited to comedies than to heavy drama. However, Alfred Hitchcock didn't think so. The Missouri-born actor told them that Hitchcock had just signed him to star in *Saboteur* (1942).

Just as Reagan hated flying, Cummings had a passion for it, and kept urging Reagan to "come fly with me." Sheridan had told him that their fellow actor, who was to marry five times and father seven children, "Liked an occasional boy." Reagan assumed that Cummings' invitation "to come fly with me" was actually a sexual pass.

To attend a cast party, Sheridan made Cummings up and let him wear her clothes to the informal event.

In the controversial adaptation of the novel *Kings Row*, Reagan played Drake, a young trust-fund philanderer, a radical change of pace for him.

Robert Cummings *(left)* was cast as Parris, his close friend from childhood.

In later life, Reagan was saddened to see Cummings, an advocate of natural foods and a healthy diet, succumb to drug addiction.

Within a year after making *Kings Row,* Cummings would join the U.S. Army Air Corps, becoming a flight instructor.

Reagan recalled, "Robert fell for all that Warners publicity crap about what an ace pilot I was. In all my talks about flying with him, never once did he see through the ruse. I must have sounded like the aviator I certainly wasn't."

"Young Reagan was such an easy-going and fun person to be around that he was clearly the best-loved actor on the set," said Coburn. "I really hated it later when I had to amputate his legs," he joked.

Rising from the swamps of Georgia, Charles Coburn, born in 1877, said he started his theatrical career handing out programs in the local Savannah Theater. He'd made his debut on Broadway back in 1901. He often performed on stage with his first wife, actress Ivah Wills. After his wife died in 1937, he came to Hollywood to begin film work. Today, he is best remembered for his appearance opposite Marilyn Monroe in the 1953 *Gentlemen Prefer Blondes.* At the time he met Reagan, he'd just finished *The Lady Eve* (1941), with Barbara Stanwyck.

In the same year that he played a sadistic doctor in *Kings Row,* he also made *In This Our Life.* Reagan kidded him: "As Bette Davis' pathetic uncle, you seemed to display an unnatural interest in your niece."

An associate producer, David Lewis, was on the set almost every day. As Sheridan noted, "David seems to follow Ronnie around with panting tongue."

[But did Reagan keep his promise to let Lewis give him nude massages during filming? The only source for that is Wood, who claimed he walked in one day on Reagan as he lay nude on a cot receiving a sensual massage from his associate producer.

"I told the boys to carry on and left," Wood told Sheridan. "I suspect it's one of those George Cukor/Clark Gable director/actor seductions.]

Reagan later recalled that two of the most formidable actresses he ever worked with were Maria Ouspenskaya and Judith Anderson. Born in 1876 during the days of the Russian Empire, Ouspenskaya became an acting teacher and a stage star. She came to Hollywood and had early success in *Dodsworth* (1936), which brought her an Oscar nomination as Best Supporting Actress. When she met Reagan, she was at the peak of her career, appearing as an old Gypsy fortuneteller in the horror film, *The Wolf Man* (1941). She had had other hits in *The Rains Came* (1939), with Tyrone Power, and in *Waterloo Bridge* (1940) with Robert Taylor and Vivien Leigh.

Anderson, an Australian, had just been nominated as Best Supporting Actress for her portrayal of the malevolently lesbian Mrs. Danvers (the housekeeper) in Alfred Hitchcock's *Rebecca* (1940). After *Kings Row*, she would go on to appear in many memorable films, including *Laura* (1944), and in Tennessee Williams' *Cat on a Hot Tin Roof* (1958), with Elizabeth Taylor and Paul Newman.

A major-league sadist masquerading as a decent, small town doctor: Charles Coburn.

London-born Claude Rains had first thrilled Reagan in his appearance in *The Invisible Man* (1933). "From *Casablanca* (1942) to *Mr. Smith Goes to Washington* (1939), Claude was one of the most talented actors who ever appeared before a camera," Reagan claimed.

Nancy Coleman, who came from Washington State, was a minor actress who played Louise Gordon (the daughter of Coburn's character, the sadistic Dr. Gordon) in *Kings Row.* Her early romance with Reagan prompts the doctor to (sadistically and unnecessarily) amputate his legs after an accident at the railroad tracks.

Coleman would work with Reagan and Errol Flynn in their upcoming movie, *Desperate Journey* (1942).

Three talented technicians contributed greatly to the success of *Kings Row.* They included a Chinese American cinematographer, James Wong Howe, a master of the use of shadow and one of the first to use deep-focus cinematography.

An American composer of Austro-Hungarian birth, Erich Wolfgang Korngold was one of the leading composers of Hollywood's Golden Age, rivaled by Max Steiner and Alfred Newman.

For the film's production design, there was no one better than a Connecticut Yankee, William Cameron Menzies. At Hollywood's first Academy Awards ceremony in 1929, Menzies had won an Oscar for Best Art Direction for his work on *The Dove* and *the Tempest.*

Reagan knew his most challenging moment would be the scene where he wakes up to discover that the sadistic doctor had amputated his legs. "I had to find out how it really felt, short of actual amputation," he said. "I woke up in the morning, rehearsing the line, looking up at the ceiling. I even rehearsed in front of mirrors in the men's rooms of restaurants. I consulted doctors and psychologists. Anything to summon up the cauldron of emotions a man must feel who wakes up one sunny morning to find half of himself gone. Ann worked with me over and over again on the scene. I had to get it right."

He later said, "Perhaps I never did quite as well

Maria Ouspenskaya, a relic of the Romanov Empire.

again in a single shot."

The day he walked onto the set in pajamas and a nightshirt, Jane had come, with little Maureen, to greet him and wish him well.

He discovered that the prop men had cut a hole in the mattress and installed a structural support, with a void, beneath the opening. Reagan had to sink his legs into that hole.

"Lights! Camera! Action!" the director commanded at the beginning of the shot

Then Reagan, as Drake, screams, "Randy!" Again, "Randy! Randy!" In desperation, his hand reached down, grasping for but not finding his thighs. He quivers like a slain animal in his death throes. "Where's the rest of me?"

With the delivery of that line, Reagan entered screen immortality.

Wood pronounced it a wrap after the only one take.

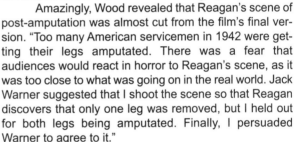

Also cast in *Kings Row,* Judith Anderson had previously appeared in an even more famous movie as Mrs. Danvers, the cold, imperious, and ultimately, psychotic, housekeeper in *Rebecca* (1940).

Cummings later recalled, "When Ronnie delivered that line to movie audiences, across the country, at first, they thought his genitals had been cut off, too. There were gasps of horror."

Amazingly, Wood revealed that Reagan's scene of post-amputation was almost cut from the film's final version. "Too many American servicemen in 1942 were getting their legs amputated. There was a fear that audiences would react in horror to Reagan's scene, as it was too close to what was going on in the real world. Jack Warner suggested that I shoot the scene so that Reagan discovers that only one leg was removed, but I held out for both legs being amputated. Finally, I persuaded Warner to agree to it."

Claude Rains told Reagan "I am Bette Davis' favorite actor."

Reagan replied, "I'm her least favorite."

In the movie, unlike events as they transpired within the book, when Drake dies of cancer, Reagan recovers from a deep depression and finds personal redemption through the love and support of his beloved Randy (Sheridan). She helps him become a successful real estate developer, and he recognizes that life is worth living, even without legs.

In 1945, the year of his death, the novelist, Bellamann, was working on his novel's sequel, *Parris Mitchell of Kings Row.* Katharine, his wife, finished the novel for him, publishing it posthumously in 1948.

Although *Kings Row*—Reagan's greatest screen role—became a classic, it did not get good reviews. Bosley Crowther, writing for *The New York Times* described it as "gloomy and ponderous."

Harrison's Reports defined it as "A powerful but somewhat depressing drama."

In spite of the attacks, *Kings Row* was nominated

Playing an almost demented, deeply repressed daughter: Nancy Coleman

for three separate Oscars: Best Picture, Best Director, and Best Black and White Cinematography. But MGM's *Mrs. Miniver* carried off all three of those prizes.

In general, Reagan fared better than Cummings. Crowther, for example wrote, "Cummings looks and acts like a musical-comedy juvenile trying to find his bearings in this heavy Ibsenesque plot."

There was talk that Reagan might be nominated for an Academy Award, but Warners decided to throw its powerful support behind *Yankee Doodle Dandy,* starring James Cagney, instead.

The American Medical Association strongly attacked the movie because of its portrayal of doctors in such an unflattering glare.

"*Kings Row* was the finest picture I ever appeared in, and it elevated me to the degree of stardom I had dreamed of when I first came to Hollywood in 1937," Reagan said.

The film developed something of a negative image after its release in February of 1942. "America had gone to war, and *Kings Row* was hardly a morale booster," Reagan said. "All the other studios were rushing into production of pictures to lift the American spirit and imbue us with hope of winning the war. Our picture presented a depressing view of small town America, quite unlike those Andy Hardy films with Mickey Rooney. I bet Hitler would have loved *Kings Row* if Josef Goebbels could slip a pirated copy into Berlin."

Before Reagan could really capitalize off his breakthrough role, he'd have to join the Army. He failed to take advantage of his new position as a top star at Warners, and noted to his severe disappointment the juicy roles he lost between 1943 and 1946.

After the war, his film career would never regain the momentum it had momentarily achieved.

Kings Row had another downside. Jane Wyman later confessed to Joan Blondell. "It may ultimately have contributed to my divorce from Ronnie. He screened it countless times, every time someone came over, although they might have seen it already. Night after night, I had to watch that film. I came to know every line every actor in it delivered. I got so I couldn't take it anymore. Finally, I told Ronnie, 'Why in hell don't you make another movie instead of reliving your one moment of screen glory?' That pissed him off."

Reagan to Ann Sheridan, in reference to his amputated legs: "Where's the Rest of Me?"

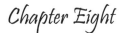

Chapter Eight

After His Success in Kings Row, Reagan Becomes MCA's "Million Dollar Baby"

Drafted into the Army, Reagan Objects to Medical Personnel Fondling "The Family Jewels"

In a mink coat with some strings of pearls, Jane Wyman salutes 2nd Lt. Ronald Reagan, of the Army Air Force Personnel Office, in the autumn of 1942. Granted referrals, he had continued to make movies that year until he was finally called up for duty.

Since he was "blind as a bat," he was not fit for active duty. Instead, he'd begin to make war propaganda movies.

In *Juke Girl* (a secret reference to a prostitute), Ronald Reagan gave Ann Sheridan, his sometimes mistress, the most passionate kiss of his screen career.

When Jane Wyman saw this publicity still, she lamented, "If only he kissed me this way at home!"

In the summer of 1941, with Europe at war, many young American men faced being drafted into the military. Millions of Americans believed that the United States could stay out of the war—but not Reagan. He was convinced that an American involvement in World War II was inevitable. But because of his poor vision, he didn't think he would ever be drafted.

291

Actually, he didn't want to go into the Army. At long last, he was on the verge of major stardom, a dream cherished for so long, and he had a beautiful wife and a baby girl.

To his chagrin, during the making of *Kings Row,* his status as a member of the U.S. Cavalry reserve was revoked, thereby making him immediately eligible for active duty.

He was devastated. As he complained to Dick Powell, "I've worked and labored for this moment, and now that it's here, it seems that the government has other plans for me. If I'm drafted into the Army and spend several years away from Hollywood, I won't have any fans left when I get back."

"That's always a possibility," Powell said. "In Hollywood, our replacements are always pounding on studio doors. The old-timers like Clark Gable will return to face a new crowd of good-looking guys at Warners, MGM, Paramount, whatever. By the end of the 1940s, a whole new generation of younger guys will be enlisted as replacements for Errol Flynn, Tyrone Power, and Robert Taylor. The stars of the 1930s will be viewed as over the hill, long in the tooth, and washed up."

"Stop!" Reagan said. "You're just too depressing."

A uniformed movie star with wholesome, Midwestern roots and a mother, Nelle, who adores him.

Nelle paid a visit in September of 1943 to "Fort Roach," the headquarters of Reagan's film production unit. He always responded in anger when someone accused him of "being a draft dodger avoiding danger."

He cited how valuable to the war effort war propaganda films were.

In response to a letter he received, Reagan got up early one morning, kissed Jane goodbye, and drove to March Field for his physical. His athletic body passed the medical examination. As he later said, "I didn't like some young guy, just out of medical school, fondling my balls, but it's all in the game."

Two doctors later, however, bluntly informed him that although he'd passed the physical, "You're as blind as a bat. If we gave you a gun, you'd probably end up accidentally shooting at General Eisenhower."

"And based on your lousy vision, you'd probably miss," the other doctor said.

Reagan was given a copy of his medical report. It recommended "Limited service—eligible for corps area service command, or War Department Overhead only."

At the time, men so designated were rarely drafted. Reagan told friends, "It's highly unlikely I'll ever be called."

However, while he was still asleep, on Sunday, December 7, 1941, a call came in from Neil (Moon) Reagan. "Wake up, Dutch!" he shouted into the phone. "We're at war. The Japs attacked Pearl Harbor this morning."

At the time of America's entry into World War II, Reagan was only thirty years old—and still draftable. Within a week, he was instructed to report to Fort Mason at the port of San Francisco, where warships were launched for action in the Pacific.

Right after the Japanese attack, young men across America, many of them either outraged or in a state of numbed disbelief and/or shock, lined up at their local draft boards. Based on his association with Warners, Reagan, however, was not among them.

Lew Wasserman, Reagan's agent at MCA, called on Jack Warner, asking him to write a letter to the Assistant Secretary of the War Department, seeking temporary deferment. Warner claimed that Reagan was vital to the financial security of his studio. He also stated that he planned to cast Reagan in "propaganda films," conceived to boost the morale and resolve of the American public.

Within thirty days, Reagan received notice from the War Department that he would be deferred until April of 1942. Then, after reappraisal, if inducted into the Army, he'd be assigned the rank of second lieutenant.

The implications of Reagan being drafted meant that Jane would, in essence, become the breadwinner of the household. Wasserman, who was also her agent, managed to renegotiate her contract, raising her salary to $750 a week, although she was still mired in B pictures—and would be for some time.

With that increase in salary, she could easily afford the $15,000 mortgage they'd taken on their new home in the Hollywood Hills. It called for a payment of only $125 a month.

Although Reagan's contract with Warners wouldn't expire until 1944, Wasserman urged him to let him try to re-negotiate his movie contract anyway. During Wasserman's subsequent meeting with Jack Warner, the agent pressed his case. "I think that when *Kings Row* is released, Ronnie is going to move into the top tier of male movie stars. You'd better sign him for another seven years, or I'll let his contract expire and I'll freelance him. Louis B. Mayer has already hinted to me that he'd like to make Reagan a boy star at MGM."

Warners had seen a sneak preview of *Kings Row* and agreed with Wasserman's assessment. The new contract called for him to pay Reagan $758,000 over a seven-year period.

Reagan had an ally in Col. Lewis B. Hershey, director of the Selective Service, who viewed morale-boosting movies as "essential to the national health, safety, and interest of America."

He cited war movies under production as a virtual "second front" in its propaganda wars against both Japan and the Nazis. Now that America was no longer neutral, Hershey requested that all studios, including Warners, make "the Japs the most evil monsters who ever inhabited the Earth and Hitler's Nazis devil worshippers intent on enslaving the world."

Warner told Reagan, "I want to get deferments

for you until you've made three more pictures after *Juke Girl* (1942) and *Desperate Journey* (also 1942). I'll try to convince the War Department that it's more vital to have you turning out American propaganda movies that taking some desk job in the Army. With your eyesight, that's exactly what you'll become, a paper pusher."

"If you can make a lot of films, at least five in 1942 and 1943, I'll release one a year. That way, your fans won't forget you. You know, those jerks are a fickle lot, but they keep us in pussy, potatoes, and Porsches."

***

Reagan immediately went into production on *Juke Girl* with his favorite actress and sometime lover, Ann Sheridan. She had married George Brent on January 5, 1942.

Originally, Warner had cast Ida Lupino in the lead, but when *Kings Row* opened with such success, he wanted to reteam Sheridan with Reagan. "I probably should make five or six pictures teaming you and your Ronnie boy, our answer to MGM's Spencer Tracy and Hepburn, the faggot and the lesbian," Warner said to Sheridan. "At least you and Reagan are heterosexuals—as far as I know. In Hollywood, of course, you can never be sure."

After Reagan read the script, he was disappointed. So was Sheridan. "This is not exactly a great wedding present from Warners," she told Reagan.

As a follow-up to his success as Drake in *Kings Row,* he had wanted something stronger. *Juke Girl* was a dreary story about a slovenly group of itinerant crop pickers in Florida, highlighting conflicts between laborers in the field and management's taking advantage of them.

"I'd call it the truck farmer's version of Steinbeck's *The Grapes of Wrath,*" Sheridan said. "A grim melodrama."

A.I. Bezzerides and Kenneth Gamet had adapted the story from Theodore Pratt. Although Pratt had originated in Minnesota, most of his novels were set in Florida, where he lived. Originally, he'd entitled his story "Jook Girl." Jook was a reference to a small roadside joint in the southeastern United States where one could eat, drink, and dance to music from a jukebox.

After reading the script, Reagan called Sheridan. "What in hell is a Juke Girl?"

"It's a euphemism for whore," she answered. "It's not spelled out in the script, but juke gals work a tavern catering to farm workers."

"Sounds like we're making a filthy picture," he said.

"Not at all," she answered. "It's more about crops than cocks."

Once again, Reagan was helmed by the German director, Curtis Bernhardt, who did not seem happy with his latest assignment. He later said, "I did not like either of the pictures I made with Mr. Reagan, nei-

ther *Million Dollar Baby* nor *Juke Girl*. He was a sort of unimportant, pleasant, healthy, typically American boy, nothing special about him at all. I did not expect much of a future for him in films. He had a nice smile that might work better if he were an insurance salesman."

"The only time he heated up on camera was when he made love to Annie Sheridan," Bernhardt claimed. "In one love match, shooting began on Wednesday and ended on Friday. She'd just come off her honeymoon, but it looked like she was getting ready for a second honeymoon with Reagan. When I finally finished the scene, I advised the two of them to get a room. It appeared to me that they took my advice, but I suspected that something was going on between those two long before they came together in *Juke Girl*. I hoped George Brent wouldn't find out."

Cast as Steve Talbot, Reagan played a drifter who arrives in Florida with his friend, Danny Frazier (Richard Whorf). They seek work in the tomato fields. Their friendship is strained when Steve sides with a farmer, Nick Garcos (George Tobias), in his struggle with Henry Madden (Gene Lockhart), who controls a fruit farm and packaging plant.

In a complicated plot, the story moves forward with violence, killings, commercial intrigue, even mob justice. Reagan would forever remember the battle of the tomatoes. At one point, he squashed a big, fat, juicy tomato into Lockhart's face.

In one scene, hired thugs try to break the resolve of an independent farmer by smashing truckloads of his tomato crates. After wallowing in squashed tomatoes for three nights, Reagan said, "With all the misconceptions about pampered stars, none is so far afield as the belief that physical discomfort isn't tolerated. On the first night, we used real tomatoes in the trucks. A crew placed them back in the trucks for the filming on the third and fourth nights. By this time, the tomatoes were rotten and stunk like hog heaven. Not only that, but I always despised tomatoes."

The film was supposed to take place among crop pickers in the humid heat of Florida. But actually, it was shot in the wintry cold of Central California, the temperature dropping one night to 27° F. Since the actors needed to have sweaty faces, they often rubbed glycerine on their skin to create the illusion. Bernhardt asked some of the men to smoke cigarettes to explain the vapor in the night air. When the breath vapor became too visible, Bernhardt would have to call for a halt in filming.

Sheridan was given star billing as Lola Mears, the *Juke Girl* herself. Steve (i,.e, Reagan) romances Lola, but she seems reluctant to commit because of her shady past. She takes a job in Atlanta, Georgia, telling Steve he'll be better off without her. However, they become closer when a lynch mob goes after them both. Before the final curtain, Lola and Steve, united in love, agree to settle down on their own farm and give up their tumbleweed lives.

In *Juke Girl,* Reagan appears in a scene in a bar with George Tobias (*center*) and Richard Whorf. The dwindling members of his fast-fading fan clubs considered this the "lustiest" picture of him ever taken. "He's got a gleam in his eyes," said Brenda Fairfield, president of his Los Angeles Fan Club. "He was never more beautiful, and he seems to be looking at a stripper."

When not occupying his time with Sheridan, Reagan spent evenings with William Hopper, Hedda's son. He'd been cast in *Juke Girl* in an uncredited role as a postal clerk. "Stardom seems to have eluded me," he told Reagan.

On location, he asked to bunk with Reagan as he'd done before, and Reagan agreed. He no longer felt as uncomfortable around William as he had before. He was free to undress in front of him, take a shower, and share a bed with him. At one point, he asked William, "Have you gotten over your crush on me?"

"Far from it," William proclaimed. "When Ronnie Reagan is old and gray, he can put his shoes under my bed any night he wants."

Sheridan claimed that, in some perverse way, "I think Ronnie gets off on the adulation Bill heaps on him. After all, it's pretty god damn hard to reject being adored. Bill flattered him constantly. After even the simplest scene, Bill would praise him, calling him the most brilliant actor in films today."

Sometimes, as Reagan sat with William and Sheridan around a campfire, they listened to music composed and performed, informally, by Lockhart. Although he played the villain in the film, off screen, he was polite and charming. He wrote lyrics for songs, and sang many of his creations for them.

He told Reagan, "I'm in the bio period of my career—*Abe Lincoln in Illinois* (1940); *Edison the Man* (1940); *Billy the Kid* (1941); and *The Devil and Daniel Webster* (1941). He had just filmed *They Died With Their Boots On* (1941) with Errol Flynn cast as General Custer.

Reagan told him, "I'm seriously pissed off that I didn't get to play General Custer. After all, I was Custer in *Santa Fe Trail*. I think Jack Warner fucked me by not giving me the role again."

"Win some, lose some," Lockhart said.

Reagan was distressed to learn that Howard da Silva had been cast as Cully in *Juke Girl*. He had detested that actor ever since he'd told him that Jane was having an affair with Dennis Morgan during their work together on *Bad Men of Missouri*.

Two weeks into the shoot, Reagan also had a reunion of sorts with Faye Emerson, who had flirted outrageously with him when they'd shot *Nine Lives Are Not Enough*. Once again, she flirted with him, and once again, he showed no interest in her at all.

Cast as a fellow drifter and itinerant worker, Whorf was very talented, later becoming an author, director, and designer. At the time he met Reagan, he was appearing in far better A-list pictures, including *Yankee Doodle Dandy* with James Cagney (1942); and *Keeper of the Flame* (1943), with Spencer Tracy and Katharine Hepburn.

One night at a local tavern, Reagan and Whorf joined Alan Hale, Sr., and associate producer Jack Saper, who were also involved in the filming of *Juke Girl*. Both Saper and Hale told Reagan they looked forward to working with him and Flynn on their upcoming movie, *Desperate Journey*.

Reagan had recently made *Tugboat*

In one of the more dramatic moments of *Juke Girl*, Reagan smashes a big, rotten tomato in the face of Gene Lockhart, who plays the vicious owner of a fruit farm and packing plant.

Reagan was the most physically violent of all U.S. presidents—that is, on the screen.

Annie Sails Again with Hale. Reagan later said, "There was one thing Hale could do—and that was drink. He played a drunk on *Santa Fe Trail* with Errol and me, and he wasn't acting. I could nurse a drink for an hour or two. Hale could drink all night. He obviously had a hollow wooden leg. He told me that once in Texas, he'd drunk for thirty-six uninterrupted hours. I told him, 'That's impossible.' He claimed that every hour or so, he went to the toilet and threw up and then came back for more. What a man! What a disaster!"

In Reagan's view, Tobias, a New Yorker, was pleasant and easy to work with. He had signed with Warners in 1939, playing supporting roles in such movies as *Yankee Doodle Dandy (1940),* with James Cagney, and in *Sergeant York* (1941) with Gary Cooper. Tobias said he'd gotten his start by appearing as a Russian visa officer in Greta Garbo's 1939 *Ninotchka.*

Otherwise deeply involved in wartime film and propaganda production, Jack Warner had given producer Hal B. Wallis a clear hand without any interference during the shooting of *Juke Girl.* At first, based on the title, Warner thought it was a musical. That was partially true: In the movie, as Lola, Sheridan is a singer, warbling "I Hates Love."

But when Warner was screened a rough cut of the film, he was horrified at its pro-union stance. During his long and turbulent battles with union workers, Warner had sided with Walt Disney's anti-labor stance.

Juke Girl marked the beginning of the end of Warner's long association with Wallis He would make only one more movie for Warners, *Casablanca* (1942), before leaving the studio.

Reviews were lackluster, if not hostile, when *Juke Girl* opened across the country. *The New York Times* defined it as "another Warner's semi-social life-in-the-raw-drama, where a lot of slangy lingo is tossed fast and loose. As a cynic, Sheridan contrasts with Reagan, an idealist, who is stanch *(sic)* as a young hero. The whole smacks too much of the synthetic. It's like a tune that comes out of a jukebox."

No sooner was Reagan back in Hollywood, than he received a call from Warner, who with his typical vulgarity, said, "Get yourself some pussy and head out again. You don't want to keep Errol Flynn waiting on his *Desperate Journey."*

***

On location for *Juke Girl,* Reagan had come to know Ann Sheridan as he never had before or would ever again in the future.

It was obvious to him that she was very unhappy about her recent marriage to George Brent, with whom Reagan had co-starred in *Dark Victory.* "George's marriages usually don't make it through the honeymoon," she said. "I also suspect that he's resumed his affair with Bette Davis."

"He's a real penny pincher," Sheridan complained. "He recently told a reporter, 'I'm saving my money. You can't play Shirley Tem-

Sheridan and Brent on their honeymoon in May of 1942.

297

ple forever.' He told me I had to buy all my own clothes and that I had to pay half of the household expenses."

"That's a better deal than I'm offering to my poor Jane," he told her. "If I go into the Army, she'll have to pay all of the household expenses, including bringing up Baby Maureen. On a soldier's pay, Jane can't expect me to buy her expensive gowns."

"Oh, you men," Sheridan answered. "Excuses, excuses." It's more than the money thing. George is very withdrawn at times, going into deep, dark moods. He'll lock himself away and not speak to me for days. I think he hits the bottle during those periods of isolation. Right before marrying me, he had this affair with Ilona Massey when they made *International Lady* (1941). Apparently, he likes her Hungarian goulash. The picture should be retitled *An International Affair.*"

"You know better than most that all of us—the handsome hunks of the screen—face impossible temptations," he said. "After all, we're horny guys and they cast us with the most desirable women on the planet—and that means you, sugar."

"You're right, she said. "I didn't really expect a womanizer like George to be faithful. Frankly, I'm a 'man-nizer' if there's such a word. I think an actor and an actress should not marry. I wonder at times how you and Jane will make it. It's inevitable that one star will become a bigger star than the other—call it professional jealousy. I've already become a bigger star than he is. You saw *A Star is Born,* of course. George is low octane; I'm high octane. Some reporters are already referring to him as a has-been of the 1930s with a career in decline. Annie Gal is going up, up, just like you."

"As Hollywood stars, you and me, baby, the King and the Queen of the Bs, are going to become the King and Queen of Warners—forget that smokestack, Bette Davis. As for Flynn, he'll probably end up in jail for raping an eight-year-old girl...or boy, perhaps."

During the course of the evening, she admitted that she went to Jack Warner to protest against having to appear in *Juke Girl.*
"He threatened me with suspension again."

On location, both of them shared their dreams. She had learned that Warner had acquired the rights to Edna Ferber's sprawling novel, *Saratoga Trunk.* She was "burning with desire" (her words) to play the heroine of the novel, whom she described as a Creole version of Scarlett O'Hara.

Reagan was astonished to learn that she'd recommended him to Jack Warner, suggesting that he play the male lead, a cowboy, in *Saratoga Trunk.* He'd never read the novel, and she told him she'd lend him her copy.

"I'm already working in Hollywood with a French teacher," she said. "Right now, he's got me speaking 'Franco-Texan.' I'm even willing to don a blonde wig for my screen test."

[Reagan did read the novel and, indeed, thought he could play the role of the cowboy. But his getting drafted into the Army ended that possibility. As for Sheridan, she made a screen test, which, according to Jack Warner, was "so god damn awful I couldn't even show it to her."

Two bathing beauties, Ronald Reagan and Jane Wyman, on their honeymoon in Palm Springs, 1940.

In 1945, Saratoga Trunk *was released, the role of the Creole vixen having gone to a Swede, Ingrid Bergman, playing opposite cowboy Gary Cooper. One critic claimed that "at times, it is unbearable to sit through this disaster." That made Reagan feel better that he'd lost the role.]*

On long, lonely nights, Reagan and Sheridan talked about their upcoming projects—*Desperate Journey* for him, and the flag-waving *Wings for the Eagle* (1942) for her. "My co-star is that dreamboat, Dennis Morgan," she told him. "He's got all the starlets at Warners salivating."

"I know that Morgan has been married for years," he said. "Do you think he messes around with his leading ladies?"

"Do you think a bear shits in the woods?" she answered. "Sure, he does. He's a prize catch. Just ask such leading ladies as Ginger Rogers and Merle Oberon."

He didn't want her to know that their co-star, Howard da Silva, had told him about rumors of an affair between Morgan and Jane. He was, in essence, fishing for information.

Sheridan was trying to escape the *Oomph Girl* image and wanted to be viewed more seriously as an actress. "I don't know if this recent publicity will help me," she said.

She showed him an article that defined her as "a hash house version of Carole Lombard who combines comedy with sex appeal." The article also noted that it was appropriate that she was working on a movie with truck drivers. "Sheridan is known for her foul language and can outcurse any truck driver."

He noticed that on her dressing table she kept a picture of herself as Clara Lou from Denton, Texas. "I was all pudgy fat with kinky hair and a space between my teeth. But in a few months, I turned myself into a beauty contest winner, even though I've got no tits."

I think you're lovely, and your tits are just fine with me."

"I like your balls, too," she said.

[George Brent drove up from Los Angeles and made a surprise visit to the set of Juke Girl, *where Curtis Bernhardt was shooting a scene at night.*

What happened is not exactly known, except it became fodder for Hollywood gossip. All that is known for sure is that Brent gave Reagan a black eye. Someone told him that Reagan was having an affair with his wife. The culprit was the gossipy Howard da Silva, who had revealed Jane's earlier indiscretion with Dennis Morgan.

What is known is that Bernhardt had to order heavy makeup to camouflage Reagan's black eye. "Fortunately, I was shooting night scenes, and I could cast his left eye in shadow," the director said. "He told me he bumped into a door when he got up one night to take a piss. Brent told me he punched 'the hell out of Reagan.' I prefer to believe Brent."]

Not wanting to alert Jane to the incident, Sheridan temporarily quit accepting invitations to the Reagan household for dinner. Sheridan and Jane would make two more pictures together in the 1940s. Apparently, Jane never learned of the affair between Sheridan and her husband. If she did, she never confronted Sheridan about it.

According to Joan Blondell, when rumors of Reagan's infidelity reached Jane, she had a tendency to brush them aside.

As she once told Blondell, "How can I expect fidelity from him when he can't expect it from me? The pot can hardly call the kettle black."

***

Paulette Goddard picked up the phone to hear Jane's voice bubbling over with excitement, even though it held a hint of anxiety. "You won't believe this, but that Russian bear, Gregory Ratoff, has cast me in *Footlight Serenade* (1942) with John Payne as my leading man. Betty Grable and Victor Mature are in it, too."

"I heard that Grable and Mature are really going at it," Goddard said. "With them teamed up with lovebirds like you and John, the film should be retitled *Lovers Quartet.* You might steal Mature away from Grable one night just to find out what the excitement is all about."

"Your suggestions are always so outrageous—that's why I adore you so," Jane said.

"You are one lucky girl," Goddard said. "John Payne and Mature are the two sexiest men in Hollywood. I got John Wayne on my last picture. What a dud! Guess what? I'm now making another movie. Are you sitting down? It's called *The Forest Rangers* (1942)."

"Who's in it?" Jane asked.

"That red-haired bitch, Susan Hayward, is the other leading lady. In the movie, and perhaps later in real life, too, we've got to fight it out for Fred MacMurray. I saw a picture of

Betty Grable *(left)* and Jane Wyman duke it out in *Footlight Serenade.* Jane worried that her legs weren't as beautiful as those of Grable.

him shirtless. He's got a great body, and I must investigate below the belt. Did you have to duke it out with Hayward for Ronnie boy?"

"I did and you can declare me the winner," Jane said. "He promised he'd never see her again."

"I met Regis Toomey," Goddard said. "He's in my picture, too. You and Regis, as you know, hold the world's screen kiss record. Frankly, I wouldn't even let that loser kiss me on the cheek."

"I did it for a day's pay," she said. "He knows he has no future as a leading man. He actually said something smart. He told me, 'I'd rather be a supporting actor than a star—supporting actors last longer.'"

"True, true," Goddard said. "But he left out something. A true female movie star, after the blush of youth fades, can always marry a very rich man and live in luxury for the rest of her life. Men love to marry movie stars."

Incidentally, my divorce from Charlie *[Chaplin]* is coming through in June *[1942]*. I'm a bachelor gal once again—thank God. I'm playing the field, darling."

While preparing for her third picture in 1942, Jane read Robert Ellis' script of *Footlight Serenade.* "Hell in a basket," she told Reagan and others. "Here I am, playing Betty Grable's sidekick. Always a sidekick, never a star. I get to rub Grable's ankles when she's tired from dancing. Betty and I started out in the chorus line with Goddard and Lucille Ball. Now Betty's heading for the bigtime, and I'm still taking the leftovers."

"It's not so bad," Reagan assured her. "At least you're drawing a fine paycheck."

When Reagan read the script, he said, "I see that John Payne plays your husband. I worked out with him when you guys did *Kid Nightingale.* My god, that guy practically did a striptease on camera. I hear the gals really go for him. But in this flicker, he's got to compete with a guy they call 'The Body Beautiful.'"

[The reference was to Victor Mature, cast as a conceited heavyweight boxing champion who wants to put on a Broadway show with a part for Betty Grable. Unknown to Mature, Jane, in a secondary role, is secretly married to Payne, also in the cast. The predictable complications ensue. No one ever accused Ellis of being a great screenwriter.]

Cast as a conceited boxer, a shirtless Victor Mature is interviewed by an admiring news reporter.

"Ellis must have been on something when he came up with the name of my character," Jane said. "Flo La Verne. Isn't that just too precious for words?"

Ellis gave Jane a line that would have no special meaning for 1942 audiences, but which would get a laugh when shown to audiences in the Reagan 1980s. At one point, Grable tells Jane that she plans to become the understudy to the star of the show. Jane quips, "You have as much of a chance of being the understudy as I have of being the First Lady."

[As Jane told Goddard in the early 1980s, "Had I stayed married to Ronnie, I'd be First Lady now, going down in the history books. The way it is, history will shine on that little MGM starlet, instead. What was the poor dear's name? Nancy something? I went to see one of her movies only because it had

Torn between two hunks, John Payne *(left)* and Victor Mature, Betty Grable called herself "The luckiest girl in the world. I had both of them. Jane Wyman prefers John."

my friend, Barbara Stanwyck, in it. I fell into a deadly coma."]

Although Jane had met Grable at the same time she had been introduced to Goddard and Lucille Ball, she'd never been as close to Grable as she was to the other two actresses.

Ratoff told Jane that Darryl F. Zanuck at Fox had granted Grable some leeway in the selection of her female co-star. Ironically, the two choices were Jane and Ball. Grable chose Ball because she said, "Her career has fallen into the briar patch."

When Ball arrived for lunch with Jane and Grable, Grable was not available, as she had retreated with Mature.

At table, Ball said to Jane, "Long time no see, kid."

"I heard you turned down my role," Jane said. "Is my part that bad?"

"It was okay, rather routine," Ball said. "My real reason is that I wanted to star in *The Big Street* (1942). If I'd accepted *Footlight,* I wouldn't be available for *The Big Street.* By the way, I hear RKO is not going to renew my contract."

"I hope that's just a rumor and that it isn't ture," Jane said. "All of us live in fear of losing our contracts. I think you're great, and I loved you and Desi *[Arnaz]* in *Too Many Girls* (1940)."

"I did, too," Ball said, "and at least I met Desi. I'm mad about the boy. So are a hundred other women. Darling Desi likes to service all of us, including, on occasion, the cocksucking mouth of César Romero."

Both women shared memories of the early 1930s and their struggles at the time, remembering when they'd been cast in the chorus line of *The Kid From Spain*. Although Jane wasn't delighted with her current role, she vowed to make the best of it.

"For me, the highlight of the movie will be when I put on boxing gloves and duke it out with Betty," Jane said. "My anxiety is that we've both got to wear shortie short shorts, and her legs were voted most beautiful in the world."

"We all fall short in some department," Ball said. "As for me, I'm always getting cast with well-stacked broads, and I'm known as the 'No Tit Wonder.'"

For the most part, Jane and Grable got along during the shoot. So far, it seemed that Jane was still unaware of any involvement with the blonde goddess and her husband.

Jealousy did arrive on one occasion, and that was when the costume designer, Earl Luick, presented Grable with a very sexy gown. Grable rejected it. "I'd prefer to wear skunk," she told Luick.

He then crossed out Grable's name on the garment's design sketch and wrote in Wyman's name in its place. After the gown was made, Jane wore it in a scene. At its conclusion, the crew "wolf-whistled" her. In Jane's words, "Betty was seriously pissed off."

Four days later, Grable had recovered from her upset and invited Jane to go with her to Zanuck's office. "I want you to sit outside the door in the secretary's office. If Zanuck tries to rape me, and if you hear me screaming, call security."

Grable remained in Zanuck's office for nearly an hour, and Jane heard no screaming. When she finally emerged, Grable's face was beaming. "No rape, darling, but I got a pay raise to $2,000 a week. Also, a promise to shoot all my future films in Technicolor. And you know how gorgeous I look in Technicolor. He told me he would have shot *Footlight Serenade* in color, but he was in short supply of color stock because of the war."

Jane later said to friends, "I adore Betty, but the green bug bites me, hard, ever so often. Especially that afternoon when she left Zanuck's office. It was not just the pay raise, but she told me she was getting some 5,000 fan letters a week, mostly from servicemen."

Grable had a tough dancing number with her song, "I Heard the Birdies Sing." She had to (cheerfully) engage in a boxing match with her own shadow. For help, she called in her sometimes boyfriend, George Raft. Jane had been seduced by him during the production of *Rumba*, when she had a bit part opposite the female lead, Carole Lombard. Jane came over to him to shake his hand. She later complained to Grable, "The conceited bastard once fucked me. Now he doesn't know me."

"What does it matter?" Grable asked. "By the way, I think he's a latent homosexual. He lived with Valentino in New York, and I heard those roomies really went at it. During my so-called affair with George, about the only time he ever touched me was to beat me up."

As always, director Ratoff rattled off instructions in his thick Russian accent filled with more malapropisms than Samuel Goldwyn. When he saw

Former lovers who hustle—George Raft *(left)* and Rudolf Valentino.

302

that Jane didn't like her role, he suggested, "You should become a bobcat (perhaps he meant 'wildcat'?) like Olivia de Havilland and Bette Davis. They barged into Jack Warner's office and demanded stronger parts. They're getting them."

"I can't do that," Jane said. "Frankly, I'm glad to be employed. Let's face it: Those wisecracking blondes of the 30s, of which I was one, are being shown to the door. Take Glenda Farrell and Joan Blondell, for instance. I fear I might be next. At least, I'm occasionally given the female lead, as when I co-starred with Edward G. Robinson. It's better to work than it is to stand at the gate of Warners looking through the iron bars."

Jane found herself appearing with Phil Silvers again, after having co-starred with him and Jimmy Durante in *You're In the Army Now.*

"This time around, poor ugly Phil, a scene stealer himself, had to compete with two handsome hunks, and he was no match for John and Victor," Jane said. She introduced him around, presenting him as a comedian. He corrected her. "I'm a comic actor. I don't do stand-up." Because he'd just completed filming *My Gal Sal* (1942), he needed no introduction to that picture's male star, Mature himself.

Many envious stars had become profoundly bored with the constant barrage of fan magazine fluff about what an ideal couple Jane Wyman and Ronald Reagan were. Consequently, they were eager for news of infidelities associated with either member of the marriage of "America's Sweethearts."

One case emerged when Jane invited singer Joy Hodges to the Fox commissary for lunch. Reagan remembered Hodges fondly for her help in snagging his first screen test. Involved in a car accident, Hodges couldn't make it to the luncheon, but Mature wandered in and asked Jane if he could share her table.

He had been freed of Grable that afternoon because she and John Payne were meeting with director Irving Cummings about their next co-starring vehicle, *Springtime in the Rockies* (1942). "I don't envy Payne," Mature told Jane. "In this upcoming movie with Betty, he's got to fight off the sexual advances of both César Romero and Carmen Miranda."

Throughout most of the luncheon, Mature was quite flirtatious with Jane. She didn't exactly welcome his advances, but didn't reject them either. A photographer snapped a picture of the two of them as he was holding her hand. The next morning, when it appeared in the papers, the rumor mill began grinding out tales of a torrid affair that Mature was conducting with Jane during the filming of the picture. Jane was not as upset as she might have been, because the *faux* romance with Mature threw "the hounds off the scent of John and me," as she told Goddard.

In front of his assembled cast, Ratoff predicted that *Footlight Serenade* would become the hit musical of 1942. He was wrong. Nonetheless, it attracted a reasonable box office success, in large part because of Grable's marvelous dancing and the authentic-looking backstage sets.

Footlight Serenade marked a key moment in Grable's increasing visibility as the box office champion of World War II. Based partly on the success of that film, "The Girl With the Million Dollar Legs" would become the most famous pinup queen of World War II.

***

Juke Girl wrapped late on a Saturday night. By Monday morning, Reagan was rushed into shooting *Desperate Journey,* a sort of anti-Nazi action/adventure/propaganda film with Errol Flynn as his co-star. The script depicted Nazis as dunderheads and nincompoops.

303

With the exception of Michael Curtiz, Reagan didn't always get a first-rate director, certainly not for his B pictures. That changed with *Desperate Journey,* directed by Raoul Walsh.

Walsh, a New Yorker, had worn an eyepatch ever since his was driving through the Utah desert and a jackrabbit crashed through his windshield, spraying his face with shattered glass and putting out his right eye.

Prior to his accident, Walsh had portrayed John Wilkes Booth, Lincoln's assassin, in D.W. Griffith's *The Birth of a Nation* (1915). As an actor, he had also interpreted the role of Gloria Swanson's boyfriend in *Sadie Thompson* (1928). After the loss of his eye, this hard-core Hollywood veteran directed such stars as John Wayne, James Cagney, and Humphrey Bogart.

[Marlene Dietrich told people that Walsh was the biggest "pain in the ass I've ever known."]

Reagan wasn't thrilled at being directed by Walsh, who had just completed *They Died With Their Boots On* (1941) with Errol Flynn cast as General George Armstrong Custer.

Reagan still resented losing the role to Flynn,

Jean Douchet summed up the screen character of director Raoul Walsh, who's depicted above:

"His characters are projected on the world by their own energy and committed to a space that only exists for ther actions, fury, spirit, craft, ambition, and unbridled dreams."

after he'd portrayed Custer in *Santa Fe Trail.* Reagan's resentment—jealousy, really—increased when he learned that Walsh and Flynn were contemplating five more films in their immediate future—*Gentleman Jim* (1942); *Northern Pursuit* (1943); *Uncertain Glory* (1944); *Objective, Burma!* (1945); and *Silver River* (1948).

Ironically, although many of these upcoming Walsh films contained roles that could have been handled by Reagan, he had to serve in the military. Cynically, he frequently wondered, "If Flynn were such a 'perfect specimen' (as the title of one of his movies had implied), why hadn't he been drafted, too?"

He'd heard rumors of Flynn's ill health, but didn't believe them. "The guy's body looks too terrific to have anything wrong with it," Reagan told his friends. "Walsh and Flynn are so close, they look like brothers...or should I say, lovers? They've got their arms around each other, and they go out at night lowering Hollywood's liquor supply and bursting maidenheads even if there aren't many of them around these days."

Flynn called Walsh "Uncle," the director referring to his star and best friend as "The Baron."

"He's my kind of man," Flynn said to Reagan. "He was an athlete, a stunt rider, a man's man. He's also a man's director, the exact opposite of cocksucking George Cukor, the so-called Women's Director."

Reagan was provocative when he discussed Flynn privately with Walsh. "Does Flynn's homosexuality bother you?"

"Hell, no!" Walsh said. "A stiff prick has no conscience. A hole is a hole is a hole. If it provides sexual relief, it does its job. Why would the gender of a person matter if either one brings sexual satisfaction?"

"I've never heard it put that way before," Reagan said.

"I don't know how many times Flynn has told me he's in love," Walsh said. "Right now, he has the hots for Helmut Dantine. This weekend it will be someone else. He doubles his chances by not being gender specific."

Unusual for him, Reagan was also provocative when he talked privately with Flynn. "You look in great shape, man," he said. "But Walsh told me you were classified 4-F."

"I've been examined by private doctors and Army doctors," Flynn said. "My decadent lifestyle has caught up with me—too much sex, too much liquor, too much opium and cocaine, too many cigarettes. I was told that my heart and lungs are irreparably damaged. One doctor predicted that I have only two years to live."

Flynn leaned over to Reagan and whispered, "I don't want this to get around, but I occasionally have recurrent bouts of venereal disease, although I'm clean for now, at least. I have a heart murmur and recurrent malaria. Get this: I also have tuberculosis in my right lung."

"Sorry to hear that," Reagan said. "You'd never know any of that crap by looking at you. How are you going to handle all this?"

"I'm going to double up on my smoking and drinking," he said. "I'm thirty-two years old now, and if I have to leave this earth so soon, I'm going to have sex three times a day—twice with women, the other with some boy ass. If I get horny in between, I'm going to take it out and masturbate, regardless of who's looking. Would you like me to demonstrate, sport?"

As Flynn started to unzip, Reagan protested, "Not today...maybe a week from now."

Flynn admitted that he had specifically requested Reagan for the role, even though he resented any scene where he might shine. "I found on *Santa Fe Trail* that you and I blend in well together on the screen—good chemistry. Frankly, if you weren't such a square, we could blend together perfectly off screen, too, as we're well matched."

"Errol, I told you—it was NO yesterday, NO today, and NO tomorrow."

"You're really missing out on the time of your life, sport," he answered.

As shooting progressed, Reagan began to take Flynn's health claims seriously. Before the picture wrapped, his weight had dropped to just 165 pounds. Wardrobe had to re-tailor his wardrobe and in some cases, use padding.

"They don't have to pad me in the crotch, though," he told Reagan. "That remains as fat as ever."

In spite of his bravado, he often didn't make it to the set until noon, which inevitably brought a lashing from Walsh.

"But 'Uncle' was the eternal forgiving father," Reagan said. "No matter how many times Flynn fucked up in this preposterous Rover Boy-like saga we were making."

Of the many pictures snapped of Errol Flynn, dressed or undressed, this was his all-time favorite.

He had only one complaint: "It doesn't show my most celebrated asset."

***

305

In its production of *Desperate Journey*, a film that was increasingly interpreted as a useful propaganda film suitable for viewing by audiences within each of the nations allied against Hitler, Warners made it a point to include portrayals of aviators from most of the Allied Nations.

In the movie, the leader of the mission is an Australian, Flynn himself, playing Flight Lieutenant. Forbes. Reagan got second billing—in letters as big as Flynn's—cast as the American flight officer, Johnny Hammond. Alan Hale, Sr. played an R.A.F. veteran, Flight Sergeamt Kirk Edwards, who hailed from Scotland. As flying officer Jed Forrest, Arthur Kennedy represented Canada; and a very young Ronald Sinclair portrayed an Englishman, Lieutenant Flight Sergeant Lloyd Hollis II, the "baby" of the crew.

The plot contained no real love interest, but Nancy Coleman was cast as Kaethe Brahms, who comes to the aid of the downed pilots. Reagan had appeared with her in *Kings Row,* in which she'd been cast as his first girlfriend. He told Walsh, "With Nancy, there is no way I'm going to come down with my usual disease of *Leadinglady-itis.* You've dressed her up to look like a dyke librarian."

The villain of the piece was the veteran actor Raymond Massey, playing Major Otto Baumeister, no longer John Brown or Abe Lincoln from Illinois. Wearing a monacle, no less, and menacing, he interpreted his role as a Nazi commander of a prison for Allied soldiers in a sneering, utterly unconvincing way.

The mission of the Allied pilots involved flying over Schneidemühl, close to the Polish border, and bombing the railway junction that channeled Nazi munitions trains on to other parts of the Western and Eastern Fronts.

After successfully bombing their target, the heroes' plane is shot down and they are rounded up and imprisoned. They are interrogated and threatened in Massey's office. But through a ruse, they escape and begin a cross-country trek through Germany, with the Nazis hot on their trail. At one point, they slip aboard a train and secretly enter Hermann Göring's private railroad car, where they break into the Nazi's private stocks of food and liquor until

In *Desperate Journey,* Errol Flynn *(left)* and Ronald Reagan, wearing Nazi uniforms, make nincompoops out of the Germans in this preposterous, implausible yarn.

Ronald Reagan: the only U.S. President to publicly impersonate a Nazi.

306

they're discovered.

As part of the process, they unveil a treasure trove of secret Nazi documents, including the locations of secret *Messerschmidt* factories manufacturing planes to bomb Britain.

As they cross Germany, they leave a trail of destruction, including setting fire to chemical works in Berlin and mowing down hundreds of Nazis.

Flynn declares, "We're going to be the first invasion to hit Germany since Napoléon." Their feats, as later appraised by critics, "would put even Superman to shame."

As Bosley Crowther of *The New York Times* put it, "The frenzied action is filled with hair-raising, side-splitting adventures, a wild goose trek across Germany, including slugging guards, knocking out Raymond Massey, car chases, and incidental sabotage. You need to turn to the comics to see action like this."

At the end, only three of the original crew, depicted as "The Three Musketeers," remain alive. In a feat of astonishing daring, they manage to mow down fields of armed Nazis as part of their plan to commandeer a German aircraft ready for a bombing attack on the waterworks of England.

After subduing the Nazi security guards protecting the plane, the three Allied airmen take off. But before they reach the English Channel, they release a bomb aboard the plane to destroy a German munitions factory.

At the end of the movie, Flynn proclaims, "Now for Australia and a crack at those Japs."

Flynn had to memorize many lines in German, which he delivers fluidly and smoothly during scenes depicting his friends' interrogation by Nazi guards.

At one point, Flynn tells Reagan, "I don't want you to upstage me. I've become used to sharing co-billing with females like Ann Sheridan or Bette Davis. But sharing such a billing with a male is a bit hard for me to take, sport."

Ultimately, Flynn demanded that Reagan's best scene be transferred to him, a demand that eventually led to a widely observed argument between Flynn and Walsh. Of course, the two men later made up, but Walsh nonetheless insisted he wanted Reagan to interpret the scene. In it, Massey has prisoner Reagan brought into his office, hoping that the American might reveal the secrets of a newly developed American bomber plane.

Although the character played by Massey speaks English, Reagan uses double-talk, inventing works such as "thermacockle" and "dermodyne." He later knocks Massey out, eats his breakfast, and helps the other prisoners escape from the heavily guarded Nazi compound.

Reagan delivers a few good quips, although some of them come at inappropriate times. The Allied soldiers are being chased by a Nazi patrol intent on killing them. When the pilots' stolen German car runs out of gas, Reagan says, "This is the first time I ever ran out of gas with a couple of guys."

There was a certain irony in one of Reagan's lines. He is awakened by a member of his crew. He complains, "Why do you have to wake me up when I was having a date with Ann Sheridan?" He'd just completed *Juke Girl* with Sheridan, with whom he had had shared intimacies that went way beyond those of a mere "date."

Desperate Journey's incarnation of a malicious but incompetent Nazi: Raymond Massey.

When Kennedy, a co-star in *Desperate Journey,* lunched one day with Reagan, he had just completed *They Died With Their Boots On* with Flynn.

"I heard on every picture, Flynn has some young actor following him around panting," Kennedy said. "On this one, it's not Helmut Dantine, but Ronald Sinclair. In the General Custer movie, it was a young man named William Meade. He was a rich kid set to inherit a fortune and was a great guy, just the kind Flynn likes—handsome, athletic, fabulous body, and a crack polo player. In spite of all his money, he wanted to act. Flynn got him a job as an extra. Then tragedy struck. During the filming of the massacre of Custer and his army at the Little Bighorn, Meade fell from his horse onto his sword, which pierced his heart. Flynn went into mourning, and rightfully so. The whole cast was saddened by the passing of that kid."

Alan Hale, Sr. was by now a familiar face to Reagan, having worked with him before, most recently on *Juke Girl.* He usually liked to have lunch with Flynn, but that ritual was put on hold whenever Flynn retreated at noontime to his dressing room with Sinclair.

Hale amused Reagan, telling of his adventures making movies with Flynn. "Once I, along with three other actors, were chatting and having a few nips with Flynn in his dressing room. All of a sudden, Lupe Velez appeared. She just walked right in, ignoring us, and unzipped Errol and went down on him. As she was sword swallowing, she looked up and saw this statuette of the Madonna and Child on his dressing table. She broke off her suction to cross herself and beg for forgiveness from the Madonna, then resumed her work. She's a complete exhibitionist."

[On December 14, 1944, Velez, despondent over her latest unsuccessful love affair, took an overdose of sleeping pills and died.]

Flynn kept badgering Reagan to come to his Mulholland Farm, high above Los Angeles on Mulholland Drive, for drinks and dinner. Finally, Reagan agreed, but insisted on bringing Jane, warning Flynn, "My wife is a lady—so cool it."

Flynn obviously must have found that amusing, as he'd seduced Jane long before her husband ever did.

Later, Jane and Flynn pulled off the charade, never letting Reagan know that, years prior to their get-together, she'd been an overnight visitor.

An article in *Photoplay,* quoting Reagan, revealed his newest impression of the Aussie: "Here was not a swashbuckler's eyrie, but the home of a man with quiet culture. Books on philosophy, adventure, the best fiction, copies of bespoke travel in foreign lands, a musical library of the best symphonic records, everywhere the evidence of taste and thoughtful living. I had to revamp my image of Errol. Here was a man with a capacity—and a need—for friendship."

In *Desperate Journey*, unlike in most Flynn pictures, romantic entanglements almost didn't exist, since the cast was mainly male except for Coleman. Nonetheless, Flynn maintained his reputation as an ace seducer, although he ran into trouble with Dantine.

The handsome, gracious Austrian was twenty-five years old.

He told Reagan, "It's so ironic. Here I am playing a *Luftwaffe* pilot and also a Nazi pilot in *Mrs. Miniver*, and I'm one of the most anti-Nazi men around."

Biographer David Bret summed up Flynn's sexual dilemma during the filming of *Desperate Journey.*

"Dantine, like actor Patric Knowles, soon found himself fighting off Errol's amorous advances—though had Errol been aware that the young man was Jewish, he most definitely would not have been interested. Dantine had long since set his sights on Tyrone Power, and according to a statement given at the time by his friend, Tallulah Bankhead, as Power was away fighting in the war, Dantine was 'saving himself' for his lover's return."

Back on the set, Flynn turned his sexual attention onto the youngest actor on the set, Ronald Sinclair, who was only "barely legal" at the time. A native New Zealander, he was known as a pretty boy with a baby face.

Flynn confided in Reagan, "Unlike you, *this* Ronnie is a hell of a lot more cooperative in satisfying my sexual desires. He's a sodomite's dream fantasy come true. I think he's straight, and he complains that I hurt him, but he always gives in to me. He wouldn't dare turn down the star of the picture."

In the middle of filming, the U.S. government sent word to Reagan that he had only two weeks to finish his work on *Desperate Journey.* Jack Warner had not succeeded in getting him a more extended deferment. Walsh had to reschedule his shooting, and begin to film scenes out of sequence. There was great pressure. Reagan later wrote: "Long shots of my back were saved for a double after I was gone."

A minor actor, David Casey, later said, "My claim to fame is that I once played Ronald Reagan in a movie, but only my back."

To Reagan's amazement, he learned that Wasserman had renegotiated an even more profitable contract than his recent one, this one authorizing a salary of $3,500 a week for forty-three weeks of work annually.

"But I thought Warner contracts usually called for forty weeks of work, annually. Why the extra three weeks?" Reagan asked.

Wasserman explained, "I knew that Warner wouldn't go higher than $3,500 a week. That's more than he's paid any star, including Flynn. Those forty-three weeks, spread out over seven years, will eventually total more than a million dollars. As you know, you once made a film called *Million Dollar Baby,"* Wasserman said. "Thanks to this contract, you, Mr. Reagan, are now MCA's Million Dollar Baby."

At long last, success," Reagan lamented. "The moment it happens, I go into the Army on a soldier's pay of $250 a month."

***

Unlike Jane Wyman, Reagan often liked to stay home at night, reading newspapers or listening to the war news. In contrast, she wanted to go dancing almost every night. Before he went into the Army, he made a deal with her, agreeing to take her out as often as possible.

With a nanny looking after Maureen, Reagan and Jane became regulars at the Brown Derby, followed by dancing at the Cocoanut Grove or the Trocadero. Chasen's became their favorite dining venue, as Reagan considered its chefs the finest in Los Angeles.

Increasingly, they went out with other couples, especially Barbara Stanwyck and Robert Taylor. Apparently, neither Stanwyck nor Reagan ever learned

Baby Maureen and Jane tell Reagan goodbye as he heads out early to report for duty at the War Propaganda Department. For a while, at least, Jane's parting sally to him was, "Win one for the Gipper."

that their respective spouses had had a brief fling together during the filming of *The Crowd Roars.*

Sometimes, particularly at Chasen's, Jane and Reagan were seen dining with their boss, Jack Warner, and his wife, Ann Page. They were also friendly with agents Lew Wasserman and his wife, the former Edith Beckerman, and with Jules Stein and his wife, the former Doris Jones.

But Jane detested Reagan's new friend, director Sam Wood, who'd helmed him in *Kings Row.* Politically, she viewed him as "to the right of Josef Goebbels." Still a liberal Democrat, Reagan seemed to enjoy endless political debates with the virulently anti-communist Wood. Perhaps this was the beginning of Reagan's training for his presidential debates of the 1980s.

Finally, Jane told him, "I've had it! I've got other things to do than sit around listening to you guys go at it. From now on, count me out. I'll make other plans."

It was at that time that Jane began to "date" Van Johnson, the strawberry blonde, freckle-faced singer, actor, and dancer, who was being groomed to appear in all those "Boy-Next-Door" roles in World War II-era movies.

Her friend, Lucille Ball, had introduced them. Ball had been instrumental in launching Johnson's movie career. He'd appeared with her and with Desi Arnaz in the movie, *Too Many Girls* (1940).

She told Jane, "I just adore Van, and he'd be the perfect escort to take you dancing. Not only is he a good dancer, but he won't put the make on you...ever! He plays ball for the opposite team."

"Oh, I see," she said.

Jane explained the situation to Reagan about her need for an escort, telling him that "Van is harmless, although I doubt if I can trust him around you."

He told her, "This Johnson boy sounds like a fine choice for you."

Johnson and Jane became intimate friends on their first date. She later said, "Van is marvelous. He's dedicated to having a movie career, but he's also a lot of fun. He's a fabulous dancer, but I kept up with him. I was flattered when he complimented me on my dancing. In some clubs, we took over the floor, the other couples standing back to watch us go. I felt the years disappear from my age. At the end of the evening, I got a peck on the cheek."

Over the next few months, Jane was photographed with Johnson many times. Insiders such as Hedda Hopper and Louella Parsons knew that Johnson was a "vanilla date," but much of the public began to believe that Jane was cheating on her husband while he was at home changing Baby Maureen's diapers. There were rumors that "Hollywood's Most Ideal Couple," as they were dubbed in the press, were actually on the dawn of breaking up.

Reagan knew that he would be away from Jane for weeks at a time during his military service, and it seemed that Jane's arrangement with Johnson would be most suitable.

Johnson was often invited to the Reagan's house for one of her home-cooked dinners, since he was leading the bachelor life. He jokingly kidded Jane in private, "If you ever decide to dump that handsome hunk of yours, I get first grabs."

"Oh, Van," she answered. "How you boys talk."

Jane and Johnson had reasons other than dancing as motivations for their dating.

Each served as a "beard" for the other. Johnson was carrying on a clandestine affair with the dancer/actor Gene Kelly. On Broadway, Johnson had been Kelly's understudy during his hit show, *My Pal Joey,* where he played a womanizing louse. With a Hollywood contract, Kelly had made *For Me and My Gal* (1942) with Judy Garland, in

310

which he'd played another heel trying to avoid the draft.

Jane and Johnson deliberately were seen together in the early part of any given evening. But often, they slipped away and separated before the night was over. Sometimes, Jane didn't arrive home until two o'clock in the morning. Apparently, Reagan never questioned the lateness of her returns home.

Johnson often disappeared into the arms of Gene Kelly, Jane preferring the arms of Dennis Morgan or John Payne. This arrangement would continue through the war years and beyond.

No one seemed to suspect what was really going on behind the scenes, with the possible exception of Reagan, who had already been alerted to his wife's dalliances with both Payne and Morgan.

Unlike her own slow rise to fame, Johnson seemed to be "storming through 1942" (Jane's words) in his movie career. He'd been cast as a cub reporter opposite Faye Emerson in the filming of *Murder in the Big House* (1942), during which he was asked to dye his eyebrows and hair black. He'd also had a small role in MGM's *Somewhere I'll Find You,* starring Clark Gable and Lana Turner.

"Gable and I played poker a lot," Johnson later said, "although he told me in the beginning, 'I don't like fags.' Not so Lana. She adores us boys. Problem was, the damn director, Wesley Ruggles, terrified me so much I kept blowing my lines."

On a few nights, Jane was seen with both Johnson and his new friend, Keenan Wynn, who had made his screen debut in *Somewhere I'll Find You.*

Wynn had married Eve Lynn Abbott, but in the beginning—for obvious reasons—she was not included in their outings. Kelly was usually involved with actress Betsy Blair (his eventual wife) and wasn't always free. Johnson admitted, "Keenan is not the prettiest face in the world, but I love him dearly. We're an item. In spite of his looks, he's a hot number in bed."

Johnson, when not with Jane, was often seen out with "Keenan and Evie," as he called them. Rumors spread that they were a threesome, as Jane revealed to Reagan one night.

"That's My Boy!" by VAN JOHNSON'S DAD

Modern Screen

Reagan gave Jane permission to "date" handsome Van Johnson, with his clean-cut boy-next-door look. Perhaps Van's gender preference for men reassured everyone that he wouldn't pose any serious threat to the Reagan marriage.

Since Broadway, Gene Kelly had been dancing into the arms of Van Johnson.

Keenan Wynn...Van Johnson's secret love.

311

"That's fine with me," he said, "providing you don't make it a foursome."

***

Before heading to Warners to play a supporting role in Olivia de Havilland's latest movie, *Princess O'Rourke,* Jane complained to the ever-patient Reagan: "I detest Olivia. I don't have anything against her personally, but I envy her roles, which I think should have gone to me. On the set, I'm going to be ever so polite to her. After all, I'm an actress and can pull that off. It wouldn't do me any good to let her know how I feel about her. I'll have to talk to her sister one day. I hear

Amour and Scandals Royal: Princess O'Rourke (Olivia de Havilland), disguised as a "commoner," is helped and hosted by the kindly Jane Wyman, who is married, as part of the plot, to Jack Carson.

Joan Fontaine loathes Olivia. Maybe Joan could deliver the real story about her sister."

"It sounds like you have the same kind of envious relationship with Olivia that I have with Errol Flynn. We don't want to be them, we want merely to take over their movie roles."

When Jane reported to work at Warners for the filming of *Princess O'Rourke*, the first person she encountered was De Havilland, who had arrived early. The star of the picture graciously invited Jane for a morning coffee in her dressing room. To Jane's astonishment, she discovered that De Havilland envied the choice roles being funneled to Bette Davis, just as much as Jane envied parts going to De Havilland. In spite of her envy, however, De Havilland maintained an uneasy friendship with Davis.

"Jack Warner still thinks of me as an *ingénue* and doesn't give me the meaty roles I want." De Havilland complained. "I wanted to star in *The Letter,* a role which, of course, went to Bette. I even wanted the role she played in *The Man Who Came to Dinner* opposite Monty Woolley. I think Ida Lupino often gets better roles than mine. I wanted her part in *The Hard Way* (1942), but I was turned down."

After enough Hollywood gossip, De Havilland became very businesslike. "Now, let's go over this script. It not only will be directed by Norman Krasna, but he wrote its script. That will make it extra difficult for me when I have to tamper with some of his lines."

Before even going over the script, De Havilland told Jane, "Remember, I'm of royal blood in the movie, and I act regal even when *incognita* as a princess. You are a commoner—in fact, I want you to act drab and common, married to a slob like Jack Carson. At no point are you to take the spotlight off me. Imagine yourself as a lady-in-waiting in my shadow."

Originally, Fred MacMurray had been slated for the Robert Cummings lead, and he probably would have been more convincing as an airplane pilot studly enough to produce male heirs, the hope of the princess' uncle (Charles Coburn). MacMurray, however, dropped out, pleading previous commitments to Paramount.

When she'd first read Krasna's script, De Havilland rejected the role of the princess, claiming that she would not report to work if she was assigned the part. Confronted with her defiance, Jack Warner ordered that she be suspended. As her replacement, he contacted Alexis Smith, asking her to test for the role and go through a wardrobe fitting. But before a contract could be drawn up with Smith, De Havilland had a change of mind and reported back to work, adhering to an erratic, diva-driven schedule that forced Krasna on many a day to shoot around her.

Princess O'Rourke was a Cinderella-in-reverse tale, evoking a precursor of a roughly equivalent movie released in 1953, *Roman Holiday,* that starred Audrey Hepburn as a demure but rebellious princess in Rome.

Princess O'Rourke was a light comedy set in wartime Washington, D.C., with Olivia de Havilland cast as Princess Maria, fleeing from an unnamed European country after being driven out by the Nazis.

She is on a visit to the nation's capital with her Uncle Holman (Charles Coburn). Claude Rains had lobbied for the role, but lost it to Coburn.

Love, American style: Jack Carson and Jane Wyman set a good example for a lonely, misguided monarch.

Disappointed with the traditional and tired blood lines of conventional European royalty, Coburn is seeking a fresh, "virile" American as a proper consort prince for Maria.

Traveling incognito, and presumably terrified of flying, she swallows some sleeping pills aboard a flight piloted by Eddie O'Rourke (Robert Cummings). When the flight has to turn back because of bad weather, Cummings can't arouse Maria from her pill-induced slumber, so he graciously hauls her off to his apartment, where she will presumably recover, unharmed, from the effects of the pills.

From there, the plot thickens. When the Princess awakens, Cummings assumes that she is "Mary Williams," an impoverished European refugee. "Mary" is subsequently befriended by a very down-to-earth couple, Jean Campbell (Jane), the wife of Dave Campbell (Jack Carson.)

The mistaken identity plot thickens and complications ensue.

Finally, it all ends happily, with a White House wedding presided over by Harry Davenport, playing a Supreme Court Justice. A lookalike for the president's dog, Fala, makes his screen debut.

In the film, the princess writes a note to her suitor, Cummings, which the little Scottie dog delivers to his room. The setting, which accurately replicated the interior of the White House, was created by designers on Warner backlots.

A New Yorker, Norman Krasna was a playwright, screenwriter, pro-

In the early 1940s, Fala was the most famous dog in America. He's depicted here beside his owner, Franklin Delano Roosevelt.

In *Princess O'Rourke,* the role of Fala as a symbol of the president himself was assigned to a (canine) stand-in.

ducer, and film director. Jane had first met him when she had a bit role on his movie, *The King and the Chorus Girl.*

Krasna was mostly known for writing screwball comedies involving mistaken identity. For his script of *Princess O'Rourke,* he won an Academy Award.

Not only did Carson and Jane lead a strong supporting cast, but they were joined by other major talent, notably an elegant Londoner, Gladys Cooper, playing a governess and secretary to the princess. Jane frequently had tea with her at four o'clock.

She later recalled, "Dame Gladys was the most impressive actress I ever worked with."

Born in 1888, Cooper had begun her career on the stage as a teenager in Edwardian musical comedies before going into dramatic roles in silent films. She delayed her arrival in Hollywood until 1940, where she began to play a series of character parts, often cast as a disapproving,

Gladys Cooper: Aristocratic and domineering.

snobbish, aristocratic society woman. Famous roles include her casting in *Rebecca* (1940), starring Laurence Olivier and Joan Fontaine. The year Jane met Cooper, she was also cast as the domineering mother of Bette Davis in *Now, Voyager* (1942), which would bring Cooper an Academy Award nomination as Best Supporting Actress.

Jane chatted briefly with Julie Wilson, who had been cast as a stewardess. She was terribly disappointed in her reduced status as an actress. As Jane well knew, she'd been one of Reagan's leading ladies in *International Squadron.*

During the year he'd filmed *Princess O'Rourke,* Coburn also starred in *The More the Merrier* for which he would win a 1943 Oscar as Best Supporting Actor.

"Because Ronnie has screened *Kings Row* countless times, I must confess I've come to hate you," Jane said. "You seem so nice in person, but such a monster on screen."

"Don't let my niceness fool you," Coburn said, jokingly. "I have a black heart—in fact, I'm just a dirty old man."

During the making of *Princess O'Rourke,* Carson, in later life, admitted that he'd served once again as the "beard" for Jane during her illicit romance with Dennis Morgan. Ostensibly, Morgan made frequent visits to the set to see his best friend, Carson. "We lunched with Jane in the commissary and later retreated to my dressing room," Carson recalled. "I'd slip out discreetly and leave Dennis and Jane to pursue whatever perversions they wanted to—just kidding, folks. The meetings with Jane and Dennis became easier in the future because Warner cast all of us in pictures together. In fact, my next picture was with Jane."

De Havilland conflicted on several occasions with Cummings. He ran into frequent scheduling conflicts, as he was also filming *Between the Girls* at Universal. Knowing that he was a secret cross dresser, film crews teased him endlessly about the title of the movie.

When De Havilland did show up on the set, she was infuriated to find that Cummings was shooting at Universal. Often, she'd have to deliver her lines to a stand-in. She was also frustrated that Coburn kept forgetting his lines, calling for numerous retakes in his scenes with her.

The tension between De Havilland and Warners intensified as shooting progressed, or didn't progress, on *Princess O'Rourke.* Suffering from low blood pressure, De Havilland began to arrive late and leave early. Some days, she called in sick.

Her frustration with Warners led to a lawsuit. Unlike Bette Davis, who lost her own bitter legal battles with Warners, De Havilland ultimately prevailed.

The production of *Princess O'Rourke* was one of the most troublesome vehicles ever turned out by Warners. Although filmed mostly in 1942, its release was held up for almost a year because of legal issues, most of them revolving around De Havilland and her lawsuit to get out of her contract.

Before the eventual release of *Princess O'Rourke,* a firestorm of criticism came from Washington and its wartime Bureau of Motion Pictures. A copy of the film was shipped for screening. Within a day, a strongly worded letter of objection arrived from BMP officers, citing that the script had not been pre-approved. Nelson Poynter, the director of the BMP Office in Hollywood, called on Warner at Burbank. He accused Warner Brothers of "recklessly using the war for background incidents in an opportunistic attempt to capitalize off America's epic battle rather than to interpret it."

He also objected to the depiction of the President, who remained looming somewhere in the background. "You make him sound like a busybody," Poynter charged. "You've also caricatured the Secret Service and made fun of our Allies among European nobility." In spite of these stern objections, BMP did nothing to stop the eventual release of the picture.

In general, Jane was mostly singled out for decent reviews, and in some ways, *Princess O'Rourke* marked a turning point in her career as it provided a showcase for her comedic talents. She was especially good and appraised as "Sparkplug capable with her foil, Jack Carson." For the most part, the picture got good reviews, *Variety* defining it as a "spritely, effervescing, and laugh explosive comedy-romance." It enjoyed moderate success in its day. When it was re-released decades later, modern viewers were not as kind.

***

It was early morning in the household of Barbara Stanwyck and her husband, Robert Taylor. Pouring her morning coffee, Stanwyck went to the phone to hear Reagan's cheerful voice. "You're always so god damn pleasant," she said to him. "Not me in the morning. I'm like a caged tiger who hasn't been given any red meat in four days."

"It's my fault for calling so early, but I wanted to alert Bob that I'm on my way to pick him up."

She put down the phone and walked down the long hallway toward the bathroom. "Junior, she shouted through the closed bathroom door, over the sound of running water, "your boyfriend is on the phone."

"Coming!" Taylor shouted back.

"I bet that's what you say to him," she said, sarcastically.

Stanwyck had always taunted him about his homosexuality, and she accused him of having a crush on Reagan. Taylor had repeatedly denied that.

Reagan was driving Taylor south, to a local marina, where their mutual friend, actor Robert Stack, had rented a small yacht to take them on a weekend sail to

When gossips got word of Robert Taylor's entry into the armed forces, they joked that an even more effective fighter might be his wife, Bloody Babs, shown here brandishing scissors in the tough, lady-like but macho style for which she had become infamous.

Catalina. Jane didn't want to go, and Stanwyck wasn't invited.

Over a quickie breakfast, Stanwyck demanded to know why she couldn't come along. "I know that the late, much-lamented Carole Lombard used to accompany Gable, you, and the other guys on hunting trips."

"This is different," Taylor told her. "It's like boys' night out. The guys will be nude on the boat wanting to get a suntan all over. No place for a woman."

"God knows what you boys will do with your dicks hanging out," she snapped.

At the sound of a honking horn, he jumped up from the table and grabbed his bag. "Take care, Queen!" He always called her that.

"Aren't you going to kiss me?" she asked.

"Later, when I come back," he said, heading out the door and racing toward Reagan's car, since they were running late for their rendezvous with Stack, an actor as handsome as they were.

Reagan was much closer to Taylor than he was to Stanwyck, an actress he found intimidating, although Jane seemed to admire her style and commanding presence. Since their marriage in 1939, Taylor and Stanwyck had become Reagan's closest friends, included in their inner circle of Joan Blondell, Dick Powell, James Stewart, Claudette Colbert, and Eddie Albert from their *Brother Rat* movies.

Fan magazines propagandized the marriage of Barbara Stanwyck and Robert Taylor as another ideal couple, evocative of the marriage of Ronald Reagan and Jane Wyman.

Here, Stanwyck poses with Lt. Robert Taylor at home from active duty in the Navy.

The night before picking Taylor up, Reagan had told Jane, "Barbara treats Bob like an unruly child, and she always humiliates him, suggesting he's not a real manly man. You know, unlike us, they occupy separate bedrooms."

"Even on their honeymoon?" she asked. She'd heard rumors that Taylor and Stanwyck had a "lavender marriage," Both of them were known for sleeping with others on the side. Taylor had had affairs with Howard Hughes, Errol Flynn, and Tyrone Power, but with some females, too, including Virginia Bruce and even Greta Garbo, when he'd made *Camille* with her. He'd just completed *Johnny Eager* (1942), in which he'd been intimate with Lana Turner. Stanwyck had had her own affairs, dating from the A-list with Marlene Dietrich and Joan Crawford.

"Bob and Barbara must come together sometime," Reagan told Jane. "The other day, Bob told me that she always wants to control the fuck. As for their honeymoon, Bob claimed he'd found her so overpowering and commanding that he became impotent—and she'd mocked him."

"That's a sure-fire way to give a man an erection," Jane said.

"Evenings with them can be rough," he said.

"Better than time out with the Battling Bogarts," she said. "Mayo Methot, as you remember, once pulled out a revolver and threatened to kill him."

He recalled an evening at dinner when Stanwyck was on a rampage, attacking her husband's masculinity.

"No wonder the press is hailing us instead of them as the ideal couple," Jane said. "It looks like we're going to remain unchallenged as Hollywood's most ideal couple," he said. "Me in uniform while you're staying behind."

"I guess the press will write about all your daring aerial combats shooting down

Göring's *Luftwaffe* pilots," she said. "Of course, you'll still be in California behind a desk somewhere."

On the boat to Catalina Island, about a mile offshore, Reagan, Stack, and Taylor sailed with a three-man crew. The rental of the yacht was a gift from Howard Hughes, the aviator and billionaire. Reagan had heard rumors that both Stack and Taylor on occasion were "Hughes' boys."

It was Stack who first stripped down and suggested that Taylor and Reagan drop their trunks, too. "Let's get a suntan all over."

Not afraid to take off his trunks, Reagan stripped down and headed for a mat on the deck. Taylor was the most reluctant, but, he too, took off his trunks.

On the trip to Catalina, Stack had talked about his friend, John F. Kennedy, who had just left Hollywood for Navy duty. Reagan was familiar with Ambassador Joseph P. Kennedy, but knew nothing of his children. Stack said that, "After the war, he plans to get into politics from his home state of Massachusetts. Probably run for Congress. After that, the Senate. And, then, the Presidency."

"I wouldn't take that ambition too seriously," Reagan said. "Doesn't every red-blooded American boy want to be President of the United States, even me?"

***

To Blondell, Jane recalled the last dinner party she had hosted for Stanwyck and Taylor. "It was a disaster."

"Ronnie held back, but Bob and Barbara were drinking heavily. Bob teased Ronnie about his first days in Hollywood when Ronnie was touted as "the next Robert Taylor."'

"I'm still working on it," Reagan had retorted.

At the party, Taylor had revealed that he'd never seen the 1940 movie, *Waterloo Bridge,* in which he'd played a soldier and Vivien Leigh had played a ballet dancer/prostitute in London.

"I don't get off on too many of my pictures," Taylor said. "When Louis B. Mayer learned I'd not seen *Waterloo Bridge,* he held a special screening of it in his living room in front of friends."

"You seem so casual about the movies you make," Jane said. "How unlike Ronnie. When tour buses stop by our house, Ronnie runs out the door and invites them in for a screening of *Kings Row.*"

"Jane exaggerates," Reagan said, looking embarrassed. "I have shown it on occasion to a very select few of our friends."

"Yeah, right," Jane retorted. "He defines 'friends' as anyone listed in the Los Angeles phone book."

"I understand why Junior doesn't want to see his own films," a rather drunk Stanwyck had chimed in. "After all, I've made a couple with the guy myself. I prefer to work with a real man. I've just finished *Ball of Fire* with Gary Cooper (1942). Talk about a real man."

Robert Stack *(seen above with Barbara Stanwyck)* often went swimming with Stanwyck, Jane Wyman, Reagan (when available), and Robert Taylor.

The first time Stanwyck saw Stack in a bathing suit, she told him, "Your body is perfect, a piece of sculpture when compared to Bob or Ronnie."

Then she looked over at Reagan. "You look like a real man," she said. "Not like pretty boy over there. How about it, Reagan? Why don't you and I make a movie together one day?"

"I'd love it, but I don't see that happening."

On the night before Reagan's departure for San Francisco and his new post with the U.S. Army, Jane threw an intimate dinner party for him, inviting Joan Blondell, Dick Powell, Jack Benny, and Mary Livingston. Pat O'Brien showed up with his wife, Eloise, and George Brent escorted his wife, Ann Sheridan. Reagan and Brent had made up in the aftermath of Brent giving him a black eye when he and Sheridan were filming *Juke Girl*.

Taylor said he was anxious to put on a uniform, but that his wife objected.

"You're too old," Stanwyck told him. "They want young men, not grandfathers."

Taylor was only thirty-one.

[In February of 1943, Taylor would be sworn into the U.S. Navy under his original name of Spangler Arlington Brugh. Although he would apply several times for active duty, he was turned down because of his age. Instead, the Navy sent him to Livermore, California, to make seventeen training films for Naval Air cadets. Reagan, in contrast, would find himself making films for the U.S. Army Air Force.]

***

Upon the release of *Desperate Journey, The New York Times* referring to it as "comic book stuff," but the fast-paced action scenes, under Walsh's direction, were generally singled out for praise.

Warner was horrified that *Desperate Journey* opened at the same time as Flynn's notorious trial on charges of statutory rape, where the term "in like Flynn" was coined.

The fear was not real. The courtroom revelations about Flynn's romp with underage girls actually generated publicity that sent audiences flocking to movie houses. *Desperate Journey* earned more than $2 million, considered a big success in 1942 dollars.

By the time the film was released, Reagan was not wearing a military uniform from the Warners' wardrobe department, but a real one issued by the U.S. Army.

Hollywood, 1942: Lt. Ronald Reagan shows up in uniform with his wife, Jane Wyman, for the premiere of *Tales of Manhattan* at Grauman's Chinese Theatre.

Chapter Nine

Jane and Reagan Go to War

Drafted Into the U.S. Army,

Reagan Becomes a

"Bloodless Celluloid Commando"

His Popularity Roars to an All-Time High,
Even Though Jane Refers to Him as a "Has-Been"

Ronald Reagaon, on the ranch with his favorite horse, "Baby," took an athlete's pride in the grace of his body's "mechanics." But his poor eyesight kept him off the battlefields in World War II, although he promised to "kill as many Nazi beasts as I can."

He made propaganda films instead.

During a War Bond fundraising tour with John Payne, Jane wrote to her close friend, Paulette Goddard. "I'm traveling with the obscenely handsome John Payne. Men as sexy as he is should be rounded up and placed in a male harem for the girls to enjoy, especially me."

The day after Jane hosted Reagan's farewell party at their newly christened "dream house," she drove him to Glendale, where he caught the night train north to San Francisco. During their tearful farewell, he left her with a *cliché*: "Jane, keep the home fires burning, and take care of yourself and our baby girl."

Aboard the train, his identity shifted from that of a Hollywood movie star to a commissioned officer in the Army Air Corps, the predecessor of the U.S. Air Force.

As his train headed north during the frightening month of April, 1942, the publicity department at Warners was ordered, in cooperation with the U.S. Army, to inaugurate a massive buildup for Reagan and Jane. "We're going to use them as our propaganda couple to promote the U.S. War effort," Warner said.

Almost within the week, the studio's publicity department launched a campaign with such

MORE COLOR THAN ANY OTHER MOVIE MAGAZINE

Modern Screen

OCTOBER
15¢

CAPT. RONALD REAGAN

Poster Boy: America, in league with Hollywood as symbolized by Ronald Reagan, goes to war.

headlines as "MR. AND MRS. AMERICA FIGHTING THE WAR." One feature story was headlined, "REAGAN & WYMAN—SO LONG BUTTON NOSE."

In spite of how it misled the public, Reagan and Jane aided Warners' publicity campaign with zeal. *Variety* reported: "Ronald Reagan left today to join an Army unit in San Francisco, leaving behind his beloved young wife (Jane Wyman), and their daughter, Maureen. She told the press, 'I will wait for him, pray for him, and live for the day when Ronnie comes marching home.'"

Before heading out, Reagan had been photographed looking at horrific pictures of the swollen bodies of dying boys and girls being deliberately starved to death by Nazi soldiers in the ruins of Warsaw. "I hate war," Reagan told the press. "But the scourge of Hitler's Nazism has to be wiped from the face of the earth."

He would never be sent to fight on the battlefields of Europe or the Pacific. He did not reveal that his poor eyesight would keep him stationed in California throughout the duration of the war.

Jane was quoted as saying, "Now the war is real for us. Now it's Ronnie's war, and it's also my war."

Although Jack Warner had powerful political influence in Washington, time had run out on his ability to get any more deferments for Reagan. In his final call to Reagan, Warner held out a titillating promise: "There's a hell of a lot of buzz going around that you're a shoo-in for the Oscar for your performance in *Kings Row*."

Northbound on that train, Reagan was saddened to think that the lucrative contract that Lew Wasserman had negotiated with Warners wouldn't help him now. Household and living expenses would have to come out of Jane's salary. It was clearly understood that studio paychecks ended whenever an employee entered the Armed Forces.

Jane Finds "My True Love" in the Arms of John Payne.

As reported by *Screenland* magazine, "Just when Reagan's career and his personal life are rich with fulfillment comes his call to duty. If he is called, the one hindrance may be his deficiency of eyesight. Without his glasses, he can't see clearly more than five feet from him. Ronnie's adoring wife, Jane Wyman, isn't saying a word. But there's a hurt in her face as she goes gaily around Hollywood these days. Little Maureen Elizabeth, the Baby Reagan, is too young and healthy to realize the scope of the drama."

Arriving at Fort Mason, Reagan had to submit to another physical, a medical procedure which he continued to define as "jiggling my balls." He was assigned the job of supervising the loading of convoys heading for Australia. "Our strategy was to build up a force there to prevent Japan from pinning down its flank on Australia and then being able to turn that attack onto the West Coast of the United States."

He often chatted with soldiers heading out to the Pacific. "They talked the same lingo," Reagan said. "They were enraged at the attack on Pearl Harbor. Most of them had the same goal. To quote them, 'I want to kill as many Japs as I can before they

In the spring of 1943, Reagan took his orders like any other man in military service. They included early morning calisthenics. Surely he could not have imagined at the time that one day, he would be Commander-in-Chief.

come for us.' Never in my life have I met so many young Americans seeking revenge—and they'd get it, too."

At the time, the somewhat archaic Fort Mason was configured mainly as a Cavalry post, and Reagan felt at home there, as he went horseback riding in his riding breeches, boots, and spurs. Men not in the Cavalry often mocked "these cowboys on horseback," reminding them that the Polish Army on horses had been "systematically slaughtered by the mechanized might of Nazi tanks."

Long after he left Fort Mason, Reagan recalled his most terrifying experience there. "I had to stand in line in my underwear with a long line of guys waiting to get vaccinated. The day before, seven of our men had died from inoculation from a faulty vaccine. I could only pray that the problem had been solved. When that needle was jabbed into my arm, I paused for a silent moment, waiting to see if I were going to drop dead. Obviously, I survived. But now I know what is meant when someone says, 'I was sweating blood.'"

On his second day at Fort Mason, Colonel Bob Ferguson came out to greet him. They were friends, from having served together in the 11th Cavalry. Ferguson had worked on Reagan's movie, *Sergeant Murphy*, way back in 1938. After warm greetings,

Ferguson turned Reagan over to his supervisor, Colonel Philip Booker.

In his memoirs, Reagan described the colonel as "a small, slim man with the wiry physique of a horseman…blunt, quiet, and all business." He soon learned that Booker was a fan of his Brass Bancroft films, in which he'd played an agent of the Secret Service. "But just because I'm a fan of yours doesn't mean that you can give me any shit."

One night, Booker invited Reagan and three of his fellow lieutenants to his home for dinner. At table, Reagan learned that Booker was a graduate of the Virginia Military Institute, as had been depicted in Reagan's movie, *Brother Rat.* Reagan brought this up at table.

The reaction from the colonel came as a shock to him. "I saw that piece of crap," Booker raged. "Nothing has made me so god damn mad in my whole life. You guys libeled my *Alma Mater.*"

At Fort Mason, Reagan avidly followed the war news from Europe and the Pacific. It was grim—in fact, 1942 was the darkest year of the war for America. Reagan's fellow officers and enlisted men were despondent over bulletins coming in from the Pacific. Bataan had surrendered "to the Japs," the papers said, and that stunning defeat was followed by the fall of Corregidor. The Japanese attacked Mandalay *[the second-largest city and the last royal capital of the country then known as Burma],* forcing the colonial British to flee from Indo-China to India. In Europe, the news was consistently horrible. The Nazis had launched V-2 rockets onto war-torn London, thereby obliterating massive acreage in the British capital's densely populated East End.

Among his fellow servicemen, Reagan could not escape the fact that he was a movie star, the only one serving at Fort Mason. Many of his fellow soldiers asked for his autographed picture and posted it on the inside of the door of their locker. When quizzed about the implications of that by Colonel Booker, Reagan said, "I'd feel more comfortable if their pinup was Betty Grable instead of me."

"I would, too," replied the colonel. "I guess it takes all kinds to make up an Army."

At night, the horny young men quizzed Reagan endlessly about what they inelegantly termed "Hollywood pussy." They wanted to know which female stars "put out" and what their bust measurements were. He answered each question with his usual good nature, without giving too many specific details and definitely avoiding insights into any of his own sexual relationships with the stars at Warner Brothers.

Sometimes the questions were very provocative, even salacious. Larry David of St. Louis said, "I once saw a picture of you in the paper with Lana Turner. I heard this rumor that one night in New York, uptown in a night club in Harlem, she sucked off five big, dark-skinned bucks in the men's room. Is that true?"

"That's a new one on me," Reagan said. "I know Miss Turner. She's really a fine lady."

On some nights, Reagan—even though he didn't really seem to belong—went out "on the town" with his fellow servicemen, trying to fit in with their pursuit of hell raising, female flesh, and liquor.

Back in Los Angeles, he shared some of those memories with Dick Powell, telling him that San Francisco was crawling with prostitutes who'd flocked there to service the military men shipping out. "Any guy could get laid, providing he had at least ten bucks in his pants," Reagan said.

He recalled meeting a "dyed blonde vixen" (his words) from his native Des Moines. She tried to pick him up, and when he turned her down, she focused on a handsome young lieutenant instead. "She told a bizarre story that one night, she seduced a man with two penises. I guess when it comes to a man's body, anything is possible, certainly a freak. She disappeared that night with the lieutenant, although he assured her he had

322

only one dick."

"The town was also crawling with homos," Reagan said. "They, too, were flocking in droves to San Francisco, and they scored plenty. Unlike the prostitutes, they didn't charge. Men turned to them when they had spent their monthly stipend from the government."

He later said, "I was always opposed to gays in the military, although realizing, of course, that they were already there and had been since the days of Alexander the Great. There was a lot of stuff going on in the Fort Mason barracks at night, but I said nothing. It was a touchy issue, and I didn't want to get involved. 'Hear no evil, See no evil'—that's who I am."

[In the closing years of Reagan's presidency, the nation's chief executive was challenged for a statement from a journalist about his stand on gays in the military. He had no comment. Later, he told Donald Regan, his chief of staff, "That's a problem I'll leave for George Herbert Walker Bush. Let him stick his neck out."

In the late 1940s, Reagan recalled another issue associated with his experiences at Fort Mason. One night in a bar, he was approached by a homosexual with a Southern accent who told Reagan he was a playwright and had written a drama for Tallulah Bankhead. "He was drunk and volunteered to give me a blow job," Reagan said to Powell. "After the guy told me I was the best-looking thing in pants, he reached out and felt me up and I almost punched him, but then, decided not to. He didn't look like the violent type."

"I thought nothing of the matter until I was introduced to Tennessee Williams at a Hollywood party. I was divorcing Jane Wyman, and he told me that she was being considered as the star of the (1950) movie version of his stage play, The Glass Menagerie. *Williams claimed we'd met during the war in San Francisco and that he'd unsuccessfully propositioned me in a bar. Then I remembered that nasty little encounter."*

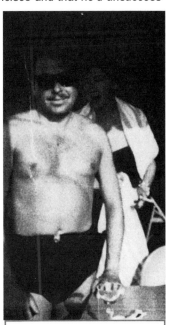

"I thought you were very aggressive just reaching out and feeling a man like that," Reagan told Williams. "For copping that feel, I want you to write a great role for me, the equal of that Stanley Kowalski part you gave to Brando."

"Your request is my command," Williams later quoted himself as having said to his friend, the author Donald Windham. "As a movie star, I'd place Reagan in the same position I put Lana Turner when MGM assigned me to write a movie scenario for her."

"I remember that," Windham said. "You called it 'a celluloid brassiere.'"

"In Reagan's case, let's change that to a celluloid jock strap," Williams said.

Reagan later admitted to Dick Powell and Robert Taylor, "I was sometimes overcome with guilt as I watched these scrawny little boys boarding ships heading for the war in the Pacific while I, robust, virile, and more than six feet tall, stood by, sending at least some of them to their deaths."

Sometimes, Reagan's duties included showing teenage schoolboys around the public areas of Fort Mason. "If the war had lasted long enough, some of

Tennessee Williams in Key West, Florida, 1947. He once propositioned Reagan.

these guys with pimples would have been drafted into the Army themselves," Reagan recalled.

"I was usually asked three questions: How many Nazis have you mowed down? How many Japs did you kill? Did you ever date Betty Grable?"

Despite his rank as an Army lieutenant, Reagan never escaped his status as a movie star. His superior officers ordered him to give interviews to the press and to deliver short speeches at local benefits and War Bond rallies. His big night came at the San Francisco premiere of *Kings Row.* Colonel Booker ordered him to deliver a morale-boosting pep talk before the first-night audience. Seats for the first showing of his proudest cinematic achievement would be reserved for select members of the Armed Forces. From the podium, Reagan faced a sea of combat-ready men in uniform.

Near the end of his tour of duty at Fort Mason, Reagan was ordered back for three days in Los Angeles to help launch the USO program, spearheaded by, among others, Bette Davis and John Garfield, with such stars as Joan Crawford and Marlene Dietrich lending their support as well.

Entertaining the troops: Marlene Dietrich at a USO show...trying to make the boys happy.

Back from her War Bond tour of the Southeast, Jane welcomed him home, but he later expressed concern about her dark mood. "She was polite and loving on the surface, but seemed strangely distant as if her interests were elsewhere," he said. "Something was on her mind, and I didn't know what. It seemed that without my presence, she had done just fine on her own. On the train back to San Francisco, I was left feeling rather empty about my homecoming."

He confided these concerns to his agents, Lew Wasserman and Jules Stein, and to Dick Powell, who may or may not have known that Jane had fallen deeply, perhaps hopelessly, in love with John Payne.

Back at Fort Mason, Reagan claimed, "I smelled trouble," when he was ordered to report at once to Colonel Booker's office. There, he was told that he'd been summoned to the office of the commanding general of the post. Booker thanked him for his help with the USO program before warning him, "In the presence of the general, you'll address him in the third person, and you stand at attention and salute."

"Yes sir!" Reagan snapped.

***

Reagan recalled that he was very nervous when he was summoned into the office of the Commanding General. When it came time to write his memoirs, the general's name escaped him.

"In fairness to you, I've heard complaints that you're sick and tired of being a showhorse for all our starstruck Cavalry brass," the General said. "You are, after all, our only resident movie star here, eating cauliflower and hot dog stew with the rest of us."

"With your permission, sir," Reagan said. "I only make personal appearances when ordered to do so by my superior officers. In the future, sir, I will refer all such requests to your office for your approval. You can decide whether the request is from some starstruck fan wanting an autographed photo and a look at a movie star. You know best, sir, what is needed for morale and the War Effort."

"That sounds about right to me, Reagan," the General said. "I thought all these appearances were just your attempt to keep your name before the public. A lot of fans will forget a lot of you stars by the end of the war."

"I hope not, sir," Reagan said. "Sir, right now, I've been placed in the position of 'Ronald Reagan, have uniform, will travel.' I do, sir, what I am ordered to do."

"Good to hear that, Reagan," the General said, "because I have an order of my own. I have a directive from the office of President Roosevelt. He has declared that throughout the country, cities are to celebrate 'I Am an American Day,' with military parades, entertainment, and pep rallies with morale-boosting speeches. All of that will be followed by a War Bond sale. It's all for the War Effort, of course. And we'll need a major Hollywood star to sing the National Anthem."

"Sir, my wife, Jane Wyman, is a singer, and I'm sure she'd love to fly to San Francisco to sing the National Anthem."

The General cast his most disapproving look on Reagan. "I'm sorry to deny you a conjugal visit, but I had something else in mind. Frankly, I'm a Jeanette MacDonald fan myself. I never miss one of her pictures with Nelson Eddy, although I find him a piece of fluff. I have no idea what she sees in that silly fart. I understand you've bedded most of the Hollywood beauties. I'm sure you know Miss MacDonald."

"Sir, she's an MGM star," Reagan said. "I worked with the women of Warner Brothers."

"I don't give a flying fuck what studio she works for," the General said. "All I know is I want Miss MacDonald in San Francisco to sing the National Anthem and to meet me. Otherwise, it's your ass, Reagan. DISMISSED!"

After leaving the General's office, Reagan, as instructed, reported to Colonel Booker. He had already received a report from one of his liaison officers. "Good work, Reagan," Booker said. "I understand you pulled the General's stinger before he even got warmed up."

Back in his office, Reagan immediately placed a call to Louis B. Mayer in Culver City. Getting his secretary on the phone, he told her that he had an official request from the Commander General of the U.S. Army base in San Francisco. His call was put through to Mayer right away. In the conversation that ensued, Reagan conveyed the General's request for the services of MacDonald.

"I'm the wrong man to ask for any favors from Jeanette," Mayer said. "She hates my guts. I just terminated her contract. But I'll have a friend of hers convey the request."

"Thank you, Mr. Mayer," Reagan said.

"Anything for the War Effort," Mayer answered. "Otherwise, Hitler will be burning Jews on Hollywood Boulevard."

Within two days, MacDonald called

Singing sensation Jeanette MacDonald, shown here with Clark Gable in *San Francisco*.

325

Reagan, claiming that she would appear. Assuming that she would, he had by then worked out arrangements for her appearance.

Reagan and members of the press were on hand to greet the singing star at the San Francisco airfield where her plane landed. In front of reporters, she told Reagan, "You're far more handsome in person than you are on the screen, and you look good in your movies, too."

"Flattery will get you anywhere with me," he said, jokingly.

It seemed that half of San Francisco turned out for the holiday celebration. MacDonald gave the grandest rendition of "The Star Spangled Banner" he'd ever heard. "Her voice could be heard all the way to Tokyo," Reagan recalled.

She agreed to another performance, one that Reagan had arranged just for men in uniform.

Throughout San Francisco, thousands of men were waiting to be shipped out from temporary housing in, among others, the mammoth Cow Palace and abandoned factory buildings. The soldiers had been confined to these dreary quarters and, in most cases, weren't allowed off base, based on the government's fear that they might accidentally reveal classified information. In those days, San Francisco was crawling with spies for the Japanese.

The venue for MacDonald's performance, and the 17,000 servicemen slated for attendance, was the infield of San Francisco's Greyhound racing track.

When Reagan announced MacDonald, she was received with wild applause. "Maybe you guys would have preferred Betty Grable," MacDonald said from center stage. "But what you see is what you get." At that, the servicemen applauded even more loudly, as she launched into a repertoire of hit songs from her movies.

At first, Reagan had been concerned that the singer would be "too operatic, too high brow" for the audience, but she won them over.

Of course, "The Battle Hymn of the Republic" was mandatory, but she got the most applause when she sang "San Francisco," the name of the song and the title of her hit 1936 movie with Clark Gable and Spencer Tracy. In the film, MacDonald had belted out her anthem, cheerfully and defiantly, in the dusty, earthquake-ravished ruins of San Francisco, "singing in that hokey but entertaining way," Reagan said. "Although Judy Garland had mocked Jeanette's performance in that film, the boys loved the song."

"The soldiers were so young, so full of hope," Reagan later said. "For hundreds of them, it would be their last night in America. Jeanette knew that. I knew that. Tears were in our eyes as Jeanette and I embraced at the end of her concert."

Without his knowing it, the brass was about to end Reagan's days as an officer at Fort Mason. One morning, Colonel Booker demanded his appearance in his office. "Kid, we're shipping you back home to Los Angeles. In your new assignment, you'll be able to spend most nights in the bed of that beautiful wife of yours, the one the press calls 'Pug Nose.'"

"What gives?" Reagan asked. "I got the impression that the Army deliberately likes to assign soldiers to bases away from home."

"This is a special case, a whole new Division," Booker said. "On orders from General George Kenny, you've been assigned to the Air Force base in Los Angeles. You're going to make training and propaganda films for the Army."

Booker filled him in on the details: Although Jack Warner, who had been assigned the rank of Lieutenant Colonel, had not succeeded in getting yet another deferment for Reagan, he had nonetheless used his considerable influence to get him transferred to a newly created propaganda division of the Army Air Corps. It was called the First Motion Picture Unit (FMPU). Its task involved the production of morale-boosting films. Lew

Wasserman, Reagan's agent, had also been instrumental in arranging Reagan's new assignment on his home turf.

"At last the Army got something right in your new assignment," Booker said. "In my thirty-four years in the Army, this is the first time I've seen the brass make sense by putting a square peg into a square hole."

[Reagan later claimed, "I've been called a square several times, but that was never seen as something to be proud of. I just wish the Colonel had used a different image, calling me a round peg fitted into a round hole."]

New films!! From a wartime production company whose government-sanctioned, government-funded mission rocked Hollywood. It's the U.S. Army's FMPU (First Motion Picture Unit)!

After a final salute, and as Reagan was heading out the door, the Colonel called him back. "I never told you this, kid, but I liked you a hell of a lot more than I ever let on. In my short time with you, I came to think of you as my son. Now get the hell out of my sight before I get too god damn sentimental."

***

Before departing for San Francisco, Reagan had given Jane a public relations lecture. "Exchange that mink coat for an apron from the kitchen. No more dancing with Van Johnson at the Troc. Hide that costume jewelry, even though it's fake. Wear sensible clothes and shoes, none of that glamorous stuff that will look whorish to soldiers fighting in the mud. At all times, appear as a dutiful housewife and loving mother. After all, you and I are the poster young man and woman of Hollywood at war."

"As much as I dislike what you're ordering me to do, I think you're right—god damn it and to hell and back," she answered.

For the most part, Jane followed Reagan's suggestion and toned down her nightclubbing and partying. But she had another boss, too, and that was Jack Warner.

The call from her mogul boss had come in at ten o'clock on Saturday morning. That was an unusual hour for Warner to call, but he said it was an emergency. She thought some star had fallen ill, and that she was being summoned to replace her on a film set.

A star had, indeed, fallen ill, and Jane was being summoned to replace her, but not in a film. Warner had been informed by the Victory Committee that Rita Hayworth had become ill just prior to her scheduled departure on a War Bond fund-raising, month-long tour of America's Southeast. Warner wanted Jane to replace her.

"You're to tour with John Payne," Warner said. "I loved you two together in *Kid Nightingale* (1939). You both are singers and can both entertain a crowd. You get along with him okay, right?"

"I admire his talent and found him pleasant to work with," she said, demurely, concealing the depth of her passion for her upcoming traveling companion. She agreed to the tour and its terms, and Warner gave her the names of the people to contact about transportation and logistics.

After concluding the call with her boss, bubbling over with enthusiasm, she phoned Joan Blondell. "If there's any man who can make me forget that Ronnie is away, it's

John Payne," she said. "For me, that's like winning Lotto. I could have gotten César Romero for a traveling mate. I'll really get to know what it's like to be the wife of John on this tour."

"Have fun, kid," Blondell said.

Before leaving on her tour, Jane met with actor William Demarest, who had been her agent in the 1930s. He weighed in on his opinion of Reagan's tour of duty in the Army. "I don't think he minds it as much as some of the guys like Robert Taylor and Jimmy Stewart. They are leaving booming careers. In spite of *Kings Row,* Reagan is still mired in B pictures, so he's not giving up that much. Of course, he'll miss you and the baby."

"I'm not sure Ronnie agrees with you," she said. "He thought his career was about to blast off like a rocket. Also, he'd just signed a million dollar contract, and now the money's been cut off."

After talking to Demarest, she had only a day to pack and make herself ready for the tour, leaving instructions with Maureen's nanny. In a call to Payne, she learned that he, too, was eager to depart.

On September 9, 1942, Jane embarked on a month-long tour of the South, beginning in the bluegrass State of Kentucky.

At many of the rallies, Payne auctioned off his necktie and was forced to keep buying new ones, many of them selected by Jane. One woman offered to pay $1,000 for Payne's underwear—"or $2,000 if it's soiled a bit." He politely declined.

Unlike Reagan, she did not suffer from a fear of flying. "I flew a few overcrowded crates during that tour," she recalled, "but I wasn't afraid. John was by my side, and he gave me security. Occasionally, I had nightmares about my friend, Carole Lombard, going down in that plane. Clark (Gable) was still mourning, despite the tons of mail from women around the world, many of them willing and able to replace Carole as his fourth wife."

In every town in which they stopped, there were endless luncheons, usually with the town mayor, the councilmen, and anybody viewed as a local dignitary. "But why must they always serve chicken *à la king*?" Jane asked Payne.

From the very beginning, she had been served chicken wings in hot sauce. She found the dish usually made her ill, and she complained later that the food was too greasy. "Southern cooks seem to cook all their vegetables in what they call fatback," she said. Complaining of stomach troubles, she switched to hot tea, fruit juices, and unbuttered

Help Win the War! Buy a Bond! Wyman with Payne in *(top photo)* Spartanburg, SC and *(lower photo)* in Burlington, NC.

328

toast, losing fifteen pounds before the end of the tour.

The question most asked of Payne was, "How's your love life?" He had a pat response: "How's yours?" The most frequent question put to Jane was, "What is Ronald Reagan really like?"

Her pat answer was, "A scholar and a gentleman…in all, a very nice and kind man. Great husband. Great father."

Payne usually sang first, followed by a song from Jane, then a duet from their joint appearance in *Kid Nightingale.*

Because of hotel room shortages, Jane and Payne were not always able to get a suite, or even adjoining rooms. Sometimes, they were on separate floors. No matter, he planned to slip into her room at night to sleep with her, leaving before dawn and heading back to his own quarters.

As Jane later told Goddard, "I fell in love with John in Kentucky and even more in love with him when we visited his native Virginia. We did shows in Roanoke. In the South, John reverts to his Southern gentleman accent. They love *chittlin'* talk in these parts. The only time he is not a gentleman is when he makes love. Then he becomes Tiger Man."

"What a lucky gal you are," Goddard said. "You get Payne and I'm settling for Burgess Meredith."

At one point, Jane found herself in the same airport with her longtime friend, Lucille Ball. "It took a god damn war for Hollywood to recognize me as a singer," Jane complained. "Instead of getting cast as the lead in a musical, like Betty Grable, I'm allowed to sing in bond rallies. They're lining up camp shows for me, too."

"Even so, we're late to the game," Ball said. "Bob Hope was shaking his butt and Dorothy Lamour was bouncing her twat before servicemen even before Pearl Harbor."

"I hear they're even sending Hedy Lamarr on tour," Jane said. "She can't sing, can't dance, and can't tell jokes."

"All she has to do is stand before an audience and let the guys look at her," Ball said. "Perhaps she can take off her clothes like she did in *Ecstasy.* Or, better yet, she might tell the guys what it's like to get fucked by both Mussolini and Hitler."

"My friend, Jack Carson, can tell jokes," Jane said.

"Don't forget Orson Welles," Ball said. "He can do magic tricks. Astaire can dance, and Veronica Lake, the midget, can show off her peek-a-boo hairdo."

Sometimes Jane was asked "Who is taking care of Baby Maureen?" She answered that it was Nelle Reagan, her mother-in-law.

As the tour progressed, Jane began to part with some of the possessions in her handbag, beginning with a tube of lipstick which she gave to a woman who bought a $1,000 War Bond. Later on, she sold her earrings, telling Payne they were costume jewelry. She even gave away her compact and her gold cigarette case, a gift from Reagan, as an incentive to persuade someone to buy $2,000 worth of War Bonds.

In Norfolk, Virginia, at their most successful bond rally, she and Payne netted $52,000 worth of War Bond sales.

[Greer Garson later infuriated Jane when she reminded her that her War Bond rally in Huntington, West Virginia, drew a crowd of 12,000 fans, larger than any of the rallies where Jane and Payne appeared.]

In North Carolina, one man asked if they had a War Bond worth $15,000.

"Business must be good for you," Jane said to him.

"I'm a gambler," he told her. "Like marines and doctors, we gamblers also contribute to the War Effort. Therefore, I'm glad to invest some of my profits in War Bonds. By the way, I cheat at cards."

"You come up here with that $15,000, and I'll give you a kiss," Jane promised.

That promise of a kiss inspired her with an idea: She'd heard that some of the stars were selling mouth-to-mouth kisses on their tours. Hedy Lamarr had once sold a kiss for $25,000. When Jane tried that, there were no bidders.

Later, she suggested that Payne should try to sell a $25,000 kiss. Amazingly, at one stop, he got a taker—a rather effeminate man. "I'm loaded and I'm buying."

The crowd booed him and Payne rejected the offer. "You should have gone for it," Jane scolded him that night. "As you kissed the guy, you could have said to yourself, 'I'm doing this for god and country.'"

After heading a War Bond rally in Spartanburg, South Carolina, Jane retired to her hotel suite, where Payne joined her within the hour. For the first time, he talked to her extensively about his recent divorce from Anne Shirley, with whom he had not been living during the final turbulent months of their marriage.

Anne Shirley...John Payne's wife, and Jane Wyman's competition.

Throughout the tour, but especially on this evening in Spartanburg, Jane expected a proposal of marriage from Payne, with a recommendation that she divorce Reagan. But, as she'd later confide to Goddard, "He never asked me—not once—even though he told me he couldn't live without me."

"How like a man," Goddard quipped.

Throughout the remainder of World War II, Payne enjoyed his life as a bachelor. Shirley's public image as a sweet, dewy-eyed innocent was beginning to wear thin with the public, and her audience was dwindling. In 1944, she abandoned her screen career.

For Jane, the highlight of her tour, other than the love-making of one of Hollywood's greatest studs, was a luncheon at the White House sponsored by Eleanor Roosevelt as a means of thanking the entertainers for their contributions to the War Effort. Years later, Jane remembered the event with a certain irony. "I never became First Lady, but at least I married a future President of the United States."

At the end of the tour, Payne revealed his plans. He was only a year younger than Reagan, so he knew he wouldn't be sent to fight the war in Europe or the Pacific. But he decided he was going to enlist as an Army pilot. He was already an expert aviator. "I'll teach young guys how to fly planes, at least the mechanics of it. War veterans will teach them how to handle themselves in aerial combat."

Three weeks after his return to Hollywood, he showed up to take her dinner in uniform. "He looked like a poster boy for Uncle Sam," she said.

Upper photo: A hardworking First Lady (Eleanor Roosevelt) and *(lower photo)* a First Lady "who might have been"—shown here dressed with a 1940s sense of military chic.

He told her that he'd been assigned to the base at Long Beach, California, where, as it turned out, he remained for the next two years. She promised she'd slip away and drive down to see him every chance she got.

***

No sooner had Jane returned from her tour of the South than she received a call from Bette Davis, who informed her that she and John Garfield were opening the Hollywood Canteen in premises that had originally been conceived as a stable. The premiere of "this home away from home" for servicemen was scheduled for October 3, 1942.

Davis wanted Jane to be there at least one or two nights a week to entertain the servicemen, dance with them, and serve coffee and doughnuts.

Jane agreed, and Dennis Morgan was often her escort. Singing with him at the canteen provided the perfect cover for their continuing affair.

One night, Morgan told her about some casting news at Warners that surprised her. "As you know, I was supposed to be the freedom fighter in *Casablanca,* opposite Reagan and Ann Sheridan. Of course, that didn't happen. You may remember that I replaced Bogie as Cole Younger when he bolted from our film, *Bad Men of Missouri.* But did you know that I was the original player slated to appear as the star of *The Sea Hawk?* But Jack Warner decided that Errol Flynn would play a better swashbuckler. I was also set to play General Custer in *Santa Fe Trail* opposite Flynn, but that part went to Reagan."

"Well, now that Ronnie and a lot of other stars are in the military, you can clean up as Warners' leading actor," Jane said.

She was right. Two years older than Reagan, and therefore not immediately eligible for the draft, Morgan did not enter the service, and continued to make movies throughout the war, beginning with *Wings of the Eagle* (1942) in which he co-starred with Jack Carson and Ann Sheridan. "It was a real flag-waver," Morgan told Jane. His last such film was the controversial World War II drama, *God Is My Co-Pilot* (1945).

As Jane later said, "Dennis fought the war on the screen, not off it."

Only weeks before she departed for her tour with Payne, the Treasury Department in Washington had launched its War Bond tours, calling on Hollywood stars to provide the entertainment. Stars were assigned to seven separate units, each sent to various destinations that included 353 cities and towns during the month of September alone.

Jane was notified that she'd been assigned to Group 5, whose other players included Veronica Lake, Greer Garson, and Payne. At a launch party, Jane chatted with Garson and Lake and with some of the stars from Unit 6, which comprised her friend, Goddard, along with James Cagney, Reagan's friend, as well as Hedy Lamarr and Irene Dunne.

Jane also became a performer at the USO's Camp Shows. She preferred not to travel too far afield, and she therefore confined her appearances to bases in California, where she was joined by stars who included Lucille Ball, Betty Hutton, Lena Horne, and the Andrew Sisters.

From 1941 to 1947, the USO sponsored some 400,000 shows with such stars as Bing Crosby, Judy Garland, Frank Sinatra, and even Hattie McDaniel—"Mammy" of *Gone With the Wind.* As Jane remembered it, "Danny Kaye was a tough act to follow."

Wayne Broyhill, an enlisted man, had a different point of view. "Danny was okay telling jokes and all. But we were surrounded by guys all day. We wanted female flesh, and that was provided by Jane Wyman. She did a sexy number and showed us her gams. The boys yelled and hooted until they were hoarse. That Ronald Reagan is a lucky bastard."

Jane never went overseas for camp shows, although she was often invited to do so by the likes of Edward G. Robinson, her former co-star, or such luminaries as Martha Raye, Merle Oberon, and Al Jolson. Demurring, she said she needed to be near her young daughter.

Many stars were asked to appear in film clips slated for screening in theaters across the country. A Newsreel Division of the War Activities Committee of the Motion Picture Industry was formed in connection with this War Bond drive. Payne was asked to make one of these clips with Dorothy Lamour. On the day of the shooting, Jane went with him to the studio.

"My God," she later told Goddard. "Lamour practically tore John's pants off him. She was one hot-to-trot bitch, who wouldn't control her horny paws. He actually seemed to enjoy the attention. He'll pay for that."

Beginning with Carole Lombard in 1942, twenty-eight performers lost their lives during their War Bond and morale-building tours because of illness, diseases, and plane crashes. In 1943, a plane carrying a USO troupe crashed outside Lisbon, Portugal, severely injuring Broadway singer Jane Froman. Despite her confinement at the time to a wheelchair, she fought her way back to the stage to entertain again.

[Jane later noted that Hollywood was adapting Froman's story into a Technicolor movie entitled With a Song In My Heart *(1952). She lobbied aggressively for the role, only to lose it to Susan Hayward. "I desperately wanted that part, almost more than any other role. But it went to Susan Hayward, that red-haired bitch. At least I managed to tear Ronnie away from her entangling web. Hayward can't sing. They had to dub her with Froman's voice."]*

***

Leaving Fort Mason, Reagan reported to work in Hollywood, joining the newly created First Motion Picture Unit (FMPU), created by General Henry H. Arnold, who was nicknamed "Hap." He commanded the Army Air Corps, which later morphed into the U.S. Army Air Force.

Reagan would stay at this command post throughout the duration of the war, never leaving the United States, although many of his fans were made to believe that he was fighting with Allied troops in Europe.

As the months passed, Reagan was amazed at the growth of the Air Corps. In 1939, at the beginning of the armed conflicts in Europe, it had some 25,000 men and fewer than 3,900 planes. By the time of the June, 1944 D-Day invasion of Normandy, Arnold commanded some 2.5 million men. American factories were turning out 150,000 planes per year.

Photoplay carried the news that "Jane Wyman and wee daughter are probably the happiest people in town, since husband and daddy Ronald Reagan has been temporarily sent back to Burbank to make government film shorts."

Before Reagan signed on, Warner had already been making propaganda films for the War Department, including such releases as *The Tanks are Coming* and *Service with the Colors,* each targeted at young men who had not enlisted.

When Reagan went into the army, only three percent of men in the movie colony had signed up. Dozens upon dozens of directors, actors, screenwriters, sound engineers, producers, cameramen, and other technicians had not joined.

Reagan's first office was at the old Vitagraph Studios in Los Angeles until that location proved too small. At that point, he and the vast crew were transferred to the Hal

Roach Studios in Culver City. Because of the undisciplined crew there, and reports of "outrageous behavior" among the former movie people, locals referred to it as "Fort Wacky." It also became better known as "Fort Roach."

At Fort Roach, Reagan faced 1,000 enlisted men and officers, most of whom had had no military training except for what they'd received working on war pictures at the various studios. As one technician, Ralph Davidson, told Reagan, "We know how to stage a war only if it's called for in the script."

Reagan's superior officer was Paul Mantz, who had been the most famous stunt pilot in Hollywood. In 1937, he'd helped Amelia Earhart learn navigational skills, but had rejected her offer to fly with her as co-pilot during her ill-fated (final and disastrous) attempt to fly around the world.

Star Power as Hollywood Goes to War: Lieutenant Reagan (who defined himself, facetiously, as "the American Goebbels" after Nazi Germany's notorious propaganda chief), at the FMPU, organizing propaganda and training films.

Mantz had once run an air charter service dubbed, "The Honeymoon Express" because it carried so many illicit lovers to secret rendezvous destinations. His clients had included Howard Hughes, Clark Gable, James Cagney, and Errol Flynn. "I should write a tell-all," Mantz told Reagan. "You won't believe some of the love duos—even trios—I flew, with genders getting all mixed up." Mantz had also worked on flight scenes for such pictures as *Test Pilot* (1938), starring Clark Gable and Spencer Tracy.

During his tenure at Fort Roach, Reagan constantly appeared on the covers of magazines. He was always in full uniform, always with a smile, and most often with the Stars and Stripes waving behind him. In the history of the Presidency, no man, other than Dwight D. Eisenhower, had ever been photographed so frequently in uniform.

Reagan met many young recruits who complimented him on his daring aerial exploits as depicted in such films as *Murder in the Air* and *International Squadron*. He didn't tell them that those scenes had been faked, and that any daring aviation feats had been performed by stunt pilots.

Hollywood at War: Hollywood's most celebrated stunt pilot (Paul Mantz) found a huge demand for his services at Reagan's FMPU. Much of it involved staging aerial dogfights for the Army's propaganda and training films.

During Reagan's first week at Fort Roach, Jack Warner arranged for him to meet General Henry Arnold, nicknamed "Hap," the chief of staff of the Army Air Corps. These two men had jointly developed the idea of the First Motion Picture Unit for the production of Army training and P.R. films. Hap and Reagan blended harmoniously and learned to work well together. Hap told Warner, "The Reagan boy is my kind of soldier, my kind of man, a sharp shooter. I hear he's a real lady's man, too."

"That's putting it mildly," Warner replied. "During his first three years at Warners, all our starlets lost their virginity."

Arnold had several long talks with Reagan, focusing on military issues and convincing him that the future of the United States as a world power depended on its supremacy in the air. Amazingly, Arnold never learned that Reagan, one of his chief protégés, was plagued with an irrational terror of flying.

He viewed Reagan as one of his most effective propagandists. During his time at Fort Roach, FMPU would produce some 225 films, most of them with a running time of 30 minutes, although some lasted on the screen for only nine minutes. The cheaper ones were completed for less than $5,000, although longer ones cost as much as $15,000. Reagan starred in some of these films and narrated dozens more. Many of them have been lost or destroyed in the years since the war ended.

During his first months at Fort Roach, Reagan was deeply troubled about moral issues associated with the war and his films. He told Jane and some of his closest friends, such as Dick Powell, "Sometimes I lie awake thinking about these guys: Our films are shown to high school and college students. We glorify flying—just read our press releases. We claim flying is full of inspirational splendor, the roaring engines of bomber formations gliding through the clouds. In reality, as any R.A.F. pilot can tell you, flying is a grim and dangerous business. A man can die—in fact, he usually does."

Warner told Reagan that the U.S. government had more or less taken over the direction of his studio, using its facilities, when needed, to make propaganda and training films. The Army also provided outlines for A-list feature movies for them to shoot. "At our peak in 1939, we were turning out about a hundred films a year. In 1943, we were reduced to making only about three or four dozen. Of course, that means less work for Jane. Naturally, the war has really cut into our profits."

On most nights at Fort Roach, Reagan was allowed to go home to spend the night with Jane. On many a night, she wrote him a note that she'd be late, leaving Baby Maureen in the care of a nanny. Jane never explained where she was, and he was too polite to ask. Occasionally, she'd mention casually, "Oh, I was out with some friends, and forgot how late it was getting."

Reagan had met Oklahoma-born Owen Crump when he was a writer at Warner Brothers. In his new role with FMPU, Reagan found himself taking orders from Crump. A dynamic, rather overpowering personality, Crump was described by Reagan as "terse and tough."

At the time Reagan worked with him, Crump had wed Lucile Fairbanks, which made him the nephew-in-law to Douglas Fairbanks, Sr., and Mary Pickford. In time, that would lead to Reagan being invited to Pickfair, the home of the reclusive Pickford, America's former sweetheart, and her husband, Buddy Rogers.

Crump took Reagan to the screening of a picture he'd co-directed with John Huston. Called *Winning Your Wings* (1941), it starred Jimmy Stewart. "The aim of Jimmy's film was to inspire young men to forget baseball games, summer romances, football in autumn, and family vacations," Crump said. "The suggestion was that men should abandon those pursuits and enlist in the Air Force." Crump then uttered a statement that appeared to be outrageous: "When that film was shown in theaters, it incited 500,000 young men to enlist. I want you to turn out films as powerful as Jimmy's."

"It's a tough act to follow, but I'll try," Reagan said.

***

During the war, magazines were brimming with stories of male stars who had either been enlisted, been drafted, or somehow managed "to elude Uncle Sam."

Reagan came into contact with many of them, and read about those he didn't encounter. Among Reagan's closest friends was Robert Taylor, who appeared in war movies such as *Bataan* (1942), but he was told too old to be drafted. Nonetheless, in 1943, he enlisted in the Naval Air Corps and became a flight instructor. He also narrated the 1944 wartime documentary, *The Fighting Lady*.

Too old to enlist, Bob Hope and Reagan's friend, Pat O'Brien, traveled thousands of miles to entertain the troops.

James Stewart was one of the actors who became a genuine hero during the war. He joined USAAC in 1940, although initially he was refused entry because he was five pounds under the required weight of 148 pounds. But he talked his recruitment officer into ignoring his weight. He became a colonel and flew combat missions, eventually awarded the Distinguished Flying Cross.

It was Jimmy Stewart, who made the most successful American propaganda film, *Winning Your Wings*.

Repeatedly honored by the military, he rose to the rank of Brigadier General by 1959.

After seeing some of Reagan's training films. Stewart told him, "Real war is not like you depicted it. It's more deadly and insane, at times without reason or any type of morality, nothing but senseless death. It was execution in the air of young men who would never be allowed to finish their lives, either in Germany or in America."

Cary Grant and Errol Flynn each avoided military service, but David Niven volunteered and left Hollywood to return to war-torn England where he became a hero, his exact role in the service never fully explained.

Frank Sinatra avoided the draft and never served in any branch of the military.

A World War I veteran, Humphrey Bogart was in his 40s and too old to be drafted, although he frequently appeared in war movies, including the classic *Casablanca*.

Reagan said, "Bogie was in, the king of Warner Brothers, and I was out. And damn it, I didn't win the Oscar for *Kings Row*. Neither did Bogie, but his time would come again. Mine would not."

On August 12, 1942, the "King of Hollywood," Clark Gable, turned down a commission and entered the Army as a private. Perhaps as a swipe at Reagan and others, he said, "I don't want to entertain. I just want to be sent where the going is tough."

In January of 1943, after his involvement in a training program known as one of the Army's "90-day wonders," Gable graduated as a second lieutenant and aerial gunner. In England, he became part of a flying squadron, the 351st heavy Bombardment Group, known as "Hatcher's Chickens," named in honor of their colonel.

Gable did not escape the attention of Josef Goebbels' Nazi propaganda machine.

From Berlin, a broadcast was made: "Welcome to England, Hatcher's Chickens, among them the famous American cinema star, Clark Gable. We'll be seeing you soon in Berlin, Clark."

Before the war, Gable had been Hitler's favorite male movie star. *Der Führer* issued a specific order to try, if possible, to capture Gable alive, especially if his plane was shot down behind enemy lines. "If not that, I want his dead body brought to me."

While based in England, Gable carried out dangerous missions over Germany, including the bombing attack on the synthetic oil plants at Gelsenkirchen. In that raid alone, twenty-five Allied bombers were lost. Gable's plane returned safely, but riddled with five bullet holes. He was so daring in combat that many of his crew members felt—perhaps as a reaction to the fatal plane crash of his wife, Carole Lombard, in circumstances not associated with active combat—that he harbored a secret death wish.

After his military service in England, Gable asked to be transferred to the continuing war in the Pacific against the Japanese. He waited and waited until, as he said himself, "I felt discarded." After serving for nearly two years, he asked for a discharge from active duty. Ironically, that request was granted by a captain, Ronald Reagan, at Fort Roach.

Film star Ronald Reagan: Dealing with delicate ideological issues AND looking good while he was doing it. His fear of flying was not visible in this publicity shot for FMPU.

Lower photo: evidence of the growing military might of the US's wings of war.

[In the closing months of the War, Jane and Reagan visited Gable after his return to California. Jane had never mentioned her sexual encounter with Gable so long ago. At Gable's ranch in Encino, they discovered an aging movie star, graying at the temples and putting on weight. They learned that he consumed a quart of Scotch a day, having purchased an entire truckload of it when war had first erupted in Europe.

Gable told Reagan, "If Hitler had caught me, the son of a bitch would have put me in a cage like a gorilla and exhibited me throughout Germany. If my plane were going down, I would not have bailed out and allowed my capture by the Nazis for delivery to whatever fate lay in store for me."

Hermann Göring of the Luftwaffe had designated Gable as "one of the most wanted of war criminals."

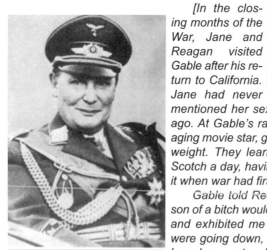

An effeminate pic of the director of Germany's *Luftwaffe*, the sadist, art collector, and morphine addict, Hermann Göring.

336

***

An upcoming king of Hollywood—at least in terms of box office receipts— was John Wayne.

Having met during the late 1930s, when both of them were struggling for stardom, Reagan and Wayne knew each other only casually. It wasn't until the late 1940s and early 50s that they finally bonded in their mutual goal of ferreting out communists who were allegedly "infiltrating" the movie industry.

But these two men did have a few tense encounters during World War II, when both of them remained in Hollywood. Across the country, boys in their late teens or young men in their early 20s flocked to see Wayne ("The Duke") in the movies. During the war he made some movies, including *The Fighting Seabees* (1944); *Back to Bataan* (1945), and *They Were Expendable* (1945).

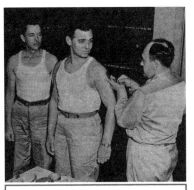

The King of Hollywood enlists! Clark Gable gets inoculated, just like every other guy, during his basic training.

These movies once prompted Reagan to quip, "To judge by his movies, John won the war against the Nazis and the Japs single-handedly."

When The Duke heard that, he told Ward Bond, "When you see Reagan again, tell him I'm going to rip out his right eyeball and eat it as an appetizer. I haven't seen him mowing down any Japs in this man's war."

Owen Crump called Reagan to his office one day to "bounce an idea off your head. "What about setting up recruiting desks in the lobbies of movie theaters, nationwide, that happen to be screening any of Duke's films?"

"I think it would work," Reagan said.

"John is even more of a hero to young boys than Jimmy Stewart is, and look at all the recruits he enlisted with his propaganda film"

Reagan rendezvoused with Wayne for dinner one night at the Cock n' Bull in Hollywood to feel him out on Crump's idea.

This military magazine documents how appealing the idea of Clark Gable's capture would have been to the Nazi propaganda machine. Hitler wanted him tortured and paraded, nude, and in chains, through the streets of Berlin.

Over steaks, Wayne became very defensive about not having enlisted. "You know I'm too old for the draft. I'm classified 3-A, which is a family deferment."

"I talked to your man John Ford, and he thinks you should do more for the war effort. That led Crump to come up with this idea about the lobby enlistments."

"I wish Ford would shut his god damn mouth about my status," Wayne said, flashing anger. "He's always urging me to enlist."

"That's what Ford told me, but he claims that you always come up with the excuse that you've got two more pictures to complete."

"It's not so easy," Wayne said. "Over at Republic, Herbert J. Yates is threatening to sue me if I walk out on my contract. He's even called the War Department seeking a permanent deferment for me."

Wayne also confessed a personal reason for not wanting to enlist. "I know it's selfish of me, but I've been waiting for years for my big break in films, and it's finally here. If I walk out now, I may never get this chance again. Don't you see the gamble I'm taking if I enlist?"

"I see it clearly," Reagan said. "I faced the same thing after *Kings Row,* but the War Department would not grant me any more deferments. I was carted off willingly."

"Hooray for you, the American hero," Wayne said, mockingly. "You've got to understand something. Some of the leading men of Hollywood, stars like Robert Taylor and Clark Gable, are in the military. All sorts of roles are opening up for leading men, and I want to take advantage. Hell, I've appeared with Marlene Dietrich and Joan Crawford, even Claudette Colbert. I got to fuck Marlene and Crawford. Not Colbert, of course. She's as much of a duke as I am."

He wasn't always overweight, pompous and jowly: John Wayne in a studio publicity shot for *Back to Bataan* (1945).

Before the end of Reagan's dinner with Wayne, Duke had agreed to the theater lobby enlistment campaign and even promised to go on a three-month tour of U.S. bases and Army hospitals in the South Pacific.

Years later, when Ford talked to Reagan about his dinner with Wayne, the director said, "I think the Duke has become a superpatriot mainly as an attempt to atone for sitting out World War II."

Not just Ford, but a lot of men Reagan knew in the movie industry had enlisted, including Robert Montgomery and Fox producer Darryl F. Zanuck.

In 1942, Jane and Reagan had attended the wedding of Wayne Morris, their *Brother Rat* co-star and Jane's former lover, to Patricia O'Rourke, an Olympic swimmer and sister to B-movie actress Peggy Stewart.

That same year, Morris became a Navy flier, piloting F6F Hellcats off the aircraft carrier *USS Essex.* A daring pilot, he shot down seven Japanese planes and contributed to the sinking of five large ships in service to the Japanese Empire. For his daring feats, he would be awarded four Distinguished Flying Crosses and two air medals.

Back at Fort Roach, Reagan met Brooklyn-born Dane Clark and co-starred with him in a wartime propaganda movie. Reagan later told Meredith, "Dane calls himself 'Joe Average,' but he really isn't. He has a law degree, and during the Depression, he was a boxer, baseball player, construction worker, and nude model. He told me as a model he got a lot of propositions, especially from homosexuals."

Previously stationed at Fort Roach, Clark had managed to make such war movies as *Action in the North Atlantic* (1943) with Humphrey Bogart, and *Destination Tokyo* (1943) with Cary Grant. Reagan arranged for both of these films to be shown at his military base.

[After the war, as Reagan floundered to find a suitable movie role, he noted that Clark at Warner Brothers shot way ahead of him, playing the surly artist opposite Bette Davis in A Stolen Life *(1946). He'd just appeared in* God Is My Co-Pilot *(1945) with Jane's good friend, Dennis Morgan. Exhibitors in 1945 named him the 16th most popular star at the box office.*

Clark was one of the first Hollywood actors to appear on television, which in the late 1940s was just emerging. He advised Reagan to do the same, but Reagan told him, "I can't see myself appearing on that little box."

How wrong he was.]

Actor Arthur Kennedy, who had played Jane's boyfriend in *Bad Men of Missouri,* was assigned to a post in the FMPU's wardrobe department, but he disliked his sergeant. When he applied for a transfer, he was very polite in describing his plight to Reagan. "Sir, my sergeant isn't the type to stand on a blood-soaked beach and yell, 'Onward men!'"

"I understand," Reagan said. "I'll see what I can do.' He obtained Kennedy a new post as assistant to the gardener at Fort Roach. "He spent a lot of time clipping hedges, but usually sneaked off the base at three o'clock and never got caught. That way, he could keep up with his drinking."

Reagan would appear for the first and last time in a movie, made on base, with Burgess Meredith.

Meredith admitted to Reagan, "I'm not a dashing swain, but in a kind of mongrel way, I chased the foxes." Over a period of time, that had included a group of A-list stars such as Hedy Lamarr, Ingrid Bergman, Olivia de Havilland, Peggy Ashcroft, Ginger Rogers, and Norma Shearer, plus a *ménage à trois* with a wealthy German lady and her lesbian lover.

Meredith was filled with amusing stories, telling Reagan that during sex with Tallulah Bankhead, she had shrieked, "For god's sake, don't come inside me! I'm engaged to Jock Whitney!"

Meredith was arguably the most accom-

Diminutive Dane Clark, a former nude model and boxer in New York, hit Hollywood in 1943. He tried to promote himself as a sex symbol, but suffered from the stigma of labels defining him as "the poor man's John Garfield."

plished actor Reagan ever appeared with, having starred in some of Hollywood's biggest movies and also achieving success on Broadway. Before joining the Army, he had scored big in the 1939 film adaptation of the John Steinbeck novel, *Of Mice and Men,* a story about hope, despair, migrant workers, and marital infidelity during the Great Depression.

As a means of avoiding confusion with a certain politician, the actor, John Kennedy of Massachusetts *(photo above)* opted to bill himself as Arthur Kennedy.

A talented, brooding actor of great intensity, Kennedy was assigned by Reagan the task of clipping hedges on their Army base.

"Most of the time, the guys thought Reagan was a square," Meredith said. "Very formal, very stiff, a man who obeyed the rules. But he had his ribald moments. His favorite (comedy) routine, believe it or not, involved demonstrating the Seven Stages of a Man's Life through a pissing routine."

Edmund Morris, in his biography of Reagan, described it as follows: "First, Reagan would imitate the Little Boy with bursting bladder, hoisting himself high on tiptoe. Then the furtive adolescent, a copy of *Esquire* in hand, making vague masturbatory motions. Next came Mr. Regular Fella, who unzipped, peed, zipped, washed, and exited whistling. The pansy followed, mincing up to the wall and ogling to the left and right, while taking as much time as possible *in flagrante.* He was pushed aside by the Athlete, who unfurled a prodigious member (he used the full length of this tie) and hosed the mahogany with such force that he staggered in recoil. Then the wobbling Drunk, spraying everybody in sight. Finally and pathetically, the Old Man doddered in, fumbling at his fly buttons—here he became cruel."

Arthur Kennedy, Burgess Meredith, and Dane Clark weren't the only actors working at Fort Roach. Reagan became lifelong friends with the strikingly handsome George Montgomery. After he married singer Dinah Shore in 1943, the newlyweds often doubled dated with the Reagans.

Reagan became aware of an argument percolating its way through Fort Roach, mostly in the makeup department, as to which was the better-looking actor, Reagan or Montgomery. Standing 6'3" and weighing 210 pounds, Montgomery usually won. Much of his well-muscled body had been developed by riding horses and working cattle on his family ranch in northern Montana, where he'd been born the youngest of fifteen children to Ukrainian immigrant parents.

As he told Reagan, he'd landed a job as a stunt man on an MGM Greta Garbo picture in 1935, only two days after his arrival in Hollywood. That had led to stunt work in cowboy films, and by the early 1940s, he was co-starring with such stars as Ginger Rogers and Gene Tierney. Coincidentally, he'd also co-starred with—and been seduced by—two of Reagan's girlfriends, Carole Landis and Betty Grable. Just prior to joining the U.S. Army Air force, Montgomery completed a wartime movie, *Bomber's Moon* (1943), in which he and Kent Smith escape from a prison camp.

While at Fort Roach, Reagan made future best friends in the most unlikely of places.

"I hated the son of a bitch when I first met him," said William Holden, who, during the war, became a Second Lieutenant in the U.S. Army Air Force, working in collaboration with the First Motion Picture Unit.

He recalled an early episode of his involvement in the Armed Services: "My friend, Richard Webb and I, from Paramount, went to Reagan's office at Fort Roach to present our credentials. He ordered us to stand at rigid attention while the fucker read laboriously all the regulations. I hated his guts. Once freed from this god damn dictator, I called him a son of a bitch when I left his office."

Holden had really wanted to join active service, and he resented having to report to the Motion Picture Unit. Its only advantage, he maintained at the time, was that he got to go home every night to his wife, the American actress Ardis Ankerson, who acted under the name of Brenda Marshall.

He related a memorable incident when, early one morning, Reagan and a camera crew were roughly

Tall, rugged, and handsome, George Montgomery wanted to be an interior decorator, but became a boxer instead. Drifting to Hollywood, he became a movie star.

He frequently went out on romantic dates with Reagan. Don't get the wrong idea: Singer Dinah Shore and Jane Wyman went along for the fun.

shuttled into the desert for a training mission. "It must have been 120° F., and our bodies were soaked with sweat," Holden said. "At noon, we were given a horrible lunch, Spam or something, and some rotting cabbage."

Hours later, back at the base, Holden said, "There must have been something wrong with the Spam. Every guy in the unit got the runs. At the barracks, there was a stampede to the urinals where 18 toilet bowls with no seats were lined up. In a mad dash it was first come, first dump. At one point, the noise sounded like fiesta night in Guadalajara."

"On the seat, I turned to look at the guy unloading next to me. It was Mr. Ronald Reagan, our captain. After that, Ronnie and I became best friends, or more aptly, 'asshole buddies' as Southern boys say. It was the beginning of a beautiful friendship."

Sometimes, Reagan was embarrassed that he had not served on the front, even though his eyesight had prohibited it. That was especially true when he had a reunion with his *Brother Rat* star, Eddie Albert.

It was the beginning of a beautiful, life-long friendship between William Holden and Reagan. But it began under unlikely circumstances.

"Ronnie and I were sitting on the can, side by side, suffering bouts of diarrhea from rotten Spam."

Albert's career with the Army had begun long before the United States entered the war, and even before the beginning of his film career. As a clown and high-wire artist with the Escalante Brothers' Circus, he had performed in Mexico. Privately, he was working for U.S. Army Intelligence, photographing Nazi U-Boats in Mexican harbors.

On September 9, 1942, he'd enlisted in the U.S. Navy, later becoming a lieutenant in the U.S. Naval Reserve, where he was awarded the Bronze Star for his bravery in the invasion of Tarawa in November of 1943. He rescued some 75 Marines under heavy enemy machine gun fire.

Back in Hollywood, Albert presented Reagan with an intricately carved fastener *[netsuke]* removed from the "uniform of a dead Jap." Reagan accepted the gift with a red face.

***

Reagan immersed himself in his latest gig as a military propagandist.

"Even when he came home, he talked about nothing but the war, speculating how the world was going to line up politically when victory came," Jane told her friends. "He detested Josef Stalin, our ally, telling me that politics make strange bedfellows. He hated communists, especially home-grown Reds."

At Fort Roach, Reagan found himself making films again. Either in front of the camera, or as a narrator, his film and radio experience was highly valued.

In his first Army film, he interpreted the title role of *Mr. Gardenia Jones* (1942), even though he objected to his character's name. "Somehow, Gardenia doesn't strike me as a fit name for a man." Lending their talents was an impressive cast, beginning with Laraine Day, his leading lady from when both of them had starred in *The Bad Man* (1941).

Supporting players included Charles Winninger, Fay Bainter, and Chill Wills. The director was George B. Seitz, whose career had begun in the Silents when he'd directed

The Perils of Pauline (1914).

Mr. Gardenia Jones was a documentary depicting the work of the USO, showing how it provided both recreational and morale-boosting services for American troops. In the movie, Gardenia has enlisted before the Japanese attack on Pearl Harbor. When the invasion occurs, Reagan is seen in aerial combat, mowing down Japanese planes, a bit of fantasy for a man afraid to fly.

In a surprise to both the cast and their director, this flag-waving war propaganda film ran into threatened censorship problems with the War Department. Despite the film's patriotic overtones, their objections almost prevented MGM from releasing it. The War Department censors objected to scenes that depicted soldiers jumping up with joy at the opportunity of taking a shower in the canteen, or sitting in overstuffed, comfortable chairs. "This Army," as noted by *The New York Times,* "feels this is not good for morale, as it implies that there are no showers or other comforts for soldiers in military camps."

After expressing its objections, the War Department allowed the film to be released anyway. Eventually, it won a nomination for an Academy Award as the Best Documentary of 1942.

***

Lewis Seiler, who had directed both Jane and Reagan in *Tugboat Annie Sails Again,* was brought in to helm Reagan and others in *Beyond the Line of Duty* (1942). Seiler seemed anxious to speed his way through production of this 22-minute film, as he wanted to move on to his next assignment directing Marlene Dietrich and John Wayne in *Pittsburgh* (1942). Even if it were a rush job, *Beyond the Line of Duty* would go on to win an Oscar as Best Short Subject (two reel).

The film is unique in that it cast both a sitting president, Franklin D. Roosevelt (in archive footage), and a future president, Reagan (as narrator).

The star of the film was a bomber pilot hero from Texas, Captain Hewitt T. Wheless, cast as himself. A week after the raid on Pearl Harbor, Wheless, as the pilot of a B-17, had attacked Japanese warships in the Philippines and shot down seven Japanese fighter planes.

In his next film, formally entitled *Recognition of the Japanese Zero Fighter (1943),* but identified around Fort Roach and to thousands of enlisted men as simply *Jap Zero,* Reagan found himself at the center of an instructional film teaching Allied airmen to correctly distinguish between enemy Japanese aircraft (the Zero) and the American P-14 fighter plane, which resembled it in many ways. Reagan played the role of a pilot who not only recognizes, but then destroys a Zero over the Pacific. He later said, "*[In making this film]* I relied on my experience filming sequences for *International Squadron* (1941).*"

Months later, after watching the film, Crump sent out a rather sour memo, stating "Ronald Reagan is too famous a face to use in films involving instructional procedures. Our job is to save lives, not entertain."

From then on, Reagan was banned from appearing in equivalent films, although Crump did not issue that mandate to such actors as Van Heflin, George Montgomery, Lee J. Cobb, Arthur Kennedy, and William Holden, whom Crump defined as "boozy and ridicu-

lously charming, a poster boy to get young men to enlist."

Reagan would, however, be allowed to work on other "War Effort" films not conceived strictly as "instruction manuals."

***

Without question, the most ambitious of all of Reagan's war propaganda shorts was *Rear Gunner* (1943), with an all-star cast headed by Burgess Meredith as Army Private Pee Wee Williams. Supporting players included Reagan himself, cast as Lieutenant Amers, along with instructor Tom Neal and Dane Clark, playing an

Reagan *(right)* teaches, instructs, commands, inspires, and urges his companions and the nation onward in *Rear Gunner.*

enlisted man who likes Coney Island shooting galleries.

When she heard that her husband was working with Burgess Meredith, Jane was concerned that Reagan might learn some of her sexual secrets. Before leaving for military duty, he'd dated her best friend, Paulette Goddard. He would marry her in 1944. Goddard was Jane's *confidante*, and she wondered how much the actress had told Meredith. As she said in a call to Goddard, "Please warn him that discretion is the better part of valor, or however the line goes."

The film traces the odyssey of Pee Wee, a shy Kansas farm boy who is transformed into a killing machine, thanks to his assignment as an aerial gunner in the tail turret of a U.S. bomber.

Ray Enright, who had recently helmed Jane and Reagan in *An Angel from Texas* (1940), was called in to direct. Reagan had to leave town to shoot the film on location, both in the desert outside Tucson and also at the Las Vegas Gunnery School.

The film was blatantly patriotic, aimed at encouraging young men to go to gunnery schools in preparation for aerial combat. Most men who enlisted wanted to be pilots, not rear gunners. Gunnery schools frequently advertised with the slogan "We are always on the lookout for men short on height, but long on ambition." These schools were in the business of training "shorties" to become killers in the sky.

One of Reagan's lines proclaimed, "The film is about creating a modern knight of fire." He defined the position of a rear gunner as "a passport into the vistas of victory." In one sequence, an instructor tells Meredith, "A rear gunner knows that the fire from your guns is the fire of freedom."

After a film sequence demonstrating a rear gunner in action, Reagan asserts, "It's shooting like this that will knock them on their Axis."

In just twenty-six minutes of frenzied aerial combat, the farmboy evolves from a hayseed to a war hero, winning the Distinguished Service Cross.

One sequence depicts Reagan in the cockpit, evoking one of his Brass Bancroft movies when he played an "Agent in the Air" for the Secret Service.

Viewed today, the film seems to have emerged from a time machine. Some references evoke a snicker, as when the dialogue includes a reference to the Air Corps having a "gay day."

Unlike most of the films from FMPU, Jack Warner paid for the cost of *Rear Gunner's* production and wanted to release it as a commercial feature, with exhibitors paying to show it. The War Department objected, claiming, "Actors such as Ronald Reagan and Burgess Meredith, who have been commissioned into the Army, should not be exploited for commercial gain by any film studio."

Consequently, *Rear Gunner* was released, without charge, to theaters nationwide as part of their regular programming. It was not, however, specifically promoted as a special feature, as Warner would have preferred.

***

With a duration of twenty-two minutes, *Target Tokyo* (1942) was narrated by Reagan. It was a glorification of the B-29 bomber, a virtual flying fortress created to bomb the Japanese homeland into submission. Before the advent of the B-29, Japanese generals had claimed that their homeland was beyond the reach of any American bomber. The B-29 proved what a false statement that was.

The film begins on an early dawn in Nebraska, where the B-29s begin their long journey, with stopovers en route

As narrator, Reagan claims that for the Japs to stop them, their task would be "as hopeless as trying to stop the flow of water at Niagara Falls."

At one point during a bombing raid, the B-29 is shown flying over a munitions factory in the environs of Tokyo. Reagan asks the pilot, "Well, bud, what are you waiting for?" Immediately, the bombs rain down, destroying the factory.

General Douglas MacArthur had to evacuate The Philippines during the epic battle for those islands against the Japanese, vowing, "I shall return!" Reagan became involved in yet another film, *Westward Bataan* (1944), which paid homage to MacArthur and his island-hopping military strategy. It depicted and dramatized the U.S. campaign to cut off supply routes to Japanese soldiers maintaining beleaguered strongholds in New Ireland and New Britain. Reagan declares, "The Japs can surrender or rot."

An officer in the movie tells his men that the Japanese should be watched "like you would a deadly rattlesnake."

The enemy is depicted as a pack of fanatics, willing to fight to the last man, woman, or child, giving up their lives for their emperor. Viewers are told that the Japanese are willing to sacrifice ten million of their people. As narrator, Reagan grimly asserts, "Well, life isn't cheap in America." A Japanese mother is shown as she is presented with a box containing the ashes of her son. "We don't raise our boys to be god in little white boxes," Reagan assures his viewers.

Tarket Tokyo promoted the technological sophistication of the B-29, a flying Superfortress with Twelve 1/2- inch (12.7 mm) remote controlled M2 Browning machine guns and 20,000 pounds of "Earthquake bombs."

The atomic bombs that later fell on Japan were delivered by this aircraft.

***

In *For God and Country* (1944), Reagan had an unusual role. Cast as a Catholic chaplain, he tells his fellow soldiers, "Guns are not for chaplains." His two closest friends are a Protestant and a Jew, both of whom are killed trying to save the life of a Native American. "We were trying to cover all religious fronts in this film, all except Moslems and atheists," Reagan said. "There was a famous saying, 'There are no atheists in a foxhole.'"

For God and Country is a plea for racial and religious harmony among men allied against a common enemy. As part of the film's narrative, the chaplain asks, "What better weapons can a soldier carry with him into battle than those of courage, of unswerving devotion to his faith, and to his fellow man? The obvious answer to Reagan's question is "a gun."

Very few of these wartime propaganda films depicted African American servicemen, who were referred to as Negroes in most World War II movies. *Wings for This Man* (1945) was an exception, as it was devoted entirely to black pilots training in Alabama at the Tuskegee Air Base.

Racial issues in the then-segregated U.S. army were touched upon delicately and lightly, very lightly.

The movie begins with Reagan as narrator dramatically depicting an outnumbered U.S. squadron in a dogfight with planes from the *Luftwaffe*. The Nazi planes are shot down. Back at the base, it is revealed that the American pilots were black. To find their place in the sun, Reagan suggests, "These airmen had to overcome misunderstanding, distrust, and prejudice."

For the most part, racial issues are not hit upon too heavily. Reagan states: "One thing was proven here: That you can't judge a man by the color of his eyes or the shape of his nose. These men were pioneers, and pioneers have never had it easy."

At the film's end, a white officer is seen decorating a black pilot, giving him "*Wings for This Man*," the title of the short.

***

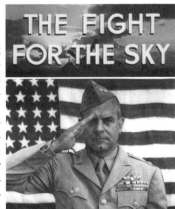

The Fight for the Sky (1945) was one of the last of Reagan's propaganda films. The documentary details the exploits of the American fighter escort pilots during bombing raids of Nazi Germany. They are depicted destroying the *Luftwaffe*.

Reagan's co-star was Jimmy Doolittle, the aviation pioneer who earned the Medal of Honor as commander of the famous "Doolittle Raid" over Japan during World War II. In 1942, Doolittle and his fellow pilots shocked the Japanese by flying the first retaliatory air raid unleashed upon the Japanese mainland. The attack force of sixteen B-25s set off from an aircraft carrier, the U.S.S. Hornet *[now permanently moored as a museum ship in Alameda, California, near San Francisco.]*

Targets of the raid included, among others, Tokyo, Yokohama, Osaka, and Kobe. After the raid,

Jimmy Doolittle salutes in Fight for the Sky. When it was released, Reagan said, "We've already beat the Krauts and the Japs. We're just waiting for the Fat Lady to sing."

Doolittle's plane, now out of fuel after twelve hours of fighting, went down in a rice paddy on the Japanese-occupied mainland of China. Rescued by Chinese guerillas, with the assistance of the American missionary, John Birch, Doolittle was smuggled into territory controlled by the Allies. Although Doolittle survived for other heroic missions and flying records, four of his crew members lost their lives as a result of being captured and tortured by the Japanese.

The Fight for the Sky focuses on Thunderbolts (B-47s), Mustangs (P-51s), and Lightnings (P-38s), planes that smashed Hermann Göring's *Luftwaffe* during its desperate attempts to maintain control of the skies of the Fatherland.

As Reagan asserts during his narration of the film, "Into these three great fighters, America poured its genius. No American fighter ever failed because of enemy odds, however great."

As bombs fall over Germany, the film ends with praise for heroic Allied pilots "who in the decisive hour smashed the *Luftwaffe* and gave freedom of the air over Europe."

The film was released in both a 20-minute version and as a longer feature with a running time of 40 minutes. Reagan narrated only the shorter version. The movies are packed with camera footage of strafing runs and aerial combat. Images of several fighter aces are shown on the screen. Each pilot survived the war, though some were captured when their planes went down and they were held as POWs.

The message sent out to these pilots was "Attack! Attack! Attack!"

One day, Reagan received a call that informed him that the Armed Services were releasing him to make a film at Warner Brothers.

***

The number of Jane Wyman films produced at Warners was greatly reduced during the closing years of World War II. She appeared in only a fraction of the movies she'd rushed through in the 1930s and early 1940s.

A highlight of her film production during World War II had included co-starring with Olivia de Havilland in *Princess O'Rourke* in 1943. Her schedule was busier in 1944 when she was cast in three B-pictures and made a guest cameo appearance in *Hollywood Canteen* alongside such stars as Bette Davis and Joan Crawford.

The war did not devastate her small family in the way it did thousands of other American homes. Reagan drove home from Fort Roach most evenings, and Baby Maureen was healthy, except for a tendency to cry hysterically at three o'clock in the morning.

Jane continued to see a lot of her personal friends, usually visiting them at their homes for private dinners or parties. Occasionally, at obscure locations, she went out dancing with Van Johnson.

As the war dragged on, Jane continued her affair with Dennis Morgan, who—because he wasn't otherwise committed to military service—was still making movies for Warners.

Also, with high anticipation and whenever she could, she drove down to Long Beach, where John Payne was a flight instructor with the Army Air Force.

After his divorce from Anne Shirley in 1942, she had fully expected him to urge her to divorce Reagan and to marry him. When they had gotten together, both of them had expressed their "undying love" for each other. But there was no talk of his eventually marrying her.

One Sunday afternoon, with no warning whatsoever, he told her that they needed to talk. Their weekend, at least in her view, had been glorious, "almost the dearest, yet

John Payne dumped Jane Wyman so he could marry Gloria DeHaven.

most passionate, I ever spent with John"

But that afternoon, as they faced a dying sun sinking in the west, Payne delivered news that devastated her. He told her that he was ending their relationship because he'd proposed marriage to the MGM music star, Gloria DeHaven. As Jane later revealed to both Blondell and Goddard, "I was in a state of shock. I had no clue this was about to happen. I guess John wants a wife more than he desires a married off-the-record gal like me hanging on to him."

At the base, after his kiss-off speech, Payne reached for her hand after opening her car door. "Maybe we'll meet again, kid, after the war is over. That is, if I grow tired of my bride and you finally get up enough courage to ditch Reagan."

"Maybe," she said, declining a farewell kiss.

She later told Goddard, "I cried all the way back to Los Angeles. I lost what was never mine in the first place."

Goddard knew DeHaven, who was the daughter of actor Carter DeHaven. He'd used his influence to get her cast in minor parts in two Charlie Chaplin films—*Modern Times* (1936) and *The Great Dictator* (1940)—made during the course of Chaplin's marriage to Goddard.

Jane had seen DeHaven in the 1943 *Best Foot Forward* with June Allyson and again with Allyson in *Two Girls and a Sailor* (1944).

Payne had told her that DeHaven, who was seven years younger than Jane, would retire from the screen after their marriage.

[DeHaven retired from filmmaking, but only briefly, making a return in the lackluster 1948 melodrama, Summer Holiday, *in which she played the sweetheart of Mickey Rooney. The picture flopped.]*

Blondell and Dick Powell also ended up in the divorce courts, freeing themselves from each other in 1944. Powell soon became involved with Allyson, whom he would marry the following year. Powell and Reagan still continued as friends. But after his marital reshuffling, instead of showing up at the Reagan home for dinner with Blondell, he appeared there with Allyson on his arm.

Jane remembered her first meeting with the short and perky MGM star. As she later told Blondell, "Right in front of Dick and me, June flirted outrageously with Ronnie."

Battling Blondes: June Allyson.

...and her nemesis, Joan Blondell.

"I'm not surprised," Blondell said. "She's a nympho, in spite of that syrupy personality of hers. The bitch lived with me for a time at my apartment in New York when she was trying to break into show business. I know *all* about that one."

After her messy divorce from Chaplin, Goddard began dating actor Burgess Meredith, who was making war propaganda films at the time with Reagan at Fort Roach. She married him in 1944, much to the consternation of Jane. "She didn't marry him for his looks or for his money, of which he had none. Surely, it wasn't because of his talent as an actor."

Meredith himself explained to Jane what had attracted him to "P.G.," as he called her.

"She walks into a room and you feel a sinuousness about her, a sense of danger. On top of that, she produces a nonstop flow of speech that is witty, cunning, and touching."

After witnessing the marital debris of her closest friends, Jane consoled herself over the loss of Payne, whom she continued to maintain as "the greatest sexual thrill of my life."

"Grab him, darlin', if he's in uniform." Burgess Meredith marries Paulette Goddard.

She told Blondell, "I still have the affection of Ronnie and Dennis Morgan, the two handsomest men at Warners. Not bad for a working gal like me. Who knows? In my next film, I may imitate Ronnie and develop *Leadingman-itis.*"

"Jane, dear, there are those—not me, of course—who claim you came down with that disease back when we made all those silly pictures for Warners in the 30s."

***

The first picture Jane made in 1944 had the less-than-enticing title of *Make Your Own Bed*. She was teamed with the robust, 220-pound Jack Carson, who had first appeared on the stage in a college production playing Hercules. "I tripped," he told her, "and brought down half the set."

"That's one way to launch yourself into show business," Jane said.

In this, his latest film, Carson told her, "Here I go again, playing the clown, stooge, or whatever befuddled mess I am."

[The title of the film seemed to stem from a not-very-funny standing joke about a double

Jack Carson sleuths and schemes around Jane Wyman in *Make Your Own Bed*.

348

bed.]

Once again, her lover, Dennis Morgan, was a frequent visitor to the set, ostensibly to see Carson, his best friend. Secretly, Morgan continued to use Carson as his "beard" to meet with Jane. As Carson later confessed, years later, "I was with them only until we left the studio. Then I scrammed to leave them to tend to business. Maybe Jane was not getting enough from Reagan. How in the hell would I know?"

On the first day of shooting, she met a Londoner, her director, Peter Godfrey. She later concluded, "Peter was a bit too experimental and avant-garde for a pedestrian script like *Make your Own Bed.* He was very talented and was also at home with the classics, including both Molière and Strindberg."

The rather weak screenplay of *Make Your Own Bed* was by Francis Swann and Edmund Joseph. The plot has Walter, a gunpowder manufacturer (Alan Hale, Sr.) and Vivian, his wife (Irene Manning), living in the country and finding it difficult to keep servants. Walter solves the problem by hiring a private detective, Jerry (Jack Carson) who had been fired for arresting the local District Attorney. Walter tells Carson that his life is in danger—"Nazi spies are everywhere."

In *Make Your Own Bed,* Jerry, as portrayed by Carson, needs a cover, so he brings in his *fiancée,* Susan (Jane), to work for the household as a cook. The biggest problem involves the fact that she can't cook. Consequently, as improbable as it sounds, Walter and Vivian solve their staff problem by agreeing to take turns preparing the meals themselves, all the while keeping Jane employed.

There is another problem, however: Jerry, as a sleuth, can't even locate the Brooklyn Bridge. But by the final reel, as could be predicted, the Nazi spies are unmasked.

The most fascinating woman on the set was Irene Manning. Though born in Cincinnati, she could be made up to look like a continental *femme fatale.* She had played the diva, Fay Templeton, in *Yankee Doodle Dandy* (1942) opposite James Cagney. Jane was jealous of her, although she tried to conceal it. She'd co-starred with Morgan in *Desert Song* (1943), and Jane had heard rumors of an affair.

To make matters worse, director David Butler had cast Manning in another 1944 movie, *Shine on Harvest Moon.* It not only starred Morgan, but two of Jane's best friends, Jack Carson and Ann Sheridan. Jane lobbied to join Carson, Morgan, and Sheridan as a player within that film, but she was rejected in favor of Manning, which infuriated her and increased her distaste for the singer-actress.

Manning didn't seem jealous of or threatened by Jane, and at one point, invited her to join her on an all-girl USO tour of war-torn England for morale-boosting performances with bandleader Glenn Miller, shortly before his death in 1944.

Although at the time, Jane claimed that she was needed "to take care of Ronnie and Maureen," she regretted not having been part of that troupe.

She later said, "Had I gone, it would have made a fascinating chapter in my memoirs."

[Incidentally, those memoirs—although contemplated—would never be written.]

After it was wrapped, Jane sat with Carson and Morgan, watching the final cut of *Make Your Own Bed.* At the end, and over drinks, she claimed, "This is the worst movie I've ever made."

Perhaps it really wasn't, but that's what she said at

USO darling Irene Manning: Making her own bed, and competing with Jane for the attentions of Dennis Morgan.

the time.

Bosley Crowther, writing in *The New York Times,* panned it. "For all the contortions it goes through, the movie is a limp dishrag, a labored but failed endeavor to fetch laughs with a lot of old gags, like kitchen disasters and wrong doors. The humor is feeble and unsustained."

***

Jerome Cowan, Jane's new leading man in *Crime by Night,* may not be a household name, but the appearance of this mustachioed

Jane didn't like her role in *Crime by Night,* but loved having her name in large letters above the title. She had a scene with Jerome Cowan *(left)* and with bit player Stuart Crawford.

When Cowan told her he was having sexual fantasies about her, she snapped, "Only in your dreams, pal!"

character actor from New York had been immortalized in two film classics, which are forever being shown on TV. One was *The Maltese Falcon* (1941), in which Cowan was cast as the doomed private eye, the partner of Sam Spade, as played by Humphrey Bogart. The other famous film in which Cowan appeared was the perennial Christmas favorite, *Miracle on 34th Street* (1947). Jane would eventually see that film more than once, partly because it starred her former lover, John Payne, alongside Maureen O'Hara.

After serving in World War I, Cowan had become a vaudeville headliner until 1936 when Samuel Goldwyn brought him to Hollywood for a role in *Beloved Enemy.*

Amazingly, despite his late entry into films, Cowan became one of the most employed actors in Hollywood, appearing in some 120 movies. He was the suitor spurned by Bette Davis who consequently ended up onscreen with him as *The Old Maid* (1939). After completing his role with Jane, Cowan prepared for another face-off with Davis in her star role in *Mr. Skeffington* (1944).

During the filming of *Crime By Night,* Cowan downplayed not only his role, but that of Jane's. "It's just another Warner Brothers' private eye caper—nothing more, nothing less. The only thing it's got going for it is a trio of very beautiful actresses, beginning with you but also including Eleanor Parker and Faye Emerson."

"When I heard that you three beauties were in the movie, I had a wet dream," Cowan said. "Although I'm faithful to my wife, Helen Dodge, I dreamed that all three of you were the chief girls in my Harem."

"How flattering," Jane said, not quite disguising her sarcasm.

After dinner with Cowan, Jane shared her impression of him with Morgan. "My god, couldn't Jack Warner have come up with a younger actor to appear as my boyfriend? I looked it up. Cowan was born in the final year *[1897]* of Grover Cleveland's presidency. He's forty-seven right now and looks older. I'm twenty-seven and look like a girl out of college."

"How true," Morgan responded.

Jane also complained to the film's director, William Clemens, about his choice of her leading man, and her role. "Basically, it seems that all I have to do is feed Cowan his lines."

"But you get to kiss him in the final reel," Clemens said.

"Thanks a hell of a lot!" she snapped. "That would be like kissing my father if I had one. With Cowan as my boyfriend, he could get arrested for child molestation. Where is John Payne now that I need him in more ways than one?"

The plot of *Crime by Night* focuses on private eye Sam Campbell (Cowan) who is on vacation with his secretary-partner, Robbie Vance (as played by Jane). They become involved in a murder investigation. Harvey Carr, the father-in-law of Larry Borden (Stuart Crawford), is found dead from a blow by an ax. Borden's promising career as a concert pianist had ended in a fight with Carr, who had chopped off Borden's hand with an ax. Therefore, Borden was a prime suspect in Carr's murder, perhaps as an act of revenge for destroying his musical career.

Borden is Campbell's friend, and he and Robbie (that is, Jane), arrive to help. Eleanor Parker was cast as Irene Carr, the daughter of the murdered man and Borden's ex-wife. She arrives on the scene as another dead body, that of the gardener, turns up.

Irene shows up with Paul Goff (Charles Lang), a singer whom she intends to marry. He also arrives with his agent, Ann Marlow (Faye Emerson).

Complications ensue in the thickening plot, which spins around a Nazi spy ring. Carr, the murder victim, owned a chemical plant. At first, Goff is a suspect until he is also murdered.

SPOILER ALERT: Ann Marlow (Emerson) turns out to be the culprit, a Nazi spy. Ironically, at the time, after her marriage to Elliott Roosevelt, Emerson was set to move into the White House, the nerve center of the United States' War direction against the Nazis.

As a reviewer in *The New York Times* asserted, "The real crime in *Crime by Night* are the people who made it, forcing the audience to sit through 72 minutes of tedium. At my viewing, many patrons walked out after the first thirty minutes."

***

Leaving Fort Roach, based on wartime orders from his superiors, Reagan returned to Warner Brothers. He later wrote, "It was a thrill for me once again to be a part of the picture business." His assignment involved playing a key role in a feature film, *This Is the Army* (1943), a sometimes bizarre wartime musical produced by Hal B. Wallis and Jack Warner. The screenplay was by Claude Binyon and Casey Robinson. Robinson had written the script for *Kings Row.*

The movie was based on Irving Berlin's hit Broadway musical of 1942. He had produced a roughly equivalent show as a morale-booster during World War I called *Yip, Yip, Yaphank.* Money earned for the 1943 movie version, eventually totaling some $12 million, would be donated to the Army Emergency Relief Fund.

At the time, Reagan was drawing a monthly stipend from the Army of $250. He was told that even though he was starring in the film, he would get no additional salary from Warners. However, the non-enlisted civilian star of the movie, song-and-dance man George Murphy, would draw around $28,000.

In addition to Murphy, other major stars would be cast in the film, along with some 300 Army men and sailors from the U.S. Navy. Before the war, most of these had been singers or actors in civilian life.

For the most part, Reagan was impressed with the cast which the film's director, Michael Curtiz, had assembled. Although he considered Curtiz temperamental and difficult, he had gotten along with the Hungarian when he'd helmed Errol Flynn and him in *Santa Fe Trail.*

In addition to Murphy and Reagan, Curtiz had cast "sweetheart sweet" Joan Leslie, plus supporting players who included George Tobias (Reagan's co-star in *Juke Girl)* and Alan Hale, Sr. (Reagan's co-star in *Tugboat Annie Sails Again).*

Other veteran performers included Charles Butterworth, Rosemary DeCamp (the mother of the character portrayed by Reagan), Una Merkel, Stanley Ridges, Ruth Donnelly, and Dolores Costello, once hailed as "the goddess of the silent screen." Personalities who included Kate Smith, Frances Langford, Gertrude Niesen, Victor Moore, Joe E. Louis, and Berlin himself appeared as themselves.

On his first day back at Warners, Reagan was ushered into Curtiz' office, where he was concluding an acrimonious phone conversation with an irate Bette Davis. Curtiz slammed down the phone. "The patriotic bitch wants to be in my movie. She can't sing or dance. She's no soldier. When I cast bitch in *Cabin in the Cotton* (1932), I called

Jane claimed, "I was seriously pissed off when I didn't get to play Ronnie's girlfriend in *This Is the Army."* Instead, the part went to "sweet little Joan Leslie," depicted above.

If Jane had gotten the part, she could have worn her own uniform. In the summer of 1942, as a public relations statement partly based on her success in selling War Bonds, she was commissioned in the Army Air Corps as a 2nd lieutenant. Jane was proud of it, however, and insisted, "I deserved the part."

her a 'goddamn nothing no good sexless son of a bitch.' But we made up when I lick pussy. She likes pussy licked. We made five more films after that, but not this one, goddamn it."

At some point, Reagan asked Curtiz, "Exactly what type of boy is Johnny Jones, the one I'm to play?"

"Who gives a fuck?" Curtiz exclaimed. "No one cares about character. I make it so fast nobody notices. Don't argue with me. I'm Best Director." He pointed to a table where his Oscar for Best Director rested. He'd won it for the 1942 *Casablanca,* with Humphrey Bogart and Ingrid Bergman. "Bogie's a shit. Bergman fuck him, she fuck me, she'll fuck any round object."

"Your role no special shit," Curtiz continued. "Any actor at Warners under thirty-five can play it. You run around calling people to stage and turning down offers of Joan Leslie who wants to marry you so she can get fucked. You want to wait until war's end. You claim you don't want to make her widow. She finally wins and you get fuck. You don't actually fuck her on screen, fool. You and Leslie can stage private exhibit for me. I like to watch. Usually, I hire a big black buck to fuck young blonde gal. That's my favorite."

Curtiz told Reagan their film meant a lot to him. "I escaped from the Nazis. Members of my family not so lucky. They die at Auschwitz."

"Right now at Warners I ride high. Tomorrow, I might fall off horse. You no make dough at box office, you are tossed into gutter with garbage."

Then Curtiz summoned Joan Leslie into his office and introduced her to Reagan. A latter-day film historian would write: "Sweet, perky young things were a dime a dozen in Hollywood's heyday, but Joan Leslie stood out as a highly appealing and engaging young actress with some flashes of genuine talent."

George Murphy, who had tap-danced his way to fame in 1930s and early 40s musicals, was cast as Reagan's father. "And I never let him forget it," Reagan said. Actually, he was only nine years older than Reagan, having been born a "Connecticut Yankee."

Actors who became career politicians: Reagan with George Murphy in a scene from *This is the Army.* Murphy steered Reagan from left to right.

This Is the Army opens in 1917, with Murphy portraying a fast-talking vaudeville performer who gets drafted. In World War I, after a severe injury to his leg, he can't perform any more, although he can walk around with a cane. As Reagan admitted, "It took a lot of makeup and a gray dye job to make George look like my father."

Although the two men had known each other for years, Murphy became president of the Screen Actors Guild (SAG) in 1944. It was during this time that the two performers bonded.

[Reagan later referred to Murphy as "my own John the Baptist," whatever that meant. In time, Murphy became a politician, serving as a Republican in the U.S. Senate from 1965 to 1971, representing the State of California. He became the first notable U.S. actor to make the transition from the movies into politics, predating both Reagan and Arnold Schwarzenegger, each of whom served as governor of California.

Beginning with This Is the Army, *Reagan and Murphy became lifelong friends. "When I met Ronnie, he was a nearly hopeless hemophiliac liberal. But I changed his mind, although it took a lot of talking. As a liberal, he backed all the wrong causes. It was a struggle, but I eventually turned him into a benighted Republican. I made him realize that our Republican philosophy of self-reliance, as opposed to the welfare state, was in keeping with his own ideals and not those of mad-dog Democrats who like to give away the store."]*

Reagan experienced an embarrassing moment when he stood on a replica of a Broadway stage with Murphy and Curtiz. The director was stridently demanding the beginning of the movie's big number, which included the singing and dancing of dozens of soldiers.

[In those days, the military was segregated.]

"BRING ON THE WHITE SOLDIERS!" Curtiz bellowed.

After the men were in place, Curtiz yelled, "BRING ON THE NIGGER TROOPS!"

Murphy politely corrected him, telling him that N word was offensive, not only to blacks but to him.

"I'm sorry," Curtiz said. "BRING ON THE COLORED NIGGERS."

During the first week of filming, Reagan was introduced to Irving Berlin at least five times, in as many separate venues. "He never seemed to remember that we'd met before. One day, he sat through the rushes and greeted me with, 'Young fellow, I just saw some of your work. You've got a few things to correct—for example, the huskiness in

353

your voice—but you really should give this business some serious consideration when the war is over."

Cast in a very minor role was Craig Stevens, who was seven years younger than Reagan. Like Jane, he was from Missouri. Since 1939, he'd been cast in minor parts, although he and Reagan would co-star in a film together after the war.

As Reagan privately confessed to Murphy, "I was starting to worry a bit about Craig. I invited him to share my dressing room, but he praises my body and my looks too much, whether I'm in or out of my clothes. He also brings me gifts as if he's courting me. I was going to confront him. How wrong I would have been."

"How so?" Murphy asked.

"One day, he introduced me to this beautiful actress, Alexis Smith," Reagan said. "He's going to marry her. I'm now so comfortable with Craig that I even piss with him at the urinal without suspecting him of checking out my dick. He's definitely not a homo."

"My boy, you can be rather naïve about some things," Murphy said. "Haven't you ever heard of a bisexual?"

Reliable, stalwart and solid: Reagan as the competent but unflashy announcer for the frequently bizarre military/theatrical revue *This Is the Army*.

"Frankly, I don't believe such a thing exists. You're either straight or you're a homo. Guys who pretend otherwise are just bullshitters."

For their appearances in *This Is the Army,* Curtiz asked many of the soldiers—"I selected only pretty boys"—to appear in drag. "Many guys seemed only too eager to dress up like gals," Curtiz told Reagan. "Do you think it's possible that the Army is infested with homos?"

"Definitely not," Reagan said. "It's against Army policy to enlist homos. They weed them out at induction centers."

"So you say," Curtiz said. "I think many of them slip in anyway."

Reagan never recovered from the day Hale appeared on the set of *This Is the Army* in a blue dress with long blonde curls inspired by something from a silent Mary Pickford movie. He was not too happy being in drag. "Alan, would you go out on a date with me after the show?" Reagan asked.

"Why don't you go fuck yourself?" Hale suggested.

"Wait till Ward Bond and John Wayne hear about this," Reagan said. "I want to be the first to tell them."

With some other soldiers in drag, Hale performed in a number called "Ladies of the Chorus."

When the Breen office saw the film, wherein U.S. soldiers danced merrily together in drag, they exploded in fury and violently objected. They demanded that such scenes be cut. Jack Warner refused.

Breen also interpreted many of Berlin's songs as "too suggestive." Again, Warner refused to eliminate them from the film, and contacted the War Department, which warned the Breen office "to take a hike."

"There's a war on, in case you bluenoses never heard that," General Hap Arnold told Joseph Breen during an angry phone call. "I'll decide what our boys can see or not see, and I want them to see this picture." Then he slammed down the phone on Breen.

354

Not politically correct in today's terms, the film also included an unfunny minstrel number entitled "Manny," in which dozens of white soldiers, about half of them in drag and all of them in blackface, performed a "coeducational" song and dance number that by today's standards seems surreal.

Reagan found himself the butt of the song, "This is the Army, Mr. Jones." He had not one memorable scene, but acquitted himself well, although outclassed by the massive array of stage talent surrounding him.

All the dancing white soldiers were shown up by the film's showstopper, the black troupe of the James Cross Company performing a fast-moving and ultra-energetic number entitled "That's What the Well-Dressed Man in Harlem Will Wear," a reference to Army khaki.

At the revue's end, the soldiers learn they are being immediately shipped, that very night, to Europe. They march through the theater with rifles and full military gear, hurriedly kissing their (weeping) mothers, wives, and girlfriends *adios,* and moving out and into a waiting convoy of trucks.

The film was a big hit, earning some $12 million for the Army Emergency Relief Fund.

In spite of his lackluster performance, Reagan fitted in perfectly with the patriotic mood of the country. For the first and only time in his life, *Box Office Record,* in reference to the 1942-43 season, gave him the highest ranking of any male star in Hollywood. With 195 points, he topped a list that included runners-up James Cagney at 186, Bing Crosby at 176, Clark Gable at 171, and Cary Grant at 169.

"I'm king of the hill," Reagan shouted into a phone at Jane when notified of his standing.

Although he would hardly have believed it at the time, that moment in his life represented his peak as a Hollywood movie star. In terms of what pertained to his career as an entertainer, everything after that would run downhill.

***

For her final film of 1944, Jane Wyman found herself reunited with her friends, Ann Sheridan and Jack Carson, in *The Doughgirls,* a wartime bedroom farce about the housing shortage in Washington. Also cast were the Reagans' newly minted friends, Alexis Smith and her handsome boyfriend (soon to become her second husband), actor Craig Stevens

Carson, in the role of Arthur Halstead, has married his girlfriend, Vivian, and he books a honeymoon suite for them. But he soon learns that Jane has moved in her friends, Edna (Sheridan) and Nan (Smith), who can't find lodgings elsewhere. Not only that, but they, too, have newly minted husbands, Sheridan having hooked up with John Ridgely and Smith with Stevens.

Doughgirls: Ann Sheridan *(left)*, Alexis Smith, Jane Wyman.

355

The young women—Jane, Smith, and Sheridan—soon face complications when, for somewhat contrived reasons, the marital status of each of them is unexpectedly defined as illegal by the authorities When Vivian learns that she is unmarried, she boots Carson out of their quarters. In his frustration, he refuses to pay the hotel bill unless Vivian moves out her girlfriends. Subsequently, she is forced to pawn her earrings to settle the bill.

In the meantime, Arthur's boss, Stanley, played by Charles Ruggles, pursues Jane, although the mating of the pixie-like comic and Jane seems preposterous. He was fifty-eight at the time.

Eve Arden was cast as a Russian guerilla fighter, Natalia Moskarova, who is sent over from the Russian Embassy as yet another roommate. Although miscast, it was obvious to the other stars that Arden was a major threat as a scene stealer. She played the role in its broadest sense, lacking the subtlety of Greta Garbo's performance as a die-hard Soviet communist in *Ninotchka* (1939).

Doughgirl: Eve Arden as a gun-toting Soviet socialist.

A play by Joseph Fields, *The Doughgirls,* had been a hit on Broadway in 1942, running for 688 performances. The brother of the famous lyricist, Dorothy Fields, Joseph was both a playwright and director, having scored two previous Broadway triumphs, *My Sister Eileen* (1940) and *Junior Miss* (1941).

Although Jack Warner was willing to bid only $40,000 for the screen rights to *Gone With the Wind* (1939), he put up an astonishing (for the time) $250,000 for the movie rights to *The Doughgirls.*

Of course, he knew that the Broadway script was "too spicy" for the movies, and that he'd have to remove any suggestion that the couples were living together and having pre-marital sex. Much of the racy dialogue of the play would also have to be rewritten into something much more bland.

James V. Kern was hired to write the screenplay with Sam Hellman. For some unknown reason, Warner also designated Kern as director of this prestigious project, even though he'd had no experience in that field.

Jane expressed at the time her disappointment with Kern both as a writer and as a director. *[Later, however, she changed her mind about Kern, a New Yorker. "I met him when he was still green. He'd been a lawyer, ditching that career for show business. He really found himself when he became a director of TV series in the 1950s, doing hundreds of shows, including the* I Love Lucy *series with my friend, Lucille Ball, and in the early 60s,* My Three Sons, *with Fred MacMurray."*

At the time of her involvement with Kern in *The Doughgirls,* however, Jane complained to him about the way he'd written her character of Vivian. "You've made me a little harebrained, witless figure. I mean, some of the lines I've been given make me squirm. When I hear that Alexis and Craig are going to have lunch at the White House with FDR, I make the ridiculous claim, 'I enjoyed the president in *Princess O'Rourke.'* As you well know, I was the co-star of that movie. The President didn't appear in the film. I read the script for the Broadway play. My character of Vivian had far more spice."

Jane also complained to Mark Hellinger, the producer. "I noticed you billed me in fourth position, under Alexis. I've been a star at Warners, and Alexis is the new girl on the block."

"Sorry, Jane, but my billing stays," Hellinger said. "Case closed."

That night, Jane complained to Reagan that she hated her role so much she was considering refusing to cooperate, and subsequently being placed on suspension. Up until then, he had hardly paid attention to her concerns, but suddenly, he came alive.

"You know that Maureen and I are depending on you to bring in a weekly paycheck," he said. "We can't live on Army pay!"

"All right, god damn it," she told him. "How does it feel to be a kept boy?"

He stormed out of the house and drove over to spend the night with Ann Sheridan, who surprised him with news that she'd almost gone on suspension herself. "I saw the play on Broadway, and I decided I didn't want to play any of the three girls."

He was very persuasive, and he invited her to come to dinner the following night and talk Jane into going forward with the role of Vivian.

Sheridan agreed to do that. After about an hour, she convinced Jane to continue struggling through the role, promising her, "We'll have fun. Alexis is a great gal, and Carson is your pal."

Sheridan later told Smith, "What tempted Jane was that once again, Carson can be her beard for any rendezvous she has with Dennis Morgan."

On the set, Jane chatted briefly with Regis Toomey, with whom she had shared the longest screen kiss in history. He'd been given only a minor role in *Doughgirls* as "Agent Walsh."

"I still dream of that kiss," he told her. "I'm ready for a repeat."

"Once was enough," she quipped. "I'm still trying to catch my breath."

Cast in a minor role was Irene Manning, with whom Jane had appeared in *Make Your Own Bed.* She continued to snub Manning, believing that she was conducting a clandestine affair with Dennis Morgan.

When Jane saw the ads for *The Doughgirls*, she complained once again to its producer, Mark Hellinger. Publicity included sexy pictures of Smith, Sheridan, and Jane, but what she objected to was the prominent display of Manning, even though her role was small. "My god, you're showing her tits, a big bosom on display, and that lacy see-through lives up to its purpose."

"Sex sells," Hellinger told her.

"So that's how Manning makes her money," Jane quipped before walking away.

During the closing months of the war, Sheridan continued to spend evenings with Jane and Reagan. She recalled one evening as typical.

She said, "Ronnie was a baseball nut. The day before, he'd heard this game on the radio, and he gave us a play-by-play account, the way he used to do on the air in Des Moines. Jane begged him to stop, claiming that neither of them was interested in baseball. He politely listened to his wife's complaints, but carried on with a detailed description for all nine innings."

In the kitchen, Jane complained to Sheridan, "If it's not baseball, it's politics. Christ, he even makes speeches in his sleep."

***

In 1944, Jane got a reprieve from her marriage when the Air Force sent Reagan, with John Garfield, on a bond-selling tour across America.

Garfield later recalled, "In any town we landed in, I went out and chased the dames. Because I was John Garfield, I always scored. Once, I took three gals back with me. I invited Reagan to share in my luck. But he stayed in his room reading scripts. I'd heard what a lady-killer he'd been at Warners. That was one *serious* man."

Garfield played a large role in Jane's life. They both spent three or four nights a week at the USO, entertaining and feeding U.S. servicemen. Bette Davis and others saw Jane leave every one of those nights with Garfield. There were plenty of rumors but no smoking gun. No one was absolutely sure they were having an affair.

John Garfield with Lana Turner in a defining moment from *The Postman Always Rings Twice.*

However, when Garfield, in 1946, made the classic *The Postman Always Rings Twice,* he gave his version to his co-star, Lana Turner, with whom he was having an affair at the time.

As related to Turner, Garfield said, "I fucked Jane over a period of six weeks. After traveling on the road with her 'bookish' husband, on that war bond tour, I figured the poor gal needed it from some man who knew how to deliver the goods, namely, me."

Garfield, as even his friends would admit, was not known for his modesty.

[At the beginning of World War II, Bette Davis and John Garfield, with help from others, founded the Hollywood Canteen, a morale-booster for military men being shipped off to fight in the Pacific, or else returning after surviving military engagements on land and sea.

Garfield enlisted Jane's support, and she appeared regularly at the canteen, entertaining the young men with song, dancing with them, and serving them coffee and doughnuts. "I got a lot of propositions, but the rule was, no dating the servicemen after the canteen closed."

Of course that otherwise strict rule didn't seem to apply to either Garfield or Jane.

The entertainment center became so popular that Jack Warner ordered director Delmer Daves to make it the subject of a movie with an all-star cast. It was released in 1944 and entitled Hollywood Canteen. *The plot was thin, the main stars being Robert Hutton, Dane Clark, and Joan Leslie. Hutton becomes the millionth G.I. to enter the canteen, and consequently, he wins a date with his dream girl, Leslie.*

During the filming, Jane asked her director, Daves, to screen one of his earlier movies, the 1943 wartime adventure, Destination Tokyo, *for servicemen. It starred Cary Grant in what had been Daves' directorial debut. Daves obliged and the men applauded wildly.*

A few years later, Jane read a screenplay by Daves entitled Dark Passage, *a movie Warners released in 1947. When she heard that Daves was also directing it, and that it would star Humphrey Bogart, she went to Daves and lobbied for the female lead. "Sorry," Jane," he said, "but Bogie's already spoken for his Baby to play Irene in our movie."*

She knew, of course, that "Baby" meant Lauren Bacall.].

Foreground, *left to right;* Jack Carson, Jane Wyman, John Garfield, and Bette Davis raising the military's morale, in *Hollywood Canteen.*

The tepid "romance" of Hutton and Leslie in *Hollywood Canteen* was merely a backdrop for the appearances of a star-studded cast that included both Joan Crawford and Bette Davis.

Avowed enemies, they tried to stay in different parts of the canteen. Other stars ranged from *film noir's* Ida Lupino to Roy Rogers and Trigger. Sydney Greenstreet, Peter Lorre, and Paul Henreid represented the *Casablanca* coven. Jane convinced her friend, Barbara Stanwyck, to add her star name to the canteen, both in the movie and at the service counter.

One night, she whispered to Jane, "I see at least twenty hot guys here who would be Bob's type."

[The reference, of course, was to her bisexual husband, Robert Taylor.]

Jack Benny was in the movie and often appeared at the canteen to deliver a comedy routine, as did veteran performer Joe E. Brown. Jane still referred to Brown as "My least favorite leading man."

When Jane worked at the canteen, singing a song or two, she waited until closing time, when Garfield would volunteer to drive her home. On some nights, Garfield preferred to depart the premises with Joan Crawford on his arm. Their romance would grow hotter when they both co-starred in the 1946 *Humoresque.*

When Dennis Morgan made an appearance to entertain the troops, Jane always left the canteen with him.

Upon the release of *Hollywood Canteen,* audiences ignored the assault of the critics and flocked to see it. Jack Warner donated 40% of the ticket sales to the canteen itself.

***

Jane visited Van Johnson frequently during his recuperation from his automobile crash, and when he recovered, he asked her to go dancing with him. During the war, she'd kept a low profile and wasn't seen in clubs. But with victory almost assured, she went back to nightclubbing with Johnson.

Ironically, the movie magazines had run more pictures of Reagan and Johnson during the war than any other movie stars. Whereas Reagan represented the (married) man in uniform, Johnson had been dubbed "America's (available) Sweetheart," and frequently depicted with June Allyson.

"Jane seems to have captured both of these so-called gods," Sheridan said. "Of course, she and others knew her dates with Johnson were harmless and merely platonic outings."

Sometimes, Jane was seen out with both Johnson and a handsome young actor, Tom Drake, who had achieved fame as Judy Garland's "Boy Next Door" in *Meet Me in St. Louis* (1944). She was a "beard" to their burgeoning relationship, although Johnson also continued his affair with the married Keenan Wynn.

One night, Drake told Jane, "I don't rate the magazine coverage Van and your Ronnie get, but I'm also a favorite. I'm getting tons of mail, real gooey letters from young girls. Van gets even more mail like that."

"What would those little girls think if they could see you and Van, intimate and

An idealized portrait of small-town American virtue: Tom Drake, "The Boy Next Door," with Judy Garland in *Meet Me in St. Louis.*

together?" Jane asked.

***

Released in the summer of 1944, *The Doughgirls* picked up mostly bad reviews, one of them defining it as "More mishmash than smash." James Kern was attacked for his lack of experience as a director.

Paper after paper decided to downplay the film's other female stars and feature Jane—despite the fact that she had been billed below both Smith and Sheridan. The press had continued to define her and Reagan as "The Constant Honeymooners," and they still graced the cover of magazines. Maureen was, throughout most of the war, the most widely publicized baby in America.

The New York Times asserted, "Jane Wyman plays a priceless nitwit. The pairing of Wyman with her sidekick, Jack Carson, is threadbare." Other New York critics attacked how Hollywood had "sanitized" the original stage play, blaming its censure on a "bunch of bluenoses."

Despite its reviews, it did a respectable business at the box office, and Jane continued to get roles.

That led to a bitter row one night when Reagan came home. "You complain that all I talk about is politics. Well, all you talk about is your damn career."

"As a star, I've caught up with you in the last two years. There are those who say I've surpassed you."

"What are you trying to do?" he angrily retorted. "Replicate the plot of *A Star Is Born?*"

He was referring to the Fredric March/Janet Gaynor film released in 1937. It was the story of a rising young actress who marries a Hollywood super star. As he becomes a has-been, her star rises.

The argument became so intense that Reagan packed a bag and went to spend the next ten nights in the apartment of William Holden. He kept a small hideaway with a double bed, mainly where he brought his women.

"Ronnie and I never got off together," Holden told his friend, Glenn Ford. "We slept together. He'd fall asleep and I'd jerk off if I didn't get anything that day. When I blast off, I always let out a war whoop. I'm sure he heard me, but pretended to be asleep."

During the final months of World War II, Jane's marriage to Reagan was in serious trouble. His growing interest in politics and her near-obsession with her own career formed a deep void between them.

When she got a good review, he'd say, "That's nice, Janie," and go back to reading his newspaper, or else he'd talk politics. "Did you hear that FDR might appoint Douglas MacArthur to rule over Japan?"

"Who gives a fuck?" she'd say.

One evening, he saw her emerging in an evening gown and a mink coat. "I was told not to wear mink during the war years. But the damn war is about over, and I'm back with my mink to show off in front of the photographers."

"Where are you heading?" he asked. "You know I have to get up at 4:30 tomorrow morning."

"I can sleep late," she said. "We operate on different time clocks."

"It's not good for our marriage, your going out late at night like this," he said.

"It's good for my career," she said. "I've got to circulate, go to parties, go dancing, meet directors and producers."

"Don't climb too high," he cautioned her. "As I've told you before, I don't intend to become known as Mr. Jane Wyman."

***

Jack Warner told Reagan that throughout the war, his fan mail had continued unabated. Millions had seen him appear in or else narrate Army films. "In some weeks, your mail tops Flynn's. His fans are still loyal to him, even though he was investigated on charges of statutory rape. Judging by the mail, however, thousands of young American gals want to get raped by Flynn, not to mention the hordes of homo mail he gets from guys who are 4-F."

Day after day, Reagan viewed real combat footage sent by his crews in both Europe and the Pacific. "It was a horrible experience to sit through," he said. "One can only imagine what it was like to be in the middle of it. Plane crashes, poor guys being burned alive, massacred by the Japs or the Nazis. All the horror of war."

When at last, the Allies declared victory in Europe, Owen Crump became the first of FMPU's camera combat units to move into western Germany. Crump even beat Eisenhower in inspections of Hitler's notorious death camp at Buchenwald. Thousands had suffered and died in this camp. Newspapers made it famous as the former abode of one of her era's most notorious women, Ilse Koch, the wife of Karl-Otto Koch, commandant of the camp. After the war, this psychotic woman ("The Bitch of Buchenwald") was accused of having lamp shades crafted from the skins of murdered inmates with distinctive tattoos.

Crump sent footage of the atrocities back to Reagan and the officers of FMPU. Crump issued a warning. "The scenes depicted in these films are not fit for human viewing."

After watching what he called "the most sickening scenes I was ever to witness in my life," Reagan went outside the screening room and vomited.

He later said. "Those images are engraved on my brain forever. There will be no escaping them in my nightmares. What ghastly images to have to watch: Inmates so gaunt and emaciated you wondered how they could possibly be alive. I saw ditches being filled with their bodies and then bulldozed by the Nazis as if they could really bury their cruelty and depravity. I never knew how a country with Germany's rich cultural background could revert to such savagery."

Reagan recalled the final bitter battles of Americans fighting the Japanese as they prepared for an invasion of their homeland, where a million U.S. soldiers, it was estimated would lose their lives.

He was driving along a California highway when he heard on the radio that "a fantastic bomb has been dropped on Hiroshima."

"Suddenly, I knew my days in the Army were drawing to a close and I could return to Warners a movie star. It was the end of one aspect of my career. It was also a beginning, but none of us knew that at the time."

When he got to a phone, he called Jane.

"Your Johnny—in this case, Ronnie—will soon be marching home. Kick out all your other boyfriends and make room for Daddy."

"You're joking, of course," she said, sharply.

"Of course I am," he said.

***

To most of his fans, Reagan had shown "great courage under fire" during the war.

Actually, he'd never heard one gun fired. His reputation had been based solely on his "daring exploits" as portrayed in some of his movies, especially the wartime propaganda flicks, *Jap Zero* and *Rear Gunner.*

Reagan had served at Fort Roach for more than three years. But on September 10, 1945, he was given his discharge, thereby terminating his active duty.

After he drove home and entered his house, he secretly anticipated a "Welcome home, Ronnie" surprise party. But even though she was not involved at the time in any film project, Jane was nowhere to be found. There was no note or explanation of any kind.

Maureen and her nanny, however, were waiting to greet him.

He immediately placed a telephone call to Jack Warner, perhaps expecting him to react with joy that he was free to resume his movie career at Warners.

As Reagan later told Bill Holden, "Jack was friendly enough, and he invited Jane and me over to dinner. He also congratulated me on all those wartime propaganda movies. But his mood changed when I asked him to start sending over scripts."

"We don't have anything for you now," Warner said. "I'm sure something will turn up. We'll stay in touch. I've got to go."

As Reagan confessed to Holden, "So, this was to be my homecoming. I felt both my private life and my movie career had evaporated. I was desolate."

***

In the summer of 1944, Jane had flown to New York at the request of Jack Warner to promote *The Doughgirls.* While there, she had received a phone call that changed her life.

The second day of her arrival, Walter Winchell, in his popular column, had announced her presence in New York. That morning, at around 10AM, a call came in from director Billy Wilder. Since the success of his *Double Idemnity* (1944), starring Fred MacMurray and Jane's friend, Barbara Stanwyck, Wilder was the hottest director in Hollywood.

"What a delight to hear from you, Mr. Wilder," she said.

"I'm an early riser, and I dropped off a novel for you to read. I left it for you at the Plaza's reception desk."

"I'll read it right away," she promised.

"I'm going to make it into a film," he announced. "I want you to play the girlfriend of the hero. Perhaps I should say 'anti-hero.' He's an alcoholic."

"What is this novel called?" she asked.

"Read it! It's *The Lost Weekend.*"

Throughout the war years, despite the harmonies produced on their piano, tensions were high in the "WyReaMan" household.

Chapter Ten

Starlet Nancy Davis Joins MGM's "More Stars Than There Are in Heaven"

Nancy Gets a Reputation as "One of Those Girls Whose Phone Number Gets Handed Around a Lot."

At Manhattan's Stork Club, Clark Gable was seen dating Nancy Davis.

A columnist wrote: "Has something happened to Clark Gable, something in the form of starlet Nancy Davis, that is, changing the fitful pattern of his romantic life? Has he, in other words, finally found the Gable woman, for whom he is more than willing to give up the Gable women? The answer seems to be yes--even though, if it is love at all, it is, so far, love in hiding."

Ronald Reagan may have been Nancy's consolation prize after losing Clark Gable, but the B-picture star became the love of her life. She made up her mind long before he did.

The problem was: How to get this roving post-Wyman Romeo to quit dating every starlet in Hollywood and settle down to home and hearth with her?

363

During World War II, Ronald Reagan

(always in uniform) and Jane Wyman arguably became the most publicized couple in Hollywood, representing a fantasy version of what the American male in uniform and his wife and baby daughter on the homefront should look like. What was going on in their private lives beyond the screen was not known at the time, nor even today.

As for Nancy Davis of Chicago, she almost fell off the radar screen until after the war, when her biography could resume after a long and dormant slumber.

After Nancy's graduation from Smith College in 1943, she secured work in summer stock that was so minor it's hardly worth mentioning.

Alert, aware, intelligent, and ambitious. Nancy Davis in 1950.

Nancy still pursued a theatrical career, beginning at the lowest rung on the ladder, appearing in New England as an apprentice in mostly summer stock theaters.

"An apprentice meant you had to do everything, even clean the toilet in the star's dressing room," Nancy recalled.

"I appeared in rickety old summer stock playhouses along the Eastern Seaboard, including Bass Rocks, Massachusetts. "Sadly, most of them are gone today."

Nancy remembered her excitement when she actually had a line in one of these plays. "It wasn't much of a part. I wore a black uniform and a starched white apron. I came out and spoke my line: 'Madam, dinner is served.' Often an actress starts at the bottom, and I was following that age-old custom."

During that summer of 1943, Walter Hartwig, director of the Ogunquit Playhouse in Maine, cast Diana Barrymore in *You Can't Take It With You,* by George S. Kaufman and Moss Hart. Nancy had wanted the role for herself, but was hired as an apprentice.

Diana was the daughter of the legendary John Barrymore, an alcoholic Don Juan who had died the previous year (1942). Her mother was the poet, Blanche Oelrichs, who had been Barrymore's second wife.

Diana Barrymore, called "The Barrymore Brat" because of her Hollywood excesses, was the star, Nancy Davis the apprentice, in summer stock.

In the year of her father's death, Universal had signed Diana to a contract and promoted her as "1942's Most Sensational New Screen Personality." But within months, she'd become known as "The Barrymore Brat," because of her intake of alcohol and drugs and her lack of self-discipline.

In response to the negativity building up against her in Hollywood, and as a means of fine-tuning her dramatic technique, Diana decided to take a respite and do summer stock in 1943, where she often showed up drunk at curtain time. She was also recovering from a disastrous affair with Errol Flynn, who had housed her dissipated father during his dying days. In her memoirs, Diana denied an affair with Flynn, but friends claimed otherwise.

Ironically, when Diana's memoir, *Too Much, Too Soon* was adapted into a film, Flynn played her father, with Dorothy Malone appearing as Diana. Nancy noted the brouhahas surrounding Diana during her apprenticeship, discussing them later with Joshua Logan.

Nancy was later hired to work on Ogunquit's

summer stock production of *The Male Animal,* in which Buddy Ebsen was one of the stars. He was known for his inimitable, eccentric dancing style, with his tall, lanky frame doing rubbery gyrations. Nancy had seen him perform on the screen with both Shirley Temple and Judy Garland. He told her that he had lost out on the role of "The Tin Man" in *The Wizard of Oz* (1939), because he was allergic to the silver makeup.

Say it isn't so. When Nancy Davis worked in summer stock with Buddy Ebsen *(upper photo)*, she developed a powerful crush on him. Her taste in men later improved.

In the lower photo, hayseed Ebsen is seen in the TV series, *The Beverly Hillbillies* with Irene Ryan as possum-hunting Grannie.

John Edenstone worked on the production that summer and later claimed that Nancy developed a powerful crush on Ebsen. She admitted to that in a memoir. Edenstone recalled, "Perhaps Nancy should be forgiven for her taste in men. Ebsen was a jerk. Even though many members of the production staff were gay, he was always attacking what he called 'queers.' He

G 101   M.G.M.
NANCY DAVIS

When Nancy Davis was signed by MGM, the studio at first tried to promote her *(upper photo)* as a *femme fatale*. But she had formidable competition from true *femmes fatales* like Lana Turner, Ava Gardner, and a rapidly maturing Elizabeth Taylor.

Nancy's image *(lower photo)* did end up in a stack of movie star postcards distributed before World War II in Sweden, each of them sized and formatted like baseball fan cards.

shouldn't have been alarmed. No self-respecting homo would be attracted to that hayseed. In later years, he sure found his calling when he played the rube, Jed Clampett, in *The Beverly Hillbillies* on TV."

Nancy's job as a backstage apprentice involved switching on recorded music backstage when Ebsen, on stage, walked over to a Victrola. "I was so mesmerized by him that I ignored the cue, and he had to ad-lib while I got the stars out of my eyes, and played the music."

Since her crush on Ebsen was going nowhere, she headed back to Chicago at the end of the summer with men on her mind—one in particular.

***

Nancy was rumored to have begun a three-month affair with Dr. Daniel Ruge, the longtime partner of Loyal Davis, her stepfather. Ruge later denied it, claiming, "You reporters have gotten me mixed up with Clark Gable, whom Nancy did date. Not me, brother, although she was a nice, beautiful young lady."

Hollywood biographers such as Mart Martin have long included Dr. Daniel Ruge among Nancy's post-war lovers. "For twenty years," Ruge said, "I was loyal to Loyal, but I didn't share his racist attitudes. Neither did Nancy, She loved her stepfather and let him rant, never challenging him."

Born in Nebraska in 1917, he had earned his medical degree and a doctorate in pharmacology at Northwestern Medical School in Chicago. As a student, he had contracted tuberculosis, which had scarred his lungs. While training as a neurosurgeon in Chicago, he had worked for Loyal.

Ruge's assistant, Peter Winter, originally had wanted to be a doctor himself, but finally dropped out, having concluded that studying medical journals "was not my thing."

Winter had a front row seat to Ruge's growing interest in Nancy. "She was the one who chose to go after Daniel, in my view," Winter said. "He was an easy conquest. I think she'd lost her virginity long before they became secretly involved. I saw evidence that they were going at it hot and heavy. Very masculine, Daniel stood 6'2" and was appealing to a lot of the nurses. But Nancy got the prize."

"I don't think he was in love with her, but found her a reliable sex outlet. He was too much of a gentleman to go into clinical details, but he always came in with a smile on his face after a night out with Loyal's stepdaughter. I often saw them heading out at night, with theater tickets. Loyal knew about it and didn't object. He trusted Daniel not to get her pregnant, or, if he did, he knew how to take care of it."

Young Dr. Daniel Ruge *(upper photo)* was one of Nancy Davis' first lovers when he worked for her stepfather, Dr. Loyal Davis, in Chicago.

Later, he became Reagan's White House doctor, and was with him at the time of an attempted assassination in 1981. Dr. Ruge may, in fact, have saved the life of the President.

"The affair ended," Winter said in an interview, "when Nancy settled in New York and found many other beaux, of that I'm certain. But she and Daniel would remain friends for years to come, even in the White House.

[Fast forward to March 30, 1981. The local time in Washington, D.C., is 2:25pm, and President Ronald Reagan is leaving the Hilton Hotel after a speech before the AFL-CIO. Suddenly, six shots ring out from a .22 caliber Rohm RG-14 revolver. The assassin was the deranged, Oklahoma-born John W. Hinckley, Jr., age 26.

Reagan was not hit directly. One bullet ricocheted off the President's armor-plated, black Lincoln limousine and penetrated his left side. The bullet hit his rib and punctured and collapsed a lung before lodging in the spongy tissue an inch from his heart. The President had come close to instant death.

Reagan's press secretary, Jim Brady, received a direct shot, the bullet entering his brain. Police officer Thomas Delahanty was shot in the neck. As he was trained to do, Secret Service Agent Timothy McCarthy stood his ground and turned to face the gunfire. He took a bullet aimed at Reagan. It hit him in the chest. All the men shot around Reagan survived, through Brady remained paralyzed on the left side of his body until his death in August of 2014.

In one of the ironies of history, Dr. Daniel Ruge, Nancy's former beau, was functioning at the time as chief physician at the White House. He stood close to Reagan during the attack on the President's life.

Rushed to George Washington University Hospital with Reagan, Ruge ordered that the President be stripped naked so he could locate the entry point of the bullet. Blood transfusions were ordered at once. The President was calling out, "I can't breathe." He was suffering a massive loss of blood. Emergency surgery was performed, and some members of the staff were on the verge of rushing to their phones to announce that Reagan was dead, and that George H.W. Bush had assumed the presidency.

There was great confusion at the time as to who was running the government. Secretary of State Alexander Haig proclaimed, "I am in control here." At the time, Bush was flying to Washington from Texas.

Ruge later admitted, "I made a grave error in not notifying the proper people that, according to the 25th Amendment, Bush should have been named Acting President. Reagan was completely drugged and out of it. He was in no shape to preside over World War III, should it have come."

Rushed to the hospital, Nancy was in a state of hysteria. That night she wrote in her diary, "Nothing can happen to my Ronnie. My life would be over." Her anguish and depression lasted for months.

Ruge, still friends with Nancy after all those years, later discussed his term as chief physician at the White House. He said, "I inspected every inch of Reagan's body, inside and out. He was seven years older than me, and he was in a hell of a lot better shape than I was. He didn't smoke cigarettes and took care of himself."

He also denied that Reagan, during his first term, showed signs of his oncoming Alzheimer's disease. "He had a good memory then. I don't know about his last years in office. I never saw any signs of mental deterioration."

Ruge claimed he didn't remain in his post for a second term, because, "I found the job vastly overrated. It's not one of the glamour jobs at the White House. For example, Nancy often could not fit me in for a seat at State dinners. Dressed in a tux, I had to sit in my office solving crossword puzzles, waiting for the President to have a stroke, which never happened."

Ever faithful, Nancy was always there for Reagan throughout his hospital ordeal. In her 1989 memoir, My Turn, *she claimed she had the White House chef deliver her hus-*

band "two favorite soups: hamburger and split pea."

As Reagan recovered, the story grew more bizarre. At his trial on June 21, Hinckley was charged with thirteen offenses, but found not guilty by reason of insanity on June 21. After the trial, he wrote that the "shooting was the greatest love offering in the history of the world." In his deranged mind, he seemed to believe that his act would earn the love of actress Jodie Foster, with whom he had maintained an obsession ever since he'd seen her in the 1976 film, Taxi Driver. *In it, she played a child prostitute.*

Before heading off to kill Reagan, Hinckley considered tracking Foster down and committing suicide in front of her, but he soon rejected the idea. In his crazed mind, he figured that assassinating a President would elevate him to the level of a historical figure like Lee Harvey Oswald—and therefore, her equal. Oswald was his role model.]

***

George Batson's *Ramshackle Inn* opened on Broadway on January 5, 1944, marking the New York debut of ZaSu Pitts on the stage. The play got poor to occasionally tepid reviews. But because of Pitts' draw as a popular *comedienne*, it nonetheless ran for 216 performances. The newspaper *PM* reviewed it as "a dreary piece of hocus-pocus, with a soporific first act and a helter-skelter second and third. Batson seemed to tailor the role of "Belinda Pride" to Pitts' specific talents, with her "blinking eyes, fluttering hands, and quavering voice."

The plot concerns a retired librarian (Pitts) who buys a decaying colonial inn on the beach for only $3,000. As would be expected, it is falling apart and has a leaky roof. As one critic wrote, "Pitts is the imperturbable librarian who encounters ghosts and secret trunks, as she wanders through mysterious situations and thunderstorms, meeting both the living and the dead as innkeeper."

Most of the residents of the inn are bizarre—characters, viewers might have believed, from the twilight zone. There's a bootlegging operation going on in the basement.

Pitts liked her role so much that she persuaded the producers to take it on the road, first to Washington, then to Chicago. It was here that Nancy, along with her parents, Loyal and Edith Davis, took her to see the play, following the performance with a reunion with Pitts.

There was a small role in the play for "Alice Fisher," a gangster's moll who is kidnapped and sedated. Alice, dazed, drugged, and confused, makes only a brief appearance. The young actress interpreting that role dropped out in Chicago.

Subsequently, Pitts asked Nancy if she'd step in and take over the role as *Ramshackle Inn* headed for Detroit and points throughout the Middle West.

Nancy later wrote in one of her memoirs, "I suspect Edith had a hand in getting me the role. It was my first part in a professional production, and I grabbed my big chance. I played the role of the girl held captive upstairs. It wasn't much of a part, but it was a start, and I was on my own, with the best wishes of my parents."

In Detroit, Pitts took Nancy under her wing, even letting her share her dressing room. "It was a brand

new world for me," Nancy said, "and having a friend like ZaSu was very comforting. She had been a great beauty in her youth, and at this point in her career looked ageless. We traveled with the play across country."

During the tour, the players stopped off at the Danforth Lodge on Lake Oconomowoc in Wisconsin. Nancy was seen going out with two different beaux, described as "farm-fed, red-blooded, all-American types."

John Sheldon, a stagehand, later said, "Even though she was under ZaSu's protective eye, Nancy seemed to have a few stage door Johnnies waiting to take her out. She was not an obvious showgal cutie, but men, some much older than Nancy, seemed to find her sexually alluring. I don't know if she were putting out for these guys or not. She never said anything. But there was a lot of gossip about her backstage."

Nancy's mentor, inspiration, and unofficial guardian was a family friend and actress from the Silent era: ZaSu Pitts.

Here, she's depicted with Mary Pickford *(right)* in a 1917 scene from the silent film, *A Little Princess.*

The play returned to New York, but not to a theater on Broadway. "We played the subway circuit," Nancy said, referring to theaters in Brooklyn and the Bronx. At one point, they appeared on Long Island.

When the tour ended, Nancy decided to remain in New York, pounding the streets of Broadway, looking for a job in the theater. "I fancied myself the second coming of Helen Hayes," she said, jokingly. "I'd grown up surrounded by such great artists as Spencer Tracy and Lillian Gish. Now, I wanted to become part of their exclusive fraternity, even if it meant getting attacked by a lecherous Tallulah Bankhead."

***

Moving into the least expensive room at the Barbizon, an all-woman's hotel known for housing acting

Veteran actress ZaSu Pitts claimed, "Nancy is like a daughter to me."

hopefuls at the time, Nancy began her conquest of Broadway. To keep her from feeling alone and adrift, she lived close to family friends when she moved to a small apartment on East 51st Street, near the man she still called "Uncle Walter," Walter Huston. He urged her to date and meet people in the theater. He even arranged escorts for her with people who might get her a part in a show.

Spencer Tracy lived in the Waldorf Suites, and sometimes, Katharine Hepburn stayed with him. Nancy grew closer and closer to him, and he would play an important role in her career as it advanced.

During the day, she walked the streets, going from one casting office to another. She later denounced a lot of these casting calls as "meat markets." Horny producers often asked her to show them her legs—and many of them wanted her to lie on their casting couch or else perform fellatio on them as they sat at their desks. For the most part, she avoided such advances. "I want to be a serious actress," she told family friend, Lillian Gish. "I don't intend to become a Ziegfeld Girl."

In her first memoir, *Nancy* (1980), she admitted to having dated "a lot of actors, mostly writers, directors, assistant directors, and assistant producers." On occasion, she dated more influential producers and directors, some of whom took her to the Stork Club. "No serious romances," she recalled.

She was on a lean budget and had to "watch every penny, or at least every nickel" (her words). Visiting movie stars stopped at the Stork Club, then one of the most fashionable after-dark rendezvous spots in New York, and one night, she caught her first glimpse of the very glamorous Joan Crawford. Ethel Merman was a regular, and Nancy saw her showing up

Spencer Tracy in an early photo with his son, John, who was deaf, living "in a world of silence," as his father, with anguish, described.

on the arm of J. Edgar Hoover. When Nancy mentioned her sighting to Tracy, he said, "It's all a cover. He's a homo, and she's really a dyke."

Waiters at the Stork Club always served platters of freshly baked rolls. When Nancy thought no one was looking, she slipped two or three rolls into her evening bag—one roll for breakfast, another as an ingredient for sandwiches at lunch, if she could afford a slice of baloney to go with it.

One night, the club's savvy owner—celebrity-hunting, eagle-eyed Sherman Billingsley—sent over a pound of butter, with a note: "I thought you might enjoy some butter on my rolls."

One day at lunch, Tracy told her that his son, John, was coming to New York, and he wanted Nancy to go out with him, showing him the sights. Although Tracy maintained a suite at the Waldorf Towers, he asked Nancy if she'd invite his son to sleep on the sofa bed in the living room of her apartment. She agreed, finally deciphering why Tracy didn't want his son to stay with him. She realized that Katharine Hepburn was a frequent visitor, and he didn't' want John to report any news back to his mother, the former Louise Treadwell, who was still a loyal wife to Tracy despite his philandering.

Before John's arrival, Tracy told her, "I'm proud of the boy. I don't like to talk about his deafness, but know that he leads a fairly normal life in spite of it. He went to college, and his classmates were very fond of him. He often went out on dates with the prettiest campus queens. He's a great dancer—no Fred Astaire—but he can whirl you around a dance floor. He's making a career as an artist. Walt Disney is my friend, and he's hired John at his studios."

"He has the makings of a great polo player and could have been a champ," Tracy said. "Too bad polo has gone more or less out of style in Hollywood."

He also vowed, "As for his deafness, I will never give up. Somewhere, some place, I'll find a doctor who can restore his hearing."

John had been a polio victim and in addition to his deafness, had poor eyesight.

Nancy followed Tracy's guidance and treated John like one of her regular boyfriends. Since they were living together in such close proximity, it was assumed by those who knew her that she was having an affair with Tracy's son, especially since they were seen out together every night. Huston certainly thought so, and suggested to his friends, "My dear little girl, or so I think, is going to marry Spence's son. He's a god damn nice boy, and I believe he'd make a suitable husband for Nancy. Spence always uses John's having been born deaf as an excuse for his drinking, which is pure bullshit, of course."

John and Nancy did the rounds together, strolling along Fifth Avenue and through museums, and visiting the theater. At night, they went dancing, and Tracy didn't exaggerate the talent of his son on the dance floor. Every day, with Tracy, they took a walk in Central Park. Nancy noticed that he seemed to love his son very much, but seemed incapable of displaying his affection.

John preferred musicals instead of dramas, as it was hard for him to decipher the plot. As for musicals, he told Nancy he could sense the music through vibrations.

One night, John and Nancy went to see Tracy perform in a Broadway Play, *The Rugged Path,* written by Robert E. Sherwood, the dean of American dramatists. The play had opened to critical attacks, most of them directed at Sherwood. Even though Tracy's acting was praised in most reviews—"a good actor in a bad play," Hepburn still urged him to drop out.

Tracy had showed Nancy a review by John Chapman in the *Daily News*: "The sooner Spencer Tracy goes back to Hollywood, the better—and he should stay there!"

The Rugged Path opened on Broadway in November of 1945, closing in January after eighty-one performances. In brief, it was the story of a newspaper editor who becomes a liberal activist after time spent in London as the English were plunged into World War II. He clashes with the paper's conservative owners, including his brother-in-law, before leaving to fight in the Pacific.

One night, Hepburn entertained John, Nancy, and Tracy at her own small apartment. Fellow guests included writer/director Garson Kanin and actress Ruth Gordon. It turned out to be John's farewell dinner.

As Spencer Tracy said about his son, John Tracy, depicted above as a young adult: "But he bravely carried on in spite of his deafness, including dating my little friend, Nancy Davis."

"Did they go at it, living together in the same small apartment?" Spencer mused. "I don't know. Sometimes, the father is the last to find out such things."

Katharine *("La Divinissima")* Hepburn.

The next morning, a driver from MGM, as arranged by Tracy, arrived to take John to the airport. At her door, she reached down to pick up his suitcase. "No, let me do that," he said. "You are my princess and I am your slave."

After kissing him goodbye, she later claimed, "I closed the door and wept."

Huston was wrong about any lasting romantic link between John and Nancy, although he insisted they did have an affair. "A hot-to-trot young man and a hot-to-trot young lady living in such close quarters," he said. "The inevitable must have happened. At least I think it did."

***

In 1946, with World War II at an end, Broadway experienced its apogee in both drama and musicals. Ethel Merman had a smash hit in *Annie Get Your Gun,* and *Oklahoma!* was in its third season; *Carousel* in its fourth. *I Remember Mama* was a big hit at the Music Box, and *The Magnificent Yankee* was being staged at the Royale.

The year before, Tennessee Williams had premiered *The Glass Menagerie.* Later, it became a movie that starred Jane Wyman. On Broadway in 1946, *The Voice of the Turtle,* a play by John Van Druten, was in its third season. A year later, it would be made into a film starring Ronald Reagan.

In comedy, Judy Holliday scored a hit in *Born Yesterday.* When she repeated her performance on the screen, she would win an Oscar for it, beating Bette Davis' performance in *All About Eve* and Gloria Swanson's star role in *Sunset Blvd.*

Into this firestorm of success arrived Mary Martin, opening *Lute Song* at the Plymouth, a lyrical musical based on a very old Chinese play, *PiPa-Ji.*

[Set during the Han Dynasty (206 b.c.–220 a.d.), PiPa-Ji (The Lute), by Gao Ming, tells the story of a loyal wife who is impoverished when her husband is forced to marry another woman. She spends the next 12 years searching for him, earning her living by playing the pipa (lute). In the Broadway adaptation of this ancient Chinese opera, the two are eventually reconciled and live out their lives happily.]

Martin had scored a big success three years earlier on Broadway in *One Touch of Venus.*

The director of *Lute Song* was John Houseman. Born in Romania, the British-American actor was known for his collaboration with director Orson Welles in projects that included both *Citizen Kane* and for their launch of New York's acclaimed Mercury Theatre in 1937.

Prior to landing a small role on Broadway in *Lute Song*, Nancy had been hired as an actress in a gig that lasted for only four days. She later wrote that she could not remember the name of the play or its director. "He called me out into the garbage-strewn alley," she recalled. "He told me that I was wrong for the role and did not understand the character."

"I've got to let you go," he said. "Good luck in your theatrical ambitions, but, frankly, your legs are too thick

Post-war Broadway audiences might have enjoyed *Lute Song* if they could accept Mary Martin as an abandoned Chinese wife and Nancy Davis as a Chinese flower maiden.

372

for the theater."

She was too embarrassed to go back inside, so she asked him to retrieve her coat and purse, which he did. Nancy later wrote, "It was the first and last time I was ever fired from anything. I found out how painful it is to be rejected."

Out of work again, she'd made extra money modeling for the Conover Agency. She was often asked to model hats, because the agency suggested that she didn't have the physique for a full-figure model, especially if she had to show off her legs.

For the Broadway stage, *Lute Song* was adapted by Sidney Howard and Will Irwin, with a score by Raymond Scott and lyrics by Bernard Hanighen. Accessorized with lavish sets and music, it was an avant-garde mood piece, the story of a young wife, Tchao-Ou-Niang (Martin), who is married to Tsai-Yong (Yul Brynner). He leaves his wife and goes away to become a highly visible magistrate. He marries Princess Nieou-Chi (Helen Craig) and loses contact with his original family.

His parents, played by Mildred Dunnock and Augustin Duncan, die of starvation, and Martin, as his wife, although abandoned, nonetheless has to sell her hair to pay for her in-laws' funeral expenses. Ultimately, Brynner's character is reunited with Martin's character, and the princess welcomes her into the royal palace as Tsai-Yong's No. 1 wife.

[Craig, star of film, TV, and radio, had created the role of the deaf mute in the original Broadway production of Johnny Belinda *in 1940. Ironically, the movie version (1948) would bring Jane Wyman an Oscar.]*

Before opening on Broadway, Martin had been a houseguest of Edith and Loyal Davis in Chicago. Edith no doubt gave the star a slight nudge, which led to the casting of Nancy in a minor role as a Chinese handmaiden, *Si Tchun* (spelled by Nancy in a memoir as *Tsi Chun*). It marked her first and last appearance on Broadway. She later said, "I looked about as Chinese as Betty Grable." Oddly enough, even though they remained lifelong friends, Martin didn't even mention Nancy in her memoir, *My Heart Belongs* (1976), a strange omission.

Houseman later claimed in a memoir, "I wanted to fire Nancy, but Martin intervened and prevented me from doing so."

His star confronted the director, "I have a very bad back, and Nancy's father is the greatest neurosurgeon in America. Nancy stays in the play! Or else I walk!"

He later wrote: "At Mary's behest, to play the princess's flower maiden, we engaged a pink-cheeked, attractive but awkward and amateurish virgin by the name of Nancy Davis." He may have been off his mark with that virgin appraisal.

In preparation for her role, Nancy dyed her brown hair black and worked her makeup so that her eyebrows were set at an angle. "I hope this would make me look more like a Chinese Princess's flower maiden, really a lady-in-waiting. In spite of that, I still never won the favor of Houseman."

In contrast to his negative critique of Nancy, Houseman almost seemed to be in love with Brynner, describing him as "dynamic and strangely beautiful, and young man of Russian-Chinese origin. He was very sexy, an exotic leading man with an interesting speech and a vaguely Oriental look." Before the beginning of dress rehearsal, he invited Houseman to his dressing room, where he stood completely nude. "I am yours to do with as you wish. Dress me from my skin outward…or whatever you had in mind."

Before signing for *Lute Song,* Brynner did modeling work, having been photographed in the nude by George Platt Lynes. Nancy confessed in a memoir that "all the girls in the cast had a crush on Brynner," who had hair then and a magnificent physique. A photograph of him in all his uncut glory was circulated backstage. The original negative was later acquired by gay pop artist Andy Warhol.

Nancy never admitted that she was among those who had a crush on Brynner. She didn't have to: Too many others in the cast were already spreading that rumor.

In later life, Brynner had only compliments for Nancy. "If she'd stuck it out, I think she would have become a first-rate star."

He later confided in Houseman, who was not always discreet. He'd told his director that he had not actually seduced Nancy, but that she'd "serviced" him. There is only his word for that. However, throughout his career, he was known for summoning the most beautiful young men and women to his dressing room, where they found him waiting in the nude to be serviced.

[Once, when he was asked about that custom of his during his star role in The King and I, *Brynner said, "I'm the King of Siam, with unlimited power. I am merely taking monarch's privilege."*

Regardless of what happened (or didn't happen) with Nancy, Brynner, as a major star, went on to world class seductions, an impressive array that included Deborah Kerr, who found him "very, very sexy," and even Tallulah Bankhead. The list is long: Anne Baxter, Ingrid Bergman, Claire Bloom, Joan Crawford, Yvonne De Carlo, Judy Garland, Gina Lollobrigida, Maria Schell, and ultimately, Marilyn Monroe. When he was dying of cancer, Marlene Dietrich said, "Goody, goody—serves him right." He had abruptly dropped her.

Brynner also had a number of homosexual affairs, especially with a very young Sal Mineo, when they appeared together in The King and I *on Broadway. In France, the author, painter, and designer, Jean Cocteau, often fellated Brynner when they smoked opium together.]*

Immediately adjacent to the theater presenting *Lute Song* was a competing theater showcasing *Three to Make Ready,* starring Gordon MacRae, Ray Bolger, and Arthur Godfrey. Nancy had befriended two future stars, Patricia Neal and Jean Hagen. Hagen would one day star in a movie with Nancy called *Night Into Morning,* and Neal would co-star with Reagan in *The Hasty Heart.* The three aspiring actresses often visited the theater next door.

Sexy, exotic Yul Brynner had hair when he appeared in *Lute Song* and discovered the charms of Nancy Davis. He'd posed for an infamous nude, half of which is shown above, taken by a photographer depicting Brynner in all his uncut glory.

In the lower photo, he is seen in his iconic role as the King of Siam in *The King and I.*

Later, MacCrae boasted that "Nancy and I saw some action in my dressing room." Hagen said she doubted that, because she felt that MacCrae exaggerated his conquests. "He was always bragging about the women he had. One night, he even forced himself onto me. I resisted, but didn't put up all that much fight. I figured it was easier to give in. He was so god damn good looking. He later became an old drunk, singing in motel restaurants in Indiana."

Many of the cast members of *Lute Song* were heavy drinkers, but not Nancy. During the run, Richard Davis, her stepbrother, arrived in New York to stay with her. He was accompanied by three Princeton men into heavy boozing. After one all-night binge, Richard came into her apartment and was so sick he threw up in her bathtub. He later said, "It took two years before she would speak to me again."

Both Edith and Loyal Davis flew in from Chicago to attend the opening night of *Lute Song*.

The highlight of the show was Martin singing "Mountain High, Valley Low." *Time* magazine defined *Lute Song* as "The season's loveliest production and its most charming failure. There should have been either less spectacle or less story." The play opened on February 6, 1946 and closed on June 8 after 142 performances.

Lute Song was viewed as only moderately successful, surviving as long as it did because of the box office appeal of Mary Martin. For Brynner, it led to the career breakthrough of his life. Martin eventually recommended him to her friends, Richard Rodgers and Oscar Hammerstein, to play the Siamese despot in the classic musical, *The King and I*, a role that would be indelibly associated with him.

In spite of *Lute Song's* bad reviews, Brynner won the Donaldson Award as "the most promising new Broadway star of 1946."

Later, Nancy would be asked to go with it on tour, but she rejected the offer. An offer for another road tour with a play had come in from her dear friend, ZaSu Pitts.

The studly singer/actor Gordon MacCrae, who was appearing in a theater next door to *Lute Song,* later boasted to Patricia Neal and Jean Hagen that he'd seduced Nancy Davis.

Hagen wasn't sure if MacCrae ever accomplished that or not, "But he sure got around to me!"

***

Before Broadway, the cast of *Lute Song* tried out their musical in both New Haven and Boston. Nancy bonded with its lead dancer, Ron Fletcher, who was also a choreographer. She later described him as "effervescent, high strung, and very, very stylish."

As described in Fletcher's memoirs, "There was a quality Nancy had that drew her to me and I never was that interested in girls. I find her a curious mixture, on the one hand vulnerable yet I sensed a strength and a resolve in her that was iron willed. She seemed very determined."

"We went out every night because she made me laugh, and she had this amazing little chortle. Her voice had a touch of whimsy, rather adorable. I often took her ballroom dancing. We glided across the floor like Vernon and Irene Castle."

Fletcher said that during the Boston tryouts, they were virtually penniless. "Both of us were readers, and we pooled our money, five dollars in all, and joined a rental library. One night, we were determined to go ballroom dancing, but had no money to buy tickets. Since we hadn't rented any books yet, we went back to the rental library and withdrew our deposits. After that, we danced the night away."

Fletcher and Nancy were introduced to Dolly Haas, who was married to the famous newspaper caricaturist, Al Hirschfeld. She was a star of both German and American films, and was planning to take over Mary Martin's role for the road show tour of *Lute Song.*

[*Martin would later candidly admit, "Dolly was much better in the part than I was."*]

Haas recalled Fletcher and Nancy showing up one night in her dressing room. "She was an enchantingly beautiful young girl, and I think they were very interested in getting married. They even asked my opinion about what they should do. They seemed so young, so very much in love. I told them to go for it."

Many years later, Fletcher admitted he had had a sexual relationship with Nancy. "She was one of only three women that I slept with in my entire life."

In later years, Fletcher referred to Nancy as "a delightful creature. She was bright and curious. However, she didn't seem worldly at all, and I liked that about her. I would tell her tacky, obscene stories, and that wonderful laugh of hers could be heard."

"Although we had a little romance on the road, I don't think she was in love with me, and I was not in love with her. After we came back to New York, we slowly drifted apart. However, when I opened an exercise studio in California, she was a frequent visitor, showing up with her socialite friend, Betsy Bloomingdale, for my special exercises."

[A former Martha Graham modern dancer, Fletcher was also a disciple of the health and exercise regimes of Joseph and Clara Pilates, the original developers of the Pilates exercise regime, a movement that later attracted millions of devotees. It combined calisthenics and yoga with orthopedically savvy exercise equipment that to one pupil resembled instruments from a medieval torture chamber.

In 1972, Fletcher opened his health and exercise studio in Los Angeles, and his first customer was the novelist, Judith Krantz, who wrote bestsellers that included Scruples. *When he met her, he told her, "I am a gay man recovering from an addiction to alcohol." Krantz found him charming and soon spread the word among the Hollywood elite. Patrons who began showing up at his studio included Barbra Streisand, Candice Bergen, Ali MacGraw, and, as mentioned, "Nancy and Betsy," who were Fletcher's favorite customers.]*

As author Kitty Kelley noted, "Most of Nancy's closest friends and relationship were with homosexual men, both as friends and lovers. Homosexuality seemed to envelop her world. For the rest of her life, she enjoyed platonic friendships with well-dressed gay men who became her mentors in the arts, fashion, cuisine, and interior design, shaping her tastes and pointing her toward sophistication."

When Fletcher drifted out of her life, Nancy took up with Roger Fryer, an aspiring young producer. She went out with him almost every night, accompanied by his lover, a young actor named James Carr. She referred to them as "Bobby and Jimmy." In summer, the three of them could be seen in her small back garden barbecuing hot dogs on a grill.

Fryer and Nancy would become lifelong friends, and he went on to achieve great success on both Broadway and in Hollywood. "I make movies to pay the rent," he told her. "But the stage is my true love."

Ron Fletcher, the celebrated dancer and choreographer, was one of many intimate relationships "Broadway Nancy" formed with homosexual men.

In the lower photo, in Los Angeles, he is seen teaching one of his famous Pilates classes, lessons which attracted A-list stars from the movie community.

"The theater world and the film world are both strange," Fryer said, "in that you don't keep your relationship usually beyond the run of the show or the making of a film. But Nancy was one of the people that kept her friends closely held."

In time, Fryer would produce such Broadway hits as *A Tree Grows in Brooklyn, Auntie Mame*, and *Sweeney Todd*, his blockbuster films including *Mame, The Boys from Brazil*, and *The Shining*. He brought to the Los Angeles stage such luminaries as Katharine Hepburn, Elizabeth Taylor, Carol Channing, Angela Lansbury, and Mary Martin. He also presented plays by Arthur Miller, Eugene O'Neill, Tennessee Williams, and Lillian Hellman.

Biographer Bob Colacello also noted Nancy's affinity for homosexual men. "If she had stayed in show business instead of marrying an actor who went into politics, it would hardly have been noteworthy. She was close to a number of lesbian and bisexual women over the years, starting with her godmother, Alla Nazimova, and her circle of friends. But this is not unusual in the world of entertainment. If gay men were attracted to the young Nancy Davis, it was probably for the same reason that straight men were: She was pretty, lively, well-dressed, a good dancer, a good listener, and, like her mother, a natural-born coquette. She knew how to flirt with a man in ways that were flattering and unthreatening, which may explain why gay men felt especially comfortable around her."

***

Following the success of *Ramshackle Inn,* George Batson wrote another play, *Cordelia,* for ZaSu Pitts, who asked Nancy if she'd accept a small part in it and take it on the road with her. Nancy accepted without reading the script, because she trusted Pitts' judgment completely. The aging actress not only wanted to star in the play, but she believed in it so much, she'd invested a lot of her own money in producing it. *Cordelia* went on tour in the summer of 1946, hoping for a premiere on Broadway that autumn.

As the plot unfolds, ZaSu is raising two sisters whose mother walked out on them. She also rents rooms in a shack at the end of a wharf in New England, one of which is occupied by a gambler. Cast as Millicent, Nancy plays an upper-class young woman who falls in love with the street-smart gambling man.

Once again, she was on tour with Pitts, sharing her hotel rooms and helping organize Pitts' wardrobe, much of it designed by Edith Head. To the cast, they appeared extremely close, sleeping together, dining together, and going home with each other every night during tryouts in both Boston and New Haven.

Although it was wild speculation, with no real evidence, many cast members assumed that Pitts and Nancy were engaged in a lesbian affair. It was well known to them that Nancy's godmother, Alla Nazimova, the Silent Screen goddess, was a lesbian. In reality, Pitts viewed Nancy almost like her own daughter and was very protective of her.

The reviews were lackluster, critics evaluating the play as "amateurish and hoked-up."

As a last resort, a play doctor was summoned. He immediately changed the name of the play from *Cordelia* to *Dangerous Woman*. Pitts stuck up her nose at that title. "Sounds like a Joan Crawford movie."

Ironically, in 1952, Crawford would make a film, *This Woman Is Dangerous.*

Jack Kirkland was a "play doctor" and a man of many talents—playwright, producer, director, and screenwriter. At the time, he was best known for adapting Erskine Caldwell's controversial play, *Tobacco Road*, to the screen. Nancy met him, remembering that he'd penned one of her favorite movies, *Now and Forever* (1934), with Gary Cooper, Carole Lombard, and Shirley Temple.

But even a talented writer such as Kirkland could not rescue *Cordelia,* and Batson's play closed on the road, never making it to Broadway.

***

After the failure of *Cordelia,* Pitts wanted a "surefire guarantee of success," and with that in mind, she selected a much-reprised comedy workhorse, *The Late Christopher Bean,* written by Sidney Howard from an original French farce. Many other actresses had already interpreted that play, including Lillian Gish, Edith Evans, and the formidable Marie Dressler.

In the summer of 1947, Pitts, along with Nancy, still sharing her hotel room, toured with the play on the summer stock circuit. That autumn, Pitts took the play to major cities that included Philadelphia, Boston, Milwaukee, and Cleveland. At the opening at Chicago's Civic Theater on October 20, 1947, Nancy received more congratulatory telegrams than Pitts, with acknowledgments from such established stars as Spencer Tracy, Walter Huston, Mary Martin, and Lillian Gish.

On opening night, Edith Davis appeared, wearing a mink coat with an orchid pinned to it. On her arm was Loyal Davis, who was now the president of the Society of Neurological Surgeons.

After the show, Edith threw a gala opening night party, inviting the elite of Chicago, including Dwight Green, the Governor of Illinois.

The next day, reviews of Nancy's role were not as enthusiastic as those of her parents. In her role as an *ingénue,* Nancy was called "a sweet, decorous girl." Another critic found her "unusually attractive and talented." She carried a copy of that review in her purse for months, although later admitting, "I wasn't exactly setting show business on fire, yet I was doing work I really liked."

The producer, Michael Myerberg, had signed screen actor Guy Kibbee as the star of the play. Bald, pot-bellied, and rosy-cheeked, Kibbee was familiar to film-goers of the 1930s, as he'd starred with almost every major performer from Errol Flynn to Shirley Temple. He was cast as a country doctor who takes in roomers, one of whom is Christopher Bean, an artist. During the course of the play, Bean dies, bequeathing the household a number of paintings. Although at first they're thought to be worthless, as the plot develops, it's revealed that they're masterpieces. Nancy was cast as

ZaSu Pitts in Erich von Stroheim's silent classic, *Greed* (1924), her most controversial performance.

Ingénue Nancy Davis onstage with ZaSu, in a performance of *The Late Christopher Bean.*

378

the country doctor's older daughter, who is in love with a local paperhanger who turns out to be an artist himself. By Act Three, we learn that Pitts, the doctor's housekeeper, had been secretly married to Bean, and that in her capacity as his widow, all those masterpieces belong to her.

On the road, Kibbee and Pitts got all the critical attention, and Nancy was virtually ignored. One critic, however, called her performance "nicely sweetened without saccharine."

When the play opened at the Olney Theater in Olney, Maryland, outside Washington, Nancy received a note backstage, requesting a visit with her after the show. It was from General and Mrs. Omar Bradley, who had recently been entertained at home in Chicago by Edith. Bradley, of course, had commanded the American Army in Normandy, and was slated to become President Harry Truman's chairman of the Joint Chiefs. Nancy welcomed them warmly, realizing that her mother still had the kind of allure that attracted famous people.

The next day, the local paper asserted, "Nancy Davis took the role of a sappy, cloying girl and turned it into a real person."

During the play's run in Olney, James Karen, a young actor, part of the Olney Theater Company, congratulated Pitts on her star role in the controversial four-hour long *Greed* (1925), a pet project of the temperamental director, Erich von Stroheim. "That god damn picture," Pitts muttered to Karen. "Don't mention that film to me. As far as I'm concerned, Stroheim can shove every single reel of it where the sun don't shine." Then she turned and walked away.

Nancy was shocked, as she'd never heard her mentor use such strong language. "To provoke her like that, *Greed* must have brought back a lot of painful memories."

***

After her return New York, Nancy attended a party given by Mary Martin. For a starlet, an invitation to one of Martin's parties was a great honor, as she knew all the luminaries on Broadway, including Alfred Lunt, Lynn Fontanne, Helen Hayes, and playwrights such as George Kaufman.

At the party, she was introduced to actor/singer Alfred Drake, who, with his rich baritone voice, had become the King of Broadway musicals, particularly after his spectacular performance as Curly, male lead in the 1943 production of *Oklahoma!* With macho pizzazz, he'd opened each performance with a rousing rendition of "Oh What a Beautiful Mornin'."

Nancy had first seen him playing Marshall Blackstone in the original production of *Babes in Arms* (1937), in which he'd sung the title song. She found him very handsome in a virile, masculine way, and it was obvious that he was attracted to her, too. Despite his marriage in 1944 to Esther Harvey Brown, he was still known for his seductions of "songbirds

Two views of the man who at the time was the most dashing romantic lead on Broadway—Alfred Drake, known for "draking" women.

379

and starlets." Boastfully, he relayed to his friends the names of the stars or starlets who had been "draked," and which of them remained for him to "drake."

Nancy had heard that in spite of his name, he was actually Italian, having been born Alfred Capurro of parents who had emigrated to New York from Genoa. Somewhere along the way, according to those who knew Drake, he began seeing Nancy on the side. "It had to be a back alley affair," said Cole Porter, who himself had a crush on Drake, "because Alfred was married, and he didn't want word to get back to his Esther."

From unverified reports, including from Porter, the affair lasted for only a season. "I think the Davis girl objected to the fact that she couldn't be seen in public with him and especially couldn't go to A-list parties, where he had to show up with his wife. I also think that she wasn't convinced that he'd get her a part on Broadway."

Suddenly, Drake was out and Max Allentuck was her man of choice, at least for a little while.

Allentuck was way down the line when it came to Broadway luminaries, but he nevertheless had the power to get an aspiring actress cast in a play. His career had begun in vaudeville. After that, he worked for major producers such as Kermit Bloomgarden, who was currently presenting Lillian Hellman's *Another Part of the Forest* (1946), and who would later produce *The Diary of Anne Frank* (1955), and *The Music Man* (1957).

Years later, Helen Tiers, the former secretary to Allentuck, was interviewed by reporter Joan Evert. The secretary remembered Nancy's arrival in Allentuck's office. "She didn't look like a young actress seeking a job in the theater," Tiers claimed. "She was dressed like a movie star. She owned a fur coat and always wore tasteful, well-tailored clothes. She was also beautifully groomed, not a hair out of place. Unlike most showgirls of that day, Davis believed in 'The Fashion House Style,' which promoted 'good lines and quiet, subdued colors.' Even though very busy, Max always made time for Davis, most often slipping out the back door with her to do whatever they did together. Frankly, I think Nancy Davis was hotter for Max than he was for her…His first marriage to Peggy Phillips had crashed. By 1949, he would wed the actress Maureen Stapleton, no great beauty, but one of the most talented stage actresses on Broadway. She had made her debut in the 1946 *Playboy of the Western World*."

In her column, Dorothy Kilgallen wrote, "Max Allentuck, general manager for producer Kermit Bloomgarden, is often seen after the curtain goes down with rising brunette starlet, Norma *(sic)* Davis. Do I hear wedding bells?"

Wedding bells did not toll. Soon, Nancy, in the opinion of Allentuck, was "pursuing bigger game in the Hollywood jungle."

[Although Stapleton divorced Allentuck in 1959, in 1981, she seemed fully aware of her ex-husband's involvement with Nancy Davis, when Stapleton attended a reception in Washington with Tennessee Williams. She had been one of his favorite actresses since the 1951 production of The Rose Tattoo.

In the reception line, Nancy Davis Reagan, now First Lady, greeted the actress.

"Hello, Maureen," Nancy said. After she had passed on down the line, Tennessee whispered to Stapleton, "I didn't know you knew Nancy Reagan. Not enough to call her by her first name."

"I never met her before. But, like me, she's an actress,

Maureen Stapleton in the urban canyons of NYC's Theater District, late 1940s.

"Nancy Davis was screwing around with my husband, Max Allentuck, before I got to him."

and we always call each other by our first names. Besides, we have something in common: She used to fuck my former husband, Max Allentuck.]

***

In July of 1948, Nancy's gay friend, Roger Fryer, turned producer, asked her to play the daughter in a stage revival of *The Little Foxes* by Lillian Hellman. The role of the formidable, evil Regina Giddens had originated as a Broadway hit in 1939, starring Tallulah Bankhead. In 1941, producer Samuel Goldwyn and director William Wyler had cast Bette Davis in the movie version. That film had starred Teresa Wright as Regina's daughter. In the Chicago stage revival of 1948, Nancy was given that role.

She accepted the role from her friend, Fryer, although there is evidence that there was tension between them during rehearsals. At one point, an exasperated Nancy said, "Teresa Wright is a hard act to follow."

Ruth Chatterton, the former wife of George Brent, was asked to take on an even more daunting challenge and interpret the role of Regina Giddens in the footsteps of Bankhead and Davis, each of whom had stamped powerful images into one of the genuine "bitch roles" of the stage and screen.

A star during the early Talkies, Chatterton's career had already peaked by the time she accepted the role of Regina. Her last American movie, William Wyler's *Dodsworth,* had been released in 1936.

Nancy Davis was virtually ignored by reviewers. However, John Davidson wrote: "The role of Regina Giddens, a soulless and sadistic vixen, an unmitigated murderess, is so overpowering that it seems to devour poor little Nancy Davis, who struggled to hold her own in this Southern nest of cottonmouths and rattlers."

***

In September of 1948, back in New York, pounding the dirty sidewalks of Broadway,

Three distinguished actresses, Tallulah Bankhead (left); Bette Davis (center); and Ruth Chatterton appeared either on stage or the screen as the Southern hellion, Regina Giddens, in *The Little Foxes.*

Nancy Davis was cast as Chatterton's daughter.

Living in a shadowy existential hell with an evil dragon for a mother. *Above, left*: Teresa Wright and Bette Davis in *The Little Foxes*.

In Chicago, Nancy *(right)* dreaded stepping into Teresa Wright's shoes in this gothic tale of family anguish and female duplicity. She got tired of hearing, "Teresa Wright did it better." Her performance went virtually unnoticed.

Nancy was once again looking for work and finding none, although Roger Fryer told her she might gain experience working in television, then in its pioneering stage. He told her he'd see if he could line up something for her. Spencer Tracy was also looking for a role for her. When he called her apartment, she thought it was to report on a possible role. But it involved something else. He told her that his friend, Clark Gable, was coming into town later that month, and he wondered if she'd be free to date him. "I highly recommended you."

"It would be the greatest honor of my life, but I can't imagine the King of Hollywood walking up three flights of steps to date an unknown starlet. I mean, he could have his pick of any woman in New York."

"Great!" he said. "You'll do it. I'll give Clark your phone number."

After putting down the phone, Nancy immediately called Edith in Chicago. "I'm going to date Clark Gable! *The* Clark Gable!"

"Oh, my dear, you're delusional," Edith said.

Nancy often turned to astrology as her guiding light, and subsequently, she consulted an astrologer. The stars were right in the heavens, or so it seemed, for her date with "The King."

Three days later, Gable called and invited her for dinner and dancing at The Stork Club. She later said, "I was in a state of shock when I put down the phone. My heart was palpitating. I had worshipped him on the screen. I could not believe that I had actually spoken to him."

From reading fan magazines, Nancy was awed by the glamorous women Gable had conquered, including his late, doomed wife, Carole Lombard. The list included some of the most glamorous stars of the Golden Age—Lana Turner, Mary Astor, Joan Crawford, Jean Harlow, Hedy Lamarr, Merle Oberon, Norma Shearer, Lupe Velez. "What would a man who'd had all those queens want with a mere handmaiden?" *[Her reference was inspired by the role she'd played in* Lute Song.*]*

The slim, brown-eyed beauty from the Windy City paraded into the Stork Club on the arm of Gable himself. Photographers at the entrance snapped their pictures. In a memoir, Nancy would later rave about how "sexy, handsome, and affectionate," he was. In the club, he held her hand, and she found him "romantic and fun-loving."

"A flood of women walked by our table on the way to the powder room," she wrote.

She claimed that she didn't know how many friends she had until Gable invited her to dance. "Oh, Nancy, darling, how wonderful to see you!" many of the women said, wanting to be introduced to Gable.

The evening presumably ended with a kiss on the mouth. On many an occasion, his dates had complained about his bad breath, because of the false teeth he wore. Nancy had no complaints, and accepted his offer to be booked during every night of this stay in Manhattan.

The World Series was being played at the time, and he invited her to Yankee Stadium following lunch the following day. At ten o'clock, a lovely bouquet of red roses arrived at her apartment before he picked her up. Actually, Gable did not cut as dashing a figure as he had when he'd played Rhett Butler back in 1939. Gore Vidal, whose mother, Nina Vidal, had once had an affair with him, wrote, "At this point in his life, Gable had put on weight, and he drank heavily. After a few drinks, he would loosen his false teeth, which were on some sort of peg, and then shake his head until they rattled like dice. His post-war movies had flopped at the box office, but he was still a big name to his public."

At Yankee Stadium, Nancy and Gable were mobbed. Four policemen had to escort Gable and Nancy to their box seats. Earlier, they had been seen lunching at the exclusive "21."

Walter Winchell, in his popular column, wrote: "At long last, Clark Gable had found a replacement for his beautiful doomed wife, who went down in that plane crash in 1942. He went into mourning, but now seems to have emerged. If anyone can bring him out of his depressive shell, it is a cute little brunette starlet whom he's taking to all the hot spots of Manhattan."

Other reporters heard the sound of wedding bells, which had rung, at least in print, for Nancy before, but which had always stopped ringing before she was able to march up the aisle to an altar.

Gable and Nancy continued their high-profile

Nancy Davis, as a postwar Broadway *ingénue*, looked, acted, and dressed like a major-league star before she became one.

When Clark Gable made *The Hucksters* (1947) with Ava Gardner *(see above)*, he told her "I'm not feisty Mickey Rooney, but there's still fire in the engine."

To Sydney Greenstreet, he recalled dating Nancy Davis. "Something might have happened if I'd stayed in New York. But I went back to Hollywood, where I already had an over-full card of women—and Ava can't be beat."

dating, attending a hot ticket Broadway musical, *High Button Shoes.* The musical starred Phil Silvers and Nanette Fabray, with music by Jules Styne and lyrics by Sammy Cahn. Its director was George Abbott. As Gable walked in with Nancy, the audience stood up and gave him an ovation.

Word of an affair reached Chicago. Edith telephoned one morning. "What in hell is going on between Gable and you?"

"We're just good friends," Nancy said.

"Like hell. I've talked to Spencer Tracy. As you know, he's Gable's confidant. Gable told Spence that he's fucking you."

"Spence exaggerates."

"Well, if he's plugging my daughter and you get knocked up, make sure you get a wedding ring."

Tracy seemed to fancy himself a matchmaker. He told Katharine Hepburn, George Cukor, Garson Kanin, and Ruth Gordon, "Clark is banging Nancy. She's seen late at night leaving his suite at the Waldorf. He's not much of a lay, as he freely admits himself, but she couldn't do any better than wed the King of Hollywood. Actually, that title belongs to me, but I forgive Clark for using it."

Nancy more or less denied the affair, without actually saying so. Back in Hollywood, Joan Crawford, Gable's steadfast friend and lover over the years, claimed that he had admitted to an affair with Nancy—"Whoever in hell she is."

Joan Crawford in a publicity still for *Mildred Pierce,* a role coveted and lost by Jane Wyman.

Crawford was Clark Gable's part-time lover. He confessed to her that in New York, he had "strayed with Nancy Davis."

"Nancy, who?" Crawford asked.

In a memoir, Nancy hinted that Gable may have indirectly proposed to her. One night he asked her, "How would you feel about living on a ranch?" He was obviously referring to his ranch in Encino, California.

She later claimed that she fumbled her response. She said, "Gee, I don't know. I never have." On looking back at that moment, she wondered, "Was Clark sounding me about a possible future together? And, if so, how should I have responded? I wasn't in love with him, but if we had seen more of each other, I might have been."

And then, suddenly, it was over.

Gable flew back to Hollywood and to the arms of Ava Gardner, with Grace Kelly and Marilyn Monroe looming in his future. A year later, he entered into an unsuccessful marriage (1949-1952) to Sylvia, Lady Ashley, a socialite.

Tracy told his gossipy friend, the director George Cukor, that "Clark was Nancy's first choice for a husband. Ronald Reagan was just the consolation prize."

***

Long before Ronald Reagan and Jane Wyman became big stars on television, Nancy broke into the medium during its infancy. As she recalled, "I had to wear green makeup and black lipstick! TV was very new, and you had to wear some strange colors if you wanted to look good on those early, primitive black-and-white TV sets."

An offer came through for her to appear in a telecast called *Broken Dishes,* set to air on May 12, 1948, on Kraft Television Theatre. Some biographers have suggested that this was a new script. Actually, it had been around for years. *Broken Dishes* had premiered as a Broadway play in 1929 when it had introduced another newcomer to the theater, also named Davis—Bette in this case. The screen diva defined November 5 of that year as "the greatest triumph of my professional career, the night I first saw my name on a Broadway marquee."

Far from being an unknown property, *Broken Dishes* had already been adapted into three separate Hollywood movies, each with a different title: *Too Young to Marry,* with Loretta Young (1931); *Love Begins at Twenty* with Patricia Ellis (1936); and *Calling All Husbands* with Lucile Fairbanks (1940). When Nancy starred in the teleplay, the property was viewed in Hollywood as "a tired old workhorse."

It was a comedy focusing on a henpecked husband in the Middle West, with a nagging wife always talking about "the man I should have married." The daughter, as played by Nancy, seeks independence from her domineering mother by marrying a man her mother finds objectionable. At the finale, that man the mother idealized turns up. Ironically, he has become a penniless fugitive, desperately fleeing from the police.

Benny Thau, head of casting at MGM, had flown to New York to confer with Tracy at his temporary home at the Waldorf Towers. Nancy had alerted Tracy to watch her debut on TV. He invited Thau for drinks with him and to view the telecast as well. Thau detested television and feared future competition from the new medium, so he sat, visibly suffering, through the telecast. Apparently, however, the fifty-one-year-old man, unmarried at the time, became quite fascinated with the twenty-eight year-old actress, Nancy herself.

At the end of the broadcast, Thau expressed his interest in dating Nancy. Tracy agreed to call her, finding her excited when she heard he was in charge of casting at MGM, "The Tiffany of Studios."

After his first date with Nancy, Thau discussed with Tracy that he might arrange a screen test for her. "We need another clean cut, girl-next-door type at Metro," Thau said. "We've already got enough sultry types—take Lana Turner and Ava Gardner, for example. Of course, for class, we already have your beloved Katharine Hepburn."

In her memoirs, Nancy doesn't even mention Thau, although he became one of the most influential men in her screen career. According to unconfirmed reports, Thau's long affair with Nancy actually began in New York.

She wanted to believe Thau when he told her he would arrange a screen test for her at MGM. If the studio bosses liked it, a seven-year contract would follow. "I could hope and dream," she recalled.

In the meantime, while awaiting that contract, she did more live television. ZaSu Pitts cajoled once again and asked Nancy to repeat their roles in *Ramshackle Inn* as part of a telecast for Philco Television Playhouse. It aired on January 2, 1949.

Nancy's performance went over so well with the Philco producers that she was invited to repeat her role in *The Late Christopher Bean,* the play in which she had toured with Pitts. However, she was not available for the telecast, and the Davis' family friend, Lillian Gish, took the star role. That telecast was premiered on February 6, 1949.

Star Maker Benny Thau: When the MGM Lion roared, starlet Nancy Davis answered the call.

385

By that time, Nancy's screen test at MGM had been scheduled. She often had long talks on the phone with Thau.

When her air tickets arrived, she organized the details of her departure and packed her luggage.

She told her friends, perhaps in exaggerated jest, "Greer Garson replaced Norma Shearer as Queen of MGM. Now I'm on my way to dethrone Garson." Nancy never actually "dethroned" her, but she did replace Garson in one of her roles: The British actress had been Thau's mistress.

Although Nancy arrived on the scene at the end of Hollywood's Golden Age, she still managed to win a seven-year contract at a time when more established MGM contract players were being let go. As she set foot on California soil, many stars were desperately free-lancing in search of acting jobs.

Although Edith encouraged her daughter's film career, Loyal did not, claiming, perhaps correctly, that Hollywood was "an unsavory place."

Spencer Tracy had contacted his gay friend, director George Cukor, known as the best women's director in Hollywood, and asked him to direct Nancy's screen test. That was unheard of; Cukor didn't do screen tests. But for Tracy, he agreed to supervise Nancy's try-out.

Tracy also placed a call to Dore Schary, a former screenwriter now in charge of production at MGM. He would soon replace Louis B. Mayer. Schary had written the script for *Boys Town* (1938), which brought Tracy an Oscar. "Nancy knows how to look like she's thinking when she's on stage," Tracy said. "I'm told you want to make message pictures. Nancy would be ideal for those."

When Nancy heard that Schary suffered back pains, she put him in touch with her stepfather, Loyal Davis, a high-profile neurosurgeon. The doctor relieved the executive's pains, which made him grateful to Nancy.

Before her screen test, Nancy spent three weeks with Lillian Burns, MGM's drama coach, who rehearsed the starlet in voice, dancing, acting, deportment, and appearance.

For the test, Thau arranged for Nancy to have as her cameraman George Folsey, who was said to photograph women more beautifully than anyone in his field. "I can turn a snaggle-toothed hag into a sultry, classical dame," he proclaimed.

Sent to makeup, Nancy found herself sitting between June Allyson and Elizabeth Taylor. Both of them would eventually become her friends.

The top hair stylist in Hollywood, Sydney Guilaroff, was assigned to tangle with her hair. William Tuttle, acclaimed as the leading makeup artist in Hollywood, rivaled only by Perc Westmore, did her face. He told her, "We'll have to do something about your eyes: They are too big for pictures."

She walked onto the set with her eyes half closed until the cameraman, Folsey,

Women who drove Benny bananas: Greer Garson *(left)* and Nancy Davis.

386

asked, "Did you get enough sleep last night?"

She explained what Tuttle had said.

"It was a fucking joke. You can't have eyes too big for the movies. Ever see a Joan Crawford picture?"

As her leading man, Howard Keel was selected to appear opposite her. The handsome, strapping, macho baritone from Illinois would become the movie equivalent of Alfred Drake on Broadway, eventually appearing in such upcoming musicals as *Annie Get Your Gun* (1950) and *Show Boat* (1951). He was known for his big, booming voice. Nor was he modest, claiming, "I'm big in all departments."

Keel and Nancy were given a script for an upcoming MGM film, *East Side, West Side* (1949). Ironically, when shooting began for that film, Nancy would be assigned a role in it.

During the filming of her screen test, Nancy admitted, "I was terribly nervous, but Howard talked to me and made me calm down." During a break, he told her of his background, asserting that he'd come from a coal-mining town where his father had committed suicide when he was a young boy.

Macho, magnetic, and charismatic: Howard Keel "wiving it wealthily" in *Kiss Me Kate*.

As he grew in stature in the coming years, he would become a sex symbol at MGM, and he boasted of having scored with his leading ladies. They had included Kathryn Grayson, Ava Gardner, and Esther Williams. He said that before that, he'd seduced Norma Jeane Baker (Marilyn Monroe) when she was only thirteen and he was twenty-one. He referred to Monroe as "San Quentin jail bait."

Four years after his screen test with Nancy, Hedda Hopper asked Keel, "You appeared on camera with both of Reagan's wives, Nancy and Jane Wyman. You are known in Hollywood as quite a ladies' man Did you get lucky with Nancy or Jane?...Maybe both?"

"I can answer your question with a question," Keel said. "Does a bear shit in the woods?"

After the screen test, Nancy had to fill out a questionnaire about herself. She shaved two years off her age, defining it as twenty-six. Among her phobias, she listed that she hated "vulgarity, untidiness of mind, and cigars."

When she signed with MGM, Nancy stood 5'4" and weighed 116 pounds. She named her favorite actors as Walter Huston and Spencer Tracy, her favorite female star as Laurette Taylor, the older, Irish-American actress. In 1944, on Broadway, she had been the first to interpret the key matriarchal role of Amanda in Tennessee Williams' *The Glass Menagerie.*

Nancy also asserted that her greatest ambition was "to have a successful marriage."

Although he masked it, Cukor took an instant dislike to Nancy. Privately, he told Tracy, "She has ab-

George Cukor: Very outspoken in his negative impression of Nancy.

387

solutely no talent."

[Throughout the rest of his life, Cukor made nasty remarks about her. In his most notorious comment, he claimed, "If I had a nickel for every Jew Nancy was under, I'd be rich."]

Cukor showed her screen test to producer Pandro S. Berman, who had dealt, frequently, with such über-luminaries as Katharine Hepburn. He told Cukor, "Nancy Davis just doesn't have star material."

Nancy later recalled, "I escaped the usual star buildup, having to pose in bathing suits and the like. From the beginning, I was cast either as a young girl with children, or I was padded to appear as pregnant more times than I can recall. From 1949 to 1956, I would make eleven films, but, except for a few of them, I hardly remember what happened during the shoot."

Unlike Reagan's first wife, Jane Wyman, Nancy didn't seem to be particularly susceptible to *"Leadingman-itis."* Male stars who failed to light her fire included Van Heflin, James Mason, Zachory Scott, James Whitmore, Ray Milland, Ralph Meeker, and George Murphy, Reagan's best friend. "Glenn Ford was attractive enough, but he was involved," she said. In one of her final films, however, her leading man really turned her on—Reagan himself. By then, she'd already married him.

During her first interview with Louella Parsons, the aging gossip maven asked her, "Is there one man in your life?"

"Not yet," Nancy said. "I don't want to sound trite, but I'm married to my career, and that's pretty much the truth."

Actually, the first journalist to interview Nancy after she signed her contract was columnist Ines Wallace. What she wrote was rather bland. Privately, she had a sharper opinion: "My impression of her was dismal. She was more like a character actress than a leading lady. She looked a bit long in the tooth. Mayer liked to sign young girls—take Elizabeth Taylor, Judy Garland, or Lana Turner, for example. I was told that MGM planned to build Nancy up. Up for what? Oblivion? The fans won't go for this one. Trust me!"

Nancy also realized that within MGM, she couldn't compete with those "child-woman" stars, the rosy-cheeked "girl next door" type. June Allyson and Jane Powell were already under contract for those parts, with Debbie Reynolds looming on the horizon.

"I had to be something in between," Nancy said. Thau told wardrobe and makeup that he wanted them to create "that respectable lady look, an image of manicured prettiness."

"Nancy was not glamorous," Thau said, "and she knew that."

"After I put my "Jane Henry" on that contract, I started receiving a weekly paycheck," Nancy said. "No longer would I have to depend on Edith and Loyal for support."

[In later years, Nancy, in her real-life role as a mother, would have to provide money for her son, Ron Reagan, Jr., during the early stages of his career as a ballet dancer.]

Although her starting salary was low, Nancy seemed pleased with it. "Of course, "she remarked, "Lassie, that beautiful collie, was pulling in $1,000 a week at the time."

Thau had previously informed Nancy that Lassie, in the dog's capacity as a star, was equivalent to "Greer Garson with fur."

Berlin-born Gottfried Reinhardt was the son of the fabled Austrian theater director, Max Reinhardt. The son had produced *Two-Faced Woman* (1941), the final film of Greta Garbo.

When Nancy first encountered Reinhardt as part of a chance meeting, he was in preparation for his classic 1951 film, *The Red Badge of Courage,* the epic Civil War drama starring war hero Audie Murphy.

According to Reinhardt "Benny Thau always made his directors cast the girl he was sleeping with at the time. Nancy was a horrible actress, and I knew she got her contract by devious means. Benny called me into his office and asked me to cast her in my next picture. Sidney Franklin had already rejected her. I said I would get back to him, but I never did. Of course, Benny could have insisted, but he didn't. Even with no talent, Nancy had a lot going for her, giving Benny blow jobs and having Loyal Davis take care of Dore Schary's back."

Dore Schary represented a new breed of mogul, making decisions and sponsoring movies that would have driven his domineering predecessor (Louis B. Mayer) crazy.

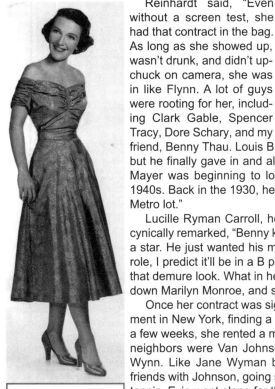

Taffeta Fashion Glam: In this *haute* fashion shot arranged by MGM, the hope was that Nancy would evoke an allure as pronounced as that of Lana or Ava. But as her resumé was scrutinized, she seemed less and less suited for sultry.

Reinhardt said, "Even without a screen test, she had that contract in the bag. As long as she showed up, wasn't drunk, and didn't upchuck on camera, she was in like Flynn. A lot of guys were rooting for her, including Clark Gable, Spencer Tracy, Dore Schary, and my friend, Benny Thau. Louis B. Mayer didn't like her screen test, but he finally gave in and allowed her contract to go through. Mayer was beginning to lose a lot of his power in the late 1940s. Back in the 1930, he would have ordered Davis off the Metro lot."

Lucille Ryman Carroll, head of MGM's talent department, cynically remarked, "Benny knew the Davis girl would never be a star. He just wanted his morning blow job. If he gives her a role, I predict it'll be in a B picture. Of course, Schary goes for that demure look. What in hell does he know? He even turned down Marilyn Monroe, and she went over to Fox."

Once her contract was signed, Nancy evacuated her apartment in New York, finding a similar one in Santa Monica. After a few weeks, she rented a modest house in Beverly Glen. Her neighbors were Van Johnson and his wife, the former Evie Wynn. Like Jane Wyman before her, Nancy became close friends with Johnson, going swimming with him or else playing tennis. Evie went along for the outings.

[Johnson's boss, Louis B. Mayer, had ordered him to get married as a means of putting a stop to rumors that he was a homosexual. "I became 'It,' meaning the only safe choice woman for Van to marry," Evie later said. "I was told to divorce Keenan, Van's best friend, and then marry Van. To save his career at MGM, Keenan also agreed to Mayer's harsh terms. Boy, did we make a lot of sacrifices to hold onto an MGM contract."]

Not the big stars, but the minor ones, resented Nancy at MGM and spread rumors about her. When Nancy arrived in Hollywood, she perhaps thought that Clark Gable would continue dating her, as he had in New York. But except for a lunch or two in the MGM commissary, he did not.

She'd heard that he was seeing an MGM blonde, Audrey Totter, who had signed with the studio in 1944, playing a floozy who makes her dough by rolling drunken soldiers and sailors in *Main Street After Dark*. Totter took up with Gable when they were cast together in *Any Number Can Play* (1949). She and Nancy would later come into jealous conflict over actor Robert Walker.

[Ironically, Totter would also get into jealous tangles with Jane Wyman over the affections of John Payne and Lew Ayres.]

Totter referred to Nancy as "Benny's little *protégée* from New York." She had taken an instant dislike to Nancy on first sight. She spread the story around the studio that one morning, she had an appointment with Thau, claiming she had entered his office and found his secretary out. She opened the door to Thau's office without knocking, and discovered someone going down on him as he sat behind his desk. She claimed that quickly and quietly, she shut the door and left his office's

Ernst Lubitsch *(left)*, a brilliant director of savvy and wit, is seen with Gottfried Reinhardt, the talented son of the celebrated theater impresario, Max Reinhardt.

When Benny Thau asked him to cast Nancy in his next picture, he was horrified.

anteroom. "I waited in the hall to see who had been performing fellatio. After twenty minutes, Nancy Davis, looking prim and proper, emerged."

MGM's casting director had an enormous influence on her brief film career. As vice president of MGM, he had been in charge of casting since 1928. He was one of MGM's "College of Cardinals," who reported directly to the boss of bosses, Louis B. Mayer. The

Nancy-Hater: Audrey Totter

other so-called cardinals included Eddie Mannix, Lawrence Weingarten, and Hunt Stromberg.

"Nancy is in good hands with Benny," Tracy told Gable and others. "Mayer is bombastic, but Benny is more the quiet type—in fact, his voice is so soft, you have to strain to hear the fucker. If two stars are waging war on the set, Benny is called in as the peacemaker."

In his early fifties, Benny had a tendency to early baldness and was developing a paunch. He always ate a large piece of cake for dessert at lunch, and repeated that order for dinner, always *à la mode*.

As he said himself, "I was constantly surrounded by the most beautiful men and women in the world. I never pretended to be a looker myself."

Elizabeth Taylor claimed that "Benny was like a surrogate father. I turned to him for advice...and perhaps a little more." The final phrase within that statement was deliberately enigmatic.

Actually, Thau could have been a second father to Nancy, too, as he was four years older than her birth father, Kenneth Robbins.

Thau was very popular among the male stars at MGM, often lining up prostitutes for them. He was especially known for his Christmas Eve orgies.

In spite of his unprepossessing looks and personality, Thau was rumored to have "the busiest casting couch at MGM," rivaling that of Harry Cohn at Columbia and Darryl F. Zanuck at Fox. Greta Garbo adored him and trusted him so much that she worked without a formal contract. "Benny's handshake was enough for me," she said.

His list of conquests was long—often starlets like Nancy, but sometimes, big name actresses such as Jean Harlow, Rosalind Russell, Jeanette MacDonald, Mary Astor, Joan Crawford, Loretta Young, and Norma Shearer.

He willingly abandoned all of these ladies when a red-haired Londoner arrived at MGM. She was Greer Garson, born in 1903 and, consequently, far closer to Thau's own age—he was born in 1898—than Nancy.

Nancy Davis in 1949: A new starlet outside her home on Beverly Glen, rushing to get ready for a hot date.

Garson became Thau's mistress. He closely supervised her career. In 1941, she was nominated for an Oscar for *Blossoms in the Dust,* that soggy Technicolor soap opera.

Usually, MGM did not sign actresses as old as Garson for their star roles, only for character parts. But Garson's style, manners, and ageless beauty seemed to overcome that prejudice. In 1942, she appeared in her biggest box-office hit, *Mrs. Miniver,* which earned an Oscar for her. When she received it, she delivered the longest acceptance speech (5 ½ minutes) in Hollywood history, a liberty that would not be tolerated during Academy Award ceremonies today.

During the filming of *Mrs. Miniver,* a young (age 26) and very handsome actor, Richard Ney, played her son. "When I saw Richard in uniform, I fell madly in love with him," Garson said. "So I married the boy." She was 39.

No longer with Garson as his mistress, Thau was a free agent when he encountered Nancy. "She was sweet and appealing," he recalled. "Except for some jealous actresses, she was very popular at MGM."

During her first weeks in Hollywood, Thau was Nancy's constant escort, although eventually, both of them expanded their date calendars.

[Thirty years after his affair with Nancy and long after his retirement from MGM, Thau was an invalid, confined to a wheelchair, a permanent resident of the Motion Picture and Television Hospital outside Los Angeles. He would die

An MGM publicity photo: Tennis anyone? Nancy, anyone?

there in 1983 when Nancy was First Lady, presiding over the White House.

Several members of the Hollywood elite came to visit the dying man. Reporters were shocked to find him so outspoken. "I don't have to protect any star's reputation at this point," he claimed. "Even my own." He admitted that at one point, there had been talk of marriage with Nancy. "But I didn't pursue it. First, I was a much older man. I was also aware that Edith and Loyal were anti-Semites, and I was a Jew. So marriage was something to think about, but it just wasn't realistic."

Among those interviewing Thau was the well-known biographer, Anne Edwards, author of Early Reagan (1987). She visited Thau during the closing months of his life. As reported by Kitty Kelley, Thau confided to Edwards that Nancy was renowned in Hollywood for giving oral sex. "She not only slept around, she performed that act and she performed it not only in the evening, but in offices. That was one of the reasons she got her contract, and one of the reasons she was popular at MGM." Edwards said she did not print Thau's claim because it was "too scandalous, too tasteless," and because her book was about Reagan, not Nancy.

Greer Garson, the original "cougar," with Richard Ney. Their marriage lasted four years.

Peter Lawford, one of Nancy's lovers, also claimed, "She was known for giving the best head in Hollywood."

Another biographer, Laurence Leamer, who wrote Make Believe: The Story of Nancy and Ronald Reagan (1987), also claimed that Benny Thau's receptionist alleged that she found used condoms in Thau's wastepaper basket after every one of Nancy's visits. That suggested that their sex acts may have extended beyond fellatio, since in the late 1940s, few women used condoms when giving oral sex back in those halcyon days before AIDS.

Other books—not just Kitty Kelley's—have suggested that Nancy became known as "the fellatio queen of Hollywood" long before the release of Linda Lovelace's Deep Throat in 1972.

A free-lance reporter, Daniel Burns, visited Thau at his retirement home and later claimed that he made a "deathbed confession." Perhaps unknown to Burns, that confession had already been expressed to others.

Thau told Burns, "Nancy was the undisputed Queen of Fellatio in Hollywood. The champion had been Faye Emerson before her marriage to Elliott Roosevelt. In the 1950s, after Nancy got married to what's his name, Marilyn Monroe was, more or less, the undisputed queen, even though she didn't hold the title. Of course, all critics agree that by the early 70s, Linda Lovelace was the oral expert. During her brief fling with William Holden, she tried to get Reagan's pal to fix her up with the man himself."

In Linda's view, only Reagan could determine "which of us is better, Nancy or me."

So far as it is known, Holden never complied with Lovelace's request.

Later, when asked about the role of Thau in her life, Nancy claimed, "I liked him as a friend, but that is as far as it went. I was not his girlfriend."]

In heavily sanitized latter-day evaluations," Nancy proclaimed, "Joining the studio was like walking into a dream world." But because of her understated manner and her somewhat distant approach to acting, MGM often found her hard to cast. In the early 1950s, roles that might have gone to Nancy went instead to Janet Leigh, Leslie Caron, Jane Powell, and, most definitely, Debbie Reynolds.

Almost as a foreshadowing of her future as Ronald Reagan's wife, if a role called for "a gentle, plain, and understanding spouse," it went to Nancy, in Thau's opinion.

***

The legacy of Nancy's movies appear minor, indeed, when compared to the distinguished list of those of Oscar-winning Jane Wyman, and to the many (less stellar) films made by Reagan. One of the few positive things that a film critic might say about Nancy's film repertoire is, "They're not as bad as rumor has it."

The first film Nancy made was a mystery thriller, *Shadow on the Wall,* co-starring Ann Sothern and Zachory Scott. Many movie-goers thought it was her third picture, because, although it was shot early in 1949, it was not released until more than a year later, after she'd appeared in two other films, *The Doctor and the Girl* and *East Side, West Side.* The reason for the delayed release of *Shadow on the Wall* is not known. Perhaps MGM had made a similar B picture and wanted to hold back the premiere of *Shadow on the Wall* as a means of reducing the competition.

Although George Cukor had directed her screen test, for her first film, Nancy was assigned a relatively untried Englishman, Patrick Jackson, to helm her. He'd made documentaries in the 1930s and had directed *Western Approaches,* a fictional account of 22 sailors marooned in a lifeboat, in 1944. Much of that film had been shot in the Irish Sea. Real sailors rather than professional actors were used.

"Pat was patient with me, knowing how scared I was," Nancy said. "He told me the movie was based on a novel, *Death in a Doll's House,* and he gave me a copy which I read in one night. I think I got more understanding from the book than from the director."

Sothern usually played sassy but sympathetic characters, but in *Shadow on the Wall,* she was cast as the villain, Dell Faring, who, in a jealous rage, shoots her sister, Celia (Kristine Miller), when she learns she's involved in an affair with her boyfriend. Suspicion for the murder falls on Celia's husband (Zachory Scott), who—if he's found guilty—may be sent to the electric chair.

The only witness to the murder is a nine-year-

Reflections in a Mirror? Or just a *Shadow on the Wall*? Nancy Davis gets *noir*-ish in her film debut.

393

old child, the stepdaughter of the victim, played by Gigi Perreau. She saw only the shadow of the killer, projected on a wall, and she was so traumatized by what she witnessed that her memory is blocked.

The girl is sent for consultations with a psychiatrist (as played by Nancy), who races to unblock the child's memory before the wrong man dies.

In a chat with Nancy, Sothern told her, "Studios sell stars on their good looks and personality buildups. It will happen to you. You'll be asked questions like, 'Do you sleep in the nude?' A star is just a big name to a studio, nothing more. Publicity will give you a fake bio. If you don't deliver at the box office, you're out the door."

The cast of *Shadow on the Wall*, *left to right*: Ann Sothern, Zachory Scott, Gigi Perreau, and Nancy Davis.

Who was the real killer? Sothern or Scott? Psychiatrist Nancy held the clue, which was locked inside the traumatized brain of little Gigi.

One of Sothern's most visible hits had been Fox's *A Letter to Three Wives* (1949), wherein she played an ambitious writer married to a younger man (Kirk Douglas).

Years later, Sothern expressed a dim view of Nancy to tell-all biographer Kitty Kelley. "I remember her as quite soft and pudgy, looking like she'd had a nose job. Although she was pleasant enough, she seemed rather devious to me. I can't tell you exactly why—it was just a feeling I had. Maybe it was because she was so ambitious. She was a tough lady who definitely knew where she wanted to go. She didn't impress me much."

"She was well connected with Benny Thau, if you get my drift. He sometimes appeared on the set to see how things were coming along for his Nancy."

Sothern viewed all female newcomers to the screen with a certain disdain, seeing them as "tomorrow's competition." Also, at the time she expressed her negative opinions of Nancy, she was in the process of divorcing her actor husband, Robert Sterling, and she had recently been dropped from MGM after her final appearance in a series of Maisie movies in which she had starred as a wisecracking secretary, Maisie Ravier, since 1939. *[Sothern's last exposure to the role was in* Undercover Maisie *(1947).]* She was worried about her future in movies—and rightly so. In the months ahead, she would turn to television.

As a type, Scott, in real life, reminded Nancy too much of the sleazy character (Monty) he had played opposite Joan Crawford in *Mildred Pierce* (1945). She later thanked him in a memoir for being supportive of her as she struggled through her first movie role.

Off screen, she noticed that Scott wore a gold earring. He claimed he'd worn one ever since 1938, when the captain of a fishing boat he'd hired off the coast of Mexico had worn one.

Scott wore it in spite of an attack by Walter Seltzer, a publicist at Warners, who claimed, "Scott has a quality of effeteness about him, a slight effeminacy. There is talk that he is a ho-

Gigi Perreau, screaming and traumatized, by *Shadow on the Wall*.

mosexual, and that he really doesn't fit into Hollywood."

Nancy could not help but notice an enormous tension between Sothern and Scott. Jackson had told her, "It's good that they don't have to play any love scenes. I've known directors who had to helm love scenes between bitter enemies. Imagine having to passionately kiss one of your worst enemies?"

At one point, Jackson explained why Scott was feuding with Sothern: He blamed her for interfering in his marriage to the former Elaine Anderson. In November of that year, Elaine would file for divorce from Scott, citing mental cruelty.

While Scott was away from Hollywood, on location, Sothern had introduced Elaine to the novelist, John Steinbeck, asking him to escort her to dinners and parties. As their courtship continued, Steinbeck fell in love with Elaine and continued their off-the-record affair even after Scott returned. Alienating Scott further, Sothern often served as a "beard" to mask their adulterous relationship.

During the shooting of *Shadow on the Wall,* the homosexual Latino, César Romero, was a frequent visitor to the set. After he'd been locked away with Scott in his dressing room for more than an hour, Sothern loudly remarked, "César is helping Scott mend a broken heart by offering his own special physical comfort. The use of his expert mouth."

On the set, Nancy befriended Perreau. A few years before, as a four-year-old, she had played the daughter of Claude Rains and Bette Davis in *Mr. Skeffington* (1944).

Nancy seemed aware that Perreau's career as a child actress was suffering from comparisons to a far more talented juvenile, Natalie Wood, who was three years her senior.

Jackson predicted that Nancy and one of the movie's supporting players, Barbara Billingsley, could usually be interchanged "as the same housewifey types."

[Barbara later hit it big when she was cast as June Cleaver in the long-running (1957-1963) sitcom, Leave It to Beaver. *Nancy, who would probably have been adept at portraying an American mom from the 1950s, might also have been ideal as Beaver's mother.]*

The New York Times praised Nancy's performance in *Shadow on the Wall*, finding it "beautiful and convincing." It could not, however, accept Sothern's radical change of screen image, suggesting that she was better suited for musicals or light comedies. *Newsweek* claimed that both Sothern and Scott handled their "high-voltage roles with effective restraint."

Nancy got her best review from *Variety,* which defined her performance as a standout, claiming "This actress is definitely a comer."

MGM brass, however, interpreted *Shadow on the Wall* as "just another cheap B-picture thriller."

Thau would later tell Nancy that it was just as well that the release of *Shadow on the Wall* had been delayed, because he believed that her two other films, *The Doctor and the Girl* (1949) and *East Side, West Side*

Tyrone Power *(left)* with César Romero.

Carmen Miranda, friends to both men, said, "These two guys committed what the public might call acts of unspeakable perversion, but what I might view as just having a wild party."

395

(also 1949), were, in the long run, better showcases for her talent.

***

As evidence of how small a town Hollywood was in the late 1940s, MGM designated, as director for Nancy's next film (*The Doctor and the Girl*), Curtis Bernhardt.

[Coincidentally, in 1940, he had helmed Jane Wyman in My Love Came Back. *A year later, he had directed Reagan in* Million Dollar Baby. *Now, it was his turn to work with Nancy in a minor role.]*

The stars included Glenn Ford and Janet Leigh, with Gloria DeHaven appearing in a supporting role. At the time, she was married to John Payne, Wyman's "true love" from earlier in the decade.

Originally entitled *Bodies and Soul,* the movie had an array of talented supporting players, most notably Charles Coburn, cast as a famous doctor and the father of the screen characters played by Ford, DeHaven, and Nancy. Other players included Bruce Bennett, Warner Anderson, and Arthur Franz. Nancy was typecast, playing the daughter of a famous neurosurgeon (Coburn), which—as the daughter of Loyal Davis—she was in real life.

Like Nancy, Leigh would also write an autobiography. Entitled *There Really Was a Hollywood,* it was published by Doubleday in 1984 when Nancy was one of the most famous and powerful women in the world. Many fans wondered why, within its pages, Leigh deliberately eliminated any mention of Nancy, with whom she'd played pivotal scenes.

"The Doctor" (Glenn Ford) and "The Girl" (Janet Leigh). Nancy, to her regret, was NOT the romantic lead. "Off screen, Janet got Glenn—not me," Nancy said.

But as the daughter of a real-life doctor, she knew how to play it. Here, with a sense of gritty realism, is Nancy with Glenn Ford, "The Man Who Got Away" from her.

"The choice was deliberate," Leigh in later years revealed to reporter George Hills. "I detested Nancy Davis. Not only did she make a play for my then beau, Glenn (Ford), but she went after most of my roles at MGM."

"Alfred Hitchcock claimed that Nancy's name was submitted for my landmark role in *Psycho* (1960)," Leigh continued. "After all, I received an Oscar nod—and should have won instead of Shirley Jones—for that terrifying scream, the most famous in film history. Demure little Nancy would have fucked up that scene for sure. Hitch told me, 'I turned Miss Davis down, of course. The idea of casting her was absurd.'"

"She went after my roles, regardless of what they were—everything from an *in-génue* to a tragic heroine. Perhaps a widow romanced by Robert Mitchum, a Russian spy opposite John Wayne, a naïve Southern girl, Gene Kelly's girlfriend, Carleton Carpenter's love interest (can you imagine such a thing?) or even Robert Ryan's gun moll," Leigh claimed.

In her own memoirs, Nancy wasn't as petty as Leigh. She did at least mention her as a member of the cast, but it wasn't even a case of damning by faint praise. All that she wrote was, "Janet played Glenn's wife." Privately, she was said to have thought that Leigh's role would have been better suited for her.

Actually, Bernhardt cast their respective roles correctly. Leigh was seven years younger than Nancy, and as such was physically better suited for the role of "The Girl" in the film.

Ford was cast as a young doctor who suffers from a difficult relationship with his father (Coburn), and pursues a romance with a young female patient (Leigh) in all her dewy freshness, *[Leigh had been "discovered" by Norma Shearer, the former Queen of MGM.]*

Dore Schary wanted gritty realism and consequently, he ordered Bernhardt to shoot the scenes "on the fly" in New York City. That involved setting up cameras on the actual streets and sidewalks "to film the natives," as Bernhardt defined them.

Years later, although Ford hardly remembered being in the movie with Nancy, he had nothing but praise for Leigh. "She had ability, brains, and ambition. I got to know her."

Bernhardt described their relationship in more cynical terms. "Ford got to know her all right, like David knew Bathsheba. Janet Leigh ingratiated herself with Ford by launching their romance one afternoon when she pissed all over him."

He was referring to a scene where Ford and Leigh played a newly married couple. On their wedding night, he has to carry her up two flights of stairs. As he does, he whispers to her, "I don't think I can make it."

"The more he struggled, the more I laughed," Leigh wrote, "until finally, I passed the threshold of restraint and wet my pants, which only made me laugh harder—and it kept coming (I swear). I could see a spot on my skirt in the actual film."

Ford, at the time, was married to singer-dancer Eleanor Powell, who had retired from the screen to marry an unfaithful husband. Like Reagan, Ford came down with "Leadinglady-itis," as provoked by Rita Hayworth. Along the way, he managed to seduce Eva Gabor, Joan Crawford, Judy Garland, Margaret Sullavan, and Barbara Stanwyck. He even had a one-night stand (*surprise!*) with Marilyn Monroe, as he confessed to his son, Peter Ford. The question is still out as to whether Bette Davis seduced him when they co-starred together in *A Stolen Life* (1946).

After meeting Ford, playwright Clifford Odets, the lover of Cary Grant, issued a strange pronouncement. "It is an easily won bet that in a few years, Ford will get just like the other movie people: Bored, sprawling, careless, an overly relaxed fallen angel—They are all affable boys out here, almost tramps."

In *The Doctor and the Girl*, DeHaven was cast as the most rebellious of Coburn's three daughters, running off to live in Greenwich Village. Her character was described as "flouncy and indiscreet." After falling ill from an illegal, back alley abortion, she arrives, near death, on her brother's doorstep. She has lost much blood and dies shortly afterward, in spite of what one critic called "the desperate ding-dong struggle on the table to save her."

397

[In another of the ironies of Hollywood, Nancy found herself working closely with DeHaven, who was the 'blood enemy" of Jane Wyman, having stolen John Payne from her.]

In somewhat nerdy contrast, Nancy played Coburn's dutiful daughter, who marries a successful pediatrician (Warner Anderson). Bernhardt ordered that one of her scenes be reshot: After Nancy greeted Ford, cast as her brother, with unseemly emotion, the director admonished her with, "Please remember that you're playing Glenn's sister, not his lover."

In another memorable scene, Nancy, clad in mink, arrives one wintry day at her brother's dingy third-floor walkup. Before leaving, she gives Leigh (playing her sister-in-law) her mink coat. After she's gone, Ford tells his wife, "She has plenty more mink coats at home."

Also cast as a doctor, Arthur Franz was introduced to Nancy. He would co-star with her again in *Hellcats of the Navy* (1957), the only movie she ever made with Reagan.

Bernhardt claimed, "Janet had Glenn tied up, so Nancy went after Bruce *[Bennett],* or so it

It has been said that Nancy Davis, as a lonely young girl, learned the power of fantasy and self-creation from her actress mother and theatrical godmother, each of them larger-than-life actresses who ate up the scenery.

seemed to me. I think she struck out, but who knows? I know that Virginia Mayo fell for Bruce big time when they made *Smart Girls Don't Talk* in '48."

Although the film contained "two male beauties," Bennett and Ford, neither of them gave Nancy a tumble, so it was alleged. Off screen, she was pursued by Coburn, then in his seventies, perhaps rehearsing for his role in *Gentlemen Prefer Blondes* (1953), when, as a millionaire, he lecherously chased after Marilyn Monroe.

Nancy later claimed, "Charles invited me to dinner, and I spent the rest of the evening fighting him off."

The 98-minute film made a profit of $184,000 on a budget of slightly more than a million dollars. It opened on September 29, 1949 in theaters around the country. Nearly all critics ignored Nancy's performance, the focus being on Ford, Leigh, and Coburn. *Variety* was an exception, faintly praising it with the evaluation: "Nancy Davis is to be favorably noted."

The New York Times critiqued *The Doctor and the Girl* as "a nice little bedside tearjerker—slightly gruesome, of course, but full of hope. In the role of the noble young doctor, who shuns a Park Avenue practice to help the working poor, Ford does a satisfactory job of solemnly carrying the torch flung by Dr. Kildare in that film series. *Suture! Suture tie! Sponge!"*

***

Director Gottfried Reinhardt later claimed, "With all the talent on tap, I didn't want to cast Nancy Davis in a picture, so I palmed her off on Dore Schary."

Consequently, it was Schary who ordered the producer, Voldemar Vetluguin, to cast Nancy in *East Side, West Side,* an A-list picture top heavy with stars—Barbara Stanwyck, James Mason, Ava Gardner, Van Heflin, and Cyd Charisse.

The MGM film was set for a Christmas (1949) release and came in on schedule.

Nancy joined an array of very talented supporting players, including the communist sympathizer Gale Sondergaard, William Conrad, Douglas Kennedy, and William Frawley. Cast as a supporting figure was Beverly Michaels, the sexpot of sexpots. "If it has blonde floozy written on it, I got the part," Michaels said. She also captured the producer, Vetluguin, who married her that year.

Mervyn LeRoy, the film's director, always claimed that he had "discovered" Jane Wyman when he'd cast her in a very minor role in *Elmer the Great* (1933). "Ironically, I was the same director who helmed Reagan's other wife, Nancy, in her first A-list picture," as he bragged in later years.

East Side, West Side was a melodramatic mystery thriller about a high society couple, the Bournes, (as portrayed by Stanwyck and Mason) on the verge of breaking up their marriage. The interloping mistress in the film is Ava Gardner, cast as Isabel Lorrison, who is eventually murdered.

East Side, West Side: Nancy Davis in a "one-take" scene with Barbara Stanwyck, who, according to director Curtis Bernhardt, "had the hots for little Miss Nancy."

As a *femme fatale*, Gardner undulates across the screen, claiming that with the crook of a finger, she can lure Mason away from Stanwyck. Gardner later said that her performance was inspired by Joan Crawford's attempt to steal Norma Shearer's husband in *The Women (1939)*.

[In a touch of irony, whereas in 1949 Gardner played a home wrecker on the screen, she was defined as a home wrecker offscreen because of her well-publicized affair with Frank Sinatra. At the time, he was still famously married to his high school sweetheart, Nancy Sinatra.

During the film's conception, Gardner had been slated to play the lead role of Mason's wife. But when Stanwyck became available, Gardner was demoted to the role of Mason's mistress. Later, Gardner said, "At the time, I was seriously pissed off. But it turned out to be the better role, and certainly the more flamboyant one."]

Van Heflin and Barbara Stanwyck appeared together in *East Side, West Side*. He told her, "If you'd like to know me better and get acquainted with all my body parts, and I yours, all you have to do is invite me over tonight. I take loving a woman as seriously as I do sailing the high seas, and I view love-making as an art form. I like to make a woman feel as if she'd been loved from the tip of her brow to her big toe."

"An enchanting offer," Stanwyck said. "You should pitch those lines to Ava Gardner."

Mason is the primary murder suspect. After many complications and mixed alliances, Heflin finds a woman's broken fingernail, a clue that eventually sets Mason free.

Nancy was cast in the film as Hazel Lee, the best friend of the character played by Stanwyck, who remains elegantly attired throughout the film, evoking a model for Christian Dior's 1949 "New Look."

Her portrayal as a meddlesome tattle-tale wasn't designed to populate any Nancy Davis fan clubs. Fully aware of Mason's philandering, she deviously asks Stanwyck, "Is everything all right between you and Brandon?" She then reveals a string of details associated with her husband's infidelities.

In another scene, Nancy hosts a party for the character played by Heflin, a foreign correspondent launching his first book. It is he who will eventually crack the mystery of who murdered the character played by Gardner.

LeRoy remembered Nancy as having two things on her mind, "Snaring a famous husband and having a big career. Gable had eluded her and she could only let her mouth water when Sinatra came after work to pick up Ava. Nancy told me she wanted to be bigger than both Stanwyck and Gardner. She didn't have the talent of Stanwyck or the beauty of Gardner, so I suggested she'd set her goalpost too high."

Nancy and other cast members could not help but notice that Sinatra showed up most evenings to haul Gardner away for the night. It is not known for sure, but this may have been Nancy's first encounter with Ol' Blue Eyes. She developed a crush on him that would endure for decades. When she was First Lady, she frequently invited the singer to gala affairs at the White House.

Nancy admired Mason from afar, especially his "languid but impassioned" speech patterns. The Yorkshire-born actor was married at the time to actress Pamela Mason, who sometimes visited the set with her friend, Zsa Zsa Gabor.

During a chat with Mason, Nancy learned that he was a devoted cat lover. The year he made the film with Nancy, he and Pamela had published a book, *The Cats in Our Lives.*

Nancy had heard rumors that Mason had a gay streak in him. During the shoot, two of the handsomest and most well-built young men on the film crew made extended visits to his dressing room. The DO NOT DISTURB sign was exhibited during each of their visits.

In her memoirs, Nancy recalled that her one big scene was with Stanwyck. "I was nervous working with a star of her reputation and especially because I had to give a long speech. But when I got it right on the first take, she applauded and congratulated me, which, of course, made me feel marvelous."

One day, Stanwyck's husband, Robert Taylor, was scheduled for an arrival on the set. Stanwyck told Nancy that she and Taylor had been invited to dinner at the home of Ronald Reagan and Jane Wyman. "They are our close friends," Stanwyck asserted.

When Taylor appeared, Gardner, notified in advance of his arrival, retreated to her dressing room. "Watch the bitch go," Stanwyck muttered to Nancy. "In this film, I'm playing the cuckolded wife. It happened to me in real life. Bob was fucking Gardner when they made *The Bribe* (1949) together. Now Gardner is getting murdered in our movie. It couldn't happen to a more deserving person."

When Gardner heard that Stanwyck was badmouthing her on the set, she told LeRoy, "I notice that Bloody Babs is being nice to that Davis girl. She'll be lucky if Stanwyck doesn't seduce her. The little thing is Stanwyck's type, just like Nancy Sinatra. Stanwyck adores Frankie's wife, and he suspects something…"

"Maybe Stanwyck just likes gals named

Two closeted bisexuals, Barbara Stanwyck and James Mason, cozy up to each other in *East Side, West Side.* But it was just make-believe.

Nancy?" LeRoy said.

In a memoir, Nancy described Gardner as "...so beautiful, she took my breath away." She met her at the MGM newsstand when Gardner wore no makeup. The actress complimented Nancy on her performance in *The Doctor and the Girl*. Those were the last kind words Gardner would ever say about Nancy. Soon after that, someone told Gardner that Nancy was lusting after her man, Sinatra.

Ironically, Nancy eventually found herself emotionally involved with two of Gardner's boyfriends, actors Robert Walker and Peter Lawford. Gardner had co-starred with Walker in *One Touch of Venus* (1948). That had led to Gardner's involvement with Walker's best friend, Lawford. As he explained it, "Bob and I like to share."

Eventually, as her relationship with Sinatra deepened, Gardner dumped both Lawford and Walker. Following in her footsteps, Nancy began to date both young men herself, which turned Gardner against her, even though she'd discarded the men.

"Of course, Ava got pissed off at Nancy," LeRoy said. "Nancy was greedy, wanting Peter, Bob, and Frank. What a coincidence that each of them was or had been involved with Gardner. I don't think it just a coincidence."

Gardner, by then engaged to Sinatra, became friends with Mason and his wife, Pamela, and frequently went out as a foursome. It was at table with the Masons at the Sugar Hill Club in Harlem that Gardner got into a terrible fight with Sinatra over his liaison with a New York prostitute. During one of the argument's most memorable moments, she removed her diamond engagement ring and tossed it across the club.

Of the cast, it seemed that the beautiful, talented dancer, Cyd Charisse, was the only member who, like Caesar's wife, was above reproach.

As a child, she suffered from polio, but went on to become a dancer with Fred Astaire and Gene Kelly. At the time that Nancy met her, she was married to the singer, Tony Martin. As she'd tell anyone interested, "With Tony in your bed, a girl has no need of any other man." They remained married until her death in 2008.

As was her custom on a film set, Nancy made a point of ingratiating herself with the supporting players of *East Side, West Side*. She often appeared even when she wasn't needed. "She was learning, learning, learning, watching the pros go at

Ava, beautiful Ava Gardner, with James Mason in *East Side, West Side*.

Faced with such female pulchritude, and the acting talent of Stanwyck, Nancy *(cheesecake photo, below)* simply faded into the background.

it," LeRoy recalled.

One of the first persons she met and chatted with was Gale Sondergaard, who had won an Oscar for her film debut in *Anthony Adverse* (1936). She was later nominated for an Academy Award for her role as "the first wife" in *Anna and the King of Siam* (1946). She told Nancy that originally, she had been slated to play the evil witch in *The Wizard of Oz* (1939). "The first script called for the witch to be glamorous," she told Nancy. "But then the script was changed to make the witch hideous. I bowed out. I thought that my wearing such disfiguring makeup would damage my career. Margaret Hamilton had none of my reservations."

During the months ahead, the actress would view Reagan with "total disgust." She later accused Reagan of turning in a report to the FBI about her and her husband, producer Herbert J. Biberman, alleging that both of them were card-carrying communists. Biberman became one of the notorious "Hollywood Ten" of the early 1950s. This led to Sondergaard being blacklisted in Hollywood. When screen roles dried up, she fled to New York to find work in the theater.

Devoted actress, Neo-Pinko and Reagan Hater: Gale Sondergaard.

Nancy noticed that another actor, Douglas Kennedy, a New Yorker, was paying a lot of attention to Stanwyck. His adulation must have paid off because she was instrumental in getting him cast as the Sheriff in her hit TV series for ABC, *The Big Valley* (1965-69).

Also cast in the movie was veteran actor William Frawley, who had made more than a hundred movies. He told Nancy he was finding it harder and harder to find character roles. She was pleased to read that in 1951, Desi Arnaz and Lucille Ball had cast him as the cantankerous, miserly landlord, Fred Mertz, in their hit TV series, *I Love Lucy*.

When *East Side, West Side* opened across the country, Nancy gave it a good review, praising it as "outstanding." The rest of the country did not. The attack was led by Bosley Crowther of *The New York Times*. "It's a picture that just about hits the low water mark of interest, intelligence, and urgency."

Marica Davensport had co-written the screenplay, which was based on her novel. But even she said she was not going to see the picture because she'd heard that it was horrible.

Cyd Charisse in a dance routine ("Sombrero") that was a lot less demure than her role in *East Side, West Side*. Faced with the choreographic brilliance of this dance icon, it became increasingly clear that Nancy could not compete.

Stanwyck's biographer, Dan Callahan, summed up the film in his book, *The Miracle Worker*. "Mason and Heflin are stuck in dull roles, and Stanwyck herself is saddled with the worst role of the kind of sniveling, stoic wifey who does nothing but worry about her husband's infidelities. She's up against young Amazons like Cyd Charisse and the ultimate big blonde, Beverly Michaels, who acts as a *deus ex machina* in the last third. Sitting beside Charisse in a car at one point, Stanwyck is photographed like a grizzled old frontierswoman. The resplendent Ava Gardner, playing the hellcat trying to break up her marriage, dominates the whole stultifying enterprise through sheer physical splendor."

MGM records revealed that *East Side, West Side* garnered $1,518,000 in North America and slightly more than one million in overseas rentals. But because of the expenses and the all-star talent, the profits generated were only $31,000.

LeRoy later summed up the cast of *East Side, West Side,* claiming, "They were a bunch of whores, faggots, cocksuckers, dykes, tramps, commies, pederasts, dopers, panty sniffers, rimmers, pillheads, floozies, and male hustlers selling it by the inch." He told this at a party given for colum-

Postwar Bad Girls: What's an ambitious *starlette* to do? Go "Goody-Good" or "Baddy-Bad" on screen?

Pictured above: Beverly Michaels, a girl whose public image Nancy wanted to avoid.

nist Hedda Hopper, who, in her picture hat, laughed loudly. Of course, he knew she could not print such a provocative comment.

*[**Fast forward** to late 1963 in Puerto Vallarta, Mexico, where Gardner was co-starring with Richard Burton and Deborah Kerr in Tennessee Williams'* The Night of the Iguana, *directed by John Huston.*

Elizabeth Taylor, who had accompanied her husband, often joined Burton, as well as Tennessee, Gardner, and Huston, for a tequila-soaked night. At the time, Gardner had turned on Nancy, because of her interest in Sinatra.

Gardner surprised her fellow drunks one night by claiming, "I got to Ronnie's uncut inches before Nancy." She then related an incident that took place at William Holden's private home when his wife, Brenda Marshall, was away. At the time, Holden had been Reagan's best friend.

"I was jaybird naked in the pool with my companions, the black model, Maddy Comfort, and the artist, Paul Clemens," Gardner said. "Reagan came out wearing a polo shirt and slacks to see what all the raucous laughter was about. We grabbed him and tossed him in the pool with us. He put up a struggle, but we stripped him. Maddy and Paul later wandered off, and I lured Ronnie into Bill's cabana. He wouldn't fuck me, but I went down on him and he rose to the occasion."

Later, after Gardner went back to her villa, Tennessee asked Huston, "Do you think Ava is telling the truth, or is she just getting back at Miss Nancy?"

"Hell, how would I know?" Huston asked. "Whether it's true or not, the story makes a good yarn."]

***

Nancy's stepson, Michael Reagan, reportedly once said, "If Nancy knew that one day she'd be First Lady, she would have cleaned up her act in the late 1940s.:"

He was obviously referring to her notorious sex life. To read her two memoirs, you get the impression she was a demure virgin when she married Reagan.

It is not known how many men Nancy dated during the starlet years at MGM that preceded her first and only marriage. Only the "marquee names" of Nancy's dating lists have emerged, and that is because some of them lived to see Nancy become famous. Men, being men, like to brag, particularly about their sexual conquests. There are even web sites today devoted to Nancy's list of suitors, many of whom have privately praised her alleged "oral talents."

***

It is not entirely certain if Marlon Brando ever had an affair with starlet Nancy Davis. If he did, it was of short duration and occurred shortly before she nabbed Reagan as her husband. Nancy omitted any mention of Marlon within her autobiographies, as she did each of her other lovers.

Marlon, however, told two producers— Charles Feldman and Elia Kazan—that he'd made love to Nancy, whom he found "kinda cute with her brown eyes and hair just the color I like it."

In the early 1950s, Nancy was known to have composed a list of unattached marriageable males. At the top of her list was Ronald Reagan. Other men on the list included actors, producers, and directors. Surely Nancy knew enough about Marlon to realize that he was "not marriage material." She allegedly told Ava Gardner that "Marlon is just too wild and bohemian for me."

"But not for me, *honey child*," Ava was supposed to have countered. "Been there, done that."

Nancy had first met Marlon in Manhattan when she was dating Clark Gable, a short-term romance that never got off the launch pad. When she reunited with Marlon in Hollywood, Nancy was in the throes of a torrid affair with Benny Thau, head of casting at MGM.   Thau was said to be deeply in love with Nancy during a period when she was dating other men.

One of Thau's assistants reportedly saw Nancy and Marlon dining at Chasen's, a restaurant that Marlon had never visited before, as he hated formal dining rooms. She was elegantly attired in a black Chanel dress, a large white hat, and a corsage of small orchids. Having (temporarily) abandoned his blue jeans, Marlon wore a sports jacket and slacks but no tie.

When Thau heard that the woman he loved had been seen out with Brando, he was furious, threatening that Marlon would never make a picture for Metro-Goldwyn-Mayer. "By trying to move in on Nancy, the cocksucking queer has ruined himself in this town—I'll see to that."

Whatever relationship existed between Marlon and Nancy fizzled quickly, because she was soon seen dating others.

Brando, the quintessential Postwar Bad Boy. His dining with Nancy at Chasen's supposedly drove MGM's casting director, Benny Thau, into a jealous rage.

Marlon told Kazan that Nancy would never appear opposite him in one of his films—"That is, if I ever make another film. But if you know of any roles calling for 'the perfect wife,' then Nancy's your gal. She's the exception to every other actress in Hollywood. Instead of some big-time career, she wants to

His relationship with Nancy, if one developed at all, fizzled quickly.

settle down in a rose-covered cottage, raise three kids, and greet hubbie with a Scotch and soda every night at six o'clock, as the smell of fried chicken wafts through the house."

Marlon may have accurately interpreted Nancy's feelings at the time. She later confessed to just such a dream, hardly knowing that the "cottage" would turn out to be the White House. There, in 1981, she would suffer the highest disapproval rating of any First Lady in modern times.

When Marlon was informed of Nancy's marriage to Reagan, he sarcastically told Feldman, "It's a perfect match. I hear Reagan brushes his teeth every time he kisses a woman. I can even suggest a theme song for their marriage. Make it George Gershwin's 'Our Love Is Here to Stay.'"

In the years to come, Marlon would always speak kindly of Nancy, "even when she was single-handedly running the Free World." On the other hand, he consistently deplored Reagan for what he claimed was "His witch hunting of so-called Communists."

***

Since Nancy had been a teenage girl, Spencer Tracy had always defined her as "my favorite daughter." He was her mentor, someone she loved and respected. But Tracy got drunk a lot and became very indiscreet, lacking in judgment. His friend, director George Cukor, later claimed that at some point in the late 1940s, Tracy's platonic relationship with Katharine Hepburn hit rocks in the road. "In a way, Nancy Davis was blamed."

Tracy rented a cottage on Cukor's estate, with Hepburn a frequent visitor. To his intimates, the gossipy director later described the Tracy-Hepburn conflicts about Nancy.

Hepburn had originally befriended Nancy, but whereas Tracy had encouraged her to become an actress, Hepburn did not.

She wrote Nancy a letter, warning her "How damn awful the acting profession is: Perhaps you think it's all too glamorous, and it's all about socializing with rich and famous stars. Most young girls who dream of being an actress end up waiting tables or else are found at the switchboard."

One night, according to Cukor, Tracy became "Fed up with Kate bossing me around." He turned on her and ordered her out of his cottage. At one point during their argument, Tracy is reported to have said, "If you don't get out, I'll give you a boot in your bony butt."

Tracy had become hostile at the end of the filming of *Adam's Rib* (1949), in which bisexual Hepburn had taken an "undue interest" in her co-star, Judy Holliday, another bisexual actress.

As Tracy relayed to Cukor about Hepburn, "Sometimes when I hear the sound of that out-of-control voice, my whole body cringes. I encourage her to smoke more,

HOLLYWOOD QUIZ: What (or who?) was one of the wedges (discounting their respective bisexuality) that tested the widely publicized loyalty of Spencer Tracy to Katharine Hepburn? ANSWER: Nancy Davis!

Depicted above are Tracy and Hepburn in one of their scenes from *Adam's Rib* (1949).

since that lowers her voice register."

Before kicking her out, and perhaps as a means of making her jealous, and to infuriate her, Tracy confessed, "I've found an adoring woman, one who understands me, respects me, and gives in to me on any issue. How unlike you! She's the woman I've been looking for all my life and never found. Believe it or not, it's someone I've known for years, but have never thought of in that special way before—that is, until now. Hell, I'm even a friend of her mother's."

"Who might this Goddess of Virtue be?" Hepburn had asked, sarcastically.

"Nancy Davis."

A week later, Hepburn called Cukor, claiming, "Spence has all but given up. He'll end up one day all alone except for the bottle. I won't be there for him."

At the time of her dismal assessment, she seemed unaware that Tracy was experiencing renewed vigor with Nancy.

Cukor told his close gay friend, Anderson Lawler, an early lover of a young Gary Cooper, "Spence is enjoying the comforts of the damned—a bottle of whiskey. He's not in good health. He's no longer a champ at the box office. He looks like shit. He's a walking tub of suet. He sucks off hustlers but won't admit he's a homo. Yet he's still a big enough name he can get a date on a Saturday night, even if it's Nancy Davis. I directed her in her screen test. I know how limited she is."

Even though she'd headed East in 1950 to rehearse her Broadway performance of Rosalind in *As You Like It,* Hepburn still called Cukor for news of the Nancy Davis/Spencer Tracy liaison.

Cukor later said, "Kate has always been aware of Tracy's affairs with other women, and even of his affairs with a number of men. The ratio was about ten women to every one male. But the mere mention of Nancy Davis' name made her explode."

"Spence is a big name in Hollywood, and Nancy will date anybody with a big name," Hepburn charged. "She likes to associate with important people. She is not the only actress in Hollywood who thinks she can sleep her way to the top. There are some actresses, myself included, who get there on talent alone."

Nancy dated Tracy, although not exclusively, for at least three months. He seemed to know she was trying to advance her career. As he admitted to Cukor, "I encourage her in a film career, although I secretly know she doesn't have what it takes to be a star like Kate and me. Her biggest hope in life is to hook up with a producer, director, or perhaps a rich actor. The thing with Gable didn't work out, but there are others."

Eventually, after she started dating Reagan, Tracy and Nancy drifted apart. Tracy loathed Reagan, calling him a "Red baiter always looking for a pinko in the haystack."

"Miss Nancy is laying a trap for this Reagan guy," Tracy told Cukor. "I think the two of them deserve each other. I just hope Ronnie goes in for oral sex like I do. If he does, he'll be happy as a pig in shit."

Years later in a memoir, Nancy wrote: "Spence was the most charming man I've ever known."

As for Hepburn, Nancy claimed that her friendship with the aging actress just (inexplicably) ended. "To this day, I don't understand why. I made several attempts to revive our relationship, but got nowhere."

***

Nancy's brief fling with Norman Krasna hardly rates a blip on the radar screen, even though it led to a proposal of marriage. He was a talented screenwriter, playwright, producer, and director, who had garnered an Oscar for writing the screenplay of *Princess*

O'Rourke, in which Jane Wyman had a co-starring role. At the time Nancy met him, he was writing a play, *John Loves Mary,* which would later be released as a movie (in 1949) with Reagan.

Krasna was only three years older than Nancy, and, like her, he too had worked in a department store, Macy's, in Manhattan. Dropping out of law school, he'd turned to writing. When she dated him, he was in the throes of divorcing the former Ruth Frazee.

If Nancy had a selfish motive in going after him, it was to advance her career.

Marriages that might have been: Producer/mogul Norman Krasna, with fresh and dewy Nancy Davis, as shown in a publicity shot from way back in 1943 from a drama production at Smith College.

Krasna, in collaboration with producer Jerry Wald, had signed a $50 million deal with Howard Hughes, the owner of RKO, to produce a dozen movies. Krasna promised Nancy that if she'd marry him, he'd make her the "Queen of RKO," and offer that Hughes had previously made to Ingrid Bergman, who had turned him down.

On October 13, 1949, the Hollywood columnist, Edith Gwynn, wrote: "Nancy Davis and her whole family are thinking over a proposal of marriage from Norman Krasna. He is so *currazy* about her that he's already popped the all-important question."

When Reagan showed up on Nancy's doorstep, two days before Christmas, she had already rejected Krasna's proposal. Reagan, as head of SAG, congratulated her on having being assigned her own dressing room at MGM, and delivered to her a gold key, compliments of the studio, that had been commissioned as a symbolic honor from Ruser Jewelers in Beverly Hills.

After being dumped by Nancy, Krasna fell into the arms of Erle Chennault Galbraith, the former wife of Al Jolson, marrying her in 1951, the union lasting until his death in 1984. When he met Nancy years later at a party, he told her, with modesty and humor, "Any man would look great in my wife's eyes after having been married to Al Jolson!"

***

Rumor has it that when actor comedian Milton Berle, once known as "Uncle Miltie," or "Mr. Television," first submitted his memoirs, *Milton Berle, An Autobiography* in 1974 to Delacorte Press, it contained a lengthy section devoted to Nancy Davis.

At that time, there was talk that Reagan might have a good chance of winning the presidency in 1976, and that Nancy might become First Lady. Either Berle's agent or his editor apparently asked him to remove the section on Nancy, which was labeled "tasteless and vulgar."

When Nancy dated Berle, he was just emerging from two marriages to actress Joyce Compton (1941-1948 and, after a divorce and remarriage, 1949-1950).

He may have dated Nancy three times. "Any more than that, and my mother figured out some way to put a stop to it," Berle said. "She didn't want me to get serious over just one woman. She wanted me to play the field."

On his first date with Nancy, he told her, "I am both a Jew and a Christian Scientist."

Long before meeting Nancy, he had generated a notorious past loaded with sexual exploits. He even claimed to have seduced evangelist Aimee Semple McPherson. If true, he would be following in the foot-steps of Reagan.

In addition to encounters with anonymous starlets and chorines, he often dated from the A-list. His part-ners had included Reagan's girlfriend, Ann Sheridan, Lucille Ball, Linda Darnell, and Betty Hutton.

In Miami, during conversations with Darwin Porter, Veronica Lake was very graphic about her se-duction by Berle: "It was at least a foot long and be-came at least two inches more when erect. I'd never seen anything like it, and I had once been seduced by Porfirio Rubirosa."

Berle often boasted about it, even in public set-tings: "I've got the biggest *schlong* in Hollywood. I've got Forrest Tucker and John Ireland beat by two or three inches, maybe more."

Standing beside him at a urinal, fellow comedian Phil Silvers quipped, "You'd better feed that thing or it's liable to turn on you."

The comedian's adopted son, Bill Berle, once shopped a *Mommie Dearest* type memoir about his fa-ther, a tell-all inspired by Christina Crawford's exposé of her mother, Joan Crawford. Entitled *Near You,* it re-layed tales about his notoriously well-endowed father, calling him a "domestic tyrant, a habitual gambler, and a physically gifted ladies' man with an aberrant sex life." In it, he claimed that Berle, invited to a function at the White House, was overheard telling a group of men, "I fucked Nancy Davis back in the Stone Age."

Overhearing him, Merv Griffin, one of Nancy's closest friends, approached Berle and cautioned him to "Cool it—Nancy might hear you."

Berle turned on him in fury: "Shut your cocksuck-ing mouth, faggot." Then he grabbed his crotch, as he did so often, "or else I'll choke you with this club of mine."

Griffin turned and walked away.

Bill Berle also wrote, "I wasn't there to see my fa-ther put his 14-inch thing of his to use on Rita Hay-worth, Marilyn Monroe, even Nancy Davis, but I hoped they had a good time."

He also wrote, "In time, my father went from being the biggest celebrity in the world to a 'couldn't-get-ar-rested' has been."

"Here I am, dancing with Marilyn Monroe, butt to butt," Milton Berle said.

He also claimed, "I seduced a fu-ture First Lady (an obvious refer-ence to Nancy) and a First Lady *wannabee*. Marilyn told me that JFK had promised to divorce Jackie and marry her, thereby making MM First Lady. God, what a story that would have been!"

Merv Griffin in 1945, just after he began working as an announcer at KFRC Radio in San Francisco.

Merv later became one of Nancy Reagan's best friends and a de-fender of her reputation "against the vile, tasteless attacks of Uncle Miltie."

***

One of Nancy's suitors was Mike Wallace, the journalist, game show host, actor, and media personality remembered chiefly today for appearing as the host of CBS's *60 Minutes,* which had its debut on television in 1968. In the years that followed, he interviewed some of the most prominent people in the world.

His origins with the Davis family go back to when he was a freelance radio announcer in Chicago in the early 1940s before he enlisted in the U.S. Navy in 1943.

Although a Jew who knew about prejudice, legendary broadcaster Mike Wallace, who dated Nancy, was accused at one time of being "a homophobe, a racist, and anti-Mexican."

It is not clear when Nancy dated Wallace, perhaps after his divorce from his first wife, Norma Kaplan in 1948 and before his marriage to his second wife, Buff Cobb, in 1949.

Wallace first encountered Edith Davis in Chicago in 1941 when he was broadcasting the evening news on Chicago's WBBM, and she was performing live, on radio, as an actress. After their broadcasts, they often went to the Wrigley Building for drinks.

He became a guest at the Davis home, where he met both Loyal and Nancy. "I got to know Edith and her child," he later said. He was interviewed by author Bob Colacello. "Her child was very ladylike, a Smith girl with a Peter Pan collar and the black patent leather shoes and the white gloves and pearls. Nancy was her father's darling. Utterly unlike her mother, who could drink and be very bawdy in a funny way."

When Nancy matured into an attractive young starlet during her MGM days, Wallace recalled, "She wanted to be rich and famous, but things weren't happening fast enough for her."

Nancy reportedly found Wallace one of the most informed and intelligent men she'd ever dated. They didn't always agree, although their friendship lasted until he died, as did his loyalty to Edith and Loyal. "I'm the son of Russian Jews," Wallace said. "Loyal and Edith were called anti-Semitic, but I never saw any sign of that."

Wallace had his own prejudices, as revealed in 1967 during his documentary, *CBS Reports; The Homosexuals.* During the now notorious broadcast, he asserted, "The average homosexual, if there be such, is promiscuous. He is not interested or capable of a lasting relationship like that of a heterosexual marriage. His sex life, his love life, consists of a series of chance encounters at the clubs and bars he inhabits. And even on the streets of the city—the pick-up, one-night stand, and these are the characteristics of the homosexual relationship."

Reportedly, Nancy saw the broadcast, watching in horror. There were some subjects on which she was more informed and sophisticated.

By 1992, Wallace said, "Of all my broadcasts, I have come to regret that one most of all. I'm far better informed today. I was just parroting what I heard from doctors and psychiatrists. They were wrong, and I was wrong to fall for their shit. I know differently today. Gay people by the millions have long-lasting relationships and even raise loving families."

Although she continued to maintain respect for Wallace, as she did for her anti-Semitic, racist parents, he did cause her more embarrassment. During the first year of the Reagan presidency in 1981, he had to apologize for a racial slur he made against blacks and Hispanics. At a break in *60 Minutes,* he was caught on tape during his delivery of a broadcast about how a bank duped low-income workers in California. He said, "You bet your ass their contracts are hard for them to read over watermelon or tacos."

He later apologized, saying, "We Jews felt a kind of kinship with blacks, but, Lord knows, we weren't riding the same slave ship."

Wallace went to visit Edith and Loyal at Scottdale's Biltmore Estates. Loyal was 84 at the time, Edith 92. A CBS-TV co-worker who was with Wallace at the time reported on how their reunion went. Loyal and Edith were standing in their doorway.

Edith called out, "Mike, how in the fuck are you?"

After exchanging greetings, she is alleged to have pulled her dress up over her head to show him her recent surgical scars. "Look what those fucking cocksuckers did to me."

Later, she revealed that whenever a doctor was examining her, "I always grab his crotch to see what kind of man he is."

When Nancy became First Lady, Wallace interviewed her. He ungallantly asked her to confirm her birth year—either 1921 or 1923. "Your son, Ron Junior, said it was 1921."

"He wasn't there," she snapped.

"Well, which year was it?" Wallace asked again.

"I haven't made up my mind yet," she said.

Months later, Wallace attended a gala dinner on Martha's Vineyard thrown by Katharine Graham of *The Washington Post.* He was seated between a former First Lady (Jacqueline Kennedy Onassis) and Nancy, the current First Lady. He recalled Nancy inviting her to revisit the White House.

"Jackie was very polite," Wallace later said, "but it was obvious to me that she didn't want to go back again."

"I'll think about it and get back to you," Jackie said.

***

Late in 1948, before Nancy arrived in Hollywood, her actress friend, Colleen Moore, gave her a letter of introduction to a handsome young actor, Robert Stack. She'd seen him in his screen debut in 1939 when he gave Deanna Durbin, the teenage singing sensation, her first smooch on camera in *First Love,* a charming, Cinderella-like tale. The cinematic event made frontpage news and heralded Stack into stardom.

"If you play your cards right," Moore told Nancy, "you might learn what caused Durbin to swoon."

In a phone call to Stack, Nancy heard a warm, inviting voice: "Colleen is a great friend of my family. If she says you're adorable, that's good enough for me. Let's go out on a date and test the waters."

Reportedly, Nancy was "awed by Robert's male beauty." In 1980, when Reagan was running for President, Stack published his autobiography, *Straight Shooting.* He was more subdued about Nancy, calling her "attractive and well-mannered. She had this little laugh that was quite enchanting. She even had a sense of humor about herself…and everybody else. My family invited some of the Hollywood elite to their parties. Because of Nancy's background and social graces, she glided through the parties

Millionairess Colleen Moore: Robert Stack's matchmaker and a flapper-star from the Silent Era.

410

like the most graceful swan in the room, with her hair in place and always tastefully dressed, even one night when a drunken Veronica Lake almost threw up on her."

Although they weren't offensive to Nancy in any way, Stack's editor at Macmillan reportedly chose to remove all references to Nancy. In a curt note, he (or she) wrote: "In the Davis revelations, let's remove Nancy and stick with two other Davis names—Bette and Sammy."

Because Nancy was viewed as such hot copy at the time, with Reagan running for President, the editor made Xerox copies of Stack's comments, and circulated them through the Macmillan offices.

Stack's mother had been a dazzling Hollywood socialite who had attended the 1923 wedding of Rudolph Valentino to Natasha Rambova. His father was an advertising executive who created the slogan, "The beer that made Milwaukee famous." The family regularly entertained such celebrities as Frank Sinatra, Enzio Pinza, Edward G. Robinson, Nelson Eddy, Clark Gable, and Robert Taylor.

In the late 1930s, the seventeen-year-old Stack, with his golden blonde hair, was called an Adonis. He captivated the attention of Howard Hughes, the billionaire bisexual, studio mogul, and aviator.

Stack was always awed by power and money, but he really preferred women, and the list of his conquests is long: Elizabeth Taylor, Betty Grable, Diana Barrymore, Yvonne De Carlo, and Lana Turner, plus a treasure trove of starlets. After World War II, when Anne Frank's attic *[where she'd hidden from the Nazis]* was searched, Allied soldiers found a romantic photograph of Stack among her treasured possessions.

During the summer of 1940 in his bachelor apartment in the Hollywood Hills, Stack and John F. Kennedy, newly arrived in town and seeking sexual adventures, entertained a bevy of starlets but also big name stars on occasion. "I've known many of the great male stars of Hollywood, including Clark Gable," Stack said. "But none of them compared to Jack. He literally could charm the pants off a gal."

In 1940, Robert Stack, once known for having "the most perfect male physique in Hollywood," shared the same bed with a future President, JFK. They were rarely alone in this bed.

Reportedly, he also got a future First Lady under the sheets, too.

It was through Stack that Nancy first heard of JFK. "He was the only man in Hollywood better looking than me," he immodestly proclaimed. "All the hot *tamales* on the West Coast took notice. He really needed a date book. I've known him to have sex in the afternoon, sex at cocktail time, sex after dinner, and even a sleepover after midnight—all with a different woman."

Stack and his socially connected parents once took over the former home of Colleen Moore, a Mediterranean style house, vintage 1928, at 345 St. Pierre Road in Bel Air. It had been built with money earned when Moore was number one at the box office during the peak of the Jazz Age in the 1920s. At one point, when he was dating Nancy, he took her there. There were pictures in the hall of the star with her Dutchboy haircut and shapeless dresses, taken when she was the personification of the flapper.

Stack told Nancy, "This is a lovely house with terrible memories—attempted murder, rape, and just about every sexual deviation in the book."

He showed her the blue-painted room which had been his bedroom. "This is the bedroom where Errol Flynn was accused of the rape of Betty Hansen. For a time," Stack told Nancy, "the police sealed off the room to ensure that no one disturbed the evidence, which they hoped would incriminate Flynn." *[With the help of fabled attorney, Jerry Giesler, Flynn was eventually judged not guilty.]*

As a couple, Stack and Nancy soon drifted apart, in spite of finding each other "congenial company."

When a group of fan clubs voted Stack as "The Sexiest Man in the World," he moved on to virtually dozens of beautiful women who were throwing themselves in his pathway.

Two horny bachelors, Robert Stack and a young John F. Kennedy, on the prowl in postwar Hollywood. JFK told his pal, Stack, "I've come to Hollywood on a poontang hunt."

As for Nancy, she became involved in the tormented life of actor Robert Walker and, by extension, his best friend, Peter Lawford.

***

One of Nancy's favorite wartime movies was *Since You Went Away* (1944), starring Claudette Colbert, Jennifer Jones, Joseph Cotten, and Shirley Temple. Nancy had been moved by the brief performance of Robert Walker in the film. His heartbreaking smile signaled "to all those little people sitting out there in the dark" that the character he was playing, that of a very young soldier, was inescapably doomed.

In the movie, he was earnest, lean, and likable as the boyfriend of the character played by Jennifer Jones. Ironically, although the scenes between this married-in-real-life couple were effective, their relationship was collapsing. Producer David O. Selznick had already begun his affair with Jones, and, after her divorce from Walker, he would marry her. There are those who say that Walker never recovered from his loss of his wife.

Complicating Walker's life, even though he claimed that he hated himself for doing so, he often indulged in homosexual affairs. Perhaps in a misguided attempt to wreak revenge on Jones during the filming of *Since You Went Away*, he had sexual liaisons with two of the handsomest young men, each in a minor role, who ever graced the movie screens of the 1940s. They were Guy Madison (making his film debut) and John Derek.

During the closing months of World War II, Walker used his quiet charm, good looks, and sincere voice to convince audi-

Love Lost: Then-newlyweds Jennifer Jones with Robert Walker.

While he was mourning the loss of Jennifer to Hollywood kingpin David O. Selznick, Nancy caught Walker on the rebound.

ences that he really was the boy next door. He was most endearing in pictures as a young soldier at war. His main competitor for that title was another handsome actor, Tom Drake, who became Judy Garland's "boy next door" in the 1944 *Meet Me in St. Louis,* a role originally cast with Walker in the part.

In another instance that illustrates the extreme complications of Hollywood relationships, Walker became involved with Peter Lawford. In the throes of his affair with Lana Turner, he had taken up with Walker when not dating Drake and Reagan's estranged wife, Jane Wyman.

After filming *One Touch of Venus* (1948) with Ava Gardner, Walker and the Tarheel beauty had a brief fling. Lawford also had a fling with Gardner. The plot thickens. At the same time, both Walker and Lawford also began to date Nancy.

After the collapse of his marriage to Jones ("the love of my life"), Walker had entered into a disastrous marriage to Barbara Ford, the daughter of the well-known director, John Ford. Its annulment after only five weeks intensified his depression and heavy drinking.

On October 22, 1948, Walker was arrested in Los Angeles on a charge of drunken driving. A candid snapshot of him at the time of his arrest was flashed around the world, even appearing in *Life* magazine. In the photograph, the actor is obviously intoxicated, his suit rumpled, his right hand balled into a threatening fist, his face contorted with rage.

"I feel Bob is crying out to the world to save him," his friend, Katharine Hepburn, told Irene Mayer Selznick when she saw the photograph.

According to Irene, "Kate had a protective feeling whenever she encountered a lost soul"—Spencer Tracy was an example of that. She'd befriended Walker during the filming of *The Sea of Grass* (1947) when he'd played the nasty offspring of Tracy and herself. Their friendship had deepened in their next picture together, *Song of Love* (also 1947) when, as Johannes Brahms, Walker had pined for her.

After Walker's arrest on the drunk and disorderly charge, Dore Schary at MGM warned the actor that he had two choices—either quit films or else undergo psychiatric treatment at the Menninger Clinic in Kansas, where stars often went to "dry out."

Walker opted for the clinic, where he spent seven months in rehabilitation. Eager to see how he was responding to treatment, Hepburn remained in constant touch. After his return from Kansas, beginning the moment he stepped off the plane, the press mobbed him. Walker announced. "I'm able to work again—eager to live."

After his return to Hollywood, Walker began dating Nancy. Hepburn was very upset with Nancy—"First, she moves in on Spence, and now on Bob, as if he didn't have enough trouble."

Soon after his return to Los Angeles, he renewed and repeated his self-destructive habits, including the consumption of inordinate amounts of alcohol. His love life grew even more complicated, especially with men. As for women, he concentrated on Nancy.

At one point, Walker confided to his friend and

Robert Walker *(left)* and Peter Lawford were each cynical, opportunistic, gossipy, and, as the years advanced, spectacularly unstable.

Both of them enjoyed the alluring charms of Ava Gardner and each got to enjoy Nancy Davis' "specialty."

sometimes lover, Merv Griffin (when he was still young trim, and handsome) that he had proposed marriage to Nancy. He later became one of Griffin's closest friends.

"Obviously, she didn't accept," Griffin said to Walker.

"She told me that over the course of a lifetime, she thought Reagan would be the better provider," Walker said.

Lawford, who by now had his own key to Walker's home, came over late one afternoon with their mutual friend, producer Joe Naar. Walker was not supposed to be there, having told Lawford he'd arrive in time for dinner.

As later relayed to Cukor, Lawford claimed that when they came into the living room, he first encountered Nancy in the nude and Walker half dressed on his sofa. "It appeared to me that they were engaged in some sort of sex act—guess what?" Lawford said. "Nancy rushed to the bathroom to get dressed. At the time, she seemed terribly embarrassed, but she recovered quickly. It wasn't long after that she began to date both Bob *and* me. As you know, I was already deep into my affair with Bob."

"The whole town's talking," Cukor said, "about a *ménage à trois.*"

[Naar later became the best and most reliable source for information about the sexual trysts among Walker, Nancy, and Lawford. A former William Morris agent, he later produced the hit (1975-1979) TV series, Starsky and Hutch. *As an agent, his clients included not only Lawford, but Steve McQueen, Ali MacGraw, Raquel Welch, and Marilyn Monroe.*

At one point, Naar double-dated with Lawford and Monroe. He remembered their first date, but didn't recall the young starlet he was with at the time. "At one point, Peter urged me to switch dates, and I ended up taking Marilyn home. She became not only my temporary lover, but my lifelong friend, confidante, and client."

Naar's friendship with Lawford led to his becoming a member of Camelot's inner circles. The Kennedys accepted him, and he became known for jetting around the country with them and the likes of Frank Sinatra and Sammy Davis, Jr.

Ironically, one of Naar's most successful ventures was as a producer for the General Electric Hour, *which was hosted by none other than Ronald Reagan.]*

Nancy was added to the marquee names of Lawford's seductions, which included a lot of A-listers, notably June Allyson, who also seduced Reagan, as well as Lucille Ball, Anne Baxter, Noël Coward, director George Cukor ("Peter was such a lousy lay—strictly oral"), Ava Gardner, Judy Garland, Rita Hayworth ("she had bad breath"), Sal Mineo ("my all-time best"), Marilyn Monroe ("there was a problem with hygiene")' Lee Remick, Clifton Webb ("I let him do all the work"), Van Johnson and his lover, Keenan Wynn, whose divorced wife, Evie, Johnson had married, on orders from Louis B. Mayer.

The dean of Hollywood biographers, Lawrence J. Quirk, who knew Lawford "from way back when" asserted that he went out with women "to help dispel rumors about his relationships with men—and there were several of them. These relationships worried him; they were often a sexual release rather than a romance. When he fell in love with or entertained romantic feelings toward a man, Peter grew inescapably depressed. This side of his erotic life he found ominous, threatening, baleful, yet he needed it, too."

Author Mart Martin claimed that from his investigation, Lawford often patronized "young male extras and studio messengers."

Supposedly, Nancy was aware of Lawford's journeys

Emmy Winner Joe Naar

414

into the gay world, but for her it didn't seem a problem. She had dated and even had affairs with gay men during her New York days.

When Lawford married Patricia Kennedy, and became part of the Kennedy clan, his wife did not seem unduly concerned with his trysts in the gay world. While he was away, she was having her own flings, including one with Porfirio Rubirosa, the Dominican playboy known for his international charm; his links to the brutal Dominican dictator, Trujillo; his failed marriages to Doris Duke and Barbara Hutton; and for his stupendous sexual endowment.

Apparently, Walker had many soul-searching talks with Nancy. As he told her and so many other friends, "Even as a kid, I knew I was not meant to be born into this world. It was an accident. I've spent my life trying to escape the world, wanting to go back to the peace I knew before I entered it."

After the collapse of his Hollywood career, Drake, no longer the pretty boy at MGM, worked selling used cars in Los Angeles. In the late 1940s and early 50s, he and Lawford often slipped away to wherever Lawford had access to privacy.

"I'd heard stories that Peter was having a fling with both Walker and this starlet, Nancy Davis," Drake said. "I found that out during my final weekend with Peter. He showed up in Palm Springs with Walker and Nancy. Privately, he told me that she had taken turns fellating them during their transit from Los Angeles to Palm Springs.

"She worked on one of us in the back seat," Lawford said. "The other had to drive. We took turns."

"I was heartbroken that weekend," Drake said. "Peter had dumped me, and I was still madly in love with him."

In another biography appeared an account that Lawford and Walker drove all the way to Arizona with Nancy so that she could visit her parents, then living in their retirement residence. Lawford may have relayed the incident to one of his wives, but that appears not to be true. Those who knew Nancy doubted very seriously if she would show up in Arizona with not one, but two lovers.

Young lovers Peter Lawford and Nancy Davis.

Whereas he married into a First Family (the Kennedys), she became the iron-gloved matriarch of a First Family of her own.

Handsome Tom Drake, "the boy next door" to Judy Garland in *Meet Me in St. Louis,"* had a lament about his years-long affair with Peter Lawford:

"Imagine, I had to fight off Robert Walker, Lana Turner, Ava Gardner, and ultimately, Nancy Davis for squatter's rights to this elusive Brit."

Drake's account seems far more plausible. Of course, Lawford could have fabricated the Arizona tale as a means of masking his sexual tryst with Drake.

Alfred Hitchcock may have been type casting when he starred Walker as the smiling psychopath and repressed homosexual in *Strangers on a Train* (1951). It became Walker's most memorable role and one of the British director's grandest creations.

The year the picture was released, Nancy was saddened by Walker's sudden death.

On the night of August 28, 1951, Walker's housekeeper found the actor ranting, raging, and threatening violence. She summoned his psychiatrist, who examined him, then sedated him with amobarbital. The sedative, combined with the alcohol in Walker's bloodstream, caused immediate respiratory failure. He was dead at the age of thirty-two.

During the years that followed, Nancy followed Lawford's saga, especially the episodes associated with his role as brother-in-law of John F. Kennedy, based on his marriage to Patricia Kennedy. Lawford would marry three more times as he drifted into alcoholism and hired call girls, who viewed him as a "quick $50 oral sex trick," plus a series of male hustlers upon whom he performed fellatio and quickly dismissed them.

By then, Nancy was far, far away, her world orbiting around Ronald Reagan.

Her relationship with Reagan began when Mervyn LeRoy was directing Nancy in *The Doctor and the Girl*. She had a matter she wanted to take up personally with Reagan, who at the time was the President of the Screen Actors Guild. Nancy knew that LeRoy and Reagan were friends.

Although she had to wait for days, the call from Reagan finally came through.

***

The films of Nancy Davis, if they are remembered at all today, are highlighted by *The Next Voice You Hear,* released by MGM in 1950. Her co-star was James Whitmore, with whom she'd make another movie in 1951. Child actor Gary Gray was cast as their son. Based on a preposterous script by Charles Schnee, the movie was produced by Dore Schary and directed by William A. Wellman, popularly known in Hollywood as "Wild Bill." The plot could easily have dipped into camp were it not for the screen sincerity of Nancy and Whitmore.

The film's unlikely premise focused on the voice of a man claiming to be God. His declarations would pre-empt every radio program, worldwide, for six broadcasts over the same number of days. On Sunday, as an anxious world awaited his words, he was silent, presumably resting on the Sabbath.

Whitmore and Nancy portrayed a typical American couple with the *clichéd* names of Joe (played by Whitmore) and his pregnant wife Mary (Nancy). They hover beside their radio, listening to "God" broadcasting from "Heaven."

A New Englander, Wellman was the most talented of the directors who ever helmed Nancy. His 1927 silent film, *Wings,* was the first movie to win an Academy Award as Best Picture. He'd go on to direct *A Star Is Born* (1937), with Janet Gaynor and Fredric March; *Nothing Sacred* (also

Nancy's ultimate "Mom" role: *Left to right*, James Whitmore, Gary Gray, and the future First Lady of the United States.

416

1937) with Carole Lombard; and *Beau Geste* (1939) with Gary Cooper.

Before directing Nancy, he had just scored a big hit with his World War II drama, *Battleground* (1949). Coincidentally, that film had also starred Nancy's friend, Van Johnson, and featured Whitmore in a supporting role.

Nancy dreaded reporting to the set to face Wellman, as his reputation had preceded him. He was known as brusque and aggressive. Louise Brooks had described him as "sadistic."

He did not immediately endear himself to Nancy. "I hate all actresses," he told her. "I detest their narcissism. I prefer to direct men. Women take up so much time worrying about their hair, their makeup, their wardrobe."

"He knew I just wasn't the big-bosom, sweater girl type like Lana Turner," Nancy said. "So we got that out of the way. I couldn't have looked more drab than I did in my $12.95 maternity smock."

She was one of the first actresses to appear on screen as openly pregnant. Before that, actresses tried to conceal their pregnancy, as if it were something vulgar, an embarrassing condition not to be flaunted before audiences. But Wellman wanted realism in Nancy's character, insisting that she wear no makeup and not to benefit from the ministrations of a hairdresser. When MGM commissioned Hollywood's leading hairdresser, Sydney Guilaroff, to style Nancy's hair, Wellman chased him off the set.

An affable, plain-looking actor from New York, Whitmore, with Nancy, closely resembled a typical middle-class American couple. He had recently appeared with Marilyn Monroe in *The Asphalt Jungle* (1950). Monroe was just emerging as a screen siren. Whitmore would later appear with Reagan's first wife, Jane Wyman, in one of the episodes on her *Jane Wyman Presents the Fireside Theatre.*

Whitmore had been a dedicated student at the Actors Studio in New York, and when he moved to Los Angeles, he opened his own acting workshop. One of his new pupils was James Dean. One hot afternoon, the young actor, sloppily dressed, showed up on the set of *The Next Voice You Hear.* When later queried, Nancy reportedly claimed she did not remember meeting Dean, who would later threaten a character portrayed by Reagan with a gun in one of the episodes on his *General Electric Theater.*

In front of Nancy and Wellman, Dean said, in reference to Whitmore, "I owe a lot to Jimmy here. He has much to teach an actor. So far, he's the only person I've met in Hollywood who hasn't demanded to suck my cock in return for a favor."

Working with Wellman did not turn out to be the ordeal for Nancy that she had feared—in fact, they became friends. She recalled, "The tiger turned out to be a pussycat."

When it was completed, MGM sent Nancy to New York to promote *The Next Voice You Hear.* She recalled "my greatest thrill" involved standing in front of the Radio City Music Hall's grand marquee, where for the first time, she saw her name, NANCY DAVIS, posted in big letters. She remembered standing for an entire hour looking up at the marquee.

At the film's premiere on September 12, 1950, she was escorted by her new beau, Ronald Reagan, whom she had already begun to date. *[More about that later…]* The occasion marked the first time the couple had ever been photographed together.

Regrettably, Radio City Music Hall was not the proper venue for a message picture from Dore Schary. Movie fans were used to coming to the grand showcase for spectacles and later, to see the Rockettes performing their stunning precision dance numbers.

The New Yorker pounced on the film, attacking it as a "meandering, maudlin affair." *The New York Times,* however, cited Nancy's role as "a cheerful and considerate pregnant wife."

In Los Angeles, her friend, Spencer Tracy, went to see the movie. To Katharine Hepburn, George Cukor, and others, he said, "Nancy projected the passion of Good Humor ice cream—frozen, on a stick, and vanilla."

In spite of its controversial subject and nation-wide reviews, the film failed at the box office, losing $65,000 for MGM.

But what did Nancy's newest boyfriend think of *The Next Voice You Hear*? After its premiere, Reagan invited Nancy to dinner and gave her some advice. "Send that wardrobe you wore in the picture to the cleaners and then lose the claim check."

What for Nancy began as a romantic evening ended on a sour note. He told her, "I'm still in love with Jane, even though she's divorced me. I still think we'll get back together one day. I plan to grow old with her."

***

Before being cast in *The Next Voice You Hear,* Nancy had made two screen tests, hoping to play the female leads in two films, each scheduled for release in 1950.

She first wanted to appear as the wife of Cary Grant in *Crisis*. In it, he played a renowned brain surgeon vacationing in South America with his wife, a role Nancy coveted. The surgeon becomes inadvertently embroiled in a revolution when the country's dictator, played by Oscar-winning José Ferrer, urgently needs life-saving brain surgery. The dictator demands that it be performed, by the American doctor, with utmost secrecy.

Dore Schary screened Nancy's test, later defining it as "The worst screen test in the history of motion pictures." He told aides, "Nancy will be perfect playing the simple plain housewife to a bloke like James Whitmore. But for Cary Grant's wife, let's cast Paula Raymond. She's a hell of a lot sexier than Nancy."

[Since Grant took no part in denying the role to Nancy, she did not hold a grudge against him. In fact, in 1981, as First Lady, five weeks after the attempted assassination of Reagan, she invited Grant to a gala event at the White House in honor of the U.K.'s Prince Charles.

For that event, she selected what she called "a fun group," consisting not only of Grant, but Audrey Hepburn, right-winger William F. Buckley, her close friends Alfred and Betsy Bloomingdale, and fashion doyenne Diana Vreeland.

The evening erupted into a media controversy when Nancy was photographed curtseying before Prince Charles. It set off a firestorm, one newspaper claiming, "No First Lady should be caught bowing her knees in front of royalty. Actually, in her current role, Nancy Reagan has far more power than Prince Charles."]

The next role Nancy sought and appeared in a screen test for was the part of the wife of Chief Justice Oliver Wendell Holmes. A friend of the Davis family, Louis Calhern, had already been cast as the justice in *The Magnificent Yankee* (1950). He would win an Oscar nomination for his role, which required him to age from 61 to 90 during the course of the film.

"I knew the part was a difficult one for me, too," Nancy said. "I, too, had to age considerably for the role."

Once again, studio personnel evaluated her as "totally unsuited to play the wife," the part going to Ann Harding, who had both the talent and the presence to pull off the demanding role.

Nancy learned later that this time around, Schary had endorsed her for the role, as had Ardie Deutsch, the film's producer. However, when John Sturges was assigned to direct *The Magnificent Yankee,* he sat through Nancy's test, which seemed to infuriate him. He wrote a memo to Schary, claiming that Nancy was "WRONG! WRONG!

418

WRONG!" for the part.

[Nancy never shared a story with Calhern that she'd learned from Dr. Loyal Davis. At one point, in Chicago, he had performed surgery on the ailing actor. In the middle of the procedure, as he lay on the operating table, Calhern's heart stopped. Desperately, Davis massaged his heart and resuscitated his breathing. Although he revealed details of the incident to both Edith and Nancy, the doctor chose never to tell his most famous patient.]

***

After the failure of *The Next Voice You Hear,* and her "bombing" in two separate screen tests, Nancy's future as a movie star looked dim. A whole roster of new stars was on the horizon, dozens of whom were far more talented and beautiful than she was. She would limp through only a few more pictures before fading into oblivion, only to evolve decades later into one of the most powerful behind-the-scenes women of the 20th Century.

She claimed that her next movie, *Night Into Morning* (1951)*,* was her favorite film, in spite of the similarity of its title to *Night Unto Night,* a film made in 1949 by Reagan. She was hoping that her latest film would salvage her dimly flickering career. Her fantasy was that by starring with Ray Milland, it would lead to a breakthrough equivalent to that of Jane Wyman when she co-starred with him in *The Lost Weekend* (1945). That film had propelled Wyman into an A-list career and had brought Milland an Oscar for his portrayal of a tormented alcoholic.

Milland expressed his hope that with his appearance once again as an alcoholic, he would score another triumph, this time as a college professor who becomes a drunk and a possible suicide after his wife and ten-year-old son are burned to death in a freak fire.

A Canadian, Fletcher Markle (the director), would praise Nancy's performance. "If only the critics had taken notice," he said. "She is a gifted actress, although typecast as a nice, steadfast war widow. In her one big scene, where she tries to prevent Milland from committing suicide by jumping out of a hotel window, she was superb. She had one page of dialogue, and she pulled off this difficult scene in just one shot. After that, I called her 'One Take Nancy.'"

In the film, John Hodiak played an academic, a junior colleague of Milland's at his college. Engaged to be married to the widowed character played by Nancy, he becomes jealous of the attention she pays to Milland.

Nancy would recall, "This was one of the few times I played a *fiancée* and not a wife."

Markle had emigrated to the land of sunshine and palm trees

Lightning did not strike twice. Ray Milland *(left),* shown above with Nancy and John Hodiak, had immortalized himself opposite Jane Wyman by playing an alcoholic in*The Lost Weekend.*

Six years later, now cast with Nancy Davis as his leading lady, he hoped for his second Oscar. Alas, his performance, and the picture, failed.

from the cold winds of Winnipeg, Manitoba. He was multi-talented: Actor, screenwriter, TV producer, and director. He had contributed to the screenplay of Orson Welles' *The Lady from Shanghai* (1947), starring Rita Hayworth as a blonde.

One day Markle's lover, Mercedes McCambridge, appeared on the set. Having divorced his first wife, the former Helen Blanche Willis, in 1949, Markle was rushing into a marriage to McCambridge. She met Nancy, later asking Markle, "Where did you find that little mouse?"

In November of 1950, McCambridge triumphed over Nancy when she was designated as number four in *Photoplay's Choose Your Stars* contest. In spite of her sagging career, Nancy came in fifth. McCambridge seemed delighted that fans favored her over Nancy. Topping both of them was starlet Piper Laurie, who had just had a fling with Reagan, as she later confessed in her autobiography.

McCambridge on the verge of shooting Joan Crawford in *Johnny Guitar.*

Born in Wales, Milland, to Nancy, at least, seemed rather cynical, having appeared on the screen since 1929. She suspected that he might have interpreted a co-performance with her as a comedown. During his long career, he would star opposite Gene Tierney, Lana Turner, Marlene Dietrich, Ginger Rogers, Loretta Young, and Veronica Lake, sometimes seducing his leading ladies, as he did with Jane Wyman in *The Lost Weekend* and later as the murder-plotting husband in *Dial M for Murder* (1954), co-starring Grace Kelly, with whom he fell in love. That threatened one of the most enduring marriages in Hollywood, that of Milland to the former Muriel Weber.

Nancy, emoting with John Hodiak in *Night Into Morning.*

He told Nancy, "From now on, acting to me is just taking home a paycheck. I think it's downhill for me from now on."

John Hodiak, involved at the time in a disintegrating marriage to Anne Baxter, laughed as rarely as Greta Garbo. In one scene within *Night Into Morning,* Nancy was called upon to make this stoic Ukrainian laugh. In take after take, his laugh—to the director, at least—sounded fake. The scene took place when they were mounting a flight of stairs. During Nancy's final take, she spontaneously whispered, "belly button," in response to which Hodiak laughed uproariously. His cackles met with the director's approval.

Nancy's friend, Jean Hagen, was also in the picture. She and Nancy bonded more than ever and had lunch together. Hagen had seduced Ralph Meeker during the filming of their previous picture, and now she turned her seductive charms onto Hodiak. She later told Nancy,

Nancy with John Hodiak: Is he barring her entrance? Or signaling that it's OK to enter?

"Getting fucked by Johnny is like getting plowed with a beer bottle."

While making the film, Hodiak seemed very depressed. Not only was his marriage failing, but the year before, he had been voted "box office poison" by movie exhibitors across the country.

[At the age of 41, Hodiak would suffer a fatal heart attack in his bathroom and die.]

That curmudgeon of *The New York Times,* Bosley Crowther, attacked *Night Into Morning,* appraising it as "a morbid swirl of sentiment and self-pity" *Variety,* however, cited Nancy's performance as showing "warmth and understanding."

[Nancy appreciated the kind words, but told Hagen, "those words doth not a star make."

***

Nancy made only a brief appearance with Fredric March in the 1952 *It's a Big Country,* Dore Schary's flag-waving salute to America. An all-star cast, a glittering roster, was assembled by MGM, including personalities already familiar to Nancy—Ethel Barrymore, Gary Cooper, Van Johnson, Gene Kelly, Janet Leigh, Marjorie Main, George Murphy, Lewis Stone, and James Whitmore. An anthology of vignettes, it depicted scenes from American lives. It was directed by a committee whose members included Richard Thorpe, Charles Vidor, Don Weiss, Clarence Brown, John Sturges, and William A. Wellman.

In Nancy's segment, "Four Eyes," she plays a schoolteacher who becomes aware that one of her pupils cannot see very well. She tries to persuade his father (March), improbably cast as an Italian immigrant, to purchase of pair of eyeglasses for the boy— hence the title, "Four Eyes." She meets passionate resistance from a father who thinks it's unmanly for his son to wear glasses. She triumphs in the end. She later said, "I wish my segment with March could have been a whole picture. I'm sure I could have learned a lot from him."

At first, Nancy had been leery of working with March because of the reputation that had preceded him. He had already seduced many of his costars, including Tallulah Bankhead, Clara Bow, Olivia de Havilland, Ann Harding, and Miriam Hopkins. He was notorious as "the most lecherous fanny-grabber in Hollywood."

Back when she was still speaking to Nancy, Katharine Hepburn told of her experience with March when he'd been cast opposite her as her tartan-wearing lover, the Earl of Bothwell, in *Mary of Scotland* (1936). Knowing that he was going to glide his hand up her 16th-century costume, she was prepared for him. "When he came to my dressing room, I had taken the largest banana in my fruit bowl and put it into my bloomers. When his hand went up my dress, he discovered a very large phallic object and retreated. Case closed."

A much older and not-so-horny March encountered Nancy when they worked together in 1952. "He treated me like a lady and was a perfect gentleman in every way."

In spite of Schary's high expectations for *It's a Big Country,* audiences stayed away in droves. Ultimately, it lost $677,000 for MGM.

Despite Nancy's praise for March, most critics found his performance as a *Papa Italiano* hammy, a caricature. Bosley Crowther of *The New York Times* thought it a role that J. Carroll Naish might have pulled off. In his autobiography, Schary never even mentioned his once pet project. Nancy also cut mention of it when she penned her second memoir.

It seemed that both MGM and its stars wanted to forget the film as a fiscally disastrous embarrassment.

***

In her first memoir, *Nancy,* she made an astonishing claim: "I also did *Rescue at Sea,* which may have appeared as *The Frogmen* in 1955, if it came out at all. I played opposite Gary Merrill, and it's another picture I'd just as soon forget. Every performer has a few of these in the closet."

Everybody is entitled to a lapse of memory, but it's surprising that Nancy didn't compose her memoirs with a scrapbook of newspaper clippings and memorabilia about her movies on her desk. It's true that she appeared in a movie originally entitled *Rescue at Sea,* but its title was later changed—that particular film was never called *The Frogmen.*

There was a movie released n 1951 called *The Frogmen,* and it did star Gary Merrill (at the time, Mr. Bette Davis) in third billing. The two big-name stars involved with the project were Richard Widmark and Dana Andrews, but no women ever appeared in *The Frogmen.* It was the story of the U.S. Navy's Underwater Demolition teams battling the Japanese Army and Naval forces in the Sea of Japan during World War II.

For some strange reason, Nancy, in her memoirs, remembered appearing in *The Frogmen,* co-starring Gary Merrill.

Although Merrill had indeed been in the movie, Nancy had not. The film's two major stars were Richard Widmark *(left)* and Dana Andrews.

In neither the script nor the final footage, not a single female was waiting for them after their successful demolition of underwater obstacles for the U.S. Navy in the Sea of Japan during World War II.

Why would Nancy connect herself with this all-male underwater adventure film? The mystery may have been solved when director Henry Hathaway was tracked down. He had been the original director of *The Frogmen,* and a major director in Golden Age Hollywood, helming such stars as Clara Bow, Gary Cooper, Marlene Dietrich, and Nancy's friend, Walter Huston. Its original script had called for some women's roles, the type who waited on the shore for their lovers to return from the dangers of The Deep.

"I vaguely remember—and I could be wrong about this—but I think I called Nancy in for a reading for one of the female roles," Hathaway said. "Instead of Merrill, Richard Conte was to have been her leading man. Later, both Conte and I dropped out, and the script was rewritten with no roles for women at all."

Lloyd Bacon was called in to direct *The Frogmen.* He had helmed Reagan in *Knute Rockne—All American* (1940).

Even though she wasn't in it, Nancy said she was ashamed of *The Frogmen.* She need not have been. It was the first A-list movie to depict SCUBA diving and clandestine underwater demolition activities during wartime, and it became a big cultural hit. Many young men cited this movie as their inspiration for becoming Navy SEALS.

***

Often missing from the list of Nancy's movies was the 1952 release of *Shadow in the Sky,* a financial disaster that cost MGM $644,000, in spite of its relatively low production costs. Her co-stars were James Whitmore, her close friend Jean Hagen, and a self-styled "sex bomb" and bad boy, Ralph Meeker.

The film was directed by Fred M. Wilcox, a Virginian better known for his two dog movies, *Lassie Come Home* (1943), and *Courage of Lassie* (1946). He'd also had a hit directing Margaret O'Brien in *The Secret Garden* (1949).

Nancy's work with him went smoothly for both of them.

Its plot centers around Burt (Meeker), who is in a mental institution after having undergone traumatic experiences while serving as a Marine in the South Pacific during World War II. His girlfriend, Stella, is played by Hagen. Wilcox couldn't help but see that Hagen was Meeker's girlfriend offscreen as well. "She was seen coming and going from Meeker's dressing room" he recalled.

A decision was made by the studio to sell *Shadow in the Sky* as a sexy movie. Publicity did not think Nancy, or even Jean Hagen, should be the focus of the ad. Instead, it was decided that Ralph Meeker, clad in skinny bathing attire, would attract a wider audience.

Nancy was cast as Betty, Burt's sister, married to Lou (Whitmore). The suspense of the movie, if it could be called that, derives from whether Burt, as a mentally wounded warrior, can be stabilized enough to return to a normal life outside the asylum.

Whitmore often lunched with Nancy and she came to consider him "a good family man." Before he divorced his wife, the former Nancy Mygatt, in 1971, the couple had three sons. After that, he married three more times. His final marriage, launched when he was a senior citizen, lasted until his death in 2009.

Nancy seemed to have no memory of making that movie, devoting only sixteen lines to it in her memoirs, *Nancy.* Maybe she blanked it out because while working on the film, she received very distressing news.

She learned that Reagan had proposed marriage to actress Christine Larson, and he was said to be deeply in love with the beautiful starlet.

"Lightning struck twice for Nancy," Wilcox later said. "While filming our movie, she learned that Metro didn't plan to renew her contract."

Although Meeker was unmarried at the time, he was out of the running because of his affair with Hagen," Wilcox said. "At any rate, he'd soon be off to Broadway to star in William Inge's *Picnic,* where he was said to have taught

Ralph Meeker might have added Nancy to his impressive roster of A-list seductions.

Actually, he spent more time applying his "magnificent woman-killing weapon" (as he immodestly described it) to Jean Hagen.

his understudy, Paul Newman, 'Who's the Man,' if you get my drift."

***

Talk About a Stranger (1952) was Nancy's last film for MGM, which, as she had predicted, soon after dropped her from its roster of contract players. That was hardly surprising. Faced with the loss of revenue as audiences stayed home to watch TV, the once-fabled studio was releasing hordes of its stars and staff. The Golden Age of Hollywood had come to a whimpering end. Once big name stars like Bette Davis were advertising for jobs.

The star of *Talk About a Stranger* was George Murphy, who called himself Reagan's best friend, an honor also claimed by both Robert Taylor and William Holden.

Playing the son of Nancy and Murphy was the rumor-spreading child actor, Billy Gray. The Vienna-born actor, Kurt Kasznar, one of Hollywood's closeted gays, was cast as the mysterious stranger.

Directed by David Bradley, *Talk About a Stranger* tells the story of Bud Fontaine, Jr. (as interpreted by Gray), who suspects a strange new neighbor (Kasznar) of poisoning his dog. The boy launches a smear campaign and spreads vicious rumors about the man, which turn out to be based on false impressions. In time, Bud comes to realize that people are not always what they appear to be, learning one of life's lessons, but not before he endangers crops in the valley by his vandalism of the neighbor's oil tank. Murphy and Nancy cope as best they can with their irrepressible son.

Bradley seemed an odd choice as a director. He was an actor, a collector of vintage films, and a university lecturer. At the Art Institute of Chicago, he'd cast a 17-year-old wannabee actor, Charlton Heston, in his feature length 16mm version of *Peer Gynt*.

In 1963, he would direct *Madmen of Mandoras*, a short feature film that was expanded, in 1969, into the notorious made-for-television movie, *They Saved Hitler's Brain*, a sci-fi romp that some critics define as one of the most absurdly campy (but unfunny) films ever made.

After George Murphy *(right)*, one of Reagan's closest friends, co-starred with Nancy in *Talk About a Stranger*, he gave Reagan some advice: "Dump Nancy, and marry Doris Day."

Producer Richard Goldstone shared his memories of working with Nancy: "At MGM, she was on her way out the door, yet at the commissary she was table-hopping, talking to all the big names, sitting at one point with Clark Gable before hopping over to share a drink with Spencer Tracy and to give him a big kiss. I had never seen a starlet dare do that before."

All that Nancy remembered about Gray was that he had a fascination with motorcycles. The year she'd met him, he had

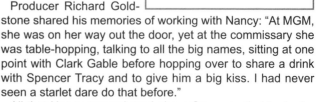

Evil neighbors who turn out to be benign and innocent: gay actor Kurt Kasznar.

424

appeared as the boy version of the Native American athlete and protagonist of *Jim Thorpe—All American.* Burt Lancaster had been cast as the adult version of Jim Thorpe. Later that year (1951), Gray would make a science fiction film, *The Day the Earth Stood Still,* starring Michael Rennie and Patricia Neal, a future girlfriend of Reagan's.

Gray went on to achieve fame in the long-running (1954-1960) TV series, *Father Knows Best.* He later denounced the plots and characters of this sitcom as "totally false," blaming the series for "a lot of problems between men and women today."

Talk About a Stranger: George Murphy, Billy Gray *(center)* and again, another "worried mother" role for Nancy.

Talk About a Stranger was advertised as a film that would send "chills down your spine." It did not. Nancy was later reported to have said, "George and I both agreed: *Talk About a Stranger* was MGM's way of giving us the pink slip."

Murphy himself later quipped: "Every year since then, around Christmastime, I have promised Nancy that I would get a print and run it—but thus far, she has been spared that pleasure. I do hope that the Democrats don't get hold of the film and run it on *The Late, Late Show* during my 1970 campaign for the Senate. It might be more than I could overcome."

Murphy also wrote, "Nancy met Ronnie about the time we were making *Talk About a Stranger.* He had succeeded me as President of the Screen Actors Guild and in that capacity, Nancy paid him a visit. She was repeatedly being embarrassed by the fact that the name 'Nancy Davis' kept popping up on Communist Front lists, and she was receiving invitations to attend radical meetings. That was difficult to bear, since Nancy was decidedly anti-communist. At director Mervyn LeRoy's suggestion, she sought out Reagan for his counsel. He not only straightened out the matter, but a year later, he married the girl."

What Murphy did not put into his memoir was a final line, "against my wishes."

***

After her sagas at MGM, Nancy wanted to bow out of films, particularly after her marriage to Reagan in 1952, but "I had some bills to pay, so I hung in there a little longer. I made *Donovan's Brain* (1953), a low-budget sci-fi picture, but it was not a class act."

Based on a novel by Curt Siodmak, it was released by United Artists in 1953. The screenplay was both written and directed by Felix E. Feist, an MGM executive who had directed both Deanna Durbin and her younger rival, Judy Garland, in *Every Sunday* (1936).

Nancy recalled that *Donovan's Brain* "was silly but popular, and must have been particularly amusing to my father." *[She was referring to her stepfather, Dr. Loyal Davis.]*

She recalled the first morning she reported to work, driving at 4:30am through the deserted streets of Beverly Hills one wintry, pre-dawn day. Suddenly, the flashing dome lights of a police squad car signaled for her to pull over. Two officers were suddenly flanking her car. One of them demanded her license, the other searched the back seat with his flashlight. They demanded answers: "Where are you going? Where have you come from? How much money do you have in your purse?"

That night, after she returned home from the studio, she told Reagan what had happened to her. He laughed at her encounter. "Honey, the cops saw a good-looking woman driving a convertible at that time of the morning. They thought you were returning from a hard night's work."

"What kind of work?" she asked.

"Those cops thought you were a prostitute."

Nancy's co-star in *Donovan's Brain* was Lew Ayres, who by now had descended to the nadir of his career. He was no longer the beautiful young German soldier depicted in the classic *All Quiet on the Western Front (1930)*.

Ironically, he had starred with Jane Wyman in her Oscar-winning portrayal in *Johnny Belinda* (1948). When she had divorced Reagan, it was with the belief that Ayres would marry her. He had dumped her instead.

Donovan's Brain, like *The Next Voice You Hear*, is regarded today as high camp. When Nancy was First Lady, it was sometimes shown at midnight. Audiences, nearly always composed of young people, would "hoot and holler" at the screen.

Its plot spins around an attempt by Dr. Patrick Cory (as played by Ayres) to keep alive the brain of a multi-millionaire megalomaniac, "the man you love to hate," W.H. Donovan. He had gone down in a fatal plane crash, and his body had been removed temporarily for safe-keeping to the nearby home of Dr. Cory. Cory, surgically and illegally, removes his brain and attempts to keep it alive. His long-suffering wife, Janice, is played by Nancy. The brain eventually takes possession of Cory and transforms him into an evil blackmailer.

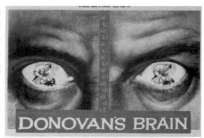

For Ayres, it was a humiliating comedown. For Nancy, it was a final (doomed) opportunity for stardom:

Photo above shows Nancy with her co-star, Lew Ayres (Jane Wyman's former love fantasy from *Johnny Belinda*) in *Donovan's Brain*, a weak but campy sci-fi thriller that caused embarrassment during her tenure as First Lady

In her memoirs, Nancy recalled her upcoming film, *Hellcats of the Navy* (1956), as her final film and the only one in which she ever co-starred with Reagan. By the time of its production, they had been married for four years.

She was wrong. She made one more film after *Hellcats of the Navy*.

***

Her last film, *Crash Landing* (1958), was made for Columbia. It was the one that Nancy had confused with *The Frogmen*. Originally, *Crash Landing* was entitled *Rescue at Sea*. [*Nancy had recalled it as the original title of* The Frogmen.]

She had remembered Gary Merrill as her co-star in *The Frogmen*. Actually, he became her co-star in *Rescue at Sea*, whose title was eventually altered to the more dramatic *Crash Landing*.

The 76-minute film was one of the first major aerial disaster films. Nancy was cast as Merrill's devoted wife. He plays a pilot crossing the Atlantic with a plane full of passengers. Midway across the ocean, he is forced to make an emergency landing. Fortunately, a U.S. Navy vessel is nearby to rescue the crash victims.

The film was a forerunner of *Airport* (1970), the hit movie that starred Burt Lancaster and Dean Martin, bringing a Best Supporting Actress Oscar to Nancy's friend, veteran Helen Hayes, cast as a stowaway.

As in all subsequent aerial disaster films, *Crash Landing* focused on a diverse group of passengers making true confessions as they prepare to die. The film was created by Fred Freiberger (aka Charles Woodgrove), the future producer of the third season (1968-69) of *Star Trek*.

Merrill spent most of his time complaining about his marriage to Bette Davis, which at the time was on the rocks.

*[**Movie trivia**: Merrill had replaced José Ferrer in the Broadway hit,* Brother Rat *(1937), the play that inspired the subsequent movie starring Jane Wyman and Ronald Reagan. Merrill told Nancy that he had appeared as one of the soldiers in* This Is the Army, *also starring her husband, Reagan. Reagan had also co-starred with Merrill's estranged wife (Bette Davis), playing her gay suitor in* Dark Victory *(1939).]*

For Nancy, it was another "Home and Hearth, Postwar U.S. Mom" role, an image that would serve her well during her husband's later campaigns.

She's shown here in *Crash Landing* with her man in uniform (Gary Merrill) and their onscreen son, Kim Charney.

Nancy met the second female lead, Irene Harvey, sizing her up as competition, as she frequently did. Harvey had made her screen debut in *The Stanger's Return* in 1933, starring Lionel Barrymore. After divorcing her first husband, William Fenderson, she had fallen in love with *matinée* heartthrob Robert Taylor, who had broken from Thelma Ryan after taking her virginity. Thelma later became First Lady, Patricia Nixon.

Taylor moved on to the bisexual aviator, Howard Hughes, and Errol Flynn, even Greta Garbo, before settling in to marry Barbara Stanwyck. ("Her balls are bigger than mine," he'd told Reagan).

The fourth lead was played by Roger Smith, a handsome, debonair leading man from California. His greatest film exposure was yet to come, when he'd play Patrick Dennis, the nephew of *Auntie Mame* (1958), starring Rosalind Russell in her classic, lighthearted hit.

He would go on "to do what a million other men only dreamed about," and that was marrying sexpot Ann-Margret in 1967. He became not only her husband, but her manager.

Fred F. Sears, a Bostonian, directed Nancy's final film. He was about the same age as Reagan and had made the *Durango Kid* series of westerns, starring Charles Starrett. At the time he helmed Nancy, he was known as a quickie director, always bringing a picture in way before deadline. He was also called "the fast buck director," turning out juvenile crime films, action thrillers, rock musicals, and sci-fi "epics."

427

He would later become notorious for making one of the worst movies of all time, *The Giant Claw* (1957), "a clunky mishmash of hideous special effects. The giant claw turns out to be a spectacularly inept marionette that looks like a mutant turkey and sounds like a crow choking to death," in the words of one critic.

Most movies seem to have some kind of sexual relations going on between and among the cast and crew. But, from all reports, *Crash Landing* was rather pristine. There was an attempt at sex on the part of a drunken Merrill. He sent a messenger to Nancy's dressing room, requesting her to come to his trailer to go over some scenes with her.

He later said, "I'd heard from my buddies that she gave great head. That was her reputation in Hollywood. I knew she was married, but I hoped she still played around. I was married to Bette, but I let the bitch know she didn't own my dick. Bette used to go down on Howard Hughes, and I wanted to see how my wife, as a cocksucker, stacked up against Reagan's wife. I stood jaybird naked in my trailer waiting about twenty minutes for Nancy. She didn't show up."

When it came to sex talk, the gutsy New Englander, with his dour demeanor and dark brow, wasn't known for his subtlety.

Merrill, boorish and frequently drunk, was a man with a personal and onscreen past. Here he is with Bette Davis, in mink, during filming of *All About Eve*.

Nancy, whose screen image was to an increasing degree that of the kind of girl an American ex-GI would want to marry, simply didn't project an onscreen image with as much fun or drama.

***

During her involvement in those many B-pictures, Nancy had had only one role in mind, and that was to become the wife of a successful and presentable man. At the time, it was inconceivable that such a role would morph her one of the world's most famous women.

She once said, "I was following in some big, big footsteps—Martha Washington, Dolley Madison. For great humanitarian achievement, there was no lady who ever came close to Eleanor Roosevelt. For style, Jackie Kennedy won all honors. But in movie terms, my role of First Lady would be like remaking *Gone With the Wind* and casting me in the Vivien Leigh role of Scarlett O'Hara."

Chapter Eleven

Jane Wins an Oscar—At Last, Big-time Stardom for the Hey-Hey Girl

"Jane Deserves a Fling...and I Intend to Let Her Have It." —Ronald Reagan

"I'm In Love with Lew Ayres—and He Wants to Marry Me."

The Weekend Wasn't Entirely Lost.	Can a Girl Really Have It All?
Her road to stardom began with scenes like this from *Lost Weekend*, where glam Jane, accessorized with (now endangered) Somalian leopardskin, emotes with an alcohol-blocked novelist, as played by Ray Milland.	With *Johnny Belinda* came stardom and a wrenching emotional resonance with a former army chaplain bruised from the horrors of active duty on the blood-soaked Pacific front. Here, plain Jane as the reclusive deaf-mute, Belinda, with one of her true loves, Lew Ayres.

Throughout the war years, Joan Blondell and Paulette Goddard had remained Jane's steadfast *confidantes*. Alexis Smith was a newer friend, and also devoted to Jane, just as her new husband, Craig Stevens, seemed to hang on Reagan's every utterance.

One morning, Jane, in tears, called Goddard. "Ronnie and I had a big fight last night, and he stormed out of the house. The fan magazines still call us 'The Constant Honeymooners,' but nothing could be farther from the truth. We're at odds over something all the time."

Their latest conflict involved Reagan's desire to have another child. A very precocious four-year-old Maureen was virtually demanding a little brother as a playmate.

"Unless Billy Wilder has misled me, *The Lost Weekend* will be my breakthrough role," Jane said. "As you know, I've waited fifteen years for something like this. I don't want to fuck it up now, get pregnant, and let my career fade away."

"Tell that fucker of yours that if he wants a baby, adopt one," Goddard advised.

Like many couples trying to pick up their threads of marital bliss in the aftermath of the many changes brought on by WW2, Reagan and his then-wife present an illusion of compatibility at the California State Military Guard Ball of 1945.

"I might do just that," Jane said. "Maybe tonight, if he ever stops talking about politics and the menace of communism, and reverts to his demand that we have a child, I'll bring up the adoption idea. As for dirty diapers, the nanny can change them."

"You're in luck working with Ray as your leading man," Goddard said. "I seduced him on the set of *Reap the Wild Wind* (1942). He was ten times better than our co-star, Johnny boy *[a reference to John Wayne]*. Ray and I have just filmed *Kitty* (1945). It's a sort of Eliza Doolittle costume drama set in the 1780s. I'm this guttersnipe walking the sidewalks of London. Ray discovers me, coaches me, and turns me into a duchess."

"Sounds like fun," Jane said.

"On the set, we resumed our affair, and he's hotter and better looking than ever," Goddard said. "He's the best kisser in Hollywood. Ever notice those luscious lips of his? His Welsh dick is in good working order, and he never pulls out until a woman is completely satisfied."

"What about his wife?" Jane asked. She was referring to the former Muriel Weber, whom Milland had wed

"Every girl deserves the chance to spend one night of her life with Gregory Peck."
— *Jane Wyman*

Expensive Accessories for an A-list Celebrity: Satin and very good mink...What else would a movie star wear?

Jane arrives at the premiere of *Johnny Belinda*, the film that would eventually win her an Oscar.

back in 1932.

"Oh, her!" Goddard said, contemptuously. "She's that long-suffering dishrag who knows Milland seduces his leading ladies like your Ronnie used to. But Ray told me he long ago became bored pumping the same old piece night after night."

"How you talk, gal," Jane said. "I wish Ronnie wasn't such a gentleman, and could get lowdown and dirty once in a while. Put some steam into our sex life. Are you through with Ray for the moment? Can I move in?"

"Full speed ahead," Goddard said. "That fucking husband of mine [Burgess Meredith] is so horny, he demands it once or twice a day. I've got plenty of action on the side, even with Clark Gable, now that he's no longer in the service. I think you told me you've had him, too. He's nothing to write home to mother about. But I'll soon be making another 18th-century costume drama, this time with that divine Gary Cooper. [Her reference was to The Unconquered (1947).] Coop and I shacked up together when we made Northwest Mounted Police (1940). Yes, he indeed deserves his nickname, 'The Montana Mule.'"

Ray Milland was filled with emotional intensity when he filmed this scene with Jane Wyman in *The Lost Weekend*.

"It wasn't the script," he later said. "It was my anger at that bitch, Hedda Hopper. When I refused to go on her *Hedda Hopper Show*, she called me 'a limey son-of-a-bitch, the worst kind of ingrate.' She also threatened to spread the word about what she called 'My true sexual proclivities.'"

"I'm still young and life has got to offer more than Ronnie and babies," Jane said. I've still got Dennis [Morgan] and thank God for that. I call him always reliable and dependable. My nickname for him is EverReady."

"Say no more, doll," Goddard said.

"I still long for John Payne," Jane said.

"Honey, a sexual thrill like him comes to a girl only once in a lifetime, if that. But get over it. Ever onward. Maybe one day you'll make a movie with David Niven. I've had him. Ever had a dick that's six inches thick? Try it. You'll like it."

"Before I ring off," Jane said, "I've been dying to ask you a question. Why in hell did you ever marry a guy like Burgess Meredith?"

"Darling, I've always wanted to ask you a big question," Goddard said. "What in fuck were you thinking when you married Ronald Reagan?"

***

Jane received a phone call from Billy Wilder. "The Breen office is fighting every aspect of *The Lost Weekend* project. Fucking bluenoses. But Warner, the son of a bitch, said we'll make the film anyway. Report Monday morning to wardrobe."

That Monday, Jane stopped at Warners to retrieve some possessions from her dressing room before driving over to Paramount.

By coincidence, she encountered Jack Warner, who still called her "Little Janie." He had given the OK to lend her to Paramount. "So, you're off to make that drunk movie. Don't get your hopes up, gal. I'm an old showman. I always believed that drunks on film should be for comic relief. Depicting an alcoholic as a serious character will mean a big bomb at the box office. But it will be Paramount's loss, not mine. By the way, give my luck to Ronnie. When he gets back, come over and dine with us like you guys used to do."

When Jane reported to Paramount to co-star in *The Lost Weekend* (1945) with Ray Milland, its director, the Austria-born and deeply respected Billy Wilder, came out to greet her. That represented "star treatment" that he usually bequeathed to the more established actresses he'd directed, such as Barbara Stanwyck during her collaboration with him on *Double Idemnity* (1944).

She'd heard a lot about Wilder and was anxious to be directed by him. She knew that he was Jewish and had fled the Nazis in 1933, emigrating to Hollywood, where he'd had a successful career. He'd co-authored the script for the screwball comedy, *Ninotchka* (1939) with Great Garbo, as directed by Ernst Lubitsch. It had been widely advertised as GARBO LAUGHS.

Over coffee in the Paramount commissary with Wilder and his co-writer (Charles Brackett), while discussing their *Lost Weekend,* Jane learned from Wilder that "You were not our first choice. We offered

To effectively portray these scenes of progressive drunkenness, Milland said, "I knew that when the camera came close, nothing could be hidden or faked."

He praised Wilder for his help, citing his "prying, probing, intuitive touch of genius," and Brackett for his "kindly calm and sociological insight."

the part to Stanwyck, but she turned it down, thinking it was Milland's movie. Then we decided to ask another friend of yours, Paulette Goddard, but we decided she was too sexy."

"I didn't know any of this," a distressed Jane said. "Neither of them said anything to me about it."

"Actually, Milland was not our first choice either," Brackett said. "To play the stressed-out and alcoholic writer, Don Birnam, we went first to José Ferrer. But he was just too ugly, and we became convinced that to win the sympathy of movie audiences, we had to go for someone handsome. Then, at first, Milland didn't want to appear in a movie of such human degradation."

Wilder and Brackett informed Jane that the location scenes on the streets of post-war New York had already been filmed. "Even scenes of an unshaven Milland rattling the doors of a pawn shop to get a loan," Brackett said. "We even captured the grit and grime of Bellevue Hospital." She was told this with the understanding that her scenes in the movie would be filmed in a studio.

Brackett assured her that she would get co-star billing, her name appearing in the same size letters as Milland's.

"It took Billy and me two months to write the screenplay," Brackett said. "We wrote it with our blood. Enormous changes had to be made from the novel."

He was referring to Charles R. Jackson's bestseller with the same title. In distinct contrast to what had been portrayed in the novel, Don Birnam's repressed homosexuality was trivialized into a case of writer's block. To provide more of a love interest than what had appeared within the novel, Jane's character of Helen St. James was virtually invented for the film.

During their second cup of coffee, Jane learned that MGM, Fox, and Columbia had each rejected the script, defining it as "too downbeat, too grim."

She quickly summed up both Brackett and Wilder as being widely different personalities. She later said, "Charles was the classy façade, Billy the guts."

[In Hollywood, the frequent and usually inspired collaborators, Wilder and Brackett, were known as "the Gold Dust Twins," "the Katzenjammer Kids," or "Hansel and Gretel."]

"It's good working with Billy, although we fight a lot," Brackett said. "We're from completely different backgrounds. My roots go back to 1629 and the Massachusetts Bay Colony. Billy was conceived one night when his prostitute mother was raped behind a sleazy beerhall in some back alley. I appeal to the better side of human nature. He prefers the dark side of man."

Finally, perhaps with a sense that its *noir* theme of repressed anguish and alcoholism was very *avant garde* for a nation recovering, often with the assistance of alcohol, from the ravages of war, Wilder handed her the latest revisions to the script. Then he suggested that she spend the rest of the morning reading them, since she wouldn't be called onto the set until after lunch.

Before noon, a leopardskin coat was delivered to her dressing room, with instructions to wear it when called for, as it configured into the plot. *[It was the prop that brought Helen and Don together at the beginning of the movie. Toward the end, Don pawns it in a pawn shop in exchange for a gun, with which he plans to commit suicide.]*

Talking him out of his death wish would be the focal point of Jane's big scene. Her character would succeed in that awesome task. She would convince him to give up liquor and return to writing his novel, *The Bottle.* At the end of the film, Milland drops a lit cigarette into a glass of whiskey, as a means of making it undrinkable and as proof that he is cured.

Wilder had arranged for her to have lunch in the commissary with Milland, presumably to discuss the nuances of their respective roles. In person, the Welshman was far handsomer and more charming than he was on the screen in any of his light comedies. "Paulette has told me wonderful things about you," Jane gushed.

"Why take her word for it?" Milland answered. Then he raised an eyebrow. "Why not investigate for yourself?"

Almost from the beginning, he established the tone of their relationship by openly flirting with her. She no doubt had heard the many rumors associated with his prowess at seducing his leading ladies.

He confessed to her, "My character is unsettling—so unlike me—and personally, I find the subject of alcoholism distasteful. I'm afraid that as a drunk, I'll dip into caricature and be laughed off the screen."

"Fortunately, my character stays sober throughout the run of the film. I think I can pull it off unless Billy starts screaming and cursing me," she said.

"Filming on the streets of New York was a nightmare," he said. "I spent a night in the ward at Bellevue where patients were delirious during their withdrawal from alcohol. Many of them were having these hideous hallucinations like the one I have to have in this damn movie. I fled at three o'clock that morning. I couldn't stay there all night. At times like now, I feel I was not psychologically cut out to be an actor," he confessed.

"Neither was I," she said. "But I had no choices—either be a showgirl or a prostitute."

"But my dear, they're the same profession," he said.

He amused her with stories of his life, beginning when he was in the Household Cavalry of the British Army and became an expert marksman, horse rider, and airplane pilot. "I'd like to go riding with you one Sunday afternoon."

"Maybe Ronnie could join us," she said. "He's an expert rider."

"How nice, but that's not exactly what I had in mind," he said. "I prefer to go riding with just you."

"Oh, I see," she said.

"I have nothing but fond memories of the horse stables," he said. "When I was fifteen, I lost my virginity one evening in an empty stable stall. I surrendered it to a very determined blonde two years older than me."

Before luncheon was over, he reached over, took her hand, and kissed it. "I have always believed that an actor and an actress, playing lovers on the screen, should rehearse that love in private. What do you think?"

"I completely agree," she said. "I've always become intimate with and demonstrated my affection for my leading men. That's except for Joe E. Brown and Phil Silvers."

Milland looked mildly surprised until he realized that she might be joking. But in the days ahead, he came to know that she had been serious. In a call to Goddard, after about four days of working with Milland, she confessed, "We did the dirty deed. You were right about him. What a contrast to Ronnie, who comes to bed smelling like a bar of soap. Ray gives off a real he-man scent. A true male aroma, and that's a turn-on."

As Milland admitted in his memoirs, *Wide-Eyed in Babylon,* "There had been a few previous peccadilloes, nothing serious, just the normal male revolt against his convenient chains. It was very easy to succumb to in those days."

He also said that whenever his homelife was deteriorating, he would pack a suitcase and check into the Sunset Towers. "My wife thought my depression was a dramatically staged excuse to shack up with some blonde Hollywood dame, and not without reason." While making *The Lost Weekend,* that statement perhaps reflected his involvement with Jane.

During the filming of *The Lost Weekend,* Jane had a sad experience during her brief reunion with Craig Reynolds. He had been "my dream man, my Adonis" when they had appeared together in movies in the 1930s. Both of them were dreaming of stardom, and at the time, there was talk of marriage.

She learned that he was appearing in an uncredited role in her film. "I'm afraid that the stardom I dreamed about isn't going to happen for me," he told her. He'd joined the Army during the war and had won a

At an afterparty celebrating the Oscar victories of *The Lost Weekend,* Jane embraces director Billy Wilder. Ronald Reagan looks on, indulgently, from the left, while Ray Milland, on right, appears inebriated.

434

Purple Heart. "But now that I'm back in Hollywood, the phone isn't ringing."

She seemed rather embarrassed to have run into Reynolds in such reduced circumstances. His star had flickered out, and hers was just beginning to shine brightly. She kissed him on the cheek and moved on after wishing him good luck. She was deeply saddened to learn of his death in 1949 in a motorcycle accident.

Right before Christmas in 1944, Jane received a call from Wilder, who had obviously been drinking. "The shitheads over at Paramount have decided not to release *The Lost Weekend.* 'It's too god-damned depressing,' the assholes said. But I know the real reason. The liquor industry is willing to part with $5 million for the negative of this film. They want to destroy it, claiming that showing it will cut into their profits."

But in the weeks ahead, the president of Paramount, Barney Balaban, overruled his executives. "I don't make pictures to flush them down the toilet," he said. "Open the god damn film across the country, and to hell with the liquor industry. Bogie's baby *[Lauren Bacall]* is called 'The Look.' After *The Lost Weekend,* Milland will be known as 'The Kidney.'"

The Lost Weekend was eventually nominated for seven Academy Awards, winning four of them: Best Picture, Best Director (Wilder), Best Actor (Milland), and Best Writing of an Adapted Screenplay (won jointly by Brackett and Wilder).

After his win, Milland reached the pinnacle of his career, becoming the highest paid star at Paramount.

When shooting was finished on *The Lost Weekend,* Milland told Jane goodbye. He headed north for a two-week vacation with his wife, Muriel. As a farewell to Jane, he told her, "Maybe we'll meet again."

***

As World War II was coming to an end, Reagan faced an uncertain future in films. In contrast, based on the acclaim heaped on her performance in *The Lost Weekend,* Jane's career had skyrocketed.

To her friends, Joan Blondell, June Allyson, and Paulette Goddard, Jane complained constantly. She had always wanted a father figure to compensate for the dad she never had. For a time in the early 1940s, Reagan was that to her, plus also a lover. "Now I'm the breadwinner," she proclaimed. "Do you gals know what an Army captain's pay is?"

The general public remained under the impression that Reagan and Jane were the happiest married couple in Hollywood, although "Ray and Muriel" were also cited as an equivalent example of marital bliss. Ironically, all of this publicity was happening at the time Jane and Milland were conducting an illicit affair.

But occasionally, a reporter was more realistic, as was a wartime writer for *Modern Screen.* "If things at the studio upset Jane Wyman, she gripes about them at home. And she is upset a lot. She flies off the handle. When Ronald Reagan is around, he tries to calm her down. But she doesn't want to be calm, she wants to storm. 'You don't know what things are like,' she tells her husband. 'You've been away too long.' When she cools off, she realizes that Reagan has his own problems and that it can't be fun to come home on a weekend pass and listen to her beef."

Months later, *Modern Screen* filed another report, suggesting that there was trouble in paradise and hinting that Jane may have a secret lover. Rumors were rampant at the time in Hollywood, many believing that Jane and Van Johnson were having an affair, as had been hinted before in the past. At the time, the world did not know that the handsome, freckle-faced, blonde-haired actor was a homosexual. And only the most deeply entrenched insiders knew that Jane's secret lover was actually Dennis Morgan.

Reagan was infuriated when he read *Modern Screen.* He threatened to hunt down the reporter who had written the article, and "throttle" him if he didn't retract the statements printed about Jane. As it happened, the accusations were never retracted, and Reagan did not attack the reporter.

Jane did not want another baby, but Reagan and Baby Maureen did. On a shopping trip with her mother at Saks Fifth Avenue, Maureen placed an order for a baby brother with the store clerk.

Within a few days, the issue was finally resolved: Jane and Reagan would adopt a baby boy.

In his arguments for adoption, Reagan issued a statement to the press, citing that because of the disruption of World War II, thousands of unwanted children were homeless and desperately in need of loving parents.

On March 21, 1945, shortly after he was born, Michael Edward Reagan was brought to the Reagans' home. At last, Maureen had

As the Reagan/Wyman marriage crumbled, a beaming Reagan, with a smiling Jane, posed for this "happy home" shot with blonde-haired Maureen and a new member of the family, an adopted son they named Michael Edward Reagan.

a baby brother. Reagan welcomed the newcomer to the household, calling him "our real child."

Jane later said, "I never thought of Michael as an adopted child, and as he grew up, I never thought of myself as an adoptive mother, but as his own mother. The way I see it, we're blood. I have no more to say, except that he is my baby boy."

A few fan magazines ran pictures of Reagan, Jane, and Michael, but many devoted photos to just Reagan and the baby.

Despite the presence of two small, demanding children within their home, Reagan and Jane, after the war, became fixtures on the Hollywood party circuit. As columnist Hedda Hopper wrote, "At parties, Ronnie talks politics while Jane perches atop the piano and makes like Helen Morgan."

Her role as a fixture, with her husband, on the party circuit lasted no more than a few months before Jane grew bored. She wanted her old life back, but with newer escorts. By this time, Reagan had given up partying and was devoting his nights instead to the politics associated with the Screen Actors Guild. In 1947, he was elected as the organization's President.

June Allyson, married to Dick Powell at the time, was a close observer of the Reagan marriage. She hid her own attraction to him from Jane, but she told other friends, "One day, I'll get my man, Ronnie. Probably when he leaves Janie. I want him. And Lola gets what Lola wants."

An older, more mature man, Powell had begun overlooking his errant wife's many indiscretions, including her love affair with Alan Ladd and, later, her off-the-record weekends in Las Vegas with Dean Martin.

Allyson predicted that the Wyman/Reagan marriage would end in the divorce courts. "Her career is on the rise. His is going to hell."

***

Jane was delighted to learn from the British director, Peter Godfrey, that she'd be starring once again in the 1946 release of *One More Tomorrow*. Her passion for Dennis Morgan had continued unabated, although here were long periods of separation. As she and Reagan had grown farther and farther apart, she welcomed the tenderness and love that Morgan provided, though he was still married and kept telling her he did not plan to divorce his wife.

Godfrey would soon be directing Reagan in two of his movies, *That Hagen Girl* (1947) and *The Girl from Jones Beach* (1949).

Jane was pleased to hear that she'd also be co-starring with two of her girlfriends, Alexis Smith and Ann Sheridan. Morgan would also be working once again with "my best pal," Jack Carson. Ironically, Carson's character in the movie was named "Regan."

One More Tomorrow was a reincarnation of Philip Barry's socially conscious play, *The Animal Kingdom,* which had been filmed in 1932 with three A-list stars, Ann Harding, Leslie Howard, and Myrna Loy.

In this latest version, Sheridan was cast in the star role as Christie Sage, a photographer for *The Bantam,* a publication going bankrupt. Once again, Jane played Sheridan's 'sidekick.

Morgan played Tom Collier, a rich playboy pursuing Sheridan. When she turns him down, he is ensnared by Cecilia Henry (Smith), a scheming gold-digger who eventually marries him. Still pining for Christie (Sheridan), it's clear that he doesn't really love Cecilia.

On the set, reunited with Morgan, Jane discov-

After completing *One More Tomorrow,* Jane said, "It's a picture I'm ashamed of—and I don't shame easily."

Jack Warner agreed. He delayed its release until it could benefit from all the favorable publicity Jane received for *The Lost Weekend.*

Although it wasn't her fault, Dennis Morgan, her co-star, became angered when marquees across the country took down his name and displayed hers instead. "Oh, my god," she told Joan Blondell. "I'm experiencing with Dennis what I'm going through with Ronnie. Dennis was the hottest male star on the lot, and now he's falling. His star is dimming. Ronnie's star is also dimming. I'm shining brighter than ever, and I think they resent me."

"Of course they do, darling," Blondell said. "How like a man. They're all no good!"

Hollywood insiders always wondered if Jane Wyman (*left*) ever found out about Ann Sheridan's long-enduring affair with her husband.

It was a romantic liaison that began long before Reagan's marriage to Wyman.

ered a more mature actor, one more self-assured. He had become the leading man at Warner Brothers, a position Reagan coveted but never achieved. Morgan's peak years were from 1943 to 1949. Later, he fell out of favor with 1950s audiences.

During the shoot of *One More Tomorrow,* she got to know him better than ever, learning more about his background. Unlike her, he'd had a normal childhood as the son of a baker. His mother had studied music before her marriage and had transmitted her love of singing to her son. They often sang duets together. As a teenager, he took singing lessons, and he often sang at solo recitals and church socials. In high school, he'd played the trombone in the school band.

At Carroll College in Waukesha, Wisconsin, he'd fallen in love with Lillian Vedder, later marrying her, but not abandoning his pursuit of some of his leading ladies.

When *One More Tomorrow* was released, the critics, if they noticed Jane at all, claimed she was "sadly wasted in another sidekick role." One reviewer wrote, "The original version of *The Animal Kingdom* with Leslie Howard was oversexed and heavy handed, while the one with Dennis Morgan is simply flat. Although the cast is likable, they couldn't save a dull script."

Ginger Rogers, who would appear in movies starring both Reagan and Morgan, later commented on these two being afflicted with *"Leadinglady-it is."*

"In most cases, Ronnie and Dennis moved on once the picture was over," Rogers said. "From the grapevine, I heard that the one exception to their fickle wars is their continuing fascination with Jane Wyman. Her particular appeal has always eluded me. But she must send out some siren call, because both Dennis and Ronnie keep coming back to her charms."

"As for Jane herself, I was fairly neutral about the dame," Rogers said. "That is, until she decided to dig her greedy claws into Lew Ayres. He was my ex, but I still resented the bitch for moving in on him."

***

During the months after the war, Alexis Smith and her husband, Craig Stevens, were spending a lot of their free time with Jane and Reagan, now that he was no longer in the Army.

Alexis' career at Warners seemed on a quick rise to stardom. "I'm no longer window dressing," the actress from British Columbia told the Reagans. She had made *Gentleman Jim* (1942) with Errol Flynn; *The Constant Nymph* (1943), with Joan Fontaine and Charles Boyer; and she'd played an unsympathetic part in Humphrey Bogart misfire, *Conflict* (1945). She was set to make yet another film with Bogart, *The Two Mrs. Carrolls* (1947). She had previously appeared with Jane in *The Doughgirls* (1944) and now, in the buoyant aftermath of the Allied victories in Europe and the Pacific, she was on the screen with Jane once again in *One More Tomorrow* (1946).

One night during one of their communal

A vanilla, and unconvincing, portrayal of a "marriage of convenience" inspired by the life of Cole Porter. Despite the film's shortcomings, the casting department at least got something right: Like Porter himself, both of the film's stars, Cary Grant and Alexis Smith, were bisexuals.

dinners, Alexis announced, "I'm going to play Cole Porter's wife, Linda, in my latest film, *Night and Day* (1946)," Alexis told the Reagans. "My leading man is Cary Grant. Of course, he's not as handsome as Craig is."

As a means of maintaining her friendship with Alexis, Jane tried to conceal her jealousy.

The Lost Weekend had not been released yet, and Jane's career appeared to be going nowhere. She had left word with Jack Warner. "Please notify me of any roles that Joan Crawford or Bette Davis turn down. I'm your gal."

So far, he had not heeded her desperate call.

Two days after the dinner with Alexis and Stevens, a call came in for Jane from Michael Curtiz, the director of *Night and Day. [He had only recently directed Joan Crawford in Mildred Pierce, a role Jane had coveted.]* To Jane, Curtiz said, "Girlie, I promise you role. I deliver role to you. Cole Porter story. Well, not the faggot's real story. Movie is *Night and Day.* Part for you."

"But I was told you'd already cast Alexis Smith as Porter's wife," she said.

"Not the female lead, dummy," Curtiz said. "That of song-and-dance cutie. You get to work with Grant. A big shit. Best of all, you get me. Greatest director west of Budapest."

Was the real Cole Porter as good-looking as Cary Grant? Actors up and down Broadway responded with a resounding NO!

In *Night and Day,* Jane played a good hearted turn-of the Gilded Age cutie, but resented having such a small role while Alexis Smith got the star part.

"Send over the script," she said. Within two hours, a studio messenger from Warners arrived on her doorstep with the script for *Night and Day.* She studied it for a few hours, and was greatly disappointed with her role of showgirl Gracie Harris. At the time, she appeared only briefly at the beginning of the film, although her role was later expanded.

She was pleased that her part as a showgirl gave her a chance to show off her talent as a singer and dancer. Her big number in *Night and Day* was "Let's Do It," with all its risqué suggestions. The role called for her impersonation of a gold-digging hooker, pursuing millionaires, each of whom she called "Peaches," so she wouldn't have to remember their names.

The ultimate curmudgeon: Monty Woolley.

Under contract, and needing money for her recently expanded family, she accepted the role and showed up the next day at the studio. By then, the complete cast had been assembled, including Eve Arden, her friend from *The Doughgirls,* who relayed scandalous stories about having co-starred with Crawford in *Mildred Pierce.*

Also cast was a friend of both Cary Grant and Cole Porter, character actor, Monty Woolley, known as "The Beard" for obvious reasons.

"I had given up being blonde," Jane recalled. "But the role called for a blonde. I headed to my hairdresser and a bottle of bleach. I was back to being a blonde cutie like I was in the 30s. Although I was a ripe old thirty-two years old, I was once again a cho-

439

rus girl."

Even though her appearance in *Night and Day* was brief, Jane's bubbly personality came out. Grant defined her performance as "vivid," as opposed to the more demure Alexis, cast in the role of Porter's long-neglected wife, as indeed the real Linda had been during the course of marriage to her gay husband.

Jane was shocked to learn that Warner had paid Porter $300,000 for what turned out not as an accurate overview of his life story, but a fictionalized, sanitized overview. Porter had specifically requested that Grant play himself onscreen, even though physically, the two men did not resemble one another at all.

[Ironically, two other famous figures would request Grant to play themselves on the screen—notably John F. Kennedy in PT 109, and gangster Lucky Luciano in the film version of his crime-soaked life. Grant said, "Even I would like to play me on the screen."

Porter also demanded that his longtime friend, character actor Monty Woolley, be cast as himself in the film. The white-bearded actor had achieved his own measure of screen stardom when he had appeared with Bette Davis and Ann Sheridan in *The Man Who Came to Dinner* (1941).

On the set, Jane met Woolley, who greeted her with a kiss on the cheek. "I hope you're here to welcome me to Hollywood, he said. "It's rather like living on the moon, wouldn't you say?"

Publicly, Jane expressed admiration for Grant's talent. Privately, she asserted that she "loathed" him. To Reagan and her girlfriends, she called him "a queenie prima donna." Her troubles with him began on June 14, 1945, during the early filming of *Night and Day* on a back lot at Warners, where a simulation of the New Haven railway station had been crafted.

"In stifling heat, I was dressed in this period costume fit for a winter in Alaska," Jane recalled. "Grant demanded that our scene be reshot, reshot, reshot, and then reshot again. He didn't like his dialogue, although he'd previously approved it. He objected to our costumes, claiming they were not authentic to the period. He objected to what he called 'my fucking rotten characterization in this stinker.' Since he was facing Technicolor cameras for the first time, he objected to his makeup, claiming that it was giving him skin rash. By quitting time, all of us were in a piss poor mood—and hating Grant. He was one leading man who didn't capture my heart—and a homo to boot."

After the release of *The Lost Weekend* and its subsequent acclaim, Warner ordered Jane back into the studio. Her role in *Night and Day* had been expanded, and as such, her character was needed for additional sequences which would appear near the ending of the film.

She acquiesced, but regrettably for her, she had already been cast as Ma Barker in *The Yearling*. "Sometimes, on the same day, I had to be a chorus girl in the morning and then in the afternoon appear as a drab frontierswoman. I nearly had a nervous breakdown."

She confessed to Paulette Goddard and others, "I've ordered Ronnie out of my room at night. I can't be his sex slave and make two movies at once."

In the final weeks of shooting *Night and Day*, Curtiz finally lost his patience with Grant, with a screaming denunciation in front of cast and crew. The director called his star "a limey faggot," and then walked off the picture. Warner persuaded him to return the following day.

At long last, filming ended. On the final day of the shoot, Grant confronted Curtiz: "If I'm ever stupid enough to work with you again, you'll know I'm either broke or I've lost my mind." Then he stormed off the set.

When the film was released, Porter praised it. But privately, he said, "It was a plot of absurdities concocted by a string of Hollywood hacks. But I wouldn't want the truth depicted anyway."

Film historian Lawrence J. Quirk later wrote: "Of course, the real Cole Porter, bitchy, tormented, wildly homosexual, compulsive promiscuous, never got to the screen—to his own secret amusement."

Screenland accurately summed it up: "Movie audiences who elect to see this Technicolor extravaganza will have a delicious feast of Cole Porter songs, as well as notable personalities."

[A 2002 film, De-Lovely, *starring Kevin Kline and Ashley Judd, dealt more frankly with Porter's homosexuality.]*

***

In 1939, Marjorie Kinnan Rawlings had won the Pulitzer Prize for Fiction, based on her coming-of-age novel, *The Yearling,* the tender story of a young boy in the late 19th century wilds of north-central Florida. He adopts an orphaned fawn with disastrous consequences. It was also the story of a family's struggle against the elements of nature.

MGM acquired the novel's film rights, with Sidney Franklin set to produce it. His attempt, begun in 1941, failed. He had cast Spencer Tracy in the lead role, opposite Anne Revere, who was later blacklisted during the Joseph McCarthy witch hunt era. Cast as the young boy, Gene Eckman was thirteen years old and from Georgia.

Although MGM invested half a million dollars in location shooting near Ocala, Florida, the production eventually shut down. Tracy feuded with director Victor Fleming of *Gone With the Wind* fame. He complained, "The god damn insects devoured our flesh and then ate our bones."

Eckman was deemed wrong for the role.

The Yearling remained shelved throughout most of the war until Franklin revived it in 1945. This time, he demanded an all-new cast. Penny Baxter, the story's patriarch, had been originally conceived as a small-time farmer and game hunter, warm-hearted and loving. In contrast, the novel was very clear that the boy's

Said to be the toughest woman in Florida, hard-drinking, hard-scrabble Marjorie Kinnan Rawlings became a literary legend in the Southeast.

mother, Ora, is deeply embittered by the death of her three previous children, and profoundly resents the harsh frontier conditions in which they live.

The boy, Jody, raised in the bug-infested scrub country of north central Florida, is desperate for love, which he is not getting from his mother. He showers affection on the fawn, nicknamed "Flag." Penny had to kill the fawn's mother as part of a folk-medicine ploy that involved using her internal organs to draw the poison out of his bloodstream after he was bitten by a rattlesnake. Jody takes the fawn home with him, but as it ma-

441

tures, the deer become destructive, damaging the family's meager crops. Flag has to be put down, which catalyzes tragic consequences for Jody.

After he'd seen *The Lost Weekend,* Benny Thau thought Jane might be possible, as part of a remarkable change-of-pace role for her, as Ma Baxter.

One Friday afternoon, Jane was summoned to Thau's office, receiving instructions that she was to read *The Yearling* over the weekend. Thau wanted her to audition, the following Monday, for the role of Ma Baxter.

She bought two copies of the novel, one for herself, the other for Reagan to read. This time, he showed an interest in one of her roles. He thought it could mean a breakthrough for her, telling her, "You might even win an Oscar like Luise Rainer did for *The Good Earth,* another film about survival against powerful odds."

Jane mentioned that Thau was known for his infamous "casting couch."

Child star Claude Jarman, a Tennessee hillbilly boy, snuggles up to his movie father, Gregory Peck. Jarman had to beat out 12,000 other Southern boys for the coveted role.

"Go over there and say you'll do the part. But let me know if the bastard gets fresh with you. I'll storm over there and kick some ass."

That Monday, with trepidation, she arrived at 10AM at Thau's office. Although she desperately wanted the part, the idea of doing it terrified her. At this point in her life, she felt very insecure.

Introduced to Thau, she found him "a perfect gentleman speaking in a soft voice." He spent about half an hour discussing the role with her before summoning the producer, Sidney Franklin, and the film's director, Clarence Brown, into his office.

When Brown shook Jane's hand, he appeared shocked. "I thought you were a brunette."

She explained that she had to have her hair dyed blonde for her role as a showgirl in *Night and Day.*

"If you get the role in *Yearling,* you've got to dye it back," Brown told her.

"Not so fast here," Thau said. "If we cast Gregory Peck in the lead, he's already very dark. The boy we're considering, Claude Jarman, Jr., is very blonde. If Jane is a blonde, it would explain how Jarman came along."

Peck was summoned back to Thau's office the next day. He was currently making David O. Selznick's *Duel in the Sun,* a Technicolor West-

Jane, glamour queen of the 30s and early 40s, went plain, "care-worn, and embittered" on this testament to the survival instincts and grit of the impoverished American Frontier.

In this case, the "Frontier" was the insect-and-alligator-infested scrublands and swamps of north-central Florida.

ern. He had complained, "It's difficult making love to Selznick's woman [a reference to Jennifer Jones] while your boss is looking on."

In Thau's office, Peck was told that MGM wanted him for the role of Penny Baxter opposite Jane Wyman.

"Surely, you don't mean Wyman!" Peck asked in astonishment. "Wouldn't she be better in light comedy?" He had not seen *The Lost Weekend.*

"The gal has untapped possibilities," Thau assured him.

At first, Thau had considered the young British actor, Roddy McDowall, to play the boy, Jody. But Thau eventually rejected him as "too prissy," deciding to launch a nationwide talent search. That led to the discovery of Claude Jarman, Jr., who at the time was a fifth grader in Nashville. He was tested and signed for the role.

Brown might have seemed an odd choice to direct *The Yearling.* After all, he was famous for having helmed Greta Garbo in seven movies and Joan Crawford in six. Although born in Massachusetts, he had grown up in Tennessee and was familiar with rural America. That had been amply demonstrated in such films as *Of Human Hearts (1938),* a saga of pioneer life.

Once again, an MGM crew journeyed to Ocala, where filming on *The Yearling* began on March 15, 1945. There, they faced the same problems as before: Rainstorms, oppressive heat, humidity that drenched clothing and caused makeup to run, and endless attacks by swarms of insects.

Casting the fawn proved especially difficult. The deer grows during the course of the film, changing his body shape. Before shooting ended in January of 1946, a total of 72 different deer had been used, and since none of them could act on cue, endless retakes were necessary. Peck recalled that for one scene, Brown had to shoot the scene in 72 takes, which was the same number of deer used in the depiction of Flag.

As Ora, Jane had never looked so drab on film. Although still in her early 30s, she appeared to be at least forty, maybe more. But she didn't object. "I wanted to be taken seriously as an actress. I knew that would only happen if I showed Hollywood I could take on a major dramatic role."

One day, Jane received an unexpected visitor to the set, Marjorie Kinnan Rawlings herself. After asking Jane if she had any rotgut liquor, she settled onto Jane's sofa, where she endlessly chain-smoked unfiltered Lucky Strikes. Very outspoken, she candidly said, "Back home, I pound my typewriter day and night while in my bathroom, I make bathtub gin and float red roses in my toilet. The problem is that every time I take a crap, I have to replenish them."

"I've got to tell you!" Rawlings continued. "You and Peck don't look like the characters in my novel. Penny is a runty little frontiersman, a farmer and game hunter, and Ma Baxter is as big as a barn. I figured the only way you got the part was because Brown is fucking you."

"I hope Greg and I will surprise you," a flustered Jane stammered, diplomatically.

A rather drunk Rawlings departed three hours later, but only after demanding a kiss on the lips from Peck. He and Jane were then introduced to Jarman, their "son."

"The Kid [a reference to Jarman] worked increasingly well with both Greg and me," Jane said. "He even got a Juvenile Oscar for his performance. But I feared that after *The Yearling,* there would be no more great

A ballsy, *über*-extroverted hurricane of male flash: Forrest Tucker. Jane said "no."

roles for him."

The Yearling's third male lead was played by the rugged Forrest Tucker, cast in the film as a member of the redneck Forrester family, distant neighbors of the Baxters. In the early 40s, Jane had seen Tucker in two movies, *The Westerner* (1940) with Gary Cooper, and *Keeper of the Flame* (1942) with Spencer Tracy and Katharine Hepburn.

"He seemed perfect for the role of backwoods Lem," Jane said. "He stood 6'4", weighing 200 pounds. He was famous for his endowment, said to be one of the largest in Hollywood. Although married to the former Sandra Jolley, he had plenty of girlfriends coming and going. Word about his big attraction traveled fast in Hollywood. With Tucker, the line of beauties formed on the left and right."

Tucker kept inviting Jane to go out drinking with him, but she refused, claiming, "I fear I'll lose my virginity."

Their romance (and their affair) continued beyond the filming of *The Yearling*.

Here, Peck and Plain Jane appear in deliberately soiled—and historically accurate—scrub-farmer garb.

"How could that be?" he asked. "Aren't you married to that Reagan fellow?"

"I am," she said, "but he hasn't gotten around to deflowering me yet."

"You're such a bullshitter, Janie, but I like you, a gal with spirit."

The supporting players didn't mean much to Jane during the shoot. Her interest involved bonding with Peck. "He looked absolutely gorgeous in spite of his frontier rags. After meeting this tall, sturdy, and urbane young actor, she told her girlfriends, "He is the handsomest man in Hollywood—the new Gary Cooper."

In 1942, Peck had married Greta Kukkonen, a Finnish hairdresser. They would have three sons. As a means of learning more, Jane put through a call to Paulette Goddard, the world's expert on the bedtime habits of stars, both male and female, who played around.

"He cheats on his wife only on that rare occasion," Goddard told her. "Of course, that nympho, Ingrid Bergman, got him on the set of *Spellbound*. Hitch *[Alfred Hitchcock]* told me that the Swede would fuck a doorknob if nothing else were available."

Jane told Goddard "If Bergman can seduce Greg, so can I."

As always, Goddard urged her on. "Go, Girl, Go."

At first, Peck was too busy to spend any time with Jane. Like her, during her early involvement in filming *The Yearling*, he'd have to race between the sets of two separate pictures, *Duel in the Sun* and *The Yearling*. He later defined that period of his career as "a kind of cinematic schizophrenia. The film sets were a mile apart. I'd get out of my Florida cracker overalls and put on my sexy cowboy stud clothes and practice my Texas drawl on the way to make love to Jennifer Jones. What a contrast in characters! Jane faced the same dilemma in *Night and Day,* doing her final scenes as a showgirl before getting all drab for Ma Baxter in *The Yearling*."

On a professional level, Jane had nothing but praise for Peck. "He was my alltime favorite leading man, very easy to work with, a real gentleman, very serious about his acting, always wanting to get his every scene right."

Near the end of the shoot, the cast and crew traveled to Lake Arrowhead, east of San Bernardino and about 100 miles from Los Angeles. Jane rented a cabin on one side of the lake, the Pecks rented one on the other.

Whenever he was not involved with the Screen Actors Guild, Reagan came to stay with Jane, Maureen, and Baby Michael. The Pecks and the Reagans often dined together, with Reagan at the barbecue, grilling steaks in the backyard.

When their respective spouses, Greta and Reagan, returned to Los Angeles, both Jane and Peck decided to stay on in their respective rented cabins for solitude and brief vacations. It was during this period that Peck got into his speedboat at night and crossed Lake Arrowhead for dinner at Jane's. "I loved her cooking. I put on twenty pounds, ending up weighing 184 pounds on a 6'3" frame."

On quiet evenings, he told her about his early struggles trying to break into acting. "I was often homeless in New York, sleeping in Central Park on a bench. I got a lot of offers from guys wanting me for a sleepover, sometimes just in exchange for a good meal. I turned them down except once or twice when I'd do anything for a big juicy steak."

He told her he'd been exempt from military service because of a back injury he suffered while receiving dance instruction from Martha Graham.

"Fox didn't think it was macho to promote the idea that I'd been in a dance class, so Publicity claimed that I injured myself while rowing when I was at my university," he said.

"The Welsh playwright, Emlyn Williams, got me my big break as the lead in his play, *The Morning Star,* in 1942. He believed in the casting couch," Peck remembered.

It was in the Reagans' cabin that Jane and Peck became intimately involved. "Those moonlit nights on the lake under a full moon were very romantic," director Brown said. "I knew what was going on behind the backs of Greta and Reagan. The whole crew knew."

Jane told her girlfriends, Goddard and Blondell, "I followed in Ingrid Bergman's footsteps. Greg is hypnotic. A gal can fall for him. That deep, well-modulated voice of his is pure seduction. He told me that he'd been a male model before going to Hollywood. He posed for underwear ads, but, as he told her, "the underwear ads were rejected."

"Tell me why!" she asked.

"I'm too embarrassed," Peck said. "The advertiser instructed the ad agency to find another model. He didn't want me giving men a case of penis envy."

"Men exaggerate so," Goddard said.

"But in Greg's case," Jane said, "he told the truth. He's a great lover, a woman's dream. He's going to have a big career in Hollywood. He's getting fan mail from women and homos all over America. He has to give in to temptation once in a while. He's only human—and all man!"

In the only statement Peck made in an interview about Jane, he said, "She's a great woman. Very talented and a hell of a lot of fun to be with."

The Yearling was released in Los Angeles very late in 1946, in December, as a means of making it eligible for Oscar consideration in that year. Its official premiere was celebrated during January of 1947 at Manhattan's Radio City Music Hall, where it was a big hit.

Most reviewers and columnists lauded Jane's performance. *Photoplay* claimed that "*The Yearling's* chief acting honors belonged to Jane Wyman as Ma Baxter. Devoid of glamorizing makeup, she *is* a care-worn, embittered woman with one goal in life: Food and shelter, and maybe a well outside her door so she need not trek a mile for every precious drop."

Parents Magazine stated, "It is Jane Wyman as Ma Baxter who does the most creative acting, for she suggests a whole lifetime of denial in the mother's fear of losing Jody if she loves him too openly. Her intense pride in rising above poverty and being beholden to no one is true of pioneer dignity. And she makes understandable the bitterness of backwoods women."

Columnist Dorothy Kilgallen wrote: "Jane Wyman, demonstrating an amazing versatility, is the surprise of the picture. She plays the drab, nagging, miserable farm wife with such authority and definition as to make it almost impossible to believe that this weary creature and the glamorous little cookie of *Night and Day* came from the repertoire of the same actress."

Peck himself pronounced *The Yearling* as "a bit too saccharine for me, too many Walt Disney elements." Despite his reservations, he was nominated for Best Actor, although he lost to Fredric March for his performance in the box office hit, *The Best Years of Our Lives.* Jane was nominated for an Oscar as Best Actress of the Year, only to lose to her longtime rival, Olivia de Havilland, cast as the long-suffering mother in *To Each His Own.*

The Yearling was also nominated as Best Picture and Best Director (Brown) of 1946 and Harold F. Kress was nominated for Best Film Editing.

In addition to its many nominations, the film went on to win a pair of Oscars, one for Best Art Direction and Interior Decoration; another for Best Color Cinematography.

Based on the acclaim accorded to Jane after the release of two of her recent films, *The Lost Weekend* and *The Yearling,* she had self-confidence for the first time in her life. "I found I had a new self. I was no longer afraid, no longer shy. If people didn't understand the new me, the hell with them. Regrettably, I don't think Ronnie understood that I was going to the top rung on the Hollywood ladder, in spite of what happened to his career. From that moment on, my turned-up button nose became something that nature had placed in the center of my face. Period."

***

"What a comedown," Jane said, when she learned that she'd been cast in a Western named *Cheyenne* (1947), *[It was retitled* The Wyoming Kid *for TV.]* "A god damn Western," she railed.

Reagan tried to console her, reminding her that most of the big female stars at Warners had also appeared in Westerns. "Did you forget that you were in *Bad Men of Missouri* with Dennis Morgan?"

"I didn't forget," she said. "In fact, he's my co-star in *Cheyenne.*"

She tried to conceal her delight at being with Morgan again, since, during her filming of *The Yearling,*

Jane, Bruce Bennett, & Janis Paige in *Cheyenne.*

446

she'd almost lost touch with him.

On the first day of shooting on the set of *Cheyenne,* Morgan lunched with her, each of them trying to console the other for the failure of *One More Tomorrow.* Later, he visited her in her dressing room, perhaps proving that her allure for him was still as strong as ever.

She found him "as sweet as ever." She told Joan Blondell, "He reminds me of a naughty little boy who's caught sticking his hand in the cookie jar. Critics call his acting wooden, but I find he's versatile and not appreciated by Jack Warner."

Other than Michael Curtiz, Jane had never worked with a director as powerful as Raoul Walsh. Before leaving one morning for work, Reagan told her, "Errol *[Flynn]* and I survived Raoul in *Desperate Journey.* So can you."

Morgan said, "Walsh has directed John Wayne, Errol Flynn, James Cagney, Edward G. Robinson, Humphrey Bogart, and Marlene Dietrich. Now us. He'll make mincemeat of us."

Actually, he didn't. Walsh seemed to realize that *Cheyenne* would be one of his minor efforts, and he didn't overly extend himself. One afternoon, he flatly told Jane and Morgan, "Direct yourselves today. I'm going to get drunk. If you don't want to do that, go fuck each other, which sounds like a hell of a lot more fun than starring in this picture."

In *Cheyenne,* Morgan played a card shark in trouble with the law. A Wells Fargo agent approaches him and offers him a deal. "Find a stagecoach robber known as "The Poet," and all charges against you will be dropped.

Morgan sets out on his mission, where he encounters Jane, cast as Ann Kincaid. She is secretly married to "The Poet," a swaggering folk hero played by Bruce Bennett, a former Tarzan. Arthur Kennedy, her boyfriend in *Bad Men of Missouri,* played his stagecoach-robbing sidekick, the Sundance Kid. Singer Janis Paige plays a saloon singer, and did so badly.

Jane later said, "I have only a distant memory of that movie. I know that moviegoers stayed away in droves."

Throughout most of the film, Jane and Morgan are at odds on the screen. At one point, they are forced to sleep together in a small cabin. He says, "Put your foot where it belongs."

In response, she quips, "Don't tempt me!"

In their reviews of the Western, most critics were cruel, although some thought Jane was cool and Morgan jaunty as an amateur sleuth trying to unmask a quixotic stagecoach bandit. The heavies in the film, Bennett and Kennedy, were labeled as "dour," and Bosley Crowther of *The New York Times* found Paige "ridiculous as the dance hall girl."

Variety claimed that Jane's role sweetened toward the end when she falls for Morgan.

In Jane's summation, "Just when I got the ball rolling on my career, I fumbled the pass."

***

In 1947, Jane assessed herself as being, "On top of the world." She said that in spite of her continuing marital conflicts with Reagan. Her marriage was deteriorating rapidly, even though, as she told her confidantes, "Ronnie doesn't seem to realize that. After years of pursuing every dame at Warners, he seems to be settling down to a comfortable, middle-class family life. He even wants a third child."

Of course, he has SAG," she told both Dick Powell and June Allyson. "At times, I think he's more married to the Guild than to me."

Powell tried to apologize for him. "With all the union troubles, with everything coming down on his head, it's no wonder."

Later that evening, when Powell was outside talking to Reagan, Allyson joined Jane in the kitchen. "Darling, do what I do," Allyson said. "Have an affair on the side. Right now, I'm making *Good News* with Peter Lawford. We had an affair, but it's over now."

"He's very handsome," Jane said.

"I'll introduce you."

***

Jane was excited by her next picture, *Magic Town* (1947), mainly because her co-star was James Stewart, with whom she had had a fling back in the 1930s. William Wellman, its director, told her that he was hoping for the kind of critical success that "Jimmy enjoyed after *It's a Wonderful Life.* That picture flopped at the box office, but it got great reviews. I know you want to continue your winning steak after *The Lost Weekend* and *The Yearling.* If you and Jimmy perform like I think you can, both of you might carry off Oscars for *Magic Town.*"

"You certainly have high hopes for us," she said. "I hope Jimmy and I can live up to your expectations."

Once, when she failed to deliver a certain scene, Wellman yelled at her, "You stinking deer killer! Do it again!" Throughout the filming, he kept calling her "Deer Killer," a reference to her role in *The Yearling.* It was an ongoing joke with him, one she didn't appreciate.

RKO, it turned out, was only the distributor. *Magic Town* was an independent production created by the Oscar-winning screenwriter, Robert Riskin, who had married Fay Wray. He had been a frequent collaborator of Frank Capra, having worked with him on *It Happened One Night* (1934) which had brought Oscars to Claudette Colbert and Clark Gable.

In *Magic Town,* Stewart was cast as Rip Smith, a failed pollster who hoped to jump-start his career by finding the "public opinion capital of America," where he could test views that reflected the American mindset at the moment.

He settled on the small town of Grandview, where everybody was typical. Everyone that is, except Mary Peterman (as played by Jane), a crusading newspaper editor who wants the town to evolve, expand and grow. Stewart prefers it to remain in a time capsule.

Naturally, they fall in love. Before shooting began, Stewart told Wellman, "I want to generate as much heat with Jane as Katharine Hepburn and I did in *The Philadelphia Story* (1940).*"

Generally known as "Wild Bill," the director had assembled an impressive supporting cast. Jane had a reunion with Regis Toomey. Together, they still held the record for the longest screen kiss. This time, he got only a peck on the

James Stewart and Jane Wyman in *Magic Town*: Sexy but coyly romantic icons of small-town virtue.

cheek.

Meeting Jane again after a long absence, her co-star, Stewart, warmly embraced and kissed her. Over lunch in the commissary, they had time for an update of their lives. "I'm amazed you haven't gotten married yet," she said. "You know what happens to an unmarried actor in Hollywood who turns forty. Hedda and Louella will spread rumors that you're queer."

"How wrong they'd be," he answered. "I keep a little book. In it, I record my every conquest. To date, I've reached 201."

"Please tell me just the marquee names," she said. "If you don't, I'll call Paulette Goddard, and she'll keep me up to date."

"I'm not a Kiss-and-Tell guy, but if you insist: "Jane Wyman, first and foremost. Wendy Barry, Diana Barrymore, Olivia de Havilland, Jean Harlow, Rita Hayworth, Katharine Hepburn. Must I go on?"

"Don't stop now," she said.

"Okay. Jeanette MacDonald, Ginger Rogers, Rosalind Russell, Norma Shearer, Lana Turner, Loretta Young, Margaret Sullavan, and Marlene Dietrich. When Marlene and I made *Destry Rides Again* in '39, I knocked her up. She had an abortion."

"How unfortunate," she said. "I'd have loved to see what a kid by you and Marlene looked like."

Stewart may have been off in his math. Before he entered the Air Corps during World War II, a Hollywood columnist estimated the number of his conquests to be "263 different glamour girls of Hollywood."

He still had the stammering delivery and gangly physique she remembered, and although he'd matured, he remained boyishly attractive. She told Lucille Ball, "Jimmy has a somewhat eagle-beaked appearance, but he's handsome in an offbeat way."

"I may soon get married, but I've loved my bachelor days," he said. "Let me tell you, they were wonderful…just wonderful. Boy, did I have some hot times. It would be hard to give it up and settle down."

Over dessert, he asked her, "Do I have to apologize for that night when Hank *[Henry Fonda]* and I took advantage of your innocence? You were so young, so pretty."

"Don't kid yourself, big boy," she said. "I wasn't all that innocent. I was fucking Errol Flynn, Robert Taylor, and Clark Gable, for openers: You're not the only one who can drop marquee names. And let me add the great James Stewart and Henry Fonda to that impressive roster. Speaking of that, do you go in for repeats?"

"We'd better not," he said. "Let's just confine it to flirting with each other and kissing on camera. You see, I'm close friends with your Ronnie. I'd feel guilty about it."

"It's your loss," she said with a sigh.

When it was released, *Magic Town* didn't find its audience, although later generations usually tended to appreciate it.

As for her performance in it, *Photoplay* gave Jane a plug, writing, "It's unusual enough to rate a cheer. It's unrealistic enough to rate a brush-off. Wyman is a good actress; her quiet handling of the role of the small town newspaperwoman is apt enough to sometimes put the mannered Stewart at a disadvantage."

Faced with a lackluster reception, RKO publicity agents went to work and devised a series of provocative new ads. Within a context and using a pose having nothing to do with the movie, Stewart was depicted holding Jane in a sexy embrace with her shapely legs on ample display. The headline blared "THEIR LOVE JEOPARDIZED THE HAPPINESS OF THOUSANDS."

Reagan went to see the film, later critiquing it to Jane with the comment, "Where was Frank Capra when you and Jimmy needed him?"

Jane also got her share of negative reviews, one critic writing, "I was never sure who Jane Wyman was impersonating. Surely it wasn't Irene Dunne. No, Jean Arthur. No, I've got it. Claudette Colbert."

***

Jane accepted June Allyson's invitation and visited her on the set of *Good News* (1947), a movie she was co-starring in with Peter Lawford. Six years younger than Jane, the good-looking British star was a known bisexual in Hollywood.

Peter Lawford is seen on a night club outing to Slapsie Maxies, with Jane Wyman as his date.

At the time, he was no longer dating Allyson, but was juggling affairs with another MGM starlet, Nancy Davis, as well as with Van Johnson and Tom Drake. He was also managing an affair with Robert Walker, and had broken up with Lana Turner. Before that, he'd had a fling with Rita Hayworth.

Reagan heard of this, but didn't seem to be threatened. "Everybody knows this limey bastard is a pansy. You'll be safe with him. He's so effete. Not just the way he talks, but the way he walks and acts..."

When Allyson and Jane got together, they discussed one favorite topic—and that was men. Jane revealed "a cute story" about when she'd first called Reagan for a date. "I invited him to drop by my place for cocktails. He asked me, 'What for?'"

After meeting her, Lawford asked Jane out one Friday night. He met her at the studio and drove her up to Malibu, asking, "You made some excuse to your husband?"

"I don't remember if I did or not, but he's used to my going out."

"You and June must spend a lot of time making excuses to your husbands," he said.

Lawford, cruising.

Jane chose not to view that as an insult and threw herself into the fun of the evening. He admitted, during their drive up the coast, that he had been surprised when Allyson had responded to his advances during their work co-starring together in *Two Sisters from Boston* (1946).

"I guess I believed all that fan magazine pulp that depicted Dick Powell and her as the perfect couple. I was crazy about her. She was like a little china doll, so sweet, so nice, so intelligent. She even invited me to her home for parties. She insisted I bring a date to throw Dick off her trail."

"He's only a good detective in the movies, not in real life."

"June and I finally had to cool it because Louis B. Mayer found out about us and threatened our careers," Peter said.

Allyson later recalled, "I sort of presented Peter as a present to Jane when we broke off. She was so frustrated in her marriage to Ronnie. I had been fond of Peter in a very romantic way. I loved his devil-may-care attitude, and his British accent fascinated me."

According to Allyson, "Jane and Peter became intimate on their first date."

In Malibu, Lawford invited her to a little tavern that on Friday nights featured an open mike. "I'm having to sing and dance in *Good News,"* Lawford said. "I'm neither a singer or dancer. Tonight, I'd like to sing a few songs with you to get over my shyness about singing in public. I know you're a singer. We can do the familiar favorites that both of us know, like 'Bye, Bye Blackbird.' If I can sing before strangers, I'll be better prepared to do so on camera."

He and Jane sang five songs, and the crowd in the tavern cheered, demanding more. Jane called out to the audience, "We have so many requests, we'll stay here all night and sing them all!" That brought even more cheers.

Later, she told Allyson that after midnight that evening, Lawford brought her back to his living quarters. "I think Lady May Lawford lived in another part of the house. He calls his mother 'The Bitch.' Peter is very oral."

After only five dates, as Jane was about to start filming *Johnny Belinda* with Lew Ayres, both Lawford and Jane were ready to move on to other conquests. She told Allyson the real reason she broke from Lawford: "I heard that he goes to whorehouses since his regular dates won't do all the oral stuff he demands. He's also said to patronize male hustlers that he pick up in toilets. I'm afraid that if I keep dating him, I'll catch something."

About a month after they broke off from one another, Jane received a call from Lawford. Apparently, he'd given a blow-by-blow description of their affair to his newly minted and very gossipy friend, Frank Sinatra. "Frank wants a date with you," Lawford said. "Are you game?"

"Let me get back to you on that," she told him. Then she hung up the phone, never to use it again to call Lawford.

***

June of 1947 represented one of the darkest moments in Reagan and Jane's troubled marriage. During the course of that month, Reagan was stricken with pneumonia. When he began gasping, "I can't breathe," he was rushed to the emergency ward of Los Angeles' Cedars of Lebanon Hospital. There, he was diagnosed with a fever of 104°. When Jane was allowed to visit him the following morning, his doctors told her that he had a rare strain of pneumonia that resisted so-called miracle drugs. They suggested that he might die.

Coming as it did on top of her mounting woes, she worked herself into a state of hysteria. Months before, her own doctor had told her that she was pregnant again. That was about the last news she wanted to hear, as she'd been cast as the star of *Johnny Belinda,* her most important role to date.

During a talk with Joan Blondell, she accused Reagan of tricking her and getting her pregnant. "He thinks that by knocking me up, he can save our marriage," Jane said. "All he's done is make me hate him." Before ringing off, she told Blondell that she'd had sex with Reagan for the last time. "We're going to separate."

Early on the morning of June 26, Maureen's nanny summoned an ambulance to rush Jane to the Queen of Angels Hospital. There, at 11:26AM, she gave premature birth to a pathetically frail and undersized wraith, a baby girl, whom she'd already named Christine Reagan. Days later, when Reagan recovered from his pneumonia, he incorrectly informed the press that Jane had had a miscarriage. She had not. The girl was born, but had died of cardiac arrest at 8:45PM on the evening of her birth.

Reagan did not console Jane on their loss. Neither did she offer him any comfort.

On her orders, the authorities cremated the body six days after Christine's death.

***

When Reagan, after a prolonged fight for his life, was released from the hospital, he was seventeen pounds lighter. And whereas he resumed work on the filming of *That Hagen Girl* with Shirley Temple, Jane began to train for the role of the deaf mute in *Johnny Belinda.*

To master sign language, Jane hired Elizabeth Gessner, an expert, who spent weeks teaching her how. She had a hard time mastering it, but finally, she realized what her problem was. The fact that she could hear was reflected in her reactive timing and in the expression on her face. She solved that problem by stuffing wax into her ear canals during rehearsals, a technique she'd continue during the actual shooting of the film. Using that device, and by remaining silent for hours at a time, she gave the illusion of being lost within a context of total deafness.

Reagan was still occupying the same home with her, Maureen, and Michael. At first, he didn't know that her ears were plugged, thinking she was refusing to speak to him.

As she remembered, "We often passed each other in the hallway. He came and went, usually involved in SAG business at night. He had moved out of our bedroom and slept in the guest room. Under the same roof, we lived in separate worlds."

***

During pre-production, before Jane's casting as Belinda, there had been many intense debates, all of them stressful, with various stars considered for the role. Joan Crawford called producer Jerry Wald, who was responsible for the green-lighting of *Johnny Belinda.* "I need another Oscar to match the one I won for *Mildred Pierce,"* she asserted.

Wald was impressed with the way Jean Negulesco had helmed Crawford in *Humoresque* (1946). Of course, Wald knew she was too old for the role, as was Bette Davis, who was also in the running.

"The new girl on the block," Eleanor Parker, was deemed most suitable, but she had already signed to appear in other pictures, *Escape Me Never* with Errol Flynn, and *The Voice of the Turtle* with Reagan, both in 1947.

Finally, after all the Warner executives had seen a screening of *The Yearling,* Jane emerged as the final selection. Somewhere along the way, two of Jane's closest friends, Alexis Smith and Ann Sheridan, had also been discussed as possible candidates.

Yet even after Jane signed for the role, the casting debates continued. Samuel Goldwyn, presumably meddling in the affairs of a competing studio, called Wald, telling him, "You know in your heart that there's only one actress who'd be the ideal choice for Belinda—and that's my little Teresa Wright. Even though you've already cast Wyman, you know I'm right. With her, it might be a stretch. With Wright,

A sensitive movie brilliantly acted, and marketed with lurid overlays from MGM's publicity department.

Despite condemnations from censors, audiences were drawn to it.

452

it's a natural."

Wright had already won an Oscar for Best Supporting Actress in *Mrs. Miniver* (1942), and had delivered a brilliant performance in *The Best Years of Our Lives* (1946). For a very brief time, Wald considered removing Jane from the project and signing Wright instead, but Goldwyn demanded too much money for a loan-out.

Bringing *Johnny Belinda* to the screen had required a long period of gestation. In 1940, it had opened on Broadway as a play starring Helen Craig, the wife of actor John Beal, who had been Katharine Hepburn's co-star in the film, *The Little Minister* (1934).

An abused deaf-mute, as portrayed by Jane, emerging—with the help of Lew Ayres, seen here from behind—from her prison and shell.

At the time, Jane had attended a performance of the play with Reagan and Louella Parsons during one of their cross-country promotional tours. Parsons predicted "This play will never be made into a film because the plot centers on a rape. That is forbidden for display on screen."

Parsons opinion reflected a conservative application of the values and standards of her era, but *Johnny Belinda* would defy the Code and become the first A-list picture of its kind to feature rape since 1934, when the Production Code had begun strict enforcement of its self-defined moral imperatives.

World War came and went before Wald unearthed the property and told Warner, "It'll make a hell of a movie." It took a lot of persuading before Warner purchased the rights for $50,000. Even then, the studio faced the major task of rewriting and reconfiguring it. To that effect, Warner hired two screenwriters of minor importance. One of them was Irma von Cube, a German-American who, after an early career working on films in Berlin, had penned the script for *Song of Love* (1947), starring Katharine Hepburn, Paul Henreid, and Robert Walker. Her partner in the scriptwriting of *Johnny Belinda* was a writer/actor, Allen Vincent, who had starred in minor films in the 1930s. As a scriptwriting team, they went through eight versions before one of them was finally deemed acceptable.

Johnny Belinda had originated as a play by Elmer Blaney Harris, who based it on an incident that had occurred at his summer home on Prince Edward Island off the eastern coast of Canada. Lydia Dingwell (1852-1931), a deaf mute, had been brutally raped and impregnated, with dire consequences, including murder. The story not only dramatized the horror of rape, but the consequences of spreading rumors and lies in a small town of fishermen and their families.

Jane was cast as Belinda McDonald, the victim of the rape, who is befriended by a new doctor, Robert Richardson. He realizes that Belinda, though treated like a dummy by the townspeople, is very intelligent. Her father is Black McDonald, and she lives with him and her Aunt Aggie. Belinda rarely ventures into town, where she is likely to be mocked.

The doctor's secretary is in love with him, but when he spurns her advances, she marries a local lout, Locky McCormick, the villain of the piece. He gets drunk at a dance, goes to the farm where Belinda is alone, and rapes her, which causes her to become pregnant.

When news of her pregnancy spreads through the town, the doctor is suspected as the father. The baby boy is named Johnny.

When Locky, now married to Richardson's secretary, decides he wants to claim (and kidnap) the baby, he is shot (and killed) by Belinda after a struggle. Subsequently, she's put on trial for murder, but eventually, news of who actually committed the rape is aired in the open light of day. Richardson saves the day, taking Belinda and Johnny to their new home and a new life.

As director of this controversial screenplay, Jean Negulesco became available when Errol Flynn refused to accept him as director on the set of *The Adventures of Don Juan* (1948).

Negulesco proposed to Wald that Brian Aherne should be shoehorned into the role of the doctor. "If not Brian, how about Robert Donat or Ronald Colman?"

Wald, however, had a different vision: He had seen Marlon Brando interpret the brutish role of Stanley Kowalski in Tennessee Williams' *A Streetcar Named Desire,* and as the doctor, he wanted the handsome, talented young actor. Warner, however, adamantly disagreed. He, too, had seen *Streetcar*. "I understand Brando is a secret faggot. Besides that, he mumbles. I didn't understand a god damn word he said except 'STELLA! STELLA! STELLA!'"

As a 1930s "Pretty Boy on Celluloid," Lew Ayres had a certain androgynous appeal, attracting the hearts of such diverse personalities as Spencer Tracy or Ginger Rogers, and ultimately, Jane Wyman herself.

Finally, the name of Lew Ayres was put forth, based on his having played a doctor in a series that included nine *Dr. Kildare* movies from 1938 to 1942.

Although his fame had derived from roles he had played before the war, Ayre's career was far from over. He had already made a successful post-war comeback playing an empathetic doctor in *The Dark Mirror* (1946).

When Ayres was first contacted about the role, he said. "Although I hear you signed Jane Wyman, who is all wrong for the part, I hope you cast Teresa Wright as my leading lady."

Wald responded, "You leave the casting to us, okay?"

At the time Ayres made that statement, he had seen neither *The Yearling* nor *The Lost Weekend.* He remembered Jane, if at all, as the wisecracking "Hey-Hey Girl" of the 1930s. He didn't learn until later that she didn't want him for her leading man either, preferring Joseph Cotten.

The studio's first choice for the rapist was sexy, stoically handsome Rory Calhoun, who had served a three-year jail term for several incidences of armed robbery before he was twenty-one. His gay agent, Henry Willson, was heavily promoting him and taking sexual advantage of his new discovery. Calhoun would go on to become a star, making two pictures with Marilyn Monroe, *How To Marry a Millionaire* in 1953, and *River of No Return* in 1954, which also co-starred Robert Mitchum.

Warner ruled against Calhoun. A newly emerging, malevolent-looking "menace" on the screen, Stephen McNally, was selected instead. *[Ironically, when the actor was billed as "Horace McNally," he had played the kindly doctor, Robert Richardson, on Broadway in the stage version. He kept the name of Horace until he was cast in Johnny Belinda.*

Henceforth, he would be billed as Stephen McNally.] Wald had been impressed when he'd played the villain in Judy Garland's *The Harvey Girls* (1946).

When McNally first met Jane on the set, he asked her, "Can we go somewhere private and rehearse the rape scene?"

She denied his request.

A New Yorker, like McNally, Jan Sterling would become one of the best known of the cinematic blondes of the 1950s. She'd be nominated for an Academy Award as Best Supporting Actress for her performance in *The High and the Mighty* (1954).

At the time Jane met her, she was married to the British actor, John Merivale, who would later become famously associated with Vivien Leigh, becoming her lover after her divorce in 1960 from Lord Laurence Olivier. Sterling herself would become married to the likable lug, the "character leading man," Paul Douglas.

Originally, Janis Paige, a singer/actress, was selected for the role of the doctor's jealous secretary, Locky's wife, but Wald interpreted her screen test as unacceptable.

Agnes Moorehead was cast in the role of Belinda's aunt and flinty guardian. Moorehead had made her debut in *Citizen Kane* (1941), one of the greatest films ever made. Before that, she'd worked in The Mercury Theatre with Orson Welles. Moorehead's performance in *Johnny Belinda* was eventually nominated for an Academy Award as Best Supporting Actress.

Charles Bickford was offered the role of Belinda's father. Wald later said, "He held me up. It was highway robbery. But we finally hired him for $5,000 a week." At the time, Bickford was among the hottest character actors in Hollywood, and there was talk that he might win the Oscar for his recent appearance in *The Farmer's Daughter* (1947), co-starring Loretta Young and Ethel Barrymore.

***

Cast and crew of *Johnny Belinda* were moved to the village of Mendocino, some 42 miles north of San Francisco, along the 42-mile-long Big River. This rustic setting had been selected by Wald with the understanding that more than any other village in California, it matched the terrain of a fishing hamlet in the Maritime Provinces of Canada.

On the set, Jane came face to face with her leading man, Lew Ayres.

She had first seen him on the screen in 1929 when he'd starred opposite Greta Garbo in *The Kiss* and she'd "thrilled at his male beauty" when he played the young soldier on *All Quiet on the Western Front* (1930).

Ever since, he'd been a media event, and she followed his life and career in the fan magazines. They had reviewed his marriages, first to Lola Lane and later to Ginger Rogers.

From the first night, Jane and Ayres became almost inseparable. "I'm not saying that Lew drove the nails into the coffin of my marriage to Ronnie," she later told June Allyson. "Lew was not to blame. But he moved into my heart. I would probably have divorced Ronnie anyway. There is no way I wanted to become the wife of a politician."

In record time, both Ayres and Jane became *confidants*. Reagan had offered her no comfort following the cremation of their infant daughter, but Ayres did. At first, he came on to her like a priest, which he had wanted to be at one time in his life. But by the third night, her "father confessor" had become her lover.

As she later claimed, "he became almost overnight the love of my life."

Jane had to tell someone, and she chose Agnes Moorehead, who, based on their work on the same movie set every day, became an eyewitness to Jane's fast-developing love affair. Jane told her, "John Payne thrilled me sexually, Dennis Morgan is a darling. But Lew is something else. I have an actual glow when I'm around him. I know I sound like a silly schoolgirl, but he touches my heart in a way no man has ever done before."

During their time off, they would wander off together. Sometimes, they shared a picnic along the banks of the Big River, finding a secluded spot. She took up painting, with a preference for landscapes. He drove her around in a battered pickup truck rented from a local farmer with funds provided by the studio.

They found an escapist retreat in the fern-banked canyons of Russian Gulch, amid copses of redwood trees. Sometimes, they explored the rocky coastline around Fort Bragg, finding a hidden cove where he made love to her. She painted scenes of the Noyo River, with its small fishing craft, while he read the theology-based existentialism of Søren Kierkegaard.

"Often, we would sit for hours at a time, when we weren't needed for a scene," she told Moorehead. "Like Belinda in our picture, I could communicate silently with Lew."

He told her of his much-publicized experiences during World War II. In March of 1942, following the Japanese attack on Pearl Harbor, he had refused to bear arms and consequently, registered as a conscientious objector. In reaction, many theaters boycotted his films, especially films in his *Dr. Kildare* series. Along with other conscientious objectors, he was sent to Cascade Locks, an internment center in Oregon. "I believe in praising the Lord, but not passing the ammunition," he said at the time.

He left the internment camp by volunteering as a medical corpsman and chaplain's assistant serving on the front lines in the South Pacific. Once there, he earned the respect of his fellow servicemen, exposing himself to danger, aiding the wounded, and comforting the dying.

He told Jane, "The horrors of war were worse than I'd imagined. I held little children in my arms as they were bleeding to death, with only a minute or so to live. I saw other children standing by to watch their parents be buried in a mass grave. I held soldiers whose intestines had been ripped out by a bomb. I listened to their dying word. Often it was, 'Tell my mother that I will always love her from Heaven.'"

Ayres showed her a column written by right winger Hedda Hopper shortly after his return to Hollywood. She commended him for his service during the war, the terms of which had originally inspired frontpage ridicule. "Ayres faced professional suicide, but to crucify a man who stands up to his own convictions is un-Christian and un-American," Hopper wrote.

He kept his body in good shape at the age of thirty-eight, two years older than Reagan. Often, Jane and Ayres swam nude together in the waters of Big River. He told her he liked the role he was playing. "I stand up against a bigoted, self-righteous town. The role was made for me."

"Ronnie is pragmatic," Jane told Moorehead. "Lew is idealistic. Ronnie reads about politics, Lew devours books on religion and philosophy."

On Sunday afternoons, on a riverbank, Ayres would play his jazz banjo for Jane. She didn't know that he'd been trained as a musician in his native Minnesota. His father had played the cello.

Jane also said, "He doesn't indulge in Hollywood gossip like I love to do. In addition to being a brilliant actor, he can also whittle, sculpt, write anti-war plays, and compose a symphony—he's a true Renaissance man. I find him a wonderful companion and a great and most satisfying lover. When he seduces a woman, he makes her feel like a goddess. He also has a good sense of humor, very much like my own."

"His eyes convey a sadness," she told Moorehead. "He's very quiet. When he does speak, it's with a warm, caring voice that I find very soothing. He's a vegetarian. I haven't had a steak since I met him. At night, he holds me in his arms."

"Girl, you sound like you're in love," Moorehead answered.

***

When Jack Warner saw the first rushes of *Johnny Belinda,* he exploded in fury. "What is this? Some fucking mood piece about fog and seagulls from Sweden?" He had just returned from a vacation in France. When Jane came on the screen, he was even more horrified. "I can't stand the sight of her. She's ugly. People don't buy tickets to see an ugly woman on the screen. Put some makeup on her. You've got too much of this deaf-and-dumb shit. Have a voice over to narrate and let us know what she's thinking. Silent pictures went out, already. In fact, Warners invented the talking picture."

Negulesco did not listen to the demands of his boss and went on shooting the picture as he'd conceived it.

Late one afternoon, Reagan arrived unexpectedly in Mendocino. He hadn't informed Jane that he was coming. Was he on the scene because he'd heard rumors that she was having an affair with Ayres? Moorehead and Negulesco noticed that Reagan got a chilly reception from Jane. She did not allow him to sleep in her cabin, claiming that it would break her concentration for the role. Ironically, he ended up bedding down in Ayres' cabin, because it was the only place with an available bed.

As Negulesco later said, "I would love to have been a fly on the wall to hear what those two guys had to say about each other."

Reagan left early the next morning, but the director noticed that Jane did not kiss him goodbye. However, Reagan shook Ayres' hand and thanked him for putting him up for the night.

Within two days, another unexpected visitor arrived on the scene to confront Ayres. It was his girlfriend, the blonde-haired actress, Audrey Totter. Unknown to Jane, she and Ayres had been engaged in an affair.

Unlike Reagan, who had been discreet and had caused no trouble, Totter was "itching for a fight," as she told Negulesco.

Their confrontation took place in Jane's cabin in the presence of Ayres. "The screams between the two jealous women could be heard across the river," Negulesco said.

In a rage, Totter left Mendocino, vowing never to speak to Ayres again.

"Totter got kicked out on her ass," Negulesco recalled. "I had a member of my crew drive her to San Francisco and put her on a plane back to Los Angeles. Her fling with Lew was over. Obviously, he'd found a new gal, a married one at that. I figured that if Totter knew that, then the word had already spread across Hollywood. America's ideal couple of World War II was that no more. The title had passed."

***

After their completion of *Johnny Belinda*, Jane told the cast and crew goodbye, hugging and kissing Moorehead. She told her newly made friend that she was going for a short vacation in New York. After telling Negulesco farewell, Ayres drove Jane to San Francisco, where they boarded a plane together to New York.

Once in Manhattan, they booked a suite together at The Plaza, but for the most part avoided the usual celebrity haunts, such as the Stork Club. However, Harrison Carroll, the Hollywood reporter for the *Herald-Express,* caught up with the romantic couple one night.

Perhaps he came upon Jane in an unguarded moment. She almost never made comments about Reagan to the press. But on this afternoon in December of 1947, she did. "There is no use lying. I am not the happiest girl in the world. It's nothing that happened recently. It's an accumulation of things that have been coming down for a long time. When I return to Los Angeles, I will talk things over with Ronnie. I hope and believe that we will solve our problems and avoid a separation."

Later, when columnist Gladys Hall cornered her, she had been drinking and was even more indiscreet, delivering a far more candid appraisal of her marriage. "Ronnie and I are through. We're finished! It's all my fault."

When she read these statements, Louella Parsons called Reagan at once. These two former residents of Dixon, Illinois, had long been allies and friends. He told her, "I love Jane and I know she loves me. I don't know what this is all about, and I don't know why Jane has done it. For my part, I hope to live with her for the rest of my life."

Then he uttered a shocker, "Jane very much needs to have a fling, and I intend to let her have it."

Hedda Hopper managed to reach Reagan for brief statement. He said, "If it comes to divorce, I'll name *Johnny Belinda* as my co-respondent."

Back in Hollywood, Jane asked Reagan to move out, and he took his luggage to a hotel. Even so, she seemed to realize how indiscreet her comments in New York had been.

She wrote an "open letter" to him, which was sent to and then published in a movie magazine.

"Dear Ronnie,
You and I have been married for seven years. During this period, at least once a week, you've reminded me (kiddingly), how lucky I am to have you for a husband. I thing I am lucky. All kidding aside, there isn't a single thing about you I'd want to change. You've been wonderful to me in many ways."

Apparently, she didn't mean a word of what she'd written.

To squelch rumors about an affair with Ayres, Jane called Reagan and invited him to be her escort at the premiere of *Johnny Belinda*. He told George Murphy, "I think this means a reconciliation. I'll be sleeping in my own bed tonight."

It was a glittering affair. In contrast to her drab appearance in the film, Jane showed up in a satin gown and a mink coat, looking almost as glamorous as she'd ever appeared.

Although the lavish event went smoothly, and she was smothered in congratulations, the evening ended in disaster. After he'd taken her to dinner at Chasen's, a fight erupted between Reagan and her on the sidewalk when the valet was retrieving Reagan's car.

Jane was heard shouting at Reagan, "I got along without you, and I damn well can get along without you now, you fucking has-been."

Also waiting for her car, actress Jane Greer overheard the altercation.

Wyman asked the doorman to hail a taxi for her. As she was getting into the cab, Greer also heard Reagan call after her, "Who are you fucking tonight?"

Johnny Belinda opened across the country to rave reviews. Warners, however, decided to take out full page ads emphasizing the rape. A drawing pictured a menacing man moving toward a frightened young woman. Headlines blared "SHAME CAME OUT OF THE SHADOWS AND CHANGED A YOUNG GIRL'S LIFE" Some of the ads suggested that Ayres, as the doctor, was the culprit who raped her. "HER DOCTOR WAS

THE FIRST TO SHARE HER SHAME."

In spite of Jack Warner delaying the film for months, he relished its success when it became the studio's biggest money-maker of the year. "Sometimes, it's great to be wrong. I'm laughing all the way to the bank."

In Hollywood, Parsons reviewed *Johnny Belinda* for *Cosmopolitan,* "If stardom is what Jane Wyman wants most, *Johnny Belinda* will guarantee her this eminence. Jane as the deaf mute is real and very touching. She rises to every demand of tenderness and warmth."

Seen together at the Oscar Ceremony, waiting for an announcement about *Johnny Belinda*: Lew Ayres and "no longer plain" Jane Wyman.

Reagan was noticeably absent.

Jane expected to be on the list of Best Actress Academy Award nominations, although she didn't expect to win. On Oscar night, Ayres, not Reagan, was her escort. Irene Dunne was nominated for *I Remember Mama;* Olivia de Havilland for *The Snake Pit;* Ingrid Bergman for *Joan of Arc;* and Jane's friend, Barbara Stanwyck, for *Sorry, Wrong Number.*

With Ayres in the seat beside her, she listened as Ronald Colman came forward to read off their names. "I slumped in my seat," Jane later said. "Two rows in front of me, I could see the neck of Dunne. She was preening, probably already mouthing her acceptance speech. Then I heard the name of JANE WYMAN ring out in the hall. I was speechless. I nearly fainted. I couldn't believe it. Lew gave me a big kiss and hug in front of the world, and urged me to get up on my feet and go forward. I dropped my handbag, and everything, including my lipstick, went rolling out on the floor. On the way to the stage, I thought of the damnest things, like 'did I remember to wear my girdle?'"

Lovemaking on Oscar Night.

Accepting the Oscar, she gave one of the shortest speeches in the history of the Academy. "I accept this award very gracefully for keeping my mouth shut. I think I'll do that again."

Backstage, she was congratulated by Ayres, who hugged and kissed her again. She consoled him for his own loss. He had been nominated as Best Actor of the Year, but lost to Laurence Olivier for *Hamlet.*

An hour later, Jane showed up for a gala celebration honoring her in the Champagne Room of the Mocambo. On one of her arms was Jack Warner himself; on the other, Lew Ayres.

Warner took the occasion to announce that Jane was being considered for two upcoming pictures. The first was the film version of Tennessee Williams' *A Streetcar Named Desire* that at the time, on Broadway with Marlon Brando, was eliciting raves throughout the theatrical world.

[The film role ultimately went to Vivien Leigh, bringing her her second Oscar.]

The second movie Warner announced at Jane's Oscar Night party was the filming of *Ethan Frome,* the 1911 novel by Edith Wharton, a story about tragedy, irony, and repression set in rural New England.

[Bette Davis for years had urged Warners to film the Wharton novel. But she'd left the studio. Warner briefly considered co-starring Joan Crawford with Humphrey Bogart, but the project was eventually shelved.

In 1922, it would finally reach the screen with Liam Neeson and Patricia Arquette as co-stars.

Reagan got his own silent revenge for being left out of the festivities surrounding Johnny Belinda. *When he published, in 1964, his autobiography of his years in Hollywood, he didn't even mention the film or his estranged wife's Oscar win.]*

That night, with her Oscar beside her bed, Ayres made love to her "until the *cock* crowed," as she remembered it to June Allyson.

She received yet another prize before morning. Somewhere in the middle of the night, in the pre-dawn hours, he proposed marriage. "I can't think of living apart from you."

She remembered his exact words, as she later relayed them to Allyson. Holding her close, Ayres told her, "I want you to be my bride for the next fifty years. And then we'll talk about it."

Chapter Twelve

Jane Wyman Dumps Reagan for Lew Ayres, Leaving Him Broken-Hearted and Suicidal

Pleasuring Marilyn and Doris Day, a Liberated Bachelor Goes on the Prowl

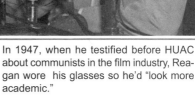

Ronald Reagan and Diana Lynn stand on their heads as part of a training exercise for their pet chimp in the notorious *Bedtime for Bonzo*.	In 1947, when he testified before HUAC about communists in the film industry, Reagan wore his glasses so he'd "look more academic."
"Katharine Hepburn and Cary Grant raised a feisty leopard in *Bringing Up Baby;* James Stewart had an invisible six-foot rabbit named *Harvey,* and Donald O'Connor had *Francis, the Talking Mule.* I thought I could get away with raising Bonzo. But my enemies used my performance against me politically in the years ahead, and I was forever ridiculed and haunted by the memory of appearing in that farce. Bonzo sure made a monkey out of me."	"I will defend the right of any American to openly practice and preach any political philosophy from monarchy to anarchy. But this is not the case with regard to the communist. He is bound by subversion and stealthy to impose on an unwilling people the rule of the International Communist Party, which is, in fact, the government of Soviet Russia."

Reagan had spent nearly four years in the U.S. Army Air Force making war propaganda films. No longer drawing a captain's pay, he was finally back on the payroll at Warner Brothers, with a salary of $3,500 a week, an large amount in 1945 currency. There was no immediate role for him, so he spent most of his days working on the construction of an unfinished ranch house surrounded by eight acres in Northbridge in the San Fernando Valley, which he and Jane had recently purchased.

Postwar Reagan: He's no longer the newest, hottest, or youngest actor in town.

"In my absence from the screen, a lot of new faces had emerged," he said. "Roles were going to Peter Lawford, Tom Drake, Robert Walker, Cornel Wilde, and there was talk that my friend, William Holden, and Burt Lancaster were going to become super stars."

According to George Murphy and Dick Powell, Reagan viewed Gregory Peck "as the hottest new kid on the block." Ironically, Peck was co-starring with his wife, Jane Wyman, in what would become a classic, *The Yearling*.

Although he had not yet found "the proper comeback picture for Ronnie," Jack Warner invited him to dinner. He later said at a dinner party, "A very different looking Ronald Reagan arrived at my door. He'd lost that pretty boy look he had when all the hot little starlets at my studio were chasing him. He'd become a man, with broader shoulders. He was also heavier. That boyish air he'd had was completely gone. After the war, Robert Taylor, Errol Flynn, Clark Gable, and Tyrone Power just weren't the pretty boys that caused women and teenage girls to swoon in the 1930s. Ronnie now numbered in that old group. The word handsome could still be used to describe these men, however."

Actually, in the ensuing years, Reagan became more interested in politics than he did in filmmaking, since the great roles he'd anticipated had eluded him, the ones he had expected after his appearance in *Kings Row*. He told actor Robert Montgomery, "The super stardom I'd dreamed about is not going to happen—and I know that."

"I can say the same thing about myself," Montgomery answered.

Despite his falling popularity, he could still point to a hefty paycheck. In 1946, he earned $150,000 a year as opposed to Humphrey Bogart who brought home "to my Betty" (Bacall) $432,000. Also at Warners, Errol Flynn earned just one dollar under $200,000, with Bette Davis, still queen of the lot, hauling away $328,000.

Pistol-Packin' Reagan Faces Death Threats from Union Brass, Then Outs Hollywood "Commies" to the FBI.

462

"I set about joining "every organization I could find that would guarantee to save the world, although later, to my great regret and shame, I learned that many of these were nothing but communist front groups." Reagan wrote in a memoir.

"At the time, my aim was to save the world from Neo-Fascists. I overlooked the on-coming world nightmare of communist takeovers. Actually, in the beginning, I viewed many communists as liberals like myself. Some communists I considered misguided; others, of course, were far more dangerous. At the time, I was trying to separate a good communist from a bad communist, but I soon learned there was no good communist."

On the homefront, Reagan had a lot to overcome. He'd later write, "I was a bit in-troverted. I've been inclined to hold back a little of myself. In some ways, I think this re-luctance to get close to people never left me completely."

Jane Wyman would certainly agree with that assessment, as would his children, Maureen and Michael, and later, even his future children with Nancy Davis: Patti Davis (who didn't want to use his last name as her own) and Ron Reagan, Jr. His son would eventually become a liberal like his father had been in the 1930s and 40s.

Reagan still defined himself as a "hemophiliac liberal," but the blood flow of his "bleeding heart" had been slowed down somewhat by the waste and greed he'd wit-nessed firsthand in government spending in World War II.

***

In the immediate post-war years, as he saw how corrupt Hollywood was, Reagan lost many of his idealistic beliefs. To an increasing degree, he began to express his fear that Communists were trying to take over the film industry for use as a propaganda vehicle, worldwide. At the time, 95% of the movies shown worldwide were conceived, scripted, and produced the United States. American films were drawing a weekly audi-ence, worldwide, of 500,000,000, a staggering figure that's especially impressive, con-sidering the population at the time.

Years later, Reagan recalled his own political shift to the right, "The light went on in some obscure region of my head. It took me a long time, but reality dawned. I came to condemn liberals, *[one of which I had been]*, as lost in their own ideological myopia."

***

Reagan received a mysterious midnight visit at his home from three agents of the FBI. He'd been an informant to the FBI on a very casual basis since 1941, reporting on wartime conditions in Hollywood when he was making propaganda films for the gov-ernment.

Until that late night meeting, Reagan's role had been only casual. But since the

---

Middle Aged, but Still a "Babe Magnet," Reagan Sees the Decline of His Movie Career Before Warner Brothers Boots Him.

---

end of the war, J. Edgar Hoover had noticed the actor's increased political power and wanted him to become a weekly informant for information about—in the director's words—"Who's Red in Hollywood, and who's taking his marching orders from old Joe Stalin."

Reagan later asserted that his four-hour early dawn meeting with the FBI "opened my eyes about Moscow's attempt to take over the film industry and to use it for their own propaganda purposes."

In the months to come, during the "witch hunt" of communists in the film industry, Reagan—now identified internally, within the F.B.I. as "Agent T-10"— filed weekly reports with Hoover.

Under the Freedom of Information Act, his role was eventually made public, although not a lot was ever learned. Many pages, perhaps vital for understanding exactly what he did, were missing from the mass of documents As for those people in the industry whom Reagan had cited as communists, their names were blacked out.

As regards his role as a domestic spy for the FBI, he told Powell and Murphy, "I felt like I was acting out my Brass Bancroft Secret Service roles in the movies."

***

Before the war, Reagan had served on the Board of Directors of the Screen Actors Guild. After his discharge from the Army, Jane Wyman was influential in getting him reinstated. He would devote much of his time and energy during the next few years to the political activities of SAG, putting more energy into them than he did into his film career.

Reagan became its third vice president in 1946. In 1947, Robert Montgomery resigned as president, because subsequent to becoming a film producer hiring actors, he viewed his duties at SAG as a conflict of interest. A special election awarded Reagan with the organization's presidency. Later, he was formally elected

The two most dangerous and deeply closeted homosexuals in America: FBI Director J. Edgar Hoover *(left)* and his *protégé* and long time companion, Clyde Tolson.

SAG reunion *(left to right)*: Jane Wyman, Henry Fonda, Ronald Reagan, Boris Karloff, and Gene Kelly.

More drama as SAG's administration grows increasingly hostile to anything associated with socialism: *(Left to right)* George Murphy, Gene Kelly, Ronald Reagan, and William Holden.

as SAG's full-time president, serving terms from 1947 to 1952, and again in 1959 to 1960, eventually serving an unprecedented six terms.

Director John Huston delivered a harsh appraisal of Reagan's presidency of SAG. "I think he hooked up with SAG for purely selfish reasons. He used it as a road to power and political influence. He only went into politics because he was washed up as an actor, appearing in horrible B pictures."

Reagan later confessed, "Although Jane was helpful in getting me back on the board, I didn't pay much attention to her suggestions. Perhaps I also ignored Anne Revere ("too radical"); Louise Beavers ("a champion of civil rights"); and Agnes Moorehead ("I never took to lesbians very much").

He paid more attention to the men, "even Frankenstein" (*i.e.,* Boris Karloff), Edward Arnold, Walter Pidgeon, Pat O'Brien, and Dick Powell. "They made a lot of sense, but James Cagney, Henry Fonda, and John Garfield were leaning too far to the left," Reagan said.

"Of course, I listened to old friends, Robert Taylor and George Murphy, who were very conservative Republicans, as was Dick Powell."

A series of crippling strikes loomed in the film industry. In an emergency meeting, the SAG board, and later the membership, voted by a vast majority to adopt a no-strike policy, which Reagan endorsed. But the issues that would later divide Hollywood into warring camps were just beginning.

Since Reagan appeared to be anti-union, and had enormous influence within SAG, he developed powerful enemies, placing himself at risk of bodily harm.

When his positions became known, he was viewed as "anti-labor." This led to a series of threats against him, He received anonymous calls late at night, pressuring him to publicize the riots as a working class protest about wages, benefits, and hours, and not just an intra-mural battle between two competing unions, the CSU (Conference of Studio Unions) and IATSE (International Alliance of Theatrical Stage Employees). One caller shouted at him, "If you don't play ball, we'll throw acid in your face, and unless it's a remake of *Frankenstein,* you won't be able to make any more of your rotten movies*."*

The morning after receiving what he viewed as a very serious threat, Reagan drove to the security office at Warner Brothers. There, the staff issued him a .32 Smith & Wesson handgun. He mounted it in a holster strapped to his chest, inside his jacket.

From then on, during a period of seven months, he never went anywhere without it. Every night, a Burbank police officer stood outside his house until dawn. "If approached and threatened by a would-be assassin, I was prepared to shoot to kill," Reagan said.

He was later credited as one of the major forces that ended the labor strife. Jack Warner said, "Ronnie turned out to be a tower of strength, not only for the actors, but for the whole industry. He is to be praised by anyone working in the film industry."

"Ronnie was a worthy successor to Bob Montgomery and me as president of SAG," Murphy said. "He was well aware of the strange creatures crawling out from under make-believe rocks in our make-believe town. He was on the front line in exposing those in the industry who are as Red as a May Day Parade in Moscow."

The strikes slowly came to an end in 1947. "The communist-dominated unions dissolved, in Reagan's words, "like sugar in a hot cup of coffee."

Jack Warner loudly proclaimed, "I will fire anyone suspected of being a communist."

In all, Reagan calculated that the post-war strikes had cost the studios $150,000,000, with a loss of wages set at $28,000,000.

465

A week after reporting for work again at Warner Brothers, Reagan was summoned to the office of Jack Warner to discuss his future career.

"I've been mulling over what kind of movies you should make. Movie audiences have changed since your Brass Bancroft days."

"What do you think I'm best at?" Reagan asked. "I've got my own ideas, but you're the bossman."

"You're not romantic enough to step into Errol Flynn's shoes," Warner said. "I see you as Warners' answer to Cary Grant, in film scripts of parlor, bedroom, and bath."

"Personally, I like Westerns and outdoor pictures like what you've assigned for me in *Stallion Road,*" Reagan said. "I'd like to appear in historical Civil War dramas. I'm a U.S. Cavalry/Indian buff, that kind of stuff. John Wayne will be rattling his saber as a Yankee soldier, I'm sure. I hear Ray Milland is getting in on the act, and you can bet your ass that Gregory Peck will do adventure stories, riding off into the setting sun, the wind blowing the cavalry guidons."

"Well, I'm not one to talk to so much about Civil War dramas," Warner said. "I turned down *Gone With the Wind.*"

"What about putting me in baseball or football pictures?" Reagan asked. "I like films about sportsmanship, America's pioneering spirit, courage under fire. I'm for depicting the violence needed to settle the West with all those redskins wanting our scalps. I'm sure your boy, Errol Flynn, will be making those kind of adventure films."

"Speaking of Flynn, he was set to star in *Stallion Road,* but I heard that he was drunk that day and the following night of his first appearance on the set. Some boys from the studio are trying to sober him up so I can bring him back to work on some other picture. I decided to drop Flynn when I heard that Bogart and Bacall each wanted to star in *Stallion Road.* They're almost guaranteed box office these days. With them in the movie, you can make a comeback in a hit."

To his chagrin, Reagan left Warner's office with no clear guidance or insight into what his film future held. That afternoon, he met the director of *Stallion Road.* A New Yorker, James V. Kern seemed "an odd choice to direct a hoss opera" (Reagan's words). He was known as a singer, songwriter, screenwriter, and actor. He'd previously helmed Jane Wyman, Ann Sheridan, and Alexis Smith in *The Doughgirls* (1944). He'd later achieve far greater success as one of the resident directors of the hit TV series of the 1950s, *I Love Lucy.*

Right before he left the studio, Kern introduced Reagan to the acclaimed Southern novelist, William Faulkner, who had been hired to write the script for *Stallion Road.*

Later, when Reagan was alone with Faulkner, the novelist told him, "I hate this god damn script based on that Stephen Longstreet novel. I'm working on this piece of shit for only one reason. I'm dead broke. I'm always dead broke. Why not lend me two-hundred dollars? But I'm warning you: I'll forget to pay you back."

466

Ten days before shooting began, Reagan received an emergency call from Kern. "Bogie and Bacall have dropped out of the picture."

"Any reason given?" Reagan asked.

"Bogie told Jack Warner he doesn't like Westerns, and also that he didn't want to work with you. He said he doesn't like your witch hunt politics. I've replaced them with Zachory Scott and your friend, Alexis Smith. I worked smoothly with Jane and her in *The Doughgirls.*"

Within the week, Warner bluntly rejected Faulkner's script and brought in Longstreet to try to write the screenplay from his own novel.

"It seemed that Longstreet had a lot of pokers in the fire," Reagan said. "Before he left Warners that day, he gave me a copy of an unpublished novel of his. He told me it would make a great movie with me in the lead. I promised to read it over the weekend."

During his first week of work, Reagan was disappointed that Warner had cut the budget in half and would shoot *Stallion Road* not in Technicolor, as originally announced, but in black and white. "The loss of color was a pain in the ass," Reagan told Kern. "Color would have given the crew a chance to shoot the beautiful scenery of the Sierra Madre Range, north of Los Angeles, with its lush setting of alpine meadows sweeping down to the waters of the Pacific."

In this publicity photo, the film's male leads Zachory Scott *(left)* and Reagan, are standing on either side of "Baby," Reagan's own horse. The men are each reading the original novel from which the movie script had derived.

Reagan with Alexis Smith, with whom he used to socialize as part of a double-dating ritual with his then-wife, Jane. After a misunderstanding with just the four of them together in Palm Springs, their friendship ended.

Reagan talked privately with Kern about the loss of Bogie and the subsequent casting of Scott. "I was hoping to ride Bogie's shirttails to a big box office success to tell the world—REAGAN IS BACK!"

"At least you're getting star billing," Kern said. "With Bogie and Bacall, you'd have been reduced to the third lead."

"Don't get me wrong," Reagan said. "Zach is a fine actor and, I'm sure, a pleasure to work with, even though he's a homo."

In the latest conception for *Stallion Road*, Reagan was cast as Larry Hanrahan, a horse breeder and a veterinarian, with Alexis interpreting the role of a rancher, Rory

467

Teller, who visits Larry hoping that he can cure her ailing prize mare. He falls for her. So does his arriving friend, Stephen (as played by Scott), who is visiting the ranch as a setting for his next novel.

Along the way, Stephen and Rory have a falling out. Subsequently, Stephen steps in to form the third leg of a love triangle.

Stephen comes down with life-threatening anthrax. Rory to the rescue. She injects him with an untested serum, and he miraculously recovers. So does her love for him.

Nelle Reagan visited the set for three days in a row. She later told her son, "From what I've seen, *Stallion Road* will be a bigger picture than *Gone With the Wind.*"

"Ronnie and I both decided that the horrible old Production Code would work against luring people into movie theaters after the war," Alexis said. "The reality of war increased the sophistication of audiences who wanted more realism in the movies. All over America, women were having children out of wedlock, for example. Also, segregation was breaking down."

One scene Reagan remembered called for Alexis and him to get down from their horses, lie down under a tree, and kiss. She was lying beside him on the grass as his lips came down over hers.

Suddenly, Kern called out, "CUT! You look like you're fucking her! Raise yourself up a bit and rest yourself on one elbow!"

"We reshot the scene," Reagan said. "I had to make love to Alexis on one elbow."

During the filming of *Stallion Road,* Reagan was introduced to Count Nino Pepitone by Dan Dailey, the singer/actor. Pepitone had been an officer and expert equestrian in the very stylish Italian Cavalry during World War II. The two men bonded. Reagan eventually hired Pepitone as his riding coach and later as manager of his eight-acre ranch in the San Fernando Valley. He'd named the place "Yearling Row" after Jane's successful movie with Gregory Peck.

He and Pepitone constructed paddock fences and a quarter-mile racetrack. "Every post hole for the inner rail posts was dug by me," Reagan said.

In the future, Pepitone would also manage Reagan's second ranch, which lay in the more distant Malibu Hills.

Pepitone sold Reagan his alltime favorite horse, a black thoroughbred which Reagan named Baby. "I fell in love with that horse," Reagan said. "It was that horse I used in *Stallion Road.*" At the ranch, he and Pepitone began to breed thoroughbreds, selling them at yearling sales.

Stallion Road took only 109 days to shoot, a record for Reagan. It was wrapped in March of 1947.

The box office was poor. In Mississippi, Faulkner went to see the movie, and later wrote Reagan a note: "The horses stole the picture from you guys."

***

In a direct confrontational style usually associated with Bette Davis in her dealings with Warner Brothers, Reagan, instead of passively waiting for his next role, entered a meeting with Jack Warner armed with two script proposals of his own. He had never been this bold before.

Still hoping to make him a big star, Warner listened patiently. Reagan had read the script of Bogie's next movie, *The Treasure of the Sierra Madre* (1948), a Warner project slated for direction by John Huston, who had also written its screenplay. It wasn't the lead, but Reagan wanted to play a character named Cody, who tries—with an evil coven—to find gold in the mountains. In the film, he dies during his efforts to do so.

One morning over coffee at his breakfast table, Reagan read that the role had gone to Bruce Bennett, who, billing himself as Herman Brix, had played Tarzan. Reagan had last seen him on screen as Joan Crawford's discarded husband in her Oscar-winning *Mildred Pierce.*

[Years later, during their co-starring gigs as competitive brothers in The Last Outpost *(1951), Reagan and Bennett would laugh about their having competed for the role.]*

Reagan also had read Stephen Longstreet's latest script and pitched it to Warner, claiming that it would be ideal as a Western for him. It was the Civil War drama that Reagan had mentioned he'd like to film one day. Warner had promised to review the script.

At a glittering Hollywood gala, Jane Wyman presented a united front, disguising her alienation from her then-husband, Ronald Reagan.

Once again, to his disappointment, Reagan read in *Variety* that the picture, based on the Longstreet project, was scheduled for filming and direction by two men well known to him, Raoul Walsh and his wartime Army boss, Owen Crump. Warner had decided that the role, with its exciting Civil War scenes, would go to none other than Errol Flynn, the star he'd previously rejected for *Stallion Road.*

Had Reagan succeeded in getting the role, he would have co-starred with Ann Sheridan, with whom he'd had a long-enduring affair and with whom he was still on friendly terms.

Reagan would never get cast in a Western at Warners. After he was dumped by his boss, he starred in Westerns made by other studios during his declining years in the movies.

***

During the filming of *Stallion Road,* Reagan had many long talks with Alexis Smith. She was not only his friend, but Jane's *confidante,* and one of the few people in Hollywood who knew about his disintegrating marriage to Jane.

At one point, he pleaded with her, asking her for some guidance, with the purpose of "getting Jane to come back to me. As you know, we're secretly separated, although she comes around to see our kids."

Alexis warned him not to pressure Jane. "She and Lew Ayres have this thing going, and you've got to let it play out, for better or worse. Her affair with him may lead to your divorce, but, again, it may not. It may peter out—forgive the pun—and she'll come back to you."

"You mean, I've got to wait and see, since it seems our future is entirely in her hands."

Jane did not want the press to learn about her marital difficulties. While Reagan was filming *Stallion Road,* she was queried about a dual-career marriage. When America's young men were returning from the war, the questions most often being asked was, "Will women become wives and mothers, leaving business to the male breadwinners?"

Jane defended working women: "Thousands of nice young couples all over the country have two jobs in one family, and they do all right. They adjust to it and to one another because they want to get along. There's no reason why two actors can't do the same thing if they're in love and don't start thinking themselves big. Our marriage is working for us."

Obviously, she didn't believe in being truthful. She also claimed, "Having children is not a reason for a woman to give up work."

Reagan faced a lonely time in his life, although he had support from his friends, Robert Taylor, William Holden, George Murphy, and Dick Powell, all of whom found him depressed and defeated. "He was a builder-upper, not a tearer-downer," Murphy said. "He'd put his heart into his marriage to Jane. She was the bedrock of his family, which had included Michael and Maureen growing up. Both of them still mourned the loss of Christine, the infant who died."

***

At one of the lowest points in his life, "an English Rose," actress Patricia Roc, entered Reagan's life. Beautiful and alluring, she was hailed by producer J. Arthur Rank as "the archetypal British Beauty, the Goddess of the Odeons, a blue-eyed brunette with porcelain skin."

Before meeting Reagan, Roc, in London, was referred to as "Bed Roc," because of her numerous affairs. One of them was with actor Michael Wilding, with whom she'd filmed *The Farmer's Wife* in 1941. As Roc recalled, "I had him long before Elizabeth Taylor."

Roc later said, "I was surprised that a man of Ronnie's dignity would stoop so low as to marry such a little, loud, brassy blonde like Jane Wyman. He deserved a woman of more finesse and dignity, with more sophistication. He found me warm, earthy, and sexually inviting."

On her second day in Hollywood, Roc dined with Walter Wanger, producer of *Canyon Passage* (1946), at the celebrity-haunted Brown Derby. Two tables away she spotted Reagan talking with Adolphe Menjou. Throughout the meal, Reagan kept looking at her. When Wanger noticed, he warned her, "Don't bother. He's a bore. I'm sure he and that Right Winger Menjou are talking about Reds under the bed."

Finally, Menjou left and so did Wanger, but Roc chose to remain behind. So did Reagan. After their respective dining companions left, he got up and came over to her table, asking if he could join her.

Some of her fans defined Patricia Roc as "the most beautiful woman in England, our answer to Hedy Lamarr." Her notorious affairs earned her the nickname "Bed Roc."

Reagan was among her conquests. She later claimed that she prevented him from committing suicide.

470

"It's about time," she said. "You looked at me like a *Tyrannosaurus rex* hungry for his next meal."

He told her that during the war, when he'd worked in propaganda films, his staff had been sent some of the patriotic movies she'd made in Britain, including *Let the People Sing* (1941) and *We'll Meet Again* (1943), co-starring Vera Lynn, the title based on her biggest World War II hit when she was "the most beloved songbird in Britain." He congratulated her for her contribution to the war effort.

He asked for her phone number. She told him, "I'll give that to you and a lot more. But why don't we drop by your place, and you may get more than my phone number."

She later admitted, "He seemed shy, and I made it easy for him. He didn't seem happy cheating on his wife, but a man's desire won out. I left the next morning."

Roc was not only beautiful, but a *femme fatale* who specialized in seducing married men. She was always the epitome of elegance, style, and fashion.

In 1945, the year Reagan met her, she'd scored hits in two English-made studio melodramas about Thomas Gainsborough, the 18th-century English portrait and landscape painter. They included *Madonna of the Seven Moons*, and the aptly named *The Wicked Lady*.

After that, she came to Hollywood to film *Canyon Passage* (1946), the only movie she'd make there. The stars of that picture were Dana Andrews, Susan Hayward (Reagan's former girlfriend), Ward Bond, Andy Devine, and Lloyd Bridges.

"I found Ronnie very personable, good looking, but depressed," Roc later said in an interview. "He was still very much in love with his wife, yet became fascinated with me. We went to bed on our first date together, and after that, he wanted to monopolize me. But I was dating others."

"If I went to dinner with another man, Ronnie would tip the waiter to get a table next to mine, where he would sit alone and just stare at me."

"I became deeply fond of him, but rather as one becomes fond of a lost child. We became lovers because, quite frankly, I was scared and lonely on my arrival in Hollywood, and sex seemed the only thing to alleviate his utter misery. I was seriously concerned that he might do something to himself if I didn't make him feel that somebody wanted him, because his wife sure as hell didn't."

"Of course, we had to be extremely careful how and where we met, especially as he was still locked into one of the highest profile marriages in Hollywood. We could both have lost our contracts had we been caught. He really fell in love with me, even though expressing his deep love for Wyman. He even followed me on location where I was making *Canyon Passage*. I couldn't turn around without falling all over him."

While waiting for Roc to finish her scene for the day, Reagan accidentally came face to face with the film's star, Susan Hayward, whom he had not seen since their torrid affair of the late 1930s. According to the film's director, Jacques Tourneur, "Susan walked right past Reagan and didn't speak to him. Later, I found out why. He'd dumped her for Jane Wyman back in 1940."

Unknown to Reagan on the afternoon of his visit, Roc had just spent two hours in the dressing room of the male star of the picture, Dana Andrews.

A "fair damsel" as "sex crazed" as Roc did not want to confine her amorous pursuits just to Reagan. She was also seen dating Lloyd Bridges, Cary Grant, Errol Flynn, and Brian Donlevy. Character actor Ward Bond developed a powerful crush on her, but she tried, perhaps unsuccessfully, to keep "Uncle Ward" at bay.

As her biographer, Michael Hodgson, noted, "In real life, Patricia's effect on men was to prove devastating. Had things gone differently, Nancy Davis might never have become Reagan's wife, and he might not have survived to enter the White House."

Reagan told Dick Powell, "Patricia Roc has instant sex appeal, I don't know what it is. This stunning, blue-eyed brunette has put a spell over me. At least she can make me forget about Jane for a while."

It was during his affair with Roc that Reagan suffered a nervous breakdown, which led to thoughts of suicide. He conveyed to Roc that at times in the middle of the night, he thought about killing himself, leaving Nelle and Jane to take care of Maureen and Michael.

"I found him just wretched and miserable," she said. "He adored Wyman and his family, and just couldn't understand why or how she had completely lost interest in him. She was bored with his political interests and his intense involvement in the Screen Actors Guild. She resented what she called 'his obsession with the threat of communism.'"

"If I had been older and more experienced, I would have realized how deeply he was suffering and would have urged him to seek psychiatric help. He told me, 'Life just isn't worth living anymore. I don't see the point of going on.' Night after night, I tried to talk him out of suicide. His depression affected our love life. On many a night, he was unable to perform like a man should."

"I hate to say this, but when Ronnie is in love, he looks like a sick parrot," Roc later told her biographer, Michael Hodgson.

"Sometimes, after he left my place, Ronnie told me he would drive over to Lew Ayres' home, park his car across the street from his doorway, and just sit there until three or four o'clock in the morning. Just waiting and looking, either watching the lights go on or off in the house or Wyman and Ayres returning home late from some nightclub."

"When I left him in Hollywood, he seemed heartbroken," Roc claimed. "He begged me to stay. He had taken up heavy drinking, often in the company of his friend, William Holden. I don't know how good a friend Bill was. He was very charming, very sexy. Once, when Ronnie was called away for a night shoot, he asked Bill to pick me up and escort me to a premiere. Behind Ronnie's back, he propositioned me after taking me to dinner and the show. Did I go to bed with Bill Holden? I'll never tell!"

For the premiere of the British film, *Scott of the Antarctic*, Reagan had a reunion with Roc at the film's Royal Command Film Performance at the Odeon on London's Leicester Square in November of 1948. Both he and Roc appeared on the stage. *[Reagan was in London at the time filming* The Hasty Heart *with Patricia Neal, whom he was also dating.]*

That night, he presented Roc with a beautiful ruby ring. Backstage at the Royal Film Performance with her, Christine Norden, the British sex symbol, overheard Roc claim, "I love rubies. They are so hot. Just like sex!"

"Reagan came back to live with me at my London flat on Hallam Street, where he repeatedly asked me—begged me, really—to marry him." Roc said. "He told me that before leaving America, Wyman had denounced him. 'She called me a bore and told me she wanted a divorce.' Ronnie looked utterly damaged. I had to have a lot of sex, and, as was the case with him in Hollywood, he often could not perform."

"We said our goodbyes and it was obvious that he was suffering during his departure from London. I

Britannia Rules!

Ultimately Reagan lost the battle for the affections of Patricia Roc to Anthony Steel, England's "Mr. Beefcake," depicted above.

felt sorry for him, but I didn't love him. A new man had entered my life."

He turned out to be André Thomas, a French cameraman, who became her second husband in 1949.

Despite the bonds of her recent marriage, Roc soon fell under the spell of Anthony Steel, England's "Mr. Beefcake," during their making of the film, *Something Money Can't Buy* (1952). "Tony had this animal magnetism that Ronnie didn't possess, and he was very, very *very* good in bed, unlike Ronnie. We didn't always use protection, which led to the birth of my son. André forgave me for my indiscretion, but I suspect that he always believed that Ronald Reagan was the father of my son."

When Roc was interviewed shortly before her death, a reporter noted a "wicked twinkle in her eye" at the mention of Reagan's name. "I think I saved his life. And you know, had I accepted his proposal, I would have made a rather good First Lady, wouldn't I? But the thought of living the rest of my life in America was more than I could bear."

At her home in Minusio, overlooking Lake Maggiore in Switzerland, Roc always kept a photograph of Reagan and herself, each of them gazing deeply into the other's eyes. It was still resting on her piano right after Christmas in 2003, when she died at the age of 88.

Today, Patricia Roc is defined by British film historians as "The Fairest of the Fair, the most beautiful girl ever to appear in British cinema."

***

"I was ashamed of my next picture," Reagan told Dick Powell. "I could not bear to sit through it."

He was referring to *That Hagen Girl* (1947), whose co-star had been Shirley Temple, the most famous child star of the 1930s.

"From the moment I first read the script, I did not like my role of Tom Bates, a man in love with a girl half his age. Jack Warner insisted I do it. So did the director Peter Godfrey. I didn't want to lose that weekly paycheck, which was keeping me going, so I went for it."

"The picture didn't help Shirley either," Reagan said. "She was transitioning from a beloved child actress to a teenager in love, and the public didn't quite accept her. To them, she was still sailing on *The Good Ship Lollipop.*"

David O. Selznick, who held Temple's contract, later met Reagan at a party. "I lent her to Jack Warner because, quite frankly, I didn't know what in hell to do with her anymore now that she'd filled out."

Warner was hoping to achieve the success of Irving Reis' *The Bachelor and the Bobby Soxer* (1947), which had teamed Temple with Cary Grant. But in that movie, Temple merely had a puppy crush on Grant. His real romantic interest centered on (the fully adult) Myrna Loy.

Charles Hoffman had to draft three separate scripts before Godfrey agreed to green-light the movie.

In the film, Mary Hagen was

rumored to be the illegitimate offspring of a union between a demented heiress and a local war hero. She finds friendship in a teacher (Lois Maxwell) and with a young would-be suitor (Rory Calhoun). Mostly, she is shunned by the judgmental, gossipy townspeople.

After the war, lawyer Tom Bates (Reagan) returns to town a decorated war hero. Slowly he falls in love with the very young Mary in spite of the circulating rumors that he was her father. Predictably, a scandal ensues.

The first day he met Temple, Reagan joked with her: "I hope you're no longer a communist." He was referring to a ridiculous report back in 1938 when at the age of ten she was called to testify before HUAC. It was all a mistake, and she was exonerated and later became a friend of J. Edgar Hoover, at one time sitting on his knee within F.B.I. headquarters.

Temple's opinion of Reagan? "If only he looked younger, or I older."

As released in Holland, the film was retitled *"Scandale!"* a prophetically apt name.

At one point near the end of the film, Reagan had to jump into cold water eight different times to rescue the character being played by Temple from a suicide attempt. By the time the scene finally pleased the British director, Reagan had caught viral pneumonia and was hospitalized. He nearly died. It was at this same time that Jane gave birth to Christine, their daughter who died a few hours later.

Reagan's hospitalization caused serious delays in the film's production. Matters became more complicated when Shirley announced that she was pregnant, her condition growing more obvious by the day. *[She had recently, and impetuously, married a philandering heartthrob, John Agar.]* As a means of viewers looking too closely at her thickening frame, her scenes and the delivery of her lines had to be rushed, often ruining the shreds of dramatic flair they might have conveyed. In faraway shots, her (non-pregnant) double was used.

When he was finally able to return to work, Reagan strenuously objected to the ending, in which he leaves town, with Tem-

An unlikely, and ultimately disastrous, screen duo: A post-adolescent Shirley Temple, shown here with her middle-aged romantic interest, Ronald Reagan.

ple, aboard a train, presumably with the intention of marrying her. Reagan would have preferred that his character board the train alone, with the understanding that she'd then be free to marry her young lover, as played by Calhoun.

Godfrey, however, saw nothing wrong with the original script's ending. "After all," Reagan said, "he was married to jail bait himself. His wife was young enough to be his daughter."

An audience's reaction at a sneak preview proved that Reagan was right. When he appeared in a scene with Temple near the end of the film and said, "I love you," some viewers walked out; others booed. "I sank down in my seat and waited for the audience to file out before I dared show my face outside," he recalled.

Based on that informal survey, Godfrey ordered that the offending scene be deleted from the film's final version. Its deletion reduced an already confusing movie into something almost incomprehensible.

Ex-con and serial seducer, Rory Calhoun, with "that horny eternal virgin," *Rebecca of Sunnybrook Farm*.

"At least," censors noted, "he was closer to her age than that lecherous character played by Reagan."

"Of all my leading ladies, I had the least chemistry with Shirley than I ever had with any actress in the past." Reagan claimed. "Elizabeth Taylor might have pulled it off. In spite of all those years in front of a camera, Shirley could not act."

Temple ultimately had the last word about *That Hagen Girl:* "As movie kissers go, Reagan is not bad at all. In fact, he was very, very good."

The reviews generated by the film were so devastating that they hastened the end of Temple's screen career. *That Hagen Girl* was defined as "a foamy dud" and "an uninspired soap opera." Temple's acting was dismissed as "wooden," and Reagan was cited as "hopelessly miscast."

Time magazine, in its November 10, 1947 issue, lacerated the picture. "Moviegoers with very strong stomachs may be able to view an appearance of rebated incest as a romantic situation."

In Moscow, *The Daily Worker* wrote: "Shirley is just Shirley. But Reagan! A philosophic father and sweetheart to the same girl. Odd."

One critic wrote: "In one scene, Shirley Temple attempts suicide. Too bad she did not succeed."

The New York Times wrote, "Poor, put-upon Shirley looks most ridiculous through it all. She acts with the mopish dejection of a school child who has just been robbed of a two-scoop ice cream cone."

That Hagen Girl was featured in the 1978 anthology *The Fifty Worst Films of All Time.* When Reagan ran for political office, all prints of the film mysteriously disappeared, but a few of them re-emerged in 1990 and were subsequently shown on Turner Classic Movies. Its resurrection vastly amused Reagan's political enemies, who subsequently mocked him as a "child molester."

As a footnote, during the filming of *That Hagen Girl,* Reagan had dated Lois Maxwell, who was cast in the movie as a sympathetic teacher, Julia Kane, a figure who might have made a more suitable romantic choice for Reagan, as Tom Bates, to romance.

Instead, Reagan dated her off screen, going out with her on about four dates during the course of the filming. On their first date, she told him that her original name had been Lois Ruth Hooker.

"No wonder you changed it," he said.

During one of their outings, he escorted her to a *Life* magazine photo shoot in which she posed with an up-and-coming actress. Reagan found himself shaking the hand of a striking blonde. He held her hand for an extended time, and seemed mesmerized by her allure.

He would remember her long after the photo shoot. He and Marilyn Monroe would meet again many times in his future.

***

The outdoor adventure film that Reagan had been promised never happened. Jack Warner called him and told him that his attempt to hire Cary Grant had failed, and that Reagan was needed at once to report to London-born director Irving Rapper for a role as an army sergeant on leave during World War II in New York.

The script was based on one of the most successful of Broadway plays in the 1940s, *The Voice of the Turtle.* "It was written by that British fag, John Van Druten," Warner told Reagan.

As the play's star on Broadway, Margaret Sullavan, who had been married to Henry Fonda, had generated rave reviews. "I've tried to negotiate with the bitch, but to no avail," Warner lamented. "What a whore! She never met a highway pickup she didn't go for. You wouldn't want to work with a dame like that."

"Then who are you going to cast as my leading lady?" Reagan asked. "I think June Allyson would be ideal if you can get Louis B. Mayer to release her."

"I'm casting Eleanor Parker," Warner answered.

At the time, Parker was one of the stars at Warners who had emerged during the war. Reagan had not seen her performance in the remake of *Of Human Bondage* (1946), in which she played W. Somerset Maugham's mean-spirited waitress-prostitute.

Reagan protested, wanting to co-star with a bigger name. "Listen, Ronnie, my boy," Warner said. "You used to be very cooperative. Now you're protesting everything like some grand diva. You don't have box office clout, not that you ever did. If you want that paycheck to continue coming in, you'll let me direct your career. Also, to put it mildly, I'm god damn pissed off at your union activities."

That Monday morning, Reagan reported to work and was greeted by Rapper, who had previously scored a hit helming Bette Davis in *Now, Voyager* (1942).

During their talk together, Rapper told him

Because of the wide variety of roles she played, Eleanor Parker was called "the woman of a thousand faces." Here, depicted romantically with Reagan in The *Voice of the Turtle,* her makeup and hairdo evoke Margaret Sullavan.

that he'd recently talked with Davis. "I told her I was directing you in your new movie. She said. "Watch out for little Ronnie Reagan.'"

"What in hell did she mean?" Reagan asked.

"Only Bette knows what Bette means," Rapper said. "We have this love-hate relationship."

"What I have with Bette I wouldn't call love," Reagan said.

Rapper gave him the finished script from Van Druten, who had also written the screen version. Rapper said that within a few days, Reagan would meet the co-stars. They included Eve Arden, Wayne Morris, Kent Smith, John Emery, and Nino Pepi-

Playing a wannabee actress, Eleanor Parker *(center)* tries to separate man-eating Eve Arden from her soldier boyfriend (Reagan).

tone, Reagan's horse-breeding friend from the Italian cavalry. Pepitone needed a job, and Reagan had used his influence to get him cast in the movie as a headwaiter.

The Voice of the Turtle revolves around an aspiring actress, Sally Middleton (Parker), who has come to New York to conquer Broadway. Her friend is Olive Lashbrooke (Arden), a promiscuous man-chaser who doesn't believe in chastity.

Because Olive's weekend date, Bill Page (Reagan), can't find any hotel space in wartime New York, Olive maneuvers Sally into housing him in her new apartment. Despite their mutual reserve, love wins in the end, and Bill and Sally become romantic.

When he first met Parker, Reagan thought she was Margaret Sullavan. *[In a nod to Sullavan's success in the Broadway version, Warner had ordered that Parker's hair and makeup be inspired by that of her predecessor.]*

"What in hell does 'Voice of the Turtle' mean?" he asked Parker.

"Rapper told me it comes from the Old Testament's *Song of Solomon*," she said, and that it's a reference, like many other of the passages within that book, to erotic love."

For, lo, the winter is past, the rain is over and gone; the flowers appear on the earth; the time of the singing of birds is come, and the voice of the turtle is heard in our land.

"Oh, I see…Turtle as in turtle dove," he said. "Well, here I am, back in my military clothes again. But in the army, we didn't have such well-tailored uniforms."

He later recalled, "After I played my first scene with Parker, I had no more reservations about her. The question became, could I hold my own with such a talented actress?"

Over lunches and between takes, they got to know each other. Although he admitted to Rapper that he found her "extremely attractive," there would be no *Leadingladyitis.* She had recently married film producer Bert E. Friedlob, and "she seemed very involved on the home front," Reagan said. "And, of course, I had my ongoing woes with Jane. The air was not made for a romantic attachment, although it might have been diverting…for me, at least."

On his last day on the set, Reagan wished her luck in her future. "Perhaps we'll work together again."

"Perhaps," she said. "Things have a way of working out for me. I maintain that if you work, believe in yourself, and do what is right for you without stepping all over others, the way somehow opens up."

"That is the most un-Hollywood philosophy I have ever heard in my life, especially in dog-eat-dog Hollywood," he said.

On the set of *The Voice of the Turtle,* he was reunited with Wayne Morris, with whom he'd made those *Brother Rat* movies. The former Golden Boy of Warners never regained his footing in films after the war. He told Reagan, "If you hadn't come along, I would have won Jane for myself."

For Reagan, *The Voice of the Turtle* was a modest success. His reviews were tepid. "At least I wasn't attacked." A typical overview appeared in *Newsweek.* "Ronald Reagan turns in a pleasantly sensitive performance as the sergeant."

***

J. Edgar Hoover, with a lot of right-wing help, launched the most sweeping and penetrating witch hunts in American history. He saw Red everywhere, a river of conspiratorial corruption whose tentacles, he claimed, incorporated the highest offices in Washington, as well as most of the movie studios and film stars in Hollywood. The hunt was on to ferret out communists in all walks of life, but mostly in politics and the film colony. In the "Red Scare" that J. Edgar spearheaded in the aftermath of World War II, lives, friendships, reputations, and careers would be destroyed.

The very conservative J. Parnell Thomas, a former stockbroker, had been elected seven times as New Jersey's representative in Congress before being sent to prison for nine months on charges of corruption. Prior to his downfall, he was an avowed anti-communist. He claimed that the Federal Theatre Project presented nothing but "sheer communism propaganda."

He seemed to have a special aversion to Hollywood. When Thomas became chairman of the House Un-American Activities Committee, J. Edgar supported him totally. The FBI fed Thomas a constant stream of accusations as to who was a communist and who might make a friendly witness before HUAC.

In May of 1947, Thomas and his chief aides visited Hollywood on a "fact-finding" mission. He held several secret meetings with Reagan, who promised his full support in "weeding out the Hollywood garden of Red weeds."

Thomas returned to Washington to launch his investigations of HUAC, with America's radios and early televisions tuned in. At first only friendly witnesses were called. Many of the spectators wanted not only to hear who was a communist, but to view the testimonial performances of movie heartthrobs who included Gary Cooper and Robert Taylor.

Reagan arrived days before the hearings for secret meetings with Hoover and his lover, Clyde Tolson, Hoover's chief aide at the FBI. Reagan promised his full cooperation. Because of his connections with SAG, he claimed "I'm in the ideal post to go after the commies polluting our industry."

Accompanied by the sound of popping flashbulbs, Reagan's appearance before HUAC hardly prompted the heartthrob hysteria brought on by the testimonies of sexpots Taylor and Cooper.

Having already promised to combat the movie industry's "domination by communists, radicals, and crackpots," Reagan had volunteered to appear before HUAC.

He looked rather studious in a white gabardine suit complete with thick glasses. As president of SAG, he claimed he had always opposed communist propaganda. "I do not believe that the communists have ever at any time been able to use the motion picture screen as a sounding board for their ideology." He contradicted testimony by Robert Taylor in that regard.

Before the committee, he seemed to be undergoing a major political change, drifting uncomfortably from an FDR New Deal liberal into a conservative Republican. On some weeks he would take one position, appealing to his liberal friends, and at another time he would be turning them in as suspected communists.

Earlier, he'd told Hoover that "I am firmly convinced that the Congress should declare the Communist Party illegal."

After his testimonies, he hurriedly left Washington for a return to Hollywood and his marital woes.

***

After Reagan's return to Hollywood, Alexis Smith tried to bring about a reconciliation between Jane and her distraught husband. Along with Smith's husband, Craig Stevens, she invited the estranged couple to drive east with them into the desert for a long weekend of rest in Palm Springs. Friends had made their vacation home available to Alexis and Stevens.

"I had to do a lot of persuading, but Jane has agreed to come with us," Alexis said. "I used the argument, 'You must do it for the children if not for Ronnie.' She was very hesitant, but finally agreed. Actually, to tell the truth, I think she wants to make Lew Ayres jealous."

Reagan had won the sympathy of Alexis when they had co-starred together in *Stallion Road,* his first picture after the war. As for Stevens, he was up for a major role in one of Reagan's upcoming pictures, *Night Unto Night.*

At the time of the ill-fated trip to Palm Springs, Alexis and Stevens had become Jane and Reagan's closest friends, and both of them were saddened at Jane's separation from her husband.

As Jane once told Ann Sheridan, "Alexis and I often drift off somewhere to indulge in girl talk, but Craig hangs out with Ronnie. He seems to worship him."

Stevens had told Jane, "Everything I ever knew about politics I learned from Ronnie."

Reagan seemed pleased to have such a devoted person listening to his political views. But Jane was suspicious. "Craig and Ronnie sometimes went for an occasional weekend together, like a sailing trip to Catalina," Jane told Sheridan. "When he gets back, I always ask Ronnie what happened."

"If you're implying anything, don't," Reagan warned her. "I had initial suspicions about Craig, but not now. He's had plenty of chances if he wanted to move in on me, and he's been a perfect gentleman. When we've been in a small cabin and had to share the same bed, nothing happened. Forget your fears. He's married to one of

In Hollywood, Good Friends Should Swing Together. (*aka* "Going Too Far with Ronnie and Jane."

Depicted above, Craig Stevens and his wife, Alexis Smith.

the most beautiful women in Hollywood. What makes you think he wants a man?"

"I didn't have the heart to tell you, but Joan Crawford told me that Alexis is a lesbian," Jane said. "Crawford thinks Craig and Alexis have a lavender marriage."

"I only learned what that meant a few weeks ago," he said. "You know the same is said about our friends, Bob Taylor and Babs Stanwyck. I don't believe it's true. I've also gone away with Bob. He's all man, with an eye for the ladies."

"Crawford told me more," Jane said. "She suspects that Craig had an affair with her husband, Phillip Terry. As for Terry himself, Crawford told me he had an affair with Bob Taylor."

"You're nothing but a little Hedda Hopper today," Reagan said. "Okay, since you're spreading rumors, let me reveal a few about you. It was rumored that when you made *Magic Town,* you had an affair with Jimmy Stewart. That's not all. You were said to also have had an affair with Wild Bill Wellman" *[i.e., director William Wellman].*

"Well, maybe I did, smart ass," Jane said, walking out of the room.

"Now that you've become a big star, you'll be hearing a lot more rumors spread about yourself, and you'll get bad press."

[Reagan's prophecy came true.]

Jane still managed to enchant both Louella Parsons and Hedda Hopper, but columnist Hy Gardner in the months ahead began making digs at her. He had been hired as an entertainment reporter and syndicated columnist for *The New York Herald-Tribune.*

He once wrote: "Jane Wyman, that woman unlike the genuine cream of the cinema crop, whose names are box office magic, seems to consider the approach of a reporter as an irksome intrusion upon the privacy of a high-priced public goldfish."

Jane retreated to Palm Springs that weekend with Reagan, Alexis, and Stevens. But she returned alone. Reagan later left the villa where Stevens and Alexis were staying and checked into a hotel, as he needed a few days' rest after the pressure he'd faced in Washington delivering his testimony before HUAC.

When word of this reached gossipy Hollywood, it was assumed that Reagan's attempted reconciliation with his estranged wife had failed. But Joan Blondell later reported a very different version of what happened that weekend. Blondell claimed that she heard only a very sketchy version from Jane.

"Ronnie and I did not get back together," Jane told her. "We also ended our friendship with Craig and Alexis."

"After buttering us up for months, making us think they were friends who liked our company, it turned out that they liked more than that," Jane said. "Friday night went beautifully. The house had two bedrooms. The four of us talked openly. It was suggested, and Ronnie and I agreed, that we would not share a bed our first night back together. We'd wait and see how things went that Saturday."

"But by midnight, we found out that wasn't the real reason Craig slept with Ronnie and Alexis bedded with me. As I was drifting off, she started feeling my breasts, wanting to make love to me. Ronnie experienced much the same assault. He was half asleep when he felt Craig's lips come down on his, and his hand feeling the family jewels. We both packed our bags, and I headed back to Lew Ayres. Ronnie rented a hotel room and stayed on."

Blondell responded, "The war brought a lot of changes in sexual attitudes, and in post-war Hollywood, there's a lot of that shit going on. I know there is. Wife-swapping's been around for a long time. But now there's a new game out here. It's about sexual bonding, husband to husband, and lovemaking among wives."

"Count me out!" Jane responded.

Although both Hedda Hopper and Louella Parsons had publicly forecast that the marriage of Jane Wyman and Ronald Reagan might be "everlasting," each of them was eager to rush into print with headlines. "RONALD REAGAN SCOUTS MARITAL BREAK," wrote Hopper. In even bigger headlines, Parsons announced, WYMAN, MATE IN RIFT. Jane got the focus in the headline because by then, she was by far the bigger star.

After the appearances of those "scoops," Reagan called each of the columnists directly, telling them "It's only a 'tift.' All married couples have them. I'm confident that we'll solve our problems and have a long and happy life."

When Louella Parsons heard that Jane was making indiscreet remarks about Reagan's sexual performance, she lectured her severely. In her column in a 1948 issue of *Photoplay,* the columnist wrote: "It is unfortunate but true that Hollywood can shrug off most marriage crack-ups. But when they are Jane Wyman and Ronald Reagan—well—we just can't take that. For eight years, they have shared a beautiful life that has earned them the respect and admiration even of people who did not know them personally. To those of us who are close friends, they were an ideal Mr. and Mrs. That's why this hurts so much!"

Rosemary DeCamp, the actress, had been one of the first to recognize an animosity coming from Jane, whose impatience with Reagan was clearly evident during the course of a SAG meeting. In the middle of a verbose speech by Reagan that went on and on, Jane stood up. "Oh, for god's sake, Ronnie, shut up and go shit in your hat."

Months before the actual filing of the divorce, Hollywood gossips and the town's press corps were speculating about a warring twosome who had, throughout World War II and the years leading up to it, been defined as Tinseltown's "Most Ideal Couple."

For the most part, the press took Reagan's side, concluding that he was the wronged party. In the spring of 1948, Fredda Dudley in *Silver Screen* magazine wrote: "Hollywood sympathy in this case is one hundred percent behind Ronnie, who is a prince. Jane is a moody person, temperamental, ambitious, restless, and seeking; furthermore, she is not now and hasn't been well for some time. It is to be hoped, that as her health improves, her other problems will vanish, and that two of the town's favorite people will resume their marriage."

Parsons warned Jane, "You're losing a good, decent family man. They are hard to find in Tinseltown. Most of the men out here are looking for a good man themselves."

For Reagan's birthday on February 6, 1948, Jane presented him with a turquoise-colored Cadillac, but signed the card, "Love, Michael and Maureen." Then she flew to Las Vegas for a quickie divorce.

Once in Las Vegas, she checked into the Flamingo Hotel. According to the *Los Angeles Examiner,* on February 27, 1948, "She was seen in the casinos and out dancing every night with a different man, her various beaux having one thing in common: Youth and beauty."

But within a week, she flew back to Los Angeles, telling a reporter, "I couldn't stand the wind blowing in from the desert."

Later, she told Reagan, "There is no chance for us. I'm filing for divorce and charging extreme mental cruelty."

Years later, during recollections of her years with Reagan to her Catholic priest, Robert Perrella, as well as to her girlfriends, June Allyson and Paulette Goddard, Jane claimed, "It was exasperating to awake in the middle of the night, prepare for work, and have someone at the breakfast table, newspaper in hand, expound on the far right, the far left, the conservative right, the conservative left, the middle-of-the-roader."

On June 28, 1948, the inevitable happened: Jane filed a petition for divorce. Reagan did not show up in court, but was represented by an attorney, William Berger. Jane's lawyer was Lloyd Wright, who had represented some of the biggest names in Hollywood at the time of their divorces, ranging from Mary Pickford to Charlie Chaplin, even Mae West. (Yes, the diva had once been married.)

Child support, alimony, and a property settlement were determined. Reagan was ordered to pay $500 a month in child support for Maureen and Michael, for whom Jane retained custody. As long as Jane continued to work in films, she would get no alimony. However, should she not be able to work, he

When Reagan was told that his leading lady would be Patricia Neal, he didn't know who she was.

Producer Jerry Wald told him, "Jack Warner has the hots for her. She's only twenty-two. He wants to configure this Southern belle from Tennessee as Warner's answer to Greta Garbo."

Reagan didn't think it was believable that "a hick from Tennessee would be hailed as a new Garbo."

was to pay her an additional $500 a month in support. The value of their communal property, totaling $75,000, was to be divided half and half, following the sale of their house on Cordell Drive. She later moved into a house in Malibu.

As a side note, she was given all the furniture, and he kept the horses, including his favorite, "Baby."

Her only comment, upon leaving the courthouse was to a reporter, "There is nothing between us anymore. Case closed."

When he came by to visit the kids, Jane said, "You're welcome at any time. But call first and warn me. I might not be here. Thanks for the memory. We had some good times."

"And two children," he reminded her. "Don't forget them."

At the time of their parents' separation, Maureen was seven years old, Michael only three. "Daddy told me the sad news, but promised to always be around for me when I needed him," Maureen later wrote in a memoir.

Although Jane had been such an important part of Reagan's life, in his autobiography, *An American Life,* he mentioned her as only a terse abbreviation: "I married Jane Wyman but it didn't work out, and in 1948, we were divorced."

One of his old friends recalled, "There had been warning signs, but I think the divorce horrified and shocked him. He didn't think he'd ever be divorced. His mother had put up with an awful lot from her husband, but they had remained married even though he repeatedly came home drunk."

"Small town boys grow up thinking only other people get divorced," Reagan later wrote. "The plain truth was that such a thing was so far from even being imagined by me that I had no resources to call upon."

"As soon as news of his divorce was published, Reagan's phone began to ring, the way it had when his picture was first published in the Hollywood press as Warners' new young star.

He later said, "I was still mourning Jane, but to compensate, some of the world's most beautiful women were calling me for dates."

Still proclaiming grief over the loss of Jane, Reagan entered what Dick Powell defined as his "second horndog period," the first having occurred in the late 1930s when he'd arrived at the gates of Warner Brothers. "I think he set out to fuck everything in sight."

***

Producer Jerry Wald called Reagan to inform him that Jack Warner had approved the casting of Jane Wyman and him in *John Loves Mary,* based on the hit Broadway play of the same name written by Norman Krasna. "I'll have the scriptwriters, Phoebe and Henry Ephron, write in love scenes between Jane and you. Your kissing—and I hear from the gals that you're good at that—will win Jane's heart all over again."

Reagan was stunned at the news and expressed his concern: "What will Jane think of working with me?"

He had other concerns as well. He'd already seen the Broadway stage version of *John Loves Mary,* starring William Prince as John, with the elegant Nina Foch as Mary.

"From what I saw in New York, the play is too much like *The Voice of the Turtle.* I'll be in my Army uniform again. But this time, instead of an Army sergeant on leave, I'll be a returning veteran. Don't you think, as a plot device, that this 'Returning Soldier from the War' *schtick* is wearing a bit thin as a plot device? Dana Andrews already delivered, in *The Best Years of Our Lives* (1946), the best take ever about a veteran's return to the homefront."

"Jack Warner insists that you do it," Wald answered. "And, as everybody on the lot knows, Jack knows best. David Butler will be your director. He did all right with Hope, Crosby, and Lamour in *Road to Morocco* (1942)."

Reagan learned that his supporting cast would include names familiar to him: Jack Carson, Wayne Morris, Edward Arnold, Virginia Field, Katherine Alexander, and Irving Bacon.

Two weeks later, near the time he was to report to work, Wald called him with a sense of last-minute panic. "I've just got the news from Jack. I don't know what happened. Wyman's out, Patricia Neal is in."

"Who in hell is Patricia Neal?" Reagan asked.

"You'll meet her soon," Wald answered.

That night, Reagan found an article in *Variety,* reporting that Neal had achieved success on Broadway in the Lillian Hellman play from 1946, *Another Part of the Forest.*

The play had been Hellman's prequel to *The Little Foxes* that had, in 1939, been such a successful Broadway play, with Tallulah Bankhead playing the mature Regina. The Broadway play had evolved into a 1941 movie with Bette Davis starring as Regina.

When the film script of *John Loves Mary* arrived, Reagan read it avidly in moments when he wasn't worrying about his marriage to Jane and coping with the union wars among the movie guilds.

Its farcical plot was based on the premise that the character played by Reagan would marry, "in name only," a Cockney war bride so that he could bring her to America and get her U.S. citizenship. Then, according to the plot, she would divorce Reagan and marry his war buddy (Jack Carson). Virginia Field had already been cast in the role of Reagan's English bride who arrives in New York to discover that her love interest, Carson, is already married, with a child on the way.

Reagan, as the returning veteran, comes back to the girl he left behind, Neal. She's been expecting him to marry her until she learns he's already wed. Edward Arnold, cast as Senator McKinley, her father, has plenty to say about his daughter's dilemma. The supposed setting is the senator's apartment at the St. Regis Hotel in Manhattan.

Before the beginning of shooting, Reagan was introduced to Neal at Jack Warner's New Year's Eve party. "Reagan walked over to me across a crowded room and shook my hand, telling me what wonderful things he'd heard about me. Then he went away. Shortly before midnight, I spotted him on the terrace weeping uncontrollably with some older woman. I'd heard he was all broken up over his marital difficulties with Jane Wyman."

Butler gathered the entire cast of players together for a read-through. Reagan renewed his acquaintance with this *Brother Rat* co-star, Wayne Morris. He and Morris had always viewed themselves as rivals. "I called Jane Wyman, my old girlfriend, and asked her out the other night," Morris said.

"Did she accept?"

"Hell, no!" Morris said, "But you can't put a guy down for trying."

Arnold, the burly and engaging actor

Patricia Neal recalled this scene with Ronald Reagan: "It was a trouser-challenged moment for him. He was kidded by the cameramen, who wondered how he could possibly wear such shorty-short panties without something hanging out. Ronnie defended his masculinity by claiming he wore a heavy-duty jockstrap to protect his modesty."

"with the big gut," the intimidating stare, and the deep voice, had been president of SAG from 1940 to 1942. During this tense period with the unions, Reagan spoke to him two or three times a week, viewing him as an experienced and politically seasoned "comrade-in-arms."

After the first day's shoot, Neal told Reagan, "You knew exactly what to do. Everybody seems to. I was too excited to be afraid on my first day in front of a camera."

Three days later, he attended the first rushes with her. After they had sat through them, she said, "It was purgatory. I thought I looked bad. I didn't realize that the camera adds twenty pounds. I was a caricature in those false eyelashes and that overly painted mouth. As for my voice, it was pure molasses."

Neal's sexy, seductive voice, however, recorded beautifully, Reagan comparing it to "an organ concert." Less diplomatically, Carson likened it to "a musically inclined dripping rain pipe playing the scales."

In one of his scenes with Neal, Reagan was ordered to appear in a pair of underwear assigned by the wardrobe department.

During his enactment of the scene, as the cameras rolled, and Arnold, as an irate father, walked in on a romantic interlude between Reagan and Neal, Reagan was hurriedly zipping up his pants—without a jockstrap. He yelped in pain before yelling out, "I've got my dick caught in the zipper."

The cameras kept rolling.

In his first memoir, *Where's the Rest of Me?,* published in 1965, Reagan reported on this incident, but edited out most of the graphic details. Nonetheless, that film clip entered the Warner files as "one of the most hilarious behind-the-scenes bloopers in film history."

Back in his dressing room, a pantless Reagan complained to Butler. "Look at me! These underpants are cut so short my dick hangs out. Just look!"

"I see!" Butler said. "You're uncut just like me. For God's sake, man, this is not a blue movie we're making. All actors appearing in underwear scenes should wear a jock strap. I thought you knew that."

As the new girl on the block, Neal was swamped with invitations to parties, perhaps with the assumption that many of Hollywood's more established actresses wanted to check out the latest competition. She told Reagan, "Even Bette Davis has invited me for tea. Do you know Miss Davis?"

"I've had the pleasure," Reagan said, sarcastically.

In the beginning, Wayne Morris, the fading blonde screen Adonis of the 30s, was Neal's frequent escort to these parties. There, he reportedly drank too much and fretted, publicly, about his falling star.

Eventually, Neal found Carson a lot more fun, and she began to go out with him. The press seized on this dating, and practically had the two of them walking down the aisle. In her memoirs, Neal admitted that one night, she and Carson went to bed together, but she claimed, "We were too wasted to have sex."

She also went out on three dates with Reagan, but, according to her, "I drew a blank, like I did with Carson. He spent most of our evening lamenting the loss of Jane. When it came time to go to bed, I couldn't get a rise out of him. That would have to wait until we co-starred together in *The Hasty Heart* (1949) in London."

One morning on the set, over coffee, Neal confided to Reagan that she'd met Cooper the night before. For some reason, he was accompanied by Errol Flynn. "Gary shook my hand, said he'd be glad to work with me, and walked away. Flynn—no longer the sexy Robin Hood in green tights—pursued me. Being a helpless girl, I was forced to give in to his demands. But I was still dreaming of Gary."

When Wald saw the rushes of *John Loves Mary*, he sent a memo, dated January 19, 1948, to Reagan. "The idea that you get paid for all those kissing scenes with Pat Neal is beyond my comprehension. In the new contract between producers and actors, I'm planning to have a clause inserted regarding kissing scenes, that a refund be made by the actors to the studio. You certainly put everything into your so-called 'work.'"

Unlike its Broadway predecessor, the film version of *John Loves Mary* quietly slipped in and out of movie theaters across the country without any stampedes at the box office. It did nothing for Reagan's career. Any good reviews went to "that emerging new star, the ravishing Patricia Neal."

Of course, she also came in for her share of negative reviews. Bosley Crowther of *The New York Times*, wrote, "There is little to recommend her for future comedy jobs. Her way with a gag line is painful."

***

In June of 1949, Jack Warner ordered the release of *Night Unto Night,* a film that Reagan had made in 1946, but whose exposure had been delayed. "I don't expect to make a profit with this turkey," the studio mogul said, "but I'm hoping to at least get back my production costs."

Night Unto Night was the second movie Reagan shot after his discharge from the Army. It was promoted as the American debut of the Swedish-born Viveca Lindfors.

Warners hoped that she would be the studio's answer to Greta Garbo or Ingrid Bergman. As it turned out, more Americans saw Lindfors' debut in *To the Victor* (1948), wherein she was cast as a woman with a past who falls in love with Dennis Morgan; or in the same year, in *The Adventures of Don Juan,* in which—in period costumes opposite Errol Flynn, she looked ravishing. Finally, with the much-delayed release of *Night Unto Night,* movie-goers could see her co-starring with Reagan. The only problem was, no one seemed to actually want to see the movie.

Right after his release from the Army, Reagan managed to look rather boyish in a swimsuit on a beach with his co-star, Swedish-born Viveca Lindfors, another Scandinavian *femme fatale* with hopes of becoming "the next Greta Garbo."

Night Unto Night was made during one of the most troubled periods in Reagan's life, with Jane threatening to end their marriage. Reagan found a "lot of comfort" (his words) in the friendship of his co-star Craig Stevens, back when he and Jane, along with Stevens and Alexis Smith, often comprised a quartet for dinner and dancing.

But by the time the movie was released, Reagan had broken off his friendship with the bisexual actor after Stevens had revealed the depth of his romantic attraction.

As a director, Chicago-born Don Siegel had been unknown to Reagan. So was his leading lady.

When Siegel introduced Reagan to Lindfors, she said, "Forgive me, but I've never heard of you."

"Miss Lindfors," he answered, "I can return the compliment. I have never heard of you, either."

"I was a film star in Sweden," she said.

"Well, I've heard of Greta Garbo and Ingrid Bergman, two other film stars from Sweden. But I've missed your movies."

She walked away, no doubt insulted.

Lindfors was detested by the film's second female lead, Osa Massen. She had been born in Denmark, as opposed to Lindfors' Sweden. Reagan referred to their conflicts as "The Battle of the Vikings." Massen complained to him that Siegel was favoring Lindfors in all their scenes and giving her extra close-ups. "I think he's in love with her."

"I wish he'd fall in love with me and give *me* preferential treatment," Reagan said. "God knows I need it to get through this stinker."

Once alerted by Massen, Reagan came to notice that Siegel and Lindfors were indeed having an affair. They disappeared every day at around noon into her dressing room. The director married his star in 1948.

***

Drawn from the pages of the Philip Wylie novel, the plot of *Night Unto Night* casts Reagan as John Gaylord, a biochemist who retreats to a rented beachfront home on the Gulf Coast of Florida. *[The movie was actually shot in California, a lot of the action (such as it was) taking place in the beachfront house that had been used in the production of Joan Crawford's* Mildred Pierce.*]*

It turns out that the house he's rented from Ann (Lindfors) is haunted. When he asks her about strange noises in the building, Ann admits that she sometimes heard the voice of her dead husband, killed during World War II, echoing through the house. As a scientist *[he's a biochemist],* he tries to convince her that the dead do not return to Earth.

He has a dark secret: He has epilepsy. The film seems to treat epilepsy as if it's contagious. Complications arise when Ann's

When this movie was shot, Reagan was still very close friends with Craig Stevens *(left),* one of the co-stars, along with Osa Massen *(center)* in *Night Unto Night.*

sister, Lisa (Massen), arrives and shows a romantic interest in Reagan. At this point, Lindfors, as Ann, has already fallen in love with him.

Secondary roles were played by Rosemary DeCamp and Broderick Crawford, a married couple who live nearby.

Although Reagan and Lindfors did not particularly like each other, they maintained a surface politeness and even had a few conversations together. Once, when the topic of sex came up, he told her, "It's always best in the afternoon, when you've emerged fresh from the shower."

She told him, "I'm glad I met Don *[i.e., Siegel].* Before coming here, I had not had sex with a man for several months. I was hot and hungry."

During the filming of *Night Unto Night,* Reagan, along with most of the other cast members, had to ride a bus through the gates at Warners in Burbank, where picket lines had formed. Rocks and bottles were thrown at the windows of their bus.

Both Stevens and DeCamp were sympathetic to the strains Reagan endured at the time. "He was dealing with the ugly strike through his position at SAG," DeCamp said. "He was working 18 to 20 hours a day, but he remained cheerful and loquacious when he showed up with three or four hours sleep. In contrast, Jane Wyman was seen out almost every night dancing like a son of a son. Yet the North Hollywood Women's Professional Club named her its 'Ideal Working Mother' for 1946."

Near the end of the film, when the epilepsy of Reagan's character is disclosed, he goes upstairs to commit suicide with a revolver. This is his big scene with Lindfors. He tells her, "Death isn't the worst thing in a man's life—it's only the last."

She counters, "I don't know the reason for death, but I do know that life has its own reasons—and it isn't ours to end."

Before the end of the film, she convinces him not to shoot himself.

In that, the movie's plot is different from that within Wylie's novel. In the book, John kills himself by deliberately walking into the path of an oncoming truck.

In a memoir, Reagan wrote, "If you think this was a hard story to bring to life on the screen, you're right."

Shooting the various scenes of *Night Unto Night* ended on December 29, 1946. Reagan remembered Christmas Eve on the set. "Eggnog was served and by two o'clock that afternoon, we were drunk. We needed the sun, but got threatening gray skies. I went home to the most depressing Christmas of my life." As predicted, *Night Unto Night* was an utter flop. One reviewer asserted that, "Jack Warner should have left it collecting dust in some archive." Another reviewer, in pointing out the inadequacies of Reagan's performance, asked, "Where is John Garfield, even Dane Clark, now that we need him?"

***

After viewing the drab and uncompelling *Night Unto Night,* which, based on his orders had been shelved for years, Jack Warner decided to co-star Reagan and Viveca Lindfors in yet another movie together, a casting choice he never explained. He summoned Reagan to his office: "I have this important new film I want you to make with Viveca and Claude Rains. It's called *Up Till Now,* and in it, you play a communist."

"At first, I thought he was joking," Reagan recalled. "Then I realized he was serious."

"Me, a communist?" Reagan asked Warner in astonishment. "In case you don't know, there's a Red scare on. Do you want me to get blacklisted?"

"Read the script tonight and you'll understand why I want to make this movie, particularly right now when all of us are under investigation from Washington."

That night in his library, Reagan studied the script by David Goodies, who had just signed a six-year contract with Warner Brothers to develop screen treatments. The credibility he was currently enjoyed was based on the successful transition of his novel, *Dark Passage,* into a movie co-starring Humphrey Bogart and Lauren Bacall. *[Released in 1947, it had been marketed with the tagline: TOGETHER AGAIN: BOGART AND BACALL—IN DANGER AS VIOLENT AS THEIR LOVE.]*

In *Up Till Now,* Claude Rains would be cast as a puzzled father of two sons, one of whom (Reagan) becomes a communist, and another (possibly Arthur Kennedy), a fascist.

Lindfors would play a naturalized American citizen who explains the value of democracy to the politically errant brothers. Her conversations would, before the end of the film, persuade each of them to repudiate their former political convictions.

Warner told Reagan, "You see, with this film, I can go before HUAC and repudiate communism and present myself as a defender of democracy, attacking evil communism. In the HUAC witch hunt in Hollywood, I don't want them to catch me flying a broom."

Actually, even though the movie had not been made, weeks later, Warner appeared before HUAC and cited *Up Till Now* as testimonial to his commitment to the propaganda war against the communists.

"The film will star Ronald Reagan, the truest American and the most anti-communist in all of Hollywood. With the help of its producer, Jerry Wald, *Up Till Now* will show us battling un-American ideologies. It will unmask Reds in the film industry and expose our foreign enemies. Democracy has no middle lanes, left detours, or right alleys—only the great big highway of American Liberty, sufficiently broad and straight for all to travel in peace."

Back in Hollywood, Reagan met with Goodies, finding that he was currently rewriting a script based on W. Somerset Maugham's *The Letter,* which in 1940 had been one of Bette Davis' most memorable movies. The new treatment was to be entitled *The Unfaithful.*

Goodis told Reagan that he'd written *Up Till Now* "to give people a look at themselves and their American heritage." In his own words, Goodis was "mesmerized to meet a bigtime movie star like you."

Reagan later told Wald, "That Goodis fellow practically was foaming at the mouth. It seems he worships my screen image. He wanted to date me. Imagine!"

A few weeks later, without explanation, Warner abruptly canceled *Up Till Now.*

As late as 1957, Goodis still harbored a crush on Reagan. He got in touch with him and asked him to play the male lead opposite Jayne Mansfield in an upcoming film, *The Burglar.* Reagan rejected the film role, just as he had turned down the author's sexual advances. Dan Duryea was cast as the male lead instead. Today, *The Burglar* (1957) reigns as a *film noir* classic, one of the greatest heist films ever made.

Instead of *The Burglar,* Reagan accepted the lead in *Hellcats of the Navy* opposite his wife, the former starlet Nancy Davis.

As Nathan J. Juran, the director of *Hellcats of the Navy,* later said, "Ronnie could have been making love, at least on screen, with Jayne Mansfield. Instead, he ends up with Nancy. I hope they have some off-screen chemistry. They sure didn't have any on screen in our turkey of a movie."

***

Meeting in a closed door session at the Waldorf Astoria in New York, the Motion Picture Association of America released on December 3, 1947, what became notorious as "the Waldorf Statement." In a two-page press release, studio moguls ranging from MGM's Louis B. Mayer to Columbia's Harry Cohn, attacked the "Hollywood Ten," a group of writers and directors, each of whom was facing a jail term for contempt of Congress.

Although Reagan initially had reservations about the Blacklist, knowing what harm in could cause, particularly to innocent people, he ultimately endorsed it as a necessary evil.

In a speech to SAG, Reagan lauded its members "for doing more than any other union in America to rid itself of communists" He went on to vilify producers who still hired suspected communists.

[By 1953, Reagan got what he wanted: SAG adopted a bylaw that barred communists and required new members to swear loyalty oaths.

A cynical Melvyn Douglas was still bruised from the beating which his wife, Helen Gahagan, had experienced in recent Senatorial elections at the hand of Reagan's ally in the suppression of pinkos, Richard Nixon. Douglas later commented on that: "Reagan was hardly the family values man he appeared to be. He was seducing practically every virgin in Hollywood. Before he banged them, he did not, so I heard, require them to sign a loyalty oath."]

***

Some observers defined it as "Love on the rebound." With the understanding that Jane Wyman was spending her nights in the arms of Lew Ayres, two shapely blondes were about to enter Reagan's life.

At the end of the war, Reagan and William Holden bonded as never before. Each of them turned to the other for emotional support. In many ways, Holden replaced Robert Taylor, George Murphy, and Dick Powell as Reagan's closest comrade.

In 1941, Holden had married an attractive divorced woman, actress Brenda Marshall, whose real name was Ardis Ankerson. On May 2, 1946, the couple gave birth to Scott Porter Holden.

As Holden admitted, "I was never much of a family man." He spent many nights

489

away from home, often out with Reagan as his drinking companion. When the two men walked into Ciro's on many a night, all that the waiter had to ask was, "The usual?"

In addition to their respective family problems, both of them were worried about their careers. Holden would listen sympathetically to Reagan's woes about Jane and the movies he'd been assigned, before pouring out plenty of his own pain. He admitted to Reagan, "I've hit rock bottom. I'm almost thirty and a wreck—a second-class actor in Hollywood with little hope of longevity. I'm getting shit wages, just enough to feed my family and perhaps pay my liquor bill. On most nights, I stick you with the tab, since you're drawing bigger bucks."

Holden invited Reagan to pick him up after a day's shoot at the set of his latest movie, *The Dark Past* (1948), co-starring Lee J. Cobb, Adele Jergens, and Nina Foch. It was a remake of the 1939 *Blind Alley.* As the star of this psychological thriller, Holden played an escaped convict, convicted killer, and dream-shackled gunman, who hides out with his gang in the isolated home of a psychiatrist, whose family and guests he holds hostage.

"When I joined him on the set, Bill's biggest complaint was the flat-top haircut which the film's director, Rudolph Maté, ordered him to get," Reagan said. "Bill hated it. That man was fastidious about his hair, going to the barber once a week. He told me he didn't want to play a killer, preferring to make Westerns instead. That's what I wanted to do instead of so-called romantic comedies."

It was on the set that Holden introduced Adele Jergens to Reagan. He later said, "I think I fell in love with her the moment I saw her walking across the sound stage toward me. I asked her out that very night for a date."

A "chorus girl blonde," the Brooklyn-born actress accepted. Over dinner at the Brown Derby, he learned about her background. During a stint as a Rockette at Radio City Music Hall in Manhattan, she was named "Number One Showgirl in New York."

She had also worked as a chorus girl at the Brooklyn Fox Theater and as a model for the John Robert Powers Agency. While understudying for the role usually reserved for the stripper Gypsy Rose Lee, in the 1942 stage version of the musical review *Star and Garter,* she filled in for the star one night when Lee was ill. A Columbia talent scout had chosen that particular evening to attend. His "discovery" of Jergens eventually led to a movie contract in 1944. During the months to come, she was cast opposite Rita Hayworth in *Tonight and Every Night* (1945).

In the final years of World War II, Jergens became one of the most popular pinup girls among G.I.s, rivaled only by Betty Grable and Rita Hayworth, both of whom viewed her as formidable competition.

In films, Jergens was often cast as either a blonde floozie or as a burlesque dancer. After Reagan began taking her out. Holden noted that their romance was taking a serious turn.

At the 1939 World's Fair in New York, a beautiful blonde, Adele Jergens, was voted "The Fairest of the Fair." In Hollywood, her publicists began calling her "The Girl with the Million Dollar Legs," which "seriously pissed off" Betty Grable, the holder of that title.

Subsequently, Columbia redefined Jergens as "The Champagne Blonde." When William Holden introduced her to Reagan, he admitted, "I fell in love."

One night, Reagan proposed marriage to her, and she accepted, with the understanding that they'd marry as soon as his divorce was finalized. She had never been married. Since it would not be proper for her to wear an engagement ring, as he was still wed to Jane at the time, he gave her a diamond bracelet instead. He even purchased a mink coat to go with it.

A jealous Evelyn Keyes claimed, "Jergens knew how to get ahead at Columbia. She slept with Harry Cohn, who had the hots for her. At one time, she was fucking both Ronald Reagan and Cohn."

Jergens was often seen out on the town with both Holden and Reagan. At first, Hollywood gossips assumed that Reagan was merely "The Beard," concealing the adulterous relationship Holden was having with his co-star. When Holden, Jergens, and Reagan were spotted one morning leaving his Londonderry apartment at 5AM, each of them dressed for work, word spread that the "chorus girl cutie" was having a three-way with both actors.

At this point, Jergens developed a friendship with Virginia Mayo, who, ironically, was set to co-star in *The Girl from Jones Beach* with Reagan.

In her home in Thousand Oaks, California, in 2004, shortly before her death, Mayo told author Darwin Porter, "Adele and I had many talks about Reagan. She told me that he was a "real gentleman, and he bestowed many gifts on her."

"I think I'm helping him recover from the loss of Jane," Jergens confessed to Mayo. "I think he's rushing too soon into another marriage, although I've already agreed to it. Encouraged by Bill Holden, he's going through a heavy drinking period. Even when drunk, though, Ronnie is still a gentleman, unlike Bill. When he's stinking drunk, Bill becomes a monster and sometimes hurts me. He gets very rough."

Mayo asked Jergens if the rumors about a three-way with Holden and Reagan were true.

"Adele was evasive, but I read between the lines," Mayo recalled.

Jergens told her, "I won't go into that, but I will tell you this: Bill and Ronnie are the two cleanest actors in Hollywood. I once came over to Ronnie's apartment. He'd given me the key, and I planned to meet him there later. In the living room, I poured myself a drink. I heard all this laughter coming from the shower. At first, I thought Ronnie had brought home another woman. It turned out to be Bill. Both of them came out of the shower a little later, with their bodies wrapped in towels. If you ask me, you must know, both of them smelled like a bar of soap. But they always did. I think each of them took at least four showers a day, unlike some actors, who managed to get under the water only two or three times a week, if that."

When Reagan was starring in *The Girl From Jones Beach (1949)* with Vir-

Too Many Blondes?

Adele Jergens, *(left)*, with Marilyn Monroe, her ferociously competitive co-performer in *Ladies of the Chorus*. As it happened, Reagan got involved with each of them at the same time.

491

ginia Mayo, Adele Jergens was filming *Ladies of the Chorus* (1948), at Columbia. Cast as a chorus girl, she starred opposite Marilyn Monroe in her first significant film role. The two actresses played mother and daughter, even though Jergens was only nine years older than Marilyn.

Reagan remembered that he had once met Marilyn at a photo shoot. He greeted the director, Phil Karlson, who welcomed him to the set. In the early 1950s, he would direct John Payne, Jane Wyman's former lover, in three movies, eventually helming Elvis Presley in *Kid Galahad* (1962).

Karlson liked Reagan and invited him to watch Marilyn do her big number—"Every Baby Needs a Da Da Daddy."

"I could tell that Reagan was mesmerized by Marilyn," Karlson said. "His eyes practically bulged. He told me that he felt Marilyn was heading for big stardom. Frankly, I think she gave him a hard-on. Fortunately, Adele was nowhere around. She would have been jealous."

At the end of the number, which she did in one take, Marilyn ran over to Reagan. She gave him a wet kiss on the lips. "We've met before. Don't you remember?"

"Who could forget you, kid," he said. "You were sensational."

"I'm even more sensational when you get to know me," she claimed.

Before Jergens appeared on the set, Karlson noticed that Marilyn slipped Reagan her phone number. "Come up and see me sometime, big guy," she said, imitating Mae West.

"I knew from that moment that Adele had some serious competition." Karlson claimed.

***

Lauren Bacall, backed up by Humphrey Bogart, announced that she was willing to risk suspension by refusing to appear in *The Girl from Jones Beach*. As she told friends privately, "My main objection would be having to appear in such a revealing white bathing suit."

"It was the second Ronald Reagan picture I turned down," Bacall said. "Both Bogie and I had refused to appear with him in *Stallion Road."*

The lead female role in *The Girl from Jones Beach*, a fluffy romantic comedy, went to the blonde bombshell, Virginia Mayo, to be directed by Peter Godfrey, who had previously helmed Reagan in that abject disaster, *That Hagen Girl.*

After reading the script, Reagan objected to his role, telling Jack Warner that he didn't want to do it. "I see myself sitting tall in a saddle for the camera—you know, like John Wayne or Gary Cooper. Are you, by any chance, sitting on a script like Frank Capra's *Mr. Smith Goes to Washington?* Look what it did for Jimmy Stewart."

"You're doing that *Jones Beach* thing or else," Warner warned him. "Just today, I put Bacall on suspension for refusing to play the female lead."

Reagan himself knew that it was a role that called for Cary Grant. In fact, when the movie was released, one reviewer claimed, "Cary Grant could have phoned in Reagan's role."

Reagan described his role as that "of a modern painter of the *Vargas* or *Petty Girl* type. Eddie Bracken played my sidekick. The plot called for me to romance a dozen or so gorgeous models."

In the plot, Reagan played Bob Randolph, who, as an illustrator, has drawn the perfect model, "The Randolph Girl." Bracken is hired by television producers to find the real life Randolph Girl. But Reagan, as Randolph, loudly asserts that the beautiful girl in his illustration had been inspired by a composite of a dozen or so models.

Eventually, the search leads to Ruth Wilson (Mayo), who looks like the living image of the illustrated version of the Randolph Girl. When the character played by Reagan learns that, he changes his name to Robert Venerik, claiming that he is a Czech immigrant who knows very little English. That allows him to enroll in a class where Ruth teaches English "as a second language" to new arrivals. From that point on, the plot leads to its inevitable, somewhat contrived, conclusion. The viewer easily surmises, based on dozens of clues and signals, that Reagan and Mayo will, before the film's end, fall in love.

Jones Beach: Lotsa Girls, Lotsa Flesh, Lotsa Fun.

Left to right: Ronald Reagan, Virginia Mayo, Eddie Bracken, and Donna Drake.

Mayo recalled the late morning when she had to make her first appearance in a skimpy white bathing suit. "The bathing suit is the most unfriendly garment in the wardrobe department. A girl can't keep a secret in a bathing suit."

Summoning her courage, she put on the bathing suit and walked outside her dressing room door. Reagan was waiting there for her. "He gave out a wolf whistle that could be heard in Chicago," she said. "I loved it! He restored my confidence."

He later said, "That bathing suit on Virginia would have raised the dead. The film we were making wasn't much, but Virginia's white thighs would guarantee box office."

Reagan later wrote that at one point, "Eddie Bracken got so goggle-eyed over the beauties in the film—not just Virginia—that he stepped on my heels and tripped me. It cracked my coccyx. It was my first experience with the pain of a broken bone. Unfortunately, it would not be my last."

Reagan gets *The Girl from Jones Beach*. "Mayo They Be Happy Forever."

Godfrey had to shoot around Reagan until he recovered, which caused the picture to run over budget.

Jane Wyman had taken the children, Maureen and Michael, for a holiday in Hawaii. She turned her house over to him, since she had a live-in staff there, who would take care of him during his convalescence.

One afternoon, Bracken visited Reagan. "I was filled with apologies for causing the accident. As I was heading into his bedroom, a beautiful young blonde emerged," Bracken said. "She flashed a smile at me and quickly left. After her face registered with my brain, I realized that it was that new girl, Marilyn Monroe, who had just come from Ronnie's bedroom. She was getting a hell of a lot of publicity, and I just knew it was Marilyn."

In the next room, Bracken faced Reagan who, despite being bedridden, had a smile on his face.

"That blonde," Bracken said. "That was Marilyn Monroe!"

"One and the same, but let's keep that as our little secret."

"My lips are sealed," Bracken responded.

"Thank god Marilyn's weren't," he quipped.

"For three seconds, I didn't get it, until the light dawned," Bracken said. "Marilyn had given him a blow-job, so that he wouldn't have to exert his back."

"Ronnie looked at my face as I was registering what had happened. He quickly picked up on it."

"You catch on quick, you dumb bone-crusher," Reagan said. "look what you've done to me, you fart!"

"Lying flat on your back obviously has its rewards," Bracken said.

"But Marilyn and I are going to have to delay 'number two' until my back heals, thanks to you."

***

[Film historians and movie trivia buffs have long speculated about what prompted Adele Jergens to break off her engagement to Ronald Reagan. Virginia Mayo provided the answer."Adele found out that Marilyn (Monroe) was slipping behind her back for sex with Ronnie. She called the whole thing off, but she didn't return the mink coat or the diamond bracelet."

Before her death on November 22, 2002, Jergens gave her final interview. At the time, she was living in a retirement community at Camarillo, California.

"If I had played my cards right, I might have become the first actress ever to be First Lady of America. Too bad I let Reagan slip through my fingers over a jealous spat over Marilyn Monroe. I should have forgiven him."

Today, the world, except for dieheard fans, have forgotten the dazzling blonde of the film noir *era.*

Journalist Alan K. Rode summed up her appeal: "Adele Jergens could sing, dance, strut, and act with the best of them. She will always epitomize that bygone era of hard-boiled repartee, sleek fedoras, and sequined, spangled burlesque queens. For better or worse, she was that gorgeous gal that the heavies in movies just had to have along for the ride."]

***

Reagan had serious misgivings when it was announced that he was going to co-star with Ida Lupino in a movie called *Woman in Hiding,* to be shot during the late summer of 1949.

This was to be his first picture under a new deal Wasserman had arranged with Jack Warner. Reagan still had three years to go under his contract with Warner Brothers. Under the revisions arranged for him by Wasserman, he would make only one picture a year for Warners for a pre-defined fee of $150,000. He would otherwise be free to work for other studios.

Then Wasserman arranged for yet another contract, this time between Reagan and Universal Studios. In May of 1949, an agreement had been reached that stipulated that Reagan would make five pictures for Universal over a five-year period for a salary of $75,000 per picture.

On the surface, he had maintained an uneasy friendship with Lupino, "except she

494

leans too far to the left for my tastes."

"If Lupino is not an actual Red, she's at least a deep magenta," he told William Holden.

Apparently, at the time they were scheduled to make a movie together, Lupino had not yet learned that Reagan was filing reports about her political activities with the FBI.

Twice before, he had been slated at Warners to co-star with Lupino, in both *Kings Row* and *Juke Girl,* but in each instance, she had gone on suspension rather than accept parts she disliked.

On the Saturday before shooting was scheduled to begin the following Monday, Reagan agreed to play in a for-charity baseball game for the benefit of the City of Hope Hospital. Some of the town's leading male actors were teamed against an opposing group composed of film comedians.

Before the end of the first inning, Reagan, after hitting the ground during a play, screamed out in excruciating pain.

Rushed to the hospital in an ambulance, he learned the bad news. He would not be shooting with Lupino (or with anyone, for that matter) on Monday. "My leg was sheathed in layers of tape and moleskin, with straps from these mummy wrapping hitched to a thirty-five pound weight by means of a pulley," he wrote in a memoir. "Twenty-four hours later, my eyes were swollen shut, my teeth hurt at even the touch of a tongue, and I itched and peeled all over. I was allergic to the wrappings. For more than a week, the massive histamine doses kept me only semi-conscious; then I settled down to weeks of discomfort because there was no removing the bandages."

An X-ray had shown that he had broken his right thigh bone in six different places. His hospitalization lasted for seven weeks. After that, he still would not be fully recovered. "Months in a cast was followed by a steel-and-leather brace, and that was followed by crutches. At long last, I was able to hobble around on a cane."

Initially, when Jane Wyman was in London shooting *Stage Fright*, she lent Reagan access to the home they used to share but which now, thanks to their divorce settlement, she occupied. There was a staff on site to take care of him. When she returned from England, Reagan was moved to the home of his mother. There, Nelle waited on him day and night at the house he had purchased for her on Phyllis Avenue. She was in her late sixties and ailing, but drove over to the Farmers' Market every day in her old Studebaker to buy fresh fruit and groceries for him.

"I cooked all his favorite foods and tended to him like the baby boy I had long ago given birth to," she recalled. "When he could walk again and take care of himself, he moved out. I cried all that day and half the night. I didn't want him to leave, but to stay with me."

Directed by Michael Gordon, *Woman in Hiding* went into production on schedule. The director arranged for actor Howard Duff, fresh from an affair with Ava Gardner, to replace Reagan as the male lead.

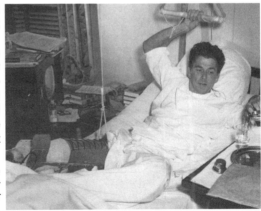

Reagan recovers from a shattered thighbone after a charity baseball game. Marilyn came to give him "lip service."

495

Lupino objected to the handsome replacement when she met him. "I don't like him," she told Gordon.

Apparently, she changed her mind. One night, Duff seduced her, and she later married him.

Months later, Reagan encountered Duff at a party. "Thank you for breaking your leg. Ida was against me until she succumbed to my masculine charm."

Years later, by the time Reagan ran for Governor of California, Lupino still retained her negative impressions: "I blamed the bastard for deserting the Democrats," she claimed.

***

During his long periods of convalescence, Reagan could count on only one visitor, Marilyn Monroe. As he told William Holden, "I never knew when she would show up. For the most part, she was always in a hurry, perhaps going off on another date. She was one busy girl, but she knew I needed sex. I was flat on my back, but I could count on her to give me lip service. That brought me some sexual relief. My back and leg might not be in working order, but at least one part of my plumbing was still satisfactory. Marilyn's a great gal. You should date her sometime, Bill. Just don't let your wife know."

During World War II, Captain Ronald Reagan was stationed in California, handling PR for the Army. In that capacity, Captain Reagan ordered his staff photographer, Private David Conover, to visit a local factory to take pictures of women on the homefront who were turning out aircraft, munitions, and parachutes. These morale-boosting photos of pretty girls contributing to the war effort were for publication in *Yank* magazine.

One of the girls he photographed that day was Norma Jeane. She could hardly know at the time that she'd eventually have an affair with Private Conover's commanding officer – or that the officer would become, long after her own death, the President of the United States. Conover later claimed that the eyes of Norma Jeane "held something that touched and intrigued me. She should be a movie star."

After lunch, he requested that she change into a red sweater, and he took more pictures of her in which her breasts were more prominent. When Conover came into the office of his boss (Reagan) a week later, he noticed that he'd pinned up that picture of Norma Jeane. Reagan said, "This young lady, not Lana Turner, should be called The Sweater Girl."

Holden, among others, including Dick Powell and June Allyson, believed that Marilyn viewed Reagan as a father figure more than a lover. "She was going through a rough period in her life," Allyson recalled. "Even though he was incapacitated, Ronnie was that shoulder for her to lean on."

Sometimes, Marilyn didn't seem so rushed, and she'd spend hours with Reagan in his Londonderry apartment during his long recuperation.

She related to Reagan that originally, Harry Cohn had held out such promises to her, even admitting that he'd put her on the casting couch. "He told me he was looking for a backup for Rita Hayworth, with whom he was having a lot of trouble," Marilyn said. She even shared some of her secrets with Reagan, including that her hairline had been lifted through electrolysis, with the intention of highlighting her widow's peak.

On one visit, she shocked him. "I thought you were my old girlfriend, Lana Turner. You look just like her."

"Only younger," Marilyn said. "I am the *new* Lana Turner, made up to look just like her."

One afternoon, she arrived heartbroken and fell into his arms. "Cohn has let me go from Columbia. His promises are shit."

"You know what Cohn's final words to me were?" she asked Reagan. "He called me a 'goddamn cunt' and told me he never wanted to see me on the Columbia lot ever again."

When Reagan had met her on the set of *Ladies of the Chorus* (1948), Marilyn had told him that the picture with Adele Jergens was going to be a big hit. It wasn't—in fact, it flopped at the box office.

She revealed that she had studied and "worked so very, very hard" for the part. At one point, she'd gone to a seedy burlesque theater in downtown Los Angeles. Billing herself as "Mona Monroe," she'd stripped for the men. She later said, "I heard from one of the ushers that whenever I came on, the men placed their coats over their genitals to do their business in the dark."

She even went to see a performance by the elegant Lili St. Cyr. This tall, buxom, and statuesque blonde brought glamour, almost a sense of refinement, to the art of striptease. Marilyn visited her performance every night and met her backstage. What she didn't tell Reagan was that she had a lesbian affair with St. Cyr.

While at Columbia, Marilyn had fallen in love with her strikingly handsome voice coach, Fred Karger, who conducted his own band. What she didn't know, but would soon find out, Karger had another woman competing for his love-making. The competition was formidable: Jane Wyman.

During her chats with Reagan, Marilyn apparently left out many details of her life. She presented only limited but often tantalizing facts about her past. She didn't tell him about her lesbian affairs, because she knew he wouldn't understand such things.

As author Michael John Sullivan once wrote in his book, *Presidential Passions,* "Reagan's understanding of sexuality was exceedingly simplistic: For him, sex was either black or white so that sexual feelings of a highly complex or conflicting nature were both threatening and incomprehensible. The inflexibility of his narrow sexual sensibilities is perhaps best seen in his unchanging attitude toward homosexuality. Working in a business that is home to a very high percentage of gays and bisexuals, he remained intimidated by the prospect of sexual diversity."

In contrast, Marilyn understood.

In addition to St. Cyr, Marilyn was also engaged in a lesbian liaison with Natasha Lytess, her drama coach at Columbia.

Marilyn had to carry around a datebook to keep abreast of her affairs, which included Karger, but also actor John Carroll and even producer Joe Schenck.

When Reagan saw a picture in *Variety* of Marilyn on a date with Pat DiCicco at the Cocoanut Grove, he warned her about this hustler, who had been married to Thelma Todd (murdered) and Gloria Vanderbilt (beaten).

It was through Reagan that Marilyn once met Holden, who was scheduled to appear in *Born Yesterday* at Columbia.

Over drinks with Holden and Reagan, Marilyn said, "You two butch numbers are excepted, but I find that most male actors are 'pansies,' because acting is a feminine art. When a man has to paint his face and pose and strut and pretend emotions, he isn't doing what is normally masculine."

"Hello, fellow pansy," Holden said to Reagan. "To prove my masculinity, I'm going out to fuck every starlet in Hollywood."

Holden seemed enchanted with Marilyn—in fact, he left Reagan's apartment that night, promising to drive her home.

When she visited Reagan again, during a discussion about Holden, she said, "Through Bill, I've discovered the dumb blonde role that will make me one of the biggest stars in Hollywood. In *Born Yesterday,* I'll play Billie Dawn, a great role. Bill thinks I'm perfect for it. He's going behind Cohn's back and arranging a test for me at Columbia. He thinks the test will convince Cohn to give me another chance."

One rainy afternoon, Marilyn arrived at Reagan's apartment, her eyes red from crying. She said that the designer, Oleg Cassini, had made a gown for her, and had presented it to her as a gift. "I returned the favor," she said.

In her gown, she attended a party at the home shared by Cassini and his wife, Gene Tierney. "The bitch threw me out the door the moment I came into the foyer," Marilyn claimed. "In front of everybody, she exploded in fury. Her exact words, and she shouted them loud enough for everybody to hear, were, 'How could you invite this tramp? She's a nothing!'"

Reagan offered her what comfort he could, and then, in return, she offered him her own kind of comfort.

Four days later, Marilyn was back in Reagan's apartment, this time telling him the bad news. Harry Cohn had refused to look at her test for Billie Dawn in *Born Yesterday.* "I won't tell you what else the bastard said about me."

Somehow, she managed to get herself cast in a cameo role in another movie, *Love Happy,* with the Marx Brothers. She asked Reagan, "Will I have to bed all the Marx Brothers?"

"Probably, but not at the same time," he answered.

That was followed by another role that year in *A Ticket to Tomahawk,* with Dan Dailey and Anne Baxter. She was delighted when the director, Richard Sale, told her, "You can sing and dance better than Betty Grable."

That Saturday, Grable herself arrived at Reagan's apartment with a gift. He hadn't seen her since her marriage to bandleader Harry James.

When June Allyson heard about their reunion, she said, "I'm only guessing, but I don't think they resumed their affair. It was just two old friends getting together to talk about their early days in Hollywood, trying to climb rungs of the ladder to stardom."

Reagan was very saddened to hear news over the radio on July 5, 1948, that Carole Landis—another blonde he'd known from his early Hollywood years—had overdosed on sleeping pills and died. It was reported that she had been despondent over the breakup of her affair with Rex Harrison.

Allyson admitted to her friends, Peter Lawford and Van Johnson, that she, too, had had a brief fling with Reagan when he came to visit her one afternoon. "He was still walking on crutches at the time. I was the one who had to seduce Ronnie. It was just a two-week fling. I was mad at Richard *[a reference to her husband at the time, Dick Powell]* at the time. Ronnie was between marriages. Nothing came of it. We remained friends."

Years later, she told Johnson, "Could you imagine? I'm one of the few women in Hollywood like Marilyn Monroe, who seduced two U.S. presidents. Although I had John F. Kennedy before Marilyn, in her case, she had Ronnie before I did."

At one point, Reagan flew Marilyn to Miami Beach. He checked into a suite at the Roney Plaza, booking her into the more modest Helen Mar Hotel, a few blocks away.

During their time together, he took her for three nights in a row to hear his favorite entertainer, Sophie Tucker, billed as "the Last of the Red Hot Mommas." She was appearing in a sold-out revue at the Beachcomber.

To end each show before the essentially Jewish audience, she sang, "*Yiddische Momme.*" For some reason, this was Reagan's favorite, although he was the least Jewish person in the night club.

Sophie also invited Reagan and Marilyn to her big birthday bash on February 9,

1950. In 1887, she had been born in the Ukraine, which had been ruled during that era by Czarist Russia. A crowd of celebrities flew in from around the country, including Al Jolson, Eddie Cantor, George Burns, and Joe E. Lewis, along with newer comedians who included Jerry Lewis and Dean Martin. Frances Langford sang.

Reagan was among the honored guests asked to say a few words at the podium. For some reason known only to himself, he called Sophie "the Whistler's Mother of Show Business." He praised her talent and congratulated her for her contribution to charity. "Sophia fled from Czarist Russia to come to our shores seeking the American Dream. That dream has come true for her."

Sophie closed her birthday gala by singing her signature song, "Some of These Days."

Backstage, as a farewell, Reagan and Sophie lip-kissed. After that, Sophie kissed Marilyn, revealing to Reagan in a broad aside, "My advice, Ronnie, is to marry this sweet little sugartit. Make an honest woman of her. Take the word of the Last of the Red Hot Mommas."

During their final dinner together on Miami Beach, Reagan told Marilyn that he'd booked her aboard a plane separate from his own flight as a means of discreetly hauling her back to Los Angeles. "It's been fun," he said, "but it's over now. Someone else has moved into my life."

"So, it's just one of those things," she said, appearing on the verge of tears. She never could stand rejection.

Back in Los Angeles, she waited two weeks before showing up on his doorstep again. He welcomed her into his apartment.

"We did our thing," she later said. "But there was never any commitment, any definition of our relationship, or whether it had come to an end. It did, eventually, of course, but I ended it...Not him! Do I know men?"

Nightclub entertainer Sophie Tucker: "Ronnie got it all wrong. What in hell did I have to do with Whistler's Mother?"

Marilyn Monroe: The last of the Red Hot Mommas urged Reagan "to make an honest woman out of her. Marry her and to hell with Jane Wyman."

***

Mobile again, no longer walking with a cane, Reagan launched one of his most serious romances, one within a series of "between marriages affairs," this time with gossip and entertainment columnist Doris Lilly. Cindy Adams, the *New York Post* columnist, once wrote, "Doris was never fond of poverty. She was meeting rich people when the rest of us were in camel's hair. She received a prized sable coat from a male admirer, who was a little bit married."

"If it were true that money grew on trees, all my friends would be married to apes,"

499

Lilly said. For years, she wrote a popular gossip column for the *New York Post.* Later, she admitted that her column was sometimes "silly," and that the people she wrote about were often "shallow." But they're pleasant and they smell good and they eat well and drink good wines—and that's all right."

Even as a young contract actress working for Cecil B. DeMille, Lilly had an eye for people already established, but also for up-and-coming millionaires. She sensed that Reagan, although a "failed actor" (her words) when she began to date him, was "really going places one day, perhaps in a field different from the movies."

Lilly told author Kitty Kelley that Reagan "liked the big, outdoor blonde, Pasadena Rose Bowl Parade queen type of California woman. I know, because I was one of them. Whenever they were in town, we went to see George Jessel or Sophie Tucker, his favorite entertainers. We went ice skating in Westwood by the old veterans' home. I listened to all his stories and his endless rants about politics. We were often separated on different coasts. Sometimes the references in his letters were sexual."

Columnist Doris Lilly was a social butterfly whom Reagan called "My Gilded Lily" as she flitted from millionaire to millionaire.

On April 28, 1948, in a letter he wrote to her, he said, "I'd like to be tossing off a 'short one' with you."

One Sunday morning, when she called him, and after a few minutes of dialogue, she accused him of having "another blonde in bed with you."

He later sent her a note. "Your call interrupted no Sunday matinee (*d--n it*: I was just fogged over and sleepy.")

He never wrote out the words "damn" or "hell." They were always abbreviated to "d—n" or "h—l."

On their dates, he was still driving that turquoise Cadillac, that birthday gift from Jane Wyman before their divorce.

"Reagan and I had a delightful little romance in 1948," Lilly claimed. "Intimately, he was nothing memorable, but he was an appealing-looking guy who was very, very sweet. I hate to say that he was weak—maybe a nicer word would be 'passive.' He loved to go out and be seen at all the nightclubs in Hollywood in those days, and he loved to drink, but was never a drunk. He was a very gentle, very square, very hayseed type of man."

She later denied that she had ever admitted to an intimate relationship with Reagan. "I don't talk about sex. That's not my generation." However, it was well known among Reagan's friends that Lilly often indulged in a sleepover with Reagan, leaving before dawn. William Holden and Reagan's best male friends were aware of the relationship, because he talked privately about his plans to marry her. He confessed to Holden and others, "The sex was great." Obviously, based on what she later said, it was greater for Reagan than it was for Lilly.

Years later, she recalled that one night, Reagan was filled with total despair, "I just can't get it right," he told her. Reportedly, he was almost sobbing. "I'm no good alone. I need someone to share my life, and Doris, you are that someone."

She said, "What I knew for sure was that he didn't love me, and I didn't love him. I could have had him if I'd wanted him. If I was willing to make the big moves, push, be there, encourage him, never leave him alone for a moment. He would never leave me if I made him think it would be wrong to do so. Those soft, vulnerable eyes staring into mine. I couldn't do it *[i.e., marry him]*. I would only bring him more misery later on. I let the moment go."

"But the day was saved," Lilly said. "Along came Nancy to save his soul."

In 1951, after she broke up with Reagan, Lilly's tongue-in-cheek novel, *How to Marry a Millionaire* was published by Putnam. Ironically, its 1953 adaptation into a film became one of the most popular movies Marilyn Monroe ever made.

Lilly later wrote a sequel, *How to Marry a Billionaire* (Delacorte, 1984). "A million dollars isn't much money these days. You can't even get a decent house for that."

Lilly is also said to have been the inspiration for the Holly Golightly character in Truman Capote's novella, *Breakfast at Tiffany's,* which evolved, in 1961, into a movie hit starring Audrey Hepburn. *[Capote had wanted Marilyn Monroe to interpret the role. Other women, not just Lilly, also claimed to have been the inspiration for Holly.]*

Lilly said, "There was a lot of wondering about who was the original Holly Golightly. Pamela Drake and I were living in this brownstone walk-up on East 78th Street, exactly the one in *Breakfast at Tiffany's*. Exactly. Truman used to come over all the time to watch me put on my makeup before I went out. There's an awful lot of me in Holly Golightly."

Lilly later said, "After me, I don't think Ronnie went out with anyone on a very serious basis. He was a new bachelor with a roving eye. From what I heard, he took out a girl only once or twice before dumping her. Some of his affairs lasted a whole week."

When Reagan became President, Lilly sold two of the love letters he'd written to her for $4,400. Financier Malcolm Forbes purchased them and presented them as a gift to Nancy Reagan. He waited until Reagan left office so that she would not have to declare them as gifts.

Lilly was furious when she heard what Forbes had done. "That bitch *[a reference to Nancy]* is so jealous of any other woman who knew Ronnie that she'll probably destroy the letters so that future generations won't know there was anyone else but her in his life. It's a damn shame that Malcolm gave them to her, because those letters should be preserved as part of history."

***

Perhaps out of friendship with Reagan, both Hedda Hopper and Louella Parsons rarely reported on his post-Wyman romances. However, columnist Sidney Skolsky ran many a juicy tidbit, detailing a number of affairs of the women in his life, including Adele Jergens, Monica Lewis, Patricia Neal, and Nancy Davis, whom he referred to as "a pretty model."

Connie Wald, who had been married to Jerry Wald, a close friend of Reagan, recalled that period of his life "between marriages."

"His career was going downhill, and he was drifting from the bed of one beautiful young woman to another. I must say, the girls really went for him. He had his pick of Hollywood beauties. He was so sweet and nice, and he still had his good looks. Yet he was a very private man. He didn't want anyone to look inside. He was never really serious about anyone until Nancy Davis came along, and even she had a hard time nailing him. She faced stiff competition from half the dames in Hollywood. Many a starlet was anxious to become the second Mrs. Ronald Reagan, president of the Screen Actors Guild."

Even the fan magazines picked up on Reagan, the new "Hollywood swinger." *Sil-*

ver Screen wrote, "Never thought we'd come right out and call Ronald Reagan a 'wolf,' but let us face it. Suddenly, every glamour gal considers him a super-sexy escort for the evening. He admits he's missed a lot of fun and is out to make up for it. Some say that the torch of Jane Wyman has finally been reduced to a feeble flame."

***

Sometimes, Reagan double dated with other married couples, particularly Robert Taylor and Barbara Stanwyck, who were having their own marital troubles. They would divorce in 1951. One night, Reagan was spotted with starlet Kay Stewart, whom he called "My Yellow Rose of Texas.

Stewart and Reagan often talked about how they got started in Hollywood in the late 1930s. She had a brief appearance in Ernst Lubitsch's 1939 *Ninotchka,* and she had worked with Preston Sturges in his comedies. Reagan said, "Kay had never really had a chance to show off her talent."

Reagan claimed his hot date, Kay Stewart, had "Betty Grable legs and Betty's blonde hair, although in this picture she had reverted to her natural "wren brown."

Both Stewart and Reagan were recovering from recent divorces. She had been married to Langdon William Proctor.

Reagan told Stanwyck, "Kay wants to be as big a movie star as you are."

Stanwyck shot back, "As if that were possible."

Actually, Stewart went on to garner nearly a hundred credits, mostly in TV series, such as *Charlie's Angels, Baretta, Medical Story,* and *The Doris Day Show.*

"My romance with Kay ended before it really began," Reagan told Taylor. "She's looking for another husband, and it isn't going to be me."

***

Penny Edwards had a small role in *That Hagen Girl* with Reagan and Shirley Temple. Three weeks after making that box office failure, he called her for a date, which led to several outings and what was rumored as a prolonged sexual fling.

At the time Reagan met her, she was appearing in *Two Guys from Texas* (1948), with Dennis Morgan and Jack Carson. He quizzed her a lot about Morgan, and she said she knew very little about him, except Jane paid at least five visits to the set to see Morgan. Ed-

Penny Edwards, shown here in full cowgirl drag with Roy Rogers. When the "King of the Cowboys" wasn't in the saddle, Reagan became the horseman.

wards later said, "I think Ronnie suspected something was going on between Dennis and Jane. I felt something was, but I'm not a blabbermouth."

Edwards was blonde and blue-eyed—"just my type," Reagan said.

Stanwyck said, "Ronnie was a gentleman who preferred blondes but married brunettes."

Edwards had appeared in 1943 in *The Ziegfeld Follies* with Milton Berle. "He took my virginity and gave me the wrong impression about men. I had never seen a nude man before, so I just assumed that all of them had a tree truck between their legs. Did I soon learn differently."

Reagan would go for long periods without calling and then suddenly, "in the middle of the night, he'd ring up for a date," she recalled.

He learned that she'd become involved on and off the screen with Roy Rogers, "King of the Cowboys." When his wife, Dale Evans, retired as "Queen of the Cowgirls," Edwards filled in for her, signing on for such pictures as *Sunset in the West* (1950). She told Reagan "You take Roy out of the saddle, and he isn't much, if you get my drift."

"I've heard the same said about John Wayne," Reagan said.

"They can't say that about you, lover boy," Edwards said. "What stamina! What endurance!"

"My thing with Ronnie might have gone somewhere had it not been for my mother," Edwards recalled. "She was a real Bible thumper, a religious zealot. She hated Ronnie, and called him a whoremonger."

He met her a few more times, including as part of a date with her right before he married Nancy Davis. She told him she was making *Pony Soldier* (1952) with Tyrone Power. "Guess what? I'm shot with an arrow, I ride in a burning wagon, I am kidnapped by Indians and thrown from a horse. I have to swim in a raging river, and I'm tied to a flaming stake to be set on fire. Otherwise, there's not much action, certainly not from Ty Power."

He later learned she'd taken up with bisexual Rory Calhoun, with whom both of them had worked on *That Hagen Girl*. But then, she abandoned her film career to join the Seventh Day Adventists. The *Los Angeles Times* headlined the news—PENNY EDWARDS CALLS WHOA TO HOSS OPERAS.

Her retreat was only temporary. In the late 1950s, she returned briefly to film some Westerns. She ended her life making appearances at Western conventions, dressed in cowgirl outfits and signing autographs for members of her dwindling fan base.

***

Reagan's involvement with starlet Peggy Knudsen was so brief it hardly counts. From Duluth, Minnesota, she arrived in Hollywood hoping to break into the movies. As she told Reagan, "I ended up working with two of the biggest bitches in Hollywood, Bette Davis in *A Stolen Life* (1946) and later, that same year, with Joan Crawford in

A veteran infighter of the diva wars: Peggy Knudsen.

Humoresque."

She also appeared with Humphrey Bogart and Lauren Bacall in *The Big Sleep.* "Don't believe all those stories about Bogie being faithful to his wife," Knudsen said.

When she dated Reagan, she had emerged from a divorce from Adrian P. Samish. She finally decided that Reagan wasn't going to marry her, so she went after and won Jim Jordan in 1949.

Reagan never saw her again, but read in *Variety* that she was appearing in *Istanbul* (1957) with Errol Flynn. Reagan had seen Flynn, drunk and extroverted, at a party a few months earlier. "Poor Peggy," he said. "She's getting Errol on his last legs, just before the lid is closed on his coffin."

***

Florida-born Dorothy Shay, known as "The Park Avenue Hillbillie," was another Reagan conquest. As part of her art, she usually dressed like a Park Avenue socialite, but when she opened her mouth, she sounded like a low-end Florida cracker from the Panhandle.

When Reagan met her, she had scored one of her biggest recording hits, "Feudin' and Fightin.'" Her 1947 *The Park Avenue Hillbillie*, rose to number one on Billboard's chart of best-selling popular albums.

Later, Shay worked with Bud Abbott and Lou Costello in the movie, *Comin' Round the Mountain* (1951). "Lou and I used to talk dirty," she said. "Real raunchy stuff. I told him that of all the guys I'd bedded, Ronnie was strictly missionary position. In contrast to him, I did everything. I think my kinky maneuvers turned him off. I don't believe he'd ever experienced any 'rosebud' foreplay. There was a part of him that he wanted to keep very, very private."

Dorothy ("The Park Avenue Hillbillie") Shay.

***

Reagan became intrigued by starlet Eileen Howe after reading about her in the newspapers. For a time in the late 1940s and early 1950s, she was hailed as "the prettiest girl in Hollywood."

In December of 1946, Louella Parsons ran a strange item in her column, claiming, "Eileen Howe is allergic to touch, and can't even hold hands with her boyfriend."

"Where in hell did Louella get that idea?" Reagan later asked after dating Howe.

A former model for the Hartford Agency in New York, Howe became fodder for gossip columnists once she'd arrived in Hollywood. In

Eileen Howe, whose "True Confessions" were promoted on the front page of this French magazine .

May of 1947, Dorothy Kilgallen claimed, "Gilbert Roland, once Constance Bennett's husband, is wooing Eileen Howe."

As a starlet in Hollywood, she was secretly dating Lew Ayres, who otherwise was expressing "undying love" for Jane Wyman.

Howe's date book was filled with suitors who included Jimmy Van Heusen, Errol Flynn, Dean Martin, and movie Tarzan Lex Barker.

Like those men, Reagan was drawn to her measurements of 35-23-35. She had to work Reagan in between calls from Howard Hughes. Ted Briskin was seen dating her after his divorce from Betty Hutton. Tony Curtis, Vince Edwards, and Scott Brady were also on her trail.

Reagan gave up the chase in January of 1952 right before he married Nancy. Columnist Hay Hoye wrote: "Gary Cooper's latest 'friend' is Eileen Howe."

Reagan's conclusion about her: "She didn't do too bad for a gal who can't stand to be touched."

***

Singer Evelyn Knight was not the most beautiful blonde Reagan ever dated, but she was talented, quite good looking, and had a bubbly personality that charmed him, at least temporarily.

Known as "The Lass with the Delicate Air," she was a popular recording artist in the 1940s and 50s, having scored a big hit with "Buttons and Bows." Her duet with country singer Red Foley, "My Heart Cries for You," was a lament heard on jukeboxes from Maine to Florida and west to Oregon.

Reagan first spotted her during a visit to the Blue Angel Nightclub in Manhattan. He waited until her final performance and then invited her out for a midnight date. She was seen leaving his hotel suite the following morning. Back in Los Angeles, he attended her shows at both Ciro's and the Cocoanut Grove.

He claimed that Knight was his favorite singer, saying that he preferred her to Jo Stafford, Peggy Lee, and Dinah Shore. He told William Holden that his greatest night with her was at a small club in San Fernando Valley, where both of them had been drinking heavily. Knight took the microphone and sang all the favorites whose names were called out to her from the audience. "She knew them all, and never missed a beat," he said. "We ended up closing the joint down."

He asked Holden, "Guess who my competition is? Tony Martin, Bing Crosby, and Gordon MacCrae. Those singers are a randy bunch." He'd heard that Ray Sinatra, a cousin of Frank Sinatra, had signed on as her musical conductor. "I wonder if Ray takes after Frank."

The last time he saw Knight was in 1954, two years after his marriage to Nancy. She told him, "I'm getting out of the business. Supper clubs are dying, and the sound of rock and roll fills the air waves."

Knight ended up living in obscurity in Phoenix, where she hired out as a babysitter, usually to people who knew nothing of her illustrious past.

Singer Evelyn Knight dedicated "My Heart Cries for You" to Reagan.

Reagan dated the Massachusetts-born Ruth Roman, a sultry brunette, before she married Mortimer Hall in 1950. When he learned that she was the daughter of immigrant parents from Lithuania, he told her, "If all the girls in Lithuania look like you, I'm taking the next boat there in the morning."

Her father had been a circus barker, who died when she was very young. As a means of supporting her family, her mother became a charwoman.

Reagan told Hedda Hopper, "Ruth has really struggled to get beyond one of those 'blink-and-you-miss-me' parts."

Roman played a supporting role to Rita Hayworth in *Gilda* (1946) and to Bette Davis in *Beyond the Forest* (1949). Finally, she nabbed a key role in *Champion* (1949) with Kirk Douglas.

Ruth Roman: "If guys like Ronnie Reagan couldn't get Ava Gardner, they settled for me."

"I love acting," she told him. "But it can break your heart. It has mine several times." She said that she had posed for stills for crime magazines at $5 an hour as a means of earning $200 to travel by train from Massachusetts to Hollywood.

One day, Reagan visited the set of *Champion* where he chatted briefly with its director, Mark Robson. While Roman was in the shower, Robson introduced Reagan to Lola Albright. Reagan then secretly asked Albright out on a date.

Eventually, after months of struggle, Roman was awarded the female lead in Alfred Hitchcock's *Strangers on a Train* (1951). Originally, the male lead was to have gone to his friend, William Holden, who pulled out at the last minute. Subsequently, that key role went to a weaker actor, Farley Granger. The second male lead was given to Robert Walker, who was dating Nancy Davis at the time.

After her completion of *Strangers on a Train,* Roman was cast with Jane Wyman in *Starlift* (1951). Reagan became a bit agitated after hearing that. Doris Day, whom he was also dating at the time, was in that movie, too, and he didn't want either Day or Roman to discuss him with his ex-wife. "Jane and I are divorced," he told Roman, "but I still feel embarrassed when she encounters women with whom I'm having an affair."

By the time she made *Starlift,* Roman was no longer bedding Reagan, but he did see her on occasion. "In my talks with Jane, your name never came up," she assured him. She told him that Gary Cooper was also in *Starlift.*

"He propositioned me, even though I heard he was still in love with Patricia Neal."

"And married, too," Reagan added.

***

Hailing from Akron, Ohio, singer/actress Lola Albright was buxom and blonde. On her first date with Reagan, she wore a gown with such low *colletage* that it left little to the imagination. She came to Hollywood in 1947, but didn't get a good role until her involvement in *Champion,* two years later.

Reagan wondered if she'd been seduced by Kirk Douglas, who was known for bedding actresses with whom he appeared.

Reagan may have gotten her a role in his own *The Girl from Jones Beach,* released the same year as *Champion.* At any rate, he admired her very much and noted that she had a fairly successful career in Hollywood without ever becoming a big star.

In time, he saw her as a nightlife singer on television's detective series, *Peter Gunn* (1958-1961), as created by Blake Edwards. Albright was cast as the romantic interest of the series' namesake, Peter Gunn, played by Craig Stevens. Reagan as a rather crass joke said, "Until you, *I* used to be Craig's love interest." Later, Reagan went to see Elvis Presley's *Kid Galahad* (1962), because he heard that Albright was in it.

Reagan also maintained another, indirect link, to Albright. In 1952, she married actor Jack Carson, the best friend and often movie sidekick to Dennis Morgan, with whom Jane had conducted her most enduring love affair.

As far as Albright's dating of Reagan, it appears that he took her out to a nightclub on perhaps two occasions as part of "a harmless encounter," he said. "Lola was very charming, a talented star who could both act and sing, and a nice person, something not always encountered in Hollywood."

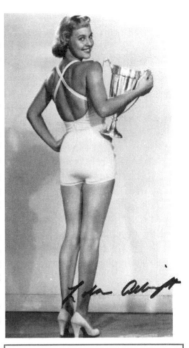

Lola Albright tried to imitate Betty Grable's celebrated World War II pinup photo, but didn't quite pull it off.

Years before, Reagan had seduced the real thing. Lola was "merely the mock."

***

Ann Sothern was acquainted with Reagan's second wife, Nancy Davis, before he was. Both of these women had appeared in *Shadow on the Wall.* If the blonde-haired Sothern had had her way, she might have been the one who married Reagan instead of Nancy.

In 1949, Sothern was in the throes of divorcing Pennsylvania-born actor Robert Sterling, whom she'd impetuously married in 1943, when thousands of other couples seemed to be rushing with equivalent wartime zeal into the bonds of matrimony.

Sterling had been a flight instructor throughout most of the war. After his release from the military, he found that his career had faltered during his absence. Likewise, after appearing in several postwar films, including as the featured actress within the popular Maisie series, Sothern's own career "was on the skids," as she put it.

Since Reagan and Sothern always seemed to be laughing and joking with each other on their "fun

Ann Sothern: "I worked with Nancy Davis, but what I did with Ronnie, I wouldn't exactly call 'work.'"

507

dates," his friends, including Dick Powell and June Allyson, thought they might eventually traipse down down the aisle together. "I knew that Ann was most willing," Allyson said.

Reagan, however, may have found Sothern too aggressive. She'd told him, "When a gal is getting rid of a husband, it's time for her to go shopping for another."

Although he dated her from anywhere from three weeks to a month, marriage was not on his agenda. She'd gained a bit of weight, and she was two years older than he was. As he told William Holden, "I like my dates to be ten to fifteen years younger than me."

"So you can be a father to them?" Holden facetiously asked.

"Yeah, right!"

"You say ten to fifteen years," Holden said. "You've got it all wrong. Try twenty to twenty-five years."

The Sothern/Reagan romance ended abruptly. Allyson thought she knew the reason why. Shortly after filming *A Letter to Three Wives* (1949), Sothern contracted infectious hepatitis after being injected with an impure serum as part of a medical procedure while she was in England for a stage performance.

Reagan didn't wait around long enough for her to recover.

***

A more serious relationship for Reagan developed with Betty Underwood, a starlet who had had a minor role in *The Girl from Jones Beach* (1949).

A former Powers model in New York, the strikingly beautiful Underwood was one of dozens of young women who had come to maturity during World War II and had migrated to Hollywood. She arrived there in 1948, and began dating Reagan, who was in the last throes of his divorce from Jane Wyman.

One night, he invited her to a premiere. "I like to arrive with a bombshell on my arm," he said. "That way, Jane won't think I'm still in mourning over her desertion of me."

In Hollywood, Underwood became better known for dating famous men than she was for her movie career. She enjoyed a romance with the former Mr. Joan Crawford (Franchot Tone), which caused a rift between her and actress Jean Wallace, who was married to Tone at the time.

Scott Brady, the brother of Laurence Tierney, was a handsome stud, the former lover of Anne Bancroft, who dated him at the same time Underwood did. "Scott was very proud of his equipment—and rightly so," Bancroft said.

Brady said, "I liked Betty a lot. But in those days, my phone was ringing off the walls, not only from hot babes, but a lot of famous male stars, too. I guess word of my gift had gotten around. I turned her over to Reagan."

That was not exactly the case. Brady didn't actually turn her over to anybody. Underwood charted her own course.

Reagan's affair with her lasted until March of

Betty Underwood. As one reporter wrote, "Betty Underwood plays Ronald Reagan like a fiddle, making him chase her all over the East Coast, from New York to Florida."

1951. The year Reagan married Nancy (1952), Underwood became engaged to Lester Deutsch, the multi-millionaire aeronautics pioneer.

At last report, she was still alive in 2013. If asked to dredge up a memory of Reagan, she recalled him as "charming, delightful, and very romantic."

If she had any regret at all, it involved her burning of his love letters, which would potentially be worth a lot of money today.

***

A Los Angeles native, the attractive starlet, Shirley Ballard, also appeared in Reagan's date book at the time. Fourteen years younger than him, she was another talented newcomer to the industry who never became a full-fledged star. After her heyday, parts were infrequent and minor, and included a brief appearance in the 1979 film *Mad Max,* starring Mel Gibson.

Shirley Ballard on Reagan: "A hard guy to nail down."

When Hedda Hopper asked Reagan about Ballard, he said, "It was nothing, Hedda, She's a fine girl. We were just ships who passed in the night without colliding."

***

Reagan was introduced to Peggy Stewart by her brother-in-law, Wayne Morris, who had co-starred with Reagan and Jane Wyman in those *Brother Rat* movies.

Growing up in West Palm Beach, Florida, Stewart, a beautiful starlet, was twelve years younger than Reagan. She'd entered a wartime marriage to actor Don ("Red") Barry, but their wedded bliss didn't make it till the Victory parades.

She became known for a string of B Westerns, in which she appeared with such cowboy stars as Sunset Carson, Wild Bill Elliott, and Gene Autry.

She broke into movies at the same time as Reagan did, making her debut in *Wells Fargo* (1937), in which she was cast as the teenage daughter of Joel McCrea.

"I've played every role from a chorus girl in *Man About Town* (1939) to a convict in *Girls in Chains* (1943)," she said.

When Reagan no longer called, she "free lanced" in the romantic department until actor Buck Young came along. She married him in 1953, and was still married to him at the time of his death in

Peggy Stewart: "After my divorce at the end of the war, I was shopping around. Ronnie fell into my cart, but hopped out."

509

2000.

In later years, Stewart often appeared dressed as a cowgirl at film festivals, where her fans remembered her. A fan would approach her, "I still remember you in *Cheyenne Wildcat* (1944)."

Stewart was still working as late as 2012, when she was cast as "Grandma Delores" in the Adam Sandler comedy, *That's My Boy.*

***

Reagan momentarily fell for "my songbird," Monica Lewis, a dimple-cheeked beauty known as "America's Singing Sweetheart." One of her biggest hits was "Put the Blame on Mame," the highlight of Rita Hayworth's movie *Gilda.* Other hits included "I Wish You Love" and "Autumn Leaves." The theme and title associated with the *Autumn Leaves* was made into a movie (1956), starring Joan Crawford.

Lewis' singing voice was later used for commercials on the TV series, *General Electric Theater,* which Reagan hosted.

Still alive at the time of this writing, Lewis wrote an autobiography, *Hollywood Through My Eyes: The Lives and Loves of a Golden Age Siren,* in which she detailed her romances with Reagan and Kirk Douglas.

She also wrote about her discovery by Benny Goodman and her ill-fated stint at MGM, where she was groomed "as a threat to Lana Turner. I was in the right place at the wrong time."

At the time Reagan dated her, Lewis was the singing voice of "Miss Chiquita Banana," a cartoon TV commercial. In 1948, she appeared on the first ever *Ed Sullivan Show.* She married record producer Robert Thiele in 1945, but divorced him in 1947. A few months later, she was seen out with Reagan. They made an attractive, compatible couple, but nothing very serious came out of their romance, since Reagan, and perhaps Lewis, too, were each "playing the field."

No, it isn't Lana Turner. It's Monica Lewis!

Reagan was reportedly shocked when he learned that Lewis had married Jennings Lang in 1956.

[In 1951, Lang had been involved in one of that year's biggest Hollywood scandals. Producer Walter Wanger discovered that his wife, the beautiful and sultry Joan Bennett, sister of Constance Bennett, was having an affair with Lang, a theatrical agent at the time. They conducted their romance clandestinely, often at vacation spots in the Caribbean. In Los Angeles, they enjoyed "quickies" at his apartment in Beverly Hills.

Wanger learned of the affair. Like a crazed cuckold, he lay in wait for them, shooting Lang in the testicles when he emerged from a car with Bennett. He

Monica Lewis with her husband, Jennings Lang, the man who delivered the only known punch to the face of Ronald Reagan.

510

later pleaded temporary insanity, eventually escaping with a four-month jail sentence.]

Reagan was acquainted with Lang, as he had become the head of MCA's West Coast TV operations.

In the halls of one of MCA's office buildings, Reagan encountered Lang during the time he was married to Lewis. "Jennings, my good fellow," Reagan said, mockingly. "I hope everything is in working order. You're the first *castrato* I've ever met."

Losing control, Lang punched Reagan in the face, bloodying his nose. Apparently, this was the first and only time Reagan had ever been struck in the face in Hollywood.

Lang later became a producer, turning out such pictures as *Airport 1975*. He never forgave Reagan for his insult. After he left MCA, he attacked him. "Reagan is the invention of that Hollywood conglomerate, MCA," he charged. "Every facet of his life, from his film career to his entry into politics, to his money in the bank, is indirectly controlled by MCA. He is the puppet, with MCA pulling his strings, with the help of the Mafia."

***

A diminutive beauty, Wisconsin-born Christine Larson graced movie screens from 1948 to 1955 in a series of grade B Westerns and long-forgotten potboilers like *Last Train to Bombay (1952) and* Valley of the Head Hunters (1953).

She became better known in TV series, including *The Cisco Kid* and *Four Star Playhouse,* and in 1950, she also starred in five episodes of *Dick Tracy*.

In Hollywood, Larson became notorious for her varied affairs with screen actors, and was often featured in the gossip columns. She had a long affair with actor Johnny Mack Brown, who had been one of the greatest halfbacks ever to play for the University of Alabama's Crimson Tide.

In Hollywood, Brown had been a romantic leading man, appearing opposite such stars as Greta Garbo, Mary Pickford, and Joan Crawford. His widely publicized affair with one of his leading ladies, Marion Davies, then mistress of William Randolph Hearst, damaged his career.

Baha'i Beauty:
Christine Larson

When Jack Carson spotted Reagan with Larson one night at the Cocoanut Grove, he quipped, "Out with a redhead for a change?"

Larson and Reagan were often spotted together going horseback riding, usually on Sunday afternoons. She was a champion equestrian and a rodeo queen. She told him, "My greatest ambition in life is to own a Lipizzaner stallion. Why don't you buy me one?"

"I thought I was stallion enough for you," he answered.

She not only went riding with him along the trails of the Hollywood Hills, but she designed his cowboy gear too. Before dating him, she had been a designer for the Western Costume Company. "I prefer to dress my men from the skin, beginning with their jockstraps," she once said. He liked the suits she gave him, except for one. It was all in red, and included red boots and a red ten-gallon hat. He refused to wear it.

William Holden said, "Christine was different from Ronnie's usual girlfriends. She was absolutely gorgeous with great legs. I slipped behind Ronnie's back and bedded her a few times. A hot little number."

Holden later claimed that "Neither Christine nor Nancy Davis knew it—at least I don't think they did—but Ronnie was also carrying on at least three other affairs when he was courting them. I screwed around a lot myself in those days. But I was more selective than he was—I mean, I went for the class dames like Audrey Hepburn and Grace Kelly."

For Reagan, at least, there was a potential problem associated with Larson's choice of religions, especially if Reagan continued his involvement in politics. She was a follower of the Bahá'í faith. It was reported that Larson got Reagan to attend at least four Bahá'í services with her.

[Ranked as one of the world's fastest-growing religions, and founded by Bahá'u'l-láh, a much-persecuted visionary who was exiled for his teaching in 19th-century Persia, Bahá'í is a monotheistic religion emphasizing the spiritual unity of humankind, asserting that there is only one God, the source of all creation, and that the human purpose is to learn to know and love God through such methods as reflection, service to humanity, and prayer. The religion, which has more than five million adherents worldwide, recognizes the link to God of such prophets and messengers as Moses, Muhammed, Jesus, Buddha, and Krishna.]

The playwright, O.Z. White, who knew both Reagan and Larson, claimed, "Reagan would talk about politics, Christine about the Bahá'í. In that religion, it is forbidden for a member to enter politics."

Even so, Larson claimed that Reagan was moved by her faith and its universal message. When he became President of the United States, he asked for a halt to the executions of the Bahá'í people in Iran.

At one point, as reported by June Allyson, "Ronnie got down on bended knee and proposed marriage to Larson the old-fashioned way. She told me she was in her twenties, but I'd heard that she was actually 33 at the time."

Along with an engagement ring, he presented her with a diamond wrist watch. She promised she'd get back to him with her answer the next day. As promised, she called him the following afternoon, rejecting his offer of marriage, but telling him that she planned to keep the wristwatch.

At the time, he was dating Larson at her apartment on North Beverly Glen, he was also dating Nancy Davis, who had an apartment on South Beverly Glen. On some days, he'd have a late afternoon session with Larson before driving over to escort Nancy to dinner.

One night, according to Larson, "Ronnie appeared on my doorstep in a state of panic. Even though I'd not accepted his marriage proposal, we had continued to see each other. He'd told me he'd just come from the apartment of Nancy Davis."

"She claims she's pregnant, and I'm the father," Reagan told Larson. "I'm not so sure. This may be just a trick to lure me into the marriage trap."

That night, Reagan left Larson's home and drove alone to Slapsie Maxie's nightclub on Wilshire Boulevard. It was one of his favorite haunts. Although she was on a date with someone else, he spotted starlet Selene Walters.

She was later described as "a big California blonde star, like one of those beautiful Rose Bowl queens Reagan always lusted after."

At some point, Walters slipped him her phone number and address. She would later become the centerpiece of one of the most notorious chapters in Reagan's "between marriages" horndog periods.

Larson later lamented having rejected Reagan's proposal of marriage. "I made a terrible mistake," she confessed. "I liked him a lot, although I was not in love with him.

512

I could not have imagined that one day, he would be Governor of California. If I had married him, I would have been First Lady of California. It never occurred to me that he'd rise that far in politics."

Larson died in 1973, and, of course, wasn't alive to see her former lover obtain an even more important government office.

Actually, what hastened the end of the Reagan/Larson affair was the day she told him that she had fallen in love with Gary Cooper and that they were engaged in a torrid affair in spite of their age difference.

In 1989, someone asked Reagan if he'd ever proposed marriage to Christine Larson. "I do not recall any person by that name," he said. "I have no memory of her whatsoever. I dated a number of young ladies in those days, but nothing serious—that is, until my dear Nancy came along."

***

Bob Thomas, author of *Jack Warner, Crown Prince of Hollywood,* said of Jacqueline Park, "Her life had been the stuff of trashy novels. Born in Philadelphia without a father; raised in New York's Hell's Kitchen by a promiscuous mother, worked as a dancer in Manhattan night spots; recruited by a madam as the plaything of millionaires; went to Hollywood for the kinky pleasures of director Edmund Goulding. She tried to be an actress, but mostly she worked nighttime for well-known figures including Cary Grant, who introduced her to the mind-expanding capabilities of LSD."

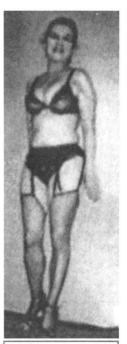

George Paley, a businessman from the Los Angeles area, introduced Park to Reagan, who seemed entranced by her beauty and her self-assured personality. He asked for her telephone number and called her the next day at the Studio Club, where she lived.

At that time, before his eventual move to a ranch in the Hollywood Hills, he was still living in the Londonderry Apartments. He made a date with her for the following night. He suggested that since he lived only a short distance away, it would be cheaper to take the bus. "Right away, I knew he was cheap, but I went over anyway."

At his apartment door, he greeted her in a red silk bathrobe with an ascot. "Our first date got off to a rough start," she later confessed. He didn't want to leave his apartment with me. When things got amorous later in the evening, it was embarrassing. He couldn't perform. He blamed it on the fact that he was still in mourning over his wife, Jane Wyman, who had divorced him."

This blurred photograph shows Jacqueline Park, dressed to receive visitors. She had a brief fling with Reagan, but a longer, more enduring affair with Jack Warner.

In spite of that disaster of an evening, Park claimed she continued to see him. "He was an important man, the president of SAG. "We both were confident that his sexual prowess would return—and it did."

"A kinky footnote in my dating career," Reagan told William Holden.

Transportation was always an issue between them. On her first date, she asked for cab fare back home. "I told him I was afraid to be out on the streets, a woman alone at two o'clock in the morning."

"He told me there were no rapists in his area, and that it was foolish to waste money on a cab. I barely had enough bus fare in my purse. It continued that way throughout our entire relationship. No cab fare...ever. He never took me to a night club. He never bought me a gift. He occasionally ordered take-out. I still don't know why he didn't want to be seen with me. I sure as hell didn't look like chopped liver. And he was divorced, after all."

Reagan had a more favorable memory of Park than she had of him. He told June Allyson, "Jackie is a curious mixture of a fragile beauty and worldly wisdom learned through the school of hard knocks."

His relationship with Park ended brusquely on the night she arrived at the Londonderry Apartments and confronted him with news that she was pregnant. "It was the worst night of my life," she recalled. "He accused me of having affairs with other men. At one point, he shouted at me, 'All you starlets are trying to entrap a man by getting pregnant and demanding marriage. First, I don't think the kid in the oven is mine. We were never seen together. There's no proof we ever had a sexual relationship. You're going to have to deal with this god damn thing yourself. I know I'm not responsible. You'll not get one cent from me. One of your other boyfriends will have to give you the money for the abortion.'"

In tears that night, she left his apartment, "taking the bus, of course. I didn't plan to go after him in court with a good lawyer. I was afraid that if I defied him, I'd lose my membership in SAG."

A friend of hers, Bentley Ryan, came to her rescue. She credited him with arranging the details of her abortion.

As was later speculated, had she given birth to Reagan's child, there might have eventually been another son (or daughter) arriving at the door of the White House, "demanding to see Daddy."

After Reagan, Park dated many famous men, including Frank Sinatra after Ava Gardner dumped him. "Frank liked orgies," she said. "I didn't. We broke up when he demanded I go to bed with him and another woman."

For a time, she conducted a secret affair with the handsome lawyer and playboy, Greg Bautzer. "One night, he told me to arrive after midnight. By then, I had a car. Before I got out of my car, I spotted a woman leaving his house. I saw him kissing her goodbye. When she walked under the streetlight, I recognized her face. It was Jane Wyman."

Ironically, in 1961, Park became the mistress of Jack Warner, Reagan's former boss. "He was just as cheap as Reagan. A lousy tipper. His underwear was torn. He patched together thin bars of soap in his bathroom. He gave me a weekly allowance of $200, but sometimes shortchanged me."

She recalled being taken to London, where they attended a reception in which he introduced her to Princess Margaret. "Jack told her Royal Highness, 'Jackie here has a heart of gold and a snatch to match.'"

"He refused to take me to the White House when he got an invitation from John F. Kennedy in 1962," Park claimed. "His excuse was, 'I can't take my mistress to the White House.' Later, when he returned to Hollywood, he told me, 'I'll be damned. Jack Kennedy slipped away with me to one of the private rooms. Waiting for us was his own mistress and a gal for me, too.'"

Years later, after Warner ended their relationship, Park recalled Reagan: "He just ran out on me when I got pregnant. He was a swinger in those days. He went out with this girl and that girl. But the moment he married Nancy, he became a Republican. He reformed, and there is nothing more boring than a reformed swinger."

514

Park later became a Manhattan "psychodramatist," *[in this case, a sex therapist]*, charging male clients $100 an hour to act out their sexual fantasies. She also wrote a book, *Memoirs of a Hollywood Mistress,* but found trouble finding a publisher.

***

When Kitty Kelley's 1991 book, *Nancy Reagan: The Unauthorized Biography,* came out, the accusations of actress Selene Walters made headlines. A typical one read GIPPER THE RIPPER. Her stunning charge was that Reagan had raped her. Only two American presidents have ever been charged with rape—first, Reagan, and later, Bill Clinton.

Walters did admit to meeting Reagan, "the lone wolf," when he appeared at Slapsie Maxie's nightclub one night when she was in the company of another man. She also claimed that she slipped him her phone number and address. Her motives may have been more career-oriented than based on any physical attraction for him.

"He was the president of the Screen Actors Guild, and I thought he might help my career. God knows, I needed some help."

She later said that she was asleep when her doorbell rang at three o'clock that morning. It was Reagan.

"I opened the door and let him in," she later told *People* magazine. "Once inside, it was the battle of the couch. I was fighting him. I didn't want him to make love to me. He's a very big man, and he just had his way. Date rape? No, that was Kelley's phrase. I didn't have a chance to have a date with him."

Based on the events of that night, Walters said she had no ill will toward Reagan. "I even voted for him for president. I don't think he meant to harm me."

Some reporters claimed that Reagan's aides managed to keep Walters' revelations from being printed in *The Washington Post, The New York Times*, and *The Los Angeles Times.*

But the week Kelley's book was released, Reagan was accosted on the steps of a church, where he and Nancy were paying one of their biannual visits.

In front of TV cameras, a reporter called out: "Did you rape Selena Walters?"

Reagan politely said, "I don't think church would be a proper place to use the word I would have to use in discussing that."

The reporter later commented, "That was not exactly a denial."

The reporter's encounter with Reagan, with Nancy clinging tightly to the arm of her husband, was broadcast on TV news across the nation.

***

Did Ronald Reagan rape Selene Walters (*shown supine, above*)?

Both Doris Day and Jane Wyman appeared in Reagan's next film, *It's a Great Feeling* (1949), a silly piece of fluff spoofing Hollywood. But none of their scenes was together. In addition to Day, the actual stars of the picture were Dennis Morgan and Jack Carson, in yet another of their movies together.

In her autobiography, *Doris Day, Her Own Story,* by A.E. Hotchner, Ernest Hemingway's friend, Day claimed that she had met Reagan through mutual friends who had moved to Los Angeles from New York.

This was at the time Reagan was divorcing Jane, and Day was in the throes of divorcing her second husband, saxophonist George Weidler. She had previously been married to trombonist Al Jorden, with whom she had a child, Terry Jorden, who later changed his name to Terry Melcher, adopting the name of Day's third husband, Martin Melcher.

Is It *Really* a Great Feeling?

Reagan appeared in a cameo with Dennis Morgan in a scene that takes place in a barbershop. It is one of the few times that Jane Wyman's former lover (Reagan) came together with her present lover (Morgan).

At the time she started dating Reagan, Day had just emerged from a romance with Jack Carson, her co-star in her first film, *Romance on the High Seas* (1948). Carson and Day had also co-starred in her next film, *My Dream is Yours* (1948). Their romance had been called "mutually therapeutic." She was trying to keep him from drinking himself into oblivion, and he was attempting to wean her from her addiction to smoking three packages of Camels a day.

"The first time I saw her, I adored this pretty blonde with the freckles," Reagan said. "She had a real bubbly personality."

Reagan's first date with Day was in May of 1948, at the time Jane was filing for divorce. Day remembered that he spent most of the first evening "talking mainly about Janie. I lamented George."

"I'm a failure," she said to him.

"Not at all!" he responded, trying to reassure her. "Jack Warner told me you're going to become one of the biggest stars in Hollywood."

"But I failed at the two things I wanted most in life—that was to be a good wife, and to have a happy marriage."

"There were two things that impressed me about Ronnie," Day wrote. "How much he liked to dance, and how much he liked to talk. Ronnie was really the only man I've ever known who loved dancing. There was a little place on Cienega that had a small band and a small dance floor, where he often took me. He danced well and had a pleasant personality, so I invariably enjoyed going out with Ronnie."

Whereas Day was a Republican, Reagan at the time was still a liberal Democrat. She listened intently to his discourses, although his points often didn't match her conservatism. She suggested he might tour the country giving speeches. "He's what I would call a political personality—engaging, strong, and very voluble."

As Day's biographer, David Bret, wrote: "The two would sneak off to his apartment high in the Hollywood Hills, and make love while marveling at the panoramic view below."

Previously, Reagan and Day had each been directed by Michael Curtiz. She complained that he had given her great insecurity. "He wants me to lose weight and have hollow cheeks like Marlene Dietrich."

"I'm back to being a bachelor again," he said. "This was my first apartment in Hollywood. When I married Jane, I took her to live with me here. But these days, or nights, it

Reagan was overshadowed by other actors in the "cattle call" that Jack Warner issued for most of his then-underused stable of movie stars.

Depicted above: Doris Day, Dennis Morgan, and Jack Carson, listening through a peephole.

gets pretty lonely wandering around this bachelor flat without anyone to love. This place brings back a lot of memories, both good and bad."

"I'm surprised you moved in again," she said. "I'd have preferred starting over again somewhere else."

As Reagan told June Allyson, "Doris needs a lot of reassurance about her looks."

She told him, "Sometimes I look at myself in the mirror, and I burst into tears at all those freckles."

"You're beautiful," he said. "So fresh-faced. The freckles add to your charm."

"I don't know," she said. "I have to spend so much time in makeup that I feel I'm wearing a plaster mask whenever I face the cameras. I'd give my soul to look like Hedy Lamarr."

He was vaguely disturbed when he learned that Alexis Smith and Craig Stevens had befriended her and welcomed her to Hollywood, asking her to parties. These included an invitation to the home of Stanley Mills Haggart, the set designer and advertising agent.

Reagan always felt that Smith and Stevens had only "set Jane and me up so that, as a bisexual couple, they could move in on us."

Even though he apparently never made his intentions known to Day, Reagan talked about the possibility of proposing marriage to her to such good friends as George Murphy. Dick Powell and June Allyson were also aware of the possibility of a marriage between the singing star and Reagan.

He even went so far as to discuss with Murphy the business angle of such a liaison. "I didn't want to become Mr. Jane Wyman, but I'm thinking over being Mr. Doris Day. That might be a career goal, as I move into middle age. The roles are already drying up. I could be very aggressive, get the best movie deals for her, the fattest recording contracts. I'd make a great manager for her."

On the set of *It's a Great Feeling,* Reagan shook the hand of the director, David Butler, who welcomed him. Butler had been a former actor himself on the stage, and later in the Silents, but he became better known for second-rate musicals. Reagan soon learned that Butler had developed an unreciprocated crush on Day.

Reagan learned that he and Jane were not alone in making a cameo appearance in Butler's film. They were joined by Errol Flynn, Gary Cooper, Joan Crawford, Sydney

Greenstreet, Danny Kaye, Patricia Neal, Eleanor Parker, and Edward G. Robinson, along with Directors Michael Curtiz, Raoul Walsh, and King Vidor. Butler even had cast himself in a cameo.

Reagan had only one scene, set in a barbershop, not with Jane, but with Morgan and Carson. There was an undercurrent of sexual rivalry. Either known or unknown to Reagan, Jane had continued her long affair with Morgan. Complicating matters, Day had broken off with Carson before landing in Reagan's welcoming arms.

In the scene, Carson is in the barbershop, lamenting his difficulties in shooting his latest film. In the seat beside him is a man whose face is covered with a hot towel. When the towel is removed, it's revealed that the mystery man is Reagan himself.

Day plays a woman trying to break into Hollywood with the help of Morgan and Carson.

Before heading back to Wisconsin, Day appears as a Parisian prostitute in a black wig, crooning, "There's Nothing Rougher Than Love." Finally, she gives up and returns to her hometown of Gurkeys Corners, where she is set to marry her local hayseed boyfriend, Jeffrey Bushfinkle. Carson finds them at the altar. The bride and bridegroom have their backs to the camera. After their marriage vows, Bushfinkle lifts the veil of his bride to kiss her. He is seen for the first time. He looks like Errol Flynn. It *IS* Errol Flynn!

Later, Carson complained to Reagan. "When I made my first picture with Doris, *Romance on the High Seas* (1948), I was the fucking star. By the time this turkey is in the can, I'll be out there as her supporting player. She'll be the star."

At the end of the shoot, Carson encountered Reagan again. "In that last scene with Flynn, he and I almost came to blows—no, not that kind…"

Reagan later speculated why he and all the stellar personalities were cast in this "lightweight fluff. Jack Warner had all of us under contract, and I think he wanted to give us something to do until something better came along."

After finalizing his cameo, he called Lew Wasserman. "Get me a Western, god damn it!"

"Not now, Ronnie, baby," his agent said. "You're going to be flown to England to make *The Hasty Heart* with Patricia Neal. If you're lucky, you'll get to fuck her, although Gary Cooper is a tough hoss to follow."

***

At the time of his cameo in *It's a Great Feeling* (1949), Reagan, as president of SAG, was facing the "growing menace" of television and its threat to the Hollywood film industry. He wrote: "Supplies of headache powder are running low, and there's moaning and groaning in the land of make believe—for Hollywood and the entire entertainment industry are caught in the throes of a revolution."

SAG entered into a dispute with motion picture producers. At one point, actors threatened to go on strike.

The dispute, as Reagan explained it, developed within a context wherein screen actors had sold their services with the understanding that movies were intended only for exhibition in theaters. "Films should not be used in television without additional payments to actors."

The producers claimed they had a right to use a film they made and paid the actors for in any medium they chose.

In the end, the producers held firm on not granting residuals from television to actors for films they had made, some dating back to 1930, long before television became an almost universal fixture.

***

Patricia Neal was not Jack Warner's first choice, nor the first choice of director Vincent Sherman, for the role of the nurse, Sister Margaret, the only female role in *The Hasty Heart*

(1950), based on the hit play by John Patrick. Originally, Eleanor Parker, who had co-starred with Reagan in *The Voice of the Turtle,* had been cast in the role, but had to drop out because she was pregnant.

Reagan seemed pleased when Neal was designated as her replacement, because he had worked so smoothly with her in *John Loves Mary.* That was a comedy. *The Hasty Heart* was a serious drama set in Burma during World War II, most of its scenes taking place in a military hospital. When Reagan signed on, he thought he was going to be cast as Latchie, a dying Scottish soldier, clearly the film's most meaty and pithy part. But he soon learned from Sherman that the role had gone to an Irish newcomer, Richard Todd. A handsome actor born in Dublin, Todd walked off with the prize, for which he would later win an Oscar nomination.

Reagan had to be satisfied with the far less charismatic role of "Yank," a compassionate American soldier recovering from malaria. In the hospital, he tries to befriend the often hostile Latchie.

Reagan and Neal, as friends and "civilians" aboard the ship returning to the US from England at the conclusion of filming.

Neal, instead of uprooting herself to London for the four-month filming, with Reagan, of *The Hasty Heart,* would have preferred to remain in Hollywood, co-starring with Gary Cooper in *Task Force,* because she was madly in love with him. Cooper promised to write her every day during their separation, which he did not do.

Neal and Reagan arrived together in bombed-out, post-war London during one of the bitterest, coldest winters in twenty or so years. "There was no heat anywhere," Reagan said.

Although jealous of his having been awarded the star role, Reagan maintained a surface politeness with Todd. Todd later recalled, in an interview, "Reagan had a lot of complaints about filming in England. After the war, England froze the amount of money a producer could take out of the country. To spend the revenue earned in Britain, movie companies were shooting in England. Reagan felt that that represented a total lack of grace on Britain's part, considering that the United States had 'saved England from

Hitler's Nazi grip' (his words)."

Filming was at the financially troubled Elstree Studio, which was being rebuilt after damage from Nazi bombardments during World War II, and slowly being adapted for use as a television production facility.

In *The Hasty Heart,* Latchie can't relate to others in the ward, although Yank tries to win his friendship, as does Neal as the nurse. At the time of his casting, Todd was thirty years old and had been a British paratrooper. He asked Reagan, "How many Nazis did you kill during the war?"

"I made propaganda films for the Americans," Reagan said, perhaps with a pang of guilt.

"We were shooting in England, but we were supposed to be in Burma, where it was hot," Todd said. "Sometimes, we had to appear

Barely Speaking:
Richard Todd, *(left)* with Ronald Reagan.

in our shorts. Reagan continued to complain about the chill and dampness. 'I'm freezing my balls off,' he told me. 'The gals back in Hollywood won't like that.' That was the first time I realized that Reagan could talk like a regular bloke."

After the first week of filming, Todd invited Reagan to go on a pub crawl with him. Reagan told Todd, "I feel my film career is about over and yours is just beginning. I envy you. But one thing I don't envy is trying to make it in post-war Hollywood. It was always a vicious place. But the deadly rattlers have been replaced with man-eating dinosaurs. I may go into politics on a national level, although my involvement in politics has damaged my film career. I made enemies of directors and producers who might otherwise have hired me."

Todd also claimed that, "The image of Jane Wyman hovered over the set of *The Hasty Heart* like she was the co-star of that picture. Reagan was still in love with her, although having dates—perhaps affairs—with others. He and Patricia Neal were together practically every night. He once told me that he thought he and Jane would get back together. Once, I jokingly asked him, 'if he got back with Jane, would he give me his cast-offs?' He had no answer for that. While shooting the film, he spent a lot of time on the phone with Jane in California. He was eager for news not only of her, but also of the children. "

Neal later credited Reagan with giving her a lot of support during the filming. "We would have dinner and even go dancing at one of the local halls. He was a good dancer. People may have been shabbily dressed and their food rationed, but at night they sang and danced with all their hearts. They were happy the war was over. English food was horrid, a lot of cardboard fish with soggy bread crumbs and exhausted vegetables. Reagan missed his steaks and had a batch flown in from '21' in New York. But when he invited Neal to a steak dinner at the Savoy Hotel, the chef came out and apologized. 'The steaks, Mr. Reagan, have gone bad.'"

Neal said, "Ronnie knew differently. The chef and the kitchen crew had eaten them."

Sherman recalled, "Both Pat and Ronnie were depressed over their affairs of the heart. They were pining for Gary Cooper and Jane Wyman. I had to put up with these two lovesick puppies."

At the Savoy, Neal and Reagan had adjoining suites. Waiters and maids noted that they kept the connecting doors open at all times. One maid reported that she'd caught them having a shower together. When Todd heard about this, he said, "My motto is, if you're not with the one you love, make love to the one you're with."

When Neal was appearing on Broadway with Anne Bancroft in *The Miracle Worker* (1959), she modified her account of her experiences in London. Bancroft was seriously dating the designer, Stanley Mills Haggart, at the time.

"I once said that Ronnie never made a pass at me," Neal said. "What I didn't say was that I made a pass at him. On several nights, we cuddled up. What else was there to do? It was so god damn cold in London after the war. Of course, I wished it were Gary in my bed. At the time, Ronnie was mourning for Janie but getting cozy with Doris Day—and with me."

In the Dining Room of the Savoy Hotel, Reagan and Neal often dined with Elizabeth Taylor and Robert Taylor, who were in London together filming *Conspirator* (1949). He still numbered Robert among his best friends. Robert confessed to Reagan, "Elizabeth and I are getting it on."

Neal formed a friendship with a young dentist, Hamish Thomson, who was in love with her friend, Helen Horton. One weekend, Thomson drove Neal and Reagan on a sightseeing tour of the Cotswolds. "We played a quiz game," Neal said. "The question was, 'What would you like to be if you could be anybody in the whole world'?"

Reagan answered, "President of the United States."

Virginia Mayo, who had made *The Girl from Jones Beach* with Reagan, attended a Royal Command Film Performance of the movie, *Scott of the Antarctic [the third most popular film at the British box office in 1949]*, starring John Mills. "Our party in London included Alan and Sue Ladd," she recalled, "along with Larry Olivier and Vivien Leigh. Vivien fell asleep during this dull and depressing movie, and her right breast popped out. I nudged Ronnie to awaken her and inform her of her tit malfunction. Instead of watching John Mills, he spent the rest of the movie staring at that exposed breast of Scarlett O'Hara, which he didn't get to see in *Gone With the Wind*."

Before the screening, Reagan had met Queen Elizabeth *(a.k.a. Elizabeth Bowes-Lyon, identified in later years as Queen Elizabeth, The Queen Mother]*, but not her daughter, Princess Elizabeth *[who ascended to the throne in 1953, and was later identified as Queen Elizabeth II]*, who was pregnant at the time. Reagan was also introduced to Princess Margaret and Prince Philip.

When not otherwise involved, and when he had time off, Reagan wandered among "the nooks and crannies of Mayfair, exploring old curiosity shops. I expected Nell Gwynne to emerge from her royal carriage at any minute."

One night, at the Bar of the Savoy Hotel, Neal heard Reagan pondering whether the United States should attack the Soviet Union and destroy it while the U.S. still had exclusive access to the atomic bomb. "We could establish for centuries to come the *Pax Americana*," he said.

Whereas Vincent Sherman had known Reagan for years—in fact, he'd directed some of the scenes from his *Juke Girl* with Ann Sheridan—Neal met the director in London for the first time. He had a reputation for seducing some of his leading ladies, such as Joan Crawford and Bette Davis. "You're next," he told her.

Reagan and Todd bonded more as filming progressed. "I think he forgave me for taking the role he wanted," Todd said. "At one point in the film, he gave me a massage on camera. If he had not become president, he could have hired out as a masseur. If I recall, he gave me an erection."

It can be assumed that Todd was joking, but perhaps not.

Todd later recalled, "Ronnie buttered me up when he heard I had been cast opposite Jane Wyman and Marlene Dietrich in Alfred Hitchcock's upcoming *Stage Fright* (1950), to be shot in London. I think Reagan wanted me to be a go-between, running messages to Jane on the set in our upcoming film. He told me he thought there was a good chance that if she would agree to meet with him, there could be a reconciliation."

"I didn't think so, but I humored him," Todd said. "I promised to put in a good word for him with Jane."

Todd later delivered a bombshell, telling Sherman, "Reagan approached me shortly before his marriage to Nancy Davis and asked me to make one final plea with Jane Wyman to re-marry him. I found this astonishing, because the grapevine claimed that Nancy was already carrying Reagan's baby on her long route with him to the altar."

According to Todd, Reagan said that he'd call off his upcoming marriage to Nancy "if Jane came through."

During the filming of *The Hasty Heart*, Sherman claimed that Reagan was "very thin skinned when I critiqued his performance. In his memoir, *Where's the Rest of Me?*, he had good words for everyone but failed to mention me."

During the four months that Reagan worked in London, Sherman noted a radical shift in his politics, as Reagan moved away from the Democrats and into the camp of the Republicans. As he'd later put it, "I spent those months in England while the Labour Party was in power. I saw firsthand how the welfare state sapped incentive to work from many people in a wonderful and dynamic country."

Sherman claimed that Reagan tried to get over Wyman by having a secret affair with a script girl on the set of *The Hasty Heart*. "She was sort of a mousy-looking creature with glasses, but she had big tits," Sherman recalled. "I heard that she joined him for shack-ups when he took a vacation after filming. They were seen together in Wales, Ireland, and France."

When Sherman returned to Hollywood, Jack Warner told him, "I want to get rid of Reagan. Most of his pictures are lousy. Did you see crap like *That Hagen Girl* and *Night Unto Night*? He was a pretty boy when he was running around Hollywood in the early 40s fucking Betty Grable and Lana Turner. But he's getting jowly and moving into middle age. I'll throw him in crappy films and maybe he'll break the contract."

As Reagan entered the 1950s, he faced the dilemma of all other actors confronting the Big 4-0. He had long talks with Jimmy Stewart, Robert Taylor, Dick Powell, and George Murphy. Hollywood was a great burial ground for young romantic leads turning middle-aged. A few of the better ones, including Stewart, Henry Fonda, and Cary Grant, could survive in the right pictures, but most of the others were cast aside.

Reagan feared that his tomb was waiting for him at Forest Lawn. If he couldn't continue a career in movies, what should he do with the rest of his life? Though he initially resisted it, did appearing on that little black-and-white box in people's living rooms loom in his future?

Reagan had signed to make five movies with Universal at a salary of $75,000 per movie. When he refused to appear in the first two movies Universal offered him, Lew Wasserman, his agent, was forced to renegotiate his contract. What emerged was a three-picture deal, beginning with *Louisa* (1950), followed by *Bedtime for Bonzo* (1951), and concluding with *Law and Order* (1953), the last finally fulfilling his dream of getting cast in a Western.

***

Universal filmed *Louisa* in 35 days for a budget of $800,000, much of which went to its "elderly talent" that included Charles Coburn, Edmund Gwenn, and Spring Byington. On the set, Reagan had a reunion with Coburn, accusing him once again of "cutting off my legs in *Kings Row*, you miserable old fucker."

It was during the making of *Louisa* that Stage 18 was converted into a mammoth party hall, marking Coburn's 60th anniversary in show business. A surprise guest at the party was Jane Wyman, who made no special overtures to the man she'd just divorced.

Even though Reagan was appearing in weak films during his postwar era, he still maintained a certain popularity among fans who cited his "likable personality." In the first poll of *Modern Screen* readers, Reagan ranked fifth in popularity, following in the wake of John Wayne, Alan Ladd, Clark Gable, and newcomer Farley Granger.

In this scene from *Louisa*, Piper Laurie evokes a rebellious teenager, Reagan a frustrated middle-aged adult. Charles Coburn looks on.

Most movies at the time were devoted to young love, but not *Louisa*. It was about the romance of a dotty grandmother (Byington), torn between two suitors. Directed by Alexander Hall, the congenial family comedy cast this plump woman as the mother of the character played by Reagan. She comes to live with her architect son. Once there, she is pursued by an elderly grocer (Gwenn). Coburn was cast

Reagan and Piper Laurie in *Louisa*. She was barely legal.

as Norton's boss, an aging, bombastic roly-poly who is also a rival for Byington's affections.

Reagan, as Norton, is the befuddled, anxious son, watching his mother's antics. Cast in the role of Reagan's wife was Ruth Hussey, sweet as his helpmate in an unchallenging role. Piper Laurie, making her film debut, is cast as Reagan's daughter, who's coping with the affections of Scotty Becket, her young boyfriend.

Some critics hailed the film as a "geriatric love story."

Reagan's role could have been played by any one of dozens of actors. It was not a showcase for his limited acting talents. Yet in spite of his lackluster role, he later said, "*Louisa* is a good and healthy plus to any list of screen credits."

Reagan found London-born Gwenn a delight, and congratulated him on his performance as Kris Kringle in the 1947 film, *Miracle on 34th Street*, for which he won a Best Supporting Actor Oscar.

Reagan had known Byington since the 1930s. She told him that she had two dreams: One involved purchasing a small coffee plantation in Brazil—she was already learning Portuguese—and another involved enrolling in flying lessons.

"Two worthy goals," Reagan told Hall. "Not a bad ambition for a woman born in 1886."

Reagan welcomed Hall's direction, telling him, "If you could do for me what you did for Robert Montgomery in *Here Comes Mr. Jordan* (1941), I'd be pleased indeed. *[For his involvement in that picture, Hall had been nominated for an Academy Award as Best Director of the Year.]*

Cast as boyfriend Jimmy Blake in the movie, Scotty Beckett was a Californian who started in show business when he was three years old. Although he had made a name for himself appearing in the *Our Gang* comedies of the 1930s. Reagan had met him when he played the child manifestation of the Robert Cummings' character in *Kings Row.*

One might assume that an off-screen as well as on-screen romance might have developed between Laurie and Beckett. He was born in 1929, she in 1932. But instead, that eighteen-year-old neophyte actress fell into the arms of a 39-year-old instead, Ronald Reagan.

Laurie accompanied Reagan on a tour to promote *Louisa* in his former residence, Des Moines, and later to his hometown of Dixon. Nelle, looking very frail, also joined the tour. In the words of one reporter, Reagan appeared in a "cocoa brown suit and tie" at the Paramount Theater in Des Moines, where he had once been a radio announcer. He introduced a stunningly beautiful Laurie, who wore an emerald green strapless gown as temperatures soared outside, within a theater that had no air conditioning.

Reagan told his audience, "Hollywood people aren't really like what you read in the gossip columns." Backstage, he whispered to Nelle, "They're even worse."

After leaving Des Moines, witnessing all the changes that World War II had brought to the town, he remarked, "You can't go home again."

It seemed that the entire town of Dixon came out to greet Reagan and his mother. The mayor presented him with a key to the city, and banners along the main street proclaimed WELCOME HOME DUTCH. He led the parade, riding down Main Street in a cowboy outfit on a palomino. Later, at a banquet, Nelle and Reagan serenaded diners with "In the Good Old Summertime."

During his dedication of a new swimming pool, Reagan addressed a crowd, calling them a "pack of sissies. We used to swim in the river."

***

A daughter of Detroit, the beautiful teenager, Piper Laurie, was making her film debut in *Louisa* with Reagan and other members of the cast. She had signed a contract with Universal, and was getting a big buildup by that studio's publicity department. The staff claimed that she bathed in milk and ate flower petals to protect her luminous skin. Her ancestors were Jewish immigrants from both Poland and Russia.

Reagan was the first big star to be captivated by Laurie's beauty, or at least he was the first to date her. But other handsome male stars lay in her future, including Paul Newman and Tony Curtis. Howard Hughes had also cast his eye on her.

One night at a premiere, Ann Sheridan introduced her to Clark Gable. As Gable later told

In 1950, Reagan *(on the right)* returned to his hometown of Dixon, where he'd been a lifeguard.

At a dedication ceremony for the town's new swimming pool, he stripped off his clothes, except for a scarlet bathing suit, and showed off a trim, fit physique, still holding up after all these years.

Sheridan, "That is a very, very pretty gal. Too bad I'm such an old man."

As Reagan turned forty, he was just at the age that many men think of seducing younger girls, even teenagers. Such was the case with Reagan and Laurie. When he had been introduced to her on the set of *Louisa*, where she played his sixteen-year-old daughter, she noted that he held her hand for an extra long time.

During the filming, Reagan chatted with the teenager, listening to her complaints about the script and the character she was playing. To live up to Universal's publicity, which had hyped her as "The Girl Who Eats Orchids," she was served flower petals for lunch in the commissary, even though she found them distasteful.

At his invitation, she became a frequent visitor to his dressing room.

One day, the film's producer, Robert Arthur, approached her, telling her it wasn't proper for such a young girl to be seen going in and out of Reagan's dressing room. Arthur reminded her, "Reagan is old enough to be your daddy."

After that, she started turning down invitations to visit Reagan in his dressing room, but he was persistent, inviting her to the Hollywood premiere of *Francis* (1949), the picture starring Donald O'Connor in the story of a talking mule. It launched a series of Francis sequels. Both Laurie and Reagan were photographed with the mule. At the event, members of the Universal staff (in theory, at least) served as their chaperones.

There was no seduction during the shooting of *Louisa*. All that Laurie got from Reagan was a kiss on the cheek.

However, the cast was asked several months later to perform *Louisa* on the Lux Radio Theater. At the end of the broadcast, Reagan invited Laurie to dinner, promising he'd serve hamburger steak instead of "those god damn orchids they force you to eat."

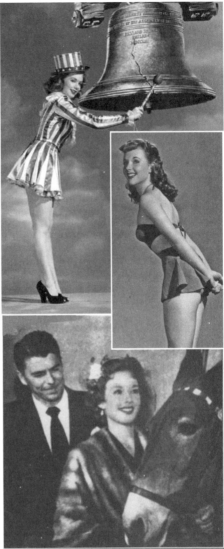

Upper photos: Piper Laurie, teenaged sex symbol, gets "cutsie patriotic."

Lower photo: Piper Laurie, having lost her virginity to Ronald Reagan, is escorted by him to a premiere of *Francis* (1949), starring Donald O'Connor with a "Talking Mule."

He had to ask permission from Laurie's mother, Charlotte Alperin. The woman seemed apprehensive, but reluctantly agreed, perhaps because Reagan was such an important figure in Hollywood.

In the car, heading to his home, Laurie noticed him looking at her. But surely, she asked herself, it wasn't in *that* way.

In his apartment, with its panoramic view, he offered her a glass of wine, turned on some romantic music, and retreated to the kitchen.

She later wrote in her autobiography, *Learning to Live Out Loud*, "I didn't know if Ronnie knew I was a virgin. I knew I wanted to make love with him. I wanted to be completed by this wonderful man who clearly desired me. He would know what to do."

The revelations she made in that memoir later made headlines. Susannah Cahalan of *The New York Post* wrote. "Ronald Reagan wasn't 'the great communicator' in the sack."

Laurie described the bedroom romp as "without grace. Ronnie was more than competent sexually. He was also a bit of a show-off. He made sure I was aware of the length of time he had been 'ardent.' It was forty minutes. And he told me how much the condom cost."

However, she claimed that he'd ruined the romantic experience she'd envisioned by telling her, "There's something wrong with you" during their drawn out intercourse. "You should have had many orgasms by now—after all this time. You've got to see a doctor about your abnormality, and maybe that doctor can find out why it hurt you so at first. There's something wrong with you that you should fix."

She later lamented, "His words to me were cold and just plain stupid. And in a moment in my life when I might have benefitted from it the most, he offered not the slightest trace of humor or kindness."

Months later, she was sent on a publicity tour with Reagan to Chicago.

A Universal executive, Charles Simonelli, who was on the tour with them, told Laurie, "He is good at making all those speeches. Do you think he's running for president or promoting *Louisa?*"

Later that night, he followed her back to her suite at the Ambassador East Hotel and asked if he could come in. She refused, but suggested a walk in the night air instead. The question of age came up, and he seemed troubled that she was only nine years older than his daughter, Maureen.

He kissed her passionately, and told her he wanted to be with her again. She said she had another *beau*, the singer, Vic Damone. "The truth was, I no longer found Ronnie to be someone I wanted to be close to. His insensitivity had been wounding, and, in retrospect, even cruel."

During the walk back to the hotel, she told him that she had been honored that such a famous movie star "had been the first." As she looked at his face, he appeared shocked. She later wondered, "Did he know I was a virgin? Didn't the stain on the sheet send him a signal?"

During the final year of Reagan's presidency, Laurie was invited to the White House for the "goodbye gala" of all of his old friends, mostly from his Hollywood days.

She cabled her regrets and later explained why she did so: "I told myself it was because I didn't agree with him at all, politically, but that wasn't the complete truth. I hadn't seen him since before he'd become Governor of California. After all those years, it seemed odd to be invited. I assume the guest list had been put together without his input, and that I would simply be among a large group of actors with whom he'd worked. That would have made me uncomfortable. As disappointing as it was, the relationship had been more important to me than that. I wished to save myself embarrassment. Who knows? I might already have been wiped from his memory."

***

Before he shot *Louisa,* Reagan had made a far more serious film, *Storm Warning* (1951), an anti-Ku Klux Klan "message picture." The last such movie Warners had made was the 1937 anti-Klan film, *Black Legion,* starring Humphrey Bogart.

But despite the fact that technically, it was an older film, *Louisa* was released before *Storm Warning.*

Jerry Wald, Reagan's long-time friend and a former screen writer, was the producer of *Storm Warning,* and he ran into trouble casting the four leads—that of a crusading district attorney, Burt Rainey, and two sisters, Marsha Mitchele (a fashion model), the other, Lucy Rice, a pregnant waitress living in a small Southern town with her brute of a husband, Hank Rice.

During the film's development, it had been tentatively entitled *Storm Center.* Wald had considered casting Bette Davis as the older sister, with Jane Wyman playing the married waitress.

Wald sent the script to Lauren Bacall, who studied it with Bogie, the star of *Black Legion* (1937), the first anti-KKK film at Warners. Bogie recommended that she

Pain, betrayal, and strife in this scene from *Storm Warning* as Steve Cochran, playing a bigoted brute, gets physical with his wife (Doris Day), and her sister (Ginger Rogers).

reject the role. She didn't feel she was right for the part, so he cabled Jack Warner. Enraged, Warner ordered that his contract player go on her sixth suspension.

He then sent the role to Joan Crawford, who had recently heated up the screen in *The Damned Don't Cry* with Steve Cochran, a story about a gangster and his moll. Crawford heard that Doris Day was about to be signed as the younger sister. Consequently, she, too, rejected *Storm Warning,* sending a memo to Wald. "Who in hell would ever believe I was the sister of Doris Day?"

Ginger Rogers was called, and she immediately accepted the role. After winning 1940's Best Actress Oscar for *Kitty Foyle,* she had long ago proved that she was a dramatic actress—and not just the dancing partner of Fred Astaire.

When Wald presented the script to Doris Day, she felt that the role of the younger sister would be a challenge, a non-singing part. She declared that "I'm not up to it." Wald had heard that her first husband, the trombone player, Al Jorden, had been abusive to her, and that she might draw upon her own horrible memories to portray the battered woman. She wanted to work with Rogers, whom she claimed had been "my idol since I was just a girl going to the movies."

"You and Ginger are both Christian Scientists," Wald said, "so when you're not due on the set, you can talk religion with each other."

Since Wald had liked Cochran so much as the gangster in *The Damned Don't Cry,* it was surprising that he did not immediately consider him for the role of Hank. He kept referring to the part as a "Stanley Kowalski type character." He'd seen Marlon Brando on Broadway and decided to offer him the role. Within a week, he'd heard from Brando. "You must be joking," was all he wrote.

Surprisingly, Wald next considered José Ferrer, who was a very different type of actor and would have been horribly miscast. Finally, he went back to what was obvious all along, and cast Cochran as the handsome, hirsute, sexual menace.

A former cowpuncher, Cochran had drifted into the theater, appearing as Mae West's co-star in the stage production of *Diamond Lil*. At night, he kept her bed warm. As West proclaimed, "It takes a big man to satisfy a big gal like me."

When Cochran learned that Wald had offered the role to Ferrer, he told the producer, "What a mistake that would have been. The role calls for a male sexpot, which Ferrer just ain't. As for me, the gals of Hollywood, and some of the cocksuckers, too, call me 'Steve the *Schvantz*.'"

Wald signed Stuart Heisler (*The Glass Key/Dallas/Tulsa*) to direct *Storm Warning*, with the stars billed as Ginger Rogers in the lead, followed by Ronald Reagan, Doris Day, and Steve Cochran. The casting of Rogers and Day would later confuse some fans, who went to see *Storm Warning* thinking that it was a lighthearted musical.

Two movie veterans, Ronald Reagan and Ginger Rogers, posed for a publicity still for *Storm Warning,* their pose suggesting the film was about a benign romance.

Far from it. The film dealt with the effect of the Ku Klux Klan and the terror it generated in a small Southern town.

Reagan had met Heisler when he'd made the 1944 wartime propaganda movie, *The Negro Soldier,* a documentary-style recruitment piece targeting African-American men. Coincidentally, Heisler had been the film editor on Jane Wyman's first movie, *The Kid from Spain* (1932). "Her part was so brief, I hardly noticed her," Heisler told Reagan.

In his casting of Reagan, Wald told him, "I'm considering various other titles—*The Violent Friends!, Cause for Alarm!, The Outraged City!, Outcry!, The Fallen!, Winner Take Nothing!, Thunder in the Night!,* and *End of the Line!,* always with an exclamation point at the end of each title."

After rejecting each of those titles, he devised the title, *Ku Klux Klan, Storm Warning,* eventually dropping the reference, within the title at least, to the KKK.

The film begins on a bizarre *film noir* note, with Marsha (as played by Rogers) arriving on a rickety bus late at night in a little town that is shutting down fast. She witnesses a man being dragged from his jail cell and murdered. Two Klansmen then remove their hoods, revealing themselves as Charlie Barr (Hugh Sanders) and Hank (Cochran).

By the time she reaches her sister's home, she learns that Lucy (Doris Day) is married to Hank, whom she'd just witnessed help murder a man.

Ironically, although the KKK is known for its anti-black stance, the two people murdered during the course of the movie included a white man and, later, a white woman.

Marsh faces a dilemma when she finds that her sister is madly in love with Hank and expecting his baby. The plot thickens when Rainey, the town's District Attorney (Reagan) learns that she actually witnessed the murder. He wants her to testify against her brother-in-law, Hank, and other members of the Klan.

The movie ends in violence, with Day getting fatally shot, the only film in which one of her characters ever dies on the screen.

Each of the principal stars had already seen the Broadway version of *A Streetcar Named Desire*, the controversial 1947 Broadway play by Tennessee Williams for which Warners had acquired the screen rights. In the filmed version—eventually released in 1951—Brando would repeat the role he had made famous on the stage, and Vivien Leigh would play Blanche DuBois.

All four of the stars of *Storm Warning* noted its similarity—with the exception of the KKK subplot—to *A Streetcar Named Desire*.

When Williams saw the movie, he accused the scriptwriters of plagiarism, although he never pressed any legal action against writers Daniel Fuchs and Richard Brooks. Brooks would go on to write and direct *Elmer Gantry* (1960) with Burt Lancaster in a classic performance.

Doris Day's biographer, Tom Santopietro, would certainly agree with Williams' assertion. He wrote: "When fashion model Marsha Mitchell arrives in town with her 'high-fallutin' ways,' she interrupts the blissfully ignorant blue-collar marriage of her younger sister Lucy and Hank Rice. Just as in *Streetcar*, Blanche DuBois' arrival intrudes upon her younger sister's marriage to Stanley Kowalski. Hank Rice is, like Kowalski, presented as a crude, bigoted roughneck, and Cochran is here outfitted like Brando's Kowalski, right down to the tight-fitting T-shirt. Most striking of all is the long-simmering sexual tension between Stanley and Blanche here mirrored in the quick-to-boil sexual attraction between Hank and Marsha, an attraction that end in an explosion of violence and death."

District Attorney Rainey (i.e., Reagan) is eager "to rid the town of a bunch of hoodlums dressed up in sheets." When Marsha confronts Lucy with what her husband has done, she claims, "I don't care what he's done. I'm not gonna leave him." Her dedication evokes Stella's devotion to Brando in *Streetcar*.

In the footsteps of Kowalski, Hank tries to rape Lucy's older sister, as Brando did to Blanche DuBois.

Storm Warning's outdoor scenes were shot in the small California town of Corona, in Riverside County, southwest of Hollywood, which the set designers had defined as the community most closely resembling a town in America's Deep South. As Reagan said in his memoirs, "It was rumored to be the center of Klan activity here on the West Coast."

He recalled that one morning, shooting a street scene at 3AM, he was approached by "a little character who sidled up to me and whispered out of the corner of his mouth, 'I hear this movie is about the Klan. I'm in the local outfit, and if you need to rent some robes, let me know.'"

In Corona, Reagan staked out "two nests for myself." One was a jailcell in which he could nap between takes. Another was the stockroom of a women's ready-to-wear shop on Main Street, where he could be made up and changed into his drab wardrobe as a small town district attorney. Wald had instructed the wardrobe department, "Don't dress him up—just off-the-rack garments that don't really fit right. He's not posing for some men's fashion magazine."

Storm Warning ends violently, as Doris Day is fatally shot, the only film in which a character she plays dies. Reagan and Rogers look on in grief.

529

When it was released, no one registered any laughs from members of the audience, but when it's viewed today, some politically savvy viewers guffaw at the words expressed by a character who (rather awkwardly) says to Reagan's, "Everything would be okay if nobody interfered with us from Washington."

On the final day of shooting, Rogers had lunch with Reagan. "Wald told me I can't help but win another Oscar for this."

"I wish you luck—Oh, just to have one Oscar!" he lamented.

During the filming of *Storm Warning,* gossip columnists published items about Day dating Reagan. Apparently, he never actually proposed marriage to her, but discussed the possibility with George Murphy. "If you want to run for high office one day," Murphy advised, "Doris would make a great choice—what a personality! She can sing, too. Even if you bore your audience with one of your long-winded speeches, they'll still show up to hear her sing 'Sentimental Journey.'"

If Reagan ever actually decided to propose marriage to Day, he waited too long. She was also dating someone else and would, in fact, marry Martin Melcher on April 3, 1951. Both were practicing Christian Scientists.

Melcher would be an unfortunate choice. When he died in 1968, Day discovered, to her horror, that he had squandered her lifetime earnings in poor investments.

Wald decided to launch *Storm Warning* in the South, but soon perceived that towns such as Atlanta and Birmingham were, in his view, "too racist." He decided on the more neutral city of Miami (Florida) where *Storm Warning* was screened in a public theater on January 17, 1951.

Wald had approved an ad that depicted a Klansman beating Rogers below a blaring headline that read—"UNDER THE HOOD, HE WAS PURE YELLOW."

Day came down with the flu and canceled her scheduled appearance at the film's premiere in Miami. Reagan had planned to continue his affair with her, but when she dropped out, he called another blonde and invited her down to Miami instead. Her name was Marilyn Monroe.

Reagan had flown Marilyn to Miami once before, stashing her on Miami Beach. Once again, he booked her into the relatively cost-conscious Helen Mar Hotel. This "second time around" ended their relationship when he refused to escort her to the premiere. "I wanted to make a grand entrance with flashbulbs popping, with you and Ginger. She's always been one of my idols."

When he still refused, she denounced him. "I'm good enough for you to fuck, but not to be seen with in public," she said.

[Eventually, Marilyn would not only get to meet her idol (Rogers) but would work with her as well. Along with Cary Grant, they starred together in Monkey Business *(1952).]*

Critical response to *Storm Warning* was essentially negative. Bosley Crowther of *The New York Times* defined *Storm Warning* as a "mechanically melodramatic film, superficially forceful but lacking real substance or depth." Critic Dennis Schwartz claimed that the film "trivializes the serious subject of race hatred with an inadequate depiction of the KKK. Surprisingly, the racial hate message of the Klan is never touched upon. These Ku Klux Klan members seem to be only interested in keeping outsiders away from their town, dressing up in their robed costumes to act tough while in disguise and using the Klan to hide their thieving criminal activities."

One critic claimed that Reagan was "his usual mediocre self." The reviewer for *Cue* liked it, calling it "a first rate melodrama—a grim, gripping story."

The film marked Wald's last effort for Warner Brothers. After his work on it was finished, he left the studio to form his own production company. His relationship with Reagan went back to his early days at Warners when Wald was a contract screenwriter.

After that, Reagan pitched many projects to Wald, describing the kind of roles he wanted. He expected to spend part of the 1950s starring in films produced by Wald. But proposals from Wald never came in. Wald did, however, contact Jane Wyman, casting her in her memorable 1951 film, *The Blue Veil.*

In the 1980s, Rogers would be invited to Reagan's White House. "I didn't get to dance with Ronnie, but Vice President George Bush told me that his 'great dream' involved dancing with me, based on his having seen Fred Astaire and me in *Top Hat* (1935)."

***

More than *Kings Row,* more than *Knute Rockne—All American,* Reagan is famous for having made *Bedtime for Bonzo* (1951) for Universal. He was cast as Peter Boyd, a psychology professor, who tries to teach human morals to a chimpanzee (Bonzo), hoping to solve the "nature versus nurture" question. To that effect, he employs Jane Linden (actress Diana Lynn) to pose as the chimp's mother, with Reagan the father. As a scientific experiment, they raise him exactly like a child growing up in the 1950s.

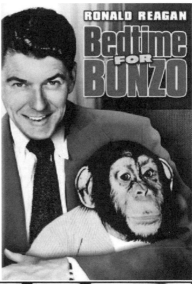

Regardless of whether any of them saw the movie, political opponents used Reagan's making of this film to mock him with such headlines as BONZO GOES TO WASHINGTON. Some critics claimed that Bonzo showed more intelligence than Reagan. A random survey taken in Los Angeles revealed that the only film most people on the street could name that Reagan ever made was *Bedtime for Bonzo.*

Frederick de Cordova was designated as director of this trifle. In time, he helmed such stars as Elvis Presley, Tony Curtis, Audie Murphy, Yvonne de Carlo, Humphrey Bogart, Bob Hope, and Errol Flynn. But he was forever mocked for having directed Reagan in *Bedtime for Bonzo.* When he directed Johnny Carson's *The Tonight Show,* the TV host frequently ridiculed Reagan and, less frequently, De Cordova for *Bonzo.*

Reagan's leading lady

Their "child," a chimp named Bonzo, causes bedroom consternation for Ronald Reagan and Diana Lynn.

When it opened, *Bonzo* got rather good reviews, *Variety* defining it as a "first-rate comedy," and *The Hollywood Reporter* labeling it as "a smash." But when Reagan's political enemies viewed it in the 80s, one Democratic candidate wrote, "Bonzo wasn't the only actor in this embarrassment with his tail hanging between his legs."

531

was a Los Angeles actress, Diana Lynn, who had been a child prodigy at the age of twelve, showing an amazing talent at the piano, and eventually developing a deep and abiding friendship with author Gore Vidal. She appeared in the comedy *My Friend Irma* (1949), in which Dean Martin and Jerry Lewis made their film debut.

A Viennese character actor, Walter Slezak, played a zoology professor, with his corpulent figure, bushy hair and mustache, his shifty eyes, and high-pitched, sneering voice.

For some reason, Reagan never saw the complete cut of *Bedtime for Bonzo* until he ordered, during the course of his presidency, that it be screened at the White House. His only comment was, "You're a chump if you make a movie with a chimp—they're born scene stealers."

***

After Bonzo, Reagan's longtime wish came true. Director Lewis R. Foster at Paramount, in a production for William H. Pine and William C. Thomas, cast him in a western, *The Last Outpost* (1951). As a "man in gray on horseback," Reagan was cast as an officer in the Confederate Army in conflict with his brother, depicted by Bruce Bennett playing a Union officer. The plot revolves around the Confederacy trying to intercept gold shipments heading East from the Southwest. Reagan insisted that the producers pay for the transport of his own horse, "Baby," to Arizona.

Other than his horse, what made the film exciting was its female co-star, Rhonda Fleming, who would also be cast as his leading lady in three future productions.

Still not married to Nancy Davis, he came down with a new bout of his chronic *"Leadinglady-itis."* Stunningly beautiful, Fleming was one of the few actresses he ever worked with who was actually born in Hollywood instead of having migrated there. At the time she met Reagan, she was between husbands.

Reagan's actual relationship with Fleming has been one of the most misunderstood in his repertoire. George Murphy claimed that he "fell in love with Rhonda during the making of *The Last Outpost.*"

June Allyson said that one night, when she invited Reagan to dine with her husband, Dick Powell, and herself, "All he did was talk about Rhonda. He may have been the first guy who called her the 'Queen of Technicolor.' He went on and on until I got jealous, praising

You'll have to see the movie to learn why Reagan, cast as the dashing leader of a Confederate cavalry unit in Arizona, ends up dressed as "a Yankee in blue." At least his dream came true: He finally got to star in a Western.

Here, he has eyes only for the ravishingly beautiful Rhonda Fleming, Hollywood's Queen of Technicolor.

532

how 'incredibly beautiful' she appeared before the color cameras with that porcelain skin and flaming red hair.'"

In Reagan's tell-nothing memoir, *Where's the Rest of Me?* he merely mentions that he was cast opposite Fleming. However, Irv Kupcinet, a columnist for the *Chicago Sun Times,* in his autobiography, published in 1988, included a curious passage. He claimed that Reagan, "the handsome bachelor, was mad about the girl" (Fleming).

"Rhonda was fond of Ronnie, but not in love. One night, Reagan was so frustrated that he pulled out his gun and fired a shot at her. I'm sure he was wide of the mark purposely, but he did scare the romance out of their idyll. I often wondered what the course of history might have been."

A year later, Fleming called Kupcinet's story "awful" and "crazy." In a statement, she claimed: "Reagan and I weren't social on or off the set. We certainly didn't have a romance."

In Edmund Morris' book, *Dutch,* he wrote: "My research cards show Reagan stepping out with at least sixteen young and beautiful actresses from Doris Day and Rhonda Fleming to the peachy and not-yet-legal Piper Laurie. God knows how many more there were or how many came back to spend the night. He was always shy about speaking of such matters when I interviewed him as an old man."

***

Since he needed money, Reagan agreed to accept a low salary of $45,000 for starring in *Hong Kong* (1952) less MCA's ten percent commission. He remembered the day at Warners when he got $150,000 per picture.

The producers of *The Last Outpost,* William H. Pine and William C. Thomas, as well as director Lewis R. Foster, and even its distributor, Paramount, were so pleased with the on-screen chemistry of Rhonda Fleming with Reagan that they cast them together in *Hong Kong* (1952).

As Reagan recalled, "This was my first time to play a bum." He was cast as Jeff Williams, an often unshaven, down-on-his-luck, American ex-soldier who decides to stay on in Hong Kong after the end of World War II. He hopes to make a lot of money selling surplus equipment left in Asia by the departing Armies.

"First a fucking chimp, now a four-year-old Chinese boy to steal the scenes." He was referring to child actor Danny Chang, who had the third lead. Reagan takes him in after discovering him wandering lost and alone.

He plots to steal a precious jeweled idol the boy possesses, and then to desert him, until his better nature, as prompted by his growing love for the very decent character played by Fleming, a Red Cross volunteer. At the time he meets her, Reagan has been embittered by his run of bad luck, but he's eventually won over by the charm and innocence of the boy and by the loving compassion of Fleming.

This movie poster is significant for one reason: The designer misspelled Reagan's last name, billing him as "Regan."

533

In an interview, Fleming said that Reagan was "more glowing and vibrant when he was telling yarns offscreen than when he was playing before the cameras. I don't think he felt very comfortable as an actor. Actually, I think he truly wanted to be in some other profession."

Reagan told director Foster, "I'll soon be forty-five years old. At this point in my life, I had hoped to be either Duke Wayne or at least Bill Holden. I should have playing the hustler, Joe Gillis, in *Sunset Blvd.*"

Reagan said "*Hong Kong,* with its paranoid politics about the communists, came and went before you could blink your eyes."

The film's review in *The New York Times* suggested that its title might more aptly have been "Ping Pong."

***

Reagan returned to Warners, his *alma mater*, for two more movies. Reunited once again with Virginia Mayo, he co-starred with her in *She's Working Her Way Through College* (1952). Shortly before she died, Mayo told author Darwin Porter, "I thought Ronnie and I had something going, and I liked him a lot. But Nancy Davis showed up all the time—and nothing came of it."

Mayo played a woman who, in an effort "to improve her mind," abandoned her career in burlesque to enroll in a Midwestern college, where she rents a room from Reagan, a professor, and his wife, as played by Phyllis Thaxter. Between classes, in an attempt to boost ticket sales for the University's floundering drama department, Mayo's character choreographs a musical, in which the very talented Gene Nelson, cast as a football star, joins her, as does another blonde beauty, Patrice Wymore, who was even more famous for her marriage (1950-1959) to Errol Flynn.

Director H. Bruce Humberstone also cast Don DeFore as Shep Slade, an obnoxious, boastful, ex-champion footballer, who still has a yen for Reagan's wife, his former sweetheart from younger days.

When Reagan went to see the final cut of *She's Working Her Way Through College,* he remarked, "It's (nothing but) a showcase for Virginia's gams."

Here, in *Hong Kong,* Reagan appears with child star Danny Chang. With a touch of bitterness, he later said, "Never appear with scene stealers like a chimp or a child."

She's Working Her Way Through College would not be the only time Reagan toiled in burlesque. At the nadir of his career in the 60s, he'd MC a burlesque act in Las Vegas.

534

***

As his farewell to Warners, Reagan starred in a baseball picture, *The Winning Team* (1952), with Doris Day as his wife. "Since you didn't become my wife off screen, I guess you can play my wife on screen," he told Day.

He was cast as Grover Cleveland Alexander, one of the foremost legends of American baseball. He later said that he enjoyed making the film as much as he did *Knute Rockne—All American.* "I also got to do some real acting dealing with Alexander's drinking problem—shades of Ray Milland in *The Lost Weekend.*"

Alexander, of course, was the baseball great who won the championship for the St. Louis Cardinals against the New York Yankees in the 1926 World Series.

Before shooting began, Reagan trained for three weeks with Cleveland's Bob Lemon and with Detroit's Harry Priddy, pitching and learning "the difference between throwing from the mound and just throwing."

Reagan cuddles up with a "working student," Virginia Mayo.

Alexander, the baseball great, nicknamed "Old Pete," had died in 1950. Although Day got star billing because of her box office clout, the real star of the picture was Reagan.

Although Reagan continued for a while to be cast in minor film roles, *The Winning Team* hastened the end of any big movie career for him as a middle-aged actor. Day's biographer, Tom Santopietro, summed up the problem: "Reagan did not have the emotional depth of acting chops to bring off the complex characterization required. He is simply not a very interesting actor, and is not up to the task of appearing in every scene. His lack of technique and resulting inability to access the required emotional complexities are evident in every scene requiring a display of emotion."

Later, Day was reported to have said, "My role required for me to do little more than appear angelic and be supportive and helpful. My God, where was Nancy Davis? She should have played my part."

Lewis Seiler, who helmed *The Winning Team,* had first directed Reagan in *Hell's Kitchen* (1939) with the Dead End Kids.

Reagan actually liked the script about Alexander, who had been a heavy boozer and suffered epileptic seizures. This was Reagan's second time playing an epileptic, beginning with "that dismal failure," *Night Unto Night* (1949).

Day and Reagan were backed up with strong support from character actor Frank Lovejoy, who defined himself as "a boy from the Bronx." At the time he met Reagan, he had just appeared with Joan Crawford in *Goodbye, My Fancy* (1951). That movie would become his best remembered. "I'm always cast as the movies' Everyman," he told Reagan.

Reagan almost faced a disaster. He had recovered from breaking his right leg in a charity baseball game. However, in one scene from *The Winning Team,* he fell and almost inflicted the same injury to his left leg. Priddy, Detroit's second baseman, had accidentally stepped on him. "I suffered a painful laceration," Reagan claimed, "and had to hobble around for days. At least he didn't break my leg."

Day later recalled, "Aimee, the wife of Grover Cleveland Alexander, was the most boring role I ever had to play. I wasn't surprised when it failed to score a home run at the box office. Ronnie was already in his 40s trying to act like a 21-year-old."

Both of them talked about their upcoming marriages, Reagan "praising Nancy as if she were a goddess fallen to earth," in Day's view.

She was more realistic about her own new spouse. "I've settled down in Toluca Lake with Martin (Melcher) to a life of non-bliss."

Time dismissed *The Winning Team,* attacking the "rookie performance" by Reagan.

Even though Day "hated myself in the thankless role," she won *Photoplay's* Gold Medal for being "the most popular actress of the year."

Reagan departed from the Warner's lot on January 28, 1952, after fifteen years of filmmaking. There was no fanfare, "not even a gold watch," he said. "I thought a good-bye from Jack Warner might be in order. I got only silence. I asked for my final paycheck. I was told, 'It's in the mail.'"

As he pulled his car out of the studio parking lot that day, he noticed an attendant removing his "permanent" nameplate from in front of what had, for years, been his parking space.

Years later, when he was running for Governor of California, Warner was approached to open his wallet for the campaign.

Refusing to contribute, he said, "No, no, no, Dennis Morgan for governor, Ronald for first friend."

***

Released from his long-enduring contract with Warner Brothers, Reagan found himself adrift in a sea of aging, unemployed actors, each of them on the verge of turning fifty. Dick Powell had told him, "The road between forty-five and fifty goes by as quickly as a summer cloudburst."

Once again, he was rescued by the same Paramount team that had cast Rhonda Fleming and him in *The Last Outpost* and *Hong Kong:* producers William H. Pine and William C. Thomas, along with director Lewis R. Foster.

The moment Reagan read the script for *Tropic Zone* (1953), he knew it would be a dud. He called it "a sand-and-banana epic," although it was hardly an epic.

"The script was hopeless, but I was grateful to the boys for hiring me before. As a favor to them, I agreed to make *Tropic Zone."*

Actually, Lew Wasserman, his agent, later revealed, "I practically had to beg Pine and Thomas to use Ronnie again."

Chapter Thirteen

Jane Battles Marilyn

for the Man Who Becomes Her Husband No. 4 and No. 5.

A "Cougar on the Prowl," Jane Seeks Young, Hot, and Handsome Male Flesh on the Hoof

Jane lamented to Paulette Goddard, "Just my luck. To win Ronnie, I had to fight off Betty Grable, Susan Hayward, and a wagon load of starlets at Warners. To get my claws into my new husband, Fred Karger *(depicted twice with Jane in photos above)*, I had another road block. Little Miss Monroe herself. Freddie is that rare specimen—a living doll!"

"But just when I thought I'd knocked Marilyn out of the race, around the bend comes another Adonis...Rock Hudson, who can offer Freddie something I can't."

"BELOVED BELINDA IN A LOVABLE NEW ROLE," proclaimed the ads at Warners. As Jane reported to work at her home studio, these ads were already in production in the art department. She had a leading role in a fluffy new comedy, *A Kiss in*

the Dark. Her co-star would be David Niven, on loan from Samuel Goldwyn. In events which transpired, the British actor's name would be billed over hers.

The second male lead would be played by Wayne Morris, her old flame from the late 1930s. But as Jane told Paulette Goddard, "With Wayne and me, the candle has already burnt out at both ends."

Over lunch with Jane, Morris told her, "I've gone from leading man to the meathead boyfriend who loses the girl—like in this thing we're making!"

"At least you've got a job, sugar," she told him. "And in the Hollywood of today, that's a damned fine accomplishment!"

The three leads would be supplemented with a strong supporting cast that included Victor Moore, Broderick Crawford, and Maria Ouspenskaya.

After reading the script, Jane told her director, Delmer Daves, "I thought that Jack Warner could come up with stronger material for an Oscar winner like me."

"Be patient," he told her. "I see another Oscar in your future. After all, you can't expect to win Oscars back to back like Luise Rainer."

A Kiss in the Dark's plot centered around a concert pianist, Eric Phillips (Niven), who returns from a tour to discover that he's inherited an apartment house with loony tenants. His favorite is a beautiful photographer's model, Polly Haines (Jane). Niven has trouble with his resident manager, the zany Victor Moore, the scene stealer of the film.

Jane remembered her role chiefly for the fact that as a photographer's model, she had to undergo more than two dozen wardrobe changes.

David Niven, whose mysterious war record as an Allied spy is still a matter of conjecture, played this love scene with Jane's full understanding of his former affair with her gossipy friend, Paulette Goddard.

She called Jane, wanting to know if she had yet succumbed to his manly charms.

"No," Jane answered. Since shooting began, he's had this sore throat and retreats to his dressing room when he's not needed on the set."

"Sorry about that, girl," Goddard said. "You're missing out on something really wonderful. I should know."

She had first met Crawford when they had appeared together in *Larceny, Inc.* with Edward G. Robinson. "What a puny role for a star like me," he told her. The events of 1949 would later represent the pinnacle of his career, as he'd win the Best Actor Oscar for his role as the crooked politician in *All the King's Men,* its script based on the bestselling book by Robert Penn Warren.

Jane had great respect for Ouspenskaya, and was later very sorry to learn that *A Kiss in the Dark* was the final role for the aging Russian actress. After many distinguished performances, she died on December 3, 1949, at the age of 73. She suffered a fatal stroke after severe burns from a fire in her house. She had ignited it after falling

She Falls in Love with Her Co-Star, Rock Hudson, Until the Night She Discovers Him in Bed With Her Husband

asleep with a lit cigarette.

In addition to being sick, Niven could not master moving his fingers across the piano keybord in any convincing way. He later admitted, "An expert played the piano with his arms through my tailcoat while I rolled my eyes and looked soulful."

She tried to put a good face on the film, saying, "The role is a test of my versatility. Comedy is as exacting as drama. It demands more of a performer technically, although audiences aren't as apt to give a good comedy performance the recognition it deserves."

The Observer in London defined *A Kiss in the Dark* as "one of the silliest and trashiest stories seen on the screen for many a long day." *Time* claimed, "The film is a daffy romantic comedy apparently intended to show that Oscar-winning Jane Wyman is not really a deaf-mute."

***

Preparations for her next film began with a call from director Michael Curtiz, telling her that Jack Warner had cast her in a comedy called *The Octopus and Miss Smith.*

"Your leading man, girlie, is Dennis Morgan. Maybe you guys will spend time on film, not all time fucking. Morgan is no more big box office. He'll play second violin to you."

"You mean, second fiddle," Jane said.

"Fiddle, violin, trumpet, who gives a fuck?"

Jane was cast as Jennifer Smith, with Morgan as Davy Jones (alias Bill Craig), who claims he's a zoologist, maneuvering an underwater vehicle. He is actually a submarine engineer on a secret government mission. After an accident at sea, he rescues Jane, but because of the secrecy associated with his job, he can't tell her who he is.

When she recounts the story of her rescue to her business partner (Eve Arden), and to representatives of the Tyson Institute, which intends to finance a project for her, they think she's crazy. Since Morgan can't tell her who he really is, the inevitable complications ensue. All ends well, however, and eventually, Jane wins her sailor both on and off the screen.

Jane blew her top when she heard that the film's title had been changed to *The Lady Takes a Sailor* (1949), but she was otherwise cooperative.

When she was criticized for accepting such a silly part, she told Louella Parsons that had she not accepted the role, a lot of employees at Warners would have been fired, based on Jack Warner's policy of laying off employees because of dwindling postwar profits. "It might have been a mistake, but I made a lot of the crew happy by accepting the role."

Curtiz had assembled a supporting cast that was stronger and more talented than the frothy and somewhat silly plot. Its members included Eve Arden, Allyn Joslyn, Fred Clark, Tom Tully, and William Frawley. Jane's former friend, Craig Stevens, was awarded a minor role, but the two of them avoided each other whenever possible. Jane and Reagan had broken from Stevens and his wife, Alexis Smith, after that weekend in Palm Springs.

She told Curtiz, "I've been away from comedy too long, and I'm off in my timing. Comedy is damn tricky. I take my hat off to anyone who

Jane maintains her resolve in this comedy about ladies, sailors, errors, and mistaken identities. *Above*, Dennis Morgan, Eve Arden, and a mystified (until the final reel) Jane.

539

can play it well. Fortunately, we've got my gal pal, Eve Arden. She's always on her mark."

On her final day on the set of *The Lady Takes a Sailor,* Curtiz told Jane she had to sail to England for her next movie, *Stage Fright,* to be directed by Alfred Hitchcock.

"Who's my leading man in this one?" she asked Curtiz.

"Marlene Dietrich," he answered.

***

Before leaving for England, Jane filmed a cameo for inclusion within the otherwise completed *It's a Great Feeling* (1939), a film in which her lover, Dennis Morgan, played the male lead. Reagan was in the picture, too, but he and Jane had no scenes together in that all-star Warner Brother's extravaganza.

In one scene of that movie, Jack Carson and Morgan are grooming Doris Day for stardom. Carson says, "I'll see to it that she's as good in this as Jane Wyman was in *Johnny Belinda."*

"She didn't even talk in that one," Morgan says.

Carson replies, "Well, you can't have everything."

It's a Great Feeling marked the film debut of Maureen Reagan.

It was positioned into a scene where Jane is called into the office of the producer (played by Bill Goodwin), and is told that Carson was going to direct her in *Mademoiselle Fifi,* her next movie. Jane faints upon hearing that she has to work with a director who, the audience learns, is notoriously temperamental.

At this point, a blonde kid (Maureen) enters with a glass of water. She hands it to Jane and says, "Here, Mommy, take this."

Maureen, in a latter-day evaluation of her first screen appearance, claimed, "I thought I was just terrible, certainly the weak link in an otherwise fine production."

***

Reagan had returned from England after making *The Hasty Heart.* Plans called for him to care for and protect Maureen and Michael while Jane went to London shooting *Stage Fright* with Alfred Hitchcock. Jack Warner promised her star billing over her co-star, Marlene Dietrich.

The two male leads were Michael Wilding and Richard Todd. Ironically, Todd had been Reagan's co-star in *The Hasty Heart.*

"When I first arrived at the studio, Marlene was the first to greet me," Jane recalled. "She was the epitome of graciousness, although I heard from Hitchcock that she bitterly resented getting second billing. Ironically, she became the most visible star of the picture."

"I admired Marlene's figure," Jane said. "She was

Jane's attempt to train her daughter Maureen, pictured above in a scene with her from *It's a Great Feeling,* sparked the child's interest in becoming an actress.

Jane later said, "If producers and casting directors were looking for 'cute' and 'perky' in the early 1950s, I was their gal."

almost fifty, yet retained her sense of glamour and enchantment. She invited me to lunch that day and stuffed herself with steak and kidney pie. I had to watch my weight and settled for a salad. Yet she never gained weight."

As it happened, according to Dietrich, Hitchcock would have preferred for an English actress to play Jane's role, and he would have been happier if Tallulah Bankhead (whom he had previously directed in *Lifeboat* (1944), had been given the part played by Dietrich. Jack Warner had personally vetoed each of those preferences.

Later, when Jane confronted the director about his preference for an English actress, he admitted that he had wanted Jean Simmons.

Stage Fright was a murder mystery, some of it relayed in flashback, based on the Selwyn Jepson novel, *Man Running,* with a screen treatment from Whitfield Cook, Ranald MacDougall, and Alma Reville (the director's wife). Dietrich rewrote some of her own dialogue.

Jane was cast as Eve Gill, an American who is studying at RADA, wanting to become an actress. She develops a crush on fellow actor Jonathan Cooper (Todd), who is secretly in love with the flamboyant stage actress and singer, Charlotte Inwood (Dietrich).

Jane befriends Todd when he claims that Charlotte came to him

Hitchcock usually opted to include a "blink of the eye" cameo of himself in each of his films. In *Stage Fright,* he opted to make that appearance in a London street scene with Jane.

Are the most menacing killers always the handsomest? Here's Jane in Stage *Fright* with the film's scariest psycho, her tormentor, Richard Todd.

in a blood-stained dress after killing her husband. When he went to retrieve a new dress for her at her home, witnesses saw him leaving the scene of the crime and he was fingered as the killer.

Eve meets Detective Wilfred O. Smith (Wilding) and is drawn into his orbit, finding out that his middle name is "Ordinary." She bribes Charlotte's cockney dresser, Nellie Goode (Kay Walsh), and Jane becomes "Doris Tinsdale," hired to be Charlotte's maid.

From that point on, the plot employs many of Hitchcock's tricks before it reaches its dramatic conclusion. It turns out that Jonathan is the real murderer after all, and that

Hitchcock tricked the audience with a *faux* flashback.

Two veterans of the English stage were cast as Jane's parents, Alastair Sim as Commodore Gil, and Sybil Thorndike as Mrs. Gill. Sim was a Scottish character actor who, in addition to his theatrical career, had been a leading star in British cinema in the 1950s, appearing in more than fifty movies. Jane was amazed at the tonal control of his voice and his sensitivity to the nuances of the English language. "Only John Gielgud rivaled him," she said.

She adored Thorndike, who had been made a Dame Commander of the Order of the British Empire. George Bernard Shaw had written *Saint Joan* specifically for her.

Others in the cast included Hitchcock's daughter, Patricia Hitchcock, in her movie debut as Chubby Bannister in a humorous vignette.

Super glamorous Marlene Dietrich lights up for demure Jane Wyman in this scene from *Stage Fright*. Jane complained to Hitchcock, "I may have an Oscar, something Marlene doesn't have, but she has everything else-- She's taken a bite out of Richard Todd, she's snared Michael Wilding, she's got the Dior wardrobe, the glamour, and the songs."

"She might be telling us she's "The Laziest Gal in Town," but she's damn busy looking after Marlene!"

Even though Dietrich detested Hitchcock, he gave her the star treatment, allowing her to bring in Cole Porter to help her with her one big song in the movie, "The Laziest Gal in Town." At first, she'd rejected it, claiming "It is too old." But it went over so big with audiences that she sang it on tour for the rest of her professional life.

For her other song, "La Vie en Rose," Dietrich purloined the signature song of her French lover, Edith Piaf. Hitchcock finally agreed to include it in the film, after protesting that the song was already too well known.

He also let Dietrich hire Christian Dior to design her wardrobe, which the diva insisted on taking home with her at the end of filming.

"Next to Marlene, I looked like a little brown wren," Jane complained.

When she saw the first rushes, Jane burst into tears, seeing herself depicted on the big screen as a drab maid. She called Jack Warner and he agreed. He phoned Hitchcock, ordering him, "Let Jane spiff herself up. After all, she is one of our studio's marquee attractions, and there is nothing to be gained by making her look like Marjorie Main on a bad day."

Hitchcock tried to reassure Jane. "You're an attractive woman in your own right. You're one type, Marlene is another. You're also twelve years younger than she is. The camera will catch that. So why worry?"

"Jane's refusal to stick to the script annoyed me," Hitchcock said. "She should have been a pimply faced girl. Wyman just refused to be that, and I was stuck with her. Suddenly, with Warner's blessing, she started showing up with more makeup. She just refused to stay in character the way it was written."

Although Jane frequently tangled with Hitchcock, their relationship remained more tranquil than his with the more temperamental Dietrich. Jane later said, "We had a pleasant uneasiness between us at all times. In other words, I didn't find him a cuddly teddy bear. I also didn't like it when he told me that he preferred to direct blondes."

As shooting progressed, Dietrich began to pay more and more attention to Jane, overcoming her initial jealousy at her star billing. As Jane recalled, "On days when Marlene had no studio call, she would come on the set just the same. She'd fix my dress, make suggestions about my hair and makeup, and help me in many ways."

Later, Jane had unattractive stories to relay to Paulette Goddard, who was no friend of Dietrich, since Goddard was jealous of the star's appeal to Erich Maria Remarque, the renowned writer whom Goddard eventually married.

Jane claimed, "At one point, when Dietrich was messing with my hair, she fondled my breasts."

It isn't known if this really happened, or whether Jane was being spiteful to Dietrich. However, the German diva had been known to pull that stunt with other female stars, as once reported by, of all people, Mae West.

Dietrich told Jane, "If the Academy gave Oscars for great performances as a lover, I would have a shelf filled with replicas of that statuette."

At first, Jane found the Irish-born stage and film actor and former soldier, Richard Todd, "Handsome enough to win any maiden's heart." That year, he would marry Catherine Grant-Bogle, whom he'd met at Scotland's Dundee Repertory Theatre. "Hitchcock told me that Marlene had already 'auditioned' the young man *[i.e., Todd]*, who was two years younger than me," Jane said.

As regards Todd, Michael Wilding said, "Dick was taking bachelor's privilege before settling down to wedding bliss. That is, of course, bedding any available lass he could. Jane seemed the most susceptible to his Irish charm and wit."

At the time of Jane's first excursion to a Mayfair pub with Todd, he turned her off by talking about his experience of working with Reagan in *The Hasty Heart.*

"If you don't mind, I'd rather close that chapter of my life."

During her filming of *Stage Fright,* Jane's attorney sent her documents defining the date of her divorce from Reagan as July 18, 1949.

Jane rejected Todd's next two invitations for pub crawls with him. Then one afternoon, she received a letter from Lew Ayres. In it, he reminded her that he'd been married twice before (to Lola Lane and Ginger Rogers), and telling her that he had no desire to repeat the process. "I may never marry again. At least you and I made a great film together, and had endearing moments of love. But it must end."

Louella Parsons was in London at the time, and she heard that Ayres had dumped Jane. Normally, the gossip maven and the actress were the best of friends, but on this occasion, Parsons told friends that "Jane was icy cold."

"I have no plans to marry *anyone,*" Jane told Parsons.

"Perhaps I got Jane on the rebound," Todd recalled to Wilding and others. "But she came to my dressing room and fell into my arms. I think she needed reassurance that she was still desirable to men. Before that night ended in her hotel suite, she was assured about just how desirable she really was. It took a loving Irishman like myself to do that job. From then on, we had this thing, although I kept it from my bride-to-be. There was a lot of sneaking around."

Dietrich got involved in details associated with Todd's upcoming marriage. She wanted to know the birth dates of both Todd and Grant-Bogle.

Astrologist Carroll Righter was Dietrich's professional stargazer. The actress consulted him at least three times a week. A cultured homosexual, he would advise her to see Jean Gabin one evening, Douglas Fairbanks, Jr. another evening, or Ernest Hemingway on a third night.

In front of Jane, Dietrich told Todd what she'd learned from her astrologer. "You must not marry that girl. The stars are never wrong. My life is ruled by the stars. If you marry her, you'll be making a ghastly error."

Todd later said, "Marlene, or rather her stargazer friend, was right. My marriage ended in divorce."

Hitchcock told Jane, "The only thing I like about Todd is his expressive eyes. You have other qualities, but I think you also have some of the most expressive eyes of any actress in film today."

"Thank you," Jane said, "but I can assure you that Richard has hidden talent—not just his eyes."

"I see, my dear," Hitchcock replied. "I will have to take your word for it. Unlike George Cukor, who is in town filming a movie, I do not put my leading actors on a casting couch."

During the making of *Stage Fright,* Wilding was ending his marriage to Kay Young, whom he would divorce in 1951, allowing him to marry Elizabeth Taylor the following year. Prior to his marriage to Taylor, he had been the fourth most popular star at the box offices of Britain.

Both Dietrich and Wilding were immediately attracted to each other. "When I introduced them, they were practically making love," Hitchcock said. "I wanted to tell them to get a room. In a sense, they did. Her dressing room."

On their first day together, Wilding was bewitched by "the world's most glamorous grandmother." As he recalled in a memoir, *The Wilding Way,* "My first sight of her was breathtaking. She was lying on a sofa, draped in furs, her lovely legs gleaming in black tights, looking like a 20th Century Venus. I was completely bewitched and tongue-tied until she broke the silence herself."

"Before Marlene took up with Michael, I got a sample of her world-famous oral talents," Todd said. "So did George Bernard Shaw, I heard, on their first meeting. After she serviced me, she told me that even though she opposed my upcoming marriage, she considered my bride to be a very lucky girl. I considered that a great compliment, considering some of the guys she had serviced. You name them, Gary Cooper, Yul Brynner, Joe DiMaggio, Kirk Douglas, Burt Lancaster, George Raft, Orson Welles, John Wayne, General George Patton, John Gilbert, Howard Hughes, Ronald Colman, John F. Kennedy, and such ladies as Colette and Barbara Stanwyck."

Before Jane met Michael Wilding *(above),* Dietrich told her, "He's the British equivalent of Jimmy Stewart."

"That's good to know," Jane answered. "I've had Jimmy, and liked him, so maybe this newly liberated bachelor gal will make a new conquest."

"Too late," Dietrich told her. "I saw him first, dear heart."

Wilding was nearly twelve years younger than Dietrich. She found him sophisticated and amusing, and he entertained her with amusing anecdotes about his life. As her biographer, Donald Spoto, wrote, "*[Wilding]* had scarcely been introduced to her when she offered herself to him, as if the way for her to feel young was to prove to herself that she could keep a young man. 'I am too old for you,' she said bluntly. Obviously, he did not agree."

During the shoot, Dietrich and Wilding became the most photographed couple in London, their romance generating tabloid fodder. But it was not destined to last. Maria Riva (Dietrich's daughter), in her memoirs, provided the reason why her mother did not remain with Wilding.

Riva wrote: "During the Wilding time, my mother kept up her devotion to Maurice Chevalier, became involved with a famous American actress known not only for her talent, pined for Jean Gabin, received her baseball player when he needed cosseting, loved Erich Maria Remarque, her charming general, Edith Piaf, a gorgeous Teutonic blonde who became her German pal, and worked full time at being indispensible to her immediate entourage."

Riva was being discreet, not revealing some of the other names with whom Dietrich was involved at the time.

After the filming, Dietrich told both Jane and Riva, "I don't like Hitchcock. Why they all think he is so great, I don't know. Josef von Sternberg was great, *Stage Fright* is bad. Maybe in cutting, he'll do all his famous 'suspense' to save it. He certainly didn't do it while we were shooting this monstrosity."

Privately, Wilding told Hitchcock, "I don't like this Wyman creature. Perhaps Ronald Reagan went for her. I'm not sure who Reagan is. I've never seen one picture of his. I hear he's a second rate actor. She suffered being the only Yank in an all-English cast."

Publicly, he said to the press, "Miss Wyman carried off her role with dignity and poise. I think she held her own beautifully."

At the end of the shoot, Hitchcock told the press, "Marlene Dietrich is a professional star. She is also a professional cameraman, art director, film editor, costume designer, hairdresser, makeup artist, composer, and producer—*and* director."

The next morning, she read in the *London Express Observer* that Marlene Dietrich had been spotted at one of the London airports while awaiting the departure of a flight to Paris. A journalist had reported that after being asked what it was like working with Jane Wyman, "Miss Dietrich merely shrugged her shoulders and walked toward the departure gate."

Upon the release of *Stage Fright,* Dietrich got rave reviews, Hitchcock, Jane, and the movie not faring well. The word used to describe Jane was often "mousy."

Critic Molly Haskell hailed Dietrich's performance as one of the greatest in her long career. The *Sunday Mirror* in New York found Dietrich "supercharged with sex appeal at her age. She makes Jane Wyman look like a Girl Scout leader."

Another reviewer mocked Jane's attempt at a Cockney accent, except when she said "mattam" for madam. "That was the only Cockney enunciation she managed to get correct," he wrote.

Years later, Jane said, "On the screen, I was supposed to be falling in love with Wilding. Nothing could have been further from the truth. In my scenes with him, I couldn't make out half of what he was talking about."

Fans today, especially those who watch *Turner Classic Movies,* seem to appreciate *Stage Fright* more than those who saw it back in 1950.

***

In an inaccurate report, the *Daily Express* ran a story asserting that Lew Ayres had flown into London and was seen dancing with Jane Wyman. The journalist wrote, "I hear wedding bells in the background."

Jane was not with Ayres, as he had previously broken off with her. She was dating her latest beau, Clark Hardwicke, described as a "millionaire sportsman." He was actually a golfer. But he did look like Ayres, so the inaccuracy in the report was based on a case of mistaken identity.

Jane's affair with the young man would continue after her return to Hollywood.

A pivotal moment came for her in London right before she left. On a sightseeing trip in a chauffeur-driven Rolls Royce provided by the studio, she asked her driver to stop in front of an imposing building. She thought it was Westminster Abbey. Actually, it was Westminster Cathedral, the largest Catholic church in England. She later told a reporter, "I'd never seen such a sight in my life."

She spent an hour inside, marking the beginning of her interest in the Catholic liturgy. She attended the Cathedral every day during the remainder of her stay in London, becoming fascinated by the rituals inside, including mass, rosaries, the wardrobe of the priests, and the panorama of church history extending back to its Old Testament beginnings. On the day of her final visit, she made a strange statement: "I'm going to become a Catholic even if it kills me."

In Hollywood, among the bills that had piled up, she first opened a letter from her divorce lawyer, Lloyd Wright. He charged her $7,500 for divorcing Reagan. She sent him a check for $5,000 and marked it "Payment in Full." He accepted her reduced fee.

Jane in 1950, on the loose with Clark Hardwicke, capturing a young man's fancy until the real thing came along.

***

Ironically, her letterhead read, "Mrs. Ronald Reagan, Hollywood, California."

When Clark Hardwicke returned to California, she was seen frequently with him. There were rumors of an upcoming marriage.

Ruth Waterbury, a former assistant to Louella Parsons and the former editor of both *Photoplay* and *Silver Screen,* didn't think so. "Let's face it: Clark Hardwicke is a cute, sexy kid with a good athlete's body. Janie was feeling light and giddy, and Clark filled the bill for that mood. She used him to distract herself. I never heard her say anything really deeply felt about him."

[The last time Jane was seen in public with her dashing young beau was in August of 1950, when Movie Life *covered the preview of* The Glass

Plain Jane, without makeup, testifying in court about her intention of divorcing Reagan.

Menagerie, *her latest film based on the hit Broadway play by Tennessee Williams. After that, Hardwicke slid into the graveyard of her forgotten beaux.]*

***

A new saga in the very dysfunctional life of the Wingfield family began when Charles Feldman and Jerry Wald, as producers, set out to bring Tennessee's *The Glass Menagerie* to the screen. They envisioned it as a 1950 release directed by Irving Rapper.

Casting was a major issue fraught with trauma. Tennessee rarely got his wish when it came to the stars who were hired for screen adaptations of his plays. Originally, he'd wanted Teresa Wright for the role of Laura. "Her sad eyes and the aching vulnerability in her voice would make her ideal as Laura," he told Feldman.

But by the time Tennessee reached Hollywood, he had changed his mind, telling Feldman, "Only Judy Garland can capture the poignancy of Laura."

The producer had his own ideas. "I'm pitching the role of Amanda *[the play's steely matriarch]* to Ethel Barrymore and the part of Laura *[Amanda's disabled and overly vulnerable daughter]* to Jeanne Crain."

In the weeks that followed, Feldman ran into more and more roadblocks and kept calling Tennessee to report on changes in his vision for the cast. In the first of these calls he announced, "I think Gene Tierney should play Laura, with Montgomery Clift in the role of the Gentleman Caller." Tennessee at least liked the idea of Clift.

Two days later, Feldman called again with another change: "How about Marlon Brando as the Gentleman Caller, and Tallulah Bankhead as Amanda?"

"As much as I adore Tallulah, don't you think she's a bit strong to play a gentle Southern belle?"

Before Feldman called again, he'd spoken to Brando. "Marlon said he'll never work with Tallulah again unless the Earth is attacked by Martians."

[In 1947, Tallulah and Brando had starred together, with frequent outbursts of spleen, rage and fury, in the Jean Cocteau play, The Eagle Has Two Heads.*]*

A week later, Feldman called again. "I've come up with the best idea of all: Miriam Hopkins, that Savannah magnolia, as Amanda, with Ralph Meeker playing the Gentleman Caller. He's less than lovable to work with, but brazenly masculine for the role."

Although it had been pre-arranged that the film would be distributed by Warner Brothers, there were rumblings from Louis B. Mayer at MGM. Enraged, he had telephoned Tennessee's literary agent, Audrey Wood, claiming he owned the rights to *The Glass Menagerie* because Tennessee, while on salary at MGM, "wrote the play on our dime. By giving this to Warner's, he's biting the hand that fed the little faggot. I'm finding it harder and harder to cast Greer Garson. But she'd be great as Amanda. I also resent Williams' criticism of my judgment at MGM."

A dysfunctional mother argues with her dysfunctional son: Arthur Kennedy with Gertrude (*"Rise & shine!"*) Lawrence.

[Tennessee had told the press that he had been dropped by MGM "in retaliation for my unwillingness to undertake another stupid assignment after I fucked up on Marriage Is a Private Affair *(1944) for Lana Turner."]*

Mayer's threat of a lawsuit did not materialize, and eventually, to his humiliation, he lived to see his own daughter, Irene Mayer Selznick, produce Tennessee's second film, *A Streetcar Named Desire*, for Warner Brothers, not MGM.

Tennessee was surprised once again when Feldman called to tell him that he'd just signed the British star, Gertrude Lawrence, to play Amanda. Tennessee knew her as a singer, dancer, and musical comedy performer. *The Glass Menagerie* would be Lawrence's only film in which she worked at an American studio with an otherwise all-American cast.

Since, contractually, Feldman had the power of casting, Tennessee relented, but nevertheless threw in a dig, "Is Lawrence bringing Daphne du Maurier to Hollywood with her?"

[Both Tennessee and Feldman knew that Lawrence and the world-famed novelist were lesbian lovers.]

When Tennessee actually met Lawrence, he was deliberately provocative: "In London, Noël Coward told me that he lost his virginity to you when he was just thirteen years old. According to Noël, the two of you did it on a train."

"That story is absolutely true," she answered. "I fear I scared off the boy from women for life."

With some reluctance, Tennessee accepted a screenwriting credit with Peter Berneis, the play's adapter.

Tennessee shuddered when he learned the details of the movie's final casting. The role of Laura went to Jane Wyman.

He feared that she was too old for the part, but the co-producer, Jerry Wald, assured him she'd be terrific. "Jane, of course, isn't fresh anymore. But she studies a character for weeks and throws herself into the part."

It was the director, Irving Rapper, who called Tennessee to tell him that the pivotal character of Tom Wingfield would be played by Arthur Kennedy, and the part of the Gentleman Caller would be given to Kirk Douglas, then in the first flush of his stardom.

Visiting the set, Tennessee met with Jane, later defining her as "a strong, cold, and determined bitch."

He remembered her divorced husband, Reagan, dropping by the set to give her a poodle for her birthday.

"I later met John F. Kennedy before he became President," Tennessee said. "I thought he was much too good looking and sophisticated to get elected. As for Reagan, there is no way in hell that I could believe this untalented actor would ever become president. It was inconceivable. I guess I don't know how to pick them in politics."

He made this statement in 1980 to Margaret Foresman of *The Key West Citizen*.

Reagan invited Tennessee to join

Kirk Douglas as the "Gentleman Caller," with Jane as the girl whose psyche is as damaged as her clubfoot.

548

Jane and him in the commissary.

As Tennessee remembered it, Reagan and Jane talked about which boarding school would be the right choice for their daughter, Maureen. "They decided on Palos Chadwick School at Palos Verdes. That's where Joan Crawford sent her daughter, Christina, instead of smothering her. I'm sure Joan would have decided on death-by-strangulation if she knew that Christina would write that horrid little memoir, *Mommie Dearest*, *[published in 1978]* about her adoptive mother."

Tennessee continued: "Maureen never wrote a *Daddy Dearest* book about Reagan, but that other daughter of his, Patti Davis, came close, or so I'd heard. I never read crap like that before."

After Reagan bid Jane and Tennessee goodbye, he headed out the door.

Ten minutes later, Tennessee left the commissary with the intention of beginning his afternoon walk. He later told Darwin Porter, "Reagan was outside, waiting to be picked up by someone. This blonde suddenly pulled up in her car. I strained my one good eye. The face was unmistakable. That blonde taking Reagan away, no doubt, for a session of love in the afternoon, was none other than perky little Doris Day."

***

Interpreting the role of Laura was a rough challenge for Jane, as she had to play the club-footed and deeply depressed daughter of the spectacularly dysfunctional Wingfield family. She lives in a world of her own, collecting fragile glass animals. She shares the apartment with her brother, Tom (as played by Arthur Kennedy), and her iron magnolia mother, Amanda (Gertrude Lawrence). Tom is a frustrated would-be writer earning a meager living laboring in a warehouse. The three survive in a tenement building in St. Louis. The absent husband of the house, a telephone repairman, "fell in love with long distance" and, years before, abandoned his family to survive as best they could.

Wanting his disabled sister to find a potential *beau*, Tom brings home a gentleman caller (Kirk Douglas) as the movie heads toward its tragic *dénouement*. At a particularly poignant moment, he informs the very vulnerable Laura that he's already engaged to another woman.

Although Rapper was the wrong director for the job—it called for an Elia Kazan—he did try to make effective use of Jane's bittersweet docility in close-ups.

She recalled, "It takes more than a limp to play a lame girl. It takes a definite frame of mind, in which you project yourself into the part so fully that you even think like a handicapped person and act like one. In *Menagerie* I wear a specially designed shoe that makes my left foot turn in and that actually forces me to limp."

Ironically, Jane's personal hobby involved collecting glass replicas of animals. She even lent Warners some

Jane used her expressive eyes to convey her character's vulnerability, living in her "world of glass." She told Rapper, "In some respects, Laura reminds me of that lonely little girl I left behind in St. Joseph."

pieces from her personal collection.

During the filming, Michael Reagan became desperately ill with some kind of flu virus and had to be hospitalized. When she wasn't needed on the set, Jane was with him at the hospital.

Rapper warned that she was risking shutting down production if she contracted the flu herself.

She later became furious that Warners publicity promoted the film like some sex drama with large lettered typeface proclaiming:

HE WAS TOO SHY FOR TOO LONG...AND THEN CAME FRESH GUY.

The filmed version of *The Glass Menagerie* (1950) did not do well at the box office. Even Douglas expressed his disappointment. "Unfortunately, the movie was not well directed," he said, "and Gertrude Lawrence's vanity had to be appeased. She insisted on a flashback, where she was young and glamorous, so no one would think she was the old lady that she actually was. The elements didn't mesh; the movie just didn't come off."

Years later, Douglas would recommend that moviegoers wanting to see *The Glass Menagerie* should, in lieu of the version he was in, catch the 1987 version directed by Paul Newman, starring his wife, Joanne Woodward.

In reference to the 1950 version, Tennessee himself later stated, "I detested the film. As I predicted, Lawrence was a dismal error in casting. The movie version was a dishonest adaptation of my play. I would soon get used to that in Hollywood's other attempts to film one of my dramas."

Bosley Crowther of *The New York Times* agreed with Tennessee about the miscasting of Lawrence. He called her "a farcically exaggerated shrew with the zeal of a burlesque comedian to see her diffident daughter wed. Her Southern accent has an occasional cockney strain."

Crowther, however, had kinder words for Jane's performance, defining her acting as "beautifully sensitive."

Time magazine wrote: "Miss Wyman is constitutionally incapable of looking so ethereal as Julie Haydon, who played the role on Broadway. But with the help of shoulder-length hair and a childlike smile, she gives the part of the girl half her age an almost equally poignant sincerity."

Jane told Rapper, "I worked harder on Laura than I did on *Johnny Belinda.*"

***

For a brief few months, Jane Wyman captured Greg Bautzer, a powerful attorney and the most sought-after bachelor in town.

She had nothng but high praise for him, telling a reporter, "He's a woman's man, thoughtful, considerate, attentive. If you ask him to the most informal dinner party, he'll send flowers the next day with a sweet note. If you go nightclubbing with him and are separated from him for so much as one dance, he'll send a waiter with a scribbled message, 'Miss you.' When you're with him, you know that for him—at that moment at least—you're the only woman in the world and the most beautiful."

A native Californian, the same age as Reagan, Greg Bautzer began to date Jane in 1950. He was one of the most prominent attorneys in Hollywood, with clients who ranged from Howard Hughes to Ingrid Bergman.

Many of his female clients—most of them top stars—were also his lovers. He seduced Lana Turner when she was just sixteen and went on to long, tumultuous on again, off again affair with Joan Crawford. His roster of seductions featured Dorothy Lamour, Ava Gardner, Ginger Rogers, Rita Hayworth, Peggy Lee, Merle Oberon, Joan Caulfield, Marguerite Chapman, and Evelyn Keyes. He finally married actress Dana Wynter in 1956.

Others seduced by him included Lucille Ball, Tallulah Bankhead, Gene Tierney, Marlene Dietrich, and Jayne Mansfield.

"I think Greg was born with really good looks," Jane said. "He stood 6'2" and was a great dancer. He was well built and took care of his athletic body. He was not only very intelligent, but a brilliant attorney with great charisma." She shared these views with the homosexual actor, Clifton Webb, with whom she co-starred in the 1959 movie, *Holiday for Lovers*.

The July, 1951 issue of *Photoplay* filed a report on the romance between Jane and Bautzer:

> *"The guy has something, there's no doubt about that. Ask any man what it is and he'll tell you. Bautzer's a man's man, virile, successful, a gentleman where he works, or where he plays. And he's out to win, wherever he is, in the courtroom, at the poker table, or on the tennis court. Yet somehow, once he has won, he seems to lose interest—as though the fun were all in the battle, and the victory anticlimactic."*

It appears that Bautzer seduced Jane long before they made any high-profile appearances, such as escorting her to the premiere of her hit movie, *The Blue Veil* (1951).

At that premiere, both of them encountered Ronald Reagan, who was dating starlet Nancy Davis at the time. After Bautzer introduced her to Nancy, he whispered to Jane, "Not my type. Maybe it's all that Reagan can get these days."

Once they went public with their affair, columnists and fan magazines speculated on the probability of an upcoming Bautzer/Wyman marriage.

Modern Screen proclaimed, "At last, a girl who can make Greg Bautzer forget about Lana and Ava, etc."

A reporter discovered that both Jane and Bautzer had taken blood tests as a prelude to marriage.

Another reporter for *Modern Screen* saw Jane and Bautzer at a party hosted by George Sanders. He wrote, "Usually Bautzer works the room. But on this particular evening they spent most of the night in the corner making goo-goo eyes at each other. They did talk to their host and later to the producer Gabriel Pascal. That was big of them, since the party was in Pascal's honor."

Then, suddenly, Bautzer was no longer seen with Jane, but with Ginger Rogers, who had recently made *Storm Warning* with Reagan. After listening to Lena Horne at her show at the Cocoanut Grove, Bautzer and Rogers danced the night away. At their booth, he frequently kissed her.

Paulette Goddard later provided the clue as to why the affair between Jane and Bautzer ended so abruptly. "Greg could charm the pants off a girl, and Hollywood cocksuckers never let him alone—notably his client, Rock Hudson. He arranged Hudson's divorce, incidentally. But there was a Jekyll and Hyde quality to Greg. He had violent fights with Joan Crawford—I mean knock down, drag-out fights. Alcoholism ran in his family. When he had too much to drink, Mr. Hyde came out."

"Jane told me that he arrived at her doorstep unexpectedly one night and caught her in bed with that handsome hunk, Howard Keel, with whom she was co-starring in *Three Guys Named Mike.* Jane said that Keel escaped, but Greg practically put Jane in the hospital. That was the end of that."

***

Lana Turner turned it down, and Ava Gardner rejected it. June Allyson accepted it, but at the last minute had to notify MGM that she had to bow out because she was preganant. "A Blessed Event is on the way. But call Jane Wyman. She's looking for something light and fluffy after *The Glass Menagerie."*

Allyson was right. Jane accepted the role in *Three Guys Named Mike* (1951), in which she played Marcy Lewis, an airline stewardess, in this black-and-white comedy directed by Charles Walters.

The three handsome "Mikes" in the film included Van Johnson, playing a research scientist; Barry Sullivan, an advertising executive; and Howard Keel, an airplane pilot. Sidney Sheldon, who in time would evolve into one of the bestselling novelists in the world, wrote the screenplay, whose theme revolved around three guys chasing after Marcy.

Walters, who was gay, had just directed Judy Garland in *Summer Stock* (1950). Garland had been fired from *Annie Get Your Gun* (1950), the title role subsequently being awarded to Betty Hutton, with Keel as her leading man.

Even though Allyson had to bow out of the film's lead role, she telephoned Jane every two or three days for updates about what was happening.

Allyson had always remained in touch with Johnson, her close friend and co-star.

As Jane told Allyson, "All that Van and I do is talk girl talk. I'm ever so grateful to him for all those nights he took me dancing

Three Guys Named Mike was made in an era when a job as a "stewardess" was considered glamorous, and when an airplane ride to anywhere was an exciting and adventurous novelty.

during the War."

A New Yorker, Barry Sullivan stood 6'3", and Jane found him "very manly, the type of guy whose shoulder a girl can lean on."

She met him during the peak career period of his life, when he'd appeared in his most famous movie, cast as a director in *The Bad and the Beautiful* (1951), opposite Lana Turner and Kirk Douglas. He had also played opposite opposite Bette Davis in *Payment on Demand* (1951).

Keel was married, having wed Helen Anderson, who had been in the chorus of his stage musical, *Oklahoma!*. In the early 1950s, at the peak of his career, he became known for seducing his leading ladies, especially Kathryn Grayson and Ava Gardner, each of whom had co-starred in *Show Boat*. Apparently, he struck out with Doris Day in *Calamity Jane* (1953).

Jane had been attracted to his macho flair, his booming baritone style, and his studly good looks. During luncheons together, they shared memories of their awful childhoods. Keel had been born the son of a poor and violent coalminer who had committed suicide when he was a young boy. Before breaking into show business, he'd been a singing waiter and other more dubious professions. He admitted to Jane that on rare occasions, "When I was broke, I sold my services to older women."

"Well, I'm two years older than you. How much do you charge?"

"For you, baby, it's free. I'll pay you."

"That's very flattering. I think I'll take you up on that offer."

She later told Allyson, "Our bopping lasted until the end of filming. Then for him it was back to Helen. How lucky she is. Howard is a man and a half, maybe even more than that."

In his memoir, *Only Make Believe,* Keel wrote, "I lost Janie at the end of the film. I guess she thought airline pilots were a wayward lot."

The movie made a tidy profit for MGM, although reviews were tepid at best. *Time* found Jane's performance perky enough, but claimed, "The plot device of three Mikes chasing her is a thin idea spread pretty thin."

***

For her next picture, Jane moved over to Paramount, wanting to take her dressing room trailer with her. However, the gates of Paramount weren't wide enough to allow it access inside.

She was looking forward to her next picture, *Here Comes the Groom* (1951). Not only would it give her a chance to sing and dance, but it would mean a reunion with Bing Crosby, one of her favorite performers.

They had seen each other infrequently over the years for "dalliances." He'd first seduced her when she had an uncredited bit part in his 1936 musical, *Anything Goes. [Ironically, Crosby appeared in the 1956 version of* Anything Goes*, too.]*

Their director assigned to *Here Comes the Groom* was Frank Capra, with whom Jane had always wanted to work, even though, since the end of the war, his career had fallen into great decline. Critics derided his style of filmmaking as old-fashioned,

overly idealistic and sentimental. More sophisticated movie fans had emerged from the ashes of World War II, calling for more cynical heroes than a Capra character.

In the Paramount commissary, Jane lunched with both Crosby and Capra until Crosby was summoned to the head office. She told Capra, "Bing's still adorable, but I've noticed a lot of changes in him. He seems deeply troubled. More temperamental. Although he's so very nice to me."

"As long as he treats you like a lady, what else matters?" Capra asked. She seemed to agree.

After their luncheon reunion, she spent the night with Crosby, inviting him to a friend's apartment. She encountered a disillusioned man, who seemed to find comfort in her arms. He was still married to the former actress and nightclub singer, Dixie Lee, but they lived in separate parts

Here Comes the Groom: Perpetuating the myth that weddings make a girl happy.

of their home, along with their four boys: Gary, twins Dennis and Phillip, and Lindsay.

For the first time, she learned that Dixie was suffering from ovarian cancer, and had been an alcoholic for years.

Crosby sensed that Jane was very unhappy to be appearing with Alexis Smith. "I thought you, Craig Stevens, and Reagan had all been great friends."

She told him she didn't want to talk about it. "That's over now."

The rest of the cast consisted of Franchot Tone, James Barton, Alan Reed, Minna Gombell, and *Wünderkind* Anna Maria Alberghetti, an opera prodigy from Italy.

Alberghetti had performed professionally since the age of six and had made her Carnegie Hall debut in New York at the age of thirteen. In time, she would appear on several occasions on *The Ed Sullivan Show*.

Jane learned that the original story of *Here Comes the Groom* by Robert Riskin had been shopped around for several years, and that it had, for a while, been considered as a vehicle for James Stewart and later for Bob Hope. Hope, Crosby's co-star in all those "Road Movies," called on the first day of shooting: "Bing, so now you're reduced to taking my rejects?"

[During the shooting of Here Comes the Groom, *Riskin, Capra's alter ego, suffered a stroke and had to undergo surgery for a blood clot in his brain. He was left partially paralyzed and confined to a wheelchair for the rest of his life. He would never write again.]*

In the plot, Crosby was cast as a newspaper reporter, Pete Garvey, stationed in Paris. He visits an local orphanage and falls in love with a young boy, Bobby, and his little sister, Suzi. He wants to adopt them and bring them back to live with him in Boston. But U.S. Immigration warns him that he must marry within five days or the adoption will be voided and the Parisian kids deported.

In the movie, the child character (Theresa) played by Alberghetti is also up for adoption. Her immediate problem gets solved when an well-meaning American couple, Mr. and Mrs. Godfrey (Alan Reed and Minna Gombell) take her away after her soulful rendition of "Caro Nome."

Back in Boston, Crosby learns that Jane, his fiancée when he left, is now engaged to her boss, the blueblooded and very rich Wilbur Stanley (Franchot Tone), and that she plans to marry him. Garvey learns that Smith, cast as Winifred Stanley, is also in love with her fourth cousin (Tone). The usual Capra complications ensue, but the public knew in advance that it could count on a happy ending with all matters resolved.

In their duet together, "In the Cool, Cool, Cool of the Evening," written by Hoagy Carmichael with lyrics by Johnny Mercer, Jane and Crosby overshadowed even their talented array of backup musicians.

When it was released by Decca Records, "In the Cool, Cool, Cool of the Evening" reached the bestseller chart on *Billboard,* landing there in September of 1951 and nesting there for six weeks.

The lyrics had Americans singing throughout the autumn:

In the cool, cool, cool of the evenin', tell 'em I'll be there.
In the cool, cool cool of the evenin', better save a chair
When the party's getting' a glow on, 'n' singin' fills the air,
In the shank o' the night, when the doin's are right, you can tell 'em I'll be there.

On screen, Jane showed such chemistry with Crosby that a reporter visiting the set wrote of a possible romance. He was right. Columnists began to pick up on that, even though Crosby was still married.

He and Jane got to know each other as never before. He confided details of his life to her which he had shared with only two or three other friends. Louis Armstrong described him as "a lost, lonely dude."

He admitted that he "suffered Catholic guilt" but had indulged in a series of extramarital affairs, calling himself a "serial adulterer" and labeling his behavior as "compulsive."

"I have no trouble finding beautiful women willing to hop into bed with me," he confessed. "Often, they just want to use me."

"Are you sure it's not your melodious voice that wins them over" she asked him, facetiously.

When Hope arrived on the set, Crosby told him, "Jane and I are considering marriage, but only after Dixie dies. We are mutually supportive of each other. She's also great in bed, a charming companion, and a rather sophisticated lady. I think she would make a wonderful wife."

"Make me best man," Hope said. "Of course, since it's a public appearance, I'll have to charge you."

"Let me put it this way," Crosby said. "Jane is the tonic in my vodka, the cream in my coffee, the caviar on my toast." As for the best man fee, I'm being generous giving you two dollars."

One day, Crosby said, "I'd like to meet Maureen and Michael. In the meantime, I've invited my four boys to lunch with us in the commissary. You might find out for yourself if you want to be the stepmother of these losers."

During the lunch, Jane sensed that his sons were afraid of their father. "He was rather sharp with them," she later told Capra. "In Gary's case, he canceled his order of a steak and selected a salad for him instead."

Jane was correct in her assessment of the tensions between Crosby and his boys. After the singer died in 1977, son Gary wrote a "Daddy Dearest" type of memoir entitled *Going My Own Way*, in which he depicted Crosby as "cruel, cold, remote, and both physically and psychologically abusive."

Crosby did admit to Jane that he reserved the harshest punishments for Gary. As the young man later wrote: "Each Tuesday afternoon, he weighed me in, and if the scale read more than it should have, he ordered me into his office and had me drop my trousers. I dropped my pants, pulled down my undershorts, and bent over. Then he went at it with a belt dotted with metal studs he kept reserved for the occasion. Quietly, dispassionately, without the least display of emotion or loss of self-control, he whacked away until he drew the first drop of blood, and then he stopped. It normally took between twelve and fifteen strokes. As they came down, I counted them off one by one, and I hoped I would bleed early."

A famously tragic American family: The four Crosby brothers in 1959. *(Left to right)* Dennis, Gary, Lindsay, and Phillip.

[Bing Crosby's sons came to tragic ends. Lindsay died in 1989 and Dennis in 1991, both of them suicides from self-inflicted gunshot wounds. Gary died in 1995, when he was 62, of lung cancer. In each case, Jane still retained fond memories of Crosby and wrote him long, heart-warming letters, addressing his grief.

None of these sons inherited any of Crosby's millions. His will created a blind trust stipulating that none of his offspring would receive inheritances until they reached the age of 65. Only Phillip lived beyond that age, dying at 69, in 2014, of a heart attack.]

Capra later said, "When I finally got Jane and Bing to walk down the aisle at movie's end, it was straight out of *It Happened One Night [released in 1934, and directed by Frank Capra]* with Clark Gable and Claudette Colbert. I decided that if I was reduced to having to steal from my own picture, it was time for me to take a long rest."

Crosby was paid $150,000 for his performance; Jane, $125,000. Capra made off with $176,000.

Jane later told June Allyson, "I withdrew from Bing's affection because stories were printed that he planned to divorce Dixie and marry me. I was getting awful letters at the studio. Homewrecker was the mildest accusation against me. I realized it was time to go."

Here Comes the Groom made money in spite of its critical reviews. Joseph McBride, Frank Capra's biographer, wrote, "The plot itself had seen better days. All Capra was able to do was magnify its flaws."

The kindest words appeared in *The New York World-Telegram* in a critique by Alton Cook: "Now that Jane Wyman has her Oscar safely tucked away, she is back at being our most pixieish comedienne and making her share of things very mirthful as a fisherman's daughter out to crash Boston's most blue blooded circles. When Frank Capra is in exactly his best mood, he and his writers have the maddest and funniest flights of fancy ever produced on this continent."

Another critic nailed it more accurately: "*Here Comes the Groom* is pure Capracorn!"

Capra later recalled, "Jane traded her crying towel for the glamour girl's raiment and became a dish to behold."

While Jane was still married to Reagan, Evelyn Keyes, "Scarlett O'Hara's Younger Sister" in *Gone With the Wind,* decided to throw a big bash to celebrate the first anniversary of her marriage to director John Huston. The co-hosts were directors Lewis Milestone *(All Quiet on the Western Front)* and Jean Negulesco *(Three Coins in the Fountain).*

Keyes wanted to hire a band to entertain her 200 guests, among whom were some of the stellar members of *tout* Hollywood.

Keyes had worked with musician Fred Karger on *The Jolson Story* (1946) and suggested that he pull together a band for the night to entertain her guests. He hurriedly agreed and knew just which of his fellow musicians was best for which instrument. After only two days of rehearsals, they were "ready for showtime," as he told Keyes.

Reagan had always wanted to work with Huston, but never got the chance after failing to nab the role he wanted in the director's *The Treasure of the Sierra Madre* (1948), starring Humphrey Bogart.

Huston and Keyes soon became very good friends of Reagan and Jane. They frequently visited each other's homes, and also went double-dating together at various clubs.

When Karger and his band took a 30-minute break, Keyes introduced him around to Hollywood hostesses.

In fact, Karger and "my boys" were such a smash success at the party that some of these show-biz hostesses, that very night, began plans to book him for their own special events.

At one point, it was not Keyes, but Judy Garland who introduced Karger to Reagan and Jane. Garland grabbed Jane's arm. "Come with me to the can. I need to take a crap!" Reagan was left talking with Karger, of whom he later said, "What a nice young man."

In the large ground floor bathroom of the Huston ranch, hawk-eyed Garland, though a bit drunk, picked up on Jane's interest in the handsome young band leader.

"Privately, I've hired Freddie for duties other than music. But he's a great musician. He's worked with me on some numbers. He's one of the music directors over at Columbia."

"Is he married?" Jane asked.

"He's divorced. Sounds like you're interested, girl! If you're like me, I never got enough when I married Vincente Minnelli. I guess he was saving it up for Gene Kelly."

"Mr. Karger is awfully handsome, even charismatic," Jane said.

"Not only that, but Freddie's hung like there's no tomorrow," Garland said. "I'll arrange for you guys to get together late one afternoon for drinks at my place."

"He's available, now that Rita has dumped him," Garland said.

[Garland was referring to the involvement of Rita Hayworth with Karger, who had worked privately with her, coaching her for scenes in Gilda *(1946) and* The Loves of Carmen *(1948).]*

After taking her self-styled "crap," Garland grabbed Jane's arm again. "C'mon, I'm going to sing *Over the Rainbow* for these drunken slobs."

Although Keyes had hired Karger and his band, the hostess had also persuaded some of the most famous entertainers in the world to sing free for her guests, including not only Garland, but Frank Sinatra. After they performed, Jane herself asked if she could sing two numbers, going into a whispered conference with Karger.

This huddle would be the first of many a *tête-à-tête* that would continue on and off until Karger's death. Or, as Jane put it to Garland on another night, "Our huddle that night at the Hustons led to a cuddle..and beyond."

In a memoir, Keyes wrote, "It was the best goddamned party I ever attended."

The next weekend, on a Sunday afternoon, Reagan and Jane arrived unannounced at the Huston ranch. It was not unusual for friends to just drop in for the weekend at the Hustons. Invitations were not necessary.

Their living room was in shambles. Upon seeing them, a hung over Huston said, "Evelyn, it's time for Bloody Marys—and don't be stingy with the vodka, darling."

Sipping drinks with her guests, Keyes related what had happened the previous night. They had invited Humphrey Bogart, Lauren Bacall, Ida Lupino, and Collier Young to join them for dinner.

"At around one o'clock this morning, John here decided he wanted to play football with the boys," Keyes said. "Bogie was barefoot at the time. For a football, he used my $1,000 ceramic vase. Bogie dropped it, and it shattered into pieces. He cut his foot on the sharp pieces. Betty *[Bacall]* while scolding him all the while picked out the slivers with tweezers."

Throughout the afternoon, Huston revealed to Jane and Reagan that he was a world class drinker. Despite becoming increasingly intoxicated, he told one fascinating story after another.

As dusk descended, when everyone agreed that they were hungry, Huston invited all four of them down to Olvera Street, the Mexican section of Los Angeles, for tacos and beer. "Jane and John had had quite a few, but Ronnie and I were restrained," Keyes recalled. "At the end of the fest, Ronnie put a giddily drunken John and Jane into the back seat and took the wheel, with me sitting up front beside him."

"We'll be the policemen, and I'll drive," Reagan announced.

In her memoir, Keyes wrote, "Ronnie was a sober-minded, responsible citizen even then. A nice Democrat. I wonder where he went wrong."

***

Jane was seen around town dating Curtis Bernhardt, a director far older than she was. It may or may not have been a romance. He'd helmed her during the war in *My Love Came Back* (1940), and they had remained friends. Now he had a new picture for her called *The Blue Veil* (1951). He wanted her to play a nun-like nursemaid.

"Me? A nun? You've got to be kidding!"

She was perplexed, but over just one night's dinner, he sold her on the role.

She told him, "Bring it on. I'll

The Blue Veil: Jane with Richard Carlson...The love that might have been.

558

play anything except lesbians, hookers, and gun molls."

She was called back to the studio for some retakes on *Here Comes the Groom*. During the course of those touch-ups, she had lunch with Bing Crosby. When he was informed of her newest film offer, he urged her to go for it.

"I don't know," she said. "It's been such fun working with you in a musical. After *Johnny Belinda* and *The Glass Menagerie,* my nerves are frayed. I'm ready for the recuperation ward. *The Blue Veil* is one tough role."

"But at least, unlike *Johnny Belinda,* you'll get to talk," Crosby answered.

A week went by before Bernhardt called again from an office at RKO. "I've got bad news. Garbo saw the French version of *The Blue Veil*. She wants to use it as a vehicle for her comeback picture."

The Blue Veil: Jane with her actor/mentor, Charles Laughton.

[Bernhardt was referring to a French picture, directed by Jean Stelli, Le voile bleu. *It had been released in German-controlled Paris in 1942 and became one of the biggest film successes during the Nazi occupation of France, an era when Germans heavily censored any film shown in their captured territories.*

But soon after her initial enthusiasm, Garbo notified Bernhardt that she was not going to accept the role.

[In the late 1940s and early 50s, Garbo occasionally accepted a script, making it known that she was contemplating a comeback, and then rejecting the roles, perhaps based on fear of facing the cameras after such a long absence from the screen. Such was the case with The Blue Veil.*]*

After Garbo's departure, Bernhardt sent the script to Ingrid Bergman, who responded, "After all those condemnations based on my love affair with Roberto *[Rossellini, whom she later married]*, I've become *persona non grata* in Hollywood. I'll have to turn it down. The public will probably mock me in a nun's role."

Only then did Bernhardt once again appeal to Jane. "You're our gal," he said. "Garbo has bolted."

The script arrived, an adaptation by Norman Corwin from a story by the French author François Campaux. Norman Krasna and Jerry Wald, Jane's old friends, were co-producers. Wald cabled, "I've been serarching for another Wyman picture after *Johnny Belinda*. I assure you, *The Blue Veil* is it. It has your second Oscar written on every page. Not only that, but I've cast your buddy, Joan

The Blue Veil: Matronly Jane with the then *ingénue* Natalie Wood.

Blondell, as a supporting role."

The title of the film came from the blue veil that French nursemaids commonly wore. The melodramatic plot centered on LouLou Mason, a war widow (played by Jane) who, after the death of her newborn baby, devotes her life to raising other people's children. The film is a series of vignettes about the families and children Jane becomes involved with as a nursemaid.

In the wake of the death of her newborn, Jane takes a job caring for the infant son of Frederick K. Begley (Charles Laughton), a corset manufacturer who lost his wife in childbirth. He proposes marriage, but she rejects his offer. Instead, he marries a woman named Fleur (Agnes Moorehead), who immediately fires Jane.

That leads her into a series of adventures in various homes, none more notable than when she begins the care and supervision of Stephanie (as played by the then-juvenile actress, Natalie Wood), the daughter of a fading musical actress Annie Rawlins (Joan Blondell).

As the teardrops fall, LouLou experiences one heartbreak after another within the various homes, even fleeing with one boy, Tony, to Florida. When his mother, Helen Williams (Audrey Totter), decides she wants him back. Jane's character is arrested.

She ends her days as a janitor working in a children's school. There, she is spotted by one of her former charges, Dr. Robert Palfrey (Don Taylor). When he finds her, lonely and nearly destitute, he takes her home with him to raise his own children.

During the first week on the set of *The Blue Veil,* Bernhardt introduced her to a strong supporting cast who included not just Blondell, Laughton, and Moorehead, but Richard Carlson, Carleton Young, Audrey Totter, Cyril Cusack, Dan O'Herlihy, and Don Taylor, fresh from having played Elizabeth Taylor's husband in *Father of the Bride* (1950) and *Father's Little Dividend* (1951).

Lunching with Blondell, Jane said, "My God, I've got to go from twenty to seventy. Only Perc Westmore, my old makeup artist, can pull that one off."

[Whereas Perc defined the pattern for her makeup, he had to be hospitalized during the shoot.]

"No actor ever impressed her as much as Laughton, a towering and portly thespian known in both America and England. He was also a notorious homosexual, his status well known within London's theater circles. "He taught me how to act, walk, and talk like an old person. I learned more in two weeks from him than I did from any director. He made me feel old, and I mean that as a compliment. But I was only thirty-seven at the time, and in the prime of my life, with hormones raging. It was a big leap from that to old lady, but I finally got there."

Jane chatted with Natalie Wood, who told her she wanted to escape the curse of such child stars as Shirley Temple, whose career ended when she turned adolescent. "Right now, I'm playing daughters to such parents as Fred MacMurray, Margaret Sullavan, and James Stewart, and I'm slated to be Bette Davis' daughter in *The Star.* As you know, I'm calling your friend, Blondell, 'mom'."

"If *The Blue Veil* flops, we'll all pick our whistlestops," Wald told her. "If not, we'll take our bows. It's a challenge for you, but you have the tal-

The Blue Veil: Jane, decrepid but dignified.

560

ent to pull it off. Better than Garbo ever could."

Jane detested the invasive press, but granted one interview during the shoot. As the statement indicates, no one ever accused her of being "The Great Communicator," as they would Reagan in later years.

"We're put into this world. No one knows why. Sometimes I don't like it. Sometimes, I'd rather be in heaven. Meanwhile, I'm here for a certain number of years. Nothing adds up for me except how much good you can show people during that span. Without a goal, you don't live, you drift. I've set myself quite a few. This is the only one that's ever made sense."

Writing in *The New York Times,* Bosley Crowther defined *The Blue Veil* "a whoppingly banal tear jerker that will lure multitudes of moviegoers who like nothing better than a good cry. Curtis Bernhardt's soupy direction stretches Wyman into a series of parchedly sunlit episodes contrived to squeeze the heart and present this lady as a quivering-lipped saint. Wyman has little to do herself except age daintily. Since, like the rest of *The Blue Veil,* Wyman is so far removed from flesh and blood, we can only leave her and it to heaven."

At awards time, for her performance, Jane won a Golden Globe Award for Best Actress and also nominated for an Oscar.

The Blue Veil grossed nearly $4 million, the most financially successful picture RKO released that year. For the first time in her long career, Jane was named one of the film industry's "Top Ten" box office draws.

Jane wouldn't take Maureen Reagan to see *Johnny Belinda* because it involved a rape, but she made it a point to escort her to a screening of *The Blue Veil.* In her memoirs, Maureen recalled the experience. "*The Blue Veil* was that movie where she loses a baby and then becomes a governess; she spends the rest of her life saying goodbye to one child after another. What a depressing movie! And she had to live with this character every day. No wonder it was sometimes difficult to get a smile out of her."

Maureen later told her friends at school, "My mother sat through the entire movie and didn't shed a tear. She has no sense of drama."

Jane's competitors for the Oscar that year (1951) included Katharine Hepburn for her role in *The African Queen;* Eleanor Parker for *Detective Story;* and Shelley Winters for *A Place in the Sun.*

All of them lost to Vivien Leigh, taking home her second Oscar for her memorable performance as Blanche DuBois in Tennessee Williams' *A Streetcar Named Desire.*

Blondell was nominated for Best Supporting Actress, but lost to Kim Hunter as Stella in *A Streetcar Named Desire. Variety* defined Blondell's performance as her best since *A Tree Grows in Brooklyn* (1945). In *The Blue Veil,* she played a neglectful show business mother of a twelve year old. One writer said, "Blondell added vinegar to a movie drowning in molasses."

It was a year of honors. Very briefly, Jane was reunited with her co-star in *The Yearling.* As he'd matured a bit, Gregory Peck looked handsomer than ever. She surely recalled her romantic nights with him. Both of them had been given *Photoplay's* Golden Award of 1951 for Favorite Actor and Favorite Actress of the year.

After the Awards Ceremony, she asked him, "If we're so goddamned popular, why not do a picture together?"

"Great idea," he said. "I'll lobby for the right script."

Their dual roles never materialized.

***

After Reagan's separation from Jane, he got to know Fred Karger before she did. When he was flirting around with the idea of marrying Adele Jergens, he often picked her up during the early evening night after she'd finished work her day's work on *Ladies of the Chorus*. In it, she played Marilyn Monroe's mother, even though she looked like her sister.

On the set of that movie, Karger was responsible for the staging of Marilyn's big number, "Every Baby Needs a Da-Da Daddy."

On three different occasions, Reagan and Jergens double dated with Marilyn and Karger. Reagan was surprised to learn that Marilyn was living with Karger's mother, Anne, and his daughter, Terry.

Karger told Reagan, "I brought Marilyn home and asked mother to take care of her, because she was lost, broke, and lonely. Anne just adores her. So does my daughter."

When Reagan started secretly seeing Marilyn, especially when he was convalescing with a broken leg, Marilyn complained to him, "Freddie doesn't love me. A man can't love a woman and feel contempt for her. He's ashamed of me and wants to change me. He says he can't take me out because I dress like a trollop."

Once, after she hadn't visited for quite a while, she showed up "slightly altered."

"Freddie told me I had this small blemish, a fleshy tip, that made my nose appear too long. He arranged for me to go to a plastic surgeon to take care of it. The surgeon also removed some cartilage and inserted it into my jaw to make my chin stronger. Before that, Freddie was calling me 'chinless'."

"You look more gorgeous than ever," Reagan assured her.

Later, when Marilyn became the roommate of Shelley Winters, she told her, "Freddie is so neat, he even keeps his pubic hair trimmed. He thought my upper teeth protruded, so he set up an appointment with an orthodontist, sending me to this Dr. Walter Taylor, who is a specialist in cosmetic surgery."

Later, when Marilyn took up with agent Johnny Hyde, she told him that, "Freddie makes me feel inadequate. After a night with him, I'm churning in frustration. He won't do certain things in bed I like."

"I'll bet he's a secret homo," Hyde said.

"He also told me that he can never marry me

Fred Karger: Babe magnet.

MM as she looked when Karger first dated her.

Her biographer, Fred Lawrence Guiles, wrote: "When Marilyn realized she was in love with Karger soon after their first dinner, she felt she must persuade him to marry her. That he didn't seem about to do so was a reality to which she finally would resign herself. Fred Karger was to have the singular distinction of being the only human being Marilyn attempted to disarm and yet who was resistant up to the end."

because I would not make a fit stepmother for his daughter, Terry. She adores me."

Maurice Zolotow, one of Marilyn's early biographers, wrote that Karger was "the epitome of courtliness. But when Marilyn fell for him, he was sour on women. When he talked of love, it was to express a world-weary hopelessness about the honor of women. He claimed that women were not capable of genuine love. He believed that no one could give herself honestly and entirely to one man for whom she cared. He said women 'were too shrewd, too practical.'"

One moonlight night on Santa Monica Beach, Karger, a bit tipsy, said those three magic words that Marilyn was longing to hear—"I love you."

She later told columnist Sidney Skolsky, "Those words were better than a thousand critics calling me a movie star. All the fame and bright lights I had dreamed about suddenly were in *me.*"

But the next day, in Marilyn's words, "Freddie forgot about what he'd told me on the beach. He was his same cynical self with all the barriers to his emotion erected around him. He even teased me about my ignorance of culture and history."

He told her, "Your mind isn't developed. Compared to your body, it's embryonic."

Joan Blondell later said, "All the problems that Freddie found in Marilyn he didn't find in Jane. Jane was more his type. Marilyn for sex, Jane for marriage."

Karger's first known outing with Marilyn as his date was at the premiere of *The Asphalt Jungle* (1950), her first breakthrough movie. "I deserved something from him," she told Skolsky. "In 1948, for his Christmas present, I bought him a $500 gold watch which I'm still paying off at the rate of $25 a month."

She later told Skolsky, "One of the reasons I fell for John Kennedy is that he looks like Freddie."

When Karger began dating Jane, Marilyn heard about it and exploded in fury. When she learned that he planned to marry Jane, she told Winters, "I will hate Jane Wyman for the rest of my life, even in heaven. I wasn't all that interested in Reagan, but I played around with him just to get even with Jane for taking Freddie from me. I'm still carrying a torch for the guy. He should have been an underwear model."

***

After *The Blue Veil,* Jane returned to Warners for a cameo appearance in *Starlift* (1951). Directed by Roy Del Ruth, its all-star cast included James Cagney, Gary Cooper, Gene Nelson, Frank Lovejoy, Virginia Mayo, Phil Harris, Gordon MacRae, Randolph Scott, Doris Day, and Ruth Roman.

At the time, Reagan was dating both Day and Roman.

"I'm not on the screen for very long," Jane said, "but at least I get to sing 'I May Be Wrong (but I Think You're Wonderful).'"

The silly plot concerned two pilots, Mike Nolan (Dick Wesson) and Rick Williams (Ron Hagerthy), who try to meet Nell Wayne (Janice Rule), a fictitious film star performing in a star-studded musical in San Francisco. Before meeting Rule, Roman introduces them to Day and MacRae, who are rehearsing, "You're Gonna Lose Your Gal."

Although *Starlift* takes place during the Korean War, Jane said that it evoked fond memories of her times at the Hollywood Canteen during World War II.

Bosley Crowther, the acerbic critic for *The New York Times,* summed it up: "The acts are unspeakably slapdash, and the romance is painful beyond words. The performances given by Janice Rule and Ron Hagerthy as the flier are as sappy as they could possibly be, and Dick Wesson as a pushy pal of the flier is downright insufferable."

Glam Jane becomes Plain Jane again, this time in *The Story of Will Rogers.*

***

Hollywood columnists were surprised when Jane accepted the role of Betty Blake Rogers, the wife of Will Rogers, Sr., the legendary humorist and lariat-twirling cowboy from the Ziegfeld Follies. The picture was *The Story of Will Rogers,* set for a 1952 release from Warner Brothers, with Michael Curtiz directing.

As columnist Sidney Skolsky noted, "The part of Rogers' wife so clearly called for that gentle lady, Phyllis Thaxter, who once played Ronald Reagan's wife in a film. Thaxter knows how to play 'nice,' without the usual spoonful of saccharine. But why did a big star like Oscar-winning Jane Wyman take such a small role—a part that could have been handled by hundreds of actresses of minor talent?"

Thanks to the passage of time, Jane's reasons for accepting the minor role can be determined. To begin with, she was planning to star in a very strong role as a movie star who returns to Broadway in an aptly titled script called *Broadway Revisited.* It was a powerful role, although there was a rumor that Jack Warner had originally offered it to Lauren Bacall, who would play a similar role in her future on Broadway in *Applause*, a stage musical based on *All About Eve.*

Jane had a secret reason for wanting the part: She hoped that, based on her performance, producers could see that she could impersonate a stage actress. She had witnessed many stars approaching forty or beyond who had extended their professional lives, after movie roles evaporated, by appearances on the stage.

There was another reason. She had just appeared with her pal and sometimes lover, Bing Crosby, in *Here Comes the Groom.* He thought he could play Will Rogers and actually submitted to a screen test. He asked Jane to co-star as his wife. However, when he saw himself on the screen, he had to admit that his own personality and the *persona* of the humorist were not a perfect fit. As he told Jane, "Will and I don't go together like love and marriage, or a horse and carriage."

Jane was ready to bow out of the role after Crosby's screen test bombed, but Warner persuaded her to accept the role as a favor to him. He had decided to cast Will Rogers, Jr. in the part of his father, but he was very inexperienced and had no marquee name.

"I need someone who can get movie fans to buy tickets," Warner told her. "If you'll go along with me on this one, I'll assure you of some big pictures coming up where I'll give you the lead. I've requested this kind of concession from Bette Davis on at least on two occasions when she was big around this studio, and she agreed."

The mogul was referring to Davis taking a secondary role in *The Man Who Came to Dinner* (1941) with Monty Woolley and *Watch on the Rhine* (1943) in which she played second fiddle to Paul Lukas.

Directed by Michael Curtiz, with whom Jane had a dreaded reunion, *The Story of Will Rogers* featured a supporting cast of now familiar faces to her, including James Gleason, Carl Benton Reid, Eve Miller, and Slim Pickens. Steve Brodie and Eddie Cantor were also in the cast.

Virtually all of America had tuned in for details about Rogers' tragic death in 1935, when he was killed in a plane crash en route from Fairbanks to Alaska's northernmost tip, Point Barrow. His close friend, Wiley Post, also died in the wreck. In the movie, Noah Beery, Jr. interpreted the role of Post.

During a dialogue with Curtiz, he told her that her role had been offered to both Eleanor Parker and Phyllis Thaxter—yes, the same housewifey actress suggested by Skolsky.

The role of Will Rogers, in addition to being offered to Bing Crosby, had been considered for both Herb Shriner and Charles Drake. Curtiz also told her that Will Rogers, Jr., the son of the subject of the film, had been screen tested and subsequently rejected for the role way back in 1942. In contrast, on this newest effort, he got the part.

"Big year for me, 1942," Curtiz said. "I was hot shit. *Casablanca,* you know. Your boy, Reagan, didn't get Bogie's part."

Jane was introduced to her leading man, Will Rogers, Jr., who had had a varied career. From January 3, 1943, to May 23, 1944, he had been a U.S. Congressman from California when he resigned to rejoin the U.S. army. Through a varied career, he'd been a minor actor, writer, and publisher.

He closely resembled his father, though lacking any of his talent. He later told the press that he found Jane "wonderful to work with, tremendously helpful and supportive. She taught me more about acting than Curtiz did."

Publicly, Jane said nothing, but complained to Curtiz, "I find him tiring to work with— retake, retake, and more retakes until he gets it right, if he ever does."

Reviewers were puzzled that the script by Frank Davis and Stanley Roberts contained so many historical inaccuracies about Will Rogers, Sr. Although his son was very familiar with his father's life, he apparently never alerted the writers about the points where they were wrong. For example, the movie depicts Rogers' father, Clem Rogers, as a delegate from Oklahoma at the 1932 Democratic convention that nominated Franklin D. Roosevelt. Clem Rogers, the grandfather of Rogers, had died in 1911, the year his grandson was born.

After a screening, Jane told Curtiz, "I don't like the way I look on the screen. As for that drab wardrobe you forced me to wear, it stinks. I refuse to do anything to promote the film."

She was right. The critics damned her performance with faint praise, using such words as "likable," "supportive," "pleasant," and "displays a gentle attitude."

She described her role as "a simpering onlooker." Years later, when she saw it on TV, she said. "I think I used Nancy Davis as my role model, you know when she gazes adoringly at Reagan when he's making one of his endless speeches."

In spite of its many weaknesses, *The Story of Will Rogers* was one of the top box office hits of 1952, grossing $2.65 million in U.S. rentals.

In later life, Rogers, Jr. appeared in several TV productions, and was one of several actors to host syndicated reruns of the hit series, *Death Valley Days,* whose original run was hosted for a season by Reagan himself.

Jane lived long enough to be saddened by the increasing deaths of people she had known. In 1993, she heard over TV news that Rogers, Jr. had committed suicide at the age of 81, after suffering heart problems, several strokes, and an ongoing series of hip replacements.

***

Jane always listened to broadcasts from Hollywood, especially roundups of news in the entertainment industry.

The date was March 4, 1952. Leading off the afternoon news was an announcement that Ronald Reagan had married the MGM starlet, Nancy Davis, in the Little Brown Church in the Valley, in Studio City, California.

Stunned, Jane turned off the TV. The next day, reporters besieged her, wanting her to reveal her feelings and reactions. It seemed that the world wanted to know.

"I wish Ronnie and his bride all the happiness—and that's all I have to say. It's not my affair."

"What do you think of Nancy Davis?" one reporter called out to her.

"I have never heard of the lady until today," she falsely claimed.

Cougar Jane with the younger and very well-heeled Travis Kleefeld, whose society mother was anything but amused.

"But she's a movie star," he yelled back.

"I doubt that," she said. "I read *Variety* from its front cover to the back page. I don't recall reading about any Nancy Davis. Excuse me, I'm late for an appointment."

Exactly thirteen days from the date of Reagan's marriage, Nancy made her own announcement to the press. She reported, "I'm engaged to Travis Kleefeld, and I'll have nothing else to say about it."

As reporters rushed back to their offices and their typewriters, the first questions on everyone's lips was, "Who in the fuck is Travis Kleefeld? Do we have a picture of this guy?"

A devastatingly handsome young man, Kleefeld was ten years younger than Jane but looked much younger even than that. When they had been secretly dating, he was often mistaken for her son.

After the announcement of his engagement to Jane, he became an overnight celebrity. The search was on to find out who he was.

No complete answer ever emerged, but there were clues. It seemed that Jane had met the dashing young man at a Christmas party, and had begun to date him right away.

Speculation was rampant. Had Jane deliberately chosen to announce her engagement so soon after Reagan's marriage? Was she rushing into something impetuous because her former spouse had beaten her to the altar? Only she knew the answers.

Very little was known about him. He was said to be rich, and that he didn't have to marry Jane for her money. He was the scion and heir to a well-known contracting family, and he worked in the family business, which he would one day inherit. His friends, however, said that his secret desire was to be a singer like Frank Sinatra.

[Five years after the announcement of his engagement, Kleefeld did launch a fairly unsuccessful singing career, billing himself as "Tony Travis." He generated little enthusiasm for his talent, despite the fact that he had quite an acceptable singing voice.]

Two weeks after Jane's wedding announcement, she was summoned to Warner Brothers. The studio mogul told her that a ton of fan mail had come in from her devotees, denouncing her decision to marry a man so much younger than herself.

"You've been called everything from a cradle snatcher to an old bag lady seeking to corrupt a handsome young man," Warner said. "You've made a laughing stock of yourself. Your fans are deserting you in droves. Hundreds claim that they will never go to see another Jane Wyman picture."

When a reporter investigated the reaction of Kleefeld's parents, it was obvious that collectively, they interpreted the upcoming marriage as horrifying. One family member said, "I hear Jane Wyman is forty-five if she's a day."

Actually, at the time, she was only thirty-eight.

When the fan magazines hit the stands, Jane was humiliated and burst into tears at the unflattering coverage.

Columnist Ruth Waterbury, a close observer of Jane's, later recalled, "The situation matched that *[of the storyline]* of her future picture with Rock Hudson called *All That Heaven Allows,* the story of an older woman falling for a young man. Was Jane in love with Kleefeld enough to withstand the hostile reaction of the public? I think she loved him in her fashion. But eventually, she started to give in. She couldn't stand up to the mounting pressure and ridicule. In a few weeks, she called off the engagement, claiming that 'Travis and I aren't right for each other.'"

Since his family controlled the purse strings, the son and heir opted to acquiesce to their complaints. *Modern Screen* wrote, "Travis Kleefeld put a down payment on a mink coat for Jane Wyman just before the engagement was called off. Incidentally, relations between Jane and Kleefeld's mother were what you might call 'strained' when we were going to press."

Jane was also quoted as saying, "Age had nothing whatever to do with our decision not to marry. I guess we're the only two people who are not conscious of the difference in our ages. It was just that we decided that marriage was wrong for us and it was silly to go into as serious a matter as matrimony without being perfectly aware it was what we both wanted. Believe me, Travis and I will always be friends. I think he is one of the finest men I've ever met. But we have both realized that we went into this thing too quick and that it's better to break up before marriage than to go into the divorce courts later."

What Louella Parsons knew and other reporters didn't was that after breaking off the engagement, Jane continued to see Kleefeld on several occasions. "He's great in bed," Jane told Parsons in a confidential aside. From then on, she saw him in secret for the next few weeks, although he dated other, younger women.

When asked why she continued to see Kleefeld after breaking off the engagement, Jane said, "It's best that way—no entangling alliances."

She admitted to Parsons that she was jealous of the starlets that Kleefeld dated, knowing that the columnist would not print that comment.

Riddled with insecurities, Jane told Ruth Waterbury, "God, I feel old looking at Travis out with all those young, beautiful women. Don't print that!"

***

In spite of the fiasco associated with her engagement to Kleefeld, Jane entered her "cougar" period, although that term was not in vogue at the time. Today, of course, "cougar" is used to describe an older woman pursuing a younger man.

Along came Tony Trabert, an extraordinary tennis player who was thirteen years younger than Jane, but looked twenty-five years her junior. In the opinion of some observers, it survived as one of the most mysterious relationships of her life.

Was it an affair, a friendship, a passing fancy, or something serious? Jane was not talking. Trabert became the World's no. 1 tennis champion, and is included in the list of the twenty-one greatest players of all time.

Standing 6'1", he was considered by reporters "cute rather than handsome." There had been speculation that Kleefeld looked like Jane's son, but Trabert, in the words of one journalist, "could pass for her grandson."

As a cynical Hedda Hopper said when she saw a picture of Jane with Trabert at a tennis match, "The next thing I'll hear is that Jane has been hanging out around kindergartens."

[Born in Cincinnati in 1930, Marion Anthony Trabert was a stand-out athlete in both tennis and basketball at the University of Cincinnati.

In 1955, three years after dating Jane, his record was one of the most spectacular ever associated with an American tennis player. He had won a trio of the most prestigious amateur tennis tournaments—the French,

Jane with the very young future tennis star, Tony Trabert. When June Allyson heard of this relationship, she sniffed, "The less said about it, the better."

Wimbledon, and American Championships en route to being ranked World No. 1 among the amateurs for that year. He turned professional that autumn of 1955.

After his retirement in 1971, he began a 33-year career as a tennis and golf analyst for CBS, covering such events as the U.S. Open. After an amazing career, Trabert retired in 2004, three years before Jane died.]

***

Originally, Judy Garland had signed with Paramount to appear as a Broadway star in a film entitled *Just for You.* Robert Carson had written its screenplay based on Stephen Vincent Benet's story, *Famous.*

But after being fired by MGM on the set of *Annie Get Your Gun,* Garland was still struggling with pill addiction. Bloated and puffy, she had failed in her diet.

Consequently, Paramount decided to rewrite the script into a vehicle for Jane Wyman and Bing Crosby, pairing them together as a team based on the success of their previous hit, *Here Comes the Groom.*

Just for You, with a reworked script, was shot within a context of speed and intense pressure beginning in mid-October of 1951, and finished shortly before Christmas for an early release in 1952.

Filming it was not a happy experience for either Jane or Crosby, who had discussed a possible marriage

Grande Dame of the American Theater, Ethel Barrymore, co-starring with *Der Bingle* and Jane in *Just for You.*

during the making of their previous film together.

This time around, however, "Der Bingle" was not in a romantic mood. Consumed by what he described as "Catholic guilt," Crosby was morbidly obsessed with the agonies of his slowly dying wife, the former star, Dixie Lee, a victim of ovarian cancer. Also, his conflicts with his sons, especially Gary, were growing increasingly wrenching and bitter.

Jane's private life was in upheaval as she drifted from beau to beau. Consumed with emotional anxieties, she also faced a health crisis, leading eventually to hospitalization because of a kidney stone.

In spite of her problems, and despite her status as a woman on the doorstep of middle age, she looked like a far younger actress than she actually was. That was fine with her, considering the skimpy costumes she'd have to wear in her upcoming picture.

Its director, Elliott Nugent, had assembled a strong supporting cast, including the formidable Ethel Barrymore, along with Robert Arthur, Natalie Wood, Regis Toomey, and veteran actress Cora Witherspoon.

Jane was cast in it *Just for You* as Carolina Hill, a musical comedy star on Broadway with a personal style evocative of Mary Martin. Carolina is the girlfriend of Jordan Blake (Crosby), a Broadway producer who is so busy and self-involved that he neglects his two children, Jerry Blake (Robert Arthur) and Barbara Blake (Natalie Wood).

In the film, Jane tries to bring harmony to the family and reconcile Crosby's character to his son and daughter.

During their first luncheon together, Jane and Crosby talked about the plight of alienated children as being "a little too close to home" to each of their individual situations. Crosby was very estranged from his four sons, and between Jane's career and her heavy dating schedule, she saw little of Maureen and Michael.

She was anxious to meet and work with "Miss Barrymore," whom she regarded as the greatest actress in the history of the American theater. Ethel had been cast as Alida De Bronkhart, the principal of a snobbish girls' school.

She found Ethel in declining health, living the last decade of her life. "I was young back in 1901, somewhat of a beauty. Look at me now, a withered rose in the summer garden, deep in December."

Whenever possible, the two actresses met for tea or else had lunch together in the commissary.

Barrymore shared many memoires of Jane during their long discussions together, revealing details about her private life that didn't get included in her autobiography, *Memories.*

Ethel tantalized Jane with tidbits from her past. "Twice in my life, two people have attempted to rape me. Tallulah Bankhead and my brother, John. Only one of them succeeded, but I won't tell you which one."

She also said that in 1900, Winston Churchill had proposed marriage to her. "Perhaps I should have accepted his proposal," she told Jane.

Jane hadn't seen Natalie Wood since they'd worked together on *The Blue Veil,* where she'd played Joan Blondell's adolescent daughter. "Here I am again playing a daughter," she told Jane. "When will I ever

"Zinging a Little Zong"...*Just for You,* with Bing and Jane.

grow up?"

[Four months later, Jane encountered Natalie at a Hollywood premiere. The young girl rushed up to her to whisper confidential secrets. "Guess what? I've had my period. The flow of blood terrified me. I screamed for my mother, thinking I was dying. Mother had never explained to me the finer points of menstruation."

"Congratulations!" Jane said. "Welcome to womanhood."

"I can't wait to check out the dicks of so many guys—Tab Hunter, Tony Curtis, Rock Hudson, maybe even Robert Wagner. Or perhaps that new guy, Jimmy Dean. I've talked it over with my mother, and she thinks it should be this hot young actor, Nick Adams. In fact, she's selected Nick to teach me the ways of the world."

"I think fourteen is an acceptable age," Jane said. "It wasn't that long ago that a four-teen-year-old was getting married and having children and following Daniel Boone into the American wilderness."]

Paramount hoped to repeat the success of a Crosby/Wyman duet, which had been such a hit in their rendition of "In the Cool, Cool, Cool of the Evening."

In response, the composers came up with "Zing a Little Zong." When it was released as a recording, it enjoyed a moderate success, but they did not replicate the sales of their previous hit.

For his appearance in *Just for You,* Crosby was paid his standard fee of $150,000, with Jane receiving $133,000. During the shoot, she also signed a contract with Decca, who wanted to promote her as "The Dinah Shore of Tomorrow."

She was rather *blasé* about a recording career, although she made some records with Danny Kaye, Groucho Marx, and Jimmy Durante. Two of her comedy releases included "Black Strap Molasses" and, on the flip side, "How Di Ye Do and Shake Hands."

Just for You enjoyed only moderate success at the box office, and was certainly not a hit the way that *Here Comes the Groom* had been.

The Christian Science Monitor wrote, "As Broadway star Carolina Hill, Jane Wyman is abundantly qualified to strike a young man's fancy—or, as the story indicates, a young man's father's fancy. She plays with genuine affection scenes in which she tries to promote better family relationships among the Blakes, and with tender understanding, the difficult passages in which she discovers that she has inadvertently encouraged the young son to fall in love with her."

Writing in *Showplace,* critic Jake Karr said, "*Just for You* is artificial hocus-pocus. Miss Wyman bobs about ingratiatingly, mainly in abbreviated togs, displaying an elegant figure. She also pipes prettily some of the film's songs."

Mae Tinee of the *Chicago Tribune* found that "Miss Wyman sparkles like Lake Michigan on a sunny morning, and the studio provides her with some of the most becoming costumes a woman could have."

[After Just for You, *Crosby and Jane went their separate ways, occasionally running into each other, but drifting apart.]*

***

On most occasions, Jane kept quiet when asked about Reagan. She'd often leave the room "to powder my nose," if she were at a private party. If cornered by a reporter, she'd say, "Excuse me, I'm late for an appointment."

But Reagan angered her when, as president of SAG, he "launched a stupid campaign" (her words). He wanted to prevent fan magazines such as *Photoplay* and *Modern Screen* from writing about the private lives of "established stars." Jane expressed her disbelief that Reagan thought such a thing was possible to achieve in a free society with a free press.

In a public statement, Reagan said, "Such stories are all right for youngsters on their way up—Natalie Wood or Tab Hunter come to mind, perhaps Tony Curtis or Janet Leigh."

"But there comes a time when established stars such as Jane Wyman and myself should have control over what is written about them, with the option of a veto."

It is not known what prompted his outrage. Jane told friends that she suspected it was an event that occurred back in September of 1951, when she, escorted by Greg Bautzer, attended the premiere of *The Blue Veil.*

On a chance encounter, the couple ran into another couple in the lobby of the theater: Reagan out on a date with the MGM starlet, Nancy Davis. He introduced his date to his former wife.

As Bautzer noted, "An iceberg came between these two ladies big enough to sink ten ships the size of the *Titanic.* But all of us were ever so polite."

When both couples arrived later at Ciro's, for some reason, Nancy and Reagan were directed to empty chairs at the table otherwise occupied by Jane and Bautzer. *[Perhaps it was a mistake from a misguided maître d'hôtel, although it was later surmised that Bautzer himself had tipped the headwaiter and asked him to do that.]* Not wanting to make a scene, Reagan and Nancy sat at the table with Jane and the handsome attorney, whom he already knew.

Bautzer said, "Reagan looked like he was sweating blood. But all of us were too well bred to make a scene. Boy, did that guy look like he wanted to crawl out of his seat. Both Nancy and Jane behaved like two proper ladies, not bitter rivals in a love triangle."

It must have been terribly awkward for Nancy, because I'm sure she'd heard all the stories about how Reagan was still moaning over the loss of Jane. Everybody ordered something, something light, that is, and this 'double date' soon broke up as we went our separate ways. My evening didn't end until Jane swore on a stack of Bibles that I was better in bed than her former husband."

When the fan magazines heard what Reagan planned to do by presenting a censorship proposal to the members of SAG, they fought back. A typical response, an open letter to Reagan, appeared in *Motion Picture Magazine,* as composed by its editors:

> "You cited fan magazines about stories of your divorce from Jane Wyman as being 'false and irresponsible' invasions of your privacy. We disagree, because you apparently didn't feel the marriage itself was a private affair. During your marriage, you opened your home to photographers and reporters and allowed pictures of your home, your wife, and your children, Maureen and Michael, to be taken. But if a happy marriage is news, then it seems to follow that the breakup of that marriage is also news. Yours is a business, Mr. Reagan, which is built on publicity. In this sense, actors are like politicians."

Most actors were horrified to learn about Reagan's position. Ida Lupino and many others at SAG advised him not to bring such a proposal to a vote.

His censorship proposal died like a victim shot in the heart.

***

Still floating from studio to studio, Jane was assigned a role in her next movie, *Love Story,* scheduled for a 1953 release through Columbia.

[Its title was later changed to the more sexually suggestive Let's Do It Again.]

She was to be reunited with Ray Milland, her co-star from *The Lost Weekend*.

Three weeks before director Alexander Hall was to begin rehearsals and shooting, Jane arrived at Columbia to work on her dance routines and songs.

As she waited in a rehearsal room, in walked Fred Karger. She'd first heard his small band at a party given by Evelyn Keyes and John Huston. "My dreamboat" she later called him. He had just come from a morning game of tennis.

As she'd later tell June Allyson, "He was the man with the Betty Grable legs, the male equivalent, of course. He wore a pair of tennis shorts, very tight, making things rather obvious. His outfit and T-shirt were sunflower yellow. I had never seen a tennis player in anything but white. He was beautifully tanned and a living doll. He told me he was going to be my vocal coach at Columbia. I'm afraid I said something obvious, an old line."

"And what was that, my dear?" Allyson asked. "Maybe I'll use it sometime myself."

"I asked him, 'Did it hurt?'"

"You mean, my tennis game?"

"No, when you fell from Heaven," she answered.

Karger had dark, wavy hair, a compelling smile, and an athletic build.

Fred Lawrence Guiles, author of *Legend, The Life and Death of Marilyn Monroe*, wrote, "Fred Karger's eyes danced with an exuberance that become mystifying only after you bumped up against his reserve."

It seemed that Jane fell in love with him almost at once, although she later confessed, "I never did break down the wall of reserve he'd constructed around himself." Dur-

Doing It Again: Jane with Ray Milland, this time in a context more flippant than the emotionally wrenching *The Lost Weekend*.

Paramount promoted movie depictions of Jane as cheesecake, wearing leotards and sexy, strapless, form-fitting tops. Fearing that he was focusing exclusively on her legs, she told the photographer, "My breasts have not altogether fallen, in case you want to photograph them—fully covered, of course—too."

572

ing the three weeks she worked with him, she got to know him "as Bathsheba knew David" (her words).

"He looks great in clothes, from tennis shorts to a tuxedo," Jane told Joan Blondell. "And he looks best of all without a stitch on. It would take a Michelangelo to sculpt a body like that."

Except for his tennis outfits, he always wore conservative, dark suits and never went out the door without putting one on. Most evenings, he wore a tuxedo when taking her nightclubbing and certainly for his public appearances as the leader of his band. Once, when he escorted Jane to a garden party, he selected a dark suit as his wardrobe to an event where other many other men were attired (his words) in "pussy pink or marigold pants."

"Almost overnight, Freddie has come to fill a void in my life," Jane told Paulette Goddard. "I think he is the man for me."

"Sounds to me you've found husband number four," Goddard said.

"I think you're right. I want to be with someone young and vital, not some grandpa like Reagan, who sits in the living room every night reading editorial pages and news magazines, not to mention endless books on politics."

"Ronnie talks politics day and night," Jane said. "Freddie and I share the same interests, including similar tastes in music. He likes to gossip about the movie colony, like I do. He also likes to spend every evening dancing in nightclubs, just like I prefer. Unlike Van Johnson, he doesn't drop you off at the end of the evening, with just a kiss on the cheek. After stripping down, he brushes his teeth, gargles, and jumps into bed to send a gal to Heaven."

***

While working with Karger during the day and spending her nights in his arms, she learned more about him. He was more than a vocal coach. She knew he had his own band, but he was also a composer and conductor.

He'd been born only a year before her, the son of the famous Maxwell Karger, a producer and director at the old Metro company before it became Metro-Goldwyn-Mayer.

In 1921, Maxwell died young, suffering a fatal heart attack aboard a train traveling from New York to Fort Wayne, Indiana. Fred's mother, Anne Karger, had lived with him at the Hollywood Hotel, and was known for staging Saturday night parties, which she called "Pops Evenings."

As a young boy, Fred moved among the Hollywood elite, getting a kiss on the lips from Rudolph Valentino, a lollipop from Charlie Chaplin, or the promise of becoming a child star from Mary Pickford. Jack Pickford, Mary's brother, always tossed him in the air, and Buster Keaton once brought him a pet baby rattlesnake. "Imagine giving a rattlesnake to a little boy," Fred said.

Fred with Jane, in love, and happy.

573

"Buster was insane."

Fred had been born a Catholic, but was not a practicing one. "I'm out all Saturday night into the wee hours. When it's time for mass, I'm sleeping it off," he told Jane.

In August of 1940, he'd married a minor actress, Patti Sachs, who eventually left show business and became a high-powered lawyer. They had one daughter, Terence Meredith, nicknamed "Terry." When Sachs and Fred separated, she used her skill as a lawyer "to fleece me," Fred told Jane. "I got custody of Terry. My daughter and I live with Anne."

During his days, Fred was the assistant to Morris Stoloff, the musical director at Columbia. But at night, he made the rounds, playing at elegant private parties, including one at the home of Jack Warner. Because of his good looks, he and his band were often booked by some of the most famous hostesses of Hollywood, including Merle Oberon. Sometimes, he'd get a booking in the Escoffier Room at the Beverly Hills Hotel. On such an occasion, Jane always had a front-row table.

Hedda Hopper summed up the attraction: "Fred Karger and Jane had music in common and had a lot of laughs together. Since he was practically her age, she didn't have to go through any more older women/younger man publicity. He was as lonely as she was, and, unlike Bautzer, wanted to remarry. He felt rootless and disoriented, and wanted to get back into domestic harness again. At the time, everyone thought he was perfect for Jane. Even Ronald Reagan approved of him."

"I'm in love with Freddie Karger," Jane said in a giddy voice over the phone to June Allyson. "He makes beautiful music on and off the stage. I'm already calling him Freddie. He's gorgeous and all the plumbing is first rate and works perfectly—a maiden's dream. He is my Prince Charming, the man I've waited for all my life and didn't think I would ever find."

"Cool it, gal," Allyson cautioned.

As Maureen Reagan later wrote, "Mother brought Michael and me home one weekend from boarding school. It was a Halloween weekend, and I met Fred and his daughter, Terry, who was about six months younger than me. Michael, Terry, and I went trick or treating. When we got back, mother and Fred were waiting in the den. We walked in, and they sat us down and told us of their plans to be married. Boom! Instant extended family! Just add water and stir. When they got back from their elopement, we had these bags of rice to throw at them. I think I might have pelted Fred with clumps of rice a bit harder than tradition called for."

***

On November 1, 1952, Jane Wyman married Fred Karger in Santa Barbara at El Montecito Presbyterian Church, although both were Catholic, a church that frowned on divorce. Fred's best man was Richard Quine, the actor and director. They had the shortest honeymoon on record, one Sunday night in a suite at a Santa Monica hotel.

Both of them got up early Monday morning to begin filming *Let's Do It Again* (1953)..

News of Jane's Infatuation Goes Out to the A-list:

Above, Ethel Merman, Jane, and Fred Karger share a meal and some gossip. But what are all three of them looking at? The formidable Bette Davis had just appeared before them.

Back in Hollywood, they quickly learned that both Louella Parsons and Hedda Hopper were furious at Jane for not giving either of them an exclusive scoop.

In another part of town, a young starlet, Marilyn Monroe, was, as she later recalled, "Crying my eyes out. I vowed to get even with Wyman if it was the last thing I ever did." There were rumors that she had contemplated suicide that day by overdosing on sleeping pills.

When Oscar Saul, the producer of *Let's Do It Again,* arrived at the set that morning, he found a party underway. "I asked my assistant director, 'What in hell is going on?'" Saul asked. "He told me that the cast and crew were giving a surprise party for Fred and Jane. They had eloped that weekend."

At lunch in the commissary, screenwriter Nunnally Johnson stopped by to congratulate Jane and Karger. Later that night, he wrote to his friend, Claudette Colbert, who was at her home in Barbados. "Met Jane Wyman's new husband—and that's all there is to that!"

After Jane and Karger had been back in Hollywood for just two nights, her friends decided to throw a private party at Chasen's, since there had been nothing festive for their actual wedding.

Ironically, also dining at Chasen's that night was Marilyn Monroe with her chief supporter, the columnist Sidney Skolsky. He had done more to promote her career than any other writer in Hollywood, performing many of the kind of PR stunts for her that Louella Parsons had crafted for Reagan.

"When Marilyn heard of the private party for Jane and Freddie, she decided to crash it," Skolsky said. "I urged her not to. That was the only bitchy thing I ever saw her do."

She jumped up from the banquette and headed for the entrance to the private party. The usher there was a fan of hers and just assumed that she was among the invited guests.

Parsons was there that night, and witnessed Marilyn slinking into the party. Hedda Hopper was also there, accompanied by her son, William, and his companion, the designer, Stanley Mills Haggart.

Haggart later said, "I had known Marilyn since the days she'd first arrived in Hollywood. I knew she was up to no good. She glided into the room in a form-fitting pink dress and headed straight for Freddie. Jane was on the other side of the room, but she, like the rest of the guests, almost came to a standstill, gazing upon Marilyn and wondering what she was up to."

"She sidled right up to Freddie and gave him one of her gooey wet ones, no doubt sticking her skilled tongue down his throat. Freddie looked completely flabbergasted, actually shocked. I looked over at Jane. She was bubbling over in fury."

"Congratulations, Freddie," Marilyn said, loud enough for the room to hear.

"That voice wasn't Marilyn's usual coo," Haggart said. "It was strident, obviously she wanted Jane to hear every word. After giving the groom another gooey one, she fluttered away, blowing kisses to Freddie as she departed."

Again, she called out in a loud voice, "Just because you're married doesn't mean you have to be a stranger. You can come knocking on my door any rainy night. I'm sure we can find something to do that will amuse you."

Then she returned to Chasen's main dining room to rejoin Skolsky.

Three weeks later, Marilyn had another run-in with Jane. Earlier, she had told Shelley Winters, "Even though Joe DiMaggio is in my life, Fred Karger is the only man I've ever loved. To hell with marriage licenses. I'll still go after him from time to time. I know he'll always give in to me. He didn't want to marry me, but he's still turned on by me. As for Wyman, that bitch will get hers."

Her revenge on Jane was enacted through a chance encounter. The event, which became notorious in Hollywood history, also occurred at Chasen's, this time in the ladies' room.

When Marilyn entered the lounge, she spotted Jane in front of a mirror, applying fresh lipstick. Details are missing. They obviously had words, and another woman in the lounge later reported that she heard Jane call Marilyn "a cheap little bleach blonde trollop."

At that point, Marilyn lunged at Jane, and ripped off her wig. Because of a scalp irritation, Jane had worn a wig that night to conceal her condition.

Jane screamed as Marilyn quickly exited from the ladies' room.

Within the week, the novelist, Jacqueline Susann, heard of the incident, which later became the most dramatic scene in her best-sell-

"Doing it Again?" Or was it the first time? Jane with Aldo Ray.

ing novel, *Valley of the Dolls.* The encounter was also depicted on the screen in 1967, with the real-life Susan Hayward cast as the diva who gets her wig ripped off.

Incidentally, that movie featured the doomed Sharon Tate, whose fate it was to be brutally murdered by a psychotic gang under the influence of Charles Manson.

Many years later, at a party in New York, a hostess introduced Jane to Susann. Jane glared at her hostess. "I'm a lady. Why should I want to meet this piece of trash?" Then she turned her back on Susann and walked away.

"If that's a lady, I'm the Queen of Sheba," Susann told her hostess.

***

Just at the point when Ray Milland had become a distant memory—like that Ellen Drew movie, *Night Plane from Chungking,* you saw back in 1943—the handsome actor came back into her life. To Jane's surprise, she was told that her upcoming film with Milland would be a remake of *The Awful Truth.* Adapted from a Broadway comedy, it had already been filmed three times, as silent movies in 1924 and 1929, and—in its most successful version, in 1937, starring Irene Dunne and Cary Grant.

Teamed with Milland for the first time since *The Lost Weekend,* Jane got star billing over him. Milland's career was in steep decline, but Jane was at her peak. The tired old script was given fresh, modern overtones. *Let's Do It Again* was the story of a composer's wife (played by Jane) who tries to make her husband jealous. Her plan backfires and catalyzes her divorce from Milland.

Directed by Alexander Hall, *Let's Do It Again* was produced by Oscar Saul, who had barged into Harry Cohn's office at Columbia saying, "Just think, Harry, we've got two Oscar winners, Wyman and Milland, in a picture together once again."

"Big fucking deal!" Cohn said. "I won't get excited until I see the box office receipts."

After greeting Hall and Saul on the set, Jane braced herself for a reunion with Milland in her dressing room, where she had already changed her outfit and adjusted her makeup three times. When he came in to greet her, she was taken aback. He had aged considerably, blaming his increasing loss of hair on the branding irons used to curl his locks when he'd co-starred in *Reap the Wild Wind* (1942) with John Wayne and Paulette

Goddard.

As before, as he had back in 1944, he flirted with her. "Shall we take the advice in the title of our movie and do it again?" he asked.

"I think not," she said, politely, kissing him on the lips. "I prefer to keep the old memory intact."

As for Aldo Ray, the second male lead of *Let's Do It Again*, Jane didn't give in to him, but he relentlessly pursued her anyway, making propositions in his "gargle voice." She remembered him as "very masculine, a bit rough around the edges but kind of sexy."

Ray had been a Navy frogman and had played football in college. He had a sizable endowment and had posed nude in a widely circulated underground photograph.

As he confessed, "I dropped trou for George Cukor, who helped me in my career." Ray also climbed the lavender ladder when he was cast with Spencer Tracy in *Pat and Mike* (1952). That movie also featured a particularly macho performance from Tracy's platonic friend, Katharine Hepburn.

After his performance with Jane, Ray fell into the arms of Rita Hayworth when they co-starred in *Miss Sadie Thompson* (1953).

Jane later recalled, "Every woman needs an Aldo Ray in her life, but never for more than six weeks. And then he has to go."

Let's Do It Again grossed $1.25 million at the box office. It was widely promoted with the advertising slogan, "Go Girl, Go!" That is what Jane did, letting loose in the role, even doing a wicked mambo, which was all the dance rage that year, and performing in such sultry song and dance numbers as "I'm Takin' a Slow Burn Over a Fast Man." Her performance brought out her farcical side, and her acting was compared favorably to that of Irene Dunne's in the film's 1937 predecessor. As for Milland's "serviceable" performance, critics pointed out that "He is no Cary Grant."

***

While Jane was still filming *Let's Do It Again*, representatives from Warners arrived to ask her to pose for advance publicity photographs for her upcoming film, *So Big* (1953). Her two male co-stars, Sterling Hayden and Steve Forrest, had already been announced, as had its director, Robert Wise. Of course, Wise's two greatest triumphs lay in his future—*West Side Story* (1961) and *The Sound of Music* (1965).

The "soaper/saga," a novel written by Edna Ferber, was reaching the screen for the third time. As a silent, it had starred Colleen Moore, Nancy Davis' close friend. Jane's own friend, Barbara Stanwyck, had made it into a talkie in a 1932 version.

One night at dinner, after Jane announced to Stanwyck that she'd signed to reprise her role as the noble, valiant woman toiling in the soil, the diva stormed out of the room. She went two weeks before speaking to Jane again. "Sorry, Jane, but I get pissed off when I hear that another actress is reprising a role for which I've given my original interpretation."

When Jane called Paulette Goddard to tell her about her next two leading men, Goddard was excited. "My God, you're getting two of the handsomest, most masculine, hot, horny, and hung actors in Hollywood—all the girls say so. Steve, you know, is the brother of Dana Andrews, and all of us have had him, at least those of us who got him when he was sober. Forrest, during the war, fought in the Battle of the Bulge against the Nazis in their last big drive into the West. I hear that the Battle of the Bulge was named after Steve."

"Since Steve plays my son in the film—a kid I've named So Big—would that be committing incest?" Jane facetiously asked.

"Follow the advice of your latest movie ad," Goddard said. "Go, Girl, Go!"

Both Goddard and June Allyson constantly advised Jane to play around. "It actually saves a marriage and keeps it from getting boring," Goddard claimed.

At the time, Jane was indulging in what she called "the revenge fuck." In 1952, although she had entered into the first of what would be two separate marriages to band-leader Fred Karger, she had heard rumors that he was still slipping around for trysts with his former girlfriend, Marilyn Monroe, who had also wanted to marry him.

When Hayden posed with Jane for the ads for *So Big*, she was immediately attracted to him.

Edna Ferber *Author* USA 83

The Literary Voice of the Great American Plain: Edna Ferber.

In the early 1940s, during his marriage to blonde god-dess Madeleine Carroll, Hayden had been billed as "the Beautiful Viking God." He was known for seducing his leading ladies—Anne Baxter in *Blaze of Noon* (1947); Dorothy Lamour in *Manhandled* (1949), and Marilyn Monroe in *The Asphalt Jungle* (1950). Apparently, he managed to elude Bette Davis when they'd appeared together in *The Star* (1952).

After Jane posed for publicity photographs with Hayden, she told Wise, "Sterling, without a doubt, belongs among the gods of Valhalla. What a man! What a god! After being with him, how can I go home at night to Fred *[Karger]* and be satisfied?"

Steve Forrest was "another blonde god" [Jane's words] but completely different in personality. He was a tall Texan, born to a Baptist minister in a family of thirteen, one member of which included his older brother, Dana Andrews. Enlisting in the Army at age eighteen, he'd returned to America and benefitted from the G.I. Bill, eventually receiving his Bachelor's degree, with honors, from UCLA. He'd majored

Vintage Americana: Abandoning all vestiges of glamor, Jane portrays a pioneer woman sod-busting with her husband (Sterling Hayden) and raising a son in *So Big*.

in theater and soon was working at the La Jolla Playhouse outside San Diego, where Gregory Peck discovered him and arranged for a screen test at MGM, which led to a contract.

Jane and he sometimes went nightclubbing together. One night at a tavern north of Santa Monica, they sang a duet together, the quality of which benefitted from his status as a trained vo-

Jane flew to New York to see Steve Forrest perform on Broadway in the aptly named *The Body Beautiful*.

calist.

She raved about him so much to June Allyson, that she, too, "sampled the wares" *[Allyson's words]* when they starred together on TV in *The DuPont Show With June Allyson,* a series that was launched in 1959. Although Forrest had married Christine Carilas in 1948 and would still be married to her at the time of his death in 2013, he still played around.

"Women found him irresistible," Jane claimed, "beginning with a seduction of Lana Turner when he'd appeared in her 1952 picture, *The Bad and the Beautiful.*"

As an actor trying to make it in Hollywood, Forrest was rumored to have "put out" for Reagan's friend, Robert Taylor, when they co-starred together in *Rogue Cop* in 1954. That same year, he was second billed to Reagan in *Prisoner of War* as one of the incarcerated G.I.s tortured by the North Koreans.

When Jane saw the publicity photographs in which she'd posed with Hayden for *So Big,* she was enraged. She personally called Jack Warner to denounce them. "This is a tender story of Selina and her love for her son, her dreams that sustained her through years of rugged farm toil."

"Sex sells, Janie," the mogul answered. "Now I've got to go. Joan Crawford's on the phone."

She later denounced the ads as the "work of a pack of vulgarians." The ads depicted her being grasped by a lustful, brutish Hayden. The copy read:

In a moment of intimacy, Jane Wyman shows her screen husband, Sterling Hayden, a new outfit for their son, who is becoming "So Big."

HE STOOD THERE SO BIG—LOVE HAD COME. INTENSE. UNASHAMED.

Jane is depicted with her "son" in the movie, *So Big.*

For the rest of his life, Hayden would be kidded about those ads. Gossipy Hollywood already knew about his endowment, the size of which was almost legendary.

Literary fans of Edna Ferber protested the advertising, but it nonetheless succeeded in herd-

Once again, as in *The Yearling,* she played a frontier woman who bravely ekes out a living in an often cruel climate, triumphing against powerful odds.

ing TV-crazed audiences of the 1950s into movie houses. Instead of listening to Jane's protests, Warner approved an equivalent ad with equivalently lurid photos, this one with the headline:

SHE WAS READY TO FORGET SHE'D EVER BEEN A LADY.

***

As a married woman, Jane felt it was her duty to move Karger out of that little bungalow he shared with his mother and daughter, Anne and Terry. "I don't trust grown-up men who still live with their mothers. Don't tell me you're another Clifton Webb who even attends parties with his mother?"

"You know I'm not that type," he answered. "Webb can't make you scream in ecstasy at night."

She found a home for them on Beverly Glen Boulevard, with small, separate bedrooms for Maureen, Michael, and Terry. Anne was left alone in her bungalow. Jane's living room was big enough to accommodate his two pianos and her one piano.

From the first, she found that their career demands often had them living in separate worlds. Sometimes, as he was staggering in from a late night gig, she was leaving to report to make-up on a film set.

When she wed Karger, whereas Jane was at the peak of her earning power, he drew a modest weekly wage and often picked up one or two hundred dollars for a gig at night. Nearly all of his money went either for alimony payments to his first wife or for the upkeep of his daughter, Terry, or to his mother, Anne.

Joan Blondell said, "Freddie in essence is a kept boy. That is not unusual in Hollywood. Many big stars like Jane support their husbands or else pay the bills of their boyfriends."

Karger enjoyed living in his new wife's luxurious world with two or three servants, including a nanny to look after their children when they were home and not away at boarding schools. On weekends, he liked to be served breakfast in bed.

After three weeks of married life with Karger, Jane got a call from June Allyson. "How's married life, kid?"

"Freddie is a man of intellect, talent, and sophistication," Jane said. "Except for the conflicts in our working schedules, I have only one complaint about him in the bedroom."

"Don't tell me he's the type of guy you have to ask, 'Is it in now?'"

"Quite the contrary," Jane said. "You have to warn him not to put in those final inches or he'll split me open. No, it's not that. He has this habit of spending thirty minutes every morning deciding on which pair of underwear he wants. I don't know why it matters, unless he's modeling his drawers for someone."

"Unlike my life with Ronnie, Freddie just can't get enough," Jane claimed to Allyson. "Sometimes he wakes me up in the middle of the night ready and raring to go. After all, I did get to know him on my aptly named film, *Let's Do It Again.*"

"Oh, if that were only true with Richard and me." She was referring, of course, to her husband, Dick Powell.

Modern Screen wrote, "Fred Karger might have had a better chance if he'd married Sarah Jane Fulks and not the great movie star, Jane Wyman. But Sarah Jane disappeared a long time ago. Wyman is said to boss him around, and Karger, from all reports, is imbued with a manly pride and not used to taking orders from a woman. Also, he wants to become a bigtime musician like Harry James, and he resents it terribly when the press refers to him as Mr. Jane Wyman."

In less than a month of marriage, Jane began to find flaws in her husband's character. She admitted to Joan Blondell, "When he's drunk, he's dangerous to be around. When he found out I'd had a fling with Bing Crosby, he became violent and started breaking things in the living room. I explain my thing with Bing was before I met him, but that didn't cool him off. I think he's jealous because Bing, as a musician, is wildly successful and Freddie is still struggling."

"As you know, I like to paint on Sunday afternoon. I had seven of my paintings decorating the walls of our living room. He was so mad, he broke a bottle of Scotch and slashed my art work."

"Even when sober, he has a violent temper," Jane told Blondell. "We attended this premiere. Some stupid fan called out to me, 'Jane, who's the guy with you? Is he important?' That really pissed off Freddie. I had to restrain him or else he'd have slugged that fan."

The most shocking revelation she learned about Karger was that he had a bad heart condition similar to that of his father, Maxwell, a condition so serious it had led to the producer's early death.

"Up to then, I thought my husband was a stallion," Jane said. "Now I know differently. He seems to go day and night, a fulltime job at Columbia and all those late night gigs with his band. He's tired, overworked, completely exhausted, which makes him irritable."

In March of 1953, he endured a mild heart attack. "We had him rushed to the hospital in an ambulance," Jane told Allyson. "The doctor warned me he had to cut back on his schedule and give up smoking those three packages of cigarettes a day. I'm urging him to give up the band, too. I didn't tell him that I'm often embarrassed to go to a Hollywood party to find Freddie and his band working as the hired hands for the night."

A big blowup in their marriage occurred right before Christmas of 1953. Jane was late arriving home, and Karger and the children were collectively decorating the living room and the Christmas tree. When young Michael was left alone in the living room, the boy began lighting candles. He accidentally set fire to the decorations on Jane's antique dining table, which was covered in heirloom lace.

A fire broke out and blazed out of control The fire department was summoned as it spread. When Jane got home, she was shocked to find her living room soaking in water, the ceilings blackened, and some of her valuable possessions destroyed.

She had such a fight with Karger that he moved out before Christmas Eve, spending two weeks in a suite at the Beverly Hills Hotel. Reportedly, Marilyn Monroe, in the aftermath of one of her frequent tiffs with DiMaggio, moved in with Karger when the former baseball player, in a rage, flew to visit his relatives in San Francisco.

Finally, Jane admitted to Blondell, "I miss the sex. I'm going over to the hotel to make up with Freddie and ask him to come home. The living room has been redone."

After a year of marriage, Jane told Blondell, "I think I had a Hasty Heart rushing into marriage to Freddie."

Her words were a reference, of course, to Reagan's movie, *The Hasty Heart.*

***

Jane received a call from director Douglas Sirk, informing her that Universal had decided to remake that tearjerker, *Magnificent Obsession,* based on Lloyd C. Douglas's bestselling novel, originally published in 1929.

Its plot had previously been adapted into a film in 1935, starring Robert Taylor and Jane's friend, Irene Dunne, in the lead roles. The script had originally been offered to Jane's other Catholic friend, Loretta Young, but she had rejected it. "Irene is my best friend. I don't want to remake the picture in which she was so glorious," Young said.

Jane's career in the mid-1950s was slipping, and Universal executives decided to give her a boost in this seminal soap. Executive Ed Muhl also insisted that "America's new heartthrob," Rock Hudson, be cast as the male lead. "The original *Magnificent Obsession* made a big star out of Robert Taylor. I think the remake can do the same for Rock. Maybe lightning will strike twice."

Jane had rehearsed how to be a deaf mute before shooting *Johnny Belinda.* A month before the filming began, on *Magnificent Obsession,* she studied how blind people react. "They just don't go around careening into the furniture and tripping over themselves," she said. The character she plays is blind throughout part of the movie.

Two days before shooting, Rock had taken an inner tube to ride the waves at Santa Monica beach. Soon, he was drifting way out to sea, where he rode the crest of a wave back toward the shoreline. Before he reached it, the crashing surf landed him on the beach with a broken collarbone.

Fearing that he'd jeopardize his big chance, he refused to let doctors put a cast on him, although he was warned that the bone would not heal properly and that he might feel pain for the rest of his life.

On the first day of shooting, Jane sensed that something was wrong with him when they came into body contact during rehearsals for a scene together. She went with him to his dressing room, where he confessed that his collar bone was broken. She promised not to tell anyone and to be careful in her love scenes with him.

Rock, born in Winnetka, Illinois, in 1925, was considerably younger than Jane. He stood 6'5" and towered over her. He was not only tall, but exceedingly handsome, wavy haired, and solidly built, a former Navy man who had become a Hollywood beefcake pin-up, thrilling millions of teenage girls and gay men of all ages.

Jane was very patient with Hudson, even when some of their scenes had to be reshot thirty or even forty times.

On the set, producer Ross Hunter huddled with Sirk and Jane, telling both of them, "I want this to be a three-hanky movie. I like to give the public what it wants—a chance to dream, to live vicariously, to see beautiful women, jewels, gorgeous clothes, and to experience melodrama."

Hunter told Jane, "I'm the world's champion crier. That's why I'm so good at producing junk like our movie. Call me the 'Sultan of Soap Operas.' Even though I find it repulsive, I hawk heterosexual romance. In fact, I worship at its altar because it makes big bucks for me."

Hunter had served in Army Intelligence during World War II. Later, this gay man became a theatrical producer and director, known for light films starring Doris Day, Lana Turner, Debbie Reynolds (the Tammy

Based on the directives of Jack Warner, the ads that promoted the tender love story portrayed by Jane Wyman and Rock Hudson were sensationalist and lurid.

Posters screamed: "A Story Of Love That Will Become One Of The Deepest Emotional Thrills Of Your Lifetime!", and "This was the moment unashamed, when this man and this woman felt the first ecstasy of their *Magnificent Obsession!*"

582

movies) and later, Julie Andrews.

A Dane, Sirk had been one of Germany's leading stage directors before the war, later working for UFA studios. He was credited with making a star of Zarah Leander in Nazi cinema. Because his second wife, Hilda Jary, was Jewish, he said, "goodbye to Adolf" (his words), leaving Germany in 1937. By 1942, he was making anti-Nazi films in Hollywood.

Hudson later told Sara Davidson, who was working with him on his autobiography, "Doug would lock his office door, have the secretary hold his calls, and come after me on his knees. It was enough to keep him hooked and eager to help my career."

In *Magnificent Obsession,* Rock was cast as a spoiled playboy, Bob Merrick. He has an accident in his speedboat, and his rescuers send for the only resuscitator in the area. Regrettably, Jane, cast as Helen Phillips, discovers her husband as he suffers a heart attack and dies. He, too, needed that resuscitator, the assumption being that if its life-saving powers hadn't been squandered on the character played by Rock, Jane's husband would have lived.

Jane's Helen refuses to accept Bob's generous offers and apologies. When he tries to pursue her by jumping inside her car, she escapes onto the street, where she is hit by an oncoming car and, as a result, becomes blind.

From then on, heartstrings are pulled. Along the way, Merrick discovers his spirituality, learning about the "magnificent obsession of helping others without making them aware of it. As only a Ross Hunter movie would dare, he even becomes a brain surgeon, not only saving Helen's life, but restoring her sight. After a long struggle and endless resistance, she falls in love with him, leading to an improbable but happy ending.

On the set, Jane was reunited with her friend, Agnes Moorehead, who had starred with her in *The Blue Veil.* In *Magnificent Obsession,* she played the role of Jane's trusted friend, Nancy Ashford.

"I can play them all," Moorehead told Jane. "Bring 'em on. Domineering mothers, comical secretaries, neurotic spinsters, puritanical matrons."

Barbara Rush, a beautiful young actress, was cast as Joyce Phillips, Jane's stepdaughter in the film. Married to actor Jeffrey Hunter, she would appear opposite such stars as Marlon Brando, Paul Newman, Richard Burton, James Mason, Frank Sinatra, and Kirk Douglas during her movie career. She affectionately called Ross Hunter "Uncle Mame."

One of the supporting players, Otto Kruger, had been a matinee idol in the 1930s, later cast as suave villains or shady fellows. He'd appeared in films starring everyone from Barbara Stanwyck to Grace Kelly.

Mae Clarke, born Violet Mary Kootz in Philadelphia, had a small supporting role. Her career had peaked in 1931 when she played Frankenstein's bride and was chased by Boris Karloff in *Frankenstein.* That same year, James Cagney in *The Public Enemy* smashed a grapefruit in her face at the breakfast table.

Hudson's romantic life was growing more and more complicated. One night, Ross Hunter invited him to Chasen's for dinner. "As Hudson entered the room, all the eyes, even the jaded ones attuned to male beauty, cast

It was during the filming that Agnes Moorehead's friend, the outrageously campy Paul Lynde, came on the set.

When Moorehead was called away, he told Jane, "The whole world knows Agnes is a lesbian—I mean classy as hell, but one of the all-time Hollywood dykes."

their gaze upon him," Hunter said.

He later told a jealous Sirk, "Rock was especially stunning that night. After two bottles of champagne, I told him that I wanted to spend the weekend with him in Palm Springs. It was even bigger than I had imagined."

"By the end of that weekend, I told him, 'I love you, Rock!'"

"Even with a broken collar bone, I was really put on the casting couch—first with Sirk, and, to top it off, now Hunter." Rock said. "I was getting a real workout."

Rock confided his being a victim on the casting couch to his friend and fellow gay actor, Roddy McDowall.

"Jane was always gracious and put me at ease in front of the camera," Hudson said. "I was nervous and didn't want to fuck up this big picture. It was my first real break. I think I brought out the mother instinct in her. Things got out of hand one night, though. What shall I call it? Mother love, perhaps? You get my drift."

"It's not that I had not had intimate contact with a woman before. In my day, I've delivered a few mercy fucks, notably with Joan Crawford at her house. Or a weekend with Tallulah Bankhead in Las Vegas. Those mercy fucks extended to fading matinee idols like Errol Flynn and Tyrone Power. I didn't mean for it to happen with Jane. I respected her too much. I think she turned to me when she heard Fred Karger was back, banging Marilyn Monroe."

When the film was released, it made ten times as much money as the original Taylor/Dunne version—in other words, it was a major hit.

Hudson got the worst reviews. Critic Doug McClelland called him, "comic strip handsome, thrashing about with no special distinction, his scenes lined up with all the depth and subtlety of great colored blocks."

The New York Times appraised Jane: "In appealing contrast to Miss Dunne's pristine languor, Miss Wyman is, as usual, refreshingly believable throughout."

Magnificent Obsession was a big hit, earning $5 million for the studio. Thousands of letters poured into Universal, citing Hudson's stunning male beauty—"and those soulful eyes."

A star was born.

Magnificent Obsession brought Jane another Oscar nomination. But that was the year (1955) that Grace Kelly won the Best Actress Award for *The Country Girl.*

***

Escorted by Fred Karger, Jane had flown to New York to promote *Magnificent Obsession.* A suite was reserved for them at the Waldorf Astoria. Rock Hudson flew in the following day and paid an early afternoon visit to their suite. It was made clear that Rock and Karger would work out together at a health club on Manhattan's Upper East Side, and that Jane would spend part of the afternoon having her hair styled in advance of their gala event that evening. All of them agreed to return to Jane and Karger's suite later that afternoon, allowing time to dress in formal wear for that evening's gala event.

After some additional chitchat, Jane departed for her appointment with the hairdresser. Twenty minutes after leaving the Waldorf, she realized she'd left a diamond bracelet—one of her most expensive pieces of jewelry—on a tabletop back at the Waldorf. She hurried back to the suite, fearing that a member of the housekeeping staff might steal it.

She entered the suite believing that she it was empty. Suddenly, she heard noises from the bedroom. When she opened the door, she found Karger and Rock engaged together in lovemaking. Karger was on the bottom, and he was the first to see her. "Oh, my God, Rock. It's Jane."

She grabbed her diamond bracelet and walked quickly toward the exit, leaving the men alone together. She didn't know what happened between them after that.

When she returned to the suite later that afternoon, she found Karger alone. He was already dressed in his tuxedo for the premiere. Rock, apparently, had left.

She said nothing. It was Karger who spoke first: "You've got to understand, honey. Both Hunter and Sirk told me that Rock is going to become the biggest star in Hollywood in just a year or so. I had to give in to him. He came on strong. With him headed for super stardom, he could get me assigned as musical director on all his films. I was doing it for career advancement…*for us,* darling."

Presumably, she assumed her most convincing mask of sophistication and tolerance. "It's okay, darling," she said. "Rock is very seductive. I, of all people, know that."

"You mean…?" He looked flabbergasted.

"I mean just that, my husband," she answered. "I had him before you. We'll have to ask him which of us he prefers."

"I can't believe this is happening," he said.

"I'm flying back to California alone," she said. "I hope you'll understand. Now let me get dressed so we can put on our best smiles as *Mr. and Mrs. Jane Wyman* on the red carpet."

***

The months ahead were rough on the marriage. Jane called it "marriage on the rocks." Karger was gone nearly every night of the week. On some of those occasions, he was appearing with his band. But she suspected many of those nights were spent at Rock's home.

Karger and Jane began a slow drift apart. Hedda Hopper and Louella Parsons were soon made aware of their marital troubles.

That summer, Jane revealed to Parsons, "There will be no reconciliation. I have decided that things aren't working out between us."

"There's no hope?" Parsons asked.

"None."

"When Parsons contacted Karger, he told the gossipy columnist, "Let Jane speak for the both of us. It's her decision."

Hopper one morning led her syndicated column with the headline WYMAN/KARGER MARRIAGE ON THE ROCKS. She had learned that Karger had gone back to living with his mother, Anne, and his daughter, Terry.

Five weeks later, Parsons spoke to Jane and had a long talk with her. "I told Jane that both of them were equally to blame. I also said that I knew they had problems, but they were not important ones. I convinced her to take him back."

In a week, Karger was sleeping in Jane's bed again, and both Hopper and Parsons were writing about their reconciliation.

It is not known who, but some gossipy "friend" of Jane's reported an incident he'd learned. According to the revelation, Karger had spent a long weekend in Palm Springs, occupying a hotel suite with both Tyrone Power and Marilyn Monroe.

Jane might have overlooked his dalliance with Rock, but bringing Marilyn back into his life was too much. She could tolerate a liaison between him and Power, but not with Marilyn, or so she told Joan Blondell.

On November 10, 1954, she filed for divorce, charging mental cruelty. Her papers came through on December 7.

The day before that, she was received into the Roman Catholic faith, which, of course, frowns on divorce.

Blondell later said, "Many stars in Hollywood, though loyal Catholics in their spiritual hearts, don't always adhere to the church's rigid teachings. The Pope is so unbending, only the most devout can follow his dictates. The church's sense of morality is too rigid for a mere human being with needs and desires. Life is about having fun. It's so damn short."

***

With movie roles drying up, Jane, in 1955, became the host of *Jane Wyman Presents the Fireside Theater,* her gig lasting for three years.

"I was following Ronnie by appearing on the little black-and-white box," she told friends.

Fireside Theater was an anthology drama series that ran on NBC from 1949 to 1958, becoming the first successful series on American television. Shooting schedules were short and budgets skimpy, but the public loved it, even though most critics panned the telecasts. For most of its run, *Fireside Theater* was among the top ten most popular shows on television.

Both Frank Wisbar and Gene Raymond predated Jane as host, but she became the most successful because of her famous name, winning the most viewers.

It wasn't that she was not getting any film roles. Offers were for movies she didn't want to make, including *Friendly Persuasion* (1956) with Gary Cooper, a role that went to Dorothy McGuire. She praised the great latitude she had working in television during her tenure. She also agreed to star in fourteen of the series' episodes, eventually appearing with Joseph Cotten, Paul Henried, and Linda Darnell. One of them was *Holiday in Autumn* (1955), wherein she co-starred with Fay Wray of *King Kong* fame. She also worked with actors she knew from earlier periods of her career, including Jack Carson and Dane Clark, even her former lover, Peter Lawford.

When she left the series, it would not be Jane's last venture into TV drama. "Bigger and better things—and a lot more money—were my distant horizon," she recalled much later.

***

Returning to the big screen, Jane starred in "a woman's picture," *Lucy Gallant,* for producers William H. Pine and William C. Thomas. It was set for release in 1955.

For the first time, she'd be working with the strikingly handsome, muscular, 6'3", square-jawed actor, Charlton Heston. On being introduced to her, Heston startled her with his opening line.

"Did you know that Ronald Reagan and I have something in common?" he asked her.

"And what might that be?" she asked.

"We both posed nude for sculpture classes," he said.

[NOTE: Whereas Reagan retained his "bloomers" during those modeling sessions, Heston, by all accounts, did not.]

The film's director, Georgia-born Robert Parrish, was a former child star. He was also a screenwriter and editor, having won an Oscar for the film, *Body and Soul* in 1947. As an actor, he'd appeared with her former lover, Lew Ayres, in the 1930 *All Quiet on the Western Front.*

Jane was supported by two talented actresses, Claire Trevor, cast as Lady Mac (short for MacBeth), and Thelma Ritter as Molly. "Any time Trevor or Ritter appeared on camera, you can be assured they'll steal the scene," Jane said to Parrish.

On the first read through of John Lee Mahin's film script, based on the Margaret Cousins novel, Jane found out just how disappointed Heston was to be co-starring with her. "This movie is nothing but trashy soap opera," he said.

Jane didn't know what Heston was getting, but she was drawing $163,000 for ten weeks' work.

"When I heard *you* were my leading lady, I thought it was one of those May-December romances," he told her. I mean, you're thirty-seven, but I'm only thirty, although I look twenty-five."

After that put-down, she struck back. "Perhaps you're right. I see you're still carrying around your baby fat in that pudgy ass of yours. Better take it off, Chuck."

Although insulted, he took her advice and slimmed down for all of his next pictures, many of which had him half nude.

During the shoot, she found him, "cold and distant," and he obviously did not like working with her in this story of marriage vs. career, the saga of a dress designer who sets up shop in a hick Texas oiltown where women, for the most part, are attired in calico and gingham.

Into her life comes Casey Cole (Heston), a lanky local rancher, who falls in love with her. Their love scenes were unconvincing. At one point, Heston joins the Army, but upon his return, he becomes an oil tycoon. Lucy's shop burns to the ground, and she faces a perennial question: Stay on and build a bigger

Off screen, Charlton Heston was cynical about his role in *Lucy Gallant*, telling Jane:

"It's basically your show, with me wandering in and out for stud duty," Heston said. "I'm contracted to make this buzzard for one reason. Dollar bills!"

Haute mode: Jane, prepping for *Lucy Gallant's* fashion promenade with designer Edith Head.

"Edith was a lesbian," Jane claimed. "She always managed to cop a feel when fitting me for one of my gowns."

store, or retreat into a marriage? Feminists hated her final choice.

Ritter's advice was "Having a man is better than ending up a rich old maid with a monogrammed water bottle."

The highlight of the movie was a spectacular fashion show. The film's costume designer, Edith Head, actually makes a rare appearance on camera. So did Alan Shiver, the actual then-governor of Texas, who introduces the fashion show.

Paramount publicity ran a promotional ad that both Heston and Jane found vulgar:

HE'S COLD—SHE'S HOT—SHE WARMS HIM UP.

Another copywriter got carried away, defining the movie as:

A STORY WITH THE FORCE AND POWER OF AN EXPLOSIVE GUSHER.

At the end of the shoot, Heston said, perhaps falsely, that "Jane's a lot of fun, down-to-earth, and unaffected."

When asked what she thought of working with Heston, Jane uttered: "No comment!" and walked away.

Bosley Crowther of *The New York Times* wrote: "Some of it catches sudden flashes and briefly revealing glints of the crudities and vulgarities of the Texas *nouveaux riche.* The ostentation of such things as lavish spending and going to backyard barbecues in evening gowns is subtly satirized."

The film, *Lucy Gallant,* limped into theaters across the country, soon disappearing with a broken leg and quickly forgotten.

***

The teaming of Jane Wyman and Rock Hudson was so successful in *Magnificent Obsession* that Universal decided to unite them again as a romantic couple in *All That Heaven Allows* (1955).

Once again, the producer was Ross Hunter, who commissioned Peg Fenwick to write the screenplay based on a story by Edna L. Lee and Harry Lee.

It was the story of a May-September romance between a wealthy widow, as played by Jane, who lives in a small, suburban New England town with two college age children. One day, an exceedingly handsome and virile young gardener arrives to prune her trees. He is Don Kirby (Hudson), an intelligent, down-to-earth passionate younger man who leads an idealistic, Thoreau-inspired, *Walden Pond*-style life outside the gossipy, mean-spirited town. Gradu-

The Rock Hudson she'd worked with on *Magnificent Obsession* (1954) was not the same actor she had encountered on the set of *All That Heaven Allows* (1955).

He had, during the interval between these films, become a big star. In the fan magazines, he and Marilyn Monroe were written about more than any other celebrities. Fan clubs had sprouted up in all the States.

ally, the couple fall in love, despite the difference in their age and class.

Her children are horrified. Son Ned (William Reynolds) accuses his mother of besmirching her late husband's memory. Daughter Kay (Gloria Talbot) is equally unenthusiastic, fearing that her mother will disgrace the family. She prefers her to wed Harvey (Conrad Nagel), a longtime family friend. In real life, Nagel, born in 1897, had been a romantic leading man on the silent screen. Jane doesn't seem attracted in any way to this older man, who could conceivably have played her father. At the time of shooting, Jane was forty-one, Rock, 29, although he looked even younger.

Jane knew that Sirk was a sometimes lover of Rock's and she felt she could discuss her embarrassment with him. She revealed that she'd walked into her suite at New York's Waldorf and had found Rock seducing Fred Karger.

"That is a problem," he said. "There will be love scenes between Rock and you."

"Don't worry, I'll pull them off regardless of how I feel about Rock's betrayal," she said. "I won't be the first actress in Hollywood who has faced this dilemma."

She decided she needed another hit, and she threw herself into this story of small town bigotry, prejudice, and narrow-mindedness.

On the set, at one of their first reunions since their embarrassment at the Waldorf, Hudson walked right over to her and kissed her on the cheek. "Great to be working with you again. Our last picture made me a biggie. People treat me different. Sometimes they just stare at me in awe. If I let out a fart after eating a bowl of chili, I get applause, like I've done something wonderful. It seems that everybody I meet thinks I can walk on water."

"I don't!" she said sharply.

"Oh, Janie, let's make this picture and forget about Freddie," Rock said. "He's trying to find himself. You must understand that in Hollywood, these things happen more than you would know."

For the sake of the picture, she told him she'd cooperate with him.

He said he'd been tapped by George Stevens to appear in his upcoming film *Giant* (1956), based on the Edna Ferber novel. His co-stars would be James Dean and Elizabeth Taylor. He claimed that both Alan Ladd and William Holden had wanted the lead role in *Giant,* but both had been rejected.

"Maybe you'll bed both of them, too," she said, sarcastically.

Jane with Douglas Sirk, who had slept with her acting partner.

Jane, backstage, with Rock Hudson, who had slept with her husband.

Cover boy William Reynolds, hailed as a "classic male beauty," played Jane's son in *All That Heaven Allows.* Director Sirk told Jane, "I'd like to direct a love scene between 'Billy Boy' and Rock, but the world isn't ready for that...Yet!"

"Actually, that's what I plan to do," he said.

During the course of the day, he told her that his gay agent, Henry Willson, was forcing him into a lavender marriage with his secretary, Phyllis Gates, who was a lesbian. "I hate the idea of getting married, but too many of the fan magazines are running stories headlined: WHY ISN'T ROCK MARRIED?"

Within the first week, Jane was either introduced or else renewed her acquaintance with the rest of the cast, particularly Agnes Moorehead, who had previously starred with Rock and herself in *Magnificent Obsession.*

When Jane filmed a scene with Reynolds playing her character's son, in reference to the character played by Hudson, he tells her, "All you see is a good-looking set of muscles."

Ironically, that is what Rock saw and appreciated when he was introduced to Reynolds.

[Many film critics have hailed Reynolds—who was native to Los Angeles and of Norwegian ancestry—as the most stunning of the so-called "pretty boys" of the 1950s, others of whom included Robert Wagner, Tony Curtis, and Tab Hunter.]

Sirk told Jane that he felt "Rock will go for this hunk big time. Billy boy is just his type. The question is, will Reynolds swing in Rock's direction?"

It is not known if Rock ever made a pass at Reynolds, as he so often did with handsome young men who worked with him on his films, once falling in love with a cameraman.

Reynolds had married Molly Sinclair in 1950 and remained wed to her until the time of her death in 1992.

The only published source attesting that Rock and Reynolds might have been lovers was a 2004 biography, *Rock Hudson,* by the prolific writer, David Bret. But there is no other confirmation, and the claim could have been just speculation.

During the filming of *All That Heaven Allows,* as Jane moved deeper and deeper into her on-screen romance, the script rekindled sad memories of how the gossips of Hollywood had destroyed her own engagement to Travis Kleefeld, a young man she'd loved at the time. As an actress, she was drawing on that experience as a means of bringing the character of the affluent older widow in love with a younger man to the screen.

When reporters came to the set, Jane put up a brave front: She said, "After working with Rock Hudson the second time around, I'd say that he's got to be the biggest thing to hit the industry."

After Sirk read that that comment in the papers, he said to her, "Rock's got the biggest thing all right."

"Oh, you size queens," Jane responded, dismissing him.

During the filming, Jane bonded with Virginia Grey, who was her same age. Born in Los Angeles, Grey told Jane that Gloria Swanson had been her first babysitter. At the age of ten, Grey had made her film debut in the silent, *Uncle Tom's Cabin* (1927).

Jane, as well as most of Hollywood, knew of Grey's long-enduring affair with Clark Gable. She confided to Jane that she was heartbroken when he married Lady Sylvia Ashley in 1949. "He'd proposed to me months earlier," she said. "I'll never marry any other man if I can't have Clark. After all, once you've gone to bed with Clark Gable, no

Virginia Grey: "It's Clark Gable or no one."

590

other man will do."

Unknown to Grey, Jane herself had long ago had an affair with Gable. Her appraisal of him as a lover was remarkably different from Grey's high evaluation.

The same year (1955) that Grey had worked with Jane, she'd also played a role in the film version of Tennessee Williams' *The Rose Tattoo,* working with the volatile and very temperamental Anna Magnani and the (calmer and more restrained) Burt Lancaster.

As Jane was leaving the studio late one afternoon, she ran into Karger, who was just arriving. At first, she thought he had come to see her, perhaps hoping for a reconciliation, although they had only recently divorced. He was courteous but distant, as she would later recall to Sirk, with whom she still confided.

It turned out that Karger was at Universal to retrieve Rock in advance of the plans they'd formulated for that evening. He explained it to Jane by claiming that Rock had hired his band as part of one of his upcoming outdoor parties.

That was the last time she saw Karger on the lot. However, Sirk and others told her that after that, Karger made it a point to wait for him across the street from the entrance to Universal. He was parked there many afternoons around the time when shooting had ended for Rock that day.

As Jane told Sirk, "Fred is obviously not playing for Rock every night of the week. Or perhaps he is, so to speak."

Don't worry," Sirk said. "Their romance won't last long. Rock is very promiscuous. I get him once or twice a week. And he usually keeps three or four studs on call at all times. The thing with Fred will blow over soon enough."

"I don't know why I'm so concerned about it," she said. "After all, I divorced him."

Critics dismissed *All That Heaven Allows* as another "soaper from Sirk." However, it scored so big at the box office that in the wake of its success, Universal wanted to cast Jane and Rock in a series of romantic comedies together.

Rock would go on to his biggest success in light, romantic comedies, but the female role would not go to Jane, but to Doris Day, as it did in *Pillow Talk* (1959), a mega-hit.

Years later, Jane lunched with Sirk. She asked, "What's a damsel like me to do? I lost my husband to Rock, but his thing with Fred is over by now. Alas, those romantic comedies featured Doris Day instead of me."

"Well, why don't you chase after Fred and remarry him?"

"That's about the dumbest idea I ever heard," she said. "You can take that idea and shove it where the sun don't shine. I'll never remarry that jerk. NEVER!"

"Jane, my darling, You're protesting too much."

***

When *All That Heaven Allows* was initially released, and dismissed as "a woman's weepie," Sirk said, "There is a short distance between high art and trash, and trash that contains an element of craziness is by this very quality nearer to art."

In the 21st Century, many film historians are inclined to agree with Sirk's assessment. *All That Heaven Allows* has won praise from such filmmakers as Rainer Werner Fassbinder and Quentin Tarantino.

In 1995, the United States' National Film Registry added it to their list of films that it defined as "culturally, historically, or aesthetically significant."

Film historians today cite the movie as a critique of the conformity-obsessed America of the Eisenhower era.

Jane's "Miracle" with Van Johnson.

Jane had a reunion with Van Johnson on the set of their latest picture, *Miracle in the Rain* (1956). Whereas she had returned to Warners (at least for the filming of this movie), he had been let go from MGM, where, in the 1940s, he'd been billed nationwide as America's Sweetheart, along with his female counterpart, June Allyson. In 1945, he had tied with Bing Crosby as America's top box office star.

Johnson poured out his frustrations to her.

Before the end of his contract with MGM, he had co-starred with Elizabeth Taylor in *The Last Time I Saw Paris* (1954). He'd also teamed with Gene Kelly as the sardonic second lead in *Brigadoon,* both pictures released in 1954.

He was still married to Evie Wynn, the former wife of Keenan Wynn, who had divorced her so that Johnson could marry her. As prompted by Louis B. Mayer, he had hoped that by doing so, he would squelch rumors about his homosexuality.

It wasn't just his declining career that troubled Johnson that particular day, but his loss of a role he coveted: He had wanted to play the Texas rancher, Bick Benedick, in the movie version of Edna Ferber's *Giant,* opposite Elizabeth Taylor and James Dean. But the coveted role had gone instead to Rock Hudson.

Jane tried to comfort him. "Rock stole that choice part from you, and he ran off with my husband, the sleep-around Fred Karger."

Perhaps with a bittersweet sense of irony, she told Johnson, "This is my last picture at Warner Brothers. I got my first screen credit here back in the 1930s—and now it's over. I don't expect Jack Warner to come out and say goodbye. He had another actor moving into Ronnie's dressing room before he had even finished packing. Things get gone and quickly forgotten around this joint."

***

The sappy plot of *Miracle in the Rain* by Ben Hecht had appeared in *The Saturday Evening Post* back in 1943. Warners had invested $75,000 for the story back then, which at the time was considered a very high price. Hecht was a successful and highly visible screenwriter, known for such hits as *His Girl Friday* (1940), so he could command top dollar for his material. Yet for some reason, his *Miracle* had never been brought before a camera.

Before Jane's picture reached the big screen, Hecht's story had already been transformed into four separate productions for live television, in 1947, 1949, 1950, and 1953, respectively.

After reading the script, Warner said, "It's such a goddamn sad ending, it's bound to bring in an Oscar or two. After all, the soldier is killed and our meek little typist also dies in St. Patrick's Cathedral, clutching the G.I.'s talisman in her palm. You can't beat crap like that!"

Miracle's plot involved a young woman who falls in love with a soldier during World War II, Weeks later, he is killed overseas. The miracle arises when she gets up from her sickbed, even though she's seriously ill, and makes her way to St. Patrick's Cathedral. Miraculously, her dead lover appears again before her, giving her a lucky coin he had taken overseas with him, which later provides "proof" that he (*i.e.*, his spirit) had really been there, and that she was not hallucinating.

Her friends felt that Jane's recent conversion to Roman Catholicism had influenced her acceptance of the role.

In Manhattan's St. Patrick's Cathedral, Jane lights a candle in memory of her dearly departed after being comforted by a (very handsome) priest.

To her chagrin, she was later advised, "Movies about Catholic miracles have gone out of style."

In Hecht's original story, Jane's character dies (presumably in a state of ecstasy) in St. Patrick's Cathedral. But Warner didn't want that to be made clear. In the wide screen version, the audience is left guessing: Did Jane's character die, or did she recover and go on with her life?

No longer flying high as Hollywood's Golden Boy, Johnson was nonetheless paid $150,000 for starring in the picture, Jane taking home $120,000.

Evocative of Reagan's departure from Warner Brothers, Jane's farewell was equally dismal. She called Jack Warner's office to tell him goodbye. She later said, "I didn't expect him to walk me to the gate. but he refused to take my call. So much for that. Hollywood has always been cruel on its aging dames. Perhaps Paramound will remake Gloria Swanson's *Sunset Blvd.* and cast me in the role of that aging screen diva, Norma Desmond."

At the gate, one man came out to greet her. An aging janitor, Hebnry Dolland, in his seventies, kissed her farewell. He'd remembered her when she was a Warners' chorus girl in the 1930s, and he told her he'd be retiring soon, too. "Not much to retire on, though."

"That's what we get for working for that tightwad, Jack Warner for all these years," she said, waving Dolland goodbye. It was her *adieu* to the studio that had employed her, sometimes traumatically, for such a long time.

***

Weeks after leaving Warners, Jane accused Jack Warner of sinking all his promotional budget into *Giant,* leaving *Miracle in the Rain* to open with relatively little advertising and almost no promotion. "It could have been a hit," she told Johnson. "It could have brought us Oscars. Instead, we were screened in front of empty houses."

The Academy ignored it at Oscar time. "At least I didn't catch pneumonia after having to act all those scenes in a god damn rain pour," Jane said.

The New York Herald Tribune joined dozens of other newspaper critics in lambasting the movie. "Miss Wyman's typist is a glum portrait unrelieved by any sense of depth of character or humor. She is sad even when she realizes she is in love. There is hardly a change of expression when she learns of the death of her soldier boyfriend, played by Van Johnson. *Miracle in the Rain* is straight-faced and uncompromisingly dull."

Hecht came under fire for his "hankie grabber, which is not typical of this tough-talking former newshound." His *Miracle* was called "a tough lump of goo to swallow."

The New York Times was gentler in its condemnation, claiming, *"Miracle in the Rain* hits high, lovely notes on occasion, but too often lapses into soap opera."

The St. Louis Post-Dispatch labeled *Miracle* "a tearjerker that is as unabashed as any we've encountered."

"My future belongs on that little black box," Jane said. "Maybe there'll be a film role every now and then, no doubt playing a mother."

***

Offers for big screen roles were few and far between. Those that came in were for what Jane called "monster pictures." When she'd gone to a screening of *What Ever Happened to Baby Jane* (1962), she was horrified, later claiming that "Bette Davis and Joan Crawford have disgraced themselves. They must have needed the money awfully bad."

Journalist Vernon Scott wrote, "Fortunately, Jane is economically independent and can afford to sit on the sidelines rather than accept distasteful pictures."

To Van Johnson, Jane said, "I refuse to play a dope addict, an aging prostitute, or, as I've told producers many times before, a lesbian. I turned down the role of a lesbian in *Walk on the Wild Side* (1962). It's going to my friend, Barbara Stanwyck."

"Takes one to play one," Johnson said.

"Now Van, be kind," she cautioned.

"Her former husband, His Lordship, Bob Taylor, once propositioned me at MGM," Johnson claimed.

"That doesn't surprise me at all," she said. "I always suspected something was going on between Ronnie and Bob. All those weekends alone together in the wilderness."

To cheer her up, Johnson invited Jane to a party he was hosting that Saturday night, promising her that there would be a surprise guest.

On the day of the event, she began dressing and working on her makeup at three that afternoon, arriving alone at the party at eight o'clock.

There were some thirty guests there, mostly male. After making the rounds and hearing endless compliments, Fred Karger emerged from Johnson's bedroom dressed in his usual dark suit.

She was mildly shocked at seeing him again, because they had not contacted each other in months. He explained that he was staying temporarily with Johnson. "We're roommates," he said.

"Roommates?" She was skeptical. "Is that what they're calling them this year?"

For part of the night, they talked about their less-than-bright careers and the problems generated by their children, Terry, Maureen, and Michael.

During the weeks ahead, she began to encounter Karger at other parties and, on occasion, when his band was hired for a gig. One night, she agreed to meet with him for dinner, and they began to see each other more regularly after that.

She later told Joan Blondell, "Our Catholic faith is bringing us together again. We

594

spend a lot of time discussing Catholicism. I've been trying to lure Freddie back into the church again. We're both at loose ends, not knowing where to go. The other night, when he brought me home, we kissed on my doorstep. I invited him in for a nightcap. He never left. It was wonderful having him make love to me again. I'm even considering re-marrying him."

"Never a good idea," Blondell warned. "If it didn't work out the first time, chances are it won't the second time on the merry-go-round either. I bet you'd face the same problems. And then there is the gay thing, hiding in the closet."

"I can't truly blame Freddie for turning elsewhere for that which I can't give him," Jane said.

***

The day Jane decided to remarry Karger, she phoned June Allyson to tell her the news. Unlike Blondell, Allyson seemed delighted. "I always thought Freddie was a living doll," she said.

"And after all," Jane continued. "He's not the only man in Hollywood who has slept with both Rock Hudson and Marilyn Monroe—take the late, lamented James Dean, for example."

Jane remarried Karger on March 11, 1961. Attending the ceremony were such dear friends as Allyson, Blondell, Paulette Goddard, Loretta Young, Irene Dunne, and Claudette Colbert. As Colbert later said to Jane, "What are we old bags to do now that movie roles are almost disappearing? I find that, unlike today, I attend more funerals than weddings."

As Colbert had noted, it was a time for burying old friends and acquaintances. Reagan's mother, Nelle, died in 1962, and Jane, accompanied by Karger, attended the funeral.

She offered her sympathies to Reagan, who looked grief stricken. "Welcome to the 1960s, Ronnie," she said. "The Hollywood we used to know is *Gone With the Wind.* I sure miss it. I know you'll also miss Nelle something awful."

When she looked into his eyes, she saw the tears welling up. He said nothing.

"Nelle was such a good woman," Jane said, in parting. "They don't make them like her any more. She belonged to an America that is fast fading, and we belong to a Hollywood that is now making all these sick movies."

Maureen Reagan summed up her family situation at that time. "Mother was re-married to Fred Karger, and the two of them shared a small apartment in Beverly Hills. Dad and Nancy were living at the house in Pacific Palisades. Michael had moved in with them to finish up high school. Ron *[i.e, Reagan, Jr.]* was in kindergarten, and Patti was eleven years old and full of resentment for a twenty-two year old woman nicknamed 'Mermie" *[i.e., Maureen herself]* who sat next to her father on the sofa."

After remaining safely at home every night during the first three months of his re-marriage, Karger got an occasional gig, but not like he'd done in his heyday. Disco had come to Hollywood, and he was no longer in such demand. But sometimes, he didn't return home until three or four o'clock in the morning. She no longer asked where he'd been.

***

Throughout the course of most of her marriage to Karger, Jane managed to star in an occasional film or teleplay. But as her marriage entered its final months, she received no offers for either the big screen or for "the little black box," as she continued to call it.

She and Karger began to argue and fight a lot. He continued to have violent outbursts of temper.

They were also having problems with their children. Michael had dropped out of Arizona State University after only one semester. Like Reagan, she had cut him off financially.

Maureen was having marital problems. She'd wed John Filippone, a police officer, in 1961 but divorced him the following year. In 1964, she married David G. Sills, an attorney and Marine Corps officer. He moved her to San Clemente while he was stationed at Camp Pendleton, demanding that she abandon her acting ambitions. She later admitted, "I was a perfectly wretched housewife."

Out of boredom, she joined her father as a Republican volunteer during the 1964 presidential race of Barry Goldwater against Lyndon B. Johnson.

By 1967, she'd divorced Sills.

Long before that, however, Jane also faced the divorce judge.

***

Other than the usual charges aired before a divorce court, Jane never spoke about the reasons for the collapse of her second marriage to Karger. But two reasons have emerged over the years, mainly gleaned from friends like Blondell.

Karger had escorted Jane to the funeral of her friend, Dick Powell, who had died on January 3, 1963. Jane offered Allyson what sympathy she could, even though she knew that her friend had never been faithful to her actor/director husband. *[Privately, Jane and many of her friends referred to Allyson as "a nympho.]*

Jane told Karger about Allyson's numerous affairs, including one with John F. Kennedy, who was later assassinated in November of the year of Powell's death.

"She sometimes seduces her leading men, including Peter Lawford," Jane claimed. "For years, Alan Ladd was the passion of her life, and later, Jimmy Stewart. She also has this thing for Dean Martin."

At first, Jane wasn't suspicious when June began to call Karger to "help me with some arrangements." She paid him $200 per consultation, and he told her, "It's about what I get for a gig."

A few times, when Karger returned home at four o'clock in the morning, Jane snapped sarcastically, "some gig." She told Blondell that she'd found lipstick on Karger's collar on more than one occasion.

Blondell said, "I'm not surprised. I've known that Allyson bitch for years, beginning in New York. She was known as 'Miss Hot to Trot.'"

What may have finally turned Jane off Karger was when he hired a twenty-two year old saxophone player, Terry Nelson, from Chicago, for his band.

Whenever Karger, with his band, went out of town on a gig, Nelson always roomed with him. In Los Angeles, Karger often spent long nights with the sexy young blonde, later informing Jane, "We had to rehearse some new numbers."

"I can imagine what those numbers were," she said. "Sixty-nine, for example."

Whenever she made accusations like that, he'd storm out the door, usually after breaking some objects.

She told Blondell, "I can't go on with him. I've got to end it, sooner than later."

One day, Nelson, through a family connection, arranged for Karger and his band to appear at a small club in his native Chicago. Bidding Jane goodbye, he and Nelson flew away.

Before the end of the gig, and before he'd flown back to Los Angeles with Nelson, Jane had moved out of their apartment. She left a brief note: "From now on, Buster, you pay the damn rent. Better yet, why not move in with Nelson? You're practically living with him anyway."

[Nelson outlived Karger, dying of AIDS in Chicago in 1984.]

In court on March 9, 1965, Karger charged Jane with desertion. Three weeks later, she countercharged, claiming "grievous mental cruelty." She also revealed that she'd been the victim of "Karger's uncontrollable temper."

***

Reagan must have been dismayed when he picked up the papers that March. He had been approached by powerful monied interests to become the Republican candidate for Governor of California in the next election. His close friend, the song-and-dance man, George Murphy, had just been elected to the U.S. Senate from California.

Although the primary wasn't until the spring of 1966, he would spend all of 1965 "gladhanding my way across the state."

He was horrified when his name was brought up and his divorce from Jane spread all over newspapers in their rehash of her divorce from him. But Murphy told him not to worry about his status as a divorcé. "This isn't fucking Alabama or Georgia in the Bible belt. This is California!"

After her (second) divorce from Karger was finalized, Jane told Blondell, "I guess I have no talent for marriage. That's the last time for me."

"Well, Reagan seems to have found his mate for life," Blondell said.

"Ronnie is the marrying kind. I'm not," Jane said. "He's found his clinging vine, the one he always wanted, but he didn't find an independent woman like me. This little former starlet creature is the kind of wife I never was."

Despite the embarrassing charges that were aired in divorce court, Jane felt no hostility to Karger. In fact, far from the prying eyes of gossips, they sporadically got together "to catch up on things," as she put it. Once, they were spotted together in San Francisco, provoking an item in a local newspaper column about the possibility of a third marriage of her to Karger.

[Jane and Karger remained friendly until the end. Three years after their divorce, he remarried. But, like his father, he had continuing heart trouble, and once had a heart attack. She visited him whenever she could.

When she heard that he was dying of leukemia, she claimed that she "went to the church every day, asking God to save Freddie."

Despite her prayers, Karger died of leukemia in 1979 at the age of sixty-three.]

Jane would outlive her "two-time" and "two-timing" husband by twenty-eight years. She would never marry again.

***

After appearing with her in some of Jane's favorite movies, Agnes Moorehead—Jane called her "Aggie"—offered an interviewer some insights into Jane's life.

"In some ways, I think Jane has entered the most contented period of her life. The intense careerism has mellowed and lessened; she has her good friendships, her rewarding sessions with the paintbrush and canvas, her pleasure in her developing children."

"I think she has given up her illusions about men and the kind of life she had hoped to live with one. She has come to realize, in a sense, that she was her own best company—and she understands herself better than any other human being. At last, she is free of the foibles and assorted demands of a mate."

Seven years of relative seclusion would pass before Jane returned to the screen, although during the interval, she would occasionally accept a role in a teleplay.

***

"I thought I'd spend the rest of my days hanging out paining landscapes in Carmel," she told Paulette Goddard. "But then came November of 1980. All hell broke loose."

She was referring, of course, to the election of her former husband, Ronald Reagan, to the office of President of the United States.

Stories about the ins and outs of their previous marriage were making headlines around the world.

As she told Goddard, "I was getting calls from Finland, Egypt, even Patagonia. Where the hell is Patagonia?"

She refused every request for interviews about her life with Reagan. She did make one statement, however: "I have no regrets about not becoming First Lady. Oh, no, the glare of the White House, with its fish-bowl existence for a First Lady, is not for me. I have perfectly wonderful memories of my years with the President. We are good friends, and we will always remain good friends."

Reagan also refused to discuss his first marriage, except for one remark: "I was divorced in the sense that the decision was made by somebody else—not by me."

An adept survivor in a fast-changing Hollywood, Jane managed, with skill and style, to revamping her image and her "look" with every decade.

Here's Jane in the early 70s, sporting a look that enhanced her appeal to golden-age fans as well as to the casting directors of made-for-TV movies, daytime TV, and sitcoms.

Jane Launches a Hit TV Series

Falcon Crest

"At Last, My Marriage to Ronnie Paid Off"

A young executive at Lorimar, one of the leading producers of TV programs, spoke to his board of directors: "If an old dame like Jane Wyman can still hobble around, and doesn't look like Phyllis Diller's grandmother, I see some real show biz marketability for her, having been married to Reagan and all that shit."

"Let's bring her back. Makeup can do wonders these days, or we could photograph her through gauze. Didn't the bitch once win an Oscar or something? Who cares? The big thing is that she was married to the President of the United States. I'm told that no one in American history ever divorced a man who went on to become President."

"We have the perfect series coming up," he continued. "Of course, the Hollywood Hills is filled with has-beens who could play the role, but there's no one who was once married to Ronald Reagan. Wasn't Hitler still alive when they got married?"

The young executive was told that in 1940, the United States had not yet entered World War II.

"My god!" he answered. "Way back then! She must have told Reagan when he walked in the door to wipe the dinosaur shit off his shoes."

***

Originally, Jane's friend, Barbara Stanwyck, had been offered the role of Angela Channing, the tyrannical matriarch of the Falcon Crest Winery in a TV soap tentatively entitled *The Vintage Years.* Flush with success from his hit series, *The Waltons,* Earl Hamner later changed the title to *Falcon Crest,* fearing that the first tag would indicate the soap was about old people.

Falcon Crest would go out on the CBS network for its first broadcast on December 4, 1981, running for nine trauma-infused seasons, shutting down on May 17, 1990.

Its lifespan more or less paralleled the two-term presidency of Ronald Reagan.

When Stanwyck bowed out, Hamner thought it would be wise to exploit the publicity generated by Jane Wyman, Reagan's first wife, who was back in the news again. He reportedly said, "Dare we bill her as 'The Woman Who Almost Became First Lady?'"

In the original pilot, Jane sported a gray wig, but that was later changed to her own dyed brown hair. "The preview audiences laughed at me for wearing that dreadful wig, and I put my foot down. Also, I told Hamner to soften my role. Originally, my character was too much of a god damn bitch."

He later called Jane "A tough broad, but she knew what she was doing. It was not her first time at the rodeo."

As a Napa Valley wine tycoon, Angela would spend the series feuding with and fighting her relatives, plus others, as a means of retaining control of the family legacy.

She battles one of the heirs to Falcon Crest, Robert Foxworth, and his wife, Susan Sullivan, but dotes on her handsome playboy grandson (Lorenzo Lamas), the real-life son of Fernando Lamas and Arlene Dahl.

Throughout the 8½ year run of the series, guest stars came and went, including Celeste Holm, still remembered for her role in *All About Eve* (1950), who nearly burns down Falcon Crest.

A good hunk of *tout* Hollywood, notably Lana Turner, showed up for guest appearances. Jane had always detested her, an enmity dating back to the time "she messed around with Ronnie."

To boost ratings, other featured notables included Gina Lollobrigida (after negotiations with Sophia Loren fell through); Robert Stack, Cliff Robertson, Kim Novak, Leslie Caron, Lauren Hutton, Eddie Albert, Eve Arden, and Ursula Andress, whose involvement caused a tiffle because of her status as one of Nancy Reagan's best friends.

One of the highlights of the series transpired when Jane, as Angela Channing, married Falcon Crest's lawyer, Phillip Ericson (Mel Ferrer). Consistent with her character, as developed by Jane, Angela does this not only for love, but for access to greater power. Ferrer's character maneuvered am-

"The Iron Lady of the Vineyards," Jane Wyman, veteran survivor of changing times in Hollywood, with the *Falcon Crest* gang in 1984.

bitiously through the politics of the family legacy until the writers of the series had him killed off in a plane crash.

At one point, Ginger Rogers, perhaps the ultimate symbol and archetype of Golden Age Hollywood, was proposed for the role of Susan Sullivan's mother. But the blonde was ruled as "not the right type" for the role. Jane Greer, star of many a 1940s *film noir,* was hired instead.

Hamner notified Jane that he was casting César Romero, as her co-star in the role of a very wealthy tycoon, who helps her "save the plantation." The script was still being written when she was told, "There will be some on-screen romancing." At the time, Romero was in his seventies and white-haired.

Although Jane had often accepted Romero as an occasional escort between her marriages—this lifelong bachelor had been the escort of many great Hollywood divas, including Joan Crawford—she was alarmed at the prospect of that new twist in the series' storyline. She was especially disturbed at the prospect of any kissing scenes between them.

Celebrity psychic John Cohan was a friend, confidant, and psychic advisor to Jane for many years. He had followed her interaction with another of his friends, Rock Hudson, during their filming of *Magnificent Obsession* and *All That Heaven Allows.*

[Cohan has been a celebrity seer and channel of wisdom to stars who have included Elizabeth Taylor for more than thirty years. During much of that time, he supplied columnist Cindy Adams with his yearly predictions, many of which turned out to be surprisingly accurate.

Many insights about the stars can be found in Cohan's tantalizing memoir, Catch a Falling Star: The Untold Story of Celebrity Secrets*, published in 2008. In it, he has much to reveal about former friends and clients, including Natalie Wood, Merv Griffin, John Kennedy, Jr., Elvis Presley, Mick Jagger, and Rudolph Nureyev. He also writes about "my dear friend" Nicole Brown Simpson as well as "the love of my life," Sandra Dee, the former wife of singer Bobby Darrin.]*

John Cohan...privy to celebrity secrets.

Cohan was also a friend of Romero, and was well aware of his long-lived crush on Desi Arnaz. When Jane learned that Romero was to be assigned as her love interest in *Falcon Crest,* she called Cohan to express her possible objections. "I don't want him on the show if there's to be a kissing scene," she said. "There's an AIDS epidemic, I don't know where his mouth has been the night before."

Cohan had a talk with her, telling her that "Cesar is a gentleman and a fine actor. I can assure you that he's as meticulous in his hygiene as he is in his grooming. You have nothing to fear."

Obviously, Cohan convinced her that Romero would present no threat, even during an embrace. She called Hamner the next day and told him, "I think Cesar will be ideal in the part of my beau."

Jane's friendship with Romero remained intact, despite her fears. A few weeks later, Romero resumed escorting Jane to various premieres or tributes to aging players in the film industry. They'd sometimes end the evening dancing. "He's a great dancer," she told Cohan, something he already knew, of course.

César Romero..."The Latin from Manhattan."

601

Starting out at $25,000 per episode, Jane's fee for her involvement in *Falcon Crest* eventually rose to $100,000 per episode, making her the highest paid woman in television.

John O'Connor, in *The New York Times,* summed up *Falcon Crest* in 1981. "And so it goes, the standard stuff of soaps, with a crisis bubble bursting at least three times between commercial breaks. At fadeout, Jane Wyman is meaningfully stroking a falcon on the grounds of her estate. The stage is set for anything."

The other actors in the series often complained to Hamner that Jane was telling them how to act. When Hamner confronted her with this, she said, "The poor dears, for the most part, have had no experience. If they're bad, I'll look bad. Now we can't have that happening, can we?"

Throughout the run of the series, Jane bitterly resented any publicity that linked her to the Reagan presidency. Her former association with the President became especially visible at the 1984 Democratic Convention, when protesters opposing Reagan's policies carried signs "JANE WYMAN WAS RIGHT" within view of television crews.

Her salary as a highly visible actress was sometimes compared to that earned by Reagan in his capacity as president, columnists suggesting that she was being paid ten times more than he was.

She didn't like it when critics jokingly referred to her series as "*Dallas* with grapes."

"We were more glamorous than *Dallas [1978-1991],* but not as outrageous as *Dynasty [1981-1989],*" she said.

Because of her declining health, Jane was absent throughout much of *Falcon Crest's* final (1989-1990) season. She rallied, however, to the point where, in defiance of her doctor's orders, she returned for the season's last three episodes. In the final scene of the series, she raises her glass to either the vineyards or the series (no one was really, sure, as the moment was richly symbolic), "A toast to you, Falcon Crest," she said, "and long may you live."

On the last day of the series' filming, she had told Hamner, "Honey, I've seen them come and go...mostly go. And now it's time for me to make my exit. I'll say this: It's been a ride to hell and back. And I'm still here. Now I want to be alone."

Golden age icon Loretta Young, Jane's then closest friend, had married the famous dress and costume designer, Jean Louis, in 1993, when she was eighty and he was eighty-four. Young had been instrumental in motivating Jane to become a member of the Third Order of Saint Dominic, informally known as "Lay Dominicans."

[Lay Dominicans define themselves as "Men and women, singles and couples, living a Christian life with a Dominican spirituality in the secular world. We find our inspiration following the same spiritual path taken by many Saints, Blesseds and other holy men and women throughout the almost 800 year history of the Dominican Order."]

As a means of living closer to her friend, Jane had moved into the upscale resort community of Rancho Mirage in Riverside County, near Palm Springs, 120 miles southeast of Los Angeles.

When Young died in 2002, Jane was very distraught. More than ever, she seemed to cling to her Catholic religion.

The year (2001) after Young's death, Jane's only biological child, her daughter,

Maureen, died from melanoma. Jane told Cohan, "There's nothing worse for a parent than to outlive her own children."

She was further devastated when Reagan died in 2004. She issued a rare statement about him. "America has lost a great President and a great, kind, and gentle man."

Cohan recalled going to see her on his final visit, when he found her bedridden and in seriously declining health.

She asked him to stay overnight with her. In her condition, that was obviously not a sexual overture. She told him she was very lonely and just wanted someone to hold her. "I need that like a plant needs water," she said.

He stayed with her and comforted her, later commenting on what a "charming, bright woman she was as a person, not just a great actress."

At the age of ninety, on the night of September 1, 2007, death came to her in her sleep. She had left instructions to be buried in her Dominican habit.

A funeral mass was held two days later at the Sacred Heart Catholic Church in nearby Palm Desert. Michael Reagan delivered a short eulogy, asserting that "Hollywood has lost the classiest lady to ever grace the silver screen."

In her later years, she had a favorite remark, "I am a little too old to be happy, but just old enough to be grateful."

Many newspapers ran banner headlines, proclaiming, "THE FIRST MRS. REAGAN DIES."

She had told Young and others, "I'm sure many headline writers will do that, but I would have preferred to be recognized as a star with my own achievements, rather than for a marriage I entered into decades ago."

Jane Wyman, on the set between takes during the final season of *Falcon Crest*. Forlorn, she looks into her future. The chorus girl cutie of the 1930s had become an aging matriarch.

Let's remember Jane Wyman and Ronald Reagan not as old and decrepit—and ill—relics who survived to see the 21st Century, but as two kids in love with each other, or at least in love with love.

Late in her life, when Jane was shown this picture, she said, "God, we were gorgeous, and about to become the most publicized happily married couple of World War II."

Hellcat Reagan & Nurse Nancy

Co-Star in a

"Jingoistic Wartime Potboiler"

"Ronnie and Nancy," as they were now called, never became the screen team they had dreamed about—a working duet equivalent to William Powell and Myrna Loy or Katharine Hepburn and Spencer Tracy.

But they did make one attempt at it in *Hellcats of the Navy,* a 1957 release from Columbia Pictures.

For *Hellcats of the Navy,* Columbia granted Reagan the usual contractual clauses allowing a star to select his own director. Subsequently, Reagan opted for Nathan Juran, who had helmed him in *Law and Order* (1953). Then Reagan successfully persuaded the studio to designate Nancy as his co-star.

Juran had been an Oscar-winning art director for such films as *The Razor's Edge* (1946). A year after his direction of *Hellcats of the Navy,* he'd achieve a rank in "camp heaven" after directing the sci-fi horror flick, *Attack of the 50-Foot Woman* (1958), a libidinous romp that seemed perfect back then for a Saturday night date at a drive-in. *[Its storyline? After an aborted murder attempt, an alluring and scantily clad socialite, massively and majestically enlarged after an encounter with Aliens, seeks revenge on her lying, abusive, and cheating husband.]*

One evening, the co-starring, co-habiting, married couple sat down in their living room to read the script of *Hellcats.* It was based on a widely publicized book by U.S. Admirals Charles A. Lockwood and Hans Christian Adamson, about a real-life Naval operation that had unfolded in 1944. The film would open with an introduction by Fleet Admiral Chester W. Nimitz, who had directed a naval campaign in the Tsushima Strait and the Sea of Japan during World War II. His mission's aim involved maneuvering a flotilla of U.S. submarines through underwater obstacles and heavy minefields. In the movie, Nimitz's character was portrayed by the actor Selmer Jackson.

The film's scriptwriters were credited as David Lang and "Raymond Marcus."

It wasn't until 1986 when an anti-communist U.S. president learned that the filmscript had actually been written by a blacklisted screenwriter, Bernard Gordon, who had opted for "Marcus" as a pseudonym.

In the screenplay, Nancy is in love with Commander Casey Abbott (Reagan). Simultaneously, she's also involved in a minor romance with a member of his crew, frogman Les Barton (Harry Lauter).

Abbott must struggle not to get his personal feelings mixed up with his high-profile role as commander.

Reagan, as Abbott, leading a fictional submarine, *U.S.S. Starfish,* is ordered to interrupt the flow of war supplies en route from Japan to voracious Japanese forces invading China. Most of the action takes place in the obstacle-studded, heavily mined waters off the Asiatic mainland.

As an actor, Reagan's worst problem was that he suffered from claustrophobia, a lifetime terror of small, enclosed spaces. For unrelenting hours at a time, he was forced to work with as many as sixteen cast and crew members, all of them packed like sardines into the tiny reconnaissance tower of a working submarine.

A dramatic point in the film occurs when Reagan, as Commander Abbott, has to make a "*Command Decision,*" evocative of the 1948

Clark Gable film of that same name. In *Hell-cats,* when Reagan makes an equivalently crucial decision, he signals its weightiness to the audience by narrowing his squinty eyes, tightening his jaw muscles, and furrowing his brow, which was beginning to wrinkle at this stage of his middle-aged years.

When a Japanese destroyer bears down on them, Reagan orders his submarine to dive into very deep waters as a means of avoiding enemy shells. Lauter, preoccupied with his duties as a frogman, and outside the sub on the waters of the wide open sea, is left to die. A few scenes later, audiences know that Reagan's competitor for the love and carnal affections of Nurse Nancy has descended to a watery, fish-bitten grave.

The submarine's chief officer, Lt. Commander Don Landon, and the film's third male lead is played by Arthur Franz, who had previously appeared in such war movies as *The Sands of Iwo Jima* (1949) with John Wayne, and *The Caine Mutiny* (1953) with Humphrey Bogart.

As Nancy studied her character of Nurse Lt. Helen Blair in *Hellcats of the Navy,* she found she'd been cast in a "Love Triangle," perhaps evoking memories of her own life and the role played in it by Jane Wyman, the third part of a competitive trio that flourished prior to Nancy's marriage to Reagan.

Unlike Reagan, Franz had been a real-life hero during World War II, serving in the U.S. Army Air Force. His plane had been shot down over Romania, and he was incarcerated in a POW, from which he escaped and made his way to freedom.

Throughout most of *Hellcats,* the characters portrayed by Reagan and Franz are locked into a bitterly competitive feud until the end, when Reagan, by now working as a frogman himself, is rescued by Franz. All is forgiven, and Reagan, without a rival in love, can at last claim Nurse Nancy.

She later wrote that the kissing scenes with Reagan were the easiest she'd ever played on screen, not that there had been that many.

In the final reel, Reagan agrees to marry Nurse Nancy. She later told Juran, "I had less trouble getting Ronnie to marry me on film

Offscreen, in the photo above, actor and co-star Arthur Franz *(left)* is all smiles with the Reagans when the cameras weren't rolling. But on screen, he and the character played by Reagan were bitter enemies.

Audiences didn't find Nancy alluring as Reagan's girlfriend in this movie. She was clad in a starched and unsexy uniform, droning her nagging lines to Reagan without a trace of charm. Obviously, she was more alluring to him as a wife in private than as his on-screen lover.

607

than I did in real life."

Reagan's assignment as commander of the Hellcats involved retrieving actual Japanese mines from enemy-patrolled waters so that Naval experts could determine, in the safety of their laboratories, why they were resistant to detection by sonar.

Reagan was disappointed when he saw the final cut of *Hellcats of the Navy.* In his first autobiography, *Where's the Rest of Me?*, he stated that he had wanted to make a film that evoked the quality of *Destination Tokyo,* a suspenseful 1943 film that had co-starred Cary Grant with John Garfield. Such was not the case. Reagan lamented that Columbia was more interested in the budget than in the script, and strongly criticized the recycling of stock footage from the studio's archives.

Edmund Morris, Reagan's authorized biographer, said that *Hellcats* was "a turkey so many-feathered it practically squawked off the screen."

After it was finished, and for a brief time, Reagan considered retiring to his little stud farm to become a fulltime breeder of race horses, a lifestyle that evoked his role, and the character he developed, in *Stallion Road* (1947).

"*Hellcats* ended movies for me," Reagan said.

[Actually, it didn't. The ill-advised The Killers *(1964), still in his future, would represent his final adieu to films.]*

Critic Glenn Erickson defined the script of *Hellcats* as "completely derivative and cornball." He also criticized the lack of realism derived from its use of stock footage. David Krauss called the production "bargain basement," and evaluated both Reagan and Nancy as "stiff." He went on to say that Juran's direction was "as dry as a military briefing."

In each of Nancy's memoirs, she had almost nothing to say about either her role or her involvement in *Hellcats*, except for a remark about kissing Reagan. In one memoir, she said the film was released in 1956; in another, she wrote 1957—and got it right that time.

Variety commiserated with Nancy for being stuck in such a thankless role.

The New York Daily News cited Nancy's performance as "providing subordinate romantic interest which does not get in the way of the film's primary offering—action."

Other reviewers were less kind, especially when the movie was released on DVD during Reagan's presidency. "Nancy and Ronnie had as much chemistry in their on-shore romance as did Wallace Beery and Marie Dressler in the 1933 *Tugboat Annie,*" wrote Kenneth David.

In his first autobiography, in reference to filming *Hellcats,* Reagan wrote: "Nancy and I had a moonlight farewell scene on the eve of my departure for the dangerous mission that was the climax of the story. The first thing I knew, Nancy was crying instead of saying the lines in the script, and then she was giggling between sobs, laughing at herself for having gotten so carried away that *[in her mind, at least]* she was really saying goodbye and sending me on a suicide mission."

Chapter Fourteen

"Ronnie and Nancy"

The Long, Tortuous Road to Marriage, &

The Dysfunctional Union of Two Competing Families

They Didn't Know It Yet, but the Fading (and Fired)
Movie Star and the Failed (and Fired) B-List Starlet
Had a Shared Rendezvous With Destiny

One blustery afternoon, Ronald Reagan in his "Bogie trenchcoat," took Nancy Davis to the marriage license bureau.

She shared her version of what love is. "It meant giving more than receiving, and it also meant sharing. I think you know you are in love when you no longer are the most important person you know. I would give my life for Ronnie. I feel lucky in that I have no doubt of my love and of my being loved.:"

Nancy Davis was disappointed that her very frugal husband, Ronald Reagan, had "deep pockets and short arms." He didn't want to spend money to hire a photographer to record the events associated with their wedding.

William Holden and his wife, the actress Brenda Marshall, however, hired a photographer to record their wedding reception and paid for a wedding cake. Knife in hand, Reagan looks like he's about to attack the symbolic bride and groom crowning the multi-tiered confection..

She Became One of the Most Fascinating, Enigmatic, and Controversial First Ladies In American History— But How Did She Lure a Reluctant Reagan Into Marriage?

Nancy's road to the altar was long and tortured, with many roadblocks and many detours. It would take two and a half years of steady pursuit on her part.

Before meeting Reagan, Nancy had composed a list of eligible bachelors in Hollywood, all of whom she considered worth marrying. Reagan's name was at the top of the list. She decided to start at the top and work her way down the chart.

She opted to reach him through his friend, film director Mervyn LeRoy. For the previous few months, she'd received a lot of mail directed to "Nancy Davis" with information about rallies and meetings of the Communist Party. It was the era of Hollywood's "Blacklist," and she didn't want to lose her chance at stardom for fear that she'd be mistaken for Red, or accused of socialist sympathies, or worse.

He told her he'd relay her concerns to Reagan, president of SAG, to see what he could do.

"But I'd prefer to speak to Mr. Reagan personally," she said.

"First, let's do it my way," he said. "After all, I'm used to directing the scene."

Reagan had never seen Nancy in a film, not even *East Side, West Side,* a 1949 flick that had starred his friend, Barbara Stanwyck, and in which Nancy had played a supporting role.

A hip Hollywood director like LeRoy knew Nancy's real motive for wanting to speak to Reagan personally. "I think she wants to date you," the director said.

"My calendar's full, but I'll consider it," he answered. "I won't ask you what she looks like, because I know that she must be attractive if she's an MGM starlet."

"Who knows? MGM might have signed her on as a threat to Marjorie Main. But, no, that's not the case. Nancy is quite attractive, I assure you. I was the first director to discover Jane Wyman when I put her in a small part in *Elmer the Great* back in 1933. Maybe lightning will strike twice for you when you meet Nancy."

Über-Assertive, Now and Forever.

"I love to wear red, but I'm not a Red," Nancy said. "If anything, I'm probably the most anti-communist starlet in Hollywood."

Reagan told LeRoy that he'd think about dating her, but first, he wanted to investigate her placement "on a commie mailing list."

"She's no Ava Gardner, but she's kinda cute," LeRoy said. "She's single. You're single. Why don't you take her out?"

"And disappoint two dozen other Hollywood cuties that night?" he said. "I may ask her out. Then again, I might not. For all I know, I'll fall for the hot little blonde I'm seeing."

"Marilyn Monroe?"

"Been there, done that," Reagan answered. "No, another Marilyn—Marilyn Maxwell."

"You're moving in on Frankie's territory, I see," LeRoy said.

Reagan took two weeks getting back to Nancy. He did discover that there was a movie extra, Nancy Lee Davis, registered as a screen worker who occasionally got a job as an extra. Her name, indeed, was on a list of movie workers who, between 1945 and 1952, were suspected of affiliations with the

Out with Nancy, Reagan, for some reason, chose to wear his glasses, although for years, he usually avoided being photographed in them.

As Nancy joked, "It's not true that women don't make passes at men who wear glasses."

Communist Party. She had also supported members of the notorious, disgraced, and blacklisted "Hollywood Ten."

Reagan reported this to LeRoy, and the director subsequently called Nancy with news that her name had been cleared of suspicion. But she still protested, claiming, "But I want to speak to Mr. Reagan myself."

Reagan warned her, in his call to her the following day, that their meeting would have to be for an early dinner, since he was due at the studio at 5AM the following morning.

She responded, "I have the same problem."

As it happened, both of them lied, since neither was involved in any film being shot at the time.

The historic meeting of the future President of the United States with his future First Lady took place in October of 1949.

When he arrived at her doorstep, she later told friends, "He had both legs. I'd seen *Kings Row,* where they were amputated. But he was on crutches."

[He was still recovering from a broken leg he had injured in a charity baseball game.]

He took her to LaRue's on the Strip, which back then was a hip gathering spot.

She claimed she was immediately attracted to him, "finding him nice looking." She also viewed his mind as "stimulating and, unlike all other actors, he could talk about something other than motion pictures."

Over dinner, he discovered that she'd never seen a performance of Sophie Tucker, "The Last of the Red Hot Mommas." Tucker was his favorite entertainer, which surprised her. She thought his favorite singer would perhaps be Doris Day,

611

his favorite comedian Jack Benny. But, no, it was Miss Sophie, with her raunchy jokes and her very Jewish humor, had been scheduled for an appearance at Ciro's later that night.

After Sophie's act, the other couples danced to the music of Xavier Cugat's band, but Reagan couldn't join in, because of his injured leg.

At the end of her show, Sophie joined them at table. "I adore Ronnie," she said to Nancy. Then she turned to Reagan. "A brunette for a change?"

The last time she'd seen him was after her performance on Miami Beach, where he'd showed up with a blonde, Marilyn Monroe, then an aspiring starlet.

He was honest with Nancy, telling her that he'd fibbed about that early morning call. "I didn't want to be trapped in a blind date that didn't go well. It'll soon be dawn, so you can say this date was a knockout."

By the time this photograph was taken, Reagan had proposed marriage to Nancy. but when he first met her, he wrote: "Bells didn't ring. Nor did rockets explode."

As he told Robert Taylor, "Nancy's pretty, but not what I expected. A bit reserved, unlike Ann Sothern or Ruth Roman. Her large hazel eyes are her best feature. Otherwise, she's a rather demure brunette."

On her doorstep, he kissed her on the cheek and left without any promise of calling her again.

When Nancy first started dating Reagan, she was twenty-eight, though claiming to be twenty-six. "That sounds better."

Although he failed to make any promises, Reagan called her at 11AM and invited her out for another night on the town. She later said, "We had dinner that night, and the next night, and the night after that. For about a month, we must have gone to every restaurant and nightclub in Los Angeles."

Rumors circulated that during their first month together, he was spending his nights in her small apartment in Westwood, a suburb west of Hollywood near the UCLA campus.

In Nancy's second memoir, she admitted that she and Reagan soon tired of going nightclubbing every night. "We started spending more of our time alone in my apartment, where we watched movies and ate popcorn." Presumably, they found other amusements, too. She looked forward to his taking her to Chasen's every Tuesday night for its weekly special, "Beef Belmont."

People who knew Reagan well, including Dick Powell, claimed, "Ronnie didn't immediately fall in love. He had to be very gently led into those pastures like a horse, and be assured that the green grass was for grazing and that he wouldn't end up in the glue factory."

After the first activity-filled month, Reagan didn't call Nancy as frequently, perhaps only once or twice a week. She feared he was losing interest.

Biographer Laurence Leamer wrote: "For a woman who sought a courtly Spenserian romance, Ronnie might seem a strange choice indeed. He was a man too scared by past romantic failures to fall easily into an impassioned union typical of youthful first love. But Ronnie was the first man Nancy had ever met who measured up to Dr. Loyal. She loved Ronnie. She wanted him, a man whom she could admire uncompromisingly, the way she admired Dr. Loyal."

"Ronnie's heart was frozen," Leamer continued. "To him, spring was not the harbinger of summer, but only of another winter. Nancy put up with all of Ronnie's ambivalence. She listened to his endless political talk, as Jane had not, and loved every word. She thought his most banal political remarks rang with profound meaning. She looked at him with pure adoration."

[When Nancy became First Lady, that loving and sometimes ferociously protective gaze became known as "The Look."]

***

When Reagan didn't call, as he

Had Nancy Davis not gotten pregnant (Patti was on the way), Reagan might have carried Doris Day across the threshold instead.

"I was a gentleman who preferred blondes, but married brunettes," he told his friend, singer/actor George Murphy.

Here he is, publicizing his second picture with Doris, *The Winning Team* in 1952 (the year he married Nancy).

It was the last picture he ever made at Warner Brothers, a studio where he'd worked since 1937.

As he later joked, "On the way out the door, I felt the pointed toe of Jack Warner's shoe in my most hidden spot."

Their 1952 baseball flick, *The Winning Team,"* choreographed a "movie version" of what a Reagan/Day nuptial might look like.

In the photo above, bride and groom—with Doris wearing white satin, a veil, and lace— dig into the fixings for a cold, Depression-era wedding supper prepared, Americana-style, by well-wishing friends.

had before, she concentrated on her career and very soon—when she learned that he was dating other women, she started going out with other men. That was all too evident one noonday in the MGM commissary, when she heard a starlet at a nearby table bragging to her friends about a recent gift of jewelry from Reagan. So far, he had never given Nancy any gift, not even flowers.

She later heard that while he was making *Storm Warning* (1951), he was seriously considering proposing to Doris Day.

Jane Wyman had heard that Reagan had been on the verge of marrying Nancy.

"Don't ask me why I'm so happy that the Davis girl is going out with other men," Jane told Joan Blondell. "I walked out on him, but I will cling to him at times for the comfort and security that only he can provide me. I know that if I ever got sick or something, and couldn't work, he'd be the first person to arrive on my doorstep."

As for Nancy, Jane learned she was still seeing Benny Thau at MGM.

"Ronnie didn't want to get too involved with Nancy," George Murphy recalled. "That's why he stopped seeing her so much. It was getting too god damn intense. Besides, I advised him to stick with blondes—no, not Marilyn Monroe but Doris Day. Doris was all that was fine and decent and would make an ideal First Lady if his dream of becoming president ever came true."

On one date, Nancy invited him to see her in *The Next Voice You Hear* (1950), wherein she co-starred with James Whitmore. After the movie, he told her, "Unpack your bags. You're going to be around Hollywood for quite a time."

On their dates, Reagan often shared his career woes with Nancy. In November of 1950, he gave a revealing interview to *Silver Screen:* "I'd love to be a louse on screen like Humphrey Bogart. You know, the kind of fellow who leers at the dolls and gets leered back. The guy who treats women rough and makes them love it. You know why I'd love to be louse? Because the public loves him. He makes money for his employers. He's talked about and swooned over. He grimaces forth from the pages of *Silver Screen* and people bring mouse traps to his doorstep. The louse business is, for sure, the open road to 'Fame in Films.'"

William Holden recognized that Reagan was in no hurry to make a commitment to another woman. "He was burned in his first marriage, and the pain still is deep. I understand why he wanted to keep dating other women. Of course, I'd call it more than dating."

Nancy discussed her own career problems with Reagan. She was featured in a number of picture layouts—in fact, *Movieland* heralded her as "A Star is Born." Despite the glamour of that connotation, she was photographed in jeans cleaning the house.

When director George Cukor saw the published version of these domestic photographs, he told friends, "The Hattie McDaniel image of a maid in *Gone With the Wind* is old-fashioned. The 1950s image of a maid should be none other than Miss Nancy Davis, who sure knows her way around a vacuum cleaner."

Hedda Hopper noted that Jane and Nancy each appeared in the same magazine. "Jane was all dolled up and looking glamorous, like a movie star should. In contrast, poor Nancy looked dowdy."

Jane and Nancy would never be mistaken for each other, although biographers over the years have noted a certain similarity in both of the "President's Ladies." Each has been perceived as a "strong-willed woman often displaying a fiery temper."

Despite the critical and commercial failure of many of her pictures, the studio insisted that Nancy continue to pose for publicity layouts. MGM sent her to the chic Amelia Gray's fashion shop in Beverly Hills for fittings of dresses from the latest Parisian designers, with the understanding that these dresses were to be borrowed for photo layouts. A sales clerk later said that "Miss Davis selected the wardrobe of a rich, thirtyish, unmarried society matron."

The stardom that Nancy had dreamed about did not come with the release of *The Next Voice You Hear* (1950). In that, she played a pregnant wife. "After that film, now I'm only offered roles for pregnant wives."

"Pregnant is something you don't want to get," Reagan cautioned.

"I noticed that when I go into a restaurant with you, the people at the other tables cast sly glances my way, checking to see if I'm showing any signs of pregnancy." Nancy said.

Rumors buzzed through Hollywood about Reagan's upcoming marriage to Nancy. In March of 1951, a columnist in *Variety* wrote: "Another date, this time for dinner at LaRue's on the Strip, adds fuel to the fires of romantic gossip raging about Ronald Reagan and Nancy Davis. Expect an announcement of marriage any day now."

That didn't happen. A year would drift by. Another year. Then another six months, even though some headlines had already announced Nancy as "THE NEXT MRS. RONALD REAGAN."

The *Hollywood Reporter* trumpeted, "Nobody's seen an engagement ring, but Ronnie is wearing his heart on his sleeve, and there's a twenty-karat sparkle in the eyes of Nancy Davis."

Modern Screen reported, "Don't look now, but here comes the bride. Ronald Reagan and Nancy Davis have had that 'about-to-be-married look' for more than a year now."

Louella Parsons weighed in with her take, writing in *Modern Screen,* "Are Ronald Reagan and Jane Wyman haunted by their perfect love? Not long ago, I went to dinner at their home, and Maureen came in to cut her birthday cake. Her mother and father stood by her side, polite to each other and respectful—so different from those gay kids who went barnstorming across the country with me years ago. I turned away so they couldn't see the tears in my eyes."

"I wonder—Do those embers of the once perfect love they shared still burn deep with haunting memories that won't let them forget?"

The report was unconfirmed, but one traumatic day, Nancy arrived to deliver something to Reagan at his apartment. It was perhaps a surprise gift she knew he wanted. After she knocked on his door, it was said to have been opened by a young actress, Christine Larson. Nancy left at once, taking the gift away with her. She was no doubt heartbroken.

During their weekends together, Reagan often shared his views with her on many subjects, as he was well informed. In most cases, even if she disagreed with him on a subject, she never argued. She was far more tolerant and sophisticated about homosexuality than he was.

He told her, "It's a tragic mistake and we should continue to view homosexuality as an illegal act. Participants should be subject to arrest and imprisonment."

When he became governor, he said, "Perhaps the only place in government that can employ homosexuals is the Department of Parks and Recreation."

In the media, that remark was widely denounced and defined as "vulgar, crude, ignorant, and tasteless." There were calls for "impeachment of the bigot."

Before Co-Ruling the Free World, Nancy Learns to Shovel Horse Manure at Her Boyfriend's Malibu Ranch

---

Nancy knew that their dating was getting more serious one night when he told her, "I really miss having someone to love—in fact, I hunger to have someone love me."

She later told her friends, "I knew at this point I had him."

***

During the final year before their marriage, Nancy and Reagan were living together, mostly at her apartment, like husband and wife. Weekends were usually spent at his Malibu ranch, sometimes with Michael and Maureen, when they weren't away at school. When they were in town, the children lived with Jane.

The ranch lay half a mile inland from the Pacific. Once there, visitors discovered a rundown old farmhouse that was gradually being fixed up. In March of 1951, Reagan had paid $85,000 for the property, on which he raised horses. When the first colt was born—he described it as "a gorgeous dapple filly"—he named her "Nancy D."

Ranching was not Nancy's thing. Her expressed distaste for it may have caused her to lose Clark Gable. She wasn't going to let that happen again. On the ranch, she threw herself into the spirit of it all, although admitting to friends, "I carried water to the horses and even shoveled manure. The closeness of animals, bugs, and dirt was a bit of a stretch for me, but at least I got to work shoulder-to-shoulder with Ronnie."

Sometimes, when Reagan drove the children back to Jane, she would invite him inside, even if Nancy were with him. "Jane was perfectly nice to me," Nancy wrote. "Not only had she been married to Ronnie, but she was very much 'The Star,' and it was her house and her children. I felt out of place, and I was a little in awe of her."

Later, as their "Love Triangle" continued, Nancy became very angry at Jane when she learned that Jane had convinced Reagan not to remarry until she did. She was dating bandleader Fred Karger at the time. Jane felt it would be embarrassing to her if Reagan remarried while she was still unwed.

When he learned about Jane's upcoming marriage to Karger, he felt he could go ahead and propose to Nancy.

As more and more people in the film industry learned about Nancy's link to Reagan, she was often asked, "What is he really like?"

She had a pat answer: "The secret is that there really is no secret. He is exactly the man he appears to be. The Ronald Reagan you see in public is the same Ronald Reagan I live with. He is not a fraud or a phony."

***

Reagan had seen Dr. Loyal and Edith many times, and both of them heartily approved of him. Loyal thought he was be "a good provider." Edith, on the other hand, told Nancy, "If I were twenty years younger, you would have me to fight off for this stud. He's a real catch."

When Nancy married Reagan in 1952, her movie career was drawing to a close. Months before the pre-defined end of her MGM contract, Nancy was told that it would not be renewed.

616

Mightier moguls than Nancy had already succumbed to the ax: Louis B. Mayer himself had resigned, more or less against his will, in the aftermath of a series of money-losing pictures he'd made.

As a means of softening the journalistic impact of her impending departure from the movie industry, Nancy preferred to tell reporters that she planned to retire from the screen and devote herself to her new role as a housewife and mother, a position that paralleled many of the beliefs and role models of the Eisenhower era.

But she still had a handful of undistinguished films to make for dwindling audiences to sit through. Worsening things was that she never really developed a fan base like Wyman and, to a lesser extent, Reagan.

***

The prospect of remarrying perplexed not only Reagan but Jane, Michael, and Maureen, too.

While he was still dating Nancy, Reagan was rumored to have spent the night of January 5, 1951, with Jane, celebrating her birthday, and, one assumes, some shared memories. The next day, he placed an excited call to Dick Powell. "Janie and I have made up. We're going to remarry."

But in just two weeks, Jane apparently changed her mind. The reasons are not known, but June Allyson speculated, "I think Ronnie told her that one day, he wanted to be President of the United States, and she didn't want to spend the rest of her life on the road to the White House."

Louella Parsons told of a private talk she'd had with Jane, not for publication. She had asked the columnist, "What's the matter with me? Will I ever find happiness?"

For a while, Reagan dated starlet Penny Edwards. According to her, he told her one night, "I like you just fine. But I think I've forgotten how to fall in love."

Another of Reagan's dates was Ann Sothern, who had once co-starred with Nancy. "When I dated Reagan, he had two things on his mind, politics and Jane Wyman. Even when he was supposed to be hot and heavy with Nancy, I noticed it was Ruth Roman he invited to the premiere of his film, *The Hasty Heart* (1949).

Sothern said, "He told me he gave Jane a small poodle with a note—'This is to keep you company until your lovin' man comes home again.'"

When Jane started work on a new movie, *Three Guys Named Mike* (1951), Reagan sent her a large bouquet of red roses. "I know you'll be safe with Van Johnson. But I don't know about Howard Keel and Barry Sullivan. Especially Keel."

One night, June Allyson and Dick Powell invited Reagan over to dinner by himself. He wanted to talk to the couple, who had remained his close friends over the course of many years. Allyson had also maintained an intense friendship with Jane until they had a falling out.

Reagan was wondering if he could more or less incorporate both Jane and Nancy into an extended family, celebrating reunions with Maureen and Michael during communal weekends at the ranch. He had promised Jane she could go to the ranch any time she wanted for horseback riding.

"Ronnie," Allyson said. "That's not going to work out. Nancy won't like it. It's a stupid idea unless you're planning to set up a *ménage à trois*. And a *ménage à trois* will only take place in your sexual fantasies."

617

As Michael later said, "Back in those days, the press was trying to promote a feud between my mother and Nancy. When I met separately with each woman, they had nothing but derogatory things to say about each other. I agreed with whichever one I was with at the time."

When friends asked Jane if theirs was a feud like that of Joan Crawford with Bette Davis, she denied it. "I have no grudge against Miss Davis. To show that there are no hard feelings, I plan to attend the funeral of the bitch."

Before and after his marriage to Nancy, Jane tried to avoid attending events or private parties and dinners where she would encounter Nancy. Reagan had stopped bringing Nancy by her home when he drove over to return Maureen and Michael to their mother.

However, on certain occasions, they were trapped together. One such event occurred in 1964, when Maureen hosted a lavish reception at the time of her second marriage (*i.e.,* to David Sills). Nancy, Reagan, and Jane stood together in the reception line to greet their guests.

Although it was all smiles in the reception line, Jane and Nancy avoided each other for the rest of the day. Jane left early, privately telling Maureen, "Better luck with your second choice of a husband. I hope it won't be as disastrous as your marriage to that policeman—what's his name."

***

Joan Blondell described a last minute drama that transpired during the planning phases of the Nancy/Ronnie wedding.

"Jane came to see me and we talked and drank until around three o'clock in the morning," Blondell said. "She wondered if she should stage an eleventh hour maneuver to get Ronnie back. She was determined to go to him in the pre-dawn hours and plead with him to remarry her. That ended when I reminded her that if she did that, she might have to get him out of bed with Nancy."

"Later," Blondell continued, "she told me that she had contacted Ronnie, and he agreed to meet her for a late breakfast at a secluded café in Santa Monica. I think she did ask him to take her back. But it was too late. He told her he was going ahead and marrying Nancy, even though he was still in love with Jane."

"Ronnie won his victory," Blondell said. "She wanted to be his wife again. Ronnie had always predicted she'd change her mind and want him back. But, according to Jane, he held out a compromise: He promised that during his upcoming marriage, he'd slip away and see her on occasion."

"We'll make love like we used to for old time's sake," he reportedly said.

Chains of love, Till death do us part: A proud, much-manipulated "Papa."

***

Before and after Reagan's marriage to Nancy, Maureen, his older offspring, revealed her fears about his upcoming marriage to Nancy. "She's still young enough to have children. Not only will I have to think about adjusting to half brothers or sisters, but I'll be torn between two families. Please understand, siblings aside, my loyalty will always be to you and my mother. I love both of you dearly."

"How are you getting along with Nancy?" Reagan asked Maureen.

"I find her sympathetic to the problems of a young girl like me growing up in Hollywood. But any motherly love I have will be reserved for mother."

"I understand that," he said.

[Maureen would later write a memoir, First Father, First Daughter, *in which she discussed the problems of Reagan marrying "The Other Woman." Adding to the complications of her family landscape, Nancy and Reagan eventually presented her with a half-sister and a half-brother.*

Maureen later said, "Dad married Nancy just in time. Patricia Ann Reagan was born by cesarean on October 21, 1952.

Years later, Maureen suggested that there was jealousy between her half sister and herself. She remembered sitting on the sofa in the Reagan living room, watching her father bounce Patti on his lap, later tossing her up in the air. Maureen wistfully, and perhaps with deep touches of envy, remembered when she sat on her dad's lap, and when he had tossed her into the air.

With Reagan, Maureen would always try to be the loyal daughter, presenting Patti in the most unfavorable light. "She even changed her name to Patti Davis," Maureen said. "I'm proud to be a Reagan. She's not!"

Indeed, Patti Davis grew up to be the "black sheep" of the family. She became known for her liberal viewpoints, many of which contrasted with her father's conservatism. She was pro-choice on abortion, and favored gay rights. Reagan did not.

Patti Davis, daughter of Ronald and Nancy Reagan, was the prodigal daughter, dumping the Reagan name and using her mother's maiden name instead to symbolize her disgust with her father's right-wing political views.

As for her own politics, she was a pot-smoking liberal. At the age of 41, she posed for the July, 1994, edition of *Playboy,* appearing on the cover with the hands of a black man cupping her (otherwise naked) breasts. She also made a direct-to-video *Playboy Celebrity Centerfold,* the tape showing her cavorting in lesbian settings outdoors, followed by a solo masturbation scene.

Patti's first novel, *Homefront,* published in 1986, recorded fictionalized events inspired by her own childhood and teenaged years, an artistic choice which seriously pissed off her father's Republican friends.

She was also an author, not portraying her family in a positive light in The Way I See It, *in which she called her father, "cold, distant, and aloof to everyone except Nancy." She also charged Nancy with physical abuse.*

Nancy's mother was horrified in 1994 when Patti posed for Playboy.

On May 28, 1958, both Maureen and Michael would be presented with another sibling, born Ron Reagan, Jr. He, too, reportedly embarrassed his father when he dropped out of Yale to become a ballet dancer.

As President, Reagan was quizzed by reporters about his son's sexual orientation. Reagan answered, "We checked him out. He's definitely straight."

One amusing incident occurred on Saturday Night Live, *during his father's presidency. In a funny skit, Ron Jr. parodied Tom Cruise's performance in* Risky Business *(1983) by dancing in his underwear—presumably while his parents were away— in a replica of the interior of the White House.*

Nancy and Reagan watched the show that night, but reportedly did not understand it. When it was explained to the President, Reagan asked, "Who is this Tom Cruise fellow?"

In 1988, one reporter confronted Reagan, "Is it true, as some have it, that your son is not only a liberal, but an atheist?"

"I'll have no comment," the President said.]

Ron Reagan, Jr. "Like father, like son" in every instance except his love of ballet.

***

Reagan's friends, Robert Taylor, George Murphy, William Holden, and Dick Powell, claimed that "Ronnie went through the jitters about marrying again."

"I'm still in love with Jane, but I also love Nancy, but in a very different way," he explained to Murphy.

"Nancy," he continued, "will be loving and supportive. I know that about her. But Jane is a seductive little vixen. She'll betray you, infuriate you, but you keep going back for more of what she dishes out. I'll share a secret

If both Tom Cruise and the President's son worked in a male strip club, which would women prefer? Your choice.

620

with you. Unlike Nancy, Jane talks real dirty in a guy's ear—What a turn-on!"

Reagan later admitted that during his courtship of Nancy, "I did everything wrong, doing everything that could have lost her if somebody up there hadn't been looking after me."

In his autobiography, he wrote, "In spite of my determination to remain foot-loose, in spite of my belief that the pattern of my life was all set and would continue without change, nature was trying to tell me something very important."

"I loved Jane, and I am still in love with her, but as a wife, she never understood me and my aspirations. Nancy is just the opposite. *She understands.*"

***

From the beginning of her relationship with Reagan, as Nancy later claimed, she sensed that acting was not providing fulfillment for Reagan. He seemed to want a career in something else, and she assumed that was politics, since he talked about that subject all the time.

Biographers have suggested that Nancy was the single most important source for leading Reagan out of the liberal camp into the right-wing den. But she denied that, claiming he was the one who got her interested in politics.

Before she married Reagan, Nancy consulted with Carroll Righter, Hollywood's reigning astrologer. He assured her that the "stars would shine on such a union." She felt confident to move ahead.

***

At long last, on February 29, 1952, that day arrived. At the marriage bureau, when they applied for a marriage license, an onlooker described their arrival.

"Ronnie looked a little pale in a turtleneck and trench coat, Nancy radiant in a white-collared black dress." It was the same black dress she'd worn on her first date with him.

Four days later, on the day of his wedding, Reagan was forty-one and had lost the youthful good looks that had drawn so many women to him during his early days in Hollywood. Nancy was thirty-one, although most of America thought she was twenty-six, because that's what was published in interviews.

In addition to their ranch, he would purchase a dream house along the Pacific Palisades.

In 1954, when he became a spokesperson for General Electric, that company would fill the house with every imaginable electric gadget designed for modern living, including a chandelier wheel with a dozen recessed colored lights, prominently positioned above their dining table.

William Holden was designated as Reagan's best man, his wife Ardis (the actress known as Brenda Marshall) serving as Nancy's matron of honor.

Nancy noticed that the Holdens weren't speaking to each other. They had had a fight the night before, after Ardis learned that her husband had had a fling with the bisexual actress, Judy Holliday, when they had co-starred together in *Born Yesterday* (1950).

Midway through the ceremony, Holden, with a few drinks in him, came up to Nancy. "Let me be the first to kiss the *new* Mrs. Ronald Reagan."

621

She quickly whispered to him. "You're jumping the gun. The ceremony's not over yet."

"No I'm not," Holden said, and kissed her anyway.

Nancy later claimed, "I certainly remembered that kiss from Bill. But I don't remember getting a kiss from Ronnie."

He had said he wanted no publicity. However, when they arrived at the Holden home for their modest reception, a photographer was waiting to record this historic event. Ardis had ordered a wedding cake.

At the reception, Reagan stood with Holden, looking over at Nancy and Ardis on the other side of the room.

"At least I know that with Nancy, I won't have a wife outshining me on the screen. No one is ever going to call me Mr. Nancy Davis, I can assure you."

"I'm with you, man," Holden said. "No one ever called me Mr. Brenda Marshall. That's what we get for marrying unimportant actresses, unlike Jane Wyman."

For their honeymoon night, Reagan drove Mrs. Ronald Reagan to the grandly historic Mission Inn in Riverside, where incognito movie stars often went for off-the-record trysts, especially on weekends. *[In 1940, Richard and Patricia Nixon had celebrated their wedding reception here.]*

After that night of passion, Reagan and Nancy set off to Phoenix to join Dr. Loyal Davis and his wife, Edith, who were vacationing there at the time.

Nancy later said, "Having a honeymoon with one's in-laws might have been a bit strange, I admit. But it worked beautifully, and Ronnie enjoyed the company of my parents who were so pleased with my choice of a husband."

As Edith told Reagan, "Honey, if you don't get it right the first time with Wyman, you're going to make it with Nancy. She'll be the best little wife a man could hope for, unlike those whores of Babylon out there in California."

During their drive from Phoenix back to Los Angeles, Reagan and Nancy were trapped in the worst sandstorm to hit western Arizona in twenty years. "The winds were harsh enough to make a coyote airborne," Reagan later said.

The winds at one point ripped the canvas of the retractable top of their convertible. For part of the ride, Nancy had to position herself on her knees on the front passenger seat, facing backwards, and holding the torn canvas together. Her hands became so frozen they had to stop periodically so that she could rub them together to help the blood circulate.

To some couples, the storm might have represented an evil omen. But for Nancy, at least, it wasn't so. She was totally optimistic.

Years later, as President of the United States, Reagan, one afternoon in the White House, told his aide (Secretary of the Treasury and later, Chief of White House Staff) the similarly named Donald T. Regan, "I found the ideal Cinderella. The shoe fit her little foot perfectly. As her Prince Charming, I promised to make her my Princess. Instead of that, I made her Milady and put her in a position more important than any damn run-of-the-mill princess. In fact, I plunged her into a life beyond her wildest dreams."

A Special Feature

White House Nights
Frank Sinatra & the Reagans
A Love Triangle

This photograph, taken on July 5, 1981 at the White House, on the occasion of Nancy Reagan's sixtieth birthday, was published on the frontpages of newspapers throughout the United States, even abroad.

Nancy was dancing, embraced in the arms of "the man of my dreams," Frank Sinatra, although he's wearing one of his worst *toupées*. She obviously regrets the intrusion of her husband, Ronald, who always suspected that "something was always going on between those two."

Originally, when he was still a pal of John F. Kennedy, Ol' Blue Eyes detested the Reagans. But when Bobby Kennedy, then Attorney General, made Frank *persona non grata* at the White House, the singer switched his political alliances.

He'd once said, "Reagan is a stupid bore who can't get a job in pictures." He'd also called Nancy, "A dumb broad with fat ankles who can't act."

But at this White House gala in 1981, he sang:

> *"I'm so proud that you're First Lady, Nancy,*
> *Also so pleased that I'm sort of a chum.*
> *The next eight years will be fancy as fancy as they come.*
> *Nancy, Nancy, Nancy, with the smiling face."*

"Gorbachev, Tear Down That Wall"

—Joyce Hodges

The 1930s-era starlet, Joy Hodges, was the woman who, early in the game, had filled Reagan in on the lowdown aspects of the entertainment industry during his first venture into Lotus Land. Consequently, she and Reagan became life-long friends. She lived through his presidency and beyond, dying on January 19, 2003, in Palm Springs, California, at the age of 88.

Hodges once told reporters, "I got Ronnie his first pair of contact lenses and his first screen test. He was the first leading man in Hollywood to wear contact lenses, and he would take them out on a regular basis to show their then-new technology to friends."

When Reagan occupied the White House, he often invited her to dinner. Later, she commented, "At one party I found myself seated next to President Mikhail Gorbachev. I turned to him and said, 'Gorby, tear down that wall—and he did! Of course, Ronnie in Berlin later stole my line and it became his most famous statement as president."

She recalled her final meeting with Reagan in January of 2001. "He looked at me and summoned up a name from somewhere deep in his memory. He called me 'Miss Jones.'"

She figured that he had recalled how she had played "Miss Jones" in the 1937 Broadway musical, *I'd Rather Be Right,* produced by Richard Rogers and George Kaufman. Its most memorable musical number was "Have You Met Miss Jones?"

The plot centered on a beautiful heroine (Miss Jones, as played by Hodges) and her boyfriend (Austin Marshall). The couple desperately needs to increase their income before they can get married. Before the final curtain, a show-biz representation of the President of the United States steps in and gracefully solves the lovers' dilemma.

"Ronnie probably remembered me from the play, or if not, at least as the subject of that song," Hodges said.

Auld Lang Syne: Two views of actress and *danseuse* Joy Hodges, from the era she welcomed then-newcomer Ronald Reagan to Hollywood.

In Memory of

Ronald Wilson Reagan

40th President (1981-1989) of the United States

February 6, 1911-June 5, 2004

At a White House Governor's Dinner, Ronald Reagan, 40th U.S. President, chats with Bill Clinton, the 42nd U.S. President, and Hillary Rodham Clinton, possibly the 45th U.S. President.

Near the conclusion of his first autobiography, *Where's the Rest of Me?,* Reagan was in a nostalgic mood. He remembered many of the people he had known, specifically acknowledging "May Robson, Alan Hale, Lionel Barrymore, Ethel Barrymore, Zasu *(sic)* Pitts, Eddy Arnold of the booming laugh, kindly Paul Harvey, roistering, scratching Wallace Beery, Charles Coburn (who amputated my legs), Adolph *(sic)* Menjou, and the greatest of all actors, Walter Huston."

Demurely, Reagan went on to label some of the less inhibited, more flamboyant actors he had known, specifically defining Ty Power, Errol Flynn, "Bogey," "Coop," Dick Powell, Wayne Morris, Clark Gable, and Jack Carson, as members of "a special breed."

Reagan ended his first (and relentlessly opaque) memoir on a reassuring, feel-good note, citing the usually rather blunt Clark Gable as saying, "The most important thing a man can know is, as he approaches his own door, that someone on the other side is listening for the sound of his footsteps."

Referencing the happiness he'd found in married life with Nancy, and the wisdom he had found after the termination of his film career, he concluded, "(At last) I have found the rest of me."

The Long Goodbye

In August of 1994, five years after his departure from the Oval Office, Ronald Reagan, with the ever faithful Nancy at his side, received the devastating news that he'd been diagnosed with Alzheimer's disease.

Reacting to that, in November of that year, as autumn winds blew in from the Pacific, he penned a handwritten message to the American people. In part, it read:

"I have recently been told that I am one of the millions of Americans who will be afflicted with Alzheimer's Disease...
"At the moment I feel just fine. I intend to live the remainder of the years God gives me on this earth doing the things I have always done...
"I now begin the journey that will lead me into the sunset of my life. I know that for America, there will always be a bright dawn ahead.
"Thank you, my friends. May God always bless you."

From there, his health and his memory continued to deteriorate.

His friend, Merv Griffin, remembered visiting Reagan in his office in Los Angeles, at Century City. During that visit, the former President picked up a photograph of the White House. "This building looks familiar," he said to the TV talk show host. "Where is it?"

Before he arrived in Hollywood, Reagan had been a gifted swimmer and lifeguard who saved 77 lives from drowning in the Rock River, near his home town of Dixon, Illinois.

But in retirement, he had to wear water wings and be propped up whenever he entered or departed from the waters of his pool by a security guard.

Flailing around for ways to fill his time, he developed and then defined a "special mission" for himself—gathering up magnolia leaves that had blown onto the pool's surface. Recognizing the importance that Reagan associated with this task, Secret Service agents routinely collected bags of these leaves from other sites, placing them onto the surface of the pool's water so he could then take credit for removing them.

Once a football star at Illinois' Eureka College, Reagan, during his retirement, began to imagine that he had to get into uniform for the big game. "The team needs me!" he urgently and repeatedly told Nancy. He began to confuse scenes from his movies with his real life. Omnipresent were scenes from his famous football picture, *Knute Rockne—All American* (1940) that produced his all-time most famous line, "Win just one for the Gipper."

One morning, the fast-deteriorating former president woke up sobbing, asking attendants nearby, "Where's the rest of me?"—a question inspired by his critically acclaimed performance in *Kings Row* (1942), after a sadistic surgeon had maliciously amputated his legs. Decades later, from the depths of his dementia, he imagined that his own legs had been surgically removed.

The aging Titan would sometimes "cry like a baby" about taunts that his brother, Neil Reagan, had hurled at him, based on his belief that "Moon" had uttered those insults only a few hours before. Preceding him to the grave, his brother had died of Alzheimer's Disease in 1996.

In reaction to her husband's deterioration, Nancy, growing increasingly frail and having lost an alarming amount of weight, said "My heart is broken."

As the first U.S. President to die during the 21st Century, Reagan passed on at his home in Bel Air, California, on June 5, 2004, not knowing that he had once been the most powerful elected leader in the World. His longevity defined him as the second longest-lived president in U.S. history, having survived 93 years and 120 days, just 45 days fewer than Gerald Ford.

After a state funeral in Washington's National Cathedral, a ceremony presided over by then-president George W. Bush, Reagan's body was flown back to the Ronald Reagan Presidential Library in Simi Valley, California.

There, at a sunset Memorial Service and Internment Ceremony, Nancy, overcome with grief, lost her composure, crying in public for the first time that week.

She accepted the folded flag that had been draped over the coffin of her one-and-only husband. As she kissed the casket, she mouthed the words, "I love you," before her sad departure.

Her final words were, "Ronnie's long journey has finally taken him to a distant place where I can no longer reach him."

* * *

Ronald Reagan did not fear departing on another journey. He added a personalized footnote to his favorite poem, Alfred Lord Tennyson's *Crossing the Bar,* verses that were read at his Memorial Service:

Sunset and evening star.

And one clear call for me!
And may there be no moaning of the bar,
When I put out to sea.

"We have God's promise that I have gone on to a better world, where there is no pain or sorrow. Bring comfort to those who may mourn my going."

—*Ronald Reagan*

"Who is this strange woman and why is she kissing me?" Reagan might have asked on February 6, 2000 the occasion of his 89th birthday.

As part of the celebration, Nancy had given him a piece of cake and a kiss. Their 45th wedding anniversary, scheduled for March 4, would transpire in less than a month. But he didn't know who she was. He had no idea that he had ever married her.

Acknowledgments

Jane Wyman, Nancy Davis, and Ronald Reagan (despite the latter two's "reveal noth-ing" memoirs) chose not to tell us very much about what used to be called their "salad days." Perhaps they were just being discreet, preferring to emphasize their triumphs rather than their compromises and indiscretions.

We at Blood Moon subscribe to Oscar Wilde's adage that there's nothing else to do with gossip but spread it around. So consequently, we have decided to do it for them.

It took some effort, actually decades of it, to assemble this portrait of the Reagans' "Love Triangle."

We were aided in our research by a vast array of collaborators in the film colony. Virtu-ally everyone who ever worked with the Reagans had opinions and insights about them, both good and bad. If we listed all of them—some of them wanted anonymity—it would fill many dozens of pages.

Those people quoted in this book were viewed as newsworthy enough to have been the subject of individual interviews over the course of many years. As the Reagans be-came increasingly famous, many "lesser souls" wanted to talk about their involvements with Nancy, Jane, and Ronald.

The list is long and convoluted, but here is a sampling of some of the contributors:

Jack Carson (who was especially insightful about his best friend, Dennis Morgan); John Payne (from a hospital bed in New York, following an accident); Susan Hayward (when she was semi-retired and my neighbor in Fort Lauderdale).

There were so many others: Glenda Farrell, Frank McHugh, Eddie Albert, Wayne Mor-ris, Pat O'Brien, Edward G. Robinson, James Cagney, Allen Jenkins, Mervyn LeRoy, Priscilla Lane, Adele Jergens, Virginia Mayo, Ida Lupino, Phillip Terry, Ann Sheridan, Kent Smith, Audrey Totter, Rock Hudson, Raoul Walsh, Bruce Bennett, John Litel, Ray Enright, Tom Drake, Peter Lawford, Milton Berle, Bryan Foy, William Clemens, Lloyd Bacon, Anita Louise, Eddie Foy, Jr., Gale Page, Lewis Seiler, Michael Curtiz, Merv Grif-fin, Richard Thorpe, Alan Hale, Sr., Curtis Bernhardt, David Lewis, Jerry Wald, Viveca Lindfors, Alexis Smith, Peter Godfrey, Shirley Temple, Eve Arden, David Butler, Lewis R. Foster, Andrew Marton, Allan Dwan, and Nathan Juran.

As everyone in the business knows, the Hollywood Hills and the canyons of Manhattan are filled with (sometimes embittered) unpublished memoirs. It seems that everyone who was anybody, along with those who wanted to be, view their lives as worthy of a memoir. Year after year, most of these go unpublished

Blood Moon, however, receives some of these at regular intervals. Some representative titles have included: *I Was Tyrone Power's Secret Male Lover, Liberace's Secret Life,* and *My Affair with Oprah Winfrey.* Fear of libel often prevents the publication of many of these revelations.

Although many of their manuscripts never saw the light of publication, we are nonetheless grateful to the literary agencies operated by Bertha Klausner, Jay Garon-Brooke, and Ilsa Lahn for letting us wade through their "slush piles."

Manuscripts on Robert Taylor, Barbara Stanwyck, and especially Paulette Goddard (written by her former secretary) were most helpful, as were portraits of Dick Powell, Dennis Morgan, George Murphy, Betty Grable, Lucille Ball, and William Holden. Long before us, other authors attempted separate manuscripts on the subjects of this book—i.e., "tell-alls" about Nancy, Jane, and Ronald.

One of our greatest contributors was Joan Blondell, a dear friend and house guest. She was very helpful about the early career of her "fellow chorine," Jane Wyman, and filled with wonderful stories about backdoor intrigue at Warner Brothers in the 30s.

Another close friend, Van Johnson, on whose Manhattan terrace I spent many hours in the company of our mutual friend, songstress Greta Keller, had known and co-starred with Jane Wyman and (to a lesser degree) Reagan since World War II.

June Allyson was filled with revelations about the Reagans, especially in her later years, after she broke with Jane over a disagreement.

No one was more helpful than Stanley Mills Haggart, my former boss. He arrived in Hollywood during the Silent era and began writing about the film colony's fun and foibles in his voluminous diary. (It was never submitted for publication, and for good reason!) In the late 30s and early 40s, he had been Hedda Hopper's "leg man." In that much-envied and highly competitive position, he was often aided by his long-time companion, William Hopper (Hedda's son). William was a close personal friend of Reagan's, and appeared in bit parts in many of his early films.

Although Hedda couldn't print many of the indiscretions that Stanley and her son uncovered, confirmed, and delivered to her, she wanted to be keenly aware of what was happening after dark and during the pre-dawn hours of the industry that employed and fascinated her.

LOVE TRIANGLE

ITS AUTHORS

DARWIN PORTER

As an intense and precocious nine-year-old, **Darwin Porter** began meeting movie stars, TV personalities, politicians, and singers through his vivacious and attractive mother, Hazel, a somewhat eccentric Southern girl who had lost her husband in World War II. Migrating from the depression-ravaged valleys of western North Carolina to Miami Beach during its most ebullient heyday, Hazel became a stylist, wardrobe mistress, and personal assistant to the vaudeville comedienne Sophie Tucker, the bawdy and irrepressible "Last of the Red Hot Mamas."

Virtually every show-biz celebrity who visited Miami Beach paid a call on "Miss Sophie," and Darwin as a pre-teen loosely and indulgently supervised by his mother, was regularly dazzled by the likes of Judy Garland, Dinah Shore, Veronica Lake, Linda Darnell, Martha Raye, and Ronald Reagan, who arrived to pay his respects to Miss Sophie with a young blonde starlet on the rise—Marilyn Monroe.

Hazel's work for Sophie Tucker did not preclude an active dating life: Her *beaux* included Richard Widmark, Victor Mature, Frank Sinatra (who "tipped" teenaged Darwin the then-astronomical sum of ten dollars for getting out of the way), and that alltime "second lead," Wendell Corey, when he wasn't emoting with Barbara Stanwyck and Joan Crawford.

As a late teenager, Darwin edited *The Miami Hurricane* at the University of Miami, where he interviewed Eleanor Roosevelt, Tab Hunter, Lucille Ball, and Adlai Stevenson. He also worked for Florida's then-Senator George Smathers, one of John F. Kennedy's best friends, establishing an ongoing pattern of picking up "Jack and Jackie" lore while still a student.

After graduation, as a journalist, he was commissioned with the opening of a bureau of *The Miami Herald* in Key West (Florida), where he took frequent morning walks with retired U.S. president Harry S Truman during his vacations in what had functioned as his "Winter White House." He also got to know, sometimes very well, various celebrities "slumming" their way through off-the-record holidays in the orbit of then-resident Tennessee Williams. Celebrities hanging out in the permissive arts environment of Key West during those days included Tallulah Bankhead, Cary Grant, Tony Curtis, the stepfather of Richard Burton, a gaggle of show-biz and publishing moguls, and the once-notorious stripper, Bettie Page.

For about a decade in New York, Darwin worked in television journalism and advertising with his long-time partner, the journalist, art director, and distinguished arts-industry socialite Stanley Mills Haggart. Jointly, they produced TV commercials starring such high-powered stars as Joan Crawford (then feverishly promoting Pepsi-Cola), Ronald Reagan (General Electric), and Debbie Reynolds (selling Singer Sewing Machines), along with such other entertainers as Louis Armstrong, Lena Horne, Arlene Dahl, and countless other show-biz personalities hawking commercial products.

During his youth, Stanley had flourished as an insider in early Hollywood as a "leg man" and source of information for Hedda Hopper, the fabled gossip columnist. On his nightly rounds, Stanley was most often accompanied by Hedda's son, William Hopper, a close friend of Ronald Reagan's.

When Stanley wasn't dishing newsy revelations with Hedda, he had worked as a Powers model; a romantic lead opposite Silent-era film star Mae Murray; the intimate companion of superstar Randolph Scott before Scott became emotionally involved with Cary Grant; and a man-about-town who archived gossip from everybody who mattered back when the movie colony was small, accessible, and confident that details about their tribal rites would absolutely never be reported in the press. Over the years, Stanley's vast cornucopia of inside Hollywood information was passed on to Darwin, who amplified it with copious interviews and research of his own.

After Stanley's death in 1980, Darwin inherited a treasure trove of memoirs, notes, and interviews detailing Stanley's early adventures in Hollywood, including in-depth recitations of scandals that even Hopper during her heyday was afraid to publish. Most legal and journalistic standards back then interpreted those oral histories as "unprintable." Times, of course, changed.

Beginning in the early 1960s, Darwin joined forces with the then-fledgling Arthur Frommer organization, playing a key role in researching and writing more than 50 titles and defining the style and values that later emerged as the world's leading travel accessories, *The Frommer Guides,* with particular emphasis on Europe, California, New England, and the Caribbean. Between the creation and updating of hundreds of editions of detailed travel guides to England, France, Italy, Spain, Portugal, Austria, Germany, California, and Switzerland, he continued to interview and discuss the triumphs, feuds, and frustrations of celebrities, many by then reclusive, whom he either sought out or encountered randomly as part of his extensive travels. Ava Gardner and Lana Turner were particularly insightful.

One day when Darwin lived in Tangier, he walked into an opium den to discover Marlene Dietrich sitting alone in a corner.

Darwin has also ghost written books for celebrities (who shall go nameless!) as well as a series of novels. His first, *Butterflies in Heat,* became a cult classic and was adapted into a film, *Tropic of Desire,* starring Eartha Kitt, among others. Other books included *Razzle-Dazzle,* about an errant female movie star of questionable morals; and an erotic thriller, *Blood Moon,* hailed as "pure novelistic Viagra, an American interpretation of Arthur Schnitzler's *La Ronde."*

Darwin's novel, *Marika,* published by Arbor House, evoked Marlene Dietrich for many readers.

His controversial novel, *Venus,* was suggested by the life of the fabled eroticist and diarist, Anaïs Nin. His novel, *Midnight in Savannah,* was a brutal saga of corruption, greed, and sexual tension exploring the eccentricities of Georgia's most notorious city.

His novel, *Rhinestone Country,* catalyzed a guessing game. Which male star was the inspiration for its lovable rogue, Pete Riddle? Mississippi Pearl praised it as "like a scalding gulp of rotgut whiskey on a snowy night in a bowjacks honky-tonk."

Darwin also transformed into literary format the details which he and Stanley Haggart had compiled about the relatively underpublicized scandals of the Silent Screen, releasing them in 2001 as *Hollywood's Silent Closet,* "an uncensored, underground history of Pre-Code Hollywood, loaded with facts and rumors from generations past."

Since then, Darwin has penned more than eighteen uncensored Hollywood biographies, many of them award-winners, on subjects who have included Marlon Brando; Merv Griffin; Katharine Hepburn; Howard Hughes; Humphrey Bogart; Michael Jackson; Paul Newman; Steve McQueen; Marilyn Monroe; Elizabeth Taylor; Frank Sinatra; John F. Kennedy; Vivien Leigh; Laurence Olivier; the well known porn star, Linda Lovelace; all three of the fabulous Gabor sisters, plus Tennessee Williams, Gore Vidal, Truman Capote, and Jacqueline Kennedy Onassis.

As a departure from his usual repertoire, Darwin also wrote the controversial *J. Edgar Hoover & Clyde Tolson: Investigating the Sexual Secrets of America's Most Famous Men and Women,* a book about celebrity, voyeurism, political and sexual repression, and blackmail within the highest circles of the U.S. government.

He has also co-authored, in league with Danforth Prince, four *Hollywood Babylon* anthologies, plus four separate volumes of film critiques, reviews, and commentary.

His biographies, over the years, have won more than 30 First Prize or runner-up awards at literary festivals in cities which include Boston, New York, Los Angeles, Hollywood, San Francisco, and Paris.

Darwin can be heard at regular intervals as a radio commentator (and occasionally on television), "dishing" celebrities, pop culture, politics, and scandal.

A resident of New York City, Darwin is currently at work on two biographies slated for release in 2015—*Peter O'Toole, Hellraiser, Sexual Outlaw, and Irish Rebel;* and *Bill & Hillary—So This Is That Thing Called Love.*

DANFORTH PRINCE

The publisher and co-author of *Love Triangle*, **Danforth Prince** is one of the "Young Turks" of the post-millennium publishing industry. He's president and founder of Blood Moon Productions, a firm devoted to researching, salvaging, compiling, and marketing the oral histories of America's entertainment industry.

One of Prince's famous predecessors, the late Lyle Stuart (self-described as "the last publisher in America with guts") once defined Prince as "one of my natural successors." In 1956, that then-novice maverick launched himself with $8,000 he'd won in a libel judgment against gossip columnist Walter Winchell. It was Stuart who published Linda Lovelace's two authentic memoirs—*Ordeal* and *Out of Bondage*.

"I like to see someone following in my footsteps in the 21ˢᵗ Century," Stuart told Prince. "You publish scandalous biographies. I did, too. My books on J. Edgar Hoover, Jacqueline Kennedy Onassis, and Barbara Hutton stirred up the natives. You do, too."

Prince launched his career in journalism in the 1970s at the Paris Bureau of *The New York Times*. In the early '80s, he resigned to join Darwin Porter in researching, developing and publishing various titles within *The Frommer Guides*, jointly reviewing the travel scenes of more than 50 nations for Simon & Schuster. Authoritative and comprehensive, they were perceived as best-selling "travel bibles" for millions of readers, with recommendations and travel advice about the major nations of Western Europe, the Caribbean, Bermuda, The Bahamas, Georgia and the Carolinas, and California.

Prince, along with Porter, is also the co-author of several award-winning celebrity biographies, each configured as a title within Blood Moon's Babylon series. These have included *Hollywood Babylon—It's Back!*; *Hollywood Babylon Strikes Again*; *The Kennedys: All the Gossip Unfit to Print*; and *Frank Sinatra, The Boudoir Singer*.

Prince, with Porter, has co-authored such provocative biographies as *Elizabeth Taylor: There is Nothing Like a Dame*.

With respect and a sense of irony about "When Divas Clash," Prince and Porter also co-authored *Pink Triangle: The Feuds and Private Lives of Tennessee Williams, Gore Vidal, Truman Capote, and Members of their Entourages*, as well as *Jacqueline Kennedy*

Onassis: A Life Beyond Her Wildest Dreams.

Prince is also the co-author, with Darwin Porter, of four books on film criticism, three of which won honors at regional bookfests across America, including Los Angeles and San Francisco. Special features within these guides included the cinematic legacy of Tennessee Wiliams; the implications associated with strolling down *Sunset Blvd.,* that "Boulevard of Broken Dreams"; behind-the-scenes revelations about the making of *Ben-Hur,* starring Charlton Heston. From *Flesh* to *Trash*, he previewed many of Andy Warhol's films and "unzipped" Marlon Brando. He also took a cinematic look at the legacy of Greta Garbo in the re-release of her movies of long ago, revisiting *Mata Hari, Anna Christie, Queen Christina, Anna Karenina, Camille,* and *Ninotchka,* among many others.

Prince, a graduate of Hamilton College and a native of Easton and Bethlehem, Pennsylvania, is the president and founder (in 1996) of the Georgia Literary Association, and of the Porter and Prince Corporation, founded in 1983, which has produced dozens of titles for both Prentice Hall and John Wiley & Sons. In 2011, he was named "Publisher of the Year" by a consortium of literary critics and marketers spearheaded by the J.M. Northern Media Group.

According to Prince, "Blood Moon provides the luxurious illusion that a reader is a perpetual guest at some gossippy dinner party populated with brilliant but occasionally self-delusional figures from bygone eras of The American Experience. Blood Moon's success at salvaging, documenting, and articulating the (till now) orally transmitted histories of the Entertainment Industry, in ways that have never been seen before, is one of the most distinctive aspects of our backlist."

Publishing in collaboration with the National Book Network (www.NBNBooks.com), he has electronically documented some of the controversies associated with his stewardship of Blood Moon in more than 50 videotaped documentaries, book trailers, public speeches, and TV or radio interviews. Any of these can be watched, without charge, by performing a search for "Danforth Prince" on **YouTube.com**, checking him out on **Facebook** (either "Danforth Prince" or "Blood Moon Productions"), on **Twitter** (#Bloodyand-Lunar) or by clicking on **BloodMoonProductions.com**.

During the rare moments when he isn't writing, editing, neurosing about, or promoting Blood Moon, he works out at a New York City gym, rescues stray animals, talks to strangers, and regularly attends Episcopal Mass every Sunday.

INDEX

640

311, 316, 326, 328, 333, 335-338, 355,
366, 382, 383, 384, 389, 390, 400, 404,
406, 411, 424, 431, 448, 449, 462, 523,
524, 556, 590, 591, 616
Gabor, Eva 397
Gabor, Zsa Zsa 134, 400
Gainsborough, Thomas 471
Galbraith, Erle Chennault 407
Galbraith, Virginia and C. Audley 15
Gallagher, Carol 232
Gambling on the High Seas 220, 221, 222
Gamet, Kenneth 294
Gamut, Kenneth 273
Garbo, Greta 60, 95, 115, 148, 221, 245,
248, 256, 297, 316, 340, 356, 388, 391,
420, 427, 432, 443, 455, 486, 559, 561
Gardner, Ava 237, 384-385, 387, 398-399,
400-403, 404, 413, 414, 495, 551- 553,
611
Gardner, Erle Stanley 80
Gardner, Hy 480
Garfield, John 131, 156, 169, 171, 176, 206,
218, 243, 257, 284, 285, 324, 331, 357,
358, 359, 465, 488
Gargan, William 107
Garland, Judy 14, 176, 187, 234, 247, 257,
310, 326, 331, 359, 365, 374, 388, 397,
413, 414, 425, 547, 552, 557, 558, 568
Garnett, Tay 282, 283
Garson, Greer 238, 277, 331, 386, 388, 391,
547
Gates, Phyllis 553, 590
Gay Bride, The 104
Gaynor, Janet 158, 360
General Electric Theater 52, 60, 190, 417,
510
Gentleman Jim 304, 438
Gentlemen Prefer Blondes 287, 398
Gering, Marion 28
Gessner, Elizabeth 452
Ghosts 17
Giant 592
Giant Claw, The 428
Gibson, Hoot 116
Gibson, Mel 509
Gielgud, John 542
Giesler, Jerry 412
Gilbert, Jane 215
Gilbert, John 221, 544
Gilda 506, 510, 557
Gipp, George 212, 214, 215, 216
Girl from Jones Beach, The 437, 491, 492,
507, 508, 521
Girl from Mexico, The 214
Girls in Chains 509
Girls on Probation 131, 132, 133
Gish, Lillian 15, 17, 369, 370, 378, 385

Glass Menagerie, The 239, 241, 372, 387,
546-549, 550, 552, 559
Gleason, Jackie 272, 564
Gleason, James 264
"God Bless America" 216
God Is My Co-Pilot 244, 331, 338
Goddard, Paulette 22, 24, 25, 39, 41, 89,
104, 134, 181, 230, 240, 241, 243-245,
261, 299, 300-303, 329, 330-332, 343,
347, 348, 429, 430-435, 440, 444, 445,
449, 538, 543, 551, 573, 577, 578, 595,
598
Godfrey, Arthur 374
Godfrey, Peter 349, 437, 473, 475, 492, 493
Godzilla, King of the Monsters! 179
Goebbels, Josef 210, 290, 310, 335
Going My Own Way 555
Going Places 139, 140, 141
Gold Diggers of 1937 80, 81, 227
Golden Boy 213, 478
Goldstone, Richard 424
Goldwater, Barry 596
Goldwyn, Samuel 23, 164, 183, 302, 350,
381, 452, 538
Gombell, Minna 554
Gone With the Wind 63, 104, 106, 113, 118,
120, 121, 136, 143, 148, 152, 154, 170,
171, 217, 242, 253, 272, 279, 284, 331,
356, 428, 441, 466, 468, 521, 557, 595,
614
Good Earth, The 442
Good News 448, 450, 451
Good, Peter 199
Goodbye Again 226
Goodbye, Mr. Chips 284
Goodbye, My Fancy 535
Goodies, David 488
Goodman, Benny 61, 63, 510
Goodwin, Bill 540
Gorcey, Leo 165, 175
Gordon-Canning, Robert 58
Gordon, Bernard 606
Gordon, Gavin 252
Gordon, Michael 495
Gordon, Ruth 371, 384
Göring, Hermann 273, 306, 317, 336, 346
Goulding, Edmund 119, 148, 149, 150, 151
Grabiner, Harry 38
Grable, Betty 4, 23, 24, 31, 32, 44, 45, 63,
73, 115, 169, 183, 219, 226, 232, 245,
246, 258, 259, 278, 281, 300-303, 322,
324, 326, 329, 340, 411, 490
Graham, Katharine 410
Graham, Martha 376, 445
Grainger, Edmund 273
Grand Hotel 148, 248
Granger, Farley 506, 523

646

647

651

655

657

BLOOD
MOON
Productions, Ltd.

661

BLOOD MOON PRODUCTIONS

Entertainment About How America Interprets Its Celebrities

Blood Moon Productions is a feisty and independent New York based publishing enterprise dedicated to researching, salvaging, and indexing the oral histories of America's entertainment industry. As described by *The Huffington Post*, "Blood Moon, in case you don't know, is a small publishing house on Staten Island that cranks out Hollywood gossip books, about two or three a year, usually of five-, six-, or 700-page length, chocked with stories and pictures about people who used to consume the imaginations of the American public, back when we actually had a public imagination. That is, when people were really interested in each other, rather than in Apple 'devices.' In other words, back when we had vices, not devices."

Reorganized with its present name in 2004, Blood Moon originated in 1997 as the Georgia Literary Association, a vehicle for the promotion of obscure writers from America's Deep South. For several decades, Blood Moon and its key players (Darwin Porter and Danforth Prince) spearheaded the research, writing, and editorial functions of dozens of titles, and hundreds of editions, of THE FROMMER GUIDES, the most respected name in travel publishing.

Blood Moon maintains a back list of more than 30 critically acclaimed biographies, film guides, and novels. Its titles are distributed by the National Book Network (www.NBNBooks.com), and through secondary wholesalers and online retailers everywhere.

Since 2004, Blood Moon has been awarded dozens of nationally recognized literary prizes. They've included both silver and bronze medals from the IPPY (Independent Publishers Association) Awards; four nominations and two Honorable Mentions for BOOK OF THE YEAR from Foreword Reviews; nominations from The Ben Franklin Awards; and Awards and Honorable Mentions from the New England, the Los Angeles, the Paris, the Hollywood, the New York, and the San Francisco Book Festivals. Two of its titles have been Grand Prize Winners for Best Summer Reading, as defined by The Beach Book Awards, and in 2013, its triple-play overview of the Gabor sisters was designated as Biography of the Year by the Hollywood Book Festival.

For more about us, including access to a growing number of videotaped book trailers, TV and radio interviews, and public addresses, each accessible via **YouTube.com,** search for key words "Danforth Prince" or "Blood Moon Productions."

Or click on **WWW.BLOODMOONPRODUCTIONS.COM;** visit our page on Facebook; subscribe to us on Twitter (#BloodyandLunar); or refer to the pages which immediately follow.

Thanks for your interest, best wishes, and happy reading. Literacy matters! Read a book!

Danforth Prince, President
Blood Moon Productions, Ltd.

In the early summer of 2015, Blood Moon will release the grittiest, most unvarnished, and most comprehensive overview of the life, accomplishments, and scandals associated with the 20th Century's most astonishing (and most alarming) actor:

Peter O'Toole

One of the world's most admired (and brilliant) actors, Peter O'Toole wined and wenched his way through a labyrinth of sexual and interpersonal betrayals, sometimes with disastrous results. Away from the stage and screen, where such films as *Becket* and *Lawrence of Arabia*, made film history, his life was filled with drunken, debauched nights and edgy sexual experimentations, most of which were never openly examined in the press. A hellraiser, he shared wild times with his "best blokes" Richard Burton and Richard Harris. Peter Finch, also his close friend, once invited him to join him in sharing the pleasures of his mistress, Vivien Leigh.

"My father, a bookie, moved us to the Mick community of Leeds," O'Toole once told a reporter. "We were very poor, but I was born an Irishman, which accounts for my gift of gab, my unruly behavior, my passionate devotion to women and the bottle, and my loathing of any authority figure."

Author Robert Sellers described O'Toole's boyhood neighborhood. "Three of his playmates went on to be hanged for murder; one strangled a girl in a lovers' quarrel; one killed a man during a robbery; another cut up a warden in South Africa with a pair of shears. It was a heavy bunch."

Peter O'Toole's hell-raising life story has never been told, until now. Hot and uncensored, from a writing team which, even prior to O'Toole's death in 2013, had been collecting under-the-radar info about him for years, this book has everything you ever wanted to know about how THE LION navigated his way through the boudoirs of the Entertainment Industry IN WINTER, Spring, Summer, and a dissipated Autumn as well.

Blood Moon has ripped away the imperial robe, scepter, and crown usually associated with this quixotic problem child of the British Midlands. Provocatively uncensored, this illusion-shattering overview of Peter O'Toole's hellraising (or at least very naughty) and demented life is unique in the history of publishing.

Coming Soon: A Pertinent Addition to the Political Rumpus of America's
2016 Elections and Beyond

Bill & Hillary

So This Is That Thing Called Love

Blood Moon, famous for its exposés of celebrity scandal in Hollywood and in the political camps of both the Kennedys and the Reagans, has AT LAST turned its focus onto the role THE CLINTONS have played in Washington's Babylon.

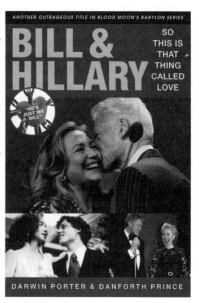

No other big-league power team has ever done it like Bill & Hillary. With the release of this book, Blood Moon will prove that Democrats can generate scandals even more provocative than their Republican counterparts.

Unprecedented and unauthorized, this book is savvy about the ways smart people sometimes compromise in affairs of the human heart. It's not about politics, but about the political world's most enduring love affair, and the role of the Clintons as the world's most famous couple. It's based on revelations from witnesses to the dramas of a hard-nosed but nonetheless romantic team who might once again take over the Free World.

Its authors have studied virtually everything about the Clintons since their days as local celebrities in Little Rock. It all began when two students, meeting at Yale in 1970, united—based on their own brand of love—to launch "The Plan," events from which have already incited tragedy, triumph, screams of protest from sometimes horrified observers, and the ongoing fascination of celebrity-watchers everywhere.

JACQUELINE KENNEDY ONASSIS
A Life Beyond Her Wildest Dreams

After floods of analysis and commentary in tabloid and mainstream newspapers worldwide, this has emerged as the world's most comprehensive testimonial to the flimsier side of Camelot, the most comprehensive compendium of gossip ever published about America's unofficial, uncrowned queen, **Jacqueline Kennedy Onassis**. Its publication coincided with the 20-year anniversary of the death of one of the most famous, revered, and talked-about women who ever lived.

During her tumultuous life, Mrs. Onassis zealously guarded her privacy and her secrets, but in the wake of her death, more and more revelations have emerged about her frustrations, her rage, her passions, her towering strengths, and her delicate fragility, which she hid from the glare of the world behind oversized sunglasses. Within this posthumous biography, a three-dimensional woman emerges through the compilation of some 1,000 eyewitness testimonials from men and women who knew her over a period of decades.

An overview of the life of Mrs. Onassis is a natural fit for Blood Moon, a publishing enterprise that's increasingly known, worldwide, as one of the most provocative and scandalous in the history of publishing.

"References to this American icon appear with almost rhythmic regularity to anyone researching the cultural landscape of America during the last half of The American Century," said Danforth Prince, Blood Moon's president and one of the book's co-authors. "Based on what we'd uncovered about Jackie during the research of many of our earlier titles, we're positioning ourselves as a more or less solitary outpost of irreverence within a landscape that's otherwise flooded with fawning, over-reverential testimonials. Therein lies this book's appeal—albeit with a constant respect and affection for a woman we admired and adored."

Based on decades of research by writers who define themselves as "voraciously attentive Kennedyphiles," it supplements the half-dozen other titles within Blood Moon's Babylon series.

JACQUELINE KENNEDY ONASSIS—A LIFE BEYOND HER WILDEST DREAMS
Darwin Porter and Danforth Prince

Paperback, Biography/Entertainment
6" x 9" 700 pages with hundreds of photos
ISBN 978-1-936003-39-6   Also available for E-readers.

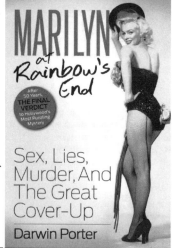

PINK TRIANGLE

The Feuds and Private Lives of Tennessee Williams, Gore Vidal, Truman Capote, and Famous Members of their Entourages

Darwin Porter & Danforth Prince

Softcover, 700 pages, with photos   ISBN 978-1-936003-37-2
Also Available for E-Readers

The *enfants terribles* of America at mid-20th century challenged the sexual censors of their day while indulging in "bitchfests" for love & glory.

This book exposes their literary slugfests and offers an intimate look at their relationships with the *glitterati*—MM, Brando, the Oliviers, the Paleys, U.S. Presidents, a gaggle of other movie stars, millionaires, and dozens of others.

This is for anyone who's interested in the formerly concealed scandals of Hollywood and Broadway, and the values and pretentions of both the literary world and the entertainment industry.

***

"A banquet... If *PINK TRIANGLE* had not been written for us, we would have had to research and type it all up for ourselves...Pink Triangle is nearly seven hundred pages of the most entertaining histrionics ever sliced, spiced, heated, and serviced up to the reading public. Everything that Blood Moon has done before pales in comparison.

"Given the fact that the subjects of the book themselves were nearly delusional on the subject of themselves (to say nothing of each other) it is hard to find fault. Add to this the intertwined jungle that was the relationship among Williams, Capote, and Vidal, of the times they vied for things they loved most—especially attention—and the times they enthralled each other and the world, [*Pink Triangle* is] the perfect antidote to the Polar Vortex." **—Vinton McCabe in the NY JOURNAL OF BOOKS**

"Blood Moon prides itself on mixing tabloid journalism, going to the source of gossip itself—okay, hearsay, or the quickly deteriorating minds of aging witnesses—with genuine moments of hard-work research (and there always is some of that in Blood Moon Productions' books) to come up with their titles.

"Full disclosure: I have been a friend and follower of Blood Moon Productions' tomes for years, and always marveled at the amount of information in their books—it's staggering. The index alone to *Pink Triangle* runs to 21 pages—and the scale of names in it runs like a *Who's Who* of American social, cultural and political life through much of the 20th century...The only remedy is for you to run out this February, in time for Valentine's Day, and buy *Pink Triangle*." **—Perry Brass in THE HUFFINGTON POST**

"We Brits are not spared the Porter/Prince silken lash either. PINK TRIANGLE's research is, quite frankly, breathtaking. PINK TRIANGLE will fascinate you for many weeks to come. Once you have made the initial titillating dip, the day will seem dull without it." **—Jeffery Tayor in THE SUNDAY EXPRESS (UK)**

ABOUT THE AUTHORS: Darwin Porter, himself an unrepentant *enfant terrible*, moved through the entourages of this Pink Triangle with impunity for several decades of their heyday. Early in 2014, he wrote a book about it.

"Every literate person in America has strong ideas about The Pink Triangle. This *exposé* of its members' feuds, vanities, and idiosyncracies will be required reading if you're interested in the literary climate of 'The American Century.'" **—Danforth Prince**

THOSE GLAMOROUS GABORS
Bombshells from Budapest
Darwin Porter

Zsa Zsa, Eva, and Magda Gabor transferred their glittery dreams and gold-digging ambitions from the twilight of the Austro-Hungarian Empire to Hollywood. There, more effectively than any army, these Bombshells from Budapest broke hearts, amassed fortunes, lovers, and A-list husbands, and amused millions of *voyeurs* through the medium of television, movies, and the social registers. In this astonishing "triple-play" biography, designated "Best Biography of the Year" by the Hollywood Book Festival, Blood Moon lifts the "mink-and-diamond" curtain on this amazing trio of blood-related sisters, whose complicated intrigues have never been fully explored before.

From *the New York Review of Books*: "You will never be Ga-bored...this book gives new meaning to the term compelling.

"Be warned, *Those Glamorous Gabors* is both an epic and a pip. Not since *Gone With the Wind* have so many characters on the printed page been forced to run for their lives for one reason or another. And Scarlett making a dress out of the curtains is nothing compared to what a Gabor will do when she needs to scrap together an outfit for a movie premiere or late-night outing.

"For those not up to speed, Jolie Tilleman came from a family of jewelers and therefore came by her love for the shiny stones honestly, perhaps genetically. She married Vilmos Gabor somewhere around World War 1 (exact dates, especially birth dates, are always somewhat vague in order to establish plausible deniability later on) and they were soon blessed with three daughters, **Magda**, the oldest, whose hair, sadly, was naturally brown, although it would turn quite red in America; **Zsa Zsa** (born 'Sari') a natural blond who at a very young age exhibited the desire for fame with none of the talents usually associated with achievement, excepting beauty and a natural wit; and **Eva**, the youngest and blondest of the girls, who after seeing Grace Moore perform at the National Theater, decided that she wanted to be an actress and that she would one day move to Hollywood to become a star.

"Given that the Gabor family at that time lived in Budapest, Hungary, at the period of time between the World Wars, that Hollywood dream seemed a distant one indeed. The story—the riches to rags to riches to rags to riches again myth of survival against all odds as the four women, because of their Jewish heritage, flee Europe with only the minks on their backs and what jewels they could smuggle along with them in their *decolletage*, only to have to battle afresh for their places in the vicious Hollywood pecking order—gives new meaning to the term 'compelling.' The reader, as if he were witnessing a particularly gore-drenched traffic accident, is incapable of looking away."

—New York Review of Books

About the Author:

Darwin Porter spent more than a half-century collecting anecdotes and interviews with virtually everyone ever associated with the Gabors, including a gaggle of Hungarian and Viennese eyewitnesses who remembered the Gabors before their American debuts. **Jolie Gabor**, the trio's mother, was a frequent guest within Porter's home in New York City, and for a period of three years, the Austrian-born cabaret singer, **Greta Keller** (Jolie Gabor's best friend and each of the three sisters' godmother) was a semi-permanent resident there. Jolie and Greta, "two shrewd and hard-nosed battleaxes from the mine fields of Old Europa," are included among the many sources which contributed to the hundreds of never-before-published revelations which permeate this astonishing triple biography.

Softcover, 730 pages, with hundreds of photos, ISBN 978-1-936003-35-8
Also available for e-readers

INSIDE LINDA LOVELACE'S
DEEP THROAT
DEGRADATION, PORNO CHIC, AND THE RISE OF FEMINISM
DARWIN PORTER

"THIS BOOK IS A WINNER!" An insider's view of the unlikely heroine who changed the world's perceptions about pornography, censorship, and sexual behavior patterns forever

The Beach Book Festival's Grand Prize Winner: "Best Summer Reading of 2013"
Runner-Up to "Best Biography of 2013" *The Los Angeles Book Festival*
Winner of a Sybarite Award from HedoOnline.com

"This book drew me in..How could it not?" Coco Papy, Bookslut.

A Bronx-born brunette, the notorious Linda Lovelace was the starry-eyed Catholic daughter in the 1950s of a police officer who nicknamed her "Miss Holy Holy." Twenty years later, she became the most notorious actress of the 20th century.

She'd fallen in love with a tough ex-Marine, Chuck Traynor, and eventually married him, only to learn that she had become his meal ticket. He forced her at gunpoint into a role as a player within hardcore porn, including a 1971 bestiality film entitled *Dogarama*.

Her next film, shot for $20,000, was released in 1972 as *Deep Throat*. It became the largest grossing XXX-rated flick of all time, earning an estimated $750 million and still being screened all over the world. The fee she was paid was $1,200, which her husband confiscated. The sexy 70s went wild for the film. Porno chic was born, with Linda as its centerpiece.

Traynor, a sadist, pimped his wife to celebrities, charging them $2,000 per session, It became a status symbol to commission an "individualized" film clip of Linda performing her specialty. Clients included Elvis Presley, Frank Sinatra, Milton Berle, Desi Arnaz, Marlon Brando, William Holden, Peter Lawford, and Burt Lancaster. The Mafia had found its most lucrative business—pornography—since Prohibition.

After a decade of being assaulted, beaten, and humiliated, Linda, in 1980, underwent a "Born Again" transformation. She launched her own feminist anti-pornography movement, attracting such activists as Gloria Steinem, and scores of other sex industry professionals who refuted their earlier careers.

Critics claimed that Linda's *Deep Throat* changed America's sexual attitudes more than anything since the first Kinsey report in 1948, that she super-charged the feminist movement, and that to some degree, she re-defined the nation's views on obscenity.

The tragic saga of Linda Lovelace changed beliefs about entertainment, morality, and feminism in America. This book tells you what the movie doesn't.

Darwin Porter, *author of some twenty critically acclaimed celebrity exposés of behind-the-scenes intrigue in the entertainment industry, was deeply involved in the Linda Lovelace saga as it unfolded in the 70s, interviewing many of the players, and raising money for the legal defense of the film's co-star, Harry Reems. In this book, emphasizing her role as a celebrity interacting with other celebrities, he brings inside information and a never-before-published revelation to almost every page.*

INSIDE LINDA LOVELACE'S DEEP THROAT
The Most Comprehensive Biography Ever Written of an Adult Entertainment Star
and Her Relationship with the Underbelly of Hollywood
Softcover, 640 pages, 6"x9", with hundreds of photos. ISBN 978-1-936003-33-4

PAUL NEWMAN
The Man Behind the Baby Blues, His Secret Life Exposed

Darwin Porter

Drawn from firsthand interviews with insiders who knew Paul Newman intimately, and compiled over a period of nearly a half-century, this is the world's most honest and most revelatory biography about Hollywood's pre-eminent male sex symbol.

If you're a fan of Newman *(and who do you know who isn't)* you really should look at this book. It's a respectful but candid cornucopia of once-concealed information about the sexual and emotional adventures of an affable, impossibly good-looking workaday actor, a former sailor from Shaker Heights, Ohio, who parlayed his ambisexual charm and extraordinatily good looks into one of the most successful careers in Hollywood.

Whereas the situations it exposes were widely known within Hollywood's inner circles, they've never before been revealed to the general public.

But now, the full story has been published, as recorded by celebrity chronicler Darwin Porter—the giddy heights and agonizing crashes of a great American star, with revelations and insights never before published in any other biography.

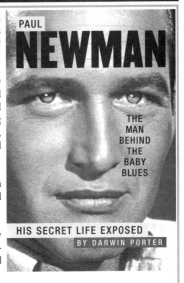

PAUL
NEWMAN

THE MAN BEHIND THE BABY BLUES

HIS SECRET LIFE EXPOSED
BY DARWIN PORTER

ABOUT THE AUTHOR: "There are guilty pleasures. Then there is the master of guilty pleasures, Darwin Porter. There is nothing like reading him for passing the hours. He is the Nietzsche of Naughtiness, the Goethe of Gossip, the Proust of Pop Culture. Porter knows all the nasty buzz anyone has ever heard whispered in dark bars, dim alleys, and confessional booths. And lovingly, precisely, and in as straightforward a manner as an oncoming train, his prose whacks you between the eyes with the greatest gossip since Kenneth Anger. Some would say better than Anger."

—**Alan W. Petrucelli,** *The Entertainment Report*
Stage and Screen Examiner, Examiner.com

Paul Newman, The Man Behind the Baby Blues
His Secret Life Exposed

Recipient of an Honorable Mention from the New England Book Festival, this is the most compelling and unvarnished biography of Paul Newman ever written.

Hardcover, 520 pages, with dozens of photos. **ISBN 978-0-9786465-1-6.** Also available for E-readers

MERV GRIFFIN

A LIFE IN THE CLOSET

Darwin Porter

Hardcover, with photos. ISBN 978-0-9786465-0-9. Also available for E-Readers.

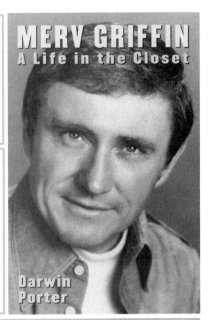

"Darwin Porter told me why he tore the door off Merv's closet.......*Heeeere's Merv!* is 560 pages, 100 photos, a truckload of gossip, and a bedful of unauthorized dish."

Cindy Adams, The NY Post

"Darwin Porter tears the door off Merv Griffin's closet with gusto in this sizzling, superlatively re-searched biography...It brims with insider gossip that's about Hollywood legends, writ large, smart, and with great style."

Richard LaBonté, BOOKMARKS

MERV GRIFFIN, A LIFE IN THE CLOSET

Merv Griffin began his career as a Big Band singer, moved on to a failed career as a romantic hero in the movies, and eventually rewrote the rules of everything associated with the broad-casting industry. Along the way, he met and befriended virtually everyone who mattered, in-cluding Nancy Reagan, and made billions operating casinos and developing jingles, contests, and word games. All of this while maintaining a male harem and a secret life as America's most famously closeted homosexual.

In this comprehensive and richly ironic biography, Darwin Porter reveals the amazing details be-hind the richest, most successful, and in some ways, the most notorious mogul in the history of America's entertainment industry.

HOT, CONTROVERSIAL, & RIGOROUSLY RESEARCHED

HERE'S MERV!